CAMBRIDGE LIBRARY

Books of enduring schola

History

The books reissued in this series include accounts of historical events and movements by eye-witnesses and contemporaries, as well as landmark studies that assembled significant source materials or developed new historiographical methods. The series includes work in social, political and military history on a wide range of periods and regions, giving modern scholars ready access to influential publications of the past.

The Book of the Farm

Henry Stephens (1795–1874) was a farmer and later a writer on agriculture. After attending lectures on chemistry and agriculture at the University of Edinburgh he boarded with a Berwickshire farmer, George Brown, and gained practical experience of agricultural work. In 1820 Stephens acquired his own farm, on which he used modern and experimental farming methods. In 1837 he sold the farm, and devoted the rest of his life to writing guides to farming for the use of inexperienced farmers. These influential volumes, first published in 1842, and reprinted many times (the 1844 edition is reissued here) contain Stephens' detailed descriptions of contemporary farming practices. He describes in meticulous detail all aspects of farming, including livestock care and slaughter, dairying, irrigation practices and crop culture. Arranged by season and including copious high-quality illustrations of farming equipment, these extremely popular and fascinating volumes were considered the standard work on practical Victorian agriculture, and were used as an 'instructional manual' on the recent BBC television series, 'The Victorian Farm'. Volume 1 describes farming tasks performed in winter.

Cambridge University Press has long been a pioneer in the reissuing of out-of-print titles from its own backlist, producing digital reprints of books that are still sought after by scholars and students but could not be reprinted economically using traditional technology. The Cambridge Library Collection extends this activity to a wider range of books which are still of importance to researchers and professionals, either for the source material they contain, or as landmarks in the history of their academic discipline.

Drawing from the world-renowned collections in the Cambridge University Library, and guided by the advice of experts in each subject area, Cambridge University Press is using state-of-the-art scanning machines in its own Printing House to capture the content of each book selected for inclusion. The files are processed to give a consistently clear, crisp image, and the books finished to the high quality standard for which the Press is recognised around the world. The latest print-on-demand technology ensures that the books will remain available indefinitely, and that orders for single or multiple copies can quickly be supplied.

The Cambridge Library Collection will bring back to life books of enduring scholarly value (including out-of-copyright works originally issued by other publishers) across a wide range of disciplines in the humanities and social sciences and in science and technology.

The Book of the Farm

Detailing the Labours of the Farmer, Farm-steward, Ploughman, Shepherd, Hedger, Cattle-man, Field-worker, and Dairy-maid

VOLUME 1

HENRY STEPHENS

CAMBRIDGE UNIVERSITY PRESS

Cambridge, New York, Melbourne, Madrid, Cape Town, Singapore,
São Paolo, Delhi, Dubai, Tokyo, Mexico City

Published in the United States of America by Cambridge University Press, New York

www.cambridge.org
Information on this title: www.cambridge.org/9781108024945

This edition first published 1844
This digitally printed version 2010

ISBN 978-1-108-02494-5 Paperback

THE
BOOK OF THE FARM,

DETAILING THE LABOURS OF THE

FARMER, FARM-STEWARD, PLOUGHMAN, SHEPHERD, HEDGER
CATTLE-MAN, FIELD-WORKER, AND DAIRY-MAID.

BY

HENRY STEPHENS, F.R.S.E.

IN THREE VOLUMES.

WITH NUMEROUS ILLUSTRATIONS.

VOL. I.

"Wherefore, come on, O young husbandman!
Learn the culture proper to each kind."
VIRGIL.

WILLIAM BLACKWOOD AND SONS,
EDINBURGH AND LONDON.
MDCCCXLIV.

PRINTED BY NEILL AND COMPANY, EDINBURGH.

ADVERTISEMENT.

On bringing the Book of the Farm to a close, the Author feels it incumbent upon him to apologize to his Subscribers for the work being extended so much beyond the original intention, and also for the occasional irregularity of its periodic appearance. The same facts will explain both circumstances; and they are these:—

Shortly after the commencement of the publication, the Author was encouraged, by the advice of his Friends, to make the Book of the Farm as perfect as he could, as it would be thus more useful to the class of young Agriculturists for whose benefit it was originally undertaken. Effectually to attain this purpose, he found it quite necessary to give the descriptions of all the primary operations of the Farm in minute detail—to increase the number of the various classes of Illustrations—and to enlarge the scale of those referring to the Implements. The Prospectus proposed to confine the illustrations simply to fifteen Plates, and two hundred Wood-Engravings; whereas, the actual number deemed necessary for the entire completeness of these departments, has been extended to thirty-three Plates, and upwards of six hundred Wood-Engravings,—the very space occupied by the latter causing a sensible increase in the bulk of the entire work.

The Author would acknowledge the assistance he has received in making the Book of the Farm what it is. In an especial manner, he would mention the name of Mr James Slight, Engineer, Leith Walk, Edinburgh, who supplied him with the descriptions of the whole Implements, great and small, noticed in the work; and also that of his Son, Mr GEORGE HENRY SLIGHT, who executed all the Drawings of the Machinery.

The Portraits of most of the Animals selected for illustration were painted, from the life, by Mr JOHN SHERIFF, A.R.S.A., Edinburgh; and the Drawings illustrative of field operations were supplied by Mr GOURLAY STEELL, Edinburgh.

To Dr HENRY R. MADDEN, Penicuik, the Author would also acknowledge his obligations for some remarks, explanatory of scientific principles, connected with the principal operations of husbandry.

REDBRAE COTTAGE,
Edinburgh, 17th September 1844.

CONTENTS OF VOLUME I.

CLASSIFIED LIST OF THE ILLUSTRATIONS.

ENGRAVINGS ON STEEL.

The Portraits of Animals were engraved by Mr THOMAS LANDSEER, London.

The Machinery was engraved by Mr W. H. LIZARS, Edinburgh.

ENGRAVINGS ON WOOD.

The Engravings were executed by MR BRANSTON, London.

THE STEADING.

FENCES.

OPERATIONS CONNECTED WITH THE CULTURE OF CORN.

OPERATIONS CONNECTED WITH TURNIP CULTURE AND USE.

HORSES.

HARNESS.

SWINE.

THE

BOOK OF THE FARM.

---

1. OF THE DIFFICULTIES WHICH THE YOUNG FARMER HAS TO ENCOUNTER AT THE OUTSET OF LEARNING PRACTICAL HUSBANDRY.

"One, but painted thus,
Would be interpreted a thing perplex'd
Beyond self-explication." CYMBELINE.

The young farmer, left to his own guidance, when beginning to learn his profession, encounters many perplexing difficulties. The difficulty which at first most prominently obtrudes itself on his notice, consists in the *distribution* of the labour of the farm; and it presents itself, in this way:—He observes the teams employed one day in one field, at one kind of work; and, perhaps, the next day in another field, at a different sort of work. He observes the persons, employed as field-workers, assisting the teams one day; and in the next, perhaps, working by themselves in another field or elsewhere. He observes those changes with attention, considers of their utility, but cannot discover the reasons for making so very varied arrangements; not because he entertains the least doubt of their propriety, but, being as yet uninitiated in the art of farming, he cannot foresee the purpose for which those labours are performed. The reason why he cannot at once foresee this, is, that in all cases, excepting at the finishing operations, the end is unattained at the time of his observation.

The next difficulty the young farmer encounters is in the *variety* of the labours performed. He not only sees various arrangements made to do the same sort of work, but various kinds of work. He discovers this difference on examining more closely into the nature of the work he sees performing. He observes one day the horses at work in the plough in one field, moving in a direction quite opposite, in regard to the ridges, to what they were in the plough in another field. On another day he observes the horses at work with quite a different implement from the plough. The field-workers, he perceives, have laid aside the implement with which they were working, and are performing the labour engaged in with the hand. He cannot comprehend why one sort of work should be prosecuted one day, and quite a different sort of work the next. This difficulty is inexplicable for the same reason why he could not overcome the former one; because he cannot foresee the end for which those varieties of work are performed. No doubt he is aware, that every kind and variety of work which are performed on a farm, are preparatives to the attainment of certain crops; but what portion of any work is intended as a certain part of the preparation for a particular crop, is a knowledge which he cannot acquire by intuition. Every preparatory work is thus perplexing to the young farmer.

Field work being thus chiefly *anticipatory*, is the circumstance which renders its object so perplexing to the learner. He cannot, possibly, perceive the connection between preparatory labours and their ultimate ends; and, yet, until he learn to appreciate their necessary connection, he will remain incapable of managing a farm. It is in the exercise of this faculty of anticipation or foresight that the experienced and careful farmer is contradistinguished from the ignorant and careless. Indeed, let the experience of farming be ever so extensive, or, in other words, let the knowledge of minutiæ be ever so intimate, unless the farmer use his experience by foresight, he will never be enabled to conduct a farm aright. Both foresight and experience are acquired by observation, though the former is matured by reflection. Observation is open to all farmers, but all do not profit by it. Every farmer may acquire in time sufficient *experience* to conduct a farm in a passable manner; but many farmers never acquire *foresight*, because they never reflect, and therefore cannot make their experience tell to the most advantage. Conducting a farm by foresight is thus a higher acquirement than the most intimate knowledge of the minutiæ of labour. Foresight cannot be exercised without the assistance of experience; though the latter may exist independently of the former. As the elements of every art must first be acquired by observation, a knowledge of the minutiæ of labour should be the first subject for acquirement by the young farmer. By carefully tracing the connection betwixt combined operations and their ultimate ends, he will acquire foresight.

The necessity of possessing foresight in arranging the minutiæ of labour, before the young farmer can with confidence undertake the direction of a farm, renders *farming* more difficult of acquirement, and a longer time of being acquired, than most other arts. This statement may appear incredible to those who have been accustomed to hear of farming being easily and soon learned by the meanest capacity. No doubt it may be acquired in time, to a certain degree, by all who are capable of improvement by observation and experience; but, nevertheless, the ultimate ends for which the various kinds of field-work are prosecuted, are involved in obscurity to every learner. In most other arts no great space usually elapses between the commencement and completion of the piece of work, and the piece is worked at until finished. The beginner can thus soon perceive the connection between the minutest portion of the work in which he is engaged, and the object for which it is intended. There is in this no obscurity to perplex his mind. He is purposely led, by degrees, from the simplest to the most complicated parts of his art, so that his mind is not bewildered at the outset by participating in a multiplicity of works at one time. He thus begins to acquire true experience from the outset.

The young farmer has no such advantages in his apprenticeship. There is no simple easy work, or one object only to engage his attention at first. On the contrary, many minutiæ connected with the various works in progress, claim his attention at one and the same time, and if the requisite attention to any one of them be neglected for the time, no other opportunity for observing it can occur for a twelvemonth. It is a misfortune to the young farmer, in such circumstances, to be thrown back in his progress by a trifling neglect. He cannot make up his leeway until after the revolution of a year. And though ever so attentive he cannot possibly learn to anticipate operations in a shorter time, and therefore cannot possibly understand the drift of a single operation in the first year of his apprenticeship. The first year is generally spent almost unprofitably, and certainly unsatisfactorily to an inquisitive mind. But attentive observation during the first year, will enable him, in the second, to anticipate the successive operations ere they arrive, and arrange every minutia of labour as it is required. Many of the events of the first year, which had left no adequate impression of their importance on his memory, crowd upon his observation in the second, as essential components of recognised operations. A familiar recognition of events, tends, in a rapid degree, to enlarge the sphere of experience, and to inspire confidence in one's own judgment; and this quality greatly facilitates the acquisition of foresight.

Let it not be imagined by those who have never passed through the perplexing ordeals incident to the first year of farming, that I have described them in strong colours, in order to induce to the belief, that farming is an art more difficult of attainment than it really is. So far is this from being the case, I may safely appeal to the experience of every person who had attained manhood before beginning to learn farming, whether I have not truly depicted his own condition at the outset of his professional career. So that every young man learning farming must expect to meet with those difficulties.

---

2. OF THE MEANS OF OVERCOMING THOSE DIFFICULTIES.

"We can clear these ambiguities."
ROMEO AND JULIET.

Experience undoubtedly dissipates doubt, and removes perplexity; but experience, though a sure and a safe, is a slow teacher. A whole year must revolve ere the entire labours of a farm can be exhibited in the field, and the young farmer satisfactorily understand what he is about; and a whole year is too much time for most young men to *sacrifice*. Could the young farmer find a monitor to explain to him, during the first year of his apprenticeship, the purpose for which every operation on a farm is performed,—foretell to him the results which every operation is intended to effect,—and indicate to him the relative progress which all the operations should make, from time to time, towards the attainment of their various ends, he would thereby acquire a far greater quantity of professional information, and have greater confidence in its accuracy, than he could possibly obtain for himself in that anxious period of his novitiate. Such a monitor would best be an experienced and intelligent farmer, were he duly attentive to his pupil. Farmers, however, can scarcely bestow so much attention as would be desired by pupils at all times; because the lapses of time occasioned by necessary engagements, in the fulfilment of which farmers are sometimes obliged to leave home, produce inattention on the part of the farmer; and inattention and absence combined constitute sad interruptions to tuition, and cannot always be avoided by the most pains-taking farmer. But a *book* might be made an efficient assistant-monitor. If expressly written for the purpose, it might not only corroborate what the farmer inculcated, but serve as a substitute in his temporary absence. In this way tuition might proceed uninterruptedly; and the pupil never want a monitor upon whom he could confidently rely. Were a book purposely so arranged put into the hands of young farmers so circumstanced, the usual deprecations against recommending the acquirement of practical farming from books alone, would not here apply. I would give no such counsel to any young farmer. Because books on farming, to be really serviceable to the learner, ought not to constitute the arena on which to study farming—the field being the best place for perceiving the fitness of labour to the purposes it is designed to attain—but as monitors for indicating the best modes of management, and shewing the way of learning those modes most easily. *By these, the practice of experienced farmers might be communicated and recommended to beginners. By consulting those which had been purposely written for their guidance, while they themselves were carefully observing the daily operations of the farm, the import of labours,—which are often intricate, always protracted over considerable portions of time, and necessarily separated from each other,—would be acquired in a much shorter time than if left to be discovered by the sagacity of beginners.*

It is requisite to explain, that by the phrase "*young farmer*," I mean the young man, who, having finished his scholastic and academical education, directs his attention, for the first time, to the acquirement of practical farming; or who, though born on a farm, having spent the greater part of his life at school, determines, at length, on following his father's profession. For the latter class of young men, tuition in farming, and information from books, are as requisite as for the former. Those who have constantly seen farming from infancy, can never be said to have been young farmers, for, by the time they are fit to act for themselves, they are proficients in farming. Having myself, for a time, been placed precisely in the position of the first description of young men, I can bear sincere testimony to the truth of the difficulties I have described as having to be encountered in the first year of apprenticeship. I felt that a guide-book would have been an invaluable monitor to me, but none such existed at the time. No doubt it is quite reasonable to expect of the farmer, ability to instruct the pupils committed to his charge in a competent manner. This is certainly his duty, which, if rightly performed, no guide-book would be required by pupils; but very few farmers who receive pupils, undertake the onerous task of instruction. Practical farming they leave the pupils to acquire for themselves in the fields, by imperfect observation and slow experience, as they themselves had previously done,—theoretical knowledge, very few, if any, are competent to impart. The pupils, being thus very much left to their own application, can scarcely avoid being beset with difficulties, and losing much time. At same time it must be acknowledged, that the practice gained by slow experience is, in the end, the most valuable and enduring. Still a book on farming, expressly written to suit his circumstances, might be a valuable instructor to the young farmer; it might guard him against the difficulties which learners are apt to encounter; and it would recompense him for loss of time, by imparting sound professional information.

Such a book, to be really a useful instructor and correct guide, should, in my estimation, possess these necessary qualifications. Its principal matter should consist of a clear narrative of all the labours of the farm, as they occur in succession; and it should give the reasons fully for which each piece of work is undertaken. While the principal operations are narrated in this way, the precise method of executing every species of work, whether manual or implemental, should be minutely detailed. The construction of the various implements by which work is performed,—the mode of using them,—the accidents to which each is liable,—should be circumstantially described. A seasonable narrative of the principal operations will shew the young farmer, that farming is really a systematic business, having a definite object in view, and possessing the means of attaining it. The reasons for doing every piece of work in one way, rather than another, will convince him that farming is an art founded on rational and known principles. A description of the implements, and of the method of using them, will give him a closer insight into the nature and fitness of field-work for attaining its end, than by any other means. A perusal of these narratives, all having a common object, will impart a more comprehensive and clearer view of the management of a farm in a given time, than he could acquire by himself from witnessing ever so many isolated operations. The influence of the seasons on all the labours of the field is another consideration which should be attended to in such a book. In preparing the ground, and during the growth of the crops, the labour appropriated to each kind of crop terminates for a time, and is not resumed until a fit season arrive. These periodical cessations from labour form natural epochs in the progress of the crops towards maturity, and afford convenient opportunities for performing the work peculiarly appropriate to each epoch; and, since every operation of the farm is made to conform with its season, these epochs correspond exactly with the *natural* seasons of the year. I say with the *natural* seasons, in contradistinction to the common yearly seasons, which are entirely conventional. This necessary and opportune agreement between labour and the natural seasons, induces a corresponding division of the labours of the farm into four great portions, or *seasons*, as they are usually termed. Labour should therefore be described with particular reference to its appropriate season.

3. OF THE KIND OF INFORMATION TO BE FOUND IN EXISTENT WORKS ON AGRICULTURE.

"Tire the hearer with a book of words."
MUCH ADO ABOUT NOTHING.

Unless the business of a farm be treated in books somewhat in the manner thus described, I consider it impossible for a young farmer to derive from them the requisite information for conducting a farm, even though he should be constantly resident upon it. By even the most careful perusal of books, which relate methods of cultivating crops and treating live stock in the most general terms and in detached sections having no relative connection with each other, the young farmer will never, in my opinion, understand how to apportion labour, and modify its application to the raising of crops and rearing of live-stock, in accordance with the nature of the season. He will never learn to know by perusing a narrative couched in the most general terms, when an operation is really well performed; because, to be able to judge of the quality of work, all its minutiæ ought previously to have been fully and carefully detailed to him. Narratives couched in general terms, to the exclusion of essential minutiæ, will never impart that precision of ideas which the mind should possess in conducting any piece of field work; and without precision of ideas in regard to labour, no man will ever be able to conduct a farm aright. But to be told how to conduct a farm aright, is the chief motive of the young farmer for consulting a book at all.

Now, on examining works of any pretensions which have, for years past, been written on practical agriculture, none will be found to have been written and arranged on the principles I have recommended, and much less for the special benefit of beginners in farming. All are so arranged as to constitute books of reference for experienced, rather than as guides for young farmers. Yet, how few of the former will condescend to *consult* agricultural works! The aversion of experienced farmers to consult books on agriculture has long been proverbial. No doubt, this aversion may be explained; but whether the explanation is to be found in a general indifference to book-farming, or in the quality of the books themselves, or in both circumstances combined, it is not easy to determine. The aversion, however, appears to be felt more towards systematic than periodical works on agriculture.

The latter class receives favour, because, possibly, they may contain something that is not generally known, and their information bears the character of freshness. As to young farmers, if they cannot find books suited to their particular state of knowledge, they have no alternative but to peruse those that are extant.

For the sake of the young farmer, the usual contents of agricultural books require further consideration. Let any systematic work on practical agriculture be examined, and it will be found to contain an arrangement of the various particulars of farming, somewhat in this order. The soil and the various methods of working it are first described. The implements are then most probably particularised, or their description deferred to a later portion of the work. The methods of raising and securing the different kinds of crops are then detailed. And the treatment of live-stock is delayed to the last. We suppose that no satisfactory reasons can be given for adopting this particular arrangement of subjects. It is perhaps considered a *simple* arrangement, because it proceeds from what is considered the elementary process of preparing the soil, to the more complicated process of cultivating the plants for which the soil has been prepared. But the simplicity of the arrangement, I apprehend, is to be found rather in what is assumed than what is apparent; for ploughing land is not a more simple process, or more elementary, than sowing seed. Indeed, some sorts of ploughing require far greater dexterity and ingenuity in the performance than any process connected with the production of crops. Perhaps it is considered a *natural* arrangement, because the ground is first prepared, and the crop is then sown. The ground, it is true, must be partially, if not wholly, prepared before the crop be put into it; but, in the cultivation of the summer crops, much of the labour bestowed on the land is performed whilst the crops are in a rapid progress towards maturity.

Although the seasons visibly influence the operations and products of the farm, systematic works on agriculture scarcely disclose the subdivision of the year into seasons, much less the very different operations performed in different seasons, and still less the difference of character of the same season in different years. For all that is given in them by way of advice, every operation may as well be performed in one season as in another. No doubt, reference is made, and cannot altogether be avoided being made, to the season in which the piece of work described should be performed; but the reference seems to allude to the season more as an accidental concomitant, than as constituting the sole influential power that regulates the order of time in which the work should be performed. The allusion to the season, in short, only forms an isolated hint, which, being singly repeated in a number of places, it is impossible for the reader to keep in mind the particular operation that should be performed in its own season. This apparent neglect of the great influential power which regulates all farm business, constitutes an insuperable objection to describing, in an uninterrupted narrative, a piece of work which is performed at intervals. Such a dissertation might bewilder the reader on its perusal, but could not satisfy the mind of the young inquiring farmer.

But the minuter arrangements in the books I am remarking on, are fully more objectionable than the general. The entire process usually adopted for working the land for a particular crop, is described in an uninterrupted narrative, before a description of the nature of the crop is given for which the soil is preparing; and, in consequence, before the connection between the preparation and the crop can be understood by the young farmer. This is not the usual procedure on farms, and cannot therefore be accounted natural; and it certainly tends to mislead the beginner. The usual practice is, that the land destined for any particular crop, is prepared to a certain degree, at stated times, in accordance with the natural seasons, and between those times many operations intervene which bear no relation to that particular crop. Every operation thus occupies a portion of time, intermittent in its season, and cannot truly be described in a continued dissertation. The finishing operation of every crop is always deferred until the appropriate season.

The descriptions of implements are very unsatisfactory, and their construction, for the most part, is very imperfectly represented. None trace their action from the first start to the entire completion of the work. Implements of husbandry having, only a few years ago, been made in the rudest manner, their actions were necessarily imperfect, and their absolute weight a serious drag on the draught. They are now constructed on true principles of mechanical science,—are light in motion, perfect in action, and elegant in form. It is remarkable that a correct description of improved implements has not ere this been undertaken by some skilful machinist.

Some works treat first of the science of agriculture, and then of the practice, as if the science of the art had been ascertained by studying abundance of facts derived from practice; or, as if its science already possesses such a superiority as to be allowed the precedence of practice. Others make science follow practice, as if the science had been derived from the practice described; whereas what is offered as science, is generally presented in isolated speculations, volunteered chiefly by theorists unacquainted with the practice of agriculture. Some authors theorise on agricultural subjects from as slight a foundation of facts, as in the experimental sciences, although they profess to give no preference to science over practice. Theorising writers, however, sometimes throw out hints which, when improved by more practical experimenters, really lead to useful results; but whatever may be the origin of the hints of theorists, the ability to give a convincing and philosophical reason for every operation in husbandry, is an accomplishment which every young farmer should endeavour to attain. Efforts to discover reasons for practice, derived from principles applicable alike to science and good husbandry, is a healthful exercise of the mind, and tend to render it capable of accommodating practice to existing circumstances. Conformity of practice with the season, exhibits in the farmer superior ability for conducting farming operations: like the experienced mariner, who renders every change in the gale subservient to the safety of his ship; navigation itself, not being more dependent on weather than is farming. By pursuing a course of observation and investigation such as this, the mind of the young farmer will soon become scientifically enlightened; but books on farming usually afford no assistance in pursuing such a course of study.

The treatment of live-stock is usually deferred to the conclusion in works on agriculture, as if it were either the most important, or the most complicated occupation, of the farm. Breeding for the improvement of a particular race of animals, and judicious crossing betwixt two fixed races, are indeed occupations which tax the judgment severely; but the ordinary treatment of live-stock is as easily managed as most of the operations of the field. The complete separation, moreover, made in books betwixt live-stock and field-operations, is apt to impress the mind of the inexperienced reader, that no necessary connection subsists betwixt stock and crop, whereas neither can be treated with advantage either to the farmer or themselves, unless both are attended to simultaneously.

From what I have stated regarding the arrangement of the subjects in systematic works on agriculture, it will be observed that they are better adapted for reference than tuition. They form a sort of dictionary or cyclopedia, in which different subjects are treated independently of each other, under different heads, though they may not be placed in alphabetical order. Being strictly works of reference, they may be consulted at any time; and are only valuable as such, in proportion to the accuracy of the information they contain: and being such, they are unfitted to impart agricultural knowledge suited to *beginners;* because, 1*st*, operations are not described in the order in which they occur on the farm;

2d, the descriptions omit many of the minutiæ of management, and yet constant attention to these constitutes an essential characteristic of a good farmer ; *3d*, they contain no precautionary warnings against the probability of failure in operations from various incidental causes, which ought to be anticipated, and attempted to be shunned ; and, *4th*, they afford no idea of the mode of carrying on various operations simultaneously in the different departments of management. Such works, therefore, impart no notion of *how* to set about to conduct a farm ; and yet, without this essential information, to obtain which the earnest young farmer toils incessantly, they can render him no assistance as guides. Indeed, the authors of such works do not profess to be teachers of young farmers.

Experience has made me well acquainted with the nature of the difficulties tyros in agriculture have to contend with ; and I clearly see that the books on farming extant, are incompetent to assist them in overcoming those difficulties. I consider it, therefore, very desirable that a work should be written for the express purpose of presenting facilities to young farmers, in the acquirement of their profession. This opinion I have entertained for many years, and see no cause to change it for all the works on agriculture that have been published of late years. To me it is matter of surprise that such a work has never yet been written by any of the prominent writers on agriculture in this prolific age of books, when assistance in the acquirement of learning is proffered in so many shapès to the youths of all classes. In most other branches of art, there is no want of facilities in books for acquiring their elementary principles and practice. On the kindred art of gardening, in particular, every possible variety of publication exists, from the ponderous folio to the tiny duodecimo, containing all the minutiæ of practice, and the elucidation of principles. It is difficult to account for the want of solicitude shewn by agricultural writers, for the early advancement of the young farmer. Perhaps many of them have never experienced the irksome difficulties of acquiring a practical knowledge of agriculture, and therefore cannot extend their sympathies to those who have ;—perhaps the exhibition of an intimate acquaintance with the minutiæ of farming appears too trivial an accomplishment to arrest the attention of general writers ;—perhaps they think when a young man begins to farm, it is sufficient for him to have a steward in whose skill he can confide ;—perhaps the tuition of young farmers is beneath their dignity, and they would rather aspire to the higher object of instructing experienced men ;—or perhaps they have never condescended to trouble themselves with practical farming, which, to judge of their lucubrations by the sterlingness of their practical worth, many of them, I dare say, never have.

4. OF THE CONSTRUCTION OF "THE BOOK OF THE FARM."

"A book? O rare one!
Be not as is our fangled world, a garment
Nobler than that it covers: let thy effects
So follow, to be most unlike our courtiers,
As good as promise."

CYMBELINE.

A book for the special purpose of instructing young farmers, such as it should be, and such as they are entitled to expect from the hands of experienced agriculturists, is yet a desideratum in the agricultural literature of this country. I am disposed to question the ability of any one man to write such a work; as its accomplishment would require a rare combination of qualities. The writer would require, as a primary qualification, to be a highly experienced agriculturist able to indite lucid instructions for conducting a farm. He should also be a clear-headed mechanician, to describe with minute distinctness the principles and construction of agricultural implements. He should, moreover, be an accomplished man of science, to explain to conviction the rationale of every operation. Onerous as the task thus appears, I shall, nevertheless, attempt to write such a book. With adequate assistance I trust, I shall be able to overcome at least the practical difficulties of the undertaking; and as to the scientific part, men of science have not yet brought science to bear upon agriculture in so satisfactory a manner as to justify them in contemning the rational explanations given of the various operations by practical men. Could I but succeed in *arranging* the various operations as they successively and actually occur on a farm, in so lucid a manner, as that any young farmer might comprehend the exact purport of each piece of work, as it developed itself in the field, I should certainly do him essential service. In accomplishing this, it is scarcely possible to invest, with sufficiently attractive interest, the descriptions of the minute details of the various operations, so that their aptitude to the purpose intended may be appreciated. Careful attention to these details, in themselves I own irksome, will the sooner enable the young farmer to understand thoroughly the connection of successive operations, and by the understanding of which he will be forewarned of the approach, and be able to ascertain the import, of the particular end for which they are preparatory. Besides shewing by anticipation the successive operations as they arrive, could I also give clear descriptions of the labour performed for each crop, as it is carried on *simultaneously* on a farm, I should achieve a still greater service for the young farmer. He would then clearly comprehend a difficult department of his art.

To accomplish these ends, I purpose to arrange the matter in the following manner, and for the following reasons. The entire business of a farm necessarily occupies a year; but that year embraces in some years more, and in others less, than twelve months. The agricultural year, moreover, both in its commencement and termination, does not correspond with that of the calendar; and those periods are determined in this way. The beginning and ending of every agricultural year are entirely dependent on the duration of the life of cultivated vegetables which constitute the chief product of the farm. In the temperate regions of the globe, vegetable life becomes dormant, or extinct, according as the vegetable is perennial or annual, at the beginning of winter. The beginning of winter is therefore chosen, in the temperate zones, to commence the agricultural year, and, of course, the labours of the farm; and when winter again approaches, the labours of the field have performed their annual revolution. The same sort of work is performed year after year. To understand those labours throughout the year is the chief aim of the young farmer; and to describe them to him satisfactorily is the principal object of this book.

Two modes of describing farm-business may be adopted. One is to arrange it under different heads, and describe all similar operations under the same head, as has hitherto been done in systematic works on agriculture. The other mode is to describe the operations as they *actually occur, singly, in succession*, as is to be done in this work. Both methods describe the general farm business, and both may be consulted for any particular part of the business. But how the relative position of any particular part of the business stands in regard to and influences any other, can only be shewn by the latter method, and it does so at a glance of the eye. Moreover, as some parts of farm business commence, and others terminate, at one or other period of the year, the latter method can clearly indicate what the other cannot so well do, in which period any particular operation is commenced, continued, or terminated; and it gives the details of each operation much more minutely than the other method.

The agricultural year, like the common year, is distinctly and conveniently divided into seasons, which regulate all farm work. I have given the seasons as full an influence over the arrangements of the matter in this book as they really possess over the business-matter of the farm. The whole business-matter is divided into four parts, each bearing the name of the season that influences the operations that are performed in it. By this arrangement every operation, whether requiring longer or shorter time for completion, is described as it takes its turn in the fields. The work that occupies only a short time to begin and complete, in any one season, is described in a single narrative. Very few of the operations of a farm, however, are begun and completed in one of the seasons, some extending over the whole four, and most into two or three. Any piece of work that extends over almost all the seasons, can nevertheless be described with great accuracy; for although, in its progress towards completion, it may altogether occupy an extended range of time, each season imposes a peculiar kind of operation towards the advancement of the work; which peculiar operation ceases, and a different kind is entered upon at the season which concludes the work. These cessations of labour, connected with the same work which extends over several seasons, are thus not mere conveniences, but necessary and temporary finishings of work, which it would be improper to resume but at a subsequent and appropriate season. In this way all the more extensive pieces of work are gradually advanced, in progressive steps, season after season, until their completion; while the smaller are concurrently brought onwards and completed, each in its proper season.

Before proceeding further, let me guard the young farmer against imbibing a misconception regarding the *length* of the seasons. In the year of the calendar, each season extends over a period of three calendar months; and the same three months every year compose the same season, whatsoever may be the nature of the weather. Every season of the calendar is thus of the same length. The seasons of the agricultural year, though bearing the same names as those of the calendar, are, on the other hand, not of the same length every year, but their duration is regulated by the state of the weather. The agricultural seasons have characteristic signs to distinguish them. The spring revives the dormant powers of vegetables; the summer enlarges their growth; the autumn develops the means of reproduction; and the winter puts a stop to vegetable energy. In the year of the calendar these characteristics are assumed to last just three months in each season, but in the agricultural year, notwithstanding that the characteristics of one season extend over, or are contracted within three months, still that season bears its proper name, whether it encroaches on or is encroached upon by another season. The spring, for example, may be encroached on by the protraction of winter on the one hand, and the earliness of summer on the other; a case in which results both a late and short spring,—a state of spring which creates very bustling work to the farmer. So with the rest of the seasons. This elastic property in the agricultural seasons contradistinguishes them from the seasons of the calendar which possess no elasticity. The commencement, continuance, and termination of field work, being therefore entirely dependent on the seasons of the agricultural year, and those seasons, in their turn, being as dependent on the weather, it follows that field operations are entirely dependent on the state of the weather, and not on the conventional seasons of the calendar. Whether an agricultural season be long or short, the work that properly belongs to it *must* be finished in it whilst it lasts. If it be of sufficient length, the work to be performed, admitting of a considerable latitude of time, may be well finished, and if not so finished, the crop runs the risk of failure. Should any season happen to be shortened by the weather, by the preceding season encroaching upon it, the work should be so far advanced during the preceding prolonged season, that, when the proper season for its completion arrives, as arrive it will, the finishing may be accomplished before its expiry. Should any season be curtailed by the earliness of the succeeding one, and the weather improve, as in the case of summer appearing before its time, no apprehension need be entertained of accomplishing the finishing work in a satisfactory manner; but should the weather prove worse, as in the premature approach of winter upon autumn, then extraordinary exertions are required to avert the disastrous consequences of winter weather upon the crops. The unusual protraction of any of the seasons in which a work should be completed is attended with no risk, except that too frequently from the consciousness of having plenty of time to complete the work, unnecessary delay is permitted, until the succeeding season unexpectedly makes its appearance. In such cases procrastination is truly the thief of time. During the protraction of a season, much time is often wasted in waiting for the arrival of the succeeding one, in which a particular work is most properly finished; but in a contracted season, a great part of the work is hurriedly gone through, and of course slovenly performed. The most perfect field-work is performed when the agricultural and conventional seasons happen to coincide in duration.

The greatest difficulty which the farmer experiences when first assuming the management of a farm is in distributing and adjusting labour. To accomplish this distribution and adjustment correctly, in reference to the work, and with ease as regards the labourer, a thorough knowledge is requisite of the quantity of work that can be performed in a given time by all the instruments of labour, animal and mechanical, usually employed. It is the duty of the young farmer to acquire this knowledge with all diligence and dispatch; for a correct *distribution* of the instruments of labour enables the work to be performed in the most perfect manner in regard to the soil,—with the smallest exertion as regards physical force,—and with the greatest celerity in regard to time; and, in the *adjustment* of those instruments, every one should just perform its own share of work. These essential particulars I shall point out, in their connection with the work in hand. In descanting on the distribution of labour, I shall incur the hazard of being prolix rather than superficial. The general reader may dislike the perusal of minute details; but the ardent student will receive with thankfulness the minutest portion of instruction, especially as he can only otherwise acquire this kind of instruction by long experience. The distribution and adjustment of labour is a branch of farm management that has been entirely overlooked by every writer on systematic agriculture.

Constant attention on the part of the young farmer to the minutiæ of labour evinces in him that sort of acuteness which perceives the quickest mode of acquiring his profession. The distribution of the larger pieces of work may proceed satisfactorily enough under the skill of ordinary work-people; but the minuter can *best* be adjusted by the master or steward. The larger operations would always be left in a coarse state, were the smaller not to follow, and finish them off neatly. There are many minor operations, unconnected with greater, which should be skilfully performed for the sake of their own results; and they should be so arranged as to be performed with neatness and dispatch. Many of them are frequently performed concurrently with the larger operations; and to avoid confusion both their concurrent labours should harmonize. Many of the minuter operations are confined to the tending of live-stock, and the various works performed about the farmstead. Attention to minutiæ, constituting the chief difference betwixt the neat and careless farmer, I have bestowed due consideration on them. They form another particular which has been too much overlooked by systematic writers on agriculture.

Implements of husbandry may be considered the right hand of the farmer; because, without their aid, he could not display the *skill* of his art. Modern mechanical skill has effected much by the improvement of old, and the invention of new implements. Modifications of construction and unusual combinations of parts are frequently attempted by mechanics; and though many such attempts issue in failure, they nevertheless tend to divulge new combinations of mechanical action. It is desirable that all mechanists of implements should understand practical agriculture, and all farmers study the principles of mechanics and the construction of machines, so that their conjoined judgment and skill might be exercised in testing the practical utility of implements. When unacquainted with farming, mechanists are apt to construct implements that are obviously unsuited to the work they are intended to execute; but having been put together after repeated alterations, and, probably, at considerable expense, the makers endeavour to induce those farmers who are no adepts at mechanics to give them a trial. After some unsatisfactory trials they are thrown aside. Were farmers acquainted with the principles of mechanics, the discrimination which such knowledge would impart would, through them, form a barrier against the spread of implements of questionable utility, and only those find circulation which had been proved to be simple, strong, and efficient. It may be no easy matter to contrive implements possessing all those desirable qualities; but, as they are much exposed to the weather, and the ground upon which they have to act being ponderous and uncouth, it is necessary they should be of simple construction. Simplicity of construction, however, has its useful limits. Most farm operations being of themselves simple, should be performed with simple implements; and all the *primary* operations, which are simple, requiring considerable power, the implements executing them should also be *strong;* but operations that are complicated, though stationary, require to be performed with comparatively complicated machinery, which, being stationary, may be used without derangement. Operations that are both complicated and locomotive should be performed with implements producing complicated action by simple means, in order to avoid derangement of their constituent parts. This last is a difficult, if not impossible problem, to solve in practical mechanics. The common plough approaches more nearly to its practical solution than any other implement; yet that truly wonderful implement, executing difficult work by simple means, should yet be so modified in construction, as to permit the ploughman to wield it with greater ease. These considerations tend to shew, that the form and construction of implements of husbandry, and the circumstances in which they may be used, are still subjects affording ample scope upon which mechanical skill can exercise itself.

Implements have not received in works on agriculture that consideration which their importance demands. The figures of them have been made by draftsmen, who have evidently had no accurate conception of the functions of their constituent parts. The descriptions given of those constituent parts are generally meagre, and not unfrequently erroneous; and as to the best mode of using implements, and the accidents to which they are liable, one would never discover that there was any peculiarity in the one, or liability to the other. In order to avoid both these classes of errors, much care has been bestowed in this work in delineating the figures, and giving descriptions of all the implements requisite for conducting a farm.

To insure accuracy in these respects, I consider myself fortunate in having acquired the assistance of Mr James Slight, Curator of the Machines and Models in the Museum of the Highland and Agricultural Society of Scotland, whose high qualifications as a describer and maker of machines are duly appreciated in Scotland. His son George, yet a very young man, is a beautiful delineator of them, as the drawings of the cuts and engravings in this work amply testify. And having myself paid close attention to the applicability of most of the implements used in farm operations, I have undertaken to describe the mode of using them, to state the quantity of work which each should perform, the accidents to which each is liable, and the precautions which should be used to avoid accidents. With our united efforts, I have confidence of giving such an *exposé* of farm implements as will surpass every other work of the kind. We have the advantage of having the field to ourselves. To assist the right understanding of the implements, they are represented by figures. Wood-cuts placed in the letter-press is the most convenient, and perhaps the most satisfactory, mode of illustration; but as the essential constituent parts of complicated implements are too much hidden for such a mode of illustration, such implements are engraved on separate plates.

So much for the practical, and now for the scientific portion of the work. Agriculture may, perhaps, truly be considered one of the experimental sciences, as its principles are no doubt demonstrable by the test of experiment, although farmers have not yet been able to deduce principles from practice. It is remarkable, that very few scientific men have as yet been induced to subject agricultural practice to scientific research; and those of them who have devoted a portion of their time to the investigation of its principles have imparted little or no satisfactory information on the subject. This unfortunate result may probably have arisen from the circumstance, that agriculture has so intimate a relation to every physical science, that, until all those relations are first investigated, no sufficient data can be offered for a satisfactory scientific explanation of its practice. The difficulty of the investigation is, no doubt, much enhanced, by husbandry being usually pursued as a purely practical art, because the facility of thus pursuing it successfully renders practical men indifferent to science. They consider it unnecessary to burden their minds with scientific research, whilst practice is sufficient for their purpose. Could the man of practice, however, supply the man of science with a series of accurate observations on the leading operations of the farm, the principles of those operations might be much elucidated; but I conceive the greatest obstacle to the advancement of scientific agriculture is to be sought for in the unacquaintance of men of science with practical agriculture. Would the man of science become acquainted with practice, much greater advancement in scientific agriculture might be expected than if the practical man were to become a man of science, because men of science are best capable of conducting scientific research, and, being so qualified, could best understand the relation which their investigations bore to practice; and, until the relation betwixt principles and practice are well understood, scientific researches, though perhaps important in themselves, and interesting in their results, tend to no practical utility in agriculture. In short, until the facts of husbandry be acquired by practice, men of science will in vain endeavour to construct a satisfactory theory of agriculture on the principles of the inductive philosophy.

If this view of the present position of the science of agriculture be correct, it may be expected to remain in a state of quiescence until men of science become practical agriculturists, or, what would still prolong its state of dormancy, until farmers acquire scientific knowledge. It is a pity to damp the ardour of scientific pursuit where it is found to exist; but, from what I have observed of the scanty services science has hitherto conferred on agriculture, and knowing the almost helpless dependency of farming on the seasons, I am reluctantly impelled to the belief, that it is less in the power of science to benefit agriculture, than the sanguine expectations of many of its true friends would lead farmers to believe. It is wrong to doubt the power of science to assist agriculture materially; and it is possible, in this age of successful art, that an unexpected discovery in science may yet throw a flood of light on the path of the husbandman; but I am pretty sure, unless the man of science become also the practical husbandman, it will be difficult, if not impossible, for him to discover which department of the complicated art of husbandry is most accessible to the research of science.

Hitherto, as it appears to me, agriculture has derived little benefit from the sciences, notwithstanding its obvious connection with many of them. A short review of the relation which the physical sciences bear to agriculture will render this opinion more reasonable. In the first place, the action of the electric agency in the atmosphere and on vegetation is yet as little understood in a practical sense as in the days of Franklin and of Ellis. No doubt, the magnetic and electric influences are now nearly identified ; but the mode of action of either, or of both, in producing and regulating atmospherical phenomena, is still ill understood ; and, so long as obscurity exists in regard to the influence of their elementary principles, the history of atmospherical phenomena cannot advance, and the anticipations of atmospherical changes cannot be trusted.

Geologists, at first engaged in ascertaining the relative positions of the harder rocks composing the crust of the earth, have only of late years directed their attention to the investigation of the more recent deposits ; but, even with these, they have afforded no assistance in the classification of natural soils and subsoils. They have never yet explained the origin of a surface-soil, almost always thin, though differing in thickness, over subsoils composed of different kinds of deposits. They have never yet ascertained the position and structure of subsoil deposits, so as to inform the farmer whether land would be most effectually drained with drains running parallel with, or at right angles to, the courses of valleys and rivers.

Systematic botany can only be useful to agriculture in describing the natural plants which are indigenous to different soils. Botanists have successfully shewn the intimate relation subsisting betwixt plants and the soils on which they grow ; but much yet remains to be ascertained of the relation betwixt different soils and trees, and the effects of different subsoils on the same kind of tree. Planting cannot be pursued on fixed principles, if planters are unacquainted with this knowledge ; and, until a fixed and generally received classification of soils and subsoils is determined on, it is impossible to comprehend, by description, what particular soil or soils the plants referred to affect.

Botanical physiology has developed many remarkable phenomena, and explained most of the important functions of plants,—investigations which tend to give a clearer insight into the growth of crops. In this department of science, too much discussion to be of benefit to agriculture has, as I conceive, been expended on what really constitutes the food of plants. Whether the food is taken up by the plant in a gaseous, a solid, or a liquid state, may in itself be a very interesting inquiry, but it tends to no utility in agriculture so long as no manures are supplied to crops in a gaseous or liquid state. All that can practically be done in supplying food to plants, is to observe the increased quantity of their secretions in a given condition from an increased given quantity of manure. Thus may the increased quantities of mucilage, farina, gluten, in the various cultivated plants, be observed. It is of little moment to the farmer whether the manure administered is taken up by the crops in a gaseous, liquid, or solid state, since all these secretions are elaborated from the same manure. The anatomical structure of plants, the situations, soils, and manures which crops affect, the secretions which they elaborate, and the prolificacy and value of their products, are the results that most interest the farmer ; and, if botanical physiologists desire to benefit agriculture, they must direct their attention to the emendation and increase of products. Again, the results from the cross impregnation of plants of the same kind, so as to produce valuable permanent varieties, may confer as valuable a boon on agriculture, as the successful crossings of different breeds of live-stock have already conferred by increasing their value. Many varieties of plants having their origin in this way have been brought into notice, and some are now established and extensively cultivated ; but most of the varieties in use have been obtained from casual impregnations effected by nature herself, and not by the efforts of man to obtain varieties possessing superior properties, as in the case of the domesticated animals. Thus botanical physiology might confer great benefit on agriculture, if its views were directed to increasing the prolificacy of valuable plants already in cultivation, and introducing others that would withstand the modes of culture and changes of climate incidental to this country.

But there is one view in which botanical physiology may be of use to agriculture, and that is, in ascertaining correctly the nature, properties, and relative values of plants. To shew the importance of such an investigation, a case may here be specified. A variety of rye-grass, called Italian, has been lately introduced into this country. It is found to be a very free grower in this climate ; and it is highly acceptable to all kinds of live-stock, whether in a green or dried state. Could this grass be rendered certainly perennial, it would be an invaluable acquisition to the pastures of this country. Its character, however, is rather capricious, for in some places it disappears after two years' cultivation, whilst in others it displays undiminished vigour of growth for four or five years, and may perhaps continue so to do for an indefinite period of time. Judging by these various results, it is probable that there is more than one variety of the plant, and distinguishing varieties seem to be known to foreigners. Keeping in view the existence of varieties, if different varieties were affected differently by the same locality, there would be nothing in the phenomenon to excite surprise ; but when the same variety, derived from the same stock, and placed in similar circumstances, exhibits different instances of longevity, there must be characteristics of the plant still unknown to cultivators. In this dilemma, the assistance of the botanical physiologist would be desirable to discover those latent characteristics. It would be desirable to know the conditions that regulate the existence of plants into permanent and temporary varieties,—a property of plants at present involved in mystery. Hitherto, no practical explanation of the subject has been proffered to the farmer; and so long as he shall be permitted to discover the true properties of plants for himself, botanical physiology cannot be regarded by him as of much use to agriculture.

The Italian ryegrass exhibits in its nature an anomaly that no other variety of ryegrass does. The *annual* ryegrass, as it is commonly called, is seldom seen in the ground, even to the extent of a few plants, in any kind of soil, and under any treatment, after the second year; and the *perennial* is as seldom observed to fail in any circumstances, except when it may have been too closely cropped by sheep to the ground too late in autumn, when it generally dies off in the following spring. But the Italian may be annual or perennial in the same circumstances. Farmers cannot account for such an anomaly. High condition of good soil may tend to prolong, whilst the opposite state of poor soil may tend to shorten, its existence. But *why* those circumstances should not produce the same effects on all varieties of ryegrass, it is for science to explain.

Entomology might be made to serve agriculture more than it has yet done. In this department of science, farmers might greatly assist the entomologist, by observing the minute, but varied and interesting, habits of insects. The difficulty of comprehending the true impulses of insects, as well as of identifying species in the different states of transformation, render the observations of farmers less exact than those of entomologists who have successfully studied the technicalities of the science. The field of observation in the insect creation being very wide, and there being comparatively but few explorers in it, a large portion of a man's life would be occupied in merely observing species and their habits, and a much larger in forming general deductions from repeated observation. The result would be, were farmers to study entomology, that a long period must elapse ere the habits of even the most common destructive insects, and the marks of their identity, would become familiarised to them. In consequence of this obstacle to the study of the farmer, the obligation ought to be the greater to those entomologists who daily observe the habits of insects in the fields and woods, and simplify their individual characteristics; and at the same time devise plans to evade their extensive ravages, and recommend simple and effective means for their destruction. The English farmer, living in a climate congenial to the development of insect life, painfully experiences their destructive powers on crops and woods; and, although in England entomologists are ever vigilant and active, yet their efforts easily to overcome the tenacity of insect life, with a regard to the safety of the plant, have hitherto proved unavailing.

Chemistry is somehow imagined to be the science that can confer the greatest benefits on agriculture. This opinion seems confirmed in the minds of most writers and agriculturists, and especially the English, most probably from the circumstance of an eminent chemist having been the first to undertake the explanation of agricultural practice on strictly scientific principles. Sir Humphry Davy has, no doubt, been the cause of bestowing on that science a character, whose influence was imagined to be more capable of benefiting agriculture than its eulogists have since been able to establish. He endeavoured to explain with great acuteness many of the most familiar phenomena of agriculture, when in possession of very limited acquaintance with practical facts; and the result has been, that whilst his own chemical researches have conferred no practical benefit on agriculture—his conclusions being in collision with practice—the field of observation and experiment which he explored and traversed has since been carefully avoided by succeeding chemists, in the conviction, no doubt, that wherein he failed, they were not likely to succeed. The idea seemed never to have struck them, that Sir Humphry had attempted to enforce a connection betwixt chemistry and agriculture which both were incapable of maintaining. Viewing the relation betwixt them merely in a practical point of view, I can see no very obvious connection betwixt tilling the soil, and forcing crops by manure for the support of man and beast,—which is the chief end of agriculture,—and ascertaining the constituent parts of material bodies, organic and inorganic,—which is the principal business of chemistry. A knowledge of the constituent parts of soils, plants, or manures, now forms a necessary branch of general chemical education, but *how* that knowledge *can improve agricultural practice*, has never yet been practically demonstrated. No doubt, chemistry informs us that plants will not vegetate in pure earths, and that those earths constitute the principal basis of all soils; but as pure earths are never found in soils, in their ordinary state, farmers can have no chance of raising crops on them. It may be true, as chemistry intimates, that plants imbibe their food only when in a state of solution; but what avails this fact to agriculture, if fact it be, when manures are only applied in a solid state? It may be quite true, as chemistry declares, that plants cannot supply, from their composition, any substance they have not previously derived from the air, earth, or decomposed organic matter; but of what practical use to agriculture is this declaration, as long as farmers successfully raise every variety of crop from the same manure? Chemistry may be quite correct in its views with regard to all these particulars, but so is practice, and yet both are very far from agreeing; and as long as this constitutes the only sort of information that chemistry affords, it is unimportant to the farmer. He wishes to be shewn *how* to render the soil more fertile, manures more effective, and crops more prolific, by the practical application of chemical principles.

There are many writers, I am convinced, who recommend the study of chemistry to farmers little acquainted with the true objects of chemical research, and not much more with practical agriculture. At all events, they expatiate, only in vague generalities, on the advantages of analyzing soils, manures, &c., but do not attempt to demonstrate *how* any practice of husbandry may *certainly* be improved by the suggestions of chemistry. The truth is, until chemists become thoroughly acquainted with agricultural facts, they cannot see the bearings of chemical principles on agricultural practice, any more than the most uncouth farmer; and until they prove the farmer's practice in any one instance wrong, and are *certain* of its being put right by their suggestions, there is no use of lauding chemistry as a paramount science for agriculture.

In this view of the science, I would rather underrate the ability of chemistry to benefit agriculture, than excite the fallacious hopes of the farmer by extolling it with undue praise. At the same time, were a chemist to recommend suggestions, promising a favourable issue, *that* might tend to excite a well grounded hope in chemical assistance, and I am sure the suggestions would even be fairly tried by farmers who entertain pretty strong suspicions against science. If, for example, on carefully analyzing a plant in common culture, it was found to contain an ingredient which it could not obviously have derived from the manure or the soil, were a suggestion made to mix a quantity of that particular ingredient with the soil or manure, it would at once be cheerfully put to the test of experiment by farmers. If, on the other hand, were the same chemist to suggest making heavy clay land friable by the mechanical admixture of sand, the physical impracticability of the proposal would at once convince the farmer that the chemist had no adequate notion of farm work. And yet propositions as absurd as this have frequently been suggested to farmers by writers who are continually maintaining the ability of chemistry to benefit agriculture. But let me appeal to facts,—to ordinary experience.

I am not aware of a single agricultural practice that has been adopted from the suggestions of chemistry. I am not speaking unadvisedly while making this unqualified statement. In truth, I do not know a single operation of the farm that has not originated in sheer practice. But is it not somewhat unreasonable to expect improvement in agricultural practice, and still more, an entirely improved system of agriculture from the suggestions of chemistry? Some chemical results may appear to bear analogy to certain operations of the farm, such as the preparation of manures; but such analogies, being chiefly accidental, are of themselves insufficient grounds upon which to recommend chemical affinity as the principle which ought to regulate a system of practically mechanical operations. How can the most familiar acquaintance with the chemical constituents of all the substances found on a farm, suggest a different mode of making them into manure, inasmuch as *practice* must first pronounce the treatment to be an improvement, before it can really be an improvement, whatever chemistry may suggest? Besides, chemistry, with all its knowledge of the constituent parts of substances, cannot foretel, more confidently than practice, the results of the combinations with the soil, of the substances analyzed amongst themselves, and the combined effects of these and the soil upon cultivated plants. I am aware that hints may be suggested by science which may prove beneficial to practise; but unless they *accord with the nature of the practice* to which they are proposed to be applied, they are certain of proving unserviceable. Many hints thrown out at random, have frequently been put to the test of experiment; but to experimentize on hints, is quite a different thing in farming, from that sort of farming which is proposed to be entirely based on theoretical suggestions, whether of chemistry or of any other science.

For these reasons, I conceive, chemists would be more usefully employed in following than in attempting to lead practical agriculture. If it were practicable, it would certainly be very desirable for the farmer to be assured that his practice was in accordance with chemical principles; if, for example, it could be explained on chemical principles *why* a certain class of soils is better suited to a certain kind of crop than other classes, and *why* animal manure is better suited than vegetable to a certain kind of crop; when chemistry shall explain *why* certain results are obtained by practice, it will accomplish much, it will elucidate that which was before obscure in principle. Were chemists to confine the first stage of their investigations of agricultural matters to this extent, farmers would be much gratified with the assurance of their practice being in unison with the principles of chemical science; and this would tend more than any other circumstance to inspire them with confidence in the utility of that science. This is the position which chemistry, in my opinion, should occupy in relation to agriculture; for how successful soever it may be in assisting other arts, such as dyeing, soap-making, and ink-making, it assists them both by synthesis and analysis; whereas it can only investigate agricultural subjects by analysis; because every substance employed in agriculture, especially a manure, is used by farmers in the state it is found in the markets, without reference to its chemical constituent parts; and, when used, should an analytical or synthetical process go on amongst those parts, or with the soil, with which they are intimately brought into contact, the process going on in the *soil* would change the chemical composition of the whole, and place them beyond the reach of chemical research. The investigation of the soil after the removal of the crop might then be curious, but nothing more. In this investigation, the farmer, the vegetable physiologist, and the chemist, would all disagree as to the extent of the influence exercised by the favourite substance of each in producing the crop. In settling the question, however, the farmer would have the same advantage over his rivals, in taking possession of the crop as the reward of *his practical* skill, as the lawyer who, in announcing the judgment of the court to two contending parties, gave a shell to each, and kept the oyster to himself.

Of all the sciences, mechanics have proved the most useful to agriculture. If implements may be characterised as the right hand of agriculture, mechanical science, in improving their form and construction, may be said to have given cunning to that right hand; for, mechanical science, testing the strength of materials, both relatively and absolutely, employs no more material in implements than is sufficient to overcome the force of resistance, and it induces to the discovery of that form which overcomes resistance with the least power. Simplicity of construction, beauty of form of the constituent parts, mathematical adjustment, and symmetrical proportion of the whole machine, are now the characteristics of our implements; and it is the fault of the hand that guides them, if field-work is not now dexterously, neatly, and quickly performed. In saying thus much for the science that has improved our implements to the state they now are, when compared with their state some years ago, I am not averring they are quite perfect. They are, however, so far perfect as to be correct in mechanical principle, and light in operation, though not yet simple enough in construction. No doubt many may yet be much simplified in construction; and I consider the machinist who simplifies the action of any useful implement, thereby rendering it less liable to derangement, does as good service to agriculture as the inventor of a new and useful implement.

These are the principles which determine the arrangement adopted in this book. In applying these principles, as the *seasons* supremely rule the destiny of every farming operation, so to them is given full sway over the whole arrangement. This is accomplished by describing every operation *in the season it should be performed*, and this condition necessarily implies the subdivision of the arrangement into *four seasons*. Authors of Farmers' Calendars divide their subject-matter into calendar or fixed months, being apparently inattentive to the influences of the seasons. Such an arrangement cannot fail to create confusion in the minds of young farmers; as any operation that is directed to be done in any month, may not, in every year, be performed in the same month, on account of the fluctuating nature of the seasons.

In adopting the seasons as the great divisor of the labours of the farm, the months which each season occupies are not specified by name, because the same season does not occupy the same number of months, nor even exactly the same months, in every year. The same work, however, is performed in the same season every year, though not perhaps in the same month or months.

In arranging the seasons themselves, the one which commences the agricultural year, which is *Winter*, has the precedence. The rest follow in the natural succession of Spring, Summer, and Autumn, in which last, all farming operations, having finished their annual circuit, finally terminate. A few remarks, illustrative of its nature, and the work performed in it, are given at the commencement of each season. By comparing these introductory remarks one with the others, the nature of the principal operations throughout the year may be discovered, and by perusing them in succession as they follow, an epitome of the entire farm operations for the year may be obtained.

Throughout the four seasons, from the commencement of winter to the end of autumn, the operations of the farm, both great and small, are described in a continued narrative. This narrative is printed in the largest type used (*small pica*). The reader will soon discover that this narrative does not extend uninterruptedly through the whole pages; portions of smaller type (*bourgeois*), intervening, and apparently interrupting it. On passing over the small type, it will be perceived that it is really written, and may be perused without interruption. The object of this plan is to permit the necessary descriptions of all the operations, performed in succession throughout the year, to be read in the large type, to the exclusion of every other matter that might distract the attention of the reader from the principal subject. A peristrephic view, so to speak, of the entire operations of the farm is thus obtained. The leading operations forming the principal subjects of the narrative, are distinguished by appropriate titles in CAPITALS placed across the middle of the page. The titles are numbered by the single Roman numeral (thus, 1.) constituting, in the aggregate, a continuous succession of *titles* running, arithmetically numbered, through all the seasons. The leading operations thus easily attract the eye. The minutiæ or minor operations forming the constituent parts of the principal operation to which they belong, each implying some specific change in the principal, is contained in a separate paragraph in the large type, and also numbered with the single Roman numeral, but between parentheses (thus, (1.)), the aggregate of which form a continuous succession of numbered *paragraphs* through all the seasons. A *word* or *words* characterising most explicitly the nature of the minor operation, are put in *italics*, at or near the beginning of each paragraph. Thus not only the principal operations, but all the minor, which they involve, may at once be ascertained. Wood-cut figures of implements, and other objects, requiring no detailed descriptions, and representing at once their form and use, are inserted in the paragraph which alludes to them in the narrative. The reasons for performing both the principal and minor operations, in the manner directed, also form a part of the matter of the narrative.

Implements, on the other hand, that require detailed descriptions to explain, and complicated figures to represent them ;—reasons for preferring one mode to another of doing the same kind of work ;—and explanations of agricultural practice on scientific principles, together constituting the subsidiary portion of the work, are given in paragraphs in the medium-sized type (*bourgeois*), and this matter in the small type is that which apparently interrupts the principal narrative. Each paragraph is numbered with a single Roman numeral inclosed within parentheses (thus, (1.)) the same as in the principal narrative, and these paragraphs carry on the numbers arithmetically with the paragraphs of the principal narrative. When references are made from the large to the small type, they are made in corresponding numerals. The words most expressively characteristic of the illustration contained in the paragraph, are placed in *italics* at or near the beginning of it.

Marking *all* the paragraphs with numerals, greatly facilitates the finding out of any subject alluded to, saves repetition of descriptions when the same operation is performed in different seasons, and furnishes easy reference to subjects in the index.

Wood-cut figures of the intricate implements, and other objects requiring detailed descriptions, are placed among the descriptions of them in the bourgeois type. Figures of implements, and other objects too intricate to be represented with sufficient distinctness in wood-cuts, or very numerous for one subject, are engraved on steel-plates. The portraits of the animals given are intended to illustrate the *points* required to be attended to in the breeding of the domesticated animals. The portraits are taken from life by eminent artists. The wood-cuts are enumerated as they occur in the order of succession, whether they belong to the large or the small type, and each wood-cut is designated by its distinctive appellation; both the numeral and appellative being requisite for quick and easy reference.

The matter in the small type appears somewhat like foot-notes in ordinary books; but in this instance, it differs in character from foot-notes, inasmuch as its occurs in unbroken pages at the end of the description of every leading operation. By this plan the principal narrative is not interfered with, and both it and its illustrations may be perused before the succeeding leading operation and its illustrations are taken into consideration. This plan has the advantage of relieving the principal narrative of heavy foot-notes, the perusal of which, when long, not only seriously interrupts the thread of the narrative, but causes the leaves gone over to be turned back again; both interferences being serious drawbacks to the pleasant perusal of any book.

Foot-notes required either for the principal narrative or illustrations, are distinguished by the usual marks, and printed at the bottom of the page in the smallest type *(Minion)* used in this work.

The paragraphs containing the matter supplied by Mr Slight, are inclosed within brackets (thus, [ ]), and attested by his initials J. S.

---

5. OF THE EXISTING METHODS OF LEARNING PRACTICAL HUSBANDRY.

> I have vowed to hold the plough for her sweet love three year.
>
> LOVE'S LABOUR LOST.

I HAVE hinted that there are three states, in one of which the young farmer will be found when beginning to learn his profession. One is, when he himself is born and brought up on a farm, on which, of course, he may acquire a knowledge of farming intuitively as he would his mother tongue. Another is when he goes to school in boyhood, and remains there until ready to embark in the active business of farming; the impressions of his younger years will become much effaced, and he will require to renew his acquaintance with farming as he would of a language that he had forgotten. Young men thus early grounded, generally make the best farmers, because the great secret of knowing practical farming consists in bestowing particular attention on minor operations, which naturally present themselves to the youthful mind before it can perceive the use of general principles. Farmers so brought up seldom fail to increase their capital; and if their education has been superior to their rank in life, frequently succeed in improving their status in society. It is to the skilful conduct and economical management of farmers so situated, that Scotland owes the high station she occupies among the agricultural nations of the world.

The third state in which the learning of farming is requisite, is, when a young man, who has been educated and entirely brought up in a town, or perhaps passed his boyhood in the country, but may have bestowed little attention on farming, wishes to learn it as his profession. In either of these cases, it is absolutely necessary for him to learn it practically on a farm; for total ignorance of his business, and entire dependence on the skill and integrity of his servants, will soon involve him in pecuniary difficulties. To meet the wishes of seekers of agricultural knowledge, there are farmers who receive pupils as boarders, and undertake to teach them practical husbandry.

The chief inducement, as I conceive, which at first prompts young men, who have been nurtured in towns, to adopt farming as a profession, is an undefined desire to lead a country life. The desire often originates in this way. Most boys spend a few weeks in the country during the school vacation in summer, on a visit to relations, friends, or school companions. To them the period of vacation is a season of true enjoyment. Free of the task,—in the possession of unbounded liberty,—untrammelled by the restraints of time,—and partaking of sports new to them and solely appertaining to the country, they receive impressions of a state of happiness which are ever after identified with a country life. They regret the period of return to school,—leave the scene of those enjoyments with reluctance,—and conceive that their happiness would be perpetual, were their hearts wedded to the objects that captivated them. Hence the desire to return to those scenes.

It is conducive to the promotion of agriculture, that young birds of fortune are thus occasionally ensnared by the love of rural life. They bring capital into the profession, or, at all events, it will be forthcoming when the scion of his father's house has made up his mind to become a farmer. Besides, these immigrations into farms are requisite to supply the places of farmers who retire or die out. Various motives operate to bring farms into the market. Sons do not always follow their father's profession, or there may not be a son to succeed, or he may die, or choose another kind of life, or may have experienced ill treatment at home, or been guilty of errors which impel him to quit the paternal roof. For these drains, a supply must flow from other quarters to maintain the equilibrium of agricultural industry. This young race of men, converted into practical farmers, being generally highly born and well educated, assume at once a superior status in, and improve the tone of, rural society. Though they may amass no large fortunes, they live in good style. In the succeeding generation another change takes place. Unless he is well provided with a patrimony, the son seldom succeeds his father in the farm. The father finds he cannot give the farm free of burdens to one son in justice to the rest of the family. Rather than undertake to liquidate *such* a burden by means of a *farm*—that is, from land that is not to be his own—the son wisely relinquishes farming, which, in these circumstances, would be to him a life of pecuniary thraldom.

The young man who wishes to learn farming practically on a farm, should enter upon his task at the end of harvest, as, immediately after that, the preparatory operations commence for raising the next year's crop, and that is the season, therefore, which begins the new-year of farming. He should provide himself with an ample stock of *stout* clothing and shoes, capable of repelling cold and rain, and so made as to answer at once for walking and riding. From the outset, he must make up his mind to encounter all the difficulties I have described under the first head. Formidable as they may seem, I encourage him with the assurance, that it is in his power to overcome them all. The most satisfactory way of overcoming them is to resolve to learn his business in a truly practical manner. Merely being domiciled on a farm is not of itself a sufficient means of overcoming them, for the advantages of residence may be squandered away in idleness, by frequent absence, by spending the hours of work in the house in light reading, or by casual and capricious attendance on field operations. Such habits must be eschewed, before there can be a true desire to become a *practical* farmer. *Every* operation, whether important or trifling, should be *personally* attended to, as there is none but what tends to produce an anticipated result. Attention alone can render them familiar, and without a familiar acquaintance with every operation, the management of a farm need never be undertaken.

Much assistance in promoting this attention should not be *expected* from the farmer. No doubt it is his *duty* to communicate all he knows to his pupils; and, as I believe, most are willing to do so; but as efficient tuition implies constant attendance on work, the farmer himself cannot constantly attend to every operation, or even explain any, unless his attention is directed to it; and much less will he deliver extempore lectures at appointed times. Reservedness in him, does not necessarily imply *unwillingness* to communicate his skill; because, being himself familiar with every operation that can arrest the attention of his pupils, any explanation of minutiæ at any other time than when the work is in the act of being performed, and when only it could be *understood* by the pupils, would only serve to render the subject more perplexing. In these circumstances the best plan for the pupil to follow, is to *attend constantly*, and *personally observe* every change that takes place in every piece of work. Should the farmer happen to be present, and be appealed to, he will, as a matter of course, immediately clear up every difficulty in the most satisfactory way; but should he be absent, being otherwise engaged, then the steward or grieve, or any of the ploughmen, or shepherd, as the nature of the work may be, will, on inquiry, afford as much information on the spot as will serve to enlighten his mind until he associates with the farmer at the fireside.

To be enabled to discover that particular point in every operation, which, when explained, renders the whole intelligible, the pupil should put his hand to every kind of work, be it easy or difficult, irksome or pleasant. Experiences acquired by himself, however slightly affecting his mind,—desirous of becoming acquainted with every professional incident,—will solve difficulties much more *satisfactorily* than the most elaborate explanations given by others. The larger the stock of these personal experiences he can accumulate, the sooner will the pupil understand the purport of every thing that occurs in his sight. Daily opportunities occur on a farm for joining in work, and acquiring those experiences. For example, when the ploughs are employed, the pupil should walk from the one to the other, and observe which ploughman or pair of horses perform the work with the greatest apparent difficulty or ease. He should also mark the different styles of work executed by each plough. A considerate comparison of these particulars, will enable him to ascertain the best and worst specimens of work. He should then endeavour to discover the cause why different styles of work are produced by apparently very similar means, in order to enable himself to rectify the worst and practise the best. The surest way of detecting error and discovering the best method, is to take hold of each plough successively, and he will find in the endeavour to maintain each in a steady position, and perform the work evenly, that all require *considerable* labour—every muscle being awakened into energetic action, and the brow most probably moistened. As these symptoms of fatigue subside with repetitions of the exercise, he will eventually find one of the ploughs more easily guided than any of the rest. The reasons for this difference he must himself endeavour to find out by comparison, for its holder cannot inform him, because he professes to have, indeed can have, no knowledge of any other plough but his own. In prosecuting this system of trials with the ploughs, he will find himself becoming a ploughman, as the mysteries of the art divulge themselves to his apprehension; but the reason why the plough of one of the men moves more easily, does better work, and oppresses the horses less than any of the rest, is not so obvious; for the land is in the same state to them all, there cannot be much difference in the strength of the pairs of horses, as each pair are generally pretty well matched, and in all probability the construction of the ploughs is the same, if they have been made by the same ploughwright, yet one ploughman evidently exhibits a decided superiority in his work over the rest. The inevitable conclusion is, that ploughman understands his business better than the others. He shews this by trimming the irons of his plough to the state of the land, and the nature of the work he is about to perform, and by training his horses more in accordance with their natural temperament, whereby they are guided more tractably. Having the shrewdness to acquire these essential accomplishments to a superior degree, the execution of superior work is an easier task to him than inferior work to the other ploughmen. This case which I have selected for an example, is not altogether a supposititious one; for however dexterous all the ploughmen on a farm may be, one will always be found to shew a superiority over the rest.

Having advanced thus far in the knowledge and practice and capability of judging of work, the pupil begins to feel the importance of his acquisition; and this success will fan the flame of his enthusiasm, and prompt him to greater acquirements. But even in regard to the plough, the pupil has much to learn. Though he has picked out the best ploughman, and knows why he is so, he is himself still ignorant of how practically to trim a plough, and to drive the horses with discretion. The ploughman will be able to afford him ocular proof *how* he places (*tempers*) all the irons of the plough in relation to the state of the land, and *why* he yokes and drives the horses as he does in preference to any other plan. Illiterate and unmechanical as he is, and his language full of *technicalities*, his explanations will nevertheless give the pupil a clearer insight into the *minutiæ* of ploughing, than he could acquire by himself as a spectator in an indefinite length of time.

I have selected the plough, as being the most useful implement to illustrate the method which the pupil should follow, in all cases, to learn a *practical* knowledge of every operation in farming. In like manner, he may become acquainted with the particular mode of managing all the larger implements, which require the combined agency of man and horse to put into action; as well as become accustomed to wield the simpler implements used by the hand, easily and ambidextrously, a great part of farm-work being executed with simple but very efficient tools. Frequent *personal* attendance at the farm-stead, during the winter months, to view and conduct the thrashing-machine, while thrashing corn, and afterwards to superintend the winnowing-machine, in cleaning it for the market, will be amply repaid by the acquisition of essential knowledge regarding the nature and value of the cereal and leguminous grains. There is, moreover, no better method of acquiring an extensive knowledge of *all* the minor operations of the farm, than for the pupil personally to superintend the labours of the field-workers. Their labours are essential, methodical, almost always in requisition, and mostly consisting of minutiæ; and their general utility is shewn, not only in their intrinsic worth, but in relation to the labours of the teams.

The general introduction of sowing-machines, particularly those which sow broadcast, has nearly superseded the beautiful art of sowing corn by hand. Still a great deal of corn is sown by the hand, especially on small farms, on which expensive machines have not yet found their way. In the art of hand-sowing, the pupil should endeavour to excel, for, being difficult to perform it in an easy and neat manner, the superior execution of it is regarded as an accomplishment. It is, besides, a manly and healthful exercise, conducive to the establishment of a robust frame and sound constitution.

The feeding of cattle in the farm-stead, or of sheep in the fields on turnips, does not admit of much participation of labour with the cattle-man or shepherd; but nevertheless, either practice will form an interesting subject of study to the pupil, and without strict attention to both, he will never acquire a knowledge of fattening live-stock, and of computing their value.

By steadily pursuing the course of observation which I have thus chalked out, and particularly in the first year of his apprenticeship, the pupil, in a short time, will acquire a *considerable* knowledge of the minutiæ of labour; and it is only in this way that the groundwork for a familiar acquaintance with them can be laid. A truly familiar acquaintance with them requires years of experience. Indeed, observant farmers are learning some new, or modifications of some old, practice every day, and such new-like occurrences serve to keep alive in them a regard for the most trivial incident that happens on a farm.

In urging upon the pupil the *necessity* of putting to his hand to every kind of labour, I do not mean to say he should become a first-rate workman. To become so would require a much longer time than he could spare in a period of pupilage. His personal acquaintance with every implement and operation should, however, enable him by that time to decide quickly, whether work is well or ill done, and whether it has been executed in a reasonable time. No doubt this extent of knowledge may be acquired *in time*, without the actual labour of the hands; but, as it is the interest of the pupil to learn his profession not only in the shortest possible time, but in the best manner, and as these can be acquired sooner through the joint co-operation of the head and hands, than by either singly, it would seem imperative on him to begin to acquire his profession by labour.

Other considerations regarding the acquisition of practical knowledge deserve the attention of the pupil. It is most conducive to his interest to learn his profession in youth, and before the meridian of life has set in when labour of every kind becomes irksome. It is also much better to have a *thorough* knowledge of farming, *before* engaging in it on his own account, than to acquire it in the course of a lease, during which heavy losses may be incurred by the commission of comparatively trivial errors, especially at the early period of its tenure, when farms in all cases are most difficult to conduct. It is an undeniable fact, that the work of a farm never proceeds *so* smoothly and satisfactorily to all parties engaged in its culture, as when the farmer is thoroughly master of his business. His orders are then implicitly obeyed, not because they are pronounced more authoritatively, but because a skilful master's plans and directions inspire that degree of confidence in the labourers as to believe them to be the best that could be devised in the circumstances. Shame is often acutely felt by servants, on being detected in error, whether of the head or heart, by so competent and discriminating a judge as a skilful master; because rebuke from such a one implies ignorance or negligence in those against whom it is directed. The fear of having ignorance and idleness imputed to them, by a farmer who has become acquainted with the capabilities of work-people by dint of his own experience, and can estimate their services as they really deserve, urges labourers to do a fair day's work in a workmanlike style.

Let the converse of all these circumstances be imagined; let the losses to which the ignorant farmer is a daily prey, by many ways—by hypocrisy, by negligence, by idleness, and by dishonesty of servants—be calculated, and it must be admitted that it is infinitely safer for the farmer to trust to his own skill for the fulfilment of his engagements, than entirely to depend on that of his servants, which he will be obliged to do, if they know his business better than he himself does. No doubt a trust-worthy steward may be found to manage well enough for him, and such an assistant is at all times valuable; but, in such a position, the steward himself is placed in a state of temptation, in which he should never be put; and, besides, the inferior servants never regard him as a master and his orders are never so punctually obeyed, where the master himself is resident. I would, therefore, advise every young farmer to acquire a *competent* knowledge of his profession, before embarking in the complicated undertaking of conducting a farm. I only say a competent knowledge; for the gift to excel is not imparted to all who select farming as their profession; "it is not in man who walketh to direct his *steps*" aright, much less to attune his *mind* to the highest attainments.

Before the pupil fixes on any particular farm for his temporary abode, he should duly consider the objects he wishes to attain. I presume his chief aim is to attain such an intimate knowledge of farming, as to enable him to employ his capital safely, in the prosecution of the highest department of his profession. This will probably be best attained by learning that system which presents the greatest safeguards against unforeseen contingencies. Now, there is little doubt that the kind of farming which cultivates a variety of produce, is more likely to be safe, during a lease, in regard both to highness of price and quantity of produce, than that which only raises one kind of produce, whether wholly of animals, or wholly of grain. For, although one kind of produce, when it happens to be prolific or high priced, may, in one year, return a greater profit than a variety of produce in the same year; yet the probabilities are much against the frequent recurrence of such a circumstance. The probability rather is, that one of the varieties of produce will succeed, in price or produce, every year, and therefore in every year there will be a certain degree of success in that mode of farming which raises a variety of produce. Take, as an example, the experience of late years. All kinds of live-stock have been reared with profit for some years past; but the case is different in regard to grain. Growers of grain have suffered greatly in their capital in that time. And yet, to derive the fullest advantages from even the rearing of stock, it is necessary to cultivate a certain extent of land upon which to raise straw and green crop for them in winter. Hence that system is the best for the young farmer to learn, which cultivates a relative proportion of stock and crop, and not either singly. This has been characterised as the *mixed* system of husbandry. It avoids, on the one hand, the monotony and inactivity attendant on the raising of grain, and subdues, on the other, the roving disposition engendered in the tending of live-stock in a pastoral district; so it blends both occupations into a happy union of cheerfulness and quiet.

Most farmers in the lowlands of Scotland practise the mixed husbandry, but it is reduced to a perfect system nowhere so fully as in the Border counties of England and Scotland. There many farmers accept pupils, and thither many of the latter go to prepare themselves to become farmers. The usual fee for pupils, in that part of the country, is one hundred pounds per annum for bed and board, with the use of a horse to occasional markets and shows. If the pupil desire to have a horse of his own, about thirty pounds a-year more are demanded. On these moderate terms, pupils are generally very comfortably situated.

I am very doubtful of it being good policy to allow the pupil a horse of his own at first. Constant attention to field-labour is not unattended with irksomeness, and, on the other hand, exercise on horseback is a tempting recreation to young minds. Besides, the desire to possess a horse of one's own, is so very natural in a young person living in the country, that, were the pupil's inclinations alone consulted, the horse would soon be in his possession. So long as the choice is given to the indifferent pupil, he will certainly prefer pleasure to duty. The risk is, that the indulgence will be confirmed into a habit that will constantly lead him astray from attending to his business. Were his equestrian excursions confined to following the hounds upon all occasions, forming acquaintances at a distance from home, and loitering about towns on market-days, the roving pupil might see the state of the country, and acquire a knowledge of the world; but the evil of this kind of life is its being introductory to one of dissipation and extravagance. This consideration should have due weight with parents and guardians, in supplying their charge with the luxury of a horse, when placing him under the roof of a farmer. It is enough for a young man to feel the removal of parental restraint, without also having the dangerous incentive of an idle life placed at his disposal. They should consider that upon young men arrived at the years when they become farming pupils, it is not in the power, and is certainly not the inclination, of farmers to impose ungracious restraints. It is the duty of their parents and guardians to impose these; and the most effectual way that I know of, in the circumstances, to avoid temptations, is the denial of a riding-horse. Attention to business in the first year, will most probably induce a liking for it in the second, and after that, the indulgence of a horse may be granted to the pupil with impunity, as the reward of diligence. Until then, the horse occasionally supplied by the farmer, to attend particular markets, or pay friendly visits to neighbours, should suffice; and, as that is the farmer's own property, it will be more in his power to curb in his pupils any propensity to wander abroad too frequently, and thereby preserve his own character as a tutor. Such precautions are, of course, only necessary against pupils who shew lukewarmness towards farming. The prudent and diligent pupil who desires to learn his profession, will daily discover new sources of enjoyment at home, far more exhilarating, both to his body and mind, than in jogging along the dirty or dusty highway, until the jaded brute he bestrides is ready to sink under his burden.

Three years of apprenticeship are, in my opinion, requisite to give a pupil an adequate knowledge of farming,—such a knowledge, I mean, as would impress him with the confidence of being himself able to manage a farm; and no young man should undertake such a management until he feels this confidence in himself. Three years may be considered by many as too long a time to spend in learning *farming;* but after all, it is much less time than that given to many other professions, whose period of apprenticeship extends to five and even seven years; and however highly esteemed those professions may be, none possess a deeper interest, in a national point of view, than that of agriculture. There is a condition attendant on the art of farming, which is common to it and gardening, but inapplicable to most other arts,—that a year must elapse before the same work can again be performed. Whatever may be the ability of the learner to acquire farming, *time* must thus necessarily elapse before he can have the opportunity of again witnessing a bygone operation. There is no doubt of his natural capacity to acquire, in two years, the art to manage a farm, but the operations necessarily occupying a year in their performance, prevents that acquisition in less time than three. This circumstance of itself will cause him to spend a year in merely observing passing events. This is in his first year. As the operations of farming are all anticipatory, the second year may be fully employed in studying the progress of work in preparation of anticipated results. In the third year, when his mind has been stored with all the modes of doing work, and the purposes for which they are performed, the pupil may attempt to put his knowledge into practice, and his first efforts at management cannot be attempted with so much ease of mind to himself, as, on the farm of his tutor, under his correcting guidance.

This is the *usual* progress of tuition during the apprenticeship of the pupil; but could he be brought to anticipate results whilst watching the progress of passing events, one year might thus be cut off his apprenticeship. Could a *book* enable him to acquire the experience of the second year in the course of the first, a year of probationary trial would be saved him, as he would then acquire in two what requires three years to accomplish. *This* book will accomplish no small achievement,—will confer no small benefit on the agricultural pupil,—if it accomplish this.

6. OF THE ESTABLISHMENT OF SCIENTIFIC INSTITUTIONS OF PRACTICAL AGRICULTURE.

" Here let us breathe, and happily institute
A course of learning and ingenious studies."

TAMING OF THE SHREW.

Although I know of no existing plan so suited to the learning of practical farming, as a protracted residence on a farm, yet I feel assured a more efficient one might easily be proposed for the purpose. An evident and serious objection against the present plan is the want of that solicitous superintendence over the progress of the pupils, on the part of the farmer, which is implied in his receiving them under his *charge.* The pupils are left too much to their own discretion to learn farming effectually. They are not sufficiently warned of the obstacles they have to encounter at the outset of their career. Their minds are not sufficiently guarded against receiving a wrong bias in the methods of performing the operations. The advantages of performing them in one way rather than another, are not sufficiently indicated. The effects which a change of weather has in altering the arrangements of work fixed upon, and of substituting another more suited to the change, is not sufficiently explained. Instead of receiving explanatory information on these and many more particulars, the pupils are mostly left to find them out by their own diligence. If they express a desire to become acquainted with these things, no doubt it will be cheerfully gratified by the farmer; but how can the uninitiated pupil know the precise subject with which to express his desire to become acquainted?

In such a system of tuition, it is obvious that the diligent pupil may be daily perplexed by doubtful occurrences, and the indifferent pupil permit unexplained occurrences to pass before him, without notice. Reiterated occurrences will, in time, force themselves upon the attention of every class of pupils; but unless their attention is purposely drawn to, and explications proffered of, the more hidden difficulties in the art of farming, they will spend much time ere they be capable of discovering important occult matters by their own discernment.

It is in this respect that farmers, who profess to be tutors, shew, as I conceive, remissness in their duty to their pupils; for all of them can impart the information alluded to, and give, besides, a common-sense explanation of every occurrence that usually happens on a farm, otherwise they should decline pupils.

It is obvious that pupils should not to be placed in this disadvantageous position. They ought to be *taught* their profession; because the art of husbandry should be acquired, like every other art, by teaching, and not by intuition. On the other hand, pupils in this, as in every other art, ought to endeavour to acquire the largest portion of the knowledge of external things by their own observation; and they should be made aware by the farmer, that he can at most only *assist* them in their studies; so that, without much study on their parts, all the attention bestowed on their tuition by the most painstaking farmer will prove of little avail. Practical experience forms the essential portion of knowledge which farmers have to impart, and it is best imparted on the farm; but they have not always the leisure, by reason of their other avocations, to communicate even this on the spot in its due time. More than mere practical knowledge, however, is requisite to satisfy the mind of the diligent pupil. He wishes to be satisfied that he is learning the *best* method of conducting a farm: He wishes to be informed of the *reasons* why one mode of management is preferable to every other: He wishes to become *familiar* with the explanations of all the phenomena that are observable on a farm.

To afford all the requisite information to the pupil in the highest perfection, and to assist the farmer in affording it to him in the easiest manner, I propose the following plan of tuition for adoption, where circumstances will permit it to be established. The more minutely its details are explained, the better will it be understood by those who may wish to form such establishments.

Let a farmer of good natural abilities, of firm character, fair education, and pleasant manners, leasing a farm of not less than five hundred acres, and pursuing the mixed system of husbandry, occupy a house of such a size as would afford accommodation to from ten to twenty pupils. The farm should contain different varieties and conditions of soil,—be well fenced,—well watered,—and not at an inconvenient distance from a town.

With regard to the internal arrangements of the house, double-bedded rooms would form suitable enough sleeping apartments. Besides a dining-room and drawing-room, for daily use, there should be a large room, fitted up with a library, containing books affording *sound* information on all agricultural subjects, in various languages; forming at one time a lecture-room for the delivery of lectures on the elementary principles of those sciences which have a more immediate reference to agriculture, and at another a reading or writing room or parlour for conversations on farming subjects. There should be fixed, at suitable places, a barometer, a sympiesometer, thermometers, one of which should mark the lowest degree of temperature in the night, a rain-gauge, an anemometer, and a weathercock. No very useful information, in my opinion, can be derived by the *farmer*, from a bare *register* of the heights and depths of the barometer and thermometer. A more useful register for him would be that of the directions of the wind, accompanied with remarks on the state of the weather, the heat of the air as indicated by the feelings, and the character of the clouds as expressed by the most approved nomenclature. The dates of the commencement and termination of every leading operation on the farm should be noted down, and appropriate remarks on the state of the weather during its performance recorded. A small chemical laboratory would be useful in affording the means of analyzing substances whose component parts were not well known. Microscopes would be useful in observing the structure of plants and insects, for the better understanding of their respective functions.

The slaughter-house required for the preparation of the meat used by the family should be fitted up to afford facilities for dissecting those animals which have been affected by peculiar disease. Skeletons and preparations for illustrating comparative anatomy could thus be formed with little trouble. A roomy dairy should be fitted up for performing experiments on the productive properties of milk in all its various states. A portion of the farm-offices should be fitted up with apparatus for making experiments on the nutritive properties of different kinds and quantities of food, and the fattening properties of different kinds of animals. A steelyard, for easily ascertaining the live-weight of animals, is a requisite instrument. The bakery, which supplies the household bread, would be a proper place for trying the relative panary properties of different kinds of flour and meal. Besides these, apparatus for conducting experiments on other subjects as they were suggested, could be obtained when required.

Another person beside the farmer will be required to put all this apparatus into use. He should be a man of science, engaged for the express purpose of shewing the relation betwixt science and agriculture. There would be no difficulty of obtaining a man of science, quite competent to explain natural phenomena on scientific principles. For that purpose, he would require to have a familiar acquaintance with the following sciences:—with meteorology and electricity, in order to explain atmospherical phenomena, upon the mutations of which all the operations of farming are so dependent:—with hydrostatics and hydraulics, to explain the action of streams and of dammed-up water on embankments, to suggest plans for the recovery of land from rivers and the sea, and to indicate the states of the weather which increase or diminish the statical power of the sap in vegetables:—with botany and vegetable physiology, to shew the relations between the natural plants and the soils on which they grow, with a view to establish a closer affinity between the artificial state of the soil and the perfect growth of cultivated plants; to exhibit the structure of the different orders of cultivated plants; and to explain the nature and uses of the healthy, and the injurious effects of the diseased secretions of plants:—with geology, to explain the nature, and describe the structure, of the superficial crust of the earth, in reference to draining the soil; to shew the effects of subsoils on the growth of trees; to explain the effects of damp subsoils, on trees, and of the variations of the surface of the ground, on climate:—with mechanics, to explain the principles which regulate the action of all machines; and which acquirement previously implies a pretty familiar acquaintance with the mathematics:—with chemistry, to explain the nature of the composition of, and changes in, mineral, vegetable, and animal substances:—with anatomy and animal physiology, to explain the structure and functions of the animal economy, with a view to the prevention of disease, incidental to the usual treatment of animals, and to particular localities. All young men, educated for what are usually termed the learned professions,—theology, law, and medicine,—are made acquainted with these sciences, and a young man from either faculty would be competent to take charge of such an establishment. Of the three I would give preference to the *medical* man, as possessing professionally a more intimate knowledge of chemistry, and animal and vegetable physiology, than the others. But the most learned graduate of either profession, will display his scientific acquirements to little advantage in teaching pupils in agriculture, unless he has the judgment to select those parts of the various sciences, whose principles can most satisfactorily explain the operations of agriculture. Ere he can do this successfully, he would, I apprehend, require to know agriculture practically, by a previous residence of at least two years on a farm. Without such a preparation, he would never become a *useful* teacher of agricultural pupils.

On the supposition that he is so qualified, his duty is to take the direct charge of the pupils. His chief business should be to give demonstrations and explanations of all the phenomena occurring during operations in the farm field. The more popular demonstrations on botany, animal and vegetable physiology, and geology, as also on meteorology, optics, and astronomy, whenever phenomena occur which would call forth the application of the principles of any of those sciences, would be best conducted in the fields. In the library, short lectures on the elementary principles of science could be regularly delivered,—conversations on scientific and practical subjects conducted,—and portions of the most approved authors on agriculture, new and old, read. These latter subjects could be most closely prosecuted when bad weather interrupted field labour. In the laboratory, slaughter-house, farm-stead, and dairy, he could command the attendance of the pupils, when any subject in those departments were to be explained.

The duty of the farmer himself, the governor or head of the establishment, is to enforce proper discipline among the pupils, both within and without doors. He should teach them practically how to perform every species of work, explain the nature and object of every operation performing, and foretel the purport of every operation about to be performed. For these important purposes he should remain at home as much as is practicable with his avocations abroad.

The duties of the pupils are easily defined. They should be ready at all times to hear instruction, whether in science or practice, within or without doors. Those pupils who wish to study practice more than science, should not be constrained to act against their inclinations, as science possesses little allurement to some minds; and it should be borne in mind by the tutors, that practical farming is what the pupils have chiefly come to learn, and that practice may prove successful in after life without the assistance of science, whereas science can never be applied without practice.

The duty common to all, is the mutual conducting of experiments, both in the fields and garden; for which purpose, both should be of ample dimensions. All new varieties of plants might be first tried in the garden, until their quantity warranted the more profuse and less exact, though more satisfactory, culture of the field. On ridges in the fallow field, with different kinds and quantities of manure, and different modes of working the soil and sowing the seeds, experiments should be continually making with new and old kinds of grains, roots, tubers, bulbs, and herbaceous plants. In course of time, the sorts best suited to the locality will shew themselves, and should be retained, and the worthless abandoned. In like manner, experiments should be made in the crossing of animals, whether with the view of maintaining the purity of blood in one, the improvement of the blood of another, or the institution of an entirely new blood. In either class of experiments, many new and interesting facts, regarding the constitutional differences of animals, could not fail to be elicited.

Any farmer establishing such an institution, which could only be done at considerable expense, in fitting up a house in an adequate manner, and securing the services of a man of science, would deserve to be well remunerated. I before mentioned that one hundred pounds a-year as board were cheerfully given by pupils to farmers under ordinary circumstances. In such an institution, less than one hundred and fifty pounds a-year would not suffice to remunerate the farmer. Supposing that ten pupils at that fee each, were accommodated on one farm, the board would amount to fifteen hundred pounds a-year. In regard to the expense of maintaining such an establishment, with the exception of foreign produce and domestic luxuries, all the ordinary means of good living exist on a farm. The procuring of these necessaries and luxuries, and maintaining a retinue of grooms and domestic servants, together with the salary of an accomplished tutor, which should be not less than three hundred pounds a-year, besides board, would probably incur an annual disbursement of a thousand pounds a-year. The farmer would thus receive five hundred pounds a-year for risk of the want of the full complement of pupils, and for interest on the outlay of capital. Such a profit may be considered a fair, but not an extravagant remuneration for the comfortable style of living, and superior kind of tuition afforded in such an establishment.

Were the particulars pitched at a lower scale, a profit might be derived from ten pupils, of not less a sum than that derived from the usual board of one hundred pounds a-year. Were two hundred a-year exacted, pupils of the highest class of society might be expected. Were different institutions at different rates of board established, all the classes of society would be accommodated.

Would farmers who have accommodation for conducting such an institution, but duly consider the probable certainty of obtaining a considerable increase to their income, besides the higher distinction of conducting so useful an institution, I have no doubt many would make the attempt. There are insuperable obstacles to some farmers making the attempt; but there are many who possess the requisite qualifications of accommodation in house and farm locality, personal abilities, influence, and capital, for instituting such an establishment. But even where all these qualifications do not exist, most of the obstacles might be overcome. In the case of the house, it could be enlarged at the farmer's own expense, for the landlord cannot be expected to erect a farm-house beyond the wants of an ordinary family; nor, perhaps, would every small landed proprietor permit the unusual enlargement of a farm-house, in case it should be rendered unsuitable to the succeeding tenant. To avoid this latter difficulty, the farmer who could afford accommodation to the fewest number, could receive the highest class of pupils, were his own education and manners competent for the highest society, while those who had more accommodation could take a more numerous and less elevated rank of pupils. In either way the profit might be equally compensatory.

In regard to other considerations, a tutor entirely competent could not at once be found. It may safely be averred, that a really scientific man, thoroughly acquainted with the practice of agriculture, is not to be found in this country. But were a demand for the services of scientific men to arise, from the increase and steady prosperity of such establishments, no doubt, men of science would qualify themselves for the express purpose. As to pupils, the personal interest of the farmer might not avail him much at first, in influencing parents in his favour, but if he possess the reputation of being a good farmer, he would soon acquire fame for his institution. I have no doubt of an eminent farmer entirely succeeding to his wishes, who occupies a commodious house, on a large farm, in an agricultural district of high repute, and possessing sufficient capital, were he to make the experiment, by engaging a competent scientific tutor, and teaching the practical department himself. Such a combination of alluring circumstances could not fail of attracting pupils from all parts of the country, who were really desirous of learning agriculture in a superior manner.

There might still be another, though less attractive and efficacious, mode of accomplishing a similar end. Let a scientific tutor, after having acquired a competent knowledge of practical agriculture, procure a commodious and comfortable house, in any village in the vicinity of some large farms, in a fine agricultural district. Let him receive pupils into his house, on his own account, in such numbers, and at such fees, as he conceives would remunerate him for his trouble and risk. Every thing relating to science within doors, could be conducted as well in such a house as in any farm-house; and as to a field for practice, let the tutor give a douceur to each of the large farmers in his neighbourhood, for liberty for himself and pupils to come at will, and inspect all the operations of the farms. In this way a very considerable knowledge of farming might be imparted. Having every article of consumption to purchase at market-price, such an establishment would cost more to maintain than that on a farm; but, on the other hand, the salary of the tutor would in this case be saved, and there would be no farmer and his family to support. To assist in defraying the extra expenses of such an establishment, let the tutor permit, for a moderate fee, the sons of those farmers whose farms he has liberty to inspect, and of those who live at a distance, to attend his lectures and readings in the house, and his prelections in the fields. A pretty extensive knowledge of, and liking for, the science of agriculture might thus be diffused throughout the country, amongst a class of young farmers who might never have another opportunity of acquiring it, because they would never become permanent inmates in any such establishment.

I have known a mode of learning farming adopted by young farmers of limited incomes, from remote and semicultivated parts of the country, of lodging themselves in villages in cultivated districts adjacent to large farms, occupied by eminent farmers, and procuring leave from them to give their daily personal labour and superintendence in exchange for the privilege of seeing and participating in all the operations of the farm.

There are still other modes than those described above of learning farming, which deserve attention, and require remark. Among these the only one in this country, apart from the general practice of boarding with practical farmers, is the Class of Agriculture in the University of Edinburgh. This Chair was endowed in 1790 by Sir William Pulteney, with a small salary, and placed under the joint patronage of the Judges of the Court of Session, the Senatus Academicus of the University of Edinburgh, and the Town-Council of the City of Edinburgh. The first professor elected by the patrons to this chair in 1791, was the late Dr Coventry, whose name, in connection with the agriculture of the country, stood prominent at one time. He occupied the chair until his death in 1831. His prelections, at the earlier period of his career as a professor, were successful, when his class numbered upwards of seventy students. When I attended it, the number of students was upwards of forty. Dr Coventry was a pleasing lecturer, abounding in anecdote, keeping his hearers always in good humour, courting interrogation, and personally shewing great kindness to every student. At the latter period of his incumbency, the class dwindled away, and for some years before his death, he delivered a course of lectures only every two years. He delivered, I understand, thirty-four courses in forty years.

The present Professor Low succeeded Dr Coventry. Since his installation into the chair, he has rekindled the dying embers of the agricultural class, by delivering an annual course of lectures suited to the improved state of British agriculture, and by forming a museum of models of agricultural implements, and portraits of live-stock, illustrative of his lectures, of the most extensive and valuable description. In Dr Coventry's time, there was no museum deserving the name, and seeing this, Professor Low had no doubt been impressed with the important truth, that without models of the most approved implements, and portraits of the domesticated animals, serving to illustrate the principal operations and breeds of animals to be seen on the best cultivated farms, and pastoral districts, a mere course of lectures would prove nugatory. This museum is attached to the University, and to shew the zeal and industry by which the present Professor has been actuated in its formation, the objects in it must be worth more than L.2000. The funds which obtained those objects were derived from the revenues under the management of the Board of Trustees for the encouragement of Arts and Manufactures in Scotland. This Board was instituted by the 15th Article of the Treaty of Union between Scotland and England. Besides forming the museum, Professor Low has, during his yet short incumbency in the chair, already contributed much important matter to the agricultural literature of the country, by the publication of his Elements of Practical Agriculture, which contain almost the entire substance of his lectures, and the series of coloured portraits of animals taken from the pictures in the museum, now coming out periodically in numbers.

There has lately been appointed a lecturer on agriculture in Marischal College, Aberdeen, at a salary of L.40 a-year. Being but an experiment, the appointment, I believe, has only been made for three years.

There is no public institution in England for teaching agriculture. Some stir is making in the establishment of an Agricultural College in Kent, the prospectus of which I have seen ; and, some time ago, I saw a statement which said that provision exists for the endowment of a Chair of Agriculture in one of the Colleges of Oxford.

An agricultural seminary has existed at Templemoyle in the county of Londonderry, Ireland, for some years. It originated with the members of the North-west of Ireland Farming Society, and the first intention was to form it on such a scale as to teach children of the higher orders every science and accomplishment, whilst those of the lower orders, the sons of farmers and tradesmen, were to be taught agriculture. But the latter arrangement only has been found to be practicable. In a statement circulated by a member of the committee, I find that " the formation of this establishment has caused its founders an expenditure of above L.4000, of which about L.3000 were raised at its commencement by shares of L.25 each, taken by the noblemen, gentlemen, and members of the North-west Society. The Grocers' Company of London, on whose estate it is situated, have been most liberal in their assistance, and have earned a just reward in the improvement of their property, by the valuable example the farm of Templemoyle presents to their tenantry.

" In sending a pupil to Templemoyle, it is necessary to have a nomination from one of the shareholders, or from a subscriber of L.2 annually. The annual payment for pupils is L.10 a-year, and for this trifling sum they are found in board, lodging, and washing, and are educated so as to fit them for land-stewards, directing agents, practical farmers, schoolmasters, and clerks. From fifteen to seventeen is the age best suited to entrance at Templemoyle, as three years are quite sufficient to qualify a student possessed of ordinary talents, and a knowledge of the rudiments of reading and writing, to occupy any of the above situations.

"Upwards of two hundred young men, natives of sixteen different counties in Ireland, have passed or remain in the school. Of these, between forty and fifty have been placed in different situations, such as land-stewards, agents, schoolmasters, and clerks, or employed on the Ordnance Survey. Nearly one hundred are now conducting their own or their father's farms, in a manner very superior to that of the olden time.

"The school and farm of Templemoyle are situated about six miles from Londonderry; about a mile distant from the mailcoach-road leading from Londonderry to Newtonlimavady. The house, placed on an eminence, commands an extensive and beautiful view over a rich and highly cultivated country, terminated by Lough Foyle. The base of the hill is occupied by a kitchen and ornamental garden, cultivated by the youths of the establishment, under an experienced gardener. The house and farm-offices behind contain spacious, lofty, and well ventilated schoolrooms; refectory; dormitories; apartments for the masters, matron, servants, &c. Each pupil occupies a separate bed; the house can accommodate seventy-six, and the number of pupils is sixty. They receive an excellent education in reading, writing, arithmetic, book-keeping, mathematics, land-surveying, and geography. This department is managed by an excellent head-master, and assistant-master, both resident in the house. The pupils are so classed that one-half are receiving their education in the house, while the remainder are engaged in the cultivation of a farm of 165 Scotch acres, in the management of which they are directed by the head-farmer, an experienced and clever man, a native of Scotland, who has a skilful ploughman under him. The pupils who are employed one part of the day on the farm, are replaced by those in the school, so that the education always advances in and out of doors *pari passu*." *

In enumerating the means of obtaining agricultural knowledge in this country, I cannot omit mentioning those co-assistant institutions, the Veterinary Colleges. Their great object is to form a school of veteri-

* Irish Farmer's Magazine, No. 51.

nary science, in which the anatomical structure of quadrupeds of all kinds, horses, cattle, sheep, dogs, &c., the diseases to which they are subject, and the remedies proper to be applied for their removal, might be investigated and regularly taught; in order that, by this means, enlightened practitioners of liberal education, whose sole study has been devoted to the veterinary art in all its branches, may be gradually dispersed over all the kingdom. The Veterinary College of London was instituted in 1791, according to the plan of Mr Sain Bel, who was appointed the first professor. Parliamentary grants have been afforded at times to aid this institution, when its finances rendered such a supply essential. It is supported by subscription. Every subscriber of the sum of L.21 is a member of the society for life. Subscribers of two guineas annually are members for one year, and are equally entitled to the benefits of the institution. A subscriber has the privilege of having his horses admitted into the infirmary, to be treated, under all circumstances of disease, at 3s. 6d. per night, including keep, medicines, or operations of whatever nature that may be necessary; likewise of bringing his horses to the college for the advice of the professor *gratis*, in cases where he may prefer the treatment of them at home.* Until last year, care was chiefly bestowed in this institution on the horse, when the Royal Agricultural Society of England, deeming it as important for the promotion of agriculture, to attend to the diseases of the other animals reared on farms as well as the horse, voted L.300 a-year out of their funds for that purpose.

The Veterinary College of Edinburgh had its origin in the personal exertions of its present professor, Mr William Dick, in 1818, who, after five years of unrequited labour, fortunately for himself and the progress of the veterinary science in Scotland, obtained the patronage of the Highland and Agricultural Society of Scotland, who have afforded him a small salary since 1823. Since then the success of his exertions have been extraordinary, not fewer than from seventy to one hundred pupils attending the college every session, of whom about twenty every year, after at least two years' study of practical anatomy and medicine, become candidates for the diploma of veterinary surgeon. Their qualifications are judged of after an examination by the most eminent medical practitioners in Edinburgh. The students enjoy free admission to the lectures on human anatomy and physiology in Queen's College by the liberality of its professors. Through the influence of the Highland Society, permission has been obtained for the graduates to enter as

* Beauties of England and Wales, vol. x. Part IV., p. 181.

veterinary surgeons into her Majesty's cavalry regiments, as well as those of the Honourable East India Company.

In recommending farmers to attend lectures on veterinary science, it must not be imagined that I wish them to become veterinary surgeons. Let every class of people adhere to their own profession. But there is no doubt that a knowledge of veterinary science is of great use to the farmer, not in enabling him to administer to the diseased necessities of his live-stock, for that requires more professional skill and experience than any farmer can attain to, and is the proper province of the regularly bred veterinary surgeon; but to enable him readily to detect a disease by its symptoms, in order to apply immediate checks to its progress until he can communicate with and inform the veterinary surgeon of the nature of the complaint, whereby he may bring with him materials for treating it correctly on his arrival. The death of a single animal may be a serious loss to the farmer, and if, by his knowledge of the *principles* of the veterinary art, he can stay the progress of any disease, he may not only avert the loss, but prevent his animal being much affected by disease. Disease, even when not fatal to animals, leaves injurious effects on their constitutions for a long time.

With regard to attending lectures on agriculture, I should say, from my own experience, that more benefit will be derived from attending them after having acquired a practical knowledge of husbandry than before; because many of the details of farming cannot be comprehended, unless the descriptions of them are given where the operations themselves can be referred to.

Abroad are several institutions for the instruction of young men in agriculture, among which is the far-famed establishment of Hofwyl, in the canton of Berne, in Switzerland, belonging to M. de Fellenberg. This establishment is not intended so much for a school of agriculture, as that of education and moral discipline. All the pupils are obliged to remain nine years, at least until they attain the age of twenty one, during which time they undergo a strict moral discipline, such as the inculcation of habits of industry, frugality, veracity, docility, and mutual kindness, by means of good example rather than precepts, and chiefly by the absence of all bad example. The pupils are divided into the higher and lower orders, among the former of whom may be found members of the richest families in Germany, Russia, and Italy. For these the course of study is divided into three periods of three years each. In the first, they study Greek, Grecian history, and the knowledge of animals, plants, and minerals; in the second, Latin, Roman history, and the geography of the Roman world; and in the third, modern languages and literature, modern history to the last century, geography, the physical sciences, and chemistry. During the whole nine years they apply themselves to mathematics, drawing, music, and gymnastic exercises. The pupils of the canton of Berne only pay M. de Fellenberg 45 louis each, and do not cost their parents above 100 louis or 120 louis a-year. Strangers pay him 125 louis, including board, clothing, washing, and masters.

The pupils of the lower orders are divided into three classes according to their age and strength. The first get a lesson of half an hour in the morning, then breakfast, and afterwards go to the farm to work. They return at noon. Dinner takes them half an hour, and after another lesson of one hour, they go again to work on the farm until six in the evening. This is their summer occupation; and in winter they plait straw for chairs, make baskets, saw logs and split them, thrash and winnow corn, grind colours, knit stockings: for all of which different sorts of labour, an adequate salary is credited to each boy's class until they are ready to leave the establishment. Such as have a turn for any of the trades in demand at Hofwyl, wheelwright, carpenter, smith, tailor, or shoemaker, are allowed to apply to them. Thus the labour of the field, their various sports, their lessons, their choral songs, and necessary rest, fill the whole circle of the twenty-four hours; and judging from their open, cheerful, contented countenances, nothing seems wanting to their happiness.

It is admitted that, on leaving the establishment, the pupils of the higher classes, are eminently moral and amiable in their deportment, that they are very intelligent, and that their ideas have a wide range; and though they may not be so advanced in science as some young men brought up elsewhere, they are as much so as becomes liberal-minded gentlemen, though not professors. The pupils of the lower classes leave at the age of twenty-one, understanding agriculture better than any peasants ever did before, besides being practically acquainted with a trade, and with a share of learning quite unprecedented among the same class of people; and yet as hard-working and abstemious as any of them, and with the best moral habits and principles. It seems impossible to desire or imagine a better condition of peasantry.

As all the instruction at this establishment is conveyed orally, a great many teachers are required in proportion to the number of the pupils. In 1819, there were thirty professors for eighty pupils. This entails a considerable expense upon M. de Fellenberg, who besides extends the erection of buildings as he finds them necessary. He is, however, upon the whole, no loser by the speculation. Each pupil of the lower orders costs him L.56 a-year to maintain and educate, which is L.3, 8s. a-year beyond the value of his work, and yet the investment is a profitable one, yielding something more than 8¼ per cent. interest, net of all charges. "The farm is undoubtedly benefited by the institution, which affords a ready market for its produce, and perhaps by the low price at which the labour of the boys is charged. But the farm, on the other hand, affords regular employment to the boys, and also enables M. de Fellenberg to receive his richer pupils at a lower price than he could otherwise do. Hofwyl, in short, is a great whole, where one hundred and twenty or one hundred and thirty pupils, more than fifty masters and professors, as many servants, and a number of day-labourers, six or eight families of artificers and tradesmen, altogether about three hundred persons, find a plentiful, and in many respects a luxurious subsistence, exclusive of education, out of a produce of one hundred and seventy* acres ; and a money income of L.6000 or L.7000, reduced more than half by salaries, affords a very considerable surplus to lay out in additional buildings."† It seems that, since 1807, two convents, one in the canton of Fribourg, and the other in that of Thurgovie, have formed establishments analogous to those of M. de Fellenberg.‡

The celebrated German institution for teaching agriculture is at Möeglin, near Frankfort on the Oder. It is under the direction of M. Von Thäer. There are three professors besides himself; one for mathematics, chemistry, and geology ; one for veterinary knowledge ; and a third for botany, and the use of the different vegetable productions in the materia medica, as well as for entomology. Besides these, an experienced agriculturist is engaged, whose office it is to point out to the pupils the mode of applying the sciences to the practical business of husbandry. Such a person would be difficult to be found in this country. The course commences in *September*, the best season in my opinion for commencing the learning of agriculture. During the winter months the time is occupied in mathematics, and in the summer the geometrical knowledge is practically applied to the measurement of land, timber, buildings, and other objects. The first principles of chemistry are unfolded. Much attention is paid to the analysation of soils. There is a large botanic garden, with a museum containing models of implements of husbandry. The various implements used on the farm are all made by smiths, wheelwrights, and carpenters, residing round the institution ; the work-

* This is the number of acres in the farm as stated in the Edinburgh Review for October 1819 ; but a correspondent in Hull's Philanthropic Repertory for 1832, makes it 250 acres.

† Edinburgh Review, No. 64.

‡ Ebel, Manuel du Voyageur en Suisse, tome ii.

shops are open to the pupils, and they are encouraged by attentive inspection to become masters of the more minute branches of the economy of an estate.

As the sum paid by each pupil, who are from twenty to twenty-four years of age, is 400 rix-dollars annually (equal to about L.60 Sterling, if the rix-dollar is of Prussian currency), and besides which they provide their own beds and breakfasts, none but youths of good fortune can attend at Moeglin. Each has a separate apartment. They are very well behaved young men, and their conduct to each other, and to the professors, is polite even to punctilio.

The estate of Möeglin consists of twelve hundred English acres. About thirty years ago it was given in charge by the King of Prussia to M. Von Thäer, who at that time was residing as a physician at Celle, near Luneburg, in Hanover, with the view of diffusing agricultural knowledge in Prussia, which it was known M. Von Thäer possessed in an eminent degree, as evinced by the translations of numerous agricultural works from the English and French, by his management in setting an example to the other great landed proprietors, and stimulating them to adopt similar improvements. His Majesty also wished him to conduct a seminary, in which the knowledge of the sciences might be applied to husbandry, for the instruction of the young men of the first families. When M. Von Thäer undertook the management of this estate, its rental was only 2000 rix-dollars a-year (L.300), and twenty years ago, the rental had increased to 12,000 rix-dollars (L.1800). This increased value, besides the buildings erected, has arisen from the large flocks of sheep which in summer are folded on the land, and in winter make abundant manure in houses constructed for their lodging.

These particulars are taken from Mr Jacob's travels, who visited Möeglin in 1819, and who, in considering of the utility of such an institution in this country, makes these remarks on the personal accomplishments of M. Von Thäer. " We have already carried the division of labour into our agriculture, not certainly so far as it is capable of being carried, but much farther than is done in any other country. We have some of the best sheep farmers; of the best cattle and horse breeders; of the best hay, turnip, potato, and corn farmers in the world; but we have perhaps no one individual that unites in his own person so much knowledge of chemistry, of botany, of mathematics, of comparative anatomy, and of the application of these various sciences to *all* the practical purposes of agriculture as Von Thäer does; nor is the want felt, because we have numbers of individuals, who, by applying to each branch separately, have reached a height of knowledge far beyond what any man can attain who divides his attention between several objects. In chemistry we have now most decidedly the lead. In all of botany that is not mere nomenclature, it is the same. In mechanics we have no equals. There are thus abundant resources, from which practical lessons may be drawn, and be drawn to the greatest advantage; and that advantage has excited, and will continue to excite, many individuals to draw their practical lessons for each particular branch of agriculture, from that particular science on which it depends; and thus the whole nation will become more benefited by such divisions and subdivisions of knowledge, than by a slight tincture of all the sciences united in the possession of some individuals." *

France also possesses institutions for the teaching of agriculture. The first was that model farm at Roville, near Nancy, founded by M. Mathieu de Dombasle.† Though it is acknowledged that this farm has done service to the agriculture of France, its situation being so far removed from the centre of that country, its influence does not extend with sufficient rapidity. Its limited capital does not permit the addition of schools, which are considered necessary for the instruction of young proprietors who wish to manage their own properties with advantage, and of agents capable of following faithfully the rules of good husbandry.

To obviate the disadvantages apparent in the institution of Roville, "a number of men distinguished for their learning and zeal for the prosperity of France, and convinced of the utility of the project, used means to form an association of the nature of a joint-stock company, with 500 shares of 1200 francs each, forming a capital of 600,000 francs (L.25,000). The first half of this sum was devoted to the advancement of superior culture, and the second half to the establishment of two schools, one for pupils, who, having received a good education, wish to learn the theory and the application of agriculture, and of the various arts to which it is applicable; and the other for children without fortune, destined to become labourers, instructed as good ploughmen, gardeners, and shepherds, worthy of confidence being placed in them." ‡ This society began its labours in 1826 by purchasing the domain of Grignon, near Versailles, in the valley of Gally, in the commune of Thiverval, and appointing M. Bella, a military officer who had gained much agricultural information from M. Von Thäer, during two years' sojourn with his corps at Celle. M. Bella travelled through France, in

* Jacob's Travels in Germany, &c. pp. 173-188.

† Annales de Roville.

‡ Rapport General sur la ferme de Grignon, Juin 1828, p. 3.

the summer of 1826, to ascertain the various modes of culture followed in the different communes. Grignon was bought in the name of the king, Charles X., who attached it to his domain, and gave the society the title of the Royal Agricultural Society for a period of forty years. The statutes of the society were approved of by royal ordonance on the 23d May 1827, and a council of administration was named from the list of shareholders, consisting of a president, two vice-presidents, a secretary, a treasurer, and directors.

The domain, which occupies the bottom and the two sides of the valley, in length 2254 metres (a metre being equal to 3 feet and 11½ lines), is divided into two principal parts; the one is composed of a park of 290 hectares (387 acres), inclosed with a stone wall, containing the mansion-house and its dependencies, the piece of water, the trees, the gardens, and the land appropriated to the farm; the other, called the outer farm, is composed of 176 hectares (234 acres), of unenclosed land, to the south of the park.

With regard to the nature of the schools at Grignon, this account has been published,—" The council of administration being occupied in the organization of regular schools, has judged that it would be convenient and useful to open, in 1829, a school for work-people, into which to admit boys of from twelve to sixteen years of age, to teach them reading, writing, arithmetic, and the primary elements of the practice of geometry. The classes to meet two hours every day in summer, and four hours in winter, the rest of the time to be employed in manual work. The fee to be 300 francs the first year, 200 francs the second, and 100 francs the third. After three years of tuition the fee to cease, when an account is to be opened to ascertain the value of their work against the cost of their maintenance, and the balance to go to form a sum for them when they ultimately leave the institution."

" Meanwhile, as the director has received several applications for the admission of young men, who, having received a good education, are desirous of being instructed in agriculture, the council has authorized the conditional admission of six pupils. But as there are yet no professors, the pupils who are at present at Grignon can only actually receive a part of the instruction which it is intended to be given. They every day receive lessons from the director on the theory of agriculture, besides lessons on the veterinary art, and the elements of botany, from the part of the veterinary school attached to the establishment; also lessons of the art of managing trees and making plantations, given by a forester of the crown forests, and some notions of gardening by the gardener. During the rest of the time, they follow the agricultural labours and other operations of the establishment. They pay 100 francs a-month, including bed, board, and washing.

"Several proprietors who occupy farms, having expressed a desire to see young farm-servants taught the use of superior implements, and the regular service on a farm, the director has admitted a few, lessening the fee to the payment of board and lodging There are two just now. To such are given the name of "farm pupils."*

The course of education proposed to be adopted at Grignon, is divided into theoretical and practical. The course to continue for two years. In the first year to be taught mathematics, topography, physics, chemistry, botany and botanical physiology, veterinary science, the principles of culture, the principles of rural economy applied to the employment of capital, and the interior administration of farms. The second year to comprehend the principles of culture in the special application to the art of producing and using products; the mathematics applied to mechanics, hydraulics, and astronomy; physics and chemistry applied to the analysis of various objects; mineralogy and geology applied to agriculture; gardening, rural architecture, legislation in reference to rural properties, and the principles of health as applicable both to man and beast.

There are two classes of pupils, free and internal. Any one may be admitted a free pupil that has not attained twenty years of age, and every free pupil to have a private chamber. The pupils of the interior must be at least fifteen years of age.

The fee of the free pupils is 1500 francs a-year; that of the pupils of the interior 1300 francs. They are lodged in the dormitories in box-beds; those who desire private apartments pay 300 francs more, exclusive of furniture, which is at the cost of the pupils.†

There is an agricultural school at Hohenheim, in the Duchy of Wirtemberg, and another at Flottbeck in Flanders, belonging to M. Voght. An account of both these institutions is given by M. Bella, in the third number of the Annals of Grignon. There are, I understand, schools of agriculture, both in St Petersburgh and Moscow, but have not been so fortunate as to meet with any account of them.

It appears to me, from the best consideration I can give to the manner in which agriculture is taught at these schools, that as means of imparting real practical knowledge to pupils, they are inferior to the usual mode adopted in this country, of living with farmers. In reference to the results of the education obtained at Möeglin, Mr Jacob says—"It

* Annales de Grignon, 2d livraison, 1829, p. 48.

† Annales de Grignon, 3d livraison, 1830, p. 108.

appeared to me that there was an attempt to crowd too much instruction into too short a compass, for many of the pupils spend but one year in the institution, and thus only the foundation, and that a very slight one, can be laid in so short a space of time. It is however to be presumed, that the young men come here prepared with considerable previous knowledge, as they are mostly between the ages of twenty and twenty-four, and some few appeared to be still older." *

Although the pupils are kept at Hofwyl for nine years, and are fined if they leave it sooner, it is obvious that the higher class of them bestow but little attention on farming, and most on classical literature. And the particulars given in the elaborate programme of the school of agriculture at Grignon, clearly evince that attention to minute discipline, such as marking down results, and to what are termed *principles*, which just mean vague theorizings, form a more important feature of tuition than the practice of husbandry. The working pupils may acquire some knowledge of practice by dint of participating in work, but the other class can derive very little benefit from all the practice they see.

---

7. OF THE EVILS ATTENDANT ON LANDOWNERS NEGLECTING TO LEARN PRACTICAL AGRICULTURE.

" ——— leaving me no sign,—
Save men's opinions, and my living blood,—
To shew the world I am a gentleman."

RICHARD II.

There would be no want of pupils of the highest class for institutions such as I have recommended for promoting agricultural education, did landed proprietors study their true interests, and learn practical agriculture. Besides the usual succession of young farmers to fill the places of those who retire, and these of themselves would afford the largest proportion of the pupils, were every son of a landowner, who has the most distant prospect of being a landed proprietor himself, to become an agricultural pupil, in order to qualify himself to fulfil *all* the onerous duties of his station, when required to occupy that important position in the country, that class of pupils would not only be raised in respectability, but the character of landed proprietors, as agriculturists, would also be much elevated. The expectant landlord should therefore

* Jacob's Travels in Germany, &c. p. 185.

undergo that tuition, though he may intend to follow, or may have already followed, any other profession. The camp and the bar seem to be the especial favourite arenas upon which the young scions of the gentry are desirous of displaying their first acquirements. These professions are highly honourable, none more so, and they are, no doubt, conducive to the formation of the character of the gentleman; but, after all, are seldom followed out by the young squire. The moment he attains rank above a subaltern, or dons his gown and wig, he quits the public service, and assumes the functions of an incipient country gentleman. In the country he becomes at first enamoured of field sports, and the social qualities of sportsmen. Should these prove too rough for his taste, he travels abroad peradventure in search of sights, or to penetrate more deeply into the human breast. Now, all the while he is pursuing this course of life, quite unexceptionable in itself, he is neglecting a most important part of his duty,—that of learning to become a good landlord. On the other hand, though he devote himself to the profession of arms or the law, either of which may confer distinction on its votaries; yet if either be preferred by him to agriculture, he is doing much to unfit himself from being an influential landlord. To become a soldier or a lawyer, he willingly undergoes initiatory drillings and examinations; but, to become a landlord, he considers it quite unnecessary, to judge by his conduct, to undergo any initiatory tuition. That is a business, he conceives, that can be learned at any time, and seems to forget that it is *his* profession, and does not consider that it is one as difficult of thorough attainment as ordinary soldiership or legal lore. No doubt, the army is an excellent school for confirming, in the young, principles of honour and habits of discipline; and the bar for giving clear insight into the principles upon which the rights of property are based, and into the true theory of the relation betwixt landlord and tenant; but whilst these matters may be attained, a knowledge of agriculture, the weightiest matter to a landlord, should not be neglected. The laws of honour and discipline are now well understood, and no army is required to inculcate their acceptableness on good society. A knowledge of law, to be made applicable to the occurrences of a country life, must be *matured by long experience;* for, perhaps, no sort of knowledge is so apt to render landed proprietors litigious and uncompromising with their tenants, as a smattering of law. Instances have come under my own notice, of the injurious propensities which a slight acquaintance with law engenders in landed proprietors, as exhibited on their own estates, and at county and parochial meetings. No class of persons require Pope's admonition regarding the evil tendency of a "little learning" to be more strongly inculcated on them, than the young barrister who doffs his legal garments, to assume in ignorance the part of the country squire:

> "A little learning is a dangerous thing!
> Drink deep, or taste not the Pierian spring;
> There shallow draughts intoxicate the brain."

I do not assert that a knowledge of military tactics, or of law, is inconsistent with agriculture. On the contrary, a *competent* knowledge of either, and particularly of the latter, confers a value on the character of a country gentleman versant with agriculture; but what I do assert most strongly is, that the most intimate acquaintance with either, will never serve as a substitute for ignorance of agriculture in a country gentleman.

One evil arising from studying those exciting professions before agriculture is, that, however short the time spent in acquiring them, it is sufficiently long to create a distaste to learning agriculture practically, for such a task can only be undertaken, after the turn of life, by enthusiastic minds. But as farming is necessarily *the profession* of the country gentleman, for all *have* a farm, it should be learned, theoretically and practically, before his education should be considered finished. If he so incline, he can afterwards enter the tented field, or exercise his forensic eloquence, when the tendency which I have noticed in these professions will be unable to efface the knowledge of agriculture previously acquired. This is the proper course for every young man destined to become a landed proprietor to pursue, and who wishes to be otherwise employed as long as he cannot exercise the functions of a landlord. Were this course always pursued, the numerous engaging ties which a country life never fails to form, rendered more interesting by a knowledge of agriculture, would tend to extinguish the kindling desire for any other profession. Such a result would be most desirable for the country; for only contemplate the effects of the course pursued at present by landowners. Does it not strike every one as an incongruity for a country gentleman to be unacquainted with country affairs? Is it not "passing strange" that he should require inducements to learn his hereditary profession,—to know a business which alone can enable him to maintain the value of his estate, and secure his income? Does it not infer a species of infatuation to neglect becoming well acquainted with the true relation he stands to his tenants, and by which, if he did, he might confer happiness on many families; but to violate which, he might entail lasting misery on many more? In this way the moral obligations of the country gentleman are too frequently neglected. And no wonder, for these cannot be perfectly understood, or practised aright, but by tuition in early life, or by very diligent and irksome study in maturer years. And no wonder that great professional mistakes are frequently committed by proprietors of land. Descending from generalities to particulars, it would be no easy task to describe all the evils attendant on the neglect of farming by landowners; for though some are obvious enough, others can only be morally discerned.

1. One of the most obvious of those evils is, when country gentlemen take a prominent share in discussions on public measures connected with agriculture, and which, from the position they occupy, they are frequently called upon to do, it may be remarked that their speeches are usually introduced with apologies for not having sufficiently attended to agricultural matters. The avowal is candid, but it is any thing but creditable to the position they hold in the agricultural commonwealth. When, moreover, it is their lot or ambition to be elected members of the legislature, it is deplorable to find so many so little acquainted with the questions which bear directly or indirectly on agriculture. On these accounts, the tenantry are left to fight their own battles on public questions. Were landowners practically acquainted with agriculture, such painful avowals would be spared, as a familiar acquaintance with it enables the man of cultivated mind at once to perceive its practical bearing on most public questions.

2. A still greater evil consists in their consigning the management of valuable estates to the care of men as little acquainted as themselves with practical agriculture. A factor or agent, in such a condition, always affects much zeal for the interest of his employer; but it is "a zeal not according to knowledge." Fired by this zeal, and undirected as it most probably is by sound judgment, he soon discovers something at fault among the poorer tenants. The rent perhaps is somewhat in arrear,—the strict terms of the lease have been deviated from,—things appear to him to be going down hill. These are fruitful topics of contention. Instead of being "kindly affectioned," and thereby willing to interpret the terms of the lease in a generous spirit, the factor hints that the rent must be better secured, through the means of another tenant. Explanation of circumstances affecting the condition of the farmer, over which he has perhaps no control,—the inapplicability, perhaps, of the peculiar covenants of the lease to the particular circumstances of the farm,—the lease having perhaps been drawn up by himself, or some one as ignorant as himself,—are excuses unavailingly offered to one who is confessedly unacquainted with country affairs, and the result ensues in interminable disputes betwixt him and the tenants. With these the landlord is *unwilling* to interfere, in order to preserve intact the authority of the fac-

tor; or, what is still worse, is *unable* to interfere, because of his own unacquaintance with the actual relations subsisting betwixt himself and his tenants, and, of course, the settlement is left with the originator of the disputes. Hence originate actions at law,—criminations and recriminations,—much alienation of feeling; and at length a settlement of matters, at best perhaps unimportant, is left to the arbitration of practical men;—in making which submission, the factor acknowledges as much as he himself was unable to settle the dispute The tenants are glad to submit to arbitration to save their money. In all such disputes, they, being the weaker parties, suffer most in purse and character. The landlord, who should have been the natural protector, is thus converted into the unconscious oppressor, of his tenants. This is confessedly an instance of a bad factor; but have such instances of oppression never occurred, and from the same cause, that of ignorance in both landlord and factor?

A factor acquainted with practical agriculture would conduct himself very differently in the same circumstances. He would endeavour to prevent legitimate differences of opinion on points of management terminating into disputes, by skilful investigation and well-timed compromise. He studies to uphold the honour of both landlord and tenants. He can see whether the terms of the lease are strictly applicable to prevailing circumstances, and judging thereby, checks every improper deviation from appropriate covenants, whilst he makes ample allowance for unforeseen contingencies. He can discover whether the condition of the tenants is influenced more by their own doings, than by the nature of the farms they occupy. He regulates his conduct towards them accordingly; encouraging the industrious and skilful, admonishing the indolent, and amending the unfavourable circumstances of the farms. Such a man is highly respected, and his opinion and judgment are greatly confided in by the tenantry. Mutual kindliness of intercourse always subsists betwixt them. No landlord, whether himself acquainted or unacquainted with farming, but especially the latter, should confide the management of his estate to any other kind of factor.

3. Another obvious evil is one which affects the landed proprietor's own comfort and interest, and which is the selection of a steward or grieve for conducting the home-farm. In all cases it is necessary for a landowner to have a home-farm, and to have a steward to conduct it. But the steward of a squire acquainted and unacquainted with farming, is placed in very dissimilar circumstances. The steward of a squire acquainted with farming, enjoying good wages, and holding a respectable and responsible situation, *must* conduct himself as an honest and skilful manager, for he

knows he is superintended by one who can criticise his management well. A steward in the other position alluded to, must necessarily have, and will soon take care to have, every thing his own way. He soon becomes proud in his new charge, because he is in the service of a squire. He soon displays a haughty bearing, because he knows he is the only person on the farm who knows any thing about his business. He becomes overbearing to the rest of the servants, because, in virtue of his office, he is appointed purveyor to the entire establishment; and he knows he can starve the garrison into a surrender whenever he pleases. He domineers over the inferior work-people, because, dispensing weekly wages, he is the custodier of a little cash. Thus advancing in his own estimation step by step, and finding the most implicit reliance placed in him by his master, who considers his services as invaluable, the temptations of office prove too powerful for his virtue, he aggrandizes himself, and conceals his mal-practices by deception. At length his peculations are detected by perhaps some trivial event, the insignificance of which had escaped his watchfulness. Then loss of character and loss of place overtake him at once. Such flagrant instances of unworthy factors and stewards of country gentlemen are not supposititious. I could specify instances of both, whose mismanagement has come under my own observation. Both species of pests are engendered from the same cause,—the ignorance of landowners in country affairs.

4. Another injurious effect it produces, is absenteeism. When farming possesses no charms to the country gentleman, and field-sports become irksome by monotonous repetition, his taste for a country life declines, and to escape *ennui* at home, he banishes himself abroad. If such lukewarm landed proprietors, when they go abroad, would always confide the management of their estates to unexceptionable factors, their absence would be little felt by the tenants, who would proceed with the substantial improvement of their farms with greater zest under the countenance of a sensible factor, than of a landlord who contemns a knowledge of agriculture. But it must be admitted, that tenants farm with much greater *confidence* under a landlord acquainted with farming, who is always at home, than under the most unexceptionable factor. The disadvantages of absenteeism are only felt by tenants left in charge of a litigious factor, and it is always severely felt by day-labourers, tradesmen, and shopkeepers in villages and small country towns.

Now, all these evils—for evils they certainly are—and many more I have not touched upon, would be avoided, if landowners would make it a point to acquire a knowledge of practical agriculture. This can best be done in youth, when it should be studied as a *necessary* branch of education, and learned as the most *useful* business which country gentlemen can know. It will qualify them to appoint competent factors,—to determine upon the terms of the lease most suited to the nature of each of the farms on their properties,—and to select the fittest tenants for them. This qualification could not fail to inspire in tenants confidence in their landlords, by which they will be encouraged to cultivate their farms in the best manner for the land and for themselves, in even the most trying vicissitudes of seasons; and without which confidence the land, especially on estates on which no leases are granted, would never be cultivated with spirit. It confers on landlords the power to judge for themselves of the proper fulfilment of the onerous and multifarious duties of a factor. It enables them to converse freely in technical terms with their tenants on the usual courses of practice, to criticise work, and to predicate the probability of success or failure of any proposed course of culture. The reproving or approving remarks of such landlords operate powerfully with tenants. How many useful hints is it at all times in the power of such landlords to suggest to their tenants, on skilfulness, economy, and neatness of work; and how many salutary precepts may they inculcate on cottagers, on the beneficial effects of parental discipline and domestic cleanliness! The degree of good which the direct moral influence of such landlords among their tenantry can effect, can scarcely be over-estimated; its primary effect being to secure respect, and create regard. The good opinion, too, of a judicious factor is highly estimated by the tenantry; but the discriminating observations of a practical and well disposed landlord go much farther in inducing tenants to maintain their farms in the highest order, and to cherish a desire to remain on them from generation to generation. Were all landlords so actuated—and acquaintance with farming would certainly prompt them thus to act—they could at all times command the services of superior factors and skilful tenants.

They would then find there is not a more pleasing, rational, and interesting study than practical agriculture; and soon discover that to know the minutiæ of farming is just to create an increasing interest in every farm operation. In applying this knowledge to practice, they would soon find it operate beneficially for their estates, by the removal of objects which offend the eye or taste, and the introduction of others that would afford shelter, promote improvement, and contribute to the beauty of the landscape of the country around. Nor would these rural pursuits be inconsistent with the exercise of those manly field-sports, in which it is the pride and boast of our country gentlemen to excel. Hunting is prosecuted with the greatest ardour in the season in which field operations are least practised, and crops can sustain the least injury. The tenantry feel great interest in the chase, many personally participate in it, and all wish it success. There is, perhaps, no single adventitious circumstance that establishes so cordial a feeling betwixt landlords and tenants in a district, as the common interest excited by fox-hunting. In prosecution of the exhilarating sport, land-owners and farmers associate together at the *meets;* or the former may fall in with the latter in a *burst* through their farms, when the hounds are in full *cry*, the scent *breast* high, and when at a *killing pace* the most experienced *fencer*, or the most *knowing one* of the *lie of the country*, will not blink a gate thrown open for him, or despise a hint to a gap in the hedge. Sportsmen know full well how much is in the power of farmers to render their sport agreeable or otherwise.

> " All now is free as air, and the gay pack
> In the rough bristly stubbles range unblam'd.
> No widow's tears o'erflow, no secret curse
> Swells in the farmer's breast, which his pale lips
> Trembling conceal, by his fierce landlord aw'd:
> But courteous now, he levels every fence,
> Joins in the common cry, and haloos loud,
> Charm'd with the rattling thunder of the field."*

Agricultural Shows afford another and a different sort of opportunity for landlords and tenants to meet. They are the most important, and at the same time the most social meetings that are held in the country; and they are now conducted on such well recognised principles, that, though all classes of persons appear at them on the same footing, the respect due to rank and station is never lost sight of.

A personal acquaintance with tenants of all classes presents to landlords a wide field for the observation of human nature under different circumstances. Coupling the observations derived from so extensive and varied a field with their own experience of practical agriculture, landowners possess peculiar advantages for collecting a store of facts, from which to be supplied with the most cogent arguments and illustrations, in every department of rural economy, and the right use of which would cause their sentiments to command attention in every public assembly in which they chose to give them utterance.

It appears extraordinary to those who have felt the difficulty of acquiring a competent knowledge of country affairs, to observe landowners, who have spent their time in learning every thing else but that, coolly undertaking to perform, without previous preparation, all the functions of country gentlemen. Granting that they are entitled to the privilege

* Somerville.

by hereditary birth, what, I would ask, would be thought of the presumption of a subaltern, who pretended to assume the command of an army, or of a student of law, to conduct an important cause before the highest tribunal? True, to command an army, or to plead a great cause, requires a higher degree of intellectual acumen, than the performance of the functions of a country gentleman in the most perfect manner. Yet, taking the most out of this admission, it is surely not intended to be maintained, that the functions of landownership may be well enough exercised without previous study, any more than to command or to plead requires no experience? Landowners, no doubt, can enjoy their incomes, in a way suitable to their tastes, without knowing any thing of agriculture, whereas the incomes derived from the army and the bar, can only be enjoyed as the rewards of service; but surely the privileges on possessing land by inheritance were bestowed by law for far higher purposes than merely expending the income derived from it. The *quid pro quo* for the privileges of inheritance is the performance of certain onerous duties. Did the privileges only imply the right of spending incomes abroad, it would be matter of little importance whether landowners understood agriculture or no; but when residing on their estates, they profess to exercise a hereditary and paternal superintendence over them,—claim a seat on the magisterial bench,—take a share in all public affairs connected with agriculture and the interests of landed property, in and out of the legislature,—it cannot be unreasonable to expect them to be endued with the attributes of the character they have assumed.

No doubt, landowners, unacquainted with agriculture, may content their minds with the assurance, that their estates are well farmed by skilful tenants,—well managed by competent factors,—and their incomes undoubtedly secured; but how do they know, who are themselves unacquainted with rural affairs, when their estates *are* well farmed, and well managed, and their incomes secured beyond a doubt? It is no infallible proof of estates being either well farmed, or well managed, to draw the rents therefrom without abatement; for rents may have been fixed at sums below their intrinsic value; or they may have been fixed unequally, in respect to relative value, whereby the excess of some rents may make good the deficiencies of others; or factors may maintain the nominal amount of rentals by annual sales of timber, stone, or other commodities which the estates may most amply afford; or all these circumstances may combine to maintain the rentals of estates; but of the correct influence of these circumstances landlords unacquainted with farming are incompetent to judge, and far less able to make comparisons of the value of their own estates with those which are under the immediate superintendence of practical landlords. Such a system of management may proceed well enough in prosperous times; but let a change occur, political or social, materially affecting agriculture, let a period of low prices prevail, or a series of bad crops diminish the capital of the tenants, and render them unable to pay their stipulated rents, and then let landlords unacquainted with rural affairs contemplate the effects of such contingencies on their incomes. How should they act under the circumstances? *They* know not. Practical landlords know at once the manner and the extent in which they should conform to the exigencies of the times; and factors under them find it a comparatively easy matter to adjust new arrangements with the tenants; and the tenants, confiding in the judgment of both, accept the well considered terms without hesitation. Inexperienced landlords, on the other hand, conduct themselves very differently in trying circumstances. Having no well founded notion of the principles which regulate the value of land, whenever a reduction of rent is demanded by the tenants, in conformity with the uncontrollably altered state of things, they have no data previously stored in their minds by which to regulate the rate of reduction; but being made aware by the factor that a reduction should be made,—more to secure the occupancy of the farms, than to maintain the solvency of the tenants,—a small per-centage is reluctantly assented to for a time, irrespective of the merits of the case of each particular farm. A settlement of affairs is thus accomplished for a season, which is most probably inapplicable to the next, when the same unpleasant business has to be negociated, or the demand for reduction peremptorily refused. Hence arises discontent; and, erewhile, the land suffers from the inability of some, and the unwillingness of the rest of the tenants, to maintain its fertility, on account of the uncertainty of their ability to retain their farms, in consequence of the distrust shewn to their representations by their landlords, and evinced by the refusal to meet their necessitous wishes in a generous spirit. No policy can be more injurious to the character of landlords than this. Ignorance, with subserviency to their factor, will be imputed to them. Were they to meet well-grounded complaints in a generous spirit, the tenants would be easily satisfied, and suffer considerable privations before they could be prevailed upon to renew them. Because they know they have bargained in specific terms with their landlords, and that they ought to fulfil their obligations as well in adverse as in prosperous times, and they are conscious that if those obligations were strictly attended to, there would be fewer occasions of collision betwixt them and their landlords. They thus feel their dependence. These are just sentiments of theory, but cannot always be maintained in practice; because many tenants, in adverse times, do not possess the means of liquidating every instant demand upon them, including rent, though their stocking may be of far greater value than the whole amount of those demands, yet, to touch upon *that* for the purpose of rent, would not only derange the economy of the farm, but ultimately injure the landlord's own interest, by neglecting the culture of the land, and depreciating its value.

> " The sweat of industry would dry, and die,
> But for the end it works to.——"

To avert so great an evil, the effects of which may be felt over the whole succeeding lease, landlords should grant such a reduction of rent at once, as will enable industrious tenants to carry on their farms to the best advantage in the altered circumstances of the times. Nor is a large reduction of rent devoid of justice; for, in prosperous times, most tenants are not in the habit of hoarding money on ordinary leases, and therefore cannot long endure adversity; and if, after bringing up their families, and providing for them, they should have earned a little spare capital, it is usually expended in prosecuting farther improvements, if required, or in extending their operations by taking other farms.

Whilst such negociations are carrying on, the factor is placed in a delicate situation. Let him be ever so well disposed towards the tenantry, he cannot convince an inexperienced landlord of the advantage of submitting to a large reduction of rent at once, rather than undergo the disagreeable task of arguing upon and yielding a petty reduction every year. Let him plead for the tenants with all the earnestness of a sympathising heart, and the force of indisputable facts, it will prove unavailing on a mind inexperienced of those facts; and in urging their case farther than the humour of the landlord will bear, he may jeopardise his own livelihood, and the case being so, his interest would rather prompt him to flatter the landlord's cupidity, than alleviate the tenant's hardships. Could the landlord be shewn that his own interest is involved in that of his tenants, there might be some hope of an equitable negociation, but to the inexperienced in country matters, how hard would be the conviction that decrease of income may promote increase of safety. Were the factor really ill-disposed to the tenants, what a glorious opportunity would such a time afford him of avenging himself upon them, by hardening the heart of the landlord against any concession, on the bare plea of inexpediency.

No doubt, landlords, though unacquainted with farming, may have their properties well managed by judicious factors, and were *implicit* reliance always placed in them, by landlords and tenants, those properties would thrive apace. But, tenants, as I have before said, always feel greater confidence under the immediate cognizance of a practical landlord, than under any factor; for, besides the question of rent, which may have to be discussed oftener than once in the currency of a lease, there are many links of attachment which bind a landlord with his tenants, that cannot subsist betwixt them and the factor. The position of tenants on very large estates, it is true, is somewhat different. Great landowners cannot be expected to become personally known to every one of their numerous tenants, even though they may be thoroughly versed in practical agriculture; and this being necessarily the case, their factors, in every portion of their estates, are endued with almost as large discretionary powers as proprietors themselves, in so far, at least, as the tenants are concerned. Still it is desirable for the most satisfactory management of even the largest estates, that landowners of the largest extent, and highest titles, should be acquainted with practical farming. Bacon says, "It is no baseness for the greatest to descend and look into their own estate." For this purpose, they should themselves be able to examine the qualifications of factors, however highly recommended they may be by testimonials. A few questions, put with the discernment which practice never fails to confer on the practical man, give a clearer insight into the actual qualifications of a factor than volumes of testimonials. The choosing of good factors is an important matter in the welfare of every estate, and much more so on one of such an extent as to preclude the possibility of the personal superintendence of the landlord himself. Practical knowledge also enables landlords at once to direct their observation to those minute circumstances which are infallible indications of land being well or ill farmed. This faculty of minute observation is invaluable to landlords and factors, in enabling them to judge of the condition of land without much trouble, and it may be easily acquired with a previous knowledge of the minutiæ of farming. The accomplishment of matured observation is well worth the landlord's while bestowing some pains to acquire.

There is also no doubt, that tenants in similar circumstances with respect to their farms, may cultivate them as well under a landlord unacquainted, as acquainted with farming. Any difficulty the tenants may have to contend with, consists not so much in the cultivation of their farms, as in obtaining similar advantages of lease from the inexperienced, as from the experienced landlord; and although as great advantages were obtained at the commencement of the lease, yet occurrences happening during it, to alter the relative position of landlord and tenant, are viewed in very different lights by the two classes of landlords, and always to the prejudice of the tenant, by the inexperienced class. There are farmers whose capital and force of character enable them to pursue an independent and successful course of farming, in spite of every obstacle that would effectually impede the career of others; but such characters, though good farmers, and therefore valuable tenants on any estate, are few in number; and when seen to make a little money, seldom fail to excite the jealousy of landlords unacquainted with farming, who, to account for their success, imagine that the land has been made to do more than it should. On the other hand, such tenants are just the men whom landlords acquainted with farming would desire to occupy *their* farms.

It is undeniable, that every advantage which tenants on estates belonging to landlords unacquainted with farming do possess, may also be possessed by those under practical landlords, besides many minor circumstances which the former class of landlords cannot appreciate as being at all conducive to the welfare and comfort of tenants.

These maxims of Bacon seem not an inapt conclusion to our present remarks: "He that cannot look into his own estate at all, had need both choose well those whom he employeth, and change them often, for new are more timorous and less subtle. He that can look into his estate but seldom, it behoveth him to turn all to certainties." *

---

8. OF EXPERIMENTAL FARMS AS PLACES FOR INSTRUCTION IN FARMING.

> "Things done without example, in their issue
> Are to be feared."
>
> HENRY VIII.

It seems to be a favourite notion with some writers on agricultural subjects, that, of all places for learning farming, experimental farms are the best. They even recommend the formation of experimental farms, with the view of affording to young men the best system of agricultural education. They go the length of confidently asserting that all the field operations and experiments, on experimental farms, could be conducted by pupils. And they are nearly unanimous in conceiving that 200 acres would be a large enough extent for an experimental farm,

* Essays, p. 106.

and that on such a farm 100 pupils could be trained to become farmers, stewards, and ploughmen.

A very slight consideration of the nature of an experimental farm, will serve to shew how unsuitable such a place is for *learning* farming. The sole object of an experimental farm is, to become acquainted with the best properties of plants and animals by experiment, and thereby to ascertain whether those properties are such as would recommend them for introduction to an ordinary farm. It is obvious, from this statement, that it is needless following, on an experimental farm, the *usual modes* of cultivating the ordinary plants and of rearing the ordinary animals of a farm. Either *new* plants, and *other* modes than the usual ones of cultivating and rearing the ordinary plants and animals, should be tried on an experimental farm, otherwise it would not be an *experimental* farm, or of more use than an ordinary farm. In witnessing new or unusual modes of culture, the pupil would thus learn nothing of the particulars of *ordinary farming.* Extraordinary modes of cultivating ordinary plants, by changes in the rotation or of manure, and the risk of failure in both—for failure is a necessary condition of experiment—would only serve to impress the minds of *pupils* with experimental schemes, instead of guiding them to the most approved plan of cultivating each sort of plant. To confound the mind of a beginner, by presenting before it various modes of doing the same thing, without the ability to inform it which is the best, is to do him a lasting injury. Were a pupil, who had been trained up on an ordinary farm, to have opportunities of witnessing varieties of experiments conducted on an experimental farm, he might then derive benefit from numerous hints which would be suggested in the course of making the experiments. But if pupils would be unfavourably placed on an experimental farm, by remaining constantly on it, much more would the farm itself be injured, by having its experiments performed by inexperienced pupils. So far from *pupils* being able to conduct experiments to a satisfactory issue, the most experienced cultivators are at times baffled by unforeseen difficulties; and so far would *such* experiments inspire confidence in farmers, that they would assuredly have quite an opposite tendency. So far, therefore, would the services of pupils in any degree compensate for the extraordinary outlay occasioned on experimental farms, by unsuccessful or unprofitable experiments, that even those of the most experienced cultivators would most probably produce no such desirable result; for no *experimenter* can command success, and failure necessarily implies extraordinary outlay. So far, therefore, could the services of pupils accomplish what those of experienced cultivators could not command, that their very presence on an *experimental* farm, with the right of co-operating in the experiments, would be a constant source of inconvenience to the experienced experimenters.

But, besides these objections, the mode of conducting experiments on so small farms as those recommended by most writers, would be quite unsuitable to pupils desirous of *learning* farming. Where varieties of culture on various sorts of plants are prosecuted on a small extent of ground, only a very small space can be allotted to each experiment. It is true, that, should any of the varieties of plants be new to this country, the seed of which at first being of course only obtainable in small quantities, to procure such being a primary object with the promoters of experimental farms, the space required for them at first must be very small. But although each lot of ground should be small, the great varieties of seeds cultivated in so many different ways, will nevertheless require a great number of lots, which altogether will cover a considerable extent of ground. How all these lots are to be apportioned on 200 acres, together with ground for experimenting on different breeds of animals, and different kinds of forest trees, is more than I can imagine. It would require more than double that extent of ground to give mere standing-room to all the objects that should be cultivated on an experimental farm, and over and above which, 100 pupils on such a farm would form a perfect crowd. Besides, the lots being so small, would require to be worked with the spade instead of the plough; and this being the case, let the experiments on such a farm be ever so perfectly performed, they could give pupils no insight whatever into real *farming*, much less secure the confidence of *farmers*.

It is the pleasure of some writers on experimental farms, to institute a comparison, or even strict analogy, betwixt them and experimental gardens. As the latter have improved the art of gardening, they argue, so would the former improve agriculture. But the truth is, there can be no analogy betwixt the introduction into common gardens, of the results obtained in experimental gardens, and the results of experiments obtained in such small experimental farms as recommended by agricultural writers, introduced into the common field culture of a farm; because, the experiments in an experimental garden having been made by the spade, may be exactly transferred into almost any common garden, and, of course, succeed there satisfactorily; whereas the experiments made by the spade in a small experimental farm, cannot be performed with the spade on a common farm; they must there be executed by the plough, and, of course, in quite different circumstances. The rough culture of the plough, and most probably in different circumstances of soil, manure, and shelter, cannot possibly produce results similar to the culture of the spade, at least no farmer will believe it; and if *they* put no confidence in experiments, of what avail will experimental farms be? Announcements of such results may gratify curiosity, but no benefit would be conferred on the country by experiments confined within the inclosures of an experimental farm. No doubt, a few of the most unprejudiced of the farmers will perform any experiment, with every desire for its success, and there is as little doubt that others will follow the example; and some will be willing to test the worth of even a suggestion; but as these are the usual modes by which every new practice recommends itself to the good graces of farmers, no intervention of an experimental farm is therefore required for their promulgation and adoption. It is the duty of the promoters of experimental farms, to disseminate a proved experiment quickly over the country, and the most efficient mode of doing so is to secure the confidence of farmers in it. To insure *their* confidence, it will be necessary to shew them, that they can do the same things as have been done on the experimental farm *by the usual means of labour* they possess, and they will then shew no reluctance to follow the example. Take the risk, in the experimental farm, of proving results, and shew the intrinsic value of those results to the farmers, and the experiments, of whatever nature, will be performed on half the farms of the kingdom in the course of the first season.

For this purpose it is necessary to ascertain the size an experimental farm should be, which will admit of experiments being made on it, in a manner similar to the operations of a farm. The leading operation, which determines the smallest size of the fields of an experimental farm, is ploughing. The fields should be of that size which will admit of being ploughed in ordinary time, and at the same time not larger than just to do justice to the experiments performed in them. I should say that *five* acres imperial is the least extent of ground to do justice to ploughing ridges along, across, and diagonally. *Three* acres, to be of such a shape as not to waste time in the ploughing, would have too few ridges for a series of experiments, and to increase their number would be to shorten their length, and lose time in ploughing. But even five acres are too small to inclose with a fence; ten acres, a good size of field for small farms, being nearer the mark for fencing. Taking the size of an experimental plot at five acres, the inclosure might be made to surround the divisions of a rotation; that is, of a rotation of four years, let twenty acres be inclosed; of five years, twenty-five acres, &c.; but in this arrangement the experiments would only prove really available to small tenants, who frequently cultivate all their crops within one fence, and the subject thus experimented on would not be individually inclosed within a fence, as is the case with crops on larger farms.

The whole quantity of land required for an adequate experimental farm may thus be estimated. New varieties of seeds would require to be increased by all the possible modes of reproduction. Old varieties should undergo impregnation,—be subjected to different modes of culture,—be preserved pure from self-impregnation,—and be grown in different altitudes. Each variety of seed already cultivated, such as wheat, barley, oats, potatoes, turnips, &c., to undergo these various modifications of treatment on five acres of land, would, including the whole, require an immense extent of ground, and yet, if each kind did not undergo all these varieties of treatment, who could then aver that all our seeds had been subjected to satisfactory *field* experiments? Only *one* kind of grain, treated as variedly as might be, on five acres for each modification of treatment, would occupy *seventy* acres; and were only five kinds of seed taken, and only five varieties of each, and the whole cultivated on both low and high ground, the quantity of ground required altogether would be 3500 acres. The extent of ground thus increases in a geometrical progression, with an increase of variety of plants. Besides, the numerous useful grasses, for the purposes of being cut green, and for making into hay, would require other 1000 acres The whole system of pasturing young and old stock on natural and artificial grasses in low grounds and on high altitudes, and in sheltered and exposed situations, would require at least 3000 acres. Then, experiments with forest-trees, in reference to timber and shelter in different elevations and aspects, would surely require 1000 acres. Improvements in bog and muir lands should have other 1000 acres. So that 9500 acres would be required to put only a given proportion of the objects of cultivation in this country to the test of full experiment. Such an extent of ground will, no doubt, astonish those who are in the habit of talking about 200 acres as capable of affording sufficient scope for an experimental farm. Those people should be made to understand that the plough must have room to work, and that there is no other way of experimentizing satisfactorily for *field* culture, on an experimental farm, but by affording it a real field to work in. If less ground be given, fewer subjects must be taken; and if any subject is rejected from experiment, then the system of experimentizing will be rendered incomplete. The system of experimentizing should be carried out to the fullest extent of its capability on experimental farms, or it should be left, as it has hitherto been, in the hands of farmers. The farmers of Scotland have worked out for themselves an admirable system of husbandry, and if it is to be improved to a still higher pitch of skill by experimental farms, the means of improvement should be made commensurate with the object, otherwise there will be no satisfaction, and certain failure; for the promoters of experimental farms should keep in mind, that the existing husbandry, improved as it is, is neither in a stationary nor in a retrograding, but in a progressive state towards farther improvement. Unless, therefore, the proposed experiments, by which it is intended to push its improvement still farther towards perfection, embrace every individual of the multifarious objects which engage the attention of agriculturists, that one may be neglected, which, if cultivated, would have conferred the greatest boon on agriculture. I come, therefore, to this conclusion in the matter: that *minute* experiments on the progressive developments of plants and animals are absolutely requisite to establish their excellence or worthlessness, and these can be performed on a small space of ground; but to stop short at this stage, and not pursue their culture on a *scale commensurate with the operations of the farm*, is to render the experimental farm of little avail to practical husbandry, and none at all to interest the farmer.

So large an extent of farm would most probably embrace all the varieties of soil. It should, moreover, contain high and low land, arable, bog, and muir land, sheltered and exposed situations, and the whole should lie contiguous, in order to be influenced by the climate of the same locality. It would scarcely be possible to procure such an extent of land under the same landlord, but it might be found in the same locality on different estates. *Such* a farm, rendered highly fertile by draining, manuring, liming, and labour, and plenished, as an experimental farm should be, with *all* the varieties of crop, stock, implements, and woods, would be a magnificent spectacle worthy of a nation's effort to put into a perfect state for a national object. What a wide field of observation would it present to the botanical physiologist, containing a multiplicity of objects made subservient to experiment! What a laboratory of research for the chemist, amongst every possible variety of earths, manures, plants, and products of vegetation! What a museum of objects for the naturalist, in which to observe the living habits and instincts of animals, some useful to man, and others injurious to the fruits of his labour! What an arena upon which the husbandman to exercise his practical skill, in varying the modes of culture of crops and live-stock! What an object of intense curiosity and unsatisfying wonder to the rustic labourer! But above all, what interest and solicitude should the statesman feel the appliance of such a mighty engine, set in motion, to work out the problem of agricultural skill, prosperity, and power.*

* Paper by me on the subject in the Quart. Jour. of Agri., vol. vii. p. 538.

9. A FEW WORDS TO YOUNG FARMERS WHO INTEND EMIGRATING AS AGRICULTURAL SETTLERS TO THE COLONIES.

"Such wind as scatters young men through the world, to seek their fortunes farther than at home."
TAMING OF THE SHREW.

For some years past the tide of emigration has set very strongly towards the shores of our colonial possessions. To attempt to ascertain the causes of this emigration, or to speculate on the probability of its success, would be quite irrelevant in this place; suffice it to be cognizant of the fact, that many people, of late years, have gone from Great Britain to settle for ever in America and Australia. Whatever may have been their former pursuits, almost the whole have emigrated with the view of becoming agricultural settlers,—either to become owners of land, or continue to be what they were in this country, agricultural labourers.

In all new countries, the price of labour for a time is high, and in consequence skilful labourers, in every department of industry, as long as they choose to engage in employment, cannot fail to earn money; for although certain sorts of provisions, that require much preparatory labour to produce them, may be dear in a new country, yet others, being more easily raised on account of their suitableness to the climate, are not exorbitant in price; and, at all events, the prices of both range comparatively lower in the circumstances than the rate of wages. Labourers, prompted by premature ambition to become owners of land,—"who hasten to be *rich*,"—entail insurmountable misery on themselves and families. Expending the little capital they had earned as servants in purchasing land, they possess no means to employ the dear labour of others; and ere the fruits of their own industry can afford them sufficient sustenance, they suffer real privations, or are obliged to obtain assistance from others on very disadvantageous terms. But however imprudently they may act in regard to their finances, and short-sightedly with respect to their future welfare, the labouring class, in all circumstances, possess the advantage of being brought up to a profession, and thus, though agricultural labourers may not have the means of employing others, they know well how to labour the land for their *own advantage.*

The same eulogium, I fear, cannot be pronounced on most of the emigrants who leave this country with the professed determination of becoming *owners* of land. Many have had no opportunities at all of becoming acquainted with agriculture; whilst others who profess to know it, know so little of it that their knowledge avails them very little when they engage in active husbandry on their settlements. Notwithstanding these exceptions, no doubt there are many emigrants who understand farming quite well. Now, I think, emigrants intending to pursue agriculture in the new country, injure their own interests very materially, by adopting the irrational plan of neglecting to learn the business they are about to engage in. They should all, without exception, know farming before they leave this country. I say without exception, for though some may, perhaps, be pretty far advanced in life, before they determine on emigrating, and though grown up persons dislike to encounter the supposed shame of learning a new trade, whilst others grudge the time and money that would cost them to learn it,—imagining that the money would be better laid out in their new speculation,—yet worse-founded opinions could not be entertained; for although advanced in life, and thereby enfeebled before leaving the land of their nativity, their new profession would be far more pleasantly acquired amidst the comforts of home, than the unavoidable inconveniences of a first settlement in a foreign land; and no man, of whatever age, should display the folly of being above learning the business he intends to pursue in future. Emigrants may be assured that they will be obliged to learn farming abroad, for it cannot come to them intuitively, and then they will discover it, when too late, to be much easier for them to exercise an acquired skill to bring in land from a state of nature to tillage, than to acquire that skill at the risk of starving their infant colony, by most probably misdirecting their efforts,—the injurious effects of which they may feel for many years to come. This is what they would term learning farming by experience, but it is very dear-bought experience, far more expensively acquired than by a little money judiciously laid out at home in learning it on another's farm. If they had learned it so, not only money, but much misdirected labour, which is equivalent to money, as well as much uneasiness of mind, would have been saved them. If emigrants possessing land are entirely ignorant of farming, they must chiefly trust to the skill and honesty of their servants, who, receiving high wages and board, and thereby being more independent in circumstances than their masters, soon become indispensable persons in their peculiar situation; and, who, imagining themselves beyond the power of the law and the chances of detection, are strongly tempted to aggrandize themselves rather than attend to the interest of their masters. Thus circumstanced, a handful of corn can be easily concealed, a drop of milk purloined every day from the cows, and a pig, or a sheep, or even a bullock, can be stolen or gone astray, when it suits their purpose.

But *young* men have no valid excuse for neglecting to learn farming before they set out to take possession of the "promised land." The plea of having plenty of time to learn farming in the colony ere old age overtake them, or plenty of cash to purchase experience of colonial agriculture, is an excuse only befitting the thoughtless and procrastinating; nor should the somewhat correct assumption, that the agriculture of the old country is not exactly applicable to the colonies, serve them as a better; for however modified field operations may be executed in different countries, the nature of land, of vegetables, and of animals, is the same in every country; and if the nature of these particulars are well understood here, there is little doubt but the knowledge may be applied with advantage in the colonies. These, however, are only plausible excuses; for though colonial farming may be learnt from old and experienced settlers,—and the plan is far better than commencing in ignorance operations on one's own account and in entire dependence on servants;—yet, it should be borne in mind, that few young emigrants will have the patience to remain so long with settlers as to acquire a competent knowledge of farming, when they perceive that they themselves might be enjoying the advantages they behold; besides, such a procedure would render abortive the determination of those emigrants who wish to take out farm-servants and implements of husbandry,—a plan which they must relinquish if they have to learn their profession in the colonies. But, I believe, there is little foundation for the assertion that colonial agriculture differs from our own. Wherever the *same kinds of crops* are raised, the *same principles* of culture must be adopted; and wherever the *same sorts of stock* are reared for the *same purposes*, the *same system* must be pursued in their management. Superior fertility of soil, amenity of climate, or nourishment in the food of animals, but slightly affect the application of principles, and only modify the application of practice. Want of efficient beasts of labour and implements may at first induce settlers to try extraordinary expedients to accomplish the desired end, but as those means improve, and the ground is by them brought into tillage, the peculiarities of colonial agriculture will gradually yield to the more matured and elastic practice of the old country. Eventually, the colonies will, I conceive, exhibit splendid examples of British agriculture, under the cherishing auspices of a fine climate. The sooner it attains that perfection, the more quickly will the prosperity of the settlers be secured; and nothing will delay its consummation so effectually as emigrants designing to engage in agriculture quitting this country in breathless haste, in total ignorance of husbandry.

Let *every* intending settler, therefore, *learn agriculture thoroughly* before he emigrates; and, if it suits his taste, and time, and arrangements, let him then study in the colony the necessarily imperfect system of agriculture usually pursued by the settlers before he embarks in it on his own account; and the full knowledge acquired here, will enable him not only to comprehend the whole system there in a very short time, but to select the part of the country best suited to his purpose, and to avoid what is erroneous. A knowledge of his profession prior to emigration, will enable him the more easily to estimate those particulars in a proper point of view. But in truth he has a much higher motive for learning agriculture here, as a thorough acquaintance of it will enable him, at once, to make the best use there of the inadequate means of culture which every emigrant must at first experience, by knowing how to apply animal labour in the culture of the new soil, when at all practicable, instead of manual, as long as wages are high,—how to suit the kind of crop to the nature and present state of the soil;—how to use expedients to gain the end in view, by accommodating labour to the existing state of the weather, the nature and condition of the crop or soil, or the state of the implements;—how to exercise ingenuity in the construction of dwellings to secure the comfort of himself and family, and accommodation of live-stock and provisions, which can best be acquired by a familiar acquaintance with farm buildings;—how to exercise a general superintendence over every department of work, so as to shew an intimate acquaintance with them, and which acquirement never fails to maintain a proper authority over every person in his employment. These are advantages which every emigrant can purchase here, but not in the colonies; but which can only be acquired by studying agriculture in one of the best districts of this country. They are advantages equivalent to capital to emigrants. No study, however lengthened, of the present state of colonial agriculture,—which may be said to have been worked out by dint of trial and failure,—will ever tutor the settler's mind so accurately as to enable him to turn every change of circumstances to the best advantage. This faculty can only be acquired at home, or with settlers in the colony, who have been experienced farmers at home; and which, acting like an additional sense, gives an insight into the management of land and stock, which those who do not possess it can have no conception. This statement may be derided by those agricultural settlers who have emigrated to the colonies, and succeeded in amassing fortunes without any knowledge of agriculture but what they had picked up by degrees on the spot, but such persons are incompetent to judge of the nature of the statement, never having been influenced by its principle; and how favourable soever the issue of their own exertions may have proved, there is no question they would have realized much larger fortunes in the time, or the same amount in a shorter time, had they brought a thorough acquaintance of the most perfect system of husbandry known to operate on the favourable circumstances which they occupied; not that a *perfect* system could at once be practised in a new colony, but its knowledge would have enabled them sooner to have brought their land into a superior state of cultivation, and their live-stock into a superior condition to yield larger profits. Deny this averment who may, will find great difficulty in disproving it.

---

10. OF THE KIND OF EDUCATION BEST SUITED TO YOUNG FARMERS.

"Between the physical sciences and the arts of life there subsists a constant mutual interchange of good offices, and no considerable progress can be made in the one, without of necessity giving rise to corresponding steps in the other. On the one hand, every art is in some measure, and many entirely, dependent on those very powers and qualities of the material world which it is the object of physical inquiry to investigate and explain."

HERSCHEL.

With respect to the education of young farmers, no course of elementary education is better than what is taught at the excellent parochial schools of this country. The sons of farmers and of peasants have in them a favourable opportunity of acquiring the elements of a sound education, and they happily avail themselves of the opportunity; but, besides elementary education, a classical one sufficiently extensive and profound for farmers, may there also be obtained. But there are subjects of a different nature, sciences suited to the study of maturer years, which young farmers should make a point of learning,—I mean the sciences of Natural Philosophy, Natural History, Mathematics, and Chemistry. These are taught at colleges and academies. No doubt these sciences are included in the curriculum of education provided for the sons of landowners and wealthy farmers; but every class of farmers should be taught them, not with a view of transforming them into philosophers, but of communicating to them the important knowledge of the nature of those phenomena which daily present themselves to their observation. Such information would make them more intelligent farmers, as well as men. The advantages which farmers would derive from studying those sciences, will be best understood by pointing out their nature.

It is evident that most farming operations are much affected by external influences. The state of the weather, for instance, regulates every field operation, and local influences modify the climate very materially. Now it should be desired by the farmer to become acquainted with the causes which give rise to those influences, and these can only be known by comprehending the laws of nature which govern every natural phenomenon. The science which investigates the laws of these phenomena, is called *Natural Philosophy*, and it is divided into as many branches as there are classes of phenomena. The various classes of phenomena occur in the earth, air, water, and heavens. The laws which regulate them being unerring in their operation, admit of absolute demonstration; and the science which affords the demonstration is called *Mathematics.* Again, every object, animate or inanimate, that is patent to the senses, possesses an individual identity, so that no two objects can be confounded together. The science which makes us acquainted with the marks for identifying individuals, is termed *Natural History*. Farther, every object, animate or inanimate, cognizable by the senses, is a compound body made up of certain elements. *Chemistry* is the science which makes us acquainted with the nature and combinations of those elements. We thus see how generally applicable those sciences are to the phenomena around us, and their utility to the farmer will be the more apparent, the more minutely each of them is investigated. Let us take a cursory view of each subdivision as it affects agriculture.

Mathematics are either abstract or demonstrative. Abtract mathematics "treat of propositions which are immutable, absolute truth," not liable to be affected by subsequent discoveries, "but remains the unchangeable property of the mind in all its acquirements." Demonstrative mathematics are also strict, but are "interwoven with physical considerations;" that is, subjects that exist independently of the mind's conceptions of them or of the human will; or, in other words still, considerations in accordance with nature. Mathematics thus constitute the essential means of demonstrating the strictness of those laws which govern natural phenomena. Mathematics must, therefore, be first studied before those laws can be understood. Their study tends to expand the mind,—to enlarge its capacity for general principles,—and to improve its reasoning powers.

Of the branches into which Natural Philosophy is divided, that which is most useful to farmers is *Mechanics*, which is defined to be " the science of the laws of matter and motion, so far as is necessary to the construction of machines, which, acting under those laws, answer some purpose in the business of life." Without mechanics, as thus defined, farmers may learn to *work* any machine which answers their purpose ; but it is only by that science they can possibly understand the *principles* upon which any machine is constructed, nor can any machine be properly constructed in defiance of those principles. Both machinists and farmers ought to be versed in mechanical science, or the one cannot make, and the other guide, any machine as it ought to be ; but, as I have had occasion to express my sentiments on this subject already, I shall abstain from dilating further upon it here. Mathematical demonstration is strictly applicable to mechanics, whether as to the principles on which every machine operates, or the form of which it is constructed. The *principles* of mechanics are treated of separately under the name of *Dynamics*, which is defined to be " the science of force and motion."

Pneumatics is the branch of natural philosophy which is next to mechanics in being the most useful to the farmer to know. It " treats of air, and the laws according to which it is condensed, rarefied, gravitates." The states of the air, giving a variable aspect to the seasons, as they pursue their " appointed course," endue all atmospherical phenomena with extreme interest to the farmer. Observation alone can render variety of phenomena familiar ; and their apparent capriciousness, arising most probably from the reciprocal action of various combinations of numerous elements, renders their complicated results at all times difficult of solution ; for all fluids are susceptible of considerable mutations, even from causes possessing little force ; but the mutations of elastic fluids are probably effected by many inappreciable causes. Nevertheless, we may be assured, that no change in the phenomena of the atmosphere, however trivial, takes place but as the unerring result of a definite law, be it chemical or physical.

Closely connected with pneumatics, in so far as the air is concerned, are the kindred natural sciences of *Electricity* and *Magnetism*. These agencies, though perfectly perceptible to one or more of the senses, and evidently constantly at work in most of the phenomena of the atmosphere, are mysteriously subtle in their operations. It is extremely probable, that one or both are the immediate causes of all the changes which the atmosphere is continually undergoing. It is hardly possible that the atmosphere, surrounding the globe like a thin envelop, and regularly carried round with it in its diurnal and annual revolutions, should exhibit so very dissimilar phenomena every year, but from some disturbing cause, such as the subtile influences of electricity, which evidently bear so large a share in all remarkable atmospherical phenomena. Its agency is the most probable cause of the *irregular* currents of the air called winds, the changes of which are well known to all farmers to possess the greatest influence on the weather.

Natural History comprehends several branches of study. *Meteorology* consists of the observation of the apparent phenomena of the atmosphere. The seasons constitute a principal portion of these phenomena. The clouds constitute another, and are classified according to the forms they assume, which are definite, and indicative of certain changes. The winds constitute a third, and afford subject for assiduous observation and much consideration. Attention to the directions of the wind and forms of the clouds will enable farmers to anticipate the kind of weather that will afterwards ensue in a given time in their respective localities. The prevalence of the aqueous meteors of rain, snow, hail, and ice, is indicated by the state of the clouds and winds.

Hydrography is the science of the watery part of the terraqueous globe. It makes us acquainted with the origin and nature of springs and marshes, the effects of lakes, marshes, and rivers, on the air and on vegetation in their vicinity; and the effects of sea air on the vegetation of maritime districts.

Geology is the knowledge of the substances which compose the crust of the earth. It explains the nature and origin of soils and subsoils; that is, the manner in which they have most probably been formed, and the rocks from which they have originated: It discovers the relative position, structure, and direction in which the different rocks usually lie. It has as yet done little for agriculture; but a perfect knowledge of geology might supply useful hints for draining land, and planting trees on soils and over subsoils best suited to their natural habits, a branch of rural economy as yet little understood, and very injudiciously practised.

Botany and *botanical physiology*, which treat of the appearance and structure of plants, are so obviously useful to the agricultural pupil, that it is unnecessary to dilate on the advantages to be derived from a knowledge of both.

Zoology, which treats of the classification and habits of all animals, from the lowest to the highest organized structure, cannot fail to be a source of constant interest to every farmer who rears stock. There are few wild quadrupeds in this country; but the insect creation itself would employ a lifetime to investigate.

Anatomy, especially *comparative anatomy*, is highly useful to the farmer, inasmuch as it explains the functions of the internal structure of animals upon which he bestows so much care in rearing. Acquainted with the functions of the several parts which constitute the corporeal body, he will be the better able to apportion the food to the peculiar constitution of the animal; and also to anticipate any tendency towards disease, by a previously acquired knowledge of premonitory symptoms. Comparative anatomy is most successfully taught in veterinary schools.

The only other science which bears directly on agriculture, and with which the pupil farmer should make himself acquainted, is *Chemistry;* that science which is cognizant of all the changes in the constitution of matter, whether effected by heat, by moisture, or other means. There is no substance existing in nature, but is susceptible of chemical examination. A science so universally applicable, cannot fail to arrest popular attention. Its popular character, however, has raised expectations of its power to assist agriculture, to a much greater degree, than the results of its investigations yet warrant. It is very generally believed, not by practical farmers, but chiefly by amateur agriculturists, who profess great regard for the welfare of agriculture, that the knowledge derived from the analysis of soils, manures, and vegetable products, would develop general principles, which might lead to the establishment of a system of agriculture, as certain in its effects as the unerring results of science. Agriculture, in that case, would rank among the experimental *sciences,* the application of the principles of which would necessarily result in increased produce. The positive effects of the weather seem to be entirely overlooked by these amateurs. Such sentiments and anticipations are very prevalent in the present day, when every sort of what is termed *scientific* knowledge are sought after with an eagerness as if prompted by the fear of endangered existence. This feverish anxiety for scientific knowledge is very unlike the dispassionate state of mind induced by the patient investigation of true science, and very unfavourable to the right application of the principles of science to any practical art. Most of the leading agricultural societies instituted for the promotion of practical agriculture, have been of late assailed by the entreaties of enthusiastic amateur agriculturists, to construct their premiums to encourage only that system of agriculture which takes chemistry for its basis.

These are the physical sciences whose principles seem most applicable to agriculture; and being so, they should be studied by every farmer who wishes to be considered an enlightened member of his profession. That farmers are quite competent to attain to these sciences, may be gathered from these observations of Sir John Herschel:—" There is scarcely any well-informed person, who, if he has but the will, has not the power to add something essential to the general stock of knowledge, if he will only observe regularly and methodically some particular class of facts which may most excite his attention, or which his situation may best enable him to study with effect. To instance one subject which *can* only be effectually improved by the united observations of great numbers widely dispersed:—Meteorology, one of the most complicated but important branches of science, is at the same time one in which any person who will attend to plain rules, and bestow the necessary degree of attention, may do effectual service." But in drawing our conclusions, great caution is requisite, for, " In forming inductions, it will most commonly happen that we are led to our conclusions by the especial force of some two or three strongly impressive facts, rather than by affording the whole mass of cases a regular consideration; and hence the need of cautious verification. Indeed, so strong is this propensity of the human mind, that there is hardly a more common thing than to find persons ready to assign a cause for every thing they see, and in so doing, to join things the most incongruous, by analogies the most fanciful. This being the case, it is evidently of great importance that these first ready impulses of the mind should be made on the contemplation of the cases most likely to lead to good inductions. The misfortune, however, is, in natural philosophy, that the choice does not rest with us. We must take the instances as nature presents them. Even if we are furnished with a list of them in tabular order, we must understand and compare them with each other, before we can tell which *are* the instances thus deservedly entitled to the highest consideration. And, after all, after much labour in vain, and groping in the dark, accident or casual observation will present a case which strikes us at once with a full insight into the subject, before we can even have time to determine to what class its *prerogative* belongs." *

Many farmers, I dare say, will assert it to be far beyond the reach of their means, and others beyond their station, to bestow on *their* sons so learned an education as that implied in the acquirement of the sciences just now enumerated. Such apprehensions are ill-founded; because no farmer that can afford to support his sons at home, without working for their bare subsistence, but possesses the means of giving them a good education, as I shall immediately prove; and no farmer, who confessedly has wealth, should grudge his sons an education that will fit them to adorn the profession they intend to follow.

It cannot be denied, that a knowledge of mathematics and natural philosophy greatly elevates the mind. Those farmers who have acquired

* Discourse on the Study of Natural Philosophy, pp. 133, 182.

these sciences, must be sensible of their tendency to do this; and they will therefore naturally wish *their* sons to enjoy what they themselves do. Those who of themselves do not know these sciences, on being informed of their beneficial tendency, will probably feel it to be their duty to educate their sons, and thereby put it in their power to raise themselves in society and at the same time shed a lustre on the profession of which they are members. The same species of reasoning applies to the acquirement of the peculiar accomplishments bestowed on the mind by a knowledge of natural history and chemistry. Neither the time nor expense of acquiring such an education is of that extent or magnitude, as to deter any farmer's son from attempting it, who occupies a station above that of a farm steward. Besides these considerations, a good education, as the trite saying has it, is the best legacy a parent can leave his child; and, on this account, it is better for the young farmer himself to bestow on him a superior education, in the first instance, with a part even of the money destined by his father to stock him a farm, than to plenish for him a larger farm, and stint his education. The larger farm would, no doubt, enable the half-educated son to earn a livelihood more easily; but the well-educated one would be more than compensated in the smaller farm by the possession of that cultivated intelligence, which would induce him to apply the resources of his mind to drawing forth the capabilities of the soil, and making himself an infinitely superior member of society. Were industrious farmers as eager to improve their sons' minds by superior education, as they too often are to amass fortunes for them,—a boon unprofitably used by uncultivated minds,—they would display more wisdom in their choice. No really sensible farmer should hesitate to decide which course to take, when the intellectual improvement of his family is concerned. He should never permit considerations of mere pelf to overcome a sense of right and of duty. Rather than prevent his son having the power to raise himself in his profession, he should scrupulously economize his own expenditure.

I shall now shew that the time occupied in the acquisition of those sciences which are expedient for the farmer to learn, is not lost when compared with the advantages which they may bestow. *Part of three years* will accomplish all, but three years are doubtless an immense time for a young man to *lose!* So it would be; but, to place the subject in its proper light, I would put this statement and question for consideration, Whether the young farmer's *time*, who is for years constantly following his father's footsteps over the farm, and only superintending a little in his absence, while the father himself is, all the time, quite capable of conducting the farm, is not as much *lost*, as the phrase has it, as it would be when he is occupied in acquiring a scientific education at a little distance from home? Insomuch as the young man's *time* is of use to the *farm*, the two cases are nearly on a par; but, in as far as both cases affect himself, there is no question that science would benefit him the more,—no question that a superior education would afterwards enable him to learn the practical part of his profession with his father, with much greater ease to himself. The question is thus narrowed to the consideration of the alternative of the cost of keeping the son at home, following his father as idly as his shadow, or of sending him to college. Even in this pecuniary point of view, the alternative consists merely of the difference of maintenance at home, and that in a town, with the addition of fees. That this difference is not great, I shall now shew.

Part of three years, as I have said, would accomplish all amply, and in this way;—the first year to be devoted to mathematics, the second to natural philosophy, and the third to natural history and chemistry; and along with these principal subjects, some time in both years should be devoted to geography, English grammar and composition, book-keeping, and a knowledge of cash transactions. The two months vacation in each year could be spent at home. There are seminaries at which these subjects may be studied, at no great distance from every farmer's home. There are, fortunately for the youths of Scotland, universities, colleges, and academies, in many parts of the country. Edinburgh, Glasgow, Aberdeen, and St Andrews, can boast of well-endowed universities and colleges; whilst the academies at Dundee, Perth, Ayr, Dollar, and Inverness, have been long famed for good tuition.

For the study of mathematics and natural philosophy, I would prefer the academies to the colleges, because their session occupies ten months, and two hours each day are devoted to each subject; whereas the college session is at most six months, and only one hour each day is appropriated to one subject. At the academies, other two hours are daily occupied with geography and English composition. The longer session, and the fuller teaching on each subject, at the same fee, are great advantages to students; and it will be found that the more fully mathematics and natural philosophy are treated, the greater fascinations they present to the student. Two sessions of twenty months might thus be profitably employed at the academy in learning mathematics, natural philosophy, geography, English grammar, and the theory of book-keeping.

Natural history and chemistry are best acquired at college, as they are not always taught, and never fully so, at the academies; and without the most ample experiments and illustrations, which cannot be expected to be afforded in provincial towns,—the seats of the academies,—these sciences cannot be profitably studied.

The cost of acquiring all those subjects at the several colleges and academies is not insurmountable, even to the limited purse of a small farmer. In any of the towns mentioned as possessing an academy, the *two* sessions of twenty months would not exceed in board at the large allowance, in a provincial town, of a guinea a-week, and fees twelve guineas, L.105; and the short session of six months at college, at a guinea a-week, and eight guineas for fees, other L.35, making in all, in twenty-six months, L.140. This is a small sum compared with the advantages to be derived from it by the young farmer, and *from it falls to be deducted the cost of keeping him at home in idleness*, which, even at ploughmen's usual wages of 10s. a-week, would amount in that time to L.56, so that his education would only cost L.84; but economy, practised by frugal habits, might make a smaller sum suffice; and, on the other hand, a larger might not be grudged to make a diligent student comfortable, by those who have no cause to economize.

---

11. OF THE DIFFERENT KINDS OF FARMING.

"I'll teach you differences."
LEAR.

Perhaps the young farmer will be astonished to learn that there are many and various systems of farming; yet so in reality is the case, and moreover, that they all possess very distinctive characteristics. There are *six* kinds of farming practised in Scotland alone; and though all are pursued under some circumstances common to all, and each kind is perhaps best adapted to the particular soil and situation in which it is practised; yet it is highly probable that one of the kinds might be applicable to, and profitably followed, in all places of nearly similar soil and locality. Locality, however, determines the kind of farming fully more than the soil; the soil only entirely determining it when of a very peculiar consistence. The comparative influence of locality over soil in determining this point will be better understood after shortly considering each kind of farming.

1. One kind is wholly confined to *pastoral* districts, which are chiefly situated in the Highlands and Western Isles of Scotland,—in the Cheviot and Cumberland hills of England,—and very generally in Wales.

In all these districts, farming is almost restricted to the breeding of cattle and sheep; and, as natural pasture forms the principal food of live-stock in a pastoral country, very little arable culture is there practised for their behoof. Cattle and sheep are not always both reared on the same farm. Cattle are reared in very large numbers in the Western Isles, and in the *pastoral valleys* among the mountain-ranges of England, Wales, and Scotland. Sheep are reared in still greater numbers in the *upper parts* of the mountain-ranges of Wales and of the Highlands of Scotland; and on the green round-backed mountains of the south of Scotland and the north of England. The cattle reared in pastoral districts are small sized, chiefly black coloured, and horned. Those in the Western Isles, called "West Highlanders," or "Kyloes," are esteemed a beautifully symmetrical and valuable breed of cattle. Those in the valleys of the Highland mountains, called "North Highlanders," are considerably inferior to them in quality, and smaller in size. The black-faced, mountain, or heath, horned sheep, are bred and reared on the upper mountain-ranges, and fattened in the low country. The round-backed green hills of the south are mostly stocked with the white-faced, hornless, Cheviot breed; though the best kind of the black-faced breed is also reared in some localities of that district, but seldom both breeds are bred by the same farmer. Wool is a staple product of sheep pastoral farming.

Pastoral farms are chiefly appropriated to the rearing of one kind of sheep, or one kind of cattle; though both classes of stock are bred where valleys and mountain-tops are found on the same farm. The arable culture practised on them is confined to the raising of provisions for the support of the shepherds and cattle-herds; and perhaps of a few turnips, for the support of the stock during the severity of a snow-storm; but the principal artificial food of the stock in winter is hay, which in some cases is obtained by inclosing and mowing a piece of natural grass on a spot of good land, near the banks of a rivulet, the alluvial soil along the river sides being generally of fine quality. All pastoral farms are large, some containing many thousands of acres,—nay miles in extent; but from 1500 to 3000 acres is perhaps an ordinary size.* Locality determines this kind of farming.

The *stocking* of a pastoral farm consists of a breeding stock of sheep or cattle, and a yearly proportion of barren stock intended to be fed and sold at a proper age. A large capital is thus required to stock at first, and afterwards maintain, such a farm; for, although the quality of the

* It is to be regretted that neither the Old nor the New Statistical Account of Scotland gives the least idea of the *size* of the farms in any of the parishes described.

land may not be able to support many heads of stock per acre, yet, as the farms are large, the number of heads required to stock a large farm is very considerable. The rent, when consisting of a fixed sum of money, is of no great amount per acre, but sometimes it is fixed at a sum per head of the stock that the farm will maintain.

A *pastoral farmer* should be well acquainted with the rearing and management of cattle or sheep, whichever his farm is best suited for. A knowledge of general field culture is of little use to him, though he should know how to raise turnips and make hay.

2. Another kind of farming is practised on *carse* land. A carse is a district of country, consisting of deep horizontal depositions of alluvial or diluvial clay, on one or both sides of a considerable river; and may be of great or small extent, but generally comprehends a large tract of country. In almost all respects, a carse is quite the opposite to a pastoral district. Carse land implies a flat, rich, clay soil, capable of raising all sorts of grain to great perfection, and unsuited to the cultivation of pasture grasses, and, of course, to the rearing of live-stock. A pastoral district, on the other hand, is always hilly the soil generally thin, poor, and various, and commonly of a light texture, much more suited to the growth of natural pasture grasses than of grain, and, of course, to the rearing of live-stock. Soil decides this kind of farming.

Being all arable, a *carse farm* is mostly stocked with animals and implements of labour; and these, with seed-corn for the large proportion of the land cultivated under the plough, require a considerable outlay of capital. Carse land always maintains a high rent per acre, whether it consists solely of money or of money and corn valued at the fiars prices. A carse farm, requiring much capital and much labour, is never of large extent, seldom exceeding 200 acres.

A *carse farmer* requires to be well acquainted with the cultivation of grain, and almost nothing else, as he can rear no live-stock; and all he requires of them are a few milch cows, to supply milk to his household and farm-servants, and a few cattle in the straw-yard in winter, to trample down the large quantity of straw into manure,—both of which classes of cattle are purchased when wanted.

3. A third sort of farming is that which is practised *in the neighbourhood of large towns*. In the immediate vicinity of London, farms are appropriated to the growth of garden vegetables for Covent-Garden market, and, of course, their method of culture can have nothing in common with either pastoral or carse farms. In the neighbourhood of most towns, garden vegetables, with the exception of potatoes, are not so much cultivated as green crops, such as turnips and grass, and dry fod-

der, such as straw and hay, for the use of cowfeeders and stable-keepers. The practice of this kind of farming is to dispose of all the produce, and receive in return manure for the land. And this constitutes this kind of farming a retail trade like that in town, in which articles are bought and sold in small quantities, mostly for ready money. When there is not a sufficient demand in the town for all the disposable produce, the farmer purchases cattle and sheep to eat the turnips and trample the straw into manure, in winter. Locality decides this kind of farming.

The chief qualification of an *occupant of this kind of farm*, is a thorough acquaintance with the raising of green crops,—potatoes, clover, and turnips; and his particular study is the raising of those kinds and varieties that are most prolific, for the sake of having large quantities to dispose of, and which, at the same time, are most suitable to the wants of his customers.

The *capital required for a farm of this kind*, which is all arable, is as large as that for a carse farm. The rent is always high per acre, and the extent of land not large, seldom exceeding 300 acres.

4. A fourth kind of farming is the *dairy* husbandry. It specially directs its attention to the manufacture of butter and cheese, and the sale of milk. Some farms are laid out for the express purpose; but the sale of milk is frequently conjoined with the raising of green crops, in the neighbourhood of large towns, whose inhabitants are whence daily supplied with milk, though seldom from pasture, which is mostly appropriated as paddocks for stock sent to the weekly market. But a true dairy-farm requires *old pasture.* The chief business of a *dairy-farm* is the management of cows, and of their produce; and whatever arable culture is practised thereon, is made entirely subservient to the maintenance and comfort of the dairy stock. The milk, where practicable, is sold; where beyond the reach of sale, it is partly churned into butter, which is sold either fresh or salted, and partly made into cheese, either sweet or skimmed. No stock are *reared* on dairy-farms, as on pastoral, except a few quey (heifer) calves, occasionally to replenish the cow stock; nor aged stock *fed* in winter, as on farms in the vicinity of towns. The bull calves are frequently fed for veal, but the principal kind of stock reared are pigs, which are fattened on dairy refuse. Young horses, however, are sometimes successfully reared on dairy-farms. Horse labour being comparatively little required thereon—mares can carry their young, and work with safety at the same time, while old pasture, spare milk, and whey, afford great facilities for nourishing young horses in a superior manner. Locality has decided this kind of farming on the large scale.

The purchase of cows is the principal expense of stocking a *dairy-farm;* and as the purchase of live stock in any state, especially breeding-stock, is always expensive, and live stock themselves, especially cows, constantly liable to many casualties, a dairy-farm requires a considerable capital. It is, however, seldom of large extent, seldom exceeding 150 acres. The arable portion of the farm supplying the green crop for winter food and litter, does not incur much outlay, as hay,—*that* obtained from old pasture grass,—forms the principal food of all the stock in winter. The rent of dairy-farms is high.

A *dairy-farmer* should be well acquainted with the properties and management of milch cows, the manufacture of butter and cheese, the feeding of veal and pork, and the rearing of horses; and he should also possess as much knowledge of arable culture, as to enable him to raise those kinds of green crops and that species of hay, which are most congenial to cows for the production of milk.

5. A fifth method of farming is that which is practised in most arable districts, consisting of any kind of soil not strictly carse land. This method consists of a regular system of cultivating grains and sown grasses, with the partial rearing, and partial purchasing, or wholly purchasing, of cattle; and no sheep are reared in this system, they being purchased in autumn, to be fed on turnips in winter, and sold off fat in spring. This system may be said to *combine the professions of the farmer, the cattle-dealer, and the sheep-dealer.*

6. A decided improvement on this system long ago originated, and has since been practised, in Berwickshire and Roxburghshire, in Scotland; and in Northumberland in England. The farmer of this improved system combines all the qualifications required for the various kinds of farming already enumerated. Rearing cattle and sheep, and having wool to dispose of, he participates in the activity of the stock-farmer. Cultivating grains and the sown grasses, he knows the culture of land as skilfully as the carse farmer. Converting milk into butter and cheese, after the calves are weaned, and indulging in the predilection for a bit of fine old pasture, he passes the summer and autumnal months as busily as the dairy-farmer. Feeding cattle and sheep in winter on turnips, he attends the markets of fat-stock as closely as the farmer in the neighbourhood of a town. Improving on the usual system of farming pursued in arable districts, by breeding and rearing *all* the stock fed on his farm—thereby eschewing the precarious trade of the dealer in stock—thus combining all the kinds of farming within the limits of his farm, he has it within his power every year to suit the particular demand of each market, and thereby enlarge the sphere of his

profits, and this he can do in any year more uniformly and certainly than any other class of his co-farmers.

To become a *farmer* of this *mixed husbandry*, a man must be acquainted with every kind of farming practised in the country. He actually practises them all. He prosecutes, it is true, each kind in a rather different manner from that practised in localities where the particular kind is pursued as the only system of farming; because each branch of his farming must be conducted so as to conduce to the welfare of the whole, and by studying the mutual dependence of parts, he produces a whole in a superior manner This multiplicity of objects requires from him more than ordinary attention, and much more than ordinary skill in management. No doubt, the farmers of some of the other modes of farming become very skilful in adapting their practice to the situations in which they are actually placed, but his more varied experience increases versatility of talent and quickness of discernment; and, accordingly, it will be found that the farmers of the *mixed husbandry* prove themselves to be the cleverest and most intelligent agriculturists of the country.

The field of their operations, on both sides of the Tweed, has long been acknowledged to be not only the most highly cultivated portion of the kingdom, but that which contains the most valuable breeds of live-stock; and as the mixed husbandry cannot be carried on within very narrow limits, there, *large farms* exist. Less than 500 acres is too limited an extent. Live-stock and grain culture being equally attended to, each comprises a large proportion of the stocking, and the capital required to furnish both is considerable, though perhaps less than the last named system, in which the entire stock are purchased every year. The rents of both systems are about the same; and though both kinds are determined by no peculiarity of soil and locality like the others, the *mixed* is adapted by a happy form of constitution to most circumstances.

---

12. OF CHOOSING THE KIND OF FARMING.

" Choice, being mutual act of all our souls, makes merit her election."

TROILUS AND CRESSIDA.

These are the various kinds of farming pursued in this kingdom; and if there be any other, its type may, no doubt, be found in the mixed system just described. One of these systems must be adopted by the aspirant pupil for his profession. If he succeed to a family inheritance, the kind of farming he will follow will depend on that pursued by his predecessor, which he will learn accordingly; but if he is free to choose for himself, and not actually restricted by the circumstances of peculiar locality, or soil, or inheritance, then I would advise him to adopt the mixed husbandry, as containing within itself all the varieties of farming which it is requisite for a farmer to know.

If he is at liberty to take advice, I can inform him that the mixed husbandry possesses advantages over every other ; and practically thus:—in pastoral farming, the stock undergoes minute examination, for certain purposes, only at distantly stated times; and owing to the wide space over which they have to roam for food in pastoral districts, comparatively less attention is bestowed on them by shepherds and cattle-herds. The pastoral farmer has thus no particular object to attract his attention at home between those somewhat long intervals of time; and in the mean while time is apt to hang heavy on his hands.—The carse farmer, after the labours of the field are finished in spring, has nothing but a little hay-making and much bare-fallowing in summer, to occupy his mind until the harvest —Dairy-farming affords little occupation for the farmer in winter.—The farmer in the vicinity of large towns, has almost nothing to do in summer, from turnip-seed to harvest —Mixed-husbandry, on the other hand, affords abundant and regular employment at all seasons. Cattle and sheep feeding, and marketing grain, pleasantly occupy the short days of winter. Seed-sowing of all kinds affords abundant employment in spring. The rearing of live stock, sale of wool, and culture of green crops, fill up the time in summer until harvest; and autumn, in all circumstances, brings its own busy avocations at the ingathering of the fruits of the earth. There is, strictly speaking, not one week of real leisure to be found in the mixed system of farming;—if the short period be excepted, from assorting the lambs in the beginning of August to putting the sickle to the corn,—and that period is curtailed or protracted, according as the harvest is early or late.

If the young farmer is desirous of attaining a knowledge of every kind of farm work,—of securing the chance of profit every year,—and of finding regular employment at all seasons in his profession he should determine to follow the mixed husbandry. It will not in any year entirely disappoint his hopes. In it, he will never have to bewail the almost total destruction of his stock by the rot, or by the severe storms of winter, as the pastoral farmer sometimes has. Nor can he suffer so serious a loss as the carse farmer, by his crop of grain being affected by the inevitable casualties of blight or drought, or the great depression of prices for a succession of years. Were his stock greatly destroyed or much deteriorated in value by such casualties, he might have the grain to rely on; and were his grain crops to fail to a serious extent, the stock might insure him a profitable return. It is scarcely within the bounds of probability, that a loss would arise in any year from the total destruction of live-stock, wool, *and* grain. One of them may fail, and the prices of all may continue depressed for years; but, on the other hand, reasonable profits have been realized from them *all* in the same year. Thus, there are safeguards against a total loss, and a greater certainty of a profitable return from capital invested in the *mixed*, than in any *other* kind of husbandry at present known.

---

13. OF SELECTING A TUTOR-FARMER FOR TEACHING FARMING.

"These are their tutors, bid them use them well."
TAMING OF THE SHREW.

After resolving to follow farming as a profession, and determining to learn the mixed, as the best system of husbandry, it now only remains for the young farmer to select a farmer who practises it, with whom he would wish to engage as a pupil. The best kind of pupilage is to become a boarder in a farmer's house, where he will not only live comfortably, but may learn this superior system of husbandry thoroughly. There is no better mode than this known at present of learning practical farming. The choice of locality is so far limited, as it must be in a district in which this particular system is practised in a superior manner. The largest district in which it is so practised, as I have already intimated, comprehends Berwickshire, Roxburghshire, and Northumberland. There, many farmers are to be found who accept pupils, amongst whom a proper selection should be made, as it would be highly injudicious to engage with one who is notoriously deficient in the requisite qualifications. The qualifications are numerous. He should have the general reputation of being a good farmer; that is, a skilful cultivator of land, a judicious breeder, and an excellent judge of stock. He should possess agreeable manners, and have the power of communicating his thoughts with ease. He should occupy a good farm, consisting, if possible, of a variety of soils, and situate in a tolerably good climate, neither on the top of a high hill, nor on the confines of a large moor or bog, but in the midst of a well cultivated country. These circumstances of soil and locality should be absolute requisites in a farm intended to be made the residence of *pupils*. The top of a hill, exposed to every blast that blows, or the vicinage of a bog, overspread with damp vapour, would surround the farm with a climate in which no kind of crop or stock could arrive at a state of perfection; while, on the other hand, a very sheltered spot in a warm situation, would give the pupil no idea of the vexations experienced in a precarious climate. His inexperience in these things will render him unfit to select for himself either a qualified farmer, or a suitable farm; but friends are never awanting to render assistance to young aspirants in such emergencies, and if their opinion is formed on a knowledge of farming, both of the farm and the personal qualifications of the farmer they are recommending, some confidence may be placed in their recommendations. And for the pupil's personal comfort, he should choose a residence where there are *no very young* children.

As a residence of one year must pass over ere the pupil can witness the course of the annual operations of the farm, his engagement at first should be made for a period of *not less* than a year; and at the expiry of that period he will, most probably, find himself inadequate to the task of managing a farm. The entire length of time he would require to spend on a farm, must be determined by the paramount consideration of his having acquired a competent knowledge of his profession.

---

14. OF THE PUPILAGE.

"A man loves the meat in his youth that he cannot endure in his age."
MUCH ADO ABOUT NOTHING.

Having settled these preliminaries with the tutor-farmer, the pupil should enter the farm—the first field of his anticipations and toils in farming—with a resolution to acquire as much professional knowledge, in as short a time, as the nature of the business which he is about to learn, will admit of.

The commencement of his tuition may be made at any time of the year; but since farming operations have a regular beginning and ending every year, it is obvious that the *most* proper time to *begin* to view them is at the *opening of the agricultural year*, that is, *in the beginning of winter*. It may not be quite congenial to the feelings of him who has perhaps been accustomed to pass his winters in a town, to participate for the first time in the labours of a farm on the eve of winter. He would naturally prefer the sunny days of summer. But the beginning of winter being the time at which every important operation is *begun*, it is essential to their being understood throughout, to *see them begun*, and in doing this, minor inconveniences should be willingly submitted to, to acquire an intimate knowledge of a profession for life. And, besides, to endeavour to become acquainted with complicated operations, after the *principal arrangements* for their accomplishment have been *completed*, is purposely to invite wrong impressions of them.

There is really nothing disagreeable to personal comfort in the business of the farm in winter. On the contrary, it is full of interest, inasmuch as the well-being of living animals then comes home to the attention more forcibly than the operations of the soil. The totally different and well marked individual characters of different animals, engage our sympathies in different degrees; and the more so, perhaps, of all of them, that they appear more domesticated when under confinement than at liberty to roam about in quest of food and seclusion. In the evening, in winter, the hospitality of the social board await the pupil at home, or at a friend's house, after the labours of the day are over. Neighbours interchange visits at that social season, when topics of conversation, common to all societies, are varied by remarks on professional occurrences and management, elicited by the modified practices of the different speakers, from which the pupil may pick up much useful information. Or should society present no charms to him, the quieter companionship of books, or the severer task of study, is at his command. In a short time, however, the many objects peculiar to the season which present themselves in the country in winter, cannot fail to interest him.

The very first thing to which the pupil should direct his attention on entering the farm, is to become well acquainted with its *physical geography*,—that is, its position, exposure, extent;—its fences, whether of wall or hedge;—its shelter, in relation to rising grounds and plantations;—its roads, whether public or private;—its fields, their number, names, sizes, relative positions, and supply of water;—the position of the farm-house and steading or farm-stead. Familiar acquaintance with all these particulars will enable him to understand more readily the orders given by the farmer for the work to be performed in any field. It is like possessing a map of the ground on which certain plans of operations are about to be undertaken. A plan of the farm would much facilitate an introduction to this familiar acquaintance. The *tutor* farmer should be provided with such a plan to give to each of his pupils, but if *he* have it not, the pupil himself can set about constructing one which will answer his purpose well enough.

15. OF DEALING WITH THE DETAILS OF FARMING.

> "Oh! is there not some patriot . . .
> To teach the lab'ring hands the sweets of toil?
> Yes, there are such."
>
> THOMSON.

The principal object held in view while making the preceding observations, was the preparation of the mind of the young person, desirous of becoming a farmer, into such a state as to enable him, when he enters a farm as a pupil, to anticipate and overcome what might appear to him great difficulties of practice, which, with an unprepared mind, he could not know existed at all, far less know how to overcome, but on being informed that he must encounter them at the very outset of his career, he might use the means pointed out to him for meeting and overcoming them. These difficulties have their origin in the pupil seeing the operations of the farm, of whatever nature, performed for the first time, in the most perfect manner, and always with a view to accomplishment at some *future* period. The only mode of overcoming such difficulties, and thereby satisfying his mind, is for the pupil to ascertain by inquiry the *purport* of every operation he sees performing; and though he may feel that he does not quite comprehend that purport, even when informed of it, still the information will *warn* him of its approaching consummation, and he will not, therefore, at any time thereafter be taken by surprise, when the event actually arrives. If I shew the pupil the importance of making inquiry regarding the purport of every operation he sees performing, I see no better mode of rendering all farming operations intelligible to his mind. In order to urge him to become familiar with the purport of every thing he sees going on around him, I have endeavoured to point out the numerous *evils* attendant on farmers, landowners, and emigrants neglecting to become thoroughly acquainted with practical husbandry, before attempting to exercise their functions in their new vocations. And, in order that the young person desirous of becoming a farmer may have no excuse for not becoming *well* acquainted with farming, I have shewn him where, and the manner how, he can best become acquainted with it,—and these are best attained, under present circumstances, by his becoming an inmate for a time in a farmhouse with an intelligent farmer. Believing that the foregoing observations, if perused with a willing mind, are competent to give such a bias to his mind, as to enable the pupil, when he enters a farm, to appreciate the importance of his profession, and thereby create an ardent desire for its attainment, I shall now proceed to describe the details of every operation as it occurs in its due course on the farm.

The description of these details, which are multifarious and somewhat intricate, will compose by far the most voluminous portion of this work, and will constitute the most valuable and interesting part of it to the pupil. In the descriptions, it is my intention to go very minutely into details, that no circumstance may be omitted in regard to any of the operations, which may have the appearance of presenting a single one to the notice of the pupil in an imperfect form. This resolution may invest the descriptions with a degree of prolixity which may perhaps prove tiresome to the general reader, but, on that very account, it should the more readily give rise to a firm determination in the pupil to follow the particulars of every operation into their most minute ramifications; and this because he cannot be too intimately acquainted with the nature of every piece of work, or too much informed of the various modifications which every operation has frequently to undergo, in consequence of change in the weather, or the length of time in which it is permitted by the season to perform it. Descriptions so minute will answer the purpose of *detailed instructions* to the pupil, and should he follow them with a moderate degree of application through one series of operations, he will obtain such an insight into the nature of field labour, as will ever after enable him easily to recognise a similar series when it is begun to be put into execution. Unless, however, he bestow considerable attention on *all* the *details* of the descriptions, he will be apt to let pass what may appear to him an unimportant particular, but which may be the very keystone of the whole operation to which they relate. With a tolerable memory on the part of the pupil, I feel pretty sure that an *attentive perusal of the descriptions* will enable him to identify any piece of work he afterwards sees performing in the field. This achievement is as much as any book can be expected to accomplish.

In describing the details of farming, it is necessary to adhere to a determinate method; and the method that appears to me most instructive to the pupil, is to follow the usual routine of operations pursued on a farm. It will be requisite, in following that routine implicitly, to describe every operation from the *beginning;* for it must be impressed on the mind of the pupil, that farm operations are not conducted at random, but on a tried and approved system, which commences with preparatory labours and then carries them on with a determinate object in view throughout the seasons, until they terminate at the end of the agricultural year. The preparatory operations commence immediately after harvest, whenever that may happen, and it will be earlier or later in the year according as the season is early or late; and as the harvest is the consummation of the labours of the year and terminates the autumnal season, so the preparatory operations begin with the winter season. Thus the winter season takes the precedence in the arrangements of farming, and doing so, that should be the best reason for the pupil commencing his career as an agriculturist in winter. In that season he will have the advantage of witnessing every *preparation as it is made* for realizing the future crops,—an advantage which he cannot enjoy if he enter on his pupilage at any other season,—but it is a great advantage, inasmuch as every piece of work is much better understood when viewed from its commencement, than when seen for the first time in a state of progression.

Having offered these preliminary remarks respecting the condition of the agricultural pupil when about to commence learning his profession, I shall now proceed to conduct him through the whole details of farming, as they usually occur on a farm devoted to the practice of the mixed, or in other words of the most perfect system of husbandry known; whilst, at the same time, he shall be made acquainted with what constitute differences from it in the corresponding operations of the other modes of farming, and which are imposed by the peculiarities of the localities in which they are practised. These details I shall narrate in the order in which they are performed, and for that purpose will begin with those of Winter,—the season which commences the agricultural year,—for the reason assigned in the paragraph immediately preceding this one.

WINTER.

> "All nature feels the renovating force
> Of WINTER, only to the thoughtless eye
> In ruin seen. The frost-concocted glebe
> Draws in abundant vegetable soul,
> And gathers vigour for the coming year."
>
> THOMSON.

The subjects which court attention in Winter are of the most interesting description to the farmer. Finding little inducement to spend much time in the fields at this torpid season of the year, he directs his attention to the more animated portions of farm-work conducted in the steading, where almost the whole stock of animals are collected, and where the preparation of the grain for market affords pleasant employment for work-people within doors. The progress of live-stock to maturity is always a prominent object of the farmer's solicitude, but especially in winter, when the stock are comfortably housed in the farmstead, plentifully supplied with wholesome food, and so arranged in various classes according to age and sex, as to be easily inspected at any time.

The labours of the field in winter are confined to a few great operations. These are ploughing the soil in preparation of future crops, and supplying food to the live-stock. The ploughing partly consists of turning over the ground which had borne a part of the grain crops, and the method of ploughing this *stubble land*—so called because it bears the straw that was left uncut of the previous crop—is determined by the nature of the soil. That portion of the stubble land is first ploughed which is intended to be first brought into requisition for a crop in spring, and the rest is ploughed in the same succession that the different crops succeed each other in the ensuing seasons. The whole soil thus ploughed in the early part of winter in each field (where the farm is subdivided with fences), or in each division (where there are no fences), is then neatly and completely provided with channels, cut with the spade in suitable places, for the purpose of permitting the water that may fall from the heavens to run quickly off into the ditches, and thereby to maintain the soil in as dry a state as is practicable until spring. Towards the latter part of winter the newest grass land, or *lea,* as grass land is generally termed, intended to bear a crop in spring, is then ploughed; the oldest grass land being earlier ploughed, that its toughness may have time to be meliorated by spring by exposure to the atmosphere.—When the soil is naturally damp underneath, winter is the season selected for removing the damp by draining. It is questioned by some farmers whether the winter is the best season for draining, as the usually rainy and otherwise unsettled state of the weather then renders the carriage of the materials for draining very laborious. On the other hand, it is maintained by other farmers that, as the quantity of water to be drained from the soil determines both the number and size of the drains, these are thus best ascertained in winter; and as the fields are then most free of crop, they are in the most convenient state to be drained. Truth may perhaps be found to acquiesce in neither of these reasons, but rather in the opinion that draining may be successfully pursued at all seasons.—Where fields are uninclosed, and intended to be fenced with the thorn-hedge, winter is the season for performing the operation of planting it. Hard frost, a fall of snow, or heavy rain may put a stop to the work for a time, but in all other states of the weather it may proceed in perfect safety.—When meadows for irrigation exist on any farm, winter is the season for beginning the irrigation with water, that the grass may be ready to mow in the early part of the ensuing summer. It is a fact well worth keeping in remembrance in favour of *winter* irrigation, that irrigation in winter produces wholesome, and in summer unwholesome, herbage for stock. On the other hand, summer, not winter, is the proper season for forming water-meadows.—Almost the entire live-stock of an arable farm is dependent on the hand of man for food in winter. It is this circumstance, which, bringing the stock into the immediate presence of their owner, creates a stronger interest in their welfare then than at any other season. The farmer then sees them classed together in the farmstead according to their age and sex, and delights to contemplate the comparative progress of individuals or classes amongst them towards maturity. He makes it a point to see them provided at all times with a comfortable bed or lair, and a sufficient supply of clean food at appointed hours in their respective apartments. The feeding of stock is so important a branch of farm business in winter, that *it* regulates the time for prosecuting several other operations. It determines the quantity of turnips that should be carried from the field for the cattle in a given time, and causes the farmer to consider whether it would not be prudent to take advantage of the first few dry fresh days to store up a quantity of them, to be in reserve for the use of the stock during the storm that may be at the time portending, for storms like other

"Coming events cast their shadows before."

It also determines the quantity of straw that should be provided from the stack-yard in a given time, for the use of the animals; and upon this, again, depends the supply of grain that can be sent to the market in any given time. For although it is certainly in the farmer's power to thrash as many stacks as he pleases at one time—provided the machinery for the purpose is competent for the task—and he is tempted to do so when prices are high; yet, as new thrashed straw forms superior provender for live-stock confined in the farmstead, its supply, both as litter and fodder, is therefore mainly dependent on its use by the stock; and as its consumption as litter is greater in wet than in dry weather, and wet weather prevails in winter, the quantity of straw used in the course of that season must always be very considerable; and so therefore must the quantity of grain ready to be sent to market. All the stock in the farmstead in winter, that are not put to work, are placed under the care of the *cattle-man*.—The feeding of that portion of the sheep-stock which are barren, on turnips in the field, is a process practised in winter. This forms fully a more interesting object of contemplation to the farmer than even the feeding of cattle, the behaviour of sheep in any circumstances being always fascinating. Sheep being put on turnips early in winter, a favourable opportunity is thereby afforded the farmer, when clearing the field partially of turnips for the sheep (in a manner that will afterwards be fully described to the pupil), to store a quantity of them for the cattle in case of an emergency in the weather, such as rain, snow, or frost. This removal of the surplus turnips that are not used by the sheep confined on the land, renders sheep-feeding a process which in part also determines the quantity of that root that should be carried from the field in a given time.—The flock of ewes roaming at large over the pastures, require attention in winter, especially in frosty weather, or when snow is on the ground, when they should be supplied with hay, or turnips when the former is not abundant. The *shepherd* is the person who has charge of the sheep flock.—The large quantity of straw used in winter causes, as I have said, a considerable quantity of grain to be sent at that season to market. The preparation of grain for sale constitutes an important branch of winter farm-business, and should be strictly superintended. A considerable portion of the labour of horses and men are occupied in carrying the grain to the market-town, and delivering it to the purchasers,—a species of work which jades farm-horses very much in bad weather.—In hard frost, when the plough is laid to rest, or when the ground is covered with snow, and as soon as

> " ——— by frequent hoof and wheel, the roads
> A beaten path afford,"

the farm-yard manure is carried from the courts, and deposited in a large heap, in a convenient spot near the gate of the field which is to be manured with it in the ensuing spring or summer. This work is carried on as long as there is manure to carry away, or the weather continues in either of those states.—Of the implements of husbandry, only a few are put in requisition in winter;—the plough is in constant use when the weather will permit,—the thrashing-machine enjoys no sinecure,—and the cart finds periodic employment.

The *weather* in winter is of the most precarious description, and being so, the farmer's skill to anticipate its changes in this season is severely put to the test. Seeing that all operations of the farm are so dependent on the weather, a familiar acquaintance with the local prognostics which indicate a change for the better or worse is incumbent on the farmer. In actual rain, snow, or hard frost, none but in-door occupations can be executed; but, if the farmer have wisely "discerned the face of the sky," he can arrange the order of these in-door operations, so as they may be continued for a length of time, if the storm threaten a protracted endurance, or be left without detriment, should the strife of the elements quickly cease.

The winter is the season for *visiting the market town* regularly, where the surplus produce of the farm is disposed of,—articles purchased or bespoke for the use of the farm, when the busy seasons arrive,—where intermixture with the world affords the farmer an insight into the actions of mankind,—and where selfishness and cupidity may be seen to act as a foil to heighten the brilliancy of honest dealing.

Field sports have their full sway in winter, when the fields, bared of crop and stock, can sustain little injury by being traversed. Although farmers should not bestow any thing like a large portion of their time to field sports,—and many have no inclination for them at all,—yet such sports may very properly be enjoyed as a recreation at times, even by farmers. When duly qualified, why should farmers not join in a run with the fox-hounds?—or take a cast through the fields with a pointer?—or sound an exhilarating whoop with the greyhounds? Either of these sports forms a pleasing incident in the week's employment, gives a fillip to the mind, and a stimulus to the circulation. That inhabiter of the country, possessing leisure and a good nag, who can remain insensible to the "joys of a tally-ho," must have a soul "dull as night." These sports can only be pursued in fresh weather, and when the ground is not very heavy with wetness; but should frost and snow prevent their pursuit, the gymnastic game of curling and the callisthenic sport of skating then afford healthful exercise both to body and mind.

Winter is the season for those in the country *reciprocating the kindnesses of hospitality, and participating in the amusements of society.* The farmer delights to send the best produce of his poultry-yard as Christmas presents to his friends in town, and in return he is invited into town to partake of its amusements. But there is no want of the attractions of hospitality nearer home. There, farmers maintain a constant intercourse of the kind with each other; while the annual county ball, in the nearest market town, or a charity one set on foot to raise a fund in support of the labouring poor who are thrown out of employment during the rigour of winter, affords a seasonable treat; and the winter may appropriately be wound up by a *ré-union* given by the hunt to those who had been conspicuous in forwarding their sport during the hunting season.

Winter is to the farmer the season of *domestic enjoyment.* The fatigues of the long summer-day leave little leisure, and much less inclination, to tax the mind with study; but the long winter evening, after a day of bracing exercise, such as those I have just described, affords him a favourable opportunity, if he have the inclination at all, of partaking in social conversation, listening to instructive reading, or hearing the delights of music. In short, I know of no class of people more capable of enjoying a winter's evening in a rational manner, than the family of the country gentleman or the farmer.

Viewing winter in a higher and more serious light,—in the repose of nature, as emblematical of the mortality of man,—in the exquisite pleasures which man in winter, as a being of sensation, enjoys over the lower creation,—and in the eminence in which man, in the temperate regions, stands, with respect to the development of his mental faculties, above his fellow-creatures in the tropics;—in these respects, winter must be hailed by the dweller in the country, as the purifier of the mental as well as of the physical atmosphere.

On this subject, I cannot refrain from copying these beautiful reflections by a modern writer, whose great and versatile talents enabling him to write well on almost any subject, have long been known to me. "Winter," says he, "is the season of nature's annual repose,—the time when the working structures are reduced to the minimum of their extent, and the energies of growth and life to the minimum of their activity, and when the phenomena of nature are fewer, and address themselves less pleasingly to our senses, than they do in any other of the three seasons. There is hope in the bud of Spring, pleasure in the bloom of Summer, and enjoyment in the fruit of Autumn; but, if we make our senses our chief resource, there is something both blank and gloomy in the aspect of Winter.

"And if we were of and for this world alone, there is no doubt that this would be the correct view of the winter, as compared with the other seasons; and the partial death of the year would point as a most mournful index to the death and final close of our existence. But we are beings otherwise destined and endowed,—the world is to us only what the lodge is to the wayfaring man; and while we enjoy its rest, our thoughts can be directed back to the past part of our journey, and our hopes forward to its end, when we shall reach our proper home, and dwell there securely and for ever. This is our sure consolation,—the anchor of hope to our minds during all storms, whether they be of physical nature, or of social adversity. * * *

"We are beings of sensation certainly; many and exquisite are the pleasures which we are fitted for enjoying in this way, and much ought we to be grateful for their capacity of giving pleasure, and our capacity of receiving it; for this refined pleasure of the senses is special and peculiar to us out of all the countless variety of living creatures which tenant the earth around us. They eat, they drink, they sleep, they secure the succession of their race, and they die; but not one of them has a secondary pleasure of sense beyond the accomplishment of these very humble ends. We stand far higher in the mere gratifications of sense; and in the mental ones there is no comparison, as the other creatures have not an atom of the element to bring to the estimate.

"The winter is, therefore, the especial season of man—*our own season*, by way of eminence; and men who have no winter in the year of the region in which they are placed, never of themselves display those traits of mental development which are the true characteristics of rational men, as contrasted with the irrational part of the living creation. It is true there must be the contrast of a summer, in order to give this winter its proper effect, but still, the winter is the intellectual season of the year—the season during which the intellectual and immortal spirit in man enables him most triumphantly to display his superiority over 'the beasts that perish.'" *

* Mudie's Winter, Preface, p. 3—5.

16. OF THE STEADING OR FARMSTEAD.

"When we see the figure of the house, then must we rate the cost of the erection."
HENRY IV. Part II.

(1.) Before proceeding to the consideration of the state in which the pupil should find the various *fields* at the beginning of winter, it will tend to perspicuity in the furnishing of a farm to let him understand, in the first instance, the *principles* on which a *steading*, or *onstead*, or *farmstead*, or *farm-offices*, or *farmery*, as it has been variously styled, intended for a farm conducted on the mixed husbandry, should be constructed, and also to enumerate its *constituent parts*. This explanation being given, and got quit of at once, the names and uses of the various parts of a farmstead will at once become familiarized to him. And before beginning with the description of any thing, I may here express it as my opinion that my descriptions of all the farm operations will be much more lucid and graphic if addressed personally to the pupil.

(2.) To present a *description* of a steading in the most specific terms, it will, in the first place, be necessary to assume a size which will afford accommodation for a farm of given extent. To give full scope to the mixed husbandry, I have already stated that a farm of 500 imperial acres is required. I will therefore assume the steading, about to be described, to be suited to a farm of that extent. At the same time you should bear in mind that the *principles* which determine the arrangement of this particular size, are equally applicable to much smaller, as well as much larger steadings; and that the mixed husbandry is frequently practised on farms of much smaller extent.

(3.) It is a requisite condition to its proper use, that every steading be *conveniently placed* on the farm. To be *most* conveniently placed, in theory, it should stand in the *centre* of the farm; for, it can be proved in geometry that of any point within the area of a circle, the centre is the nearest to every point in its circumference. In practice, however, circumstances greatly modify this theoretical principle upon which the site of all steadings should be fixed. For instance, if an abundant supply of water can be easily obtained for the moving power of the thrashing-machine, the steading may be placed, for the sake of thus economizing horse labour, in a more remote and hollow spot than it should be in other circumstances. If wind is preferred, as the moving power, then the steading will be more appropriately placed on rising ground.

For the purpose of conveying the manure downhill to most of the fields, some would prefer the *highest* ground near the centre of the farm for its site. Others, on the contrary, would prefer the *hollowest* point near the centre, because the grain and green crops would then be carried downhill to the steading, and this they consider a superior situation to the other, inasmuch as the grain and green crops are much more bulky and heavy than the manure. In making either of these choices, it seems to be forgotten that loads have to be carried both *to* and *from* the steading; but either position will answer well enough, provided there be no steep ascent or descent to or from the steading. The latter situation, however, is more consonant to experience and reasoning than the other; though level ground affords the easiest transit to wheel-carriages. It is also very desirable that the farm-house should be so situated as to command a view of every field on the farm, in order that the farmer may have an opportunity of observing whether the labour is prosecuted steadily; and if other circumstances permit, especially a plentiful supply of good water, the vicinity of the farm-house should be chosen as the site for the steading; but if a sacrifice of the position on the part of either is necessary, the farm-house must give way to the convenience of the steading.

(4.) As a farm of mixed husbandry comprises every variety of culture, so its steading should be constructed to *afford accommodation for every variety of produce.* The grain and its straw, being important and bulky articles, should be accommodated with room as well after as before they are separated by thrashing. Room should also be provided for every kind of food for animals, such as hay and turnips. Of the animals themselves, the horses being constantly in hand at work, and receiving their food daily at regular intervals of time, should have a stable which will not only afford them lodging, but facilities for consuming their food. Similar accommodation is required for cows, the breeding portion of cattle. Young cattle, when small of size and of immature age, are usually reared in inclosed open spaces, called courts, having sheds for shelter and troughs for food and water. Those fattening for sale are either put into smaller courts with troughs, called hammels, or fastened to stakes in byres or feeding-houses, like the cows. Young horses are reared either by themselves in courts with sheds and mangers, or get leave to herd with the young cattle. Young pigs usually roam about everywhere, and generally lodge amongst the litter of the young cattle, whilst sows with sucking pigs are provided with small inclosures, fitted up with a littered apartment at one end, and troughs for food at another. The smaller implements of husbandry, when not in use, are put into a suitable apartment; whilst the carts are provided with a shed, into which some of the larger implements, which are only occasionally used, are stored by. Wool is put into a cool clean room. An apartment containing a furnace and boiler to heat water and prepare food when required for any of the animals, should never be wanting in any steading. These are the principal accommodations required in a steading where live-stock are cared for; and when all the apartments are even conveniently arranged, the whole building will be found to cover a considerable space of ground.

(5.) The leading *principle* on which these arrangements is determined is very simple, and it is this:—1. Straw being the bulkiest article on the farm, and in daily use by every kind of live-stock, and having to be carried and distributed in small quantities by bodily labour though a heavy and unwieldy substance, should be centrically placed, in regard to all the stock, and at a short distance from their respective apartments. The position of its receptacle, the *straw-barn*, should thus occupy a central point of the steading; and the several apartments containing the live-stock should be placed equidistant from the straw-barn, to save labour in the carrying of straw to the stock. 2. Again, applying the principle, that so bulky and heavy an article as straw should in all circumstances be moved to short distances, and not at all, if possible, from any other apartment but the straw-barn, the *thrashing-machine*, which deprives the straw of its grain, should be so placed as at once to throw the straw into the straw-barn. 3. And, in further application of the same principle, the *stack-yard* containing the unthrashed straw with its corn, should be placed contiguous to the thrashing-machine. 4. Lastly, the passage of straw from the stack-yard to the straw-barn through the thrashing-machine being directly progressive, it is not an immaterial consideration in the saving of time to place the stack-yard, thrashing-mill, and straw-barn in a right line.

(6.) Different classes of stock require different quantities of straw, to maintain them in the same degree of cleanliness and condition. *Those classes* which require the *most* should therefore be placed *nearest* the *straw-barn*. 1. The younger stock requiring most straw, the courts which they occupy should be placed contiguous to the straw-barn, and this can be most effectually done by placing the straw-barn so as a court may be put on each side of it. 2. The older or fattening cattle requiring the next largest quantity of straw, the hammels which they occupy should be placed next to these courts in nearness to the straw-barn. 3. Horses in the stables, and cows in the byres, requiring the smallest quantity of straw, the stables and byres may be placed next farthest in distance to the hammels from the straw-barn. The relative positions of these apartments are thus determined by the comparative use of the straw. 4. There are two apartments of the steading whose positions are necessarily determined by that of the thrashing-machine, the one is the upper-barn, or thrashing-barn, which contains the unthrashed corn from the stack-yard, ready for thrashing by the mill; and the other the corn-barn, which is below the mill, and receives the corn immediately after its separation from the straw by the mill to be cleaned for market. 5. It is a great convenience to have the granaries in direct communication with the corn-barn, to save the labour of carrying the clean corn to a distance when laid up for future use. To confine the space occupied by the steading on the ground as much as practicable for utility, and at the same time ensure the good condition of the grain, and especially this latter advantage, the granaries should always be elevated above the ground, and their floors then form convenient roofs for either cattle or cart-sheds. 6. The elevation which the granaries give to the building, should be taken advantage of to shelter the cattle-courts from the north wind in winter; and for the same reason that shelter is cherished for warmth to the cattle, all the cattle-courts should always be open to the sun. The courts being thus open to the south, and the granaries forming a screen from the north, it follows that the granaries should stretch east and west on the north side of the courts; and, as has been shewn, that the cattle-courts should be placed one on each side of the straw-barn, it also follows that the straw-barn, to be out of the way of screening the sun from the courts, should stand north and south, or at right angles to the south of the granaries. 7. The fixing of the straw-barn to the southward of the granaries, and of course to that of the thrashing-machine, necessarily fixes the position of the stack-yard to the north of both. Its northern position is highly favourable to the preservation of the corn in the stacks. 8. The relative positions of these apartments are very differently arranged from this in many existing steadings; but I may safely assert, that the greater the deviation from the *principle* inculcated in paragraphs (5) and (6) in the construction of steadings, the less desirable they become as habitations for live-stock in winter.

(7.) This leading principle of the construction of a steading which is intended to afford shelter to live-stock during winter, is as comprehensive as it is simple, for it is applicable to *every size of steading.* Obviously correct as the principle is, it is seldom reduced to practice, possibly because architects, who profess to supply plans of steadings, must be generally unacquainted with their practical use. There is one consideration upon which architects bestow by far too much attention,—the constructing of steadings at the least possible cost,—and to attain this object by the easiest method, they endeavour to *confine* the various apartments in the least possible space of ground, as if a few square yards of the ground of a farm were of great value. No doubt, the necessity of economy is urged upon them by the grudging spirit of the landlord when he has to disburse the cost, and by the poverty of the tenant when that burden is thrown upon him. Now, economy of construction should be a secondary consideration in comparison with the proper accommodation which should be afforded to live-stock. Suppose that, by inadequate accommodation, cattle thrive by 10s. a-head less in the course of a winter than they would have done in well constructed courts and hammels (and the supposition is by no means extravagant), and suppose that the farmer is prevented realizing this sum on three lots of twenty cattle each of different ages, there would be an *annual loss* to him of L.30 from want of proper accommodation. Had the capital sum, of which the annual loss of L.30 is the yearly interest, been expended in constructing the steading in the best manner, the loss would not only have been averted, but the cattle in much better health and condition to slaughter or to fatten on grass. Economy is an excellent rule to follow in farming, but it should never be put in practice to the violation of approved principles, or the creation of inconveniences to live-stock, whether in the steading or out of it. I regret to observe both errors too prevalent in the construction of steadings. For example. It is undeniable that as cattle occupy the courts only in winter, when the air even in the best situations is at a low temperature, and the day short, they should in such circumstances enjoy as much light and heat from the sun as can be obtained. It is quite practicable to afford them both in courts facing fully to the south, where these influences may be both seen and felt even in winter. Instead of that, cattle-courts are very frequently placed within a quadrangle of buildings, the southern range of which, in the first instance, eclipses the winter's sun of even his diminished influence, and the whole of which, besides, converts the chilling air which rushes over the corners of its roof into the courts, into a whirlwind of starvation, which, if accompanied with rain or sleet, is sure to engender the most insidious diseases in the cattle. Beware, then, of suffering loss by similar fatal consequences to your cattle; and to prompt you to be always on your guard, impress the above simple principle of the construction of steadings firmly upon your minds. Rest assured that its violation may prove in the end a much greater loss by preventing the cattle thriving, than the paltry sum saved at first in the outlay of the buildings can possibly ever recompence you for that loss.

(8.) Fig. 1, Plate I. gives an *isometrical view* of an existing steading suitable for the mixed husbandry, somewhat though not on the precise principles which I have inculcated just now, but rather on the usual plan of huddling together the various parts of a steading, with a view of saving some of its original cost. There are many steadings of this construction to be found in the country, but many more in which stalls for feeding cattle are substituted for hammels. The north range *a a* represents the granaries with their windows, *b* the upper barn, *c c* the arches into the sheds for cattle under the granaries. The projecting building *d* in the middle, is the straw-barn, which communicates by a door in each side with the court *e* or *f* for the younger cattle. The projecting building *g*, standing parallel with the straw-barn on the right hand side of the court *f*, is the stable for the work-horses, and the other projecting building *h*, also parallel with the straw-barn on the left-hand side of the court *e*, is the cart-shed. The cow-byres *i*, and hammels *k* for feeding cattle, are seen stretching to the right in a line with the north range *a*, but too far off from the straw-barn *d*: *l* are hammels for a bull and queys: *m*, sheds for shepherds' stores: *n*, stack-yard with stacks: *o*, turnip stores: *p*, piggeries: *q*, calves' court: *r*, implement-house: *s*, boiling-house: *t*, horse-pond: *u*, hen-house: *v*, liquid manure tank: *w*, hay-loft: *x*, out-houses: *y*, slaughter-house: and *z*, hammels for young horses. This is a common disposition of the principal parts of a *modern improved* steading, and a slight inspection of the plate will convince you, that in the arrangement of its different apartments is exhibited much of the principle which I have been advocating. Many *modifications* of this particular arrangement may be observed in actual practice ;—1. such as the removal of the straw-barn *d* into the north range *a*, and the placing of hammels, such as *k*, into the courts *e* and *f*, and the conversion of one of the sheds *c* into cart-sheds. 2. Another modification incloses a large court divided into two, within a range of buildings forming three sides of a quadrangle, and retaining the north range for the granaries, of a higher altitude than the rest. 3. Whilst another comprises two large courts, each surrounded by three sides of a quadrangle, the range in the middle occupied by the thrashing-mill and straw-barn being retained at a higher altitude than the rest. 4. Another completes the quadrangle around one court. 5. Whilst another surrounds a large court, divided into two, with a quadrangle. 6. And the last modification surrounds two separate courts, each with a quadrangle, having a common side. These modifications are made to suit either large or small farms; but they all profess to follow the same plan of arrangement. In truth, however, so varied is the construction of steadings, that, I dare say, no two in the country are exactly alike. Modifications in their construction in obedience to influential circumstances may be justifiable, but still they should all have reference to the *principle* insisted on above.

(9.) Fig. 2, Plate II. contains an engraving of a *ground-plan* of the steading represented by the isometrical view in Plate I. It is unnecessary for me to describe in detail all the component parts of this plan, as the names and sizes of the various apartments are all set down. A short inspection will suffice to make you well enough acquainted with the whole arrangement. This plan has been found, by extensive use, to constitute a commodious, convenient, and comfortable steading for the stock and crop of 500 acres, raised by the mixed husbandry, and those properties it possesses in a superior degree to most similar existing steadings of the same extent in this country, and in a much greater degree than any of the modified plans to which I have just alluded.

(10.) The *steading I would desire to see erected* would be exactly in accordance with the principle I have laid down. I do not know one, nor is there probably in existence one exactly on that principle, but I have seen several, particularly in the north of England, which have impressed me with the belief, that there *is* a construction, could it be but discovered, which would afford the most excellent accommodation, the greatest convenience, and the utmost degree of comfort to live-stock ; and live-stock being the principal inhabitants of steadings, too much care, in every respect, cannot, in my opinion, be bestowed on the construction of their habitations, so as to insure them in the inclement season the greatest degree of comfort. I shall describe both an isometrical view and ground-plan of a steading of imaginary construction, in strict accordance with the above principle—the principle itself having been brought out by the promptings of experience. I shall minutely describe these plans, in the sanguine hope that the obvious advantages which they exhibit, will recommend their construction for adoption to all proprietors and tenants who feel desirous of obtaining a plan of a steading for crop and stock, the arrangements of which have been suggested by matured practical experience The size of *these particular plans* is not suited to any farm, whereon the mixed husbandry is practised, of *less* extent than 500 acres; because in order to illustrate their *principle*, it was necessary to fix on some *definite* size, that the *relative* sizes and positions of the different apartments might be definitively set down; but the whole *arrangement* of the apartments is suited to any size of plan, as the size and number of the apartments may be enlarged or diminished according to the extent of the farm.

(11.) Fig. 3, Plate III. represents an *isometrical view* of such a steading, and keeping the principle upon which it is constructed in mind, you will find that this view illustrates it in every respect that has been stated. 1. A A is the principal or north range of building, of two storeys in height, standing east and west. It contains two granaries A and A, the upper-barn C, which is also the site of the thrashing-machine, the corn-barn being immediately below it is of course invisible, the sheds D D are under the granaries; E is the engine-house, and F the steam-engine furnace-stalk, where the power employed to impel the thrashing-machine is steam, G the implement-house entering from the west gable, and H the hay-house, under a granary. These several apartments, while occupying the north range, are greatly serviceable in sheltering the young stock in the large courts I and K from the north wind. 2. Immediately adjoining to the south of the corn-barn, upper-barn, and thrashing-machine, is the straw-barn L, standing north and south, contiguously placed for the emission of straw from either side into the courts I and K. 3. It is also conveniently situated for supplying straw to the feeding hammels M, to the right or eastward of the large court K, and equally so for supplying it to those at N, to the left or westward of the large court I. 4. It is accessibly enough placed for supplying straw to the work-horse stable O, and the saddle-horse stable P, to the right or eastward in a line of the principal range A. It is equally accessible to the cow-byre Q, and calves'-cribs R, to the left or westward, in a line of the principal range A.—S is the stackyard, from which the stacks are taken into the upper-barn C, by the gangway T; U is the boiling-house; V the cart-shed, opposite and near the work-horse stable O; W is the wool-room, having a window in the gable, and its stair is from the straw-barn L; XX comprise two small hammels for bulls; Y is the servants' cow-house, in the hammels N; Z is the gig-house, adjoining to the riding-horse stable P. *a* are four sties for feeding pigs therein; *b* is a small open court, with a shed for containing *young* pigs after they have just been weaned; *c* are two sties for brood-sows while lying-in. *d* are three apartments for the hatching and rearing of fowls. *e* and *f* are turnip-stores for supplying the hammels M; *g* is the turnip store for supplying the large court K; *h*, that for the small hammels X, and the servants' cow-house Y; *i*, that for the large court I; and *p* and *q* are those for the hammels N. *k* is the open court and shed, with water-trough for the calves; *l* the open court, with water-trough for the cows. *m* is the turnip-shed for the cow-house Q, and calves'-cribs R. *n* is the hay-stack built in the stackyard S, near the hay-house H. *o* and *o* are straw-racks for the centre of the large courts I and K. *u* is the ventilator on the roof of the boiling-house U; *r*, that on the cow-house Q; *s*, that on the calves'-cribs R; *t* and *w*, those on the roof of the work-horse stable O and *y*, that on the riding-horse stable P. *x* is the liquid manure-well to which drains converge from the various parts of the farmstead. *z* are feeding-troughs, dispersed in the different courts and hammels. *v* is the open court for the servants' cows. And *f'* and *f'* are potato stores.

(12.) A very little consideration of the arrangement just now detailed, will suffice to shew you that it completely illustrates the principle I have been advocating for the construction of farmsteads. Still, looking at the isometrical view, in fig. 3, Plate III., it will be observed that the thrashing-machine C,—the machinery for letting loose the straw,—is situated in the middle of the great range A, ready to receive the unthrashed crop behind from the stack-yard S, and as ready to deliver the straw thrashed into the straw-barn L standing before it. The store of straw in L, being placed exactly in the centre of the premises, is easily made available to the large courts I and K and the sheds D and D by its four doors, two on each side. The straw can be carried down the road on the right of the straw-barn L, to the hammels M; and along the farther end of the court K, through the gate at H to both the stables O and P. It can with as much facility be carried across the eastern angle of the large court I, through the gate at the bull's hammels X, to the range of hammels at N, and to the servants' cow-house Y, by its door near the turnip-store *h*. It can also be carried right across the same court I, through the gate behind Y to the cow-house Q, and the calves'-cribs R. The hammels X, the pigs in *a b* and *c*, and the fowls in *d*, can easily be supplied with straw. You may observe in the arrangement of these apartments, that the stables O and P, and the cow-house Q, and the calves'-cribs R, are situated *behind* the hammels M and N, and they are there for these reasons:—Hammels for feeding cattle requiring much more straw than stables and byres, according to the foregoing theory, should be placed *near* the straw-barn; and hammels, moreover, being only occupied in winter by stock, should derive, during that season, the fullest advantage that can be given them of the light and heat of the sun. The servants' cow-byre Y being placed nearer the straw-barn than the hammels N, may seem to contravene the principle laid down; but the cow-byre, if desired, may be removed to the other end of the hammels, though, in the case where young horses and queys in calf are intended to occupy the small hammels N, it may conveniently remain where it is, as they do not require so much straw as cows. If these hammels are to be destined to the accommodation of *feeding* stock, then the byre ought to be removed to the extreme left of the building.

This form of steading is amply *commodious*, for it can accommodate *all* the working and breeding stock, together with four generations of young stock in different stages of growth. A more *convenient* arrangement than this for a farmstead, as I conceive, can scarcely be imagined, and all the parts of it are of such a magnitude as not only to afford ample room for every thing accommodated within it, but with proper fittings up, the arrangement is capable of conferring great *comfort* on its inmates. Its commodiousness will be the more apparent after the ground-plan has been considered in detail.

(13.) Fig. 4, Plate IV. is the *ground-plan* of the steading, of which the preceding plate that has just been described is the isometrical view. The *straw-barn* L is seen at once, running north and south. It is purposely made of the height of the upper barn to contain a large quantity of straw, as it is often convenient in bad weather to thrash out a considerable quantity of corn, when no other work can be proceeded with, or when high market prices induce farmers to reap advantage from them There is another good reason for giving ample room to the straw-barn. Every sort of straw is not suited to every purpose, one sort being best suited for litter, and another for fodder. This being the case, it is desirable to have always both kinds in the barn, that the fodder-straw may not be wasted in litter, and the litter-straw given as fodder to the injury of the bestial. Besides, the same sort of straw is not alike acceptable as fodder to every class of animals. Thus wheat-straw is a favourite fodder with horses, as well as oat-straw, whilst the latter only is acceptable to cattle. Barley-straw is only fit for litter. To give access to litter and fodder straw at the same time, it is necessary to have a door from each kind into each court. Thus four doors, two at each side near the ends, are required in a large straw-barn. Slit-like openings should be made in its side-walls, to admit air and promote ventilation through the straw. A sky-light in the roof at the end nearest the thrashing-machine, is useful in giving light to those who take away and store up the straw from the thrashing-machine when the doors are shut, which they should be whenever the wind happens to blow too strongly through them into the machine against the straw Instead of dividing straw-barn doors into two vertical leaves, as is usually done, they should be divided horizontally into an upper and a lower leaf, so that the lower may always be kept shut against intruders, such as pigs, whilst the upper admits both light and air into the barn. One of the doors at each end should be furnished with a good stock-lock and key and thumb latch, and the other two fastened with a wooden hand-bar from the inside. The floor of the straw-barn is seldom or never flagged or causewayed, though it is desirable it should be. If it were not so expensive, the asphaltum pavement would make an excellent floor for a straw-barn Whatever substance is employed for the purpose, the floor should be made so firm and dry as to prevent the earth rising and the straw moulding. Mouldy straw at the bottom of a heap, superinduces throughout the upper mass a disagreeable odour, and imparts a taste repugnant to every animal. That portion of the floor upon which the straw first alights on sliding down the straw-screen of the thrashing-machine, should be strongly boarded, to resist the action of the forks when removing the straw. Blocks of hard-wood, such as the stools of hard-wood trees, set on end, causewaywise, and sunk into the earth, form a very durable flooring for this purpose. Stone flagging in this place destroys the prongs of the pitchforks. The straw-barn should communicate with the chaff-house by a shutting door, to enable those who take away the straw to see whether the chaff accumulates too high against the end of the winnowing-machine. The communication to the wool-room in this plan is by the straw-barn, by means of the stair *c′*, made either of wood or stone. The straw-barn is represented 72 feet in length, 18 feet in breadth, and 15 feet in height to the top of the side walls.

(14.) C is the *corn-barn*. Its roof is formed of the floor of the upper barn, and its height is generally made too low. The higher the roof is, the more easily will the corn descend to be cleaned from the thrashing-machine down the hopper to the winnowing-machine Nine feet is the least height it should be in any instance. The plan gives the size of the corn-barn as 31 feet by 18 feet, but taking off 5 feet for partitioning off the machinery of the thrashing-mill, as at *s*, the extent of the workable part of the barn floor will be 26 feet by 18 feet. In that space I have seen much barn-work done, but it could be made more by diminishing the size of the shed D of the court K. The corn-barn should have in it at least two glazed windows to admit plenty of light in the short days of winter, and they should be guarded outside with iron stanchions. If one window cannot be got to the south, the door when open will answer for the admission of sunshine to keep the apartment comfortably dry for the work-people and the grain. The door is generally divided into upper and lower halves, which, as usually placed, are always in the way when the winnowing-machine is used at the door. A more convenient method is to have the door in a whole piece, and when opened, to fold back into a recess in the outer wall, over the top of which a plinth might project to throw off the rain. In this case the ribets and lintel must be giblet-checked as deep as the thickness of the door, into which it should close flush, and be fastened with a good lock and key, and provided with a thumb-latch. The object of making the corn-barn door of this form is to avoid the inconvenience of its opening into the barn, where, unless it folds wholly back on a wall, is frequently in the way of work, particularly when winnowing roughs, and taking out sacks of corn on men's backs As to size, it should not be less in the opening than 7½ feet in height and 3½ feet in width. A light half-door can be hooked on, when work is going on, to prevent the intrusion of animals, and the wind sweeping along the floor. The floor of the corn-barn is frequently made of clay, or of a composition of ashes and lime; the asphaltic composition would be better than either; but in every instance it should be made of wood,—of sound hard red-wood Drahm battens, ploughed and feathered, and fastened down to stout joists with Scotch flooring sprigs driven through the feather-edge. A wooden floor is the only one that can be depended on being constantly dry in a corn-barn; and in a barn for the use of corn, a dry floor is indispensable. It has been suggested to me that a stone pavement, square-jointed, and laid on a bed of lime over 9 inches of broken stones; or an asphaltum pavement, laid on a body of 6 inches of broken stones, covered with a bed of grout on the top of the stones, would make as dry and more durable barn-floor than wood, and which will not rot. I am aware that stone or asphaltum pavement is durable, and not liable to rot; but there are objections to both, in a corn barn, of a practical nature, and it is certain that the best stone pavement is not proof against the undermining powers of the brown rat; whilst a wooden floor is durable enough, and certainly will not rot, if kept dry in the manner I shall recommend over the page. The objections to all stony pavements as a barn-floor are, that the scoops for shovelling the corn pass very harshly over them,—that the iron nails in the shoes of the work-people wear them down, and raise a dust upon them,—and that they are hurtful to the bare hands and lighter implements, when used in taking up the corn from the floor. For true comfort in all these respects in a barn-floor, there is nothing like wood. The walls of this barn should be made smooth with hair-plaster, and the joists and flooring forming its roof cleaned with the plane, as dust adheres much more readily to a rough than to a smooth surface. The stairs to the granaries *s* and *s* should enter from the corn-barn, and a stout plain-deal door with lock and key placed at the bottom of each. And at the side of one of the stairs may be enclosed on the floor of the barn, a space *t* to contain light corn to be given to the fowls and pigs in summer when this sort of food is scarce about the steading.

(15.) As the method of hanging doors on a giblet-check, should be adopted in all cases in steadings where doors on outside walls are likely to meet with obstructions on opening inwards, or themselves becoming obstructive to things passing outwards, the subject deserves a separate notice. In fig. 5, *a* is a strong door, mounted on crooks and bands, fully open, and thrown back into the recess of the wall *b*; the projecting part of the lintel *c* protecting it effectually from the rain; *d* is the giblet-check in the lintel, and *e* that in the ribets, into which the door shuts flush; *f* is the light movable door used when work is going on in the corn-barn.

Fig. 5.

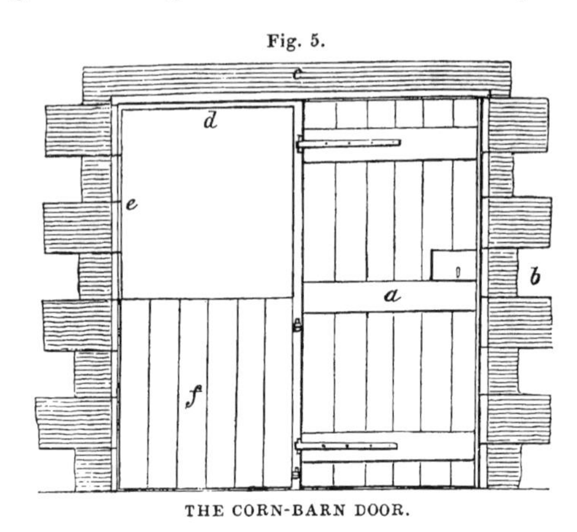

THE CORN-BARN DOOR.

(16.) The wooden floor of the corn-barn is liable to decay unless precautions are used to prevent it, but a much too common cause of its destruction is vermin—such as rats and mice. It is discreditable to farmers to permit this floor to remain in a state of decay for any length of time, when an effectual preventive remedy is within their reach; and the more certainly preventive that remedy is, the more it should be appreciated. I used a most effectual method of preventing the destructive ravages of either vermin or damp, by supporting the floor in the particular manner represented in fig. 6. The earth, in the first instance, is dug out of the barn to the depth of the foundations of the walls, which should be two feet below the door soles, and in the case of a new steading this can be done when the foundations of the walls are taken out. The ground is then spread over with a layer of sand, sufficient to preserve steadiness in the stout rough flags *b b* which are laid upon it and jointed in strong mortar. Twelve-inch thick sleeper walls *a a* of stone and lime are then built on the flags to serve the purpose of supporting each end of the joists of the floor. The joists *c*, formed of 10 by $2\frac{1}{2}$ inch plank, are then laid down 16 inches apart, and the spaces between them filled up to the top with stone and lime. The building between the joists requires to be done in a peculiar way. It should be done with squared rubble stones, and on no account should the mortar come in contact with the joists, as there is nothing destroys timber, by superinducing the dry rot, more readily than the action of mortar upon it. For this reason great care should be observed in building in the joists into the

Fig. 6.

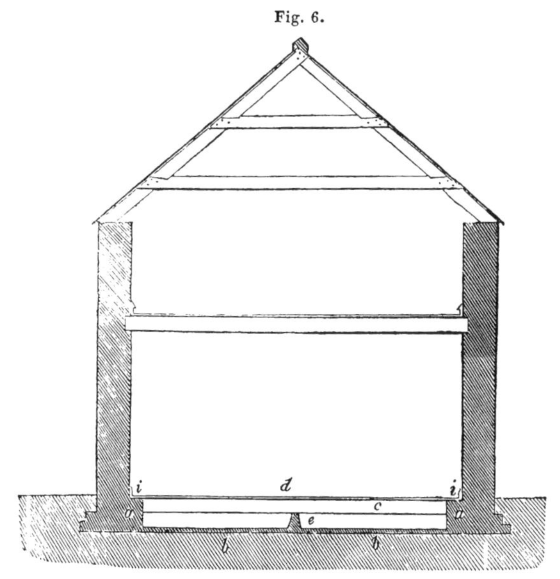

SECTION OF THE CORN-BARN FLOOR.

walls, in placing the safe-lintels over the doors and windows, the stones being dry-bedded over them, and in beam-filling between the couple-legs. The floor *d* is then properly laid on a level with the door-sole, and finished with a neat skifting board *i i* round the walls of the barn. By this contrivance the vermin cannot possibly reach the floor but from the flags, which are nearly 2 feet under it. A hewn stone pillar *e*, or even two, are placed on the flags under each joist to support and strengthen the floor. This construction of floor admits of abundance of air above and below to preserve it, and affords plenty of room under it for cats and dogs to hunt after the vermin. This figure also gives a section of the building above the corn-barn, including the floor of the upper barn, the outside walls, and the coupling, slating, and ridging of the roof of the middle range of building.

(17.) The *chaff-house*, *r*, stands between the corn and straw barns. It is separated from the former by a wooden partition, and from the latter by a stone-wall. Its height is the same as that of the corn-barn, the floor of the upper barn forming a roof common to both. It is 18 feet in length and 14 feet in width. It contains the winnowing-machine or fanners of the thrashing-machine, from which it receives the chaff. It has a thin door with a thumb-latch into the straw-barn, for a convenient access to adjust any of the gearing of the fanners; as also a boarded window hung on crooks and bands, fastened in the inside with a wooden hand-bar, and looking into the large court K; but its principal door, through which the chaff is emptied, opens outwards into the large court I. This door should be giblet-checked, and fastened from the inside with a wooden hand-bar. The space between the head of the fanners and the wall should be so boarded up as not to interfere with the action of the fanner-belts, but merely prevent the chaff being scattered among the machinery, and any access by persons being effected by the machinery into the upper barn.

(18.) D D are two *sheds* for sheltering the cattle occupying the courts I and K from rain and cold, by night or day, when they may choose to take refuge in them. The shed of the court I is 52 feet in length by 18 feet in width, being a little longer than that of the court K, which is 47 feet in length and 18 feet in width, and their height is 9 feet to the floor of the granaries, which forms their roof. The access to these sheds from the courts is by arched openings of 9 feet in width, and 7½ feet in height to the top of the arch. There should be a rack fastened against one of the walls of each shed to supply fodder to the cattle under shelter in bad weather, as at *h'*. As when a large number of cattle are confined together, of whatever age, some will endeavour to obtain the mastery over the others, and to prevent accidents in cases of actual collision, it has been recommended to have two openings to each shed, to afford a ready means of egress to the fugitives; and as a further safety to the bones and skins of the unhappy victims, the angles of the hewn pillars which support the arches should be chamfered. In my opinion, the precaution of two openings for the reason given is unnecessary, inasmuch as cattle, and especially those which have been brought up together, soon become familiarized to each other; and two openings cause draughts of air through the shed. If holes were made in the faces of the pillars opposite to each other in the openings, so as bars of wood could be put across them, the cattle could at any time be kept confined within the sheds. This might at times be necessary, especially when the courts are clearing out of the manure. The shed of the court K has a door *d'* in the back wall for a passage to the work-people when going from the corn to the upper barn, by the gangway T.

(19.) E is the engine-house for the steam-engine, when one is used. It is 18 feet in length and 8 feet in width, and the granary-floor above forms its roof It has a window looking into the large court I, and a door into the boiler and furnace-house F which house is 24 feet in length and 8 feet in width, and has an arched opening at the left or west end. The chimney-stalk is 6 feet square at the base, and rises tapering to a height of 45 feet. If wind or horses are preferred as the moving power, the windmill-tower or horse-course would be erected on the site of F.

(20.) G is the *implement-house* for keeping together the smaller implements when not in use, when they are apt to be thrown aside and lost. The intrinsic value of each implement being small, there is too generally less care bestowed on them than on those of more pecuniary value; but in use each of them is really as valuable as the most costly, and even their cost in the aggregate is considerable The implement-house is 18 feet in length by 14 feet in width, and its roof is formed of the granary-floor. This house should be provided with a stout plain-deal door with a good lock and key, the care of which should only be entrusted to the farm-steward. It should also have a partly glazed window like that of the cow-house, as sometimes this apartment may be converted into a convenient work-shop for particular purposes. The floor should be flagged or laid with asphaltum pavement. Beside the implements, this apartment may contain the barrel of tar, a useful ingredient on farms where sheep are reared, and where cart-naves require greasing; the grindstone, a convenient instrument on a farm on many occasions for sharpening edge-tools, such as scythes, axes, hay-knife, dung-spade, &c. A number of wooden pins and iron spikes driven into the walls, will be found useful for suspending many of the smaller articles upon. The walls should be plastered.

(21.) H is the *hay-house* at the east end of the north range A, and corresponding in situation to the implement-house. It is 18 feet in length, 17 feet in width, and its roof is also formed of the floor of the granary above. Its floor should be flagged with a considerable quantity of sand to keep it dry, or with asphaltum. It should have a giblet-checked door to open outwards, with a hand-bar to fasten it by in the inside; it should also have a partly glazed window, with shutters, to afford light, when taking out the hay to the horses, and air to keep it sweet As the hay-house communicates immediately with the work-horse stable O by a door, it can find room for the work-horse corn-chest *y*, which may be there conveniently supplied with corn from the granary above by means of a spout let into the fixed part of the lid. For facilitating the taking out of the corn, the *end* of the chest should be placed against the wall at the side of the door which opens into the stable, and its back part should be boarded up with thin deals to the granary-floor, to prevent the hay coming upon the chest. Its walls should be plastered. This hay-house is conveniently situated for the hay-stack *n* in the stack-yard S.

(22.) The *form* of the *corn-chest*, *y*, is more convenient and takes up less room on the floor when high and narrow, than when low and broad. When of a high form, a part of the front should fold down with hinges to give easier access to the corn as it gets low in the chest. Part of the lid should be made fast, to receive the corn-spout from the granary, and to lighten its movable part, which should be fastened with a hesp and padlock, and the key of which should be constantly in the custody of the farm-steward, or of the man who gives out the corn to the ploughmen, where no farm-steward is kept. A fourth part of a peck-measure is always kept in the chest for measuring out the corn to the horses. You must not imagine that because the spout supplies corn from the granary when required, that it supplies it without measure. The corn appropriated for the horses is previously measured off on the granary-floor, in any convenient quantity, and then shovelled down the spout at times to fill the chest; besides, lines can be marked on the inside of the chest indicative of every quarter of corn which it can contain.

(23.) O is the *stable* for the *work-horses*. Its length of course depends on the number of horses employed on the farm; but in *no instance should its width be less* than 18 feet, for comfort to the horses themselves, and convenience to the men who take charge of them. This plan being intended for a definite size of farm contains stalls for 12 horses, and a loose box besides, the whole length being 84 feet. Few stables for work-horses are made wider than 16 feet, and hence few are otherwise than hampered for want of room. A glance at the particulars which should be accommodated in the width of a work-horse stable, will shew you at once the inconvenience of this narrow breadth. The entire length of a work-horse is seldom less than 8 feet; the extreme width of the hay-rack is about 2 feet; the harness hanging loosely against the wall occupies about 2 feet; and the gutter occupies 1 foot; so that in a width of 16 feet there are only 3 feet left from the heels of the horses to the harness, on which to pass backward and forward to wheel a barrow and use the shovel and broom. No wonder when so little space is left to work in, that cleanliness is so much neglected in farm-stables and that much of the dung and urine are left to be decomposed and dissipated by heat in the shape of ammoniacal gas, to the probable injury of the breathing and eye-sight of the horses, when shut up at night. And what aggravates the evil, there seldom is a ventilator in the roof; and what is still worse, the contents of the stable are much contracted by the placing of a hay-loft immediately above the horses' heads. Whatever may be the condition of a work-horse stable in reference to size and room, its walls should always be plastered with good haired plaster, as forming the most comfortable finishing, and being that most easily kept clean.—Some people imagine that twelve horses are too great a number to be in one stable, and that two stables of six stalls each would be better. Provided the stable is properly ventilated, there can no injury accrue to a larger than to a smaller number of horses in a stable ; and besides, there are practical inconveniences in having two work-horse stables on a farm. The inconveniences are, that neither the farmer nor farm-steward can personally superintend the grooming of horses in two stables ; that the orders given to the ploughmen by the steward must be repeated in both stables; and that either all the ploughmen must be collected in one of the stables to receive their orders, or part of them not hearing the orders given to the rest, there cannot be that common understanding as to the work to be done which should exist among all classes of work-people on a farm.

(24.) Another particular in which most work-horse stables are improperly fitted up, is the narrowness of the *stalls*, 5 feet 3 inches being the largest space allowed for an ordinary sized work-horse. A narrow stall is not only injurious to the horse himself, by keeping him peremptorily confined to one position, in which he has no liberty to bite or scratch himself, should he feel so inclined, but materially obstructs the ploughman in the grooming process, and while supplying the horse with food. No work-horse, in my opinion, should have a narrower stall than 6 feet from centre to centre of the travis, in order that he may stand at ease, or lie down at pleasure with comfort. If " the labourer is worthy of his hire," the work-horse is deserving of a stall that will afford him sound rest.

(25.) It is a disputed point of what form the *hay-racks* in a work-horse stable should be. The prevailing opinion may be learned from the general practice, which is to place them as high as the horses' heads, because, as it is alleged, the horse is thereby obliged to hold up his head, and he cannot then breathe *upon* his food. Many more cogent reasons, as I conceive, may be adduced for placing the racks low down. In the first place, a work-horse does not require to hold his head up at any time, and much less in the stable, where he should enjoy all the rest he can get. 2. A low rack permits the position of his neck and head, in the act of eating, to be more like the way he usually holds them, than when holding them up to a high one. 3. He is not nearly so liable to pull out the hay among his feet from a low as from a high rack. 4. His breath cannot contaminate his food *more* in a low than in a high rack, because the greatest proportion of the breath naturally ascends; though breathing is employed by the horse to a certain degree in choosing his food by the sense of smell. 5. He is less fatigued eating out of a low than from a high rack, every mouthful having to be pulled out of the latter, from its sloping position, by the side of the mouth turned upwards. 6. Mown-grass is much more easily eaten out of a low than a high rack. 7. And lastly, I have heard of peas falling out of their straw, when eaten out of a high rack, into the ears of the horse, and therein setting up a serious degree of inflammation.

(26.) The *front rail* of the *low-rack* should be made of strong hard wood, in case the horse should at any time playfully put his foot on it, or bite it when groomed. The front of the rack should be sparred for the admission of fresh air among the food, and incline inwards at the lower end, to be out of the way of the horses' fore-feet. The bottom should also be sparred, and raised about 6 inches above the floor, for the removal of hay seeds that may have passed through the spars. The *corn-trough* should be placed at the near end of the rack, for the greater convenience of supplying the corn. A spar of wood should be fixed across the rack from the front rail to the back wall, midway between the travis and the corn-trough, to prevent the horse tossing out the fodder with the side of his mouth, which he will sometimes be inclined to do when not hungry. The *ring* through which the stall collar-shank passes, is fastened by a staple to the hard-wood front rail. I have lately seen the manger in some work-horse stables in steadings recently erected made of stone, on the alleged score of being more easily cleaned than wood after the horses have got prepared food. From my own observation in the matter, I do not think wood more difficult of being cleaned than stone at any time, and especially if cleaned in a proper time after being used,—daily, for instance. As ploughmen are proverbially careless, the stone-manger has perhaps been substituted on the supposition that it will bear much harder usage than wood; or perhaps the landlords, in the several instances in which stone-mangers have been erected, could obtain stone cheaper from their own quarries than good timber from abroad: but either of these reasons are poor excuses for the carelessness of servants on the one hand, or the parsimony of landlords on the other, when the well-being of the farmers' most useful animals is in consideration; for, besides the clumsy appearance of stone in such a situation, and its comfortless feel and aspect, it is injurious to the horses' teeth when they seize it suddenly in grooming, and it is impossible to prevent even some work-horses biting any object when groomed; and I should suppose that stone would also prove hurtful to their lips when gathering their food at the bottom of the manger. I have no doubt that the use of stone-mangers will have a greater effect in grinding down the teeth of farm-horses, than the "tooth of old Time" itself.

(27.) The *hind posts* of *travises* should be of solid wood rounded in front, grooved in the back as far as the travis boards reach, sunk at the lower ends into stone blocks, and fastened at the upper ends to battens stretching across the stable from the ends of the couple legs, where there is no hay-loft, and from the joists of the flooring, where there is. The *head-posts* are divided into two parts, which clasp the travis boards between them, and are kept together with screw-bolts and nuts. Their lower ends are also sunk into stone blocks, and their upper fastened to the battens or joists. The *travis boards* are put endways into the groove in the hind-post, and pass between the two divisions of the head-post to the wall before the horses' heads; and are there raised so high as to prevent the contiguous horses troubling each other.

(28.) The *floor* of all stables should be made hard, to resist the action of the horses' feet. That of a work-horse stable is usually causewayed with small round stones, embedded in sand, such as are to be found on the land or on the sea-beach. This is a cheap mode of paving. When these cannot be found, squared blocks of whinstone (trap rock, such as basalt, greenstone, &c.) answer the purpose fully better. Flags make a smoother pavement for the feet than either of these materials, and they undoubtedly make the cleanest floor, as the small stones are very apt to retain the dung and absorb the urine around them, which, on decomposition, cause filth and a constant annoyance to horses. To avoid this inconvenience in a great degree, it would be advisable to form the gutter behind the horses' heels of hewn freestone, containing an entire channel, along which the urine would flow easily, and every filth be completely swept away with the broom. The channel should have a fall of at least 1½ inch to the 10 feet of length The paving on both sides should incline towards this gutter, the rise in the stalls being 3 inches in all. In some stables, such as those of the cavalry and of carriers, the floor of the stalls rise much higher than 3 inches, and on the Continent, particularly in Holland, I have observed the rise to be still more than in any stables in this country. Some veterinary writers say that the position of the feet of the horse imposed by the rise, does not throw an unnecessary strain on the back tendons of the hind-legs.* This may be, but it cannot be denied that, in this position, the toes are raised above the heels much higher than on level ground. I admit that a rise of 3 inches is necessary in stalls in which geldings stand, as they throw their water pretty far on the litter; but in the case of mares, even this rise is quite unnecessary. It is indisputable that a horse always prefers to stand on level ground, when he is free to choose the

* Stewart's Stable Economy, p. 17.

ground for himself in a grass-field, and much more ought he to have level ground to stand on in a stable, which is his place of *rest.*

(29.) Fig. 7. gives a view of the particulars of such a *stall for work-horses* as I have described. *a a* are the strong hind-posts; *b b*, the head-posts, both sunk into the blocks *c c c c*, and fastened to the battens *d d*, stretching across the stable from the wall *e* to the opposite wall; *f f* the travis-boards, let into the posts *a a* by grooves, and passing between the two divisions of the posts *b b*; the boards are represented high enough to prevent the horses annoying each other; *g g* curb-stones set up between the hind and fore posts *a* and *b*, to receive the side of the travis-boards in grooves, and thereby secure them from decay by keeping them beyond the action of the litter; *h* is the sparred bottom of the hay-rack, the upper rail of which holds the ring *i* for the stall collar-shank; *k* the corn-manger or trough; *l* the bar across the rack, to prevent the horse tossing out the fodder; *m* the pavement within the stall; *n* is

Fig. 7.

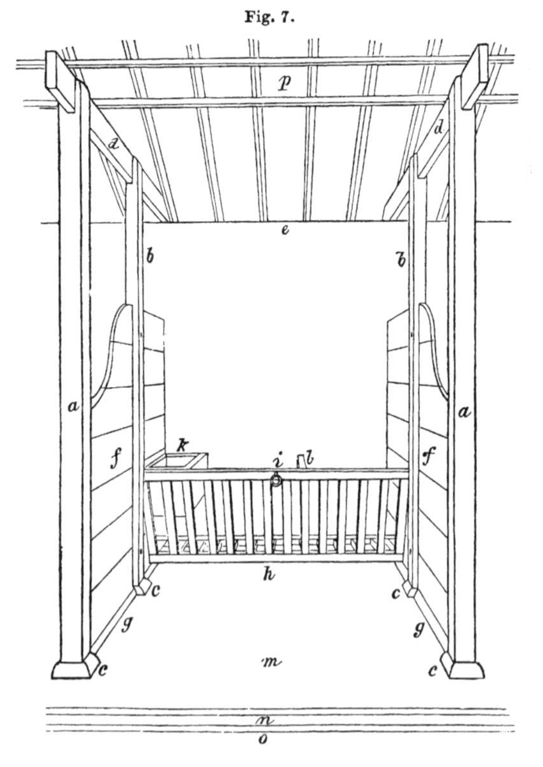

STALL FOR WORK-HORSE STABLE.

the freestone gutter for conveying away the urine to one end of the stable; *o* the pavement of the passage behind the horses' heels; *p* are two parallel spars fastened over and across the battens, when there is no hay-loft, to support trusses of straw or hay, to be given as fodder to the horses in the evenings of winter, to save the risk of fire in going at night to the straw-barn or hay-house with a light.

(30.) The *harness* should all be hung against the wall behind the horses, and none on the posts of the stalls, against which it is too frequently placed to its great injury, in being constantly kept in a damp state by the horses' breath and perspiration, and apt to be knocked down among the horses' feet. A good way is to suspend harness on stout hard-wood pins driven into a strong narrow board, fastened to the wall with iron holdfasts; but perhaps the most substantial way is to build the pins into the wall. The harness belonging to each pair of horses should just cover a space of the wall equal to the breadth of the two stalls which they occupy, and when windows and doors intervene, and which, of course, must be left free, its arrangement requires some consideration. This mode of arrangement I have found convenient. A spar of hard wood nailed firmly across the upper edge of the batten *d*, fig. 7, that supports both the posts of a stall, will suspend a collar on each end, high enough above a person's head, immediately over the passage. One pin is sufficient for each of the cart-saddles; one will support both the bridles, while a fourth will suffice for the plough, and a fifth for the trace harness. Thus 5 pins or 6 spaces will be required for each pair of stalls, and in a stable of 12 stalls, deducting a space of 13 feet for 2 doors and 2 windows in such a stable, there will still be left, according to this arrangement, a space for the harness of about 18 inches between the pins. Iron-hooks driven into the board betwixt the pins will keep the cart-ropes and plough-reins by themselves. The curry-comb, hair-brush, and foot-picker may be conveniently enough hung up on the hind-post betwixt the pair of horses to which they belong, and the mane-comb is usually carried in the ploughman's pocket.

(31.) Each horse should be bound to his stall with a *leather stall-collar*, having an iron-chain collar-shank to play through the ring *i* of the hay-rack, fig. 7, with a turned wooden sinker at its end, to weigh it to the ground. Iron-chains make the strongest stall-collar-shanks, though certainly noisy when in use; yet work-horses are not to be trusted with the best hempen cords, which often become affected with dry-rot, and are, at all events, soon apt to wear out in running through the smoothest stall-rings. A simple stall-collar, with a nose-band, and strap over the head, is sufficient to secure most horses; but as some have a trick of slipping the strap over their ears, it is necessary to have either a throat-lash in addition or a belt round the neck. Others are apt, when scratching their neck with the hind-foot, to pass the fetlock joint over the stall-collar-shank, and finding themselves thus entangled, to throw themselves down in the stalls, bound neck and heel, there to remain unreleased until the morning, when the men come to the stable. By this accident, I have seen horses get injured in the head and leg for some time. A short stall-collar-shank is the only preventive against such an accident, and the low rack admits of its being constantly used.

(32.) The *roof* of a *work*-stable should always be open to the slates, and not only that, but have openings in its ridge, protected from the weather by a particular kind of wood-work, called a ventilator. Such a thing as a ventilator is absolutely necessary on the roof of a work-horse stable. It is distressing to the feelings to inhale the air in some farm stables at night, particularly in old steadings economically fitted up. It is not only warm from confinement, moist from the evaporation of perspiration, and stifling from sudorific odours, but cutting to the breath, and pungent to the eyes, from the decomposition of dung and urine by the heat. The windows are seldom opened, and many can scarcely be opened by disuse. The roof in fact is suspended like an extinguisher over the half stifled horses. But the evil is still farther aggravated by a hay-loft, the floor of which is extended over and within a foot or less of the horses' heads. Besides the horses being thus inconvenienced by the hay-loft, the hay in it, through this nightly roasting and fumigation, soon becomes dry and brittle, and contracts a disagreeable odour. The only remedy for these inconveniences in work-horse stables is the establishment of a complete ventilation through them.

(33.) Fig. 8. represents one of these *ventilators*, in which the Venetian blinds *a* are fixed, and answer the double purpose of permitting the

Fig. 8.

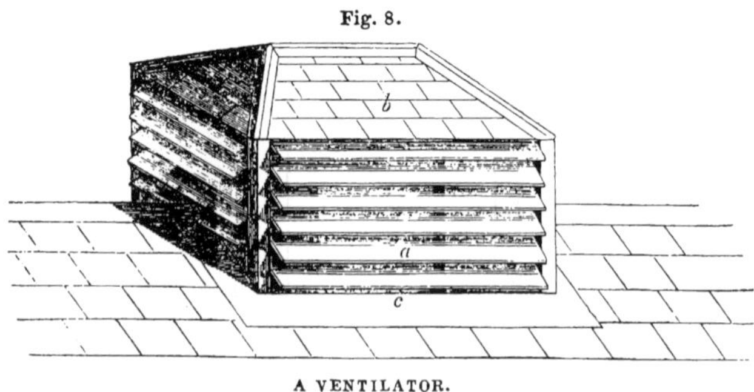

A VENTILATOR.

escape of heated air and effluvia, and of preventing the entrance of rain or snow The blinds are covered and protected by the roof *b*, made of slates and lead ; *c* is an apron of lead. Such a ventilator would be more ornamental to the steading than fig. 8, and more protective to the blinds, if its roof projected 12 inches over. One ventilator of the size of 6 feet in length, 3 feet in height in front, and 2 feet above the ridging of the roof, for every four horses in a work-horse stable, may perhaps suffice to maintain a complete ventilation. But openings in the roof will not of themselves constitute ventilation, unless there be an adequate supply of fresh air from below, to enforce a current; and this supply should be obtained from openings in the walls, including the chinks of doors and windows when shut, whose gross areas should be equal to those of the ventilators. The openings should be formed in such situations, and in such numbers, as to cause no draught of cold air to be directed against the horses. They might conveniently be placed, protected by gratings of iron on the outside to prevent the entrance of vermin, in the wall immediately behind the harness, through which the air would pass, and cross the passage towards the horses; and the air on thus entering the stable should be made to deflect to both sides of each opening, by striking against a plate of iron placed before the opening, at a short distance from the wall. I observe other forms of ventilators in use in steadings, one consisting of large lead pipes projected through the roof, with the ends turned down; and another having a portion of the slating or tiling raised up a little, and there held open. Either of these plans is much better than no ventilation at all, and I dare say either mode may be cheaply constructed; but neither is so effectual for the purposes of ventilation as the one I have figured and described.

(34.) Besides the ordinary stalls, a *loose-box*, *u*, will be found a useful adjunct to a work-horse stable. A space equal to two stalls should be railed off at one end of the stable, as represented at *u* on the plan, fig. 4, Plate IV. It is a convenient place into which to put a work-mare when expected to foal. Some mares indicate so very faint symptoms of foaling, that they frequently are known to drop their foals under night in the stable, to the great risk of the foal's life, where requisite attention is not directed to the state of the mare, or where there is no spare apartment to put her into. It is also suitable for a young stallion, when first taken up and preparing for travelling the road; as also for any young draught-horse, taken up to be broke for work, until he become accustomed to a stable. It might be, when unfortunately so required, converted into a convenient hospital for a horse, which, when seized with an unknown complaint, might be confined in it, until it is ascertained whether the disease is infectious, and then he should be removed to an out-house. Some people object to having a loose-box in the stable, and would rather have it out of it; but the social disposition of the horse renders one useful there on the occasions just mentioned. It is, besides, an excellent place in which to rest a fatigued horse for a few days.

(35.) Adjoining to this I have placed the *stable* for *riding-horses*, as at P on the plan, fig. 4, Plate IV, not that those stables should always be together, for the riding-horse stable can be placed at any convenient part of the farmstead, or near the farm-house. It may be fitted up in the form of three stalls of 6 feet each, or two loose-boxes of 9 feet each, according to inclination, that is, a size of 18 feet square will afford ample room for all the riding-horses a farmer will require. The high rack is always put up in riding-horse stables, to oblige the horse to keep up his head, and maintain a lofty carriage with it. The long manger, stretching from one travis to another, is frequently used where the high rack is approved of. But the neatest mode of fitting up the stall of a riding-horse stable is with a hay-crib in one of the corners, and a corn-box in the other, both being placed at convenient heights from the ground. The stall-posts in riding-horse stables are fastened into the ground in a body of masonry, and not to the roof, as that should be made as lofty as the height of the balks of the couples will admit, and it should be lathed, and all the walls plastered, for the sake of appearance, warmth, and cleanliness. The corn-chest may be placed either in the recess of the window, where its lid might form a sort of table, or in a corner. One door and a window are quite enough for light and entrance. The door should open outwards on giblet-checked ribets, and provided with a good lock and key, and spring latch with a handle, so as not to catch the harness. The height and width of both riding and work-horse stable-doors are usually made too low and too narrow for the easy passage of ordinary sized horses in harness; 7½ feet by 3½ feet are of the least dimensions they should ever be made. A ventilator is as requisite in a riding as in a work-horse stable, and, to promote ventilation, the under part of the window should be provided with shutters to open. The neatest floor is of droved flags; though I have seen in stables for riding horses very beautiful floors of Dutch clinkers.

(36.) The lowest part of a *high rack* is usually placed about the height of a horse's back, in contact with the wall, and the upper part projecting about 2 feet from it. This position is objectionable, inasmuch as the angle of inclination of the front with the wall is so obtuse as to oblige the horse to turn up the side of his mouth before he can draw a mouthful of provender out of it, though the front be sparred at such a width as to permit hay and grass to pass easily through. A better plan is to have the front nearly parallel with the wall, and the bottom sparred to admit the falling out of dust and seeds.

(37.) The *long manger*, which is always used with the high rack, is chiefly useful in permitting the corn to be thinly spread out, and making it more difficult to be gathered by the lips of the horse, and on that account considered an advantageous form of manger for horses that are in the habit of bolting their corn. I doubt whether horses really masticate their corn more effectually when it is spread out thin, though no doubt they are obliged to take longer time in gathering and swallowing it, when in that state.

(38.) The *hay crib* fixed up in one of the corners of the stall, usually the far one, is not large enough to contain fodder for a work-horse, though amply so for a riding-horse. A work-horse will eat a stone of hay of 22 lb. every day, which, when even much compressed, occupies about a cubic foot of space. To make a quadrifid hay-crib contain this bulk, would require the hay to be hard pressed down, to the great annoyance of the horse, and the danger of much waste by constant pulling out. Ploughmen require no encouragement by small racks to press fodder hard into racks. This they usually do, with the intention of giving plenty of it to their horses; but were racks generally made capacious enough, they would have less inducement to follow a practice which never fails to be attended with waste of provender. Such hay-cribs are usually made of iron.

(39.) With regard to the *relative advantages* of *stalls* and *loose-boxes* in riding-stables, there is no doubt that, for personal liberty and comfort to the horse, the latter are much to be preferred, as in them he can stand, lie down, and stretch himself out in any way he pleases; but they require more litter and a great deal of attention from the groom to keep the skin of the horse clean, and preserve the horse-clothes from being torn,—considerations of some importance to a farmer who has little use for a regularly-bred groom to attend constantly on his riding-horse; unless he be a sportsman.

(40.) The *floor* of the riding-horse stable may be paved either with small stones, and a gutter of freestone to carry off urine, like the work-horse stable, or, what is better, with jointed flags; but the neatest form of flooring is of jointed *droved* flags, grooved across the passage from the door to the stalls, to prevent the slipping of the horses' feet. This plan has also the advantage of being the cleanest as well as the neatest, but it is obviously more suited to the stables of the landlord than the tenant.

(41.) If you use a wheeled vehicle of any kind, the *coach-house* should adjoin the riding-horse stable. Of 18 feet square in size it will contain two light wheeled carriages, and afford ample room besides for other purposes, such as the cleaning of harness, &c. As the utmost precautions of ventilation and cleanliness cannot prevent deposition of dust in a riding-horse stable, the harness should be placed beyond its reach in the coach-house, where it should be hung upon pins against a boarded wall. To keep it and the carriages dry in winter, there should be a large *fire-place* in the coach-house. The floor should be flagged, and the roof and walls lathed and hair-plastered. A door should open from the riding-horse stable, provided with lock and key, and the large coach-house door should open outwards on a giblet-check, and be fastened with bolts and a bar in the inside. Z in plan fig. 4, Plate IV. is the coach-house; with the large fire-place *i* in it. Coach-houses having to be kept dry in winter, to prevent the moulding of the leather-work, are frequently kept so by *stoves*, which, when not in use in summer, become rusted and out of working order; and when again lighted in that state, never fail to smoke and soil every thing with soot.

(42.) The *cow-house* or *byre* Q, is placed on the left of the principal range, in a position corresponding with that of the work-horse stable. It is 53 feet in length, and 18 feet in width. The stalls of a cow-house, to be easy for the cows to lie down and rise up, should, in my opinion, never be less than 5 feet in width. Four feet is the more common width, but that is evidently too narrow for a large cow, and even 7 feet are considered by some people as a fair-sized stall for two cows; though, in my opinion, every cow should have a stall for herself, for her own comfort when lying or standing, and that she may eat her food in peace. The width of the byre should be 18 feet;—the manger is 2 feet in width, the length of a large cow about 8 feet, the gutter 1 foot, leaving 7 feet behind the gutter for the different vessels used in milking the cows and feeding the calves. The ceiling should be quite open to the slates, and a ventilator, moreover, is a useful apparatus for regulating the temperature and supplying fresh air to a byre. A door, divided into upper and lower halves, should open outwards to the court on a giblet-check, for the easy passage of the cows to and from the court, and each half fastened on the inside with a hand-bar. Two windows with glass panes, with the lower parts furnished with shutters to open, will be quite sufficient for light, and, along with the half-door, for air also. The walls should be plastered for comfort and cleanliness.

(43.) The *stalls* are most comfortably made of wood, though some recommend stone, which always feels hard and cold. Their height should be 3 feet, and in length they should reach no farther than the flank of the cow, or about 6 feet from the wall. When made of wood, a strong hard-wood hind post is sunk into the ground, and built in masonry. Between this post and the manger should be laid a curb-stone, grooved on the upper edge to let in the deals of the travis endways.

The deals are held in their places at the upper ends by a hard-wood rail, grooved on the under side, into which the ends of the deals are let, and the rail is fixed to the back of the hind-post at one end, and let into the wall at the other, and there fastened with iron holdfasts. Stone travises are no doubt more durable, and in the end perhaps more economical, where flag-stones are plentiful; but I would in all cases prefer wood, as feeling warmer, being more dry in winter, and less liable to injure the cows coming against them, and within doors will last a long time. The plan of the stalls may be seen at Q and Y in the plan fig. 4, Plate IV.

(44.) The *mangers* of byres are usually placed on a level with the floor, with a curb-stone in front to keep in the food, and paved in the bottom. This position I conceive to be highly objectionable, inasmuch as, when breaking the turnips, the head of the animal is depressed so low that an undue weight is thrown upon the fore-legs, and an injurious strain induced on the muscles of the lower jaw. A better position is, when the bottom of the manger, made of flag-stones or wood, resting on a building of stone and mortar, is raised about 20 inches from the ground, and a plank set on edge in front to keep in the food. This plank should be secured in its position with iron rods batted into the wall at one end, and the other end passed through the plank to a shoulder, which is pressed hard against the plank on the opposite side by means of a nut and screw. This form of manger may be seen in fig. 18, p. 146. In this position of the manger, the cow will eat with ease any kind of food, whether whole or cut, and all feeding-byres for oxen should also be fitted up with mangers of this construction. Mangers are generally made too narrow for cattle with horns, and the consequence is the rubbing away of the points of the horns against the wall.

(45.) The method of *supplying green food* to cattle in byres may be various, either by putting it into the manger from the inside, or from the outside through holes in the wall made exactly opposite their heads. Either way is equally serviceable to the cattle, but the latter is the more convenient for the cattleman. Its construction may be easily understood by fig. 9, which represents the door shut in the opening of the wall on the outside. But, convenient as this mode of supplying food is, I prefer giving it by the stall, when that is as wide as 5 feet, because, in cold weather in winter, the draught of air occasioned by the opening of the small doors at the heads of cows may endanger their health. There is another method by having a passage of 3 feet in width betwixt the stalls and the wall, from which both turnips and fodder

Fig. 9.

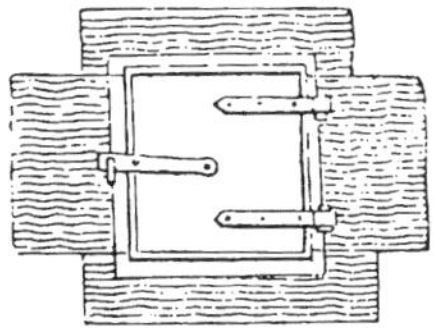

DOOR THROUGH WHICH TO SUPPLY MANGERS WITH TURNIPS.

may be supplied to the cows. In this case the space behind the cows is reduced to 4 feet in width.

(46.) The *floor* of byres should be paved with small round stones, excepting the gutter, which, being as broad as an ordinary square-mouthed shovel, should be flagged at the bottom, and formed into the shape of a trough by two curb-stones. A gutter of this form can be quickly cleaned out. A similarly formed gutter, though of smaller dimensions, should run from the main one through the wall to the court, to carry off the urine. The causewaying of the stalls of a cow-house should go very little farther up than the hind-posts, because, in lying down and rising up, cattle first kneel on their fore-knees, which would be injured in the act of being pressed against any hard substance like stones. This inner part of the stall should be of earth, made softer by being covered with litter. The urine gutters may be seen in the plan at Q and Y in fig. 4, Plate IV.

(47.) Fig. 10. represents a section of a *travis and manger of a byre*, where *a* is the wall, *b* the building which supports the manger *c*, having a front of wood, and bottomed with either flags or wood, *d* the hard-wood hind-post, sunk into the ground, and there built in with stones and mortar, *e* the hard-wood top-rail, secured behind the post *d*, and let into and fixed in the wall *a* with iron holdfasts, *f* the stone curb-stone, into

Fig. 10.

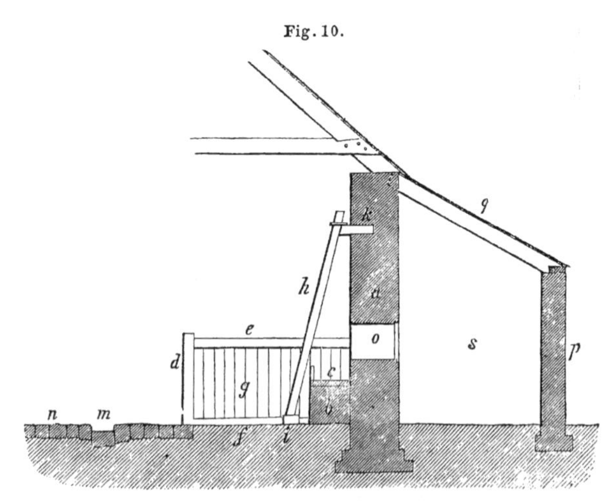

BYRE TRAVIS, MANGER, AND STAKE.

which the travis-board is let, *g* the boarding of wood, let endways into the curb-stone below, and into the top-rail above, by a groove; *h* is a hard-wood stake, to which the cattle are fastened by binders, the lower end of which is let into a block of stone *i*, and the upper fastened by a strap of iron to a block of wood *k* fixed into the wall *a*; *m* is the gutter for the dung, having a bottom of flag-stones, and sides of curb-stones, *n* the paved floor, *o* the opening through the wall *a* by which the food is supplied into the manger *c* to the cattle, from the shed *s* behind. This shed is 8 feet wide, *p* being the pillars which support its roof *q*, which is just a continuation of the slating of the byre roof, the wall *a* of which is 9 feet, and the pillars *p* 6 feet, in height. But where no small doors for the food are used, the shed *s*, pillars *p*, and roof *q*, are not required, a small turnip store being sufficient for the purpose, and to which access may be obtained by the back door, seen in Q, at the right hand of the stalls in fig. 4, Plate IV.

(48.) Cattle are bound to the stake in various ways. 1. One way is with an iron chain, commonly called a *binder* or *seal.* This is represented in fig. 11, where *a* is the large ring of the binder which slides up and down the stake *h*, which is here shewn in the same position as it is by *h* in the section of the stall in fig. 10. The iron chain being put round the neck of the beast, is fastened together by a broad-tongued hook at *c*, which is put into any link of the chain that forms the gauge of the neck, and cannot come out again until turned on purpose edgeways in reference to the link of which it has a hold. This sort of binder is in general use in the midland and northern counties of Scotland.

Fig. 11.

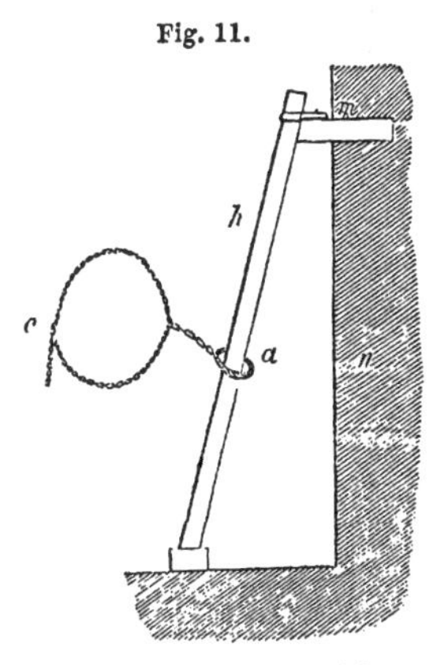

CATTLE SEAL OR BINDER.

2. Another method of binding is with the *baikie*, which is made of a piece of hard wood *e*, fig. 12, standing upright and flat to the neck of the beast; a rope *g* fastens the lower end of it to the stake, upon which it slides up and down by means of a loop which the rope forms round the stake. This rope passes *under* the neck of the animal, and is never loosened. Another rope *k* is fastened at the upper end of the piece of wood *e*, and, passing *over* the neck of the animal and round the stake, is made fast to itself by a knot and-eye, and serves the purpose of fastening and loosening the animal. The neck being embraced between the two ropes, moves up and down, carrying the baikie along with it. This method of binding animals to the stake, though quite easy to the animals themselves, has this objectionable property, which the *seal* has not, of preventing the animals turning round their heads to lick their bodies,

Fig. 12.

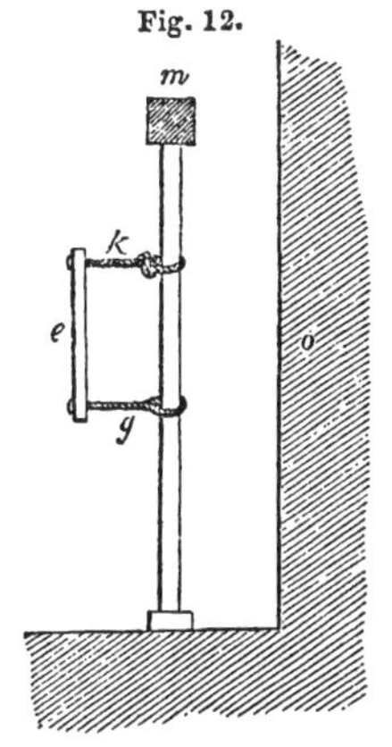

A BAIKIE.

which they can do with the seal pretty far back, and yet are unable to turn round in the stall. The seal being made of iron, is more durable than the baikie. The top of the stake of the seal is inclined towards the wall *n*, and fixed as represented by *m* in fig. 11; the baikie stake is held perpendicular, and is fixed to a log of wood *m*, fig. 12, stretching parallel to the wall *o* across the byre, of which log the cross section only is here shewn. The seal-stake is placed in an inclined position to allow its top to be fastened to the wall, and in regard to it the animal is comparatively loose; but as the neck is always held close to the baikie-stake, that stake must be placed in a perpendicular position to allow the animal to move its neck up and down to and from the manger.

(49.) This construction of byre with its fittings up, is quite as well suited to *fatten oxen* as to accommodate *milch-cows*. Feeding byres are usually constructed much too small for the number of oxen confined in them. When stalls are actually put up, they seldom exceed 4 feet in width; more frequently two oxen are put into a double stall of 7 feet, and not unfrequently travises are dispensed with altogether, and simply a triangular piece of boarding is placed across the manger against the wall, to divide the food betwixt each pair of oxen. In double stalls, and where no stalls are used, even small-sized oxen, as they increase in size, cannot all lie down together to chew their cud and rest, whereas, the fatter they become, they require more room and more rest; and large oxen are hampered in them from the first. In such confined byres, the gutter, moreover, is too near the heels of the oxen, which prevents them standing back when they desire. Short stalls, to be sure, save the litter being dirtied, by the dung dropping from the cattle directly into the gutter, and this circumstance no doubt saves trouble to the cattle-man; but in such a case the litter is saved by the sacrifice of comfort to the animals. Such considerations of economy are quite legitimate in cowkeepers in town, where both space and litter are valuable, but that they should induce the construction of inconvenient byres in farmsteads indicates either parsimony on the part of the landlord or ignorance on that of the architect; and no farmer who consults the well-being of his animals, and through them his own interest, should ever originate such a plan, or sanction it where he finds it to exist. The truth is, these confined structures are ordered to be erected by landlords unacquainted with agriculture, to save a little outlay at first. Expenditure to them is a tangible object; but in dealing thus with their tenants, they seem not to be aware they are acting with shortsightedness towards their own interests; for want of proper accommodation in the farmstead certainly has, and should have, a considerable influence on the mind of the farmer, when valuing the rent of the farm he wishes to occupy. Should you have occasion to fit up a byre for the accommodation of milch-cows or feeding oxen, bear in mind that a small sum saved at first, may cause you to incur a yearly loss of much greater amount than the saving, by not only preventing your feeding cattle attaining the perfection which a comfortable lodging would certainly promote in them; but in affecting the state of your cows by want of room, the calves they bear in such circumstances are sure to prove weak in constitution.

(50.) Immediately adjoining the cow-house should be placed the *calves' house.* This apartment is represented at R of the plan in fig. 4, Plate IV, fitted up with cribs. It is 35 feet in length, and 18 feet in width, and the roof ascends to the slates. Calves are either suckled by their mothers, or brought up on milk by the hand. When they are suckled, if the byre be roomy enough, that is, 18 feet in width, stalls are erected for them against the wall behind the cows, in which they are usually tied up immediately behind their mothers; or, what is a less restrictive plan, put in numbers together in loose boxes at the ends of the byre, and let loose from both places at stated times to be suckled. When brought up by the hand, they are put into a separate apartment from their mothers, and each confined in a loose-box or crib, where the milk is given them. The superiority of separate cribs over loose boxes for calves is, that calves are prevented sucking one another, after having got their allowance of milk, by the ears, or teats, or scrotum, or navel, by which malpractice, when unchecked, certain diseases may be engendered. The crib is large enough for one calf at 4 feet square and 4 feet in height, sparred with slips of tile-lath, and having a small wooden wicket to afford access to the calf. The floor of the cribs may be of earth, but the passage between them should be flagged, or of asphaltum. Abundance of light should be admitted, either by windows in the walls, or sky-lights in the roof; and fresh air is essential to the health of calves, the supply of which would be best procured by a ventilator, such as is represented in fig. 8, p. 128, already described. There should be a door of communication with the cow-house, and another in two divisions, an upper and a lower, into a court furnished with a shed, as *k* in fig. 4, Plate IV, which the calves may occupy until turned out to pasture. The cribs should be fitted up with a manger to contain cut turnips, and a high rack for hay, the top of which should be as much elevated above the litter as to preclude the possibility of the calves getting their feet over it. The general fault in the construction of calves' houses is the want of both light and air, light being cheerful to creatures in confinement, and air particularly essential to the good health of young animals. When desired, both can be excluded. The walls of the calves' house should be plastered for the sake of neatness and cleanliness. Some people are of opinion that the calves' house should not only have no door of communication with the cow-house, but should be placed at a distance from it, in order that the cows may be beyond the reach of hearing the calves. Such an objection could only have originated from an imperfect acquaintance with the nature of these animals in the circumstances. A young cow even that is at once prevented smelling and suckling her calf, does not recognise its voice at any distance, and will express no uneasiness about it after the first few minutes after parturition, and after the first portion of milk has been drawn from her by the hand.

(51.) The front of one of these *calves' cribs* is represented by fig. 13, in which *a* is the wicket door which gives access to it, *b b* are the hinges, and *c* is a thumb-catch to keep the door shut. You will observe that this kind of hinge is very simple and economical. It consists of the rails of the wicket being a little elongated towards *b*, where they terminate in a semicircular form, and the lower face of which is shaped into a pin which fills and rotates in a round hole made in a billet of wood, seen at the lower hinge at *b*, securely screwed to the upright door-post of the crib. Another billet *d* is screwed immediately above the lower rail, *b*, to prevent the door being thrown off the hinges by any accident. Cross-tailed iron hinges of the lightness suited to such doors, would soon break by rusting in the dampness usually occasioned by the breath of a number of calves confined within the same apartment.

Fig. 13.

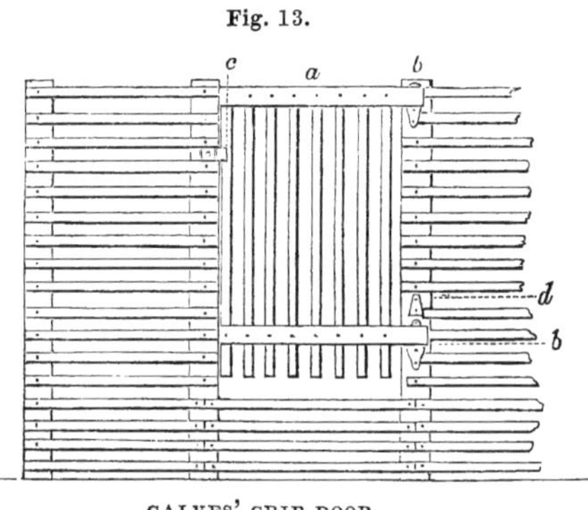

CALVES' CRIB DOOR.

(52.) A pretty large *court* should be attached to the *cow-house*, in which the cows can walk about for a time in the best part of the day in winter, basking in the sun when it shines, rubbing against a post that should be set up for the purpose, drinking a little water provided for them in a trough *w*, and licking themselves and one another. Such a court is besides necessary for containing the manure from the byre, and should have a gate by which carts can have access to the manure: *l* is such a court on the plan, fig. 4, Plate IV, being 58 feet in length by 30 feet in width.

(53.) *k* in the plan, fig. 4, Plate IV, is the *court* attached to the *calves' house*, 30 feet in length by 25 feet in width, in which should be erected, for shelter to the calves in cold weather, or at night before they are turned out to pasture, or for the night for a few weeks after they are turned out to pasture, a *shed k*, 30 feet in length by 12 feet in width, fitted up with mangers for turnips, and racks for hay. A trough of water *w*, is also requisite in this court, as well as a gateway for carts by which to remove the dung.

(54.) On the left of the cow-house is the *boiling-house* U, for cooking food in, and doing every thing else that requires the use of warm water. The boiler and furnace *b'* should be placed so as to afford access to the boiler on two sides, and from the furnace the vent rises to the point of the gable. A fire-place *a'* is useful for many purposes, such as melting tar, boiling a kettle of water, drying wetted sacks, nets, &c. One door opens into the byre, and another, the outer one, is in the gable, through which access to the byre may be obtained, or, if thought better, through the gate and court of the byre. There should be a window with glass, and shutters in the lower division, to open and admit air, and a ventilator *u*, fig. 3, Plate III, on the roof may be advisable here as a means at times to clear the house of steam. The walls of the boiling-house should be plastered. As proximity to water is an essential convenience to a boiling-house, water is quite accessible in the trough of the cows' court *l*, or, what is still better, in a trough connected with it outside, as at *l'*, in fig. 3, Plate III, or *w*, in fig. 4, Plate IV.

(55.) Windows should be of the form for the purpose they are intended to be used. On this account windows for stables, and for other apartments, should be of different forms. 1. Fig. 14 represents a window for a stable. The opening is 4½ feet in height by 3 feet in width. The frame-work is composed of a dead part *a* of 1 foot in depth, 2 shutters *b b* to open on hinges, and fasten inside with a thumb-catch, and *c* a glazed sash 2 feet in height, with 3 rows of panes. When panes are made under 8 inches square, there is a considerable saving in the price of glass. The object of this form of a stable window is, that generally a great number of small articles are thrown on the sole of a work-horse stable window, such as short-ends, straps, &c. which are only used occasionally, and intended to be there at hand when wanted. The consequence of this confused mixture of things, which it is not easy for the farmer to prevent, is, that, when the shutters are desired to be opened, it is scarcely

Fig. 14.

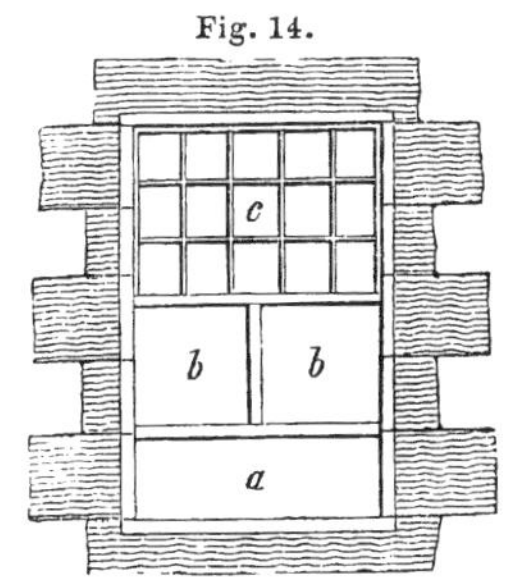

STABLE WINDOW.

possible to do it without first clearing the sole of every thing, and rather than find another place for them, the window remains shut. A press in a wall might be suggested for containing these small articles; but in the only wall, namely, the front one of the stable O, in which it would be convenient to make such a press, all its surface is occupied by the harness hanging against it; and besides, no orders, however peremptory, will prevent such articles being, at throng times, thrown upon the window-soles; and where is the harm of their lying there at hand, provided the windows are so constructed as to admit of being opened when desired? When a dead piece of wood, as *a*, is put into such windows, small things may remain on the sole, while the shutters *b b* are opened over them. 2. In other apartments, such as byres, corn-barn, calves' house, boiling-house, implement-house, hay-house, where there is no chance of an accumulation of sundry articles in the window-sole, the shutters of the windows, *if desired*, may descend to the bottom of the frame, as in fig. 15. The size of the window may still be the same, 4½ feet in height and 3 feet in width. The frame consists of two shutters *a a* 2 feet in height, with a glazed sash *c* 2½ feet in height, having 4 rows of panes. Such a form of window will admit a great deal of light and air.

Fig. 15.

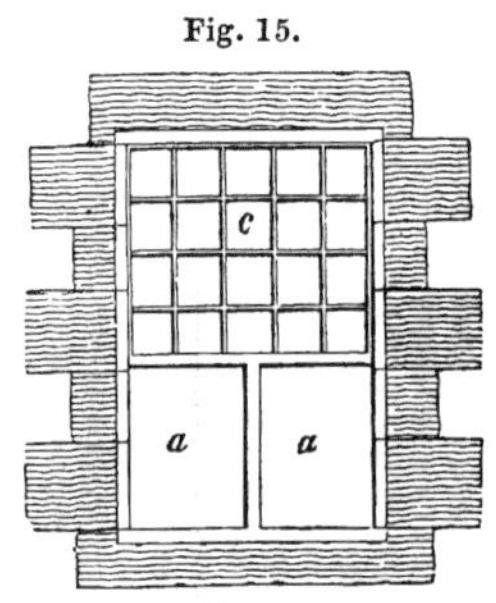

BYRE, &C. WINDOW.

(56.) The *upper barn* B, as seen in fig. 16, occupies the whole space above the corn-barn and chaff-house. It is 32 feet in length and 30 feet in breadth, and its roof ascends to the slates. It has a good wooden floor like the corn-barn, supported on stout joists. It contains the principal machinery of the thrashing-machine, and is wholly appropriated to the storing of the unthrashed corn previous to its being thrashed by the mill. For the admission of barrows loaded with sheaves from the stack-yard, or of sheaves direct from the cart, this barn should have a door towards the stack-yard of 6 feet in width, in two vertical folds to open outwards, on a giblet-check, one of the folds to be fastened in the inside with an iron cat-band, and the other provided with a good lock and key. It is in this barn that the corn is fed into the thrashing-mill, and to afford light to the man who feeds in, and ample light to the barn when the door is shut, which it should be when the wind blows strongly into it, a sky-light should be placed over the head of the man. The large door should not be placed immediately behind the man who feeds in, as is frequently the case in farmsteads, to his great annoyance when the sheaves are bringing in. There should be slits in the walls for the ventilation of air among the corn-sheaves, which may not at all times be in good order when taken into the barn. A hatchway *a*, 3 feet square, in the floor, over the corn-

Fig. 16.

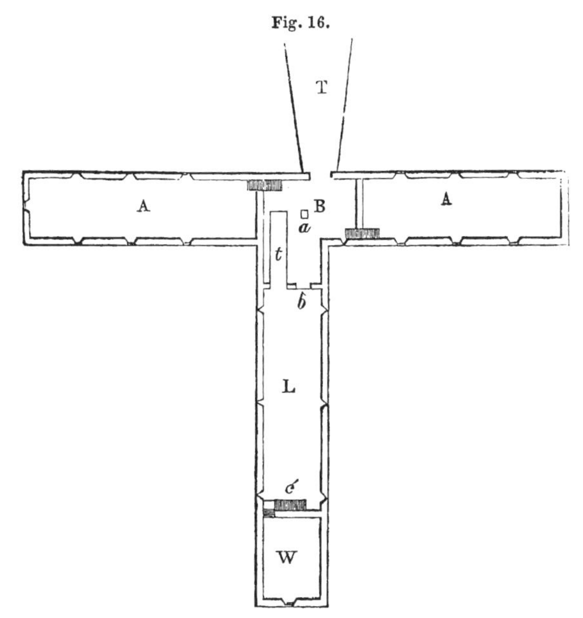

PLAN OF UPPER BARN, GRANARIES, AND WOOL-ROOM.

barn below, is useful when any corn or refuse has to be again put through the mill. Its hatch should be furnished with strong cross-tailed hinges, and a hasp and staple, with a padlock and key, by which to secure it from below in the corn-barn. An opening *b* of 4 feet in height and 3 feet in width, should be made through the wall to the straw-barn, for the purpose of receiving any straw from it that may require to be put through the mill again. This opening should be provided with a door of one leaf, or of two leaves, to fasten with a bar, from the upper barn. The thrashing-machine is not built on the floor, but is supported on two very strong beams extending along the length of the barn: *t* is the site of the thrashing-machine in the figure.

(57.) Immediately in connection with the upper barn is the *gangway* T, fig. 4, Plate IV, and fig. 16. It is used as an inclined plane, upon which to wheel the corn-barrows, and form a road for the carriers of sheaves from the stack-yard. This road should at all times be kept hard and smooth with small broken stones, and at the same time sufficiently strong to endure the action of barrow-wheels. Either common asphaltum or wood pavement would answer this purpose well. To prevent the body of the gangway affecting the wall of the corn-barn with dampness, it should be kept apart from that wall by an arch of masonry. Some farmers prefer taking in the corn on carts instead of by a gangway, and the carts in that case are placed alongside the large door, and emptied of their contents by means of a fork. I prefer a gangway for this purpose; because it enables the farmer to dispense with horse-labour in bringing in the stacks if they are near at hand, and they should always be built near the upper-barn for convenience. Barns, in which flails alone are used for thrashing the corn, are made on the ground, and the barn-door is made as large as to admit a loaded cart to enter and empty its contents on the floor.

(58.) In fig. 16, AA are two granaries over the sheds DD, implement-house G, and hay-house H, in fig. 4, Plate IV. That on the left is 76 feet in length and 18 feet in width, and the other 65 feet in length and 18 feet in width. The side walls of both are 5 feet in height. Their roofs ascend to the slates. Their wooden floors should be made strong, to support a considerable weight of grain ; their walls well plastered with hair plaster ; and a neat skifting-board should finish the flooring. Each granary has 6 windows, three in front and three at the back, and there is one in the gable, at the left hand over the door of the implement-house. These windows should be so formed as to admit light and air very freely, and I know of no form of window so capable of affording both, as this in figure 17, which I have found very serviceable in granaries. The opening is 4½ feet in length and 3 feet in height. In the frame *a* are a glazed sash 1 foot in height, composed of two rows of panes, and *b* Venetian shutters, which may be opened more or less at pleasure: *c* shews in section the manner in which these shutters operate. They revolve by their ends, formed of the shape of a round pin, in holes in the side-posts of the frame *d*, and are kept in a parallel position to each other by the bar

Fig. 17.

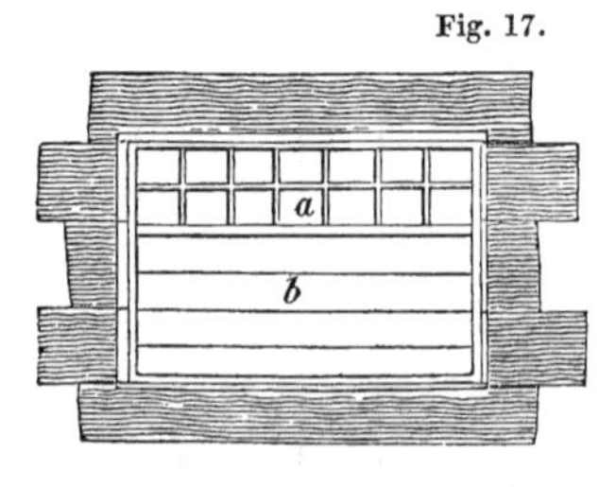

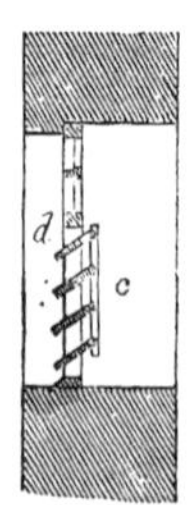

GRANARY WINDOW AND SECTION OF SHUTTERS.

c, which is attached to them by an eye of iron, moving stiff on an iron pin passing through both the eye and bar *c*. The granary on the right hand being the smallest, and immediately over the work-horse corn-chest, should be appropriated to the use of horse-corn and other small quantities of grain to be first used. The other granary may contain seed-corn, or grain that is intended to be sold when the prices suit. For repairing or cleaning out the thrashing-machine, a large opening in the wall of this granary, exactly opposite the machinery of the mill in the upper barn, will be found convenient. It should be provided with a large movable board, or folding doors, to close on it, and to be fastened from the granary. This opening is not shewn in fig. 16.

(59.) At the end of the straw-barn L is the wool-room W, fig. 16, its site being indicated by W on the roof of the isometrical view, fig. 3, Plate III. It just covers the small hammels X, and is therefore 25 feet in length and 18 feet in breadth. It enters from the straw-barn L by means of the stone or wooden trap-stair *c*. Its floor should be made of good wood, its walls and roof lathed and hair-plastered. Its window should be formed like that of the byres, with a glazed sash above, and opening shutters below. A curtain should be hung across the window to screen the light and air from the wool when desired. The door need not exceed 6 feet in height, but should be 3½ feet in width, to let a pack of wool pass easily through. As the wool is most conveniently packed in this room, there should be provided in the roof two strong iron hooks, for suspending the corners of the pack-sheet in the act of packing it, and another from which to suspend the beam and scales for weighing the fleeces. Although the wool will usually occupy this room only when the cattle are in the field, yet in case it should be found expedient to keep it over year, or have animals in the small hammels X in summer, and in case their breath should ascend into the wool through any openings of the joinings of the deals of the floor, it will be a safe precaution for preserving the wool in a proper state, to have the roof of the hammels below lathed and plastered. This room could be entered by a door and stone hanging-stair in the gable.

(60.) M and N in the plan, fig. 4, Plate IV. are *hammels* for the feeding of cattle, rearing of young horses, and tending of queys in calf until they are tied up in the cow-house. 1. Hammels consist of a shed, and an open court, communicating by a large opening. The shed part need not be so wide as the rest of the apartments in the farmstead, in so far as the comfort of the animals is concerned; and in making them narrower, considerable saving will be effected in the cost of roofing. 2. There is no definite rule for the *size* of hammels; but as their great convenience consists in conferring the power to assort cattle according to their age, temper, size, and condition, while at liberty in the fresh air, it is evident that hammels should be much smaller than courts, in which no assortment of animals can be attempted. 3. The courts of hammels, from which the dung is proposed to be taken away by horse and cart, should not be less than 30 feet in length by 18 feet in breadth, and their entrance gates 9 feet in width; and this size of court will accommodate 4 oxen that will each attain the weight of 70 stones imperial. This is the size of the courts of the hammels M. Should it not be thought inconvenient to take the dung out of the courts with barrows, then they need not be made larger than 20 feet in length by 17 feet in width, and this is the size of the courts of the hammels N, which will accommodate 3 oxen of the above size. 4. The sheds to both sizes of courts need not exceed 14 feet in width, and their length will be equal to the width of the courts. Of these dimensions, 4 oxen in the larger will have just the same accommodation as 3 oxen of the same size in the smaller hammels. 5. All hammels should have a trough, *z*, for turnips, fitted up against one of the walls of the court. The side-wall is the most convenient part, when a large gate is placed in front, through which the carts are backed to clear away the dung from the courts. In the case of the smaller courts, the turnips may be supplied to the trough over the top of the front wall. 6. To give permanency to hammels, the sheds should be roofed as effectually as any of the other buildings, though to save some expense at first, many farmers are in the habit of roofing them with small trees placed close together on the tops of the walls of the sheds, and of building thereon either straw, corn, or beans. This is certainly an excellent place upon which to stack beans or pease; but the finished building is that which should be adopted in all cases. Temporary erections are constantly needing repairs, and in the end actually cost more than work substantially executed at first. 7. The division betwixt the shed and court forms the front wall of the shed, through which an opening forms the door betwixt them. This door, 6 feet in width, should always be placed at one side and not in the middle of the hammel, to retain the greatest degree of warmth to the interior of the shed. The corners of its scuncheon should be rounded off to save the cattle being injured against sharp angles. The divisions betwixt the respective courts should be of stone and lime walls, 1 foot in thickness, and 6 feet in height. Those within the sheds should be carried up quite close to the roof. Frequently they are only carried up to the first balk of the couples, over which a draught of air is generated along the inside, from shed to shed, much to the discomfort of the animals; and this inconvenience is always overlooked in hammels which are built with the view of saving a little cost in building up the inside division walls to the roofs. 8. Racks for fodder should be put up within the sheds, either in the three spare corners, or along the inner end. 9. In my opinion there is no way so suitable for feeding oxen, bringing up young horses in winter, or taking care of heifers in calf, as hammels; and of the two sizes described above, I would decidedly prefer the smaller, as permitting the fewer number of animals to be put together 10. X X are two small hammels at the end of the straw-barn L for accommodating a bull, or stallion, or any single animal that requires a separate apartment for itself. These are each 18 feet in length and 12 feet in width within the sheds, the roofs of which are formed of the floor of the wool-room W; and 29 feet in length and 12 feet in width in the courts. The doors into them should be made to open outwards, on giblet-checks. The courts are furnished with turnip-troughs *z*, and one water-trough *w* will serve both courts, as shewn in the plan, fig. 4, Plate IV. A rack should be fitted up for fodder in the inside of each shed.

(61.) It should be observed that a part of the hammels N is fitted up as a byre Y This byre is intended to accommodate the servants' cows. There are 8 stalls, 6 for the ploughmen's, one for the farm-steward's, and one for the shepherd's cows, and they are nearly 5 feet in width. The length of the byre is 38 feet and its width is only 14 feet, which gives a rather small space behind the cows; but as servants' cows are generally small, and the milk from them immediately carried away, if there is just sufficient room for feeding and milking them, and adequate comfort to the cows themselves, a large space behind them is unnecessary. This byre has a ventilator *r'*. The cows are furnished with an open court *v*, 38 feet in length and 20 feet in width, and a water-trough *w*.

(62.) I and K of the plan, fig. 4, Plate IV, are *two large courts for young cattle*, both in the immediate vicinity of the straw-barn L, and both having a shed D under one of the granaries; I is 84 feet in length and 76 feet in width, and K 84 feet in length and 77 feet in width. Troughs for turnips should be fitted up against one or more of the walls surrounding the courts in the most convenient places, such as at *z* in both courts. Besides racks for fodder, *h'*, against one of the walls within the sheds DD, there should racks be placed in the middle of the courts, that the cattle may stand around and eat out of them without trouble. The square figures *o o* in the middle of the courts I and K indicate the places where the racks should stand, and their form may be seen at *o o* in the isometrical view, fig. 3, Plate III. Around two sides of K is a paved road *e'*, 13 feet in width, for carts going to be loaded with grain at the door of the corn-barn C. Though the cattle have liberty to walk on this pavement, it should be kept clean every day. Such courts are quite common in steadings for the rearing of young cattle in winter, and even for feeding large lots of cattle together, as is practised by most farmers who do not rear calves; but, for my part, I prefer hammels for all classes and ages of cattle; for although cattle are restricted in them in regard to space, still the few in each hammel have plenty of room to move about. There is no hardship to the animals in this degree of confinement, while they have the advantage of quietness amongst themselves in the open air, produced by being assorted according to temper, size, sex, and age. On abolishing large courts altogether out of steadings, I would substitute in their place hammels of different sizes, and convert the cattle-sheds D and D into cart-sheds and receptacles for the larger class of implements. It is probable that the use of large courts will not soon be dispensed with in farmsteads, and for that reason I have retained them in the plan, but I have no doubt that a period will arrive when farmers, to *ensure* to themselves larger profits from cattle, will see the advantage of taking the utmost care of them, from the period of their birth until disposed of in a ripe condition at an early age; and then hammels will be better liked than even courts are at the present day, and farmers will then universally adopt them.

(63.) Fig. 18 represents a *trough for turnips suited both for hammels and courts*, where *a* is the wall against which the trough is built, and

Fig. 18.

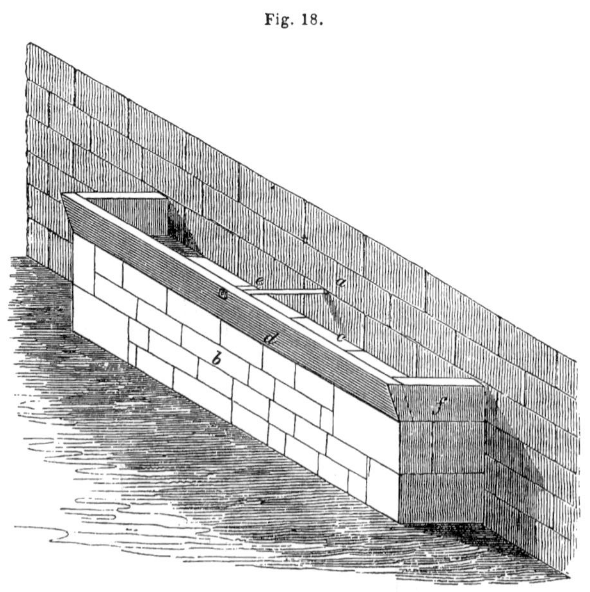

TURNIP TROUGH.

b a building of stone and lime 2 feet thick. The lime need not be used for more than 9 inches in the front and sides of the wall, and the remaining 15 inches may be filled up with any hard material; *c* is the flagging placed on the top of the wall, and forming the bottom of the trough. Some board the bottom with wood, where wood is plentiful, and it answers well enough; but of course flags, where easily obtained, are more durable, though wood is pleasanter for the cattle in wet and frosty weather in winter. *d* is a plank 3 inches thick and 9 inches in depth to keep in the turnips. Oak planking from wrecks, and old spruce trees, however knotty, I have found to make cheap and very durable planking for the edging of turnip troughs. The planks are spliced together at the ends, and held on edge by bars of iron *e* batted with lead into the wall, in the manner already described in (44.) p. 133; and the figure clearly shews this mode of fastening the plank. The masonry represented in the figure is finer than need be for the purpose; and the trough, though here shewn short, may extend to any length along the side or sides of a court.

(64.) The *straw-racks for courts* are made of various forms. 1. On farms of light soils, where straw is usually scarce, a rack of the form of fig. 19, having a movable cover, will be found serviceable in preserving the straw from rain, where *a a* is the bottom inclined upwards to keep the straw always forward to the front of the rack in reach of the cattle. Through the apex of the bottom, the shank which supports the movable cover *b* passes, and this cover protects the straw from rain. The shank with its cover is worked up and down, when a supply of straw is given, by a rack and pinion *c*, to which pinion is attached the lying shaft, on which is shipped a handle *d*. A rack of this kind is made of wood, and should be 5 feet square, and 5 feet in height to the top of the corner posts; and sparred all round the sides as well as the bottom to keep in the straw 2. A more common kind of rack is represented by fig. 20, which is of a square form, and sparred all round the sides to keep in the straw. The cattle draw the straw through the spars as long as its top is too high for

Fig. 19.

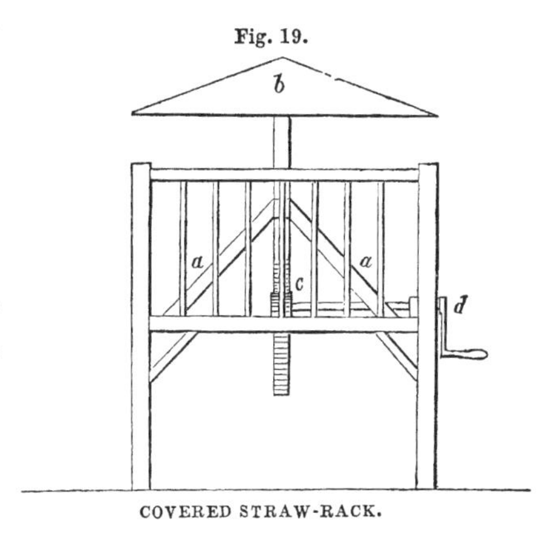

COVERED STRAW-RACK.

Fig. 20.

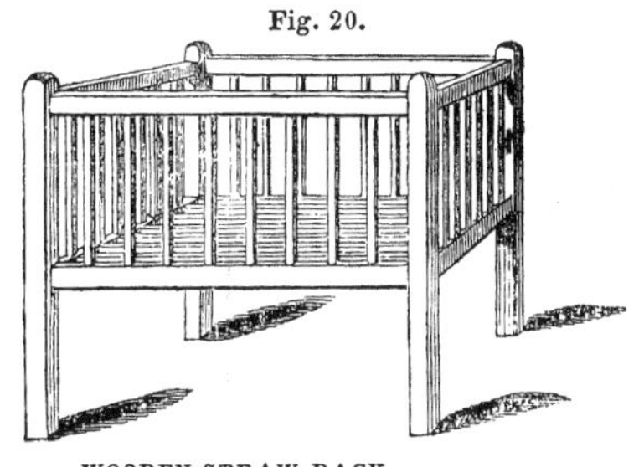

WOODEN STRAW-RACK.

them to reach over it, but after the dung accumulates, and the rack thereby becomes low, the cattle get at the straw over the top. This kind is also made of wood, and should be 5 feet square and 4 feet in height. 3. Fig. 21 represents a rack made of malleable iron, intended to supply the straw to the cattle always over its top, and is therefore not sparred but rodded, in the sides, to keep in the straw. In use it remains constantly on the ground, and not drawn up as the dung accumulates, as in the case of the other kinds of racks described.

Fig. 21.

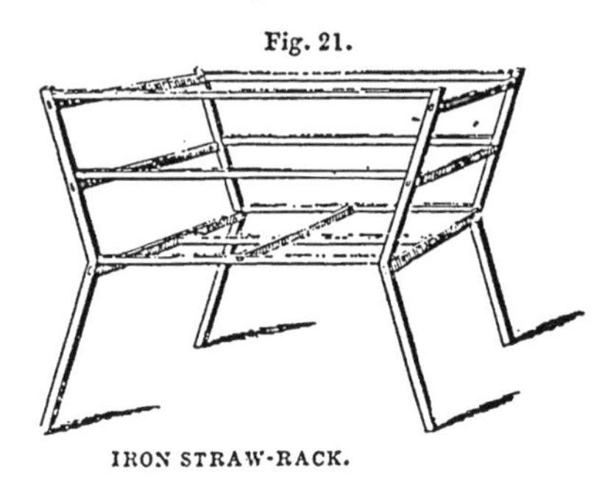

IRON STRAW-RACK.

This kind is 5½ feet in length. 4½ feet in breadth, and 4½ feet in height; the upper rails and legs are made of iron 1 inch square, and the other rails ¾ inch. Iron is of course the most durable material of which straw-racks for cattle can be made.

(65.) There are few things which indicate greater care for cattle when housed in the farmstead, than the erection of *places for storing turnips* for their use. Such stores are not only convenient, but the best sort of receptacles for keeping the turnips clean and fresh. They are seen in the isometrical view, fig. 3, Plate III, and in the plan, fig. 4, Plate IV, at *e* and *f* for the use of the hammels M; at *g* for that of the court K; at *h* for the hammels X, and servants' cow-house Y; at *i* for the use of the court I; at *m* for that of the cow-house Q, and calves' cribs R; and at *p* and *q* for the hammels N. The walls of these turnip-stores should be made of stone and lime 8 feet by 5 feet inside, and 6 feet in height, with an opening in front, 2 feet and upwards from the ground, for putting in and taking out the turnips thereat; or they may be made of wood, where that is plentiful, with stout upright posts in the four corners, and lined with rough deals. They may be covered with the same material, or with straw, to protect the turnips from frost. They should be placed near the apartments they are intended to supply with turnips, and at the same time be of easy access to carts from the roads. These receptacles may of course be made of any convenient form.

(66.) The supply of *water* to all the courts where as many turnips as they can eat are not given to the cattle, is a matter of paramount consideration in the fitting up of every farmstead. In the plan fig. 4, Plate IV. troughs for water are represented at *w*, in the large courts I and K, in those of the cow-houses *l* and *v*, and calves' cribs *k*, as well as in those of the bulls' hammels X. The troughs may be supplied with water either directly from pump-wells, or by pipes from a fountain at a little distance, the former being the most common plan. As a pump cannot conveniently be placed at each trough, there is a plan of supplying any number of troughs from one pump, which I have found to answer well, provided the surface of the ground will allow the troughs being *nearly* on the same level, when placed within reach of the animals. The plan is to connect the bottoms of any two or more troughs set on the same level, with lead pipes placed under ground; and on the first trough being supplied direct from the pump, the water will flow to the same level throughout all the other troughs. There is, however, this objection to this particular arrangement, that when any one of the troughs is emptying by drinking, the water is drawn off from the rest of the troughs, that it may maintain its level throughout the whole; whereas if the trough which receives the water were placed a few inches *below* the top of the one supplying it, and the lead pipe were made to come from the bottom of the supply trough over the top of the edge of the receiving one, the water would entirely be emptied from the trough out of which the drink was taken, without affecting the quantity in any of the others. 1. To apply these arrangements of water-troughs to the plan fig. 4, Plate IV. Suppose that a pump supplies the trough *w*, in the court I, direct from a well beside it, a lead pipe passing, on the one hand, from the bottom of this trough under ground to the bottom of the trough *w*, in the court K, and, on the other hand, to that of the trough *w* in the calves court *k*, and thence to that of the trough *w* in the court *l* of the cow-house Q; and in another direction to the bottom of the trough *w* in the court *v* of the servants' cow-house Y; and suppose that the troughs in K and *k* and *l* and *v* are placed on the same level as the supply trough in the court I. it is obvious that they will all be supplied with water as long as there is any in the supply trough, and the emptiness of which will indicate that the water from it had been drawn off by the other troughs, and that the time had fully arrived when it was necessary to replenish the trough in the court I direct from the pump. The supply trough, in such an arrangement, should be larger than either of the other troughs. The trough of the bulls' hammels X, might be supplied by a spout direct from the pump in the court I. In this way a simple system of watering might be erected from one pump to supply a number of troughs in different courts. It may be proper to illustrate this mode of connecting water-troughs by a figure Let *b*, fig. 22, be the supply trough at the pump, and *f* the receiving one, and let both be placed on the same level; then let *g* be a lead pipe connecting the bottoms of both troughs, the ends of which are protected by hollow hemispherical drainers, such as *c*. It is here obvious, from the law which regulates the equilibrium of fluids, that the water, as supplied by the pump to *b*, will *always* stand at the same height in *f*. 2. I shall now illustrate the other method of supplying troughs also by a figure. Let *a*, fig. 22, be the supply trough immediately beside the pump; let *b* be the trough in any other court to be supplied with water from *a*, and for that purpose it should be placed 3 inches below the level of *a*. Let a lead pipe *d* be fastened to the under side of the bottom of *a*, the orifice of which, looking upwards, to be protected by the hemispherical drainer *c*. Let the lead pipe *d* be passed under ground as far as the trough *b* is situated from *a*, and emerge out of the ground by the side of and over the top of *b* at *e*. From this construction it is clear, that when

Fig. 22.

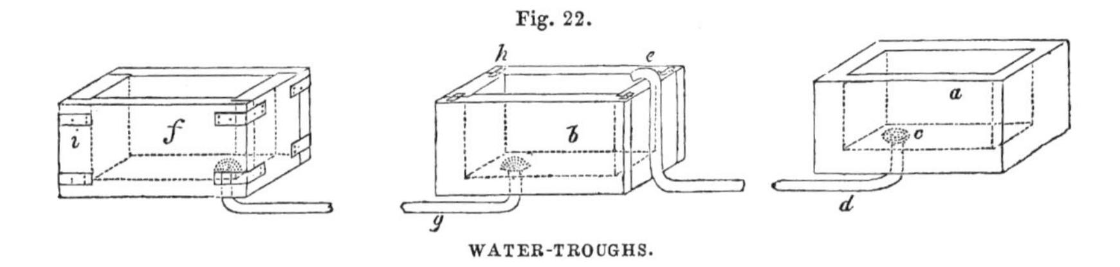

WATER-TROUGHS.

a is filling with water from the pump, the moment the water rises to the level of the end of the pipe at *e* it will commence to flow into *b*, and will continue to do so until *b* is filled, if the pumping be continued. The water in *a*, *below* the level of the end of the pipe at *e*, may be used in *a* without affecting that in *b*, and the water in *b* may be wholly used without affecting that in *a*. 3. Water-troughs may be made of various materials; the form of *a* is that of one hewn out of a solid block of freestone, which makes the closest, most durable, and best trough; that of *b* is of flag stones, the sides of which are sunk into the edges of the bottom in grooves filled with white lead, and there held together with iron clamps *h*. This is a good enough kind of trough, but is apt to leak at the joints. Trough *f* is made of wood dove-tailed at the corners, and held together by clamps of iron *i*. These troughs may be made of any size and proportions. 4. In some steadings, the water-troughs are supplied from a large cistern, somewhat elevated above their level, and the cistern is filled with water from a well either by a common or a force-pump. But in this arrangement, either a cock or ball and cock are requisite at each trough: in the case of a cock, the supply of water must depend on the cock being turned on the trough in due time, and in that of a ball and cock, the supply depends on the cistern being always supplied with water from the pump. There is great inconvenience and expense in having a ball and cock at each trough. 5 In steadings where there is an abundant supply of water from natural springs, accessible without the means of a pump, lead-pipes are made to emit a constant stream of water into each trough, and the surplus is carried away in drains, perhaps to the horse-pond. 6. There is still another mode which may be adopted where the supply of water is plentiful, and where it may flow constantly into a supply-cistern. Let the supply-cistern be 2 feet in length, 1 foot wide, and 18 inches in depth, and let it be provided with a ball and cock, and let a pipe proceed from its bottom to a trough of dimensions fit for the use of cattle, into which let the pipe enter its end or side a little way, say 3 inches, below the mouth of the trough. Let a pipe proceed from this trough, from the *bend* of the pipe, as from the bend of the right-hand pipe *e* at the bottom of the trough *b*, fig. 22, to another trough, into whose end it enters in like manner to the first trough, and so on into as many succeeding troughs, from trough to trough, on the same level, as you require; and the water will rise in each as high as the mouth of the pipe, and when withdrawn by drinking from any one of them, the ball and cock will replenish it direct from the supply-cistern; but the objection to a ball and cock applies as strongly to this case as to the other methods, although there is economy of pipe attending this method.

(67.) In most farmsteads a *shed for carts* is provided for, though many farmers are too regardless of the fate of these indispensable machines by permitting them to be exposed to all vicissitudes of weather. The cart-shed is shewn at V in the isometrical view fig. 3, Plate III., and by V in the plan, fig. 4, Plate IV., immediately behind the hammels M, facing the work-horse stable O, and looking to the north, away from the shrinking effects of the sun's heat. It is 80 feet in length, 15 feet in width within the pillars, and 8 feet in height to the slates in front. The roof slopes from the back-slating of the hammels, and is supported at the eave by a beam of wood resting on 7 stone and lime pillars, and a wall at each end. The pillars should be of ashler, 2 feet square, and rounded on the corners, to avert their being chipped off with the iron rims of the wheels by the carelessness of the ploughmen, when backing the carts into the shed. For the same purpose, a pawl-stone should be placed on each side of every pillar. This shed is longer than what is actually required where double-horse carts are only used, 6 ports being sufficient for that number, but single-horse carts are now so much in use, that more of these are required, perhaps not fewer than 8. Two single-horse carts can stand in each port, one in front of the other. Any spare room in the shed may be employed in holding a light cart, the roller, the grass-seed-machine, the turnip-sowing-machine, the bodies of the long carts, and other articles too bulky to be stowed into the implement-house G.

(68.) Though swine are usually allowed to run about the steading at pleasure, yet, to do them justice, they should be accommodated at times with protection and shelter, as well as the rest of the live-stock. *Piggeries* or *pig-sties* are therefore highly useful structures at the farmstead. They are of three kinds, 1. Those for a *brood-sow with a litter of young pigs*. This kind should have two apartments, one for the sow and the litter to sleep in, covered with a roof, and entered by an opening, the other an open court in which the feeding-trough is placed. For a breeding-sty each apartment should not be less than 6 feet square. This kind of sty is represented by *c c* in the plan, fig. 4, Plate IV, and at *c* in the isometrical view, fig. 3, Plate III. 2. Those for *feeding-pigs;* these should also have two apartments, one with litter for sleeping in, covered by a roof and entered by an opening; the other an open court for the troughs for food. A sty of 4 feet square in each apartment, will accommodate 2 feeding pigs of 20 stones each. Of this kind of sty 4 are represented at *a* in the isometrical view, fig. 3, Plate III., and in the plan fig. 4, Plate IV. These two sorts of sties may each have a roof of its own, or a number of them may have a large roof over them in common. The former is the usual plan, but the latter is the most convenient for cleaning out, and viewing the internal condition of the sties. 3. The third kind is for the accommodation of weaned young pigs, when it is considered necessary to confine them. These should have a shed at one end of the court, to contain litter for their beds. The court and shed are represented at *b* in the plan, fig. 4, Plate IV., and isometrical view, fig. 3, Plate III. They extend 25 feet in length and 21 feet in width. 4. The floors of all these kinds of sties should be laid with stout flags to prevent every attempt of the swine digging into the ground with their snouts. 5. As swine are very strong in the neck, and apt to push up common doors,

Fig. 23.

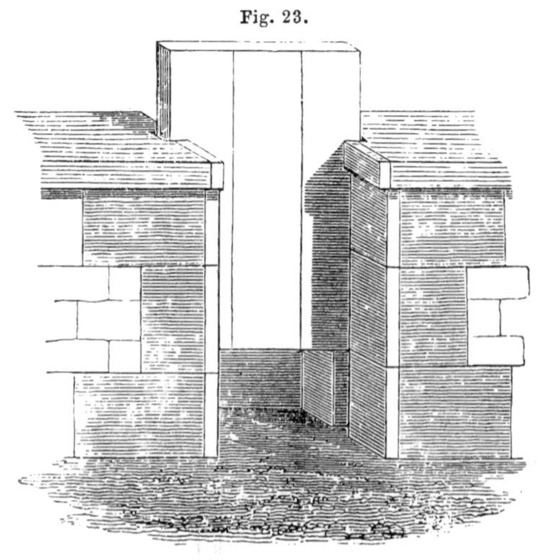

DOOR OF PIG-STY.

the best kind of door which I have found for confining them by, is that formed of stout boards, made to slip up and down within a groove in hewn stones forming the entrance in the outside wall. This form of door may be seen in fig. 23, and seems to require no detailed description.

(69.) *Domestic fowls* require accommodation in the steading as well as other stock. 1. They should be provided with *houses for hatching their eggs in*, as also for *roosting* in undisturbed, and both kinds should be constructed in accord with the nature of the birds, that is, those fowls which roost on high should be kept in a different house from those which rest on the ground. The roosts should be made of horizontal round spars of wood, and spaces of 18 inches cube should be made of wood or stone at a height of 1 foot or 18 inches from the ground, to contain the straw nests for those which are laying. The hatching-houses should be fitted up with separate compartments containing large nests elevated only 3 or 4 inches above the level of the floor. 2. The foundations should be of large stones and the flooring of strong flags, firmly secured with mortar above a body of small broken stones, and the roofs completely filled in under the slates to prevent the possibility of vermin lodging either above or below ground. 3. Good doors with locks and keys should be put on the houses, windows provided for the admission of light and air, and an opening made in the outer wall of the roosting-house, 4 feet above the ground, to admit the fowls which roost on high by a trap-ladder resting on the ground, as at *d* in fig. 3, Plate III. The roof should be water-tight at all times, and lathed and plastered in the inside, for warmth and cleanliness. The fowls' house may be seen at *d* in the isometrical view, fig. 3, Plate III, and in the plan, fig. 4, Plate IV. 4. It is not absolutely necessary that either the hen-houses or pig-sties should be placed where they are represented in the plan; but as they do not there interrupt the free entrance of the sun into the court K, and therefore do not interfere with the comfort of more important stock, they are there of easy access, themselves quite exposed to the sun, which they should always be, and they square up the front of the farmstead. The hen-house has been recommended by some people to be built near the cow-byre to derive warmth from it; but all the heat that can be obtained from mere juxtaposition to a byre is quite unimportant, and not to be compared to the heat of the sun in a southern aspect.

(70.) S, in both the plan, fig. 4, Plate IV, and isometrical view, fig. 3, Plate III, is part of the *stackyard.* 1. As most of the stacks must stand on the ground, the stackyard should receive that form which will allow the rain-water to run off and not injure their bottoms. This is done by ridging up the ground. The minimum breadth of these ridges may be determined in this way. The usual length of the straw of the grain crops can be conveniently packed in stacks of 15 feet diameter; and as 3 feet is little enough space to be left on the ground between the stacks, the ridges should not be made of less width than 18 feet. 2. The stackyard should be inclosed with a substantial stone and lime wall of 4½ feet in height. In too many instances the stackyard is entirely uninclosed and left exposed to the depredation of every animal. 3. It is desirable to place the outside rows of the stacks next the wall on *stools* or *stathels*, which will not only keep them off the wet ground, should they remain a long time in the stackyard, but in a great measure prevent vermin getting into the stacks. These stathels are usually and most economically made of stone supports and a wooden frame. The frame is of the form of an octagon, under each angle and centre of which is placed a support. The frame-work consists of pieces of plank *a a*, fig. 24, one of which is 15 feet, and the others 7½ feet in length, 9 inches in depth, and 2½ inches in thickness; and the supports consist of a stone *b*, sunk to the level of the ground, to form a solid foundation for the upright support *c*, 18 inches in height, and 8 inches square, to stand

Fig. 24.

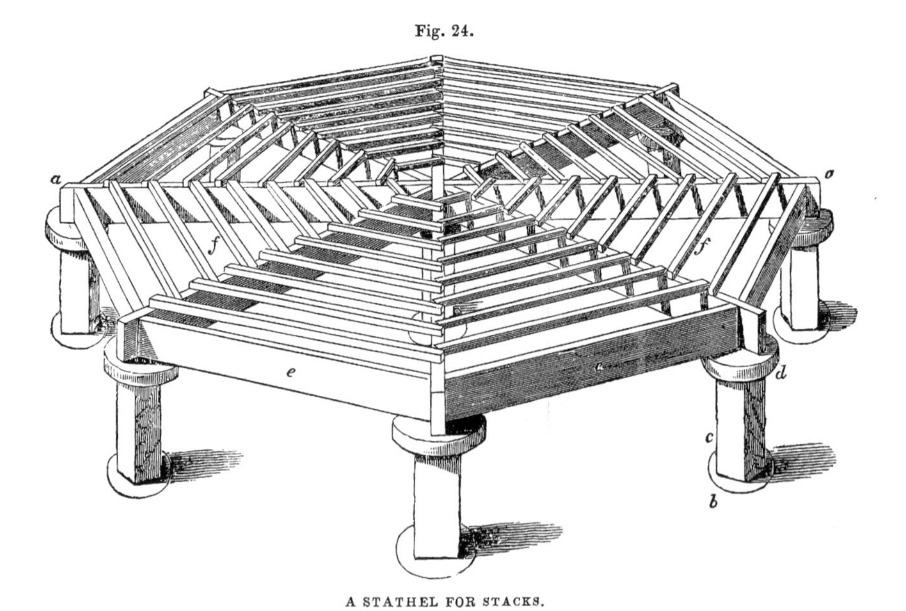

A STATHEL FOR STACKS.

upon, and on the top of this is placed a flat rounded stone or bonnet *d*, of at least 2 inches in thickness. The upright stone is bedded in lime, both with the found and bonnet. All the tops of these stone supports, 8 in number around the ninth in the centre, must be on the same level. Upon them are then placed on edge the scantlings *a*, 9 inches in depth, to each side of which is fastened with strong nails the bearers *e e*, also 9 inches in depth and 2 inches in thickness. In this way each support bears its share of the frame-work. The spaces between the scantlings *a* are filled up with fillets of wood, *f f*, nailed upon them. If the wood of the frame-work were previously preserved by Kyan's process, it would last perhaps twenty years, even if made of any kind of home timber, such as larch or Scots fir. 4. There should be a wide gateway into the stackyard, and where the corn is taken on carts to the upper barn to be thrashed, the same gateway may answer both purposes, but where there is a gangway to the upper barn, the gate may be placed in the most convenient side of the stackyard. Where carts are solely used for taking in the corn to the upper barn, the rows of stacks should be built so widely asunder as to permit a loaded cart to pass at least between every two rows of stacks, so that any particular stack may be accessible at pleasure. When a gangway is used, this width of the arrangement of the stacks is not necessary, the usual breadth of 3 feet between the stacks permitting the passage of corn-barrows, or of back-loads of sheaves. Thus, where a gangway is used, the stackyard is of smaller area to contain the same bulk of grain. 5. Stack-stools, or *stathels*, or *staddles*, as they are variously called, are sometimes made of cast-iron; but these, though neat and efficient, are very expensive and liable to be broken by accidental concussion from carts. Stacks on stathels are represented in fig. 3, Plate III. by figures of stacks, and in fig. 4, Plate IV. by circles. Stathels should also be placed along the stackyard wall from *m′* to *n′* and from *n′* to *o′* in fig. 3, Plate III.

(71.) A *pigeon-house* is a necessary structure, and may be made to contribute a regular supply of one of the best luxuries raised on a farm. As pigeons are fond of heat at all seasons, there seems no place in the farmstead, especially in winter, better suited for the accommodation of their dwelling than the upper part of the boiling-house. A large pigeon-house is not required, as, with ordinary care, pigeons being very prolific breeders, a sufficient number for the table may be obtained from a few pairs of breeding birds. I have known a pigeon-house not exceeding 6 feet cube, and not very favourably situated either for heat or quietness, yield 150 pairs of pigeons in a season. For a floor, a few stout joists should be laid on the tops of the walls. The flooring should be strong and close, and the sides, front, and roof, in the inside, lathed and plastered. A small door will suffice for an entrance, to which access may be obtained from the boiling-house by a ladder. The pigeon-holes may be seen in the gable of the boiling-house U, in the isometrical view, fig. 3, Plate III.

They may be formed of wood or stone, and should always be kept bright with white paint. The cells in this sort of pigeon-house should be made of wood. and placed all round the walls. I think that 9 inches cube are large enough for the cells. Another site for a pigeon-house may be chosen in the gable of the hay-loft above the riding horse stable, in fig. 1, Plate I.

(72.) Although potatoes are best kept in winter in pits, yet an apartment to contain those in use for any of the stock, will be found very convenient in every steading. For convenience, the *potato-store* should be near the place of their consumption or their preparation into food. In the latter case, proximity to the boiling-house is convenient. 1. Accordingly one potato-store will be found at *f'*, just at the door of the boiling-house U, in the isometrical view, fig. 3, Plate III, and plan fig. 4, Plate IV. It is 30 feet in length and 10 feet in width, and its door being placed in the centre, two kinds of potatoes may conveniently be stored in it at the same time, without the chance of admixture. The door should be provided with a good lock and key. 2. Another store of potatoes may be placed in the apartment *f'* next the cart-shed V, 18 feet by 15 feet, to supply them to the feeding beasts in the hammels M, or to the young stock in the courts; but should this apartment not be required for this, it can be used for any other purpose.

(73.) *Rats and mice* are very destructive and dirty vermin in steadings, and particularly to grain in granaries. Many expedients have been tried to destroy them in granaries, such as putting up a smooth triangular board across each corner, near the top of the wall. The vermin come down any part of the walls to the corn at their leisure, but when disturbed run to the corners, up which they easily ascend, but are prevented gaining the top of the wall by the triangular boards, and on falling down either on the corn or the floor, are there easily destroyed. But preventive means, in this case, are much better than destructive, inasmuch as the granaries are thereby always kept free of them, and consequently always sweet and clean. 1. The great means of prevention is, to deprive vermin of convenient places to breed in above ground, and this may be accomplished in all farmsteads by building up the tops of all the walls, whether of partitions or gables, to the sarking, or the slates, or tiles, as the case may be, and beam filling the tops of the side walls, between the legs of the couples, with stone and mortar; taking care to keep the mortar from contact with the timber. These places form the favourite breeding-ground of vermin in farmsteads, but which delightful occupation will be put a stop to there, when occupied with substantial stone and mortar. The top of every wall, whether of stables, cow-houses, hammels, and other houses, should be treated in this manner: for, if one place be left them to breed in, the young fry will find access to the corn in some way. The tops of the walls of old as well as of new farmsteads can be treated in this manner, either from the inside, or, if necessary, by removing the slates or tiles until the alteration is effected. One precaution only is necessary to be attended to in making beam-fillings, especially in new buildings, which is, to leave a little space *under* every couple face, to allow room for subsidence or the bending of the couples after the slates are put on. Were the couples, when bare, pinned firmly up with stone and lime, the hard points would act as fulcra, over which the long arm of the couple, while subsiding, with the load of slates new put on, would act as a lever, and cause their points to rise, and thereby start the nails from the wall plates, to the imminent risk of pushing out the tops of the walls, and sinking the top of the roof. 2. But besides the tops of the walls, rats and mice breed under ground, and find access into apartments through the floor. To prevent lodgment in those places also, it will be proper to lay the strongest flagging and causewaying upon a bed of mortar spread over a body of 9 inches of small broken stones, around the walls of every apartment on the ground-floor where any food for them may chance to fall, such as in the stables, byres, boiling-house, calves' house, implement-house, hay-house, pig-sties, and hen-house. The corn-barn has already been provided for against the attacks of vermin; but it will not be so easy to prevent their lodgment in the floors of the straw-barn and hammels, where no causewaying is usually employed. The principal means of prevention in those places are, in the first place, to make the foundation of the walls very deep, not less than two feet, and then fill up the interior space between the walls with a substantial masonry of stone and lime mixed with broken glass; or perhaps a thick body of small broken stones would be sufficient, as rats cannot burrow in them as in earth.

(74.) It is very desirable, in all courts occupied by stock, to prevent the farther discharge of rain-water into them, than what may happen to fall upon them directly from the heavens. 1. For this purpose all the eaves of the roofs which surround such courts should be provided with *rain-water spouts*, to carry off the superfluous water, not only from the roofs, but to convey it away in drains into a ditch at a distance from, and not allow it to overflow the roads around, the farmstead. 2. With a similar object in view, and with the farther object of preserving the foundations of the walls from damp, *drains* should be formed along the bottom of every wall not immediately surrounding any of the courts. These drains should be dug 3 inches below the foundation-stones of the walls, a conduit formed in them of tile and sole, or flat stones, and the space above the conduit to the surface of the ground filled up with broken stones. These broken stones receive the drop from the roofs, and carry away the water; and, should they become hardened above the drains, or grown over with grass, the grass may be easily removed, and the stones loosened by the action of a hand-pick. Rain-water spouts should be placed under the front-eaves of the building A A, and on both sides of the straw-barn L, and along the front-eaves of the stables O and P, of the byre Q, calves' cribs R, and of the hammels M and N. These lines of eaves may easily be traced in the isometrical view, fig. 3, Plate III. The spouts may be made either of wood or cast-iron, the latter being the more durable, and fastened to the wall by iron-holdfasts. Lead spouts are, I fear, too expensive for a steading, though they are by far the best. The positions of the rain-water drains around the steading may be traced along the dotted lines, and the courses the water takes in them are marked by arrows, as in the plan, fig. 4, Plate IV.

(75.) But it is as requisite to have the means of conveying away superfluous water *from* the courts, as it is to prevent its discharge *into* them. 1. For this purpose, a *drain* should enter into each of the large courts, and one across the middle of each set of hammels. The ground of every court should be so laid off as to make the lowest part of the court at the place where the drain commences or passes; and such lowest point should be furnished with a strong block of hewn freestone, into which is sunk flush an iron grating, having the bars only an inch asunder, to prevent the passage of straws into the drain. Fig. 25 gives an idea of such a grating, made of malleable iron, to bear rough usage, such as the wheel of a cart passing over it; the bars being placed across, with a curve *downwards*, to keep them clear of obstructions for the water to pass through them. A writer, in speaking of such gratings, says, "they should be strong, and have the ribs well bent *upwards*, as in that form they are not so liable to be choked up."* This remark is quite true in regard to the form gratings should have in the sewers of towns, for with the ribs bent *downwards* in such a place, the accumulated stuff brought upon them by the water would soon prevent the water getting down into the drains; but the case is quite different in courts where the straw covers the gratings

Fig. 25.

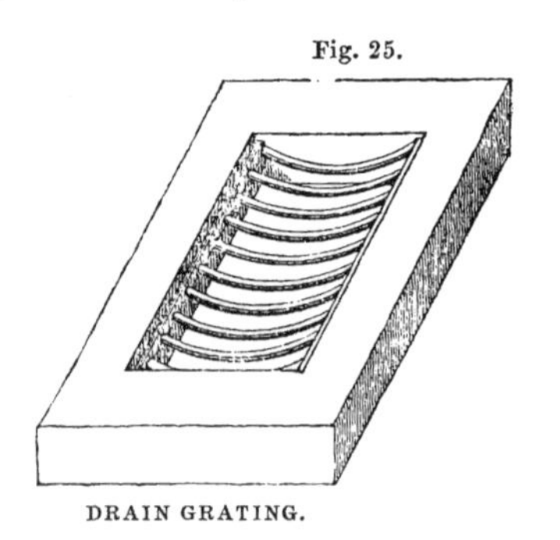

DRAIN GRATING.

* Highland and Agricultural Society's Prize Essays, vol. viii. p. 375.

from the first, and where being loose over the grating whose ribs are bent downwards, it acts *as a drainer*, but were the gratings bent upwards, as recommended, the same straw, instead of acting as loose materials in a drain through which the water percolates easily, would press hard against the ribs. and prevent the percolation of water through them. Any one may have perceived that the straw of dunghills presses much harder against a raised stone in the ground below it, than against a hollow. The positions of these gratings are indicated in the plan, fig. 4, Plate IV, by *x* in the different courts; and in fig. 2, Plate II. they are seen at the origin of all the liquid manure drains, in the form of small dark squares. 2. Drains *from* the courts which convey away *liquid manure* as well as superfluous water, should be of a different construction from those described for the purpose of carrying away rain-water. They should be built with stone and lime walls, 9 inches high and 6 inches asunder, flagged smoothly in the bottom, and covered with single stones. Fig. 26 shews the form of this sort of drain, and sufficiently explains its structure. As liquid manure is sluggish in its motion, the drains conveying it require a much greater fall in their course than rain-water drains. They should also run in direct lines, and have as few turnings as possible in their passage to the *reservoir* or *tank*, which should be situate in the lowest part of the ground, not far from the steading, and at some convenient place in which composts may be formed One advantage of these drains being made straight is, that, should any of them choke up at any time by any obstruction, a large quantity of water might be poured down with effect through them, to clear the obstruction away, as none of them are very long. These drains may be seen in the plan, fig. 4, Plate IV, to run from *x* in their respective courts in straight lines to the tank *k'*. It would be possible to have a tank in each set of hammels and courts, to let the liquid manure run directly into them; but the multiplicity of tanks which such an arrangement would occasion, would be attended with much expense at first, and much inconvenience at all times thereafter in being so far removed from the composts. Were the practice adopted of taking the liquid manure to the field at once, and pouring it on the ground, as is done by the Flemish farmers, then a tank in every court would be convenient.

Fig. 26.

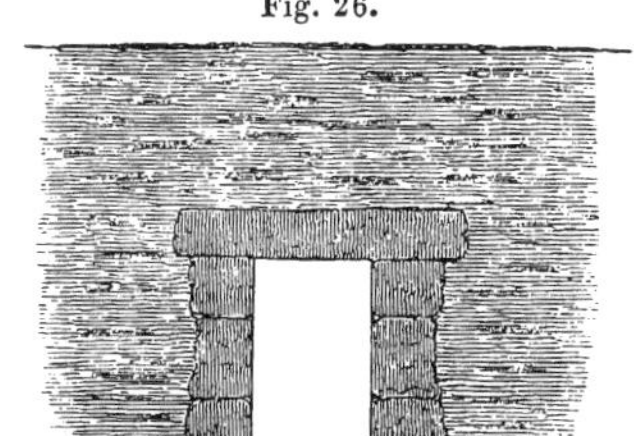

LIQUID MANURE DRAIN.

(76.) The *liquid manure tank* should be built of stone or brick and lime. Its form may be either round, rectangular, or irregular, and it may be arched, covered with wood, left open, or placed under a slated or thatched roof, the arch forming the most complete roof, in which case the rectangular form should be chosen. I have found a tank of an area of only 100 square feet, and a depth of 6 feet below the bottoms of the drains, contain a large proportion of the whole liquid manure collected during the winter, from courts and hammels well littered with straw, in a steading for 300 acres, where rain-water spouts were used. The position of the tank may be seen in the plan, fig. 4, Plate IV, at *k'*. It is rectangular, 34 feet in length and 8 feet in width, and might be roofed with an arch. The tank *x*, in the isometrical view, fig. 3, Plate III, is made circular, to shew the various forms in which tanks may be made. A *cast-iron pump* should be affixed to one end of the tank, the spout of which should be as elevated as to allow the liquid to run into the bung-hole of a large barrel placed on the framing of a cart.

(77.) *Gates* should be placed on every inclosed area about the steading. Those courts which require the service of carts, should have gateways of not less width than 9 feet, the others proportionally less. 1. The more common form of gate is that of the five-barred, and which, when made strong enough, is a very convenient form. It is usually hung by a heel-crook and band. I am not fond of gates being made to shut of themselves, particularly at a steading, for whatever ease of mind that property may give to those whose business it is to look after the inclosure of the courts, it may too often cause neglect of fastening the gate after it is shut; and unless gates are constantly *fastened* where live-stock are confined, they may nearly as well be left altogether open. The force of the contrivance of gates to shut of themselves, has often the effect of knocking them to pieces against the withholding-posts. 2. Sometimes large boarded doors are used as gates in courts, and especially in a wall common to two courts. They are at best clumsy looking things, and are apt to destroy themselves by their own intrinsic weight. 3. Sometimes the gate is made to move up like the sash of a window, by the action of cords and weights running over pulleys on high posts, the gate being lifted so high as to admit loaded carts under it. This may be an eligible mode of working a gate betwixt two courts in the peculiar position in which the dung accumulating on both sides prevents its ordinary action, but in other respects it is of too complicated and expensive a construction to be frequently adopted. I shall have occasion afterwards to speak at large on the proper construction of gates.

(78.) I wish to *suggest some slight modifications* of this plan of a steading, as they may more opportunely suit the views of some farmers than the particular arrangements which have been just described 1. I have already suggested that, if the large courts I and K are to be dispensed with and hammels adopted in their stead, the hammels M could be produced towards the left as far as the causeway *e'*, on the right hand of the straw-barn L; and so could the hammels N be produced towards the right as far as the south gate of the court I. By this arrangement the cart-shed V, and store-houses *g* and *f'*, would be dispensed with, and the cattle-sheds D D converted into cart-sheds and a potato-store. 2. The piggeries *a*, *b*, and *c*, could then be erected in the middle of the court at K, and the hen-houses in the middle of the court I, respectively, of even larger dimensions than I have given them in the places they occupy. 3. If desired, the work-horse stable O might be separated from the principal range A by a cart-passage, as is the case with the byre-range Q, by which alteration the hay-house and stable would have doors opposite, and the present north door of the hay-house dispensed with. It would be no inconvenience to the ploughmen to carry the hay and corn to the horses across the passage. 4. If the stable were disjoined, the right-hand granary may have a window in the east gable, uniform with that in the west over the implement-house G. 5. It may be objected to the boiling-house U being too far removed from the work-horse stable O. As there is as little inherent affinity betwixt a boiling-house and byre as betwixt one and a stable, the boiling-house might be removed nearer to the stable, say to the site of the riding-horse stable P, and the coach-house Z could then be converted into a potato-store, with a common door. 6. The gig-house and riding-horse stable could be built anywhere in a separate range, or in conjunction with the smithy and carpenter s shop, should these latter apartments be desired at the steading. 7. The servants' cow-byre Y, could be shifted to the other end of the hammel range N, to allow the hammels to be nearest the straw-barn. 8. Any or all of these modifications may be adopted, and yet the principle on which the steading is constructed would not be at all affected. Let any or all of them be adopted by those who consider them improvements of the plan represented on Plate IV.

(79.) As I have mentioned both a *smithy* and *carpenter's shop* in connection with the steading, it is necessary to say a few words regarding them. It is customary for farmers to agree for the repairs of the iron and wood work of the farm with a smith and carpenter respectively at a fixed sum a-year. When the smithy and carpenter's shops are near the steading, the horses are sent to the smithy, and every sort of work is performed in the mechanic's own premises; but when they are situate at such a distance as to impose considerable labour on horses and men going to and from them, then the farmer erects a smithy at the steading for his own use, fitting it up with a forge, bellows, anvil, and work-bench. Such a smithy, to contain a pair of draught-horses when shoeing, would require to be 24 feet in length and 15 feet in width, with a wide door in the centre, 7½ feet high, and a glazed window on each side of it. As the time of a pair of horses is more valuable than that of a man, a smithy is often erected at the steading, whilst the carpenter's shop is at a distance.

(80.) All the roads around the steading should be properly made of a thick bed, of not less than 9 inches, of small broken whinstone metal, carefully kept dry, with proper outlets for water at the lowest points of the metal bed, and the metal occasionally raked and rolled on the surface until it becomes solid.

(81.) The best way of building such a steading as I have just described, is *not to contract for it in a slump sum*, because, whatever alterations are made during the progress of the work, the contractor may take advantage of the circumstance, and charge whatever he chooses for the extra work executed, without your having a check upon his charges. Nor, for the same reasons, should the mason, carpenter, or slater work be contracted for separately in the slump. The *prices per rood or per yard, and the quantities of each kind of work, should be settled beforehand between the employer and contractor*. The advantage of this arrangement is, that the work is finished according to the views and tastes of the individual for whose use the farmstead has been built, he having had the power of adopting such slight modifications of the plan, during the progress of the work, as experience or reflection may have suggested. The contractor is paid according to the measurement of the work he thus executes. A licensed surveyor, mutually chosen by both parties, then measures the work, and calculates its several parts according to the prices stipulated for betwixt the contractor and his employer, and draws up a report of the value of each kind of work, the total sum of which constitutes the cost of the farmstead. Instalments of payment are of course made to the contractor at periods previously agreed upon. This plan may give you no cheaper a steading than the usual one of contracting by a slump sum, but cheapness is not the principal object which you should have in view in building a steading. Your chief object should be the convenience of your work-people, and the comfort of your live-stock. This plan enables you to erect a steading in accordance with your own views in every respect, and you can better judge, in the progress of the work, of the fitness of the plan for the accommodation required, than by any study of the plans on paper, which, upon the whole, may appear well enough adapted to the purposes intended, but may nevertheless overlook many essential particulars of accommodation and comfort.

(82.) What I mean by essential particulars of accommodation and comfort in a steading are such as these:—In giving a foot or two more length to a stable or byre, by which each animal may have two or three inches more room laterally, more ease would be given to it, and which is a great comfort to working stock: A window, instead of looking to the cold north, may be made with as much ease to look to the warm south: A sky-light in the roof, to afford a sufficient light to a place that would otherwise be dark: An additional drain to remove moisture or effluvia, which, if left undisturbed, may give considerable annoyance: A door opening one way instead of the other, may direct a draught of air to a quarter where it can do no harm: These little conveniences incur no more cost than the incongruities of arrangement which are often found in their stead, and though they may seem to many people as trifles unworthy of notice, confer, nevertheless, much additional comfort on the animals inhabiting the apartments in which they should be made. A door made of a whole piece, or divided into leaves, may make a chamber either gloomy or cheerful; and the leaves of a door formed either vertically or horizontally, when left open, may either give security to an apartment, or leave it at liberty to the intrusion of every passer by. There are numerous such small conveniences to be attended to in the construction of a steading before it can be rendered truly *commodious* and *comfortable.*

(83.) Before the prices of work to be executed can be fixed on between the employer and contractor, *minute specifications* of every species of work should be drawn up by a person competent for the task. A vague specification, couched in general terms, will not answer; for when work comes to be executed under it, too much liberty is given to all parties to interpret the terms according to the interest of each. Hence arise disputes, which may not be easily settled even on reference to the person who drew up the specifications, as he possibly may by that time have either forgotten his own ideas of the matter, or, in adducing his original intentions under the particular circumstances, may possibly give offence to one party, and injure the other; and thus his candour may rather widen than repair the breach. Whatever are the ideas of him who draws up the specification, it is much better to have them all embodied in the specifications, than to have to explain them afterwards.

(84.) The *principle* of *measuring* the whole work after it has been executed, is another consideration which it is essential you should bear in mind. It is too much the practice to tolerate a very loose mode of measuring work; such as measuring *voids*, as the openings of doors and windows are termed, that is, on measuring a wall, to include all the openings in the rubble-work, and afterwards to measure the lintels and ribets and corners. In like manner, chimney-tops are measured all round as rubble, and then the corners are measured also as hewn work. Now the fair plan obviously is to measure every sort of work as it stands by itself; where there *is* rubble let it be measured for rubble, and where there *is* hewn-work let it be measured for as such. You will thus pay for what work is actually done for you, and no more; and more you should not pay for, let the price of the work be what it may. This understanding regarding the principle of measurement should be embodied in the specifications.

(85.) To see if the *principle* I have endeavoured to enforce in the arrangement of the component parts of a steading for the mixed husbandry be applicable to steadings for other modes of husbandry, you have only to apply it to the construction of steadings usually found in the country.

(86.) In *pastoral* farms, the accommodation for stock in the steading is generally quite inadequate to give shelter, in a severe winter and spring, to the numbers of animals reared on them. For want of adequate accommodation, many of both the younger and older stock suffer loss of condition,—a contingency much to be deprecated by the store-farmer, as the occurrence never fails to render the stock liable to be attacked by some fatal disease at a future period. In the steadings of such farms, the numerous cattle, or still more numerous sheep, as the stock may happen to be, should have shelter. The cattle should be housed in sheds or hammels in stormy weather, supplied with straw for litter and provender, or, what is still better, supported on hay or turnips. For this purpose their sheds should be quite contiguous to the straw-barn. Sheep should either be put in large courts bedded with straw, and supplied with hay or turnips, or so supplied in a sheltered spot, not far distant from the steading. The particular form of steading suitable to this species of farm seems to be that which embraces three sides of a double rectangle, having the fourth side open to

Fig. 27.

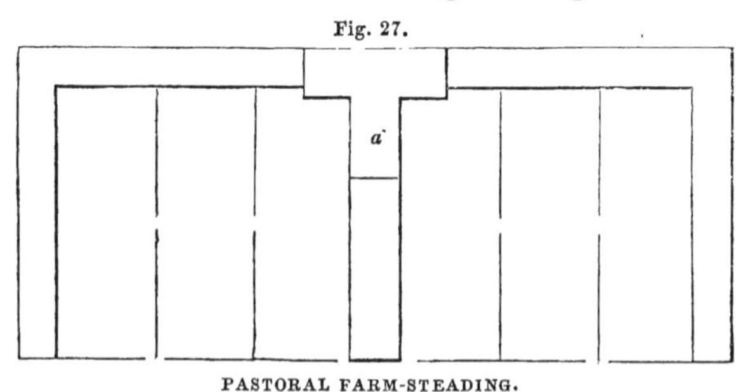

PASTORAL FARM-STEADING.

the south, each rectangle enclosing a large court, divided into two or more parts, on each side of the straw-barn, which should form a side common to both rectangles. This form answers to the modification pointed out at 3. in paragraph (8.), p. 111, and it is shewn in fig. 27, where *a* is tho straw-barn, with but the courts placed on each side of it.

(87.) In the steadings of *carse* farms, comfortable accommodation for stock is made a matter of secondary import. In them it is not unusual to see the cattle-courts facing the north. As there is, however, great abundance of straw on such farms, the stock seem to be warm enough lodged at night. Where so much straw is required to be made into manure, the courts and stables should be placed quite contiguous to the straw-barn. The form of steading most suitable to this kind of farm seems to be that of three sides of a rectangle, embracing a large court, divided into two or three parts, facing the south, and having the upper and corn barn projecting behind into the straw-yard, as described in modification 2. (8.), p. 111, and shewn in fig. 28, where *a* is the straw-barn, near the courts, and contiguous to which should be the byres and stables.

Fig. 28.

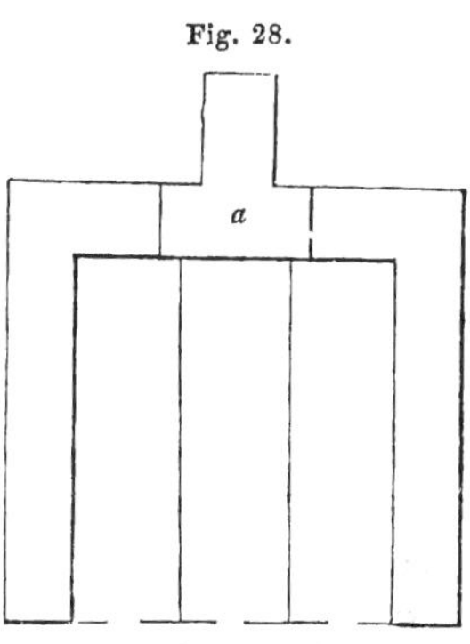

CARSE FARM-STEADING.

(88.) In farms in the *neighbourhood of towns*, the cow-houses, feeding byres, or hammels, being the only means of converting the straw into manure, which is reserved for home use from the sale of the greatest part to the cowfeeders and stablers in towns, should be placed nearest the straw-barn. The very confined state in which cows are usually kept in the byres of such farms, and especially in those near the largest class of towns, makes them very dirty, the effects of which must injure the quality of the dairy produce. In constructing a steading for a farm of this kind, such an inconvenience should be avoided. The most convenient form of steading is that of the three sides of a rectangle, embracing within it a set of feeding-hammels facing the south; the thrashing-mill and straw-barn being in the north range, the work-horse stable in one of the wings, and the cow-byre in the other, from both of which the dung may be wheeled into their respective contiguous dunghills, as is described in modification 1. (8.), p. 111, and shewn graphically in fig. 29, where *a* is the straw-barn, on both sides of which are the byres and stable, and *c* are hammels inclosed within the rectangle.

Fig. 29.

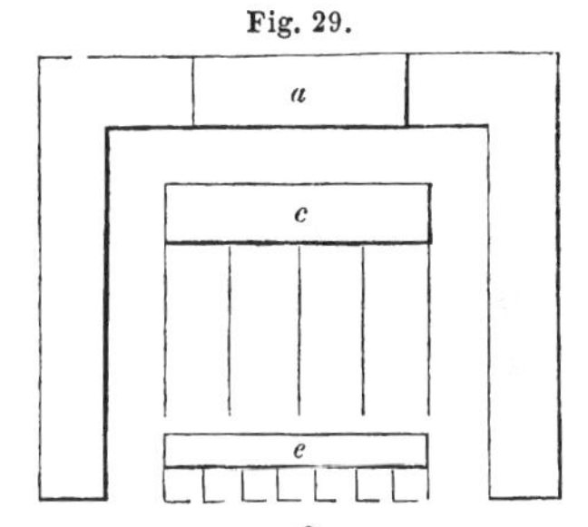

DAIRY FARM, &c. STEADING.

(89.) In *dairy* farms, the cows being the greatest means of making manure, their byres, as well as the hammels for the young horses and young queys, and the sties for the swine, should be those most contiguous to the straw-barn. It should be the particular study of the dairy farmer to make the byre roomy and comfortable to the cows, the thriving state of that portion of his stock being the source from which his profits are principally derived. The form of steading recommended for farms in the neighbourhood of towns seems well adapted to this kind of farming, in which the hammels could be occupied by the young horses and young queys, and beside which the pig-sties could also be placed, such as are shewn in fig. 29, where *c* are the hammels, and *e* the hog-sties, but which may be placed elsewhere if desired.

(90.) It may prove of service to inquire, whether this principle of constructing steadings for every sort of farm is inculcated by the most recent or authoritative writers on agriculture. 1. In the collection of designs of farm-buildings, in the Prize Essays* of the Highland and Agricultural Society of Scotland, the absolute necessity for the contiguity of cattle-sheds, hammels, and stables to the straw-barn, is a matter not sufficiently attended to. When hammels are placed in front of the principal buildings, as in No. 1. of the designs, doors are required in the back of the hammels for taking in the straw. These doors not only incur additional cost in the making, but, being placed in the shed, induce the animals to escape through them, and, when open, occasion an uncomfortable draught of air. The openings, too, betwixt the sheds and courts of the hammels being placed in the centre, cold easily circulates through the sheds. And the separation of the calves'-house from the cow-byre, as in design No. 2., must be very inconvenient in rearing calves. 2. In "British Husbandry," the principle of constructing a steading is thus laid down:—"The position of a thrashing-mill should decide that of almost every other office; for it cuts, or ought to cut, the hay into chaff, together with much of the straw; and the house that immediately receives this chaff ought to be so placed as to admit of a convenient delivery to the stalls and stables. Thus the straw-barn, chaff-house, ox-stalls, and horse-stables, with the hay-stacks and the sheep-yard (if there be any), should be dependent on the position of the thrashing-mill, as they will be attended with waste and expense of labour." † If the chaff-cutting machine is to be employed for preparing much of the straw for the use of the stock, it should be placed in the *straw-barn*, otherwise the straw must be carried to it, which would entail a considerable deal of labour. It is thus the position of neither the chaff-cutting or thrashing-machine, that should determine the site of the rest of the steading. The thrashing-machine cannot conveniently be placed near the centre of a steading, because it would then be necessarily removed to a distance from the stack-yard, and the carriage of the sheaves from which would also entail considerable labour. In the examples of existing steadings given in this recent work from pages 85 to 109, being chiefly the plans of steadings on the properties of the Duke of Sutherland, the position of the straw-barn seems in them to be considered a matter of secondary importance. In the plans in pages 85, 86, 100, 103, 107, 108, and 109, the straw-barn is surely placed at an inconvenient distance from the apartments occupied by the live-stock, and the carriage of straw from it to them must "be attended with waste and expense of labour." 3. Professor Low inculcates the principle more correctly where he says, "Barns, being the part whence the straw for fodder and litter is carried to the stables, feeding-houses, and sheds, they should be placed so as to afford the readiest access to these different buildings. It is common to place them as near the centre of the range as the general arrangement of the other buildings will allow." ‡ This is quite correct in principle; but, in referring to the figure, it is said that, "In the design of the figure, in which are represented the barns, this principle of arrangement is observed;" yet, on inspecting the figure at p. 624, it will be observed, that the feeding-hammels are placed at a greater distance from the straw-barn than even the pig-sties and poultry-yards. It does not appear that the yard behind the sties is intended to be occupied by anything but manure; so, if the hammels had occupied the more eligible site of the hog-sties, they would not have interposed betwixt the sun-light and any

* Prize Essays of the Highland and Agricultural Society, vol. viii. p. 365.

† British Husbandry, vol. i. p. 97.

‡ Low's Elements of Practical Agriculture, 2d edition, p. 623.

stock. It may also be observed, that the cow-houses, which require less straw than feeding stock, are placed nearer the straw-barn than the hammels on the right. 4. Mr Loudon, in treating of the " fundamental principles for the construction of the various parts which compose a farmery," recommends the houses for the various kinds of stock to be constructed according to the size and shape of the animals to be accommodated, and *assuming* the horse, the ox, and the sheep, to be of the form of a wedge, he draws these two conclusions; " first, that the most economical mode of lodging the first two of these quadrupeds must be in houses the walls of which form concentric circles, or segments of circles parallel to each other; . . . . and, secondly, that in all open yards where quadrupeds are allowed to run loose, and eat from racks and mangers, ... when the rack or manger is to be in a straight line, the breadth of the broad end of the wedge must be allowed for each animal, and when it is to be curved, the radius of the curve must be determined by the breadth of the smaller end of the wedge. From this theory it may also be deduced, that there must be one magnitude, as well as one form, more economical than any other, for lodging each of these animals; and that this magnitude must be that circumference of a circle which the narrow end of the wedges completely fill up, and no more." * And figures are given of both curved and straight mangers and racks to illustrate these principles. Now, independent of the acknowledged inconvenience of accommodating any circular or curved form of apartment or building in a steading, as is universally felt in regard to the usually circular form of the horse-course of a thrashing-mill, the very data on which this theory is founded are incorrect; for, although it is true that many horses and oxen are of the form of a wedge, yet the higher bred and better stock, to which all improving breeders are desirous of assimilating their own, are not wedge-shaped. The Clydesdale draught-horse, the short-horn ox, and the Leicester sheep, the nearer they attain perfect symmetry of form, the nearer they approach the form of a parallelopipedon, instead of a wedge, in the carcass. This theory is, therefore, not universally applicable. Indeed, Mr Loudon afterwards says (p. 375), that " these principles for the curvilinear arrangement of stalls, racks, and troughs, we do not lay down as of very great importance; but rather with a view to induce the young architect to inquire into the reasons of things; and to endeavour in every thing to take principles into consideration rather than precedents." The object is laudable, but its aim will scarcely be attained by the young architect having his attention directed to questionable data. He is at all times much more disposed to follow his own crude fancies, in the construction of steadings, than to improve on precedents suggested by the farmer's experience.

(91.) It may be interesting to inquire *why* the quadrangular form of steading was so much in vogue some years ago. It was, doubtless, adopted on account of its compactness of form, admitting it to be erected at a considerable saving of expense, at a time—during that of the war—when building-materials of every kind, and wages of every description of artizans, were very high. I do not believe that the value of all the ground on which the largest steading could stand, formed any inducement for the adoption of the compact form of the quadrangle, but rather from the wish of the landlord to afford no more than bare accommodation to the tenant's stocking. An economical plan, furnished by an architect, would thus weigh more strongly with him than a mere regard for the

* Loudon's Encyclopædia of Architecture, p. 373.

comfort of his tenant's live-stock, whose special care he would consider more a tenant's than a landlord's business. It is not so easy to account for the tenant's acquiescence in such a form of steading, for although it must be owned that at that period very imperfect notions were entertained of what were requisite for the comfortable accommodation of animals, yet the tenant's own interest being so palpably involved in the welfare of his stock, might have taught him to desire a more comfortable form of steading. Thus an imperfect state of things originated in the parsimony of landlords, and was promoted by the heedlessness of tenants. The consequences were, that cattle were confined in courts inclosed all around with high buildings, eating dirty turnips off the dunghill, and wading or standing mid-leg deep in dung and water; and frequently so crowded together, and stinted of food, that the most timid amongst them were daily deprived of their due proportion of both food and shelter. Is it any matter of wonder that cattle at that time were unequally and imperfectly fed? In the steadings of the smaller tenants, matters were, if possible, still worse. The state of the cattle in them was pitiable in the extreme, whether in the courts, or while "cabin'd, cribb'd, and confin'd" in the byres. Though those in the latter were, no doubt, under the constant shelter of a roof, they were not much better off as to cleanliness and food; and much worse off for want of fresh air, and in a state of body constantly covered with perspiration. But these unmerited hardships which the cattle had to endure every winter, have been either entirely removed or much ameliorated within these few years, by the adoption of conveniences in the construction of steadings on the part of landlords, and superior management, acquired by experience, on the part of tenants. Troughs are now erected along the walls of courts, at convenient places, for holding turnips, now given clean to the cattle. Rain-water spouts are now put along the eaves of the houses surrounding the courts. Drains are now formed to carry off the superfluous moisture from the courts. The courts themselves are opened up to the meridian sun, and really made comfortable for cattle. And hammels are now built for cattle in steadings where they were before unknown. Still, notwithstanding the decided improvement which has undoubtedly taken place in the construction of steadings, there are yet many old steadings which have not been amended, and too many modern ones erected, in which all the improvements that might have been have not been introduced. Should it be your fate to take a farm on which an old steading of the quadrangular form is standing, or a new one is proposed to be built, in repairing the one, and constructing the other, be sure never to lose sight of *the leading principles* of construction inculcated above, and insist on their being put into practice. A little pertinacity on your part on this point will most probably obtain for you all your wishes, and their attainment to the full will vindicate you in offering a higher rent for the farm, without incurring risk of loss.

(92.) It is now time to enter minutely into the *specifications* upon which every kind of work in the construction of a substantial steading should be executed, and those below will be found applicable to every size and plan of steading. As they accord with my own experience and observation in these matters, and both have been considerable, I offer them with the greater degree of confidence for your guidance. They embrace the particulars of mason-work, carpenter-work, slater-work, plumber-work, smith-work, and painter and glazier-work; but they are not drawn up in the formal way that specifications are usually done, the various subjects as they are specified being illustrated by examples and the elucidation of principles.

(93.) Of the specifications of *mason-work*, the first thing to be done is the *digging of the foundations of the walls*. When the site of the steading is not obliged to be chosen on a rock, the depth of the foundations of all the outside-walls should never be less than 2 feet. Judging by usual practice, this may be considered an inordinate depth, and as incurring much expense in building an unnecessary quantity of foundation walls, which are immediately after to be buried out of sight; but this depth is necessary on account of the drains which should be made around the outside walls, to keep all the floors dry in winter, and it is scarcely possible to keep them dry with drains of less depth than 27 inches, which afford the water a channel of only 3 inches below the bottom of the foundations. The ground-floor of dwelling-houses may be kept in a dry state by elevating it a considerable height above the ground; but such an expedient is impracticable in a steading where most of the apartments, being occupied by live-stock, must be kept as near as possible on a level with the ground; and it is not wood-floors alone that must be kept dry, but those of sheds, barns, and byres, whether made of composition, or causeway, or earth. The injurious effects of damp in the floors of stables, byres, and hammels, on the condition of the animals inhabiting them in winter, or of barns on the state of the straw, corn, or hay in them, are too much overlooked. Its malign influences on the health of animals, or in retarding their thriving, not being apparent to the senses at first sight, are apt to be ascribed to constitutional defect in the animals themselves, instead of, perhaps, to the truer cause of the unwholesome state of the apartments which they occupy. The truth is, the floor of every apartment of the steading, whether accommodating living creatures, or containing inanimate things, cannot *be too dry*; and, to render them as much so as is practicable, there seems no way of attaining the end so effectually as to dig the foundations of the walls deep, and to surround them with still deeper drains. This position I shall here endeavour to prove to you satisfactorily. There are many substances upon which walls are usually founded, which, from their nature, would make walls constantly damp, were expedients not used to counteract their natural baleful properties. Amorphous rocks, such as granite, which are impervious to water;—whinstone rocks, which, though frequently containing minute fissures, being deliquescent, become very damp in wet weather;—clay, and tilly clay even more than the unctuous, retains a great deal of water;—all these substances form objectionable ground upon which to found any building. Stratified rocks, such as sandstone, not retaining the water long, form drier substances for a foundation than any of the amorphous rocks or clays. Pure sand is not always dry, and it is apt to form, in some situations, an insecure foundation. Pure gravel is the driest of all foundations, but not the most secure. From the nature of these various substances, excepting the gravel, it would appear that no wall founded on them can assuredly be kept dry at all seasons; and therefore drains are necessary to render and keep them dry at all seasons. Moreover, a foundation made in a bank of even the driest gravel will prove damp, unless the precaution of deep draining betwixt the foundation and the rise of the bank is resorted to. Rather than choose a site for your steading which is overhung by a bank, make a deeper foundation on more level ground, and drain it thoroughly, or even build some height of waste wall, and fill up a part of the ground that is low around the steading. I have experienced the bad effects of digging a foundation for a steading in a rising ground of tolerably dry materials, and also the good effects of filling up low ground at a part of another steading, and have found the air in the apartments of the latter at all seasons much more agreeable to the feelings than in the former. The bad effects of the former I endeavoured to counteract by deep draining, though not so effectually as in the latter case. I am therefore warranted in concluding that dry apartments are much more healthy for animals, and better for other things, than are those which feel cold and damp. A circling, however, of substantial drains around the steading, between it and the bank, will render the apartments to the feelings, in a short time, in a comparatively comfortable state.

(94.) The *outside walls should be founded with stones* 3 feet in length, 2 feet in breadth, and 8 or 9 inches in thickness, so laid, in reference to the line of foundation, as to form a scarcement of 6 inches on each side of the wall above them. The low walls may stand on one course of such foundation, whilst the higher walls should have two such courses.

(95.) *All the walls*, both external and internal, *should be built of the best rubble-work*, the stones being squared, laid on their natural beds, closely set in good lime mortar, and well headed and packed. Headers should go through the thickness of the walls at not more than 5 feet apart in every third course. The walls should only be built one course in height on one side, before the other side is brought up to the same level, the first of the courses to go through two-thirds of the wall, besides the headers or band-stones.

(96.) The *external walls should be* 2 *feet in thickness*, and the *internal* division-walls, as also the walls composing the fronts and subdivisions of the courts and hammels, 1 *foot*. The low external walls should be raised 9 feet, and the high external walls of the middle range, as well as that of the straw-barn, 15 feet above the ground. All the gables of the external walls, and all the internal division-walls, should rise to the pitch of their respective roofs, and be entirely filled up to the sarking or tiles, as the case may be. The front and side walls of the large courts and bulls' hammels, and the subdivision walls of the courts of the hammels, should be raised 6 feet, and the front-walls of the hammels, as also those of the cows' and calves' courts and pig-sties, 5 feet above the ground. All the walls which carry roofs should be beam-filled with rubble-work, with the precaution given in (73.), p. 157.

(97.) The *external fronts* of all the outside walls, as well as those of the front walls of the courts and hammels, should be faced with *hammer-dressed rubble in courses*, not exceeding 6 inches in thickness, with the vertical and horizontal joints raised or drawn in hollow. The tops of the front and subdivision walls of the courts and hammels should be finished with a *coping* of hammer-dressed round-headed stones, 12 inches in diameter, firmly set close together in good lime mortar.

(98.) To *test* if rubble masonry is well built, step upon a levelled portion of any course, and, on setting the feet a little asunder, try by a searching motion of the legs and feet whether any of the stones ride upon others. Where the stones ride, they have not been properly bedded in mortar. To ascertain if there are any hollows, pour out a bucketful of water on the wall, and those places which have not been sufficiently packed or hearted with small stones, will immediately absorb the water.

(99.) The *width of all the doors* should be 3 feet 6 inches, and their height 7 feet, with the exception of those of the work-horse stable, corn-barn, straw-barn, and saddle-horse stable, which should be 7 feet 6 inches. The width of the arches of the cattle-courts should be 9 feet; that of those of the hammels 6 feet, and that of the ports of the cart-shed 8 feet, and all 7 feet 6 inches in height. The *width of all the windows* should be 3 feet, and their height 4 feet, with the exception of those of the granaries, which should be 4 feet in width and 3 feet in height. The windows should have a bay inside of 6 inches on each side. Slits of 1 foot 3 inches in height and 3 inches in width in front, with a bay inside like the windows, should be left in the walls of the straw and upper barns for the admission of air to the straw and the corn in the straw. All the voids should have substantial discharging arches over the timber-lintels to be able to support the wall above, even although the timber-lintels should fail.

(100.) All the *door-soles* should be laid 3 inches above the ground or causeway, and those of the stables and byres and calves'-house should be bevelled in front, that the feet of the animals going out and in may not strike against them.

(101.) The *corners* of the buildings should be of *broached ashler*, neatly squared, 2 feet in length, 12 inches of breadth in the bed, and 12 to 18 inches in height, having 1 inch chisel draught on both fronts. The *windows and doors should have ashler ribets*, the outbands 2 feet in length, and the inbands at least two-thirds of the thickness of the walls, and both 12 inches of breadth in the beds, and 14 or 15 inches in height. They should have 1 inch of the front, 5 inches of ingoings, and 4 inches of checks, clean droved. The tails of the outband ribets should be *squared and broached*. The doors of the work-horse and saddle-horse stables, upper and corn barns, hay-house and bulls' hammels, should have droved giblet-checks, to permit them opening outwards. The *window-sills* should be droved, projecting 1½ inch, and 6½ or 7 inches in thickness. The *lintels* of both the doors and windows should have 1 inch of the front, 5 inches of ingoings clean droved, and be from 14 to 15 inches in height. The *skews* should be broached when such are used, having 1 inch chisel-draught on both margins of the front, and the inner edge with a 4-inch check-plinth, having an inch back-rest under it. The *holes in the byre-wall*, through which the turnips are supplied, should be 20 inches square, with ashler ribets, flush sills and lintels, having broached fronts and droved giblet checks to receive their shutters. The side *corners of the arched openings* of the cattle-courts and hammels, and those of the ports of the cart-shed, should be regular out and inband, 2 feet in length, 12 inches of breadth in the bed, and 12 inches in height, and dressed in a manner similar to the other corners, but should be chamfered on the angles. The *arches* should be elliptical, with a rise of 2 feet, with broached soffits on both fronts, an inch-droved margin, and radiated joints. In the plan, fig. 4, Plate IV., the cart-shed ports are not arched, there being no room for such a finishing in the peculiar form of the roof. The *pillars* of the cart-shed, the byre, turnip-shed, and calves'-shed, should be 2 feet square in the waist, of broached ashler, with inch-droved margins, and built of stones 12 inches in height. Those of the two former should have a droved base course, 12 inches in depth, with 1½ inch washing, chamfered on the angles. The *tops of the walls* of the pig-sties, calves'-shed, hen-house, and potato-store, should have a 6-inch droved plinth, 12 inches in the bed. The *fire-places* in the boiling-house and coach-house should have a pair of droved jambs and a lintel, 3 feet 6 inches of height in the opening, and a droved hearth-stone 5 feet in length and 3 feet in breadth. The *boiler* should have a hearth-stone 4 feet 6 inches in length, and 2 feet 6 inches in breadth, and it should be built with fire-brick, and have a cope of 4 inches in thickness of droved ashler. The *flues* from both the fire-places and the boiler, should be carried up 12 inches clear in the opening, and should have chimney-stalks of broached ashler, 2 feet in height above the ridges of the respective roofs, 2 feet square, and furnished with a droved check-plinth and block 12 inches in depth. The *gates* of all the cattle and hammel courts should be hung on the droved ashler corners when close to a house, but on droved built pillars when in connection with low court-walls. The riding-horse-stable, if laid at all with *flags*, should have them 4 inches thick, of droved and ribbed pavement behind the travis-posts, having a curved water channel communicating with a drain outside. The travis-posts of the work-horse-stable should be provided with droved stone *sockets* 12 inches in thickness, and 18 inches square, founded on rubble-work, and a droved *curb-stone* should be put betwixt the stone sockets of each pair of head and foot travis-posts, provided with a groove on the upper edge to receive the under edge of the lower travis-board. For the better riddance of the urine from the work-horse-stable, there should be a droved curved *water-channel* 6 inches in breadth, wrought in freestone, all the length of the stable, with a fall at least of 1½ inch to every 10 feet of length. The water-channel in the cow-byres and feeding-houses should be of droved curb-stones 6 inches thick, 12 inches deep, and laid in the bottom with 3-inch thick of droved pavement, placed 6 inches below the top of the curb-stones. If stone is preferred for *water-troughs*, which it should always be when easily obtained, the troughs should not be of less dimensions than 3½ feet in length, 2 feet in breadth, and 18 inches in depth over all, or they may be made of the same dimensions of pavement-flags put together with iron-batts. Wood may be substituted for stone when that cannot be easily obtained. The liquid-manure *drain* should be 9 inches in height and 6 inches in width in the clear, with droved flat sills and hammer-dressed covers. A stone 2 feet in length, 18 inches in breadth, and 8 or 9 inches in thickness, with an opening through it, giblet-checked, will contain a *grating* 15 inches in length and 9 inches in breadth, with the bars one inch asunder, at the ends of the liquid-manure drains in the courts. The liquid-manure *tank* sunk into the ground, will be strong enough with a 9-inch brick or rubble wall of stone and lime-mortar, having the bottom laid with jointed flag-pavement. If the ground is gravelly, a puddling of clay will be requisite behind the walls, and below the pavement of the bottom. The bottom of the *feeding-troughs* in the byres, courts, and hammels, should be of 3-inch thick of flag-pavement, jointed and scabbled on the face, or of wood. All the *window-sills* in the inside should be finished with 3-inch droved or scabbled pavement.

(102.) The *walls in the front of the courts* are intended to be quite *plain;* but should you prefer ornamental structures, their tops may be finished with a 6-inch droved cope, 15 inches in breadth, with a half-inch washing on both fronts; and with a droved base-course 12 inches in depth, having a washing of 1½ inch. The pillars of the gates to the larger courts may be of droved ashler, in courses of an octagonal form, of 15 inches in thickness, and 2 feet by 2 feet, with 12-inch base, and a 12-inch checked plinth and block, built at least 18 inches higher than the wall. And if you prefer an outside hanging-stair to the upper-barn instead of the gangway, or to the wool-room, the steps should be droved 3 feet 6 inches clear of the wall, with 6 inches of wallhold. And, further, you may substitute droved crow-steps on the gables for the broached skews, with an inch back rest under them. These crow-steps, in my opinion, are no ornaments in any case, in a steading. They are only suited to a lofty castellated style of building.

(103.) The floors of the cow-byres, work-horse-stable, stalls of the riding-horse-stable, passage of the calves'-house, coach-house, boiling-house, implement-house, hay-house, and turnip and potato stores, should be laid in *causeway* with whinstone, or with small land stones, upon a solid stratum of sand, with the precaution of a bed of broken stones under the flagging as formerly recommended in (73), p. 157. A causeway, 13 feet in breadth, should also be made in the large court K to the corn-barn door, round to the gate at H, for the use of loaded carts from the barn, with a declivity from the wall to the dung area of 2 inches in the 10 feet. Causeways are usually formed in steadings with round hard stones found on the land, or in the channels of rivers, or on the sea-shore, imbedded in sand. In those situations the stones are always hard, being composed of water-worn fragments of the primitive and secondary as well as of trap-rocks; but round boulders of micaceous sand-stone, usually found in gravel pits, are unfit for the purpose of causeways, being too soft and slaty. A more perfect form of causeway is made of squared blocks of trap, whether of basalt or greenstone, embedded in sand, such as is usually to be seen in the streets of towns. The ready cleavage of trap-rocks into convenient square blocks render them valuable depots, where accessible, of materials for causeways and road metal. The floors of the pig-sties and poultry-yards should be laid with strong thick jointed stones imbedded in lime-mortar, having broken glass in it, upon a bed of 9 inches thick of small broken stones, to withstand not only the digging propensities of the pigs on the surface, but also to prevent vermin gaining access from below through the floor to the poultry. The areas of the cattle-courts, and floors of the sheds, hammels, and cart-shed, will be firm enough with the earth beaten well down.

(104.) There is a plan of making the floors of outhouses, recommended by Mr Waddell of Berwickshire, which deserves attention. It is this: Let the whole area of the apartment be laid with small broken stones to the depth of 9 inches. Above these let a solid body of masonwork, of stone and lime properly packed, be built to the height of 12 or 14 inches, according to the thickness of the substance which is to form the upper floor. The lime, which is applied next the walls, should be mixed with broken glass. If a composition is to form the floor, it should be laid on 3 inches in thickness above the masonry; but if asphaltum, 1 inch thick will suffice, the difference in the height being made up in the masonry.* This plan of Mr Waddell's seems well adapted for making a solid and secure foundation against vermin for the causewaying of the several apartments mentioned above; but it is not so well adapted for wood-floors either as a preservative against damp, or preventive against vermin, as the plan described at p. 118, (16).

(105.) While treating of the subject of causewaying, I may as well mention here the various sorts of flooring and pavement which may be formed of other materials than those already mentioned; and the first is *concrete*, which forms a very good flooring for indoor use. It is formed of a mixture of coal-ashes obtained from furnaces, and from a fourth to a third part or more, according to its strength, of slaked lime, and worked into the form of paste with water. A coating of clay of 2 or 3 inches is first laid on the ground levelled for the pur-

* Prize Essays of the Highland and Agricultural Society, vol. viii. p. 373.

pose and upon the clay, while in a moist state, the concrete is spread 2 or 3 inches in thickness, and beaten down with a rammer or spade until the under part of the concrete is incorporated with the upper part of the clay. The surface of the concrete is then made smooth by beating with the back of a shovel, and when left untouched for a time, that substance assumes a very hard texture. This is a cheap mode of flooring, labour being the principal expense attending it.

(106.) Another sort of pavement is that of *asphaltum*, suitable either for indoor use, or for outdoor purposes, where no cartage is to be employed upon it. It is a composition of bitumen, obtained from coal-tar after the distillation of naphtha, and small clean gravel. When applied, the bitumen and gravel in certain proportions are melted together in a pot over a fire, and when sufficiently liquefied and mixed, the composition is poured over the surface of the ground to be paved, which is previously prepared hard and smooth for the purpose, about an inch or more in thickness, and is spread even and smoothed on the surface with a heated iron roller. When completely dry, the asphaltum becomes a perfect pavement, as hard as stone, and entirely impervious to water. It would form an excellent flooring for the straw-barn, servants'-houses, boiling-house, potato stores, and the passages in the cow-byre and calves'-house. It might also make roofing to outhouses, where there is no chance of the roof being shaken. As made at the Chemical Works at Bonnington near Edinburgh, it costs 5d. per square foot when laid down, which makes it an expensive mode of paving. Whether this asphalte will bear heat, or the trampling of horses' feet, I do not know; but it seems there is a sort of asphaltum pavement in France which will bear 100° of heat of Fahrenheit, and is employed in flooring the cavalry barracks of that country. The substance of which this pavement is made, is called "The Asphaltic Mastic of Seyssel," and for the manufacture and sale of which a company has been formed in Paris to supply pavement for various purposes. The substance is a natural asphalte found at Pyrimont, at the foot of the eastern side of Mount Jura, on the right bank of the river Rhone, one league north of Seyssel. In chemical composition this asphalte contains 90 per cent. of pure carbonate of lime, and 9 or 10 per cent. of bitumen. To form the asphalte into a state fit for use, it is combined with mineral pitch, obtained at the same place, in the proportion of 93 per cent. of the asphalte to 7 per cent. of the mineral pitch. The pitch when analyzed contains of resinous petroliferous matter from 69 to 70 per cent,, and of carbon from 30 to 35 per cent. The preparation of this asphalte being tedious, its cost is greater than that mentioned above. For foot-pavements or floors it is about 6½d., and for roofs 8¼d. per square foot.*

(107.) Another mode of causewaying is with blocks of wood, commonly called *wood-pavement*. Portions of the streets of London have been laid with this kind of pavement, the blocks having been previously subjected to the process of Kyanizing, and they are found to make a smooth, clean, quiet, and durable causewaying. This would be a desirable method of paving the road round the large court K, Plate IV., the straw-barn, work-horse-stable, hay-house, cow-byres, passage in the calves'-house, riding-horse-stable, coach-house, and potato-stores. It would be expedient, when used in a stable or byre, that some other substance than sand be put between the blocks, for that is apt to absorb urine too readily. Grout formed of thin lime and clean small gravel, or asphalte poured in between the

* Simm's Practical Observations on the Asphaltic Mastic or Cement of Seyssel, p. 3.

blocks, might repel moisture. This latter expedient has already been tried, as may be seen at p. 14 of Mr Simm's observations on asphalte. There are various methods of disposing of the blocks of wood so as to make a steady and durable pavement. 1. The earliest plan adopted in London, in 1838, was that of Mr Stead, a specimen of laying which I had an opportunity of seeing in the Old Bailey, London, in 1839. It consisted of hexagonal blocks of wood set on end upon a sandy substratum. The blocks had the Kyan stamp on their side. Since then the substratum upon which the blocks rest has been made of Roman cement and what is called Thames ballast, which I suppose means Thames river sand. The cost of this mode is 9s. the square yard for 6-inch blocks, and 2s. the yard for the concrete. 2. Another plan is that of Mr Carey, which consists of setting cubical blocks on end, a mere modification of that of Mr Stead. The cost is for 8-inch blocks, 12s. 6d.; 9-inch blocks, 13s. 6d.; and 10-inch blocks, 14s. 6d. the square yard. 3. Mr Grimmans' is another mode of wood-paving. It consists of the blocks forming oblique parallelopipedons at an angle of 77°, and they are so cut as to set from right to left and from left to right, presenting a sort of herring-bone work. The blocks are chamfered at the edges to prevent the slipping of horses' feet. With the concrete of Roman cement and Thames ballast, this paving is charged 12s. the square yard. 4. Mr Rankin's method secures the safety of the horses' feet in slipping, but is too elaborate a mode for general adoption. It consists of a number of small blocks, cut out of the same piece of wood, lying above one another in a complicated fashion. With concrete, its cost is 16s. the square yard. 5. Of all the modes of wood-paving yet invented, that of the Count de Lisle is the best. It consists of placing beside each other oblique cubes of 6 inches, having an inclination of $63° \, 26' \, 5\frac{8}{10}''$, a number derived by calculation from the stereotomy of the cube. " These blocks are cut and drilled by machinery, mathematically alike; and are so placed in the street, that they rest upon and support each other from curb to curb, each alternate course having the angle of inclination in opposite directions. These courses are connected to each other, side and side, by dowels, which occupy the exact centres of two isosceles [equilateral?] triangles, into which each block is divisible. This arrangement affords the means of connecting every block with four others, and prevents the possibility of one being forced below the level of another. Pressure and percussion are therefore distributed, in effect, over large surfaces, and a perfect cohesion established. Nor is this cohesion advantageous only as a means of resistance against superincumbent force. It is of equal value in withstanding any effort to break up the uniformity of surface by undue expansion. The concrete foundation having a slight elliptical curve given to it, and the wood-paving being so laid as to correspond with that curve, for the purposes alike of strength and surface drainage, there is naturally a slight tension on the dowels in an upward direction, which the pressure from above tends to relieve; whilst the lower ends of the blocks abut so closely together in one direction, and every block is so kept in its position by two dowels on each side in the other direction, that the whole mass will take any increased curve consequent upon expansion, without the slightest risk of either partial or general displacement." There is much facility in replacing these blocks, especially since " the dowelling of them together at the manufactory in panels of 24 each, 6 in length by 4 in width, the blocks at the sides of which being connected by iron cramps. Thus prepared, the process of covering a street is exceedingly rapid and simple. One end of a panel is cut off at an angle to agree with that of the curb and the curve of the street, and is then abutted against it; each panel, containing four courses, in alternate angles, another dovetails precisely with the first, and thus panel after panel is laid until the street is crossed, and the last cut off to abut against the other curb." To prevent slipping, grooves are cut across the street at about 6-inches apart, and others are formed along the street, to prevent rutting, and the joinings of the longitudinal grooves are broken. The substratum upon which this mode of wood-paving is made to rest is a concrete formed of "blue lias lime, a metallic sand, and Thames ballast," which becomes permanently solid and impervious to water after two or three days, by the oxidation of the metallic sand. The cost of this mode is 13s. the square yard for 6-inch blocks and concrete complete, and 6d. a yard every year for keeping it in perfect repair for 10 or 20 years; 12s. for 5-inch blocks; 11s. for 4-inch blocks, and proportionately for repairs.

(108.) Of these various modes of wood-paving the following are the quantities of each which have been tried in London up to November 1841, viz.:—

Of Stead's hexagons, . . .	8,710	square yards.
De Lisle's oblique cubes, . .	19,838	... ...
Carey's squares, . . .	1,750	... ...
Grimman's oblique parallelopipedons,	650	... ...
Rankin's inverted pyramids, . .	492	... ...
	31,440	

The Metropolitan Wood-paving Company have adopted De Lisle's system.

(109.) As to the durability of wood-paving, it is reasonable to suppose that "a structure of wood, instead of resisting the pressure or percussion of passing vehicles, like such an incompressible substance as granite, yields to it sufficiently to counteract friction, from its inherent property of elasticity. Hence in Whitehall, where the blocks have been down about two years, they are not reduced in depth $\frac{1}{8}$ of an inch on an average; and this reduction being more the result of compression than of abrasion, is not likely to continue even at that ratio; for the solidity of the blocks is increased even if the volume be thus slightly reduced. Indeed, paradoxical as it may at first appear, the traffic, which is destructive of wood-paving in one way, contributes to its preservation in another; and may thus be explained:—The wood-paving is put down in a comparatively dry state, and if it were always perfectly dry would be much more susceptible of destruction from accidental or mechanical as well as from natural causes. But soon after it is constructed, it becomes perfectly saturated from rain and other causes, and continual pressure forces more and more water into the blocks, until every pore is completely filled. In this state, the water assists in supporting superincumbent weight, whilst it effectually preserves the wood from decay. For in fact, of the 6 sides of a block of the given form, only the upper one is exposed to the action of the atmosphere; below the surface the whole mass is as thoroughly saturated as if it were immersed in water; and the surface itself becomes so hardened by pressure and the induration of foreign substances, such as grit and sand, as to be impervious to the action of the sun, especially in a northern climate; and that water is a preservative against decay may be proved in a variety of cases. . . . . . . Dry rot, therefore, can never affect good wood-paving, nor can any other secondary process of vegetation, in consequence of the preservative qualities of water, the shutting out, in short, of atmospheric influence; and it is questionable if, under other circumstances, the incessant vibration to which the blocks are subjected, by traffic, would not have a strong preservative tendency."

(110.) On the comparative cost of laying down and maintaining wood-paving with other sorts, a statement which has been made regarding wood-paving and paving with granite, in the parish of St Mary le Strand, in London, for the last 7 years, tells in favour of the wood. It is this :—

Granite-paving and concrete cost . .	L.0	12	6	the square yard.
Repairs for 7 years at 3d. the yard, .	0	1	9	... ...
	0	14	3	... ...
Deduct the value of the stones for streets of lesser traffic, ...	0	3	0	... ...
Actual cost of 7 years, . . .	0	11	3	... ...

Wood-paving cost .	L.0	13	0	the sq. yd.				
Repairs for 7 years at 6d. the yard, . .	0	3	6	... ...				
	L.0	16	6					
Deduct value of the wood for paving streets of lesser traffic, . .	0	3	0					
					0	13	6	... ...
					L.0	2	3	... ...

Giving an apparent advantage of 2s. 3d. the square yard to the granite-paving for the first 7 years; but were the comparison continued for an indefinite period onward, it would be found that the same blocks of wood would last longer than the same blocks of granite, and hence the wood would be cheaper in the long run.

(111.) On comparing its cost with macadamisation, it is found that macadamised roads of much traffic, such as Oxford Street, Piccadilly, cost from 2s. 6d. to 3s. the square yard every year, besides the expense of the original formation; whereas wood-paving can be laid down and kept in repair for a rent-charge of 2s. 3d. the square yard every year, being a saving of from 10 to 30 per cent. per annum.*

(112.) I have dwelt the longer on the subject of wood-paving, because I am persuaded that it would make a much more durable road about steadings, and to the fields of farms, than the materials usually employed for such purposes; and as to their comparative condition under traffic, there would be a decided superiority on the side of the wood-paving, for farm roads are usually in the most wretched state of repair, every hour of time, and every ton of metal expended on them being grudged, as if they were an item with which the farmer had nothing whatever to do. I do not say that wood-paving would be cheap where wood is scarce and carriage long, and of course dear, but in those parts of the

* Stevens's Wood-Paving in London.

country where larch-wood is in abundance, and where it realizes low prices, it might be, I conceive, profitably employed in not only making farm roads, but in paving every apartment in the steading.

(113.) Another method still of causewaying is with *Dutch Clinkers*, a kind of very hard brick made in Holland, of about the breadth and thickness of a man's hand. They are used in paving roads and streets in that country. They are set lengthways on edge and imbedded in sand, and are laid so as to form a slight arch across the road. Most of the great roads in Holland are paved with this brick, and more beautiful and pleasant roads to travel on cannot be found anywhere, except perhaps in the heat of summer, when they become oppressively hot. I had an opportunity of seeing a part of the road near Haarlem laid with these clinkers, and observed, as a part of the process, that, as a certain piece of the causewaying was finished, bundles of green reeds were laid lengthways across the road over the new laid bricks, to temper the pressure of the wheels of carriages upon the bricks on going along the roads, until the bricks should have subsided firmly into the stratum of sand. As these clinkers are small, they can be laid in a variety of forms, some as a beautiful kind of Mosaic work. The import duty on Dutch clinkers was reduced to 3s. per 1000 on 1st January 1834; in 1819 it was 16s. 8d.* The present price of clinkers (1842) in London is 35s. the 1000.

(114.) Fine smooth durable pavement is made of the beautifully stratified beds of the inferior grey sandstone, a rock nearly allied to greywacke. It is a rock of fine texture, hard, and perfectly impervious to water. It occurs in abundance in the south-east part of Forfarshire, and being chiefly shipped at Arbroath in that county, it has received the appellation of "*Arbroath Pavement.*" Hard flags from the counties of Caithness and Orkney also form very durable, though not always smooth, pavement. Some, however, of this, as well as of the Arbroath pavement, requires very little, if any, dressing with tools on the face. The Caithness pavement is cut on the edge with the saw, the Arbroath pavement with common masons' tools. In a paper read to the British Association at their meeting at Glasgow in 1840, Professor Traill described this flag as belonging to the red sandstone series, although its appearance as pavement would lead one to suppose it to belong to an older formation. Pavement is also formed of the stratified portions of the sandstone of the coal-formation. Most of the foot-pavement of the streets of Edinburgh is of this kind. Its face requires to be wrought with tools, and its texture admits water. Arbroath pavement costs from 2d. to 4d. per square foot at the quarry, according to thickness. Both it and Caithness pavement cost 10d., and common stone pavement 6d. per foot in Edinburgh. When jointed and droved, the cost is 9d. per square foot additional.

(115.) In connection with the subject of masonry, I may advert to the *sinking of wells* for a supply of water. 1. In trap and other amorphous rocks, little water may be expected to be found, and the labour of sinking by blasting with gunpowder renders a well sunk in these substances a very expensive undertaking. When there is probability of finding water in stratified rocks under trap, the latter may be penetrated by boring with a jumper, with the view of forming an artesian well; but before such a project is undertaken, it should be ascertained beforehand that stratified rock or diluvium exists below the trap, and

* Macculloch's Commercial Dictionary, Art. *Tariff.*

that the dip of either is towards the site of the well. Of so much importance is one good well on a farm, that a considerable expense should be incurred rather than want, at any season, so essential a beverage as water to man and beast. When insuperable obstacles exist against finding water on the spot, perhaps the better plan will be either to go a distance to a higher elevation, where a common well may succeed in finding water, and then convey it to the steading by a wood or iron or lead pipe; or to descend to a lower site and throw the water up to the steading by means of a force-pump. Either of these plans may be less expensive, or more practicable than the boring through a hard rock to a great depth. The well in Bamborough Castle, in Northumberland, was sunk upwards of 100 feet through trap to the sandstone below; and at Dundee, a bore was made through trap, 300 feet, to the inferior sandstone below, by means of a steam-engine, to obtain water for a spinning-mill. 2. In gravel and sand, a well may be sunk to a considerable depth before finding water. Being desirous of a supply of water to three adjoining fields of dry turnip land, resting on a deep bed of pure gravel, and which had no watering-pool, I fixed on the most likely spot to contain water, near the foot of a rising ground of diluvial clay, in which to dig a well, and it happened to be a spot common to all the fields. After persevering to the depth of 22 feet without success, at the imminent hazard of overwhelming the men with gravel, as a despairing effort, at night-fall, I caused a foot-pick to be thrust down into the bottom of the pit as far as the handle, and on withdrawing the instrument, water was seen to follow it. Next morning 3 feet more were dug, when the water excavating the gravel around the bottom of the pit, rendered further digging a dangerous operation for the men, so the ring of the well was there begun to be built with stones. The water afterwards would rise no higher in the well than the level where it was first found, but the supply nevertheless was sufficient for the use of the three fields. On finding water in this case, in the midst of very hopeless symptoms, I would recommend perseverance to diggers of wells, and success will most probably reward their efforts. 3. In very unctuous clay, such as is found in carse land, water is difficult to be obtained by digging to ordinary depths; but as such a country is usually situate near a large river, or on the side of a broad estuary, by digging to the depth of the bed of the river, some sand will most probably be found through which the water will find its way to the well; and though brackish in the estuary, it may come into the well sweet enough for all domestic purposes. 4. Wells dug in stratified rocks, such as sandstone, may be supplied with water at a moderate depth, perhaps 6 or 8 feet; but amongst regular strata there is as much risk of losing water as there is ease in obtaining it. To avoid disappointment, it will be necessary to puddle the seams of the rock on that side of the well in which it dips downwards. 5. The substance which most certainly supplies water on being dug into is diluvial clay, a substance which forms the subsoil of the greatest extent of arable land in this kingdom. This clay is of itself impervious to water, but it is always intersected with small veins of sand frequently containing mica, and interspersed with numerous small stones, on removing which, water is found to ooze from their sites, and collect in any pit that is formed in the clay to receive it. The depth to be dug to secure a sufficiency of water may not be great, perhaps not less than 8 feet or more than 16 feet; but when the clay is homogeneous and hard, and there is little appearance of water, digging to upwards of 40 feet in depth will be required to find water. I knew a remarkable instance of a well that was dug in such clay in

Ireland, in which 40 feet were penetrated before any water was found; but immediately beyond that depth, so large a body of pure water was found in a small vein of sand, that the diggers escaped with difficulty out of the well, leaving their tools behind. A force-pump was obtained to clear the well of water, in order to allow the ring to be built; but it was unable to reduce the bulk of water, so that the ring remains unbuilt to this day, the water always stands within three feet of the top of the well, and the clay is not much affected by it. 6. Suppose, then, that the well is to be dug in clay containing small stones and veins of sand. Let a circle of 8 feet in diameter be described on the surface of the ground, from whose area let the ground-soil be removed to be used elsewhere. After throwing out a depth of 8 or 9 feet with the spade, let a winch and rope and bucket be set up to draw the stuff out of the well. While the digging is proceeding, let a sufficient quantity of flat stones be laid down near the winch, by which to let them down to build the ring. A depth of 16 feet will most probably suffice, but if no water is found, let the digging proceed to the requisite depth. A ring of 3 feet in diameter will be a large enough bore for the well, the rest of the space to be filled up with dry rubble masonry, and drawn in at the top to 2 feet in diameter. Whenever the building is finished, the water should be removed from the well with buckets, if the quantity is small, and with a pump, if it is large, to allow the bottom to be cleared of mud and stones. A thick flat stone, reaching from the side of the ring to beyond the centre, should be firmly placed on the ground at the bottom of the well, for the wooden pump to stand upon, or for the lead pipe to rest on. If a wooden pump is used, a large flat stone, having a hole in it to embrace the pump, should be laid on a level with the ground upon the ring of the well; but if a lead pipe is preferred, the flat stone should be entire and cover the ring, and the *clayey* earth thrown over it. The cost of digging a well in clay, 8 feet in diameter and 16 feet deep, and building a ring 3 feet in diameter with dry rubble masonry, is only L.5, exclusive of carriage and the cost of the pumps. A wooden-mounted larch pump of from 15 feet to 20 feet in length costs from L.3 to L.3, 10s, and a lead one L.2, 10s., with 1s. 2d. per lineal foot for pipe of the depth of the well. The wooden pump will last perhaps twenty years, and the lead one a lifetime, with ordinary care, and the lead at all times is worth something.

(116.) The making of the well naturally suggests the subject of *water*. The different kinds of water receive names from the sources from which they are derived. Thus there is *sea-water*, the water of the ocean; *rain-water*, the water which falls from the atmosphere; *river-water*, the water which flows in the channels of rivers; *spring-water*, the water as it naturally issues from the ground; *well-water*, the water collected in wells; *pond-water*, the water collected in an artificial hollow formed on the surface of the ground; and *marsh-water*, the stagnant water collected in swamps and bogs. All these sorts of water possess different properties, acquired from the circumstances from which each is derived.

(117.) *Pure-water* is not found in nature, for all the sorts of water accumulated on or near the surface of the earth, though differing in purity in regard to each other, are none of them pure in the chemical sense of the term; that is, free of the admixture of other matter, such as gases, salts, earths. Pure water is colourless, and insipid to the taste. Its specific gravity is 1000 ounces per cubic foot. It is made the standard of gravity, 1 being its equivalent mark. It is an inelastic fluid. It consists of hydrogen and oxygen, the combination by weight being 8 of oxygen and 1 of hydrogen,—by volume, 1 of oxygen to 2 of hydrogen,—and by equivalent or atom, 1 of hydrogen with 1 of oxygen; its chemical symbol being $H + O$ or HO. Pure water is obtained by the distillation of rain or river water, and, to retain it so, it must be kept in closed bottles filled to the stopper, as it has a strong affinity for common air, oxygen, and carbonic acid gas.

(118.) Water from the condensed vapour of fresh water, is the purest that can be obtained by natural means. Hence, rain-water collected after rain has fallen for a time, at a height above the ground, in the country, and at a distance from any dwelling of man, or new-fallen melted snow, is the purest water that can be collected in a natural state; but nevertheless it is not pure, inasmuch as it contains oxygen, nitrogen, carbonic acid, and earthy matter, which it has met with in the atmosphere, besides nearly as much common air as it can absorb. Procured from the roofs of buildings, rain-water is always contaminated with many additional impurities, derived from the channels through which it has flowed: It is generally very dark-coloured, and, when allowed to stand, deposites a quantity of earthy ingredients. It is not in a proper state for domestic purposes until it has got quit of as much of these impurities as it can by deposition.

(119) Rain-water for domestic purposes is collected in cisterns. The form of a *rain-water cistern*, represented by fig. 30, I have found an useful one for allowing the undisturbed deposition of impurities, and at the same time the quick flowing off of the purer water, without disturbing the deposition. Let *a b b c* be a cistern of stone or wood, placed at a convenient spot of the steading or farm-house, for the reception of rain-water. I have found that such a cistern, of the capacity of 12 cubic feet, holds a sufficient quantity of rain-water for the domestic purposes of an ordinary family. A cistern of 2 feet square at the base, and 3 feet in height, will just contain that quantity; but, as the size of an ordinary wash-tub is 2 feet in diameter, the space betwixt *d* and *d* must be made 2 feet 6 inches at least, and the height of the cistern *b* could be 2 feet; but if more water is required than 12 cubic feet, then the height should be 3 feet, which gives a capacity to the cistern of 18 cubic feet. Suppose the cistern represented in the figure to contain 18 cubic feet, then the area of *a* will be 2½ feet square, and *b* 3 feet in height, supported on two upright stones *d d* of the breadth of the cistern and 2 feet high. The cistern may either be made of a block of freestone hewn out to the dimensions, or of flags, of which the sides are let into grooves in the bottom and into each other, and imbedded in white-lead, and fastened together with iron clamps, having a stone movable cover *c*. Or it may be formed of a

Fig 30.

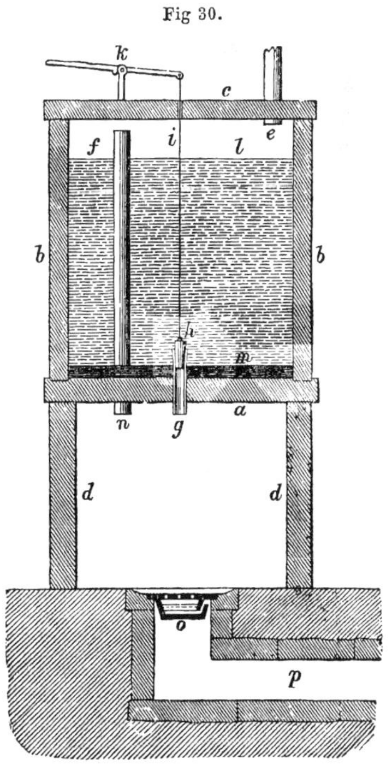

RAIN-WATER CISTERN.

box of wood, securely fastened at the corners to be water-tight, with a cover of wood, and resting on the stone supports *d d*. Stone, being more durable, is, of course, preferable to wood for a cistern that stands out in the open air. A hollow copper cylinder *g* is fastened perpendicularly into the bottom *a*, having its lower end projecting 1 inch below, and its upper 3 inches above, the respective surfaces of the bottom. The upper end of the copper cylinder is formed to receive a ground truncated cone of copper called a plug or stopper, which is moved up and down with the lever *k*, by means of the stout copper rod *i*. The plug must be made watertight with grease, the rod of which passes through a hole in the cover, to be connected with the lever, whose support or fulcrum is fixed on the cover. These parts are all made of copper, to withstand rusting from the water, with the exception of the lever, which may be of iron, painted. The rain-water is supplied to the cistern by the pipe *e*, which descends from the rain-water conductor, and is let through a hole in the cover. The water is represented standing as high as *l*, but in case it should rise to overflow, it can pass off by the lead waste-pipe *f*, which is secured and movable at pleasure in a ground-washer *n*, whose upper end is made flush with the upper surface of the bottom *a*. After the water has entered the cistern, it gets leave to settle its sediment, which it may do to the height of the upper end of *g*. The sediment is represented by *m*, and when it accumulates to *h*, the cover *c* should be taken off, and the waste-pipe *f* removed, and it can then be cleaned completely out by the washer *n*. The waste water runs away through the air-trap *o*, and along the drain *p*. It is more convenient to have two small than one large cistern, as, while the water is rising in the one, that in the other gets leave to settle. The cost of such a cistern, with droved stones, and to contain 18 cubic feet, with the proper mountings, may be about L.5. I think it right to say, in commendation of this form of water-cistern, that in no case have I known the water about the plug to be frozen, in consequence, perhaps, of the non-conducting power of the mud in the bottom of the cistern. The rod *i* has sometimes become fast to the ice on the top of the water, but a little boiling water poured down by the side of the rod through a funnel soon freed it from restraint.

(120.) Rain-water, besides containing gases in solution, becomes impregnated with many saline substances in its passage through the ground; and hence the water of springs and rivers always contains many ingredients. The purest spring-water is that which has passed through gravelly deposites, such as of granite, sandstone, quartz, because the component parts of those stony substances being insoluble, the water cannot take up much of them. In the same way the water of old wells is purer than that of new, because the long continued action of the water has removed or gradually dissolved the soluble matters in the same passages through the ground to the well. "The matters generally contained in spring, well, and river water," says Mr Reid, "are carbonate of lime, sulphate of lime, muriate of lime, sulphates of potash and soda, muriate of soda, and sometimes a little magnesia. 'In rain-water,' says Dr Murray, 'the muriates I have found generally to form the chief impregnation, while in spring-water the sulphates and carbonates are predominant, and in the former the alkalies,' potash and soda, 'are in larger quantity, while the earths, particularly lime, are more abundant in the latter.'"* It is in its combination with one or more of these salts that water becomes *hard*, chiefly with the sulphate of lime or gypsum,

* Reid's Chemistry of Nature, p. 195.

and the carbonate of lime or limestone. Water is said to be hard when it will not dissolve but decompose soap. *Soft* water, on the other hand, does not decompose, but combines easily with soap and dissolves it. Hard water is not so fit as soft for many culinary purposes, such as making tea and boiling vegetables. It is therefore of importance for you tó know when water is in a hard or soft state. By placing a few thin slices of white soap in a clean tumbler of the water to be examined, its *hardness* will be indicated by *white flakes* or *curdy particles around the soap*, the effect of decomposition, the acids of the salts in the water combining with the alkali of the soap and leaving the fatty matter. A very small quantity of either of the salts enumerated above will render water hard. Water can dissolve $\frac{1}{500}$ part of its weight of gypsum; but according to Dr Dalton $\frac{1}{1000}$ part is sufficient to render it hard; and Mr Cavendish says, that 1200 grains of water containing carbonic acid will hold in solution 1 grain of limestone. Limestone is insoluble in pure water; but water containing carbonic acid in solution can dissolve it.

(121.) "To discover whether the hardness be owing to the presence of limestone or gypsum, the following chemical tests," says Mr Reid, "may be applied. A solution of the nitrate of barytes will produce a white precipitate with water containing either gypsum or limestone; if limestone have been present in the water the precipitate will be dissolved, and the liquid rendered clear on adding a few drops of pure nitric acid; if the presence of gypsum caused the precipitate, this will not be dissolved by the nitric acid. A solution of the sugar of lead may be used in the same way, but the nitrate of barytes is preferred."*

(122.) As to a practical remedy for hard water, boiling will remove the lime. The carbonic acid in excess in the water is converted into the gaseous form, and the carbonate of lime then becoming insoluble, falls to the bottom of the vessel. Hence the incrustation of tea-kettles. If the hardness is caused by gypsum, a little pearl ash or soda (carbonate of potash or carbonate of soda) will remove it, and the lime of the water will also be precipitated with the carbonic acid of the pearl ash or soda.

(123.) River-water is always softer than spring or well-water, because it deposites its earthy ingredients when flowing in contact with common air, which it absorbs in considerable quantity. By analysis the water of the river Clyde yielded $\frac{1}{35}$ of its bulk of gases, of which $\frac{19}{20}$ were common air. "All that is necessary," remarks Mr Reid, "in order to render river-water fit for use is to filter it: This is rather a mechanical than a chemical operation, and is done by causing the water to pour through several layers of sand, which intercepts the muddy particles as the liquid passes through. Filtering stones, made of some porous material, such as sandstone, and hollowed out so as to be capable of containing a considerable quantity of water, have sometimes been employed to purify water. Compressed sponges have also been employed for this purpose. Sand and charcoal form the chief elements in the construction of the filters now so much employed for purifying water, the powdered charcoal acting not only mechanically in detaining any muddy particles, but having a chemical effect in sweetening the water (rendering it fresh) if it be at all tainted, or even in retarding putrefaction, if it have any tendency that way."†

(124.) Water, as a beverage, would be insipid or even nauseous without the gases and saline matters usually found in it. They give a natural seasoning and

* Reid's Chemistry of Nature, p. 199. † Ibid. p. 201.

a sparkling appearance to it, thereby rendering it agreeable to the taste. Every one knows the mawkish taste of boiled water when drank alone.

(125.) As I am on the subject of water, a few words should here be said on the making of *horse-ponds*. The position of the horse-pond will be seen in figs. 1 and 2, in Plates I. and II. When a small stream passes the steading, it is easy to make a pond serve the purpose of horses drinking and washing in it, and the water in such a pond will always be pure and clean. But it may happen, for the sake of convenience, when there is no stream, that a pond should be dug in clay, in which case the water in it will always be dirty and offensive, unless means are used to bring water by a pipe from a distance. If the subsoil is gravelly, the water will with difficulty be retained on it, on which account the bottom should be puddled with clay. Puddling is a very simple process, and may be performed in this manner. Let a quantity of tenacious clay be beaten smooth with a wooden rammer, mixing with it about one-fourth part of its bulk of slaked lime, which has the effect of deterring worms making holes in it. After the mass has lain for some time souring, let large balls of it be formed and thrown forcibly on the bottom of the pond, made dry for the purpose, and beaten down with the rammer or tramped with men's feet, until a coating 6 or 7 inches in thickness is formed, or more, if there is plenty of clay. Then let a quantity of clean gravel be beaten with the rammer into the upper surface of the clay before it has had time to harden. Should the pond be large, and the weather at the time of making it so dry as to harden the clay before its entire bottom can be covered with it, let the puddling and gravelling proceed together by degrees. Above the coating of gravel, let a substantial causeway of stones and sand be formed to resist the action of the horses' feet, and which, if properly protected at the ends, and finished on the open side of the pond, will withstand that action for a long time. I have seen a sort of pond recommended to be made, into which the horses enter at one end, and pass through it by the other. This is a convenient shape of pond, in as far as it admits of the uninterrupted passage of the horses *through* the pond, but it is liable to serious objections. Being contracted laterally, the pair of horses which first descend to drink will occupy the greatest proportion of its whole breadth, and, while in that position, the succeeding pair must drink the muddy water at their heels; and, as the contracted form precludes easy turning in the deepest part of the water, none of the rest of the horses can be permitted to block up the opposite or open end of the pond. A much better form of pond, I conceive, is with an open side, having the opposite side fenced, and the water supplied clean at the upper end, and made to flow immediately away by the lower. At such a pond a number of horses can stand in a row to drink at the same time, and easily pass each other in the act of washing the legs after drinking. As to the depth, no horse-pond should ever exceed the height of the horses' knees. The water should on no account reach their bellies; for although I am quite aware of ploughmen being desirous to wade their horses deep, and of even wishing to see their sides laved with water, to save themselves some trouble in cleaning, that is no reason why you should run the risk of endangering the health of your horses by making the pond deeper than the knee.

(126.) With regard to the *kind of stone* which should be employed in the building of a steading, it must be determined by the mineral product of the locality in which it is proposed to erect it. In all localities where stone is accessible, it should be preferred to every other material; but where its carriage is distant, and of course expensive, other materials, such as brick or clay, must be taken. In large flat tracts of country, stone is generally at too great a distance; but in those situations, clay being abundant, brick may be easily made, and it makes an excellent building material for walls, and far superior to the old-fashioned clay walls which were in vogue before brick became so universally used for building. Of stone, any kind may be used that is nearest at hand, though some rocks are much better adapted for building purposes than others. 1. Of the primitive rocks, grey granite forms a beautiful and durable stone, as is exemplified in the buildings in Aberdeenshire, Cornwall, and Newry in Ireland. Gneiss, mica-slate, and clayslate, do not answer the purpose well. They give a rough edgy fracture, frequently rise too thin in the bed, especially in the case of clayslate; are not unfrequently curved in the bed, and at the same time difficult to be dressed with the hammer. 2. Of the transition series, greywacke makes a beautiful building stone, as may be seen in the houses at Melrose. The old red sandstone, though a good building-stone, has a disagreeably sombre aspect, as seen at Arbroath; but the inferior grey sandstone which prevails in the neighbourhood of Dundee, is a beautiful and durable building-stone. 3. All the sandstones of the coal formation form excellent materials for building, as is exemplified in Edinburgh, and many other places. 4. The limestones, from marble to the mountain carboniferous limestone, make fine building-stone, as at Plymouth; but in case of fire they are apt to be calcined by heat, as exemplified in the cathedral at Armagh, before it was repaired. And 5. Even the trap-rocks are employed in building houses where sandstones are scarce, though the two classes of rock are frequently located together. Whinstone is objectionable, inasmuch as it throws out dampness in wet weather, and the walls require to be lathed and plastered on the inside, to render the house even comfortable. Frequently where whinstone is near at hand, and sandstone can be obtained at a little distance, the latter is employed as corners, ribets, and lintels, though the contrast of colour betwixt them is too violent to be pleasant to the eye. If sandstone, therefore, can be procured at a reasonable cost of carriage, you should give it the preference to whinstone, for the sake of comfort to your live-stock in their habitations in wet weather. You may, indeed, choose to incur the expense of lathing and plastering all the insides of the walls of the steading; but a lathed wall in any part of a steading would be apt to be broken by every thing that came against it, and is, on that account, an unsuitable finishing for a steading. 6. The worst sort of building-stone are landfast boulders of the primitive and trap rocks, which, although reduceable by gunpowder, and manageable by cleavage into convenient shaped stones, incur great labour in their preparation for building; and even after the stones are prepared in the best manner they are capable, their beds are frequently very rough, and jointings coarse, and the variety of texture and colour exhibited by them, render them at the best unsightly objects in a building. They are equally unsuitable for dry-stone dykes as for buildings, for in the case of dykes, they must be used very nearly in their natural state, as the usual charge for such work will not bear labour being bestowed on the preparation of the material. Still, after all, if no better material for building houses is near at hand than those boulders, they must be taken as the only natural product the country affords. There is a class of boulders, composed chiefly of micaceous sandstone, found in banks of gravel, which answer for dry-stone dykes admirably, splitting with ease with a hand-pick into thin layers, and exhibiting a rough surface on the bed, very favourable to their adherence together in the wall. This species of building material is abundant in Forfarshire, where specimens of dry-stone building may be seen of a superior order. In these remarks of the general choice of building-stones by Mr G. Smith, architect in Edinburgh, there is much truth:—"The engineer and architect," says he, "go differently to work in choosing their stones. The former, in making his experiments for his piers and bridges, selects the strongest and hardest as most suited to resist great pressure. The latter, for his architectural decorations, chooses not only the most beautiful as to texture and uniformity of colour, but those which may be easily cut into the most delicate mouldings, and which, moreover, will stand the winter's frost and the summer's heat. It may be remarked, that the hardest stones are not always those which hold out the best against the effects of weather." *

(127.) I may here observe, in concluding my observations on the specifications of masonry, that any lime that is used on a farm, for the purpose of steeps for grain or for mortar, gets leave to lie about in the most careless manner, either under a shed, or at some place contiguous to water, where it had been made up into mortar. In either case there is waste of a useful article; and in many parts of the country, where carriage is far distant, it is a high-priced article. The lime that is to be used in a dry state should be kept under cover; and all that is required in a season could be held in a cask or small hogshead to stand in a corner of the cart-shed or potato store, but not in the straw-barn, where a little damp may cause it to ignite the straw. With regar d to mortar, no more should be made at a time than is used, or it should be carefully heaped together in a convenient place, and covered with turf.

(128.) In Sweden mortar is made and kept in a convenient form of cart, represented by fig. 31, a practice which might with propriety be followed in this

Fig. 31.

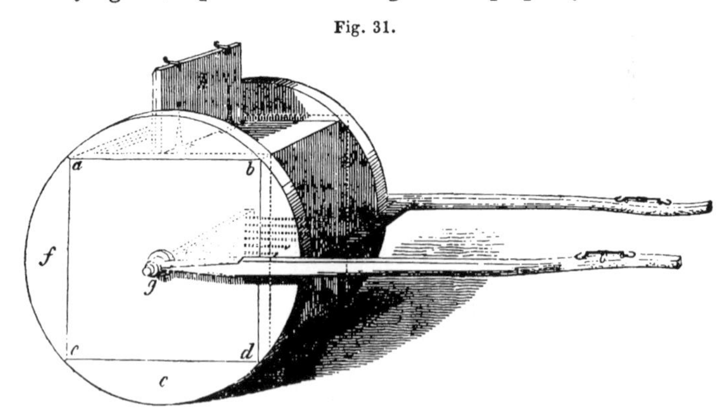

SWEDISH MORTAR CART.

country. The cart consists of a cube *a b c d* of a side of 3 feet made of 2-inch thick battens. The wheels are formed of the two sides of the cube, on which are fixed circular segments such as *e* and *f*, made of strong battens 3 inches thick, secured by a screw at each end into the side of the cube, and the circles are shod with iron as common wheels. The axle *g*, inside and outside, is closely

* Prize Essays of the Highland and Agricultural Society, vol. x. p. 85.

passed through the cube, so as not to allow any of the mortar to come out. The axle moves in a small iron nave attached to the shafts of the cart. On it are screwed iron bars *i*, which pass through one of the sides of the cube, and fastened to it by screws *k*. The use of these bars is to break the mortar when too tough; and if one set of bars is found insufficient for that purpose, similar ones should be put through the opposite side of the cube. A lid *h* is well secured to the cube by hinges, and kept fast by means of a hasp. When the shafts are drawn, the whole cart revolves with the wheels.

(129.) The lime is put into the cart by the lid, and sprinkled over with a little water, about half a gallon of which to the bushel of lime will be enough the first time. The cart is then driven round a while; and when the driver, who must often look to the mortar, finds that all the water is imbibed, a little more must be poured in, and the cart again driven round. Water is poured in in small quantities until the lime forms coagulated masses or balls, and then it is worked until no dry lime is seen in the mass. The success of making good mortar depends on the skill of the driver, who will soon learn to do it well after a cart-ful or two of driving. Three bushels of lime and sand can be prepared in this way in a short time, but the sand should not be put in till after the lime has been sufficiently wrought with water.*

(130.) Of the specification of *carpenter-work*, the first timber that is used in building consists of *safe-lintels*, which should be 4 inches thick, of such a breadth as to cover the space they are placed over, and they should have a solid bearing at both ends of 12 inches.

(131.) The *scantlings* or *couples* for the roofs vary in size with the breadth of the building. When the building is 18 feet wide, the scantlings should be 8 inches wide at bottom, 7 inches at top, and 2½ inches thick. Those for 15 feet wide buildings should be 7½ inches wide at bottom, and 6½ inches at top. All scantlings should be placed 18 inches apart from centre to centre, upon *wall-plates* 8 inches wide by 1½ inch thick, firmly secured to *bond-timber* built into the tops of the walls. These dimensions of scantlings are suitable for a roof of blue slates. For a tile-roof the scantlings are placed 2 feet apart from centre to centre. For roofing with grey-slates, which are very heavy, the scantlings should be 3 inches thick. With tiles and grey-slates the roofs require a higher pitch than with blue slates, and this is given by making the scantlings 1 foot longer.

(132.) The *balks* of an 18 feet wide building should be 7½ inches broad by 2½ inches thick, and for the 15 feet one, 7 inches by 2½ inches. In both cases the balks should be of the length of one of the scantlings, which will bring its position so low down on the scantlings as to be only a little more than 3 feet above the wall-heads. It is generally supposed that one balk is sufficient for the support of the scantlings; but it will be seen in fig. 6, p. 119, that I have represented a vertical section of the principal range of the steading with two balks, because I would always prefer two balks to one, and the only objection to the two is the expense. When two balks are employed, the lower one will be about 2 feet, and the upper one about 5 feet, above the wall-heads.

(133.) If a slated roof is adopted, there should be a *ridge-tree* 10 inches broad by 2 inches thick, and the tops of the scantlings should be bound with *collar-pieces*, 5 inches broad, and 2 inches thick, half checked into the scantlings.

* Quarterly Journal of Agriculture, vol. xi. p. 245.

If a tile-roof is preferred, it is sufficient that the tops of the scantlings be checked in with collar-pieces, as just described.

(134.) The whole roof should be covered with *sarking*, ⅝ inch thick, and clean jointed. A tile roof requires *tile-lath*, 1¼ inch square, and 11 inches apart, excepting at the eaves, which should have a boarding from 12 inches to 15 inches broad, and ⅝ inch thick for slates. Tile-lath is also employed with grey-slates.

(135.) The *peands* and *flankers* should be 9 inches broad at bottom, and 7 inches at top, and 3 inches thick, properly backed to receive the sarking or tile-lath of the respective sorts of roofs.

(136.) The *joists* of the flooring in the part of the buildings that is 18 feet wide, should be 10 inches deep by 2½ inches in thickness, placed 18 inches asunder from centre to centre, and having a wall-hold or rest of 12 inches at each end. When the bearings of joists exceed 8 feet, it is a more secure and economical plan to have beams, instead of battens, laid across the building, 13 inches deep, and 6½ inches in width, with a wall-hold of 12 inches at each end. Upon these should rest joists 7 inches deep, and 2½ inches in breadth, and not more than 16 inches apart from centre to centre, dove-tailed into the beams with a hold of 9 inches at each end. These joints are best cut out of Memel log of first or second quality, the difference of price between the two qualities being 2d. the cubic foot.

(137.) The *floors* of the upper and corn-barn and granaries should be of 1¼ inch thick, of red or white wood battens, grooved and tongued, and well seasoned when wrought and laid. The under side of the floor, and the joists which support the floor of the upper-barn, forming the roof of the corn-barn, should be clean dressed, to prevent the adherence of dust.

(138.) In some parts of the country, and especially in East-Lothian, the floor of the corn-barn is made of composition; but in order to leave a part of the floor clean upon which to winnow the grain, a space, 12 feet square, is usually left in the middle of the floor. This space is laid with sleeper-joisting, 7 inches deep by 2½ inches thick, and 18 inches apart from centre to centre, supporting a flooring of deal 2 inches thick, grooved and tongued. As a precaution against vermin, as well as the enjoyment of cleanliness while winnowing and otherwise handling the grain, I would always recommend an entire wooden floor for the corn-barn, to be laid down in the manner described in (16), and represented in fig. 6, p. 119.

(139.) The *windows* of the stables should be of the form of fig. 14, p. 139. Those of the other apartments of the steading, with the exception of the granaries, should be of the form of fig. 15, p. 140; and those of the granary should be of the form of fig. 17, p. 142. The *astragals*, if not made of wood, may be of cast-iron or zinc. Cast-iron astragals cost 1s., and zinc 9½d. the square foot.

(140.) The *exterior doors*, 7½ feet high, should be of 1¼ inch deal, grooved, and tongued, and beaded, having three back-bars, 7 inches broad by 1¼ inch thick; those of the corn-barn, cow-byre, and boiling-house being in two horizontal leaves, that of the upper-barn in two vertical leaves, and those of the rest of the apartments being entire.

(141.) If desired, small windows of one or two rows of panes may be placed above all the outside doors; in which case, the voids of these doors should be made proportionally high, say 8 feet.

(142.) The *inside doors* should be 7 feet high, of ¾ inch deal, with three back-bars 6 inches broad and 1 inch thick, grooved, and ploughed, and beaded. They should have checks 6 inches broad by 2½ inches thick, and keps and facings 4½ inches broad by ¾ inch thick.

(143.) The *travis boarding* of the work-horse-stable should be 1½ inch thick, 9½ feet long, 7 feet 6 inches high at the fore and 4 feet 6 inches high at the heel posts, dowelled in the joints with oak pins, and of an ogee form on the top, let into a 2-inch deep groove in the heel-post, and coped with beading. The *heel-posts* should be 6 inches square, beaded, the *fore-posts*, on both sides, 5 inches by 2½ inches, and both fixed at the top to *runtrees*, 6 inches deep by 2 inches broad. The side-walls of the end-stalls should be finished in the same manner, and firmly secured to wall-straps and bond-timbers.

(144.) The travis-boarding of the riding-horse-stable should be of the same strength as just described; but the heel-posts should be turned 5 feet high above the ground, with moulded caps and balls, and let from 18 inches to 2 feet into the ground, through a stone frame 18 inches square and 12 inches thick, firmly built with stone and mortar. The fore-posts should be 3 inches in diameter on both sides to the height of the travis boarding. Heel-posts are also made of cast-iron, which cost 22s. each.

(145.) The *hay-racks* of the work-horse-stable should have a hardwood rail, 3 inches deep by 2½ inches wide, and the spars of fir, 2 inches broad by 1½ inch thick, placed 2½ inches apart. These spars should be put on both front and bottom.

(146.) The hay-racks of the riding-horse-stable should be of hardwood, and placed high up, with rails, 3 inches deep by 2½ inches wide, and turned rollers, 2 inches of diameter, set 2½ inches apart. Cast-iron racks are frequently used in the corner of the stall, and they cost 10s. each.

(147.) The *mangers* of the riding-horse-stable should be of rounded battens in front, of full breadth of the stalls, placed at a convenient height above the floor, and bottomed and lined with 1¼-inch deal.

(148.) In the work-horse-stable, *corn-boxes* are placed in the near angle of the hay-racks.

(149.) The *stalls* of the cow or feeding byres should be made of 1¼ inch deal, beaded, grooved, and tongued. They should be 6 feet long, and 4 feet high, with 1 inch beaded coping, let into stakes or heel-posts, 5 inches to 6 inches diameter, and held to the wall at the head with a 2-inch fillet, and iron hold-fasts on each side. The heel-posts should either be taken to the height of the byre-wall, and secured to runtrees, 6 inches deep by 2 inches broad, or fastened into the ground with masonry like those of the riding-horse-stable.

(150.) The doors of the *feeding-holes* of the byres should be of ¾-inch deal, of two thicknesses, crossed.

(151.) The *stairs* from the corn-barn to the granaries, if of wood, should have 11 inches of tread and 7 inches of height of steps. A stair or trap of similar dimensions may lead to the wool-room.

(152.) The floors of the granaries, upper and corn barns, and wool-room, should have an angular *skirting*, 3 inches by 3 inches, around them.

(153.) Should the upper-barn, or granaries, or wool-room, be ascended by outside stone stairs, they should be furnished with plain ¾-inch iron *railing*, carried around the outer edge of the steps and platform, with a hardwood hand-rail, or be inclosed with ¾-inch deal lining, the whole height above the steps, and properly framed.

(154.) The interior of the *hen-house* should be fitted up with rough ¾-inch deal shelves and divisions, and roosting-trees 3 inches deep by 2 inches broad.

(155.) The doors of the hen-house should be of 1¼-inch deal, beaded, grooved, and tongued.

(156.) *Wooden ventilators* should be placed upon the roof above every alternate pair of horses and cattle, of the form and dimensions of fig. 8, p. 128; or they may consist of ¾-inch deal, 6 inches square, in an opening above every alternate stall, and furnished, on the upper part above the roof, with bent tubes of lead, 6 lb. to the square foot, or with zinc ones of the same dimensions. The zinc ventilators vary in price, according to size, from 4s. to 7s. each.

(157.) The ceilings of the stables, boiling-house, granaries, where tile are used for roofing, wool-room, and hen-house, should be *lathed* with Baltic split-lath $\frac{3}{16}$ of an inch in thickness. "Laths are sold by the bundle, which is generally called a hundred; but 7 score, or 140, are computed in the 100 for 3-feet laths; 6 score, or 120, in such as are 4 feet; and for those which are denominated 5 feet, the common 100, or 5 score."* Lath is also made of home wood, usually Scots fir, sawn up into ⅝-inch plank, and split irregularly with the axe, and, when nailed on, the splits are kept open by means of a wedge. The duty on foreign lath-wood is from L.4, 5s. to L.3, 12s., and on that from the colonies from 15s. to 25s., on the bulk of 6 feet wide by 6 feet high, according to the length of the timber.

(158.) The riding-horse-stable should have *saddle-brackets* of ¾-inch deal, firmly supported, and two pins let into rails 6 inches wide, and 1½ inch thick, for each horse. The work-horse-stable should have two similar rails, with large and small pins for each horse.

(159.) Every court and hammel should be provided with a *gate*, the forms and dimensions of which I will afterwards give, when I come to speak of the subject of gates in general, in spring.

(160.) The entrance to the piggeries should be furnished with doors of 1-inch deal, of two thicknesses, crossed, as represented in fig. 23, p. 152.

(161) All the varieties of *fir timber* imported into the country are employed in the building of steadings, and those kinds are most used in localities which are obtained from the nearest sea-ports. For example, along the east coast of this country Memel logs and Baltic battens are used for all rough purposes, while on the west coast no timber is to be seen in the construction of steadings but what is brought from America. 1. Norway and St Petersburgh battens being cut to proper lengths and breadths, form cheap and very durable timber for all farm purposes. The price is, for red from 3d. to 3½d., for white from 2⅝d. to 3d. the lineal foot. The Norway battens are a shade cheaper. The red or white-wood battens make excellent floors, and plain deal doors for inside use. Such flooring is beautifully dressed by planing machinery at Mr Burstall's mills at Leith. 2. Memel logs are admirably fitted for joisting, windows, outside doors, and all outside work, it being composed of strong and durable fibre, surrounded with resinous matter. It sells for from 2s. 4d. to 2s. 6d. the cubic foot. The greatest objection to its use for small purposes is its knottiness, on which account the Norway battens make handier small scantlings and cleaner door-work. 3. The American red-pine is excellent timber, being clean, reedy, and resinous. It is seldom or never of so large dimensions as Memel log. It fetches from 2s. to

* Macculloch's Dictionary of Commerce, art. *Lath.*

2s. 2d. the cubic foot. It is fitted for beams, joists, scantlings, windows, and outside doors. 4. American yellow-pine is well suited to all inside work, and especially that which requires the highest finish, such as bound-doors, window-fittings, and mantel-pieces. There is no wood that receives paint so well. The logs are generally of immense sizes, affording great economy of timber in cutting them up. Its price is, for small sizes 1s. 8d., and for large 2s. 3d., the cubic foot. 5. Swedish 11-inch plank is good and useful timber, but its scantlings are not very suitable for farm-buildings. I have seen stout joists for granaries made of it, with a $\frac{5}{8}$ draught taken off the side for sarking. It forms excellent planking for wheeling upon, and for gangways. It sells, the white wood for from 5d. to 6d., and the red from 6d. to 7d., the lineal foot.

(162.) In the interior of the country, at a distance from sea-ports, *home* timber is much used in farm buildings. Larch forms good scantlings and joists, and is a durable timber for rough work, and so does well grown Scots fir of good age, and cut down in the proper season; but its durability is not equal to larch, or generally any good foreign timber for rough purposes.*

(163.) All the timber I have referred to is derived from the trees belonging to the natural order of *Coniferæ*, or cone-bearing trees. 1. The Scots fir, *Pinus sylvestris*, is a well known tree in the forests of this country, and few new plantations are made without its aid, as a nurse for hardwood trees. In favourable situations it grows to a large size, as is evidenced in the Memel log, which is just the produce of the Scots fir from the forests of Lithuania. I have seen Scots fir cut down at Ardovie, in Forfarshire, of as good quality and useful sizes as the best Memel. 2. The Swedish plank is of the spruce, *Abies excelsa*, or *communis*, a tree which, as it is treated in this country, comes to little value, being rough and full of knots. Inspection of a cargo from Sweden, which arrived at Hull in 1808, convinced Mr Pontey that the white deal, which fetched at that time from L.14 to L.15, 10s. the load of 50 cubic feet, was of common spruce, the planks having been recently sawn, and a small branch left attached to one of them.† 3. Whether the Norway pine is the same species as the pine found in some of the forests of the north of Scotland, I do not know. I observe that some writers speak of the Norway batten as of the Norway spruce, called by them *Pinus Abies*. It may be that the white-wood battens are derived from that tree; but the red-wood kind has, very probably, the same origin as the red-wood of the north of Scotland, which is from a variety of the *Pinus sylvestris*, or *horizontalis* of Don.‡ 5. The red pine of Canada is the *Pinus resinosa*. 6. And the yellow pine is the *Pinus variabilis* or *Pinus mitis* of Michaux, which towers in lofty height far above its compeers. It grows to the gigantic height of 150 feet, and must require great labour to square it to the sizes found in the British market, large as these sizes unquestionably are. 7. The larch, *Larix europæa*, is a native of the ravines of the Alps of the Tyrol and Switzerland, where it shoots up, as straight as a rush, to a great height.

* In vol. ix. p. 165 of the Prize Essays of the Highland and Agricultural Society, you will find a long account of the Larch Plantations of Atholl, drawn up by me from the papers of the late Duke of Atholl; and in vol. xii. p. 122, of the same work, is an account of the native pine forests of the north of Scotland, by Mr John Grigor, Forres.

† Pontey's Profitable Planter, p. 41, 4th edition, 1814; and at p. 56 he relates an anecdote of a person who, though long accustomed to attend on sawyers, was deceived by some Scots fir, which he considered excellent foreign plank.

‡ See Quarterly Journal of Agriculture, vol. xi. p. 530.

(164.) In regard to the composition of wood, and its chemical properties, "It is considered by chemists that dry timber consists, on an average, of 96 parts of fibrous and 4 of soluble matter in 100; but that their proportions vary somewhat with the seasons, the soils, and the plant. All kinds of wood sink in water when placed in a basin of it under the exhausted receiver of an air-pump, shewing their specific gravity to be greater than 1.000," and varying from 1.46 (*pine*) to 1.53 (*oak*). . . . "Wood becomes snow-white when exposed to the action of chlorine; digested with sulphuric acid it is transformed first into gum, and, by ebullition with water, afterwards into grape sugar. . . . . . Authenreith stated, some years ago, that he found that fine sawdust, mixed with a sufficient quantity of wheat flour, made a cohesive dough with water, which formed an excellent food for pigs; apparently shewing, that the digestive organs of this animal could operate the same sort of change upon wood as sulphuric acid does. . . . . The composition of wood has been examined by Messrs Gay-Lussac and Thenard, and Dr Prout. According to Dr Prout, the oxygen and hydrogen are in the exact proportions to form pure water; according to the others, the hydrogen is in excess"*

(165.) "When minutely divided fragments of a trunk or branch of a tree," as M. Raspail observes, "have been treated by cold or boiling-water, alcohol, ether, diluted acids and alkalies, there remains a spongy substance, of a snow-white colour when pure, which none of these reagents have acted on, while they have removed the soluble substances that were associated with it. It is this that has been called *woody-matter*, a substance which possesses all the physical and chemical properties of cotton, of the fibre of flax, or of hemp."

(166.) "On observing this vegetable *caput mortuum* with the microscope, it is perceived to be altogether composed of the cells or vessels which formed the basis or skeleton of the living organs of the vegetable. They are either cells which, by pressing against each other, give rise to a net-work with pentagonal or hexagonal meshes; or cells with square surfaces; or else tubes of greater or less length, more or less flattened or contracted by drying; sometimes free and isolated, at other times agglomerated and connected to each other by a tissue of elongated, flattened, and equilateral cells; or lastly, tubes of indefinite length, each containing within it another tube formed of a single filament spirally rolled up against its sides, and capable of being unrolled under the eye of the observer, simply by tearing the tube which serves to support it. We find the first in all young organs, in annual and tender stems, in the pith of those vegetables that have a pith, and always in that of the monocotyledons. It is in similar cells that the fecula is contained in the potato. The second is met with in all the trunks and woody branches of trees. The tubes and the spirals (*tracheæ*) are found in all the phanerogamous plants. These are the organs which constitute the fibre of hemp, of flax, &c."

(167.) "Experiment, in accordance with the testimony of history, proves that, if excluded from the contact of moist air, woody matter, like most of the other organized substances, may be preserved for an indefinite period." The plants found in coal-mines, the wood, linen cloths, bandages, and herbs and seeds found in the coffins of Egyptian mummies, have all their characters undecayed, and yet these tombs are in many cases nearly 3000 years old. "But, if the woody matter be not protected against the action of air and moisture, the case is very

* Ure's Dictionary of the Arts, art. *Wood*.

different. By degrees its hydrogen and oxygen are disengaged, and the carbon predominates more and more. Thus the particles of the texture are disintegrated gradually, their white colour fades, and passes through all the shades till it becomes jet-black; and if this altered woody matter be exposed to heat, it is carbonized without flame, because it does not contain a sufficient quantity of hydrogen. Observe, also, that the cells of woody matter contain different sorts of *substances tending to organize*, and that these are mixed and modified in many different ways." . . . "Woody matter, such as I have defined it, being formed of 1 atom of carbon and 1 atom of water, as soon as it is submitted to the action of a somewhat elevated temperature, *without the contact of air*, experiences an internal reaction, which tends to separate the atom of water from the atom of carbon. The water is vaporized, and the carbon remains in the form of a black and granular residue."*

(168.) Now, if any means could be devised by which the substances in the cells of woody matter could be deprived of their tendency to organize, when in contact with common air, wood might be rendered as permanently durable, and even more so, than the grains of wheat which have been found undecayed in Egyptian mummies. This discovery seems to have been made by Mr Kyan. In contemplating the probability of the use of home timber being much extended in the construction of steadings, when the young woods at present growing shall have attained their full growth, it may be proper that the growers of wood, and the farmers on the estates on which wood is grown, be made aware of this mode of preventing timber being affected by the dry-rot. What the true cause of dry-rot is, has never yet been determined, but it frequently shews itself by a species of mildew, which covers the timber, and the action of which apparently causes the wood to decay, and crumble down into powder. The mildew, however, is neither the dry-rot, nor its cause, but its effect. It is distinctly seen by the microscope to be a fungus; and as the fungus itself is so minute as to require the aid of the microscope to be distinctly seen, its seeds may be supposed to be so very minute as to be taken up by the spongeoles of trees. But whatever may be the *cause* of dry-rot in timber, there is not a doubt now of the fact, after years of successful experience, that the process discovered by Mr Kyan of simply steeping timber in a solution of corrosive sublimate, bichloride of mercury, preserves timber from dry-rot.

(169.) The principle upon which the chemical action of the corrosive sublimate upon vegetable matter, preserves the timber, is easily explained. All plants are composed of cellular tissues, whether in the bark, alburnum, or wood. The tissue consists, as you have seen, of various shaped cells; and although they may not pass uninterruptedly along the whole length of the plant, as M. de Candolle maintains, yet air, water, or a solution of anything, may be made to pass through the cells in their longitudinal direction. Experiments with the air-pump have proved this beyond dispute. Those cells, and particularly those of the alburnum, contain the sap of the tree, which, in its circulation, reaches the leaves, where its watery particles fly off, and the enlarging matter of the tree, called the albumen, remains. Albumen is the nearest approach in vegetables to animal matter, and is, therefore, when by any natural means deprived of vitality, very liable to decomposition, particularly that which is connected with the alburnum or sap-wood. Now, corrosive sublimate has long been known to

* Raspail's Organic Chemistry, translated by Henderson, pp. 141–164.

preserve animal matter from decay, being used to preserve anatomical preparations; and even the delicate texture of the brain is preserved by it in a firm state. The analogy between animal and vegetable albumen being established, there seems no reason to doubt the possibility of corrosive sublimate preserving both substances from decay; and, accordingly, the experiments of Mr Kyan with it, on albuminous and saccharine solutions, have confirmed the correctness of this conjecture. The prior experiments of Fourcroy, and especially those of Berzelius, in 1813, had established the same conclusions, though neither of these eminent chemists had thought of their practical application to the preservation of timber. Berzelius found that the addition of the *bichloride* (corrosive sublimate) to an albuminous solution produced a *protochloride* of mercury (calomel), which readily combined with albumen, and produced an insoluble precipitate. This precipitate fills up all the cellular interstices of the wood, and becomes as hard as the fibres.*

(170.) Even after timber has been subjected to this process, it is requisite to give the air free access to it by means of ventilation, and for that purpose, where timber is covered up, which it is not likely to be in a steading, small openings, covered and protected by cast-iron gratings in frames, should be made through the outside walls.

(171.) With regard to the expense of this process, which is a material consideration to those who have large quantities of timber to undergo the treatment, it costs for steeping L.1 the load of 50 cubic feet. But persons having tanks for their own use only, and not for the purposes of trade, pay 5s. for each cubic foot of the internal contents of the tank. A tank, fitted up to steep large scantlings and logs, costs about L.50, and the process may cost 3d. or less the cubic foot to those who construct a tank for themselves.

(172.) Other means have been devised for preserving timber from decay, such as pyroligneous acid, derived from the smoke of burning wood; naphtha, obtained by distillation of coal-tar; and in 1839 a patent was taken out by Sir William Burnett, of the medical department of the Navy, for steeping wood in a solution of the chloride of zinc;† but experiment has not yet had time to decide whether any of these methods possesses any superiority over the valuable process practised by Mr Kyan.

(173.) The pine tribe, of which I have been speaking as of so much use in our farm buildings, is also highly useful in the arts. It is from the *Pinus sylvestris* and the *Abies excelsa* that *tar* is obtained in the largest quantities, for the use of all nations; and it is a substance which is of great utility in a farm, though not requisite in large quantity. The tar of the north of Europe is of a much superior description to that of the United States. It is obtained by a process of distillation, which consists of burning, in a smothering manner, roots and billets of fir-timber, in pits formed in rising ground for the purpose, and covered with turf.

(174.) The quantity of tar imported into this country in 1837, was 11,480 lasts, of 12 barrels per last, each barrel containing 31½ gallons. The duty is 15s. per last, 12s. upon tar from the British possessions, and 2s. 6d. per cwt. upon Barbadoes tar. " Tar produced or manufactured in Europe is not to be imported for home consumption, except in British ships, or in ships of the coun-

* See Paper by me on this subject in vol. viii. p. 385 of Quarterly Journal of Agriculture.

† Repertory of Patent Inventions, New Series, vol. xii. p. 346.

try of which it is the produce, or from which it is imported, under penalty of forfeiting the same, and L.100 by the master of the ship." *

(175.) Besides tar, most of the pines afford one or other of the turpentines. Common turpentine is extracted by incision from the *Abies excelsa* and the *Pinus sylvestris*.

(176.) Of the *specifications of plumber-work*, the kind of work done after the carpentry, the *flanks* and *peands* should be covered with sheet-lead, weighing 6 lb. to the square foot, 18 inches broad. The ridges should be covered either with droved angular freestone ridge-stones, or with 6 lb. lead, 18 inches broad, supported on 2½ inches in diameter of ridge-rolls of wood. Platforms and gutters should have 7 lb. lead. In cisterns, it should be 8 lb. in the bottom and 6 lb. in the sides. Rain-water spouts of 4½ inches in breadth, and conductors of 2½ or 3 inches diameter should be of 6 lb. lead.

(177.) The lead of commerce is derived from the ore *galena*, which is a sulphuret, yielding about 87 per cent. of lead and 13 of sulphur. Galena is found in greatest quantity in transition rocks, and of these the blackish transition limestone contains the largest. The ore is more frequent in irregular beds and masses than in veins. The galena lead-mines of Derbyshire, Durham, Cumberland, and Yorkshire, are situate in limestone, while those of the Leadhills, in Scotland, are in greywacke. Great Britain produces the greatest quantity of lead of any country in the world, the annual produce being about 32,000 tons, of which the English mines supply 20,000. The rest of Europe does not supply 50,000 tons. The export of lead has fallen off considerably, and its price has experienced a corresponding depression for some years past, on account of the greatly increased production of the lead mines of Adra in Granada, in Spain.†

(178.) As *zinc* has been substituted in some cases for lead in the covering of buildings, although sufficient experience has not yet been obtained as to their comparative durability, it may be proper to give here the sizes and prices of covering flanks, peands, and ridges with zinc. The flanks are covered with zinc, weighing 16 ounces to the square foot, at a cost of 6½d. the square foot. The peands and ridges are covered with 12-inch sheet zinc, weighing 18 ounces in the square foot, at a cost of 7d. the square foot. The zinc covers for the peands and ridges are so prepared that they clasp by contraction, and thereby hold fast by the wooden ridge-rolls, and this is so easily done, that any mechanic may put them on. Where soldering is required in zinc-work, such as the laying on of platforms on roofs, the cost of the sheet of 18 ounces to the square foot is enhanced to 9d. the square foot. Zinc in all jobs costs about half the price of lead.

(179.) Zinc is not very suitable for gutters and platforms, on account of its thinness, the wood below warping in warm weather, and tearing up the sheets of zinc.

(180.) Zinc is an ore which occurs in considerable quantity in England. It is found in two geological localities, in the mountain limestone and in the magnesian limestone. It occurs in veins, and almost always associated with galena or lead-glance. It is of the greatest abundance in the shape of a sulphuret or blende, or *black-jack*, as the miners call it. There is also a siliceous oxide of zinc, and a carbonate, both called calamine. In North America, the red oxide of zinc is found in abundance in the iron mines of New Jersey. The zinc of commerce is

* Macculloch's Dictionary of Commerce, art. *Tar*.

† See Ure's Dictionary of the Arts, and Macculloch's Dictionary of Commerce, arts. *Lead*.

derived, in this country, from the blende and calamine. It is naturally brittle, but a process has been discovered by which it is rendered malleable, and it retains its ductility ever after. It is this assumed ductility which renders the metal useful for domestic purposes. " It is extensively employed for making water-cisterns, baths, spouts, pipes, plates for the zincographer, for voltaic batteries, filings for fire-works, covering roofs, and a variety of architectural purposes, especially in Berlin; because this metal, after it gets covered with a thin film of oxide or carbonate, suffers no farther change from long exposure to the weather. One capital objection to zinc as a roofing material is its combustibility." *

(181.) The most malleable zinc is derived from Upper Silesia, under the name of *spelter*, which is sent by inland traffic to Hamburgh and Belgium, where it is shipped for this country. The quantity imported in 1831 was 76,413 cwt., and in 1836 it had fallen off to 47,406 cwt. A considerable portion of these quantities was exported to India and China, amounting, in 1831, to 62,684 cwt. The duty is L.2 a ton on what is formed into cakes, and 10s. per cwt. on what is not in cakes.†

(182.) The *slater-work* is then executed. Of its specifications, if blue slates are to be employed, they should be selected of large sizes, well squared, and have an overlap of ⅔, gradually diminishing to the ridge, and well bedded and shouldered with plaster-lime. The slates are fastened to the sarking with malleable iron nails, weighing 15 lb. to the 1000, after being steeped when heated in linseed oil. These nails cost 3s. 4d. the 1000, 1300 being required for a rood of 36 square yards. Cast-iron nails were used for slating until a very few years ago, and which were also boiled in oil.

(183.) Slating is performed by the rood, and from 1000 to 1200 blue slates should cover a rood. The cost of the slates, in towns, including carriage, and putting them on with nails, is L.4, 4s. the rood.

(184.) Blue slate is derived from the primitive rock clay-slate. It occurs in large quantities through the mountainous parts of the kingdom. Good slate should not absorb water, and it should be so compact as to resist the action of the atmosphere. When it imbibes moisture, it becomes covered with moss, and then rapidly decays.

(185.) The principal blue slate quarries in Great Britain are in Wales, Lancashire, Westmoreland, Cumberland, Argyle, and Perthshires. The most extensive quarry is in Caernarvonshire, in Wales, near the town of Bangor, on the Penrhyn estate. It employs 1500 men and boys. The Welsh slate is very large and smooth, and much of it is fit for putting into frames for writing-slates. When used very large, being thin, it is apt to warp on change of temperature. The English slates at Ulverstone, in Lancashire, and in the counties of Westmoreland and Cumberland, are not so large as the Welsh, but equally smooth and good. The Easdale slates, in Argyleshire, are small, thick, waved on the surface, and contain many cubical crystals of iron-pyrites, but its durability is endless. Being a small and heavy slate, it requires a stout roofing of timber to support it. The Ballihulish slates are rather smoother and lighter than the Easdale, though also small, and containing numerous crystals of iron-pyrites, and is equally durable. The slates in Perthshire are of inferior quality to either

* Ure's Dictionary of the Arts, art. *Zinc*.

† Macculloch's Dictionary of Commerce, art. *Zinc*.

of these. " The ardesia of Easdale," says Professor Jameson, " was first quarried about 100 years ago; but was for a long time of little importance, as sandstone flags and tiles were generally used for roofing houses. As the use of slates became more prevalent, the quarries were enlarged, so that 5,000,000 slates are annually shipped from this island. The number of workmen is at present (in 1800) about 300, and they are divided into quarriers and day-labourers. The quarriers are paid annually at a certain rate for every 1000 slates, from 10d. to 15d., I believe, as their work has been attended with more or less difficulty. The day-labourers are employed in opening new quarries, and have from 10d. to 1s. a-day."*

(186.) Slates are assorted into sizes at the quarry. The sizes at Bangor vary from 36 inches in length to 5½ inches in breadth. Their weight varies from 82 to 12 cwt. the 1000, and the prices from 140s. to 10s. the 1000 for the smaller, and from 55s. to 35s. the ton for the larger sizes.

(187.) Cisterns, with sides and ends 1 inch thick, 1s. 10d. the cubic ft. contents.
... ... 1½ ... 2s. 2d. ... ...

(188.) The *export* of slates from England to foreign ports has increased from 2741 tons in 1828, to 6061 tons in 1832. That of framed slates has decreased in number, in the same period, from 37,034 to 15,420.

(189.) The shipping expenses of slates at Bangor are 6d. the ton, and bills of lading 3s. 6d.†

(190.) When the roof is to be covered with *tile*, it should be laid with lath 1¼ inch square to a gauge of 10 or 11 inches. There should be 3 or 4 courses of slates along all the eaves. The flanks, peands, and ridges, should be covered with tile. The whole under joints of the tiling should be pointed with plaster-lime.

(191.) Tiling is executed by the rood of 36 square yards, and as pan-tiles are obliged to be made of a certain size, namely, 13½ inches long, 9½ inches wide, and ½ inch thick, by 17th Geo. III. c. 42, under a penalty of 10s. for every 1000, a rood will just contain 576 tiles. Tiles should be smooth on the surface, compact, and ring freely when struck, when they will resist water. When they imbibe moisture by porosity, they soon decay in winter by the effects of rain and frost.

(192.) There were, in 1830, 5369 brick and tile manufacturers in England and Wales, and 104 in Scotland, and must have greatly increased since.

(193) The duty on tiles was abolished in 1833, the revenue derived from that source being very trifling. The duty on foreign pan-tiles is L.15 the 1000. The export of tiles is inconsiderable, not having exceeded, in 1830, 803,742.‡

(194.) *Grey-slates* require the roof to be lathed in the same manner as tile, but, not being of an uniform size like tile, they are assorted to sizes in the quarry. The larger and heavier slates are put next the eaves, and gradually diminish in size to the ridge. The course at the eaves is laid double, slate above slate. Every slate is hung upon the lath by a wooden pin being passed through a hole at the upper end, and, on being laid on, the slates are made to overlap at least ⅓. Grey-slates should either be bedded and shouldered in plaster-lime, or laid on moss, the latter making the warmer roof.

(195.) Grey slates are pretty smooth on the surface, and, when so compact in texture as to resist moisture, form a durable though very heavy roof.

* Jameson's Mineralogy of the Scottish Isles, vol. i. p. 195.

† Macculloch's Dictionary of Commerce, art. *Slates.*

‡ Ibid., art. *Bricks and Tiles.*

(196.) The flanks are made of slate, but the ridge is covered with droved angular ridge-stones of freestone. As this species of roofing is not adapted to pavilion roofs, the peands should be covered with lead, but the safest form of roof with grey-slates is with upright gables.

(197.) The cost of grey slating depends on the locality where it is wished to be done. At Edinburgh it costs L.6 a rood; whereas in Forfarshire, the matrix of the grey-slate, it can be done, exclusive of carriage, for L.2, 10s. the rood. In Forfarshire the slates cost L.4 per 1000; 360 are required for a rood; the putting them on, including dressing, holing, pins for the slates, and nails for the laths, costs only 15s.; and with moss for bedding 1s., and lime for teething 3s., 22s. the rood. The droved angular freestone ridging-stone, including carriage, costs 6d. a lineal foot, or 10s. the rood.

(198.) Grey-slates are obtained in best quality from grey slaty inferior sandstone belonging to the old red sandstone series. They are derived from the same quarries as the far-famed Arbroath pavement, being, in fact, formed by the action of frost on pavement, set on edge for the purpose. A mild winter is thus unfavourable to the making of slates. From Carmylie to Forfar, in Forfarshire, is the great field for the supply of grey-slates; and as blue-slates can only be obtained there by sea and long land carriage, and there is little clay fit for tiles, they constitute the chief roofing of cottages and small farm-houses in that part of the country, their aspect being cold and unpicturesque, though snug enough.

(199.) Of all sorts of slating, there is none equal to blue-slate for appearance, comfort, and even economy in the long run. When a blue-slate roof is well executed at first, with good materials, it will last a very long time. Tile roofs are constantly requiring repairs, and the employment of grey-slate is a sacrifice of, and a burden upon, timber. Of the blue-slates, the Welsh give the cheapest roofing, being larger and much lighter than Scotch or English slates.

(200.) As the *plaster-work* of a steading does not require to be of an ornamental nature, its *specifications* should be simple. The ceilings of the riding-horse-stable, boiling-house, wool-room, hen-house, and granaries, when tile-roofing is employed, should be finished with two coats of the best haired plaster, hard rubbed in. The walls of the granaries, corn-barn, work-horse-stable, cow-byre, boiling-house, calves'-house, wool-room, gig-house, and hen-house, should be finished with one coat, hard rubbed in. The walls of the riding-horse-stable should have three coats, hard rubbed in. Plaster-work is measured by the square yard, and costs for one coat 3d., for two coats from 4d. to 4½d., and for three coats from 5d. to 6d., the square yard.

(201.) It is necessary to say something regarding the *specifications of smith-work*, although there is not much of this kind of work required in a steading. All the outside doors, including those on the feeding-holes at the byre, should be hung with crooks and bands; the crooks should be fastened into the ingoings of the ribets with melted lead. The larger crooks and bands cost 10s., and the smaller 5s., the pair. The inside doors should be hung with T hinges, 18 inches long, and the opening parts of the windows, with 9-inch T hinges. The former are 1s. and the latter 9d a pair. The outside doors should have good 10-inch stock-and-plate locks, which cost 2s. 6d. each, except where there are more than one outside door to the same apartment, in which case all the doors but one can be fastened by bars from the inside. The inside doors should have the same sort of locks; the common stock-lock, which cost 1s. 6d. each, not being worthy of commendation. Thumb-latches are convenient for opening and keeping shut doors that do not require to be constantly locked, such as the doors of the corn-barn, granary, boiling-house, cow-byre, and hen-house. These latches cost from 5d. to 7d. each. A wooden bar of hard-wood, to open and shut from both sides, is a convenient mode of fastening inside doors. The upper-barn door, of two vertical leaves, requires an iron stay-band to fasten it with. The doors of the riding-horse and work-horse stables should be provided with sunk flush ring-handles and thumb-latches, to be out of the way of catching any part of the harness. The mangers of the riding-horse-stable, and the upper rail of the hay-rack of the work-horse-stable, should be provided with rings and staples for the stall-collar-shanks to pass through. These cost 1d. each.

(202.) Various descriptions of *nails* are used for the different parts of work in a steading. The scantlings of the roofs are fastened together with *double-doubles*, which cost 5s. per 1000. Deals of floors are fastened down with flooring-nails, 16 lb. weight, and 4s. 6d. per 1000. The bars of the plain-deal doors are put on with 10 lb. nails, which cost 3s. 6d. the 1000. For finishing, *single-flooring* nails at 2s. 6d., and 2-inch springs at 2s. to 2s. 3d. the 1000 are used.

(203.) As a security against robbery, iron stancheons, $\frac{7}{8}$ inch in diameter, should be fixed on the outside of the low windows of the corn-barn and implement-house. Such stancheons cost 3d. per pound.

(204.) Iron is chiefly found among the members of the coal-formation, in bands composed of nodules, which are called compact clay-ironstone, a carbonate of iron. It is abundant in the west of Scotland and in South Wales. Its annual worked production is probably not less than 1,000,000 tons.*

(205.) The windows of all the apartments should be *glazed* with best 2d crown-glass, fastened in with fine putty. Glazing is executed for 2s. the square foot.

(206.) A *skylight* in blue slating is made of a frame fastened to the sarking. In tile-roofing, tiles are made on purpose to hold a pane of glass. In grey-slating, a hole is made in the slate to suit the size of the pane. A dead skylight of zinc, to answer any kind of roofing, costs 4s.

(207.) There is a duty of 73s. 6d. the cwt. on good window, and 30s. on broad or inferior window-glass, which is returned in drawback on exportation to foreign countries. When glass intended for exportation is cut into panes, it must be in panes of less than 8 inches in the side, to enable it to claim the drawback.

(208.) Glass of small sizes, though of good quality, such as is fit for glazing hot-houses and forcing-frames, costs only from 8d. to 10d. the square foot; whilst in ordinary sized panes it costs 1s. 3d., and in still larger sizes it is charged 1s. 6d., the square foot. I am not sure but the sort fit for hot-houses would answer the purpose of glazing the windows of a steading.

(209.) "The researches of Berzelius having removed all doubts concerning the acid character of silica, the general composition of glass presents now no difficulty of conception. This substance consists of one or more salts, which are silicates with bases of potash, soda, lime, oxide of iron, alumina, or oxide of lead; in any of which compounds we can substitute one of these bases for another, provided that one alkaline base be left. Silica, in its turn, may be replaced by the boracic acid, without causing the glass to lose its principal characters."*

(210.) Rain-water spouts, or *runs* as they are technically termed, may be made of wood, cast-iron, lead, or zinc. Wooden ones may be made out of the

* Ure's Dictionary of the Arts, art. *Iron.*

solid or in slips nailed together. When made out of the solid, with iron holdfasts, they cost 1s., and when pieced together 6d. the lineal foot. The conductors from both kinds cost 8d. the lineal foot. Wooden spouts should be pitched inside and painted outside. Cast-iron ones are heavy, but they cost no more than 2s. a yard if of 4½ inches diameter, and the conductors, of from 2 to 4 inches diameter, from 8s. to 18s., of 9 feet in length, each. Lead makes the best spout, but it is very expensive, being 1s. 6d. a foot. Zinc ones, on the other hand, are very light. Stout 4-inch zinc spouts cost 9½d. the foot, and a 2½ pipe, as conductor, 7½d. the foot. The lowest part of this pipe is made strong enough to resist accidents. Every sort of water-spout should be cleaned at least once a-year, and the wooden ones would be the better of an annual coat of paint.

(211.) The outsides of all the outside doors and windows, all the gates of the courts and hammels, and the water-troughs in the various courts, if made of wood, should receive *three coats of good paint*. Painting costs 3d. or 4d the square yard, but three coats can be done for 8d. the square yard. The best standing colours, and they happen to be the cheapest too, are grey, stone, or slate-blue; the last seems to be most commonly preferred. Green is dear and soon fades, and red seems very distasteful in buildings. But the truth is, that white-lead and oil are the principal ingredients in paint, and all the colouring matter has no power to preserve timber from the effects of the weather. A substance called *lithic paint* has recently been found to answer well for country purposes. The lithic, which costs 2½d. per lb., is ground to powder, and mixed, in a certain proportion, with cold coal-tar, and the mixture is applied with a brush. This paint deprives the coal-tar of its noxious smell, and hardens it into a durable paint in a few days.

(212.) White lead of commerce is a *carbonate of lead*, or *ceruse*, as it is called, artificially formed from pure lead. It has long been made with great success at Klagenfurth, in Carinthia, and large quantities are made in England. The compound is 1 equivalent of lead, 1 of oxygen, and 1 of carbonic acid; or by analysis, of lead 77.6, oxygen 6, and carbonic acid 16.4 in 100 parts. White-lead, when it enters the human system, occasions dreadful maladies. Its emanations cause that dangerous disease the *colica pictonum*, afterwards paralysis, or premature decrepitude and lingering death. All paints are ground into fine powder in a mill, as being a safer plan for the operator, as well as more expeditious, than by the hand.†

(213.) I have said (81.), (82.), (83.), that when the building of a steading is to be measured, the work that has actually been executed should alone be measured, and no *allowances*, as they are called, should on any account be permitted to increase the amount of cost. The correctness of this rule will appear obvious, and its adoption reasonable, after you have learnt the sort of claims for allowances made by tradesmen in various sorts of work.

(214.) In the first place, in regard to *masonry*, double measure is claimed on all circular work. Claims are made for allowance on all levellings for joists, bond-timbers, and wall-heads. The open spaces or voids left in the walls for doors and windows, are claimed to be measured along with rubble-work. Girthing around the external walls of rubble-work is claimed in measurement, the effect of which is, to measure the square pieces of building in each corner twice over. Scontions of all voids are claimed to be measured over and above the rub-

* Ure's Dictionary of the Arts, art. *Glass.*

† Ibid. arts. *White-lead, Paint.*

ble-work. The ashlar for the hewn-work is first measured with the rubble, and then it is claimed to be measured by itself. In like manner, chimney-tops are first measured as rubble, and then claimed to be measured again as ashlar. In short, wherever any sort of mason-work differs from the character of the general work under the contract, allowances are claimed.

(215.) In regard to *carpentry*, the claims are equally absurd. For the cuttings connected with the peands and flanks of roofs, 18 inches of extra measurement are claimed. The same extent is claimed for angles in the flooring, and in all such unequal work. In window-making, a claim is made for 3 inches more than the height, and 4 inches more than the width of windows, which is more than the voids; whereas the measurement should be confined to the mere daylight afforded by the windows. In many instances 1½, and even double measure, is claimed for round work, according to its thickness. Where plain deal is cleaned on both sides, such as the under part of the floor of the upper-barn, which forms the roof of the corn-barn, or shelving, 1½ measure is claimed.

(216.) In *slating*, claims are made on the making of peands and flanks, from 18 inches to 3 feet in width, and for eaves, from 12 inches to 18 inches in width, more than the actual work done. For all circular work, such as the slating of a round horse-course of a thrashing machine, double measure is claimed.

(217.) In *plaster work*, double measure is claimed for all circular work. There is an allowance made in plastering which is, however, quite reasonable, and that is, in the case where new work is joined to old, an allowance of 1 foot is made around the new work, as the old part has to be wetted and prepared for its junction with the new.

(218.) A perusal of these statements naturally suggests the question, how could such claims have originated? If a workman execute the work he agreed to undertake, and gets payment for what work he executes, he is not entitled to ask more. But what proves an aggravation of such demands is, that modes of measurement differ in different counties—that different allowances are made on different kinds of work—and that those allowances differ in different counties. So it appears that those allowances are based on no principle of equity. But it may be urged, in justification of these allowances, that the prices of work, as usually estimated, are too low to remunerate the contractor for his labour, and that allowances are therefore requisite to insure him against loss. To this specious statement it may be replied by asking, why should any *honest* contractor estimate work at such rates that he knows will not remunerate him? A rogue will do so, because he wishes to have possession of a job at all hazards, in order to make up his foreseen loss by exorbitant claims for allowances. If employers will not pay sufficiently for good work, as is alleged against them, and perhaps with truth, let them understand that they shall receive insufficient work as an equivalent for *their* stinted money. But it is very unfair to take advantage of an honourable employer, by capricious and absurd allowances, when he is all the while desirous to pay his workmen well for their labour. So much dependence is sometimes placed on allowances by contractors, that I have heard of a case where a surveyor was obliged to reduce the claims made against a single steading, to the extent of L.800! Such a fraudulent system ought to be entirely abolished, and it is quite in the power of those who employ tradespeople to abolish it.

(219.) It would be completely abolished were contracts to contain stringent clauses prohibiting all allowances whatsoever; and to consist of detailed measurements, and specified prices for every species of work to be executed. If more work happens to be executed than was expected, its value can easily be ascertained by the settled measurements and prices, and if less, the contractor is still paid for what he has actually executed. Were such a form of contract uniformly adopted, proprietors and farmers could measure the work done as well as any surveyor, whose services might, in that case, be dispensed with, but, what would be still better, the measurements of the surveyor could be checked by the proprietor or the tenant if either chose to take the trouble of doing it. Where any peculiar kind of work is desired to be executed, it could be specified in a separate contract.

(220.) Having thus amply considered all the details which should form a part of all specifications of the different kinds of work required to build a steading, I shall now give the particulars which should be specified in all contracts, and that these may not be imaginery, but have a practical bearing, I shall take the steading as shewn in the plan, fig. 4. Plate IV., as the example. In order that the data furnished in the proposed specifications shall be generally applicable, I shall first give the measurements of the various kinds of work proposed to be executed,—then the quantity of materials required for constructing the same,—and lastly, the prices paid for the different sorts of work in Edinburgh, both including and excluding the cost of carriages, that you may have a criterion by which to judge of the cost of doing the same kind of work in other parts of the country. You may reasonably believe, that the prices of labour and materials are higher in Edinburgh than in the country; but, on the other hand, you must consider the superiority of the workmanship obtained in so large a town. These must affect the total amount of the estimate to a certain extent, but to what exact per centage I cannot say. I am told that carpenter-work is very little dearer in Edinburgh than in the country, but that mason-work, smith-work, and plaster-work, are all considerably higher; but of smith-work, as I have already said, little is required in building a steading.

MEASUREMENT OF THE PLAN OF A PROPOSED STEADING IN FIG. 4. PLATE IV.

Mason-work.

6225	Cubic yards of	Foundations, and wheeling the earth not farther than 60 yards distance.
207	Ditto	of Drains with sills and covers.
85	Cubic roods of	Rubble-walls, 2 feet thick.
47	Ditto	of Division rubble-walls, 12 to 15 inches thick, including dykes.
42	Lineal feet of	Chimney-vents.
400	Ditto	Corners of buildings.
80	Ditto	... for archways.
50	Ditto	Arched lintels for archways.
1528	Ditto	Ribets, sills, lintels, and steps.
75	Ditto	Arched lintels over doors.
24	Ditto	Ringpens of archways to granary.
80	Ditto	Corners, sills, and lintels of feeding-holes of byres.
60	Ditto	Corners of gateways to courts.
286	Ditto	Corners or hammer-dressed scontions for gates in dykes.

Mason-work (continued).

20	Lineal feet of	Coping of chimney-stalks.
110	Ditto	Ashlar pillars for sheds, from 18 to 20 inches square.
294	Ditto	Skews on gables.
1671	Ditto	Semicircular hammer-dressed coping on dykes.
100	Ditto	Gutters in byres.
94	Ditto	Coping round liquid-manure-tank.
300	Ditto	Steps of stairs to granaries.
45	Ditto	Brick stalk for steam-engine, 6 feet square at the base.
152	Square roods of	Rubble-causeway.
287	Lineal yards of	Causewayed gutters around the buildings outside.
2	Pairs of jambs and lintels.	
	Building in boiler, including boiler and furnace complete.	
17	Droved stones, with gratings for liquid-manure-drains.	
8	Water-troughs in courts.	
31	Stones for heel-posts of stalls.	
31	Stones for curbs of stall-boardings.	

Carpenter-work.

540	Square feet of	4-inch thick safe lintels.
2768	Square yards of	Roofing, with balks and sarking.
583	Ditto	Joisting and flooring of granaries and corn-barn.
762	Lineal feet of	Ridge-battens.
192	Ditto	Dressed beams for pillars of roofs of sheds.
1141	Ditto	Door-checks or fixings, 6½ inches by 2½ inches.
1366	Ditto	Door-keps or stops and facings.
2132	Square feet of	1¼-inch deal doors.
1360	Ditto	1½-inch divisions of stalls.
829	Lineal feet of	Heel and fore-posts.
18	Ditto	Manger in riding-horse-stable.
18	Ditto	Hay-rack in ditto.
96	Ditto	Hay-racks, low, in work-horse stable.
84	Ditto	Feeding-troughs in byres.
670	Ditto	... ... courts.
36	Ditto	Racks in cattle-sheds.
432	Square feet of	Daylight of windows.
760	Ditto	Sparred divisions of cribs for calves.
669	Lineal feet of	Rain-water spouts.
87	Ditto	Conductors from ditto.
10	Small doors of feeding-holes of byre.	
14	Corn-boxes for work-horse-stable.	
2	Square racks for centre of courts.	
1	Corn-chest for work-horses.	
1	Ditto	for riding-horse-stable.
7	Luffer-board ventilators for roofs.	
8	Sparred gates, from 9 feet to 10 feet wide.	
12	... ... 5 ...	
	Rails, harness-pins, and saddle-trees.	
	Stathel-frames for stacks.	
	Pump with mounting.	

Slater-work.

77 Square roods of Blue-slating, grey-slating, or tiling.

Plumber-work.

1084 Square feet of Lead on ridges, flanks, and peands.
669 Lineal feet of Lead rain-runs or spouts.
87 Ditto Lead-pipes or conductors from runs.

Plaster-work.

1507 Square yards of 1st, 2d, and 3d coat plaster.

Smith-work.

22 Stock-and-plate locks.
28 Pairs of crooks and bands.
9 Pairs of cross-tailed hinges.
35 ... ... small.
2 Sets of fastenings for double doors.
3 Locks for small courts.
10 Pairs of crooks and bands for feeding-holes.
10 Sneck-fastenings for ditto.
33 Thumb-latches.
18 Manger-rings.
17 Seals for fastening cows, or feeding cattle.
Stanchions for windows.
Cast-iron runs and conductors, ... travis-posts, ... hay-racks for riding-horse-stable, ... window-sashes, } when used.
Boiler and furnace.
Mounting for gates.

QUANTITIES OF MATERIALS AND NUMBERS OF CARRIAGES IN STEADING.

108½ cubic roods of 2-feet walls, each rood containing 36 cubic yards of building, requiring 40 cart-loads of rubble-stones, 2 cart-loads of lime, and 4 or 5 cart-loads of sand, besides water.
710 Ashlar corners.
1004 Ribets.
100 Sills and lintels, from 4 ft. to 4½ ft. long.
20 ... ... 30 inches long.
31 Steps, from 3½ feet to 4 feet long.
60 ... ... 4½ ... 5 ...
20 Lineal feet of Coping of chimney-stalks.
2 Pairs of chimney-jambs, 3½ ft. by 2 ft. long.
2 Lintels for ditto, from 3½ ft. to 4 ...
110 Ashlar stones for pillars, from 18 inches to 20 inches square.
294 lineal feet of Skews.
200 Ditto Curbstones.
100 Ditto Sills for gutters in byres.
94 Ditto Coping round liquid-manure-tank.

17 Stones for gratings to drains.
31 ... heel-posts.
8 ... water-troughs.
31 ... curbstones below boarding in stables and byres.
160 Square roods of Causeways.
77 Ditto Slating.
136 Loads of Timber.
326 Square feet of Glass for windows.

On ascertaining the quarry-mail, or prime cost of the stones, and the cost of carriage, in the locality in which you intend to build your steading, the cost of each of the above quantities of materials will easily be ascertained.

(221.) The following schedule gives the prices of those materials in Edinburgh, and they are stated both inclusive and exclusive of carriages.

Mason-work.	Including Carriage.			Excluding Carriage.		
	L.	S.	D.	L.	S.	D.
Digging foundations, ... per cubic yard	0	0	6	0	0	4
Rubble-foundations, reduced to 2 feet thick, ... per rood of 36 cubic yards	10	0	0	8	0	0
Rubble building, 2 feet thick, per ditto	8	8	0	7	0	0
... ... 18 inches thick and under, reduced to 1 foot thick, per ditto	5	0	0	4	6	0
Rubble drains, with dressed flags, sills, and covers, 12 inches square in the opening, ... per lineal yard	0	3	0	0	2	4
Ditto, 15 inches by 18 inches in the opening, ... , . . . per ditto	0	5	0	0	4	0
Hammer-dressed coursed-work, with raised or hollow joints, . . . per square foot	0	0	3			
Where bricks are used for building the walls, the prices are for—						
2½ thick brick on edge walls, . . per square yard	0	1	9	0	1	6
4½ ... ... bed ... ... per ditto	0	3	0	0	2	6
6 ... ... per ditto	0	5	0	0	4	8
Chimney-vents, plastered, . . per lineal foot	0	0	6			
Droved ashlar, from 7 to 8 inches thick, ... per square foot	0	1	2	0	1	0
Broached ditto, ditto, per ditto,	0	1	0	0	0	10
... corners, averaging 3 ft. girth, per lin. ft.,	0	2	6			
... supports for stacks, from 2 feet to 2½ feet in girth, . . . per ditto	0	2	0			
Droved ribets, front and ingoing with broached tails, 2 feet long and 1 foot in the head, ... per ditto	0	2	6			
Droved projecting sills, 7 inches thick, per ditto	0	2	0			
Sills and lintels dressed similar to the ribets, ... per ditto	0	1	6			

Mason-work (continued).	Including Carriage.			Excluding Carriage.		
	L.	S.	D.	L.	S.	D.
Droved cornices for chimney-stalks, 6 to 7 inches thick, ... per lineal foot	0	1	6			
Droved block-course for chimney-stalks, 6 inches deep, . . . per ditto	0	0	9			
Droved skews, 2½ to 3 inches thick, per square foot	0	0	9			
Broached ditto, ditto, per ditto	0	0	8			
Corners for coach-house doors, with droved giblet-checks, . . . per lineal foot	0	1	8			
Elliptical arched lintels for ditto, per ditto	0	1	9			
Segmental ditto, per ditto	0	1	9			
Broached pillars for cart-sheds, &c., per square foot	0	0	10			
Droved jambs and lintels, . . . per ditto	0	0	9			
... Arbroath pavement and hearths, ... per ditto	0	0	9	0	0	8
... freestone pavement, . . per ditto	0	0	9	0	0	8
Broached ditto, ... per ditto	0	0	8	0	0	7½
Dressed and jointed flagging, . . per ditto	0	0	7	0	0	6½
... hanging steps, ordinary sizes, per lineal foot	0	2	4	0	1	3
... common steps, ditto, . . per ditto	0	1	6	0	1	3
... plats of hanging stairs, single measure, ... per square yard	0	1	5½	0	1	4½
... stone-skirtings, 4½ inches deep, ... per lineal foot	0	0	4	0	0	3¾
... ridge-stones, common form, per ditto	0	0	7½	0	0	7
... socket-stones for travis-posts, each	0	5	6	0	5	0
... feeding troughs, . . . per square foot	0	1	1	0	1	0
... stone water-troughs, . . per ditto	0	1	0	0	0	11
Curb-stones for gutters in byres, . per lineal foot	0	0	6	0	0	5½
Droved curb-stones for stalls, . . per ditto	0	0	6	0	0	5
Semicircular coping for dykes, hammer-dressed, from 12 inches to 14 inches diameter, ... per ditto	0	0	6½	0	0	6
Square dressed whinstone-causeway, per rood of 36 square yards	7	7	0	7	0	0
Rubble causewaying, . . per ditto	2	14	0	2	7	0
When ornamental masonry is introduced into steadings, these are the prices :—						
Droved base-course and belts, 12 inches deep, ... per lineal foot	0	1	1			
... wall-head plinths, 6 inches thick, ... per ditto	0	0	10			
... cornices, 9 to 10 inches thick, per ditto	0	2	6			
... block-course, 12 inches deep, per ditto	0	1	1			
... checked plinth and block for chimney-stalks, 1 foot deep, per ditto	0	1	2			

Mason-work (continued.)	Including Carriage.			Excluding Carriage.		
	L.	S.	D.	L.	S.	D.
Polished hanging steps, ordinary sizes, per lineal foot	0	2	6	0	2	5
Polished plats of hanging stairs, single measure, . . . , . . . per square foot	0	1	6	0	1	4
Broached copings, with droved edges, for dykes, ... per ditto	0	0	9	0	0	8
Droved pillars for small gates to hammels, &c., ... per ditto	0	0	10	0	0	9
Building in boiler and furnace complete,	0	18	0			
Bricks, ... per 1000	1	17	0	1	10	0
Rubble stones, ... per load	0	3	0	0	0	6
Carpenter-work.						
Safe-lintels and rough beams, . . per cubic foot	0	3	6	0	3	4
Dressed beams, ... per ditto	0	4	0	0	3	10
Scantling for roofs, 7 inches by 2½ inches, and 18 inches from centre to centre, ... per square yard	0	2	4	0	2	2
Scantlings for roofs, 7¾ inches by 2½ inches, and 18 inches from centre to centre, ... per ditto	0	1	6	0	1	2
Balks, 6 inches by 2 inches, and 18 inches from centre to centre, . per ditto	0	1	9	0	1	7
Balks, 5 inches by 2 inches, and 18 inches from centre to centre, . per ditto	0	1	6	0	1	4
Wall-plates for roofing, 7 inches by 1¼ inch, ... per lineal foot	0	0	4	0	0	3½
Ridge-trees, 10 inches by 2 inches, per ditto	0	0	9	0	0	8
Ridge and peand battens, 2½ inches diameter, ... per ditto	0	0	3	0	0	2½
⅝ inch thick Baltic sarking, . . . per square yard	0	1	10	0	1	9
Tile-lath, 1¼ inch square, and 11 inches apart, ... per ditto	0	0	6	0	0	5½
Bond-timber, 3½ inches by 1¼ inch, and 20 inches apart, . . . per ditto	0	0	6	0	0	5½
Baltic split lath, $\frac{3}{16}$ inch thick, . per ditto	0	0	6	0	0	5½
Plain joisting, 7 in. by 2½ in., and 18 inches from centre to centre, . per ditto	0	2	4	0	2	2
... ... 8 in. by 2½ in., . per ditto	0	3	6	0	3	4
... ... 9 in. by 2½ in., . per ditto	0	4	0	0	3	10
... ... 10 in. by 2½ in., . per ditto	0	4	6	0	4	4
... ... 12 in. by 2½ in., . per ditto	0	5	0	0	4	10
1⅛ Batten flooring, grooved and tongued, per ditto	0	3	4	0	3	2
Door-checks, 6 inches by 2½ inches, per lineal foot	0	0	6	0	0	5
Checked window grounds, 2 in. by 1¾ in., per ditto	0	0	2½			
Finishing grounds, 2 inches by ¾ inch, per ditto	0	0	1½			
Windows for barns and byres, of the form in fig. 15, ... per square foot	0	1	8	0	1	6

Carpenter-work (continued).		Including Carriage.			Excluding Carriage.		
		L.	S.	D.	L.	S.	D.
Windows for stables, of the form in fig. 14, ...	per square foot	0	1	8	0	1	6
Windows for granaries, of the form in fig. 17, ...	per ditto	0	1	6	0	1	4

		Including Carriage.		
1½ Travis-boarding, for riding-horse and work-horse stables, dowelled, ...	per square foot	0	0	8
1¼ travis-boards, grooved and tongued and beaded, for byres, ...	per ditto	0	0	6
1¼ inch deal lining, grooved and tongued, for end stalls of riding-horse stable, with fixtures, .	per ditto	0	0	5
¾ inch deal linings, beaded in walls, over and under the mangers in the riding-horse stable, . .	per ditto	0	0	3
Turned travis-posts, for riding-horse stable, . . .	each	0	8	0
Beaded travis-posts, fore-posts, and runtrees, for work-horse stable, reduced to 3 inches square,	per lineal foot	0	0	5
Stakes and runtrees of byres, 4 inches to 5 inches in diameter, ...	per ditto	0	0	6
Hardwood high hay-racks, with turned rollers, 2 inches diameter and 2½ inches apart, for riding-horse stable, ...	per ditto	0	3	0
Fir sparred low hay-racks for work-horse stable,	per ditto	0	1	0
Mangers for riding-horse stable, ...	per ditto	0	1	6
Corn-boxes for work-horse stable, ...	each	0	3	0
1¼ inch deal beaded outside doors, with 3 backbars,	per square foot	0	0	7
¾ inch deal beaded inside doors, with three 1-inch backbars, ...	per ditto	0	0	6
Sparred calves' cribs, ...	per ditto	0	0	5
Facings, keps, skirting, and coping, reduced to 4 inches broad, ...	per lineal foot,	0	0	3
Ogee copings for travises, ...	per ditto	0	0	2
1 inch beaded coping for lining, ...	per ditto	0	0	2¼
Rain-spouts of wood, out of the solid, . . .	per ditto	0	1	0
... ... when pieced, ...	per ditto	0	0	6
Conductors from rain-spouts, ...	per ditto	0	0	8
Small doors for feeding-holes of byres, . . .	each	0	1	0
Racks for centre of courts, ...	ditto	0	12	0
Corn chest for work-horses, ...		0	15	0
Stout 5 barred gates, 9 feet wide, for courts, .	each	1	10	0
... 4 ... ... 5 ... ... hammels,	ditto	0	14	0
Rails, harness-pins, and saddletrees, ...		2	10	0
Luffer-board ventilators, 6 feet long by 4 feet wide, and 2½ feet high in front, ...	per square foot	0	1	6
Octagonal stathel-frames for stacks, 15 feet diameter,	each	1	15	0
Pump with mounting, 20 feet long, ...		3	10	0

		Including Carriage. L.	S.	D.
Slater-work.				
Blue-slating, ...	per rood of 36 square yards	4	4	0
Grey, ...	per ditto	2	11	0
Tiling, ...	per ditto	2	10	0
Blue slates, ...	per 1000	3	10	0
Grey slates, ...	per ditto	4	10	0
Tiles, ...	per ditto	2	17	0
Plumber-work.				
6 lb. per square foot lead on peands, flanks, and ridges (25s. per cwt), ...	per square foot	0	1	3½
5 lb. lead for aprons to ventilators, &c. . . .	per ditto	0	1	1
Mastic for raglets, ...	per lineal foot	0	0	1½
Rain-water pipes of 6 lb. lead, ...	per ditto	0	1	6
6-inch open runs of 6 lb. lead, supported with iron straps or holdfasts, 2 feet apart, ...	per ditto	0	1	6
Lead-pump, with mounting, ...		2	10	0
Lead-pipe for ditto, ...	per lineal foot	0	1	2
Smith-work.				
Cast-iron travis heel-posts, ...	each	1	2	0
... corner hay-racks for riding-horse stable, .	ditto	0	10	0
... pump for liquid-manure tank, with 6 feet pipe, . .		3	0	0
Stock and plate-locks for outside doors, 10 inches long,	ditto	0	2	6
18-inch cross-tailed hinges, ...	per pair	0	1	3
9	per ditto	0	0	9
Thumb-latches, ...	each	0 0 5 to 0 0 7		
Manger rings, ...	ditto	0	0	1
Seals for binding cattle, ...	ditto	0	2	6
Cast-iron rain-spouts, 4½ inches diameter, . .	per lineal yard	0	2	0
Pipes from ditto, 2 inches diameter, } 9 feet long, .	each	0	8	0
... ... 4 inches diameter, } 9 feet long, .	each	0	18	0
Gate-mountings, ...	ditto	0 12 0 to 0 15 0		
36-inch boiler, with furnace complete, } or 14s. per cwt.		2	10	0
30 ... ... } or 14s. per cwt.		2	7	0
24 ... ... } or 14s. per cwt.		2	4	0
Crooks and bands for outside doors, ...	per pair	0	10	0
... ... feeding-hole doors in byres, .	per ditto	0	5	0
Stanchions, ⅞ inch diameter, ...	per pound	0	0	3
Cast-iron window sashes, ...	per square foot	0	1	0
Plaster-work.				
Best 3-coat plaster, ...	per square yard	0 0 5 to 0 0 6		
... 2	per ditto	0	0	4½
... 1	per ditto	0	0	3

o

		L.	S.	D.
Glazier-work.				
Best second crown-glass in small panes, . .	per square foot	0	0	10
... ... large panes, . .	per ditto	0	1	3
Painter-work.				
White-lead, coloured grey, stone, or slate-blue, 3 coats,	per sq. yard,	0	0	8

(222.) There is a simple rule for determining the *pitch* which a roof should have for the various sorts of slating. In blue slating the rule is, that the roof should be in height $\frac{1}{3}$ of the breadth of the building. Suppose that a building is 18 feet inside in width like the middle range of the steading, the walls are each two feet thick, which gives a breadth of 22 feet over walls. Deduct 6 inches on each wall for an escarpment on its top, upon which the scantlings or couple-legs rest upon the wall-plates, and $\frac{1}{3}$ of 21 feet gives 7 feet for the height of the roof above the walls. Old fashioned houses have a pitch of the square, that is, the height is equal to half the breadth, which, in the supposed case, would be 10½ feet. In grey slating the pitch is fixed at 1 foot below the square, or the height would be 9½ feet. In tiling, the pitch may be lower than even in blue slating, and it is determined according to circumstances; and even blue slate roofs are made as low in the pitch as $\frac{1}{4}$ of the breadth, that is with large Welsh slates. Taking the rise at 7 feet, the scantlings should be 13 feet long each, and the balk, of course, as long. Taking the rise at 9½ feet, the scantlings should be 14 feet long. (131.) and (132.), p. 187.

(223.) A liquid-manure tank can be constructed at little cost. An excavation being made in clay, a lining should be built all round. The lining may be either of rubble masonry, of stone and mortar, or of brick and mortar. If the subsoil is not of a retentive nature, a plastering of Roman cement will suffice to render the building retentive. A 9-inch wall, or a brick in length, will make a lining of sufficient strength to contain the liquid. The tank should be covered over in any of the various ways I have mentioned in (76.), and paved in the bottom with flags or bricks secured by cement. A cast-iron pump should be inserted at one end of the tank when it will be ready for use.

(224.) The cost of constructing such a tank, with brick in length and cement, will be somewhat as under, exclusive of drains:—

	Feet.	Inches.			
Inside length of tank, . .	13	6			
... width, ...	6	6			
... depth, ...	6	0=19½ cubic yards.			
Cutting the bed of the tank, at 3d. per cubic yard,			L.0	7	6
Building wall, including bricks and mortar, ...			6	8	0
Plastering and cement, ...			0	16	0
Covering with flags, ...			2	15	0
			L.10	6	6

Such a size of tank is said to be sufficient for a farm of from 150 to 200 acres. A receptacle of a more simple and inexpensive nature might be constructed, which would answer some of the ends of a more complete tank. It might be made under a shed, and composed of walls of clay, and covered with slabs of boarding. The expense of such a receptacle would be somewhere as under, the dimensions being as in the preceding case :—

Cutting the clay, at 3d the cubic yard, . . .	L.0 7 6
Clay and carting, ...	0 14 0
Boards, and expense of covering, ...	0 5 0
	L.1 6 6

Such a tank, however, would suffer in frost or drought. A cask sunk into the ground, with open channels to it, forms a sufficient tank for a cottager.*

17. OF THE FARM-HOUSE.

"Do you but mark how this becomes the house."

LEAR.

(225.) In alluding to the *farm-house* at all, it is not my intention to give a full plan of one, as I have given of the steading; because its internal arrangements are generally left to the fancy of architects or of its occupiers, and with little regard to their adaptation to a farm. Any specific plan which I would recommend of a farm-house, would therefore, I fear, receive little attention from either landlord or tenant. But the part of it which is exclusively devoted to labour, has so intimate a connection with the management of the farm, that I must give my opinion upon it. The part I mean includes the kitchen and dairy, and their accompanying apartments. Now, it may frequently be seen in the plans furnished by architects, that to give the farm-house a fashionable and airy appearance, the working portion of it is too often contracted and inconveniently arranged. The principle of its construction should be, to make this part of the house thoroughly commodious in itself, and at the same time prevent its giving the least annoyance to the rest from noise or disagreeable effluvia, which cannot at all times be avoided in the labours of the kitchen. Both objects would be accomplished by placing it independent of the main body of the house, and this is best effected by a jamb. Whatever may be the external form given to the house, the relative positions of its two parts may easily be preserved, whether in the old-fashioned form of a front tenement and back jamb, or the more modern and beauteous form of the Elizabethan style.

(226.) The ground-plan which I recommend of the kitchen and the other parts of the farm-house in which work is performed, may be seen

* Prize Essays of the Highland and Agricultural Society, vol. xiv. p. 280.

in fig. 32, where *a* is the *kitchen*, 18 feet in length, 16 feet in breadth, and 10 feet in height, provided with a door to the interior of the house, in

Fig. 32.

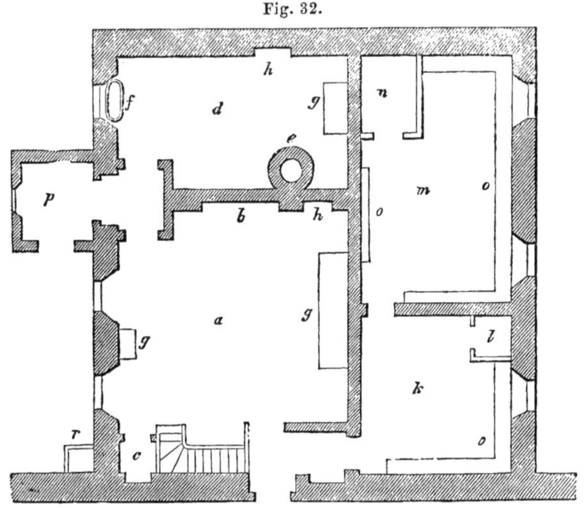

GROUND-PLAN OF A KITCHEN, &C. OF A FARM-HOUSE.

the wall nearest to you, another to the kitchen pantry *k* and dairy *m*, and a third to the scullery *d* and porch *p*. It contains two windows, one on each side of *g* on the left, a large kitchen range, oven, and furnace-pot at *b*, a commodious lock-up closet *c*, a wall-press *h*, and a dresser and table *g*. There is a stair at *c* to the servants' and other apartments above, and which also leads to the principal bed-rooms in the upper storey of the house. Beyond the kitchen is the *scullery d*, which contains a large furnace-pot *e*, a sink in the window *f*, a wall-press *h*, and a dresser *g*. This apartment is 18 feet in length, 10 feet in breadth, and 10 feet in height. A door from it, and another from the kitchen, open on a lobby common to both, and which lobby gives access by another door to the principal kitchen entrance-door through the porch *p*. The porch *p*, 6 feet square, is erected for the purpose of screening both the kitchen and scullery from wind and cold, and it contains the back entrance-door, and is lighted by a window. On the outside, and in front of the porch-door, is *r*, the rain-water cistern, fig. 30, p. 181. On going to the right from the kitchen to the *kitchen-pantry k*, is a wall-press in the passage. The pantry *k* is provided with a door; a window, which should look to the east or north; a larder *l*, and abundance of shelving at *o*; it is 12 feet square, having a roof of 10 feet in height. Within this pantry is the *milk-house or dairy m*, having two windows also facing to the north or east; a lock-up closet *n*, and shelving *o* around the walls; it is 18½ feet in length, 12 feet in breadth, and 10 feet in height.

(227.) These are the different apartments, and their relative positions, required for conducting the business of a farm within the house, and in the fitting up of which are many particulars which require attention. The *floor* of the kitchen should be of *flagged pavement polished*, that it may be cleaned with certainty and ease. The outside wall and ceiling should be lathed, and all the walls and ceiling plastered with the best hair-plaster. Iron hooks, both single and double, should be screwed into the joists of the roof, from which may be suspended hams or other articles. The dressers *g* are best made of plain-tree tops and black American birch frames, the chairs of the latter wood, and the stools of common fir. In case of accidents, or negligence in leaving them unfastened at night, it would be well to have the lower sashes of the windows of the kitchen and scullery fast, and the upper ones only to let down for the occasional admission of fresh and the escape of heated air.

(228.) In the *scullery*, the sink *f* should be of polished free-stone, made to fit the window-void, with a proper drain from it, provided with a cess-pool. The floor should be of the same material as that of the kitchen, for the sake of cleanliness. The outside wall and ceiling should be lathed, and all the walls and roof plastered. There should be a force-pump in the scullery to fill a cistern with water at the upper part of the house, to contain a constant supply for the sink. A boiler behind the kitchen fire, provided with a small cistern and ball-cock and ball in connection with the upper cistern, for the supply of cold water into the boiler; and a cock from it in the kitchen, and another from it in the scullery, for drawing off warm water when required, could be fitted up at no great cost, and would be found a most serviceable apparatus in a farm-house.

(229.) The large furnace-pot *e* should be built in with fire-brick surrounded with common brick, plastered and protected with cloth on the outside, rubbed hard into the plaster, and the mouth of the pot protected with a 4-inch pavement polished. To carry off the superfluous steam, a lead-pipe should be fastened into a narrow immovable portion of the pot-lid, and passed through the wall into the flue. An iron bar should project from the stone-wall about 3 feet or so above the furnace-pot, having a horizontal eye at its end directly over the centre of the pot, to be used when making the porridge for the reapers' morning meal in harvest, as shall be described afterwards. The dresser *g* should be of the same material as that of the kitchen. There should be iron hooks fastened into the roof for hanging any article thereon. Shelving is also useful in a scullery.

(230.) The outside walls and ceiling of the *kitchen-pantry* should be lathed, and all the walls and ceiling plastered. The flooring should be of the same material as that of the kitchen, or of hard brick. The shelving *o* should be of wood of several tiers, the lowest row being 3½ feet above the floor. The movable portion of the window should be protected with fly zinc-gauze, and so also the side and door of the larder *l*. A few iron hooks in the roof will be found useful for hanging up game or fowls. A set of steps for reaching above an ordinary height is convenient in a pantry.

(231.) The outside walls and ceiling of the *milk-house* should be lathed, and the walls and roof plastered. The flooring should be of polished pavement, for the sake of coolness. The windows should be protected in the moveable part with fly zinc-gauze, which is much better than wire-gauze; and the side and door of the lock-up closet *n* should also be lined with zinc-gauze. The best shelving for a milk-house is marble, and though this substance may appear extravagant in a farm-house, the price of marble is now so much reduced, that it is worth the extra expense, the import of foreign marble being now free. Marble is always cool, and easily cleaned and freed of stains. Scottish marble is hard and unequal of texture. The grey-veined marble from Leghorn is therefore preferable, though the black marble of the county of Galway in Ireland is equally good; but the grey colour has a coolness and freshness about it in a dairy, which the black does not possess. Polished pavement is the next best material for coolness, but it is very apt to stain with milk or butter, and the stains are difficult of removal. I speak from experience, and know the labour required to keeping stone-shelving in a milk-house always sweet and clean; and, let me say farther, unless it is so kept, any other material is preferable to it. If marble be rejected on account of expense, I would recommend stout shelving of beech or plane-tree, as being smooth, and hard, and easily kept clean. This shelving should be 2 feet broad, 1½ inch thick, and, to be convenient, should not exceed the height of 3 feet from the floor.

(232.) It is necessary to make the wall which separates the kitchen and scullery from the milk-house and pantry of brick or stone, to keep the latter apartments more cool, and less likely to be affected by the heat and vapour, which must of necessity sometimes escape from the former. It would no doubt be *convenient* for the removal of dishes to have a door communicating between the scullery and milk-house; but it is much better to avoid every risk of contamination from a place which must at times be filled with vapours injurious to milk,—a substance which is at all times delicately susceptible of injury.

(233.) The windows of all the apartments should be provided with *shutters on the inside;* and it may be a safe precaution against nocturnal intruders, to protect those of the milk-house and pantry with iron stancheons on the outside, as they should, occasionally at least, be left open even all night.

(234.) On this side of the kitchen will be observed a stair. It is 4 feet in width, and intended to lead to the storey above the kitchen floor, as also to the upper storey of the principal part of the house. The storey above the kitchen may be subdivided in this way. Let a continuation of the brick or stone wall which separates the kitchen and scullery from the milk-house and kitchen-pantry be carried up, in the form of a partition of lath and plaster, to the roof of the second storey, which may be 9 feet in height, as seen on the right of *g*, fig. 33. The

Fig. 33.

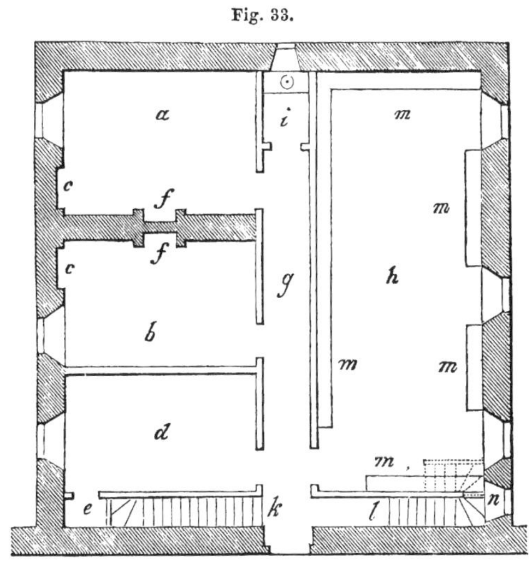

CHEESE-ROOM, &C. OF FARM-HOUSE.

wall of the kitchen flue *b* should, of course, be carried up to a chimney-stalk above the ridging, containing at least 4 flues from below, one of the kitchen fire, one of the small furnace-pot of the kitchen, one of the oven, and one of the large furnace-pot in the scullery; but there should also be one from the room above the scullery, and one from one of the rooms above the kitchen; and, to render both kitchen and scullery as wholesome by ventilation as possible, there should be a small flue from the ceiling of each to carry off heated air and vapour. The kitchen stalk would thus contain 6 flues from below and 2 from above.

(235.) The upper storey should be partitioned off in the way as seen in fig. 33. Let the apartment *a* above the scullery be fitted up with a fire-place *f* as a *bed-room* for the female servants, having a closet *c* in the outer wall. After taking off a passage *g* of 3½ feet in width along the whole length of this part of the house, this room will be 14 feet long and 10 feet wide. The space above the kitchen may be divided into 2 *bed-rooms*, one *b*, 14 feet in length, by 9 feet in width, and 9 feet in height, with a fire-place *f* and window, and closet *c*. This might be occupied as a sitting-room and bed-room by the housekeeper, if the services of such a person are required; if not, it might serve as a large store-room, with a fire-place which would be useful for various purposes. The other room *d*, 14 feet in length by 8 feet 3 inches in width, and 9 feet in height, having a window in it, but no fire-place, might be fitted up as a *bed-room for occasional stranger servants.* This latter apartment has a closet *e* in it, 3 feet in width by 2 feet in depth, directly above the lock-up closet *c* off the kitchen.

(236.) At the end of the passage is a *water-closet i*, lighted by a window in the gable of the jamb. The size of the water-closet is 5 feet 3 inches by 3½ feet. Its cistern is supplied with water from the cistern that supplies the sink in the scullery, and its soil-pipe could descend in an appropriate recess in the wall. The window of the water-closet could give light to the *passage g* by a glass-window above the water-closet door, or the passage could be lighted by a cupola in the roof, or it could be lighted from the cheese-room *h* by two windows in the lath and plaster wall, each of which could have a pane to open into the cheese-room for the purpose of ventilation.

(237.) The entire space above the kitchen-pantry and milk-house may be appropriated to a *cheese-room h*, 29 feet 3 inches in length on the floor, 12 feet in width, and 9 feet in height, having 3 windows in it. Besides the floor, proper shelving *m* should be put up for the accommodation of the cheese, in its various stages towards maturity; and the lower halves of the windows should be provided with Venetian shutters, outside of the glass, to regulate the air into the room when the windows are opened.

(238.) If there is sufficient room in the roof above these various apartments for a *garret*, access can be obtained to it by a stair at *l*, which would have to return upon itself in ascending the 9 feet, the height of the storey, and both this stair and the one *k* down to the kitchen could be lighted by the window *n*. If there is no garret, then the cheese-room will be 32 feet 3 inches in length, by dispensing with the stair *l*. The window *n* could then be also dispensed with.

(239.) These dimensions of kitchen and other apartments would be suited to the farm-house of a farm of from 500 to 1000 acres, under the mixed husbandry. The milk-house may, perhaps, be large enough for even a dairy-farm of ordinary extent; but should it be too small for that purpose, it might easily be enlarged by increasing either or both the length and breadth of the building.

(240.) It is, I dare say, well enough known, that the milk-house and cheese-room windows in farm-houses are *exempt from window-tax*, if the names of the apartments are painted, in conspicuous letters of not less than one inch in height, over their respective windows.

(241.) After going so fully into the specifications required for building a steading, it is quite unnecessary for me to do the same in regard to that part of the farm-house which contains the kitchen, milk-house, &c. Suffice it to enumerate a few articles which are particularly required for this part of the house.

(242.) The prices of these requisites, including the cost of carriage, are:—

Masonry.

		L.	S.	D.
Polished jambs and lintels for kitchen and rooms,	per square foot	0	0	10
... Arbroath hearths and pavement, .	per ditto	0	1	0
... stone skirting, 6 inches deep, . .	per lineal foot	0	0	6
... stone sink in scullery, 2 feet 6 inches long by 1 foot 9 inches broad, . .	per square foot	0	1	3
... shelves and supports for milk-house, single measure, ...	per ditto	0	1	0
... Marble-shelves, 1 inch thick, . .	per ditto	0	6	0

Carpentry.

		L.	S.	D.
Wall-straps, 1 inch square by 12 inches from centres,	per sq. foot	0	0	6
Standard walls, 3½ inches by 2 inches, and 16 inches from centres, ...	per ditto	0	1	6
Sills and runtrees for ditto, 3½ inches by 2 inches.	per lineal foot	0	0	2½
Boards and fillets for deafening, . . .	per square yard	0	1	1
Borders for hearths, 3 inches by 1¼ inch, .	per lineal foot	0	0	3
Corner beads, ¾ inch diameter, . . .	per ditto	0	0	2½
Ceiling-joisting, 3 inches by 1½, and 16 inches from centres, ...	per square yard	0	1	6
Windows with ¾ astragal bars, double hung, and glazed with best second crown-glass, . .	per square foot	0	2	9
2-inch flush and bead-bound outer back-door,	per ditto	0	1	4
2-inch bound room-doors, with sunk planted mouldings on both sides, ...	per ditto	0	1	0
1½-inch bound doors for closets and presses, with planted mouldings outside, and sunk mouldings on back, ...	per ditto	0	0	10
1¾-inch bound moulded doors for kitchen, &c.,	per ditto	0	0	11
1½-inch bound moulded doors for closets and presses, ...	per ditto	0	0	10
1½-inch bound shutters, and 1-inch bound back-folds, with planted mouldings in face, .	per ditto	0	0	10
1¼-inch bound breasts, elbows, soffits, and door jamb-linings, with planted mouldings, .	per ditto	0	0	9½
1½ bound moulded shutters, ...	per ditto	0	0	10
¾-inch backfolds with cross-beads, . .	per ditto	0	0	6

Carpentry (continued).

		L.	S.	D.
¾-inch deal linings for breasts, elbows, soffits, and jambs of doors, with fixtures,	per square foot	0	0	5
Jamb mouldings, with grounds,	per lineal foot	0	0	6
Double-faced architraves, 6 inches broad,	per ditto	0	0	7
Single-faced architraves, 5 inches broad,	per ditto	0	0	5
Facings, keps, skirtings, and copings, reduced to 4 inches broad	per ditto	0	0	3
1½-inch base moulding, with plinth, 6 inches by 1 inch,	per ditto	0	0	7
Plain plinth, 6 inches by ¾ inch,	per ditto	0	0	4
Black-birch handrail, 3 inches by 2 inches, moulded,	per ditto	0	1	0
Wooden chimney-pieces for bedrooms,	each	0	10	6
Fitting up wood-work of the seat of the water-closet, 3½ feet, complete,		1	10	0
Ditto, if done with black birch,		3	0	0
1½-inch deal cistern for scullery, properly supported, to contain 120 gallons,		1	0	0
1¼-inch deal cistern for water-closet, properly supported, to contain 80 gallons,		0	12	0
Kitchen-dresser, with 3 drawers, stout framing, sparred bottom, front doors, and 2-inch hardwood top,		3	0	0
1½-inch hardwood shelving for milk-house, when preferred to stone,	per square foot	0	1	0
Steps for pantry, 2½ feet high,		0	5	0
6 Black American chairs,	each	0	6	0
3 Stools,	ditto	0	2	6
			to	
		0	3	6
Stout deal table, 5 feet long by 4 feet broad, with drawer,		1	0	0
Small cupola, glazed with best second crown-glass, for passage,		3	0	0

Iron and Brass Work.

		L.	S.	D.
8-inch Scotch made iron rim-lock for back-door, with barrel-bolt, and 7-inch double joints,		0	18	0
7-inch iron rim-locks, Scotch make, and 6-inch double joints,	each	0	10	0
Fine press-locks, with brass mountings, and 5-inch joints,	ditto	0	4	6
Common ditto,	ditto	0	3	6
Fine water-closet latch, with snibbing-bolt and 5-inch joints,		0	6	0
Diagonal back-bar for kitchen, &c., shutters,	ditto	0	4	6
Back-bars for other windows, 12 inches by 18 inches long,	ditto	0	2	6
Strong hook-and-eye fasteners,	ditto	0	1	6
Brass sash-lifters,	per pair	0	0	9
Brass counter-check spring fasteners,	each	0	1	6
Common screw fasteners,	ditto	0	1	0
1¼-inch brass shutter-knobs,	per pair	0	0	9
3-inch shutter hinges,	ditto	0	0	6
1½-inch backfold hinges,		0	0	6
Plain ¾-inch iron ballustres for stair,	per lb.	0	0	3
¾-inch ball-cock and ball,	each	0	9	0

Iron and Brass Work (continued).

		L.	S.	D.
$2\frac{1}{2}$-inch brass waste and washers for cisterns,	each	0	5	0
$2\frac{1}{2}$-inch brass table-washer and chain for sink,	ditto	0	3	0
$\frac{3}{4}$-inch brass nose-cocks,	ditto	0	4	6
Boilers,	per cwt.	0	14	0
3-inch cess-pools,	each	0	5	6
Force-pump, $2\frac{1}{2}$ inch,		4	15	0

Plumber-work.

		L.	S.	D.
Large moulded cistern-heads,		0	18	0
Lining 120-gallon cistern with 7 lb. lead on the bottom, and 6 lb. lead on the sides,		3	0	0
Lining 80-gallon cistern, as ditto,		1	11	0
$2\frac{1}{2}$-inch waste-pipe, of 6 lb. lead,	per lineal foot	0	1	4
$\frac{3}{4}$-inch supply-pipe, of 6 lb. lead,	per yard	0	0	8
$4\frac{1}{2}$-inch soil-pipe, of 6 lb. lead,	per lineal foot	0	2	0
Service-boxes,	each	0	6	0
Patent water-closet, complete,		3	3	0
$1\frac{1}{2}$ inch lead pipe for force-pump,	per lineal foot,	0	1	3

Plaster-work.

		L.	S.	D.
Best 3 coat plaster,	per square yard,	0	0	5 to
		0	0	6
Composition deafening for floors run over with thin lime,	per ditto,	0	1	0
Plain cornices, runbeads, and arises, 12-inch girth and under,	per lineal foot,	0	0	$3\frac{1}{2}$
Base-mouldings, plinths, &c. plastered with plaster-lime,	per ditto	0	0	3

Zinc-work.

		L.	S.	D.
Fly-cloth for milk-house windows, larder, &c.,	per square foot	0	0	9
Window-sashes for ditto,	per ditto	0	0	$9\frac{1}{2}$
Folding skylights to hold 4 panes,	each	0	10	0
18-inch milk-pails, a good average size,	ditto	0	3	9
Others are 3d. per inch, more or less as the diameter increases or diminishes from this size.				
Milk-sieves,	ditto	0	1	0

(243.) In regard to the relative positions which the farm-house and steading should occupy, it has been remarked by a recent writer, that " It is generally advised that the farm-house should be placed directly in front: to which, however, it may be objected that it casts a shade over the southern entrance of the yard if very near, and if too far off, its distance will be found to be inconvenient. Perhaps the best situation is on one side of the farm-yard, with the common parlour and kitchen opening nearly into it: farmers may talk as they like about unhealthy odours arising from the stables and yards, but there never was any one injured by them, and they cannot keep too close an eye upon their servants and stock."* If farmers " cannot keep too close an eye upon their ser-

* British Husbandry, vol. i. p. 86.

vants and stock," and if the position of their houses will enable them to do so, they should do something more than place them " on one side of the farm-yard:" they must remain constantly in them, and cause "their servants and stock" to be continually in sight in the farm-yard, otherwise their watching will be of no avail; for when the servants come to know that the house has been placed there merely to watch their proceedings, they at least, if not the stock, can and will easily avoid the particular place constantly overlooked by the house. The truth is, and every farmer knows it, that it is not the spot occupied by his house, whether here or there, that maintains his authority over his servants: he knows that he himself must be " up and doing" in the fields, in the farm-yard, everywhere—" be stirring with the lark,"

" From morn to noon, from noon to dewy even,"—

ere he can ascertain whether his servants are doing their work well, and his stock thriving well. Inconvenience to himself in going a great distance betwixt his house and the steading, will induce the farmer to place his house *near* rather than at a distance from the steading. He wishes to be within call,—to be able to be on the spot in a few seconds, when his presence is required in the farm-yard, the stable, the byre, or the barn; but more than this he does not want, and need not care for. Place your house, therefore, if you have the choice, on some pleasant spot, neither " direct in front" nor much in the rear of the steading. If there be no such spot at hand, make one for your house, place it there, and dwell in it, with the comfortable assurance that your servants will not regard you the less, or your stock thrive the worse, because you happen to live beyond the influence of the " unhealthy odours arising from your stables and yards,"—odours, by the way, of the unpleasantness of which I never heard a farmer complain. No one of that class but a sloven would place his house beside a dunghill.

---

18. OF THE PERSONS WHO LABOUR THE FARM.

" *John.* Labour in thy vocation :—
Geo. Thou hast hit it: for there's no better sign of a brave mind than a hard hand."

HENRY VI. *Part II.*

(244.) Those who labour a farm form the most important part of its materiel; they are the spirit that conducts its operations. You should, therefore, become early acquainted with those functionaries. They are the farmer himself, the steward or grieve, the ploughman, the hedger or labourer, the shepherd, the cattle-man, the field-worker, and the dairy-maid. These have each duties to perform, which, in their respective spheres, should harmonize and never interfere with each other. Should any occurrence happen to disturb the harmony of labour, it must arise from some misapprehension or ignorance in the interfering party, whose aberrations must be rectified by the presiding power. I shall consider the duties in the order I have mentioned the respective agents.

(245.) And first, those of the *farmer*. It is his province to originate the entire system of management,—to determine the period for commencing and pursuing every operation,—to issue general orders of management to the steward, when there is one, and if there be none, to give minute instructions to the ploughmen for the performance of every separate field operation,—to exercise a general superintendence over the field-workers,—to observe the general behaviour of all,—to see if the cattle are cared for,—to ascertain the condition of all the crops,—to guide the shepherd,—to direct the hedger or labourer,—to effect the sales of the surplus produce,—to conduct the purchases conducive to the progressive improvement of the farm,—to disburse the expenses of management,—to pay the rent to the landlord,—and to fulfil the obligations incumbent on him as a residenter of the parish. All these duties are common to the farmer and the steward engaged to manage a farm. An independent steward and a farmer are thus so far on the same footing; but the farmer occupies a loftier station. He is his own master,—makes bargains to suit his own interests,—stands on an equal footing with the landlord in the lease,—has entire control over the servants, hiring and discharging them at any term he pleases,—and possesses power to grant favours to servants and friends. The farmer has not all those duties to perform in any one day, but in the course of their proper fulfilment, daily calls are made on his attention, and so large a portion of his time is occupied by them, that he finds little leisure to go far from home, except in the season when few operations are performed on a farm, viz. the end of summer. These are the professional duties of the *farmer;* but he has those of domestic and social life to fulfil, like every other member of society. If a farmer fulfils all his duties as he ought to do, he cannot be said "to eat the bread of idleness."

(246.) The duty of the *steward*, or *grieve*, as he is called in some parts of Scotland, and *bailiff* in England, consists in receiving general instructions from his master the farmer, which he sees executed by the people under his charge. He exercises a direct control over the ploughmen and field-workers; and unreasonable disobedience on their part of his commands is reprehended as strongly by the farmer, as if the affront had been offered to himself: I say *unreasonable* disobedience, because the farmer is the judge of whether the steward has been reasonable in his demands. It is the duty of the steward to enforce the commands of his master, and to check every deviation from rectitude he may observe in the servants against his interests. Although he should thus protect the interests of his master from the attacks of any servant, yet it is not generally understood that he has control over the shepherd, the hedger, or the cattle-man, who are stewards, in one sense, over their respective departments of labour. The farmer reveals to the steward alone the plans of his management; intrusts him with the keys of the corn-barn, granaries, and provision-stores; delegates to him the power to act as his representative on the farm in his absence; and takes every opportunity of shewing confidence in his integrity, truth, and good behaviour. When a steward conducts himself with discretion in his master's absence, and exhibits at all times a considerate mind, an active person, and an honest heart, he is justly regarded as a valuable servant.

(247.) Personally, the farm-steward does not always labour with his own hands; verifying, by his judicious superintendence, on a large farm at least, the truth of the adage, that "one head is better than two pair of hands." He should, however, always deliver the daily allowance of corn to the horses. He should, moreover, be the first person out of bed in the morning, and the last in it at night. On most farms he does work: he sows the seed-corn in spring, superintends the field-workers in summer, tends the harvest-field and builds the stacks in autumn, and thrashes the corn with the mill, and cleans it with the winnowing-machine, in winter. On some farms he even works a pair of horses, like a common ploughman; in which case he cannot personally sow the corn, superintend the workers, build the stacks, or thrash the corn, unless another person takes charge of his horses for the time. This is an objectionable mode of employing a steward; because the nicer operations,—such as sowing corn, &c. or the guidance of his horses,—must be intrusted to another, and most likely inferior, person. But in by far the greatest number of cases, the steward does not work horses: on the contrary, when a ploughman qualifies himself to become a steward, it is chiefly with the view of enjoying immunity from that species of drudgery. In any event, he should be able to keep an account of the work-people's time, and of the quantity of grain thrashed, consumed on the farm, and delivered to purchasers.

(248.) Stewards are not required on all sorts of farms. On pastoral farms, his species of service would be of no use, as it is on arable land that these are really required. Anywhere, his services are the most valuable where the greatest multiplicity of subjects demand attention. Thus, he is a *more* useful servant on a farm of mixed husbandry, than on one in the neighbourhood of a town, or on a carse farm. But even on some farms of mixed culture, the services of a steward are dispensed with altogether; in which case the farmer himself gives his orders directly to the ploughmen, or indirectly through the hedger or cattle-men, as he may choose to appoint to receive his instructions. In such a case the same person is also intrusted to corn the horses; for the ploughmen themselves are never intrusted with that business, as they are apt to abuse such a trust by giving too much corn to the horses, to their probable injury. The same person performs other parts of a steward's duty; such as sowing corn, superintending field-workers, and thrashing corn; or those duties may be divided betwixt the cattle-man and hedger. On the large farm in Berwickshire on which I learned farming, there was no steward, the cattle-man delivering the master's orders and corning the horses, and the hedger sowing the corn, building the stacks, and thrashing the corn. The object of this arrangement was to save the wages of a steward, when the farmer himself was able to undertake the general superintendence. I conducted my own farm for several years without a steward.

(249.) The duties of a *ploughman* are clearly defined. The principal duty is to take charge of a pair of horses, and work them at every kind of labour for which horses are employed on a farm. Horse-labour on a farm is various. It is connected with the plough, the cart, sowing-machines, the roller, and the thrashing-mill, when horse-power is employed in the thrashing of corn; so that the knowledge of a ploughman should comprehend a variety of subjects. In the fulfilment of his duties, the ploughman has a long day's work to perform; for, besides expending the appointed hours in the fields with the horses, he must groom them before he goes to the field in the morning and after he returns from it in the evening, as well as at midday between the two periods of labour. Notwithstanding this constant toil, he must do his work with alacrity and good will; and when, from any cause, his horses are laid idle, he must not only attend upon them as usual, but must himself work at any farm-work he is desired. There is seldom any exaction of labour from the ploughman beyond the usual daily hours of work, these occupying at least 12 hours a day for 7 months of the year, that being a sufficient day's work for any man's strength to endure. But occasions do arise which justify the demand of a greater sacrifice of his time, such as seed-time, hay-time, and harvest. For such encroachments upon his time, many opportunities occur of repaying him with indulgence, such as a cessation from labour, especially in bad weather. It is the duty of the ploughman to work his horses with discretion and good temper, not only for the sake of the horses, but that he may execute his work in a proper manner. It is also his duty to keep his horses comfortably clean. Ploughmen are never placed in situations of trust; and thus, having no responsibility beyond the care of their horses, there is no class of servants more independent. There should no partiality be shewn by the master or steward to one ploughman more than to another, as it is the best policy to treat all alike who work alike. An invidious and reprehensible practice exists, however, in some parts of the country, of setting them to work in an order of precedency, which is maintained so strictly as to be practised even on going to and returning from work, one being appointed *foreman*, whose movements must guide those of the rest. Should the foreman prove a slow man, the rest must not go a single bout more than he does; and if he is active, they may follow as best they can. Thus, whilst his activity confers no benefit to the farmer beyond its own work, his dulness discourages the activity of the others. This consideration alone should be sufficient ground for farmers to abolish the practice at once, and put the whole of their ploughmen on the same footing. I soon saw the evils attending the system, and put an end to it on my own farm. When one ploughman displays more skill than the rest, it is sufficient honour for him to be intrusted to execute the most difficult pieces of work; and this sort of preference will give no umbrage to the others, as they are as conscious of his superiority in work as the farmer himself can possibly be. The services of ploughmen are required on all sorts of farms, from the carse-farm to the pastoral, on which the greatest and the least portion of arable culture are practised.

(250.) The *hedger*, the *spade-hind*, the *spadesman*, as he is indifferently called, is a useful servant on a farm. He is strictly a labourer, but one of a high grade. His principal duty is to take charge of the hedge fences and ditches of the farm, and cut and clean them as they require in the course of the season. He also renews old fences, and runs new ones betwixt fields. He makes cuts with the spade across ridges, for the surface-water to find its way to the ditches. He is an experienced drainer. He is dexterous in the use of the spade, the shovel, and the pick, and he handles the small cutting-axe and switching-knife with the force and neatness with which a dragoon wields his sabre. As the principal business of a hedger is performed in winter, he has much leisure in the other seasons to assist at other work. He can sow corn and grass-seeds in spring; shear sheep and mow the hay in summer; and build and thatch stacks in autumn. He can also superintend the field-workers in summer, and especially in the weeding of the hedges. The hedger is a very proper person to superintend the making of drains, which, when done on a large scale, is generally executed by hired labourers on piece-work. It is thus obvious, that the hedger is an accomplished farm-servant. It may truly be said of him, what cannot be said of all farm-servants,—

" That worlds of earth are only clods,
Compared with him who digs their sods."

Hedgers are not required on all sorts of farms. They would be of little use on pastoral farms, where fences are few, and most of them elevated beyond the growth of thorns; nor on farms whose fences are formed of stone-walls; nor on carse-farms, which are seldom fenced at all. On the last class of farms, they might be usefully employed as ditchers and makers of channels for surface-water; but on such, ploughmen are usually employed as ditchers when the land is wet. The usual practice on carse farms of transforming ploughmen into spadesmen, and laying horses idle, I would say is one "more honoured in the breach than the observance," inasmuch as the labour of horses is always more valuable than that of men. On this subject, Sir John Sinclair has a few just remarks. " In a considerable farm," he says, " it is of the utmost consequence to have servants specially appropriated for each of the most important departments of labour; for there is often a great loss of time, where persons are frequently changing their employments. Besides, where the division of labour is introduced, work is executed not only more expeditiously, but also much better, in consequence of the same hands being constantly employed in one particular department. For that purpose, the ploughmen ought never to be employed in manual labour, but regularly kept at work with their horses, when the weather will admit of it."* In the combination of arable with stock culture, the services of the hedger are indispensable. Still, the farm that would give him full employment should be of large extent. A *small* farm cannot maintain either a steward or a hedger. In a choice of the two servants, on a small farm, I would recommend the hedger as the more useful servant of the two, provided the farmer himself understands his business thoroughly. I make this proviso, because the hedger *may not* understand every department of husbandry, although he generally does, having most probably worked a pair of horses in his youth; while a steward must of necessity understand farming, otherwise he can have no pretensions to the appellation; but it is certain that he can in no case be a substitute for a hedger.

(251.) The services of a *shepherd*, properly so called, are only required where a flock of sheep are constantly kept. On carse-farms, and those in the neighbourhood of large towns, he is of no use; nor is he required on those farms on which sheep are bought in to be fed off in winter. On pastoral farms, on the other hand, as also those of the mixed hus-

* Sinclair's Code of Agriculture, p. 71.

bandry, his services are so indispensable that they could not be conducted without him. His duty is to undertake the entire management of the sheep, and when he bestows the pains he should on his flock, he has little leisure for any other work. His time is occupied from early dawn, when he should be among his flock before they rise from their lair, and during the whole day, to the evening, when they again lie down for the night. To inspect a large flock at least three times a day over extensive bounds, implies a walking to fatigue. Besides this daily exercise, he has to attend to the feeding of the young sheep on turnips in winter, the lambing of the ewes in spring, the washing and shearing of the fleece in summer, and the bathing of the flock in autumn. And over and above these major operations, there are the minor ones of weaning, milking, drafting, and marking, at appointed times; not to omit the unwearied attention to be bestowed, for a time, on the whole flock to evade the attacks of insects. It will readily be seen from this summary of duties, that the shepherd has little time to bestow beyond the care of his flock. As no one but a shepherd, thoroughly bred, can attend to sheep, there must be one where a standing sheep-flock is kept, whatever may be the extent of farm. On a *small* farm, his whole time may not be occupied in his profession, when he can make as well as mend nets, prepare stakes for them, and assist the hedger (if there be one) to keep the fences in repair; or he may act as groom, and take charge of the horse and gig, and go errands to the post-town; or he may undertake the duties of steward. On *large* pastoral or mixed husbandry farms, more than one shepherd is required. The establishment then consists of a *head* shepherd, and one or more young men training to be shepherds, who are placed entirely under his control. The office of head shepherd is one of great trust. Sheep being individually valuable, and in most instances consisting of large flocks, a misfortune happening to them, from whatever cause, must incur great loss. On the other hand, the care and skill of the shepherd may secure a good return for the capital invested in sheep. The shepherd acts the part of butcher in slaughtering the animals used on the farm. The only assistance which he depends upon in personally managing his flock, is that of his faithful dog, whose sagacity in that respect is little inferior to his own.

(252.) The services of the *cattle-man* are most wanted at the steading in winter, when the cattle are all housed. He has the sole charge of them. It is his duty to clean out the cattle-houses, and supply the cattle with food, fodder, and litter, at appointed hours every day, and to make the food ready for them, should prepared food be given them. The business of tending cattle being matter of routine, the qualifications of a cattle-man are not of a high order. In summer and autumn, when the cows are at grass, it is his duty to bring them into the byre or to the gate of the field, as the case may be, to be milked at their appointed times; and it is also his duty to ascertain that the cattle in the fields are plentifully supplied with food and water. He should see the cows served by the bull in due time, and keep an account of the cows' reckonings of the time of calving. He should assist at the important process of calving. As his time is thus only occasionally employed in summer, he frequently undertakes the superintendence of the field-workers. In harvest, he is usefully employed in assisting to make and carry food to the reapers, and may lend a hand at the taking in of the corn. As cattle occupy the steading in winter on all kinds of farms, the services of the cattle-man appear indispensable; but all his functions may be performed by the shepherd, where only a small flock of sheep are kept. The office of the cattle-man is not one of trust nor of much labour. An elderly person answers the purpose quite well, the labour being neither constant nor heavy, but well-timed and methodical. The cattle-man ought to exercise much patience and good temper towards the objects of his charge, and a person in the decline of life is most likely to possess those qualities.

(253.) *Field-workers* are indispensable servants on every farm devoted to arable culture. They mostly consist of young women in Scotland, but more frequently of men and boys in England; and yet, there are many manual operations much better done by women than men. In hand-picking stones and weeds, in filling drains, and in barn-work, they are far more expert, and do them more neatly, than men. The duties of field-workers, as their very name implies, are to perform all the manual operations of the fields, as well as those with the smaller implements, which are not worked by horses. The *manual* operations consist chiefly of cutting and planting the sets of potatoes, gathering weeds, picking stones, collecting the potato crop, and filling drains with stones. The operations with the smaller implements are pulling turnips and preparing them for feeding stock and storing in winter, performing barn-work, carrying seed-corn, spreading manure upon the land, hoeing potatoes and turnips, and weeding and reaping corn-crops. A considerable number of field-workers are required on a farm, and they are generally set to work in a band. They work most steadily under superintendence. The steward, the hedger, or cattle-man, should superintend them when the band is large; but when small, one of themselves, a staid person, who is capable of taking the lead in work, may superintend them well enough, provided she has a watch to mark the time of work and rest. But field-workers do not always work by themselves; being at times associated with the work of the horses, when they require no particular superintendence. On some farms, it is considered economical to lay the horses idle, and employ the ploughmen at their labours rather than engage field-workers. This may be one mode of avoiding a little outlay of money; but there is no true economy in allowing horses "to eat off their own heads," as the phrase has it; and besides, ploughmen *cannot* possibly do light work so well as field-workers. In manufacturing districts field-workers are scarce; but were farmers generally to adopt the plan of employing a few constantly, and hire them for the purpose by the half year, instead of employing a large number at times, young women would be induced to adopt field-labour as a profession, and become very expert in it. It is steadiness of service that makes the field-workers of the south of Scotland so superior to the same class in other parts of the country.

(254.) The duties of the *dairy-maid* are well defined. She is a domestic servant, domiciliated in the farm-house. Her principal duty is, as her name implies, to milk the cows, to manage the milk in all its stages, bring up the calves, and make into butter and cheese the milk that is obtained from the cows after the weaning of the calves. The other domestics generally assist her in milking the cows and feeding the calves, when there is a large number of both. Should any lambs lose their mothers, the dairy-maid should bring them up with cow's milk until the time of weaning, when they are returned to the flock. At the lambing season, should any of the ewes be scant of milk, the shepherd applies to the dairy-maid to have his bottles replenished with warm new milk for the hungered lambs. The dairy-maid also milks the ewes after the weaning of the lambs, and makes cheese of the ewe-milk. She should attend to the poultry, feed them, set the brooders, gather the eggs daily, take charge of the broods until able to provide for themselves, and see them safely lodged in their respective apartments every evening, and let them abroad every morning. It is generally the dairy-maid, when there is no housekeeper, who gives out the food for the reapers, and takes charge of their articles of bedding. The dairy-maid should be an active, attentive, and intelligent person.

(255.) These are the duties of the respective classes of servants found on farms. You may not require all these classes on your farm, as you have seen that some sorts of farms do not require the services of all. You have seen that a pastoral-farm has no need of a steward, but of a shepherd; a carse-farm no need of a shepherd, but of a steward; a farm in the neighbourhood of a town no need of a hedger, but of a cattle-man;

and on a dairy-farm, no need of a shepherd but of a dairy-maid; but in the case of a farm of mixed husbandry, there is need of all these classes.

(256.) And now that you have seen how multifarious are the duties of them all, you will begin to perceive how intricate an affair mixed husbandry is, and how well informed a farmer should be of every one of these varieties of labour, before he attempts to manage for himself. To give you a stronger view of this, conceive the quantity and variety of labour that must pass through the hands of these various classes of work-people in the course of a year, and then imagine the clear-headedness of arrangement which a farmer should possess, to make all their various labours coincide in every season, and under every circumstance, so as to produce the most desirable results. It is in its variety that the success of labour is attained: In other words, it is in its subdivision that the facility of labour is acquired, and it is by the intelligence of the labourers that perfection in it is attained. And vain would be the endeavours of any farmer to produce the results he does, were he not ably seconded by the general intelligence and admirable efficiency of his labourers.

---

19. OF THE WEATHER IN WINTER.

> " See Winter comes to rule the varied year,
> Sullen and sad, with all his rising train
> Vapours, and clouds, and storms. Be these my theme."
>
> THOMSON.

(257.) As the weather, at all seasons, has undeniably a sensible power to expedite or retard the field operations of the farm, it becomes an incumbent duty on you, as pupils of agriculture, to ascertain the principles which regulate its phenomena, in order to anticipate their changes and avoid their injurious effects. It is, no doubt, difficult to acquire an accurate knowledge of the laws which govern the subtile elements of nature; but experience has proved that *accurate observation of atmospherical phenomena* is the chief means which we possess of becoming acquainted with those laws.

(258.) In saying that the weather has power to alter the operations of the farm, I do not mean to assert that it can entirely change any great plan of operations that may have been determined on, for that may be prosecuted even in spite of the weather; but there is no doubt that the weather can oblige the farmer to pursue a different and much less efficient treatment towards the land than he desires, and that the amount and quality of its produce may be very seriously affected by the change of treatment. For example, the heavy and continued rain in autumn 1839 made the land so very wet, that not only the summer-fallow, but the potato-land, could not be seed-furrowed, and the inevitable consequence was, that sowing of the wheat was postponed until the spring of 1840, and in many cases the farmers were obliged to sow barley instead of wheat. The immediate effect of this remarkable interference of the weather was restriction of the breadth of land appropriated to autumnal wheat, and the consequent extension of that intended for barley and spring wheat,—a change that caused so much work in spring, that it had the effect of prolonging the harvest of 1840 beyond the wished-for period, and of otherwise deranging the calculations of farmers.

(259.) Now, when such a change is, and may in any season be, imposed upon the farmer, it becomes a matter of prudence as well as of desire to become so acquainted with usual atmospherical phenomena as to anticipate the nature of the weather that is to come. If he could anticipate particular changes of weather by observing peculiar phenomena, he could arrange his operations accordingly. But is such anticipation in regard to the weather attainable? No doubt of it; for, although it is not as yet to be expected that minute changes of the atmosphere can be anticipated, yet the *kind* of weather which is to follow—whether rainy or frosty, snowy or fresh—may be predicted. We all know the prescience actually attained by people whose occupations oblige them to be much in the open air and to observe the weather. In this way shepherds and sailors, in their respective circumstances, have acquired such a knowledge of atmospherical phenomena as to be able to predict the advent of important changes of the atmosphere; and to shew that the sort of knowledge acquired is in accordance with the circumstances observed, it is obvious that, even among these two classes of observers, great difference of acquirements exists on account of diversity of talent for observation. For example. A friend of mine, a commander of one of the ships of the East India Company, became so noted, by observation alone, for anticipating the probable results of atmospherical phenomena in the Indian seas, that his vessel has frequently been seen to ride out the storm, under bare poles, while most of the ships in the same convoy were more or less damaged. As an instance of similar sagacity in a shepherd, I remember in the wet season of 1817, when rain was predicted as inevitable, by every one engaged in the afternoon of a very busy day of leading in the corn, the shepherd interpreted the symptoms as indicative of wind and not of rain, and the event completely justified his prediction.

(260.) I conceive that greater accuracy of knowledge in regard to the changes of the weather may be attained on land than at sea, because the effects of weather on the sea itself enters as an uncertain element into the question. It is generally believed, however, that seamen are more proficient than landsmen in foretelling the weather; and, no doubt, when the imminent danger, in which the lives of seamen are jeopardized, is considered, the circumstance may reasonably be supposed to render them peculiarly alive to *certain* atmospherical changes. To men, however, under constant command, as seamen are, it is questionable whether the *ordinary* changes of the atmosphere are matters of much interest. In every thing that affects the safety of the ship, and the weather among the rest, every confidence is placed by the crew in the commanding officer, and it is he alone that has to exercise his weather wisdom. On the other hand, every shepherd has to exercise his own skill in regard to the weather, to save himself, perhaps, much unnecessary personal trouble, especially on a hill-farm. Even the young apprentice-shepherd soon learns to look out for himself. The great difference in regard to a knowledge of the weather betwixt the sea-captain and the farmer, though both are the sport of the same elements, consists in this, that the captain has to look out for himself, whereas the farmer has his shepherd to look out for him: the sea-faring commander himself knowing the weather, directs his men accordingly; whilst the farmer does not know it nearly so well as his shepherd, and probably even not so well as his ploughmen. See the effects of this difference of acquirement in the circumstances of both. The captain causes the approaching change to be met by prompt and proper appliances; whereas the farmer is too frequently overtaken in his operations from a want of the knowledge probably possessed by his shepherd or ploughmen. You thus see the *necessity of farmers acquiring a knowledge of the weather*.

(261.) It being admitted that prescience of the state of the weather is essential to the farmer, the question is, how the pupil of agriculture is to acquire it? No doubt it can best be attained by observation in the field; but as that method implies the institution of a series of observations extending over a long period of years, a great part of the lifetime of the pupil might pass away ere he could acquire a sufficient stock of knowledge by his own experience. This being the case, it is but right and fair that he should know what the experience of others is. This I shall endeavour to communicate, premising that he must observe for himself, after being made acquainted with the *manner of conducting* his own observations.

(262.) The simplest way for me to communicate what has been established in regard to the observation of atmospherical phenomena, is, in the first place, to describe to you the various instruments which have, from time to time, been contrived to indicate those phenomena; and to put these instruments into a right use, you should become well acquainted with their respective modes of action, which are all dependent on strictly scientific principles. All the instruments required are the *barometer, thermometer, weathercock, hygrometer, and rain-gauge.* The principles upon which these instruments operate shall be separately explained; the phenomena of the clouds and winds, upon which the diversity of the states of the atmosphere appear so much to depend, shall be described; and the efficacy of the electric agency, which seems to affect so many of the phenomena observed, shall be noticed. The general principles of atmospherical phenomena being thus considered in this place, I shall have no more occasion to recur to them, but will only have to notice the characteristic phenomena of each season as they occur.

(263.) *Atmospherical phenomena being the great signs by which to judge of the weather*, instruments are used to detect their changes which cannot be detected by the senses. These instruments possess great ingenuity of construction, and they all indicate pretty accurately the effects they are intended to recognise. But though they tell us nothing but the truth, such is the minute diversity of atmospherical phenomena, that they do not tell us all the truth. Other means for discovering that must be used; and the most available within our reach is the converting of the phenomena themselves into indicators of atmospherical changes. In this way, we may use the transient states of the atmosphere, in regard to clearness and obscurity, dampness or dryness, as they affect our senses of sight and feeling, the shapes and evolutions of the clouds, and the peculiar state of the wind, into means by which to predicate the changes of the weather. But this kind of knowledge can only be acquired by long observation of natural phenomena.

(264.) The most important instrument, perhaps, the most popular, certainly, for indicating changes of the atmosphere, is the *Barometer*, an instrument so universally known and used by farmers, that a particular description of it is here unnecessary. This instrument is formed to be placed either in a fixed position or to be portable. As it is only used in the portable shape to measure the altitude of mountains, the method of using it need not be here described. For a fixed position, the barometer is made either of the figure of an upright column or of a wheel. Whether it is because that the divisions on the large circular disc, pointed out by the long index of the wheel-barometer, are more easily observed than the variations of the column of mercury in the perpendicular one, is the reason which renders the wheel-barometer more popular among farmers, I know not; but were they to consider that its indications cannot be so delicate as those of the upright form, because of the machinery which the oscillations of the mercury have to put in motion before the long index can indicate any change, the upright form would always be preferred. It is true that the tube of the upright barometer is generally made too small, and is perhaps so made to save mercury and make the instrument cheaper, but a small tube has the disadvantage of increasing the friction of the mercury in its passage up and down the tube. On this account, the mercury is apt to be kept above its proper level when falling, and to be depressed below its proper height when rising. To obviate this inconvenience, a tap of the hand against the case of the instrument is required to bring the mercury to its proper position. The tendency of the mercury to rise may be observed by the convex or raised form of the top of the column; and the hollow or concave form indicates its tendency to fall.

(265.) In observing the state of the barometer, too much regard should not be had to the numerals and words usually written on the graduated scale, placed along the range of the top of the column of mercury; because it is the rising or falling of the mercury alone that is to be taken as indicative of a change of weather, whatever may be its actual height in the tube. The greatest height attained by the column is entirely determined by the height of elevation of the place of observation above the level of the sea. The higher the place is above the sea, the mean height of the column will be the lower. For example, on comparing two barometers at the same time, at two places of different heights in the same part of the country, and subject to the same general climate, one may stand as high as 30 inches, and the other only at 29½ inches. According to the usual markings of barometers, the mercury at the first place would stand at "Fair," whereas, at the other place, it would be at "Changeable." This difference of the mercury is in itself important, but it does not arise from any difference in the state of the air, as indicative of a change of weather, but merely from the difference of elevation of the two places above the level of the sea. The mercury is as near its greatest height at 29½ inches at the higher place, as it is at 30 inches at the lower place, in reference to their respective positions above the sea; and this being the case, and other circumstances equal, it will be the same weather at both places. This difference of the height of the mercury is explained in this way. The barometer being the instrument which indicates the weight or pressure of the atmosphere, as its name implies, it is found on trial that the mercury stands highest at the level of the sea, and that it descends as elevation above the sea increases. The depression has been found by experiment to be $\frac{1}{10}$ of an inch for about every 88 feet of elevation, or more correctly as given in this table.*

TABLE SHEWING THE NUMBER OF FEET OF ALTITUDE CORRESPONDING TO DEPRESSIONS OF THE BAROMETER.

Depression.	Altitude in feet.	Depression.	Altitude in feet.
.1	87	.6	527
.2	175	.7	616
.3	262	.8	705
.4	350	.9	795
.5	439	1 inch.	885

(266.) It becomes, then, a matter of some importance for you, in order to place explicit reliance on the changes indicated by your barometer, to ascertain the height of your farm above the level of the sea. If you know that by other means, namely, by trigonometry, then the allowance in the table will give you its true elevation; but should you not be acquainted with its elevation, which is usually the case with farmers, the mean height of the barometer can be ascertained by a series of simple observations, made at a given time, over a year or more. For example, "the sum of one year's observations, made at 10 A.M. and 10 P.M. in 1827 was 21615.410 inches, and this number divided by the number of observations, 730, or twice the number of days in that year, gave 29.610 inches as the mean height or changeable point of the barometer."† Now, taking the mean height of the barometer at 29.948 inches at the mean level of the sea, where the atmosphere always indicates the greatest density, deduced from nine years' observations at the mean temperature of the air, with a range from 28 inches to 31 inches, it is seen that the instance adduced above of 29.610 inches gives .338 of an inch less than the mean, which, by the table, indicates an elevation of the place of observation of about 265 feet above the mean level of the sea. It is from the mercury being above or below this point of 29.610 inches in the supposed place of your farm, that you are to conclude what

* Quarterly Journal of Agriculture, vol. iii. p. 5.

† Ibid. p. 3.

weather may be expected at that place, from the changes of the barometer. From the want of this knowledge, farmers are generally led into the mistake of supposing that the words "Fair," "Change," "Rain," engraved on the scale of the barometer, indicate such weather in all places, when the mercury stands at them. The best way to correct this mistake is to have these words engraved at the heights truly applicable to the particular place of observation. Notwithstanding this source of common error, the barometer is a generally useful instrument, inasmuch as its indications foretel the same results at all seasons, with perhaps only this exception, those of the effects of heat in summer, which cannot of course be noticed in winter.

(267.) The general indications of the barometer are few, and may easily be remembered. A high and stationary mercury indicates steady good weather. A slow and regular fall indicates rain; and if during an E. wind, the rain will be abundant. A sudden fall indicates a gale of wind, and most probably from the W. Good steady weather must not be expected in sudden depressions and elevations of the mercury. A fine day may intervene, but the general state of the weather may be expected to be unsteady. An E. or NE. wind keeps up the mercury against all other indications of a change. A W. or SW. wind causes a fall when the wind changes from E. or NE.; but should no fall take place, the maintenance of the height, in the circumstances, is equivalent to a rise, and the reverse of this is equivalent to a fall. The quantity affected by these particular causes may be estimated at $\frac{2}{10}$ of an inch.* The barometer, at sea, is a good indicator of wind but not of rain. When the barometer is used within doors, the best situation for it is in any room where the temperature is equal, and not exposed to sunshine. The cost of a perpendicular barometer of good workmanship is from L.1 : 11 : 6 to L.2 : 12 : 6, according to taste and finish; that of a wheel-barometer from L.2, 2s. to L.5, 5s. The barometer was invented by Torricelli, a pupil of Galileo, in 1643.

(268.) Among the variable causes which affect the barometer is the direction of the wind. The maximum of pressure is when the wind is NE., decreasing in both directions of the azimuth till it reaches the minimum between S. and SW. This difference amounts to above $\frac{3}{10}$ of an inch at London. The variation occasioned by the wind may be owing to the cold which always accompanies the E. winds in spring, connected as they probably are with the melting of the snow in Norway; but it is not unlikely to be owing, as Mr Meikle suggests, to its opposition to the

* Quarterly Journal of Agriculture, vol. iii. p. 2.

direction of the rotation of the earth causing atmospherical accumulation and pressure, by diminishing the centrifugal force of the aerial particles.*

(269.) The accidental variations of barometric pressure are greatly influenced by latitude. At the equator it may be said to be nothing, hurricanes alone causing any exception. The variability increases towards the poles, owing probably to the irregularity of the winds beyond the tropics. The mean variation at the equator is 2 lines,† in France 10 lines, and in Scotland 15 lines, throughout the year, the quantity having its monthly oscillations. These do not appear to follow the parallels of latitude, but, like the isothermal lines, undergo inflections, which are said to have a striking similarity to the isoclinal magnetic lines of Hansteen. If so, it is probably by the medium of temperature that these two are connected. More lately, M. Kämtz has pointed out the connection of the winds with such changes, and he has illustrated the influence of the prevalent aerial currents which traverse Europe, though not with apparent regularity, yet, at least, in subjection to some general laws.‡

(270.) The *Sympiesometer* was invented by Mr Adie, optician in Edinburgh, as a substitute for the common barometer. Its indications are the same, with the advantage of having a longer scale. For the measurement of heights this instrument is very convenient, from its small size admitting of its being carried in the coat-pocket, and not being subject to the same chances of accident as the portable barometer. The height is given in fathoms on the instrument, requiring only one correction, which is performed by a small table engrayed on its case. It is stated to be delicately sensible of changes at sea, particularly of gales. Not being an instrument which has been brought into general use, though Professor Forbes is convinced it might be, I need not allude to it farther here.§

(271.) The next instrument which claims our attention is the *Thermometer*. As its name implies, it is a measurer of heat. It is undoubtedly the most perfect of our meteorological instruments, and has been the means of establishing the most important facts to science; but being a mere measurer of temperature, it is incapable of indicating changes of the atmosphere so clearly as the barometer, and is therefore a less

* Edinburgh New Philosophical Journal, vol. iv. p. 108.

† A line = twelfth part of an inch.

‡ Forbes' Report on Meteorology, vol. i. p. 235-6.

§ See Edinburgh Journal of Science, vol. x. p. 334, for a description of this ingenious instrument; and New Series, vol. iv. pp. 91 and 329.

useful instrument to the farmer. Regarding the ordinary temperature of the atmosphere, the feelings can judge sufficiently well; and as the condition of most of the productions of the farm indicates pretty well whether the climate of a particular locality can bring any species of crop to perfection, the farmer seems independent of the use of the thermometer. Still, it is of importance for him to know the lowest degree of temperature in winter, as certain kinds of farm produce are injured by the effects of extreme cold, of which the feelings are incapable, from want of habit, of estimating their power of mischief. For this purpose, a thermometer self-registering the lowest degree of cold will be found a useful instrument on a farm. As great heat does no harm, a self-registering thermometer of the greatest heat seems not so useful an instrument as the other two.

(272.) "The thermometer, by which the temperature of our atmosphere was determined," says Mr John Adie of Edinburgh, "was invented by Sanctario in 1590. The instrument, in its first construction, was very imperfect, having no fixed scale, and air being the medium of expansion. It was soon shewn, from the discovery of the barometer, that this instrument was acted upon by pressure as well as temperature. To separate these effects, alcohol was employed as the best fluid, from its great expansion by heat, but was afterwards found to expand unequally. Reamur first proposed the use of mercury as the expansive medium for the thermometer. This liquid metal has great advantages over every other medium; it has the power of indicating a great range of temperature, and expands very equally. After its introduction, the melting point of ice was taken as a fixed point, and the divisions of the scale were made to correspond to $\frac{10}{1000}$th parts of the capacity of the bulb. It was left for the ingenious Fahrenheit to fix another standard point that of boiling water under the mean pressure of the atmosphere, which is given on his scale at 212°; the melting point of ice at 32°. This scale of division has almost universally been adopted in Britain, but not at all generally on the Continent. The zero of this scale, though an arbitrary point adopted by Fahrenheit, from the erroneous idea that the greatest possible cold was produced by a mixture of common salt and snow, has particular advantages for a climate like ours; besides being generally known, the zero is so placed that any cold which occurs very rarely causes the mercury to fall below that point, so that no mistake can take place with regard to noting minus quantities. The only other divisions of the thermometer between the two fixed points in general use, are those of Reaumur and the centesimal; the former divides the space into 80 equal parts; the division of the latter, as indicated by its name, is into 100 parts. In both these scales the zero is placed at the melting point of ice, or 32° Fahrenheit."* The self-registering thermometers were the invention of the late Dr John Rutherfurd, and his are yet the best. The tube of the one for ascertaining the greatest degree of heat is inclined nearly in a horizontal position and filled with mercury, upon the top of the column of which stands an index, which, on being pushed upwards, does not return until made to descend to the top of the mercury by elevating the upper end of the thermometer. This index was first made of metal, which became oxydized in the tube, and uncertain in its motions. Mr Adie, optician in Edinburgh, improved the instrument, by introducing a fluid above the mercury, in which is floated a glass index, which is free from any action, and is retained in its place by the fluid. "The other thermometer, for registering the lowest degree," says Mr John Adie, "is filled with alcohol, having an index of black glass immersed in the liquid. This index is always carried down to the lowest point to which the temperature falls; the spirit passes freely upwards without changing the place of the index, so that it remains at the lowest point. This instrument, like the other, turns upon a centre, to depress the upper end, and allow the index, by its own weight, to come into contact with the surface of the spirit, after the greatest cold has been observed, which is indicated by the upper end of the index, or that farthest from the bulb. In both cases, the instruments are to be left nearly horizontal, the bulb end being lowest. This angle is most easily fixed by placing the bulb about ¾ of an inch under the horizontal line."†

(273.) Thermometers of all kinds, when fixed up for observation, should be placed out of the reach of the direct rays of the sun or of any reflected heat. If at a window or against a wall, the thermometer should have a northern aspect, and be kept at a little distance from either; for it is surprising through what a space a sensible portion of heat is conveyed from soil and walls, or even from grass illuminated by the sun. The maxima of temperature, as indicated by thermometers, are thus generally too great; and from the near contact in which thermometers are generally placed with large ill-conducting masses, such as walls, the temperature of the night is kept up, and the minima of temperature are thus also too high. The price of a common thermometer is from 5s. 6d. to 14s.; and of Rutherfurd's minimum self-registering thermometer 10s. 6d.

(274.) Many highly interesting results have been obtained by the use

* Quarterly Journal of Agriculture, vol. iii. p. 5.

† Ibid. p. 7.

of the thermometer, and among the most interesting are those regarding the mean temperature of different localities. In prosecuting this subject, it was found that a diurnal oscillation took place in the temperature as well as the pressure of the atmosphere, and that this again varies with the seasons. Nothing but frequent observations during the day could ascertain the mean temperature of different places; and in so prosecuting the subject, it was discovered that there were hours of the day, the mean temperature of which, for the whole year, was equal to the mean of the whole 24 hours, which, when established, would render all future observations less difficult. The results exhibit an extraordinary coincidence.

Thus the mean of 1824 gave	13′ past	9	A. M.	and	26′ past	8	P. M.
... ... 1825 ...	13′ ...	9	...	...	28′ ...	8	...
Giving the mean of the 2 years	13′ ...	9	...	...	27′ ...	8	...

These results were obtained from a series of observations made at Leith Fort in the years 1824 and 1825 by the Royal Society of Edinburgh.* Some of the other consequences deducible from these observations are, "that the mean hour of the day of minimum temperature for the year is 5 A. M., and that of maximum temperature 40 past 2 P. M.: that the deviation of any pair of hours of the same name from the mean of the day is less than half a degree of Fahrenheit, and of all pairs of hours, 4 A. M. and P. M., are the most accurate: that the mean annual temperature of any hour never differs more than 3°.2 from the mean of the day for the whole year: that the mean daily range is a minimum at the winter solstice, and a maximum in April: and that the mean daily range in this climate is 6°.065."† The mean temperature at Leith Fort for the mean of the two years, at an elevation of 25 feet above the mean level of the sea, was found to be 48°.36. The mean, taken near Edinburgh, at an altitude of 390 feet above the mean level of the sea, at 10 A. M. and P. M., with a common thermometer, and with the maximum and minimum results of self-registering thermometers, gave these results when reduced to the mean level of the sea:—with the self-registering thermometers 48°.413, and with two observations a-day with the common thermometer 48°.352, which correspond remarkably with the observations at Leith Fort. These observations were taken at 10 A. M. and 10 P. M., which were found to be the particular hours which gave a near approximation to the mean temperature of the day; but had they

* Edinburgh Philosophical Transactions, vol. x.

† Forbes' Report on Meteorology, vol. i, p. 212.

been made at the more correct periods of 13′ past 9 A. M. and 27′ past 8 P. M., it is probable that the results with those at Leith Fort would have corresponded exactly.* The mean temperature of any place may be ascertained pretty nearly by observing the mean temperature of deep-seated springs, or that of deep wells. Thus the Crawley Springs, in the Pentland Hills, which supply Edinburgh with abundance of water, situated at an elevation of 564 feet above the level of the sea, give a mean temperature of 46°.3, according to observations made in 1811 by Mr Jardine, civil-engineer, Edinburgh; and the Black Spring, which is 882 feet above the level of the sea, gave a mean temperature of 44°.9, by observations made in the course of 1810–11–15–18–19. A well in the Cowgate of Edinburgh gave a mean temperature of 49°.3, by observations made every month in the year 1794, of which the temperature of the month of June approached nearest to the mean temperature of the year, being 49°5.†

(275.) The measurement of the humidity of the atmosphere is a subject of greater importance in a scientific than in a practical point; for however excellent the instrument may be for determining the degree of humidity, the atmosphere has assumed the humid state before any indication of the change is noticed on the instrument, and in this respect it is involved in the same predicament as the thermometer, which only tells the existing heat, and both are less useful on a farm than the barometer, which indicates an approaching change. No instrument has yet been contrived by which the quantity of moisture in the air can be ascertained from inspection of a fixed scale, without the use of tables to rectify the observation. The instrument used for ascertaining the moisture of the air is appropriately termed a *Hygrometer*. Professor Leslie was the first to construct a useful instrument of this kind. His is of the form of the differential thermometer, having a little sulphuric acid in it; and the cold is produced by evaporation of water from one of the bulbs covered with black silk, which is kept wetted, and the degree of evaporation of the moisture from the bulb indicates the dryness of the air.

(276.) Another method of ascertaining the moisture of the atmosphere, is by the dew-point hygrometer of Professor Daniells; but this instrument is considered rather difficult of management, except in expert hands.

(277.) The best hygrometer is that of Dr Mason, which consists of two thermometers, fastened upright to a stand having a fountain of wa-

* Quarterly Journal of Agriculture, vol. iii. p. 9.

† Ibid., p. 10–11.

ter in a glass tube placed betwixt them, and out of which the water is taken up to one of the bulbs by means of black floss silk. When the air is very dry, the difference between the two thermometers will be great, if moist, less in proportion, and when fully saturated, both will be alike. The silk that covers the wet bulb, and thread which conveys the water to it, requires renewal about every month, and the fountain is filled when requisite with distilled water, or water that has been boiled and allowed to cool, by immersing it in a basin of the water till the aperture only is just upon the surface, and the water will flow into it. For ordinary purposes of observation, it is only necessary to place the instrument in a retired part of the room away from the fire, and not exposed to weather, open doors, or passages; but for nice experiments the observations should always be made in the open air and in the shade, taking especial care that the instrument be not influenced by the radiation of any heated bodies, or any currents of air. When the hygrometer is placed out of doors in frosty weather, the fountain had better be removed, as the freezing of the water within may cause it to break; in this case, a thin coating of ice may soon be formed on the wet bulb, which will last a considerable time wet, and be rewetted when required.

(278.) Very simple hygrometers may be made of various substances, to shew whether the air is more or less humid at any given time. One substance is the awn of the Tartarian and wild oats, which, when fixed in a perpendicular position to a card, indicates, by its spiked beard, the degree of humidity. A light hog's bristle split in the middle, and riding by the split upon the stem of the awn, forms a better index than the spike of the awn itself. To adjust this instrument, you have only to wet the awn and observe how far it carries round the index, and mark that as the lowest point of humidity, and then subject the awn to the heat of the fire for the highest point of dryness, which, when marked, will give betwixt the two points an arc of a circle, which may be divided into its degrees. I have used such an instrument for some time. When two or more are compared together, the mean of humidity may be obtained. The awns can be renewed at pleasure. With regard to confiding in the truth of this simple hygrometer, the precaution of Dr Wells is worth attention. "Hygrometers formed of animal and vegetable substances," he says, "when exposed to a clear sky at night, will become colder than the atmosphere, and hence, by attracting dew, or, according to an observation of Saussure, by merely cooling the air contiguous to them, mark a degree of moisture beyond what the atmosphere actually contains. This serves to explain an observation made by M. de Luc, that in serene and calm weather, the humidity of the air, as determined by a hygrometer, increases about and after sunset with a greater rapidity than can be attributed to a diminution of the general heat of the atmosphere." * The principle of this sort of hygrometer may serve to explain a remarkable natural phenomenon. "Hygrometers were made of quills by Chiminello, which renders it probable that birds are enabled to judge of approaching rain or fair weather. For it is easy to conceive that an animal having a thousand hygrometers intimately connected with its body, must be liable to be powerfully affected, with regard to the tone of its organs, by very slight changes in the dryness or humidity of the air, particularly when it is considered that many of the feathers contain a large quantity of blood, which must be alternately propelled into the system, or withdrawn from it, according to their contraction or dilatation by dryness or moisture." † Does Virgil allude to a hygrometric feeling in birds when he says—

> "Wet weather seldom hurts the most unwise,
> So plain the signs, such prophets are the skies:
> The wary crane foresees it first, and sails
> Above the storm, and leaves the lowly vales." ‡

(279.) The *Weather-cock* is a very useful instrument to the farmer. It should be erected on a conspicuous part of the steading, which may readily be observed from one of the windows of the farm-house. Its position on the steading may be seen in fig. 1, Plate I., and fig. 3, Plate III. Its cardinal points should be marked with the letters N. E. S. W., to shew at a glance the true points of the compass. The vane should be fitted up with a ball or box containing oil, which may be renewed when required. There is not a neater or more appropriate form for a vane than an arrow, whose dart is always ready to pierce the wind, and whose butt serves as a governor to direct it to the wind's eye. The whole should be gilt, to prevent the rusting of the iron. Mr Forster had such a vane erected at his place of residence, which had a small bell suspended from its point which struck upon the arms pointing to the direction of the compass, and announced every change of wind.§ Such a contrivance may be considered a conceit, but it has the advantage of letting you know when the wind shifts much about, as when it does, there is as little chance of settled weather as in the frequent changes of the barometer. A better contrivance of the bell would be to have a hammer suspended from the dart by a supple spring, and a bell of different tone attached

* Wells on Dew, p. 64.

† Edinburgh Encyclopædia, art. *Hygrometry.*

‡ Dryden's Virgil, i. Georgics, 514.

§ Forster's Researches into Atmospherical Phenomena, p. 203.

to each of the arms which indicate the point of the compass, and the different toned bells, when struck, would announce the direction in which the wind most prevailed. Besides bells, there is a contrivance for indicating the directions of the wind by an index on a vertical disc, like the dial-plate of a clock, an instance of which may be seen in the western tower of the Register-House in Edinburgh. This would be a very convenient way of fitting up a weather-cock.

(280.) With regard to the origin of the name of *weather-cock*, Beckmann says, that vanes were originally cut out in the form of a cock, and placed on the tops of church spires, during the holy ages, as an emblem of clerical vigilance.* The Germans use the same term as we do, *wetterhahn;* and the French have a somewhat analogous term in *coq de clocher*. As the vane turns round with every wind, so, in a moral sense, every man who is " unstable in his ways," is termed a weather-cock.

(281.) In reference to the wind is another instrument called the *Anemometer*, or measurer of the wind's intensity. Such an instrument is of little value to the farmer, who is more interested in the direction than the intensity of the wind, as it is that property of it which has most effect in promoting changes of the weather. It must be admitted, however, that the intensity of the wind has a material effect in modifying the climate of any locality, such as that of a farm elevated in the gorge of a mountain pass. Still, even there its direction has more to do in fixing the character of the climate than the intensity; besides, the anemometer indicates no approach of wind, but only measures its force when it blows, and this can be sufficiently well appreciated by the senses. The mean force of the wind for the whole year at 9 A. M. is 0.855, at 3 P. M. 1.107, and at 9 P. M. 0.605.

(281.) The best instrument of this class is Lind's anemometer, which, although considered an imperfect one, is not so imperfect, according to the opinion of Mr Snow Harris of Plymouth, who has paid more attention to the movements of the wind than any one else in this country, as is generally supposed. Lind's anemometer " consists of two glass tubes about 9 inches long, having a bore of $\frac{4}{10}$ of an inch. These are connected, at their lower extremities, by another small tube of glass, with a bore of $\frac{1}{10}$ of an inch. To the upper extremity of one of the tubes is fitted a thin metallic one bent at right angles, so that its mouth may receive horizontally the current of air. A quantity of water is poured in at the mouth, till the tubes are nearly half full, and a scale of inches and parts of an inch is placed betwixt the tubes. When the wind blows in at the

* Beckmann's History of Inventions, vol. i.

mouth, the column of water is depressed in one of the tubes, and elevated in the same degree in the other tube; so that the distance between the surface of the fluid in each tube is the length of a column of water, whose weight is equivalent to the force of the wind upon a surface equal to the base of the column of fluid. The little tube which connects the other two is made with a small aperture, to prevent the oscillation of the fluid by irregular blasts of wind. The undulations produced by sudden gusts of wind would be still more completely prevented by making the small tube, which connects the other two large ones, of such a length as to be double between the other two, and be equal to the length of either. The same effect might also be produced by making a thin piece of wood float upon the surface of the fluid in each tube."*

(283.) Another meteorological instrument is the *Rain-gauge*. This instrument is of no use to the farmer as an indicator of rain, and, like some of the rest which have been described, only professes to tell the quantity of rain that actually has fallen in a given space, yet even for this purpose it is an imperfect instrument.† "The simplest form of this instrument," says Mr John Adie, "is a funnel, with a cylindrical mouth, 3 or 4 inches high, and having an area of 100 square inches, made of tinned iron or thin copper. It may be placed in the mouth of a large bottle for receiving the water, and, after each fall, the quantity is measured by a glass jar, divided into inches and parts. A more elegant arrangement of the instrument is formed by placing the funnel at the top of a brass cylindrical tube, having at one side a glass tube, communicating with it at the under part, with a divided scale placed alongside of it. The area of the mouth is to that of the under tubes as 10 : 1; consequently 1 inch deep of rain falling into the mouth will measure 10 inches in the tubes, and 1 inch upon the scale will be equal to a fall of $\frac{1}{10}$ of an inch, which quantities are marked upon the scale, and the water is let off by a stop-cock below. The instrument should be placed in an exposed situation, at a distance from all buildings and trees, and as near the surface of the ground as possible. . . . In cases of snow-storms the rain-gauge may not give a correct quantity, as a part may be blown out, or a greater quantity have fallen than the mouth will contain. In such cases, the method of knowing the quantity of water is, to take any cylindrical vessel, such as a case for containing maps, which will answer the purpose very well; by pressing it perpendicularly into the snow it will bring out with it a cylinder equal to the depth. This,

* Edinburgh Encyclopædia, art. *Anemometer*.

† See Thomson's History of the Royal Society, p. 509.

when melted, will give the quantity of water by measurement. The proportion of snow to water is about 17 : 1, and hail to water 8 : 1. These quantities, however, are not constant, but depend upon the circumstances under which the snow or hail has fallen, and the time they have been upon the ground."* The cost of a rain-gauge, according as it is fitted up, is L.1, 5s., L.2 : 12 : 6, and L.4, 4s.

(284.) These are the principal instruments employed by meteorologists to ascertain atmospherical changes, and seeing their powers and uses, as now described, you can select those which appear to you most desirable to possess. Of them all, only two are *indicators of approaching changes*, the barometer and the weather-cock, and these, of good construction, you will of course have, whichever of the others you may choose to possess.

(285.) Besides these two instruments, there are objects in nature which indicate changes of the weather. Of these the *Clouds* are eminent premonitors. It may at first sight be supposed that clouds, exhibiting so great a variety of forms, cannot be subject to any positive law; but such a supposition is erroneous, because no phenomenon in nature can possibly occur, but as the effect of some physical law, although the mode of action of the law may have hitherto eluded the acutest search of philosophical observation. It would be unphilosophical to believe otherwise. We may therefore depend upon it, that every variety of cloud is an effect of a definite cause. If we cannot predict what form of cloud will next ensue, it is because we are unacquainted with the precise process by which they are formed. But observation has enabled meteorologists to classify every variety of form under only three primary figures, and all other forms are only combinations of two or more of these three.

(286.) 1. The first simple form is the *Cirrus*, a word which literally means a curl, or lock of hair curled. 2. The second is the *Cumulus* or heap. 3. And the third is the *Stratus* or bed or layer. Combinations of these three give the four following forms, the names of which at once indicate the simple forms of which they are composed. 1. One is *Cirro-Cumulus*, or combination of the curl and heap. 2. Another is the *Cirro-Stratus*, or combination of the curl and stratus. 3. A third is the *Cumulo-Stratus*, or combination of the heap and the stratus. 4. And, lastly, there is the combination of the *Cumulo-Cirro-Stratus*, or that combination of all the three simple forms, which has received the name of *Nimbus* or rain-cloud. The English names usually given by writers to some of these forms of clouds are very singular, and seemingly not

* Quarterly Journal of Agriculture, vol. iii. p. 13.

very appropriate. The curl is an appropriate enough name for the cirrus, and so is the rain-cloud for the nimbus; but why the heap should be called the *stacken-cloud,* the stratus the *fall-cloud,* the curled heap the *sonder-cloud,* the curled stratus the *wane-cloud,* and the heaped stratus the *twain-cloud,* is by no means obvious, unless this last form, being composed of *two* clouds, may truly be denominated a *twain*-cloud; but, on the same principle, the cirro-cumulus and the cirro-stratus and the cumulo-stratus may be termed *twain*-clouds. We must, however, take the nomenclature which the original and ingenious contriver of the classification of clouds, Mr Luke Howard of London, has given.

(287.) The first form of clouds which demands your attention is the *Cirrus* or curl-cloud. This is the least dense of all clouds. It is composed of streaks of vapour of a whitish colour arranged with a fibrous structure, and occurring at a great height in the atmosphere. These fibrous streaks assume modified shapes. Sometimes they are like long narrow rods, lying quiescent, or floating gently along the upper region of the atmosphere. At other times one end of the rod is curled up, and spread out like a feather; and, in this shape, the cloud moves more quickly along than the other, being evidently affected by the wind. Another form is that familiarly known by the " grey mare's tail" " or goat's beard." This is more affected by the wind than even the former. Another form is in thin fibrous sheets, expanded at times to a considerable breadth, like the gleams of the aurora borealis. There are many other forms, such as that of net-work, bunches of feathers, hair, or thread, which may respectively be designated reticulated, plumose, comoid, and filiform cirri.

(288.) In regard to the relative heights at which these different forms of cirri appear, I would say that the fibrous rod assumes the highest position in the air; the rod with the turned up end the next highest; the bunch of feathers is approaching the earth; the mare's tail is descending still farther; and the sheet-like form is not much above the denser clouds. Sometimes the fibrous rod may be seen stretching between two denser clouds, and it is then supposed to be acting as a conductor of electricity between them.

(289.) As to their relative periods of duration, the fibrous rod may be seen high in the air for a whole day in fine weather; or it vanishes in a short time, or descends into a denser form. When its end is turned up, its existence is hastening to a close. The plumose form soon melts away; the grey-mare's tail bears only a few hours of pretty strong wind; but the broad sheet may be blown about for some time.

(290.) The sky is generally of a grey-blue when the fibrous rod and hooked rod are seen; and it is of the deepest blue when the plumose watery cirrus appears. It is an observation of Sir Isaac Newton, that the deepest blue happens just at the changes from a dry to a moist atmosphere.

(291.) The cirrus cloud frequently changes into the complete cirro-cumulus, but it sometimes forms a fringed or softened edge to the cirro-stratus; and it also stretches across the heavens into the density of a cirro-stratus. Of all the seasons, the cirrus appears least frequently in winter.

(292.) The *Cumulus* may be likened in shape to a heap of natural meadow hay. It never alters much from that shape, nor is it ever otherwise than massive in its structure; but it varies in size and colour according to the temperature and light of the day, becoming larger and whiter as the heat and light increase; hence it generally appears at sun-rise, assumes a larger form by noon, often screening the sun from the earth, and then melts away towards night. On this account it has received the designation of the "cloud of day." Its density will not allow it to mount very high in the air; but it is, nevertheless, easily buoyed up for a whole day by the vapour plane above the reach of the earth. When it so rests it is terminated below by a straight line. It is a prevailing cloud in the daytime at all seasons, and is exceedingly beautiful when it presents its silvery tops tinted with sober colours against the bright blue sky. Cumuli sometimes join together and as suddenly separate again, though in every case they retain their peculiar form. They may often be seen floating in the air in calm weather, not far above the horizon; and they may also be seen driving along with the gale at a greater height, casting their fleeting shadows on the ground. When in motion, their bases are not so straight as when at rest. Cumuli, at times, disperse, mount into the air, and form cirri, or they descend into strati along the horizon; at others a single cumulus may be seen at a distance in the horizon, and then increasing rapidly into the storm-cloud, or else overspreading a large portion of the sky with a dense veil. Does the poet allude to the cumulus, as seen in a summer afternoon, in these breathing words?

> "And now the mists from earth are clouds in heaven,
> Clouds slowly castellating in a calm
> Sublimer than a storm; which brighter breathes
> O'er the whole firmament the breadth of blue,
> Because of that excessive purity
> Of all those hanging snow-white palaces,
> A gentle contrast, but with power divine."*

* Wilson.

(293.) The *Stratus* is that bed of vapour which is frequently seen in the valleys in a summer evening, permitting the trees and church spires to stand out in bold relief; or it is that horizontal bank of dark cloud seen to rest for a whole night along the horizon. It also forms the thin dry white fogs which come over the land from the sea with an east wind in spring and summer, wetting nothing that it touches. When this dry fog hangs over towns in winter, which it often does for days, it appears of a yellow hue, in consequence, probably, of a mixture with smoke. It constitutes the November fog in London. The stratus is frequently elevated by means of the vapour plane, and then it passes into the cumulus. On its appearing frequently in the evening, and its usual disappearance during the day, it has been termed the "cloud of night." Having a livid grey colour when the moon shines upon it, the stratus is probably the origin of those supposed spectral appearances seen at night by superstitious people in days of yore. The light or dry stratus is most prevalent in spring and summer, and the dense or wet kind in autumn and winter.

(294.) "*Cirrus*," remarks Mr Mudie, "is the characteristic cloud of the upper sky; and no cloud of denser texture forms, or is capable of being sustained there. *Cumulus* is, in like manner, the characteristic cloud of the middle altitude; and although it is sometimes higher and sometimes lower, it never forms at what may be called the very top of the sky, or down at the surface of the ground. *Stratus* is the appropriate cloud of the lower sky, and it is never the first formed one at any considerable elevation; and, indeed, if it appears unconnected with the surface, it is not simple stratus, but a mixed cloud of some kind or other."*

(295.) The forms of the clouds which follow are of mixed character, the first of which that demands our attention is a compound of the cirrus and cumulus, or *cirro-cumulus*, as it is called. The cirrus, in losing the fibrous, assumes the more even-grained texture of the cumulus, which, when subdivided into small spherical fragments, constitute small cumuli of little density, and of white colour, arranged in the form of a cirrus or in clusters. They are high in the air, and beautiful objects in the sky. In Germany this form of cloud is called "the little sheep;" which idea has been embodied by a rustic bard of England in these beautiful lines:—

> " Far yet above these wafted clouds are seen
> (In a remoter sky, still more serene,)

* Mudie's World, p. 263.

> Others, detach'd in ranges through the air,
> Spotless as snow, and countless as they're fair;
> Scatter'd immensely wide from east to west,
> The beauteous 'semblance of a flock at rest."*

Cirro-cumuli are most frequently to be seen in summer.

(296.) Another form of cloud, compounded of the cirrus and stratus, is called *cirro-stratus*. While cirri descend and assume the form of cirro-cumuli, they may still further descend and take the shape of cirro-stratus, whose fibres become dense and decidedly horizontal. Its characteristic form is shallowness, longitude, and density. It consists at times of dense longitudinal streaks, and the density is increased when a great breadth of cloud is viewed horizontally along its edge. At other times it is like shoals of small fish, when it is called a "herring sky;" at others, mottled like a mackerel's back, when it is called the "mackerel-back sky." Sometimes it is like veins of wood, and at other times like the ripples of sand left by a retiring tide on a sandy beach. The more mottled it is, the cirro-stratus is higher in the air, and the more dense and stratified, the nearer it is the earth. In the last position, it may be seen cutting off a mountain top, or stretching behind it, or cutting across the tops of large cumuli. Sometimes its striated lines, not very dense, run parallel over the zenith, whose opposite ends apparently converge at opposite points of the horizon, and then they form that peculiar phenomenon named the "boat," or "Noah's ark." At times cirro-strati cut across the field of the setting sun, where they appear in well-defined dense striæ, whose upper or lower edges, in reference to their position with the sun, are burnished with the most brilliant hues of gold, crimson, or vermilion. Sometimes the cirro-stratus extends across the heavens in a broad sheet, obscuring more or less the light of the sun or moon, for days together, and in this case a halo or corona is frequently seen to surround these orbs. In a more dense form, it assumes the shapes of some small long-bodied animals, and even like architectural ornaments; and in all its mutations it is more varied than any other form of cloud. The streaked cirro-strati are of frequent occurrence in winter and autumn, whereas the more delicate kinds are most seen in summer.

(297.) A third compound cloud is formed of the cumulus and stratus, called *cumulo-stratus*. This is always a dense cloud. It spreads out its base to the stratus form, and, in its upper part, frequently inosculates with cirri, cirro-cumuli, or cirro-strati. In this form it is to be seen in the plate of the three cows. With all or either of these it forms a large

* Bloomfield.

massive series of cumulative clouds which hang on the horizon, displaying great mountain shapes, raising their brilliantly illuminated silvery crests towards the sun, and presenting numerous dusky valleys between them. Or it appears in formidable white masses of variously defined shapes, towering upwards from the horizon, ready to meet any other form of cloud, and to conjoin with them in making the dense dark-coloured storm-cloud. In either case, nothing can exceed the picturesque grandeur of their towering dazzling forms, or the sublimity of their masses when surcharged with lightnings, wind, and rain, and hastening with scowling front to meet the gentle breeze, and hurrying it along in its determined course, as if impatient of restraint, and all the while casting a portentous gloom over the earth, until bursting with terrific thunder, scorching with lightning some devoted object more prominent than the rest, deluges the plain with sweeping floods, and devastates the fields in the course of its ungovernable fury. A tempest soon exhausts its force in the temperate regions; but in the tropics it rages at times for weeks, and then woe to the poor mariner who is overtaken by it at sea unprepared. Of the cumulo-stratus the variety called "Bishops' wigs," as represented near the horizon in the plate of the draught-mare, may be seen at all seasons along the horizon, but the other and more imposing form of mountain scenery is only to be seen in perfection in summer, when storms are rife. It also assumes the shapes of larger animals, and of the more gigantic forms of nature and art. Is the cumulo-stratus the sort of cloud described by Shakspeare as presenting these various forms?

> "Sometime, we see a cloud that's dragonish;
> A vapour, sometime, like a bear or lion,
> A tower'd citadel, a pendant rock,
> A forked mountain or blue promontory
> With trees upon't, that nod unto the world,
> And mock our eyes with air :———
> That, which is now a horse, even with a thought,
> The rack dislimns, and makes it indistinct,
> As water is in water."*

(298.) The last compound form of cloud which I have to mention is the *cirro-cumulo-stratus*, called the *nimbus* or rain-cloud. A showery form of the cloud may be seen in the plate of the draught-horse. For my part I cannot see that the mere resolution of a cloud into rain is of sufficient importance to constitute the form into a separate and distinct cloud; for rain is not so much a form as a condition of a cloud, in the final state in which it reaches the earth. Any of the three compound forms of clouds just

* Anthony and Cleopatra.

described may form a rain-cloud, without the intervention of any other. Cirro-strati are often seen to drop down in rain, without giving any symptoms of forming the more dense structure of the nimbus; and even light showers fall without any visible appearance of a cloud at all. The nimbus is most frequently seen in summer and autumn.

(299.) There is a kind of cloud, not unlike cumuli, called the *scud*, which is described usually by itself as broken nimbus. It is of dark or light colour, according as the sun shines upon it, of varied form, floating or scudding before the wind, and generally in front of a sombre cumulo-stratus stretching as a background across that portion of the sky, often accompanied with a bright streak of sky along the horizon. The ominous scud is the usual harbinger of the rain-cloud, and is therefore commonly called "messengers," "carriers," or "water-waggons."

(300.) On looking at the sky, forms of clouds may be observed which cannot be referred to any of those, simple or compound, which have just been described. On analyzing them, however, it will be found that every cloud is referable to one or more of the forms described. This defectiveness proves two things in regard to clouds. 1. That clouds, always presenting forms which are recognizable, must be the result of fixed laws. 2. That the sagacity of man has been able to classify those forms of clouds in a simple manner. Without such a key to their forms, clouds doubtless appear, to common observers, masses of inexplicable confusion. Clouds thus being only effects, the causes of their formation and mutations must be looked for in the atmosphere itself; accordingly, it has been found, that, when certain kinds appear, certain changes are taking place in the state of the atmosphere; and beyond this it is not necessary for a common observer to know the origin of clouds. It is sufficient for him to be aware of what the approaching change of the atmosphere will be, as indicated by the particular kind of cloud or clouds which he observes; and in this way clouds become guides for knowing the weather. In endeavouring thus to become a judge of the weather, you must become an attentive observer of the clouds. To become so with success in a reasonable time, you must first make yourself well acquainted with the three simple forms, which, although not singly visible at all times, may be recognised in some part of those compound clouds which exhibit themselves almost every day.

(301.) That clouds float at *different altitudes*, and are *more or less dense*, not merely on account of the quantity of vapour which they contain, but partly on account of their distance from vision, may be proved in various ways. 1. On ascending the sides of mountains, travellers frequently pass zones of clouds. Mountains thus form a sort of scale by which to estimate the altitude of clouds. Mr Crossthwaite made these observations of the altitude and number of clouds in the course of five years :—

Altitude of Clouds.	Number of Clouds.
From 0 to 100 yards,	10
100 to 200 ...	42
200 to 300 ...	62
300 to 400 ...	179
400 to 500 ...	374
500 to 600 ...	486
600 to 700 ...	416
700 to 800 ...	367
800 to 900 ...	410
900 to 1000 ...	518
1000 to 1050 ...	419
	3283
Above 1050,	2098

Hence the number of clouds above 1050 yards were, to the number below, as 2098 : 3283 or 10 : 16 nearly. The nomenclature of Howard not having been known at the time, the forms of the various clouds met with at the different altitudes could not be designated. 2. Another proof of a difference of altitudes in clouds consists in different clouds being seen to move in different directions at the same time. One set may be seen moving in one direction near the earth, whilst another may be seen through their openings unmoved. Clouds may be seen moving in different directions, at apparently great heights in the air, whilst those near the ground may be quite still. Or the whole clouds seen may be moving in the same direction with different velocities. It is natural to suppose that the lighter clouds—those containing vapour in the most elastic state—should occupy a higher position in the air than the less elastic. On this account, it is only fleecy clouds that are seen over the tops of the highest Andes. Clouds, in heavy weather, are seldom above ½ mile high, but in clear weather from 2 to 5 miles, and *cirri* from 5 to 7 miles.

(302.) Clouds are often of *enormous size*, 10 miles each way and 2 miles thick, containing 200 cubic miles of vapour ; but sometimes are even 10 times that size. The size of small clouds may be easily estimated by observing their shadows on the ground in clear breezy weather in summer. These are usually *cumuli* scudding before a westerly wind.

The shadows of larger clouds may be seen resting on the sides of mountain ranges, or spread out on the ocean.

(303.) You must become acquainted with the agency of *Electricity*, before you can understand the variations of the weather. The subject of atmospherical electricity excited great attention in the middle of the last century by the experiments and discoveries of Franklin. He proved that the electric fluid,* drawn from the atmosphere, exhibits the same properties as that obtained from the electrical machine, and thus established their identity. Since that period, little notice has been taken of its powerful agency in connection with meteorology; but brilliant are the discoveries which have since been made in regard to its powers in the laboratories of Davy, Faraday, and others. They have clearly identified electricity with magnetism and galvanism, and, in establishing this identity, they have extended to an extraordinary degree the field of observation for the meteorologist, though the discovery has rendered meteorology much more difficult to be acquired with exactness. But the science should, on that account, be prosecuted with the greater energy and perseverance.

(304.) It must be obvious to the most indifferent observer of atmospherical phenomena, that the electric agency is exceedingly *active in the atmosphere*, how inert soever may be its state in other parts of the earth. Existing there in the freest state, it exhibits its power in the most sensible manner; and its freedom and frequency suggest the interesting inquiry, whence is derived the supply of the vast amount of electricity which seems to exist in the atmosphere?

(305.) Of all investigators of this interesting but difficult inquiry, M. Pouillet has directed his attention to it with the greatest success. He has shewn that there are two sources from which this abundant supply is obtained. The first of these is *vegetation*. He has proved, by direct experiment, that the combination of oxygen with the materials of living plants, is a constant source of electricity; and the amount thus disengaged may be learned from the fact that a surface of 100 square metres (or rather more than 100 square yards), in full vegetation, disengages, in the course of one day, as much vitrous electricity as would charge a powerful battery.

(306.) That some idea may be formed of the sort of action which takes place between the oxygen of the air and the materials of living plants, it is necessary to attend, in the first place, to the change produced on

* "Electricity, though frequently called a fluid, has but little claim to that designation: in using it, therefore, let it be always understood in a conventional sense, not as expressing any theoretical view of the physical state of electric matter."—Dr GOLDING BIRD.

the air by the respiration of plants. Many conflicting opinions still prevail on this subject; but "there is no doubt, however, from the experiments of various philosophers," as Mr Hugo Reid observes, "that at times the leaves of plants produce the same effect on the atmosphere as the lungs of animals, namely, cause an increase in the quantity of carbonic acid, by giving out carbon in union with the oxygen of the air, which is thus converted into this gas; and it has been also established that at certain times the leaves of plants produce a very opposite effect, namely, that they decompose the carbonic acid of the air, retain the carbon and give out the oxygen, thus adding to the quantity of the oxygen in the air. It has not yet been precisely ascertained which of these goes on to the greater extent; but the general opinion at present is, that the gross result of the action of plants on the atmosphere is the depriving it of carbonic acid, retaining the carbon, and giving out the oxygen, thus increasing the quantity of free oxygen in the air."*

(307.) It being thus admitted that both carbonic gas and oxygen are exhaled by plants during certain times of the day, it is important to ascertain, in the next place, whether electricity of the one kind or the other accompanies the disengagement of either gas. Towards this inquiry M. Pouillet instituted experiments with the gold-leaf electroscope, whilst the seeds of various plants were germinating in the soil, and he found it sensibly affected by the *negative* state of the ground. This result might have been anticipated during the evolution of carbonic gas, for it is known by experiment that carbonic gas, obtained from the combustion of charcoal, is, in its nascent state, electrified *positively*, and, of course, when carbonic gas is evolved from the plant, the ground should be in a state of negative electricity. M. Pouillet presumed, therefore, that when plants evolve oxygen, the ground should be in a positive state of electricity. He was thus led to the important conclusion, that vegetation is an abundant source of electricity.†

(308.) The second source of electricity is *evaporation*. The fact of a chemical change in water by heat inducing the disengagement of electricity, may be proved by simple experiment. It is well known that *mechanical* action will produce electricity sensibly from almost any substance. If any one of the most extensive series of resinous and siliceous substances, and of dry vegetable, animal, and mineral produce, is rubbed, electricity will be excited, and the extent of excitation will be shewn by the effect on the gold-leaf electroscope. Chemical action, in like man-

* Reid's Chemistry of Nature, p. 100.

† Leithead on Electricity, p. 150.

ner, produces similar effects. If sulphur is fused and poured into a conical wine-glass, it will become electrical on cooling, and affect the electroscope in a manner similar to the other bodies mechanically excited. Chocolate on congealing after cooling, glacial phosphoric acid on congealing, and calomel when it fixes by sublimation to the upper part of a glass vessel, all give out electricity; so, in like manner, the condensation as well as the evaporation of water, though opposite processes, gives out electricity. Some writers attribute these electrical effects to what they term a change of form or state; but it is obvious that they may, with propriety, be included under chemical action. This view is supported by the fact of the presence of oxygen being necessary to the development of electricity. De la Rive, in bringing zinc and copper in contact through moisture, found that the zinc became oxidized, and electricity was evolved. When he prevented the oxidation, by operating in an atmosphere of nitrogen, no electric excitement followed. When, again, he increased the chemical action by exposing zinc to acid, or by substituting a more oxidable metal, such as potassium, the electric effects were greatly increased. In fact, electrical excitation and chemical action were observed to be strictly proportional to each other. And this result is quite consistent with, and is corroborated by, the necessary agency of oxygen in evolving electricity from vegetation.* But more than all this, " electricity," as Dr G. Bird intimates, " is not only evolved during chemical decomposition, but during *chemical combination;* a fact first announced by Becquerel. The truth of this statement has been, by many, either altogether denied or limited to the case of the combination of nitric acid with alkalies. But after repeating the experiments of Becquerel, as well as those of Pfaff, Mohr, Dalk, and Jacobi, I am convinced that an electric current, certainly of low tension, is really evolved during the combination of sulphuric, hydrochloric, nitric, phosphoric, and acetic acids, with the fixed alkalies, and even with ammonia."†

(309.) As evaporation is a process continually going on from the surface of the ocean, land, lakes, and rivers, at all degrees of temperature, the result of its action must be very extensive. But *how* the disengagement of electricity is produced, either by the action of oxygen on the structure of living plants, or by the action of heat on water, is unknown, and will perhaps ever remain a secret of nature. It is easy, however, to conceive how the electricity produced by these and other sources

* Leithead on Electricity, pp. 9 and 10.

† Bird's Elements of Natural Philosophy, p. 241.

must vary in different climates, seasons, and localities, and at different heights in the atmosphere.*

(310.) It thus appears that the sources of electricity are found to be *evolved in every possible form of action.* It is excited by almost every substance in nature, by friction, which is a mechanical action; it is as readily evolved by chemical action, as you have just learned; as also in the cases of condensation and evaporation of liquids; and it has also been proved to be excited by vital action, as in the case of vegetation: and as the action of oxygen is the same in the animal as in the vegetable function, it is as likely that the respiration of animals produces electricity as that of vegetables. When the sources of this mysterious and subtle agent are thus so numerous and extensive, you need not only not be surprised at its extensive diffusion, but the universality of its presence indicates that its assistance is necessary to the promoting of every operation of nature. Its identity in all cases is also proved by the fact, that though the means employed for its excitation are various, its mode of action is always the same. In every case of excitation, one body robs the other of a portion of its electricity, the former being *plus* or *positive*, the other *minus* or *negative* of its natural quantity. "The two species, or negative and positive electricity," says Dr Bird, "exist in nature *combined*, forming a neutral combination (in an analogous manner to the two magnetic fluids) incapable of exerting any obvious physical actions on ponderable matter: by the process of friction, or other mechanical or chemical means, we decompose this neutral combination, the negative and positive elements separate, one adhering to the surface of the excited substance, the other to the rubber; hence, in no case of electrical excitation can we obtain one kind of electricity without the other being simultaneously developed. We do not observe any free electricity on the surface of metallic bodies submitted to friction, in consequence of their so readily conducting electricity, that the union of the negative and positive fluids takes place as rapidly as they are separated by the friction employed."†

(311.) The *natural state* of every body in regard to its electricity is thus in a *state of quiescence or equilibrium*, but this equilibrium is very easily disturbed, and then a series of actions supervene, which illustrate the peculiar agency of electricity, and continue until the equilibrium is again restored.

* Forbes' Report on Meteorology, vol. i. p. 252.

† Bird's Elements of Natural Philosophy, p. 162.

(312.) The *force* of the electrical agency seems to be somewhat in the proportion to the energy with which it is roused into action. Dr Faraday states, that *one grain* of water " will require an electric current to be continued for $3\frac{3}{4}$ minutes of time to effect its decomposition ; which current must be strong enough to retain a platina wire $\frac{1}{104}$ of an inch in thickness red-hot in the air during the whole time." " It will not be too much to say, that this necessary quantity of electricity is equal to a very powerful flash of lightning."* When it is considered, that, during the fermentation and putrefaction of bodies on the surface of the earth, water is decomposed, and that to effect its decomposition such an amount of electric action as is here related is required to be excited, we can have no difficulty in imagining the great amount of electricity which must be derived from the various sources enumerated being constantly in operation.

(313.) In mentioning the subject of electricity, I will take the opportunity of expressing my opinion that the *electrometer* is a meteorological instrument of much greater utility to you than some of the instruments I have described; because it indicates, with a great degree of delicacy, the existence of free electricity in the air; and as electricity cannot exist in that state without producing some sort of action, it is satisfactory to have notice of its freedom, that its effects, if possible, may be anticipated. The best sort of electrometer is the " *condensing electroscope*:" it consists of a hollow glass sphere on a stand, inclosing through its top a glass tube, to the top of which is affixed a flat brass cap, and from the bottom of which are suspended two slips of gold-leaf. At the edge of the flat brass cap is screwed a circular brass plate, and another circular brass plate, so as to be parallel to the first, is inserted in a support fixed in a piece of wood moving in a groove of the stand which contains the whole apparatus. This is a very delicate instrument, and, to keep it in order, should be kept free of moisture and dust.

(314.) In regard to the *usual state* of the electricity in the atmosphere, it is generally believed that it is positive, and that it increases in quantity as we ascend. In Europe the observations of M. Schübler, of Stutgardt, intimate that the electricity of the precipitating fluids from the atmosphere is more frequently negative than positive, in the proportion of 155 : 100; but that the mean *intensity* of the positive electricity is greater than that of the negative in the ratio of 69 : 43; and that different layers or strata of the atmosphere, placed only at small distances from each other, are

* Faraday's New Researches, 8vo edition, p. 250.

frequently found to be in different electric states.* It appears also, from recent observations of M. Schübler, that the electricity of the air, in calm and serene weather, is constantly positive, but subject to two daily fluctuations. It is at its minimum at a little before sunrise: after which it gradually accumulates, till it reaches its first maximum a few hours afterwards,—at 8 A. M. in May: and then diminishes until it has descended to its second minimum. The second maximum occurs in the evening about two hours after sunset: and then diminishes, at first rapidly, and next in slower progression during the whole of the night, to present again on the following day the same oscillations. It is probable that the exact time of its increase and decrease is influenced by the seasons. The intensity increases from July to January, and then decreases; it is also much more intense in the winter, though longer in summer, and appears to increase as the cold increases.† These fluctuations may be observed throughout the year more easily in fine than in cloudy weather. "Among the causes modifying the electric state of the atmosphere," observes Dr Bird, "must be ranked its hygrometric state, as well as probably the nature of the effluvia which may become volatilized in any given locality. Thus, Saussure has observed that its intensity is much more considerable in elevated and isolated places than in narrow and confined situations; it is nearly absent in houses, under lofty trees, in narrow courts and alleys, and in inclosed places. In some places the most intensely electric state of the atmosphere appears to be that in which large clouds or dense fogs are suspended in the air at short distances above the surface of the earth; these appear to act as conductors of the electricity from the upper regions. Cavallo ascertained, from a set of experiments performed at Islington in 1776, that the air always contains free *positive* electricity, except when influenced by heavy clouds near the zenith. This electricity he found to be strongest in fogs and during frosty weather, but weakest in hot weather, and just previous to a shower of rain; and to increase in proportion as the instrument used is raised to a greater elevation. This, indeed, necessarily happens," continues Dr Bird, "for as the earth's surface is, *cœteris paribus*, always negatively electrified, a continual but gradual combination of its electricity with that of the air is constantly taking place at its surface, so that no free positive electricity can be detected within 4 feet of the surface of the earth." ‡

* Forbes' Report on Meteorology, vol. i. p. 253.

† Journal of Science and the Arts, No. IV.

‡ Bird's Elements of Natural Philosophy, p. 209.

(315.) A comparative view of the fluctuations of the barometer and electrometer may tend to shew, that, in their mode of action, all the physical agencies may be governed by the same law. The mean results of many observations by various philosophers are as follow:—

	1st Maximum.		1st Minimum.		2d Maximum.		2d Minimum.
Density,	· 10 A.M.	...	4–5 P.M.	...	10–11 P.M.	...	4–5 A.M.
Electricity,	8–9 A.M.	...	4 P.M.	...	9 P.M.	...	6 A.M.

(316.) These are all the general remarks which are called for at present on the subject of atmospherical electricity. As electrical phenomena exhibit themselves most actively in summer, observations on particular ones will then be more in season than in winter; and the only electrical excitation that is generally witnessed in winter is the *aurora borealis* or northern lights, or "merry dancers," as they are vulgarly called. It mostly occurs in the northern extremity of the northern hemisphere of the globe, where it gives forth almost constant light during the absence of the sun. So intense is this radiance, that a book may be read by it, and it thus confers a great blessing on the inhabitants of the Arctic Regions, at a time when they are benighted. The aurora borealis seems to consist of two varieties; one a luminous quiet light in the northern horizon, gleaming most frequently behind a dense stratum of cloud; and the other of vivid corruscations of almost white light, of a sufficient transparency to allow the transmission of the light of the fixed stars. They are sometimes coloured yellow, green, red, and of a dusky hue. The corruscations are generally short, and confined to the proximity of the northern horizon; but occasionally they reach the zenith, and even extend to the opposite horizon; their direction being from NW. to SE. It seems now undeniable, that the aurora borealis frequently exercises a most marked action on the magnetic needle; thus affording another proof of the identity of the magnetic and electric agencies.

(317.) It is not yet a settled point amongst philosophers, whether the aurora borealis occurs at the highest part of the atmosphere, or near the earth. Mr Cavendish considered it probable, that it usually occurs at an elevation of 71 miles above the earth's surface, at which elevation the air must be but $\frac{1}{148567}$ time the density of that at the surface of the earth, a degree of rarefaction far above that afforded by our best constructed air-pumps. Dr Dalton conceives, from trigonometrical measurements made by him of auroral arches, that their height is 100 miles above the earth's surface. His most satisfactory measurement was made from that of the 29th March 1826. As the peculiar appearance of aurora and its corruscations precisely resemble the phenomena which we are enabled to produce artificially by discharges of electricity between two bodies in a receiver through a medium of highly rarefied air, the opinion of Lieut. Morrison, R. N., of Cheltenham, a profound astronomer and meteorologist, is deserving of attention, as regards the position of the aurora at the time of its formation. He states, that long light clouds ranging themselves in the meridian line in the day, at night take a fleecy aurora-like character. " I believe," he says, " that these clouds are formed by the discharges and currents of electricity, which, when they are *more decided*, produce aurora." Mr Leithead conjectures that the aurora becomes "visible to the inhabitants of the earth upon their entering our atmosphere."* If these conjectures are at all correct, the aurora *cannot be seen beyond our atmosphere*, and therefore cannot exhibit itself at the height of 100 miles, as supposed by Dr Dalton, since the height of the atmosphere is only acknowledged to be from 40 to 50 miles. This view of the height of the aurora somewhat corroborates that held by the Rev. Dr Farquharson, Alford, Aberdeenshire, and which has been strongly supported by Professor Jameson.†

(318.) There are other atmospherical phenomena, whose various aspects indicate changes of the weather, and which, although of rarer occurrence than the clouds or electricity, are yet deserving of attention when they appear. These are, Halos around the discs of the sun and moon ; Coronæ or *broughs*, covering their faces ; Parhelia, or mock suns ; Falling Stars ; Fire-balls ; and the Rainbow. Of these, the halo and corona only appear in winter : the others will be noticed in the course of the respective seasons in which they appear.

(319.) A *halo* is an extensive luminous ring, including a circular area, in the centre of which the sun or moon appears. It is formed by the intervention of a cloud between the spectator and the sun or moon. This cloud is generally the denser kind of *cirro-stratus*, the refraction and reflection of the rays of the sun or moon at definite angles through and upon which, is the cause of the luminous phenomenon. The breadth of the ring of a halo is caused by a number of rays being refracted at somewhat different angles, otherwise the breadth of the ring would equal only the breadth of one ray. Mr Forster has demonstrated mathematically the angle of refraction, which is equal to the angle subtended by the semidiameter of the halo.‡ Halos may be double and triple ; and there is one, which Mr Forster denominates a *discoid* halo, which constitutes the boundary of a large corona, and is generally of less diameter than usual, and often coloured with the tints of the rainbow. " A

* Leithead on Electricity, p. 264.

† Encyclopædia Britannica, 7th edition, art. *Aurora Borealis*.

‡ Forster's Researches into Atmospherical Phenomena, p. 107.

beautiful one appeared at Clapton on the 22d December 1809, about midnight, during the passage of a *cirro-stratus* cloud before the moon."* Halos are usually pretty correct circles, though they have been observed of a somewhat oval shape; and they are generally also colourless, though they sometimes display faint colours of the rainbow. They are most frequently seen around the moon, and acquire the appellation of *lunar* or *solar* halos, as they happen to accompany the particular luminary.

(320.) The *corona* or *brough* occurs when the sun or moon is seen through a thin *cirro-stratus* cloud, the portion of the cloud more immediately around the sun or moon appearing much lighter than the rest. Coronæ are double, triple, and even quadruple, according to the state of the intervening vapours. They are caused by a similar refractive power in vapour as the halo; and are generally faintly coloured at their edges. Their diameter seldom exceeds 10°. A halo frequently encircles the moon, when a small corona is more immediately around it.

(321.) Hitherto I have said nothing of rain, snow, wind, or hail—phenomena which materially affect the operations of the farmer. Strictly speaking, they are not the cause, but only the effects, of other phenomena; and on that account, I have purposely refrained alluding to them, until you should have become somewhat acquainted with the nature of the agencies which produce them. Having heard of these, I shall now proceed to examine particularly the familiar phenomena of *rain*, *snow*, and *wind*. Rain and wind being common to all the seasons, it will be necessary to enter at once into a general explanation of both. Snow is peculiar to winter, and will not again require to be alluded to. And hail will form a topic of remark in summer.

(322.) You must be so well acquainted with the phenomenon of *rain*, that no specific definition of it is here required to be given. It should, however, be borne in mind, that the phenomenon has various aspects, and the variety indicates the peculiar state of the atmosphere at the time of its occurrence. Rain falls at times in large drops, at others in small, and sometimes in a thick or thin drizzle; but in all these states, it consists of the descent of water in drops from the atmosphere to the earth. In reflecting on this phenomenon, how is it (you may ask yourselves) that the air can possibly support *drops of water*, however minute? The air cannot support so dense a substance as *water*; and it is its inability to do so, that causes the water to fall to the ground. The air, however, can support vapour, the aggregation of the particles of which

* Forster's Researches into Atmospherical Phenomena, p. 101.

constitutes rain or water. Vapour is formed by the force of the heat of the sun's rays upon the surface of land, sea, lakes, and rivers; and from its easy ascent into the atmosphere, it is clear that water is rendered lighter than air by heat, and, of course, vastly lighter than itself. The weight of 1 cubic inch of distilled water (with the barometer at 30 inches, and the thermometer at 62° Fahrenheit) is 252.458 grains; that of 1 cubic inch of air is 0.3049 of a grain; of course, vapour must be lighter than this last figure. Heat has effected this lightness by rendering vapour highly elastic; and it is not improbable that it is electricity which maintains the elasticity, after the vapour has been carried away beyond the influence of its generating heat, and there keeps it in mixture with the air. The whole subject of evaporation is instructive, and will receive our attention in summer, when it presents itself in the most active condition to our view, and is intimately connected with the phenomenon of dew.

(323.) The *quantity of vapour in the atmosphere is variable.* This Table shews the weight in grains of a cubic foot of vapour, at different temperatures, from 0° to 95° Fahrenheit.

Temperature.	Weight in grains.	Temperature.	Weight in grains.	Temperature.	Weight in grains.	Temperature.	Weight in grains.
0	0.856	24	1.961	48	4.279	72	8.924
1	0.892	25	2.028	49	4.407	73	9.199
2	0.928	26	2.096	50	4.535	74	9.484
3	0.963	27	2.163	51	4.684	75	9.780
4	0.999	28	2.229	52	4.832	76	10.107
5	1.034	29	2.295	53	5.003	77	10.387
6	1.069	30	2.361	54	5.173	78	10.699
7	1.104	31	2.451	55	5.342	79	11.016
8	1.139	32	2.539	56	5.511	80	11.333
9	1.173	33	2.630	57	5.679	81	11.665
10	1.208	34	2.717	58	5.868	82	12.005
11	1.254	35	2.805	59	6.046	83	12.354
12	1.308	36	2.892	60	6.222	84	12.713
13	1.359	37	2.979	61	6.399	85	13.081
14	1.405	38	3.066	62	6.575	86	13.458
15	1.451	39	3.153	63	6.794	87	13.877
16	1.497	40	3.239	64	7.013	88	14.230
17	1.541	41	3.371	65	7.230	89	14.613
18	1.586	42	3.502	66	7.447	90	15.005
19	1.631	43	3.633	67	7.662	91	15.432
20	1.688	44	3.763	68	7.899	92	15.786
21	1.757	45	3.893	69	8.135	93	16.186
22	1.825	46	4.022	70	8.392	94	16.593
23	1.893	47	4.151	71	8.658	95	17.009

Dr Dalton found that the force of vapour in the torrid zone varies from 0.6 of an inch to 1 inch of mercury. In Britain, it seldom amounts to 0.5 of an inch, but is sometimes as great as 0.5 of an inch, in summer ; whereas, in winter, it is often as low as 0.1 of an inch of mercury. These facts would enable us to ascertain the absolute quantity of vapour contained in the atmosphere at any given time, provided we were certain that the density and elasticity of vapours follow precisely the same law as that of gases, as is extremely probable to be the case. If so, the vapour will vary from $\frac{1}{60}$ to $\frac{1}{100}$ part of the atmosphere. Dalton supposes that the medium quantity of vapour in the atmosphere may amount to $\frac{1}{70}$ of its bulk.*

(324.) The *theory* propounded by Dr Hutton, that rain occurs from the mingling together of great beds of air of unequal temperatures differently stored with moisture, is that which was adopted by Dalton, Leslie, and others, and is the current one, having been illustrated and strengthened by the clearer views of the nature of deposition which we now possess.

(325.) On the connection of rain with the *fall of the barometer*, Mr Meikle has shewn that the change of pressure may be a cause as well as an effect; for the expansion of air accompanying diminished pressure, being productive of cold, diminishes the elasticity of the existing vapour, and causes a deposition.†

(326.) M. Arago has traced the progress of *decrease* in the annual amount of the fall of rain *from the equator to the poles;* and these are the results obtained by various observers at the respective places :—

Coast of Malabar, in . .	Lat. 11° 30′ N.,	the quantity is	135.5 inches.
At Grenada, Antilles, . .	... 12° ...	...	126. ...
At Cape François, St Domingo,	... 19° 46′ ...	...	120. ...
At Calcutta, . . .	... 22° 23′ ...	...	81. ...
At Rome, ...	... 41° 54′ ...	...	39. ...
In England, . . .	... 53° ...	...	32. ...
At St Petersburgh, . .	... 59° 16′ ...	...	16. ...
At Ulea, ...	... 65° 30′ ...	...	13.5 ...

On the other hand, the number of rainy days *increases from the equator to the poles*, according to the observations of M. Cotte. Thus,

From N. Lat.	12° to 43°,	there are 78	rainy days.
... ...	43° to 46°,	... 103	...
... ...	46° to 50°,	... 134	...
... ...	50° to 60°,	... 161	...

* Philosophical Magazine, vol. xxiii. p. 353.

† Royal Institution Journal.

(327.) There is a great variation in the quantity of rain that falls in the same latitude on *the different sides of the same continent,* and particularly of the same *island.* Thus, to confine the instances to our own island, the mean fall of rain at Edinburgh, on the east coast, is 26 inches; and at Glasgow, on the west coast, in nearly the same latitude, the amount is 40 inches. At North Shields, on the east coast, the amount is 25 inches; while at Coniston in Lancashire, in nearly the same latitude on the west coast, it is as great as 85 inches.*

(328.) A remarkable variation takes place in the fall of rain at *different heights;* the quantity of rain that falls on high ground exceeding that at the level of the sea. This fact may be easily explained by the influence of a hilly country retaining clouds and vapour. At Lancaster, on the coast, the quantity that falls is 39 inches; and at Easthwaite, among the mountains in the same county, the amount is 86 inches. By a comparison of the registers at Geneva and the convent of the Great St Bernard, it appears, that at the former place, by a mean of 32 years, the annual fall of rain is 30.70 inches; while at the latter, by a mean of 12 years, it is 60.05 inches. Dr Dalton clearly points out the influence of hot currents of air ascending along the surface of the ground into the colder strata which rest upon a mountainous country. The consequence is, that although neither the hot nor the cold air was accompanied with more moisture than could separately be maintained in an elastic state, yet when the mixture takes place, the arithmetical mean of the quantities of vapour cannot be supported in an elastic state at an arithmetical mean of the temperatures; since the weights of vapour which can exist in a given space increase nearly in a geometrical ratio, while the temperatures follow an arithmetical one.† But the amount of rain at stations abruptly elevated above the surface of the earth, diminishes as we ascend. For example, at Kinfauns Castle, the seat of Lord Gray, on the Tay, in Perthshire, by a mean of 5 years, 22.66 inches of rain fell; whilst on a hill in the immediate neighbourhood, 600 feet higher, no less than 41.49 inches were collected, by a mean of the same period. This is an instance of a high elevation rising pretty rapidly above the castle, but in a natural manner; and it is adduced as a contrast with an artificial elevation of a rain-gauge at the Observatory at Paris, when the rain that fell on the town, at a vertical height of 28 metres (rather more than as many yards), was 50.47 inches, while,

* Table of the quantity of Rain that falls in different parts of Great Britain. By Mr Joseph Atkinson, Harraby, near Carlisle.

† Manchester Memoirs. New Series, vol. v. p. 233.

according to the observation of M. Arago, it was 56.37 inches in the court below.*

(329.) The variation in the amount of rain in the *seasons* follows, in a great measure, the same law as that propounded by Dalton in reference to the heights of mountains. The greatest *quantity* of rain falls in autumn, and the least in winter. Thus, according to M. Flaugergues, taking the mean amount as 1,—

In winter, there falls	0.1937	inches, including	December, January, and February.
In spring, ...	0.2217	... ...	March, April, and May.
In summer, ...	0.2001	... ...	June, July, and August.
In autumn, ...	0.3845	... ...	September, October, and November.

It may be useful to give the proportional results of each month. Again, taking the mean amount of the year as 1, the proportional result for

January, is .	0.0716	July, . . .	0.0544
February, .	0.0541	August, . .	0.0679
March, . .	0.0557	September, .	0.1236
April, . .	0.0802	October, . .	0.1370
May, . . .	0.0847	November, . .	0.1250
June, . . .	0.0765	December, . .	0.0693

As M. Flaugergues observes, the maximum belongs to October and the minimum to February, and May comes nearest to the mean of 40 years.† Taking these proportional results by the months which constitute the seasons of the agricultural year as I have arranged them, the mean of the seasons will be respectively thus :—

Winter,	November, .	0.1250	Summer,	May, .	0.0847
	December, .	0.0693		June, .	0.0765
	January, .	0.0716		July, .	0.0544
		0.2659			0.2156
Spring,	February, .	0.0541	Autumn,	August, .	0.0679
	March, . .	0.0557		September,	0.1236
	April, . .	0.0802		October,	0.1370
		0.1900			0.3285

This method of division still gives the maximum of rain to autumn, though it transfers the minimum from the winter to the spring ; which,

* Forbes' Report on Meteorology, vol. i. p. 250.

† Encyclopædia Metropolitana, art. *Meteorology*.

as I think, approaches nearer to the truth in reference to Scotland than the conclusions of M. Flaugergues, which specially apply to France.

(330.) The last table but one gives the proportional amount of rain that fell, in a mean of 40 years, in each month. It may be useful to know the mean *number of rainy days in each of the months.* They are these :—

In January, .	14.4 days.	In July, .	16.1 days.
February, .	15.8 ...	August, .	16.3 ...
March, .	12.7 ...	September,	12.3 ...
April, .	14.0 ...	October, .	16.2 ...
May, . .	15.8 ...	November,	15.0 ...
June, . .	11.8 ...	December,	17.7 ...

These tables shew, that though the *number* of rainy days is nearly equal in the vernal and autumnal equinoxes, the *quantity* of rain that falls in the autumn is nearly double of that in spring. If this last table is arranged according to the months of the agricultural seasons, the number of rainy days in each season will stand thus :—

In Winter,	November,	15.0 days.	In Summer,	May, .	15.8 days.
	December,	17.7 ...		June, .	11.8 ...
	January,	14.4 ...		July, .	16.1 ...
		47.1 days.			43.7 days.
In Spring,	February,	15.8 days.	In Autumn,	August,	16.3
	March, .	12.7 ...		September,	12.3 ...
	April, .	14.0 ...		October,	16.2 ...
		42.5 days.			44.8 days.

In all 178.1 days of rain. This arrangement shews that the greatest number of rainy days is in the agricultural winter, and the least number in the spring, which seems to agree with experience.

(331.) Mr Howard remarks, that, on an average of years, it rains every other day; and, by a mean of 40 years at Viviers, M. Flaugergues found 98 days of rain throughout the year.*

(332.) With regard to the question, Whether *more rain falls in the night than in the day?* Mr Howard's statement bears, that of 21.94 inches—a mean of 31 lunar months—rain fell in the day to the amount of 8.67 inches, and in the night to 13.27 inches. Dr Dalton also says,

* Encyclopædia Metropolitana, art. *Meteorology.*

that more rain falls when the sun is under the horizon than when it is above it.*

(333.) It has not been ascertained whether, on the *whole amount over the globe, rain is increasing or diminishing in quantity.* As M. Arago justly observes, it is very difficult to know how many years of observations are necessary to get a mean value of the fall of rain, the amount being extremely variable. There are, no doubt, several causes which may tend to change the amount of rain in any particular spot, without forming part of any general law, such as the destruction or forming of forests, the inclosure and drainage of land, and the increase of habitations. M. Arago has shewn that the fall of rain at Paris has not sensibly altered for 130 years, and that although an *increase* was supposed to have been proved at Milan, by observations for 54 years, yet the extremes of the annual results, between 1791 and 1817, were 24.7 and 58.9 inches. The observations of M. Flaugergues, at Viviers, establish an increase there in 40 years. The number of rainy days throughout the year is 98, but dividing the 40 years into decades, the number sensibly increases. Thus—

From 1778 to 1787,	there were	830	days.
1788 to 1797,	...	947	...
1798 to 1807,	...	1062	...
1808 to 1817,	...	1082	...

But this result must arise from local circumstances, as at Marseilles there has been a striking *decrease* in 50 years.

(334.) Notwithstanding the *enormous annual fall of rain at the equator*, particular instances of a great depth of rain in a short time have occasionally occurred in Europe, which probably have seldom been equalled in any other part of the globe. At Geneva, on the 25th October 1822, there fell 30 inches of rain in one day. At Joyeuse, according to M. Arago, on the 9th October 1827 there fell 31 inches of rain in 22 hours.† With regard to remarkable variations in the quantity of rain in different places, among the Andes it is said to rain perpetually; whereas in Peru, as Ulloa affirms, it never rains, but that for a part of the year the atmosphere is obscured by thick fogs called *garuas*. In Egypt it hardly ever rains at all, and in some parts of Arabia it seldom rains more than two or three times in as many years, but the dews are heavy, and refresh the soil, and supply with moisture the few plants which grow in those sunny regions.

* Encyclopædia Metropolitana, art. *Meteorology*.

† Forbes' Report on Meteorology, vol. i. p. 251-2.

(335.) According to a statement of observations by Mr Howard, there appears a *relation to exist betwixt the winds and the annual amount of rain.* This is his statement—

YEAR.	WIND.				Calm days.	Annual Rain in inches.
	NE.	ES.	SW.	WN.		
1807	61	34	113	114	43	20.14
1808	82	38	108	103	35	23.24
1809	68	50	123	91	33	25·28
1810	81	72	78	83	41	28.07
1811	58	59	119	93	36	24.64
1812	82	66	93	91	34	27.24
1813	76	53	92	124	20	23.56
1814	96	65	91	96	17	26.07
1815	68	36	121	107	33	21.20
1816	64	66	106	102	28	32.37
	74	54	105	100	32	25.18

The remarks which this statement seems to warrant are, that in regard to the E. winds, in the dry year 1807, the class of N.—E. winds is nearly double of the class of E.—S. winds; in 1815, the next driest year, is the same result; and in 1808, the next driest to that, the result is rather more than double. Still farther in regard to E. winds, in the wettest year, 1816, the class of E.—S. winds exceeds that of N.—E.; in 1814 they were $\frac{2}{3}$ of the latter; in 1812, $\frac{3}{4}$, and 1810, $\frac{7}{8}$. With regard to the classes of W. winds, the class of W.—N. winds falls off gradually from 1807 to 1810 inclusive, while the annual amount of rain increases from year to year, and in three of the six remaining years the amount is drier than the average in the dry years, and wetter than the wet ones.

(336.) Mr Howard says, that 1 year in every 5 in this country may be expected to be extremely dry, and 1 in 10 extremely wet.

(337.) The mean annual amount of rain and dew for England and Wales, according to the estimate of Dr Dalton, is 36 inches. The mean quantity of rain falling in 147 places, situated between north lat. 11° and 60°, according to Cotte, is 34.7 inches. If the mean fall over the globe be taken at 34 inches, it will, perhaps, not be far from the truth.

(338.) The *influence of the lunar periods on the amount of rain* deserves attention. Professor Forbes believes that there is some real connection between the lunar phases and the weather. M. Flaugergues, who has observed the weather at Viviers with the greatest assiduity for a quarter of a century, marked the number of rainy days corresponding with the lunar phases, and found them at a maximum at the first quarter, and a minimum at the last.

(339.) It almost always happens that rain *brings down foreign matter from the air.* It is known that the farina of plants has been carried as far as 30 or 40 miles, and the ashes of volcanoes have been carried more than 200 miles. We can conceive that when the magnitude of the particles of dry substances is so reduced as to render them incapable of falling in any given velocity, that their descent may be overcome by a very slight current of the air; but even in still air a sphere of water of only the almost inconceivable size of $\frac{1}{600000}$ part of an inch in diameter falls 1 inch in a second, and yet particles of mist must be much larger than this, otherwise they could not be visible as separate drops; the least drop of water that is discoverable by the naked eye falls with a velocity of 1 foot in the second, when the air is still. Although it is probable that the resistance opposed to the descent of small bodies in air, may be considerably greater than would be expected from calculation, still the wonder is how they are supported for any length of time.* In this difficulty there is much inclination to call in the aid of electricity to account for the phenomenon. Mr Leithead accounts for it in this way: "When the earth is positive and the atmosphere negative, the electric fluid, in endeavouring to restore its equilibrium, would cause a motion amongst the particles of the air in a direction from the earth towards the higher region of the atmosphere; for the air being a very imperfect conductor, the particles near the earth's surface can only convey electricity to the more remote particles by such a motion. This would, in effect, partly *diminish* the downward pressure of the air, which is due to its actual density;" and, in doing this, might it not, at the same time, counteract in some degree the gravity of any substance in the air by surrounding it with an electrical atmosphere? "When, on the contrary," continues Mr Leithead, "the earth is negative and the air positive, this motion of the particles will be reversed; thus increasing the pressure towards the earth, and producing the same effect as if the air had actually *increased in density*;"† and would it not thereby be more capable of supporting any foreign body in it?

(340.) Rain falls at all seasons, but *snow* only in winter, and it is just frozen rain; whenever, therefore, there are symptoms of rain, snow may be expected if the temperature of the air is sufficiently low to freeze vapour. Vapour is supposed to be frozen into snow at the mo-

* Polehampton's Gallery of Nature and Art, vol. iv. p. 143.

† Leithead on Electricity, p. 373. This explanation Mr Leithead also gives to account for the changes in the density of the atmosphere, as indicated by the oscillations of the barometer.

ment it is collapsing into drops to form rain, for we cannot suppose that clouds of snow can float about the atmosphere any more than clouds of rain. Snow is a beautifully crystallized substance when it falls to the ground, and it is probable that it never falls from a great height, otherwise its fine crystalline configurations could not be preserved.

(341.) The *forms of snow* have been arranged into 5 orders. 1. The *lamellar*, which is again divided into the *stelliform*, *regular hexagons*, *aggregation of hexagons*, and *combination of hexagons* with radii, or spines and projecting angles. 2. Another form is the *lamellar* or *spherical nucleus* with spinous ramifications in different places. 3. Fine *spiculæ* or 6-sided prisms. 4. *Hexagonal pyramids.* 5. *Spiculæ*, having one or both *extremities* affixed to the *centre* of a *lamellar* crystal. There are numerous varieties of forms of each class.* All the forms of crystals of snow afford most interesting objects for the microscope, and when perfect no objects in nature are more beautifully and delicately formed. The crystals ramify from a centre, or unite with one another under the invariable angle of 60°, or its complemental angle of 120°. The lamellated crystals fall in calm weather, and in heavy flakes, and are evidently precipitated from a low elevation. The spiculæ of 6-sided prisms occur in heavy drifts of snow accompanied with wind and intense cold. They are formed at a considerable elevation; and they are so fine as to pass through the minutest chinks in houses, and so hard and firm that they may be poured like sand from one hand into another, with a jingling sound, and without the risk of being melted. In this country they are most frequently accompanied with one of the varieties of the lamellar crystals, which meet their fall at a lower elevation; but in mountainous countries, and especially above the line of perpetual snow, they constitute the greatest bulk of the snow, where they are ready at the surface to be blown about with the least agitation of the air, and lifted up in dense clouds by gusts of wind, and precipitated suddenly on the unwary traveller like a sand-drift of the torrid zone. These spiculæ feel exceedingly sharp when driven by the wind against the face, as I have experienced on the Alps. How powerless is man when overtaken in such a snow-storm, as

———————" down he sinks
Beneath the shelter of the shapeless drift,
Thinking o'er all the bitterness of death!"†

The other forms of snow are more rare.

(342.) All other things being equal, Professor Leslie supposes that a

* Encyclopædia Metropolitana, art. *Meteorology*.

† Thomson.

flake of snow, taken at 9 times more expanded than water, descends 3 times as slow.

(343.) From the moment snow alights on the ground it begins to undergo certain changes, which usually end in a more solid crystallization than it originally possessed. The adhesive property of snow arises from its needly crystalline texture, aided by a degree of attendant moisture which afterwards freezes in the mass. Sometimes, when a strong wind sweeps over a surface of snow, portions of it are raised by its power, and, passing on with the breeze under a diminished temperature, become crystallized, and, by attrition, assume globular forms. Mr Howard describes having seen these snow-balls, as they may be termed, in January 1814, and Mr Patrick Shirreff, when at Mungoswells in East Lothian, observed the like phenomenon in February 1830.* I observed the same phenomenon in Forfarshire in the great snow-storm of February 1823.

(344.) During the descent of snow, the *thermometer sometimes rises* and the *barometer usually falls*. Snow has the effect of retaining the temperature of the ground at what it was when the snow fell. It is this property which maintains the warmer temperature of the ground, and sustains the life of plants during the severe rigours of winter, in the Arctic Regions, where the snow falls suddenly, after the warmth of summer; and it is the same property which supplies water to rivers in winter, from under the perpetual snows of the alpine mountains. While air, above snow, may be 38° below zero, the ground below will only be at zero.† Hence the fine healthy green colour of young wheat and young grass, after the snow has melted off them in spring.

(345.) In melting, 27 inches of snow give 3 inches of water. Rain and snow-water are the *softest* natural waters for domestic purposes; and are also the purest that can be obtained from natural sources, provided they are procured either before reaching the ground, or from newly fallen snow. Nevertheless, they are impregnated with oxygen, nitrogen, and carbonic acid, especially with a considerable quantity of oxygen; and rain-water and dew contain nearly as much air as they can absorb.‡ Liebig maintains that both rain and snow-water contain ammonia.§

(346.) Snow reflects beautifully blue and pink shades at sunset, as is observed with admiration on the Alps of Switzerland. It also reflects so much light from its surface, as to render travelling at night a cheerful

* Encyclopædia Metropolitana, art. *Meteorology.*

† Philip's Facts, p. 440.

‡ Reid's Chemistry of Nature, p. 192.

§ Liebig's Organic Chemistry, p. 73-8.

occupation ; and in some countries, as in Russia and Canada, it forms a delightful highway when frozen.

(347.) *Hoar-frost* is defined to be frozen dew. This is not quite a correct definition; for dew is sometimes frozen, especially in spring, into globules of ice which do not at all resemble hoar-frost,—this latter substance being beautifully and as regularly crystallized as snow. The formation of hoar-frost is always attended with a considerable degree of cold, because it is preceded by a great radiation of heat and vapour from the earth, and the phenomenon is the more perfect the warmer the day and the clearer the night have been. In the country, hoar-frost is of most frequent occurrence in the autumnal months and in winter, in such places as have little snow or continued frost on the average of seasons; and this greatly from great radiation of heat and vapour, at those seasons occasioned by a suspension of vegetable action, which admits of little absorption of moisture for vegetable purposes.‡

(348.) Dr Farquharson, Alford, Aberdeenshire, has paid great attention to the subject of hoar-frost or rime, which frequently injures the crops in the northern portion of our island long before they are ripe. The results of his observations are very instructive. 1. He has observed, that the mean temperature of the day and night at which injurious hoar-frosts may occur, may be, relatively to the freezing-point, very high. Thus, on the nights of the 29th and 31st August 1840, the leaves of potatoes were injured, while the lowest temperatures of those nights, as indicated by a self-registering thermometer, were as high as 41° and 39° respectively. 2. Hoar-frost, at the time of a high daily mean temperature, takes place only during calm. A very slight steady breeze will quickly melt away frosty rime. 3. The air is always unclouded, or nearly all of it so, at the time of hoar-frost. So incompatible is hoar-frost with a clouded state of the atmosphere, that on many occasions, when a white frosty rime has been formed in the earlier part of the night, on the formation of a close cloud at a later part, it has melted off before the rising of the sun. 4. Hoar-frosts most frequently happen with the mercury in the barometer at a high point and rising, and with the hygrometer at comparative dryness for the temperature and season; but there are striking exceptions to these rules. On the morning of the 15th September 1840, a very injurious frost occurred, with a low and falling barometric column, and with a damp atmosphere. 5. In general, low and flat lands in the bottom of valleys, and grounds that are in land-locked hollows,

* Mudie's World, p. 254.

suffer most from hoar-frost, while all sloping lands, and open uplands, escape injury. But it is not their relative elevation above the sea, independently of the freedom of their exposure, that is the source of safety to the uplands; for provided they are inclosed by higher lands, without any wide open descent from them on some side or other, they suffer more, under other equal circumstances, than similar lands of less altitude. 6. A very slight inclination of the surface of the ground is generally quite protective of the crops on it from injury by hoar-frost, from which flat and hollow places suffer at the time great injury. But a similar slope downward in the bottom of a narrow descending hollow does not save the crop in the bottom of it, although those on its side-banks higher up may be safe. 7. An impediment of no great height on the surface of the slope, such as a stone-wall fence, causes damage immediately above it, extending upwards proportionally to the height of the impediment. A still loftier impediment, like a closely-planted and tall wood or belt of trees, across the descent, or at the bottom of sloping land, causes the damage to extend on it much more. 8. Rivers have a bad repute as the cause of hoar-frosts in their neighbourhood, but the general opinion regarding their evil influence is altogether erroneous; the protective effect of *running* water, such as waterfalls from mill-sluices, on pieces of potatoes, when others in like low situations are blackened by frost, is an illustration which can be referred to. 9. The severity of the injury by hoar-frost is much influenced by the wetness or dryness of the soil at the place; and this is exemplified in potatoes growing on haugh-lands, by the sides of rivers. These lands are generally dry, but bars of clay sometimes intersect the dry portions, over which the land is comparatively damp. Hoar-frost will affect the crop growing upon these bars of clay, while that on the dry soil will escape injury; and the explanation of this is quite easy. The mean temperature of the damp lands is lower than that of the dry, and on a diminution of the temperature during frost, it sooner gets down to the freezing point, as it has less to diminish before reaching it. 10. Hoar-frost produces peculiar currents in the atmosphere. On flat lands, and in land-locked hollows, there are no currents that are at all sensible to the feelings; but on the sloping lands, during hoar-frosts, there is rarely absent a very sensible and steady, although generally only feeble, current towards the most direct descent of the slope. The current is produced in this way. The cold first takes place on the surface of the ground, and the lower stratum of air becoming cooled, descends to a lower temperature than that of the air immediately above, in contact with it. By its cooling, the lower stratum acquires a greater density, and cannot rest on an inclined plane, but descends to the valley; its place at the summit of the slope being supplied by warmer air from above, which prevents it from getting so low as the freezing temperature. On the flat ground below, the cool air accumulates, and commits injury, while the warmer current down the slope does none; but should the mean temperature of the day and night be already very low before the calm of the evening sets in, the whole air is so cooled down as to prevent any current down the slope. Injury is then effected both on the slope and the low ground; and hence the capricious nature of hoar-frost may be accounted for.*

(349.) *Frost* has been represented to arise from the absence of heat; but it is more, for it also implies an absence of moisture. Sir Richard Phillips defines cold to be "the mere absence of the motion of the atoms called heat, or the abstraction of it by evaporation of atoms, so as to convey away the motion, or by the juxtaposition of bodies susceptible of motion. Cold and heat are mere relations of fixity and motion in the atoms of bodies."† This definition of heat implies that it is a mere property of matter, a point not yet settled by philosophers; but there is no doubt that, by motion, heat is evolved, and cold is generally attended by stillness or cessation of motion.

(350.) Frost generally originates in the upper portions of the atmosphere, it is supposed, by the expansion of the air carrying off the existing heat, and making it susceptible of acquiring more. What the cause of the expansion may be, when no visible change has taken place, in the mean time, in the ordinary action of the solar rays, may not be obvious to a spectator on the ground; but it is known from the experiments of Lenz, that electricity is as capable of producing cold as heat, to the degree of freezing water rapidly.‡

(351.) The most intense frosts in this country never penetrate more than one foot into the ground, on account of the excessive dryness occasioned in it by the frost itself withdrawing the moisture for it to act upon. Frost cannot penetrate through a thick covering of snow, or below a sheet of ice.

(352.) *Ice* is water in a solid state, superinduced by the agency of frost. Though a solid, it is not a compact substance, but contains large interstices filled with air or other substances that may have been floating on the surface of the water. Ice is an aggregation of crystals subtending with one another the angles of 60° and 120°. It is quickly formed in shallow, but takes a long time to form in deep water, and it cannot become very thick in the lower latitudes of the globe, from want

* Prize Essays of the Highland and Agricultural Society, vol. xiv. p. 250.

† Phillips' Facts, p. 395.

‡ Bird's Elements of Natural Philosophy. p. 232.

of time and intensity of the frost. By 11 years' observations at the Observatory at Paris, there were only 58 days of frost throughout the year, which is too short and too desultory a period to freeze *deep* water in that latitude.

(353.) The freezing of water is effected by frost in this manner. The upper film of water in contact with the air becomes cooled down, and when it reaches 39°.39 it is at its densest state, and of course sinks to the bottom through the less dense body of water below it. The next film of water, which is now uppermost, undergoes the same condensation, and in this way does film after film in contact with the air descend towards the bottom until the whole body of water becomes equally dense at the temperature of 39°.39. When this vertical circulation of the water stops, the upper film becomes frozen. If there is no wind to agitate the surface of the water, its temperature will descend as low as 28° before it freezes, and on freezing will start up to 32°; but should there be any wind, then the ice will form at once at 32°, expanding at the same time $\frac{1}{9}$ larger than in its former state of water.

(354.) It is worth while to trace the progress of this curious phenomenon—the expansion of ice. In the first place, the water *contracts in bulk* by the frost, until it reaches the temperature of 39°.39, when it is in its state of greatest density, and then sinks. It then resists the freezing power of frost in a calm atmosphere, until it reaches 28°, *without decreasing more in bulk*, and it remains floating on the *warmer* water below it, which continues at 39°.39. When so placed, and at 28°, it freezes, and suddenly starts up to the temperature of 32°, and as suddenly *expands* $\frac{1}{9}$ more in bulk than *at its ordinary temperature*, and of course more than that when in its most condensed state at 39°.39. It retains its assumed enlarged state of ice until it is melted.

(355.) So great is the force of water on being suddenly expanded into ice, that, according to the experiments of the Florentine Academy, every cubic inch of it exerts a power of 27,000 lb. This remarkable power of ice is of use in agriculture, as I shall illustrate when I come to speak of the effects of frost on ploughed land.

(356.) It is obvious, that no large body of *fresh* water, such as a deep lake or river, can be reduced in temperature below 39°.39, when water is in its densest state, as what becomes colder only floats upon and covers the denser, which is at the same time warmer, portion; and as ice is of larger bulk, weight for weight, than water, it must float above all, and, in retaining that position, prevent the farther cooling of the mass of water below 39°.39. On the other hand, *sea*-water freezes at once on the surface, and that below the ice must retain the temperature it had when the ice was formed. Frost in the polar regions becomes suddenly intense, and the polar sea becomes as suddenly covered with ice, without regard to the temperature of the water below. The ice of the polar sea, like the snow upon the polar land, thus becomes a protective mantle against the intense cold of the atmosphere, which is sometimes as great as 57° below zero. In this way sea animals, as well as land vegetables, in those regions, are protected against the effects of the intensest frosts.

(357.) Ice *evaporates moisture as largely as water*, which property preserves it from being easily melted by any unusual occurrence of a high temperature of the air, because the rapid evaporation occasioned by the small increase of heat, superinduces a greater coldness in the body of ice.

(358.) The *great cooling powers of ice* may be witnessed by the simple experiment of mixing 1 lb. of water at 32° with 1 lb. at 172°, the mean temperature of the mixture will be as high as 102°; whereas 1 lb. of ice at 32°, on being put into 1 lb. of water at 172°, will reduce the mixture to the temperature of ice, namely, 32°. This perhaps unexpected result arises from the greater capacity of ice for caloric than water at the temperature of 32°; that is, in other words, more heat is required to break up the crystallization of ice than to heat water.

(359.) It may be worth while to notice, that *ponds and lakes are generally frozen with different thicknesses of ice*, owing either to irregularities in the bottom, which constitute different depths of water, or to the existence of deep springs, the water of which, as you have seen, seldom falls below the mean temperature of the place, that is, 40°. Hence the unknown thickness of ice on lakes and ponds until its strength has been ascertained; and hence also the origin of most of the accidents on ice.

(360.) The phenomenon of *Fog* or *Mist* occurs at all seasons, and it appears always under the peculiar circumstances explained by Sir Humphry Davy. His theory is, that radiation of vapour from land and water sends it up until it meets with a cold stratum of air, which condenses it in the form of mist,—which naturally gravitates towards the surface. When the radiation is weak, the mist seems to lie upon the ground, but when more powerful, the stratum of mist may be seen elevated a few feet above the ground. Mist, too, may be seen to continue longer over the water than the land, owing to the slower radiation of vapour from water, and it is generally seen in the hollowest portions of ground, on account of the cold air as it descends from the surrounding rising ground and mixes with the air in the hollow, diminishing its capacity for moisture.

(361.) Mist also varies in its character according to its electric state; if negatively affected, it deposites its vapour more quickly, forming a heavy sort of dew, and wetting everything like rain; but if positively, it continues to exist as fog, and retains the vapour in the state in which it has not the property of wetting like the other. Thin hazy fogs occur frequently in winter evenings after clear cold weather, and they often become so permanently electric as to resist for days the action of the sun to disperse them. Thick heavy fogs occur also in the early part of summer and autumn, and are sometimes very wetting.

(362.) The *fogs in hollows* constitute the true stratus cloud. We see vapour at a distance in the atmosphere, and call it cloud; but when it sinks to the earth, or will not rise, and we are immersed in it, we call it mist or fog. When immersed in a cloud on a mountain, we say we are in a mist; but the same mist will be seen by a spectator, at a distance in the valley, as a beautiful cirro-stratus resting on the mountain.

(363.) The *magnifying power of mist* is a well-known optical illusion. Its *concealing* and *mistifying effects* may have been observed by every one; and its causing distant sounds to be heard as if near at hand, may also have been noticed by many. The illusive effects of mist are very well described in these lines:—

> "When all you see through densest fog is seen,
> When you can hear the fishers near at hand
> Distinctly speak, yet see not where they stand,
> Or sometimes them and not their boat discern,
> Or half conceal'd some figure at the stern;
> Boys who, on shore, to sea the pebble cast,
> Will hear it strike against the viewless mast;
> While the stern boatman growls his fierce disdain
> At whom he knows not, whom he threats in vain."*

(364.) The last atmospherical phenomenon which I have to mention is the *Wind*, and, though here considered last, it is a subject which, in my opinion, chiefly affects the interest of the farmer, for I am persuaded that the variations in the nature and direction of the winds are the best indices to the changes of weather that you can study. In the temperate zone, and particularly in this island, surrounded as it is with great oceans, and not far removed from an extensive continent, the variations of the wind are so great, and apparently so capricious, as to baffle all inquiry; whereas in the tropics, the periodic winds correspond exactly with the uniform course of the seasons, and the limited range of the barometer—phenomena which are characteristic of that portion of the globe.

(365.) This disparity of phenomena betwixt the different zones can be accounted for. In the tropics, the direct influence of the solar rays upon a portion of the globe, comprehending the breadth of the ecliptic,

* Crabbe.

23° 18′ on each side of the equatorial line, seems to cause and guide the aerial current within certain limits. This is done by a uniform rarefaction of the air, as the earth regularly presents a portion of its surface to the direct action of the solar rays in its diurnal rotation round its axis. This being in constant action, and exercised on a pretty uniform surface, the current generated to supply the regular and constant rarefaction must be also constant and regular. In the temperate zones, on the other hand, the solar action is always oblique and comparatively weak, and the aerial current becomes subject to secondary influences, which, operating in different degrees at different times, cause irregularities in its course. It is probable that the electric agency has a more powerful influence in the atmosphere in the temperate than in the torrid zone, by reason, perhaps, of the diminished powers there of the solar influence; and as its mode of action is more varied and unequal than that of the sun, the state of the atmosphere is thereby rendered more varied.

(366.) This intricate and not yet well understood subject may perhaps be made more clear to your mind by considering, in the first place, the origin of the *regular winds* of the torrid zone. In the zone of greatest heat, the air is more rarefied than it is any where else. "In consequence of this," says Mr Mudie, "the rarefied air ascends into the upper part of the atmosphere, and its place is supplied by cooler and less rarefied air from the north and south at the same time, and it is rarefied in its turn, and ascends in the air. Hence there is a constant ascent of the atmosphere from the point where the sun's heat is greatest, and this travels westward round the globe, every 24 hours, at a rate from 900 to 1000 miles an hour in the tropical zone, which, of course, has no *definite* boundary, but extends on each side of the zone. In this way, all along this zone, the general motion of the atmosphere is upward away from the surface of the earth; and little or no wind or current blows in any direction *within* it, unless from disturbance produced by terrestrial causes, such as the land, islands, and mountains. *Without* the indefinite boundaries of this zone, however, there is a motion of the surface atmosphere, both from the N. and from the S., which extends farther into either hemisphere, in proportion as the sun has more declination in that. But as the atmospheric air, when undisturbed by currents on the surface of the earth, is carried eastward with the same velocity as the surface itself, that is, less than 1000 miles an hour, in the proportion of the cosines of the latitude as we recede from the equator, this real motion of the air eastward along the earth's surface, is the counterpart of the apparent motion westward, as indicated by the progress of the sun in the point of highest temperature; and though these motions are exactly equal on the same parallel, the rate of motion in the hour, the day, or any fraction of it, is less and less as the latitude increases. Therefore, when the current from the N. and from the S. from the high latitudes, besides the time it takes to travel, has less real motion eastward, or apparent motion westward, than the tropical zone into which it arrives, the consequence is, that it is deflected westward in both hemispheres, and becomes a wind from the SE. on the south side of the parallel of greatest heat, and from the NE. from the north of the same. This is what is usually termed the *trade-wind*, and would be perfectly palpable all round the globe were its surface uniform, but, like all other phenomena of the earth, this wind is so much modified by surface-action, that the actual result accords but little with what might be inferred from principles alone. Still this is the grand cause which puts the currents of the atmosphere in motion; and notwithstanding all its modifications, it has great influence in determining the climate and productiveness of the different regions of the earth." * This cause of the trade-winds was first assigned by Hadley in 1734.

(367.) The importance of this tropical influence on the currents of the atmosphere everywhere will become more apparent, when we investigate the courses of those currents in the higher latitudes. "This *surface*-current from the N. and from the S. towards the equator," continues Mr Mudie, "necessarily requires, and therefore produces, a counter-current in the *higher atmosphere*. The air, which is continually drawn towards the parallel of greatest heat, either in a palpable trade-wind, or a silent current, cannot accumulate over the Equator, because as it ascends it gets into a cold region, and is there condensed. After this it descends towards the poles along the upper part of the atmosphere, and ultimately replaces that which finds its way to the tropical zone, producing a general motion in each hemisphere towards the tropical zone near the surface of the earth, and a counter-current from the equator at a higher elevation. This counter-current is the reverse of that from the poles, and therefore the different rate of motion in the different parallels of latitude has a contrary effect upon it. As it gets into higher latitudes it has more eastward motion than the surface there, and thus it is converted into a current from the SW. in the northern hemisphere, and a current from the NW. in the southern. In latitudes near the equator, this counter-current in the atmosphere is not observed on the surface of the ground, because both the southward and northward currents occupy the surface, and indeed the whole atmosphere to a considerable altitude. When, however, we come to the middle latitudes, the SW. wind, at least in countries to the east of the Atlantic, descends

* Mudie's World, p. 101-3.

so low, that it is not only felt on the mountain-tops throughout great part of the year, but the effects of it are seen in the bleaching or wearing away of the western sides of mountains of bold escarpement, by the wind from this quarter, and the rain which this wind often brings along with it; for it is to be understood, that though, in many such countries, the E. wind is the surface-wind, which precedes or ushers in the rain, the SW. wind being the warmer one, and as such holding the greater quantity of moisture in a state of vapour, is really the one out of which the rain is elaborated by the friction of the E. wind against it."*

(368.) The force of the wind caused by the diurnal action of the sun's rays in the tropics, is still farther increased by this other circumstance. Since the attraction of the sun and moon produces the remarkable effect of an oceanic wave, we cannot but suppose that an effect equally great at least is produced upon the atmosphere by its forming an atmospheric wave. Indeed, as the atmosphere is nearer to both those attractive objects than the ocean, the effect upon it should be greater. When we add to this the elasticity of the air, or that disposition which it has to dilate itself when freed from any of its pressure, we cannot but conclude that the atmospheric tides are considerable. Now, since the apparent diurnal motion of the moon is from E. to W., the atmospheric tides must follow it, and consequently produce a constant motion in the atmosphere from E. to W. This cause was first assigned by D'Alembert.

(369.) Another species of regular wind are the *monsoons*,—a word said to be derived from the Malay word *moossin*, signifying a season,—which occur within the limits of the tropics. The SW. monsoon blows from April to October; and its cause is the rarefaction of the air over the land as the sun proceeds northward to the tropic of Cancer, while its supply of cold air is from the Indian Ocean. The one that blows from the NE. from October to April, is caused by the cold air of the Indian Ocean flowing towards the land of New Holland, when the sun travels southward to the tropic of Capricorn. Great storms prevail at what is called the breaking up of the monsoons, that is, at the equinoxes, when the sun is in the parallel of the equator, as may be expected to be the case when any system of atmospheric phenomena, which has continued for six months together, is undergoing a great and opposite change. There are many more and greatly modified monsoons besides these regular ones, along all the southern coasts of land that are bounded by the Indian Ocean within the limits of the tropics.

(370.) There still remains to be mentioned another regular form of

* Mudie's World, p. 103-4.

wind in the Tropics, and that is the *land* and *sea breeze*. In all maritime countries of any extent between the Tropics, the wind blows during a certain number of hours every day from the sea, and during a certain number towards the sea from the land. The *sea*-breeze generally sets in about 10 A.M., and blows till 6 P.M.; then there is a calm. At 7 P.M. the *land*-breeze begins, and continues till 8 A.M., when it dies away to a calm. These phenomena are thus accounted for. During the day, the cool air of the sea, loaded with vapour, flows in upon the land, and takes the place of the rarefied land air; but as the sun declines, the rarefaction of the land-air diminishes, an equilibrium is restored, and a calm ensues. The sea is not so much heated during the day as the land, neither is it so much cooled during the night, because it is constantly exposing a new surface to the atmosphere. As the night approaches, therefore, the cooler and denser air of the *hills* (for where there are no hills there can be no land and sea breezes) falls down upon the plains, and, pressing upon the now comparatively lighter air of the sea, causes the land-breeze.

(371.) This is the rationale of the origin of regular winds, and it is simple and satisfactory; but, nevertheless, it cannot explain the many anomalies which are found to exist in various parts of the temperate regions. Thus, there is no apparent constancy or intensity in the *direction* of winds; and yet, amidst much apparent confusion, extended observation has discovered some general results. It is undoubted, for example, that SW. winds predominate in Europe, and this may be an expected result from the foregoing observations; while it is also an ascertained fact, that E. winds in spring are characteristic of a periodical occurrence in the climate of Great Britain; and this, though only a local affection, may be connected with the general observation in the preceding paragraph.

(372.) In many countries to the east of the Atlantic, the E. wind is the surface-wind, and is the forerunner of rain for the reason above specified. M. Schouw has also shewn, that the W. winds diminish as we advance to the east of Europe, which is still in conformity with the general remarks given above. Thus, the W. winds of London exceed those of the E. in the ratio of 1.7 : 1; at St Petersburgh, they exceed only in the ratio of 1.3 : 1. These variable winds stamp the nature of every climate; for although they are most apparent in their effects in the temperate regions, they nevertheless also exist in the tropics, as may be experienced along every coast and large island in the Indian Ocean. Their nature, therefore, depends on causes which act with uniformity, notwithstanding all their apparent irregularities. They may be all intimately connected with one another, and they probably succeed each other in a certain order, though that order has not hitherto been ascertained. All these causes may, and probably will, be discovered; the circumstances in which they take place, and the effects which they produce, may become familiar to us; and whenever this is the case, the winds of any place might, in some measure, be reduced to calculation.*

(373.) In regard to the *direction* of the wind, I may mention only, in reference to this country, that the predominant winds are from the westerly direction, and of these the SW. prevails, and it prevails most in the months of July, August, and September. The NE. wind blows always in the spring and early summer months, as in April, May, and June; but they are most severely felt on the east coast. This table shews the comparative prevalence of the westerly and easterly winds in Great Britain, the former comprehending all those from N. to S. by the W., and the latter those from N. to S. by the E.

Years of Observation,	Places.	Wind.	
		Westerly.	Easterly.
10	London, ...	233.	132.
7	Lancaster, ...	216.	149.
51	Liverpool, ...	190.	175.
9	Dumfries, ...	227.5	137.5
10	Branxholm, near Hawick, . .	232.	133.
7	Cambuslang, ...	214.	151.
8	Hawkhill, near Edinburgh, .	229.5	135.5
	Mean,	220.3	144.7

(374.) It may prove useful to enumerate a few places at which registers of the wind are kept, to shew you the results in different parts of the kingdom. 1. In London, by a mean of 10 years of the register kept by the Royal Society, these results were obtained:—

Of SW. winds, .	112 days.	Of SE. winds, .	32 days.
NE.	58 ...	E.	26 ...
NW.	50 ...	S.	18 ...
W.	53 ...	N.	16 ...

It appears from the particulars of this register, that the SW. winds blow, at an average, more frequently than any other wind during every month of the year, but that it blows longest in July and August; that the NE. winds blow most constantly in January, March, April, May, and June, and most seldom in February, July, September, and December; and

* See Polehampton's Gallery of Nature and Art, vol. iv. p. 185-205; in which an interesting collection of accounts of varieties in the phenomena of the winds is given.

that the NW. winds blow oftener from November to March, and more seldom during September and October than any other months. 2. The following table is an abstract of 7 years' observations made by Dr Meek, at Cambuslang, near Glasgow :—

Of SW. winds, .	174 days.	Of NE. winds, .	104 days.
NW.	40 ...	SE.	47 ...

From this register, it appears that the NE. winds blow more frequently in April, May, and June ; and the SW. in July, August, and September.* 3. These are the results of a register of the winds kept by Admiral Sir David Milne, at Inveresk, near Edinburgh, in the years 1840 and 1841.

	1840.	1841.		1840.	1841.
Of N. winds,	43	77 days.	Of S. winds,	39	79 days.
NNE. ...	20	12 ...	SSW. ...	38	62 ...
NE. ...	41	49 ...	SW. ...	127	113 ...
ENE. ...	15	14 ...	WSW. ...	38	45 ...
E. ...	28	38 ...	W ...	138	105 ...
ESE. ...	13	7 ...	WNW. ...	33	29 ...
SE. ...	32	29 ...	NW. ...	45	37 ...
SSE. ...	19	20 ...	NNW. ...	13	13 ... †

4. By a register kept by Mr Atkinson, at Harraby near Carlisle, these results of the wind were obtained in 1840.

N. . .	12¼ days.	S. . .	19½ days.
NNE. .	14½ ...	SSW. .	24¾ ...
NE. . .	14½ ...	SW. .	39¼ ...
ENE. .	20¼ ...	WSW. .	70¼ ...
E. .	20¾ ...	W. .	42 ...
ESE. .	7 ...	WNW. .	16 ...
SE. .	20½ ...	NW. .	11½ ...
SSE. .	22½ ...	NNW. .	10¾ ...

Total westerly, 132¼ days ; total easterly, 233¾ ; calm, 56 ; moderate, 248¼ ; breeze, 27¾ ; strong breeze, 13¾ ; stormy, 20.‡

5. As it is of importance for you to compare the state of the weather in the hilly with that of the low country, I shall transcribe two tables of observations made in the parish of Yarrow, Selkirkshire ; the one by Mr Ballantyne, Tinnis, at an elevation of 470 feet above the level of the sea, and deduced from an average of 6 years from 1826 to 1831, the barometer and thermometer being observed at 8 A.M. and 10 P.M. :—

* Polehampton's Gallery of Nature and Art, vol. iv. p. 192–4.

† Edinburgh Evening Post, January 1842.

‡ Jameson's Edinburgh New Philosophical Journal, vol. xxx. p. 422.

Number of Days of Wind from each point of the Compass.								Fair.	Rain.	Snow.	Mean of Barometer.	Mean Heat of	
W.	NW.	N.	NE.	E.	SE.	S.	SW.						
68	46	23	30	40	22	25	92	175	154	36	29.57	Spring,	39°.
												Summer,	53°.13
												Autumn,	50°.81
												Winter,	36°.89
												Mean,	44°.96

and the other by Mr Alexander Laidlaw, Bowerhope, at an elevation of 560 feet above the sea, which gives these results, on an average of 10 years from 1821 to 1831.*

Number of Days of Wind from each point of the Compass.								Fair.	Rain.	Snow.	Mean of Barometer.
W.	NW.	N.	NE.	E.	SE.	S.	SW.				
71	35	15	22	40	16	28	101	154	169	42	29°.44

(375.) The *direction of the winds* is greatly affected by the configuration of the country, their general direction being modified so as to coincide with the natural lines of elevation and depression of the earth's surface; and it is probably on this account that the winds in Egypt are generally either N. or S.; the former prevailing nine months of the year. When the climate is tolerably regular, as in the south of Europe, the direction of the wind makes all possible difference in its character. The transition from a *sirocco* to a *tramontana*, at Rome and Naples, is as great as 10° of latitude.† A remarkable effect of local configuration on the direction of winds is thus related: "When the wind is NW. at Manchester, it is N. at Liverpool; when N. at Manchester, it is NE. at Liverpool; when NE. at Manchester, it is E. at Liverpool; and when E. at Manchester, it is SE. at Liverpool. Of course the SW. wind comes the same to both towns, as there are no hills to the S. such as are to the N. and E. of them."‡

(376.) The *force and velocity of winds* are instructive subjects of inquiry. They have been attempted to be calculated with great care and ingenuity by Mr Rouse, who constructed tables of the results. His tables

* New Statistical Account of Scotland. Yarrow—Selkirkshire, p. 30

† Forbes' Report on Meteorology, vol. i. p. 247.

‡ Morning Herald, 19th June 1839.

have been much improved and considerably augmented by Dr Young, a philosopher of profound erudition, but whose researches are not so generally known as they should be from the condensed form of expression which he used in communicating them. He compared Mr Rouse's observations with the results of Dr Lind's scale, and constructed the following table :—

TABLE OF THE FORCE AND VELOCITY OF DIFFERENT WINDS.

Force of the wind on the square foot in			Velocity of the Wind, computed from Rouse's Experiments.		Denominations of Winds.
lb.	oz.	dr.	Feet in 1 second.	Miles in 1 hour.	
0	0	1.2	1.43	1.	Hardly perceptible. *Rouse.*
0	0	5.1	2.93	2.	Just perceptible. *Rouse.*
0	0	11.2	4.40	3.	
0	1	4.2	5.87	4.	Gentle winds. *Lind.*
0	1	15.4	7.33	5.	
0	2	1.2	10.67	5.14	A gentle wind. *Lind.*
0	4	2.5	14.67	7.27	Pleasant wind. *Lind.*
0	7	13.9	15.19	10.	Pleasant brisk gale. *Rouse.*
0	8	5.3	22.0	10.35	Fresh breeze. *Lind.*
1	1	11.3	29.34	15.	Brisk gale. *Lind.*
1	15	7.8	33.74	20.	Very brisk. *Rouse.*
2	9	10.6	36.67	23.	
3	1	3.2	44.01	25.	
4	6	13.8	47.73	30.	High wind. *Rouse.*
5	3	5.2	51.34	32.54	High wind. *Lind.*
6	0	6.9	58.68	35.	
7	13	10.6	66.01	40.	Very high. *Rouse.*
9	15	6.5	67.5	45.	Great Storm. *Derham.*
10	6	10.4	73.35	46.02	Very high. *Lind.*
12	4	12·8	82.67	50.	Storm or tempest. *Rouse.*
15	10	0.	88.02	56.37	Storm. *Lind.*
17	11	7.	95.46	60.	Great storm. *Rouse.*
20	13	5.2	96.82	65.08	Great storm. *Lind.*
21	6	15.3	106.72	66.	Great storm. *Condamine.*
26	0	10.4	117.36	72.76	Very great storm. *Lind.*
31	7	13.4	116.91	80·	Hurricane. *Rouse.*
31	4	0.	126.43	79.71	Hurricane. *Lind·*
36	8	12.2	135.	86.2	Great hurricane. *Lind.*
41	10	10.7	143.11	92.04	Very great hurricane. *Lind.*
46	14	0.	146.7	97.57	Most violent hurricane.
49	3	3.2	150.93	100.	A hurricane that tears up trees.
52	1	5.2	158.29	102.9	
57	4	11.	160.	107.92	
58	7	3.2	165.34	109.	
62	8	0.		112.73	

With regard to the nomenclature here given to some of the varieties of winds, a few remarks seem called for. Whatever may be the accuracy of the higher rates of velocity I cannot say, for there is no ordinary means of judging of them, except by seeing the shadows of clouds passing along the ground, but the accuracy of the smaller velocities may very easily be judged of. It is said that wind moving 2 miles an hour is "just perceptible;" and at 3 and 4 miles it constitutes what are called "gentle winds." Let us test these. Suppose the air to be perfectly calm when you are walking at the rate of 3 miles an hour, do you feel anything like a "gentle wind" blowing upon you? Are you, in fact, in the least sensible of the action of the air upon you? I think you cannot be. The air is so insensible to you in that state that you can neither hear nor feel it, and were you to stand still when it moves at the rate of 3 miles an hour, you would feel it as little. Before you feel it at all, therefore, you may safely conclude that the air is moving at a greater velocity than 3 or 4 miles an hour, whatever indication anemometers may give, for the human skin is a much more delicate instrument for this purpose than any artificial one can possibly be. On this view of the subject, Sir Richard Phillips makes these pertinent remarks: "If wind blows 100 miles an hour, that is 528,00 feet, then as water is 833 times heavier than air, water moving at the rate of 635 feet, or 1 furlong per hour, would be equal to it, which is absurd. There must be some mistake. Water at 5 miles an hour would scarcely bend a twig, whereas a West India hurricane has been known to blow heavy cannon out of a battery. Balloons have travelled 60 miles an hour, when the anemometer shewed but 8 miles."* When I have observed the shadows of clouds flying over the land in a windy day in spring or summer, I have felt convinced that the wind must move hundreds of miles per hour in this country, where the velocity of wind is small compared to what it sometimes is in the Tropics. It is recorded, that such was the noise occasioned by the hurricane that took place at Pondicherry on the 29th October 1768, that when the signal guns were fired to warn the ships off the coast, their reports were never heard by the inhabitants within the fort.†

(377.) The subject of *Storms*, in their origin and direction, after a long period of neglect, has of late again attracted the attention of philosophers. So long ago as 1801, Colonel Capper, of the East India Company's service, in his work on winds and monsoons, gave it as his opinion that hurricanes would be found to be *great whirlwinds*. This

* Phillips' Facts, p. 455.

† Capper on Winds and Monsoons.

idea was adopted and confirmed by Mr W. C. Redfield of New York, in a memoir on the prevailing storms of the Atlantic coast of North America, which appeared in Silliman's Journal in 1831. Colonel Reid, of the Royal Engineers, has since then placed the subject in a prominent position before the public, by his more recent dissertation. His attention was first directed to it in 1831. He arrived, in military service, at Barbadoes, immediately after the desolating hurricane of that year, which, in the short space of seven hours, destroyed 1477 houses on that island alone; and having been for two years and a half daily employed as an engineer officer amidst the ruined buildings, was thus naturally led to the consideration of the phenomena of hurricanes.

(378.) The NE. storms on the coast of America did not escape the notice of Franklin, who devoted so much of his time to the observation of atmospherical phenomena. He was prevented by one of them from observing an eclipse of the moon at Philadelphia, and was astonished to find that it visited Boston after that, though Boston lies to the NE. of Philadelphia. Such an occurrence was not lost on so inquiring a mind as Franklin's, but he died before he made any progress in the investigation. Mr Redfield, however, following up his observations, ascertained that while the NE. storms were blowing on the shores of America, the wind, with equal violence, was blowing from the SW. on the Atlantic. He found, throughout their course, that the wind on the opposite sides of the shore, over which the storm prevailed, blew in opposite directions,—that, in fact, the entire storm was a progressive whirlwind, and that all these whirlwinds revolved constantly in the same direction. Colonel Reid, after much investigation, was impressed with the regularity with which storms appear to pass toward the north pole, and always revolved in the same direction, that is, opposite to the hands of a watch, or from the E. round by the N. W. S. to E. From this circumstance he was anxious to ascertain whether the revolution would not be in an opposite direction in the southern hemisphere; and this point was also illustrated by the disastrous storm in the Indian sea of 1809, in which nine sail of Indiamen foundered. He found the general phenomenon of these storms to be as a great whirlwind, represented by a circle, whose centre is made to progress along a curve or part of a curve, which is, in most cases, of a form approaching the parabolic, the circles expanding as they advance from the point at which the storm begins to be felt, the rotatory motion in the northern hemisphere being in a contrary direction to that in which the hands of a watch go round, while in the southern hemisphere the rotation is in the same direction as that in which the hands of a watch revolve; and the diameter of these circles, over which the whirl of the storm was spread, often extend from 1000 to 1800 miles. In the centre of the whirl is a comparative calm, while in its circumference the storm rages, and the wind blows from every conceivable quarter.*

(379.) There are concomitant circumstances attendant on storms which are worth relating. Major Sabine has found the magnetic intensity least at St Helena, where there are no violent storms; his line of least intensity appearing to be the true Pacific Ocean. The lines of greatest magnetic intensity, on the contrary, seemed to correspond with the localities of hurricanes and typhoons; for the meridian of the American magnetic pole is found to pass not far from the Caribbean sea, and that of the Siberian pole through the China sea. He found two instances of water-spouts, one in the northern, the other in the southern hemisphere, in which the revolutions moved in opposite directions, and both in contrary directions to great storms. He explains the variable high winds of our latitudes, by the storms expanding in size, and diminishing in force, as they approach the poles, the meridians at the same time nearing each other, and occasioning a huddling together of the gales.†

(380.) A rival theory of storms, supported by Professor Bâche, has been proposed by Mr Espy of Philadelphia. This theory supposes that the wind blows from all quarters towards a centre. Its explanation has been given by Professor Bâche; ‡ but it is the opinion of Sir John Herschell that this theory, however ingenious, is not tenable against the indications of the barometer; whereas the oscillations of the barometer, being in opposite directions in the northern and southern hemispheres, strongly confirm the correctness of Colonel Reid's views.

(381.) Mr Snow Harris of Plymouth has discovered that there is a *connection betwixt the force of the wind and the hororary oscillations of the barometer.* Thus the mean force of the wind for the whole year, at 9 A.M. was 0.855, and at 9 P.M. 0.605; but at 3 P.M. it was 1.107 of Lind's anemometer.§

(382.) M. Schübler has shewn that *winds have a characteristic electric power.* The precipitations during the wind from the northern half of the circle of azimuth, have a ratio of positive to negative electricity, which is a maximum, and in the other half it is a minimum, the negative precipitations when the wind is S. being more than double the positive ones. The mean intensity of electricity, independent of its sign, is greatest in N. winds.||

* Edinburgh New Philosophical Journal, vol. xxv. p. 342.

† Ibid.

‡ Caledonian Herald, No. i. p. 3.

§ Forbes' Report on Meteorology, vol. i. p. 248.

|| Ibid.

(383.) Capper attempts to give a *methodical arrangement of winds*, which, whether strictly correct or not, serves to shew that there are varieties in the currents of the air which may produce very different effects. As to the necessity of such an arrangement, he says—' Those who would now wish to be perfectly understood, when treating of the winds, must previously make a new catalogue of them, including all such as have been lately discovered, and this addition made, they may then venture to inquire into their several causes and effects. In this manner it is my intention to proceed; and to begin by making a new division of those with which I am acquainted into four different classes or rather genera, of which, the first excepted, there are many different species, namely, the perennial, the periodical, the topical, and the general. 1. The *perennial* is the only wind which blows the same way throughout the year, as the trade winds. 2. The *periodical* includes principally the monsoons, the Mediterranean etesian, the tropical land wind, the khumsan, the sirocco, the harmattan, and the land and sea breezes. 3. The *topical* includes the samyel, the mistral, and the Bengal north-wester, which are all of them irregular and temporary, blowing always from the same point at particular places, in sudden gusts, but of short duration. 4. The *general* winds are those which prevail in all parts of the world beyond the tropics, and might with equal propriety be called *variable* winds. These can only be discriminated from each other by the different degrees of velocity with which the current of air moves."*

(384.) As there is an atmospherical wave occasioned by the gravitation of the sun and moon, and particularly the latter, as well as a tidal wave, and as any elevation of the atmosphere cannot fail to produce a change in the part immediately below the elevated part, there seems no reason to doubt that an *analogy exists betwixt the tides and the winds, and also with rain.* It seems that if high tides at London Bridge happen at 12 or 1 noon, there is more frequently rain than at other periods, if the wind is in the E., which is not often; so it is probable that when the changes of the wind can be calculated more perfectly, we shall have more correct tide tables. It thus appears that the nearer the high tide is to noon the greater is the probability of rain, because the breeze from the sea is then strongest.

(385.) Air being very mobile, and of greatest density at the surface of the earth, when any cause produces a current in it, it is reasonable to suppose that it will be guided in its direction by the hills which it may meet with in its course, first being retarded in its velocity by their tops,

* Capper on Winds and Monsoons.

then deflected from their sides, and at length made to flow uninterruptedly down the valleys, acquiring a greater velocity the farther it pursues its course unmolested; so that we find among hills, as among streets in a town, the wind blowing different ways in adjacent places. "Hills also attract the clouds to them. The effect of this varies according to the size of the hills and their number. If rather numerous, but only moderately high, they produce frequent rains throughout the neighbourhood, being high enough to attract and stop, but not high enough to retain and absorb, the clouds. Hence Kendal in Westmoreland, and Moffat in Dumfriesshire, are found to be exceedingly rainy. If the hills are very numerous, they produce rather more uncertainty than rain; for, as the wind varies, every hill has equal chance of attracting the clouds. Hence the uncertain weather in Wales and the Highlands of Scotland. The barometer is also found to vacillate in those countries as much as the weather. If the hills are still higher, they retain the clouds often in the form of snow-clouds, which may remain till warm clouds come to dissolve them, and they then pour down the mountains in the form of brooks and rivulets. If very high, they retain clouds to such an extent as actually to prevent rain altogether, as in the neighbourhood of the west of the Andes, which is free from rain. The effect there is very much increased by the wind, which clears the windward country from rain, while the water flows down in streams on the opposite sides of the mountains, producing the most gigantic rivers in the world, as the Amazon, which has 200 tributary streams as large as the Nile or the Danube."*

(386.) Being thus made acquainted with the most approved instruments used by scientific men for ascertaining the changes of atmospherical phenomena, and thereby made to reflect on the nature and varieties of those phenomena, you will be the better able to direct your attention to those classes of them which act so prominent a part in producing the states of the atmosphere called the *weather*. This word does not mean any one state of things, but a succession of states, and their changes, which follow each other in the atmosphere, without our being able to tell why they should succeed one another in one particular order rather than another. Could the *why* and the *wherefore* of these changes be ascertained, as many other intricate facts in philosophy have been discovered, traced, or ascertained, we should know the approaching state of the weather as certainly as we can foretel the result in any science on being made acquainted with its elements. Could this desirable end

* Legh's Hints in his Weather Almanack for 1841.

be attained, farming would become one of the fixed sciences, producing necessary results, for there really seems no other obstacle to that attainment but the uncertain knowledge of the changes in the state of the weather. This, no doubt, exerts an overwhelming influence over our present state of ignorance, and as long as our acumen can penetrate no farther into what at present is a secret of nature, its effects will never be anticipated; but in proportion to the extent of obscurity in which it is involved should scientific scrutiny be exercised for its discovery. "Though one of the most interesting subjects connected with the economy of our globe, and its use and comfort to man," Mr Mudie well observes in regard to the subject of the weather, "this is one of the most difficult subjects that can engage his enquiry. One reason of this is, the vast number of elements that have to be studied and taken into account; the different laws which each of these obey; the indeterminable nature of many of them; and the modifying influences which they have upon each other in their joint working. Thus, the daily and seasonal motions of the earth, and the action of the sun and moon; the reciprocating influences of the hemispheres, those of sea and land, of plain, or valley and mountain, and of surfaces covered with vegetation of different characters are all causes of the weather; but, in most instances, particularly in such variable climates as present themselves about the middle latitudes of the quadrant, and near the shores of the sea—more especially in small countries surrounded by it—these causes are so blended with each other, that it is impossible so to analyze the result as to assign to each of them its due state in bringing about the particular weather of any day, any week, or any period, longer or shorter."* Although there is too much truth in these observations to afford any hope that the subject of the weather will be soon reduced to the capacity of every farmer, yet every farmer may contribute a little towards collecting facts connected with the atmospherical phenomena which come within the sphere of his observation; and you may have observed, from what I have said in the preceding pages regarding this subject, that the series of phenomena which affect the farmer's operations are confined to a few classes of them. In short, the currents and vapour of the atmosphere are the *immediate* causes which give rise to changes of weather. If the origin of these could be reduced to certainty, the other elements of heat, light, and gravitation would soon become better known, because they produce more steady results. The winds and clouds thus form prominent objects of study to the farmer, and on this account I have dwelt

* Mudie's World, p. 243.

longer on their properties than on any other phenomena. Should winds and clouds be under the immediate influence of the electric agency, as many suppose, a long period indeed may elapse ere certainty can be gained in regard to them. Meantime, it is your duty as well as interest to collect well observed facts, and to assist those scientific men who are labouring in this field of observation.

(387.) You will now see what part these respective elements of the atmosphere perform in the phenomena of the weather. The indications which they present are called *prognostics*, and, in enumerating these, I shall transcribe only those in which I have confidence as being most consonant with my own observation. Some writers affect to despise prognostics of the weather, classing them with quackery and superstition; but though designing persons may have employed some of them to serve their own wicked purposes, at a time when most remarkable phenomena in nature, now well known, were regarded with religious awe and dread, that is no reason for denying that natural objects may indicate symptoms of change in the atmosphere before any actually takes place in it to the extent to affect our senses. If *we* fail to anticipate changes, that should rather be ascribed to our ignorance of their nature, and our mode of observation, than to any failure in the purpose of the economy of nature. We should " never despise the day of small things" in the acquisition of knowledge, especially when our discernment has never yet discovered the mode of action of any of the primary agents in nature by which the least important change in any one atmospherical phenomenon is produced.

(388.) Prognostics may be divided into two classes,—those of a *general character*, which apply to every, and those which apply only to a *particular season*. Whether of general or particular application, they may all be deduced from the appearances of the heavenly bodies and of the sky, the state of meteorological instruments, and the motions and habits of certain plants and animals. As this is the first opportunity I have had of speaking of prognostics, it seems proper that I should allude to those of a *general* character before adverting to those *particularly applicable to winter*.

(389.) A beginning may appropriately be made with the great luminary of our planetary system—the *sun*. When the sun rises red, wind and rain may be expected during the day; but when, on the contrary, he rises unclouded, attended with a scorching heat from his beams, cloudiness and perhaps rain will ensue before midday. When he rises clouded with a few grey clouds, they will soon dissipate, and a fine day follows. When his light is dim, vapour exists in the upper region of the air, and may be expected to descend shortly after in the form of dense clouds. When his light, after rain, though it be clear enough, is of a transparent watery hue, rain will soon again fall. When his direct rays have a scorching and enervating effect on the human body, throughout the greater part of the day, the next day will be cloudy, and perhaps rainy. When the sun is more or less obscured by a thicker and thinner cirro-stratus cloud, and when he is said to be *wading* in the cloud, rain may come—if the cloud indicates rain, it will come; and if, at the same time, a *coloured* corona surround his disc, rain will certainly come; but a *colourless* corona may not be followed by rain, though it is a proof of much vapour being in the atmosphere. I have known wind follow this phenomenon, though rarely. A halo surrounding the disc of the sun is almost always sure to precede rain. A red sunset without clouds indicates a doubt of fair weather; but a good day may be expected after a red sunset in clouds. A watery sunset, diverging rays of light, either direct from the sun or from behind a cloud, is indicative of rain. After a dull black sunset rain may be expected.

(390.) There are many proverbial sayings among country people regarding the state of the weather, which, having been derived from long observation, have become axioms, and were designated by Bacon "the philosophy of the people." This is one of these—

> "An evening red, or a morning grey,
> Doth betoken a bonnie day;
> In an evening grey and a morning red,
> Put on your hat, or ye'll weet your head."

(391.) Whatever effects the *moon* may have in producing the general state of the weather, there are not many prognostics connected with her appearances. The changes of the moon produce greater effects than at any other period. With a clear silvery aspect, fair weather may be expected. A pale moon always indicates rain. A red one is the forerunner of wind. Seeing the "old moon in the new one's arms," as the phrase has it, is a sign of stormy weather, as we learn from the old ballad of Sir Peter Spens, which says,

> "I saw the new moon late yestreen, wi' the auld moon in her arm,
> And, ever alack, my master dear, I fear we'll suffer harm."

Seeing the new moon very young, "like the paring of a nail," is also indicative of wet; but when the horns of the new moon are blunt, they indicate rain, and fair weather when sharp. There is a true metrical proverb regarding the moon—

> "In the wane of the moon,
> A cloudy morning bodes a fair afternoon."

And this is equally so—

> "New moon's mist
> Never dies of thirst."

Halos and coronæ attend the moon more frequently than the sun, and their prognostics are exactly the same in both cases.

(392.) It has long been thought that the moon exercises some influence on the human system, and it is supposed that the new and full moons produce greater irritability on it than at the quarters. This may perhaps be accounted for by the influence of electrical causes at those periods when the atmospheric tide is at the highest, and the rarity of the atmosphere over the zenith at the greatest. This state of things will cause a deposition of clouds which will convey away the surrounding positive electricity, and leave every object in the neighbourhood in the opposite condition; and it is well known that a negative electric state of the body is always attended with very unpleasant feelings. *East* winds are always unpleasant to the feelings, and particularly so when the moon is new or at the full, and probably from this cause.

(393.) The *stars* appearing dim indicate rain. Very few stars seen at one time, when there is no frost, indicates a similar result.

(394.) When the *sky* is of deeply coloured blue, it indicates rain. When it is of a crystalline transparency, after rain, more rain will follow. If distant objects appear very distinct and near through the air, it indicates rain. When the air feels oppressive to walk in, rain will follow; when it feels light and pleasant, fair weather will continue.

(395.) When distant *sounds* are distinctly heard through the air in a calm day, the air is loaded with vapour; and rain may be expected when the tolling of bells, barking of dogs, talking of people, waterfalls, or rapids over mill-dams are loudly heard. The sea is often heard to roar, and loudest at night, as also the noise of a city, when a cloud is seen suspended a very short way above head. When the noise of the sea passes to the S. of the mouth of a river or estuary, rain will follow in 12 hours, but if to the N., then fair weather.

(396.) If *smoke* rise perpendicularly upwards from chimneys in calm weather, fair weather may be expected to continue; but if it fall toward and roll along the ground, not being easily dispersed, rain will ensue. If the smoke from a tobacco-pipe hang in or scent the air long, it is an indication of rain, but it also indicates a good scenting day for hounds.

(397.) When a *halo* appears, with little indication of a cirro-stratus cloud, the rain will be gentle, but of long continuance. When a part of halo is imperfectly formed, which is owing to the unequal thickness of the cirro-stratus, it indicates the quarter from which a storm will approach.

(398.) *Falling stars* and *fiery meteors* always indicate a change to stormy weather, generally wind. When falling stars are numerous, a storm will certainly appear at the break of next morn.

(399.) Much *lightning* in the night either with or without clouds, announces unsettled weather, especially if it be of pale colour.

(400.) The *aurora borealis* is most likely to appear in changeable weather, from good to bad and from bad to good.

(401.) Attentive observation will shew you, that as *vapour* is the most easily affected element of the atmosphere, so its transmutations perform an important part in producing atmospherical phenomena, and in no class is it more remarkable than in the *clouds*. The changes indicated by the different varieties of cloud are numerous and important.

(402.) When *cirri* appear in a clear settled sky, a change in the weather is taking place. When they appear like goats' hair or grey mares' tails, wind will ensue, and it will blow from the quarter to which the tufts point. When cirri unite and form cirro-strati at a comparatively low elevation, rain is indicated. When cirri are seen through a broken cloud, in deep blue sky, after rain, the rain will continue. Cirri extending on both sides of the zenith forbode a storm of wind of some days' duration.

(403.) Round well-formed *cumuli* indicate settled weather; when ragged on the edges, rain may be looked for. If their edges curl inwards, a storm is brewing. When blown outwards, wind will follow. When cumuli remain during the evening, and increase in size, they indicate rain; but when they form in the morning and disappear at night, they indicate steady weather.

(404.) If *stratus* evaporates before the mounting sun, there will be a fine day, but if it makes its way to the mountain tops, and lingers about them, rain will come in the afternoon. If it creeps down mountain sides into the valley during the day, rain will certainly fall.

(405.) The presence of *cirro-cumuli* indicates increase of temperature. Those which are dense and compact forbode storm. When cirro-cumuli surmount nimbus, an increase of temperature takes place, and frequently without rain. If grey coloured cirro-cumuli prevail in the morning, fair weather; but if red, then rain will ensue.

(406.) The presence of *cirro-stratus* indicates a change. When it forms a veil across the sky, whether thin or dense, it indicates rain, and it does so when it accumulates of a dark colour in the evening; but if edged with brilliant colours, it forbodes fair weather. When cirro-strati rest on mountain tops, the hills are said "to have put on their nightcaps," and also, when they rest on cumuli-strati, rain is indicated. When cirro-strati are white, and of positive outline, in a deep blue sky, a storm is sure to come.

(407.) When cumuli change rock-like into *cumulo-strati* rain will follow, and the exception is when rain does not follow.

(408.) When *clouds* attach themselves to others, or to mountain tops, they give indication of rain. When they form and disappear again soon, fair weather ensues.

(409.) The *most wholesome weather* is when W. winds and day cumuli prevail—when a stratus evaporates as the sun rises—during the formation of well-defined cumuli throughout the day, most abundant in the afternoon, and disappearing again in the evening—to be succeeded by strong dew and the stratus—and accompanied with westerly breezes, which fall away towards evening. In these circumstances the barometer is always steady, and the thermometer always high. When other points of wind accompany this weather, they will be attended either with frost or heat according to the season of the year.

(410.) The weather is always remarkably *unwholesome* when clouds of all denominations have undefined edges.

(411.) *Scud* is the sure precursor of a deposition from the atmosphere.

(412.) When *mist* first appears on the hills, and then moves down to the valley, rain will fall shortly afterwards, or, as more extensively expressed in this metrical stanza,—

> "When mist takes to the hill,
> Then gude weather it doth spill,
> When the mist takes to the sea,
> Then gude weather it will be."

It always *feels* cold in misty weather, and particularly in easterly *haar*.

(413.) With reference to *winds*, it may generally be said that N. winds are dry, E. winds cold, S. winds wet, and W. winds warm. The intermediate points will partake of the character belonging to the cardinal point it is nearest for the time. The same observations are thus put in quaint metre—

> "When the wind's in the west,
> The weather's at the best;
> When the wind's in the east,
> It's neither gude for man nor beast
> When the wind's in the south,
> Of rain there will be fouth;
> When the wind's still,
> No weather's ill."*

* Henderson's Scottish Proverbs, by Motherwell, p. 153.

In very wet places, such as Plymouth, it has been jokingly said that

> " The S. wind always brings wet weather,
> The N. wind wet and cold together,
> The W. wind always brings us rain,
> The E. wind blows it back again."

(414.) The greatest quantity of *rain* falls from the S. and SW Though heavy showers come from the W. they are never of long duration. The E. wind seldom brings rain, but when it does, it is of long continuance, sometimes three days. A gradual fall of the barometer indicates a long continuance of rain. When it suddenly sinks and rises alternately there will only be showers. When the depression is more sudden and great, a storm will ensue. To very wet places, the quatrain, which I have given regarding the effects of the sun rising and setting in grey and red, has been thus humorously applied—

> " If the sun in red should set,
> The next day surely will be wet;
> If the sun should set in grey,
> The next will be a rainy day."

(415.) Prognostications of changes in the weather may be derived from the habits and feelings of *animals*. With regard to man, headach, toothach, rheumatism, pains in corns, old bruises, and fractures, frequently indicate in him the approaching storm. Before thunderstorms, many have a feeling of listlessness, oppression, and uneasiness. What may be the immediate cause which actuates those feelings, it is not easy to apprehend, but it is not improbably derived from the influence of electric causes. If by any means the body is put into a negative state of electricity, whilst the inanimate objects around are in the positive state, unpleasant feelings are very likely to arise until the equilibrium is restored, either by the fall of rain or the occurrence of a thunderstorm. It is not unlikely that the inferior animals are affected by similar causes, and to a much greater degree, in consequence of their covering being either of hair or of feathers, substances both highly susceptible of electric excitement, and which, when extraordinarily affected by the electric agency, cannot fail to produce sensible effects on them,—being creatures of immediate impulse, and hence exhibiting, by external signs, the most delicate operations of exciting causes.

(416.) These are indications of *rain*,—When cattle snuff the air and gather together in a corner of the field with their heads to leeward, or take shelter in the sheds—when sheep leave their pastures with reluctance—when goats go to sheltered spots—when asses bray frequently and shake their ears—when dogs lie much about the fireside and appear drowsy—when cats turn their backs to the fire and wash their faces—when pigs cover themselves more than usual in litter—when cocks crow at unusual hours and flap their wings much—when hens chaunt—when ducks and geese are unusually clamorous—when pigeons wash themselves—when peacocks squall loudly from trees—when the guinea fowl makes an incessant grating clamour—when sparrows chirp loudly, and clamorously congregate on the ground or in the hedge—when swallows fly low, on account of the descent of the flies upon which they feed towards the earth, and when they skim their wings in waters—when the carrion crow croaks solitarily —when water wild-fowl dip and wash unusually—when moles throw up hills more industriously than usual—when toads creep out in numbers—when frogs croak—when bats squeak and enter houses—when the singing birds take shelter—when the robin approaches nearest the dwellings of man—when tame swans fly against the wind—when bees leave their hives with caution and fly only short distances—when ants carry their eggs busily—when flies sting severely and become troublesome in numbers—when earthworms appear on the surface of the ground and crawl about—and when the larger sorts of snails appear.

(417.) The approach of *wind* may be anticipated from the following prognostics:—when cattle appear frisky, and toss their heads and jump—when sheep leap and play, boxing each other—when pigs squeal, and carry straw in their mouths—when the cat scratches a tree or a post—when geese attempt to fly, or distend and flap their wings—when pigeons clap their wings smartly behind their backs in flying—when crows mount in the air and perform somersets, making at the time a garrulous noise—when swallows fly on one side of trees, the flies taking the leeward side for safety against the wind—and when magpies collect in small companies and set up a chattering noise.

(418.) *Fine weather* may be expected to continue when cattle lie in the open field, or in the courts instead of the sheds—when sheep take up their lair for the night on the brow of a knoll—when pigs lie down for the night without covering themselves up in litter—when peacocks roost on the tops of houses—when the raven sails round and round high up in the air—when song birds carol late in the evening—when the corn-crake (*Rallus Crex*) ventriloquises in the corn or grass—when the partridge calls in the evening to his mate—and when the snipe (*Scolopax gallinago*) booms in the air in the evening.

(419.) These are indications of *storm*:—When the merle thrush (*Turdus viscivorus*) sings loud and long, on which account this bird has received the name of storm-cock—when sea-gulls come in flocks on land, and make a noise about the coast,—and when the porpoise (*Phocæna communis*) comes near the shore in large numbers.

(420.) Some *plants* indicate a change of the weather as well as animals. When the common chickweed (*Stellaria media*) expands freely, no rain will fall for many hours, if it continue open, no rain need be feared for some time; in showery days the flowers appear half concealed, and when entirely shut, we may expect a rainy day. When the Siberian sow-thistle (*Sonchus alpinus ?*) remains open all night, rain will come next day. The broad-leaved red clover, the convolvulus, and many other plants, contract their leaves before showers. The stem of the red clover becomes more erect in rain. This arises most probably from the property of hygroscopicity, or the property to absorb humidity from surrounding water, which M. De Candolle says is possessed by many inorganic as well as organic bodies.* When the pimpernel (*Anagallis arvensis*) opens in the morning we are assured of a fine day.†

(421.) These instances of general prognostics are sufficient in number to enable you to appreciate their importance. I have observed every one of them in the course of my observations, and believe that many have escaped my memory. Most of them may be observed on a single farm, and they are all peculiarly applicable to the low country. They have been observed in ancient as

* De Candolle's Physiologie Vegetale, chap. ii. § 4.

† See Bacon's Sylva Sylvarum, cent. ix. cap. 823–830; and Forster's Researches into Atmospherical Phenomena, p. 130–142, for numerous prognostics indicated by plants.

well as modern times; and, indeed, as has been justly remarked by Mr Forster, " it is their being familiar to almost every age and country that affords the strongest confirmation of their correctness to those who have not had constant experience of them."

(422.) I shall now enumerate a few *prognostics peculiar to the season of winter.* When the *sun* sets red and hazy, it is an indication of frost. Sharp horns of a new *moon*, and a clear moon at any time, are characteristics of coming frost. In frost, the *stars* appear small, clear, and twinkling, and not very numerous. When few in number in fresh weather, it is probable that much vapour exists in the upper portion of the atmosphere. When very numerous in fresh weather, and having a lively twinkle, rain is indicated; the transparent vapour, in the act of subsiding into clouds, causing the twinkling. *Falling stars* are meteors which occur pretty frequently in winter, appearing in greatest number when the stars are very numerous, and are therefore indicative of a deposition of vapour, accompanied with wind from the point towards which they fall. Dull sun, moon, and stars,—occasioned by a thin cirro-stratus, almost invisible, —are all indicative of a change to rain in fresh, to snow in frosty weather. *Coronæ* appear frequently in winter upon both the sun and moon's disc, but particularly on the latter; and they always indicate the fall of vapour, whether in rain, snow, or hail, according to the warmer or colder state of the air at the time. *Coloured coronæ* and *halos* are sure indications of an approaching fall of rain in fresh, and snow in frosty, weather.

(423.) The *most common cloud in winter* is the *cirro-stratus*, whether in the state of a shrouding veil, more or less dense, across the whole sky for days, or in heavy banked clouds in the horizon before and after sunset. Whenever this form of cloud is present, there must be a large amount of vapour in the air, coming nearer to the ground as the power that suspends it is by any means weakened. Rain mostly falls direct from the cirro-stratus; but ere snow fall in any quantity, the cirro-stratus descends to the horizon into cumulo-stratus, from whence it stretches over the zenith in a dense bluish-black cloud.

(424.) A heavy fall of snow generally commences in the evening, continues throughout the next day, and at intervals in succeeding days. Snow-showers may fall heavily for the time; and when they fall, and the sky clears up quickly but is again overcome with another shower, this is said to be a "*feeding storm*." In such a case, the air always feels cold. In moonlight, masses of cumulo-strati may be seen to shower down snow at times, and then roll across the face of the moon with the most beautiful fleecy and rounded forms imaginable. The forms of the flakes of snow are pretty correct indications of the amount of fall to be; as when large and broad, and falling slowly, there will not be much, and the probability is that a thaw will soon follow; but when they fall thick and fast, and of medium size, there may be a fall of some inches before it fairs, and may lie some time. Should the flakes be spicular and fall very thick and fast, then a heavy fall, or a "*lying storm*" as it is called, may be expected, and this last sort of fall is always accompanied with a firm breeze of wind, varying from NE. to SE., and constitutos minute drift, which penetrates into every crevice that is open in doors, windows, or sheds.

(425.) *Hail*, consisting of soft, snowy, round, spongy masses, frequently falls after snow in winter.

(426.) The *appearance of the blue sky* indicates the nature of the fall; for if of a deep blue, in fresh weather, rain will fall; if of a yellowish or greenish colour near the horizon in frost, snow will certainly fall; and if a clear watery blue opening occurs in fresh weather near the horizon in the south, a heavy rain may soon be expected; as the old adage says,

> " A blue bore in the south
> Will drown the ploughman and his plough."

(427.) But the true character of all these changes is stamped upon them by the *direction of the wind*. In winter, it may be generally stated as a fact, that when the wind blows from the NW. to SE. by the N. and E., cold and frost may be looked for as certain, and if there are symptoms of a deposition from the air, snow will fall; but if the wind blows from the SE. to NW. by the S. and W., fresh weather and rain will ensue. Heavy falls of snow occur, however, with the wind direct from the S.; but they are always accompanied with cold, and such are usually termed " *Flanders' storms*." In this case, the wind veers suddenly from the N. or NE. to the S., which causes the lower stratum of vapour to give way by the introduction of warm air, and the cold vapour above then descends in quantity. The characters of the winds in winter are very well described by old Tusser in these lines :—

> " N. winds send hail, S. winds bring rain,
> E. winds we bewail, W. winds blow amain ;
> NE. is too cold, SE. not too warm,
> NW. is too bold, SW. doth no harm."*

In winter, the N. wind is firm, powerful, cold, and bracing; the NE. howling, deceitful, cold, but disagreeable, and may bring either a heavy fall of snow or rain; the E. wind is cold and drying, causing a quick evaporation; the SE. feels cold, damp, and thin, and causes a shiver; the S. wind is soft and undecided, and sometimes causes shivering; the SW. generally blows a loud and steady gale for hours, frequently accompanied with heavy battering showers; the W. wind is bluffy and buoyant; and the NW. pouring and steady, and often cold. Any wind that blows for a considerable length of time, such as two or three days, always brings down the temperature of the air. When any wind blows a good way over-head, it will be fair weather for some time, or until a change of the wind takes place; but when it blows low and very near the ground, and feels raw, cold, and thin to the feelings,—which is frequently the case in winter with the SW., S., and SE. winds,—rain will follow in fresh weather, and thaw in frost. Mostly all winds begin to blow in the upper portion of the atmosphere; and whether they will descend to the earth or not depends on the quantity, first, of the cirri, and then of the cirro-strati, in the air. Very frequently, different currents of air, at different elevations, may be seen in winter at the same time by means of the clouds. When this is observed, it may be relied upon that the uppermost current will ultimately prevail. It is characteristic of winds in winter to shift much about,—sometimes to all points of the azimuth in the course of twenty-four hours, and seldom remaining more than three days in one quarter. Winter winds are heavy, overpowering, stormy.

(428.) On the other hand, the calm of winter partakes of the stillness of death, whether in foggy and fresh, or clear and frosty, or misty and frosty, weather.

* Tusser's Five Hundred Points of Good Husbandry, Introduction, p. xxxviii.

The fresh fog hangs over towns, whose smoke, mixing with it, gives the sun or moon a copper-colour, when viewed through it. This is the noted London November fog. Clear calm air, admitting much sunshine at the middle of the day, is very bracing, healthy, and agreeable; but in the evening of such a day, the sun usually sets in red, and a heavy dew falls, which is frozen into *rime* or *hoar-frost*, incrusting every twig and sprig of trees and shrubs into the semblance of white coral. When the cold is intense, the dew is frozen before it reaches the objects on which it is deposited, and it then appears like smoke or mist, and is called "*frost-smoke*," which, when deposited on the naked branches of trees and shrubs, converts them into a resemblance of the most beautiful fillagree-work of silver. This mist may last some days during the day, as well as the night, and then new depositions of incrusted dew takes place on the trees and walls every night, until they seem overloaded with it. The smallest puff of winter-wind dispels the enchanting scene, as described by Phillips in his Letter from Copenhagen.

> "When, if a sudden gust of wind arise,
> The brittle forest into atoms flies;
> The crackling wood beneath the tempest bends,
> And in a spangled shower the prospect ends."

Winter-fog, as long as it hovers about the plains, is indicative of dry weather; but when it betakes itself to the hills, a thaw may be expected soon to follow, according to the old couplet,

> "When the clouds are on the hills,
> They'll come down by the rills."

Nothing can be truer than the saying, that "He that would have a bad day, may gang out in a fog after frost;" for no state of the air can be more disagreeable to the feelings than a raw rotten fog after frost, with the wind from the SE.

(429.) *Thunder-storms* are of rare occurrence in winter, owing, probably, to the generally humid state of the atmosphere at that season carrying off the superfluous electric matter silently, and not allowing it to accumulate in any one place. Sometimes, however, they do occur, and then are always violent and dangerous; at times setting fire to dwellings, rending trees, and destroying elevated buildings, such as the storm which occurred on the 3d January 1841. These storms are almost always succeeded by intense frost, and a heavy fall of snow in the line of their march. Flashes of white lightning near the horizon are sometimes seen in clear fresh nights, when stars are numerous and twinkling and falling stars plentiful, and they always indicate a coming storm. In reference to thunder in winter, there is a saying, that "winter's thunder bodes summer's hunger;" but with what truth I cannot say.

(430.) The electric phenomenon of the *aurora borealis* is, however, most frequent in winter, and perhaps acts as a substitute for thunder-storms in the economy of the atmosphere. It appears in different forms, either as a gleam of light in the horizon of the north issuing out from behind a dark bank of cloud, or as corruscations, which, from their sportive motions, have been designated "*merry dancers*," or "*streamers*." According to the form in which it appears, the aurora is indicative of the future weather. When exhibiting itself in a gleam of light in the north, it is indicative of good, steady weather; when it corruscates a little, the weather may be changeable; but when the corruscations reach the zenith and beyond, they augur cold stormy wind and rain. It has been long alleged, that the aurora borealis has the effect of producing a certain direction of the wind. Mr Winn stated, as long ago as 1774, that the aurora, in the south of England, was constantly followed by a SW wind and rain, and that the gale always began three hours after the phenomenon ;* and in 1833, Captain Winn observed in the English Channel, that the aurora shifted the wind to SW. and S., and that the gale began 24 hours after the phenomenon. The apparent discrepancy in the two accounts, in the same locality, of the time when the gale commenced, may perhaps have arisen from calculating the time from different periods of the phenomenon. Captain Winn further remarks, that the intensity of the storm and the time it appears may perhaps depend on the intensity of the aurora.† From long observation of the effects of the aurora borealis in one of the midland counties of Scotland, I never saw any change of the wind effected by it, except in frost, when the aurora seldom occurs, and then a SW. wind followed with gales. Coloured aurora borealis is always indicative of a change of weather, whether from good to bad or bad to good.

(431.) With regard to *rain*, there falls not so much in winter as in autumn, and the character of the winter-rain has more of cold and discomfort than of quantity. When frost suddenly gives way in the morning about sunrise, it is said to have " leapt," and rain may be looked for during the day. If it do not actually fall, a heavy cloudiness will continue all day, unless the wind change, when the sky may clear up. If a few drops of rain fall before midday after the frost has leapt, and then it fairs, there will be a fair, and most likely a fine day thereafter, with a pleasant breeze from the N. or W., or even E.

(432.) *Frost* is always attendant on winter, though seasons do occur in which very little occurs. The winters of 1834–5–6 may be remembered as seasons remarkably free from frost. Frost is a useful assistant to the farmer in pulverizing the ground, and rendering the upper portion of the ploughed soil congenial to the vegetation of seeds. It is obvious that it acts in a mechanical manner on the soil, by freezing the moisture in it into ice, which, on expanding at the moment of its formation, disintegrates the indurated clods into fine tilth. Frost always produces a powerful evaporation of the pulverized soil, which renders it very dry on the surface; and the affinity of the soil for moisture putting its capillary attraction into action, the moisture from the lower part of the arable soil, or even from the subsoil, is drawn up to the surface and evaporated, and the whole soil is thus rendered completely dry. Hence, after a frosty winter, it is possible to have the ground in so fine and dry a state as to permit the sowing of spring wheat and beans, in the finest order, early in spring. Frost never penetrates deep into the soil in the severest winters of northern countries —not more than one foot; but in this country much less, the covering of grass on the pasture-land, and the fine tilth on the ploughed land, acting as efficient non-conductors against the extension of its influence. Frost being favourable to the exhibition of the electric agency, may also prove useful to husbandry by stimulating the electric influence, not only in the soil itself, but in vegetation, in the manner formerly described in M. Pouillet's experiments (305). This is a subject worthy of extended investigation. *Rain*, too, is useful in hus-

* Thomson's History of the Royal Society, p. 513.

† The Field Naturalist, vol. i. p. 108.

bandry by consolidating light soils, and dissolving and carrying down solutions of manure *into* the soil—when sheep are feeding on turnips, for example—and placing them beyond the reach of dissipation; but its chief utility in winter it supplying the thrashing machinery with abundance of water. *Snow* also renders important services to husbandry. If it fall shortly after a confirmed frost, it acts as a protective covering against the farther cooling effects of frost on soil; and in this way, it protects the young plants of wheat and of clover from destruction by intense frosts. On the other hand, frost, and rain, and snow, may all retard the operations of the fields in winter very materially, by rendering ploughing and the carriage of turnips impracticable. Neither frost nor snow will last long, if either come when the ground is in a very wet state in consequence of rain. When the moon shines on ground that is very wet, it may be remarked how very black are the shadows of objects, which is a sign of continuance of rain, and of an unsettled state of the wind. Rain sometimes falls with a rising barometer; and when this happens, it is usually followed by fine healthy weather, which is attended with circumstances that indicate a strong positive state of the electricity of the air. This often occurs in winter. "We have," says Mr Forster, "usually a warm and agreeable sensation of the atmosphere with such rain, which is strikingly contrasted to the cold and raw sensation occasioned by the fall of thick wet mists or rain, which happens when, even with a N. or E. wind, the barometer and thermometer sink together, and when the air has previously been found to be either negatively or non-electrified; and the cause of this is most probably occasioned by a supervening current of colder or supersaturated air; and the rise of the thermometer, which accompanies the fall of the barometer in this case, may be owing to the increase of temperature produced by the condensation of the vapour in the case of rain."* "Gusts of *wind*, in some high windy weather," says Mr Forster, "seem to fluctuate in a manner somewhat analogous to the undulatory motion of waves. This fact may easily be seen by a pendulous anemometer. When the wind is accompanied by the rain, the periods of the gusts may be counted by the intervals of the more or less violent impulses of the water on the windows opposed to the wind, or the leaves of any tree twined across them."†

(433.) There are a few proverbial prognostics regarding winter weather, which I may transcribe for your information and amusement. "Hard winters are often succeeded by luxuriant summers." "A green Yule makes a fat kirk-yard," alluding to a mild Christmas proving a sickly one.

"A January spring
Is worth naething."

"If Janiveer's calends be summerly gay,
'T will be winterly weather till the calends of May.

"Hail brings frost in the tail." "A snaw year, a rich year." "Under water dearth, under snaw bread."

(434.) The prognostics which I have enumerated, both general and particular, are applicable to the low country. The prognostics among the hills differ somewhat from these; and as some of you may take up your abode in such a

* Forster's Researches into Atmospherical Phenomena, p. 247. † Ibid. p. 342.

locality, it may be desirable that I should also give you a few prognostics peculiarly applicable to them. In attempting this, I cannot do better than transcribe a part of those enumerated by the Rev. James Russel of Yarrow.

(435.) " When there is a copious deposite of dew," says Mr Russel, " and it remains long on the grass—when the fog in the valleys is slowly dissipated by the sun's heat, and lingers on the hills—when the clouds apparently take a higher station; and especially when a few cirro-strati appear loose or slightly connected, lying at rest or gently floating along, serene weather may be confidently expected. A change of this settled state is presaged by the wind suddenly rising, by close continuous cirro strati gathering into an unbroken gloom, and by that variety (of cirrus) known as the goat's hair or grey mare's tail. Sometimes a few fleecy clouds skim rapidly between the superincumbent vapour and the earth's surface, and are the forerunners of snow or rain" (the scud). " Should the cirri not pass away with the immediate fall, but extend towards the horizon, and present their troubled edges towards the zenith, there will be stormy weather for some time. When a modification of the cirro-stratus is formed to leeward, thick in the middle, and wasting at both ends, with its side to the wind like a ship *lying to*, it indicates continued wind. After a clear frost, we sometimes see long whitish-coloured streaks of cirrus (cirro-stratus), whose two extremities seemingly approach each other as they recede from the zenith. This appearance is vulgarly called Noah's ark; and if it point from SW. to NE., we expect a thaw from SW. Small blackish boat-shaped clouds rising in the W., and moving sideways, indicate a thaw, with little or no rain. A short glare of red in the E., about sun-rising, portends a rainy and windy day. When the sky shines from the watery exhalations around the mid-day sun, rain or snow will soon follow; when it has a green appearance to the E. or NE., frost and snow. A *crimson* red in the W., after sunset, indicates fair weather; a *purple* red indicates sleet. Atmospheric changes are more likely to happen a few days after new and full moon than in the quarters. The point when she changes seems to have little influence; if in the NW or NW. by W. it is often succeeded by boisterous weather. When her horns are sharp and well defined, we look for frost; when she is whitish and not very clear, for rain or snow. If the new moon seems to embrace the old, very stormy weather is likely to follow. . . . Halos are seen only when the cirro-strati are slightly but equally diffused over the sky; the sun or moon seems " to wander through the storm," which is at no great distance. One side of the halo is often open or imperfectly formed, owing to the denseness of the vapour, and points to the quarter from which the storm is approaching. . . . Aurora borealis is most likely to appear in changeable weather, and is often followed by a SW. wind. From the appearance of falling stars, it may be inferred that the equilibrium of the atmosphere, held probably by the agency of electricity, is destroyed. They generally forebode wind, and when many of them are seen, they are faithful though silent monitors, warning us to prepare, with the earliest dawn, for the coming storm. There is often much lightning in the night, both with and without clouds, which announces unsettled weather, especially if it be whitish in colour. . . . When the wind shifts to the W. after rain from S. or SW it generally fairs up, or there are but a few showers. Frost and snow from SW. are forerunners of bad weather. If the wind turn suddenly from SW. or S. to NNE., while this is accompanied with a smell resembling that of coal smoke, a severe storm will follow. . . . The lower animals, but such especially as are in a state of nature, or exposed to the open fields, are very susceptible of atmospheric changes. Sheep eat greedily before a storm, and sparingly before a thaw. When they leave the high parts of their range,—when they bleat much in the evening or during the night, we may expect severe weather. Goats seek a place of shelter, while swine carry litter and cover themselves better than ordinary, before a storm. Wind is foretold by the cat scratching a post or wall—and a thaw, when she washes her face, or when frogs come from their winter concealment. The gathering of grouse into large flocks, the diving of sparrows in dry dust, the fluttering of wild-ducks as they flap their wings, the dismal lengthened howl of sea-gulls in an inland place or around lakes, the mournful note of the curlew, the shrill whew of the plover, the *whet-whet-whet* of the chaffinch perched upon a tree, the crowing of the cock at unusual times,—all prognosticate rain or snow. When the fieldfare, redwing, starling, swan, snowfleck, and other birds of passage, arrive soon from the north, it indicates an early and severe winter. When gnats bite keenly, when flies keep near the ground (shewn by swallows, who feed upon the wing, flying low), we look for wind and rain. But the most wonderful instance of atmospherical changes is upon those creatures that burrow in the ground. The earth-worm appearing in abundance indicates rain. In like manner, the mole seems to feel its approach, as, a day or two before, he raises more hillocks than usual; and when, after a long severe frost, he begins again to work, it will soon become fresh. The effects of electricity are well known both on the atmosphere and on animals; and the deposition of aqueous vapours, with the relaxing damp near the surface of the earth which in certain states takes place, may give rise to this increased activity."* "In the middle of the hill-country, snow does not fall so heavily as in the low or either side, the storm being exhausted before reaching that distance from the sea. In that case, the stock of sheep are not so long deprived of grass as might be expected."†

(436.) There was a set of rules published about a hundred years ago by which to judge of the weather, by the Shepherd of Banbury, many of which are much akin to some that have been given above; but there are a few expressed in such definite terms in regard to the wind, that they must have been the result of patient observation for many years, and therefore deserve attention. He says: "When the wind turns to NE. and it continues two days without rain, and does not turn S. the third day, nor rains the third day, it is likely to continue NE. for 8 or 9 days, all fair, and then to come to the S. again. If it turn again out of the S. to the NE. with rain, and continues in the NE. two days without rain, and neither turns S. nor rains the third day, it is likely to continue NE. for two or three months. The wind will finish these turns in 3 weeks. After a N. wind, for the most part two months or more, and then coming S., there are usually 3 or 4 fair days at first, and then, on the fourth or fifth day, comes rain, or else the wind turns N. again, and continues dry. If it return to the S. in a day or two without rain, and turn N. with rain, and return to the S. in one or two days as before, two or three turns together after this sort, then it is like to be in the S. or SW. two or three months together, as it was in the N. before. The wind will finish these turns in a fortnight. Fair weather for

* New Statistical Account of Scotland, Yarrow—Selkirkshire, p 31-4.

† Ibid. Tweedsmuir—Peeblesshire.

a week, with a S. wind, is like to produce a great drought, if there has been much rain out of the S. before. The wind usually turns from N. to S. with a quiet wind without rain, but returns to the N. with a strong wind and rain. The strongest winds are when it turns from S. to N. by W. When the N. wind first clears the air (which is usually once a-week), be sure of a fair day or two."*

(437.) You must not suppose that all the prognostics of the weather enumerated here will *invariably* hold true, and that you will be as certain of recognising every phenomenon here described, as if you had contemplated it before you in a picture; or that a great number of them can be observed at one time. Such certainty cannot as yet be attained in predicting and describing the changes of the atmosphere, which are generally presented to us again with such modifying circumstances, as, though the character of the kind may be distinctly preserved, the species or variety of the phenomenon may differ considerably; still, by acquiring at first the leading features of these phenomena, you will afterwards be able, by attentive observation, to recognise most of the particulars which go to make up their distinctive characters. A long-continued state of any kind of weather strongly influences the character of that which is to follow. Thus the barometer sometimes sinks, and even all the clouds present every appearance of rain, and yet no rain follows, and the symptoms subside, and clear weather returns, provided the weather had been long *dry* before. And, on the other hand, symptoms of drought will fail after a long continuance of wet. Nevertheless, these are only exceptions to the general rule; be assured that every authenticated symptom is correct, and may be regarded as the forerunner of its effects; and you should be prepared to provide against these, if the symptoms are injurious, although it may happen that the forebodings have not been realized.

(438.) Many of these prognostics were well known to the ancients. One of the most eminent writers on them was Aratus, a Greek poet, who was born at Soli, in Cilicia, and flourished about 270 years before the Christian era. He was profusely quoted by Virgil in his Georgics, and Cicero translated his poems into Latin.†

(439.) The atmosphere being so essential an agent in producing the varieties of weather which the farmer experiences in his practice, it appears to me that a few observations on its nature and constitution will not be here irrelevant. And, first, with regard to its nature and importance, these observations of Mr Mudie convey their true value. "Atmospheric air," he says, "remains a gas at all the natural temperatures of the surface of our globe; and, therefore, it is of all substances the most serviceable, especially in the economy of the vegetable and animal kingdoms, as no member of either of these kingdoms can be developed, brought to maturity, or even exist, without its presence. Reaching far above the summits of the highest mountains, and penetrating downwards into the depths of the ocean, probably far beneath the lowest glimmer of the solar light, it appears to be the stimulating principle of the whole of organic nature, and one which is everywhere present."‡

* Claridge's (Shepherd of Banbury) Rules for judging of the Weather. Edition 1827, p. 23-25.

† Anthon's Lempriere's Classical Dictionary. The classical scholar may consult Watts' Bibliotheca Britannica for a list of all the editions of the poems of Aratus.

‡ Mudie's World, p. 218.

(440.) The atmosphere is anything but the simple substance which it appears. It is composed of these materials, which vary in their proportions of measure and weight in each 100 parts:—

	By measure.	By weight.
Nitrogen	77.5 . .	75.55
Oxygen	21. . .	23.32
Carbonic acid	0.08 . .	0.10
Watery vapour . . .	1.42 . .	1.03
	100. parts.	100. parts.

(441.) These substances, in reference to each other, exist in a very remarkable state in the atmosphere. " They do not form what is called a chemical compound, in which any strong degree of action is required, either to mix the different substances, or to separate them from the mixtures; but, on the contrary, each exists in this remarkable fluid, with the same perfect freedom to obey the laws of its own nature, as if only that one were present, and all the rest absent. . . . The growth of plants and the life of animals require oxygen, and the first, and probably both, require carbonic acid, while nature generally requires aqueous vapour, and probably many parts of it require nitrogen, though our knowledge of the natural effects of this particular substance is a little more obscure. But whichever of these substances any one operation requires, the requisite portion of that substance may always be obtained from the atmosphere, without effort, and by the most delicate organization. Thus, for instance, the smallest of the infusorial animals, or animalculæ, of which thousands would not amount to the dimensions of a pin's head, derive the oxygen, or the breath of life, as easily from the atmosphere as the elephant or whale; and the smallest lichen, which stains an old stone or the bark of a tree, takes its requisite atmospheric supply as certainly as the most stately tree of the forest, and with not a jot more of effort. . . . Therefore the study of the atmosphere becomes, in no inconsiderable degree, the most interesting of any which is connected with the economy of the world."*

(442.) Light as the air feels to us, the atmosphere presses with a considerable force on the earth's surface. " The whole of the atmosphere exerts the same pressure on the surface of the globe as if, instead of air, it were enveloped with water to the height of 33.87 feet above the surface" (hence the limit of the draught of a common pump), " or with quicksilver to a height of 30 inches" (hence the limit of the range of the column of mercury in the barometer). " That pressure is calculated to be equal to a weight of 12,022,560,000,000,000 lb. avoirdupois, or 5,367,214,285,714,285 tons, or to be the same as that which would be exerted by a globe of lead 60 miles in diameter. To state it in another way, this pressure is equal to a weight of 14.7 lb. on every square inch of surface."†

(443.) At the mean temperature of 60°, a cubic foot of atmospheric air weighs 527 grains troy, and a cubic foot of water 437,500 grains; so that, weight for weight, air occupies 830 times the bulk of water. The resistance which the atmosphere affords at the mean temperature, at that weight, being

* Mudie's World, p. 218 and 219.

† Reid's Chemistry of Nature, p. 52.

14.7 lb. per square inch, is equivalent to a column of mercury of 30 inches in height, or a column of water 33.87 feet. If we estimate this height in hundredths of parts for greater nicety of expression, that is, if we call the column of mercury 3000, the pressures of the several parts of which the air is made up will be—nitrogen 2336, oxygen 618, vapour of water 44, and carbonic acid gas 2.

(444.) Besides pressure, the air has the property of elasticity. "The four substances which we have enumerated are the only ones of which the atmosphere is composed, and they are pressed by nothing but their own weight—as the atmosphere is the uppermost substance upon the globe, and as such, can be subjected to no pressure but its own; therefore, our question resolves itself into an inquiry as to what should be the law of pressure in a substance which, but for pressure, would expand without limit, and whose own weight is the only pressure to which it can be subjected? Now, if we take a column of the atmosphere, beginning at the mean level of the earth's surface, and suppose it divided into portions of equal height, as, for example, portions of 1 foot, 1 fathom, 1 mile, or any other measure, it is obvious that the whole column will press on the surface of the earth, that the lowest portion will be pressed by the whole wanting 1, the next by the whole wanting 2, and so on; and that, as the base of each presses as a surface, expressible by the square of a line, if we take the height above the surface in the order of the numbers 1, 2, 3, 4, &c., the pressure will diminish in the ratios of the squares of these numbers, that is, 1, 4, 9, 16, &c., and so on. In consequence of this, we have a regular law of the diminution of pressure as we ascend in the atmosphere; and this law gives us the density or quantity of the ingredients of the atmosphere, in equal measures of space at different heights."* "In consequence of the atmosphere being confined to the earth's surface by gravitation, we find it much denser near the level of the sea, than at any distance above it. As we ascend above the surface of the earth, the density of the atmosphere rapidly decreases; thus, at an elevation of 3 miles it is $\frac{1}{2}$ the density on the earth's surface; at 6 miles it is $\frac{1}{4}$; at 9 miles $\frac{1}{8}$; and at 15 miles $\frac{1}{30}$ of that density: the greatest part of the atmosphere is thus evidently always within 20 miles of the surface of the globe, although, from certain astronomic phenomena, it is supposed to extend to a distance of 40 or 45 miles; and here is, in all probability, its utmost limit."†

(445.) "If we take the weight of the ingredients of the atmosphere, and suppose that also to consist of 3000 equal parts, the weights have not the same proportions as the pressures; for the nitrogen is about 2266.5, the oxygen 699.5, the vapour of water 31, and the carbonic acid 3. Thus the resistance of the nitrogen is more than 3 per cent. greater in proportion than its weight; that of the oxygen is 12 per cent. less; that of the vapour of water is about 42 per cent. greater; and that of the carbonic acid is 50 per cent. less than the weight. Thus each of those four substances follows a different law, and is therefore differently acted upon by those changes of heat and pressure which affect the atmosphere."‡ It is thus not the mere pressure of the air which affects the barometer, but also the different ways which its constituent parts are affected by ex-

* Mudie's World, p. 220.

† Bird's Elements of Natural Philosophy, p. 99.

‡ Mudie's World, p. 223.

ternal causes. Hence the pressure of the atmosphere, as indicated by the column of mercury in the barometer, is not an absolute and invariable measure of the quantity of matter in the atmospherical column, as that quantity is affected by the different laws to which the constituent parts of the atmosphere are subject.

(446.) Of the four ingredients of the atmosphere, the vapour of water undergoes changes which the others do not undergo. "From the great tendency to expansion or tension of the vapour of water, this is perhaps the most variable of all its ingredients, and one which has more influence on the changes of weight or barometric pressure than any of the others. This arises from the more powerful action of heat on water than upon any other of the constituents of the atmosphere; and from the fact that the more rare and attenuated the air is, in respect to the other parts of its composition, water disperses itself through it more readily. The lowest temperature of which we have any knowledge, or even any conception, has no tendency to change any of the other components of the atmosphere into the solid or even the liquid state; but the change of water to a solid in the atmosphere is a very easy and frequent process, as we find by the formation of hail and even masses of ice in the clouds in warm countries, and at comparatively warm seasons of the year. This ready action of the changes of heat upon the vapour of water in the atmosphere, is one of the most important points in the whole science of meteorology—that is, of the weather; but it is one, the right understanding of which requires the induction of several other elements."*

(447.) When cirrus, cumulus, or stratus appears alone, and in its own appropriate region, none of these clouds can be regarded as an immediate indication of rain, or other foul weather. The cirrus is at first visible in a dry state of the air, and being situated in the highest portion of the atmosphere, it can only be observed from the earth when the air is clear. But its non-observance from the earth during the obscuration of low clouds, is no proof that it does not exist. At all events, when it is seen through the openings of large and dense clouds, it is an indication of the air becoming dry, whereas, when it is seen first in clear weather, an indication is held out that a change is taking place above, and that some deposition of moisture is going on. Cirrus is an indication of the positive state of electricity in the air, and it is conceived that its great office is the diffusion of electric matter throughout the air, so that it cannot be seen when the air is surcharged with thunder-clouds. Its pointed form is favourable to transmitting electricity from one cloud to another, and it sometimes appears to perform this office betwixt cumuli. "When two or more of these simple species of cloud meet upon the confines of their respective regions, or otherwise mingle in the sky, a greater extent of atmospheric derangement is indicated, and foul weather may usually be expected, unless the disturbed atmosphere shall be carried away by a general seasonal current; and this is the case in great part of the British islands, after the dry countries to the south and east of the Baltic have reached the maximum of their summer heat. This removal of disturbed air by the general current, is the cause which has given rise to the popular maxim, 'that all signs of rain fail in fine weather,' and certainly it much depends on the ge-

* Mudie's World, p. 225.

neral character of the season, whether a moderate degree of atmospheric disturbance, and formation and blending of clouds of different species, shall or shall not be followed by rain." *

(448.) The blue colour of the sky gives so much delight to every spectator, that a few remarks on its cause cannot fail to prove interesting to you. " When we look at the sky in a clear day, it appears like a large light-blue arch set over our heads, and seen through the (supposed) invisible substance called air. But this is not the case: there is no blue dome above us, and when the sky is viewed from any elevated region of the earth, as the top of a high mountain or in a balloon, and where we would expect that this supposed blue vault would be more distinct, and manifest its blue tint more decidedly, it appears not more blue but dark or black. In proportion as the spectator rises above the surface of the earth, and *has less air above him, and that very rare*, the blue tint gradually disappears, and if he could attain a height at which there is *no air*, the sky would be perfectly black—there would be total darkness all around—except in the direction in which the sun's rays fall upon him. This is the appearance which, from the laws of optics, it is known would be presented where there is no air: and the observations of travellers who have ascended to great elevations in the Alps and Andes confirm this. Again, when we look at a distant mountain on a tolerably clear day, it will appear of a blue colour, somewhat like the sky, but a little deeper in the tint; and yet, when we approach the mountain, we see that it is of a very different colour. When we look at a forest not very far from us, it appears of a green colour; but if we recede to a great distance from it, it will acquire a bluish tint, which gradually deepens as our distance from it increases. . . . If not itself of this colour, it must acquire the hue from being seen through a blue-coloured medium. These well-established facts lead naturally to the inference that the *air itself is a blue colour*." . . . But, " why is not the blue colour seen in the air surrounding us when we look towards a house or wall not so far removed, or even in the air of a room, or in the air contained in what we call an empty glass?" . . . Because, " though the great body of air which is opposed to us, when we look at a clear sky or any distant object, transmits a sufficient quantity of blue rays to produce an impression of that colour on the eye, the small quantity in a glass, in a room, or even within the compass of a few miles, cannot convey enough of blue rays to the eye to produce the colour which the air manifests in a large body. The differences in the depth of the blue tint which are observed at different times and places, its faintness at the horizon as contrasted with its appearance at the zenith, its increasing depth at the torrid zone, and faintness at sea, depend upon the varying quantity and transparency of the watery vapour in the air. Indeed, it is upon this ingredient of the air that the blue colour is supposed to depend." †

(449.) You have seen that the mean annual fall of rain on the surface of the globe may be taken as being near the truth at 34 inches. On estimating the area of the globe, the quantity of rain that annually falls at this rate will be found to be almost incredible. The mean diameter of the earth may be taken at 7913½ miles, its mean circumference is of course 24,871 miles, and the area of its surface is 196,816,658 square miles, or 790,117,416,537,766,800 square

* Mudie's World, p. 264.

† Reid's Chemistry of Nature, p. 61-3.

inches, which, at 34 inches of rain, give 26,863,991,162,284,071,200 cubic inches, or 15,546,290,603,173,652 cubic feet of water, which, at 1000 ounces per cubic foot, give 431,033,808,959,644 tons 6 cwt. of rain per annum.

(450.) According to the estimate of Professor Rigaud of Cambridge, the sea bears to the land a ratio of 36 : 13, so the land has an area of 52,353,231 square miles, which will receive 155,684,431,013,204½ tons of rain per annum. What renders this result the more surprising is, that all this enormous quantity of rain could not have fallen unless it had before been evaporated from the ocean, seas, lakes, rivers, and the land by the heat of the sun, and been sustained in the air until it was precipitated.

(451.) These observations on weather have far exceeded their intended limits; but the subject is of so much importance to every farmer that he cannot bestow too much attention upon it; and he cannot know upon what class of phenomena he should particularly bestow his attention, unless the various particulars which go to make up the sum of all atmospherical phenomena are placed before him: He may then discover which class affects his own locality the most, or, in other words, what constitutes his own local climate. Much of what has been given will not require to be again noticed, but only referred to when we come to consider the weather of the respective seasons.

---

20. OF CLIMATE.

" Betwixt th' extremes, two happier climates hold,
The temper that partakes of hot and cold."

DRYDEN.

(452.) This seems a favourable opportunity for saying a few words on climate, a most interesting subject to the farmer, inasmuch as it will enable him to discover the favourable and unfavourable particulars connected with the site of the farm which he may wish to occupy. This is a point, in looking at farms, which I am afraid is entirely overlooked by farmers, much to their disappointment and even loss, as I shall have occasion to observe when we come to be on the outlook for a farm. Meantime let us attend to a few general principles.

(453.) Climate may be divided into *general* and *local*. The former affects alike all places in the same parallel of latitude; it is measured from the equator to the polar circles in spaces, in each of which the longest day is half an hour longer than that nearer the equator; and from the polar circles to the pole, it is measured by the increase of a month. It is obvious that the breadth assumed for those spaces is quite arbitrary, and it is equally clear that each space is subject to a different temperature. In fact, a difference of temperature constitutes the chief distinction in the general climate of places; and it is this great distinction which has given rise to the division of zones on the surface of the globe into the torrid, temperate, and frigid, names indicative of different degrees of temperature.

(454.) The *torrid zone* embraces that space of the globe on both sides of the equator in which the sun passes across the zenith during the year. Being under the perpendicular direction of the sun's rays, this is the hottest portion of the globe. It comprehends 23½° on each side of the equator, or 47° in all.

(455.) The *temperate zones* extend 43° on each side of the torrid, and being acted upon by the sun's rays in an oblique direction, are not so warm in any part of them as the torrid, and the temperature of their several parts, of course, decreases as they are situated farther from the torrid. Besides this, these zones being entirely intercepted by the torrid, the temperature of their northern and southern divisions is hotter and colder as the sun is farther off or nearer to the northern or southern extremes of his declination.

(456.) The *frigid zones* extend from the temperate to the poles. They are intercepted by both the torrid and temperate zones. The sun's rays affect them at a still more oblique angle than the temperate, and, of course, their mean temperature is yet lower than theirs. They are so far removed from the sun, that in winter the sun is never seen in them above the horizon, while, in summer, he is never under the horizon; and it is this accumulation of the sun's rays in summer, that in a degree compensates for the entire deprivation of them in winter, and has the effect of raising the mean temperature of those zones to a height in which both human life and vegetation may exist. The frigid zones extend 47°

(457.) The three zones occupy these relative proportions of space—

The torrid, . .	47°
The temperate, .	86°
The frigid, . .	47°
	180° from pole to pole.

" The climates of different parts of the earth's surface are unquestionably owing in great measure to their position with respect to the sun. At the equator, where the sun is always nearly vertical, any given part of the surface receives a much greater quantity of light and heat than an equal portion near the poles; and it is also still more affected by the sun's vertical rays, because their passage through the atmosphere is shorter than that of the oblique rays. As far as the sun's mean altitude is concerned, it appears from Simpson's calculations, that the heat received at the equator in the whole year is nearly 2½ times as great as at the poles; this proportion being nearly the same as that of the meridian heat of a vertical sun, to the heat derived, at 23½° from the poles, in the middle of the long annual day at the poles. But the difference is rendered still greater by the effect of the atmosphere, which intercepts a greater proportion of the heat at the poles than elsewhere. Bouguer has calculated, upon the supposition of the similarity of the effects of light and heat, that in lat. 45°, 80 parts of 100 are transmitted at noon in July, and 55 only in December. It is obvious that, at any individual place, the climate in summer must approach in some degree to the equatorial climate, the sun's altitude being greater, and in winter to the climate of the polar regions."*

(458.) From what has just been observed, it is obvious that the temperature of the air diminishes gradually from the equator to the poles; and it also becomes gradually colder as we ascend in height above the surface of the ground. Here, then, are two elements by which to judge of the general climate of different latitudes. Moreover, the diminution of heat from the equator to the poles is found to take place in an arithmetical progression, that is, *the annual temperature of all the latitudes are arithmetical means between the mean annual temperature of the equator and the poles.* This law was first discovered by M. Meyer, but by means of an equation which he founded on it, and afterwards rendered more simple, Mr Kirwan calculated the mean annual temperature of every degree of latitude between the equator and the poles. The results were, that the mean temperature at the equator is 84°, that at the poles 31°, and that in N. lat. 54°, 49°.20.

(459.) From Mr Kirwan's calculations of the mean temperatures of every month, it appears that January is the coldest month in every latitude; and that July is the warmest month in all latitudes above 48°. In lower latitudes, August is the warmest month; while the difference in temperature between the hottest and coldest months increases in proportion to the distance from the equator. Every habitable latitude enjoys a mean heat of 60° for at least two months; and this heat seems necessary for the production of corn. Within 10° of the poles the temperature differs little, and the same is the case within 10° of the equator. The mean temperature of different years differs very little near the equator, but it differs more and more as the latitudes approach the poles.

(460.) As the temperature of the atmosphere constantly diminishes on ascending above the level of the sea, the temperature of congelation

* Polehampton's Gallery of Nature and Art, vol. iv. p. 42.

must be attained at a certain height above every latitude; consequently mountains which rear their heads above that limit must be covered with perpetual snow. The elevation of the freezing region varies according to the latitude of the place, being at all times highest at the equator and lowest at the poles. In the higher regions of the atmosphere, especially within the tropics, the temperature varies but little throughout the whole year; and hence, in those brilliant climates, the line of perpetual congelation is strongly and distinctly marked. But in countries remote from the equator, the boundary of frost descends after the heat of summer as the influence of winter prevails, thus varying its position over a belt of some considerable depth.

(461.) But beyond the line of congelation is another which forms the boundary of the ascent of visible vapour, and this point it is obvious must be less liable to change than the point of congelation. At the equator the highest point of vapour is 28,000 feet, at the pole 3432 feet, and in N. lat. 54° it is 6647 feet. In tracing this point successively along every latitude, we learn that heat diminishes, as we ascend, in an arithmetical progression. Hence it follows, that the heat of the air above the surface of the earth is not owing to the ascent of hot strata of air from the surface, but to the conducting power of the air itself.*

(462.) The question of *local* climate presents a much greater interest to the farmer than that of the general climate of the country which he inhabits. Local climate may be defined to signify that peculiar condition of the atmosphere in regard to heat and moisture which prevails in any given place. The diversified character which it displays has been generally referred to the combined operation of several different causes, which are all reducible, however, to these two; *distance from the equator*, and *height above the level of the sea*. Latitude and local elevation form indeed the great basis of the law of climate; and any other modifications have only a partial and very limited influence.†

(463.) The climate of every individual country may be considered local in reference to that of all other countries in the same degrees of latitude. Islands are thus warmer than continents. The E. coast of all countries is colder than the W., though the latter is moister. Countries lying to the windward of great ranges of mountains or extensive forests are warmer than those to leeward. Small seas are warmer in summer and colder in winter than the standard portion of great oceans, as they are in some degree affected by the condition of the surrounding land. Low countries are warmer than high, and level plains than mountainous

* For tables of the altitudes of the points of congelation and vapour, see Encyclopædia Britannica, 7th edition, art. *Climate*.

† Ibid.

regions. Plains present only one species of climate, which differs in its seasonal characters alone, but mountains exhibit every variety, from their latitude to the pole along the meridian of the quadrant. In this way, high mountains, situate in the tropics, present every variety of climate. "If we take each mountain," says Mr Mudie, "which rises above the line of perpetual snow, as the index to its own meridian, we shall find that each one expresses, by its vegetation, all the varieties of climate between it and the pole; and thus these lofty mountains become means of far more extensive information than places which are situated near the main level of the sea, and more especially than plains, which, when their surfaces are nearly flat, have no story to tell, but the same uniform and monotonous one, for many miles." But although the high tropical mountains are thus indices of climate reaching from the equator to the pole, they are not subject to the seasonal differences which the climates are along the meridian of the quadrant. "Although," continues Mr Mudie, "the temperature does ascend and descend a little, even upon the mountains immediately under the equator, and although the seasonal change becomes more and more conspicuous as the latitude increases, either northward or southward, yet, within the whole tropical zone, the seasonal difference is so slight, that there is no marked summer or winter apparent in the native and characteristic vegetation. . . . From the small change of seasons in this region, they are almost all plants of uniform growth throughout the year, and have no winter for repose, so that, at great elevations, their growth is at all times much slower than that of plants in polar latitudes, during the perpetual sunshine of the summer there. . . Say that the altitude of the mountain under the equator, upon which the seasonal action is displayed, is a little more than 3 miles. Then, estimating in round numbers, 1 foot of altitude on the mountain will correspond to about 16,000 feet on the meridian, that is, a single foot of elevation on the mountain is equivalent, in difference of temperature, to about 3 miles, or more nearly 3 minutes of a degree in latitude, and therefore 20 feet are equal to a whole degree; and when one once arrives at the mean temperature of London, 400 feet more of elevation will bring one to the climate of Lapland." *

(464.) From these facts and reasonings, it appears that a slight difference of elevation in a mountainous district of this country, which stands upon so high a parallel of latitude, may make a considerable difference of climate, and that, other things remaining the same, that farm which is situated on a high elevation has a much greater chance of being af-

* Mudie's World, p. 132–6.

fected by changes of climate than one at a lower level. Yet certainly local circumstances have a material effect in rendering the general position of any farm less desirable, such as, vicinity to a lake or marsh, or a leeward position to a hill or large wood in reference to the direction from which the wind generally blows, as these tend to lower the temperature below that of the mean of the country. So, in like manner, any position in a long narrow valley, or on the side of a large isolated hill, or in a pass betwixt two mountains separating plains, is more subject to the injurious effects of wind than the mean of the country, as the wind acquires an accelerated motion in such localities. An elevated table-land is subject to a lower temperature and higher winds than a plain of the same extent on a lower level; hence most situations amongst hills are colder and more windy than on plains. On the other hand, the being on the windward side of a hill or large wood, or on flat ground backed with hills and woods to the N. and E., or being in the midst of a cultivated country, all insure a higher temperature and less injurious winds than the mean of the country. An extensive plain or valley, through which no large river passes, or in which no large lake or wood exists, is subject to very little violent wind. In the former exposed situations, the snow lies long, and the winds are cutting keen; while in the more sheltered positions the snow soon disappears, and the wind is less violent and keen. All these differences in circumstances have a sensible effect on the local climate of every country, and in a small one like Great Britain, varied as it is in its physical geography, and surrounded on all sides by water, they have the effect of dividing the country into as many climates as there are varieties of surface and differences of position in regard to the sea. These local influences, in most seasons, have a greater effect on the time of growth, quantity, and quality of the produce of the earth, than the general climate of the country; although, no doubt, the latter exercises such a predominating influence in some seasons, by excessive heat or rain, as to overcome all local influences, and stamp an universality of character over the season. "According to Cotte's aphorisms, local heat becomes greater on plains than on hills; it is never so low near the sea as in inland parts; the wind has no effect on it; its maximum and minimum are about 6 weeks after the solstices; it varies more in summer than in winter; it is least a little before sunrise; its maxima in the sun and shade are seldom on the same day; and it decreases more rapidly in autumn than it increases in summer."*

(465.) Besides all these causes, there is another phenomenon which has

* Polehampton's Gallery of Nature and Art, vol. iv. p. 74.

a material effect on local climate, and that is, the darting of cold pulsations downwards from the upper region of the atmosphere, and of warm pulsations upwards from the earth. This is a different phenomenon from radiant heat. These pulsations of temperature are detected by a new instrument called the *æthrioscope;* and although the experiments with it have as yet not been sufficiently numerous to insure implicit confidence in its results, yet the experience of all who have paid attention to the varieties of circumstances which affect climate, can tell them that many causes are evidently at work in the atmosphere, to produce effects which have not yet been recognised by the instruments in common use. "The æthrioscope opens new scenes to our view. It extends its sensations through indefinite space, and reveals the condition of the remotest atmosphere. Constructed with still greater delicacy, it may perhaps scent the distant winds, and detect the actual temperature of any quarter of the heavens. The impressions of cold which arrive from the N. will probably be found stronger than those received from the S. But the facts discovered by the æthrioscope are nowise at variance with the theory already advanced on the gradation of heat from the equator to the pole, and from the level of the sea to the highest atmosphere. The internal motion of the air, by the agency of opposite currents, still tempers the disparity of the solar impressions; but this effect is likewise accelerated by the vibrations excited from the unequal distribution of heat, and darted through the atmospheric medium with the celerity of sound. Any surface which sends a hot pulse in one direction, must evidently propel a cold pulse of the same intensity in an opposite direction. The existence of such pulsations, therefore, is in perfect unison with the balanced system of aerial currents. The most recondite principles of harmony are thus disclosed in the constitution of this nether world. In clear weather, the cold pulses then showered entire from the heavens will, even during the progress of the day, prevail over the influence of the reflex light, received on the ground, in places which are screened from the direct action of the sun. Hence at all times the coolness of a northern exposure. Hence, likewise, the freshness which tempers the night in the sultriest climates, under the expanse of an almost azure sky. The coldness of particular situations has very generally been attributed to the influence of piercing winds which blow over elevated tracts of land. This explication, however, is not well founded. It is the altitude of the place itself above the level of the sea, and not that of the general surface of the country, which will mould its temperature. A cold wind, as it descends from the high grounds into the valleys, has its capacity for heat diminished, and consequently becomes apparently warmer. The prevalence of northerly above southerly winds may, however, have some slight influence in depressing the temperature of any climate. In our northern latitudes, a canopy of clouds generally screens the ground from the impressions of cold. But within the Arctic Circle, the surface of the earth is more effectually protected by the perpetual fogs which deform those dreary regions, and yet admit the light of day, while they absorb the frigorific pulses vibrated from the higher atmosphere. Even the ancients had remarked that our clear nights are generally likewise cold. During the absence of the sun, the celestial impressions continue to accumulate; and the ground becomes chilled to the utmost in the morning, at the very moment when that luminary again resumes its powerful sway. But neither cold nor heat has the same effect on a green sward as on a ploughed field, the action being nearly dissipated before it reaches the ground among the multiplied surfaces of the blades of grass. The lowest stratum of air, being chilled by contact with the exposed surface, deposites its moisture, which is either absorbed into the earth, or attracted to the projecting fibres of the plants, on which it settles in the form of dew or hoar-frost. Hence the utility, in this country, of spreading awnings at night, to screen the tender blossoms and the delicate fruits from the influence of a gelid sky; and hence, likewise, the advantage of covering walled trees with netting, of which the meshes not only detain the frigorific pulses, but intercept the minute icicles, that, in their formation, rob the air of its cold. It has often been observed as an incontrovertible fact, that the clearing of the ground, and the extension of agriculture, have a material tendency to ameliorate the character of any climate. But whether the sun's rays be spent on the foliage of the trees, or admitted to the surface of the earth, their accumulated effects, in the course of a year, on the incumbent atmosphere, must continue still the same. The direct action of the light would no doubt more powerfully warm the ground during the day, if this superior efficacy were not likewise nearly counterbalanced by exposure to the closer sweep of the winds, and the influence of night must again re-establish the general equilibrium of temperature. The drainage of the surface will evidently improve the salubrity of any climate, by removing the stagnant and putrifying water; but it can have no effect whatever in rendering the air milder, since the ground will be left still sufficiently moist for maintaining a continual evaporation, to the consequent dissipation of heat."*

(466.) The particulars of the *geographical distribution of plants and*

* Encyclopædia Britannica, 7th edition, art. *Climate.*

animals tend to shew the action of general climate on the vegetable and animal functions; the effects of latitude and of elevation above the earth's surface being similar upon both, although most sensibly felt in the vegetable economy. M. Humboldt, the celebrated philosophical traveller, paid great attention to this subject, and, from his own researches, constructed tabular views of the range of animal and vegetable being in both conditions of the globe; but as his observations are more particularly applicable to America, it is not necessary to repeat them here, interesting as they really are.*

(467.) It has been said already, that "the effect of elevation is equivalent to latitude; but it must be recollected that plants will not thrive equally in places with the same mean temperature. Some require a strong ephemeral heat. Hence, in judging of the aptitude of any place for rearing particular plants, we must compare the mean temperature of the summer, as well as of the whole year, before we decide. Thus, we are enabled to explain why the pistacio nut ripens in Pekin, but will not ripen in France, where the isothermal line for the whole year is the same. But though the Chinese winter be more severe than that of France, the summer heat is far greater. Innumerable other instances might be adduced of the same fact. The moisture of a climate has much influence upon its vegetation. Water is the vehicle of the food of plants, and perhaps yields a great proportion of it; so, if moisture be deficient, plants die; but they require water in very different proportions. Those with broad, smooth, soft leaves, that grow rapidly and have many cortical pores, require much water to maintain their vitality; on the other hand, plants with few cortical pores, with oily or resinous juices and small roots, will generally thrive best in dry situations. Exposure to light is necessary for most plants. The green colour of plants is only formed in light, as is shewn by blanching; and light appears to be the cause of certain movements which are remarked in the flowers of most plants, and in other parts of some delicately organised individuals, which open and close their leaves according to the degree of light. This last property is chiefly seen in tropical plants. Light appears to be necessary to the decomposition of carbonic acid, and the fixation of carbon in their tissues; and it is indispensable to the right performance of the function of reproduction. The influence of soil on vegetables is seen in the preference which many plants have for a calcareous soil; some affect silicious sands, others clay retentive of water; some plants thrive best in the clefts of slaty rocks; some delight to dwell amid granitic rocks; and others on a saliferous

* See Edinburgh Philosophical Journal, vols. iii. iv. and v.

soil. Earthy matters enter largely into the composition of some vegetables; and in the epidermis of the gramineæ, silica is invariably found. The presence of animal matters in soils is necessary to many plants, and is generally nutritive to all. Iron and copper are found in small quantities in some plants. The *stations* of particular plants have often been determined by these peculiarities of soil; and when a soil and climate are equally suitable for many *social plants*, we find them growing together, until the strongest obtains the mastery, and chokes the others. The common heath appears to have usurped, in Europe, a space once occupied by other genera, if we may judge from what generally happens on exterminating heath; for then other plants very speedily make their appearance, the seeds of which seem to have long preserved their vitality in the earth, and only to have wanted room to spring into visible existence. A continuation of these causes no doubt influences the distribution of particular species." . . . "On comparing the two Continents, we find in general, in the New World under the equatorial zone, fewer Cyperaceæ and Rubiaceæ, but more Compositæ; under the temperate zone, fewer Labiatæ and Cruciferæ, and more Compositæ, Ericeæ, and Amentaceæ, than in the corresponding zones of the Old World. The families that increase from the equator to the pole, according to the method of fractional indications, are Glumeaceæ, Ericeæ, and Amentaceæ. The families which decrease from the pole to the equator, are Leguminosæ, Rubiaceæ, Euphorbiaceæ, and Malvaceæ. The families that appear to attain their maximum in the temperate zone are Compositæ, Labiatæ, Umbelliferæ, and Cruciferæ."*

(468.) In regard to the geographical distribution of animals, the slightest acquaintance with zoology is sufficient to shew that animals do not indiscriminately spread themselves over every part of the habitable globe. "But the natural limitation of species has been, in some measure, affected by human agency. The domesticated animals have been, by man, imported from different parts of Asia into Europe, and finally into America. At the discovery of that continent, it was without the horse, the cow, the sheep, the hog, the dog, and our common poultry, all which are spread over it in innumerable herds, and in some places have relapsed into the wild state, in countries well suited for their subsistence. The same useful animals have been, by Europeans, within the last half century, carried to the larger islands of the Pacific, where they were previously unknown. How many insects may have been propagated by the cargoes of our ships in distant lands, it is easier to conjecture than to es-

* Encyclopædia Britannica, 7th edition, art. *Physical Geography.*

timate ; how many have been imported with the cerealea and other gramineæ of Europe into newly discovered regions, it is impossible to say. Human agency has sometimes been the means of propagating in Europe disgusting or destructive species from foreign regions. Thus, the commerce of the Dutch wafted the *Teredo navalis* to the dyke-defended coasts of Holland, to the imminent hazard of that country ; the brown rat and the *blatta*, which now infest this country, are believed to be importations from the East Indies ; and the white bug, that now lays waste our orchards, is stated to have reached us with American fruit-trees."*

(469.) The definition of the limits of the zoological divisions on the globe has first been attempted by Mr Swainson, an eminent English naturalist. "He contends that *birds* of any district afford a fairer criterion of the limits of a geographical distribution than any other class of animals. Quadrupeds he believes to be too much under the dominion of man, and liable to have their geographic limits disturbed by human interference ; and the other classes of animals are either too numerous or too few, to afford the means of determining the limits of such divisions ; whilst birds, though seemingly fitted by nature to become wanderers, are surprisingly steady in their localities, and even in the limits of their annual migrations. These migrations are evidently caused by scarcity of food. Thus, our swallows leave us when their insect-food begins to fail, and they naturally pursue that route which is shortest, and affords subsistence by the way. The distance from the shores of the Baltic to Northern Africa is not half so great as between England and America ; and during the migration over land, the winged travellers find food and resting-places as they proceed to more genial climates."†

(470.) Before concluding the subject of climate, I may advert to the very general received opinion among farmers and others who are much exposed in the air, that the weather of Great Britain has changed materially within the memory of the present generation. I am decidedly of this opinion ; and I observe that Mr Knight, the late eminent botanical physiologist, expressed himself on this subject in these words. "My own habits and pursuits, from a very early period of my life to the present time (1829), have led me to expose myself much to the weather in all seasons of the year, and under all circumstances ; and no doubt whatever remains on my mind, but that our winters are generally a good deal less severe than formerly, our springs more cold and ungenial, our summers—particularly the latter part of them—as warm at least as they formerly were, and our autumns considerably warmer." He adds, that

* Encyclopædia Britannica, 7th edition, art. *Physical Geography*. † Ibid.

"I think that I can point out some physical causes, and adduce rather strong facts in support of these opinions."

(471.) Of the physical causes of these changes, Mr Knight conceives that the clearing of the country of trees and brushwood, the extension of arable culture, and the ready means afforded by draining to carry off quickly and effectually the rain as it falls, have rendered the soil drier in May "than it could have been, previously to its having been inclosed and drained and cultivated; and it must consequently absorb and retain much more of the warm summer rain (for but little usually flows off) than it did in an uncultivated state; and as water, in cooling, is known to give out much heat to surrounding bodies, much warmth must be communicated to the ground, and this cannot fail to affect the temperature of the following autumn. The warm autumnal rains, in conjunction with those of summer, must necessarily operate powerfully upon the temperature of the succeeding winter." Hence, a wet summer and autumn are succeeded by a mild winter; and when NE. winds prevail after these wet seasons, the winter is always cloudy and cold, but without severe frosts; probably, in part, owing to the ground upon the opposite shores of the Continent and of this country being in a similar state. The fact adduced by Mr Knight in support of this opinion is that of the common laurel withstanding the winter, notwithstanding its being placed in a high and exposed situation, and its wood not being ripened in November.

(472.) "Supposing the ground," continues Mr Knight, "to contain less water in the commencement of winter, on account of the operations of the drains above mentioned, as it almost always will and generally must do, more of the water afforded by the dissolving snows and the cold rains of winter, will be necessarily absorbed by it; and in the end of February, however dry the ground may have been at the winter solstice, it will almost always be found saturated with water derived from those unfavourable sources; and as the influence of the sun is as powerful on the last day of February as on the 15th day of October, and as it is almost wholly the high temperature of the ground in the latter period which occasions the different temperature of the air in those opposite seasons, I think it can scarcely be doubted, that if the soil have been rendered more cold by having absorbed a larger portion of water at very near the freezing temperature, the weather of the spring must be, to some extent, injuriously affected." Hence, the springs are now more injurious to blossoms and fruits than they were thirty years ago. Hence, also, the farmers of Herefordshire cannot now depend on a crop of acorns from their extensive groves of oaks.*

* Knight's Horticultural Papers, p. 307–9.

21. OF OBSERVING AND RECORDING FACTS.

> "Facts are to the mind the same thing as food to the body. On the due digestion of facts depend the strength and wisdom of the one, just as vigour and health depend on the other. The wisest in council, the ablest in debate, and the most agreeable companion in the commerce of human life, is that man who has assimilated to his understanding the greatest number of facts."
>
> BURKE.

(473.) THESE words of the "the greatest philosophical statesman of our country," as Sir James Mackintosh designated Burke, convey to the mind but an amplification of a sentiment of Bacon, which says, that "the man who writes, speaks, or meditates, without being well-stocked with *facts* as landmarks to his understanding, is like a mariner who sails along a treacherous coast without a pilot, or one who adventures on the wide ocean without either a rudder or a compass." The expression of the same sentiment by two very eminent men, at periods so far asunder and in so very different conditions of the country, should convince you of the universal application of its truth, and induce you to adopt it as a maxim. You can easily do so, as there is no class of people more favourably situated for the observation of interesting facts than agricultural pupils. Creation, both animate and inanimate, lies before you; you must be almost always out of doors, when carrying on your operations; and the operations themselves are substantial matters of fact, constantly subject to modification by the state of the land and the atmosphere. It is useful to observe facts and to familiarize yourselves with them, as, when accumulated, they form the stores from which experience draws its deductions. Never suppose any fact too trivial to arrest attention, as what may at first seem trivial, becomes, in many instances, far from being so; it being only by the comparison of one circumstance with another, that their relative value can be ascertained; and familiar knowledge alone can enable you to discriminate between those which influence others, and those which stand in a state of isolation. In this point of view, observation is always valuable; because at first the pupil must necessarily look upon all facts alike, whatever may ultimately be found to be their intrinsic or comparative importance. The unfoldings of experience alone can shew to him, which classes are to be regarded by themselves, and which are not only connected with, but form the character of others. Remember, also, that to observe facts correctly is not so easy a matter as may be at first supposed; there is a proper time for the commencement of the investigation of their history, which, if not hit upon, all the deductions will be erroneous; and this is especially the case when you are performing experiments instituted for the purpose of corroborating opinions already adopted; for, in this way, many an acute experimentalist has been proselytized into an erroneous system of belief. But as *pupils* you should have no preconceived notions to gratify, no leanings to any species of prejudice. Look upon facts as they occur, and calmly, cautiously, and dispassionately contrast and compare them. It is only thus that you will be able to discriminate causes from consequences to know the relative importance of one fact to another, and to make the results of actual observation in the field, subservient to your acquiring a practical knowledge of agriculture.

(474.) The facts to which you should, in the first instance, direct your attention, are the *effects of the weather at the time*, not only on the operations of the fields and on their productions, but also on the condition of the live stock. You should notice any remarkable occurrence of heat or cold, rain or drought, unpleasant or agreeable feeling in the air; the effects following any peculiar state of the clouds, or other meteors in the air, as storms, aurora borealis, halos, and the like; the particular operation of rain in retarding or materially altering the labours of the field, and the length of time and quantity of rain that it has taken to produce such an effect; as well as the effects on the health or growth of plants, and the comfort and condition of animals. The effects of cold, or snow, or drought, upon the same subjects, deserve equal attention.

(475.) You should particularly observe the *time* at which each kind of crop is committed to the ground; how long it is till it afterwards appears above it; when it comes into ear; and the period of harvest. Try also to ascertain the quantity of every kind of crop on the ground before it is cut down, and observe whether the event corroborates your judgment. In the same way, try to estimate the weight of cattle by the eye at different periods of their progress towards maturity of condition, and check your trials by measurements. The very handling of beasts for the purpose of measuring them will convey to you much information regarding their progressive state of improvement. When sheep are slaughtered, attend to the weight of the carcass, and endeavour to correct any errors you may have committed in estimating their weights.

(476.) Keep a *register* of each field of the farm; note the quantity of labour it has received, the quantity of manure which has been applied, and the kind of crop sown on it, with the circumstances attending these operations—whether they have been done quickly and in good style, or interruptedly, from the hinderance of the weather or other circumstances; and whether in an objectionable or favourable manner. Ascertain, in each field, the number of ridges required to make an acre, and whether the ridges be of equal length or not. By this you will the more easily ascertain how much dung the field is receiving per acre, the time taken to perform the same quantity of work on ridges of different length, and the comparative value of crop produced on an acre in different parts of the field. The subdivision of the field into acres in this manner will also enable you to compare the relative values of the crops produced on varieties of soil, if any, in the same field, under the same circumstances of treatment.

(477.) The easiest and most satisfactory mode of preserving and recording all these facts is in the *tabular form*, which admits of every fact being put down under its own proper head. This form not only exhibits a full exposition of the whole facts at a glance, but admits of every one being recorded with the least trouble of writing. The advantage of *writing* them down consists not entirely in recording them, but also of impressing them more strongly on the memory.

(478.) The tables should consist of ruled columns, in a book of sufficient size of leaf to contain columns for every subject. There should also be a *plan of the farm*, with every field represented, having its figure, dimensions, and name, the direction of the ridges, and the number of ridges required to make an acre visibly marked upon it. It would be advisable to enter each field into the book. in which could be noted the various sorts of labour it has received, and the produce it has yielded; so that the whole transactions connected with it for the year could be seen at a glance. There should also be a *plan of the stack-yard* made every year, with each stack represented in it by a circle, the area of which should contain the name of the field upon which the crop in the stack was grown, the quantity of corn yielded by the stack, and in what way the produce was disposed of; and even the cash (if any) which the produce realized, should be marked down. This plan of the stack-yard should be comprehended on a single page of the book.

(479.) To render the whole system of recording facts complete, a summary of them in regard to the weather in each season, together with the produce and value of the crop and stock, should be made up every year to the end of autumn,—the end of the agricultural year. In this way, an immense mass of useful facts would be recorded within the narrow compass of a single book. Comparisons could thus be easily made between the results of different seasons, and deductions drawn which could not be ascertained by any other means.

(480.) The *only objection* you can possibly urge against the adoption of this plan, is the time required to record the facts. Were the records to be made twice or thrice a-day, like the observations of a meteorological register, the objection would be well founded; because I cannot conceive any task more irksome than the noting down of dry and (in themselves) unmeaning details. But the variations and effects of the weather assume a very different importance, when they possess an overruling influence over the progress of the crops. The recording of these and such like facts can only be required at occasional times, of perhaps an interval of days. The only toil connected with the scheme would be the drawing up of the abstract of the year; but when the task, even if irksome, is for your professional benefit, the time devoted to it should be cheerfully bestowed.

---

22. OF SOILS AND SUBSOILS.

"I wander o'er the various rural toil,
And know the nature of each different soil."
GAY.

(481.) HAVING expatiated on every subject with which it seemed to me expedient that you should be acquainted, to prepare your mind for the reception of lessons in practice, we shall now proceed together to study farming in right earnest. The first thing, as regards the farm itself, which should engage your attention, is the kinds of *soil* which it contains. To become acquainted with these, so as to be able to identify them anywhere, you should know the external characters of *every* soil usually met with on a farm; because very few farms contain only one kind of soil, and the generality exhibit a considerable variety.

(482.) *Practically*, a knowledge of the external characters of soils is a matter of *no great difficulty;* for however complex the composition of any soil appears to be, it possesses a character belonging to its kind, which cannot be confounded with any other. The leading characters of ordinary soils are derived from only two earths, *clay* and *sand*, and it is the greater or less admixture of these which stamps the peculiar character of the soil The properties of either of these earths are even found to exist in what seems a purely calcareous or purely vegetable soil. When either earth is mixed with decomposed vegetable matter, whether supplied naturally or artificially, the soil becomes a *loam*, the distinguishing character of which is derived from the predominating earth. Thus, there are *clay-soils* and *sandy soils*, when either earth predominates; and when either is mixed with decomposed vegetable matter, they are then *clay-loams* and *sandy loams*. Sandy soils are divided into two varieties, which do not vary in kind but only in degree. Sand is a powder, consisting of small round particles of siliceous matter; but when these are of the size of a hazel-nut and larger,—that is, gravel,—they give their distinguishing name to the soil; they then form *gravelly soils* and *gravelly loams*. Besides these, there are soils which have for their basis another kind of earth—*lime*, of which the *chalky soils* of the south of England consist. But these differ in agricultural character in nothing from either the clay or sandy soils, according to the particular formation from which the chalk is derived. If the chalky soil is derived from flinty chalk, then its character is like that of a sandy soil; but if from the under chalk-formation, its character is like that of clay. Writers on agriculture also enumerate a peat-soil, derived from peat; but peat, as crude peat, is of no use to vegetation, and when it is decomposed, it assumes the properties of *mould*, and should be considered as such; and mould, which forms the essential ingredient of loams, is decomposed vegetable matter, derived either from nature or from artificial application. So, for all *practical* purposes, soils are most conveniently divided into clayey and sandy, with their respective loams.

(483.) *Loam*, in the sense now given, does not convey the idea attached to it by many writers; and many people talk of it, as if it must necessarily consist of clay. Thus, Johnson, in defining the verb "to loam," gives as a synonyme the verb "to clay;" and Bacon somewhere says, that "the mellow earth is the best, between the two extremes of clay and sand, if it be not *loamy and binding*;" evidently referring to the binding property of clay. Sir Humphry Davy defines loam as "the impalpable part of the soil, which is usually called *clay or loam*."* And Mr Reid defines the same substance in these words: "The term 'loam' is applied to soils which consist of about one-third of finely divided earthy matter, containing much carbonate of lime. Other soils are peaty, containing about one-half of vegetable matter."† Professor Low gives a more correct though, in my opinion, not the exact idea of a loam. "The decomposed organic portion of the soil," he truly says, "may be termed *mould*;" but he continues to say, and this is what I doubt, that "the fertility of soils is, *cæteris paribus*, indicated by the greater or smaller proportion of mould which enters into their composi-

* Davy's Agricultural Chemistry, 8vo edit. 1839, p. 150.

† Reid's Chemistry of Nature, p. 276.

tion. When soils are thus naturally fertile, or are rendered permanently so by art, they are frequently termed *loams*."* You thus see what diversity of opinion exists as to what loam is. Loam, in my opinion, has changed its meaning so far since the days of Johnson, as to consist of any kind of earth that contains a *large admixture of decomposed vegetable matter*,—I say a large admixture of vegetable matter, because there is no soil under cultivation, whether composed chiefly of clay or principally of sand, but what contains some decomposed vegetable matter. Unless, therefore, the decomposed vegetable matter of the soil so preponderates as to greatly modify the usual properties of the constituent earths, the soil cannot in truth be called by any other name than a clayey or sandy soil; but when the vegetable matter so prevails as materially to alter the properties of those earths, then a *clay-loam* or a *sandy loam* is constituted—a distinction well known to the farmer. But, if it is necessary that clay should have a preponderance in *loam*, then a *sandy* loam must be a contradiction in terms. Again, a soil of purely vegetable origin—such as crude peat or leaf-mould—cannot be called loam; for admixture of an earth of some sort is required to make loam, under every recorded definition of that term. Nor is the fertility of soils dependent on the greater or smaller proportion of mould or decomposed vegetable matter in their composition; for there are soils, with apparently very little mould in them, such as sharp gravels, which are highly fertile; and there are moulds, apparently with very little earth in them, such as deaf black mould, which are far removed from fertility. Thus, then, all soils have the properties of clayey or sandy soils, and a considerable quantity of decomposed vegetable matter converts them into loam. Hence it is possible for husbandry to convert an earthy soil into a loam, as is exemplified in the vicinity of large towns.

(484.) A pure *clay*-soil has very distinctive external characters, by which you may easily recognise it. When fully wetted, it feels greasy to the foot, which slips upon it backwards, forwards, and sideways. It has an unctuous feel in the hand, by which it can be kneaded into a smooth homogeneous mass, and retain any shape given to it. It glistens in the sunshine. It retains water upon its surface, and makes water very muddy when mixed with it or runs over it, and is long of settling to the bottom. It is cold to the touch, and easily soils the hand and any thing else that touches it. It cuts like soft cheese with the spade, and is then in an unfit state to be worked with the plough, or any other implement. When dry, clay-soil cracks into numerous fissures, feels

* Low's Elements of Practical Agriculture, 2d edit. p. 2.

very hard to the foot, and runs into lumps, which are often large, and both large and small are very difficult to be broken, and indeed cannot be pulverised. It soils the hand and clothes with a dry, light coloured, soft dust, which has no lustre. It is heavy in weight, and difficult to labour. It absorbs moisture readily, and will adhere to the tongue. When neither wet nor dry, it is very tough, and soon becomes very hard with a little drought, or very soft with a little rain. On these accounts, it is the most ticklish of all soils to manage; being, even in its best state, difficult to turn over with the plough, and to pulverise with other implements. A large strength of horses is thus required to work a clay-land farm; for its workable state continues only for a short time, and it is the most obdurate of all soils to labour. But it is a powerful soil, its vegetation being luxuriant, and its production great. It generally occurs in deep masses, on a considerable extent of flat surface, exhibiting only a few undulations. It is generally found near a large river, towards its estuary, being supposed to have been a deposition from its waters. Examples of this kind of soil may be seen, in Scotland, in the Carses of Gowrie, Stirling, and Falkirk. It may be denominated a naturally rich soil, with little vegetable matter in it, and its colour is yellowish-grey.

(485.) When a little *sand and gravel are mixed with clay*, its texture is very materially altered, but its productive powers are not improved. When such a clay is in a wet state, it still slips a little under the foot, but feels harsh rather than greasy. It does not easily ball in the hand. It retains water on its surface for a time, which is soon partially absorbed. It renders water very muddy, and soils every thing by adhering to it; and, on that account, never comes clean off the spade, except when much wetted with water. When dry, it feels hard, but is easily pulverised by any of the implements of tillage. It has no lustre. It does not soil the clothes much, and, though somewhat heavy to labour, is not obdurate. When betwixt the states of wet and dry, it is easily laboured, and can be reduced to a fine tilth or mould. This kind of soil never occurs in deep masses, but is rather shallow; is not naturally favourable to vegetation, nor is it naturally prolific. It occupies by far the larger portion of the surface of Scotland, much of its wheat is grown upon it, and it may be denominated a naturally poor soil, with not much vegetable matter in it. Its colour is yellowish-brown.

(486.) *Clay-loam*—that is, either of those clays mixed with a large proportion of naturally decomposed vegetable matter—constitutes a useful and valuable soil. It yields the largest proportion of the fine wheats raised in this country, occupying a larger surface of the country than the carse-clay. It forms a lump by a squeeze of the hand, but soon crumbles down again. It is easily wetted on the surface with rain, and then feels soft and greasy ; but the water is soon absorbed, and the surface is again as soon dry. It is easily laboured, and may be so at any time after a day or two of dry weather. It becomes finely pulverised, and is capable of assuming a high temperature. It is generally of some depth, forming an excellent soil for wheat, beans, Swedish turnips, and red clover. It is of a deep-brown colour, often approaching to red.

(487.) All clay-soils are better adapted to fibrous-rooted plants than to bulbs and tubers ; but it is that sort of fibrous root which has also a tap-root, such as is found in wheat, the bean, red clover, and the oak. The crops mentioned bearing abundance of straw, the plants require a deep hold of the soil. Clay-soils are generally slow of bringing their crops to maturity, which in wet seasons they never arrive at; but in dry seasons, they are always strong, and yield quantity rather than quality.

(488.) A pure *sandy* soil is as easily recognised as one of pure clay. When wet, it feels firm under foot, and then admits of a pretty whole furrow being laid over by the plough. It feels harsh and grating to the touch. When dry, it feels soft; and is so yielding, that every object of the least weight sinks in it: it is then apt to blow away with the wind. In an ordinary state, it is well adapted to plants having fusiform roots, such as the carrot and parsnip. It acquires a high temperature in summer. Sandy soil generally occurs in deep masses, near the termination of the estuaries of large rivers, or along the sea-shore ; and in some countries in the interior of Europe, and over a large proportion of Africa, it covers immense tracks of flat land, and is evidently a deposition from water.

(489.) A *gravelly* soil consists of a large proportion of sand ; but the greater part of its bulk is made up of small rounded fragments of rock brought together by the action of water. These small fragments have been derived from all the rock-formations, whilst the large boulders, imbedded principally under the surface, have been chiefly supplied by the older formations. Gravelly deposites sometimes occupy a large extent of surface, and are of considerable depth. Such a soil soon becomes warm, but never wet, absorbing the rain as fast as it falls ; and after rain, it feels somewhat firm under foot. It can be easily laboured in any weather, and is not unpleasant to work, though the numerous small stones, which are seen in countless numbers upon the surface, render the holding of the plough rather unsteady. As an instance of its dry nature, an old farmer of gravelly soil used to joke with his ploughmen, and offer them a "roasted hen" to their dinner on the day they got their feet wet at the plough. This soil is admirably adapted to plants having bulbs and tubers; and no kind of soil affords so dry and comfortable a lair to sheep on turnips, and on this account it is distinguished as "*turnip-soil.*"

(490.) *Sandy and gravelly loams,* if not the most valuable, are certainly the most useful, of all soils. They become neither too wet nor too dry in ordinary seasons, and are capable of growing every species of crop, in every variety of season, to considerable perfection. On this account, they are esteemed "*kindly soils.*" They never occur in deep masses, nor do they extend over large tracts of land, being chiefly confined to the margins of small rivers, forming haughs or holms, through which the rivers meander from their source amongst the mountains towards the larger ones, or even to the sea; and, in their progress, are apt at times to become so enlarged with rain, both in summer and winter, as to overflow their banks to a limited extent on either side.

(491.) These are all the kinds of soil usually found on a farm; and of these, the two opposite extremes of the pure clay and the pure sand may most easily be recognised by you. The intermediate shades in the varieties of soil, occasioned by modifications of greater or smaller quantity of decomposed vegetable matter, it would be impossible to describe. Every soil, however, may be ranked under the general heads of Clayey and Sandy soils; the gravelly and sandy, as you have learned, constituting differences rather in degree than in kind; and as every soil possesses the property of either clay or sand,—be the sand derived from siliceous or calcareous deposite,—it is useless to maintain the nomenclature of chalky and peaty soils, although these distinctive terms may be retained to indicate the origin of the soils thereby implied by them.

(492.) You are now prepared to consider the question, what constitutes *the soil*—properly so called? You will perceive the propriety of such a question, when you consider the different ideas entertained of soil by persons of different denominations. The geologist considers the uppermost alluvial covering of the earth's crust as the soil, and whatever stratum that rests upon, as the subsoil. The botanist considers as the soil, that portion of the earth's surface which supports plants. People generally consider the ground they walk upon as the soil; but none of these ideas define the soil in the *agricultural sense.* In that sense, the *soil* consists only of that *portion of the earth which is stirred by the plough,* and the *subsoil* of that which is found *immediately below the plough's course.* In this way the subsoil may consist of the same kind of earth as the soil, or it may be quite different, or it may be of rock. As it is of importance for you to keep *this* distinction of soil and subsoil always in mind, the subject should be illustrated by a figure. Let *a*, fig. 34, be the surface of the ground, the earthy mould derived from the growth

Fig. 34.

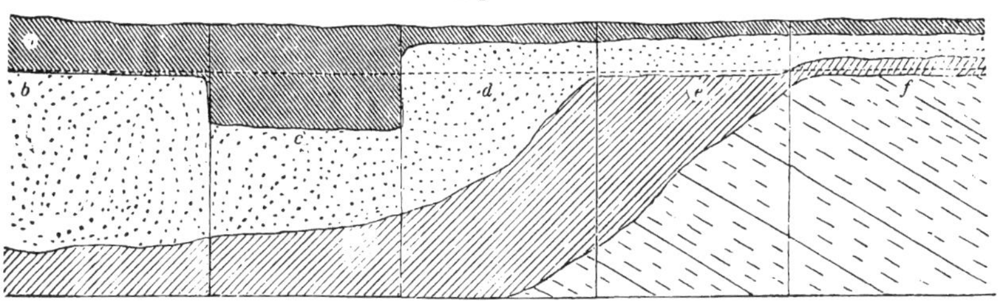

SECTIONS OF SOILS AND SUBSOILS.

and decay of natural plants; *b*, a dotted line, the depth of the plough-furrow. Now, the plough-sole may either just pass through the mould, as at *b*, when the mould will be the soil, and the earth below it the subsoil: Or it may not pass entirely through the mould, as at *c*, when the soil and subsoil will be similar, that is, both of mould: Or it may pass through the earth below the mould, as at *d*, when the soil and subsoil will again be similar, while neither will be mould, but earth: Or it may move along the surface of *e*, when the soil will be of one kind of earth, and the subsoil of another, that is, either an open subsoil of gravel, or a retentive one of clay: Or it may move upon the surface of *f*, when the soil will be earth, or a mixture of clay, sand, and mould, and the subsoil rock. These different cases of soil and subsoil are represented in the figure, each in a distinct sectional division.

(493.) The *subsoil*, then, in an *agricultural sense*, is the substance which is found immediately below the line of the course of the plough, be it earth or rock. However uniform in substance, or similar in quality, the subsoil and soil may have been at one time, cultivation, by supplies of vegetable matter, and by presentation of the surface to the action of the air, soon effects a material difference betwixt them, and the difference consists of a change both in texture and colour, the soil becoming finer and having a darker tint than the subsoil.

(494.) The *nature* of the subsoil *produces a sensible effect on the condition of the soil above it.* If the soil is clay, it is impervious to water, and if the subsoil is clay also, it is also impervious to water. The immediate effect of this juxtaposition is to render both soil and subsoil habitually wet, until the force of evaporation dries first the one and then the other. A retentive subsoil, in the same manner, renders a sandy or gravelly, that is a porous, soil above it habitually wet. On the other hand, a gravelly subsoil, which is always porous, greatly assists to keep a retentive clay soil dry. When a porous soil rests upon a porous subsoil, scarcely any degree of humidity can injure either. Rock may be either a retentive or a porous subsoil, according to its structure; its massiveness throughout keeping every soil above it habitually wet; but its stratification, if the lines of stratification dip downwards from the soil (as at *f*, fig. 34), will keep even a retentive soil above it in a comparatively dry state.

(495.) These are the *different conditions of soils and subsoils*, considered practically. They have terms expressive of their state, which you should keep in remembrance. A soil is said to be *stiff* or *heavy*, when it is difficult to cut through, and is otherwise laborious to work with the ordinary implements of the farm; and all clay-soils are more or less so. On the other hand, it is *light* or *free*, when it is easy to work; and all sandy and gravelly soils, and sandy and gravelly loams, are so. A soil is said to be *wet*, when it is habitually wet; and to be *dry*, when habitually so. All soils, especially clays, on retentive subsoils, are habitually wet; and all soils on porous subsoils, especially gravels and gravelly loams, are habitually dry. Any soil that cannot bring to maturity a fair crop, without an inordinate quantity of manure, is considered *poor;* and any one that does so naturally, or yields a large return with a moderate quantity of manure, is said to be *rich.* Thin hard clays and ordinary sands are examples of poor soils; and soft clays and deep loams, of rich. A soil is said to be *deep*, when the surface-earth descends a good way below the reach of the plough; and in that case the plough may be made to go deeper than usual, and yet continue in the same soil; and a soil is *thin*, when the plough can easily reach beyond it. Good husbandry can, in time, render a thin soil deep, and bad shallow ploughing may cause a deep soil to assume the character of a thin one. A deep soil conveys the idea of a good one, and a thin, or shallow, or ebb, that of a bad. Carse clays and sandy loams are instances of deep soils, and poor clays and poor gravels those of thin. A soil is said to be a *hungry* one, when it requires frequent applications of a large quantity of manure to bear ordinary crops. Thin poor gravels are instances of a hungry soil. A soil is said to be *grateful*, when it returns a larger produce than was expected from what was done for it. All loams, whether clayey, gravelly, or sandy,—especially the two last,—are grateful soils. A soil is said to be *kindly*, when every operation performed upon it can be done without doubt, and in the way and at the time desired. A sandy loam and even a clay-loam, both on porous subsoil, are examples of kindly soils. A soil is said to become *sick*, when the crop that has been made to grow upon it too frequently becomes deteriorated; thus, soils soon become sick of growing red clover and turnips. A *sharp* soil is that which contains such a number of small gritty stones as to clear up the plough-irons quickly. Such a soil never fails to be an open one, and is admirably adapted for turnips. A fine gravelly loam is an instance of a sharp soil. Some say that a sharp soil means a *ready* one—that is, quick or prepared to do anything required of it; but I am not of this opinion, because a sandy loam is ready enough for any crop, and it is never called a sharp soil. A *deaf* soil is the contrary of a sharp one; that is, it contains too much inert vegetable matter, in a soft spongy state which is apt to be carried forward on the bosom of the plough. A deep black mould, whether derived from peat or not, is an example of a deaf soil. A *porous* or *open* soil and subsoil, are those which allow water to pass through them freely and quickly, of which a gravelly loam and gravelly subsoil are examples. A *retentive* or *close* soil and subsoil retain water on them; and a clay soil upon a clay subsoil is an instance of both. Some soils are always *hard*, as in the case of thin retentive clays when dry, let them be ever so well worked; whilst others are *soft*, as fine sandy loams, which are very apt to become so on being too often ploughed, or too much marled. Some soils are always *fine*, as in the case of deep easy clay loams; others *coarse* or *harsh*, as in thin poor clays and gravels. A fine clay is *smooth* when in a wet state, and a thin clayey gravel is *rough* when dry. A soil is said to have a *fine skin* when it can be finished off with a beautifully granulated surface. Good culture will bring a fine skin on many soils, and rich sandy and clay loams have naturally a fine skin; but no art can give a fine skin to some soils, such as thin hard clay and rough gravel.

(496.) The *colours* of soils and subsoils, though various, are limited in their range. *Black* soils are instanced in crude peat and deep vegetable mould; and *white* are common in the chalky districts of England. Some soils are *blue* or *bluish-grey*, from a peculiar sort of fine clay deposited at the bottom of basins of still water. But the most prevailing colour is *brown*, from light hair-brown to dark chestnut, the hazel-brown being the most favourite colour of the class. The sand and gravel loams are instances of these colours. The browns pass into *reds*, of which there are several varieties, all having a dark hue; such, for instance, are some clay loams. The brown and red soils acquire high degrees of temperature, and they are also styled *warm* in reference to colour. There are also *yellow* and *grey* soils, a mixture of which makes a yellowish-grey. They are always *cold*, both in regard to temperature and colour; and are the opposite, in these respects, to brown and red soils. Colour is indicative of the nature of soils. Thus, all yellow and grey colours belong to clay soils. Grey sand and grey stones are indicative of soils of moory origin. Black soils are deaf and inert; the brown, on the other hand, are sharp and grateful, and many of them kindly; whilst the reds are always prolific. The colour of subsoils is less uniform than that of soils, owing, no doubt, to their exclusion from culture. Some subsoils are very party-coloured, and the more they are so, and the brighter the colours they sport, they are the more injurious to the soils above them: they exhibit grey, black, blue, green, bright red, and bright yellow colours. The dull red and the chestnut brown subsoils are good; but the nearer they approach to hazel brown the better. Dull browns, reds, and yellowish greys are permanent colours, and are little altered by cultivation; but the blues, greens, bright reds and yellows, become darker and duller by exposure to the air and by admixture with manures.

(497.) These are all the remarks required to be made on soils, in as far as practice is concerned; but a great deal yet remains to be said of them as objects of natural history, and subjects of chemistry, and above all as the staple of the farm. Part of the natural history, and part of their chemistry, will appear in the paragraphs immediately below, and part of both will deserve our attention when we treat of the fertility of soils; but the management of soils will occupy our thoughts through every season.

(498.) The external characters of minerals established by Werner, and recognised by mineralogists, have never been used to describe agricultural soils. It would perhaps serve no practical purpose to do so; because there are naturally such minute shades in the varieties of soils, and those shades are constantly undergoing changes in the course of good and bad modes of cultivation, that definitions, even when established, would soon become inapplicable. In respect, therefore, to a scientific classification of soils by external characters, there are as yet no data upon which to establish it, and the only alternative left is to adopt such a division as I have endeavoured to describe. In adopting that classification I have subdivided it into fewer heads than other writers on the same subject have done. In their subdivisions they include calcareous and peaty soils with the clayey and sandy. Practically, however, calcareous matter cannot be detected in ordinary soils; and as to chalky soils themselves, their management is so similar to that of light and heavy ordinary soils, according to the formation from which they are derived, that no practical distinction, as I have said, need be drawn betwixt them; and in regard to peaty soils, when reduced to earth, which they easily are by cultivation, they partake of the character of mould. The kind of mould which they form, you will learn, when I come to treat of the fertility of soils.

(499.) In regard to the relation of soils to the subjacent strata, it is held by a recent practical writer on soils that "the surface of the earth partakes of the nature and colour of the subsoil or rock on which it rests. The principal mineral in the soil of any district is that of the geological formation under it: hence we find argillaceous soil resting on the various clay formations —calcareous soil over the chalk—and oolitic rocks and siliceous soils, over the various sandstones. On the chalk the soil is white; on the red sandstone it is red; and on the sands and clays the surface has nearly the same shade of colour as the subsoil."* I do not think that this description of the position of soils is generally correct, because many instances occur to my knowledge of great tracts of soils, including subsoils, having no relation to the "geological formation under them." The fine strong deep clay of the Carse of Gowrie rests on the old red sandstone, a rock having nothing in common, either in consistence or colour, with the clay above it. The large extent of the grey sands of Barrie, and the great grey gravelly deposites of the valley of the Lunan, in Forfarshire, both rest on the same formation as the carse clay, namely, the old red sandstone; and so of numerous other examples in Scotland. In fact, soils are frequently found of infinitely diversified character, over extensive districts of rock, whose constituents are nearly uniform; and, on the other hand, soils of uniform character occur in districts where the underlying rocks are different as well in their chemical as their geological properties. Thus an uniform integument of clay rests upon the grey sandstone to the westward of the Carse of Gowrie, in Perthshire, and the same clay covers the Ochil Hills in that county and Fifeshire with an uniform mantle—over hills which are entirely composed of trap. On the other hand, a diversified clay and gravel are found to cover an uniform tract of greywacke in Perthshire. "We have grey sandstone," says Mr Buist aptly, when treating of the geology of the north-east portion of Perthshire, "red sandstone, and rock-marl, as it is called, cut by various massy veins of trap or beds of conglomerate and lime; yet I defy any man to form the smallest guess of the rocks below from the soils above them, though the ground is sufficiently uniform to give fair scope for all to manifest the influence possessed by them. There are lands whose agricultural value has been so greatly modified by the presence or withdrawal of a bed of gravel between the arable soil and tilly subsoil, which, when present, affords a universal drain, when absent, leaves the land almost unarable. But if we must shew a relation betwixt the sandstone and any of these beds, which of the three," very properly asks Mr Buist, "are we to select as having affinity with the rock?"†

(500.) In passing from practical to scientific opinion on the origin of soils, we find Mr De la Beche giving his opinion that "naturally soils are merely decomposed parts of the subjacent rock, mixed with the decomposed portions of vegetable substances which have grown or fallen upon it, and with a proportion of animal substances derived from the droppings of creatures which have fed upon the vegetation, from dead insects and worms which once inhabited the surface, and from the decomposition of animals that have perished on the land, and which have not altogether been removed by those quadrupeds, birds, and insects that act as natural scavengers."‡ This view of the origin of soils seems to corroborate the opinion of Mr Morton, quoted above; but if you look more closely into the definitions of the terms used by both writers, you will find there is not that identity of opinion between them which appears at first sight. For "the term rock," says Mr De la Beche, "is applied by geologists, not only to the hard substances to which this name is *commonly* given, but also to those various *sands*, *gravels*, *shales*, *marls*, or *clays* which form beds, strata, or masses."§

* Morton on Soils, p. 1.

† Prize Essays of the Highland and Agricultural Society, vol. xiii. p. 44-9.

‡ De la Beche, How to Observe Geology, p. 283-4.

§ De la Beche's Manual of Geology, p. 35.

Taking this correct geological definition of rock, Mr De la Beche's view is quite correct in regard to *agricultural* soils, for they certainly are decomposed portions of the rock, geologically speaking, that is, of those " sands, gravels, or clays," upon which they rest; but the impression left on the mind of the reader on perusing Mr Morton's account of the origin of soils is, that the *rocky* strata, *commonly* so called, because indurated, became decomposed to form soil; and his reference to the various geological formations of England, in explanation of the soils found above them, warrant the correctness of this impression; but it is this very impression which I wish to remove from your minds, because it conveys, in my opinion, an erroneous idea of the origin of soils.

(501.) No doubt the chemical action of the air, and the physical force of rain, frost, and wind, produce visible effects upon the most indurated rocks, but, of course, much greater effects upon incoherent rocks. We know that the action of these agents load the waters of the Ganges with detritus to the extent of 2½ per cent. of their volume, which is an enormous quantity when we consider that the water discharged by that river into the sea is 500,000 cubic feet per second, although this amount falls far short of Major Rennel's statement of 25 per cent.; yet these agents have not had sufficient power to accumulate, by their own action on indurated rocky strata, all the deposites of clay, gravel, and sand, found accumulated to the depth of many feet. Combined in their action, they could only originate a mere coating of soil over the surface of indurated rock, if the rock were situated within the region of phenogamous vegetation, because then it would be constantly covered with plants. But the plants, in their turn, would protect the rocks against the action of those agencies; and although they could not entirely prevent, they could at least retard, the accumulation of soil beyond what the decay of vegetation supplied. Even in the tropics, where vegetation displays its greatest luxuriance on the globe, the mould does not increase, though the decay of vegetables every year is enormous. " The quantity of timber and vegetable matter which grows in a tropical forest in the course of a century," says Mr Lyell, " is enormous, and multitudes of animal skeletons are scattered there during the same period, besides innumerable land shells and other organic substances. The aggregate of these materials, therefore, might constitute a mass greater in volume than that which is produced in any coral-reef during the same lapse of years; but although this process should continue on the land for ever, no mountains of wood or bone would be seen stretching far and wide over the country, or pushing out bold promontories into the sea. The whole solid mass is either devoured by animals, or decomposes, as does a portion of the rock and soil (into their gaseous constituents) on which the animals and plants are supported."* These are the causes of the prevention of the accumulation of soils in the tropics. In colder regions a similar result is thus brought about. " It is well known," continues Mr Lyell, " that a covering of herbage and shrubs may protect a loose soil from being carried away by rain, or even by the ordinary action of a river, and may prevent hills of loose sand from being blown away by the wind; for the roots bind together the separate particles into a firm mass, and the leaves intercept the rain-water, so that it dries up gradually instead of flowing off in a mass and with great velocity."†

(502.) Some other agent, therefore, more powerful than the ordinary atmospherical elements, must be brought to bear upon indurated rocks, before a satis-

* Lyell's Principles of Geology, vol. iii. p. 177.

† Ibid. p. 184-5.

factory solution of the formation of soils can be given. This other agent is water; but the moment that we assent to the agency of water being able by its great abrasive power and great buoyant property, when in motion, to transport the abraded parts of rocks to a distance, and let them fall on coming in contact with some opposing barrier, that moment we must abandon the idea of soils having been universally derived from the indurated rocky strata upon which they are found to rest. I quite agree with Mr Buist in the conclusions he has drawn in regard to soils, after he had described their relative positions to the rocks upon which they rest in a large and important district of Perthshire, where he says, " that the alluvial matters of these districts, in general, belong to periods much more remote than those ordinarily assigned to them, and came into existence under circumstances prodigiously different from those which presently obtain: that the present causes, that is, the action of our modern rivers, brooks, and torrents, and of the air and water on the surfaces now exposed to them, have had but little share in modifying our alluvial formations, or bringing them into their present form. The doctrine seems to me most distinctly demonstrable, that wherever gravel or clay beds alternate with each other, and wherever boulder stones prevail remote from the parent rock, or cut off from it by high intervening ridges, that, at the time when the surface of the solid rock became covered with such alluvium, much the greater part of it was hundreds of feet beneath the waves. The supposition of the prevalence of enormous lakes, requiring barriers only less stupendous than our highest secondary mountain-ranges, whose outbursts must have swept every movable thing before them, seems far more untenable than the assumption that the present dry land, at the era of boulders being transported, was beneath the level of the ocean, from which, by slow elevations, it subsequently emerged. Our newer alluvia, again, which are destitute of erratic boulders in general, such as our Carse of Gowrie and other clays, must have originated when the sea occasionally invaded the land to such moderate extent, that the transportation of rocky masses from great distances from our mountain-land, had been rendered impossible, by the intervention of elevated ridges, or of secondary mountain-ranges." * More than this, is it not probable that, when the stratified rocks were being deposited in water, portions of the matter, of which they were about to be formed, were carried away by currents, and, by reason of the motion given them, were deposited in eddies in a mechanical state, instead of getting leave to assume the crystalline form of indurated stratified rock? May not all diluvium have thus originated, instead of being abraded from solid strata, although it is possible that some portion may have been derived from the abrasion of rocks? It is also quite conceivable that where indurated rock, such as chalk, and sandstone, and limestone, were left bare by the subsiding waters, and exposed to atmospherical influences, part of the soil upon them may have been derived at first immediately from them.

(503.) The soil, or incoherent rocks, when complete in all their members, consist of three parts. The oldest or lowest part, not unfrequently termed *diluvium*, but which is an objectionable term, inasmuch as it conveys the idea of its having been formed by the Noachian deluge, which it may not have been, but may have existed at a much older period of the globe. This cannot be called

* Prize Essays of the Highland and Agricultural Society of Scotland, vol. xiii. p. 49.

alluvium, according to the definition of that deposite given by Mr Lyell, who considers it to consist of " such transported matter as has been thrown down, whether by rivers, floods, or other causes, upon land not *permanently* submerged beneath the waters of lakes or seas,—I say *permanently submerged*, in order to distinguish between *alluviums* and *regular subaqueous deposites*. These regular strata," he continues, " are accumulated in lakes or great submarine receptacles; but the alluvium is in the channels of rivers or currents, where the materials may be regarded as still *in transitu*, or on their way to a place of rest." * Diluvium, therefore, should rather be termed subaqueous deposites, and may consist of clay, or gravel, or sand, in deep masses and of large extent. It may, in fact, be transported materials, which, if they had been allowed to remain in their original site, would have formed indurated aluminous and siliceous rocks. When such subaqueous deposites are exposed to atmospherical influences, an arable soil is easily formed upon them.

(504.) True *alluvial* deposites may raise themselves by accumulation above their depositing waters, and art can assist the natural process, by the erection of embankments against the encroachments of these waters, and by the casting out of large ditches for carrying them away, as has been done in several places in the rivers and coasts of our country. Atmospherical influences soon raise an arable soil on alluvium.

(505.) The third member of soils is the upper *mould*, which has been directly derived from vegetation, and can only come into existence after either of the other soils has been placed in a situation favourable for the support of plants. Mould, being in contact with air, always exists on the surface, but when either the subaqueous deposite or the alluvium is awanting, the mould then rests upon the one present; or both may be awanting, and then it rests upon the indurated rocky strata.

(506.) When the last case happens, if the rocky stratum is porous, by means of numerous fissures, or is in inclined beds, the arable soil is an earthy mould of good quality for agricultural purposes; such as are the moulds upon sandstones, limestones, and trap, and the upper chalk formation; but if it rest on a massive rock, then the mould is converted into a spongy wet pabulum for subaquatic plants, forming a marsh, if the site is low, and if high, it is converted into thin peat; and both are worthless soils for agriculture. When the mould rests immediately upon clay subaqueous deposite, a coarse and rank vegetation exists upon it, and if the water which supports it has no opportunity of passing away, in time a bog is formed by the cumulative growth of the subaquatic mosses.† When mould, on the other hand, is formed on gravelly deposite, the vegetation is short, and dry, and sweet, and particularly well adapted to promote the sound feeding and health of sheep. On such deposites water is never seen to remain after the heaviest fall of rain. When mould rests on alluvial deposite of whatever nature, a rich soil is the consequence, and it will be naturally dry only when the deposite is gravelly or sandy.

(507.) Mr De La Beche seems to think that farmers do not know the reason why subsoils are favourable or unfavourable to the soil upon them.‡ I suspect

* Lyell's Principles of Geology, vol. iii. p. 218.

† For an account of the origin of Bogs, see Aiton on Moss, p. 1-120.

‡ De La Beche, How to observe Geology, p. 283.

they know more about them than he is aware of. They know quite well that a dry subsoil is more favourable to agriculture than a retentive one ;—that gravel forms a drier subsoil than clay ;—and that the reason why these results should be so, is, that clay, or a massive rock, will not let water pass through it so easily as gravel, and I presume no geologist knows more of the matter.

(508.) [We must now observe soils and subsoils in another point of view. A practical outline of the characters of various soils, and the manner in which they may be distinguished one from another, having been already pointed out to you, my intention now is, to consider them scientifically, for the purpose of preparing your minds for following me through the mazy windings of theoretical agriculture, as developed by the joint application of chemistry, mechanical philosophy, and vegetable physiology. Although, to the contemplative and still more to the speculative student, this branch of the subject will exhibit the greatest charms, still I beg you to bear in mind continually, that it is with *practice* you have to do, and that *theory* must only be used cautiously as an adjunct to well-studied and assiduously-applied *practical knowledge;* and although, by so doing, I fully believe you will not only increase greatly your interest in the whole matter, but will likewise proceed with more rapid strides in the progress of improvement, I feel equally satisfied that an opposite course, viz. the *study of theory antecedent to the application of practice*, will almost invariably be productive of just the opposite effects, viz. the retardation of your real advance in knowledge, and will, moreover, make you run a great risk of becoming speculative men, than which nothing can be more inimical to *real* improvement.

(509.) *Soil*, considered scientifically, may be described to be essentially a mixture of an impalpable powder with a greater or smaller quantity of visible particles of all sizes and shapes. Careful examination will prove to us, that although the visible particles have several *indirect* effects, of so great importance that they are absolutely necessary to soil, still the impalpable powder is the only portion which *directly* exerts any influence upon vegetation. This impalpable powder consists of two distinct classes of substances, viz *inorganic* or *mineral* matters, and *animal* and *vegetable* substances, in all the various stages of decomposition.

(510.) A very simple method may be employed to separate these two classes of particles from each other, viz. the impalpable powder and the visible particles ; and, in so doing, we obtain a very useful index to the real value of the soil. Indeed all soils, except stiff clays, can be discriminated in this manner. The greater the proportion of the impalpable matter, the greater, *cæteris paribus*, will be the fertility of the soil. (530.)

(511.) To effect this separation, the following easy experiment may be performed. Take a glass-tube about 2 feet long, closed at one end; fill it about half full of water, and shake into it a sufficient quantity of the soil to be examined, to fill the tube about 2 inches from the bottom ; then put in a cork, and, having shaken the tube well to mix the earth and water thoroughly, set the tube in an upright position, for the soil to settle down. Now, as the larger particles are of course the heavier, they fall first, and form the undermost layer of the deposite, and so on in regular gradation, the impalpable powder being the last to subside, and hence occupying the uppermost portion. Then by examining the relative thickness of the various layers, and calculating their proportions, you can make a very accurate mechanical analysis of the soil.

(512.) The *stones* which we meet with in soil have in general the same composition as the soil itself, and hence, by their gradually crumbling down under the action of air and moisture, they are continually adding new impalpable matter to the soil, and as I shall shew you hereafter the large quantity of this impalpable mineral matter which is annually removed by the crops, you will at once perceive that this constant addition must be of great value to the soil. This, therefore, is one important function performed by the stones of soil, viz. their affording a continually renewed supply of impalpable mineral matter.

(513.) When we come to consider the nourishment of plants, we shall find that their food undergoes various preliminary changes in the soil previous to its being made use of by the plants, and the aid of chemistry will prove to us that the effect is produced by the joint action of air and water; it follows, therefore, that soil must be porous. Now, this porosity of the soil is in part produced by the presence of the larger particles of matter, which, being of all varieties of shape, can never fit closely together, but always leave a multitude of pores between them; and in this manner permit of the free circulation of air and water through the soil.

(514.) As the porous nature of soil may, to a certain extent, be taken as an index of its power of retaining moisture, it is advisable to determine its amount. This is effected in the following way:—Instead of putting the water first into the tube, as directed above (511), and shaking the soil into it, take a portion of soil dried by a heat of about 200° F., and shake it into the dry tube, and by tapping the closed end frequently on the table, make the soil lie compactly at the bottom; when you have fully effected this, that is, when further tapping produces no reduction of bulk, measure accurately the column of soil, cork the tube, shake it till the soil becomes again quite loose, and then pour in the water as directed above (511). After it has fully subsided, tap the tube as before, and re-measure; the increase of bulk is dependent upon the swelling of each particle by the absorption of water, and hence shews the amount of porosity. In very fertile soil I have seen this amount to $\frac{1}{6}$ of the whole bulk.

(515.) The functions of the *impalpable* matter are far more complicated, and will require a somewhat detailed description. In this portion of the soil the mineral and organic matter are so completely united that it is quite impossible to separate them from each other; indeed, there are very weighty reasons for believing that they are chemically combined. It is from this portion of the soil that plants obtain all their mineral ingredients, and likewise all their organic portions, in so far as these are obtained by the roots; in fact, plants receive nothing from the soil, except water, which has not been associated with that portion which is at present engaging our attention.

(516.) The particles forming the impalpable matter are in such close apposition, that the whole acts in the same way as a sponge, and is hence capable of absorbing liquids and retaining them. It is in this way that soil remains moist so near the surface even after a long continued drought; and I need not tell you how valuable this property must be to the plants, since by this means they are supplied with moisture during the heat of summer, when otherwise, unless artificially watered, they would very soon wither.

(517.) Another most useful function of this impalpable portion is its power of separating organic matter from water in which it has been dissolved. Thus, for example, if you take the dark brown liquid which flows from a dunghill, and pour it on the surface of some earth in a flower-pot, and add a sufficient quantity to soak the whole earth, so that a portion flows out through the bottom of the pot, this latter liquid will be found much lighter in colour than before it was poured upon the earth, and this effect will be increased the nearer the soil approaches in its nature to subsoil. Now, as the colour was entirely owing to the organic matter dissolved in it, it follows that the loss of colour is dependent upon an equivalent loss of organic matter, or, in other words, a portion of the organic matter has entered into *chemical combination* with the impalpable mineral matter, and has thus become insoluble in water. The advantage of this is, that when soluble organic matter is applied to soil, it does not all soak through with the water and escape beyond the reach of the roots of the plants, but is retained by the impalpable portions in a condition not liable to injury from rain, but still capable of becoming food for plants when it is required.

(518.) Hitherto I have pointed out merely the *mechanical* relations of the various constituents of soil, with but little reference to their chemical constitution; this branch of the subject, although by far the most important and interesting, is nevertheless so difficult and complex, that I cannot hope for the practical farmer doing much more than making himself familiar with the *names* of the various chemical ingredients, and learning their relative value as respects the fertility of the soil; as to his attempting to prove their existence in his own soil by analysis, I fear that is far too difficult a subject for him to grapple with, unless regularly educated as an analytical chemist.

(519.) Soil, to be useful to the British agriculturist, must contain no less than 12 different chemical substances, viz. silica, alumina, oxide of iron, oxide of manganese, lime, magnesia, potass, soda, phosphoric acid, sulphuric acid, chlorine, and organic matter; each of these substances must engage our attention shortly; and as I by no means purpose to burden your memories by relating all the facts of interest connected with them, I shall confine my observations almost solely to their relative importance to plants, and their amount in soil.

(520.) *Silica.* This is the pure matter of sand, and also constitutes on an average about 60 per cent. of the various clays; so that in soil it generally amounts to from 75 to 95 per cent. In its uncombined state, it has no *direct* influence upon plants, beyond its mechanical action, in supporting the roots, &c.; but, as it possesses the properties of an acid, it unites with various alkaline matters in the soil, and produces compounds which are required in greater or less quantity by every plant. The chief of these are the *silicates of potass and soda*, by which expression is meant the compounds of silica, or, more properly, silicic acid with the alkalies potass and soda.

(521.) *Alumina.* This substance never exists pure in soil. It is the *characteristic* ingredient of clay, although it exists in that compound to the extent of only 30 or 40 per cent. It exerts no *direct chemical* influence on vegetation, and is scarcely ever found in the ashes of plants. Its chief value in soil, therefore, is owing to its effects in rendering soil more retentive of moisture. Its amount varies from ½ per cent. to 13 per cent.

(522.) *Oxide of Iron.* There are two oxides of iron found in soils, namely, the protoxide and peroxide; one of which, the protoxide, is frequently very injurious to vegetation—indeed, so much so, that ½ per cent. of a soluble salt of this oxide is sufficient to render soil almost barren. The peroxide, however, is often found in small quantities in the ashes of plants. The two oxides together constitute from ½ to 10 per cent. of soil. The blue, yellow, red, and brown colours of soil are more or less dependent upon the presence of iron.

(523.) *Oxide of Manganese.* This oxide exists in nearly all soils, and is occasionally found in plants. It does not, however, appear to exert any important influence either mechanically or chemically. Its amount varies from a mere trace to about 1½ per cent. It assists in giving the black colour to soil.

(524.) These 4 substances constitute by far the greatest bulk of every soil, except the chalky and peaty varieties, but, nevertheless, *chemically speaking*, are of trifling importance to plants; whereas, the remaining 8 are so absolutely essential, that no soil can be cultivated with any success, unless provided with them, either naturally or artificially. And when you consider that scarcely any of them constitute 1 per cent. of the soil, you will no doubt at first be surprised at their value. The sole cause of their utility lies in the fact, that they constitute the *ashes of the plants;* and as no plant can, by possibility, thrive without its inorganic constituents (*its ashes*), hence no soil can be fertile which does not contain the ingredients of which these are made up. I shall not treat of each separately, but will furnish you with one or two analyses of soil to shew their importance, and to impress them more fully on your memory. I regret that I must look to foreign works to furnish these analyses; but the truth is, we have not one single published analysis of British soil by a British chemist which is worth recording. Sir Humphry Davy just analysed soil to determine the amount of the first 4 substances mentioned, and one or two others, and failed to detect 5 or 6 of the most important ingredients. In fact, the only useful analyses we possess are those performed by Sprengel, and quoted in Dr Lyon Playfair's second edition of Liebig's Organic Chemistry applied to Agriculture, from which valuable work I quote the following examples.

(525.) Analysis of a *very fertile alluvial soil* from Honigpolder. Corn had been cultivated upon this soil for 70 years without *any manure* having been applied to it, but it was now and then allowed to lie fallow:—

	Silica with fine siliceous sand,	64.800
	Alumina,	5.700
	Peroxide of iron,	6.100
	... manganese,	0.090
	Lime,	5.880
	Magnesia,	0.840
	Potass *combined with silica,*	0.210
	Soda *combined with silica,*	0.393
	Sulphuric acid *combined with lime,*	0.210
	Chlorine *in common salt,*	0.201
	Phosphoric acid *combined with lime,*	0.430
	Carbonic acid *combined with lime,*	3.920
Organic matter,	Humus,	5.600
	Humus, *soluble in alkalies,*	2.540
	Azotised matter,	1.582
	Water,	1.504
		100.000*

* Liebig's Organic Chemistry applied to Agriculture, 2d edition, pp. 230-31.

(526.) *Alluvial soil* from Ohio, remarkable for its *fertility*—

	Silica with fine siliceous sand,	79.538
	Alumina,	7.306
	Protoxide and peroxide of iron, *with much magnetic iron-sand,*	5.824
	Peroxide of manganese,	1.320
	Lime,	0.619
	Magnesia,	1.024
	Potass, *combined with silica,*	0.200
	Soda,	0.024
	Phosphoric acid, *combined with lime and iron,*	1.776
	Sulphuric acid, *combined with lime,*	0.122
	Chlorine, *in common salt,*	0.036
Organic matter,	Humus, *soluble in alkalies,*	1.950
	Humus, *with azotised matter,*	0.236
	Resinous matter and wax,	0.025
		100.000*

(527.) Loamy sand from the environs of Brunswick, *very barren*—

	Silica, with coarse siliceous sand,	95.843
	Alumina,	0.600
	Peroxide of iron,	1.800
	Peroxide of manganese,	a trace.
	Potass and soda,	0.005
	Lime, *combined with silica,*	0.038
	Magnesia, *combined with silica,*	0.006
	Sulphuric acid,	0.002
	Phosphoric acid, *combined with iron,*	0.198
	Chlorine, *in common salt,*	0.006
Organic matter,	Humus,	0.502
	Humus, *soluble in alkalies,*	1.000
		100.000†

Here the sterility is evidently produced by the small amount of potass, soda, lime, magnesia, and sulphuric acid, all of which are essential for the ashes of most of our usually cultivated crops.

(528.) These analyses will give you some idea of the complex nature of the soil, and the necessity of most *minute* analysis if we wish to ascertain its real value. The reason for such minuteness in analysis becomes obvious when we consider the immense weights with which you have to do in practical agriculture: for example, every imperial acre of soil, considered as only 8 inches deep, will weigh 1884 tons, so that 0.002 per cent. (the amount of sulphuric acid in the barren soil) amounts to 80.64 lbs. per imperial acre.

(529.) I have purposely avoided saying any thing of the *organic* matter of

* Liebig's Organic Chemistry applied to Agriculture, 2d edit. p. 242. † Ibid. p. 212.

soil, as this is a most complicated subject, and will be far better considered under the head of manures.

(530.) All these substances, except the silica contained in the form of sand, constitute the impalpable matter of soil. It is evident, therefore, that this may differ much in chemical constitution without differing in amount, and yet have the greatest influence upon the fertility of the soil; my design, therefore, of introducing the words " *cæteris paribus*" in paragraph (510) was to induce you to bear in mind that the statement refers *solely* to soil considered *mechanically*. For fear of being misunderstood, therefore, I would paraphrase the sentence thus: —Without a certain amount of impalpable matter soil *cannot possibly be fertile*, yet while the existence of this material proves the soil to be *mechanically* well suited for cultivation, *chemical* analysis alone can *prove* its absolute value to the farmer.

(531.) *Potass* and *soda* exist in variable quantities in many of the more abundant minerals, and hence it follows that their proportion in soil will vary according to the mineral which produced it. For the sake of reference, I have subjoined the following table, which shews the amount per cent. of alkalies in some of these minerals, and likewise a rough calculation of the whole amount per imperial acre in a soil composed of these, supposing such a soil to be 10 inches deep.

Name of Mineral.	Amount per cent. of Alkali.	Name of Alkali.	Amount per Imperial Acre in a soil 10 inches deep.
Felspar, . .	17.75	Potass	927,360 lb.
Clinkstone, .	3.31 to 6.62	Potass and Soda	161,000 to 322,000 lb.
Clay-slate, .	2.75 to 3.31	Potass	80,500 to 161,000 lb.
Basalt, . . .	5.75 to 10.	Potass and Soda	37,887 to 56,875 lb.

(532.) From the above table you see the abundant quantities in which these valuable substances are contained in soil; some, however, of you, who are acquainted with chemistry, will naturally ask the question, How is it that these alkalies have not been long ago washed away by the rain since they are both so very soluble in water? Now the reason of their not having been dissolved is the following, and it may in justice be taken as an example of those wise provisions of nature, whereby what is useful is never wasted, and yet is at all times supplied abundantly.

(533.) These alkalies exist in combination with the various other ingredients of the rock in which they occur, and in this way have such a powerful attraction for each other, that they are capable of resisting completely the solvent action of water so long as the integrity of the mass is retained. When, however, it is reduced to a perfectly impalpable powder, this attraction is diminished to a considerable extent, and then the alkali is much more easily dissolved. Now this is the case in soil, and, consequently, while the stony portions of soil contain a vast supply of these valuable ingredients in a condition in which water can do them no injury, the impalpable powder is supplied with them in a soluble state, and hence in a condition available to the wants of vegetation.

(534.) In the rocks which we have mentioned, the alkalies are always associated with clay, and it is to this substance that they have the greatest attraction; it follows, therefore, that the more clay a soil contains the more alkalies will it have, but at the same time it will yield them less easily to water, and through its medium to plants.—H. R. M.]

(535.) There is another method by which soils and subsoils may be discriminated, and that is by the plants which grow upon soils. This test of discrimination is not to be trusted so confidently as the chemical composition, or especially the external characters, of soils. Their chemical and physical properties are open to observation, and can, therefore, be estimated with accuracy; but in judging of soils by the vegetation upon them, the soils themselves are excluded from our observation, while their product only is open to inspection. This, indeed, might be a fair enough mode of estimating the comparative properties of soils were their products constant, but when these change according to other circumstances than soil, the test cannot be of general application. The same rock and the same diluvium or alluvium possess the same characters throughout the globe, but the plants which grow upon them differ not only in different latitudes, but at different heights above the sea in the same latitude. Climate is thus the great agent which determines the existence of plants. The sands of the tropics yield very different plants to those of the temperate and frigid zones. But, besides climate, a great variety of plants affect the same soil, so that an inspection of the generality of plants will not enable you to detect a specific soil. Another circumstance still remains to be mentioned, which affects the relation between plants and the soils they grow upon, which is, that as *natural* plants alone indicate the natural state of the soil; so in cultivated soil plants may indicate a very different state from what the same plants would do of soils in their natural state.

(536.) Still, notwithstanding the difficulties attending the discrimination of soils by plants, it is an undoubted fact that certain plants do indicate a certain kind of soil, and often a certain condition of the same kind of soil. These plants are very limited in number, and on that account may easily be remembered. I shall enumerate those only which have fallen under my own observation, and in doing this, shall separate those plants which grow upon the respective soils, in a state of nature, from those which make their appearance after the land is in a state of cultivation. In this latter condition plants are called *weeds*, because they are then found among the cultivated corn and green crops, as also amongst the sown grasses.

(537.) You should particularly note the different kinds of weeds which affect the cultivated soils, so that you may be familiar with their names when you come to learn the different modes of destroying them, in their respective seasons, in pursuance of the various operations that will demand our attention.

(538.) On *clay-soils in a state of nature* these herbaceous plants will always be found—

Spiræa ulmaria,..............................Queen of the meadow.
Angelica sylvestris,...........................Wild angelica.
Ranunculus lingua,...........................Great spear-wort.
Rumex acetosa,................................Common sorrel.

After such soils are brought under cultivation, these weeds make their appearance, some of which are sown with the corn, and others with the grass seeds, whilst the rest are brought by the influence of the wind, or amongst dung,—

Rumex obtusifolius,..............................Common broad-leaved dock.
Senecio vulgaris,..............................Groundsel.
Lapsana communis,..............................Nipple-wort.
Agrostemma githago,..............................Corn cockle or popple.
Matricaria chamomilla,..............................Wild chamomile.
Sonchus oleraceus,..............................Common sow-thistle.

(539.) *Thin clays*, in their natural state, which become clay-loams by cultivation, yield the following plants, first in a state of nature,—

Ranunculus acris,..............................Upright meadow or bitter crowfoot.
Aira cœspitosa,..............................Tufted hair-grass.
Equisetum arvense,..............................Corn horse-tail.
Stachys palustris,..............................Marsh woundwort.

And then under cultivation,—

Tussilago farfara,..............................Common colt's-foot.
Sinapis arvensis,..............................Wild mustard.
Polygonum aviculare,..............................Knot-grass.

(540.) On a *deep strong clayey loam on an open bottom*, in a state of nature, these plants are found,—

Silene inflata,..............................Bladder campion.
Antirrhinum linaria,..............................Toad-flax.
Scabiosa arvensis,..............................Field scabious.
Centaurea scabiosa,..............................Great knapweed.
Polygonum amphibium,..............................Redshanks.
Dactylis glomerata,..............................Rough cock's-foot grass.

When the same soil is shallow, these are found,—

Ononis arvensis,..............................Common rest-harrow.
Trifolium arvense,..............................Hare's-foot trefoil.
Trifolium procumbens,..............................Hop trefoil.

After cultivation the principal weeds are these,—

Anagallis arvensis,..............................Scarlet pimpernel.
Veronica hederifolia,..............................Ivy-leaved speedwell.
Sinapis nigra,..............................Black mustard.
Ervum hirsutum,..............................Hairy tare, or fetter.

(541.) The herbaceous plants peculiar to *sandy soils*, in a state of nature are,—

Lotus corniculatus,..............................Bird's-foot trefoil.
Campanula rotundifolia,..............................Common bluebell.
Euphrasia officinalis,..............................Eyebright.
Anthoxanthum odoratum,..............................Sweet-scented vernal grass.

After cultivation these weeds appear:—

Spergula arvensis,..............................Common spurry.
Lamium purpureum,..............................Purple dead-nettle.
Fumaria officinalis,..............................Common fumitory.
Thlaspi bursa-pastoris,..............................Shepherd's purse.
Scleranthus annuus,..............................Common knawel.

Gnaphalium germanicum,...................... Common cud-weed.
Triticum repens,................................ Common couch-grass.

(542.) Upon *sandy loam on clay subsoil*, in a state of nature, these are characteristic plants,—

Juncus effusus,................................ Common or soft rush.
Achillea ptarmica,............................. Sneeze-wort.
Potentilla anserina,........................... Wild tansy or silver-weed.
Artemisia vulgaris,............................ Mugwort.

After cultivation these,—

Raphanus raphanistrum,......................... Charlock.
Rumex acetosella,.............................. Sheep's sorrel.
Chrysanthemum segetum,......................... Corn marygold.
Juncus bufonius,............................... Toad-rush.

(543.) *Sandy loam on an open bottom* in a state of nature yields these plants most abundantly,—

Genista scoparia,.............................. Common broom.
Centaurea nigra,............................... Black knapweed.
Galium verum,.................................. Hollow bed-straw.
Senecio jacobea,............................... Common rag-weed.

When cultivated, these are the most conspicuous weeds,—

Mentha arvensis,............................... Common corn-mint.
Centaurea cyanus,.............................. Blue-wort.
Sherardia arvensis,............................ Corn madder.
Lithospermum arvense,.......................... Corn gromwell.
Alchemilla arvensis,........................... Parsley-pest.
Avena elatior,................................. Tall oat-grass.
Cnicus arvensis,............................... Corn-thistle.

(544.) *Alluvial deposites in a state of nature*, yield a vegetation indicative of a wet and strong soil.

Arundo phragmites,............................. Common reed.
Juncus conglomeratus,.......................... Round-headed rush.
Agrostis alba,................................. White bent-grass.
Poa aquatica,.................................. Reed meadow-grass.
Poa fluitans,.................................. Floating meadow-grass.

All these disappear on cultivation, except the common reed, which keeps possession of the soil for an indefinite period after the best culture has been established. Where such soil is indifferently cultivated, the corn thistle, *Cnicus arvensis*, is a very troublesome weed. In other respects, the weeds are the same as in the cultivated clays.

(545.) These are the characteristic plants which are found on soils in the low country still in a state of nature, or which have been brought under the action of the plough. But, besides these soils, which may be and have been made available for the purposes of agriculture, there are other soils in the low country which cannot be rendered arable, but which, nevertheless, form the sites of numerous plants, which are peculiar to them, and which occasionally find their way into the adjoining arable soils. From the sea-beach, gravel-pits, and sandy downs, for example, plants will stray by force of vegetation, and the assistance of the wind, over the arable soil in their respective neighbourhoods;

and, on the other hand, the ordinary plants of the neighbouring pasture grounds, according to the position of the locality, will find their way to the sea-shore, or to mountains.

(546.) *Beaches*, consisting chiefly of pebbles, are maritime, lacustrine, and fluvial. The plants of maritime beaches are,—

Silene maritima,..................................Seaside campion.
Plantago maritima,...............................Sea plantain.
Glaux maritima,..................................Black saltwort.
Pulmonaria maritima,...........................Sea lungwort.
Eryngium maritimum,............................Sea holly.
Salsola kali,.......................................Glasswort.

On lacustrine beaches,—

Prunella vulgaris,.................................Self-heal.
Rubus fruticosus,..................................Common bramble.
Bellis perennis,....................................Common daisy.
Plantago media,....................................Hoary plantain.

And on beaches in rivers,—

Anthyllis vulneraria,..............................Common kidney-vetch.
Silene maritima,..................................Seaside campion.
Polygonum aviculare,.............................Knot-grass.
Achillea millefolium,..............................Common yarrow.
Alchemilla vulgaris,...............................Common lady's-mantle.
Galium verum,.....................................Hollow bed-straw.
Teesdalia nudicaulis,..............................Naked-stalked teesdalia.
Linum catharticum,...............................Purging flax.
Saxifraga aizoides,................................Yellow saxifrage.
Apargia autumnalis,...............................Autumnal apargia.

In such soils the vegetation is always thin and scanty. In wet seasons it is sometimes luxuriant enough, but in dry weather it is very liable to be burnt up by the heat of the sun.

(547.) On *gravel*, whether water worn, as usually found in the deposites of the low country, or in the shape of *grit*, that is, angular gravel, as found in the debris on the sides of mountains, occasioned by the disintegration of indurated rocks, the vegetation is somewhat different from that of the beaches. In gravel pits in the interior of the country these plants grow,—

Polygonum aviculare,..............................Knot-grass.
Rumex acetosella,..................................Sheep's sorrel.
Agrostis vulgaris,..................................Common bent-grass.
Aira caryophyllea,..................................Silvery hair-grass.
Festuca duriuscula,................................Hard fescue-grass.
Arenaria serpyllifolia,.............................Thyme-leaved sandwort.
Hieracium murorum,...............................Wall hawkweed.
Papaver dubium,....................................Long smooth-headed poppy.
Papaver rhœas,.....................................Common red poppy.
Polygonum convolvulus,...........................Climbing buck-wheat.
Chenopodium urbicum,............................Upright goose-foot.
Lolium perenne,.....................................Perennial ryegrass.
Bromus mollis,......................................Soft brome-grass.

On the sea-shore, gravel produces maritime plants,—

Cakile maritima,....................................Sea-rocket.
Chenopodium maritimum,.........................Seaside goose-foot.

Atriplex laciniata,....................................Frosted sea-arache.
Silene maritima,......................................Seaside campion.

On the sides of rivers gravel produces,—

Juncus bufonius,......................................Toad-rush.
——— *acutiflorus,*....................................Sharp-flowered rush.
Littorella lacustris,.............. ....Plantain shore-weed.

Grit, on the mountain-sides, produces alpine plants.

(548.) On *drifting sands*, or *links*, or *downs*, as they are termed, the vegetation is peculiar,—

Arundo arenaria,......................................Sea-bent.
Triticum junceum,....................................Sand wheat-grass.
Festuca duriuscula,..................................Hard fescue-grass.
Carex arenaria,.......................................Sand carex.
Galium verum,...Hollow bed-straw.

This vegetation is both mixed with and modified into one, approaching on the seaside to a maritime, and the landside to that of arable light loam.

(549.) The vegetation of *moory* ground varies according to the wetness or dryness of the subsoil. The wetness or dryness arises, of course, from the circumstance of the subsoil being composed of retentive clay or porous sand or gravel. *Wet* moory soils are characterised by these plants,—

Salix repens,...Dwarf silky willow.
Pinguicula vulgaris,.................................Butterwort.
Carex pilulifera,......................................Round-fruited carex.
Juncus squarrosus,..................................Moss-bush.
Scirpus cæspitosus,.................................Scaly-stalked club-rush.
Parnassia palustris,.................................Grass of Parnassus.

On *dry* moors, which usually contain a considerable proportion of peat-earth, these plants are found,—

Genista anglica,......................................Needle green-weed or petty whin.
Nardus stricta,..Mat-grass.
Viola lutea,...Yellow mountain-violet.
Tormentilla officinalis,..............................Common tormentil.
Gnaphalium dioicum,........... ....Mountain cud-weed.

(550.) On soils in a state of *marsh* are found,—

Lychnis flos-cuculi,..................................Ragged robin.
Menyanthes trifoliata,...............................Fringed buck-bean.
Caltha palustris,.....................................Marsh marygold.
Veronica beccabunga,...............................Brook-lime.
Comarum palustre,...................................Marsh cinquefoil.
Galium uliginosum,..................................Marsh bed-straw.

Near the sea, marshes produce—

Triglochin maritimum,...............................Sea arrow-grass.
Poa procumbens,.....................................Sea marsh-grass.
Carex pallescens,....................................Pale carex.
—— *riparia,*...Great common carex.

After marshy ground has been dried and cultivated, these weeds retain a pretty strong hold of their respective positions,—

Tussilago farfara,................................Common colt's-foot.
——— *petasites*,................................Common butter-bur.
Galium aparine,................................Goose-grass.

(551.) On *peat* or *moss* the vegetation is somewhat different, according as it is wet or dry. On dry spots of peat the

Erica tetralix,................................Cross-leaved heath,
Calluna vulgaris,................................Common ling,
Agrostis canina,................................Dog bent-grass,

establish themselves, and in wet hollow parts the

Eriophorum polystachion,........................Cotton grass,
Vaccinium oxycoccus,............................Orange-berry,

are most abundant. When peat is dried and cultivated, the weeds that most commonly affect it are—

Bromus mollis,................................Soft brome-grass.
Myosotis arvensis,................................Field scorpion-grass.
Avena fatua,................. ....Wild oats.
Galium aparine,................................Goose-grass.

(552.) On *mountain pastures* the plants are numerous, though a few only serve to shew the peculiarities of the range of elevation. At moderate heights these plants prevail,—

Calluna vulgaris,................................Common ling.
Astragalus uralensis,............................Hairy milk-vetch.
Dryas octopetala,................................Mountain avens.
Salix reticulata,................................Reticulated willow.
Gnaphalium alpinum,............................Mountain cud-weed.
Narthecium calyculatum,........................Bog asphodel.
Rubus chamæmorus,..............................Cloud-berry.
Arbutus uva-ursi,................................Common bear-berry.*

In very elevated mountain pastures these plants are found, according to the observations of Mr William Hogg, shepherd in Peebleshire,—

Calluna vulgaris, ...Common ling.
Empetrum nigrum,................................Crow-berry.
Erica tetralix,................................Cross-leaved heath.
Lycopodium clavatum, and ——— *alpinum*, } ....Club-moss.
Juncus squarrosus,................................Stool-bent.
Equisetum palustre,..............................Paddock-pipe.
Scirpus cæspitosus,..............................Deer-hair.
Narthecium ossifragum,..........................Yellow grass.
Melica cærulea, *Sesleria cærulea*, } ....Fly-bent or rot-grass.
Nardus stricta,................................Wire-bent or mat-grass.

In wet places these are found to thrive,—

Juncus effusus,................................Soft rush.
Holcus mollis,................................Soft meadow-grass or Yorkshire fog.
Carex cæspitosa,..............................Risp.
Juncus acutiflorus,............................Spratt.

* Prize Essays of the Highland and Agricultural Society, vol. vii. p. 123–35.

Carex panicea,..................................Pry.
Scabiosa succisa,..................................Devils'-bit scabious.
Hypnum palustre,..................................Marsh-fog.*

(553.) Professor MacGillivray says truly, that "no soil that we have examined has been found to produce plants peculiar to itself, excepting sand and peat; and these two soils, so different from each other in their mechanical and chemical nature, also form a striking contrast in respect to the plants growing upon them, each being characterised by a vegetation differing in aspect and qualities from each other, and scarcely agreeing in any one circumstance." † The existence of peat is invariably indicated by *Calluna vulgaris*, common ling,—*Erica cinerea*, fine-leaved heath,—and *Erica tetralix*, cross-leaved heath; and loose sand is invariably covered with *Arundo arenaria*, sand-reed, most frequently accompanied by *Triticum junceum*, sand wheat-grass, and *Galium verum*, hollow bed-straw. This remark receives additional strength from the circumstance, that all arable soils encourage a different kind of natural vegetation, which are characterised as weeds, from what they do when in a state of nature.

(554.) In so far, then, as the arable soils are concerned, the information imparted by their weeds possesses greater interest to the farmer than their natural vegetation, and these give a truer account of the *condition* of the soils, at the time, than of their nature, though the latter property is by no means overlooked. For example, clayey soils are indicated by the existence of the grasses, and of these the genera of Poa, Agrostis, and Festuca prevail; gravelly soils by *Aira caryophyllæa*, silvery hair-grass; *Aira præcox*, early hair-grass; and *Rumex acetosella*, sheep sorrel. When intermixed with a little clay, the grasses prevail. Good vegetable soil is indicated by Trifolia, Viciæ, and Lathyrus pratensis. *Thymus serpyllum*, wild thyme, indicates a vegetable mould of great thinness; and ragweed, *Senecio jacobæa*, one of depth. Purging flax, *Linum catharticum;* Autumn apargia, *Apargia autumnalis;* and mouse-eared hawkweed, *Hieracium pilosella*, indicate a dry soil; while the yellow iris, *Iris pseudacorus;* the sharp-flowered rush, *Juncus acutiflorus;* lady's smock, *Cardamine pratensis;* and ragged robbin, *Lychnis flos-cuculi*, assure us of a supply of moisture; and the purple dead-nettle, *Lamium purpureum;* and smooth naked horse-tail, *Equisetum limosum*, indicate that the subsoil is rather retentive. The common nettle, *Urtica dioica;* common dock, *Rumex obtusifolia;* mugwort, *Artemisia vulgaris;* annual poa, *Poa annua;* field poa, *Poa pratensis;* and common tansy, *Tanacetum vulgare*, grow near the dwellings of man, on the bare soil, irrespective of its kind; while in the same locality the white clover, *Trifolium repens;* red clover, *Trifolium pratense;* annual poa; hoary plantain, *Plantago media;* ribwort, *Plantago lanceolata;* purple meadow vetch, *Vicia cracca;* and common daisy, *Bellis perennis*, are found in the pasture around his house. Common chickweed, *Stellaria media;* and common fumitory, *Fumaria officinalis*, indicate a rich condition of soil; while the great ox-eye, *Chrysanthemum leucanthemum*, points out one of poverty. Wild mustard, *Sinapis arvensis*, tells of the application of manure derived from towns, and the common corn-thistle, *Cni-*

* Prize Essays of the Highland and Agricultural Society, vol. vii. p. 281–2.

† Ibid. vol. vii. p. 102.

cus arvensis, that the land is not well farmed. Whenever there is the least admixture of peat in the soil, the Erica or Calluna and spotted-bearded orchis, *Orchis maculata*, are sure to be there.

(555.) Taking a more extended view of the indications of the condition of soils, these observations of Dr Singer seem well founded. " *Green* mountains, like those of Cheviot and Ettrick Forest, abounding in grass without heath, indicate a strong soil, which is rendered productive, though frequently steep and elevated, by a retentive subsoil. This quality, and the frequent mists and showers that visit rather elevated sheep-walks, render them productive in strong grasses (*Agrostis*). . . . *Dark* mountains, clothed with a mixture of heath and grass, indicate a drier soil on a less retentive bottom. Such are many of the Highland mountains, and such also are some of those which appear occasionally among the green mountains of the southern pastoral district, in which the light soil is incumbent commonly on gravel or porous rock. On these dark-coloured mountains, a green and *grassy* part often appears where there is no heath, and the subsoil is retentive; and if the upper edge of such a spot appears well defined, this is occasioned by the regular approach of a stratum of clay or other substance impervious to water towards the surface, and the green hue disappears below, when the subsoil again becomes open. . . . On any of the mountains, whether dark or green, when the fern or bracken, *Pteris aquilina*, appears in quantities, it indicates a deep soil and a dry subsoil."* A stunted growth of heath indicates a part having been bared by the paring-spade; and when vegetation becomes of a brown colour in summer, the subjacent rock is only a little way under the surface.

(556.) Viewing the connection of plants to the soil on the great scale, we cannot but be forcibly impressed with the conviction that " the grand principle of vegetation is simple in its design; but view it in detail, and its complication astonishes and bewilders." And yet, as Professor Macgillivray justly observes, " it is the same sun that calls forth, and thus elicited, gives vigour to the vegetation, the same earth that supports it, the same moisture that swells its vessels, the same air that furnishes the medium in which it lives; but amid all these systems of general, how multiple the variations of particular constituent causes, and how infinitely diversified their results!"†

(557.) Before leaving the subject of soils at this time, it appears incumbent on me to make a few observations on their *classification*. The use of a classification would be to enable every writer who has occasion to allude to soils to indicate the particular kind which he wishes to describe so precisely, as that any one else should identify it. You are, no doubt, aware that all the plants which I have had occasion to mention may be identified in any part of the globe, so precise is their description; but the case is very different in regard to the soils I have mentioned as having a connection with those plants, not one of which, with perhaps the exception of pure sand and pure peat, could be identified by any remarks that have been made in reference to their qualities. I suspect that so much precision is not to be attained on the subject; but, nevertheless, it appears to be the general opinion that an attempt towards it should be made, and every writer on agriculture has made the attempt, in the way he has thought best.

* Prize Essays of the Highland and Agricultural Society, vol. vii. p. 464.

† Ibid., vol. vii. p. 116.

Although they have all failed in establishing such characteristics of soils as might render them easily recognized by description, yet it is worthy of remark, that they have found it necessary to adopt the same principle in their respective classifications which is practised by every farmer in raising his different crops, namely, of suiting them to the different kinds of soils. In adopting this principle, it is obvious that neither the external characters of the mineralogical system, nor their chemical composition, have been employed to describe the properties of soil, but simply their natural powers to grow the plants desired to be raised in cultivation. Still a simple description of the materials which evince those natural powers is yet a desideratum.

(558.) I observe that the Government have offered to the Royal Agricultural Society of England to make a complete and systematic analysis of all the soils of England at the public cost. The various soils to be selected from the same geological formation in different parts of the country, and particularly those which have been found by experience to be best adapted for particular crops (as wheat soils, bean soils, turnip soils, grass soils, fertile soils, barren soils, &c.), to be taken in succession from one end of the kingdom to the other. To do this in the most satisfactory manner, it is proposed to obtain 20 analyses of each particular soil, and thus procure, in the course of every year, about 1000 of such analyses, which are to be made by chemists of first-rate character for analytical investigations of the kind, and who should ascertain not only the chemical constitution, but the mechanical texture and properties of each soil, and the results to be published, as occasions demand, in the journal of the Society.* It is not improbable that these minute analyses may enable chemists or mineralogists to institute a nomenclature of soils in conformity to their true external characters, that is, to their most apparent and easily-tested properties.

(559.) Meanwhile, I shall present you with a sketch of an attempt at classification of soils by M. De Gasparin, who, although he employed chemical tests to ascertain the nature of the soil, had previously endeavoured to establish their agricultural characters. The results were, that he was led to adopt the following conclusions in regard to the relative values of the characters of soils. "It is," he says, "only after having destined a particular soil to an appropriate culture, that we can begin to consider the labour and improvement it requires. Those labours and improvements will be without an object and a bearing, if we are still ignorant of the plant to which they would be useful. And, moreover, this investigation of the appropriation of soils to particular kinds of culture, is connected with the most natural classification in a mineralogical point of view; it breaks the smallest number of affinities, and consequently renders the determination of soils more easy and more satisfactory."† I cannot help thinking that M. De Gasparin has here hit upon the *principle* upon which a true and useful classification of soils may be founded.

(560.) In his endeavour to reduce this principle to practice, he has divided soils into two great divisions; the *first* includes those having a *mineral* basis, the *second* those having an *organic* one.

* Bell's Weekly Messenger, and Mark-Lane Express, 7th March 1842.

† Comptes Rendus de l'Académie des Sciences, tome viii., No. 8, p. 285, 1839, and translated in Jameson's Edinburgh New Philosophical Journal, vol. xxvii. p. 84. I may here mention that M. de Gasparin is engaged in a work on *Agronomy*.

(561.) The first great division, consisting of soils having a mineral basis, he divides into 4 classes, comprehending *saliferous* soils, *siliceous* soils, *clays*, and *calcareous* and *magnesian* soils.

(562.) The character of *saliferous* soils is, that they have " a salt or styptic taste, containing at least 0.005 parts of hydrochlorate of soda, or sulphate of iron ;" and they consist, 1st, of *saline* soils, and, 2d, of *vitriolic* soils.

(563.) The character of *siliceous* soils is, that they produce " no effervescence with acids, affording by levigation at least 0.70 of large particles, which are deposited when the water in which the earth is dissolved is strongly shaken."

(564.) *Clays* are characterized by " not yielding effervescence with acids, and by affording by levigation less than 0.70 of the first portion."

(565.) And the characters of *calcareous* and *magnesian* soils are, that they " produce effervescence with acids; lime or magnesia, or both, being found in the solution." This class is subdivided into 5 sub-orders, namely, *chalks*, *sands*, *clays*, *marls*, and *loams*. The marls, again, are farther subdivided into 2 sections, namely, *calcareous* marls and *argillaceous* marls.

(566.) The second great division, consisting of soils having an organic basis, he divides into 2 classes, comprehending *fresh* mould and *acid* mould.

(567.) The character of *fresh mould* is, that " the water in which this mould is digested or boiled does not redden litmus paper."

(568.) That of *acid mould* being, that, under the same circumstances, it " reddens litmus paper."

(569.) It is intimated that M. De Gasparin has laid " down rules for the description of *species*, and with *examples* of all the methods of description. In reading these, we at once perceive how precise an idea of soils is conveyed in a manner that cannot be misunderstood by any agriculturist. The possibility of transmitting these clear and pointed descriptions to a distance, follows as a matter of course; and we shall in this manner be freed from all that vagueness which has been so long a just cause of complaint." This is all that is desiderated on the subject; but, useful as M. De Gasparin's services to agriculture have been in the right direction, he has not yet succeeded in establishing a faultless description of soils, for let me apply some of the rules he has given above, and test his own description by them. For example, he says, that *clay* soils are characterized by " *not* yielding effervescence with acids, and affording by levigation less than 0.70 of the first portion ;" and the character of *siliceous* soils he gives in these words, " producing *no* effervescence with acids, affording by levigation at least 0.70 for their first portion." Surely the mere difference of affording " at least" and " less" than 0.70, or any other minute proportion of any ingredient, is not sufficient to account for the great difference there is found to exist in agriculture betwixt clay and sandy soils. He does not, however, confound *loams* with *clays*, as some theoretical writers whom I have quoted have done, the loams containing clay only a little " more than 0.10 of the weight of the soil ;" whereas clays afford only a little " less than 0.70 of the first portion" of the matter separated by levigation, thereby establishing a very great difference of character betwixt them.

(570.) Little reliance, I fear, can be placed on any analyses of soils hitherto attempted, to guide us to a correct nomenclature and classification. Sir Humphry Davy, for instance, gives an example of the absorbent powers " of a celebrated soil from Ormiston, in East-Lothian,"* a given quantity of which, at a given temperature, absorbed 18 grains of moisture; whereas " a very fertile soil from the banks of the river Parret, in Somersetshire," of similar quantity and under similar circumstances, absorbed only 16 grains; thereby leaving it to be inferred, that the Ormiston soil was better than the other, which it may possibly be, but it is well known by those who know it practically, that it is far from being a fertile one. There exist, besides, many serious discrepancies betwixt authors who write on the composition of soils. M. Von Thäer gives three instances of " rich wheat-land," which contain from 74 to 81 per cent. of clay, and from 6 to 10 per cent. of sand;† while Professor Johnston, after stating that " the pure porcelain clays are the richest in alumina," adds, that " even when free from water, they contain only from 42 to 48 per cent. of this earth, with from 52 to 58 of silica."‡ Mr Loudon gives a tabular view of a classification of soils, said to have been adopted by M. Fellenberg in Switzerland, and Professor Thouin of Paris, but to remember the particular nomenclature of which would puzzle any tyro in agriculture.§

(571.) There is no doubt, however, of the truth of the opinion expressed by M. De Gasparin, were a correct nomenclature and classification of soils established, when he says that its consequence would be, " that the study of agricultural treatises would be greatly facilitated; the different methods (of culture) which are followed in distant countries will no longer appear so marvellous, and will become more intelligible; we shall comprehend better the considerations which limit or extend the several cultures; and a necessary link being established between the science of agriculture and the other natural sciences, it will become more intelligible to all, and will more readily profit by the progress of all the other branches of human knowledge."

---

23. OF ENCLOSURES AND SHELTER.

" Some husbandmen deem fences only formed
To guard their fields from trespass of their own
Or neighbours' herd or flock; and lightly prize
The benefits immense which shelter brings."

GRAHAM.

(572.) Although it may happen that the farm on which you are learning your profession, or the one which you are to occupy on your own account, may be completely enclosed, yet as the reasons for enclosing land are both numerous and cogent, it is proper that you should not only be made acquainted with them, but be able to appreciate the sound principles upon which they are founded.

* Davy's Agricultural Chemistry, 8vo edition, p. 176.

† Von Thäer's Atlas des Principes Raisonnés d'Agriculture, Tableau No. 26, p. 74.

‡ Johnston's Lectures on Agricultural Chemistry and Geology, p. 338.

§ Loudon's Encyclopædia of Agriculture, p. 312.

(573.) The *advantages derived from enclosing land* are these : 1. Enclosures shelter every kind of crop, as well as live stock, from the inclemency of the weather, and particularly against a cold and powerful wind. 2. They prevent the trespasses of men across, and animals into, fields. 3. They not only afford the most excellent and efficient shelter to live stock, but secure peace and protection to them while feeding and when at rest in the fields. 4. They enhance the value of land in every situation : an enclosed farm, in all other circumstances alike, will fetch a higher rent than an unenclosed one. From 2s. to 5s. per acre, according to the locality and nature of the ground, is not too high an estimate of their advantage on this head. 5. They greatly beautify the aspect of the country, conferring on it an undeniable sense of security, richness, and comfort. 6. They also confer ease of mind to the farmer, by securing his crops, his flocks, and his herds, from ordinary danger. 7. They impart confidence to the country gentleman in the enjoyment of his estate of land and wood, by being the means of continually improving it, so long as he maintains the fences in an efficacious manner. 8. And they improve the local climate to a sensible degree. Dr Skene Keith estimates the increase of temperature, occasioned by enclosures, to amount to from 5° to 8° Fahrenheit.

(574.) The particulars which first claim attention in commencing the enclosing of a farm, are the *nature of the soil* and the *locality of the farm ;* because these fix the system of husbandry to be adopted, and that again determines the number and size of the enclosures.

(575.) On pure clay-soil farms, enclosures are not so necessary to protect corn from the trespasses of live stock, there being only the working stock on such farms in summer, as a protection from the weather. Though clay-soils are generally situated in flat plains, margined with rising grounds; yet enclosures placed there as screens against prevailing winds, will much improve the local climate. In practice, such farms are seldom enclosed at all, on the idea that the ground is too valuable to be occupied by any kind of fence ; but this is obviously a short-sighted notion ; for all unenclosed farms are subject to being trespassed upon by live stock passing along the roads, and by people walking across the fields to shorten their journeys to church or market. Hence the prevalence of footpaths across fields in England, which had been established before the general adoption of field-enclosures. Besides all that, windy weather in harvest, in some seasons, damages more corn in one day, than the exhaustion of the soil by a well trimmed hedge would for any length of time.

(576.) Enclosures are absolutely required on all loamy soils, of which by far the greatest proportion of the surface of this country consists; because on them the finest live stock are reared and fattened.

(577.) Shelter is also requisite for the welfare of live stock on mountain-pasture. That obtained from large masses, or even belts, of planting in upland districts greatly improves the climate—prolongs the period of the duration of food, by encouraging the growth of grass both early and late in the season—and protects the live-stock from many diseases incidental to exposure to wet and cold weather.

(578.) Enclosures are of two kinds; one, which circumscribes the boundaries of farms by what is called a *ring-fence*, the other, which *surrounds each separate field*.

(579.) It will very much simplify your ideas in regard to which kind of enclosure is best suited to any particular farm, if you consider the uses to which the various kinds of farms which have already been enumerated to you are put. You can easily perceive that clay-land farms, and farms in the immediate neighbourhood of towns, which are not devoted to the rearing of live stock in summer, as well as pastoral farms, which afford a large range of pasturage to stock, do not necessarily require to be enclosed in subdivisions. It appears to be sufficient protection for them to be provided only with a *ring-fence*, and with fences along the sides of any public roads that may happen to pass through them. At the most, the subdivision of clay-land farms and those near towns need not be carried farther than dividing them into as many portions as there are numbers of the rotation of cropping pursued in each. So that only dairy and mixed-husbandry farms require to be subdivided into individual fields.

(580.) Most farms contain a variety of soils; not that the two opposite kinds of pure clay and pure sand are often found in the same neighbourhood, but varieties of soil, from clay or sand to clay-loam and gravelly loam, may be found on most farms. When clayey and sandy soils occur on the same farm, a leading fence should be run to divide them, so as each sort of soil may be fenced according to the system of husbandry most suitable for it. The clayey land will bear the best corn-crops, whilst the sandy will yield the best green crops and pastures, and rear the best live stock. Should the season prove unfavourable to the one class of soils, it may be favourable for the other; and when the markets for corn are depressed, those for live stock may be brisk. A happy juxtaposition of a variety of soils on the same farm serves to maintain its value permanently, amidst circumstances that would much depreciate it were the farm entirely composed of only one kind of soil.

(581.) Having thus ascertained the kinds of soil to be enclosed, and constituted each variety as a division of the farm, the next points for consideration, with a view to enclosure, are the site, shape, number, and size, of the fields to be made. These conditions of enclosure depend on the nature of the soil, the aspect of the ground, its inequalities, its subdivision by streams, and the rotation of crops suited to each kind of soil.

(582.) The *site* of a fence mostly depends on the aspect of the ground, and its direction is determined by that which should be given to the ridges in each field. The ridges should always, if possible, run N. and S., to allow both their sides to derive equal benefit from the solar rays. On flat ground, this direction may easily be assumed; but the inclination of the rising ground may be E. and W.; and as water detained on the surface of the ground may do more mischief than the solar rays do good to both sides of ridges at the same time, the direction of the ridges should follow the inclination of the ground, in order to secure the most rapid egress to the surface-water. Where the ground has an inclination both ways, that which comes nearest to the meridian should be preferred to the other. Where the ground rises with a compound inclination, whether facing the N. or the S., the ridges should take the N. and S. direction.

(583.) It is an essential requisite in forming enclosures, to make *all the fences which run in the direction of the ridges parallel to one another*; for whenever this parallelism is neglected, wedge-shaped ridges, or *butts*, as they are technically termed, must be formed at one or both sides of the fields, in order to work the entire surface of the ground. Owing to the inequality of the lengths of these butts or ridglets, much more time is consumed in working them, than a square piece of ground of the same area. All butts are therefore highly objectionable in fields; but as it is scarcely possible to bestow a rectangled form on every field of the farm, butts, where unavoidable, should be thrown out towards the boundaries of the farm.

(584.) To preserve neatness and uniformity in the ploughing of the fields, the fences should run parallel to one another *in straight lines*. A straight fence along the crown of a round-backed ridge of ground, affords excellent shelter to both sides of it, whether it runs N. and S. in the direction of the ridges, or E. and W. across their ends. Indeed, a fence occupying elevated ground bestows more shelter to fields than in any other situation, and such a site should always be chosen for the fence, and for a thorn-hedge, as it places it beyond the crushing power of a heavy fall of snow. But it often happens, that the lower ends of fields cannot be enclosed in straight lines, a rivulet or hollow between two rising grounds giving their terminations a serpentine form; and in such a case, the fence must follow the waving course of the rivulet or hollow ground, in order to preserve a channel for the surface-water coming down both sides of the slopes to the lowest part of the ground. A serpentine fence in a hollow, like a straight one on rising ground, affords more shelter than a straight fence in this position would against the wind, which is almost always forced down in the direction of the valley; and on this account, a thorn-hedge in the bottom of a valley has less chance of being entirely blown up with snow in winter than might be imagined. A rivulet, or where a large ditch is necessary for the conveyance of occasional large quantities of water, should run in its course along the fence, and not across the middle of the fields. In the latter position it is a great hinderance to work, by cutting short all the ridges on both sides of it.

(585.) The *shape* of fields is greatly determined by unavoidable obstacles, natural and artificial. A winding river or valley will give an irregular line to the fence at that end, and the *march-fence*, or boundary-line of a farm, may run in such a direction as to cause the adoption of butts; and another end or side of a field may abut against an old ruin, or plantation, or mural precipice of earth or rock. The corners of all fields should join at right angles with one another; because the plough can approach nearer to, and of course turn over more ground, in the square corners of a field, than in 2 obtuse and 2 acute angled corners. If every obstacle to correct enclosing can be overcome, it is demonstrable that the shape which is conducive to greatest economy in labour is the square. Thus, frequent turnings of the plough, occasioned by short ridges, consume much time; but, on the other hand, an inordinate length of ridge to obtain few turnings, fatigues the horses beyond their strength. The average strength of the horses is, in this case, the measure of the greatest length of ridge, that secures the greatest economy of labour in ploughing the field in every direction. It is, I believe, very near the mark to say, that horses can draw a plough through *cultivated lea-ground* for 250 yards, without being touched in the breath. This distance, then, is the measure of the length, and of course, too, the breadth of a field. But as ground already ploughed is of more easy draught than lea, 300 yards in the one case are as easy for horses as 250 yards in the other. The average is 275; and as there is much more loose ground ploughed in a year than lea, a higher average—say 285 yards—may be taken as the proper length of furrow on light soils. But as clay-soils are heavy, perhaps it may be near the truth to take 275 yards as the average length of draught for horses in all soils. The square shape might be profitably adopted on clay-land farms, whose extent being generally small, the break or division of land for each kind of crop cannot be large. Taking 250 yards as a long enough furrow for horses on clay-land, the divisions would be squares of 13 acres each; and as many of these could be placed together to form a principal division of the farm, as there are members in the rotation of cropping, a clayland farm can thus be laid out of any extent in divisions. But a field of 300 yards square, on loamy ground, being only about 18½ acres, is too small where live stock are reared. Preserving the proper length of ridge for the horses' easy labour, the field can be made large enough for stock—not less than 25 acres—at the same time, by giving it the shape of a right-angled parallelogram, the direction of the ridges being of course N. and S., and the longer side of the figure in the direction of E. and W.

(586.) Should a public road, or canal, or railway, pass through a farm, or an old plantation, quarry, or building, stand in the middle of the land, before it is enclosed, the irregularity occasioned by them in the fence should be placed next the obstacle; and all the butts or irregular ridges should also be placed on that side of the field. I may here mention, that a public road near enclosures is a great convenience to a farm, as it may save the making of one or more farm-roads. Easy access to and from the fields to roads, is a valuable means of maintaining uniform health and strength in horses, and of saving the wear and tear of carts and harness, especially in winter.

(587.) The *size* of the fields depends in a great measure on the nature of the farm; and yet, as you have learned, economy in labour limits both the smallness and largeness of fields. Even on the smallest class of farms on which horse-labour is at all employed, 10 acres seem a small enough space to labour land to advantage. There are many small farms on which much smaller fields than 10 acres may be observed, but such a space, fenced around, has an evidently confined-like look about it, and crops not unfrequently seem unhealthy in it. On the other hand, very large fields, such as from 50 to 100 acres each, take too much time to be finished off, even when the number of draughts of horses is ample. There is an evident attempt to do too much work at one time in such large fields. I should say that, for a successful prosecution of the mixed husbandry, a field from 25 to 40 acres is large enough, according to the extent of the farm: for it must be borne in mind that, other things being equal, the size of the fields should, in all cases, bear some proportion to that of the farm. That proportion I am not prepared to define, although I have no hesitation in giving it as my opinion that below 10 acres is too small a field for horse-labour to be employed in, and above 40 acres too large a field for quick despatch of work. The size of farm containing a variety of soils which is most in demand by farmers of mixed husbandry, is 500 acres, which would give 4 fields of 25 acres, or 100 acres for each member of a rotation of 5 crops. Placing the same kind of crop, and especially green crop and grass, in moderately sized fields, say of 25 acres each, on different parts of the farm, and most probably in different kinds of soil, a good crop in one of the fields will almost be ensured every season; and the whole labour of the farm being, for the time, confined to one moderately sized field, a good season for ploughing the land, and a safe seed-time and harvest for its crop, seem to be placed within the power of the farmer against any great or sudden change of weather.

(588.) Mountain-pastures, which are exclusively devoted to the use of live stock, should be enclosed in large divisions, because cattle and sheep are generally reared in large numbers on pastoral farms. Mountain live stock possess more active habits, and have a stronger instinct to search for food than those of the plain; and as the herbage of the mountains is always rather scanty, stock there require an ample space to roam over in order to satisfy their wants.

(589.) Although very small enclosures under constant cultivation are unwholesome both to crops and live stock, yet 2 or 3 small enclosures of from 1 to 5 acres in grass, near the farm-steading, are indispensable on every farm on which live stock is reared. These may be beneficially used by tups when out of season,—by calves when weaning from the milk,—by ewes when lambing,—by mares and foals for a few weeks until the mares regain their strength,—by a stallion at grass,—or as hospitals for sick and convalescent animals. Such fields are much more useful in grass than under the plough.

(590.) The *number* of fields depends partly on the size of the farm, and partly on the rotation of crops carried on in it. The interior of pure clay-land farms, devoted to the raising of corn alone, especially of wheat, should be no more subdivided than to have a division for each course in the rotation of crops; and this division may either be unenclosed or enclosed, according to its extent, or the exposure of the farm to particular offensive winds. If the division is of small extent, it should be unenclosed, but if large, enclosed; and in either case, it should be made up of convenient square-shaped fields of the extent determined on in a former paragraph (587): but the divisions should be enclosed under every circumstance along the march-fence, irrespective of its form or position. To subdivide a clay-land farm, on which no stock is reared in summer, into small fields, would be to devote an unnecessary waste of ground to fences. To save expense in working, and waste of ground in fences, on smaller farms of loamy soils than 125 acres, and which cannot rear much stock, the fields should correspond in number with the number of the members in the rotation of crops; and should a smaller quantity of grass or green crop be at any time wanted for a particular purpose than the contents of a whole field, a temporary fence may be used in preference to enclosing the farm into very small fields. With regard to farms of pretty large extent on soil of various loams, quite a different element enters into the consideration which determines the number of the fields. On enclosing land of this kind, the mere economy of labouring each field is not so much an object of solicitude as the welfare of the stock; and as stock always thrive best on fresh pasture, and when only a few of the same kind are herded together, it follows that the enclosures should not be of very large extent, perhaps not exceeding 25 acres each, so that 285 yards by 425 yards would embrace an enclosure of convenient size and shape of field for the grazing of cattle during the summer, and the feeding of sheep on turnips on the ground in winter. Horses will draw the plough through loam on a flat easier than on the inequality of surface usually presented by loamy ground. Suppose, then, that the enclosures contain 25 acres each, and that the 5-course rotation is followed with 2 enclosures to each member of the rotation, a farm so subdivided would contain 250 acres, which is as small extent of ground as the mixed husbandry can be advantageously practised upon; while were there 4 enclosures to each member of the course, the farm would contain 500 acres, and 6 enclosures would give 750 acres, which is as large a farm as the generality of farmers have capital to stock.

(591.) In enclosing any farm intended for the use of live stock, access to good water should never be overlooked, though it too often is. Should a rivulet not be within reach, spring-water should be obtained either by sinking pit-wells, or laying pipes, or making conduits. The best pasturage as food will never improve the condition of live stock, without the digestive aid of good water; and without an abundant supply of water graziers will never take even the best grass for cattle or horses, though it may answer sheep.

(592.) The evils of enclosing fields very closely have been urged against enclosures altogether; and it is alleged that the crops are liable to be lodged and destroyed in confined fields. The allegation is true; but it applies only to the abuse of the practice, and not to the principles, or the general practice of enclosing. Close small fields should always be kept in grass for stock; and in order to protect them from the attacks of flies which are to be dreaded in such situations, a shed to harbour in will greatly prevent the attacks of insects. Even in regard to corn, a sheltered field ripens the crops earlier than an open one.

(593.) It is also alleged that confined fields produce greater evaporation by the confined heat in them, and enclosures thereby superinduce an unusual depression of temperature. This is entirely a theoretical objection, for it is obvious that evaporation must be more promoted by exposure to wind than by confinement.*

(594.) As one object of enclosing land is protection to plants, whether trees, grains, vegetables, or grass, against the depredations of men and animals, or a protection to and place of confinement for domesticated animals, the use and necessity for enclosures could only have been felt after mankind had made considerable progress in the culture of land, and experienced the consequent depredations committed upon crops. During the pastoral state of society, when men wandered about in communities, and made any sort of fixed abode only where pasture could be obtained for their flocks and herds, their sole occupation was being shepherds. They tended the flocks and herds night and day around their own habitations. At length, fixing upon a convenient spot for themselves and animals, they constructed an enclosure or fold to confine their stock in during the night. This enclosure served the double purpose of relieving the night-watches of the shepherds and of protecting the stock against the attacks of wild animals. The first attempts at cultivating the ground were confined to a space nearest their dwellings. No enclosure was thought of for protecting the crops on the ground so long as the stock were tended by day and folded by night. In time, however, when the community increased in numbers, culture encroached upon the range of pasture, which, in consequence, became more scanty. The stock became more urgent for food, whilst the tending of them became more difficult, by the shepherds being lessened in number by the demands of cultivation. A fence then became necessary around the cultivated ground as a barrier against the predacious attempts on the stock. Hence the probable origin of the enclosing of cultivated land.

(595.) This view explains the origin of that particular mode of enclosing land which was once distinguished by the name of *infield* and *outfield*, and which prevailed in this country until a very late period, and which may yet be seen practised on the Continent in full vigour. The distant part, which was solely appropriated to pasturage by the stock, was called the *outfield*. The more contiguous portion of the land, on which was cultivated the necessaries of life for the cultivators and their families and dependents, and the fodder for the use of the cattle in winter, was called the *infield*. Cultivation was never exercised on the outfield, nor were the flocks and herds ever permitted to enter the infield. In this way was drawn a very strong line of demarcation betwixt the occupations of the shepherd and the husbandman, and which is maintained, in a remarkable degree, to this day. It was on this account, perhaps, that the agricultural Egyptians held " every shepherd an abomination" unto them.†

(596.) The broad distinction which was then established betwixt the rearing of stock and the culture of grain, served to withhold from cultivators the valuable fact that stock afford great facilities for the fertilization of land. So long

* Sinclair's Code of Agriculture, p. 171.

† Genesis, xlvi. 34.

as this fact was unknown, cultivators never imagined that the food of stock should be raised on cultivated land, or that it could be raised abundantly and economically in conjunction with their own. Whenever they perceived that grain could be more productively raised through the meliorating effect of grass on the soil, and that grass-land supported more stock when occasionally cropped with corn, and that stock could manure land much better than the hand of man, the entire unsocial system of outfield and infield was broken up. The ancient ring-fence, which only surrounded the cultivated land, was then removed to the boundaries of the possession, and in its stead were constructed suitable enclosures for the various crops about to be raised in regular succession.

(597.) Enclosures were constructed on the boundaries of possessions by the most ancient nations. It is probable that much of Egypt was never a pastoral country; for the great fertility conferred on its soil by the natural inundations of the Nile, would render it an agricultural country as soon as the first people observed their effects on vegetation. Accordingly, we find it recorded in the Sacred Writings, that, from its first mention about 2000 years before the Christian era, Egypt was a country pre-eminent for the production of corn.* Extensive canals and ditches were formed for the purpose of conveying the waters of the Nile to irrigate the parts of the country it did not naturally overflow, and these at the same time served for fences. The condition of Greece in regard to enclosures was exactly as has been above described, and from the laws which governed the limits and landmarks of landed property, it is probable that fences were only erected on the boundaries of properties like a ring-fence.† The Romans never enclosed their pasture-land for the purpose of confining cattle. They planted fences around gardens, orchards, and meadows, and also around parks for the confinement of wild animals, but in other respects their lands were enclosed much in the same manner as by the Greeks, with a ring-fence around the boundary of the farm, and they employed various kinds of fences for this purpose.‡

(598.) Most of the modern nations of Europe still enclose their land in the ancient method. Property is so much subdivided in France by the extinction of the law of primogeniture, that in at least one half of that country, all to the eastward, no field enclosures are to be seen, a few march stones, a ditch, a row of trees, or particular single trees here and there marking the boundaries of the small estates.§ Throughout Germany, Bohemia, Switzerland, and Spain, enclosures are only found near farm-houses and villages, the bulk of the corn being raised on extensive unenclosed grounds. I have seen a tract of wheat in Bohemia as far as the eye could reach, without a single fence in sight. In Lombardy the enclosures consist of the ditches which convey the waters of irrigation to the land. On the other hand, the land in Holland and Belgium is so much enclosed with trees and hedges that in many places the fields seem half choked by them. The same remark nearly applies to the south of England, where much valuable ground is occupied by beautifully luxuriant but greatly over-

* Genesis, xii. 10.

† Potter's Antiquities of Greece, p. 155, edition of 1697.

‡ Dickson's Husbandry of the Ancients, vol. ii. p. 330.

§ Young's Travels in France, p. 392.

grown hedges. The land in Ireland, particularly in the province of Ulster, is also very much subdivided by turf-dykes, which are generally in a state quite unfit to confine live-stock. It is only in the north of England and the best cultivated districts of Scotland that enclosures, suited to the improved state of agriculture, are to be found. There, farms are not only completely enclosed, but the size of the enclosure is made proportionate to the uses to which the soil is applied. There, growing crops of all kinds find shelter from the vicissitudes of the weather and protection against animals, and the stock themselves enjoy, as a recompense for confinement, peace and plenty. It is well observed by Arthur Young, that enclosed land is no decisive proof of an advanced state of husbandry; for when he saw enclosed and unenclosed land in France managed alike, he asked, "With such miserable systems of what good are enclosures? Hence we may draw this conclusion, that when we find half of France enclosed, we are not to suppose that kingdom in a state of improvement and cultivation which this circumstance implies amongst us; on the contrary, it indicates no such thing; for some of the poorest and most unimproved provinces are precisely those which are enclosed; and, for what I know, there may be visionary theorists in that kingdom, who will, from this circumstance, argue against the practice of enclosing, since no absurdities are so gross as to want advocates." *

(599.) Another object in enclosing land is to afford *shelter* to plants and animals against the changes of weather. That a fence affords shelter must be a fact cognizant to every one. Feel the warmth of a walled garden—the calm felt under the walls of even a ruin compared to the howling blast around—observe the forward grass, in early spring, on the south side of a hedge compared to that on its other side—and listen to the subdued tone of the wind under a shed to its boisterous noise heard in the open air. Sensibly felt as all these instances of shelter are, they are but isolated cases. In more extended spheres, cottages stand in a calm in the midst of a forest, come the wind from whatever quarter it may. Farm-steadings lie snug under the lee-side of a hill. Whole farms are unaffected by wind when embayed amidst encircling hills; and be the shelter, therefore, great or small, the advantages derived from it are sensibly felt. As one instance of the benefits of shelter afforded by even a low wall to a park, from the cutting effects of the sea air, I give a sketch in fig. 35, over the leaf, to shew you its effects better than words can convey. The wall and the wood next it are of the same height, but a few yards only inwards, the wood rises to a considerable height, and this is effected by a very simple contrivance, namely, the peculiar form of the cope of the wall. It is raised like an isosceles triangle, by which the wind, when it beats against its side, is reflected upwards into the air at the same angle. Had the cope been flat, the blast would have cut off the tops of the trees in a horizontal direction. But without the wood such a form of coping would afford similar shelter. Suppose land exposed on the top of a high coast, where the wind generally sweeps along the surface of the ground, injuring every plant it blows against by a momentum acquired in passing over miles of ocean. Were a wall built on the top of the crag, at such a distance from its brow, and of such a height, and with such an angle to its cope as would deflect the wind upwards, it would cause the wind to have lost most of its momentum before it again reached the ground. Such a wall, or such a belt of wood, or such a plantation without a

* Young's Travels in France, p. 393.

wall, if projected on a large scale, and planted near the top of a sloping precipice, or other rising ground, would shelter a large extent of country against the pre-

Fig. 35.

vailing winds. Were such barriers placed in lines, in suitable places, across the country, not only its local, but its general climate would be greatly ameliorated.

(600.) Instances are not awanting to shew the usefulness of such barriers. Even within the experience of the present generation, shelter has been found to amend the climate, and increase the crops of particular parts of the country. As instances of *wall shelter*, the garden of the Earl of Lauderdale at Dunbar, and the plantations along the sea-side of the Earl of Wemyss at Gosford, both in East Lothian, afford good examples. In the latter instance, the coped wall, pictured in the sketch given above in fig. 35, has afforded such a shelter, as at the distance of 20 or 30 yards the forest-trees are scarcely affected by the sea-breeze, on ground which formerly produced nothing of higher growth than sweet-briar and whins. The garden of Mr Traill of Woodwick, at Kirkwall, Orkney, affords another remarkable instance of the benefits of wall-shelter. But the benefits derived from *plantations* are far more extensive and important, not only in affording shelter, but in improving poor land. " Previous to the division of the common moor of Methven (in Perthshire) in 1793," says Mr Thomas Bishop, " the venerable Lord Lynedoch and Lord Methven had each secured their lower slopes of land adjoining the moor with belts of plantation. The year following I entered Lord Methven's service, and in 1798 planted about 60 acres of the higher moor-ground, valued at 2s. per acre, for shelter to 80 or 90 acres set apart for cultivation, and let in 3 divisions to 6 individuals. The progress made in improving the land was very slow for the first 15 years, but thereafter went on rapidly, being aided by *the shelter derived from the growth of the plantations ;* and the whole has now become fair land, bearing annually crops of oats, barley, pease, potatoes, and turnips; and in spring 1838, exactly 40 years from the time of putting down the said plantation, I sold 4 acres of larch and fir (average growth) standing therein for L.220, which, with the value of reserved trees, and average amount per acre of thinnings sold previously, gave a return of L.67 per acre."* In some situations trees will afford better shelter than stone-walls, the latter being most available near the sea-side in warding off the blighting effects of the sea-breeze. On the summit of Shotley-fell, 16 miles W. of Newcastle-upon-Tyne, Mr Burnet of Shotley-bridge enclosed 400 acres of moorland with high stone-walls, and he cropped the ground in an easy manner for the soil. The land was thus kept in good heart, but the soil being very poor, stock advanced but little, and consequently the land would not have let for above 6d. an acre, even under the best management, and after all that had been done for it; but the centre part of each field was then put within a plantation, and the improvement was then surprising. The mode of planting by the proprietor was this :—" He put the trees (nearly all larch) about 1 foot or 2 feet from the centre of each ridge, alternately on one side of the top of the ridge and on the other, and about 4 yards asunder from each tree, in the direction along the ridges. The width of the ridges varies, and also of the belts; but the ridges are just as they were when in tillage, from 10 to 15 feet wide, and the belt of the width of 2 or 3 ridges according to circumstances." A portion of ground was planted as it arrived at the end of the rotation of cropping. " That took about 1000 trees, or about one-fourth the number usually planted. He put no stock into the plantation till the trees got so high that sheep could not hurt them; he then pruned off the lower branches, and put the sheep in. Perhaps 5 or 6 years elapse between the planting and the stocking with sheep; but the consequence is, that these new plantations now carry above 4 times, and I would rather say 6 times, the stock that the same land had carried before being planted. . . . I never was more surprised than I was to see the abundance of the herbage; the cock's-foot grass 3 or 4 feet high, equal to that on lands L.3 the acre value; and in the oldest plantations, his young cattle were going to 4 times the stents the land had ever kept before it was so planted."† Besides protection, the means employed to afford shelter by plantations beautify the appearance of the country. " The plantations of Muirton" (in Ross-shire), says Mr Mackenzie, " has already (1836), and will yet in a greater degree improve the climate of the sur-

* Quarterly Journal of Agriculture, vol. xi. p. 327.

† Ibid., vol. xii. p. 51.

rounding district, as well as afford shelter and warmth. Already the plantations relieve and delight the eye, and spread a beauty and freshness around the scene. Muirton formerly looked a bleak and barren wild, while the opposite highly cultivated estates of Brahan and Coul were the delight of every passing traveller; but with these it may now vie both in richness and beauty. The hill of Muirton as a pasturage was not worth 6d. per acre, whereas, by the expending of a small sum, it may be expected to realize from 15s. to 20s. per acre of yearly rent, from the date of planting, even at the distance of 8 miles, as Muirton is, from the shipping-places of Beauly and Dingwall. Besides the price of the wood, the value of the enclosure as a wintering for sheep will be considerable." * These proofs of the advantages derivable from enclosures to stock and crop are quite sufficient, I should imagine, to prove to you the great importance of protection and shelter to both.†

---

24. OF THE PLANTING OF THORN-HEDGES.

> "Next, fenc'd with hedges and deep ditches round,
> Exclude th' encroaching cattle from thy ground."
>
> DRYDEN'S VIRGIL.

(601.) Immediately in connection with the subject of enclosures is the construction of the *fences* by which the fields are enclosed. There are only two kinds of fences usually employed on farms, namely, *thorn-hedges* and *stone-dykes*. As winter is the proper season for planting, or running, as it is termed, thorn-hedges, and summer that for building stone-dykes, I shall here describe the process of planting the hedge, and defer the description of building the dyke until the arrival of the summer season. It may be that the farm on which you have entered as a pupil, or that which you have taken on lease, may not require to be fenced with thorn-hedges. Still it is requisite that you should be made acquainted with the best mode of planting them.

(602.) The proper time for planting thorn-hedges extends from the fall of the leaf, in autumn, to April, the latter period being late enough. The state of the ground usually chosen for the process is when in lea. I recommended lea as the best state for the process, in a paper on thorn-hedges which appeared some years ago;‡ but experience has since con-

* Prize Essays of the Highland and Agricultural Society, vol. vii. p. 474.

† See paper by me on Enclosures in Quarterly Journal of Agriculture, vol. iv. p. 843.

‡ It will be found in the Quarterly Journal of Agriculture, vol. i. p. 843.

vinced me that that is *not* the best state of the ground for the purpose; because grass grows up from the turf around the young thorn-plants, and cannot be easily removed, but with the removal, at the same time, of a considerable portion of the earth upon which the young plants rest. A much better time, therefore, is after the ground has been thoroughly fallowed during the summer, that is, after it has been perfectly cleared of all weeds,—well stirred and commixed with the plough and the harrow,—and pulverised, if need be, with the roller,—freshened by lengthened exposure to the air,—amply manured with good dung, to promote the growth of the young thorn-plants,—and sufficiently limed to prevent worms traversing the soil, and, in consequence, moles mining in quest of them. If the field in which the line of hedge is proposed to be planted is not intended to be thoroughly fallowed,—that is, by a bare fallow or a crop of potatoes or turnips,—the part to be occupied by the hedge should be so treated, in order to render the soil as clean, and fresh, and fertile as possible; and the expense incurred by this treatment of the soil will be repaid by the increased health and strength of the hedge for many years thereafter. There is no doubt that lea-sod affords a firmer bed for the young thorn-plants to rest upon than fallowed ground; but it is of much greater importance to secure the ground from weeds, and health and strength to the young plants, than mere firmness of soil under them, but which peculiar advantage may be attained, too, partly by allowing the fallowed ground to consolidate for a time before commencing the operation, and partly by trampling the soil thoroughly while in the act of planting.

(603.) The ground having been thus prepared, the planting of the hedge may be proceeded with forthwith. If its line of direction is determined by existing fences; that is to say, if one side of a field only requires fencing, then the new fence should be made parallel with the old one that runs N. or S., and it may take any convenient course, if its general direction is E. and W. Should a field, or a number of fields, require laying off anew, then the fences should be set off according to the principles already laid down in the instructions in the preceding section on enclosures, namely, the N. and S. fences should run due N. and S., for the purpose of giving the ridges an equal advantage of the sun both forenoon and afternoon. To accomplish this parallelism a geometrical process must be gone through; and to perform that process with accuracy, certain instruments are required.

(604.) In the first place, 3 *poles* at least in number, of at least 8½ feet in length, should be provided. They should be shod and pointed with iron at one end, marked off in feet and half-feet throughout their length, and each painted at the top of a different colour, such as white, red, blue, green, or black, so as to form decided contrasts with each other when set in line. Three of such poles are required to determine a straight line, even on level ground; but if the ground is uneven, 4 or more are requisite. These poles will be found of use, not merely in lining off fences, but they will be required every year on the farm, to set off the breadths of the ridges of fields after being fallowed. 2. An *optical square*, for setting off lines at right angles, or a *cross-table*, for the same purpose, should also be provided. The optical square costs 21s., and the cross-table 7s. 6d. 3. You should also have an imperial measuring-chain, of 66 feet in length, which costs 13s., for measuring the breadth or length of the fields, in the process of fencing; or of drills, drains, and any other species of work set by piece to labourers at other times. Iron pins, for marking the number of chains measured, generally go along with the chain.

(605.) Being provided with these instruments, one line of fence is set off parallel to another in this way. Set off, in the first instance, at right angles, a given distance from near one end of the old thorn fence, if there be one, or of the ditch, and let this distance be 6 feet from the roots of the thorns, so that a space or scarcement of 1 foot on the edge or lip of the ditch be left, and there plant one of the poles. About 100 yards' distance plant another pole in the same manner, and so on along the length of the fence from which the distances are set off. If there be no fence to set off the distances from, then let a pole be set perpendicularly up in the line the new fence is intended to occupy, and at noon, in a clear day, observe the direction the shadow of the pole takes on level ground, and that is N. and S.; or a pocket-compass can give the direction required, deducting the variation of the needle, which in this country is about 27° W.; but the plan with the pole is the simplest and most handy for work-people. Poles, at about 100 yards' distance, should be set up in the line of the shadow; but you should bear in mind that the first two poles should be set up quickly, otherwise a short lapse of time will make a material difference in the line of direction of the shadow. Twenty minutes make a difference of 5° in the direction of the shadow of the poles, and 5° at the first pole will make a considerable deviation from the true line of N. and S. at the farthest end of the line of the new fence. Adjust the poles with one another to form the straight line, and this line forms the base line of your operations. This line is *c u* in fig. 36, projected by shadow in the manner just described, or set off from the old hedge *a b*. Let *c d* and *e* be 3 poles planted in that line. Let *f* be the cross-table erected in the line betwixt, and adjusted by looking at the poles *c* and *d*. Let *g*, *h*, and *i*, be poles set and adjusted to one another by the cross-table in the line *f k*, which is the breadth of the field, and which distance is measured by the chain to contain a number of ridges of given breadth, as any fractional part of a ridge left at either side of the

Fig. 36.

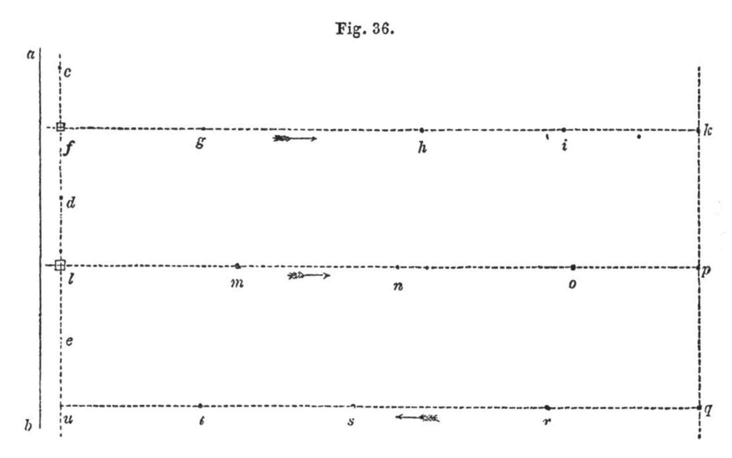

PLAN OF SETTING OFF FENCES PARALLEL TO EACH OTHER.

field afterwards proves inconvenient for work. In like manner, let the line *l p* be drawn from the cross-table at *l*, by setting the poles *m*, *n*, *o*, *p*. Then set the pole *q* in a line with the poles *k p*, and measure the distance betwixt *q* and *u*, along the line *r s t*, with the chain, which distance, if the two previous operations have been accurately conducted, should be exactly equal to the distance betwixt *f* and *k*, or *l* and *p*; but should it prove greater or less than either, then some error must have been committed, and which can only be rectified by doing the operation over again. The *arrows* shew the directions in which each line should be measured. Great accuracy should be observed in running these lines of fences parallel, for if a similar error is committed at each successive line of fence, the deviation from parallelism may prove very considerable betwixt the first and last lines. Three poles only being employed to set off the lines *f k* and *l p*, the ground may be supposed to be nearly level; but wherever such an inequality of ground is found as to cause you to lose sight of 1 of 3 poles, as many should be employed as to have 3 of them in view at one time. This point should be constantly kept in view in setting the poles.

(606.) A line of fence being thus set off, the next process is to plant it with thorns, and for this purpose certain instruments are required. 1. A strong *garden line* or *cord*, of at least 70 yards in length, having an iron reel at one end, and a strong iron pin at the other. Its use is to shew upon the ground the exact line of the fence betwixt the poles.

Its cost is, with a common reel and pin, 4s. 2. A few *pointed pins of wood with hooked heads*, to keep the cord in the direction of the line of the hedge, whether that follows a vertical curve or a horizontal one, occasioned by the inequalities of the ground. 3. A *wooden rule*, 6 feet in length, divided into feet and inches, having a piece of similar wood about 2 feet in length, fastened at right angles to one end. Its use is to measure off short distances at right angles. Any country carpenter can make such a rule. 4. No. 5 *spades* are the most useful size for hedging, which cost 4s. 3d. each. 5. A light *hand-pick*, to loosen the subsoil at the bottom of the ditch and to trim its sides, and it costs 5s. 6d. or 6s. 6. An iron *tramp-pick* to loosen the subsoil immediately under the mould, and raise the boulder stones that may be found in it. In some parts of the country this pick is unknown, but a more efficient implement cannot be employed for the purpose. This pick stands 3 feet 9 inches in height. The tramp, fig. 37, is movable, and may be placed on either side to suit the foot of the workman, where it remains firm at about 16 inches from the point, which gradually tapers and inclines a little forward, to assist the leverage of the shank. The shank is ¾ of an inch square under the eye through which the handle passes, and 1½ inch broad at the tramp, where it is the strongest. It costs 6s. 6d. 7. A *ditcher's shovel*, fig. 38. Its use is to shovel the bottom and sides of the ditch, and to beat the face of the hedge-bank. It is 1 foot broad and 1 foot long, tapering to a point, with a shaft 28 inches in length, and its cost is, No. 5, 4s. This is a useful shovel on a farm, cleaning up the bottoms of dunghills in soft ground much better than a spade or square-mouthed shovel; and yet in some parts of the country it is an unknown implement. 8. *Three* men are the most convenient number to work together in running a hedge; and they should, of course, be all well acquainted with spade-work. 9. Should tree-roots be apprehended in the subsoil, a *mattock* for cutting them will be required, and it costs 6s. 6d. 10. A sharp *pruning-knife* to each man, to prepare the plants for planting, which costs 2s. to 3s. each.

Fig. 37.

A TRAMP-PICK.

Fig. 38.

A DITCHER'S SHOVEL.

(607.) The *plant* usually employed in this country, in the construction of a hedge, is the common hawthorn. "On account of the stiffness of its branches," says Withering, "the sharpness of its thorns, its roots not spreading wide, and its capability of bearing the severest winters without injury, this plant is universally preferred for making hedges, whether to clip or to grow at large." * Thorns ought never to be planted in a hedge till they have been transplanted at least 2 years from the seed-bed, when they will have generally acquired a girth of stem at the root of 1 inch, a length in all of 3 feet, of which the root measures 1 foot, as in fig. 39, which is on a scale of 1½ inch to 1 foot. The cost of picked plants of that age is 12s. 6d. per 1000; or, as they are taken out of the lines, 10s. 6d. As thorns are always transplanted too thick in the nursery lines, in order to save room, and draw them up sooner to be tall plants, I would advise their being purchased from the nursery at that age, the year before they are intended to be planted in the fence, and of being laid in lines in ample space in garden mould, or any space of ground having a free deep dry soil. By such a process the stems will acquire a cleaner bark and greater strength, and the roots be furnished with a much greater number of minute fibres, which will greatly promote the growth of the young hedge, and thus amply repay the additional trouble bestowed on the care of the plants. But, whether the plants are so treated before they are planted or not, the bundles, containing 200 plants each, should be immediately loosened out on their arrival from the nursery, and *sheughed in*, that is, spread out upright in trenches in a convenient part of the field, and dry earth well heaped against them, to protect the roots from frost, and to keep them fresh until planted. The plants are taken from the *sheughs* when wanted.

Fig. 29.

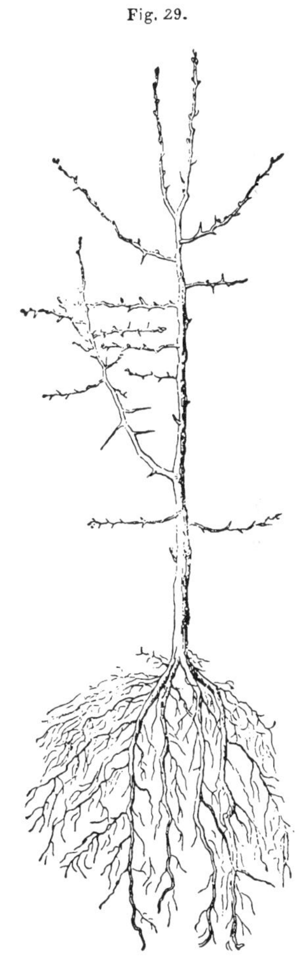

A THORN PLANT.

(608.) If the line of fence is to be straight, which should always be the case if natural obstacles do not interfere to prevent it, let the poles be set up in as straight a line as possible from one end of the fence to the other. Should the ground be a plain, this line can be drawn straight with the greatest accuracy; but should eleva-

* Withering's Botany, vol. iii. p. 561.

tions, or hollows, or both, intervene, however small, great care is requisite to preserve the straightness of the line, because on such ground a straightness of line, determined by poles, is very apt to advance upon the true line in the hollows, and recede from it in the elevations, especially if the inequalities are abrupt. Surveyors use the theodolite specially to avoid this risk of error, but it may be avoided by using plenty of poles, so that they may be set not far asunder from one another. In case evil disposed persons shift the poles in the night, and thereby alter the line of fence, pins should be driven, at intervals, well into the ground, to preserve the marks of the line. Having set plenty of poles, and so as to please the eye, take the reel and cord, and, pushing its pin firmly into the ground at the end of the line of fence where you wish to begin, run the cord out its full length, with the exception of a small piece to twist round the shank of the reel. Be sure to guide the cord exactly along the bottoms of the poles; and should any obstacle to your doing so lie in the way, such as clods, stones, or dried weeds, remove them, and smooth the ground with the spade; and then, with your face towards the cord, draw it backward towards you with considerable force until it has stretched out as far as it can, and then push the shank of the reel firmly into the ground. As the least obstruction on the ground will cause the cord to deviate from the true line, lift up the stretched cord by the middle about 3 feet from the ground, keeping it close to the sides of the poles, and let it drop suddenly to the ground, when, it is probable, it will lie as straight as practicable. Place a rather heavy stone here and there upon the cord to prevent the possibility of its being shifted from its position. With the common spade then cut, or as it is technically termed, *rut* the line of hedge-bed behind the cord, with your face towards the ditch that is to be, taking care to hold the spade with a slope corresponding to that of the sides of the proposed ditch, and not to press upon, or be too far back from, or cut the cord with the spade. Then take the wooden rule, and placing its cross-head along the cord, set off the breadth of the ditch at right angles to the rutted line 4½ feet—first, at both ends of the still stretched cord, and then here and there; and mark off those breadths with wooden pins, which will serve to check any important deviation from the true line at either end of the cord. Now, take up and stretch the cord anew along the other side of the ditch, by the sides of the pins, in the same manner, and with the same precautions as with the hedge-bed, and rut the line with your face towards, and the spade sloping like the side of the ditch. After securing a continuation of the line of the hedge-bed, remove the poles and pins along the length of the cord, and the ditch is thus marked out ready for the formation of the thorn-bed. When about forming the thorn-bed, that end of the line should be chosen for commencing the work which best suits the hand of the workman who is intrusted to make it. The rule for this is, whichever hand grasps the eye of the spade should always be nearest the thorn-bed, and the workman should work backwards.

(609.) In forming the *thorn-bed*, raise a large, firm, deep spadeful of earth from the edge of the first rutted line of the hedge, and invert it along that line, with its rutted face towards the ditch. Having placed a few spadefuls in this manner, side by side, beat down their crowns with the back of the spade, paring down their united faces in the slope given to the first rut, and then slope their crowns with an inclination downwards and backwards from you, forming an inclined bed for the thorn-plant to lie upon, as at *b c*, fig. 40. In like manner, place other spadefuls, to the end of the thorn-bed last made, taking care to join

Fig. 40.

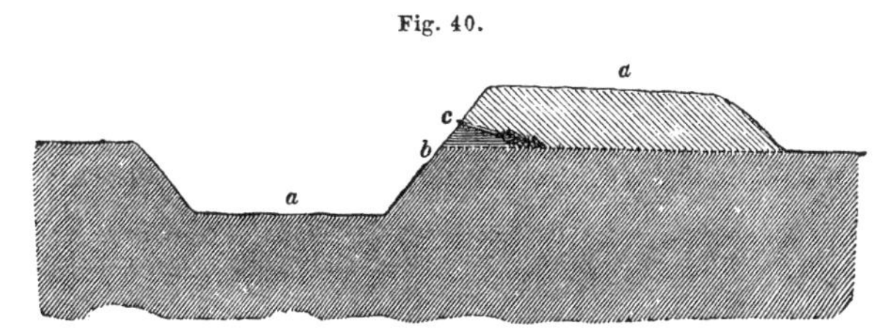

THE THORN-BED.

all the spadefuls so as to make one continued bed, and so on to the whole length of the cord of 70 yards.

(610.) Whilst the principal hedger is thus proceeding with the thorn-bed, his two assistants should prepare the thorn-plants for planting. On receiving the thorn-plants from the nursery, the usual practice is to put the bundles of plants into the soil in some convenient corner of the field, until they are wanted for planting. I have recommended the plants being purchased the year before they are to be planted, and transplanted in wide lines in good garden-mould, to enlarge and multiply the root-fibres. And now that the plants are more particularly to be spoken of, I would further recommend them to be assorted, according to their sizes, as they are taken out of the bundles, and before being transplanted in the lines. The advantage of this plan is this. Plants should be suited to the situation they are to occupy. On examining the bundles, they will be found to contain both stout and weak plants. The stoutest plants cannot derive sufficient nourishment in the poorer class of soils, however well the soils may have been previously treated for their reception; whilst weak plants will, of course, thrive well in the better soil. From this circumstance, it may be concluded that weak plants are best adapted to all classes of soils. Not so; for however well weak plants may thrive in all soils, stout plants will grow much more rapidly than weak in good soils; and were all the soil good, the most profitable fence would be obtained from the best and picked plants. But as every farm possesses soils of various degrees of fertility, although the class of its soils may be the same; and as plants in a stout and weak state are usually mixed together, the most prudent practice is to put the weaker plants in the best soil, and the stouter plants in the worse kind of soil, thus giving a chance of success to both sorts of plants and soils. Were the plants assorted when placed in transplanted lines, those could be selected which would best suit the soil which was under operation at the time. But should this trouble not be taken at first, still the plants should be assorted when being prepared for planting, according to the nature of the soil, the weaker being taken for the good soil, and the stronger for that of inferior quality. Want of attention to this adaptation of means to ends is one cause of failure in the rearing of thorn-hedges in many parts of the country; and one of those means consists in transplanting the weakest plants in good soil, and allowing them to remain there until they had acquired sufficient strength for being planted out. Although the thorn-plant may truly be said to affect every kind of soil in cultivation, yet the plant, in its different states of growth, will thrive better in one condition or kind of soil than in another; and this discrimination should be exercised by the planter, if he would have a good hedge.

(611.) The prepared thorn-plant is represented by fig. 41; and it is prepared in this way. Grasp the stem of the full plant, immediately above the root, firmly in the hand, and cut it across with a sharp knife, in an inclination towards the top of the plant at *a*; and the cut thus made will be about 6 inches above the root and fibres. Cut away the long parts of the tap-roots *b*, and any other straggling and injured roots, and even injured fibres; but preserve as many of the fibres entire as possible. Burn the tops thus cut off, or bury them deep in the ground; as they will vegetate, and are easily blown about by the wind, and very troublesome to sheep in the wool. Take great care, in frost, to cover up the prepared roots in earth until they are planted, for roots in the least affected by frost will not vegetate. The safest plan, in frosty weather, is to take but a few plants at a time out of the lines. On the other hand, in dry weather in spring, when the hedge is to be planted in dry ground, put the roots of the prepared plants in a puddle of earth and water, in a shady

Fig. 41.

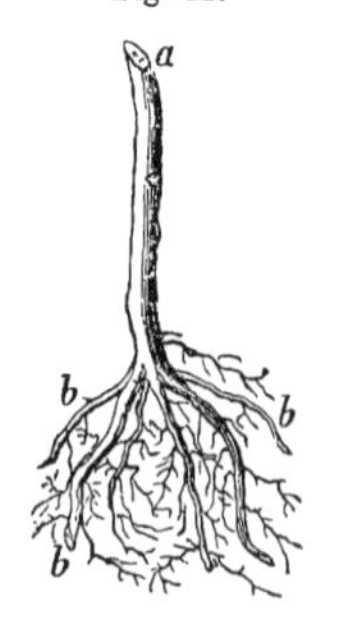

A THORN-PLANT, PREPARED FOR PLANTING.

place, for some hours before laying them in the thorn-bed, and their vegetation will thereby be much facilitated.

(612.) When both the thorn-bed and plants are prepared, the assistants lay the plants in the bed. This is done by pushing each plant firmly into the mould of the bed, with the cut part of the stem projecting not more than ¼ of an inch beyond the front of the thorn-bed, and with the root-end lying away from the ditch, at distances varying from 6 to 9 inches, the 6 inches being adapted to inferior land, and the 9 inches to good soil. Whilst the two assistants are laying the plants, the hedger takes up all the fine mould nearest the thorn-bed, and, dexterously inverting the shovel-fulls of the mould, places them above the laid plants, and secures them in their places. The two assistants having finished laying the thorns, dig and shovel up with the spade all the black mould in the ditch, throwing it upon the roots and stems of the plants, until a sort of level bank of earth is formed over them. In doing this, one of the assistants lifts the soil across the ditch, moving backwards, whilst the other proceeds forwards, face to face, shovelling up all the black mould he can find, whether in a loose or firm state, in the ditch. When the hedger has finished covering the plants with mould, and whilst the assistants are proceeding to clear all the mould from the ditch, he steps upon the top of the mound which they have thrown up above the plants, and, with his face towards the ditch, firmly compresses, with his feet, the mould above the plants, as far as they extend. By the time the compression is finished, all the mould will have been taken out of the ditch. When the thorns have received this quantity of earth above them, they may be considered in a safe state from the frost; but it is not safe, in frosty weather, to leave them, even for a night, with less earth upon them; for plants may not only be frosted in that short space of time, but the earth may be rendered so hard by frost, as to be unfit for working the next day; and should the frost prove severe and the work be altogether suspended, the plants left at all exposed will inevitably perish. In frosty weather, the plants should not be laid on the thorn-bed in the afternoon, but only in the forenoon, as in the afternoon of a short day there probably will not be time to cover the plants with a sufficient quantity of earth. Indeed, in such weather, when the ground continues hard all day, leave the work off altogether; not only because the earth is then in an unfit state for the work, but the frosted earth is apt to chill the tender fibres. On the other hand, if the weather be fresh and not too wet, such as in spring, the plants may be laid in the afternoon in safety. In very wet weather, the work should also be suspended, not only on account of the cloggy state of the ground for good work, but the inability of the men to withstand much rain in winter. The last operation of the ditch and bank will be more uniform and look better, when a considerable length of it is finished at the same time, than when joinings are visible in it at short intervals; but in frosty or in very wet weather, the sooner a piece of it is finished, the better it is for the cleanliness of the labourers and the condition of the work itself. Fig. 40 shews the progress of hedge-planting to the extent described, where *a* is the ditch with the mould all taken out, *b* the thorn-bed sloping inwards and downwards, *c* the thorn in its bed, with the end of the stem projecting a very little outwards, and *d* the mound above in its compressed state.

(613.) The rule observed for the depth of a ditch that stands well, is ½ its breadth, and the width of the bottom ⅙ of the breadth at the top. In the case of hedge-planting, the breadth is 4½ feet; the depth is, of course, 2 feet 3 inches, and the width of bottom 9 inches. The hedge-bank is always broader than the ditch, the soil lying loosely upon it, and in this case is 5 feet; and, of course, the perpendicular height of the bank is less than the depth of the ditch, being 2 feet. These are, in general, very convenient dimensions for a hedge ditch and bank, where no constant current of water has to be accommodated in the ditch; but should the ditch have to contain a stream of water, though in winter only, it should be made proportionably capacious; for if not so made at first, it will either have to be made so at last, or the force of the water will assuredly make an adequate course for itself, to the danger of destroying the thorn-bed. Ditches that are brought to a point at the bottom are objectionable in shape for many reasons. They do not afford sufficient materials out of them to form a protective bank or mound for the young thorn-plants; they are easily filled up with the mouldering of earth from the sides and tops, and the decay of vegetables; and when any water gets into them, of which there is every chance when there is an overflow of surface-water in the field, they soon get filled up in the bottom with mud. Notwithstanding the commendation of such ditches in works of agriculture,* they should be avoided when there is the probability of the least quantity of water reaching them; and no ditch in connection with a field can be exempt from the intrusion of water.

(614.) When the work has proceeded to this length, the other implements come into use. If the subsoil of the ditch, however, be a tenacious ductile clay, the spade alone is best to remove it, as picking is use-

* Communications to the Board of Agriculture, vol. ii. p. 18. Loudon's Encyclopædia of Agriculture, p. 432–3, &c.

less in such a substance, especially if somewhat moist; for it will raise no more at a time than the breadth of the face of the pick. But if it consists of hard dry clay, interspersed with veins of sand and gravel,—which compound forms a very common subsoil in this country,—picking is absolutely required; for the spade cannot get through the small stones with effect. In some parts of the country, the handpick is used to loosen such a subsoil, whilst in others the footpick is employed; and from experience in both, I would recommend the latter as being by far the more efficient implement for such work, and less laborious to the workman. Let one of the assistants loosen the subsoil with the footpick as deep as he can go for the tramp, with the point of the pick away from him; he then pulls the handle towards him, until he brings it down about half-way to the ground, and after that, he sits on it, and presses it down with the whole weight of his body, until the subsoil gives way and becomes loose, in which state he leaves it before him, and steps backwards. When the picker has thus proceeded a short way, the other assistant lifts up what has been loosened with his spade, and throws it upon the top of the mould above the thorn, taking care to place the subsoil so thrown up continuous with the slope backwards, given to the face of the bank. He also throws some to the back of the bank, to cover the whole of the black mould, with the subsoil; and endeavours to make the shape of the bank uniform. In doing all this, he works backward with his back to the face of the footpicker, but his back would be to the back of a handpicker, standing upon the subsoil which has been loosened by the footpick. He pares down the side of the ditch nearest his right hand, which, in this case, is the opposite one from the hedge. The hedger follows the last assistant, working towards him face to face, and moving forwards, shovelling up all the loose earth left by the assistant's spade, throwing it upon the top and front of the mound, making all equal and smooth, and beating the earth firmly and smooth on the face of the bank. Should the subsoil require no picking at all, the two assistants follow one another, using the spade; and the hedger brings up the rear as before, using the shovel. In this way, the hedger throws the earth fully on the face of the bank, even although some should trickle down again into the ditch, rejecting all the larger stones that come in his way, paring down that side of the ditch, giving the proper slope to the bank, and beating the face of the bank with the back of the shovel, and smoothing it downwards from its top to as far as the black mould is seen on the side of the ditch. The three men thus proceed regularly in their work. Should there be more earth at one place of the ditch than another,—which will be the case where there are inequalities in the depth of the ditch,—the surplus earth should either be thrown to the back of the bank, rather than its top be made higher at one place than another, or wheeled away to a spot on which a deficiency of earth is apprehended. Besides giving the bank an irregular appearance, it is not desirable to cover the young thorns too heavily with a superincumbent load of earth, so as entirely to exclude the air and moisture from their roots.

(615.) If going along the ditch twice finish the work, the earth in it will have been in a friable state; but with a hard subsoil the work is not so easily done. The handpick is almost always used to raise the last 4 or 5 inches of the bottom of the ditch, and in accomplishing this the same arrangement of the men, and the kind of work performed by each, will have to be gone through; only that, in this case, the assistant uses the hand for the tramp-pick, and works forward. Whilst this last picking and shovelling are proceeding, the hedger again tramps down the top of the bank before throwing up the last portion of earth. The beating with the back of the shovel is absolutely necessary to produce a skin, as it were, on the face of the bank; because the smoothened surface will resist the action of the frost, and thereby prevent the mouldering down of the earth into the ditch. A covering of clay over the bank, and the poorer it is the better for the purpose, is useful in being extremely unfavourable to the vegetation of small seeds. They will readily take root in fine mould, if that formed the external covering, and their eradication afterwards would create much trouble and cause much waste of earth. The necessity of beating the clay shews the expediency of projecting the plants but a very short way out of the bank, as that process might wound and injure the points of the stems. Indeed, I would prefer their

Fig. 42.

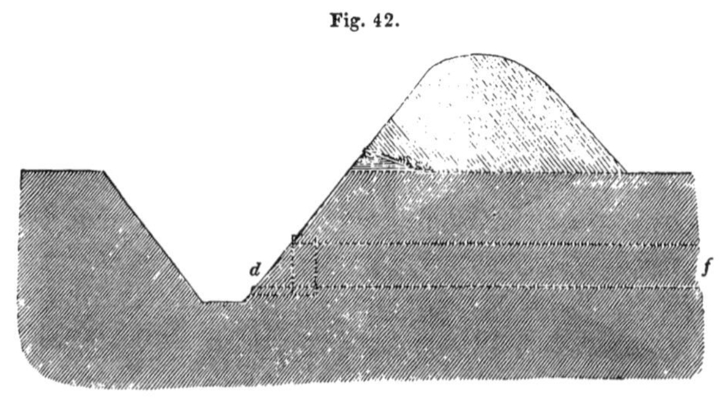

FINISHED HEDGE-BANK.

being nearly buried in the bank, so as the young sprouts had to be relieved from captivity, rather than the points should be injured; but the force of vegetation generally accomplishes their release with ease. Whilst the two assistants are preparing the cord for another stretch, and rutting off both sides of the ditch, the hedger pushes back 2 or 3 inches, less or more, of the crest of the bank with his shovel, in order to make the finished top parallel with the row of thorns, and after he has gently beaten down the front of the top into a rounded form, the process of planting thorns is finished. Fig. 42 gives an idea of a section of the whole work when finished.

(616.) Hitherto the work has proceeded quite easily, no obstacles having presented themselves to frustrate or alter the original design of a level fence; but obstacles are sometimes met with, and means should be used to avert or remove them. The obstacles alluded to generally consist of large stones, unequal ground, and stagnant water. 1. Landfast stones are frequently found in clayey subsoils, many of which can be removed with the foot-pick, but some are so large and massive as to defy removal but through the assistance of gunpowder. If you should meet with any such enormous masses, and much above ground, it would be better to carry the hedge with a sweep past them, than incur the trouble and expense of removing them with the simplest means. If they lie a short way under the thorn-bed, but have plenty of mould over them, they will do no harm to the hedge above them; but should the earth be scanty over them, it will be proper to make the earth deep enough for thorns above them, if that can be easily done, even although an elevation be thereby caused there, above the general line of hedge. 2. With regard to inequality of surface, when the ground dips in the direction of the hedge, and yet when particular undulations in it are so deep and high as to prevent the flow of water over them in the ditch, the higher parts should be cut the deeper, and the hollow parts the less, so as a continuous fall may be obtained for the flow of the water along the bottom of the ditch; but the line of the hedge should be placed on the natural surface of the ground, and thereby partake of its undulations. It is in such cases of compromise that the superabundant earth should be wheeled away from the inordinate depths, to make up for the want of earth in the hollows, and thereby equalize the dimensions of the hedge-bank. Should any hollow be so deep as that the height on either side will not allow the flow of water, a drain should be made from the hollowest part of the bottom of the ditch down the declination of the adjoining field, to some ditch or drain already existing at a lower level. 3. Undulations of the ground cause another inconvenience in hedge-planting, by retaining water in the hollows behind the hedge-bank. Such collections of water, though only of temporary existence, injure much any hedge, but especially a young one. The only effectual way of getting rid of them is fortunately a simple one, which is by constructing a conduit through the hedge-bank from each such hollow to the bottom of the ditch; and as these conduits must be founded upon the subsoil, completely under the black mould, and a little above the bottom of the ditch, they are most conveniently built after the ditch has been entirely dug out; and on this account the thorn-bed cannot be formed across these hollows until after the completion of the ditch and hedge-bank on both sides of them. Some taste and dexterity are required in the hedger to fill up the gaps thus left in the planting of the hedge, and finishing them neatly afterwards. Fig. 43 will give you an idea how to overcome the inconvenience created by these hollows, where *a* is the line of hedge upon the natural surface of the undulating ground, *b* the top of the hedge-bank parallel to the hedge, *c* the bottom of the ditch, exposed

Fig. 43.

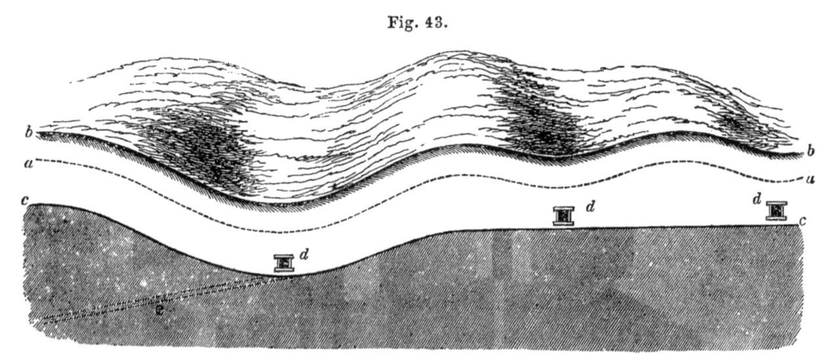

PLAN HOW TO PREVENT WATER LODGING IN HOLLOWS OF FENCES.

to view by the entire removal of the ground on this side of the ditch, and which removal also shews the positions of the conduits *d*, which carry the stagnant water away from behind the hedge-bank through below the hedge in the lowest part of the undulations of the ground, and it also shews the position of the drain *e* through the adjacent ground. It will be observed that the bottom of the ditch *c* is not quite parallel with the dotted line of hedge *a*, but so inclined from the right and left, through the heights and hollows of the ground, as to allow the water to flow in a continuous stream towards the lowest part by the drain *e*. Fig. 42 shews by the dotted lines *d* and *f* a vertical section of the position and form of the conduits formed across and below the hedge-bed. The ground behind the hedge-bank is represented in fig. 43 as declining towards the hedge, thereby giving a fall to the surface water in the same direction. To give such water an outlet, a drain should be formed along the head-ridge 2 or 3 yards behind the hedge-bank, so as to be a little out of the way of the roots of the thorns when they push outwards, and in connection with all the conduits *d*. This drain should have a conduit at bottom such as drain-tiles afford, and be filled above them with broken stones to about 1 foot from the top.

(617.) In ordinary practice, when two lines of hedges meet, the one terminates against the other, or, crossing each other, form a junction of 4 fields by the corners; and where this latter junction happens, should the land be not of much value, or should the particular situation be much exposed to the weather from an obnoxious quarter, it may be advisable to make a clump of planting of a stellar form. It is necessary in the first place, to ascertain what quantity of ground can be conveniently spared for the purpose, and that should be determined by the value of the ground, or its exposed situation. If the land is valuable, a smaller piece must suffice; but if shelter only, and not ornament, is the chief requisite, then a larger piece should be appropriated; but whatever may be the object of forming such a clump of planting, it is not worth while to enclose a smaller space of ground than $\frac{1}{4}$ of an acre, and the largest need not exceed 1 acre in the low country. Supposing the space is determined on, the inclosure of it is gone about in this manner. Ascertain the point where the two lines of hedges would intersect, and

Fig. 44.

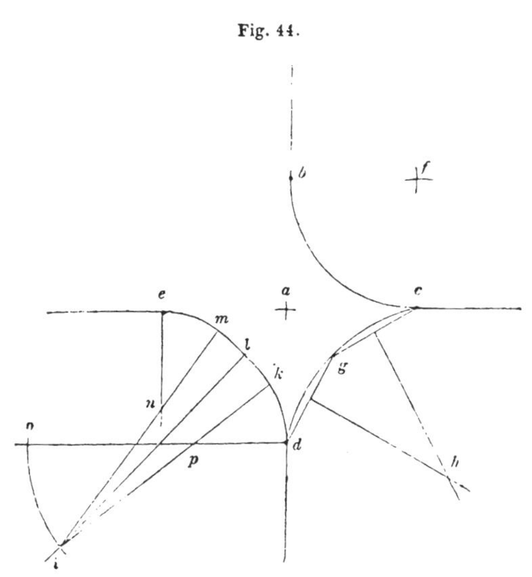

MODES OF DESCRIBING A CURVE IN THE CORNERS OF FIELDS.

fix a pole there, as at *a*, fig. 44; and from it measure equal distances with a chain along each line of fence to the points within which is to be included the space of ground allotted for the planting, as from *a* to *b*, *a* to *c*, *a* to *d*, and *a* to *e*. Then there are 3 ways of describing an arc between any two of these outward points. 1. Taking the distance *a b* from *b* as a centre, sweep an arc, and from *c* as a centre, with the same radius, sweep another arc intersecting that from *b* in *f*; and then from *f* as a centre, still with the same radius, sweep the arc *c b*. In like manner an arc of the same radius may be swept betwixt *c* and *d*, *d* and *e*, and *e* and *b*. This rule gives no pre-determined arch, but it is one which presents a pleasant curve to the eye. 2. Another plan is to fix the height of the segment which determines the point, beyond which the hedge shall not approach towards *a*. This is done by at once fixing the point *g*, which gives 3 points, *d*, *g*, and *c*, by which to find the centre of the circle *c d*. Join *g d*, which bisect, and from the point of bisection raise a perpendicular; also join *g c*, which bisect, and from the point of bisection raise a perpendicular, and where these two perpendiculars intersect at *h* as a centre, sweep the arc *d c*. This rule is founded on the corollary to the 1st problem of the 3d book of Euclid.* A simple rule which practical gardeners employ in drawing one line at right angles to another is this: From the point of bisection, as above, measure 6 feet along the line towards *c* or *g*, from the same point also measure outward 8 feet; from the further end of the 6 feet measure 10 feet, towards the end of the 8 feet, and where these two lines meet, that is the point in a perpendicular direction from the point of bisection, and a line through which, meeting a perpendicular from the other point of bisection, intersect at the centre *h* of the circle *d c*. This rule is directly founded on the celebrated 47th proposition of the 1st book of Euclid. 3. There is still another method of drawing what may be called a compound curve through two given extreme points, and other fixed points between them. The method is this. Let *d* and *e* be the terminations of the straight lines of the fences *d* and *e*, and *l* a point in the intended curve anywhere beyond the straight line between *d* and *e*, and equidistant from *d* and *e*, but within a quadrant of the two lines of fence; then set off any point *i* also equidistant from *d* and *e*, and join *i l*; from any point on the line *i l*, describe an arc of such radius as shall pass through *l*, but will fall anywhere beyond *d* and *e*. Draw *d o* at right angles to the fence *d*, and make *d o* equal to *i l*, then find a point *p* on the line *d o* equidistant from *o* and *i*. Join *i p*, and produce it to *k*, and from *p* as a centre describe the arc *d k*. For, *d o* and *i k* being equal, and *p o*, *p i* being also equal, the remaining *p d* and *p k* must be equal to one another

* See Duncan's Elements of Plane Geometry, p. 57.

and *i p k* being in a straight line, the circle of which *d k* is an arc, will touch the larger circle, of which *k m* is also an arc, according to Euclid, 3d book, 11 prob. In like manner, the arc *e m* can be described by first drawing *e n*, at right angles to the line of fence *e*, and proceed as before. If the lines of fence run at right angles to each other, the arcs *d k* and *e m* will have equal radii. This is perhaps too intricate a mode of drawing such curves for practical purposes, but it is well that your ingenuity be exercised in every possible way, so as you may never be at a loss to apply expedients according to circumstances.

(618.) A very common practice—a much too common one—and recommended by almost every writer on planting hedges, is the leaving a broad scarsement in front of the thorn-bed; and the reason given for adopting the plan is, that it is necessary to supply the young thorns with moisture. It is alleged that the sloping face of the bank conveys away the rain that falls. What although it does? The young thorn does not require to imbibe moisture by the point of its stem but by its

Fig. 45.

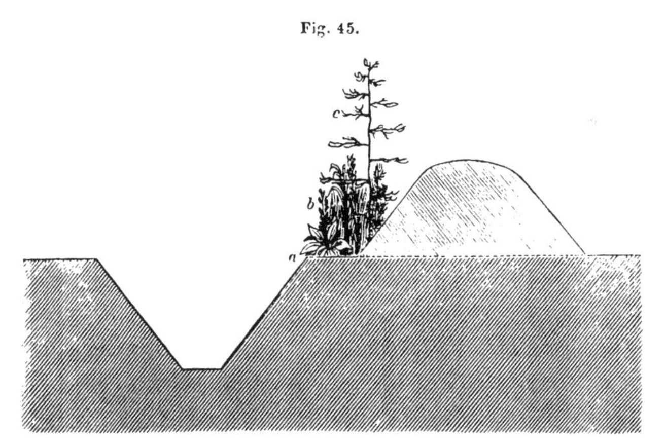

EFFECT OF A HEDGE-BANK WITH SCARSEMENT.

roots, which it can easily do through the mound, as it is loose enough for the admission of rain. But independently of that, it is obvious that a scarsement is so excellent a contrivance for the growth of weeds, that it is impossible to clean a hedge well where there is one. To be sure, earth from the bottom of the ditch may occasionally be thrown upon the scarsement to smother the weeds, but its accumulation there must be limited to the height of the thorn-bed. Besides, weeds can grow as well upon this earth as upon the scarsement; and though they may there be mown down at times, the roots of the perennial ones are quite ready to spring up again in favourable weather. The very figure which a thorn-hedge cuts on a scarsement will at once shew the impolicy of placing it in such a position. Thus, in the first place, in fig. 45, *a* is the scarsement, on which there is nothing to hinder the weeds *b* to grow in great luxuriance, vying in stature and strength with the young plant *c* itself. How true, that there " nothing teems but hateful docks, rough thistles, kicksies, burs, losing both beauty and utility ; and our hedges, defective in their natures, grow to wildness."* How is it possible in such a nursery to " deracinate such savagery ?" In the next place, such a scarsement holds out a strong temptation to travellers to make it a foot-path, so long as the hedge is young, and when it is situated by the side of a public road. And it invites the poor woman's cow, pasturing on the green road-side, to step upon it and crop the tops of the young hedge along with the grassy weeds; and it makes an excellent run for hares, in the moonlight nights, on passing along which they will not fail to nibble at the young quicks. " Fern is a great enemy to young hedge-plants," says Mr Marshall; " it is difficult to be drawn by hand without endangering the plants, and being tough, it is equally difficult to cut it with the hoe, and if cut will presently spring up again ;" and yet " in a soil free from stones and other obstructions of the spade," he says, " the planting with an offset (scarsement) is perhaps, upon the whole, the most eligible practice."† Where can fern obtain a better site for growing upon than a scarsement of a young hedge ? Such are the inconsistencies into which the acutest writers fall when they relinquish the guidance of common sense.

(619.) Where part of a hedge is desired to be carried across a water-course, an arch or large conduit is often made to span it, and its sides are banked up with sods or earth, and a quantity of mould wheeled upon it, to form the thorn-bed. I have seen such structures, but do not approve of them. If the nature of the ground will at all admit of it, it is far better to plant the thorns on the surface of the natural ground, as near as possible to the water-mark, when the water is flooded. The water-channel, which will probably be dry in summer, when the fields are only used for stock, could be fenced with paling, or, what is a much better fence in such a situation, a stone-wall, if stones can be procured at a reasonable distance, with openings left in it to allow the water to pass through in winter. These openings could be filled up in summer with a few thorns, to keep in sheep. This latter plan is a much better one than the other, for I have found that hedge-banks on a stone-building do not retain sufficient nourishment in summer to support even young thorn-plants.

* Shakspeare's Henry V.

† Marshall on Planting, p. 81 and 69.

(620.) If it is desired to plant a thorn-hedge on the top of a sunk-fence, or along the edge of a walk by the side of a shrubbery, or to enclose a shrubbery or a clump of trees in pleasure-ground or lawn, the plants may be assorted and prepared as directed above; but instead of raising a mound, which in such situations would not look well, trench a stripe of ground with the spade, in the intended line of the hedge, at least 3 feet in breadth, pointing in dung and raking in lime in adequate quantities some time before the time for planting. When that time arrives, stretch the cord in the middle of the stripe, guiding the curves with the wooden pins. First, smoothen the surface of the ground under the cord with a clap of the spade, and then notch deeply with it by the side of the cord, drawing the earth toward you. Into this furrow carefully place the roots and fibres of the thorn-plants, with their cut stems leaning against the cord, and thus, keeping the plants in their places with the left hand, fill up the furrow with earth with a trowel in the right hand. Press the plants firmly against the earth with the outside of the foot placed in a line with the stems, and make the surface level with the spade. After the removal of the cord, press the ground with the row of thorns between your feet, and finish off the work with the rake. In planting ornamental hedges, you should always bear in mind, that for whatever purpose a hedge may be wanted, the thorns should always be planted on the natural surface of the ground, for if set in travelled earth, unless it is of considerable bulk and depth, they run the risk of either being stunted in growth, or of altogether dying for want of nourishment.

(621.) In setting poles for straight lines, ordinary accuracy of eye will suffice; but in setting them in curves, where geometrical ones cannot be introduced, considerable taste is required by the planner. Such curves can only be formed by setting up large pins, and judge of their beauty by the eye, so that the sweeps may appear naturally to accommodate themselves to the inequalities of the ground, and form, on the whole, a suitable figure for the purpose they are intended to serve. Curves in fields should always be made conformable to the ploughing of the adjoining land, for if such adaptation is not attended to, land may be lost to tillage in the depth or acuteness of the curves. After the large pins are set to shew the general form of a long curve, or series of long curves, smaller ones should be employed to fill up the segments between the larger, and the cord then stretched by the side of all the pins, and the beautiful sweep of the curve carefully preserved by the small pins with the hooked heads. If a curved ditch is required, the rutting of the breadth of the ditch, as also the making of the thorn-bed, should follow the cord in its curved position; but great care is required to preserve the two sides of a curved ditch parallel; for if the cross-headed wooden rule is not held at right angles to the line of the hedge, at every point where the breadth of the ditch is measured off; that is, if the cross-head is not held as a tangent to each particular curve, the breadth of the ditch will vary considerably in different places, and, of course, the ditch will there present a twist. There is no error into which labourers are so apt to fall, as this: they measure, without thinking of the consequences, at any angle across the ditch; but they should be taught to avoid it, because, if not rectified in time, it will deprive the hedge-bank of essential covering at certain places, on account of the ditch being twisted into broad and narrow portions.

(622.) This appears to me all that is necessary to be said on the *planting* of thorns; but before dismissing the subject of hedges for the present, I must say a few words in deprecation of what are called hedge-row trees; that is, of planting forest-trees in the line of thorns. It is quite impossible, even with the greatest care, to rear thorn-plants, to become a good fence, under the drip of forest-trees. Thorns are very impatient of being overshadowed by taller trees; even trees planted on the top of a mound betwixt double hedges, rob both of moisture at the roots, and direct the drip among the branches of the thorns. "To plant trees in the line of a hedge," says Lord Kames, "or within a few feet of it, ought to be absolutely prohibited as a pernicious practice. It is amazing that people should fall into this error, when they ought to know that there never was a good thorn-hedge with trees in it. And how should it be otherwise? An oak, a beech, or an elm, grows faster than a thorn. When suffered to grow in the midst of a thorn-hedge, it spreads its roots everywhere, and robs the thorns of their nourishment Nor is this all: the tree, overshadowing the thorns, keeps the sun and air from them. At the same time, no tree takes worse with being overshadowed than a thorn."* Hedge-row trees are strongly recommended by all the old writers on agriculture, as being the best means of growing timber for the navy, and giving shelter to fields; and even a recent writer on timber seems to favour the plan of planting the oak in hedge-row, as if that tree could not be sufficiently gnarled for naval purposes, and rendered thick in the bark for the purposes of tanning, in other exposed situations than in thorn-hedges, and where they could do no injury.† Hedge-trees at a distance, no doubt, give a closely fenced appearance to a country, which then looks not unlike an extensive orchard; but they are at best formal, ill-shaped, generally stunted, and often twisted, on account of being acted on by the winds, and are injurious to roads

* Kames' Gentleman Farmer, p. 283.

† Matthew on Naval Timber, p. 359.

and crops near them, though they may yield tough timber. The oak suffers in hedge-rows in all these respects, as well as less valuable wood. It may seem ungracious treatment, after trees have grown some years amongst hedges, to root them out; but they deserve no better fate, because they are intruders, and have truly been designated "*the landlords' thieves.*" If intended for shelter, plantations and clumps are much better adapted for the purpose than single trees, and form far finer objects in the landscape than rows of stunted trees. If thorns are made to fence plantations, they should be planted on the outside of the mound, though facing the north, that the air may have free access to them; and no large forest-tree should be planted near the thorn hedge which fences the plantation; for, independent of overshadowing, thorns dislike being mixed with other plants. It is not unusual to see beech mixed with thorn as a hedge; but beech, anywhere, is no terror to live-stock in fields, and should never enter into a fence on a farm, however appropriate a beech-hedge may be near shrubberies. The sweet briar (*Rosa canina*), too, is frequently mixed with the thorn, and no doubt imparts a delightful perfume to the air after a shower in summer, but it soon kills the thorns in its vicinity. The crab apple (*Pyrus malus*) also overcomes thorns in hedges. Indeed, we have only to view the hedges in the south of England, to be convinced of the noxious effects of intermixing other plants with the thorn.

(623.) The plant commonly used in the hedges of this country is the common hawthorn (*Cratægus oxyacantha*), or sharp-thorned cratægus. The generic name is derived from the Greek κρατος, meaning strength, in reference to the hardness and strength of the wood It is the *aubépine* or *aubépin* of the French; the *hagedorn*, or hedgethorn, of the Germans.

(624.) It belongs to the natural order *Pomaceæ* of Jussieu; of *Rosaceæ*, tribe viii. *Romaceæ*, of De Candolle; and to *Icosandria*, *Di-Pentaginia* of the system of Linnæus. The *generic characters* of *cratægus* are, "calyx, with an arceolate tube, and a 5-cleft limb; petals orbicular, spreading; ovarium 2-5 celled; styles, 2-5 glabrous; pome fleshy, ovate, closed by the calcined teeth, or the thickened disk, containing a bony putamen; thorny shrubs or trees, with angular or toothed leaves, and terminal corymbs, of usually white flowers; bracteas subulate deciduous." The *specific characters* of *oxyacantha* are, "leaves obovate-cuneiform, trifid or pinnatifid, glabrous, and shining; flowers corymbose, monogynous, digynous, and trigynous; calyxes glandless, acute; native of Europe, in thickets, hedges, copses, and in high open fields; plentiful in Britain; flowers white, occasionally pink, sweet-scented; fruit nearly insipid, dark-red, occasionally yellow; its cells as many as the styles."* Height from 15 to 45 feet.

(625.) The common hawthorn is a very variable plant. Mr Loudon enumerates not fewer than 30 varieties. Of these, 7 differ from the species in the general form and mode of growth; 2 in the colour of the flowers; 4 in the de-

* Don's Miller's Gardener's Dictionary, vol. ii. p. 599–600.

velopment in structure of the flowers; 3 in the time of flowering; 5 in the colour of the fruit; 1 in having the fruit woolly; 5 in the form of the leaves; and 3 in the colour of the leaves.*

(626.) Of these varieties, the one I would prefer for field-fencing is, I believe, *digynous*. The colour of the young wood is dark purple; that of the new shoots also dark purple, spotted with minute white specks; and that of the old wood, dark orange-purple. Bark smooth and shining; leaves dark-green and shining on the upper face; spines dark purple, of medium length, fine, and sharp; the stems close together in parallel rods, stiff, and upright. Flowers rather large, and haws dark-red; neither plentiful. The plant is hardy, and will grow in any sort of soil, from clay to gravel, which is not injured by stagnant water. Near stagnant water it becomes covered with lichens and moss; will not thrive under the drip of trees, or in company with other plants. "This plant," says Mr Maclaurin truly, "branching out into innumerable ramifications, and armed in all directions with strong thorns, may be so managed, as, in a state of hedge, to present a barrier impenetrable to any kind of cattle; and not without difficulty to be passed over by such disorderly persons as might wish improperly to intrude upon the rights of others. Fitted by nature to assume a close and compact texture, which it possesses most fully during the expansion of its leaves, but retains, too, in a considerable degree, after these have fallen off, it is not without the advantage of breaking the force of stormy winds, and mitigating the severity of the weather in favour of the vegetable and animal life which it is appointed to enclose. It is so hardy and patient of direction, as easily to admit of being trained in the manner that may be desired; and unless there be some defect here, it will retain, in that state of culture, much of its native elegance and beauty."† "The wood of the hawthorn is very hard and difficult to work. Its colour is white, but with a yellowish tinge; its grain is fine, and it takes a beautiful polish, but it is not much used in the arts, because it is seldom found of sufficient size, and is besides apt to warp. It weighs, when green, 68 lb. 12 oz., and, when dry, 57 lb. 5 oz. per cubic foot. It contracts, by drying $\frac{1}{8}$ of its bulk. It is employed for the handles of hammers, the teeth of mill-wheels, for flails and mallets, and, when heated at the fire, for canes and walking-sticks. The branches are used in England for the heating of ovens; a purpose for which they are very proper, as they give out much heat, and possess the property of burning as readily when green as in their dry state."‡ "The hawthorn is manufactured into clubs for golf-playing."§ Combs were formerly made of the wood, particularly from the root. A decoction of the bark yields a yellow dye, and, with copperas, is used to dye black. "The timber of the hawthorn is often spoiled through inattention after cutting. If it be allowed to lie in the tree it soon heats, and becomes quite *frush* (brittle) and worthless. It therefore ought to be instantly cut up into planks and laid to dry."‖ The haw of the hawthorn is very apt to heat when put in heaps. It is frequently, notwithstanding, sent in large sugar hogsheads, and, of course, so great a proportion

* Loudon's Arboretum et Fruticetum Britannicum, vol. ii. pp. 830-5, a work of extraordinary labour and merit.

† Prize Essays of the Highland and Agricultural Society, vol. iv. p. 256.

‡ Loudon's Arboretum et Fruticetum, vol. ii. p. 337.

§ Cruickshank's Practical Planter, p. 394.

‖ Sang's Nicol's Planters' Calendar, p. 89.

becomes heated, that not above 1 in 20 germinates when sown. It ought to be packed in not larger quantities than bushel-hampers. When sown, it does not germinate until the second spring, and, on that account, nurserymen are in the habit of decomposing the pulp of the haw by mixing them with sandy earth, in flat heaps not exceeding 10 inches in depth, and which are frequently turned, to prevent the haws heating. Game, and many kinds of birds, particularly the thrush tribe, are very fond of the haw, and, on that account, the hawthorn forms an excellent low stunted underwood for the protection of game. It, with holly (*Ilex aquifolium*) and the dog-rose (*Rosa canina*) forms an almost impenetrable barrier against the poacher. Peasants, in many countries, eat the haws; and, in Kamschatka, they ferment them into wine. The hawthorn is a long-lived shrub, and, in some situations, attains to a considerable-sized tree. Thus, at Duddingston, in the neighbourhood of Edinburgh, is one which, in 1836, was 43 feet high, the diameter of its branches 44 feet; at a little above the roots 10½ feet in girth, and at 3 feet from the ground, 9½ feet. In Forfarshire, at Kinnaird Castle, after being 120 years planted, is one 45 feet high, 40 feet in diameter over the branches, and 35 inches across the trunk. It is growing on a sandy loam or clay.

(627.) On account of the beauty and fragrance of its flowers, the hawthorn has been a favoured plant among all nations. "It is said," remarks Mr Phillips, "that the hawthorn-flowers not only regale the spirits by their odour, but that they have the power also of counteracting poison. It has been made the happy emblem of *Hope*, because the young and beautiful Athenian girls brought branches of hawthorn-flowers to decorate their companions and friends on their wedding-day, whilst they carried large boughs of it to the altar. The altar of Hymen was lighted with torches made of the wood of this tree, and it formed also the flambeaux which lighted the nuptial chamber. The Romans had also bedecked themselves with branches of hawthorn when they seized the Sabine women." "In some parts of France, the country-people affirm to you in good faith, that the hawthorn groans and sighs on Good Friday; and, on this superstition, *they* have made it the emblem of *lamentation*. There are others who gravely adorn their hats with a bunch of hawthorn, in the belief that, during a storm, the thunder will not dare to reach them, from respect to their head-dress." "On the first of May, our ancestors never failed decorating with it the Maypole, which was permanently fixed in or near every town and village in the kingdom; and the boldest youth climbed to fix the garland of flowers on the top, whilst others, less courageous, hung festoons and wreaths of flowers through the garland, and twined them round the pole." "This rustic amusement was evidently introduced by the Romans, as we see in it the remains of their ancient games, Floralia, that were instituted in Rome as early as the time of Romulus, and which the Phoceans and Sabines observed in even earlier days."* The hawthorn is the badge of the clan Ogilvy.

(628.) The tradition regarding the famous hawthorn at Glastonbury (*C. precox* a variety of the oxyacantha) is thus recorded: "To the S.W. of the town is Weary-all-hill, an eminence," says Mr Nightingale, "which, as the monkish writers inform us, derived its name from St Joseph (of Arimathea) and his companions resting here when much fatigued in travelling through the country, during their pious mission in England for the purpose of preaching the Christian faith. Here it is recorded that St Joseph fixed his staff in the earth, which

* Phillip's Sylva Florifera, vol. i. p. 261-4.

immediately took root, and ever after put forth its leaves on Christmas day. It had, we are informed, two distinct trunks till the reign of Queen Elizabeth, when one of them was destroyed by a Puritan. The other met the same fate during the great rebellion. The blossoms of this tree were esteemed such great curiosities as to become an object of gain to the merchants of Bristol, who not only disposed of them to the inhabitants of their own city, but exported them to different parts of Europe. The probable truth with regard to this tree is, that it was brought from Palestine by some of the pilgrims, there being a species of thorn which bloooms at Christmas, a native of that country."*

(629.) The ancients were acquainted with the hawthorn as a fence. The Greeks called it pyracantha, or fire thorn. Their method of forming a thorn-hedge is thus related by Diophanes. "If you wish to have a secure hedge, having dug a trench a cubit deep (= 1 foot 6.13 inches), fix stakes in it, and stretch a rope along the trench: but let there be some vetches ground in readiness the day before; and the seed of the bramble, and of the paliarus (a species of thorn), and of the oxyacantha, being all macerated to the consistence of honey, lay the seed of the bramble, and of the paliarus, and of the oxyacantha, on the extended rope; and having besprinkled the place with the stuff, permit it to remain a short time; then lay on the earth that was thrown up out of the trench, and after 28 days it will produce shoots of 4 palms (1 palm = 4 fingers' breadth, or 1 hand), which you are to *transplant* into a trench that is not deeper than 4 palms, and they will grow more than a cubit in two months; these being drawn to a great length, they will keep off thieves. Do this at the vernal equinox."† The Greeks were not in the habit of fencing fields, but only the vineyards and orchards and meadows near their country dwellings. Homer specifies the smallness of the enclosures which were fenced:

> "Four acres was th' allotted space of ground,
> Fenc'd with a green enclosure all around." ‡

The Romans followed precisely the same practice in fencing as the Greeks, for fences around their enclosures of meadows, olive-trees, and vineyards, are only specified, whilst their stock were folded at night by the sound of the horn.§ With regard to the antiquity of fencing with thorns in our own country, it is probable that fields were fenced with thorns before Queen Elizabeth's time, and not so late as the end of the 17th century; as appears from a quotation by Marshall from Fitzherbert, when the latter complained, at the beginning of the 16th century, of landlords enclosing and thereby shutting out their demesnes and meadows from the use of their tenants. || Tusser, who lived in the 16th century, gives these directions for making hedges, which are certainly an improvement on the Greek and Roman methods:—

> "Go plough or delve up, advised with skill,
> The breadth of a ridge, and in length as you will:
> Where speedy quickset for a fence you will draw,
> To sow in the seed of the bramble and haw." ¶

And, from a quotation by Evelyn from Gerard, we would infer that, towards the

* Beauties of England and Wales, vol. xiii. part i. p. 504-5.

† Owen's Geoponika, vol. i. p. 183.

‡ Pope's Homer's Odyssey.

§ Dickson's Husbandry of the Ancients, vol. ii. p. 342.

|| Marshall's Rural Economy of Yorkshire, vol. i. p. 46.

¶ Mavor's Tusser's Five Hundred Points of Good Husbandry, p. 38.

end of the same century, the people of Herefordshire drank no other beverage than cyder, from the apple-trees in the hedgerows, which indicates a ma tured state of the trees, and of course of the hedges in which they stood.* According to Dr Walker, the first hawthorn hedges planted in Scotland were on the road leading to Inchbuckling Brae, in East Lothian, and at Finlarig, at the head of Tay, in Perthshire. They were planted at both places by Cromwell's soldiers.†

(630.) Other plants than the hawthorn have been recommended to be used for fencing fields. No doubt others, such as the black-thorn, the crab-apple, the beech, the elder, and all the forest-trees that bear pruning, might form such a fence as to mark the division of one enclosure from another; but unless the plant so employed is furnished with spines, it will prove a very inefficient fence against the outbreaks of cattle and horses, irrespective of the trespasses of evil-disposed persons. The holly (*Ilex aquifolium*) is the only other that possesses the properties of a good fencing plant. It is durable, firm, bears pruning, is highly defensive, and verdant alike in all seasons, but being very slow of growth, it would require a long time to attain a sufficient height for a fence, and, in the mean time, would incur much expense for its protection. It will, therefore, never become a substitute for the hawthorn for field-fencing, however beautiful a fence it may form near a dwelling-house or shrubbery. The cock's-spur-thorn (*C. crus galli*) and the Virginian thorn (*C. Virginiana*) have been proposed; but neither possesses any properties superior to the common kind. The juniper (*Juniperus communis*) and the whin or furze (*Ulex europæa*) have been recommended. The fitness of the whin I shall consider in the spring season. The tala plant, " a small thorny shrub," a native of South America, has been recommended as a good field-fence,‡ but there is much doubt of its thriving in our climate.

(631.) In Germany, the hornbeam (*Carpinus betulus*) is used as a field-fence. On considering it in this light, Mr Harte says, " No fence of a solid permanent kind pleases me so much as the hornbeam hedges in Westphalia and other parts of North Germany. When the German husbandman erects a fence of this nature, he throws up a parapet of earth, with a ditch on each side, and plants his hornbeam sets, raised from layers, in such a manner as that every two plants may be brought to intersect each other in the form of a St Andrew's cross. In that part where the two plants cross each other, he gently scrapes off the bark, and binds them with straw thwart-wise. Here the two plants consolidate in a sort of indissoluble knot, and push from thence horizontal slanting shoots, which form a sort of living palisado, or cheveau-de-frise; so that such a protection may be called a rural fortification. These hedges being pruned annually and with discretion, will, in a few years, render the fence impenetrable in every part. It is not uncommon in Germany to see the sides of high-roads thus guarded for 10 miles together."§

(632.) In Holland, it seems that nurserymen have *ready-made hedges* for sale. " We have seen," says Dr Neill, " that a Dutch merchant, retiring from business, may purchase fruit-trees which will yield him their produce the very first year: we found that he may also surround his garden and shrubbery with

* Evelyn's Sylva, p. 109, 5th edition, 1729.

† Walker's Essays, p. 53.

‡ Quarterly Journal of Agriculture, vol. ii. p. 408.

§ Harte's Essays on Husbandry, p. 114.

ready-formed hedges! We observed many lines of different evergreen and deciduous shrubs usually employed for this purpose, trained hedge-wise in the nursery; and these, like the fruit-trees, being frequently removed from one spot to another, may, almost without hazard of failure, be transferred to a considerable distance, and replanted."*

(633.) Thorn-plants are generally raised by nurserymen from the haw, but Lord Kames describes an economical method of rearing young plants from cuttings. "As thorns will grow pleasantly from roots," he says, "I have long practised a frugal and expeditious method of raising them from the wounded roots that must be cut off when thorns are to be set in a hedge. These roots, cut into small parts, and put in a bed of fresh earth, will produce plants the next spring, no less vigorous than what are produced from seed; and thus a perpetual succession of plants may be obtained without any more seed."† I have already mentioned that unless the cuttings are buried pretty deep in the earth, they will grow again, and it is of this propensity that his Lordship had taken advantage.

(634.) The positions are various in which thorn-plants may be placed in their bed, on planting a hedge; but there is one position which is best of all for field, and another for ornamental fencing. On this subject Lord Kames inquires, "Instead of laying the thorns fronting the ditch, would it not do better to lay them parallel to the ditch, covering the roots with 3 or 4 inches of the best earth, which would make a hollow between the plants and the sloping bank? This hollow would intercept any drops of rain that fall on the bank to sink gradually among the roots. If this is not a better position for a thorn, it must be of a singular constitution."‡ The fear of want of moisture to the young thorn-plant in an ordinary mound is groundless; for the area of the whole back of the bank, where the earth is left quite loose, is of considerable extent, and capable of absorbing sufficient moisture for the young roots. He apprehends that the face of the bank being beaten down firmly makes it impervious to water; whilst at the same time he recommends it to be made as upright as possible—a position the very best adapted for throwing off the water. He can see no good reason for thorns being laid sloping in the ground, as they might as well be planted like all other plants upright, when he thinks they would sooner become a fence. No doubt, thorns will grow very well in an upright position, and in some parts of the country, as in Yorkshire, they are so planted; but the sloping position is the most convenient for planting them with *hedge and ditch without a scarsement*, and for converting the whole stem into root. He suggests that plants 6 feet high might be planted upright; but I suspect that the transplanting of old thorn-plants is a hopeless task; besides, where are such plants to be obtained in sufficient numbers to form entire fences? He, as well as most others, recommend the plants to project as much as 1 inch from the face of the bank; but as it is necessary to smoothen the face of the bank, to prevent frost mouldering down earth into the ditch, and to plaster the poorest part of the subsoil upon it, to prevent the growth of weeds; the projecting of the plants so much is on other accounts a bad plan, as they are apt to be wounded by the rolling down of the earth and small stones, while working up and smoothing the face of the bank; and what is still worse, as the stems grow tall, they exert a greater lever power on a projecting than on an imbedded root. Hence,

* Neill's Journal of a Horticultural Tour, p. 204.

† Kames Gentleman Farmer, p. 273. ‡ Ibid, p. 277.

on examining a young thorn-hedge in autumn, when the stems are strong, and the branches long and leafy, it will be observed, that, where the plants project, the wind has caused the root to make a sort of dibbled hole around it; whereas all those which have been left even with the face of the bank, or a little below it, and been afterwards relieved from their fettered state by the force of vegetation, or the hand of care, remain quite firmly imbedded in the earth. On this account, I would much rather recommend the points of the stems being out of sight altogether, than projecting any distance from the bank. Mr Marshall mentions a method practised in Yorkshire of burying even upright plants in the soil, the shoots from which he affirms come up uniformly vigorous.

(635.) There is a very good plan of raising double hedges in Yorkshire, and it is this. A ditch is lined off, and its mould is thrown into the shape of a rounded ridglet along one of its sides. The cord is then stretched along the mound, 3 or 4 inches from the ditch, and a furrow for the thorns is chopped out with the spade in front of the cord towards the ditch. The thorns are then set nearly upright in the furrow, in the manner described in paragraph (620). A parallel line of thorns is planted in the same manner, at 3 or 4 feet apart from the first and as much farther from the ditch. Some of the subsoil from the bottom of the ditch, which is shallow, is thrown between the rows of thorns, and if it is either clayey or gravelly, weeds will not easily take root in it for some time. The advantages of this system are, that a very complete fence is formed when the thorns grow up; that there is no likelihood of gaps occurring opposite the same place in both hedges; and that when one hedge is cut down, the other continues a good fence until it grows up again. These are indubitable advantages; though the single line affords them all nearly to the same degree, with a saving of ground, but a dead fence will not be required when one of the hedges is cut down. Upon the whole, the plan is a much better one than that of the double hedges usually practised in Berwickshire and Roxburghshire, which have generally a ditch on each side, and a row of trees between the hedges. Were such double hedges confined to the boundaries of farms, they would not be so objectionable, as a single hedge is rather inconvenient betwixt two farms, because the proper time for cutting it down may not answer the cropping of both farms; but the Yorkshire plan of double hedges is a preferable one for a march fence, inasmuch as it occupies less room, and the roots of the thorns are not confined in a bank betwixt two open ditches, nor interfered with in their growth by the larger roots of trees.

(636.) Where turf is plentiful, it may be employed in this way to fence at once one side of a hedge. Let *a*, fig. 46, be the turf wall 4 feet high, 18 inches broad at the base, and 1 foot at the top, coped with a large turf; *b* the stuff thrown out of the ditch *c*, and inclined upwards towards the top of the wall. For keeping in Cheviot or Black-faced sheep, or cattle, a stake and single rail of paling *d*, will be required on the top, but not for Leicester sheep. In Norfolk, a high bank is thrown up, without a wall, from 6 to 7 feet in height from the bottom of the ditch, and the thorn-plants are set into it as at *b*, fig. 46, among the crude earth taken out of the bottom of the ditch. As might be expected in such a plan, it is no uncommon sight in that county to see the face of the bank, with the quicks in it, washed down by beating rains; and as the roots enlarge and the bank moulders down, the young plants hang their heads downwards upon the face of the bank. The reason assigned for the adoption of this objectionable practice is, that there is no wood in that county to form temporary fences until the thorns shall grow, and that being set upon the top of a steep bank, they are out of the reach of cattle at the bottom of the ditch. Even with a wall like *a* fig. 46, thorns at *b* will never grow so vigorously as when

Fig. 46.

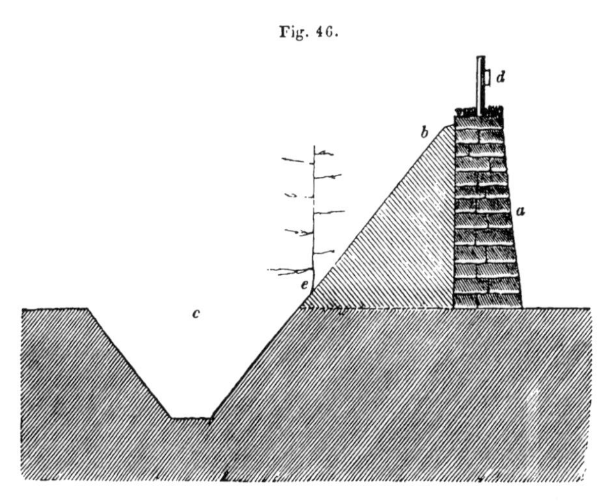

TURF FENCE TO A THORN-HEDGE.

placed at *e*; and in dry weather, they are soon stinted of moisture. Where flat stones are plentiful, a good *sheltering* fence may be formed by enclosing a space of a few feet in breadth between two walls, and on filling it with earth, an upright hedge may be planted in it, where it will thrive very well. Such fences may be seen in Devonshire, where flat stones from the primitive clay-slate formations are obtained in abundance. In connection with the mode of fencing considered in this paragraph is one recommended of building a 2½ feet wall *on the top of the bank behind the hedge* which had been thrown out of the ditch, and to make its coping of turf. There are objections to this plan; in the first place, a turf coping on a stone wall never grows well, and in consequence, turf soon becomes *there* an eyesore. In the next place, a wall founded on earth that has been thrown out of the bottom of the ditch, will not remain even but a very short time, on account of the unequal subsidence of the earth, and the consequent sinking of the stones. A 3 feet stone wall, founded upon the hard ground, on the site of the turf-wall *a* in fig. 46, with a single railed paling raised behind it, until the hedge get up, would make a far better fence both for sheep and cattle. Another mode of planting a thorn-hedge is to build a stone wall as at *a* fig. 46, in which are left holes, about the position where the letter *a* is situate in the figure, through which the thorns grow which have been planted in the bank of earth *b*. This is also an objectionable mode, inasmuch as the plants, whose roots are ramifying in the bank *b*, have no support for that portion of the stem which has to grow in a horizontal direction through the holes of the wall and the consequence is that the leverage of the part of the stem which grows upright in the face of the wall is apt to shake the roots, and should the horizontal portion of the stem rest for support upon the wall within the hole, its weight and motion soon bring down the wall, if it is constructed of dry stones, or shatter it, if built with mortar. Thorns have been recommended to be planted at the bottom of a wall, as of *a* fig. 46, with no bank such as *b* near it, but having the ditch *c* before it as a fence to the hedge, with a paling on its lip. If a *stone* wall is built in such a situation, there seems no use at all of the hedge as a fence, and if a *turf* one, then surely thorns will thrive much better with a bank of earth behind them, such as *b*, than at the bottom of a turf wall.

(637.) On considering the condition of this country and the state in which the fences are usually kept, it must be admitted that the plan of fencing the land is generally good; but, in regard to the state of the fences, it is not so well as might be. 1. With regard to the extent of fencing, the low country is sufficiently, and, in many places, too densely fenced, too much ground being occupied, to the detriment of the crops growing within them. A slight glance at the small enclosures of England will convince you of this, though the smallest enclosures are perhaps mostly occupied by meadows of permanent grass. In the north of Ireland, too, the enclosures are too small, though there the universal practice of small holdings better justify the prevalence of small enclosures. 2. The upland districts, on the other hand, are very deficient of enclosures throughout the kingdom. Most of the hill-farms have even no march-fences, the marches being marked out by natural objects, such as the water-shed point of a hill, the course of a rivulet, a ravine, or even cairns of stones. The great desideratum, however, in such farms is shelter, which cannot be afforded by any single fence in such situations. The shelter of upland districts can hardly be accomplished but on a scale that would render it of national importance; for the attempt on a comparatively small property would confer as much benefit on the property on each side of it as on itself, and the proprietor of a large estate would not incur the great expense of sheltering the whole of it. It would be desirable were proprietors of upland districts to have a mutual understanding on this subject, because plans could then be adopted which would have the effect of sheltering a great extent of country at comparatively insignificant cost. Were extensive surveys taken of the lie of alpine country, by engineers well acquainted with the prevailing winds there, and competent to suggest line fences, which would be sure to check their course, much good might be derived by live-stock; and no class of engineers could take so comprehensive a view of the subject as those engaged in the trigonometrical survey of the country.* 3. When the thorn-fences of the country are examined, we shall not find them always in a creditable state. One is allowed to grow in a rambling state, carrying a heavy head and exposing bare stems near the ground; another is far advanced in old age, and about to decay for ever; a third is entirely covered with lichens and mosses; a fourth is full of gaps, which are filled up with slabs, paling, or loose stones; a fifth is occasionally overflown with water, which gets leave to pass off of its own accord, and which it can seldom do in winter before another flood overtakes it; a sixth is completely overgrown with every weed that gets leave to shed its seeds for miles around; a seventh is almost overcome with wild plants, which have usurped the place of the thorns; such as the whin, the sloe, the crab-apple, the elder, the hazel, the mountain-ash, the holly, besides saplings and seedlings of forest trees; an eighth is so hacked and hewed with the hatchet that a greater part is a long time of recovering the butchery, whilst

* On the utility of shelter on the great scale, see Quarterly Journal of Agriculture, vol. x. p. 199—vol. xi. p. 320—and vol. xii. pp. 37 and 231.

others have died in consequence of the rain descending the split stems and rotting the roots; a ninth is so overlaid with plashing, that the already half-amputated stems die in a short time; a tenth is suspended by the principal root, after the earth has been washed away from it into the ditch; an eleventh has been cut over too high up, where it has put out innumerable twigs, whilst the stems below are quite bare; and the twelfth, the round dozen, has been so shaken at the roots, when left exposed for want of water-tabling, in consequence of the wind acting on them, by the leverage of its high stems, that after it has been cut down it dies for want of power to push out new stems. Such are the indignities to which thorn-hedges are subjected.

(638.) In conclusion on this part of the subject of hedges, no thorn-hedge ought to be switched or cut over in winter, for reasons that will be given in spring.

---

25. OF THE PLOUGH.

"Howsoever any plough be made or fashioned, so it be well tempered, it may the better be suffered."

FITZHERBERT.

(639.) The plough serves the same purpose to the farmer as the spade to the gardener, both being used to *turn over* the soil; and the object of doing this is, that this form of operation is the only means known of obtaining such a command over the soil as to render it friable and enclose manure within it, so that the seeds sown into it may grow into a crop of the greatest perfection.

(640.) The *spade* is an implement so simple in construction, that there seems but one way of using it, whatever peculiarity of form it may receive, namely, that of pushing its mouth or blade into the ground with the foot, lifting up as much earth with it as it can carry, and then inverting it so completely as to put the upper part of the earth undermost. This operation, called *digging*, may be done in the most perfect manner; and any attempt at improving it, in so far as its uniformly favourable results are concerned, seems unnecessary. Hitherto it has only been used by the hand, no means having yet been devised to apply greater power than human strength to wield it. It is thus an instrument which is entirely under man's *personal* controul.

(641.) The effect attempted to be produced on the soil by the *plough* is an exact imitation of the work of the spade. From the circumstance, however, of the plough being too large and heavy an implement to be wielded by the hand, it is not so entirely under man's controul as the spade. To wield it as it should be, he is obliged to call in the aid of horses, which, though not capable of wielding it personally, as man does the spade, can, nevertheless, through the means of appropriate appliances, such as harness, do so pretty effectually. It is thus not so much man himself as the horses which he employs that turn over the ground with the plough, they, in a great measure, becoming his substitutes in performing that operation; and they are so far his superiors, that they can turn over a greater quantity of soil with the plough in a given time than he can with the spade. Man, however, has this advantage over horses in turning over the soil, that he can do it well with a very simple instrument, the spade; whereas horses require an instrument of more complex structure—the plough—to perform the same sort of work not so well; and the reason is this, that although the spade is really a very simple instrument, the act of digging with it is not a simple operation, but requires every muscle of the body to be put into action, so that any machine that can imitate work that has called into requisition all the muscles of the body, must have a complex structure. This would be the case, even were such a machine always fixed to the same spot, and, for such a purpose, there is little difficulty in practical mechanics in imitating the work of man's hands, by complicated machinery; but it is not so simple a problem in practical mechanics, as it at first sight may appear, to construct a light, strong, durable, convenient instrument, which is easily moved about, and which, at the same time, though complex in its structure, operates by a simple action; and yet the modern plough is an instrument possessing all these properties in an eminent degree.

(642.) The common plough used in Scotland is made either wholly of iron, or partly of wood and partly of iron. Until a few years ago it was universally made both of wood and iron, but now it is generally made entirely of iron. A wooden plough seems a clumsier instrument than an iron one, though it is somewhat lighter. The plough is now made wholly of iron, partly from the circumstance of its withstanding the vicissitudes of weather better than wood; and, however old, iron is always worth something; and partly because good ash timber, of which ploughs were usually made, is now become so scarce in many parts of the country, that it fetches the large price of 3s. per cubic foot; whereas iron is now becoming more abundant and cheap (204.), being no more than L.14 per ton for common cast goods, and from L.10 to L.18 per ton for malleable iron. A wooden plough with iron mountings usually weighs 13 stones imperial, and an iron one for the same work 15 stones. The cost of a wooden one is L.3, 16s., capable of being serviceable, with re pairs, for the currency of a lease of 19 years; that of an iron one L.4, 4s., which will last a lifetime, or at least many years. Some farmers, however, still prefer the wooden one, alleging that it goes more steadily than the iron. Whatever of prejudice there may be in this predilection for the wooden plough, it must be owned that the iron one executes its work in a satisfactory manner. There is, I believe, no great difference of economy in the use of the two kinds of ploughs.

(643.) The plough, as it is now made, consists of a number of parts, which are particularly described below at (667), fig. 48, and to which you should immediately refer, in order to become acquainted with them. How well soever these different parts may be put together, if they are not all *tempered*, as it is termed, to one another, that is, if any part has more to do than its own share of the work, the entire implement will go unsteadily. It can be easily ascertained whether a plough goes steadily or not, and the fact is thus practically ascertained; and its *rationale* will be found below.

(644.) On taking hold of a plough by the handles with both hands, while the horses are drawing it through the land, if it have a constant tendency to go deeper into the soil than the depth of the furrow-slice previously determined on, it is then not going steadily. The remedy for this error is twofold, namely, either to press harder upon the stilts with the hands, and, by their power as levers, bring the sock nearer the surface of the ground, and this is called "*steeping*;" or to effect the same thing in another way, is to put the draught-bolt of the bridle a little nearer the ground, and this is called giving the plough "*less earth.*" The pressure upon the handles or stilts should first be tried, as being the most ready remedy at your command; but should it eventually fail of effecting the purpose, or the holding the stilts so be too severe upon your arms, the draught bolt should be lowered as much as required. But should both these attempts at amendment fail, then there must be some error in another part of the plough. On examining the sock, or share, its point may possibly be found to dip too much below the line of the sole, which will produce in it a tendency to go deeper than it should. This error in the sock can only be rectified at the smithy.

(645.) Again, the plough may have an opposite tendency, that is, a tendency to come out of the ground. This tendency cannot well be counteracted by the opposite method of supporting the stilts upwards with the arms, because in this condition of body you cannot walk steadily, having no support for yourself, but rather affording support to the plough. It is for this reason, that a very short man can scarcely hold a plough steady enough at any time; and hence such a man does not make a desirable ploughman. The draught-bolt should, in the first instance, be placed farther from the ground, and in so doing, the plough is said to get "*more earth.*" Should this alteration of the point of draught not effect the purpose, the point of the sock will probably be found to rise above the line of the sole, and must therefore be brought down to its proper level and position by the smith (699.)

(646.) You may find it difficult to make the plough turn over a furrow-slice of the breadth you desire. This tendency is obviated by moving the draught-bolt a little to the right; but in case the tendency arise from some casual circumstance under ground, such as collision against a small stone, or a piece of unusually hard ground, it may be overcome by leaning the plough a little over to the right, until the obstruction is passed. These expedients are said to give the plough "*more land.*"

(647.) The tendency of the plough, however, may be quite the opposite from this,—it may incline to take a slice broader than you want; in which case, for permanent work, the draught-bolt should be put a little farther to the left, and for a temporary purpose the plough may be leaned a little over to the left, and which are said to give the plough "*less land.*"

(648.) These are the ordinary instances of unsteadiness in the *going* of ploughs; and though they have been narrated singly, two of them may combine to produce the same result, such as the tendency to go deeper or come out with that of a narrower or broader furrow-slice. The remedy should first be tried to correct the most obvious of the errors; but both remedies may be tried at the same time, if you apprehend a compound error.

(649.) Some ploughmen habitually make the plough lean a little over to the left, thus giving it in effect less land than it would have, were it made to move upon the flat of the sole; and to overcome the consequent tendency of the plough to make a narrower furrow-slice than the proper breadth, they move the draught-bolt a little to the right. The ploughing with a considerable lean to the *left* is a bad custom, because it makes the lowest side of the furrow-slice, when turned over, thinner than the upper side, which is exposed to view, thereby deluding you into the belief that the land has all been ploughed of equal depth; and it causes the horses to bear a lighter draught than those which have turned over as much land in the same time, with a more equal and therefore deeper furrow-slice. Old ploughmen, becoming infirm, are very apt to practise this deceptive mode of ploughing. The plough should always move flat upon its sole, and turn over a rectangular furrow-slice; but there are certain exceptions to this rule, depending on the peculiar construction of parts of certain forms of ploughs, which will be pointed out to you afterwards.

(650.) None assume the habit of leaning the plough over to the *right*, because it is not so easy to hold it in that position as when it moves upon the sole along the land-side.

(651) Other ploughmen, especially tall men, practise the habit of constantly leaning hard upon the stilts, or of steeping; and as this practice has the tendency to lift up the fore point of the plough out of the ground, they are obliged, to keep it in the ground, to put the draught-bolt farther from the ground than it should be. A little leaning of the hands upon the stilts is requisite at all times, in order to retain a firm hold of them, and thereby have a proper guidance of the plough.

(652.) A *good* ploughman will use none of these expedients to make his plough go steadily, nor will he fall into any of these reprehensible habits. He will temper the irons, so as there shall be no tendency in the plough to go too deep or too shallow into the ground, or make too wide or too narrow a furrow-slice, or cause less or more draught to the horses, or less or more trouble to himself, than the nature of the work requires to be performed in the most proper manner. If he have a knowledge of the implement he works with—I mean, a good practical knowledge of it, for a knowledge of its principles is not requisite for his purpose,—he will temper all the parts, so as to work the plough with great ease to himself, and, at the same time, have plenty of leisure to guide his horses aright, and execute his work in a creditable manner. I have known such ploughmen, and they invariably executed their work in a masterly way; but I never yet saw a ploughman execute his work well, who had not acquired the art of tempering the irons of his plough. Until he learns this art, the best made plough will be comparatively worthless in his hands.

(653.) In the attempt to temper the irons, many ploughmen adopt a position of the coulter which increases the draught of the plough. When the point of the coulter is put forward in a line with the point of the sock, but a good deal asunder, to the left or land side, in light land that contains small stones, a stone is very apt to be caught between the points of the coulter and sock, and which will throw the plough out of the ground. This catastrophe is of no great consequence when it occurs on ploughing land preparatory to another ploughing; but it tears the ground on ploughing lea, which must be rectified instantly; and in doing it, there is loss of time in backing the horses to the place where the plough was thrown out. To avoid such an accident *on such land*, the point of the coulter should be put immediately above, and almost close upon, that of the sock; and this is the best temper of those irons, in those circumstances, for lea-ploughing. In smooth soils—that is, free of small stones—the relation of the coulter and sock to each other is not of much importance in regard to steadiness; but it is the best practice to cut the soil clean at all times, and the practicability of this should be suited to its nature.

(654.) The *state of the irons* themselves has a material effect on the temper of the plough. If the cutting edge of the coulter, and the point and cutting edge of the sock, are laid with steel, the irons will cut clean, and go long in smooth soil. This is an economical mode of treating plough-irons destined to work in clay-soils. But in gravelly and all sharp soils, the irons wear down so quickly, that farmers prefer irons of cold iron, and have them laid anew every day, rather than incur the expense of laying them with steel, which perhaps would not endure work much longer in such soil than iron in its ordinary state. Irons are now seldom if ever steeled; but whether they are steeled or not, they are always in the best state when sharp, and of the proper lengths.

(655.) An imperfect state of the mould-board is another interruption to a perfect temper of the plough. When new and rough, it accumulates the loose soil upon it, whose pressure against the turning furrow-slice, causes the plough to deviate from its right course. On the other hand, when the mould-board is worn away much below, it is apt to leave too much of the crumbled soil in the bottom of the furrows, especially in ploughing loose soils. Broken side-plates, or so worn into holes that the earth is easily pressed through them into the bosom of the plough, also cause rough and unequal work; and more or less earth in the bosom affects the balance of the plough, both in its temper and draught. These remarks are made upon the supposition that all ploughs are equally well made, and may, therefore, be tempered to work in a satisfactory manner; but it is well known that ploughs sometimes get into the possession of farmers, radically so ill constructed, that the best tempering the irons are capable of receiving, will never make them do good work.

(656.) When all the particulars which ploughmen have to attend to in executing their work,—in having their plough-irons in a proper state of repair, in tempering them according to the kind of ploughing to be executed, in guiding their horses, and in ploughing the land in a methodical way—when all these particulars are considered, it ceases to surprise that so few ploughmen should be first-rate workmen. Good ploughmanship requires greater powers of observation than most young ploughmen possess, and greater judgment than most will take time to exercise, in order to become familiarized with all these particulars, and to use them all to the best advantage. To be so accomplished, implies the possession of talent of no mean order. The ship has been aptly compared to the plough, and the phrase "ploughing the deep," is as familiar to us islanders, as ploughing the land: to be able to put the ship in "proper trim," is the perfection aimed at by every seaman, so in like manner, to "temper a plough" is the great aim of the good ploughman; and to be able to do it with judgment, to guide horses with discretion, and to execute ploughing correctly, imply a discrimination akin to sailing a ship.

(657.) [The present age is perhaps the most remarkable that time has produced, for the perfection of almost every kind of machine or tool required in the various departments of art and of manufactures. In that most important of all arts—the production of the raw material of human food—something like a corresponding progress has been effected in its machinery and tools, though certainly not to the same degree of perfection as those employed in most of our manufactures, whether they be in animal, vegetable, metallic, or mineral productions. Various causes exist to prevent, or at least retard, an equal degree of perfection being arrived at in agricultural machinery, amongst which may be noticed one pervading circumstance, that affects, more or less, almost every machine or implement employed. This circumstance is, that all the important operations of the farm are performed by *seasons* occupying comparatively short periods of time, and should the artisan be endeavouring to produce any new or important machine, he can only make trial of it in the proper season. The imperfection of human perception is too well known, to leave us in surprise at the first attempt of any improvement turning out more or less a failure. The artisan, therefore, will in all probability find that his project requires amendment; and before that can be effected, the season is past in which a second trial could be made, and, consequently, must lie over for a year, in the course of which many circumstances may occur to cause its being forgotten or laid aside. Impediments of this kind do not occur to the inventor or improver of manufacturing machinery, where constant daily opportunities are at hand to test the successive steps of his invention. One other general cause, and of another kind, exists, to supersede the necessity, or even the propriety, of employing machinery of such high and delicate finish as we see in the machines of all in-door manufactures. This is the irregularity of the media on which agricultural machinery is employed, and the numerous changes produced on these media—the soils and produce—by vicissitudes of weather and other causes, which not only affect the operation, but also the existence of many of these machines. From this cause, with its train of incidents, it may be inferred that agricultural machinery and tools must of necessity be of simple construction, which embrace nothing but the essentials of usefulness; that they have sufficient strength for their intended purpose, and free of any undue weight; that there should be no redundancy nor misapplication of materials; that all materials employed should be of the best quality, and the workmanship plain and sound—these properties, it must be admitted, are of greater importance to agricultural machinery in general, than the minute delicacy of construction and finish observable in many of those almost intellectual tools employed in some of the other arts and manufactures.

(658.) Although, therefore, agricultural machines in general do not require a high mechanical finish, yet there are amongst them those which are based on principles implying a knowledge and application of science, as well as mechanical skill in their construction; and in this class is to be ranked the plough, which in one word, is the most important of all agricultural machines.

(659.) To the *plough*, then, our attention is first to be directed, not only as standing at the head of all its fellows in the ranks of the machinery of the farm, but as being the first implement to which the attention of the farmer is called, in the commencement of this the Winter season.

(660.) Before entering upon the details of the implement as it now appears, it will be interesting to look back for a moment into its history. With the earliest stages of human industry, the tillage of the ground in some shape must be considered as coeval; and in these early attempts, some implement analogous to a plough must have been resorted to. In all ancient figures and descriptions of that implement, its extreme simplicity is to be remarked; and this is but a natural result; but with the progress of human intellect, is to be also observed deviations from the original simplicity, and an increase in the number of its parts, with a corresponding complexity in its structure. The Roman ploughs, imperfectly as they are described by different Roman authors, is an example of this. And as an example of apparently very remote origin, the *caschrom*, or plough used even at this day in some portions of the Outer Hebrides

Fig. 47.

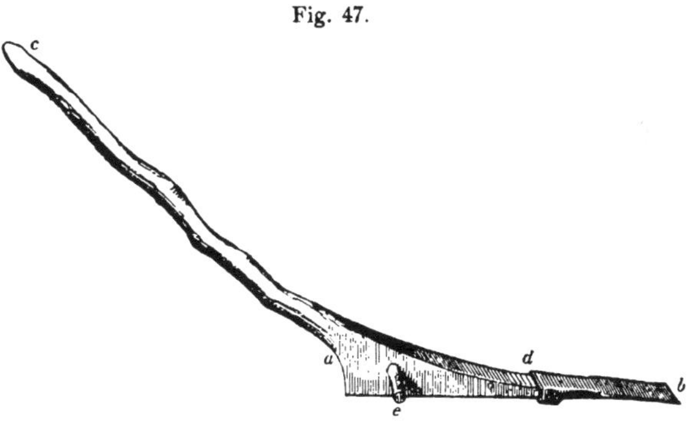

THE CASCHROM.

and in Skye, forms a very curious and interesting antiquarian relic of the ancient Celtic habits. It is formed, as in fig. 47, of one piece of wood, selected from its possessing the natural bend at *a*, that admits of the head *a b* assuming a nearly horizontal position, when the handle *c* is laid upon the shoulder of the person who wields the implement. A simple wedge-shaped share *b d* is fitted to the fore part of the sole. A wooden peg *e* is inserted in the side of the heel at *e*, which completes the implement. On this last member the foot of the operator is applied, to push the instrument into the ground. It is of course worked by the hand alone, and makes simply a rut in the ground. Yet even in this rude implement are to be traced the rudiments of a plough.

(661.) As the cultivation of the soil became more and more an object of industry, corresponding improvements would naturally follow in the implements by which such operations were performed. But in Britain, previous to the beginning of the last century, the plough appears to have continued in a very uncouth state. About that period, agriculture seems to have become more an object of improvement. Draining began to be studied, and its effects appreciated. The amelioration of the soil produced by draining would soon call for better modes of dressing such improved soils; hence, still further improvements in the plough would come into request. In accordance with this, we find the introduction of an improved plough into the northern counties of England, under the name of the Dutch, or Rotherham plough. This appears to be the foundation of all the modern improvements, and from the circumstance of engineers and mechanics having been brought from Holland to conduct the draining of the English fens, there is good reason to conclude that the Rotherham plough was originally an importation from Holland, in a similar manner as the barley-mill was, at a later period, borrowed from that country. About the middle of the past century, the Rotherham plough appears to have been partially introduced into Scotland; but until Mr James Small took up the subject, and, by his judicious improvements, gave a decided character to the plough, little or no progress had been made with it.

(662.) Small appears to have been the first who gave to the mould-board and the share a *form* that could be partially imitated by others, whereby, following his instructions, mould-boards might be multiplied, each possessing the due form which he had directed to be given to them. It is to be observed, that when Small first taught the method of construction, mould-boards were really *boards* of wood, and, for their defence, were covered with plates of iron. The method of construction being not very clearly defined, and mould-boards being necessarily constructed by many different hands, the improved system, it may be easily conceived, must have been liable to failure in practice. It was, therefore, one of those happy coincidences which now and then occur for the benefit of mankind, that the founding of cast iron was then beginning to become general. The fortunate circumstance was seized. Mould-boards, together with the head or sheath, and the sole and land-side plates, were made of cast-iron; and a model or pattern of these parts having been once formed, any number of duplicates could be obtained, each possessing every quality, in point of form, as perfectly as the original model. The plough, thus in a great measure placed beyond the power of uninformed mechanics to maltreat, came rapidly and deservedly into public esteem, under the name of Small's plough. Though originally produced in Berwickshire, the plough that seems to retain the principal feature of Small's improvements—the mould-board—is now found chiefly in East-Lothian, and, as will appear, differs very sensibly from that now generally used in Berwickshire.

(663.) Other writers, about the same period, published methods for constructing a mould-board on just principles. Amongst these, the method proposed by Bailey of Chillingham may be mentioned as approaching very near to the true theoretical form. Others less perfect have been proposed, which it is not necessary at present to notice; while several have published general descriptions of their construction of the plough, but have withheld the principles on which their mould-boards are formed.

(664.) While these improvements of the past century were going on, the plough was universally constructed with *wooden framing*; but about the beginning of the present century (the precise year cannot now be well defined), malleable iron began to be employed in their fabrication. The application of this material in the construction of ploughs came with so much propriety, that it is now, in Scotland, almost universal. It has many advantages; but the most prominent are its great durability under any exposure, and its better adaptation to withstand the shocks to which the implement is frequently liable in the course of working. In a national point of view, it is also deserving of the most extended application, being a produce for which Britain stands unrivalled. This period also was productive of an innovation on the form of mould-board and share which had been established by Small. The mould-boards hitherto referred to came under the denomination of concave, or more properly straight-lined; when Mr Wilkie, Uddingstone, near Glasgow, introduced his new form with convex lines, to be afterwards more particularly noticed, and which has been adopted in various districts in Scotland, to the exclusion of the concave form.

(665.) At a still later period, a form of plough was brought forward by Mr Cunningham, Harlaw, near Edinburgh, a practical farmer, in which are combined the properties of Wilkie's, with very slight deviation of form from that of Small's plough—the principal difference being in the form of the share.

(666.) Having, in this short sketch of the progress of the plough, brought it to the point when it has diverged into three varieties, each of which is held in equal estimation in the respective districts in which it is used, it is a remarkable circumstance that each holds its sway in its peculiar locality, to the almost entire exclusion of its compeers. The two first have undergone numerous slight changes, forming sub-varieties, but retaining the respective leading features of the concave and convex mould-boards; and as they have each spread (especially the first) over a wide extent of country, I purpose to distinguish them by the county in which they are chiefly employed. Thus, the Small's plough shall be denominated the East-Lothian, and Wilkie's the Lanarkshire, plough. The third variety is more limited in its range of application, being almost exclusively confined to Mid-Lothian, and the borders of those counties adjoining to it, throughout which it is known by the name of the Currie plough, but which it is proposed to distinguish here by the name of the Mid-Lothian.

(667.) Before entering upon the detailed description, it will be useful to the agricultural student that a nomenclature be given of the various parts of the plough. Thus, fig. 48, which is a view of a plough in perspective, presents that

Fig. 48.

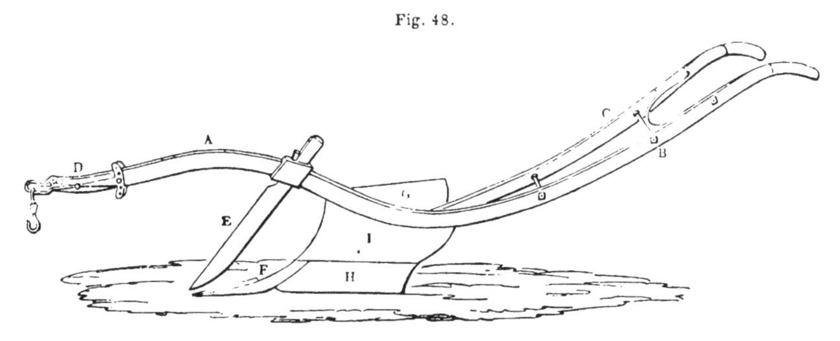

A VIEW OF THE LAND-SIDE OF A PLOUGH.

which ploughmen and agricultural mechanics denominate the *land-side*, so called because when in work it is always (except in the case of turn-wrest or right-and-left ploughs), in contact with the firm or unploughed land. The opposite or right side of the plough, being that which turns over the furrow slice cut from the firm land, is called the *furrow-side*. That member of the plough to which the animals of draught are yoked, marked A in the figure, is the *beam*. Those parts by which the ploughman holds and guides the implement are called the *stilts* or *handles*, B being the *great stilt* or *left handle*, and C the *little stilt* or *right handle;* D is the *muzzle* or *bridle* by which the horses are attached to the beam; E the *coulter*, is a cutting instrument that severs the slice from the firm land, and F the *sock* or *share* which cuts the slice below from the subsoil; G is called the *wrest* or *mould-board.* It is probable that the term wrest applied formerly to only a particular portion of the mould-board—the lower portion in the more ancient plough—which was supposed to wrest or turn aside the slice after being cut by the share; thus we find in the Kent turn-wrest plough that the wrest is a simple straight bar of wood. The mould-board, in the improved implement, receives the slice from the share, turns it gradually over, and deposites it continuously at the proper angle. H is the *sole shoe* on which the plough has its principal support, and on which it moves, and I is the *land-side plate*, only serving to complete the sheathing of the land-side, presenting a uniform smooth surface to the firm land, and preventing the crumbled earth from falling within the body of the plough. These last parts cover the body-frame from view, which will be exhibited amongst the details.

(668.) Without entering into a description of all the sub-varieties of these ploughs, it will be sufficient to attend to the type of each variety, and, first, as to their *general qualities and characteristics.*

(669.) *The East-Lothian plough*, figs. 49 and 50, Plate V.—In this plough the proper lines of the body on the land-side lie all in one plane, which, in working, should be held in the vertical position, or very slightly inclining to the left. The coulter slightly oblique to the land-side plane, the point standing towards the left, the rake of the coulter varies from 55° to 65°. In the mould-board the vertical sectional lines approximate to straight lines, giving the character of apparent concavity, and it is truncated forward. Share pointed, with a feather or cutter standing to the right, having a breadth of at least $\frac{2}{3}$ the breadth of the furrow, the cutting edge of the feather lying nearly as low as the plane of the sole. The neck of the share is prolonged backward, joining and coinciding with the curve of the mould-board, which curvature is also carried forward on the back of the feather. The character of this plough is to take a furrow of 10 inches in breadth by 7 inches in depth, cut rectangular, leaving the sole of the open furrow level and clean. The resistance to the draught is generally below the average of ploughs, and this plough is employed for every kind of soil.

(670.) *Lanarkshire plough*, figs. 51 and 52, Plate IX.—In this plough the proper lines of the land-side lie in different planes; thus when the fore-part of the land-side of the body, taken at the junction of the breast with the beam, is vertical, the hind-part, taken at the heel, overhangs the sole-line $\frac{5}{8}$ inch, and the beam, at the coulter-box, lies to the *right* of a vertical line from the land-side of the sole about 1 inch, the point of the beam being recurved towards the land-side. In working, the fore-part of the body is held in the vertical line, or slightly inclined to the left. The coulter, by reason of the bend in the beam to the right, and the point being to the left of the land side, stands very oblique, but nearly coinciding with the land-side, at the height of 7 inches from the sole. Rake of the coulter from 55° to 65°. The vertical sectional lines of the mould-board are all convex towards the furrow, giving the mould-board the character of convexity, and it is prolonged forward, covering the neck of the share. Share chisel-pointed, with the feather seldom exceeding 5½ inches broad, the cutting edge rising from the point at an angle of 8° till it is 1 inch above the plane of the sole, when it falls into the curve of the mould-board, while the neck passes under the latter. The character of this plough is to take a furrow whose section is a trapezoid, its breadth from $7\frac{1}{2}$ to 9 inches, and greatest depth $6\frac{1}{2}$ inches, the sole of the furrow being not level, and deepest at the land-side. In the finished ploughing, the laid-up furrow-slices have the acute angle upward, giving the character which I call *high-crested* to the furrow-slice, especially observable in ploughing lea. Resistance to the draught about the average, and it is considered to be well adapted to stiff clay, and to lea-land.

(671.) *Mid-Lothian plough*, figs. 53 and 54, Plate X.—This plough is always worked with a chain-bar under the beam. The proper lines of the land-side lie in different planes; thus, when the fore-part of the land-side, taken as in the former case, is vertical, the hind-part, taken at the heel, overhangs the sole line $\frac{3}{8}$ inch, but the beam is continued straight. In working, the land-side is held vertical, or slightly inclined to the left. The coulter stands rather oblique, and the point about $1\frac{1}{2}$ to 2 inches above the point of the share. Rake of the coulter varying from 56° to 80°. The vertical sectional lines of the mould-board approximate to straight lines, giving the character of concavity, and the mould-board is prolonged forward, covering the neck of the share. The share is chisel-pointed, with feather seldom exceeding 5 inches broad, and, when trimmed for lea-ploughing, the cutting-edge rises from the point at an angle of 10° to a height of $1\frac{1}{4}$ inch above the plane of the sole, when it falls into the curve of the mould-board, while the neck passes under it. The character of this plough is to take a furrow-slice whose transverse section is a trapezoid, having an acute angle with a breadth of $8\frac{1}{2}$ to 9 inches, and usually from 6 to $6\frac{1}{2}$ inches in depth. The sole of the furrow is not level, and is deepest at the land-side. In the finished ploughing the laid-up furrow-slices have the acute angle upward, forming a high crest when ploughing lea. Resistance to the draught is about the average, and this plough is considered applicable to every kind of soil, but particularly to ploughing lea.

(672.) Before entering upon the *specific details* of the three varieties into which the modern Scotch ploughs are here divided, it will be necessary to *lay down certain data, on which the details of each variety will be based.* For this purpose the figures in elevation, figs. 49, 51, and 53, in the plates of the entire ploughs about to be described, are supposed to stand upon a level plane, the heel and point of the share touching that plane, these being actually the points on which the plough is supported when in motion; this plane shall be called the *base line.* The fore-part of the land-side of the plough's body—standing in the vertical position, as seen in plan figs. 50, 52, and 54 in the plates—is supposed to be placed upon a similar line, touching the land-side of the sole-shoe and the point of the share. The base-line is divided into a scale of feet for the convenience of comparison. The zero of the scale is taken at that part of the plough's body, where a vertical transverse section, at right angles to the plane of the land-side, will fall upon a point on the surface of the mould-board, which shall be distant from the land-side plane by a space equal to the greatest breadth of the furrow taken by the respective ploughs; the height of this point above the base-line being also equal to the breadth of the slice. Or, the zero is that vertical section of the mould-board, which, in its progress under the slice, will just place the latter in the vertical position. The scale, by this arrangement. counts right and left of the zero. The dotted line marked *surface-line* in figs. 49, 51, 53, in the plates, represents the depth of the furrow taken by the respective ploughs.

(673.) This zero point has not been fixed on without much consideration; for, having experienced the inconvenience of vague generalities in stating the dimensions of the plough, as given in works on the subject, it has appeared to me desirable that some fixed point should be adopted, and this has been chosen as less liable to change than any other point in the longitude of the plough; all other points of this implement being liable to and may be changed at pleasure, without change of effect. Thus the beam or the handles may be lengthened or shortened, the position of the coulter and the length of the sole may be varied, the mould-board itself may be lengthened or shortened forward without producing any decided change in the working character of the plough, the apparent changes being easily counteracted by a corresponding change in a different direction. The lengthening of the beam, for example, would only require a corresponding change in the height of its extremity above the base line; an alteration in the length of the share, or in the position of the coulter-box, induces only a corresponding change in the angle which the coulter forms with the base line, which angle, in any case, is liable to change from the wearing of the irons themselves, but which can be rectified as required by shifting the draught bolt in the bridle. The zero point here proposed can, with tolerable exactness, be determined in any plough with the instruments that every mechanic has in his hands, *squares* and a *foot-rule.*

(674.) It may be well, also, to premise further, in regard to the contour in elevation of the different ploughs, that although the heights at the different points throughout the beam and handles are given in detail, as adopted by the best makers, which those unacquainted with the implements may follow with confidence, in the construction of implements of the same character, yet I cannot pass over the circumstance without noticing, that, with the exception of one point—the height of the beam at the draught-bolt—any part of the contour may be altered to the taste of the maker, and even the point of the beam, as already noticed, may be altered, provided the alteration is continued backward or forward in a certain angle. The change in position in the vertical direction of three other points is limited within a certain range, not from principle, however, but for convenience. These points are the *height of the beam at the coulter-box* and *at the breast-line* of the mould-board; these cannot be brought *lower* than the given dimensions without subjecting the plough to an unnecessary tendency to choke in foul ground, though they may be raised *higher* without injury, provided the corresponding parts—the mould-board and body-frame—are altered in proportion. The third point here alluded to is the *height of the handles*, which is altogether a point of convenience; but it may be affirmed of this, that it is better to be *low* than *high*, since being low places the plough more under the command of the ploughman. The different points, as given in plan, being more matters of principle, with exception of the position of the handles, cannot be deviated from without compromising the character of the plough.

(675.) With these preliminary remarks I proceed to the general description of the three varieties, taking first,

(676.) THE EAST-LOTHIAN PLOUGH.—Fig. 49, Plate V. represents an elevation of this plough, on the furrow side, drawn to a scale of 1 inch to 1 foot, and fig. 50 a horizontal plan of the same. It is found with various shades of difference, but not to the extent or of such a marked character as to require separate description from what follows. The beam and handles or stilts are almost invariably made of malleable iron, the body-frame being of cast-iron, the latter varying slightly with different makers. In its construction the beam and left handle are usually finished in one continued bar ABC, possessing the varied curvature exhibited in fig. 49, as viewed in elevation. When viewed in plan, as in fig. 50, the *axis* or central line of the beam and *left handle* are in a straight line—though in this arrangement there are some slight deviations among the different makers—the point of the beam being in some cases turned more or less to the right or furrow side, and this is found to vary from ½ inch to 2 inches from the plane of the land-side.

(677.) The *right handle*, DE, is formed in a separate bar, and is attached to the body frame at its fore end by a bolt, as will be shewn in detail, and further connected to the left handle by the bolts FFF, and the stays GG.

(678.) The *coulter* I is fixed in its box K by means of iron wedges, holding it in the proper position. Its office being that of a cutting instrument, it is constructed with a sharp edge, and is set at an angle of from 55° to 65° with the base-line.

(679.) The *mould board* L, which is fixed upon the body-frame, and to the right handle, is a curved plate of cast-iron, adapted for turning over the furrow-slice. Its fore-edge or breast MN coincides with the land-side of the plough's body; its lower edge T behind stands from 9½ to 10 inches distant from the plane of the land-side, while its upper edge P spreads out to a distance of 19 inches from B, the land-side plane. In this plough the mould-board is truncated in the fore part, and is met by the gorge or neck of the share, the junction being at the line N.

(680.) The *share* or *sock* NR is fitted upon a prolongation of the sole-bar of the body-frame, termed the head, and falls into the curves of the mould-board, of which its surface forms a continuation.

(681.) The *bridle C*, or *muzzle*, as sometimes named, is that part to which the draught is applied, and is attached to the point of the beam by two bolts, the one S being permanent, upon which the bridle turns vertically. The other bolt U is movable, for the purpose of varying the *earthing* of the plough; the *landing* being varied by shifting the draught-bolt and shackle V to right or left. The right and left handles are furnished at A and D with wooden helves fitted into the sockets of the handles.

(682.) The *general dimensions* of the plough may be stated thus, as measured on the base-line. From the zero-point O to the extremity of the heel T, the distance is 4 inches, and from O forward to the point of the share R, the distance is 32 inches, giving, as the entire length of sole, 3 feet. Again, from O backward to the extremity of the handles A is 6 feet 2 inches, and forward to the draught-bolt V′ 4 feet 7 inches, making the entire length of the plough on the base-line 10 feet 9 inches; but, following the sinuosities of the beam and handle. the entire length from A to C is about 11 feet 3 inches.

(683.) In reference to the *body* of the plough, the centre of the coulter-box K is 14½ inches, and the top of the breast-curve M 9 inches before the zero-point, both as measured on the base-line; but following the rise of the beam, the distance from M to the middle of the coulter-box will be 7 inches.

(684.) The *heights* at the different points above the base-line are marked on the figure in elevation, along the upper edge of the beam and handle; but the chief points in height are repeated here, the whole of them being measured from the base-line to the upper edge of the beam and handles at the respective points. At the left handle A the height is 3 feet, at the right handle D 2 feet 9 inches; and a like difference in height of the two is preserved till the right handle approaches the body at the middle stretcher F; from thence the difference increases till it reaches the body. The height at the point of the beam is 18 inches, and the centre of the draught-bolt, at a medium, 17 inches. The lower edge of the mould board behind, of this plough, at T is usually set about ½ inch above the base-line, and at the junction with the share about the same height.

(685.) The dimensions in *breadth*, from the land-side line, embrace the obliquity that is given to the direction of the beam and handles, compared with the land-side plane of the body taken at the sole. The amount of obliquity, as exhibited by the dotted line AC, fig. 50, which coincides with the land-side plane of the body, is, that the axis of the beam at the extremity C stands 1¼ inch to the right, and at the opposite end the left handle A stands about 2 inches to the left of the line. These points may, however, be varied slightly from the dimensions here given. In the first—the point of the beam—it is found in the practice of different makers, to range from 1 to 2 inches. In the opinion of some writers and practical men, it is held that the beam should be parallel with the land-side plane of the body. With all deference to such opinions, I apprehend that the direction of the line of draught, in a vertical plane, cannot coincide with the plane of the land-side; for the point of resistance in the plough's body cannot fall in that plane, but will pass through some point to the right of it, and which, from the nature of the subject, cannot be very precisely defined. Both reason and experience, however, point this out to the plough-maker, and especially to the observant ploughman. Hence, also, may be remarked, from the instructions laid down by Small* for the formation of the beam, which, in his time, were made of wood, that the land-side of the beam should lie in the plane of the land-side of the body, and as he directed the beam to be 2¼ inches in breadth at that point, its axis must have been 1⅛ inch to the right of the land-side plane; and in all cases, it must be admitted that the resultant of the effect will lie in the axis of the point, provided the draught-bolt is placed in that line. But, for very sufficient practical reasons, the draught-bolt has a range from right to left, by which the effects of variation of soil and other causes can be rectified at pleasure.

(686.) A similar difference of opinion has prevailed in regard to the position of the handles, in reference to the land-side plane. In the plough now under review, the left handle deviates only 2 inches from the line, whereas, as we shall see, another variety has the handle 7 inches to the left of the line; and this deviation has been advocated on the principle of allowing the ploughman to walk right in the middle between the handles, his right and left arms being equally extended.† Now I would again submit, whether the man who walks with his arms equally extended, and his body equally distant from either handle, or he who is compelled to have one handle always near his body, whereby he can, on any emergency, bring his body instantaneously in contact with the hand, or that which it grasps,—which of these men will have the greatest command over the instrument he guides? Little consideration, I imagine, will be necessary to satisfy the inquirer that the latter will have the advantage.

* Small's Treatise on Ploughs.

† Wilkie in Farmer's Magazine, vol. xii. p. 342.

(687.) The dimensions of the parts of the *frame-work* of the plough are: The beam, at its junction with the mould-board at M, is from $2\frac{1}{2}$ to $2\frac{3}{4}$ inches in depth, by 1 inch in breadth, the same strength being preserved onward to the coulter-box K. From the last point a diminution in breadth and depth begins, which is carried on to the extremity C, where the beam has a depth of $1\frac{3}{4}$ inch, and a breadth of $\frac{1}{2}$ to $\frac{5}{8}$ inch.

(688.) The *coulter-box* is formed by piercing an oblong mortice through the bar, which has been previously forged with a protuberance at this place, on each side and on the upper edge; the mortice is $2\frac{1}{2}$ by $\frac{3}{4}$ inches, and the depth $3\frac{1}{2}$ inches.

(689.) From the junction with the mould-board at M backward, the beam decreases gradually till, at the hind palm of the body at B, it is 2 inches in depth, and $\frac{5}{8}$ inch in breadth, where it merges in the left handle A. This last member retains a nearly uniform size throughout of 2 inches by $\frac{3}{8}$ inch. The right handle D is somewhat lighter, being usually $1\frac{1}{2}$ inch by $\frac{3}{8}$ inch, and both terminate in welded sockets, which receive wooden helves, of 6 or 8 inches in length. The stretchers FFF, which support and retain the handles at their due distance apart, are in length suited to their positions in the handles, and their thickness is about $\frac{3}{4}$ inch diameter, tapering towards the ends, where they terminate in a collar and tail-bolt, with screwed nut. The upper stretcher has also a semicircular stay riveted to its middle, the tails of the stays GG terminating like the stretcher with screwed tails and nuts.

(690.) Having given the general dimensions and outline-description of this

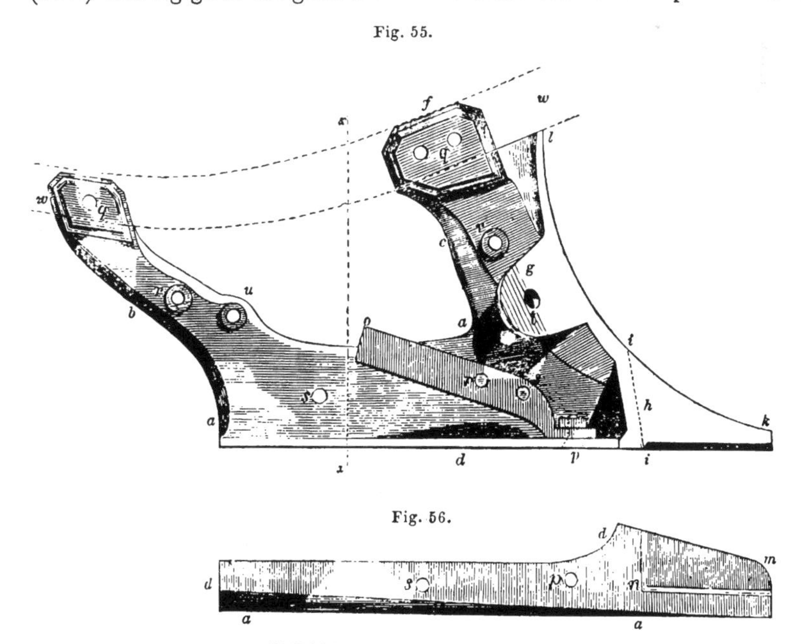

THE DETAILS OF THE BODY-FRAME.

plough, there remains to be described the *details of the body-frame and its sheathing*, all the figures of which are on a scale of $1\frac{1}{2}$ inch to 1 foot.

(691.) *The body-frame.*—The different views of the body-frame are exhibited in the annexed cuts, figs. 55 and 56, wherein the same letters refer to the corresponding parts in the different figures. Fig. 55 is an elevation of the furrow side; fig. 56, a plan of the sole-bar of the frame inverted; and a vertical section, on the line *x x*, is given in fig. 57. In all the figures, then, *a a* is the sole-bar, with two arms *b* and *c* extending upward, and having at the lower edge a flange *d* running along the right-hand side. Each of the arms *b c* terminates in a palm *e f*, by which it is bolted to the beam. The arm *c* is furnished, besides, with an oblique palm or ear *g*, upon which the fore edge of the mould-board rests, and to which it is bolted. The sole-bar *a*, with its flange, terminates forward in the head *h*, which is here made to form the commencement of the twist of the mould-board, and upon which the share is fitted, reaching to the dotted line *i i*, fig. 55. The fore edge *k, i, l* of the frame is worked into the curve answering to the oblique section of the fore edge or breast of the mould-board, and serves as a support to the latter throughout their junction. The curvature given to the arm *b* is unimportant to the action of the plough, but the general oblique direction here given to it is well adapted to withstand the thrust constantly exerted in that direction when the plough is at work. In Fig. 56, the sloping edge *d m* represents the enlargement of the sole-bar, on which the share is fitted, and where the lower part of the fore edge of the mould-board rests. The depressed portion *m n*, is that which is embraced by the flange of the share. In the frame, *o* is the lower extremity of the right handle, broken off at *o*, to shew the manner in which it is joined to the sole-flange of the frame by the bolt *p*. The bolt-holes *q q* are those by which the beam is secured to the palms of the frame; *r r* are those by which the land-side plate is attached; and *s s* those of the sole-shoe, *t* being that which secures the mould-board to the ear, and *u* that which receives the lower stretcher of the handles. (See fig. 50, Plate V. at F and O.) The letter *v* marks the second bolt-hole of the mould-board, while its third fixture is effected upon the right handle by the intervention of a bracket, or of a bolt and socket, as seen at O, fig. 50, Plate V. The dotted lines *w w* mark the position of the beam when attached to the body, the beam being received into the seats formed on the land-side of the palms *e f*, as seen more distinctly at *w*, in fig. 57.

Fig. 57.

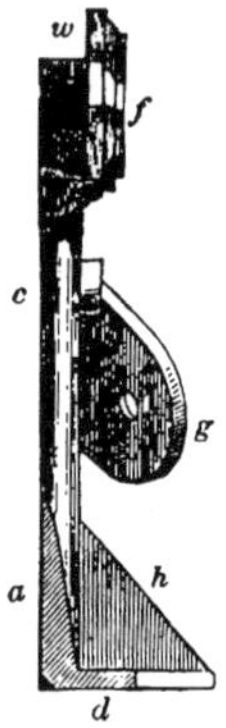

w f c g a h d

A VERTICAL SECTION OF THE FRAME.

(692.) The body-frame being an important member of the implement, regard is paid to having it as light as may be consistent with a due degree of strength; hence, in the different parts, breadth has been given them in the direction of the strain, while the thickness is studiously attenuated in such places as can be reduced with safety. The least breadth of the sole-bar *a* is $3\frac{3}{4}$ inches, of the arm *c* $4\frac{1}{2}$ inches, and of *b* $2\frac{1}{4}$ inches. The breadth of the sole-flange is 2 inches, the greatest thickness in any of the parts is $\frac{3}{4}$ inch, and the total weight of the frame is 30 lb.

(693.) *The share.*—Figs. 58–62 are illustrations of the share and its configuration; fig. 58 is a plan, 59 a geometrical elevation of the furrow-side, and 60 a direct end view looking forward, of which *a* is the *boss* adapted to the curvature of the mould-board, *b* the land-side flange which embraces the head on the land-side, *c* the sole flange, embracing, in like manner, the head below, and these three parts form the neck or socket of the share, fitting closely upon the head, and being, in effect, part of the mould-board. The part *d e f*, fig. 58, forms the share proper, consisting of *d c e* the *shield*, terminating in the point *e*, and of the part *c g e* the *feather* or *cutter* running off at the point *e*. The

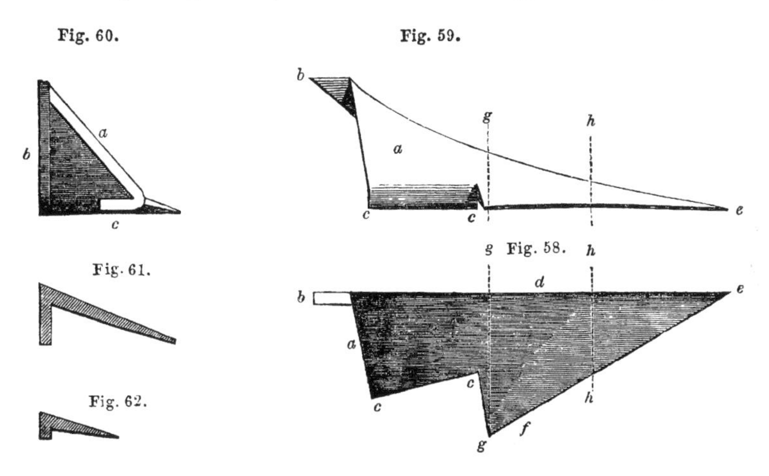

THE DETAILS OF THE SHARE.

extreme *breadth* of the share in this plough, measuring from the land-side to the point *g* of the feather, varies from 6 to 6½ inches, and its *length* in the sole, including the neck, is about 16 inches, the feather being 11 inches. The other figures 61 and 62 are transverse sections of the share on the lines *g g* and *h h* in the respective figures, exhibiting the structure and relation of the shield and the feather, as well as the position of the cutting edge of the feather in relation to the base line of the plough represented by the line A′V′, fig. 49, Plate V., where, as will be observed, the cutting edge, through its entire length, lies within less than ¼ an inch of the base line.

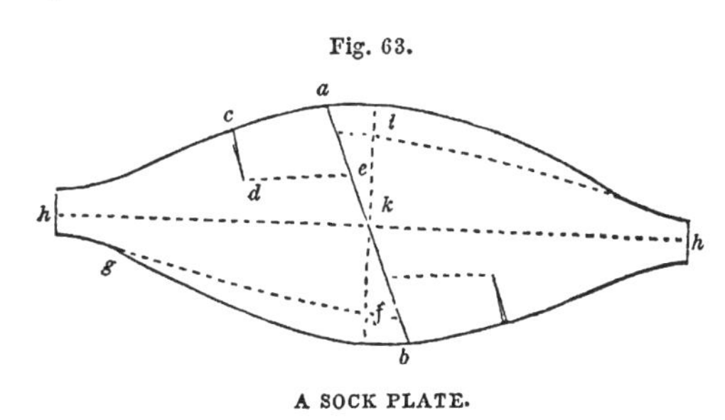

A SOCK PLATE.

(694.) The share is always formed from a plate forged for the express purpose at the iron-mills, and known in the trade by the term *sock-plate*. Fig. 63 represents the form in which these plates are manufactured, the thickness being from ½ to ¾ inches; they are afterwards cut in two through the line *a b*, each half being capable of forming a share. To do this an incision *c d* is made on the short side to a depth of 2 inches, the part *a c d e* is afterwards folded down to form the sole flange, and the part *b f g* is, in like manner, folded down to form the land-side flange. The point *h* is strengthened, when requisite, to receive the proper form of the shield and point, the latter being tipt with steel. The edge *h c* is extended to the requisite breadth to form the feather. In order to cut a sock-plate at the proper angle, so as to secure a minimum expenditure of labour and material, let a central line *h h* be drawn upon the plate, and bisect this line in the point *k*, the line upon which the plate should be cut will form angles of 70° and 110° nearly, with the line *h h*; or, mechanically, draw *k l*, equal to 5½ inches, at right angles to *h h*, and *l a* parallel to *h h*, mark off 2 inches from *l* to *a*, and, through the points *a k*, draw the line *a b*, which is the proper direction in which the plate should be cut.

(695.) *The sole-shoe.*—The figures 64–66 are illustrative of the *sole-shoe.* Fig. 64 is a plan of the shoe, *a a* being the sole flange, and *b b* the land-side

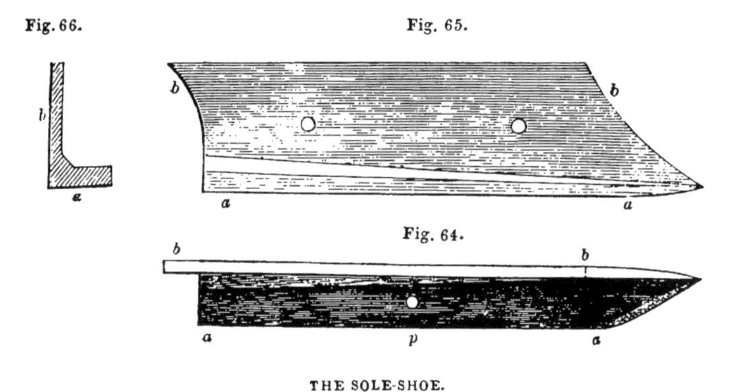

THE SOLE-SHOE.

flange. Fig. 65 is an elevation of the same, and fig. 66 a cross section, shewing the filling up of the internal angle opposed to where the greatest wear takes place. The thickness of the sole-flange at the heel *a* is ⅞ inch, diminishing forward to ⅜ inch at 3 inches from the point, and from thence it is thinned off to prevent obstruction in its progress through the soil. The breadth of the sole is 2¼ inches, and its extreme length 20½ inches. The side-flange is ½ inch thick along the edge by which it is attached to the sole, diminishing upwards to ¼ inch at the top edge, the height being 4¾ inches at the heel and 6 inches at the fore-end; weight about 14 lb. The upper land-side plate is 18 inches in length on the lower edge, being 1½ inch longer than the corresponding edge of the sole-plate, the purpose of which will be seen in the figure of the land-side, fig 71; the length on the upper edge is 21½ inches. The breadth and the contour of the upper edge must be adapted to the form that may have been given to the beam. The thickness at the lower edge must agree with that of the sole plate, and be diminished to ⅛ inch at the upper edge; weight 9 lb.

(696.) *The coulter.*—Fig. 67 is an edge and 68 a side view of the coulter of this plough, in which the same letters of reference are applied. The neck *a b* by which it is affixed in the coulter-box, is about 10 inches long, though it may, with all propriety, be extended to *c*; the neck is usually about 2 inches in breadth and $\frac{3}{4}$ inch in thickness. The blade *b c d* varies in length according to the variety of the plough to which it belongs, from 18 to 22 inches. The breadth of the blade is usually about 3 inches in the upper part, but is curved off behind and terminating in a point at *d*. The thickness of the back at the shoulder *b* is $\frac{3}{4}$ inch, and tapers gently downward to where the curvature of the back begins; from thence it diminishes towards the point to $\frac{1}{8}$ inch or less. It is formed quite flat on the land-side, and on the furrow-side is bevelled off towards the cutting edge, where it is about $\frac{1}{8}$ inch in thickness throughout the length of the edge.

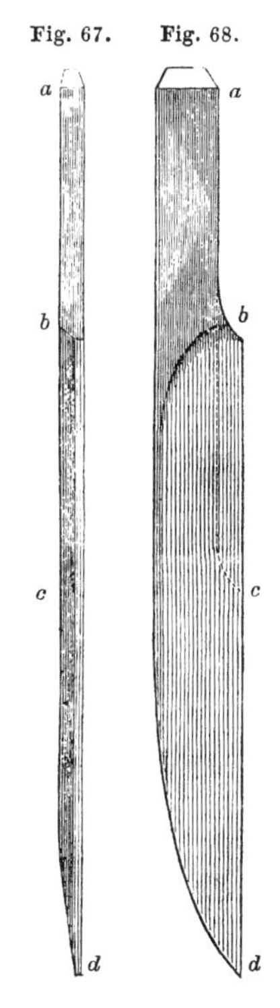

THE COULTER.

(697.) *The bridle.*—Fig. 69 is a plan, and fig. 70 a corresponding elevation of the bridle, and the manner of its attachment to the beam, where *a* is a part of the beam, *b* the cross-head, and *c c* the tails of the bridle, with their arc-heads *d* embracing the beam on the two sides; *e* is the joint-bolt on which the bridle turns for adjustment to *earthing; f* is the temper-pin or bolt, and by insertion of it into any one of the holes in the arc-heads, and passing through the beam, which is here perforated for the purpose, the bridle is held in any required position. The draught shackle *g* is held in its place upon the cross-head *b* by the draught-bolt *h* passing through both parts, and the cross-head being perforated with five or more holes, the bolt and shackle can be shifted from right to left, or from left to right, for the proper adjustment of the *landing* of the plough. To the shackle is appended the swivel-hook *i*, to which is attached the main draught-bar, or swingle-tree of the yoke.

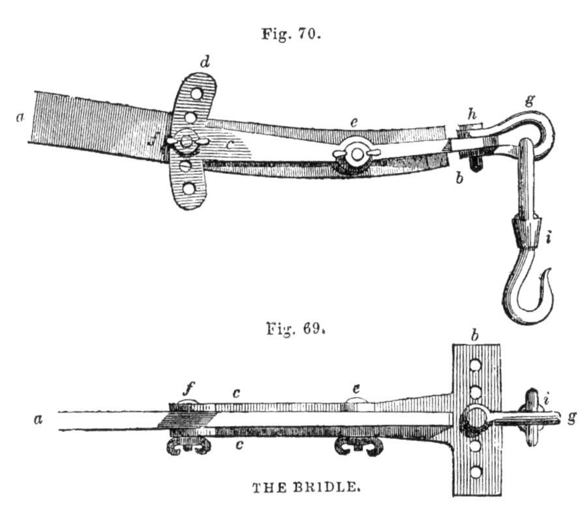

THE BRIDLE.

(698.) *The land-side.*—Figs. 71 and 72 are illustrations of the land-side, fig. 71 being an elevation of the body of this plough, represented in the working positions, but with the extremities cut off. The point of the share and the heel rest upon the base line at *a* and *b*, and the lines of the sole lying between these

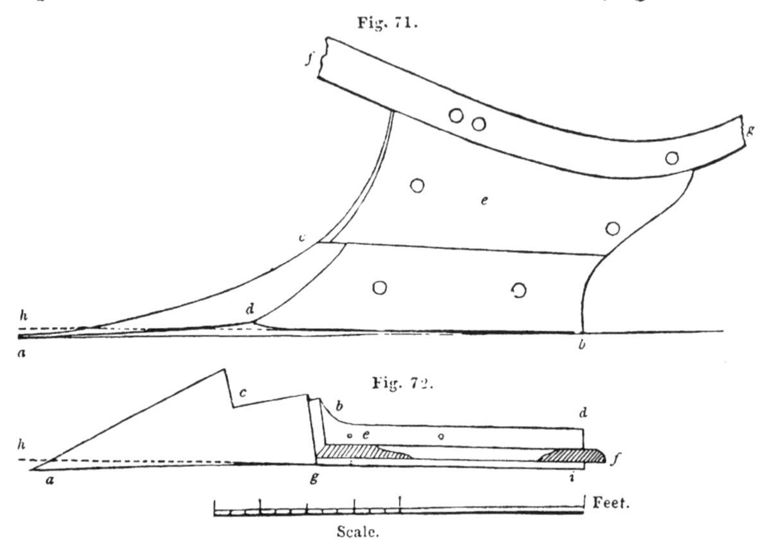

THE DETAILS OF THE LANDSIDE.

points form the very obtuse angle which obtains in the sole of this plough; *a c* is the share, and *d b* the sole-shoe; *e* is the land-side plate, and *f g* a part of the beam. The lines *a d* and *d b*, together with the base line, form the very low triangle *a d b*, whose altitude at *d* does not exceed $\frac{3}{8}$ inch, or by extending the sole line *b d* to *h*, the depression *h a* of the point of the share below this extended line will be $\frac{1}{2}$ inch nearly. Fig. 72 represents a horizontal section of the body, as if cut off at the level of the upper edge of the sole-shoe. Here *a c* is the share, *b d* the sole-flange of the body-frame, the bolt-hole at *b* being that by which the palm of the right handle is fixed to the flange; *e* and *f* the two arms of the frame, as cut across in the section *g i*, the land-side of the sole-shoe coinciding with the land-side plane, the continuation of this line, *g i* to *h*, exhibits the inclination of the share to the land-side, which in this plough may be taken at $\frac{1}{2}$ inch.

(699.) The inclination downward given to the share is intended, and experience confirms the intention, to give steadiness of motion to the implement, by giving it a lengthened base on which to stand. It is evident that if a base the converse of this were given to it—convex instead of concave—so that it should rest on the point *d*; when in motion the smallest obstruction occurring at the point of the share would give it a tendency to swerve from the horizontal line of progression, and to lose either depth of furrow or be thrown out, thus rendering the management of the plough very difficult and uncertain. Even a perfectly straight base is found not to give the requisite certainty of action, without a greater amount of exertion, as well as closer attention on the part of the ploughman. A like reason prevails for this inclination of the share landward, as does for its earthward inclination, and, for the steady motion of the plough, the latter is even more necessary than the former; but there is another reason for this landward inclination, which is, that as the plough is seldom held with its land-side truly vertical, but inclining a little landward, and it being desirable to cut the furrow-slice as near as possible rectangular, the coulter has always a slight tendency landward at the point; hence it becomes necessary to give the share a like bias. By this arrangement of the parts the incision made by the coulter will be nearly vertical. While it is admitted that these inclinations of the share afford certain advantages in the action of the plough, it must not be concealed that the practice is liable to abuse. It has been stated, that if a different arrangement were followed, a greater degree of exertion and of attention on the part of the ploughman would be called forth; thus, if the sole and land-side of the body were perfectly straight, the plough would present the least possible resistance, but as it would thus be so delicately adjusted, the smallest extraneous obstacle would tend to throw it out, unless a constant unceasing watch is kept on its movements, by the ploughman. To obviate this, he gets the share set with a strong tendency to *earth* (for it is this tendency that has most effect), greater than is requisite; and to prevent the plough taking too deep furrow, he counteracts this by adjusting the draught-bolt to an opposite tendency; the implement will thus be kept in equilibrium, but it is obtained at an additional expenditure of horse power. Under any such circumstances the plough is drawn at a disadvantage to the horses, as will be afterwards shewn, by reason of an obliquity of the line of draught to the direction of motion, and this disadvantage is augmented by every undue tendency given to the parts by which the obliquity of their action is increased; or, if not so increased, the prevention of the increase will induce a deterioration in the work performed. This point I shall be able also to establish when I come to speak of the action of the plough generally. In the mean time it may be affirmed, that all undue inclination given to the share, but especially in its *earthing*, will either produce an unnecessary resistance to the draught, or it will deteriorate the quality of the ploughing. It is, therefore, the interest of the farmer to guard against, and to prevent as much as possible, every attempt at giving any undue bias to this important member of the plough.

(700.) THE LANARKSHIRE PLOUGH.—The Lanarkshire plough, as constructed by Mr Wilkie, Uddingstone, is represented in Plate IX.; fig. 51 being an elevation, and fig. 52 a plan. Like the former, it now occurs with various shades of difference, but the leading points remain unchanged; like it, also, its framework is invariably made of malleable iron, but in the construction of this, the application of malleable iron is carried a step farther, as will appear in the details.

(701.) The *beam* and *left handle* are usually finished in one continuous bar, ABC, possessing a still more varied curvature than in the former plough, in as much as it is curved horizontally as well as vertically. When viewed in plan, and compared with the land-side plane as applied to the sole-shoe, and the forepart of the body standing vertical, it is found that the beam, where it meets the breast-curve, coincides with the land-side plane, but at the coulter-box it deviates to the right to the extent of $1\frac{1}{4}$ inch, if measured to the axis of the beam. Instead of continuing to deviate in this direction, the beam returns toward the land-side plane, till at C it is 1 inch to the right. This formation of the forepart of the beam gives a position that apparently makes the draught bear from a point within the body of the plough, that may be imagined to approximate to the centre of resistance of the body. This is, however, more apparent than real, for the beam in this case acts simply as a bar bent at an angle, and perfectly rigid, on which, suppose a power and resistance applied at its extremities, the resultant of the strain will not follow the axis of the bar through its angular direction, but in the direction of the shortest line between the two points where the power and the resistance are applied. In addition to this horizontal curvature of the beam, it will be observed that the box of the coulter is formed by an increase of thickness on the right side only, while there is even a slight depression on the left side. This double deviation to the right gives an inclination to the plane of the coulter much greater than in any other variety of plough, being about 8° from the vertical. Though this peculiarity in the form of the beam is one of the most decided characteristics of this plough, as we now find it, it does not appear to have been an original element in Wilkie's plough, for the late Mr Wilkie says, "the beam, which is 6½ feet long, is wrought quite straight on the land-side;"* and, from his data in the same paper, his coulter must have made an angle with the vertical plane of 6°, whereas, by the more modern construction, the angle is 8° Continuing the comparison with the land-side plane, it will be seen that the left handle, at its junction with the tail of the beam, overhangs the land-side plane to the left by about ⅝ inch, there being that extent of twist on the surface of the land-side, within the limits of the body and the same handle continues to recede from that plane till at the helve A it stands 7 inches to the left. This is also a *point* in construction of this plough, though it does not bear upon the principle of its actual working. As before observed regarding the position of the ploughman in relation to the handles (686), this point is one that may be liable to be questioned, but not being an essential point, its determination is of minor importance.

(702.) The *right handle* DE is formed in one bar, and attached to the body-frame, as will appear in detail; and it is connected to the left handle by the stretcher bolts FFF, and the stays GG.

(703.) The *coulter* I is fixed in its box K; the rake or angle at which the coulter stands in this plough, as before stated (270), is from 55° to 65°. The land-side face of the coulter is usually set to form an angle with the land-side plane of the plough, horizontally, of about 4°.

(704.) The *mould-board* L, fixed upon the body-frame and the right handle, is a curved plate of cast-iron, adapted to the turning of the furrow-slice. Its fore-edge or breast MN coincides with the land-side of the body; its lower edge O behind stands from 7½ to 8 inches distant from the land-side, while its upper edge P spreads out to 18 inches from B, the land-side. In this plough the mould-board is prolonged forward covering the neck of the share, meeting the shield at the root of the feather Q of the share. At this point NQ, the horizontal breadth of the mould-board is 3 inches; its height from the base line, at the same point, is from 2¼ inches to 2½ inches, according as the inclination of the share varies; the length along the lower edge from O to N is 20 inches, and from P to M 23 inches; the extreme length in a straight line from P to N is 33 inches; and the perpendicular height from the plane of the base-line to P is about 11 inches. Slight deviations from these dimensions of the mould-board are to be found in the numerous sub-varieties of this plough.

(705.) The *share* QR is fitted upon a malleable-iron head, to be afterwards described; the neck passing under the mould-board at NQ, and the shield falling into the curve of the mould-board, terminates forward in the chisel-point R.

(706.) The *bridle* C is formed in this plough by the end of the beam being converted into a fork or sheers, to which is attached the bridle proper S, by means of the draught-bolt U; the sheers forming an adjustment vertically, while the bridle yields it horizontally, by shifting the draught-shackle at S.

* Farmer's Magazine, vol. xii. p. 342.

(707.) The right and left handles are each furnished at A and D with wooden helves fitted into the sockets of the handles.

(708.) The *general dimensions* of this plough are:—From the zero-point O to the extremity of the heel T, 4 inches, and from O forward to the point R of the share is 29 inches, giving, as the entire length of sole, 2 feet 9 inches. Again, from O backward to the extremity of the handles, the distance is 5 feet 6 inches, and forward to the draught-bolt U 4 feet 4 inches, making the extreme length on the base-line 9 feet 10 inches, but following the sinuosities of the beam and handles, the entire length from A′ to U′ is about 10 feet 6 inches. In reference to the body of the plough, the centre of the coulter-box is 15 inches, and the point M of the breast-curve $6\frac{1}{2}$ inches before the zero-point O, both as measured on the base-line; but, following the rise of the beam, the distance from M to the middle of the coulter box will be $10\frac{1}{2}$ inches.

(709.) The *heights* of the different points, as measured from the base-line to the upper-line of the beam and handle, are marked on fig. 51; a few only of these may be repeated here. At the helve of the left handle, the height is 3 feet 2 inches; at the same point in the right, it is 3 feet; at the middle stretcher the difference in height is only $1\frac{1}{2}$ inch, but it again increases downward till the right handle meet the sole-bar, to which it is bolted. The height at the point of the beam is 18 inches, and at the centre of the draught-bolt U at a medium 17 inches. The lower edge of the mould-board behind is usually set at $\frac{1}{2}$ inch above the plane of the base-line, and at its junction with the share is from $1\frac{1}{2}$ to $1\frac{3}{4}$ inch.

(710.) The dimensions of the *frame-work* of this plough are in general as follows. The beam, at its junction with the mould-board at M, is from $2\frac{1}{2}$ to 3 inches in depth, by from 1 to $1\frac{1}{8}$ inch in breadth, the same strength being preserved onward to the coulter-box K; and from thence, forward to the root of the sheers, a gradual diminution goes on to about 2 inches by $\frac{5}{8}$ inch. The coulter-box is formed, as before described, by an oblique mortice being pierced through the beam; which, for this purpose, has been previously forged with a protuberance at this place, to the right side only and upward, giving it a depth of 4 inches. The opening of the coulter-box is about $2\frac{1}{2}$ by $\frac{7}{8}$ inches. From the junction with the mould board the beam begins to diminish also backward till it merges in the left handle, and here it measures only 2 inches in depth by $\frac{3}{4}$ inch in breadth. The left handle, where it joins the tail of the beam, has a depth of $2\frac{1}{2}$ inches; and here also, it forks off into the hind branch of the body; and it diminishes in depth backward, to $1\frac{3}{4}$ inch at the commencement of the helve-socket. The right handle, as in the former case, is somewhat lighter; and is connected with the left by means of stretchers, as already described (702); and both terminate in sockets for receiving the wooden helves.

(711.) *The body-frame.*—This and the succeeding figures of the details of this plough are on a scale of $1\frac{1}{2}$ inch to 1 foot. In the frame of the Lanarkshire plough, as usually constructed; those parts which in the East-Lothian plough I have called the body-frame are here formed in malleable iron. The two bars or branches of the body are welded to, and form prolongations from, the beam and left handle. Fig. 73 is an elevation of this body-frame; *a a* is a portion of the beam; *b b* a prolongation of the left handle after it merges in the beam, forming the hind-bar of the body-frame; *c c* is the fore-bar falling from the beam; each of these bars is kneed to the right hand at the bottom, forming a palm by which they are bolted to the sole-bar *d e*. This last terminates forward in the *head ef*, upon which the share is fitted. The hind-bar is forged to a breadth of 2 inches, its thickness being $\frac{5}{8}$ inch. The fore-bar is about $3\frac{1}{4}$ inches broad, and $\frac{5}{8}$ inch thick; each being respectively thinner than the beam, at the point where they spring from it, by the thickness of the land-side plate. The sole-bar *d e* is made also of malleable iron, and is 15 inches in

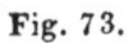
Fig. 73.

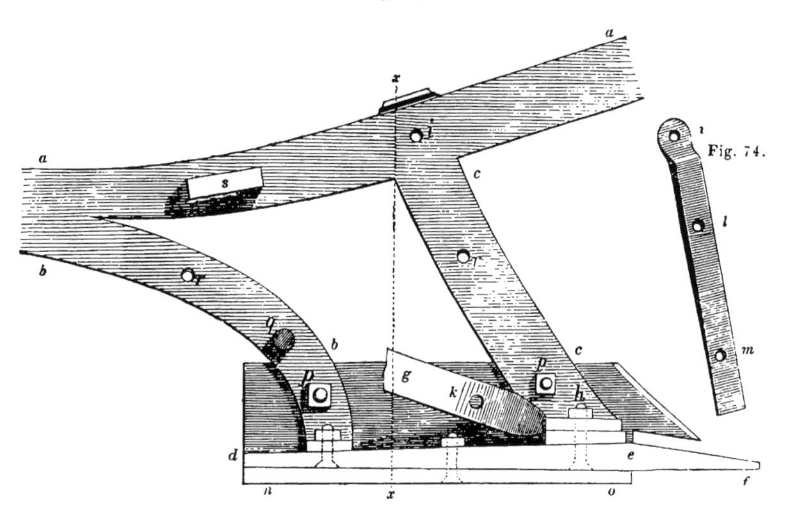

THE DETAILS OF THE BODY-FRAME.

length in the part from *d* to *e*, with a breadth of 2 inches swelled at *e*, and depth of 1 inch at *e*. The length from *e* to *f* is 8 inches, and in the depth the bar is tapered off from *e* towards *f*, where the depth is $\frac{3}{8}$ inch. From *e* it tapers backward to $\frac{1}{2}$ inch at *d*. A portion of the right handle is exhibited as broken off at *g*; the lower extremity being twisted to a right angle, so as to lie flat on the sole-bar to which it is bolted, along with the palm of the fore-bar at *h*.

(712.) To determine the position of the points, in this body-frame, let the zero-point O, as already fixed, be marked on the beam at 15 inches behind the centre of the coulter-box K, and the whole beam curved agreeably to the dimensions given fig. 52, Plate IX.; then, the height from the bottom of the sole-bar, to the top edge of the beam at the zero-point, will be $14\frac{3}{4}$ inches, as before stated, less the thickness of the sole-shoe at that point, or equal to 14 inches. The fore-part of the sole-bar at *e*, will have its position determined when a straight-edge applied to its lower side from *d*, to *e*, and extending as far as the point of the beam, will place the upper edge of the beam, where it spreads into the sheers, as at C, fig. 51, Plate IX, 18 inches above the *straight-edge*, or line of the sole-bar. The heel *d*, of the sole-bar will be 4 inches behind the zero, and its point *f*, 19 inches before it, the sole-bar being in all 23 inches. The fore-edge of the fore-bar will be 5 inches before the zero at top where it springs from the beam, and 13 inches at bottom, where it joins the sole-bar. The curvature of the fore-bar is only necessary to prevent its lying in the way of the mould-board, and a radius of 18 inches will effect this.

(713.) The provision for *fixing* the mould-board of this plough consists in a gland, fig. 74, fixed on the body-frame and right handle with bolts at *i k*, supporting the fore part of the mould-board by means of bolts at *l m*. The remaining fixture is effected by a bracket H, attached also to the right handle. as seen in fig. 52, Plate IX. The shoe, as seen in position, fig. 73, is marked *n o*, and is secured to the body-frame by the bolts *p p*. The lower stretcher, by which the right handle is connected to the left, is marked *q*, and *r r* mark the bolts for fixing the land-side plate. Fig. 74, already alluded to, is a front view of the gland on which the fore-part of the mould-board is supported, and this is seen also in profile in fig. 75, which is a transverse section of the body-frame on the line *x x*. In this figure *a* is the beam, *c* the fore-bar with its kneed palm at *h*, under which is the sole-bar *e*; *g* is the broken off part of the right handle, terminating in the palm lying over that of the fore-bar; and these three parts are secured by one bolt at *h*. The sole-shoe is seen at *o p*, with its land-side flange, which is fixed by the bolt *p*.

Fig. 75.

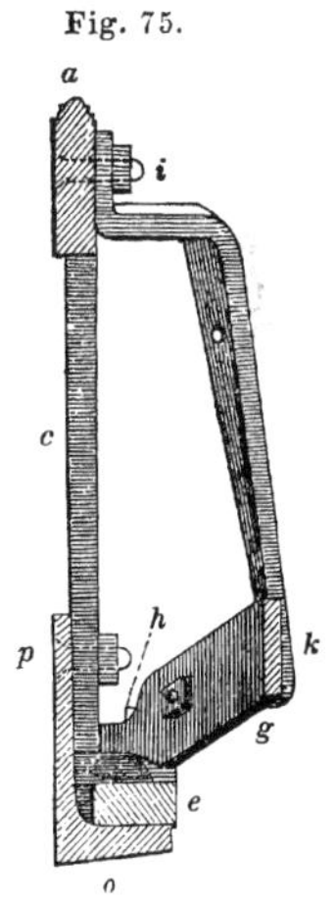

A SECTION OF THE BODY-FRAME.

(714.) *The share.*—The figures from figs. 76 to 82 are illustrative of the shares of this plough, as adapted to both fallow and lea-ploughing, where fig. 76 is a plan, fig. 77 a geometrical elevation of the furrow-side of the share; and fig. 80 a direct end-view looking forward, in all which *a b* is the neck or socket by which it is attached to the head; *c* is the shield, extending over the body and the feather, but, for distinction, I shall call the portion *e c f* in fig. 76 the body, and *b g h* the feather, *i* being the point of the share, which in this plough is always chisel-shaped. Fig. 78 is an elevation of the furrow-side of the lea-share, and fig. 79 a direct end view of the same. These views have the same letters of reference; and exhibit the rise of the cutting edge of the feather above the plane of

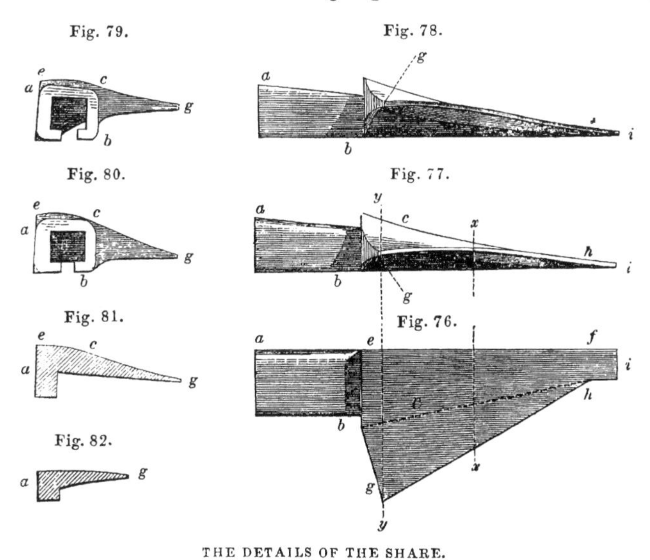

THE DETAILS OF THE SHARE.

the base-line, which, when it reaches the maximum height, stands $1\frac{1}{4}$ inch above that plane, which gives an angle equal to 8° or more with the plane of the sole in a transverse direction. The extreme breadth of this share at *e y* is 5½ to 6 inches; the length from the point to the head of the shield *i b*, 10 inches, and again from the point to the extremity of the neck *i a*, is 16 inches. A share thus formed, will necessarily cut the furrow lower at the land-side, than at the extreme edge of the feather; for, since the share must cut the slice all along its cutting edge at the same instant, that part of the slice which is cut by the chisel-point will be the lowest possible, and every succeeding point backward will be higher and higher till it reach the apex of the curved feather 1¼ inch above the true plane of the sole. Figs. 79 and 80 exhibit the opening of the neck *a b*, which fits upon the head, and *e c g* the outline of the posterior end of the shield and feather of the two shares. Figs. 81 and 82 are transverse sections of figs. 76 and 77 on the lines *y y*, *x x* respectively.

(715.) *The sole-shoe.* Fig. 83 is a plan of the sole-shoe, where *a b* is the sole-flange with its single bolt-hole, and *c d* the land-side flange. Fig. 84 is an elevation of the same, as viewed on the furrow-side, wherein *a b* is the sole-flange

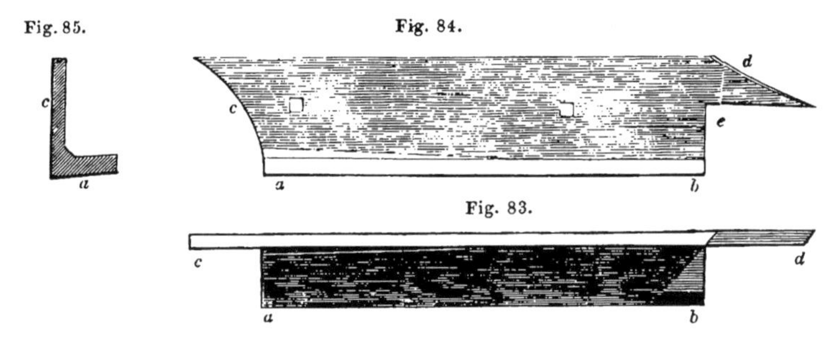

THE DETAILS OF THE SOLE-SHOE.

seen edgeways, and *c d* the side-flange, exhibiting the notch *e*, 2½ inches long and 2 inches deep, adapted to receive the neck of the share, while the slope *d* is adapted to the breast-curve of the mould-board. Fig. 85 is a transverse section of the shoe; *a* the sole, and *c* the land-side, exhibiting also the filling, in the internal angle, opposite to where the greatest wear takes place on the exterior. The land-side flange is 5 inches in height, and along the line of junction with the sole it is ½ inch thick, lessening upward to ⅜ inch at the upper edge; the sole-flange is ¾ inch in depth at the heel, diminishing forward to ½ inch at the fore-end, and retaining a uniform breadth of 2½ inches. The length of the sole-flange is 17 inches, and of the land-side flange to the extreme point 20 inches. The upper *land-side plate* in this plough is 15½ inches in length on the lower edge; its upper edge, as exhibited in fig. 90, corresponds in its outline to the beam, joining flush with the left handle. The thickness at the lower edge agrees with that of the upper edge of the sole-shoe, and is diminished at the upper edge to ⅛ inch.

(716.) *The bridle.*—Figs. 86 and 87 are two views of the bridle, the first a plan, the second a side view, with the same letters to each. *a* is a portion of the beam, the extremity of which is forked into the sheers *b b*, 2 inches wide, each cheek of the sheers being also spread out into cross-heads *c c*, 5½ inches long, each furnished with four or more perforations; they are also prevented from collapsing, by the insertion between them of a stretcher *s*. The bridle *d d* is adapted to the cross-heads of the sheers, and jointed on the draught-bolt *e*. The web *d d* of the bridle, 9 inches in length, is also provided with perforations, and furnished with the shackle *f*, which is attached to it by the bolt *g*. This arrangement affords the usual facility of changing the draught. By shifting the bridle on the cross-heads of the beam, in the vertical direction, the *earthing* of the plough

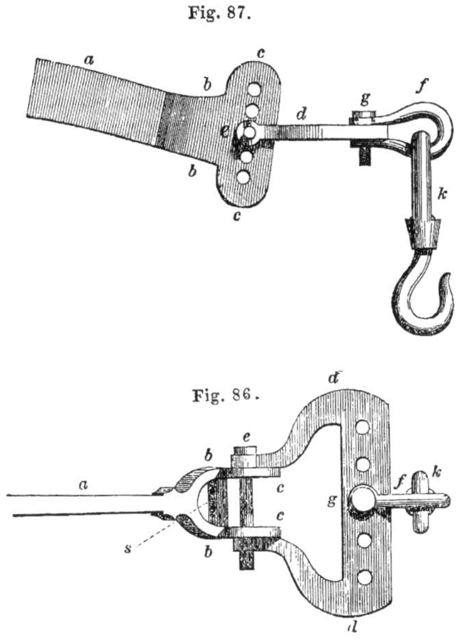

THE DETAILS OF THE BRIDLE.

is adjusted, and by the same operation on the shackle of the bridle horizontally, the *landing* is adjusted. The draught swivel-hook *k*, is attached to the shackle, as before described, to which is appended the draught-bars afterwards described.

(717.) This plough is always provided with a very useful appendage, an *iron hammer*, fig. 88. The head and handle are forged in one piece of malleable iron, the latter part being formed into a nut-key. With this simple but useful tool, the ploughman has always at hand, the means by which he can, without loss of time, alter and adjust the position of his plough-irons,—the coulter and share,—and perform other little operations, which circumstances or accident may require,—for the performance of which most ploughmen are under the necessity of taking advantage of the first *stone* they can find, merely from the want of this simple instrument. The hammer is slung in a staple fixed in the side of the beam in any convenient position, as at *s*, in fig. 73. This little appendage is confidently recommended to all ploughmen, as an essential part of the furniture of the plough.

Fig. 88.

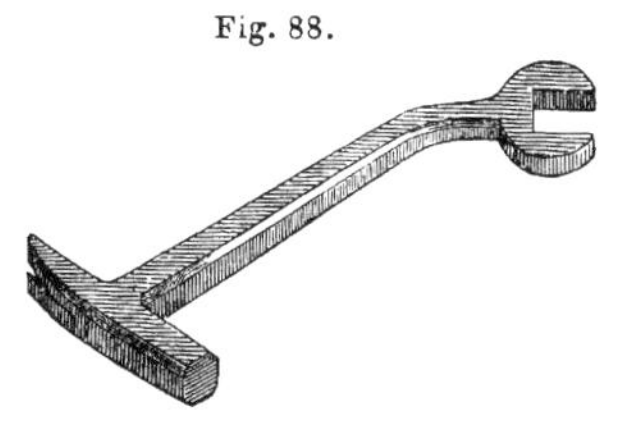

THE IRON HAMMER NUT-KEY.

(718.) *The plough-staff.*—Fig. 89 represents the plough-staff, another and a necessary article of the movable furniture of the plough. It is in form of a small shovel, having a socket, into which a helve of 5 feet in length is inserted, and in some parts of the country this is furnished with an oblique cross-head. Its position in the plough is to lie between the handles, and its use to enable the ploughman to remove all extraneous matter, as earth, stubble, roots, weeds,

Fig. 89.

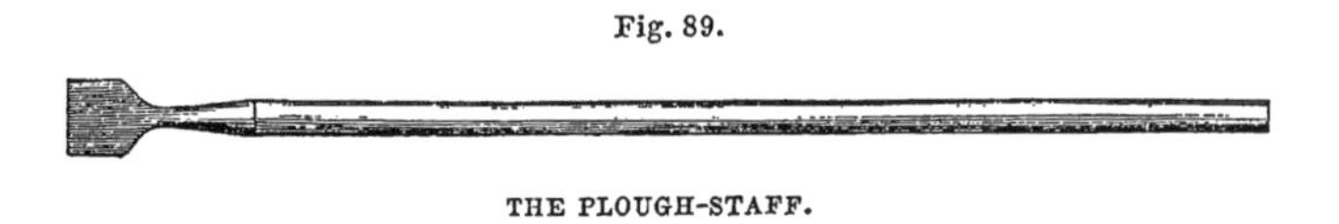

THE PLOUGH-STAFF.

&c., that may accumulate upon the mould-board or the coulter. It is common to all ploughs.

(719.) *The land-side.*—Figs. 90 and 91 are illustrations of the *land-side* of the body of this plough; fig. 90 being an elevation with the extremities cut off, the point of the share, as before, rests upon the base line at *a* and *b*, and

Fig. 90.

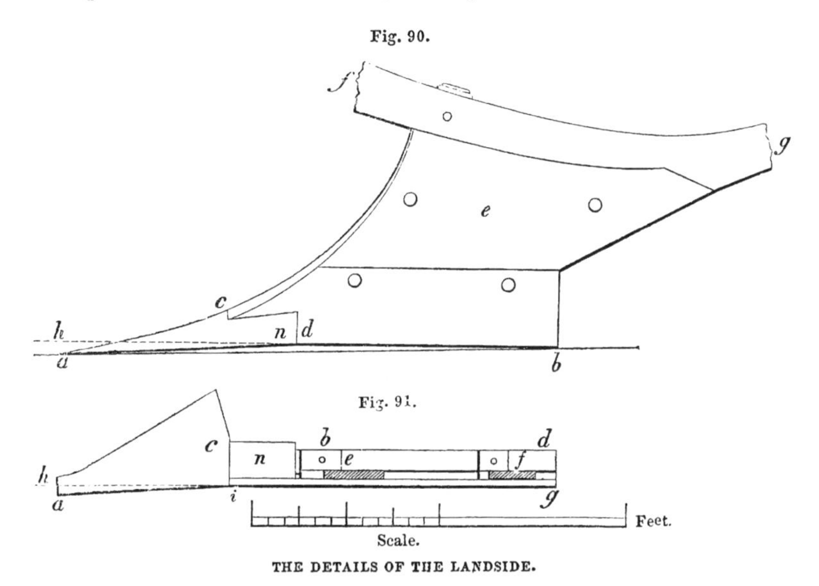

THE DETAILS OF THE LANDSIDE.

the lines of the sole lying between these points form the obtuse angle in the sole-lines; *a c* is the share, *n* its neck, and *d b* the sole-shoe; *e* is the land-side plate, which is adapted to fill up the entire space between the side-flange of the sole-shoe and the beam; the fore part being adjusted to finish with the edge of the mould-board, while the posterior part, may be worked off to the taste of the maker. The lines *a d* and *d b*, together with the base line, form a very low triangle, *a d b*; the altitude at *d*, being not more than $\frac{3}{8}$ of an inch; and by extending the side *b d* to *h*, the depression *h a* of the point of the share below the line *b d*, thus extended, will be from $\frac{1}{2}$ to $\frac{3}{4}$ of an inch. Fig. 91 represents a horizontal section of the body, as if cut off at the upper edge of the sole-shoe. Here *a c* is the share, *n* its neck; the line *g h* being a continuation of the land-side plane, indicates the inclination landward of the point of the share, which, in this plough, is usually from $\frac{1}{2}$ to $\frac{3}{4}$ inch; *b d* is the sole-bar, the bolt-hole at *b* being that by which the right handle is fixed to the bar; *e* and *f* the 2 arms or bars of the body-frame, as cut across in the section; and $g\ i$ is the land-side flange of the sole-shoe. The line $g\ i$, continued to h, exhibits the inclination of the point of the share to landward of the land-side plane. The same reasoning applies to the inclinations of the share from the sole and land side planes, as has been offered in the case of the East-Lothian plough.

(720.) THE MID LOTHIAN or CURRIE PLOUGH.—The Mid Lothian or Currie plough is delineated in Plate X., where fig. 53 is an elevation of the furrow-side, and fig. 54 a horizontal plan of the entire plough. This variety of the plough, probably from its more recent introduction, has undergone fewer changes than the two former. In one of its essential parts—the mould-board, little or no difference is to be found in all the range of this variety. In the share, greater changes are observable, and also in the coulter, as shall be noticed in due course. In the majority of these ploughs, a cast-iron body-frame is employed, and in all, the mould-board is prolonged forward over the neck of the share; and the draught is applied, through the medium of a chain-bar, placed under the beam. In respect of the mould-board of this plough, it is, in point of curvature, nearly the same as the East-Lothian, though, in its prolongation forward, it bears a resemblance to the Lanarkshire, but without possessing the characteristics of that mould-board, as will be afterwards shewn. The share, in so far as it is immediately connected with the mould-board, closely resembles the Lanarkshire, and the external parts of it takes also after that plough. The Mid-Lothian plough, therefore, may very appositely be termed a hybrid.

(721.) In the construction of the *frame-work* of this plough, the beam and left handle are usually finished in one continued bar ABC, possessing the varied curvature exhibited in fig. 53, as viewed in elevation. When viewed in plan, as in fig. 54, the axis of the beam lies in one straight line, though in this there are slight shades of variation, with different makers; and the left handle, from its junction with the tail of the beam, gradually deviates from the line of the beam's axis, till, at the extremity A, it stands 3 inches to the left of the line of that axis. With reference to the plane of the land-side, also, when the fore part of the body is vertical, the point of the beam is inclined to the right of the plane about 1½ inch, and the hind part of the body on the land-side overhangs the edge of the sole ¼ inch, there being that extent of twist upon the surface of the land-side, within the limits of the body. Some makers of this plough,—and they are those of the greatest eminence,—adopt the practice also of throwing the coulter-box to the right hand, in the beam, making the beam plain on the land-side, as in the Lanarkshire plough. This, however, is not universal, many still preferring to have the coulter in the axis of the beam. In the first case, the land-side of the coulter stands at an angle of about 7°, and the latter about 5° with the vertical line.

(722.) The *right handle* DE is formed in a separate bar, and attached to the body-frame at its fore end by a bolt, as will be shewn in detail; and it is farther connected to the left handle by the stretcher-bolts FFF, and the stays GG.

(723.) The *coulter* I is fixed in its box K by means of iron-wedges, which set and retain it in its proper position. The rake or angle that the cutting edge of the coulter in this plough makes with the base-line, takes a greater range than any of the other two, being from 45° to 80°. The land-side face, taken horizontally, is usually set to form an angle of 2° landward, with the land-side plane.

(724.) The *mould-board* L is fixed upon the body-frame, as before described, and is adapted, as in the former cases, to the turning over the furrow-slice. Its fore edge or breast MN coincides with the land-side of the body; its lower edge O, behind, stands from 8½ to 9 inches distant from the land-side; while its upper edge P spreads out to 19¼ inches from the land-side. It is, as already observed, prolonged forward, covering the neck of the share, and meeting the shield at the root of the feather Q. At the point NQ, the horizontal breadth of the mould-board is 3 inches, its height from the base line, at the same point N, ranges from 2¾ inches to 3¼ inches, according to the degree of inclination that is given to the share; but the real height from the plane of the sole-shoe is 2½ inches. The length of the mould-board along the lower edge, from O to N, is 23 inches; from P to M, along the upper edge, 26 inches; and the extreme length, from P to N, is 35½ inches. The perpendicular height, from the plane of the base line to the upper edge at P, is about 12½ inches, though trifling deviations from these dimensions may be found amongst the makers of this plough.

(725.) The *share* QR is fitted upon the head, which in general is of cast-iron, as afterwards described, the neck passing under the mould-board at NQ; and the shield, falling into the curve of the mould-board, terminates forward in the chisel-point R.

(726.) The *bridle* C of this plough is formed by a pair of straps S, appended to the point of the beam; and from the lower parts of these, the chain bar H passes to the beam, whereon it is fixed, a few inches before the coulter-box K. The bridle proper, U, is attached by the same bolt that connects the chain to the straps. Shifting the straps S up or down upon the beam, affords the requisite adjustment vertically, and the bridle U gives the horizontal adjustment.

(727.) The right and left handles are each furnished, at A and D, with *wooden helves*, fitted into the sockets of the handles. In this plough, also, there is usually applied a *brace-rod* V, fixed at the fore end to the tail of the beam, and behind to the right handle by a bolt and nut, for the purpose of supporting the right handle.

(728.) The *general dimensions* of this plough are—From the zero point O to the extremity of the heel T, the distance is 5 inches; and from O forward to the point R of the share, is 29 inches; making an entire length of 34 inches on the sole. Again, from O backward to the extremity of the handles A′, the distance is 6 feet 2 inches; and forward to the draught-bolt U′, 4 feet 3 inches; making the extreme length on the base line 10 feet 5 inches; but measuring along the sinuosities of the beam and handle, the entire length from A to U is 11 feet 6 inches.

(729.) In reference to the *body* of the plough, the centre of the coulter-box is 16 inches, and the point M of the breast curve 8 inches before the zero-point; both as measured on the base-line; but, in following the rise of the beam, the distance from M to the middle of the coulter-box is 11 inches.

(730.) The *heights* of the different points, from the base line to the upper edge of the beam and handle, are marked on fig. 53; the chief points only being expressed here. At the helve of the left handle, the height is 3 feet, the right, being 2 inches lower; the difference in height continuing nearly uniform throughout their length. The height of the point of the beam at C is 23 inches, and to the centre of the draught-bolt at a medium 16½ inches. The lower edge of the mould-board, behind, is usually set at ¼ inch above the plane of the sole; while, at its junction with the share at N, the height above the base line runs from 1½ to 1¾ inches.

(731.) For the dimensions of all the individual parts of the frame-work of this plough, it is unnecessary to repeat them here, as they correspond so nearly with those already stated in treating of the two first varieties. In this respect, therefore, reference is now made to those before described in paragraphs (687), and (710).

(732.) *The body-frame.*—The Mid-Lothian, like the East-Lothian plough, is usually constructed with a cast-iron body-frame, differing, however, in some respects, from the latter. Fig. 92 is an elevation of the furrow-side of the body-frame. It consists of a plate or web *a b c d*, of about ½ inch thick, upon which is planted the sole-bar *b e f*, the beam-flange *a h*, and also the ribs *b i* and *k l*; these last are for the purpose of strengthening the web. Fig. 93 is a direct view of the under surface of the sole-bar. Its breadth at *b* and *e* is 2¼ inches, but from *e* towards *m* it is diminished to 2 inches, where the thickness is ½ inch;

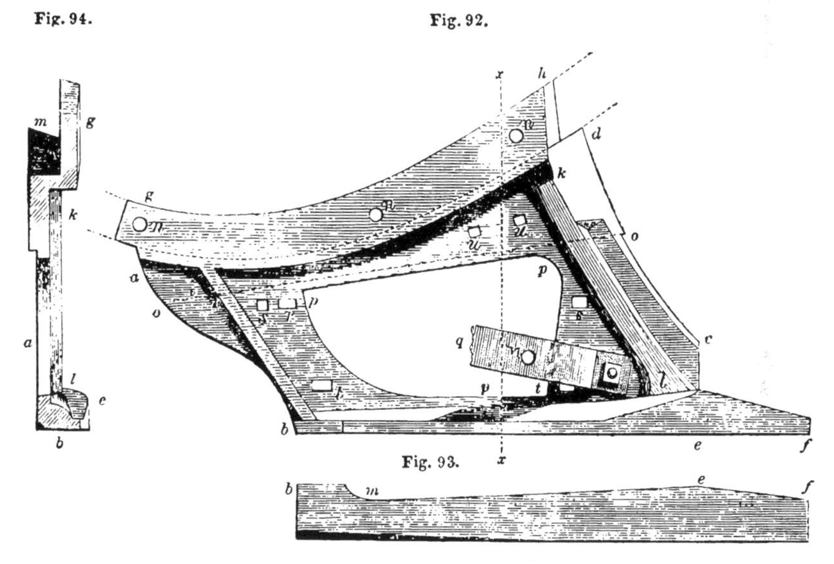

THE DETAILS OF THE BODY-FRAME.

but at *e*, where the principal strain falls, through the action upon the share, the depth is increased to 2 inches, from which it tapers forward to *f*, where it measures 1¼ inches in breadth and ¾ inches in depth. From *e*, it diminishes also backward; and from *l*, to *b*, a filling piece is inserted in the pattern, in the angle, as seen at *l*, fig. 94, to increase the strength. A filling piece is also inserted at *k*, fig. 92, to support that point where the strain from the beam falls upon the body, as well as to give a bearing to the breast of the mould-board. Fig. 94 is a transverse section of the body-frame on the line *x x*, looking forward; *a* is the web, *b e* the sole-bar, *k l* one of the ribs in fig. 92, *g* the beam-flange, and *m* the seat into which the beam is received when applied to the frame, and bolted, as at *n n n*. In the best examples of this body-frame, a part of the land-side plating is cast along with the frame; the lower edge of this portion is represented by the dotted line *o o*, fig. 92; and the frame, as here described, is always cast in one piece, but having the perforation *p p p* always formed in it. A broken off portion of the right handle is marked *q*, and is formed at the fore part into a palm, by which it is bolted to the web. The bolt-hole *r* is the place of insertion of the lower stretcher, which connects the right handle to the body-frame; *s s* are the bolts of the land-side plate; *t t* those for the land-side flange of the shoe; *u u* are the bolts for fixing a kneed bracket, on which the upper fore part of the mould-board rests, and is bolted, the lower fixture being at *v*; and a third is obtained through a bracket, bolted upon the right handle, as seen at Y, fig. 54, Plate X. The length of the beam-flange in this frame is from 19 to 19½ inches, and the height and outline of that part are obtained from the heights marked in fig. 53, Plate X, deducting 1 inch for the thickness of the sole-shoe at the heel, and ½ inch at the point.

(733.) *The sole-shoe.*—Fig. 95 is a plan of the sole-shoe; *a b* the sole-

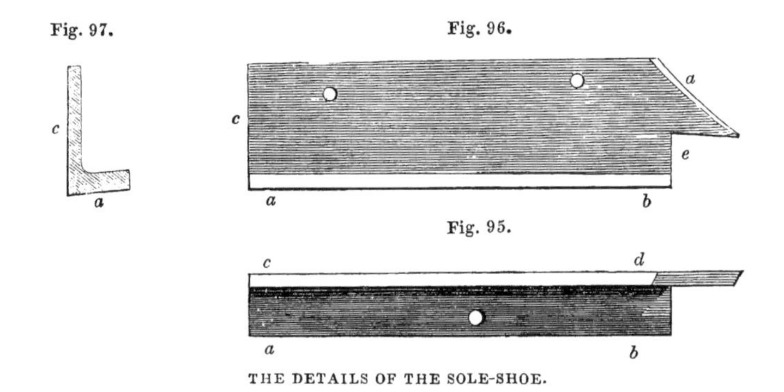

THE DETAILS OF THE SOLE-SHOE.

flange 17 inches in length, 3 inches in breadth, and 1 inch in depth at *a* the heel, but diminished to ½ inch at *b*; *c d* is the land-side flange, ½ inch in thickness at bottom, and ⅜ inch at the upper edge, the height being 4 inches. Fig. 96 is the furrow-side of the shoe, with the same letters of reference; *e* is the notch at the fore part, for the passage of the neck of the share; it is 4½ inches in length and 2½ inches in height, *d* being the curve adapted to the breast of the mould-board. Fig. 97 is a transverse section of the shoe, *a* the sole, and *c* the side-flange.

(734.) *The share.*—The share of this plough, in principle and construction, is the same as that of the Lanarkshire; but in the present case, the head being of cast-iron, the neck is necessarily somewhat larger. Fig. 98 is a plan, in

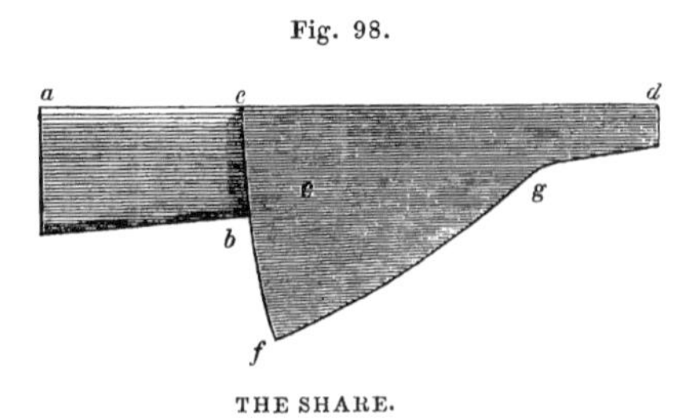

THE SHARE.

which *a b* is the neck, *a e d*, the land-side, and *c g e*, the shield; *b f g* is the feather and *g d*, the point of the share, which, in this plough, is usually chisel-pointed, and longer between the termination of the feather, and the point, than in the share of the Lanarkshire plough. In further illustration of this share, reference is made to that of the Lanarkshire plough, where fig. 78 is a direct view of the furrow-side of the share, exhibiting the rise of the cutting edge of the feather above the base-line, which, in the ploughs considered the most perfect for ploughing lea, amounts to a rise of $1\frac{1}{4}$ to $1\frac{1}{2}$ inch. The extreme breadth of this share over the feather ranges from $4\frac{1}{2}$ to $5\frac{1}{2}$ inches, the length from the point to the head of the shield, at a maximum, is 11 inches, and including the neck, 17 inches; under the same condition, the length from the extreme point to the commencement of the feather at *g*, is about $3\frac{1}{2}$ inches. Fig. 79 is an end-view of the share looking forward, in which also the same letters are applied; *a b* is the opening of the neck to receive the head, and *e c g* shews the outline of the posterior extremity of the shield and feather. This, like the Lanarkshire plough, is held as peculiarly adapted to the ploughing of lea-land; and as the share just described is that which is adapted for that purpose,—for the chief and almost sole difference between the adaptation of these ploughs for lea and stubble land lies in the configuration of the share,—it is necessary to advert to the stubble land or fallow share. In this the chief, indeed the only, difference lies in the formation of the feather, which for stubble land is made broader, and the cutting edge, instead of rising from the point at an angle of 8°, is formed so as to approach to the plane of the sole, or not exceeding an angle of 4°.

(735.) *The land-side.*—Figs. 99 and 100 are illustrations of the land-side of the body of this plough, the extremities, as in the previous cases, being cut off. Fig. 99 is an elevation, *a b* is the base-line, *a c* the share, *n* its neck, and *d b* the sole-shoe; *e e* are the land-side plates, the upper one, as before stated, being

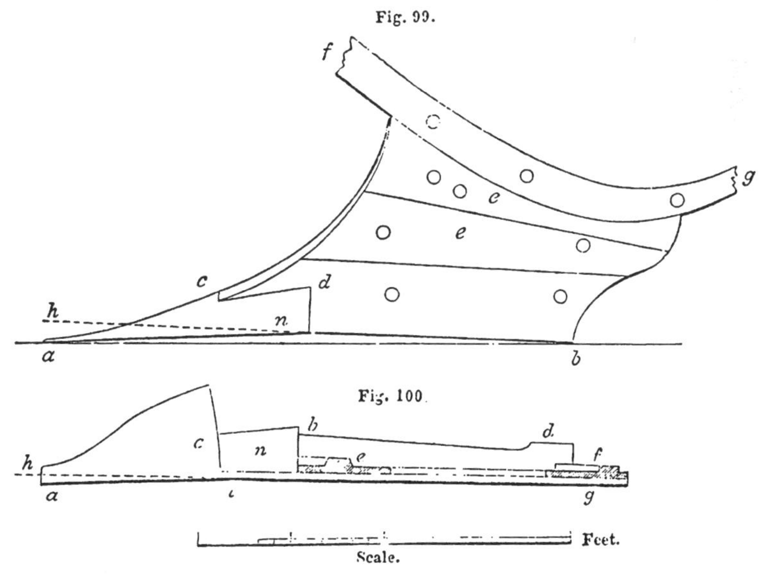

THE DETAILS OF THE LANDSIDE.

cast as a part of the body, and *f g* is a part of the beam. In the extreme cases of this plough, the altitude of the low triangle *a n b* is $\frac{3}{4}$ inch, and when the line of the sole *b n* is extended to *h*, the depression of the point of the share below that line is found to be about $1\frac{1}{4}$ inch. Fig. 100 represents a horizontal section of the body-frame, as if cut off at the upper edge of the sole-shoe; here *a c* is the share, *n* its neck, and *b d* the sole-flange; *e* and *f* are the two bars of the body-frame, and *g i* the land-side of the sole. By continuing the line of the land-side to *h*, the inclination of the share landward is found frequently to be 1 inch.

(736.) *The bridle.*—As has been already noticed, this plough differs from the others in its bridle being connected with a chain-bar, passing under and attached to the beam near the coulter-box; and for the purpose of receiving this

Fig. 101.

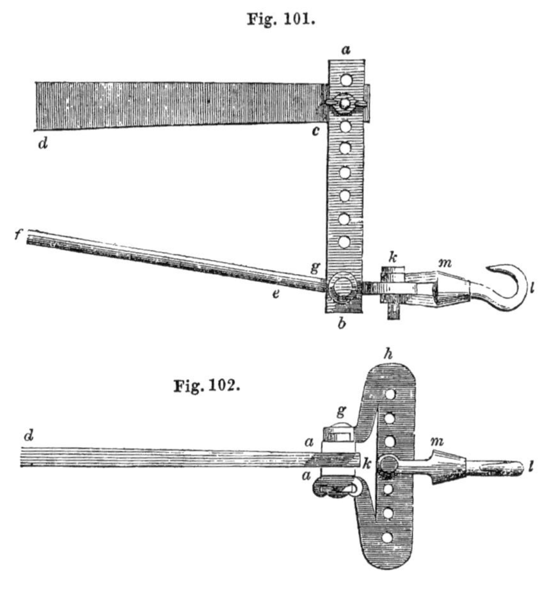

THE DETAILS OF THE BRIDLE.

equipage, the point of the beam, is elevated to the height of 23 inches above the base-line. The chain, is usually a single rod of iron, with a link and shackle behind, by which it is connected to the beam, by means of a bolt passing through the shackle and the beam at a point about 3 inches before the coulter-box. The bridle, of which fig. 101 is an elevation and fig. 102 a plan, consists of a pair of iron straps *a b*, 10 inches in length, and 1½ inch by ½ inch, each having a number of perforations by which they can be appended to the point of the beam *c d*, by means of a bolt passing through them and the beam; a strap *a b* being on each side of it. The fore end of the chain-bar *f e*, is, in like manner, received between the lower ends of the straps at *b* and secured by the draught-bolt *g*. On the same bolt is appended the bridle proper *h i*, the bolt passing through the whole of the parts. The bridle is formed with a web *h i* in front, 9 inches in length, and 1½ inches in breadth, having also a number of perforations for receiving the shackle-bolt *k*. In this equipage the draught-swivel-hook *l* and the shackle *m* are combined in one, which completes the arrangement. This combination of bridle-mounting, gives the same facility as before for shifting the direction of the draught; vertically, by raising or lowering the straps *a b* on the point of the beam, and horizontally, by shifting the shackle-bolt and shackle *k m* right and left.

(737.) Of the Action of the Plough.—The *coulter*, the *share*, and the *mould-board*, being the principal active parts of the plough, and those which supply the chief characteristics to the implement, it may be useful to the farmer as well as to the agricultural mechanic, to enter into a more minute descriptive detail of the nature and properties of these members, before entering upon the duties which each in its turn has to perform in the action of cutting and turning over the furrow-slice.

(738.) *The coulter.*—The coulter, in its construction, as well as in the duties it has to perform, is the simplest member of the plough. It is a simple bar, in form as represented by figs. 67 and 68; varying in length, according to the variety of the plough to which it belongs, from 18 to 22 inches. Simple though the form and duties of the coulter may be, there is no member of the plough whereof such a variety of opinions exist as to its position. I have shewn that in practice the rake or angle which its cutting edge makes with the base-line ranges from 45° to 80°, that of its land-side face from 4° to 8° with the vertical, and that the same face, in the horizontal direction, varies from 0° to 4° with the land-side. The objects of these variations will be duly pointed out, as mere matters of taste and convention amongst ploughmen. Two points alone, in regard to position, should be considered as standard and invariable. These are, 1st, that *the land-side face of the coulter shall be always parallel, in the horizontal direction, to the plane of the land-side of the plough's body;* and, 2d, *that at the height of 7 inches, or of 6 inches, according to the depth of furrow to which the plough is adapted, the land-side face of the coulter shall be ¼ inch to landward, or to the left, of the plane of the land-side of the body.* One other point in position is subject to a great diversity of opinion; that is, the position in which the extreme point of the coulter should stand in relation to the point of the share. In respect to *landing*, or that cause which requires the point of the coulter to be placed to landward of the share, the range of opinion is within moderate bounds, being from 0 to ¾ inch; but in the vertical direction, the range varies from ¼ inch to 2 inches; and in the longitudinal direction, a like difference of opinion exists. Thus Small recommends that the point of the coulter should be 2 or 3 inches in *advance* of the point of the share, and ½ or 1 inch *above* the plane of the sole (base-line), while it should be ½ inch or 1 inch to *landward* of the land-side plane.* The first of these propositions, as will be afterwards shewn, is very much at fault; and the almost universal practice, also, of keeping the two points nearly equal in advance, condemns the practice, and points out equality as the rule. In regard to the position of the point landward, it is liable to considerable variation, partly from the inclination that may be given to the share, and likewise from the degree of obliquity between the coulter and the land-side. This last, indeed, combined with the rule laid down, from the position of the coulter in relation to the land-side, at the height of 6 or 7 inches, is the true source from which the landward relation of the points of the coulter and share can be ascertained; hence, therefore, in whatever variety of the plough, *the coulter should have its position in regard to land determined first; and the point of the share should take its position from the coulter.* The distance to which the point of the share stands to the right of the coulter should in no case exceed ½ inch, but it were better to confine it to ¼ inch. In the vertical position, the advancing of the point of the coulter to, or retiring from, the share, violates no principle in the relation of the parts; but, to place the coulter at an undue distance above the share, leaves that portion of the slice uncut, that falls between the two points; which must produce an undue resistance, from the part being

* Small's Treatise on Ploughs, pp. 18 and 40.

forcibly pressed asunder, by a process like clipping, through the inclined action of the share upward. The nature of the soil, whether stony, or gravelly, or a loam, will, however, always have an effect on this point of the trimming of the plough; and as no principle is affected, there is no impropriety in giving a latitude in this direction, though I conceive that a distance of 1 inch, between the points of the share and coulter, ought to be the maximum, except in cases where the nature of the soil may demand a deviation from that distance.

(739.) The office which the coulter has to perform in the action of the plough, is simple and uniform; being merely to make an incision through the soil, in the direction of the furrow-slice that is to be raised. It is a remarkable fact, that in doing this, it neither increases, nor decreases, the resistance of the plough in any appreciable degree. Its sole use, therefore, is to cut a smooth edge in the slice which is to be raised, and an unbroken face for the land-side of the plough to move against in its continued progress.

(740.) In the early works on the principles of the plough, some misconceptions appear to have been formed of the influence of the coulter, under the supposition that the coulter extending 3 inches in front of the share acted beneficially; and that giving the coulter a great rake, or a low angle with the base, made it cut the soil advantageously, and with less resistance. From a series of experiments, I have satisfied myself that the first of these suppositions is erroneous, and that the projection of the coulter before the share increases the resistance in a very sensible degree. With regard to the second, the resistance seems not to be affected by the angle at which the edge of the coulter stands; and the analogy of a common cutting instrument* does not hold in the case of the coulter of the plough. With a razor or a knife in the hand, we make them pass through any object by *drawing* their cutting edge over the surface to be cut, in the manner as with a saw, which greatly increases the effect without any increase of force; and this holds, in all proper cutting instruments; but let the edge of the instrument be placed simply at an angle with the direction in which the stroke or cut is to be made, and in making the cut, let this oblique position be retained; so that the cutting edge shall proceed parallel to its original position, without any tendency to *drawing* the edge across the direction of the cut; no saving of force is obtained. This process must be familiar to every one who uses a knife for any purpose whatever. In slicing a loaf, the operator is at once sensible that, by moving the knife gently backward or forward, he is required to exert less force, while he at the same time makes a smoother cut, than he would do by forcing the knife through the loaf, with its edge either at right angles or obliquely to the direction in which the knife proceeds. The coulter of the plough acts in this last position, its cutting edge stands obliquely to the direction of motion, but has no means of drawing or *sliding*, to cross the *forward* motion; it therefore cuts by sheer force of pressure.† Where elastic substances occur, an instrument cutting in this manner has some advantages. In the case of fibrous roots, for example, crossing the path of the coulter; the latter, by passing under them, sets their elasticity in action, by which they allow the edge to slide under them to a small extent, and thus produces the *sawing* effect. In the non-elastic earths, of which soils are chiefly composed, nothing of this kind, it is apprehended, can

* Small's Treatise on Ploughs, p. 18.

† An ingenious application of the drawing action here illustrated is to be found in the subterranean cutters of Mr Parkes' steam-plough for ploughing moss-land.

occur; hence the angle of the coulter, as it affects the force requisite to move the plough, is of little importance.

(741.) I have said that the projection of the coulter in front of the share increases the resistance, and I am borne out in this assertion from the result of experiments not a little inexplicable. On a subject which has of late attracted considerable attention, I was desirous of obtaining information, from experiments alone, on the actual implement; and to attain this the more fully, I determined on analyzing the resistance as far as possible. With this view, a plough was prepared whose coulter descended 7 inches below the line of the sole, and fitted to stand at any required angle. This plough, *with its sole upon the surface of two years' old lea,* and the *coulter* alone in the *soil,* the bridle having been adjusted to make it swim without any undue tendency; the force required to draw this experimental instrument, as indicated by the dynamometer, was 26 imperial stones, or $3\frac{1}{4}$ cwt., and no sensible difference was observed in a range of angles varying from 45° to 70°. This coulter having been removed, the plough was drawn along the surface of the field, when the dynamometer indicated 8 stones, the usual draught of a plough on the surface. Another well-trimmed plough was at work in the same ridge, taking a furrow 10 by 7 inches, and its draught was also 26 stones. On removing the coulter from this plough, and making it take a furrow of the same dimensions, the draught was still the same, namely 26 stones; the furrow thus taken produced, of course, a slice of very rough ploughmanship, and though it exhibited by a negative, the essential use of the coulter—the clean cutting of the slice from the solid ground—the whole question of the operation and working effects of the coulter are thus placed in a very anomalous position. The question naturally arises, what becomes of the force, required to draw the coulter alone, through the ground; when, as it appears, the same amount of force is capable of drawing the entire plough with or without a coulter? A definite and satisfactory answer, it is feared, cannot at present be given to the question, and until experiments have been repeated and varied in their mode of application, any explanation that can be given is mere conjecture.

(742.) Since we have seen that the *same force is required to draw the plough without a coulter as with it,* and as it has been observed that the work performed without the coulter is very rough, by reason of the slice being in a great measure *torn* from the solid ground, the breast of the plough being but indifferently adapted for cutting off the slice; it is more than probable, that the tearing asunder of the slice, from the solid ground, requires a certain amount of force above what would be required, were the slice previously severed, by the vertical incision of the coulter. And though we find that the force requisite to make this incision, when taken alone, is equal to the whole draught; yet there appears no improbability in the supposition, that the *minus* quantity in the one may just equal the *plus* in the other. Be this as it may, the discovery of the anomaly presents at least a curious point for investigation, and one that may very probably, through a train of careful experiments, point out the medium through which a minimum of draught is to be obtained.

(743.) Regarding the effect of change on the angle of the edge of the coulter, though it does not directly affect the draught of the plough, it is capable of producing practical effects that are of importance. In ploughing stubble land, or land that is very foul with weeds, the coulter should be trimmed to a long rake, that is, set at a low angle, say from 45° to 55°; this will give it a tendency to free itself of the roots, and weeds, that will collect upon it, by their sliding upward on the edge of the coulter; and, in general, will be ultimately thrown off without exertion on the part of the ploughman. The accumulation of masses of such refuse on the coulter, greatly increases the labour of the horses. The amount of this increased labour I have frequently ascertained by the dynamometer, and have found it to increase the draught of the ploughs from 26 stones, their ordinary draught when clear, up to 36 stones, and immediately on the removal of the obstruction, the draught has fallen to an average force of 26 stones. It is unnecessary to add, that the prevention of such waste of muscular exertion ought to be the care of the farmer, as far as the construction of his machines will admit of.

(744.) To apply a plough with its coulter set in the position above described to lea-land with a rough surface, would produce a kind of ploughmanship not approved of; every furrow would be bristling with the withered stems of the unconsumed grasses; for, to plough such land with a coulter set in this way, would cause its partially matted surface to present a ragged edge, from the coulter acting upon the elastic fibres, and roots of the grasses, pressing them upwards before they could be cut through. The ragged edge of the slice thus produced gives, when turned over, that untidy appearance which is often observable in lea ploughing. To obviate this, the coulter should be set at a higher angle, by which it will cut the mat, without tearing it up with a bearded edge. *Crack* ploughmen, when they are about to exhibit a specimen of fine ploughing, are so guarded against this defect, that they sometimes get their coulter kneed forward under the beam so far as to bring the edge nearly perpendicular. The same cause induces the makers of the Lanarkshire plough to set the coulter with its land-side face, not coincident with the land-side plane horizontally, but at an angle with it of 4°, thus placing the *right* hand face of the coulter nearly parallel to the land-side plane, and thereby removing the tendency, of the ordinary oblique position of the right hand face, to produce a rough-bearded edge on the rising slice. The dynamical effect of such a position will be afterwards treated of.

(745.) *The share.*—The structure and position of the different shares having been already pointed out, (693.), (714.), (734.), and also their relations to the coulter; there remains to make some general remarks on the action of the share, and on the effects resulting from the varieties of that member of the plough.

(746.) We have seen that the coulter performs but a comparatively small portion of the operation required in the turning a furrow slice. The share, however, takes a more important and much more extensive part in the process; on the functions of the share, in short, depends much of the character of the plough. Its duty is very much akin to that of a spade, if pushed horizontally into the soil with a view to lift a sod of earth, but as its action is continuous, its form must be modified to suit a continuous action; hence, instead of the broad cutting edge of the spade, which in the generality of soils would be liable to be thrown out of its course by obstacles such as stones; the share may be conceived as a spade wherein one of its angles has been cut off obliquely, leaving only a narrow point remaining, adapted to make the first impression on the slice. A narrow point being liable to meet obstruction, only in the ratio of its breadth, to the breadth of the entire share, the chances of its encountering stones are extremely few; and though the oblique edge, now called the feather, has a like number of chances to come in contact with stones, yet, from its form, taking them always obliquely, and the direct resistance which the body of the plough meets with on the land-side, preventing any swerving to the left; such stones, as come in contact with the sloping edge of the feather, are easily pushed aside towards the open furrow on the right. The share thus acts by the insertion of its point under the slice intended to be raised, and this is followed up by the feather, which continues the operation begun by the point, by separating the slice horizontally, from the subsoil or the sole of the furrow; and simultaneous with this, the coulter separates the slice vertically from the still solid ground. Probably the most natural impression that would occur, at the first thought of this operation, will be, that the feather of the share should be of a breadth capable of producing the immediate and entire separation of the slice from the sole; but experience teaches us that such would not fulfil all the requisite conditions of good ploughing. The slice must not only be separated, it must be gradually turned upon its edge, and ultimately still farther turned over until that which was the upper surface becomes the lower, lying at an angle of about 45°. It is found that *if the slice were cut entirely off from the sole*, the plough would frequently *fail in turning it over* to the position just referred to; it might, in place of this, be only moved a space to the right and fall back, or, at most, it would be liable to remain standing upon its edge; in either case the work would be very imperfect, and it has therefore been found necessary to leave a portion, usually from ½ to ¼ of the slice uncut by the feather of the share. This portion of the slice is left to be *torn* asunder from the sole as it rises upon the mould-board, by which means the slice retains longer, its hold of the subsoil; turning by that hold, as upon a hinge, till brought to the vertical position, after which it is easily brought into its ultimate place. The breadth of the share is thus of necessity limited to ¾ the breadth of the slice at a maximum, though its minimum, as will appear, may not exceed ½.

(747.) The disposition of the *feather* comes next under notice. The feather having to perform the operation of cutting that part of the slice, below, that lies between the point of the share and the extremity of the feather, it is formed with a thin edge suited to cutting the soil; but the *position of that cutting edge* forms a principal feature in distinguishing the varieties of the plough, as before described. This distinguishing character is of two kinds; 1*st*, that which has the cutting edge lying parallel or nearly so to the plane of the sole, as in the East-Lothian plough, and, 2*d*, that which has this cutting edge elevated as it retires from the point of the share, rising at an angle with the base line, which is found to vary from 4° to 8° as in the Lanarkshire and the Mid-Lothian ploughs; and all the sub-varieties of these ploughs have their shares coming under one or other of these two divisions.

(748.) The share, in either of the forms above described, passes *under the* furrow-slice, making a partial separation of it from the sole of the furrow, rising as the share progresses, the rise, however, being confined entirely to the *land-side edge* of the slice, the furrow edge, as has been shewn, remaining still in connection with the solid ground; and the shield and back of the share being a continuation of the mould-board, the latter, in its progress forward, receives the slice from the share and passes it onward, or, more properly speaking, the plough passes under it.

(749.) One important consideration remains to be noticed regarding the practical effects of the two forms of feather. In the first, which has the cutting edge nearly parallel with the plane of the sole, the furrow-slice being cut below at one level over the whole breadth of the share and feather, the slice, when exposed in section, will be perfectly rectangular or very slightly rhomboidal, and the sole of the furrow will be perfectly level across. Such a share, then, will lift a slice of any given breadth and depth, which shall contain a maximum quantity of soil, and this problem can only be performed by a share so constructed.

(750.) In the second case, where the feather rises above the plane of the sole at the angles already named, the feather is found sometimes to attain a height of 1 inch and $1\frac{1}{4}$ inch above that plane. In all such cases the feather is also narrow, and, supposing that the part of the slice left uncut by it, may be torn asunder, in a continuation of the cut so made, the slice will have a depth at its furrow edge, less by about $1\frac{1}{2}$ inch or more than at its land-side edge, as cut by the point of the share. A transverse section of this slice, therefore, fig. 103, would exhibit not a rectangular parallelogram as before, but a trapezoid, whose

Fig. 103.

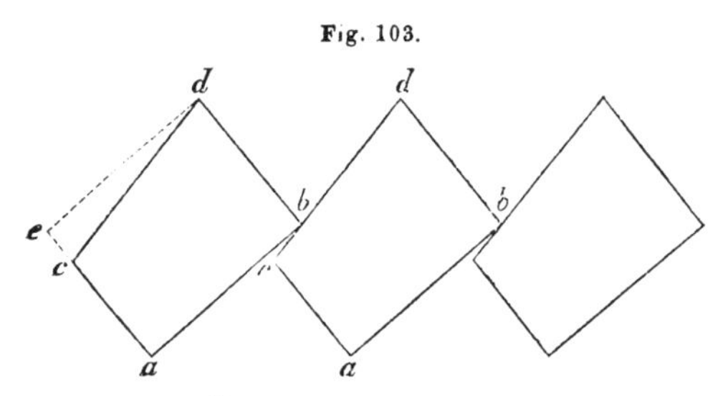

THE CHESTED FURROW-SLICE.

sides *a b*, and *c d*, might be each 9 inches, and its sides *b d*, and *a c*, 6 inches and $4\frac{1}{2}$ inches respectively. A slice of this form would therefore be deficient in the quantity of soil lifted, by a quantity contained in the triangle *d c e*, or about $\frac{1}{7}$ part of the entire slice, and this deficiency is left by the share in the bottom of the furrow as part of the solid subsoil. The absolute quantity of soil thus left unlifted by shares of this construction, will be found to vary with the elevation that is given to the feather; but wherever this form of share is adopted, results similar to that here described will invariably follow, though they may differ in degree; but the quantity left in the bottom of the furrow, will seldom fall short of 10 per cent. of the whole slice. An indirect mode of removing this defect is resorted to in practice, which will be noticed under the head of mould-board.

(751.) The *rule* which I would recommend to be followed in order to secure the maximum of useful effect in the share, as founded on practice and observation, as well as combining the theory of the share and mould-board, is, that the length from the tail of the feather to the point of the share should be from 10 to 11 inches; that the height of the shield—the surface of the share—on the land-side, opposite to the tail of the feather, be $2\frac{1}{2}$ inches above the line of the sole-shoe; that the point of the share be $\frac{1}{2}$ inch below the line of the sole-shoe, and not exceeding $\frac{1}{2}$ inch to landward of the land-side plane, this last point being more properly determinable from the coulter; and lastly, that no part of the edge of the feather should be more than $\frac{3}{8}$ inch above the plane of the sole-shoe, that plane being always understood to be at right angles to the landside plane.

(752.) *The mould-board and its action.*—Since the time that Small achieved his great improvement in the formation of the mould-board, that member has been generally held as the leading point in the plough. This, in one sense, is no doubt true; for if there is a spark of science required in the construction of the plough, it is certainly the mould-board that most requires it. Yet, for all this, I have seen a plough making work little apparently inferior to the first-rate mould-board ploughs, that had nothing to enable it to turn over the slice but a straight bar of wood.* In this case, however, the work was but apparently well done, there being nothing to consolidate the slices upon each other as they fell over by their own weight. The real state of the case seems to be this, that the share impresses the furrow-slice with its form and character, and the duty of the mould-board is to transmit and deposite that slice in the best possible manner, and with the least possible injury to the character previously stamped upon it by the share. If this view is correct, and there appears no reason why it should be questioned, the mould-board is only a medium, through which the slice is conveyed from the share to its destined position. To do this, however, in the most perfect manner, the mould-board has to perform several highly important functions; 1*st*, The transmission of the slice; 2*d*, Depositing it in the proper position; and, 3d, Performing both these operations with the least possible resistance.

(753.) The *raising* and *transmitting* the slice have frequently been described as if consisting of three or more distinct movements. With all deference to former writers, I conceive it may be viewed as having only two movements, namely, cutting the slice by the share and coulter; and, transmitting it to its appointed position through the medium of the mould-board. The first has been already discussed: I now proceed to the second.

(754.) The object of every mould-board is to transmit the slice in the best manner, and with the least possible expenditure of force; but, as might have been expected, we find considerable difference of opinion on both these points, arising from the variations in the form of the mould-board. In a general way, the *transmission of the slice* may be explained in the following manner.

(755.) In fig. 104, *a a* represents a vertical section of part of an unbroken ridge of land, and the parallelogram *a b c d* also a transverse section of an indefi-

Fig. 104.

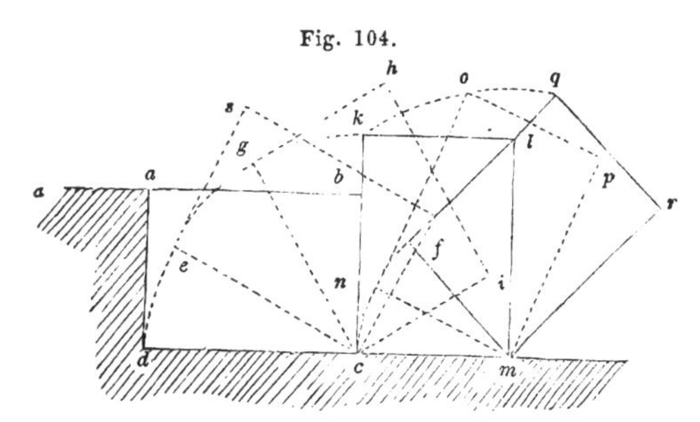

THE TRANSMISSION OF THE FURROW-SLICE.

nitely short portion of a slice which is proposed to be raised, the breadth *a b* being 10 inches and depth *a d* 7 inches; the line *d c* will be the bottom of the slice, or the line on which it is separated from the sole by the action of the share. The points of the share and coulter enter at *d*; and in progressing forward, the slice will be gradually raised at *d*, the point *c* remaining at rest, while the parallelogram revolves upon it as a centre. When the share has penetrated to the extent of the feather, the point *d* of the slice will have been raised 2½ to 3 inches. By the continued progress of the plough, the parallelogram representing the slice will be found in the position *c e s f*, and again at *c g h i*. At the fourth stage, when the zero-point of the mould-board has reached the supposed line of section, the slice will have attained the vertical position *c k l m*. During these stages of this

* A variety of the Kent turn-wrest plough which I have seen in the possession of Mr Hamilton of Carcluie, is an example of this.

uniform process, the slice has been turning on the point *c* as on a pivot, which has retained its original position, while the point *d*, in its successive transitions, has described the quadrant *d e g k*. By the continued progress of the plough, the revolution of the slice will be continued, but it will be observed, that, at this stage, it changes the centre of revolution from *c* to *m*; when the point *k* will have described the arc *k o*, the slice has then reached the position *m n o p*; and ultimately, when the posterior extremity of the mould-board has reached the line of section, the slice will have attained its final position *m f q r*, lying at an angle of 45°, and resting on the previously turned-up slice.

(756.) The *process of turning over the slice*, therefore, approximates to a *uniform motion*, provided the parts of the plough destined to perform the operation are properly constructed. The uniformity, however, is not directly as the rectilineal progress of the plough, but must be deduced from a different function to be afterwards explained. And though the process here described refers only to an indefinitely short slice, it is only necessary to conceive a continuity of such short slices, going to form an entire furrow-slice, extending to the whole length of the field; and, the lengthened furrow-slice being possessed of sufficient tenacity to admit of the requisite, and temporary, extension which it undergoes, while the plough is passing under and turning it over, is again compressed into its original length, when laid in its ultimate position. The furrow-slice, therefore, under this process, may not inaptly be compared to the motion of a wave in the ocean, keeping in view that the wave of the slice is carried forward in a horizontal direction, whereas the ocean-wave is vertical. But in both cases, though the wave travels onward, there is no translation of parts in the direction in which it seems to travel. In the case of the furrow-slice movement, it appears as in the annexed perspective

Fig. 105.

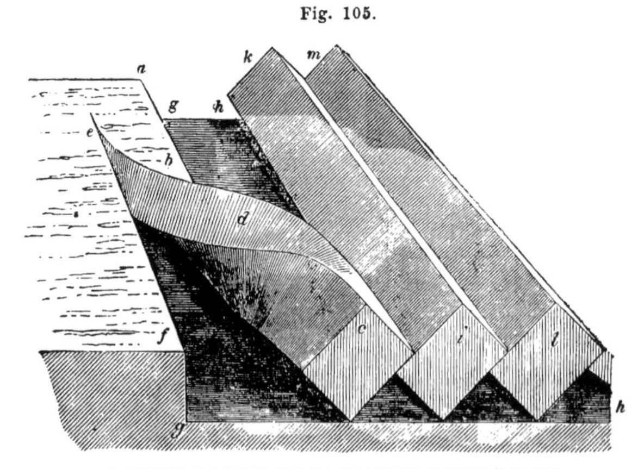

A VIEW OF THE MOVEMENT OF THE FURROW-SLICE.

view, fig. 105, where *a b* is the edge of the land as cut by the preceding furrow; *c d* the slice in the act of turning over, but from which the plough has been removed; *e f*, the edge of the land from which the slice *c d* is being cut; *g h*, the sole of the furrows, and *i k*, *l m*, slices previously laid up. A consideration of this figure will also shew, that the extension of the slice takes place along the land-side edge *e d* only, from *e* to where the backward flexure is given to it when rising on the mould-board; and where it is again compressed into its original length, by the back parts of the mould-board in being laid down.

(757.) *Of the furrow-slice.*—To accomplish efficient ploughing the furrow-slice should always be of such dimensions and laid in such position that the two exposed faces in a series of slices shall be of equal breadth; any departure from this rule is a positive fault, whether the object be a seed-furrow or intended for amelioration by exposure to the atmosphere. Furrow-slices laid up agreeably to this rule will not only present the maximum of surface to the atmosphere, but they will also contain the maximum of cubical contents, both of which propositions may be illustrated thus by fig. 106. Let *a b* represent the breadth of a 10-inch furrow slice, and describe the semicircle *a c b* upon it as a diameter. From the well-known property of the circle, that the angle in a semicircle is a right angle,* every triangle formed upon the diameter, as a base, will be right angled, and the only isosceles triangle that can be formed within it will be that which has the greatest altitude. The triangle *a c b* possesses these properties, for produce *c b* to *d*, making *c d* equal to *a b*,—the breadth of the slice, which must always be equal to the distance between the apices of two contiguous furrows. Complete the parallelogram *a c d e*, which will represent the transverse section of a rectangular slice, whose breadth is 10 inches, and whose two exposed faces *a c* and *c b* lie at angles of 45°, and their breadth, as well as the area of the triangle *a b c*, will be a maximum. In order to prove this, let a section of another slice be formed, whose exposed side *a f* shall be *greater* than the corresponding side *a c* of the former, and let this be taken at 8 inches. From *f*, through the point *b*, draw *f g*, then will *a f b* be a right angle as before; *f g* being also made equal to 10 inches, complete the parallelogram *a f g h*, which will represent the transverse section of a rectangular slice 10 inches by 8 inches, occupying the same horizontal breadth as before, and whose exposed faces will be *a f* and *f b*. Draw the line *i c k* parallel to *a b*, and passing through the apex *c* of the triangle *a c b*; and the line *i′ k′* also parallel to *a b*, passing through the apex *f* of the triangle *a f b*. Here the triangles *a c b* and *a f b* stand on equal bases *a b*; but the first lies between the parallels *a b* and *i c k*, and the second between those of *a b* and *i′ k′*, the altitude *f f′*, therefore, of the triangle *a f b*, is less than the altitude *c c′* of the triangle *a c b*. And triangles on equal bases being proportional to their altitudes, it follows that the triangle *a f b* is *less* than the triangle *a c b*, both in area and periphery. Suppose, again, a slice whose side *a l* is *less* than the corresponding side *a c*, and let it be 6 inches; from *l*, through the point *b*, as before, draw *l m*, and construct the parallelogram *a l m n*, we shall have a transverse section of a third slice of 10 by 6 inches, whose exposed faces *a l*, *l b*, occupy the same horizontal breadth as before. Here the triangle *a l b* lies between the parallels *a b* and *i′ k′*, consequently equal to *a f b* and less than *a c b*.

Fig. 106.

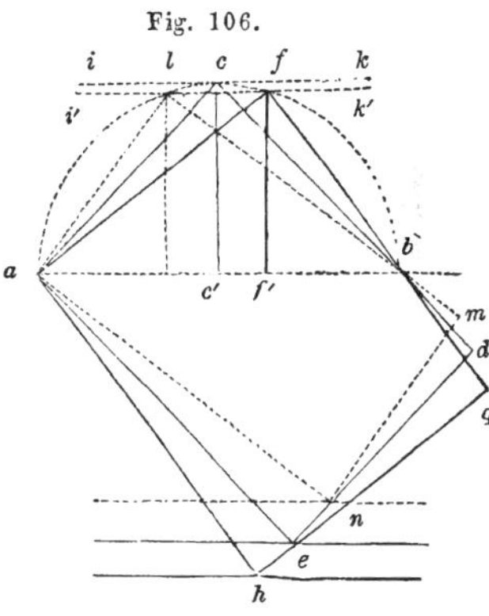

PROPORTIONAL AREAS OF THE FURROW-SLICE IN DIFFERENT POSITIONS.

(758.) This simple geometrical demonstration, as applicable to the slice, may be corroborated by the usual formula of the triangle. Thus, the altitude of the triangle *a c b* is $=\frac{a\,b}{2}=5$ inches $=c'\,c$, and the side *a c* or *c b* is $=\sqrt{a\,c'^2+c\,c'^2}$; or *a c′* and *c c′* being each equal to 5 inches, *a c* or *c b* will $=\sqrt{5^2+5^2}=7.071$

* Euclid, 31, iii.

inches, which is the *depth* due to a slice of 10 inches in *breadth*, and the sum of the two exposed faces will be $7.071 \times 2 = 14.142$ inches.

(759.) In the triangle $a f b$, $a b = 10$ inches and $a f = 8$ inches, then $a b^2 - a f^2 = f b^2$, and the $\sqrt{f b^2} = 6$ inches. The three sides, therefore, of this triangle are 10, 8, and 6 inches, and the altitude $f' f$ is easily found by the principles of similar triangles. Thus, in the similar triangles $a f f'$, $f b f'$, $a b : a f :: f b : f f'$. The perpendicular $f f'$ is therefore $= 4.8$ inches; hence the exposed surfaces are as $14.141 : 14$, and the altitudes as $5 : 4.8$. Since it turns out that $a l$ is equal to $f b$, and $a b$ common to both, it follows that $l b$ is equal to $a f$, and the periphery and altitude also equal, and *less* in all respects than the triangle $a c b$. And so of any other position or dimensions.

(760.) The slice which presents a rectangular section is not the only form which is practised in modern ploughing. Of late years, and since the introduction of the improvements by Wilkie on the plough, a system of ploughing has been revived* in which the great object seems to be that of raising a slice that shall present a *high shoulder*, as it has been called, or which I have ventured to denominate the *crested furrow*, formerly alluded to. The general impressions that prevail as to the advantages of this mode of ploughing are, that the crested furrow affords a *greater surface* to the action of the atmosphere, and a greater quantity of cover to the seed in the case of a seed furrow in lea. As there appears to me some degree of fallacy in the reasonings on this point amongst practical men, and as it does not appear to have been hitherto sufficiently investigated, I shall venture a few remarks in the hope of leading others to a more full consideration of the points involved in the subject.

(761.) The *crested slice*, instead of the rectangular section of the one already described, presents a rhomboidal but much more frequently a trapezoidal section; indeed the latter may be held as inseparable from the practice; but in comparing them I shall first take the exposed surface. In fig. 107, then, let $a b c d$ represent a transverse section of a rectangular slice of 10 by 7 inches, $a e$ the base of the triangle, whose sides $a b$, $b e$ represent the two exposed surfaces of the slice when set up with the sides at angles of 45° to the horizon, its angle at b being 90°,—its altitude $b f$ will be as before $\frac{a e}{2} = 5$ inches. Again, let $g h$ be the base of the triangle whose sides $g b$, $b h$, represent the exposed surfaces of a crested slice—whose base $g h$, equal to $g d$, may be taken at 9 inches, that being the breadth at which such ploughs take their furrow. Supposing, also, that the cresting is such as to give an altitude $f b$ of 5 inches, as in that of the rectangular slice, we shall have the sides $g b$, $b h$, from the usual formula, $g f^2 + f b^2 = g b^2$, and $g f$ being $4\frac{1}{2}$ inches $f b = 5$ inches, then the $\sqrt{4.5^2 + 5^2} = 6.72$ inches $= g b$ or $b h$, being rather more than the best practical authorities for cresting ploughs give to the depth of a slice; the dimensions recommended being from $8\frac{1}{2}$ to 9 inches broad, and from 6 to $6\frac{1}{2}$ inches in depth.

Fig. 107.

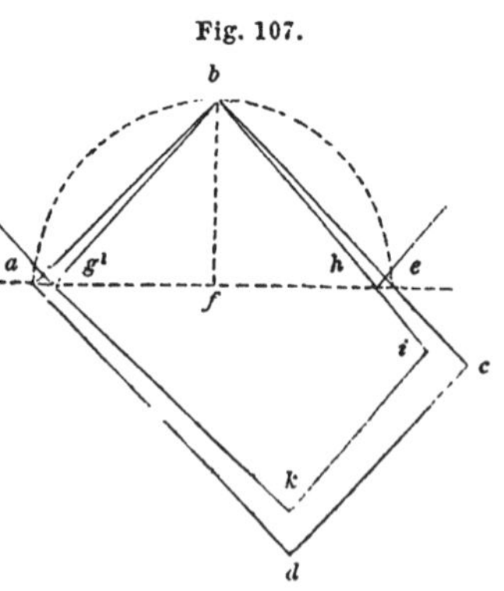

THE COMPARISON OF THE RECTANGULAR AND CRESTED SLICES.

* Blith's "English Improver Improved," p. 266, edit. 1652.

It will, therefore, always fall short in perpendicular height of the rectangular slice of 10 by 7 inches. But allowing the height to be the same, we have two triangles *a b e* and *g b h* of equal height but of unequal bases; their areas will therefore be unequal and proportional to their bases.

(762.) In bringing these two systems, however, into practice over any extent of surface, suppose a ridge of a field, the *number* of furrows of each required to turn over such ridge, will be exactly in proportion to the length of the base of the triangle, or as 9 to 10. Hence, though the individual crested slices or triangles, have an area *less* than that of the rectangular slice in the proportion of 9 to 10; yet the aggregate area of all the triangles, over any given breadth of surface, wherever the number of slices of the one exceeds that of the other in the proportion of 10 to 9, will be the same, but no more. The imaginary advantage, therefore, of a greater cover to the seed with a crested furrow falls to the ground, provided the comparison is made with a plough that takes a furrow of 10 inches wide by 7 inches deep, such as the East-Lothian plough.

(763.) It is to be admitted, that, were cresting ploughs that cut their slices 9 inches wide, to take them 7 inches deep, and still preserve the rhomboidal or trapezoidal section, they might, in that case, produce an increase of cover to the seed, as compared with a rectangular slice of 9 by 7 inches. Let us refer again to the last figure, fig. 107, and suppose $g\,b=7$ inches, $g\,f$ being, as before, $4\frac{1}{2}$ inches, then $g\,b^2-g\,f^2=b\,f^2$, or $b\,f$ will be equal to 5.36 inches, while, by the same method, the rectangular slice of 9 by 7 inches would give $b\,f$ equal to only 4.39 inches, the crested slice in this case giving a difference of height of .97 inch, and $\frac{1}{2}$ of this, or .48 inch, of greater cover of seed. But this is not a practicable case, inasmuch as the cresting plough cannot be worked in a furrow of 9 by 7 inches, and lay it at an angle that would give equal exposure to both sides of the slice, whether it possess a rectangular or rhomboidal section, the true depth being 6.36 inches nearly, for a slice whose breadth is 9 inches; and the height $b\,f$ of its triangle would be, if rectangular, only 4.5 inches. Compared with itself, therefore, the plough that takes a 9 inch furrow rectangular yields $\frac{1}{4}$ inch less cover to the seed than when it raises the crested slice; but, even with the advantage of the crest, it is not better than the plough that takes a 10-inch furrow; while, as will appear, the former labours under other disadvantages arising from that peculiarity of structure for which it is valued.

(764.) In order to exhibit the difference of effect of the rectangular and the trapezoidal slices, as lifted and laid on each other by the plough, and as they affect the real intentions of tillage, I shall consider them in separate detail. Fig. 108 is an example of the rectangular slice of 10 by 7 inches: *a b c d* may be taken as a transverse section of the body of the plough, the line *a c* being the terminal outline of the mould-board, *a f* a section of the slice which is just being laid up, and *g h* a slice previously deposited. In the triangle *i g k* the base *i k* is 10 inches, being always equal to the breadth of the slice, the angle at *g* a right

Fig. 108.

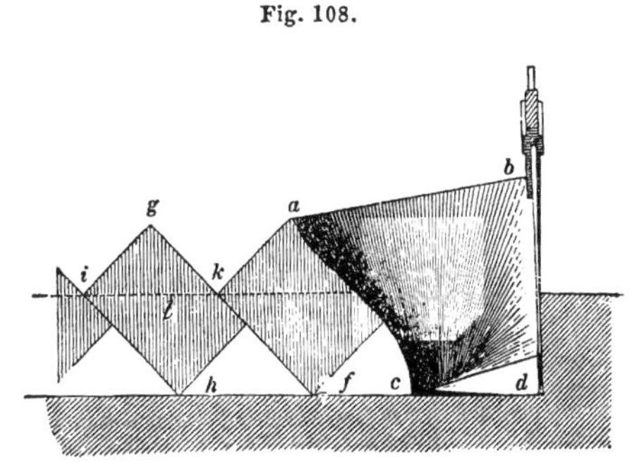

THE EFFECTS OF A RECTANGULAR FURROW-SLICE.

angle, and the sides $i\,g$, $g\,k$ each equal to 7.071 inches, the perpendicular height $g\,l$ being 5 inches, as before demonstrated. Fig. 109 is a similar representation, of a cresting plough, with its effects on the slice and the subsoil; $k\,n\,o\,p$ is a section of the plough, $k\,m$ a section of a slice in the act of being deposited on the preceding slice $c\,l$. Here the slices are trapezoidal, as they are always cut by this species of plough; and from this configuration of the slice, the broader sides are not parallel, nor do the conterminous sides of the adjacent slices lie parallel to each other in the transverse direction. The side $b\,c$ lying at an angle of 48° with the base $a\,b$, while the side $b\,m$ makes the opposite angle at b only 41°, the angle at c being 84°, and the triangle $a\,b\,c$ isosceles. The base $a\,b$ of the triangle $a\,b\,c$ is now supposed to be $8\frac{1}{2}$ inches,—the breadth recommended for a seed-furrow,—and the side $a\,c$ $6\frac{1}{2}$ inches, the opposite side $l\,h$ being $4\frac{1}{2}$ or 5 inches. The base, $a\,b$ when bisected in d, gives $a\,d = 4.25$ inches, and since $a\,c^2 - a\,d^2 = c\,d^2$, $c\,d$ will be 4.918 inches, which is less than given by the former demonstration of the crested slice; but I have observed cases still more extreme, where, still referring to the same figure, $a\,b$ was only $7\frac{1}{2}$ inches, but the angle at c became so acute as 75°, yet with these dimensions $c\,d$ is still under 5 inches; hence, in all practical cases, with a furrow less than 9 inches in breadth, the result will be a reduction in the quantity of cover for seed.

Fig. 109.

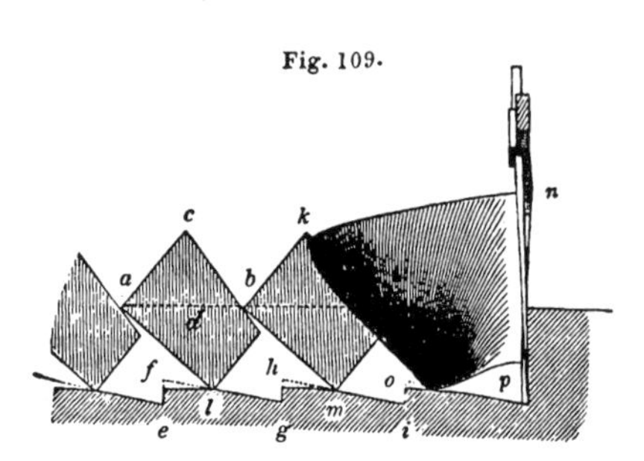

THE EFFECTS OF A TRAPEZOIDAL OR CRESTED FURROW-SLICE.

(765.) One other point remains to be noticed in reference to the two forms of slice. We have seen that the rectangular slice necessarily implies that the bottom of the furrow shall be cut upon a level in its transverse section, fig. 108; while the slice that is cut by the cresting plough leaves the bottom of the furrow with a sloping rise from the land-side towards the furrow-side at every slice, and this rise may range from 1 to $1\frac{1}{2}$ inch or more. Returning to fig. 109, the serrated line $f\,h\,o$, exhibits a transverse section of the surface of the subsoil, from which the soil has been turned up by the cresting plough. The triangular spaces $e\,f\,g$, $g\,h\,i$ represent the quantity of soil left by such ploughs at the lifting of each slice. These quantities, which, as before observed, may amount to $\frac{1}{7}$ of what the slice ought to be, are thus robbed from it, and left adhering to the subsoil, except in so far as they may be rubbed down by the abrading action of the lower edge of the mould-board, as at f and h, and the portions of soil so rubbed off are thrust into the spaces under the edge of the slices as they are successively laid up. This last process may be readily observed at any time when the plough is working in tough land or in lea. With a cresting plough, the spaces $f\,h\,o$ will be seen more or less filled up with crumbled soil; while with the rectangular plough, the corresponding spaces will be left nearly void. I cannot take upon me to say whether or not the filling in of these voids is beneficial to the land in a greater degree than if the $\frac{1}{7}$th here left below had been turned up with the slice; but this I can say, that it is more frequently left adhering to the subsoil than it is to be found stuffed under the edge of the slice. Under any view, the system of the crested furrow ploughing is not unworthy the consideration of the farmer.

(766.) In considering the question, there are two points deserving attention. 1*st*, The immediate effects upon the labour of men and horses. It may be asserted generally, that all ploughs adapted to form a crested furrow are heavier in draught than those that produce the rectangular furrow. This seems a natural inference from the manner in which they work; the tendency that they all have to *under*-cut by the coulter; the narrow feather of the share leaving more resistance to the body in raising and turning the slice; and not least, the small ridge left adhering to the bottom of the furrow, if rubbed down and stuffed under the slice, is performed by an unnecessary waste of power, seeing that the mould-board is not adapted for removing such adhering obstructions. 2*d*, The loss of time and labour arising from the breadth of furrow, compared with those ploughs that take a 10-inch furrow. Thus, in ploughing an imperial acre with a 10-inch furrow,—leaving out of view the taking up of closings, turnings, &c.—the distance walked over by the man and horses will amount to 9.9 miles nearly; with a 9-inch furrow the distance will be 11 miles; with 8½-inch furrow, it will be 11½ miles or thereby; and with a 7½-inch furrow 13¼ miles nearly.

(767.) It may, therefore, be of importance for the agriculturist to weigh these considerations, and endeavour to ascertain whether it is more for his interest that his ploughing should be essentially well done, and with the least expenditure of power and time, or that it should be done more to please the eye, with a high surface finish, though this may perhaps be gained at a greater expenditure of power and time; while the essentials may in some degree be imperfectly performed.

(768.) On this part of the subject, I cannot refrain a passing remark on the very laudable exertions that have been made all over the country in producing that emulation amongst our ploughmen, which has been so successful in producing excellence in their vocation amongst that useful class of agricultural labourers, as to give them a pre-eminence over all others of their class in any country,—I mean the institution of ploughing matches. While I offer my humble though ardent wishes for a continuance of the means which have raised the character of the Scottish ploughmen, I cannot prevent doubts rising in my mind, that, however good and beneficial these competitions are calculated to be, if the exertions of the class are properly directed; yet the best exertions of both the promoters and the actors may be frustrated by allowing a false taste to be engendered amongst these operatives. That such a false taste has taken root, I have no doubt; and the results of it are appearing in the spread of opinions favourable to that kind of ploughing which to me appears not much deserving of encouragement,—the high-crested system. I have observed, at various ploughing-matches, that the palm was awarded to that kind of ploughmanship which exhibited the highest surface-finish, without reference at all to the ground-work of it; and I have compared by actual weight, all crumbs included, the quantities of soil lifted by ploughs that gained prizes with others which did not, because their work was not so well dressed on the surface; and I have found that the one to whom the prize was awarded had not lifted so much soil by $\frac{1}{10}$ as some of those that were rejected. I am far from intending, by these remarks, to throw discredit on ploughing-matches; on the contrary, I would wish to see them meet with tenfold encouragement, and would also wish to see many more than is usually met with, of the good and the great of the land, assembled at such meetings, to encourage and stimulate by their presence the exertions of the competitors in such interesting exhibitions. With this short digression I leave this subject for the present, with the intention of resuming it in another division of the general subject.

(769.) THE PRINCIPLES AND FORMATION OF THE MOULD-BOARD.—Of the various individuals who have written upon the plough and the formation of the mould-board, Bailey of Chillingham and Small of Berwickshire are perhaps the only two who have communicated their views in a practical shape, and even in their descriptions there is somewhat of ambiguity and uncertainty, but such may be inseparable from the subject. Many other nameless artizans have varied the mould-board until almost every county has something peculiarly its own, and each district claims for its favourite all the advantages due to perfection.

(770.) I have been at great pains to analyze a considerable number of these varieties; and as the subject is not unimportant in a work of this kind, I have selected a few of those best known, and of highest character, as objects of comparison.

(771.) The method adopted to obtain a mechanical analysis of these mould-boards has been simple, but perfectly correct; and as the principle may be applied to the attainment of counterparts of other objects, perhaps more important than a mould-board, it may be deserving of a place here. As a matter of justice also to the fabricators of the different mould-boards here exhibited, I am desirous to shew the principle on which these transcripts of their works have been thus brought forward in a new form, and in contrast with each other.

(772.) The instrument employed for this purpose is a *double parallelogram* or *parallel ruler*, as represented in fig. 110, which is a perspective of the apparatus. The bars *a b*, *c d*, *e f*, are slips of hard-wood about 3 feet long, or they may be of any convenient length, and $1\frac{1}{2}$ inch broad by $\frac{3}{8}$ inch thick; each of which is perforated at *a*, *b*, *c*, *d*, *e*, *f*, the perforations being exactly equidistant in all the bars. Four similar bars, of about half the length, are perforated also at one uniform distance, and the seven bars thus prepared are jointed together upon

Fig. 110.

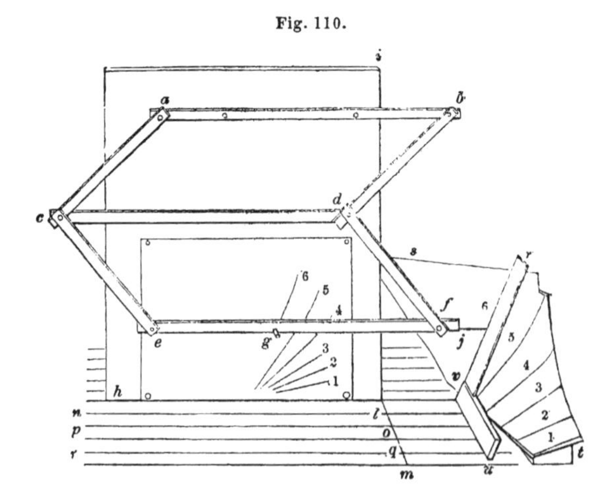

THE PARALLEL RULER.

brass studs, and secured so as to move freely at every joint, but without shake on the studs. The form, when constructed, is that of the two parallelograms *a b c d* and *c d e f*. In the end of the bar *e f* a stout wire pointer *j* is fixed of about 6 inches in length, lying in the plane of the instrument, and parallel to the edge of the bar. In a continuation of this parallel upon the bar *e f*, a socket capable of retaining a pencil or tracer is fixed anywhere at *g*. The instrument so formed is fixed upon a flat board *h i*, of about 3 feet square, by means of two screw nails passing through the bar *a b*, in a position parallel to the lower edge of the board; thus leaving all the other bars at liberty to move upon their joints; which completes the instrument. From the well-known properties of the parallelogram, as applied to the pantograph and the eidograph, it is unnecessary to demonstrate, that whatever line or figure may be traced with the pointer *j*, will be faithfully repeated by the tracing pencil *g*, upon any substance placed before it, and of the same dimensions as the original.

(773.) Another board, or table, or a level platform, is now to be selected, and a line *l m*, which may be called the fundamental, or leading line, drawn upon it. This line, to an extent of 3 feet or more, is divided into any number of equal parts, but in this case the divisions were 3 inches each; through these points of division, are drawn the straight lines *l n*, *o p*, *q r*, &c., indefinitely on each side of the line *l m*, and at right angles to it. The board carrying the instrument is provided with a foot behind, that keeps the face of the board always perpendicular to the platform on which it stands. The plough with the mould-board about to be analyzed is now set upon the table or platform upon which the leading line and the divisions have been laid down; the land-side of the plough being set parallel to the leading line, and at any convenient distance from it, suited to the instrument; presenting the mould-board in the position *s t*, and so placed in reference to the lines of division that the zero line shall coincide with one of them, provided the extremities do not overreach the divisions either way, the land-side of the plough being at the same time perpendicular. The instrument is now brought towards one extremity of the mould-board, and placed upon that parallel of the divisions that come nearest to the extremity, as No. 1 in the figure, the edge *l i* of the instrument coinciding with the leading line *l m*. A sheet of paper having been now fixed upon the board *h i* of the instrument, and a tracing pencil inserted in the socket *g*, the operation of tracing commences. The tracing point is passed in the vertical direction over the surface of the mould-board, tracing along a line No. 1; the pencil at the same time tracing a corresponding line No. 1. on the paper, which will be an exact outline of the face of the mould-board at that division, supposing the mould-board to be cut by a transverse section in that line. The instrument and board are now to be moved one division upon the leading line *l m*, the coincidence of the edge *l i* of the board with that line being still preserved. The tracing point is again made to pass vertically over the face of the mould-board, when the pencil *g* will trace on the paper a second line No. 2. This process, repeated at each successive division, 3, 4, 5, 6, &c., the corresponding lines, 3, 4, 5, 6, &c. on the paper will be traced out, exhibiting a series of perfect sectional lines of the mould-board, each line being that which would arise from an imaginary vertical plane cutting the body of the plough at right angles to its land-side at every 3 inches of its length. To prevent any inaccuracy that might arise from a misapplication of the tracing point to the oblique surface of the mould-board, a straight-edged ruler, in form of a carpenter's square *u v x*, is applied to the mould-board. The stock *u v* of the square being placed on the platform, and parallel to the line *l m*, which brings the edge *v x* always into the vertical plane, and the tracing rod must be kept in contact with this edge, while it traverses the face of the mould-board at each successive section.

(774.) This mode of analysis, it is to be observed, has not been adopted from its having any relation to the principles on which the different mould-boards have been constructed, but because it presents an unerring method of comparing a series of sectional lines of any one mould-board with those of any other; hence it affords a correct system of comparison. But it is not merely a comparative view that is afforded by it, for in the sequel it will be seen that a ground-work is thus afforded from which the mechanic may at any time or place construct a *fac-simile* of any mould-board, the analysis of which has been made after this manner.

(775.) The results of the analysis of a few of the mould-boards from the ploughs of highest character, as taken by this method, are given in the following figures. Plate XI. fig. 111 is a geometrical elevation in a plane parallel to the land-side of the mould-board of the East-Lothian plough *l d*, being its base-line. The perpendicular lines of division, commencing from the line *o o* the zero, and extending right and left, are the lines of section. Those to the right or fore-end of the mould-board, marked *a a*, *b b*, &c., and those to the left 1 1, 2 2, &c. The curved line *x y z* represents the path described on the face of the mould-board by the lower land-side edge of the furrow-slice, as the mould-board passes under it; this line I shall call the *line of transit.* Fig. 112 is a front view in elevation, of the mould-board of the same plough, and corresponding to fig. 111; *k m* is the base line of the plough; *m g* is the land-side plane in a vertical position, *m* is also the place of the point of the share; and *h i* the line of junction between the neck of the share and the mould-board, the remaining lines beyond *h i* exhibit the outline of all the sections taken by the instrument in reference to the lines in fig. 111. Thus, *o o g m* is the section of the entire body of the plough in the plane of the zero, *o y o* being the outline of the mould-board at this section, and *y* the zero point; *a a g m* the first section forward from the zero, *b b g m* the second, and so on. In like manner 1 1 *g m* is the first section backward from the zero, 2 2 *g m* the second, and so on; each section so lettered and numbered having relation to the divisions carrying the corresponding letters and numerals in fig. 111. The entire series of lines 1 1, 2 2, &c., and *a a*, *b b*, &c. thus form a series of profiles of the mould-board, supposing it to be cut vertically by planes at right angles to the land-side of the plough. In fig. 112 also the dotted line *m x y z* represents the path of the slice or line of transit, as in fig. 111, and *z k* represents a transverse section of the *slice* as finally deposited by the mould-board. Figs. 113 and 114 exhibit in the same manner the mould-board of the Currie or Mid-Lothian plough, the divisional and sectional lines being all laid off in the same manner from the zero, as in the example just described of the East-Lothian plough, and the zero point *y* in the line *o y o*, which is 9 inches from the plane of the land-side. Fig. 114 bears also the same relation to fig. 113, and as the letters and numerals in these, have the same relation and value as in figs. 111 and 112—the East-Lothian—the description given of that applies not only to the Mid-Lothian, but to the five succeeding figures, viz.:—

Figs. 115 and 116 represent the Berwickshire plough, being that which has been so successfully adopted by the Marquis of Tweeddale.

Figs. 117 and 118 are of the Lanarkshire plough.

Figs. 119 and 120, Plate XII., are of the Saline or Western Fifeshire plough.

Figs. 121 and 122 are of the FF plough of Messrs Ransome of Ipswich.

(776.) With reference to the characters of these different mould-boards it may be remarked: Of the *East-Lothian* mould-board, fig. 112, Plate XI., that those portions of the sectional lines lying between the lower edge and the line of transit are essentially straight, the two lines beyond the zero backward excepted, these being slightly concave towards the lower edge; and although the lines before the zero and above the line of transit, are concave, that part of the surface has no effect upon the furrow slice. It is, likewise, to be observed, that the parallelogram *k y*, which represents a section of the slice when brought to the vertical position, has its upper angle *y*, only touching the zero line; and no other part of the side of the parallelogram in contact with the zero line of section *o y o*; hence the mould-board, by its pressure being exerted chiefly against the upper edge of the slice, will always have a tendency to abrade the crest of its rectangular slice in its progress over the mould-board.

(777.) *In the Mid-Lothian* mould-board, figs. 113 and 114, the lines are also approximating to straight, except in the lower portions of those before the zero, where they produce a convexity of surface, but this part of the mould-board can have little influence. The chief difference, then, lies in those parts of the sectional lines, which lie above the path of the slice, and they also have no effect whatever in the formation or the conveyance of the slice; neither can the circumstance of elongation forward in this mould-board have any influence, for the same lines are to be found on the *neck of the share* of the East-Lothian as are here exhibited in the prolongation of the mould-board. We have, therefore, two ploughs in which the essential lines of the mould-board are the same, but which produce work of an opposite character. It must be kept in view, however, that in the Mid-Lothian the zero point *y* is only 9 inches from the land-side, while in the East-Lothian it is 10 inches; but the length behind the zero line being nearly alike in both, and the width at the tail also the same, the difference in distance of the zero point from the land-side produces a difference in the effect of the pressure of the mould-board on the edge of the slice. This will be perceived from the relation in which the section *k y*, representing the slice, stands to the zero line *o y o* of the mould-board; for in this case the angle at *y* formed by the side of the parallelogram and the zero line is not more than $\frac{1}{3}$ of that in the former case. This mould-board, therefore, will convey the slice in whatever form it may be cut, with less risk of injury to the crest than can be expected from the former. But as these discrepancies cannot produce the marked difference that exists in the appearance of the work performed by these two ploughs, it is not in the mould-board we are to look for the cause, but in the conformation of the share and the position of the coulter, while the mould-board, from the circumstance last pointed out, is better adapted to convey the slice unaltered.

(778.) *The Berwickshire* mould-board, figs. 115 and 116, which is also truncated forward, has the sectional lines, lying before the zero, nearly straight; but as they approach the zero they become gradually and decidedly concave, which increases towards the extremity. This concavity, it will be observed, exists only to a certain extent below the line of transit, and as the sectional lines approach the line of transit the curvature is reversed, and the surface becomes convex. This is a form well adapted to deliver a slice free of injury to the edge or crest, for, from the convexity immediately below the line of transit, the mould-board will never press upon nor abrade the edge of the slice; the pressure being exerted always within the extreme edge, as will be seen from the section *k z* of the slice, as applied at the extremity of the mould-board, though, when in the vertical position, as in *k y*, the section of the slice touches the zero line at its upper edge at an angle nearly equal to that in the East-Lothian, shewing that it is liable to abrasion until it has passed that line. But this plough, in practice, sets up a furrow of the rectangular species, with its angle or crest better preserved than in many others of this class, while, at the same time, it takes out the sole with the characteristic levelness which belongs to the class.

(779.) The *Lanarkshire* mould-board, figs. 117 and 118, has all its lines convex, the terminal edge excepted, which is nearly straight below, but preserves the convexity as it approaches the line of transit. Even above the line of transit the convexity is continued, and though not affecting the slice, it gives, in appearance, a still more decided character of convexity; and by thus making the upper edge of the mould-board retire, gives a long rake to the breast of the plough. It will be readily conceived that this mould-board, from the convexity of all its sectional lines, is essentially formed for turning up a crested furrow, more especially when the form of its share and the position of its coulter are considered. These last, being formed for cutting the slice with a very acute angle, will deliver it to the mould-board; and, from the form of the latter, the slice will pass over it uninjured; for the pressure upon the mould-board will be always greatest upon those parts of the surface of the slice lying within the edge, preventing thereby the abrasion of that tender part. These circumstances are clearly seen from the relation of the section of the slice *k y* as applied to the zero-line *o y o*, the point of contact lying considerably within the angle at *y* of the slice; and the same relation holds throughout the entire transit, up to the delivery of the slice in the ultimate position *k z*.

(780.) The *Western Fifeshire* mould-board, figs. 119 and 120, Plate XII., it will be readily perceived, belongs to the Lanarkshire class; but in this the convexity is carried so far to an extreme, as to round away the lower parts of the mould-board, till, at the lower edge behind, the width is only 6 inches. The terminal line, also, is prominently convex throughout. It differs also from its original type in having those parts of the sectional lines lying above the line of transit tending to recurvature. This, by carrying forward the upper part of the breast, gives the appearance of greater length to the mould-board; but, besides this, the part lying behind the zero is actually longer than in any of the preceding ploughs, as will appear from the sectional divisions, figs. 111, 113, 115, and 117, Plate XI. As may be anticipated, this variety of the Lanarkshire plough is famed for the acuteness of the furrow which it forms, though, in this respect, it does not excel its prototype. From the way in which the section *k y* of the slice, when in the vertical position, is applied to the zero-line, where the point of contact is seen to lie at $\frac{1}{3}$ of its breadth within the edge of the slice, it will at once appear how well this mould-board is adapted to transmit an unbroken crest. In every position of its transit up to its ultimate position, the slice will be equally secure from injury in respect to the crest; and were the crested furrow a true criterion of good ploughing, the plough that bears this mould-board, with share and coulter adapted thereto, would be the most perfect; but there are various and important arguments against it.

(781.) In *Ransome's Bedfordshire, or* FF mould-board, figs. 121 and 122, the sectional lines are of a mixed character; those in the fore part being convex, gradually diminishing in convexity to the zero, behind which they become straight lines, tending to concave—the terminal line being slightly so,—but becoming convex at the upper edge. It differs from all the Scotch mould-boards in having the terminal edge lengthened out below, instead of the usual shortening, and in having the breast cut away nearly parallel to the line of transit. The ploughs mounted with this mould-board are generally worked with cast-iron shares, having a wide-spread feather formed for cutting a level furrow-sole. The furrow usually taken with it is shallow, and, when set up, looks flat in the crest; but the work, so far as it goes, is what may be termed, in plough language, *true*: that is to say, the slice is rectangular and cut from a level sole. Though the sectional lines before the zero possess a form that would save the slice from abrasion, yet, at the zero-line and behind it, they have the opposite character in the extreme, and we accordingly find that this mould-board lays a very flat crested furrow, while the share and coulter are perfectly adapted to cut it rectangular.

(782.) With all the foregoing mould-boards, it will be observed that the section of the furrow-slice, in its ultimate position, seems to encroach upon the tail of the mould-board; and this is to be understood as arising from the circumstance of the slice being represented as incompressible, and unabraded below or above. In practice, the slice is pressed downward on the angle at *k*, and pressed home upon the preceding slice, so as to bring the face of the slice simply in contact with the terminal line of the mould-board instead of the apparent mutual interpenetration exhibited in the figures.

(783.) From the examples here given of the forms of mould-boards, and the effects which they produce when combined with any particular form of share and position of coulter, it will be easy to draw a conclusion as to the kind of work that will be performed by any plough that comes under our observation, and that without any previous knowledge of its merits; keeping in mind that the *ultimate form of the furrow* will always depend on the form of the share and position of the coulter, that the passage of the slice over the mould-board will have but a very partial effect on the form of the slice, and that this effect will be greater or less according to the form of surface. Thus, a slight convexity of surface, immediately below the line of transit, will with greater certainty secure the transit of the slice without injury to its edge, than may be expected from a surface which has a concavity crossing the line of transit, though it may be obtained, as in the Mid-Lothian and East-Lothian ploughs, with a straight-lined mould-board; but it will be more certainly obtained if the share is narrow, as in the Mid-Lothian; though this last expedient will induce disadvantages in point of draught, and risk of losing the effect, by any undue placement of the coulter. These disadvantages may arise from the coulter not being sufficiently set to landward, thereby admitting the breast of the plough to scrape upon the land, and send a small portion of earth along the mould-board, accompanying the edge of the slice, which may have the effect of abrading it so much as to injure the *appearance* of the work, though not in fact affecting its efficiency.

(784.) Having thus endeavoured to establish some data by which the agricultural mechanist, whether amateur or operative, may be assisted in determining from observation, what practical effects may be expected to result from any form of mould-board and share, I proceed to mention some rules by which he may form a mould-board on what I conceive to be the true principle, but upon which may be engrafted such deviations as taste or other circumstances may require.

(785.) Those writers who contributed to the improvement of the plough in the early stages of its modern history, laboured at a time when mould-boards of wood only were employed. Hence, their instructions related to the formation of that material alone, into mould-boards. Later writers have followed in nearly the same course, and have given rules for forming a mould-board, out of a block of wood, of sufficient dimensions to contain all the extremities of the proposed fabric. The change now pervading this branch of mechanics, wherein the introduction of cast-iron has become universal, precludes the necessity of falling back upon any of the old rules; what the agricultural mechanic is now required to furnish being not a mould-board, but, in the language of the foundry, a *pattern*, from which castings are to be obtained perfect fac-similes of the original pattern, and which may be repeated *ad libitum;* from this last circumstance, it follows that the making of a pattern will be a comparatively rare occurrence, and one which he will seldom be called upon to perform. It nevertheless appears desirable that a knowledge of the construction of such a fabric should be communicated in a manner that may enable an ordinarily skilled mechanic to construct a pattern when required, with accuracy and certainty of effect.

(786.) It has been shewn that very considerable discrepancies exist in the form given to mould-boards, and there is no doubt that peculiarities of soil may demand variations in form; but the propriety of such wide deviations may be called in question, and the actually required deviation brought within very narrow limits. It appears, indeed, that one form may be brought to answer all required purposes, if aided by a properly adjusted share and coulter.

(787.) From a careful study of the foregoing analytical diagrams, and from comparison of numerous implements and their practical effects, together with a consideration of the dynamical principles on which the plough operates, I have been led to adopt a theoretical form of mould-board, which seems to fulfil all the conditions required in the investigation, and which is capable, by very simple modifications, of adaptation to the circumstances of the medium on which it works. In the outset, it is assumed that the soil is homogeneous, and that it possesses such a degree of tenacity and elasticity as to yield to the passing form of the plough, and to resume, when laid in the due position, that form which was first impressed upon the slice, by the action of the share and coulter; the second consideration being the cutting of a slice from the solid land. In a theoretical view, this must be an operation through its whole depth and breadth; hence the share is conceived to be a cutting edge which shall have a horizontal breadth equal to the breadth of the slice that is to be raised, and that the face or land-side of the coulter shall stand at right angles to this. Another consideration is, that the slice now supposed to be cut has to be raised on one side, and turned over through an angle of 135°, the turning over being performed on the lower right-hand edge, as on a hinge, through the first 90°, the remaining 45° being performed on what was at first the upper right-hand edge. (Fig. 104.) The slice, in going through this evolution, has to undergo a twisting action, and be again returned to its original form of a right prism. To accomplish this last process, it is evident that a *wedge*, *twisted* on its upper surface, must be the agent; and to find the form and dimensions of this wedge, is solving the problem that gives the surface of the mould-board required.

(788.) We have seen, fig. 104, that the slice, in passing through the first 90°, describes the quadrant with its lower edge, and in doing so, we can conceive a continued slice to form the solid of revolution *a b c d e*, fig. 123, which is a a quarter of a cylinder, as shewn here in isometrical perspective; the radius *a b* or $a\,c$ being equal to the breadth of the slice. We have next to consider the angle of elevation of the twisted wedge; and in doing this, we must not only consider the least resistance, but also the most convenient length of the wedge. In taking a *low* angle, which would present, of course, proportionally little resistance, it would, at the same time, yield a length of mould-board that would be highly inconvenient, seeing that the generating point, in any section of the slice, must ultimately reach the same height, whether by a low or a higher angle. From experience, we find that, from the point of the share to that point in the plough's body where the slice arrives at the perpendicular position, and which I have named the zero, that 30 inches form a convenient length. The length $c\,d$ of the solid is therefore made equal to 30 inches or more, and this being divided into 10 equal parts, the parallels 1 1, 2 2, 3 3, &c. are to be drawn upon the cylindrical surface, and between the points b, d, a curve has to be described that shall be the line of transit of the slice. After investigating the application of various curves to this purpose, I have found that a circular arc is the only one that can be adopted. It presents the least attainable resistance in the first stages of the ascent, where the force required to raise the slice is the greatest, and in the last stages, where the force of raising has vanished, leaving only what is necessary to turn the slice over, there the resistance is at the greatest; and, above all, the circle being of equal flexure throughout, it is in every way best adapted to the objects here required. To determine the radius of curvature of this arc, we must evolve the cylindrical surface $c\,b\,d\,e$, and from it construct the diagram, fig. 124. Draw $e\,b$ equal to $c\,d$ of fig. 123; $e\,d$ equal to the length of the arc $c\,b$ or $d\,e$, and at right angles to $e\,b$; divide $e\,b$ into 10 equal parts, and from the points of division draw the ordinates 1 f, 2 g, 3 h, &c. parallel to $e\,d$; from b set off 10 inches for the length of the share along the line $b\,e$, which will fall 1 inch beyond the division 7, and at this distance draw the dotted line parallel to 7 m; upon this set off a distance 7 m of $2\frac{1}{2}$ inches; and through the three points, d, m, b, describe an arc of a circle, whose radius will be found equal to the circumference of the cylinder of which $a\,b\,c$, fig. 123, is a quadrant. The circular arc thus found is now to be transferred to the cylindrical surface $c\,b\,d\,e$. The transfer may be performed by drawing the arc on paper, and the paper then laid over the cylindrical surface in such a manner that the points b, m, d, shall be brought to coincide with the points b, m, d of the cylindrical surface; when the remaining points f, g, h, i, or any number more, may be marked on the cylindrical quadrant by pricking through the paper with a pointed instrument at short intervals along the arc; or, the length of the ordinates 1 f, 2 g, 3 h of fig. 124, may be transferred to the corresponding parallels of fig. 123, when the lengths of the ordinates will cut the parallels in the points f, g, h, &c. In either case, the curve can now be traced through the points b, p, n, m, &c. on the cylindrical surface. Through the points b, p, n, m, &c. draw the dotted lines $f\,f'$, $g\,g'$, $h\,h'$, &c. parallel to $c\,d$ or $b\,e$, and from the centre a draw the radii $a\,f'$, $a\,g'$, $a\,h'$, &c.; the unequal divisions of the arc $c\,b$ will thus shew the proportional angles of ascent of the slice along the line of transit now found, b, p, n, &c., for each division of the length; while the degree of flexure in the curve or line of transit remains uniform by the same, from any one point, to any other equi-distant points.

(789.) To convert the prism thus prepared and lined off into that of the twisted wedge, we have only to cut away that portion of it contained within the boundaries a, b, $c\,d$, x, preserving the terminal edges $a\,b$, $a\,x$, and $d\,x$; and the prism will thus be resolved into a form represented by a portion $a\,b\,d\,x\,e$, of fig. 125, also in isometrical perspective. Of this figure, $a\,b\,d\,x$ is the true theoretical surface of the mould-board, from the edge $a\,b$ of the share to the zero-line $d\,x$; $a\,b\,e\,x$ is the sole; the curve $b\,p\,n\,m\,l$, &c. is the line of transit of the slice; and the triangles $1'f\,1$, $2'g\,2$, $3'h\,3$, $4'i\,4$, &c. are the vertical planes, supposed to cut the solid thus reduced in the divisions 1, 2, 3, 4, &c. to the height of the line of transit, as in the analytical sections of the mould boards.

(790.) The surface now completed can only raise the slice to the perpendicular position; and to complete the operation, we have to carry the twisted wedge back till it shall place the slice at the angle of 45°. To do this we have to extend the original prism, or suppose it to have been at first sufficiently elongated towards $d\,d'$, fig. 125, and to superimpose upon its flat side the portion $d\,d'\,u\,x$, or $a\,d\,u$ of fig. 126. The part $d\,d'\,u\,x$, is now to be worked off into a part of a new cylindrical surface, whose radius is $y\,d$ or $y\,u$, fig. 126, and upon this surface, the line $d\,u$, fig. 125, is to be drawn a tangent to the curve $b\,d$ at d. A continuation of the divisions of 3 inches is to be made upon the line $d\,d'$, and the parallels $a'\,q'$, $b'\,r'$, and $u\,d'$, continued on the cylindrical surfaces. Whatever portion of the superimposed piece $a\,d'\,u$ may be found to fall within the small arc $a\,t$, fig. 126, is to be cut away, forming a small portion of an interior cylinder concentric to the point y, which being done, the remaining portions of the superimposed piece are to be cut away to the dotted lines $d\,x$, $a\,y$, $b\,z$, $u\,u'$, of fig. 125, or, what is the same thing, to the lines $d\,a$, $a'\,a$, $b't$, and $u\,t$, of fig. 126, forming tangents to the curve $a\,t$, and which will complete the surface of the twisted wedge through its entire length, and to the height of the line of transit, producing what I conceive to be the *true theoretical surface* of the mould-board.

(791.) Fig. 126 exhibits distinctly, in the quadrant $a\,b\,d$, the inequality of the angles of ascent for the slice, where the radii $a\,p'$, $a\,n'$, $a\,m'$, &c. represent the ascents to the corresponding divisions of length in the transit of the slice through the curve $b\,d\,u$, which represents the periphery of the cylindrical surfaces at the line of transit. The parts of the figure lying above that line represent those that must be superimposed above the quadrantal portion of the cylinder, to complete the upper regions of the mould-board; these parts acting merely as a preventive against the overfall of soil into the waste of the plough, are of less importance as to form, than those just described, but are quite necessary in the practice of ploughing. The parallelogram $y\,d$ exhibits the relation in which the furrow-slice stands to this form of mould-board, when the slice has been raised to the perpendicular, and $y\,u$ in its ultimate position.

(792.) Although I hold this to be a true theoretical form, it is not in this state fit to be employed as a practical mould-board; but the steps to render it so, are very simple. The broad shovel-mouth $a\,b$, fig, 125, would meet with obstructions too numerous to admit for a moment of its adoption in practice; but we have only to remove the right-hand portion of the edge $a\,b$, in the direction $b\,q$, making the breadth, $q\,m$, 6½ to 7 inches broad; that portion also contained within $7\,r\,3$ is to be cut away, leaving $m\,r$ about 4 inches broad; $b\,q\,r\,m$ will then represent the share; the mould-board being thus of the prolonged form in the fore-part. And though this form has no peculiar advantage over the truncated, in respect to working, it is better adapted to admit of the body being constructed of malleable iron, a practice which, though more expensive, is certainly the most preferable, by reason of its greater durability, and being less liable to fracture through the effect of shocks, when stones or other obstructions are encountered.

(793.) Besides the removal of these parts of the theoretical mould-board, other slight modifications are admissible. When the parts have been cut away as described, the edge *b q* of the share will be found too thick for a cutting edge. If brought to a proper thickness, by removing the parts *below*, making the edge to coincide with the curved surface; the share so prepared would have the character that belongs to the cresting ploughs. The lower edge of the mould-board from *r* to 2 would be also rather high, and would present unnecessary resistance to the lower side of the slice; both parts, therefore, require to be reduced. The surface of the feather *b q* is to be sloped down till it become straight between the points *b* and *q*, *q* not being more than $\frac{1}{4}$ inch above the plane of the sole, as at the dotted lines *n z* in fig. 126. The lower edge of the mould-board is also to be rounded off, as shewn by the dotted lines along the lower edge from *h* to *o* in fig. 128. To prevent the abrasion of the edge of the slice in passing over the mould-board, it will also be expedient to make the lines from *d* to *u*, in fig. 126, fall in, from below the line of transit upwards as shewn by the dotted lines at *d′*, *a′*, *b′*, *u*.

(794.) Other modifications may, if required by peculiar taste or otherwise, be given to this form of mould-board. If, after the points *b p n m*, &c. have been determined upon the cylindrical surface, fig. 123, or 125, and, in cutting away the parts above *a b* in the latter figure, instead of reducing the surface to the straight lines 9′ *p*, 8′ *n*, 7′ *m*, &c. we leave the surface slightly convex upon all these lines, a surface will be produced as represented by the dotted sectional lines of fig. 126, or 128, and by becoming slightly either recurved above the line of transit, as in fig. 128, or with continued convexity, as in fig. 118, Plate XI., the surface so produced would deliver the slice without risk of injury to the edge; which, though not of vital importance, is always an object in the estimation of the ploughman who performs his work with taste. The same modification would also, in the opinion of many agricultural machine-makers, render the mould-board more efficacious in the working of stiff clay soils.

(795.) Fig. 127, Plate XII, represents an elevation of the new mould-board, as now constructed by me, and fig. 128, the analytical sections of the same, taken in the same manner as described for those preceding, and having the same letters of reference. In the present case, the sectional lines are all straight to the height of the line of transit; above that line and before the zero, they are slightly concave; though, as has been shewn, this is not imperative; but behind the zero, they are convex from a little below the line of transit, as shewn by the dotted portions of the lines. The parallelogram *k y*, being a section of the slice when in the vertical position, will be seen to coincide exactly with the zero-line, as it will do through the whole passage of the slice. The letters and numerals in these two figures have the same reference as in the other figures of the mould-board.

(796.) Judging from the trials that have been made of this mould-board, and from the *uniform brightening of its surface* after a few hours' work, it promises to possess a very uniform resistance over its whole surface, which is a principal object to be aimed at in the formation of this member of the plough.

(797.) *The Mould-board Pattern.*—The instructions just given refer solely to the formation of the theoretical surface of the mould-board, including that of the share; but in the construction of a *pattern* from which mould-boards are to be cast, the process is somewhat different, though based on the principles above laid down.

(798.) In proceeding with this, therefore, the quadrant of the cylinder upon which the whole problem is grounded, may or may not be prepared. If it is to be employed, then the first process is exactly as before described in reference to the quadrant fig. 123, Plate XII., which must be formed and lined as there described; but the same process may be pursued from lines alone, without the intervention of the solid, and in the following manner. Having described the quadrant of a circle, as *a b c*, fig. 123, of 10 inches radius, construct the diagram fig. 124, as before directed, the entire length *e b* being 30 inches, divided into equal parts of 3 inches each. The arc *b d* is then to be drawn through the points *b p n m*, which points, instead of being a transfer, as before described, from the quadrant, may here be drawn at once with a beam-compass touching the three leading points *b m d*, as before, which will intersect all the divisions, converting them into ordinates 1 *f*, 2 *g*, 3 *h*, &c. to the curve *b d*. The lengths of these ordinates, from the base-line *e b*, are now to be carefully transferred to the quadrant of the circle *b d* of fig. 126, and set off in the circumference thereof; thus the point *b* in fig. 126 corresponds to the termination *b* of the base-line in fig. 124. The first ordinate *g p* is to be set off on the quadrant from *b* to *p*, the second ordinate 8 *n* is set off from *b* to *n*, the third 7 *m* from *b* to *m*, and so on through the entire quadrant of the circle. The radii *a b*, *a p*, *a n*, &c. being now drawn, will furnish the successive angles of elevation, with the sole-plane, for each division of the length throughout the quadrant.

(799.) In applying these to the mould-board, it is to be observed that the first three radii belong to the share, if it is a prolonged mould-board, or the first five if it is truncated. The quadrant, fig. 126, with its radii, being thus completely drawn out at full size upon a board, produce the line *b a* to *y*, and on *y* as a centre, with a radius of 7 inches, describe the arc *a t*, and concentric to it the arc *d u*. At an angle of 45° draw *t u* a tangent to the arc *a t*, and the point of intersection of this tangent with the arc will fix the extreme point *u* of the mould-board at the height of the line of transit; which point will be 19 inches from the land side plane *b g*, and 12 inches above the plane of the sole, or base line *y b*. From *d*, lay off divisions of equal parts on the arc *du*, each equal to $4\frac{1}{2}$ inches,—the diagonal of a square of 3 inches,—which completes the lines for the fabrication of the pattern.

(800.) The next step in the operaton is that of *building a block* out of which the pattern is to be shaped. Provide a deal-board of $3\frac{1}{2}$ feet or thereby in length, with a breadth of 10 inches; have it dressed of uniform thickness, and at least one edge and end straight and right angled, as seen at *a b c*, in the annexed fig. 129, and *a b*, fig. 126, Plate XII., forming a basement to the block, *a* being the right angle, and the continuation of the board being hid from view under the super-imposed block. Let the edge *a c* of the board be marked off in equal divisions of 3 inches, agreeing exactly with those of the diagram, fig. 124, marking the divisions with letters or numerals corresponding to the radii of the quadrant, fig. 126, the end *a b* of the board corresponding to the radius *m* of the quadrant, and to the ordinate 7 *m* of the diagram. Provide also a suit-stock or bevel of

Fig. 129.

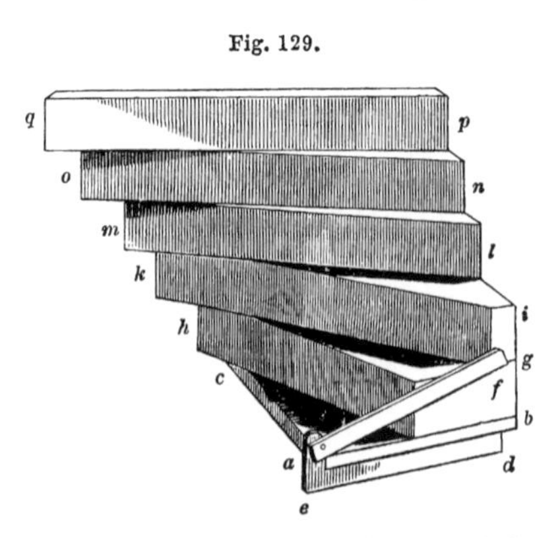

THE BUILDING OF THE BLOCK FOR THE MOULD-BOARD PATTERN.

the form represented by *d e f*, the stock *d e* being a straight bar with a head-piece at *e*, fixed at right angles to the stock, and into this the blade *a f* is to be jointed, in such a manner that when the blade and stock are set parallel to each other, they shall just receive the thickness of the basement-board betwixt them, the length of the blade being equal to the breadth of the slice. Five or more pieces of well-seasoned, clean, 3-inch Memel or yellow-pine deal are now to be prepared, each about 30 inches in length, and from 6 to 4 inches in breadth. Set the bevel to the angle *b a m*, fig. 126, and applying it at the end of the board, as in fig. 129, it will point out the position in which the first block *g h* must be placed on the board, in order that it may fill the lines of the pattern. The further end of the block, being set in like manner to fall within the lines, it is to be firmly attached to the board with screw-nails. The second block *k i*, is to be joined to the first by the ordinary method of glueing, being set, in the same manner as the first to fill the lines of the pattern at both ends, and this requires its being set obliquely to the first. The third block *l m* is set in like manner, and so on with *n o* and *p q*. The setting of the different blocks will be much facilitated by having the ends *g i l n p*, cut off to the plane of the land-side, that is, to coincide vertically with the land-side edge of the board, and by keeping in view that the terminal line *c q* lies at an angle 45°.

(801.) The block being thus prepared, the process of *working it off* is plain and easily performed in this way. Having set the bevel at the angle *b a m*, fig. 126, which answers to the end *a b* of the block, the bevel is applied as in the figure, and the surplus wood is cut away to a short distance within the end *a b* of the board, until the blade of the bevel lies evenly upon the surface, and the kneed head-piece touching the edge of the board. Set the bevel now at the angle *b a l*, and applying it at the first division on the edge of the board, cut away the surplus wood with a gouge or other tool, in a line parallel to the end of the board, or at right angles to its edge until the edge of the blade *a f* lie evenly on the surface, and the head of the stock touch the edge of the board as before. Repeating this operation at each successive division with the bevel, setting it to the corresponding angle up to the vertical or zero line, and we have a series of leading lines or draughts, each occupying its true position in the surface of the mould-board to the height of the line of transit. By continuing these lines, each in the direction already given it, until they terminate in the breast, or in the upper edge of the pattern, we have a corresponding series of points now determined, in the breast and upper edge, and by removing the surplus wood still remaining in the spaces between the lines, and reducing the surface to coincide with them, we have the finished surface from the neck of the share up to the zero.

(802.) To *complete the after portion of the pattern*, we have to form a temporary bevel with a curved blade, adapted to the small arc *a t*, fig. 126, which blade, is prolonged in a tangent *t u* at the angle of 45°. With the guidance of this bevel, its stock being still applied to the board, as in fig. 129, cut away all the wood that occurs to interrupt it behind the zero, until it applies every where behind that line without obstruction. At the third division beyond the zero, the pattern may be cut off in a right vertical, though this is not imperative, as the mould-board may be made considerably longer, and even a little shorter, without at all affecting its operation. At whatever distance in length its terminal edge may be fixed, that portion of the line of transit which lies between the zero and the terminus must leave the original curve *h m d*, fig. 123, at a tangent, and it will reach the terminus as such, or it will gradually fall into a re-entering curve, according as the terminus is fixed nearer to or farther from the zero-line; the terminus of the line of transit being always 19 inches distant from the land-side plane. That portion of the surface which now remains unfinished between the arcs *a t* and *d u*, fig. 126, is to be worked off in tangents, applied vertically to the arc *a t*, and terminating in that part of the line of transit that lies between *d* and *u*. Such portions of the interior cylindrical surface as may have been formed under the application of the temporary bevel to the arc *a t*, are now to be also cut away by a line passing through the junction of the tangents *t a′*, *t b′*, *t u*, with the cylindrical arc *a t*, forming a curved termination in the lower part behind,—as seen in fig. 127,—which completes the surface as proposed.

(803.) The *modifications* formerly pointed out, paragraph (792, 793, and 794) may now be made upon the lower and the upper parts of the pattern. The breast-curve and the form of the upper edge will now have assumed their proper curvature; and there only remains to have the whole pattern reduced to its due thicknesses. This, in the fore part, is usually about $\frac{1}{2}$ inch, increasing backward below to about 1 inch, and the whole becoming gradually thinner towards the top edge, where it may be $\frac{3}{16}$ inch. The perpendicular height behind is usually about 12 inches, and at the fore part 14 inches.

(804.) Of the Draught of Ploughs.—From the complicated structure of the plough, and the oblique direction in which circumstances oblige us to apply the draught to the implement, some misconceptions have arisen as to the true nature and direction in which the draught may be applied. The great improver of the plough has fallen into this error, and has, in some measure, been followed by others.* He asserts, " that were a rope attached to the point of the share, and the plough drawn forward on a level with the bottom of the furrow, it would infallibly sink at the point." Were this really the case, it would prove that the centre of resistance of the plough in the furrow must be somewhere below the level of the sole, which is impossible. As the centre of gravity of any body suspended from a point at, or anywhere near, the surface of that body, will always be found in a continuation of the suspending line, supposing it to be a flexible cord; so, in like manner, the centre of resistance of the plough will be always found in the direction of the line of draught. Now, if with a horizontal line of draught from the point of the share, it were found that the point of the share had a tendency to sink deeper into the soil, it would be a clear proof that the plough was accommodating itself to the general law, and that the centre of resistance is below the line of the sole. The fallacy of this conclusion is so palpable, that it would be an act of supererogation to refute it by demonstration, more especially as it never can be of any utility in a practical point of view. I have thought it necessary, however, to advert to it, as it appears to have aided in throwing a mystery over the mode of applying the *line or angle of draught*, which in itself is a sufficiently simple problem.

(805.) The reasoning hitherto adopted on this branch of the theory of the plough seems to be grounded on the two following data—the *height*, on an average, of a horse's shoulder, or that point in his collar where the yoke is applied; and, the *length* of the draught-chains that will give him ample freedom to walk. It falls out fortunately, too, that the angle of elevation thus produced crosses the plane of the collar as it lies on the shoulders of the horse when in draught, nearly

* Small's Treatise on Ploughs.

at right angles. It is my purpose, however, in this section, to shew that (keeping out of view some practical difficulties) the plough may be drawn at any angle, from the horizontal up to a little short of 90°, and that it would require less and less force to draw it as the direction of the line of draught approached the horizontal line. It would, in all cases, be required that the point of the beam, or rather the draught-bolt, should be exactly in the straight line from the centre of resistance to the point where the motive force would be applied. If this force could be applied in the horizontal direction, we should have the plough drawn by the minimum of force. This position, however, is impracticable, as the line of draught would, in such a case, pass through the solid land of the furrow about to be raised; but it is within the limits of practicability to draw the plough at an angle of 12°, and, as will be demonstrated, the motive force required at this angle would be 1 stone or 14 lb. less than is required by drawing at the angle of 20°, which may be held as the average in the ordinary practice of ploughing. A plough drawn at this low angle, namely 12°, would have its beam (if of the ordinary length) so low, that the draught-bolt would be only 10 inches above the base-line; and this is not an impracticable height, though the traces might be required inconveniently long. On the same principle, the angle of draught might be elevated to 60° or 70°, provided a motive power could be applied at such high angles. In this, as before, the beam and draught bolt would have to fall into the line of draught as emanating from the centre of resistance. The whole plough, also, under this supposition, would require an almost indefinite increase of weight; and the motive force required to draw the plough at an angle of 60°, would be nearly twice that required in the horizontal direction, or $1\frac{16}{18}$ times that of the present practice, exclusive of what might arise from increased weight. We may therefore conclude, that to draw the plough at any angle higher than the present practice is impracticable, and, though rendered practicable, would still be highly inexpedient, by reason of the disadvantage of increased force being thus rendered necessary; unless we can suppose that the application of steam or other inanimate power might require it. Neither would it be very expedient to adopt a lower angle, since it involves a greater length of trace-chains, which, at best, would be rather cumbrous; and it would produce a saving of force of only one stone on the draught of a pair of horses. Yet it is worthy of being borne in mind, that, in all cases, there is some saving of labour to the horses, whenever they are, by any means, allowed to draw by a chain of increased length, provided the draught-bolt of the plough is brought into the line of draught, and the draught-chains are not of such undue weight as to produce a sensible curvature; in other words, to insure the change of angle at the horse's shoulder, due to the increased length of the draught-chain.

(806.) In illustration of these changes in the direction of the draught, fig. 130, Plate XIII. will render the subject more intelligible. Let *a* represent the body of a plough, *b* the point of the beam, and *c* the centre of resistance of the plough, which may be assumed at a height of 2 inches above the plane of the sole *d e*, though it is liable to change within short limits. The average length of the draught-chains being 10 feet, including draught-bars, hooks, and all that intervenes between the draught-bolt of the plough and the horse's shoulders; let that distance be set off in the direction *b f*, and the average height of the horse's shoulders where the chains are attached, being 4 feet 2 inches, let the point *f* be fixed at that height above the base-line *d e*. Draw the line *f c*, which is the direction of the line of draught acting upon the centre of resistance *c*; and if the plough is in proper temper, it will coincide also with the draught-bolt of the beam; *e c f*, being the angle of draught, and equal to 20°. It will be easily perceived, that, with the same horses and the same length of yoke, the angle *e c f* is invariable; and if the plough has a tendency to dip at the point of the share under this arrangement, it indicates that the draught-bolt *b* is *too high* in the bridle. Shifting the bolt one or more holes downward will bring the plough to *swim* evenly upon its sole. On the other hand, if the plough has a tendency to rise at the point of the share, the indication from this is, that the draught-bolt *b* is *too low*, and the rectification must be made by raising it one or more holes in the bridle. Suppose, again, that a pair of taller horses were yoked in the plough, the draught-chains, depth of furrow, and soil,—and, by consequence, the point of resistance *c*,—remaining the same, we should then have the point *f* raised suppose to *f'*; by drawing the line *f'c*, we have *e c f'* as the angle of draft, which will now be 22°; and in this new arrangement, the *draught-bolt* is found to be *below* the line of draught *f' c*; and if the draught-chains were applied at *b*, in the direction *f' b*, the plough would have a tendency to rise at the point of the share, by the action of that law of forces, which obliges the line of draught to coincide with the line which passes through the centre of resistance; hence the draught bolt *b* would be found to rise to *b'*, which would raise the point of the share out of its proper direction. To rectify this, then, the draught-bolt must be raised in the bridle by a space equal to *b b'*, causing it to coincide with the true line of draught, which would again bring the plough to swim evenly on its sole.

(807.) Regarding the relative forces required to overcome the resistance of the plough, when drawn at different angles of draught, we have first to consider the nature of the form of those parts through which the motive force is brought to bear upon the plough. It has been shewn that the tendency of the motive force acts in a direct line from the shoulder of the animal of draught to the centre of resistance; and referring again to fig. 130, Plate XIII., were it not for considerations of convenience, a straight bar or beam lying in the direction *c b*, and attached firmly to the plough's body anywhere between *c* and *g*, would answer all the purposes of draught perhaps better than the present beam. But the draught not being the end in view, but merely the means by which that end is accomplished, the former is made to subserve the latter; and as the beam, if placed in the direction *c b*, would obstruct the proper working of the plough, we are constrained to resort to another indirect action to arrive at the desired effect. This indirect action is accomplished through the medium of a system of rigid angular frame-work, consisting of the beam and the body of the plough, or those parts of them comprehended between the points *b*, *h*, *c*, the beam being so connected to the body *a h*, as to form a rigid mass. The effect of the motive force applied to this rigid system of parts at the point *b*, and in the direction *b f*, produces the same results as if *c b* were firmly connected by a bar in the position of the line *c b*, or as if that bar alone were employed, as in the case before supposed, and to the exclusion of the beam *b h*.

(808.) Having thus endeavoured to illustrate the causes of the oblique action of the plough, shewing that the obliquity is a concomitant following the considerations of convenience and fitness in working the implement, I proceed to shew the relative measure of the effects of the oblique action. It is well known that the force of draught required to impel the plough, when exerted in the direction *b f*, may be taken at an average of 24 stones, or 336 lb. Analyzing this force by means of the parallelogram of forces, if we make the line *b f* to represent 336 lb., the motive force; and complete the parallelogram *b i f k*, we have the force *b f* held in equilibrium by the two forces *i b* and *k b*; the first acting in the *horizontal* direction to draw the plough forward, the second acting *vertically*, to prevent the point of the beam from sinking, which it would do were a horizontal force only applied to the point of the beam. The relation of these forces *i b* and *k b* to the oblique force will be as the length of the lines *i b* and *k b* to the line *b f*, or the line *i b* will represent 322 lb., while the oblique force is 336 lb, and the force *k b* 95 lb. This last force is represented as *lifting* the beam vertically by suspension, but the same result would follow if the beam were supported by a *wheel* under the point *b*; the wheel would then bear up the beam with the same force as that by which it was supposed to be suspended, 95 lb. But to carry out the supposition, let the draught now found be applied horizontally from the point *c*. As the plough would then have no tendency either to dip or rise, the force *k b* vanishes, leaving only the direct horizontal force *i b*; hence, were it possible to apply the draught in a horizontal direction from the point of resistance, the resistance of the plough would be 322 lb., instead of 336 lb.

(809.) But to return to the previous position of the draught, wherein, still supposing it to be in the horizontal direction, and thereby requiring that the point of the beam have a *support* to prevent its sinking too low. This support may be supposed either a *foot*, as seen in many both ancient and modern ploughs, or in the shape of a wheel or wheels, so much employed in many of the English ploughs. We see at once, under this consideration, the office that a wheel performs in the action of a plough. It has been shewn, that whether the plough be drawn in the ordinary direction of draught *b f*, in which one oblique propelling force only is exerted, or with two antagonist forces, *b i*, in the horizontal direction, and the upholding force, *b k*, in the vertical, we find that, in the latter, the difference in favour of the motive force is only $\frac{1}{24}$ of the usual resistance; but the upholding force is equal to $\frac{2}{7}$, while none of these variations has produced any change in the absolute resistance of the plough. The impelling force is theoretically less in the latter case; but since the wheel has to carry a load of 95 lb., we have to consider the effect of this load upon a small wheel, arising from friction and the resistance it will encounter by sinking less or more into the subsoil. I have ascertained, from experiment, that the difference of force required to draw a wheel of 12 inches diameter, loaded as above described, and again when unloaded, over a tolerably firm soil, is equal to 22 lb., a quantity exceeding $1\frac{1}{2}$ times the amount of saving that would accrue by adopting this supposed horizontal draught with a wheel. Having thus found the amount of draught at two extremities of a scale, the one, being the oblique draught, in common use at an angle of 20°, the other deduced from this, through the medium of the established principles of oblique forces, and the latter producing a saving of only $\frac{1}{24}$ of the motive force, while it is encumbered with an additional resistance arising from the support or wheel; it necessarily follows that, at all intermediate angles of draught, or at any angle whatever, where the principle of the parallelogram of forces finds place—and it will find place in all cases where wheels *yielding any support* are applied to the plough under the beam—there must necessarily be *an increase in the amount of resistance to the motive force.*

(810.) This being a question of some importance, the diagram, fig. 131, will render it more evident. Let *a* be the point of resistance of a plough's body, *b* the point of the beam, *c* the position of the horse's shoulder, and *a d* the horizontal line; then will *c a d* be the angle of draught equal to 20°. Let the circle *e* represent a wheel placed under the beam, which is supported by a stem or sheers, here represented by the line *e b*. In this position, the point of the beam, which is also the point of draught, lies in the line of draught; the wheel, therefore, bears no load, but is simply in place, and has no effect on the draught: the motive force, therefore, continues to be 336 lb. Suppose now the point of the beam to be raised to *g*, so that the line of draught *g c* may be horizontal; and since the line of draught lies now out of the original line *a b c*, and has assumed

Fig. 131.

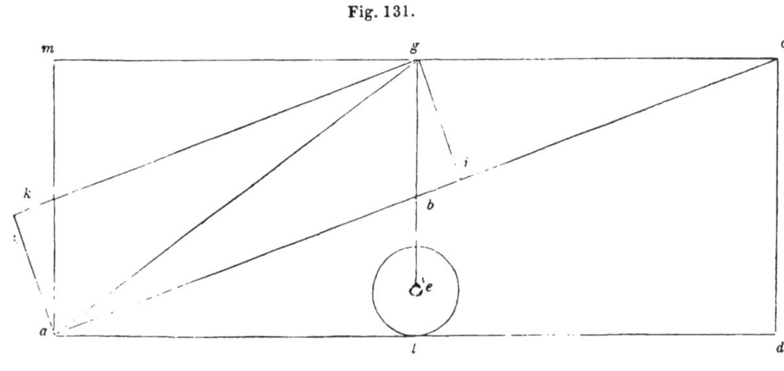

THE DRAUGHT OF WHEEL-PLOUGHS.

that of *a g c*—*g* being now supported on the produced stem *c g* of the wheel—draw *g i* perpendicular to *a c*, and complete the parallelogram *a i g k*; the side *a i* will still represent the original motive force of 336 lb., but, by the change of direction of the line of draught, the required force will now be represented by the diagonal *a g* of the parallelogram, equal to about 351 lb.; and *g c* is a continuation of this force in a horizontal direction. The draught is therefore increased by 15 lb. Complete also the parallelogram *a l g m*, and as the diagonal *a g*—the line of draught last found—is equal to 351 lb., the side *l g* of the parallelogram will represent the vertical pressure of the beam upon the wheel *e*, equal to about 200 lb., which, from experiments (809), may be valued at 40 lb. of additional resistance, making the whole resistance to the motive force 391 lb., and being a total *increase arising from the introduction of a wheel in this position, of* 55 lbs. Having here derived a maximum,—no doubt an extreme case,—and the usual angle of 20° as the minimum, we can predicate that, at any angle intermediate to *l a b* and *l a g*, the resistance can never be reduced to the minimum of 336 lb. Hence, it follows, as a corollary, that *wheels placed under the beam* can never lessen the resistance of the plough; but, on the contrary, must, in all cases, increase the resistance to the motive force more or less, according to the degree of pressure that is brought upon the wheel, and this will be proportional to the sine of the angle in the resultant *a g* of the line of draught.

(811.) The application of a *wheel in the heel* of a plough, does not come under the same mode of reasoning as that under the beam, the former becoming a part of the body, from which all the natural resistance flows; but in viewing it as a part of that body only, we can arrive at certain conclusions which are quite compatible with careful experiments.

(812.) The breadth of the whole rubbing surface in the body of a plough, when turning a furrow, is on an average about 17½ inches, and supposing, that surface to be pressed nearly equal in all parts, we shall have the *sole-shoe*, which is about 2½ inches broad, occupying $\frac{1}{7}$ part of the surface; and taking the entire average resistance of the plough's body, as before, at 336 lb., we have $\frac{1}{7}$ of this, equal to 48 lb., as the greatest amount of resistance produced by the sole of the plough. But this is under the supposition that the resistance arises from a uniform degree of friction spread over the whole rubbing surface of the body; while we have seen, on the contrary, that the coulter, when acting alone, presents a resistance equal to the entire plough. It is only reasonable, therefore, in absence of further experiments, to conclude, that the fore-parts of the body,—the *coulter* and *share,—yield a large proportion of the resistance when turning the furrow slice;* but since we cannot appreciate this with any degree of exactness, let the sole have its full share of the resistance before stated, namely, 48 lb. If a wheel is applied at or near the heel of the plough, it can only bear up the hind-part of the sole, and prevent its ordinary friction, which, at the very utmost, cannot be more than ½ of the entire friction due to the entire sole. A wheel, therefore, placed here, and acting under every favouring circumstance, even to the supposed extinction of its own friction, could not reduce the resistance by more than 24 lbs., being the half of that due to the entire sole, or it is $\frac{1}{14}$ of the entire resistance. But we cannot imagine a wheel so placed, to continue any length of time, without becoming clogged in all directions, thereby greatly increasing its own friction; and when it is considered that the necessarily small portion, of any wheel that can be so applied, will sink into the subsoil, to an extent that will still bring the sole of the plough into contact with the sole of the furrow. It will thus be found that the amount of reduction of the general resistance will be very much abridged, certainly not less than one-half, which reduces the whole saving of draught to a quantity not exceeding 12 lb., and even this will be always doubtful, from the difficulty of keeping such wheels in good working condition. This view of a wheel placed at the heel has been confirmed by actual experiments, carefully conducted, wherein Palmer's patent plough with a wheel in the heel (as patented many years ago), but in this case it was applied on the best principles, gave *indications of increased resistance from the use of the wheel, as compared with the same plough when the wheel was removed;* the difference having been 1½ stone in favour of no wheel. I hesitate not, therefore, to say, that, in no case can wheels be of service towards reducing the resistance of the plough, whether they be placed before or behind, or in both positions, and the chances are numerous that they shall act injuriously. That the use of wheels may, under certain circumstances, bring the implement within the management of less skilful hands than is required for the swing plough, must be admitted; but, at the same time, there may be a question whether, even with that advantage, the practice is commendable. I should be wanting in candour if, for myself, I answered otherwise than in the negative.—J. S]

26. OF THE VARIOUS MODES OF PLOUGHING RIDGES.

> . . . . your ploughshare . . . .
> Drawn by one pair, obedient to the voice,
> And double rein, held by the ploughman's hand,
> Moves right along, or winds as he directs.
>
> GRAHAM.

(813.) Your knowledge of soils will become more accurate after you have seen them ploughed, for as long as a crop, or the remains of one, covers soils, their external characters cannot be fully exposed to view.

(814.) On observing a plough at work you might imagine that the laying over of a furrow-slice is a very simple process; but it is really not so simple as it appears. You have already seen, in the construction of the plough, that the furrow-slice is laid over by a machine of very complicated structure, though simple in its mechanical action on the soil; and you may learn, by a single trial, that the plough is not in reality so very easily guided as it appears to be in the hands of an expert ploughman. You might also imagine that as the plough can do nothing else but lay over a furrow-slice, that the forms of ploughing do not admit of much variety, but a short course of observation will convince you that *there are many modes of ploughing land.*

(815.) The several modes of ploughing land have received characteristic appellations, and these are, gathering-up; crown-and-furrow ploughing; casting or yoking or coupling ridges; casting ridges with gore furrows; cleaving down ridges; cleaving down ridges with or without gore furrows; ploughing two-out-and-two-in; ploughing in breaks; cross-furrowing; angle ploughing, ribbing, and drilling; and the preparative operation to all ploughing is termed feering or striking the ridges.

(816) These various modes of ploughing are contrived to suit the nature of the soil and the season of the year. Heavy land requires more cautious ploughing than light, because of its being more easily injured by rain; and greater caution is required to plough all sorts of land in winter than in summer. The precautions here spoken of allude to the facilities given to surface water to flow away. The different seasons, no doubt, demand their respective kinds of ploughing; but some of the modes are common to all seasons and soils. Attention to all the methods will alone enable you to understand which kind is most suitable to par ticular circumstances of soil, and particular states of season. To give you an idea of all the modes, from the simplest to the most complicated,

let the ground be supposed to be even in reference to the state of its surface.

(817.) The supposed flat ground, after being subjected to the plough, is left in the form of *ridges* or of *drills*, each ridge occupying land of equal area, determined by similar lengths and breadths. The ridges are usually made N. and S. that the crop, as I before observed when speaking of enclosures (582), may enjoy the light and heat of the solar rays in an equal degree throughout the day, but they should, nevertheless, traverse the slope of the ground, whatever its aspect may be; and this is done that the surface water may flow easily away.

(818.) Ridges are made of the different breadths of 10, 12, 15, 16, and 18 feet, in different parts of the country. These various breadths are occasioned partly by the nature of the soil, and partly by local custom. With regard to the soil, heavy land is formed into narrow ridges, to allow the rain to flow quickly into the open furrows. Hence, in many parts of England, the ridges are only 10 and 12 feet in width, and in some localities they are in ridglets of 5 or 6 feet. In Scotland, even on the strongest land, the ridges are seldom less than 15 feet, in some localities they are from 16 to 36 feet, and in light soils a not unusual width is 18 feet. In Berwickshire and Roxburghshire, the ridges have for a long period been 15 feet on all classes of soils, being considered the most convenient width for the ordinary manual and implemental operations. In other parts of the country 16 and 18 feet are more common. More than half a century ago ridges were made very broad, that is, from 24 to 36 feet, high on the top or crown, and crooked like the letter S., from the mistaken notion that the crook always presented some part of the ridge in a right position to the sun, a form which, although it did, would remove other parts as far away from the sun's influence. In the Carse of Gowrie such broad crooked ridges still exist, but the usual practice throughout the country is to have ridges of moderate breadth, straight, and looking to noon-day. In many parts of Ireland the land is not put into ridges at all, being done up with the spade into narrow stripes called *lazy-beds*, separated by deep narrow trenches. Where the plough is used, however, ridges are always formed, though narrow, but usually of 12 feet. For the sake of uniformity of description, let it be understood, when I speak of a ridge, that an area of 15 feet of width is meant.

(819.) The first process in ridging up land from the flat surface is called *feering* or *striking* the ridges. This is done by planting 3 or more of such poles, graduated into feet and half-feet, as were recommended for setting off the lines of fence (604), and which are used both for directing the plough employed to feer in straight lines, and for measuring off the breadth of the ridges into which the land is to be made up, from one side of the field to the other.

(820.) Land is *feered* for ridging in this way. Let *a b*, fig. 132, represent the S. and E. fences of a field, of which let *x* be the *headridge* or *headland*, of the same width as that of the ridges, namely 15 feet.

Fig. 132.

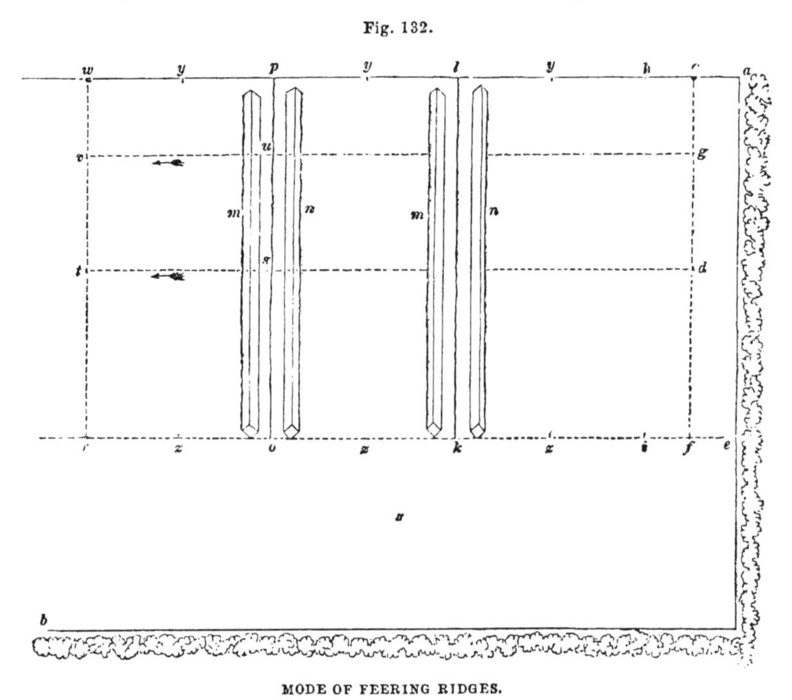

MODE OF FEERING RIDGES.

To mark off its width distinctly let the plough pass in the direction of *r e*, with the furrow-slice lying towards *x*. Do the same along the other head-land, at the opposite end of the field. Then take a pole and measure off the width of a quarter of a ridge, viz., 3 feet 9 inches, from the ditch lip *a* to *c*, and plant a pole at *c*. With another pole set off the same distance from the ditch *a* to *d*, and plant it there. Then measure the same distance from the ditch at *e* to *f*, and at *f* look if *d* has been placed in the line of *f c*, if not, shift the poles a little until they are all in a line. Make a mark on the ground with the foot, or set up the plough-staff, at *f*. Then plant a pole at *g* in the line of *f d c*. Before starting to feer, the ploughman measures off $1\frac{1}{4}$ ridge, namely, 18 feet 9 inches, from *f* to *k*, and plants a pole at *k*. He then starts with the plough from *f* to *d*, where he stops with the pole standing between the horses' heads, or else pushed over by the tying of the horses. He then, with it, measures off, at right angles to *f c*, a line equal to the breadth of 1¼ ridge, 18 feet 9 inches, towards *t* until he comes to the line of *k l*, where he plants the pole. In like manner, he proceeds from *d* to *g*, where he again stops, and measures off 1¼ ridge, 18 feet 9 inches breadth, from *g* towards *v* at a point in the line of *k l*, and plants the pole there. He then proceeds towards the other headridge to the last pole *c* from *g*, and measures off 1¼ ridge, 18 feet 9 inches, from *c* to *l*, and plants the pole at *l*. From *l* he looks towards *k* to see if the intermediate poles are in the line *l k*, if not, he shifts them to their proper points as he returns to the headridge *x* along the furrow he had made in the line *f c*. On coming down *c f* he obviates any deviation from the straight line that the plough may have made. In the line of *f c* the furrow-slices of the feering have been omitted, to shew you the setting of the poles. It is of much importance to the correct feering of the whole field to have those two first feerings, *f c* and *k l*, drawn correctly, and to attain this end it is proper to employ two persons in the doing of it, namely, the ploughman and the farm-steward or farmer himself. It is obvious that an error committed at the first feerings will be transmitted throughout the whole field. A very steady ploughman and a very steady pair of horses, both accustomed to feer, should only be entrusted with the feering of land. Horses accustomed to feer will walk up of their own accord to the pole standing before them. In like manner the ploughman proceeds to feer the line *k l*, and so also the line *o p*, but in all the feerings after the first, from *f* to *k*, the poles, of course, are set off to the exact breadth of the ridge determined on; in this case 15 feet, such as from *s* to *t*, *u* to *v*, *p* to *w*, in the direction of the arrows. And the reason for setting off *c l* at so much a greater distance than *l p* or *p w* is, that the ½ ridge *a h* may be ploughed up first and without delay, and that the rest of the ridges may be ploughed by half-ridges. The half-ridge *a h* is, however, ploughed in a different manner from the rest; it is ploughed by going round the feering *f c* until the open furrow comes to *a e* on the one side and to *h i* on the other. Then *h i* constitutes the feering along with *k l*, for ploughing the 2 half-ridges *z i* and *z k*, which, when done, the open furrow is left in the line *z y*, corresponding to the open furrow left in the line *e a*, and between which is embraced and finished the full ridge of 15 feet *e z*. The half-ridges *z k* and *z o* are ploughed at the same time by another pair of horses, and the open furrow *z y* is left between them, and the full ridge *z k z* is then completed. In like manner, the half-ridges *z o* and *z r* are afterwards ploughed by the same horses, and the open furrow *z y* is left between them, and the full ridge *z o z* is then completed. And so on with every other feering in the field. Had the feering been set off the breadth of a half-ridge, that is,

7½ feet, in the line of *i h*, from *a* to *h* and from *e* to *i*, this half-ridge could only have been ploughed by all the furrow-slices being turned over towards *h i*, and the plough returning back empty, thus losing half its time.

(821.) As a means of securing perfect accuracy in measuring off the breadths of ridges at right angles to the feerings, lines at right angles to *f c* should be set off across the field, from the cross-table and poles set at *d* and *g*, in the direction of *d t* and *g v*, and a furrow made by the plough in each of these lines, before the breadths of the feerings are measured along them. Most people do not take the trouble of doing this, and a very careful ploughman renders it a precaution of not absolute necessity, but every proficient farmer will always do it, even at the sacrifice of a little time and some trouble, as a means of securing accuracy of work.

(822.) As the plough completes each feering, the furrow-slices appear laid over as at *m* and *n*. While one ploughman proceeds in this manner to feer each ridge across the field, the other ploughmen commence the ploughing of the land into ridges; and to afford a number of ploughmen space for beginning their work at the same time, the feering-ploughman should be set to his work at least half a day in advance of the rest, or more if the number of ploughs is great or the ridges to be feered long. In commencing to plough the ridges, each ploughman takes two feerings, and begins by laying the furrow-slices of the feerings together, such as *m* and *n*, to form the crowns of the future ridges. In this way one ploughman lays together the furrow-slices of *f c* and *k l*, whilst another is doing the same with those of *o p* and *r w*. I have already described how the ½ ridge *a h* is ploughed, and stated that the rest of the ridges are ploughed in ½ ridges. The advantage of ploughing by ½ ridges is, that the open-furrows are thereby left exactly equidistant from the crowns, whereas were the ridges ploughed by going round and round the crown of each ridge, one ridge might be made by one ploughman a little broader or narrower than the one on each side of it, that is, broader or narrower than the determinate breadth of 15 feet.

(823.) A ridge, *a a*, fig. 133, consists of a crown *b*, two flanks *c*, two furrow-brows *d*, and two open furrows *a a*. An open furrow is finished at the bottom by two mould or hint-end furrows. (Fig. 134.)

(824.) After laying the feering furrow-slices to make the crowns of the ridges, such as at *f c*, *k l*, *o p*, and *r w*, fig. 132, the plan to plough up ridges from the flat ground is to turn the horses towards you on the head-ridges, until all the furrow-slices between each feering are laid over until you reach the lines *y z*, which then become the open furrows. This method of ploughing is called *gathering up*, or gathering up from the flat, the disposition of whose furrows is shewn in fig. 133, where *a a a* embrace two whole ridges, on the right sides of which all the furrows lie one way, from *a* to *b*, reading from the right to the left;

Fig. 133.

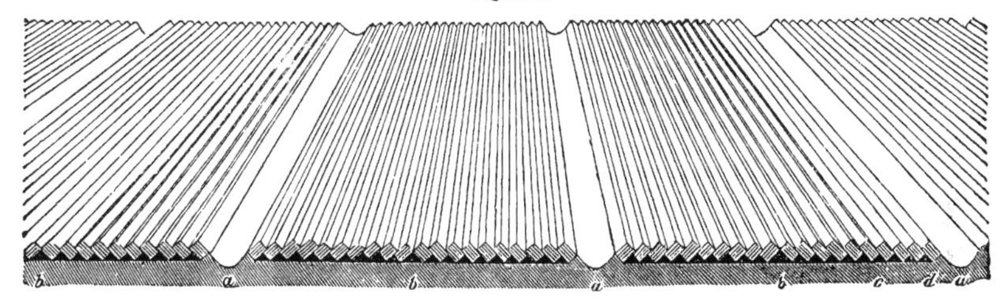

GATHERING UP FROM THE FLAT.

and on the left sides of which all the furrow-slices lie in the opposite direction, from *a* to *b*, reading from the left to the right, and both sets of furrow-slices meet in the crowns *b b b*. The open furrows *a a a* are finished off with the mould or hint-end furrows, the method of making which is described in the next figure.

(825.) The *mould* or *hint-end* furrow is made in this way. When the 2 last furrow-slices of the ridges *a a*, fig. 134, are laid over, the bottom of the open furrow is as wide as represented by the dotted line *c*, extending from *a* to *a*. The plough goes along this wide space and first

Fig. 134.

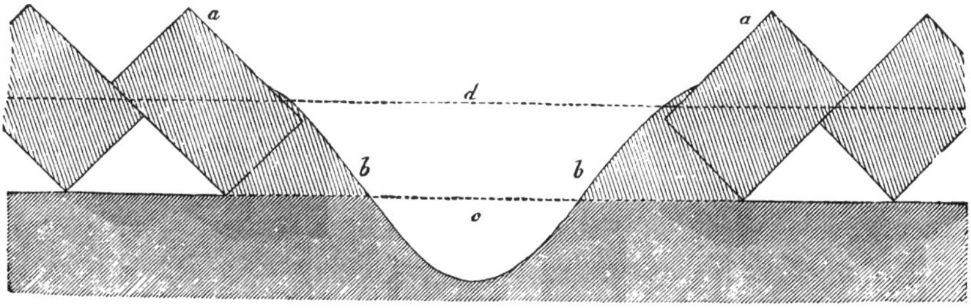

AN OPEN FURROW WITH MOULD OR HINT-END FURROW-SLICES.

lays over a triangular furrow-slice *b* on one side, and another of the same, *b* on the other side, up against and covering the lower ends of the last furrow-slices *a a*, and by which operation the ground is hollowed out in the shape represented at *c* by the sole of the plough. The dotted line *d* shews the level of the ground in its former state, before it was begun to be ridged up, and the furrow-slices *a a* shew the elevation attained by the land above its former level by ploughing.

(826.) A ridge that has been ploughed the reverse to gathering up from the flat is said to be *split*, which is the short phrase for crown-and-furrow ploughing.

(827.) This kind of ploughing of *crown-and-furrow* can easily be performed on land that has been gathered up from the flat. In this case, no feering is required to be purposely made, the open furrows answering that purpose. Thus, in fig. 133, let the furrow-brows *d* be laid over to meet together in the open furrow *a*, and it will be found that they will just meet, since they were formerly separated in the same spot; and so let each successive furrow-slice be reversed from the position it was laid when gathered up from the flat, and as represented in the figure, then *a* will become the crowns of the ridges, and *b* the open-furrows. In this mode, as well as in gathering up, the ridges are ploughed by two half ridges; and in both cases, the ploughed surface of the ridges are preserved in a flat state, there *should be* no perceptible curvature of the ground, the open furrow only forming a hollow below the level of the ploughed surface. When no surface-water is likely to remain on the land, which is the case with light soils, both these are simple modes of ploughing land; and they form an excellent foundation upon which to make drills upon stronger soils for turnips. They are both much practised in ploughing land for barley after turnips.

(828.) But when two ploughings are intended to be given to land for barley after turnips, and when it is found inconvenient to cross-furrow the land,—which will be the case when sheep on turnips occupy a field of great length in proportion to its breadth, or when the soil or season is too wet to run the risk of letting the land lie any time in a cross-furrow,—then the land should be feered so as to allow it to be gathered up from the flat, that the crown-and-furrow ploughing may afterwards complete the ridges. On looking again at fig. 133, where the ridges are represented complete, it is obvious, that were they ploughed from that state into crown-and-furrow, by making the open furrows *a a a* the future crowns, a half ridge would be left at each side of the field,—a mode of finishing off a field which no considerate farmer adopts, as it displays great carelessness and want of forethought in forming his plans. The land should therefore be so feered at first, as to leave a half ridge next the ditch when gathered up from the flat, and which the subsequent crown-and-furrow ploughing will convert into a whole one. Thus, the first feering should be made at *e a*, fig. 132, and every other should be made at the distance of the width of a ridge, namely 15 feet, from the last one, as at *y z*, *y z*, *y z*. On ploughing each feering, the open furrows will then be left at *i h*, *k l*, *o p*, and *r w*. These open furrows will form the feerings for, and the crowns of the future ridges, which, when ploughed the half ridge from *i* to *e* will have to be ploughed by itself, thereby, no doubt, incurring some loss of time in laying all the furrow-slices towards the crown *h i*, and returning with the empty plough; but that loss must be endured to get the ridges finished with a perfect form.

(829.) I may mention here, that one stretch of the plough with a furrow is called a *landing*, and going and returning with a furrow each way is termed a *bout*.

(830.) Another mode of ploughing land from the flat surface is *casting* or *yoking* or *coupling* the ridges. The feering for this mode is done in a different way from either of the two foregoing. The first feering is opened out in the line of *e a* fig. 132, close to the ditch, and every other is measured off of the width of 2 ridges from the last,—that is,

Fig. 135.

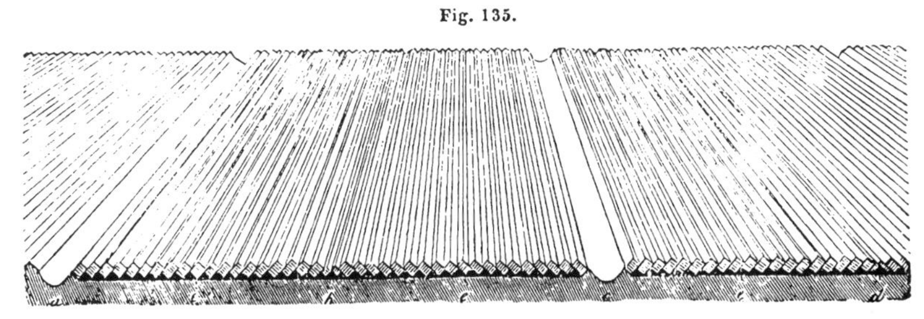

CASTING, YOKING, OR COUPLING RIDGES.

30 feet asunder—as at *y z*, betwixt *k l* and *o p*, and again at half a ridge beyond *r w*. Casting is begun by laying the furrow-slices of the feerings together, and then laying the first furrow-slice towards *e a*, on going up, and towards *y z*, betwixt *l* and *p*, on coming down, the bout; and so on, furrow after furrow, turning the horses on the head-ridges always towards you, until the open furrow is left at *y z*, betwixt *k l* and *i h*. The effect of casting is to lay the entire furrow-slices of every ridge in one direction, and in opposite directions on adjoining ridges. The proper disposition of the furrow-slices you will see in perspective in fig. 135, which exhibits 3 entire ridges, 2 of them cast or yoked together; that is, the furrow-slices of *a b* meet those of *c b* in *b*, which forms the crown of the double ridge, and those of *c d* lie in the opposite direction from *c b*, and are ready to meet those of the adjoining ridge beyond *d* at *d*, and they leave the open furrow between them at *c*; and so on, an open furrow between every 2 ridges. Ridges lying thus yoked can easily be recast, by reversing the furrow-slices of *b c* and *c d*, thereby converting the open furrow *c* into a crown of the double ridge, and making the crown *b* an open furrow. Cast ridges keep the land in a level state, and can

most conveniently be adopted on dry soils. They form a good foundation for drilling upon, or they make a good seed-furrow on dry land. Lea on light land, and the seed-furrow for barley on the same sort of soil, are always ploughed in this fashion. This is an economical mode of ploughing land in regard to time, as it requires but few feerings; the furrow-slices are equal, and on even ground; and the horses are always turned inwards, that is, towards you. Casting is best performed upon the flat surface, as then the uniform state of both ridges can be best preserved; and should the land be desired to be ploughed again, it can be cast the reverse way, and the correct form of the ridges still preserved. In this method of casting, no open furrow is more bare of earth than another.

(831.) Casting ridges is as suitable ploughing for strong as light land, provided the ridges are separated by a *gore-furrow*. A gore-furrow is a space made to prevent the *meeting* of two ridges, and as a substitute for an open furrow between them. Its effect is, in so far as the furrow-slices are concerned, like crown-and-furrow ploughing, but the difference consists in this, that it turns over a whole ridge, instead of a half ridge in each feering. It can only be formed where there is a feering or an open furrow. The method of making a gore-furrow is shewn in fig. 136. Suppose that it is proposed to make one in a feering such as is shewn by *k l* and *o p* in fig. 132. Let the dotted furrow-slices *a* and *e*, and the

Fig. 136.

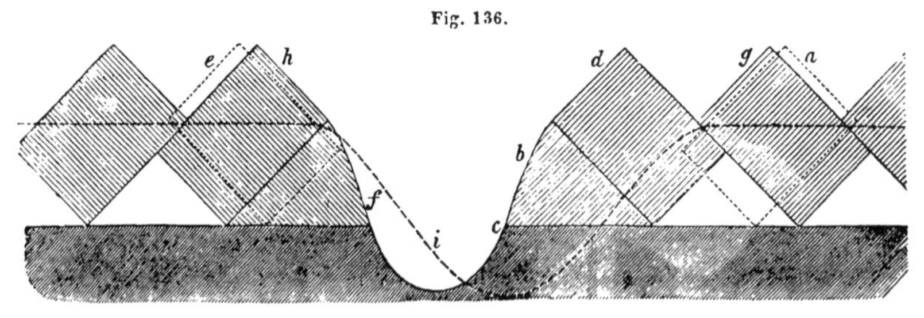

A GORE-FURROW.

dotted line *i* represent an open furrow such as in fig. 136, of which *c* is a point in the middle. Make the plough pass between the centre of the furrow-sole *c* and the left hand dotted furrow-slice *e*, and throw up to the right the triangular-shaped mould-furrow-slice *b*. Then turn the horses sharp round towards you on the head-ridge, and lay the dotted furrow-slice *a* upon *b*, which will then become the furrow-slice *d*, as seen in the fig. at *d*. Again turning the horses sharp round on the head-ridge, take the plough lightly through part of the dotted furrow-slice *e*, and convert it into the triangular-shaped mould-furrow-slice *f*, the upper end of *e* being left untouched; but a portion of *f* will trickle down towards *i*.

Turn the horses from you this time on the head-ridge, and bring down the plough behind *d*, and lay against it the ordinary furrow-slice *g*. Turning the horses again from you on the near head-ridge, lay the ordinary furrow-slice *h*, by destroying the remainder of the dotted furrow-slice *e* with some more earth, upon the triangular-shaped furrow *f*; which, when done, turn the horses *from* you again on the farther head-ridge for the last time, and come down the open furrow *i*, rubbing the soil up with the mould-board of the plough from *i* against *f*, and clearing out of the furrow any loose soil that may have fallen into it, and the gore-furrow is completed. The dotted line *i* shews the surface of the former state of the land. A gore-furrow is most perfectly formed and retained in clay-soil, for one in tender soil is apt to moulder down by the action of the air into the open furrow, which frustrates the purpose of making it a channel for running-water ; but, indeed, on light soils, gore-furrows are of little use, and, of course, seldom formed.

(832.) When land is cast with a gore-furrow upon gathered ground, it is quite correct to say that the open furrow is more bare of earth than the gore-furrow, as Professor Low intimates, but it is not so correct to say, that "this is an imperfection unavoidable in casting a ridge."* Such a remark is only applicable to cast ridges after they have been gathered up from the flat, and much more so to ridges that have been twice gathered up; but the imperfection does not belong to casting in its most legitimate form, that is, upon the flat ground. Land, in my opinion, should never be cast upon gathered ridges, to remain in a permanent form, but only for a temporary purpose ; as in the process of fallowing, for the sake of stirring the soil and overcoming weeds. For, observe the necessary effect of casting a gathered ridge. Suppose the two gathered ridges between *a a a*, fig. 133, were desired to be cast together towards the middle open furrow *a* ; the effect would be to reverse the position of the furrows from *a* to *b*, on either side of *a*. They would remain as flat as formerly ; but what would be the effect on the furrows on the other halves of the ridges from *b* to *d*? They would be gathered twice, so that the double ridge would have two high furrow-brows by two gatherings, and two low flanks by one gathering. It would, in fact, be unequally ploughed, and the open furrow on each side of it would, of course, be bared of earth, having been twice gathered. No doubt, such a distortion might be partially obviated by making the furrow-slices between *a* and *b* on each side of the middle open furrow *a* deeper and larger than those between *b* and *d*, and thus endeavour to preserve a uniform

* Low's Elements of Practical Agriculture, p. 153.

shape to the double ridge ; but this would be done by the sacrifice of sterling ploughing, and it is much better to confine casting within its own sphere, than practise it in circumstances unfavourable to the land.

(833.) The open furrow in casting does not necessarily bare the earth more than a gore-furrow. It is broader, certainly, from the circumstance of its furrow-slices being laid from each other ; but its furrow-sole is not actually ploughed deeper than the gore-furrow. In treating of casting, immediately after shewing how ridges may be gathered up once and twice, it appears to me that Professor Low seems to intimate, at page 152, that land so gathered up may be cast, and preserve its form ; but on this I would observe that casting is almost impracticable after twice gathering, at least it is unadvisable, because, in that case, the effect would be to cleave down the side *b a*, fig. 133, of the ridge on each side of *a*, that is, to throw them down again to the level of the ground ; whilst it would gather up the other two sides *b d thrice*, thereby either making the two sides of each ridge of unequal heights, or, to preserve their level, making the furrow-slices on the same ridges of unequal sizes,—practices both undeserving of commendation under any circumstances. Another author, in speaking of casting ridges together, and shewing how it may be performed by ploughing the furrow slices of two adjoining ridges in opposite directions, gives the caution that " the inter-furrow, which lies between the two ridges, unavoidably leaves a shoulder or hollow place, of more or less width, according to the expertness of the ploughman, in the centre of the crown, which defect can only be completely relieved by reploughing ;"* and informs us, that the defect may be partly prevented by using two ploughs of different mould-boards. I do not see why ploughing two furrow-slices into the open furrow in casting should be more difficult or less sterling than in any other mode of ploughing. A good ploughman will leave in the crown of the ridge, in either case, neither a shoulder nor hollow place, which are certainly not synonymous terms, as they seem to be represented here, but the opposite.

(834.) Nearly allied to casting is a species of ploughing called *two-out-and-two-in*, which can be executed on the flat ground, and requires a particular mode of feering. The first feering should be measured off of the breadth of 2 ridges, or 30 feet, from the ditch *a e*, fig. 132 ; and every subsequent feering should be measured at 4 ridges breadth, or 60 feet from the last. The land is ploughed in this way. Let *a b*, fig. 137, be the side of the field, and let *c d* be the first feering of 30 feet from *a b* ; and also, let *e f* be the next feering of 60 feet. After returning the

* British Husbandry, vol. ii. p. 46.

feering furrow-slices, begin ploughing round the feering *c d*, always keeping it on the right hand, and turning the horses from you, that is, *outwards*, on both the head-ridges, until about the breadth of a ridge is

Fig. 137.

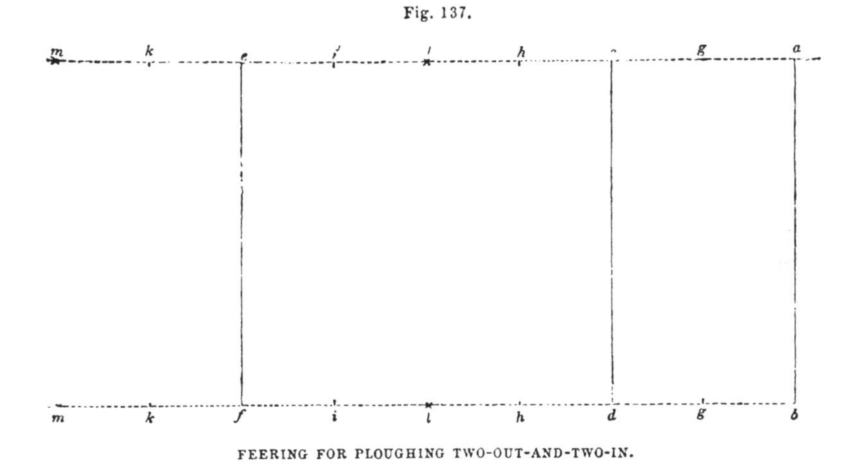

FEERING FOR PLOUGHING TWO-OUT-AND-TWO-IN.

ploughed on each side of *c d*. These 2 ridges may be supposed to be represented by *c g* on the one side, and *c h* on the other of *c d*. While this is doing, the 2 ridges *e i* and *e k* are ploughed, in like manner, towards *e f*. At this juncture, open-furrows occur at *h h* and *i i*, embracing between them the breadth of 2 ridges, or 30 feet, from *h* to *i*. Then let the ploughman who has ploughed round *c d*, plough *h* and *i*, always laying the furrow-slices first to *h* and then to *i*, and turning his horses towards him, or *in*wards, on both head-ridges, until the ground is all ploughed to *l l*, which becomes the permanent open-furrow. The next open-furrow will be at *m m*, 60 feet or 4 ridges breadth from *l l*. But as yet only 3 ridges have been ploughed betwixt *l* and *a*, the fourth ridge *g a* being ploughed along with the head-ridges *m a* and *b m*, after all the ridges of the field have been ploughed, laying its furrow-slices towards *g g*, and making the open-furrow at *a b*. The effect of this mode of ploughing is to lay all the furrow-slices in one direction from *a* to *c*, that is, across the 2 ridges *a g* and *g c*, and to lay those from *l* to *c* in the opposite direction, also across 2 ridges *l h* and *h c*, and both double ridges meeting in *c d*, which becomes the crown of the 4 ridges *l h*, *h c*, *g c*, and *a g*. In like manner all the furrow-slices over the ridges *l i* and *i e* on the one hand, and all those over the ridges *m k* and *k e* on the other hand, meet in their crown at *e f*. In ploughing by this mode, every ploughman takes in a feering of 4 ridges, which he completes before he goes to another. The reason, I suppose, that this mode of ploughing has received the appellation of two-out-and-two-in is, that 2 ridges are ploughed *towards* the feering, and the other 2 *from* the open furrow.

(835.) The appearance of the ground on being ploughed two-out-and-two-in is seen in fig. 138, where the space from *a* to *e* is 60 feet, compre-

Fig. 138.

PLOUGHING TWO-OUT-AND-TWO-IN.

hending 4 ridges, between the open-furrows *a* and *e*, 2 of which ridges, *a b* and *b c*, have their furrow-slices lying one way, towards the right, and the other 2, *e d* and *d c*, with theirs lying towards the left in the opposite way, both meeting at *c*, which is the crown of the whole break or division of 4 ridges.

(836.) This method of ploughing places the land in large flat spaces, and as it dispenses with many open furrows, it is on this account only suitable for light soils, in which it may be practised for seed-furrowing. It forms an excellent foundation for drilling upon for turnips, or even for potatoes upon gravelly soils.

(837.) The gore-furrow, described in fig. 136, might be judiciously applied to the ploughing of land two-out-and-two-in on the stronger classes of soils; but its introduction changes the character of the ridges altogether, inasmuch as the crown *c*, fig. 138, where the furrow-slices *meet*, is not only converted into an open-furrow, but the actual crown is transferred from *c* to *b*, and *d*, where the furrow-slices do *not meet* from opposite directions, but lie across the crowns of their respective double ridges in the same direction. Exactly in a similar manner, when the gore-furrow is introduced into cast ridges, as in fig. 135, the crowns *b* and *d* are converted into open furrows, and transferred to *e*, where the furrow-slices lie across the crowns in the same direction on their respective ridges, instead of meeting there.

(838.) A nearly allied ploughing to the last is that of *ploughing in breaks* or *divisions*. It consists of making feerings at indefinite distances, and ploughing large divisions of land without open-furrows. Some farmers plough divisions of 8 ridges or 40 yards; but such a distance incurs considerable loss of time to travel from furrow to furrow at the landings Instead, therefore, of distances of a given number of ridges being chosen, as is the case in the last mode of ploughing, two-out-and-two-in, 30 yards are substituted, and this particular breadth answers another purpose of deviating from the sites of the ordinary ridges, which deviation has the advantage of loosening any hard land that may have been left untouched by the plough in any of the sorts of ploughings that have yet been presented to your notice. Land is ploughed in breaks only for temporary purposes, such as giving it a tender surface for seed-furrowing, or drilling up immediately. You might easily estimate how much time would be lost in ploughing land in breaks, were the feerings made at a greater distance than 30 yards, by looking at fig 137, where the feerings *c d* and *e f* being supposed to be 60 yards asunder, the ploughs would have to go round *c d* and *e f* until they reached *h* and *i* respectively, in doing which they would have to travel in a progressively increasing distance until its extreme point from *h* to *i* reached 30 yards *for every furrow-slice laid over.* Thus is imposed on men and horses a great deal of travelling for the little work actually done.

(839.) Another mode of ploughing, which I shall now describe, is *twice-gathering-up*. Its effect may be seen by looking at fig. 139, where it will be observed that the furrow-slices rest above the level line of the ground. It may be practised both on lea and red-land. On red-land that has already been gathered up from the flat, it is begun by making feerings in the crowns of the ridges, as at *b*, fig. 133. The furrow-slices

Fig. 139.

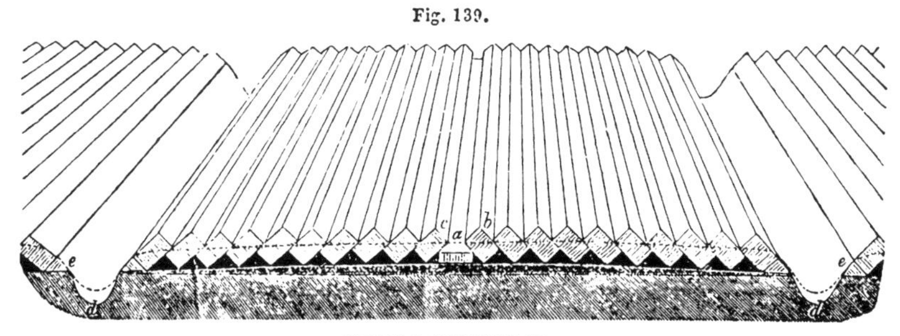

TWICE-GATHERING-UP.

of the feerings are laid together, and the ridges ploughed by $\frac{1}{2}$ ridges, in the manner of gathering up from the flat. The $\frac{1}{2}$ ridge left by the feerings at the sides of the field must be ploughed by themselves, even at the risk of losing time, because it would not do to feer the first ridge so as to plough the $\frac{1}{2}$ ridge as directed to be done in the first-gathering-up, in fig. 132, around the feering of the $\frac{1}{4}$ ridge *f c*, because the furrows betwixt *f* and *i*, if ploughed in the contrary direction to what they were before, would again flatten the ground, whereas the furrow-slices from *e* to *f* and from *z* to *i*, being ploughed in the same direction as formerly, the ground would thereby be raised above the level of *i f*, and disfigure the ploughing of the whole ridge *z e*. Gathering up from the flat preserves the flatness of the ground; and the second gathering up would also preserve the land in a flat state, though more elevated, were there depth enough of soil, and the furrow-slices preserved of their proper form, as we have seen in (827), but a roundness is usually given to the ridge in all cases of gathering up furrow-slices towards the crowns, both by the harrowing down of the precipitous furrow-brows, and the unequal size of the furrow-slices, from want of soil at the furrow-brows and open furrows. In gathering up lea the second time, no feering is required. The plough goes down a little to the left of the crown of the ridge, and lays over upon the crown a thin and narrow furrow-slice upon its back, as *a*, fig. 139, to serve as a cushion upon which to rest the adjoining furrow-slices. The horses are then turned sharp round from you, and the furrow-slice *b* is laid over so as to rest, at the proper angle of 45°, upon *a*. Turning the horses again sharp round from you, the furrow-slice *c* is also laid over at the same angle to rest on *a*, but neither *c* nor *b* should approach each other so nearly as to cover *a*, but leave a space of about 3 or 4 inches between them. The object of leaving this small space is to form a receptacle for the seed-corn, which, were *c* and *b* made to meet at a sharp angle, would slide down, and leave the best part of the ridge bare of seed. The crown of the rest of the ridges is treated in the same manner, where in fact is constituted its feering, and the ridges are ploughed in ½ ridges to the open-furrows *d*, which are finished with mould-furrows, but the ploughing of these is attended with some difficulty, in order to prevent their gradually mouldering down into the bottom of the open furrows. Twice-gathering-up is only practised in strong land, and its object is to lift the mould above the cold and wet subsoil. On dry land, no such expedient is required. In fig. 139 the dotted line *e* is meant to represent the former configuration of the ground, and now it may be seen that the open furrow at *d* is deeper than it was with once gathering-up.

(840.) The mode of ploughing exactly opposite to twice-gathering-up is that of *cleaving* or *throwing down* land. The open-furrows of twice-gathered-up land constitute deep feerings, which are filled up with furrow-slices obtained from the mould-furrows and furrow-brows of each adjoining ridge; and in order to fill them fully up, the plough should take as deep a hold of the furrow-brow as it can obtain. The furrow-slices are ploughed exactly the reverse of those of the twice-gathered-up ridges, and they are also ploughed in ½ ridges. The effect of cleaving down is to bring the ground again to the level above which it had been raised by means of the twice-gathering-up. The open-furrows are left at the crowns, as at *a*, fig. 139, the mould-furrows of which are seldom stirred, as cleaving down is usually practised to prepare the land for cross-ploughing in the spring. But when heavy land is cleaved down in winter, it is always so with gore-furrows, and these, with open-furrows, afford convenient channels, at every half ridge, for the water to flow off to the ditches. Since twice-gathering-up is only practised

Fig 140.

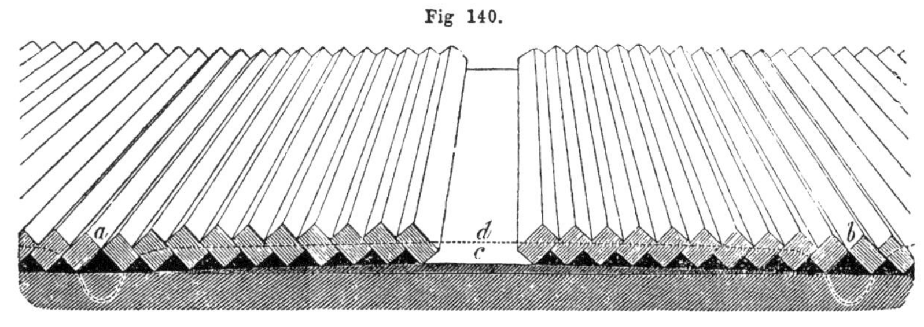

CLEAVING DOWN WITHOUT GORE-FURROWS.

on strong land, and cleaving down only succeeds twice-gathering-up, it follows that cleaving down is only practised on heavy land The effect produced by cleaving down ground may be seen in fig. 140, which represents it without gore-furrows *b* and mould-furrows *c*; but in fig. 141, the gore-furrows are shewn at *a*, and the open and mould-furrows at *b*.

Fig. 141.

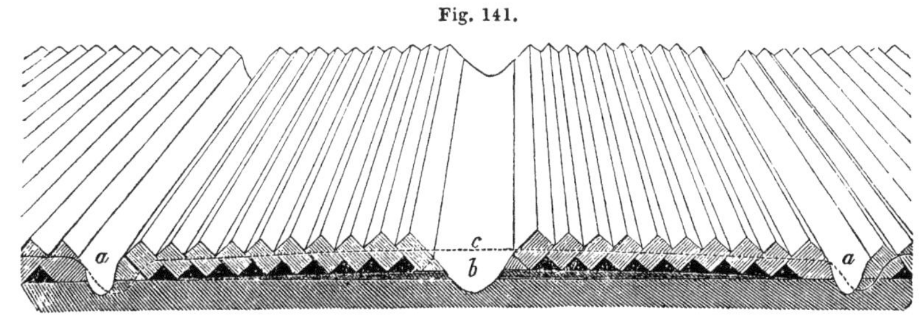

CLEAVING DOWN WITH GORE-FURROWS.

The dotted line *d*, in fig. 140, represents the surface of the former state of the ground, as does the dotted line *c*, in fig. 141. Below *a* and *b*, fig. 140, are shewn the former open furrows by the dotted line, as also does the dotted line below *a*, in fig. 141. In both figures the ground upon which the furrow-slices rest is made somewhat rounded, to shew the effect of twice-gathering it up. In the strict sense, a ridge can only be cleaved after it has been twice ploughed. It is, as I think, scarcely correct to say that a ridge is cleaved after one gathering from the flat, for it is then ploughed crown-and-furrow. With a strong furrow, a ridge that had been twice-gathered-up can be made flat by one cleaving.

(841.) What is called *cross-ploughing*, or the *cross-furrow*, derives its name from ploughing right across the furrow-slices as they lie in ridges, in whatever form those ridges may have been formerly ploughed. Its object is to cut the existing furrow-slices into small pieces, so that the land may be more easily pulverized and prepared for the future crops. It is usually executed in the spring, and should never be attempted in winter, unless the weather continue so long dry and fresh as to allow the land to be again immediately ploughed into ridges in any of the safe forms of ploughing I have described. Rain, or snow melting on land lying in the cross-furrow, is at once absorbed and retained in it, and in a short time renders it sour. But, even if cross-furrowing were executed in a proper manner in winter, and the land thereafter safely put into ridges, the land would become so consolidated during winter, that it would have to be again cross-furrowed in the spring before it could be rendered friable. The object of cross-furrowing being to pulverize land, it is practised on every species of soil, and exactly in the same manner. It is ploughed in divisions, the feerings being made at 30 yards asunder, and these are ploughed in the same manner as two-out-and-two-in, by first going round the feering, turning the horses constantly from you, until about ½ of the division is ploughed, and then turning them towards you, still laying the furrow-slices over towards the feerings, until your arrival at the open-furrow. In cross-ploughing, however, the open-furrow is never left open, but is again closed by 2 or 3 of the last furrow-slices being returned, and all marks of it obliterated by the plough shovelling the loose soil into the furrows with the mould-board, which is purposely laid over on its side, and retained in that position by a firm hold of the large stilt. The obliteration of the open-furrows is necessary to fill up the hollows that would otherwise be left by them across the ridges after they were formed.

(842.) Another mode of ploughing, having a similar object to cross-furrowing, namely, of dividing furrow-slices into pieces, is what is called *angle-ploughing* or *angle-furrowing*, and it is so named because the feerings in which it is ploughed are made in a diagonal or angular direction across the field. This mode is also ploughed in divisions of 30 yards each, and in exactly the same manner as cross-ploughing, and with the same precautions as to the season in which it is executed, and the closing of the open-furrows. It is never practised but *after* cross-ploughing, and not always then, but on strong land, or unless the cross-ploughing has failed to produce its desired effect of comminuting and stirring up the soil. It is chiefly practised in bare fallowing, and is therefore mostly confined to strong land.

(843.) I have mentioned a mode of ploughing called *ribbing* (815). In its best form it is usually performed in spring with the small plough, when it will more appropriately fall to be described than in this place; but there is a species of ploughing practised in some parts of the country in autumn or winter which bears the name of ribbing. I notice it, because it is practised in some parts, not with the view of recommending but of reprobating it. It is, I believe, called *raftering* in England; and is practised on stubble land, and consists of laying a furrow-slice on its back upon as much of the firm soil as it can cover, as seen in fig. 142,

Fig. 142.

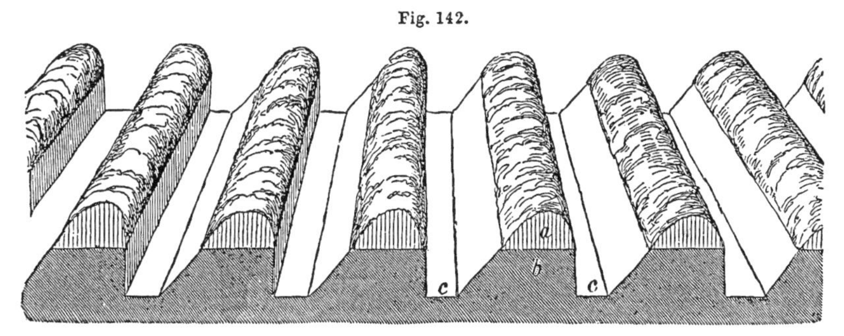

RIB-PLOUGHING STUBBLE LAND.

where *a* are the furrow-slices laid over upon the firm soil *b*, and *c* the plough-tracks. The figure represents it more compact, clean, and regular, than it is usually found in practice. It is sometimes ploughed so as the furrow-slice shall lap and hang over the piece of firm soil upon which it rests, and the plough-tracks are often very crooked. The land lies in this state all winter, and is dry enough: but the greatest proportion of the soil remaining unploughed, is none the better for this treatment. It has the advantage of being done in a short time, and without care, as it is generally done in a diagonal direction across the ridges, and without any sort of feering. It is chiefly practised on land in a very foul state, with the view of destroying the weeds; from its being believed that the under surface of the furrow-slice, where the roots of the weeds are most abundant, is thus more exposed to the action of frost than in any other position, and this opinion is no doubt correct; but if the ploughed portion of the ground is in this manner more exposed to the air, it is evident that the unploughed part cannot be exposed at all, and as the largest proportion of the land is left unploughed, any advantage attending such a mode of ploughing must be greatly counterbalanced by its disadvantages. It is practised in all sorts of soils. Its practice in Scotland is confined to the north of the Frith of Forth, and even there it is now abandoned on the large farms, though it may still be seen in the fields of the smaller tenants. When a field is so ploughed, it has somewhat the appearance of having been drilled.

(844.) The *drilling* of land being confined to summer, I shall defer any remarks on that mode of ploughing until its proper season arrives.

---

27. OF DRAINING.

> " In grounds, by art laid dry, the aqueous bane
> That marred the wholesome herbs, is turn'd to use;
> And drains, while drawing noxious moisture off,
> Serve also to diffuse a due supply."
>
> GRAHAM.

(845.) It is barely possible that the farm on which you learn your profession, or the one you may occupy on your own account, may not require draining. Nevertheless, you should be made well acquainted with this essential and indispensable practice in husbandry. But the probability is, that on whatever farm you may pass your life, some part of it at least, if not the whole, will require draining of one sort or another.

(846.) Draining may be *defined* the art of rendering land not only so free of moisture as that no superfluous water shall remain in it, but that no water shall remain in it so long as to injure or even retard the healthy growth of plants required for the use of man and beast.

(847.) On considering this definition, you may reasonably inquire why water in the soil should injure the growth of useful plants, since botanical physiologists tell us, that the greatest bulk of the food of plants consists of, or at least is conveyed to them by, water. In what way injury should arise, is certainly not very obvious; but observation has proved that *stagnant* water, whether on the surface or under the ground, does injure the growth of all the useful plants. It perhaps altogether prevents or checks perspiration and introsusception; or it may neutralise the chemical decomposition of substances which largely supply the food of plants. Be it as it may, experience assures us, that draining will prevent all these bad effects. You may conceive it quite possible for an obvious excess of water to injure useful plants; because you may have observed, that excess of water is usually indicated by the presence, in number and luxuriance, of subaquatic plants, such as rushes (*Juncus acutiflorus* and *J. effusus*), &c., which only flourish where water is too abundant for other plants; and you may even conceive that damp, dark-looking spots in the soil may contain as much water as to injure plants, though in a less degree; but you cannot at once imagine why land *apparently* dry should require draining. Land, however, though it does not contain such a superabundance of water as to obstruct arable culture, may nevertheless, by its inherent wetness, prevent or retard the luxuriant growth of useful plants, as much as decidedly wet land. The truth is, that deficiency of crops on apparently dry land is frequently attributed to unskilful husbandry, when it really arises from the baleful influence of *concealed* stagnant water; and the want of skill is shewn, not so much in the management of the arable culture of the land, as in neglecting to remove the true cause of the deficiency of the crop, namely, the concealed stagnant water. Indeed, my opinion is,—and its conviction has been forced upon me by dint of long and extensive observation of the state of the agricultural soil over a large portion of the country,—that this is the *true cause of most of the bad farming to be seen*, and that *not one farm* is to be found throughout the kingdom that would *not be much the better for draining*. Entertaining this opinion, you will not be surprised at my urging upon you to practise draining, and of lingering at some length on the subject, that I may exhibit to you the various modes of doing it, according to the peculiar circumstances in which your farm may be placed.

(848.) To the experienced eye, there is little difficulty in ascertaining the particular parts of fields which are more affected than others by superfluous water. They may be detected under whatever kind of crop the field may bear at the time; for the peculiar state of the crop in those parts, when compared with the others, assists in determining the point. There is a want of vigour in the plants—their colour is not of a healthy hue—their parts do not become sufficiently developed—the plants are evidently retarded in their progress to maturity—and the soil upon which they grow feels inelastic, or saddened under the tread of the foot. There is no mistaking these symptoms when once observed. They are exhibited more obviously by the grain and green crops, than by the sown grasses. In *old* pasture, the coarse, hard, uninviting appearance of the herbage, is quite a sufficient indication of the moistened state of the soil.

(849.) But there are appearances of moistened land, which you may easily observe without any previous tuition; and these are most apparent in soil after it has been ploughed, and more apparent still in spring, in the month of March, when the winds become dry and keen. Then you may observe, in a dry day, large patches or stripes, or belts of black or dark-brown coloured soil, in the face and near the top of an acclivity, whilst the rest of the field *seems* quite dry, of a light-brown colour; or only small spots may be observable here and there; or the flat and hollow parts of the field may be nearly covered with dark-coloured soil. You cannot mistake these broad hints of the lurking water below; but, in a few weeks, they may all have disappeared, or be reduced very much in extent, if the weather continues dry, or have become more extended in rainy weather. In the case of their disappearance in dry weather, you may conclude that any wetness of the soil which passes off as the summer advances, can do no harm to cultivated plants, and that the land, in such cases, *does not require to be drained.* Such a conclusion would be very erroneous; because it is on account of the water *remaining in the soil all winter* that the crops receive injury in summer. The amount of *wetness* which you saw pass away first in spring and then in summer, would have done no injury to the crops, for it would be all absorbed, and probably more, in the wants of vegetation; but the wetness remaining in and occupying the pores of the soil and of the subsoil all winter, render the soil so cold, that most of the summer's heat is required to evaporate the superfluous moisture out of it, and, in this very process of drying by evaporation, the heat is dissipated that should be employed in nourishing the crops all summer. No doubt, when the soil and subsoil are put into such a state as that the water that falls upon the soil from the heavens during the winter, on being conveyed quickly away in drains, does take away some of the heat from the soil, but it cannot render it cold or sour. In such circumstances, the natural heat of the weather in spring and summer would have nothing to do but to push forward the growth of the crops to early maturity, to fill them more fully, and make them of finer quality. You thus see how concealed water injures the soil in which it is retained, and you may easily conceive how it may injure the drier soil around it, by its imbibing the water in contact, by capillary attraction You thus also see the kind of good that draining effects in soil so situated. Did the symptoms of wet in spring remain as obvious to your senses throughout the summer, you would have no doubt of the land requiring draining; but you may now admit that you may be deceived by land shewing even favourable symptoms of drought. For all that you yet know to the contrary, water may be lurking under what you imagine to be dry soil Yes, and it does lurk to a very great extent in this country, and will continue to lurk in humid localities and impervious subsoils, until a vent is given to its egress.

(850.) The phenomenon of the dark spots on fields can be satisfactorily explained. Where the surface of the land is at all permeable to water, and where it rests on beds of different depths, of various lengths and breadths, and of different consistence, the water supplied from rain or snow is interrupted in its progress by the retentive beds, and becomes accumulated in them in larger or smaller quantities, according to their form and capacity; and, at length, the superfluous portion is poured from the surcharged strata, and bursts over retentive beds through the surface-soil in the form of land-springs, at a somewhat lower level. Such springs are either concentrated in one place or diffused over a large extent of surface, according as their outlet happens to be extensive or confined, and deep draining is generally required to remove these; for which purpose, deep drains are cut through alternate beds of retentive and permeable matter, and penetrate into the very seats of the springs. It may happen, however, that the surface is as retentive as the subsoil, in which case the water, not penetrating further than the surface-soil, has a free enough passage between the impervious subsoil and the loose soil; this state of soil requires mere surface-draining. Where the upper soil is pervious, and the subsoil uniformly and extensively retentive, water accumulates on the subsoil, to the injury of plants growing on the surface-soil; and to remove water from such a situation, not deep but numerous drains are required to give sufficient opportunities for it to pass away, and such drains are usually formed in the furrows. Where the soil and subsoil are both porous, the water passes quickly through them, and no draining is required to assist it in flowing away, as the entire subsoil constitutes a universal drain. In this state of soil, water is only held in it by capillary attraction, and what is not so supported sinks down through the porous subsoil by its own gravity. Capillary attraction is quite capable of supporting and bringing as much water through a permeable soil and subsoil, from rain above and sources of water from below, as is useful to vegetation, excepting perhaps under the extraordinary occurrence of excessive drought; and of all the sources from which the soil derives its supplies of water, that from springs is the coldest, most injurious to useful plants, and most permanent in its effects; and hence it is that the abstraction of water from the soil by draining does not necessarily interfere with it as a supporter of plants, as a meliorator of the soil, as a menstruum for the food, and as a regulator of temperature to plants.

(851.) These states of water in the soil and subsoil indicate that a knowledge of geology might confer a more perfect understanding of the principles of draining; and, fortunately, practice in this department of rural economy has always been consistent with the facts of geology. But a geological drainer is a character who has not yet made his appearance in the world; because no practical drainer or scientific geologist has yet explored that department of geology which is most useful to agriculture, in such a manner as to assist the art of draining. Most of our arable soils are contained within the newest rock-formations, the intricate relations of which present almost insurmountable obstacles to such a knowledge of them as to be useful in draining. The intricacy of their relations render the operations of draining uncertain; and this uncertainty, I fear, must continue to exist, until the relations of the alluvial rocks are discovered to be as unvarying as those of the more indurated. Perhaps a certainty in the matter is unattainable, because the members of the alluvial formation may not present a strictly relative position to one another. Until the fact, therefore, is ascertained one way or the other, draining must be conducted, in a great measure, by trial or experiment; and in all undertakings on trial, error must be expected to ensue, and unnecessary expense incurred. An unfortunate circumstance, arising from this uncertainty, is the comparative uselessness of the experience acquired in previous operations to guide the drainer himself and others, to the means of securing more certain results in their future efforts at draining. No drainer can affirm that the number and depth, and even the direction, of the drains which he chooses to adopt, are the best suited for drying the field he wishes to drain; nor can he maintain, that exactly similar arrangements will produce exactly similar effects in the adjoining or in any other field, at a greater or shorter distance. Every experienced drainer will coincide with the justness of these remarks, and deplore the uncertain nature of his operations; but, nevertheless, the satisfactory consolation is, that as long as he finds draining, even as it is pursued, do good, so long he will continue to practise it. Were geologists to make themselves acquainted with the practical details of draining, and then study that branch of geology which would be of greatest service to draining, it is reasonable to hope that they would confer lasting obligations on the drainer, not only by directing him to a well-grounded certainty in his object, but by shewing him how to execute his art with greater simplicity. Were they also to direct particular attention to the relation that subsists, if any, between the surface of the earth's crust and the strata immediately subjacent, their investigations might supply valuable materials for a correct nomenclature and classification of soils.

(852.) You thus perceive that a bare recital of the various modes of draining is not alone sufficient to make you an accomplished drainer; for you should know the principles as well as the practice of the art. The principles can only be acquired by a knowledge of geology, in as far as it has investigated the structure of the alluvial rocks, which are within your reach everywhere, and entirely within your power on your own farm to investigate. This knowledge, even as it is yet known, is requisite; for any difficulty in draining is found not so much in constructing a drain—most field labourers can do that—as in knowing *where* to construct it; and a correct knowledge of whether the wetness in the land arises from natural springs or from stagnant water under the surface of the soil, can alone direct you to open the kind of drain required. So generally is the practical part of the operation diffused, that every manager of land conceives he knows the whole subject of draining so correctly, that he will commence his operations with the utmost confidence of success; and this confidence has caused much money to be expended in draining, that has in great part been ill directed; not but that its expenditure has done good, but that it has not done nearly all the good that the means employed might have effected. Much money has thus been expended in many places in making a few scattered deep drains, where a greater number of smaller ones would have answered the purpose much better. A degree of success, however, has attended every attempt at draining, and it is this circumstance, more than any other, that has beguiled many into a belief that they are accomplished drainers; for no one, unfit to direct the operation in a proper manner, would have attempted it at all, unless he had actually experienced injury from wet land; or have attempted it again, unless his attempts had partially at least removed the injury; though the results have not been very successful. Were the efforts of ignorance in draining confined to the squandering of money, they might be compensated for by superior management in the other operations of the farm; but, unfortunately the sinking of valuable capital in injudicious draining cripples the means of the farmer, and at the same time prevents his reaping all the advantages derivable from draining itself Were draining an operation that could be executed at little cost and trouble, it would be of less importance to urge its prosecution in the most effectual way; but as it is an expensive operation, when conducted in the most economical manner, much consideration should be given to the matter in all its bearings, before attempting to break up ground for draining to any great extent. An examination of the earth's crust, upon which you are to operate, is absolutely necessary to direct your plans aright. Contemplate well, in the first place, the facts which such an examination unfolds to your view, and endeavour by their nature to acquire wisdom to expend your money with prudence as well as skill. Examinations of the soil and subsoil will tell you what kinds require deep draining, and what kinds may be treated with equal success under a different arrangement. Inattention to such distinctions as these has hitherto caused the inordinate application of one general principle, which, as applicable to a particular system, must receive the assent of every drainer who feels the importance of the art, but which, nevertheless, is inapplicable to every case,—I mean the system of deep draining.

(853.) You may have observed, from what has been said, that there is more than one species of draining; there is one which draws off large bodies of water, collected from the discharge of springs in isolated portions of ground; and this is called *deep* or *under-draining*, because it intercepts the passage of water at a considerable depth under the surface of the ground; and there is another kind which absorbs, by means of numerous channels, the superabundant water spread over extensive pieces of ground under the surface, and has been called *surface-draining*. This latter kind of draining subdivides itself into two varieties, the one consisting of small open channels formed on the surface of the ground in various directions for the ready use of water flowing upon the land, and this is literally *surface-draining*. The other is effected by means of small drains constructed at small depths in the ground, at short distances from one another, and into which the water as it falls upon the surface finds its way by its own gravity through the loose soil, and by which it is discharged into a convenient receptacle. But for those two species of surface-drains, the water that falls from above would remain stagnant upon the retentive subsoil at the bottom of the plough-furrow. The former kind of surface-draining is called *gaw*-cutting, so named from its resemblance to "a mark or crack left in the soil by a stroke or pressure;"* the latter kind derives its name either from the locality which it occupies, or the arrangement of its lines. From its local position, it has been called *furrow-draining* when it occupies the open furrows of the ridges of a field, though it is not necessary that such drains should always occupy the furrows. It has also been called *frequent-draining*, from the circumstance of the water finding frequent opportunities of escape; but this name, though the original one, is objectionable, inasmuch as the word may imply that the field requires draining frequently, which it certainly will not. From the arrangement of its lines, it has also been denominated *parallel-draining*, on account of the usual parallel position of the drains to one another; and yet it is not absolutely necessary to success that they shall be parallel to one another. As by this kind of draining

* See Jamieson's Scottish Dictionary. *Gaw.*

the land is thoroughly or effectually drained, it has been most appropriately called *thorough-draining ;* and this term, as a nomenclature, has the advantage of not committing the drainer to the adoption of any particular form or position of drain, but only to that form or position which renders land thoroughly dry. There are various other modes of draining, such as *wedge-draining*, *plug-draining*, *mole-draining*, each of which will receive consideration in due course.

(854.) The most superficial mode of draining is that effected by *open ditches* and *gaw-cuts*, into which the surface-water flows, and is carried off to a distance to some river or lake. This mode of draining does not profess to interfere with any water that exists under the surface of the ground, farther than what percolates through the ploughed furrow-slices, and makes its way into the open-furrows of the ridges. For the purpose of facilitating the descent of water into the open-furrows, the ridges are kept in a bold rounded form ; and that the open-furrows may be suitable channels for water, they are carefully water-furrowed, that is, cleared out with the plough after the land has been otherwise finished off with a crop. The *gaw-cuts*, small channels cut with the spade, are carefully made through every natural hollow of the ground, however slight each one may be, and the water-furrows cleared into them at the points of intersection. The gaw-cuts are continued along the lowest head-ridge furrow, and cut across the hollowest parts of the head-ridge into the adjacent open ditch. The recipient ditch forms an important component part of this system of draining, by conveying away the collected waters of the field of which it forms the boundary; and for that purpose is made as much as 4 or 5 feet in depth, with a proportional width. It is immediately connected with a larger open ditch, which discharges the accumulated waters from a number of recipient ditches into the river or lake, or other receptacle which is taken advantage of for the purpose. The large ditch is from 6 to 10 feet in depth, with a proportional width, and, when conveying a full body of water in winter, appears like a small canal. It is evident, from this description, that this is a system of pure *surface*-drainage, and is only applicable to soils that retain water for a long time on the surface, that is, on very tenacious clays; and, accordingly, it is extensively practised in such districts as the Carse of Gowrie, where it has been so for a very long period. The large ditches there are called *pows*, which literally mean *mires.* The ploughmen of the Carse are accustomed to the spade, and are yearly employed, in the proper season, in scouring out the smaller ditches ; the larger ones being only scoured occasionally. Whenever a heavy fall of rain occurs in winter or spring, they are employed in clearing out the gaws, and directing the water as fast as possible off the land along the furrows. This operation is a necessary precaution in wet weather upon strong clay land, but it constitutes a very imperfect system of *draining*, and sacrifices a large extent of good surface soil. It would be better, I think, if the Carse farmers were generally to try the effect of covered drains, which would absorb and carry away surplus water equally well as open ones, and save much time in scouring ditches, besides putting the soil into a fitter state to be worked at any season than it can be done under the present system.

(855.) The *drains* which our *forefathers made in loamy soils resting on a retentive bottom*, were placed upon the subsoil immediately under the upper soil, where that was deeper than the plough-furrow; but as the arable portion of the soil, when it is quite of a different nature from the subsoil, is never very thick, the drains were necessarily placed at a small depth; and the cut being so, experience would soon teach drainers the impropriety of placing the materials which are used to fill a drain within reach of the plough, which consisted of very few stones, often not exceeding three, and those not of large size, one being placed on each side of the cut, and another above them, forming a sort of conduit. These conduits being not far from the surface, of small area, and not very numerous in any one place, a small addition of water would carry, and the moles would force a little earth into them, sufficient to obstruct the flow of water in them, and, of course, any drain in that state would produce the very mischief it was intended to remedy. Such paltry drains have evidently been formed on the notion that a simple conduit placed between a porous soil and retentive subsoil is sufficient to render the soil permanently dry,—a notion the fallacy of which the drainers of the present day are well aware. I have met with several such drains in the course of my draining operations; and they were completely choked up, but on being opened by the cutting of the new drains, clear water flowed out of them for a considerable time. They were all beyond the reach of the plough, in the manner in which the land had been ploughed from time immemorial; but the ploughing had consisted of a mere skimming of 4 inches of the soil, and on this account the black mould immediately under the plough-track had been compressed by the sole of the plough into a thin slaty crust, under which the fine black virgin mould remained untouched, while the ploughed surface had become an effete powder by constant cropping.

(856.) Compared with this trifling method, the system of *under* or *deep-draining*, being the deepest method of any, is super-excellent. It is technically called Elkington's method, because it was first proposed and practised by Mr Joseph Elkington, Princethorp, a farmer in Warwickshire, so long ago as 1764. It is related that he discovered the mode of draining which has since borne his name by accident. His fields being very wet, and rotting many of his sheep, he dug a trench 4 or 5 feet deep, with the view of discovering the cause of the wetness. While he was deliberating what was to be done, a servant passed by chance with an iron crow-bar for fixing sheep-hurdles with in the ground. Having a suspicion that the drain was not deep enough, and desirous to know the nature of the materials under it, he forced the bar 4 feet below the bottom of the trench, and, on pulling it out, to his astonishment, a great quantity of water welled up through the hole it made, and ran along the drain. He was led to infer from this, that large bodies of water are pent up in the bowels of the earth, and are constantly injuring the surface soil, but which may be let off by tapping with an auger or rod. This discovery produced a great sensation at the time, and, in fact, introduced a complete revolution in this country in the art of draining. It served to establish draining on correct principles. It was as much more effective a method than the old system, in changing the quality of the soil, as blood-letting from a vein by the lancet affects the constitution in a greater degree than the topical application of leeches. But this method soon underwent modifications in practice. Casting a drain and tapping with an auger to catch the spring or bed of water, as in the principle of artesian wells, was the original plan; but when it was found that water did not in every case follow the auger, as it would not when disseminated through a mass of earth, and not subjected to altitudinal pressure, a modification of the plan was inevitable. It was then attempted to run deep trenches through the lowest part of the damp soil to the highest point where the supply of water was supposed to be or where it made its appearance, and lead it away as it collected by percolation through the soil and subsoil. In order to embrace the whole damp soil of any locality in the drainage, lateral branches were projected on both sides of the main branch, as far as the apparent dampness extended; and, not to omit the smallest extent of the damp soil, tributary branches were sent off to short distances from the lateral ones. The different branches were made of different sizes, according to the quantity of water which each was supposed to have to convey away. This plan of drains, when projected on the surface, looks like the trunk and branches of a tree in winter deprived of its leaves; and it might therefore be called the ramified or dendritic form. This is the plan that has been very extensively pursued since Elkington's time until about 1824, since which another system has obtained the preference. Many thousands of acres of land had been drained by that method up to that time, and there is no doubt that the country has derived much benefit from the system. I may mention the fact, as an incentive to important discoveries, and as an instance of disinterestedness, that Elkington willingly communicated all his practice to the late Mr John Johnstone, the eminent drainer, at the request of the Board of Agriculture, through whose influence the British Parliament voted him a reward of L.1000.*

(857.) It will much facilitate your conception of this system of draining, if we consider, in the first place, the *source from which the water that mars the cultivated soil is derived.* When water is evaporated by heat from the sea and land, and conveyed in vapour into an elevated part of the atmosphere, and there retained in an invisible form by the agency of electricity, it remains in that state until a change takes place in the electric equilibrium, when the vapour becomes visible in the form of clouds, which, then becoming independent bodies, become at the same time subject to the laws of physical attraction. Being attracted by the mountains, which are the highest features of the terrestrial portion of the globe, they come into contact with them, give out part of their caloric to them, and ultimately dissolving descend upon them in the shape of fog, or rain, or snow. Hence, as you have already seen (328), rain falls much more plentifully upon the mountains than the plains. The rain, as it falls upon the mountains, is absorbed at once by the soil which covers them, and when it cannot contain any more, the surplus water flows away, and forms streams and rivers. The portion of water retained by the mountain soil undergoes a very different fate. It is conveyed by its own gravity chiefly, and partly by their capillary attraction, among the mineral strata of which the mountain mass is composed, and continues to seek its way through them, until reaching a point beyond which it meets with no resistance, it comes forth to the day in the shape of a strong spring or springs, or, diffused over the whole surface of the mineral mass, it spreads over a large extent of ground. These different destinations of the same water are occasioned by a difference in the nature and positions of the geological formations of the mountain mass. For example, if the whole rising ground, from its base to the summit, is spread over with a *saddle-shaped covering of tenacious clay* the water will slide down its face, under the vegetable coating of the surface, as far as the clay descends, which may be to the plain below. This vegetable covering will be permanent grass, if the elevation of the ground is not great, or it will be heath and mosses, if the elevation exceed such a height as that the mean annual temperature of the air around it does not exceed 40° Fahrenheit, or it may be mould capable of supporting cultivated crops. Thus, in fig. 143, *a* is the clay over the hill; if rain fall on *a*, it will descend on the one side to *d* and on the other to *f*, and if

* See Sinclair's Code of Agriculture, *notes*, p. 31.

the temperature of this region is under 40°, *d e f* will form the region of heath and mosses. The water will still pass from *d* to *c*, which is the region of permanent pasture, and it will continue to flow to the plains, to *i* under *c b*, and to *h* under *f g*. The vegetable mould may be traced

Fig. 143.

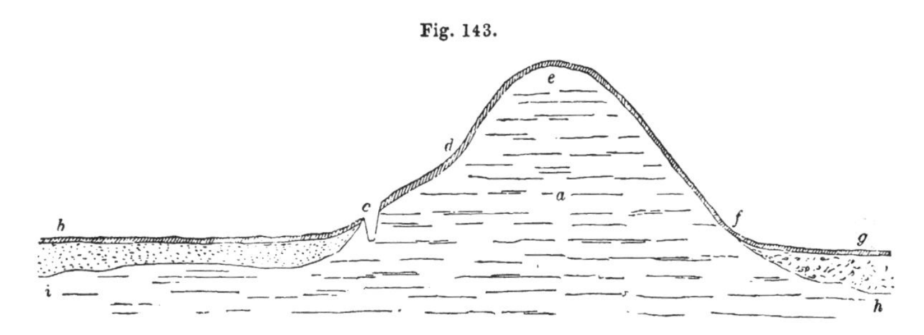

THE ORIGIN OF SPRINGS ON A UNIFORM TENACIOUS SURFACE.

from *b* by *c*, *d*, *e*, and *f*, to *g*. Should the subsoil between the mould *b* and the clay *i* be also retentive, then the water will appear at the surface at *c*, and affect all the space from *c* to *b*; but should the subsoil from *h* to *g* be porous, then the water will continue to flow from *f* upon the clay *h*, and not affect the surface-mould *f g*.

(858.) Should the mountain, however, consist of *concentric layers of different rocks arranged mantle-shaped around it*, then the water will descend between the lines of junction of the rocks; and should the masses or beds of rock be of different extents, and thickness, and consistence, which is probable, then the water will either appear at the surface of the ground as a spring, from the subjacent rock of a close texture, or it will descend yet lower, and be absorbed by the subjacent rock of a porous texture. In this manner, the harder rocks cause the springs to appear at a high elevation, while the porous ones convey the water to a lower level, until it meets with a resisting substance to cause it to come to the day. In any case the farmer cannot do any thing until the water indicates its presence on the surface of the ground, either at a high or low elevation; and then he should take measures accordingly to remove it.

(859.) To illustrate the cases now alluded to, suppose fig. 144 to represent a hill composed of different rocks of different consistence. Suppose the nucleus rock *a* to be of close texture, when the rain falls upon the summit of the hill, which is supposed not to be covered with impervious clay as in the case above, but with vegetable mould, the rain will not be absorbed by *a*, but will pass down by gravity between *a* and *b*, another kind of rock of close texture. When the rain falls in greater quantity than will pass *between* these rocks, it will overflow the upper edge of *b* and pass over its surface down to *c*, but as *c* is a continuation of the nucleus impervious rock *a*, a large spring will flow down the side

Fig. 144.

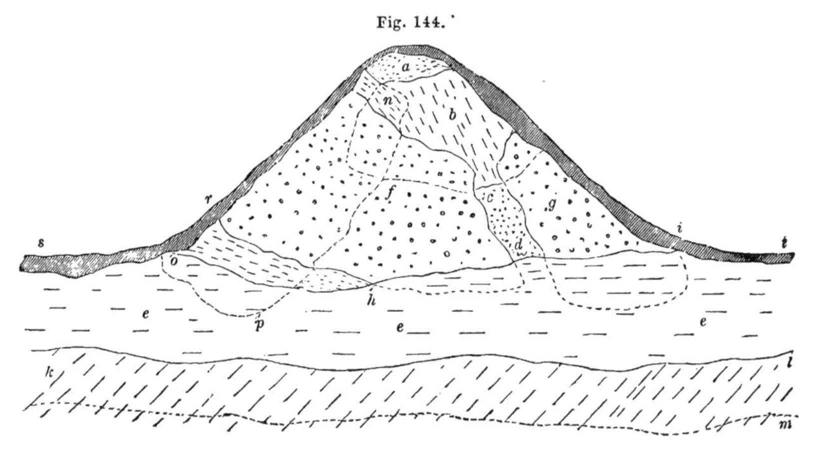

THE ORIGIN OF SPRINGS ON A VARIED SURFACE.

of the hill from *c* and render the ground quite wet to *d*, where meeting another large stratum of impervious rock, it will burst out to day a large spring at *d*, which will be powerful in proportion to the quantity of rain that falls on the mountain. On flowing down *b* part of the water will be intercepted by the rocks *f* and *g*, both of which being porous, will absorb and retain it until surcharged. The surplus water meeting with the impervious rock *e*, will be partly thrust out to day along the black line *d h* on the one hand, and *d i* on the other, when the whole line *h i* will present a long dark line of wet oozing out of the soil, with the spring *d* in the centre, and which darkness and dampness will extend down the inclined ground as far as the upper line *k l* of that porous stratum of rock. Part of the water absorbed by the porous rocks *f* and *g* will be conveyed under the impervious rock *e*, and come out at their lowest extremities, following the curved dotted lines *h d* and *d i*, and continue to flow on until it reaches the lowest extremity of *e* in the dotted line *k l*, where it will be absorbed by the porous rock *m*.

(860.) By such an arrangement of rocky strata on the side of a mountain range, will be exhibited specimens of both wetness and dryness of soils. The summit *a* will be wet, and so will the surface of *b*, but the surfaces of *f* and *g* will be dry. Again. the surface of *e* will also be wet, but less so than that of *b*, because part of the water is conveyed by *f* and *g* under *e* to the dry stratum *k l*, which being probably thicker, and, at all events, of greater extent, will be drier than either *f* or *g*. On another side of the hill another result will take effect. The rain falling on the summit *a* will descend between *a* and *n*, as far as the lowest extremity of *n* along the dotted line *o p*, which being under the impervious rock *e*, the water will continue to flow out of sight until it descends to *k l*, where it will be absorbed by the porous rock *m*, and thus never appear at all either as a spring or a line of dampness. But should the quantity of rain at any time be greater than what will pass between *a* and *n*, it will overflow *n* and be absorbed in its descent by the porous rock *f*, which, after becoming surcharged, will let loose the superfluous water in the line *h r*, upon the continuation of the rock *n*, part of which will come to day along the line *h o* of the impervious rock *e*, and part conveyed down by *o p* to the porous rock *k l*, where it will be absorbed. Thus, on this side of the hill, as long as little rain falls, none but its summit will be wet, and all the rest will be dry, though the surfaces of *f* and *k* will always be drier than those of *n* or *e*; but after heavy rains dampness will shew itself along the line *h r*, and will extend itself even to the line of *k l*, should the rain continue to fall some time

(861.) The line *s* by the summit *a* to *t* is the mould line pervious to moisture, and which is here represented as is frequently exhibited in nature, namely, a thickness of soil on the northern side of the hill as from *a* to *i*, and a thickness of soil on the southern basis, as from *r* to *s*; but a thinness of soil on the southern face, as from *a* to *r*. It is not pretended that this figure is a truly geological portrait of any mountain. Perhaps no such arrangement of strata actually exists in any single hill, but such overlying and disconnected but conterminous strata do occur over extended districts of hilly country which produce springs much in the way just described. Similar courses of water occur in less elevated districts, though it remains more hidden under the deeper alluvial rocks.

(862.) Now let us apply Elkington's method of draining to these two cases of wetness, and which are of ordinary occurrence. The hill in fig. 143 being supposed to be covered saddle-shaped with an impervious stratum of clay, no water can descend *into* it, but will flow *over* it: *a* is the clay stratum; *b* also an impervious stratum, but not so much so as *a*, containing veins of sand and nodules of stones, and forming a very common subsoil of this country. It is clear that the whole extent of ground from *e* to *b* will be wet on the surface, and the wetness will not exhibit itself in bands, but be diffused in a uniform manner over the whole surface; but as *b*, in this case, is not so tenacious as *a*, the side of the hill from *e* to *c* will always be wetter than the flat ground from *c* to *b*, because some of the water will be absorbed and kept out of sight in the looser clay *b*. The only method of intercepting the large body of water in its descent down *d* is to cut the deep drain at *c*, not only sufficiently large to contain all the water that may be supplied from above *c*, but so deep as to catch any oozing of water from *a* towards *b*. What the depth of this drain should be it is not easy to determine without further investigation, and to enable that investigation to be made, a large drain should be cut on the flat ground in the line from *b* to *c*, which will also answer the purpose of leading away the water that will be collected by the transverse drain *c*. Suppose the subsoil from *b* to *i* is 4 feet thick, then this leading drain should be made ½ foot deeper, namely 4½ feet, in order that its sole may be placed in impervious matter; and in this case the drain *c*, of the depth of 6 feet, may suffice to keep the flat ground dry. But if from *b* to *i* is 8 or 10 feet in depth, then it would be advisable to make the leading drain from *b* to *c* at least 6 feet deep, in order to drain a large extent of ground on each side of it, and the drain *c* may still do at its former depth, namely 6 feet. Should the bottom of the leading drain get softer and wetter as the cutting descends, its depth should either be carried down to the solid clay at *i*, or perhaps it would be well to try auger holes in the bottom, with the view of ascertaining whether the subjacent water might not rise to and flow along it. The expedient of boring will be absolutely necessary if the depth from *b* to *i* decreases as the distance from the hill increases, for there would be no other way of letting off the water from the basin of the clay from *i* to *c*. Should the flat ground be of considerable extent, or should the face of the plain undulate considerably from right to left, a leading drain will be required in every hollow; and each of them should be made deeper or shallower according as the subsoil is of a drawing texture or otherwise, bearing in mind that the *sole* of the drain should, if possible, rest upon an impervious substance, otherwise the water will escape through the pervious matter, and do mischief at a lower level. The subsoil between *g* and *h* being supposed to be gravel or other porous substance, it is clear that no drain is required at *f* to protect the soil between *f* and *g*, as the porous subsoil will absorb all the water as it descends from *e* to *f*.

(863.) As to the wet surface of the hill itself *c d e f*, it being composed of impervious clay, must be dried on the principle of surface-draining; that is, if the ground is in permanent pasture for the support of sheep, a number of transverse open sheep drains should be made across the face of the hill, and the water from them conveyed in open ditches into the great drain *c*; or if the ground is under the plough, small covered drains will answer the purpose best; and the contents of these can be emptied into the large drain *c*, and conveyed down the large leading drain to *b*.

Thus, in fig. 145, *a b* is the main drain along the flat ground into which the large drains *c b* and *d b* flow. It may be observed here, that when one large drain enters another, the line of junction should not be at right angles, but with an acute angle in the line of the flow of water, as

Fig. 145.

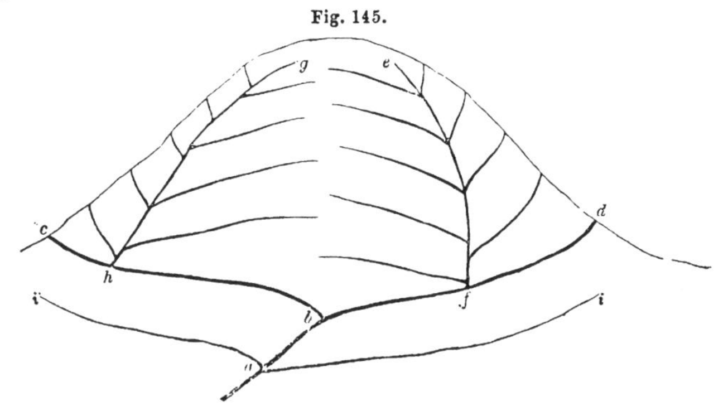

A PLAN OF SHEEP DRAINS ON A HILL OF IMPERVIOUS SUBSOIL.

at *b*. The open surface drains in permanent pasture exhibit the form as represented in this figure, where the leaders *e f* and *g h* are cut with a greater or less slope down the hill according to the steepness of the acclivity, and the feeders across its face nearly in parallel rows, into their respective leaders. In this way, the water is entirely intercepted in its descent down the hill. I may mention that where small drains enter larger, they should not only enter with an inclination, as remarked above, but where they come from opposite sides, as in this case, they should enter at alternate distances, as seen in the case of the three drains above *f*, and not as shewn in the fourth and fifth drains. The large drain *c b d* may either be left open or covered. Should it form the line of separation between arable ground and permanent pasture, it may be left open, and serve to form a fence to the hill-pasture ; but should the entire rising-ground be under the plough, this, as also the main drain *a b*, and all the small drains, should be covered.

(864.) There are *various ways of making small drains in grass.* One plan is to turn a furrow-slice down the hill with the plough, and make the furrow afterwards smooth and regular with the spade. When the grass is smooth and the soil pretty deep, this is an economical mode of making such drains, which have received the appellation of *sheep drains.* But where the grass is rough and strong, and swampy places numerous, the plough is apt to choke with long grass accumulating between the coulter and beam, and makes very rough work, and the horses are apt to overstrain themselves in the swampy ground. The lines of the drains should all be previously marked off with poles before the plough is used.

(865.) A better though more expensive plan, is to form them altogether with the spade. Let *a*, fig. 146, be a cut thrown out by the spade, 9 inches wide at bottom, 16 inches of a slope in the high side, and

Fig. 146.

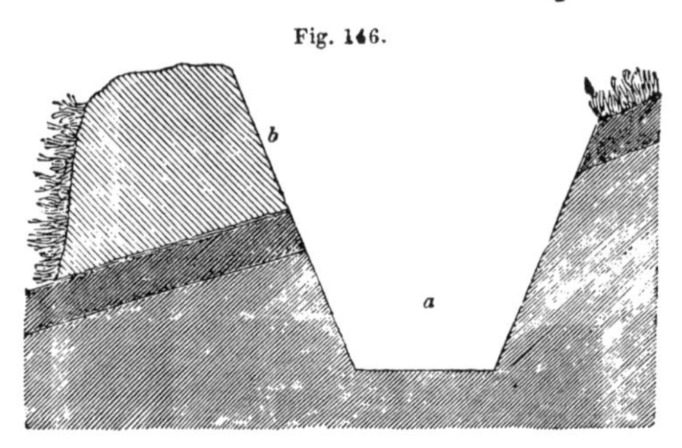

AN OPEN SHEEP-DRAIN IN GRASS.

10 on the low, with a width of 20 inches at top on the slope of the surface of the ground. A large turf *b* is removed by the spade, is laid on its grassy side downwards, on the lowest lip of the cut, and the rest of the earth is placed at its back to hold it up in a firm position, the shovellings being thrown over the top to finish the bank in a neat manner. Such a drain catches all the water that descends in the space between it and the drain above, and leads it away to the sub main drain, such as *e f* or *g h*, which is of similar construction, but of larger dimensions, running up and down the hill, and the lower end of which finds an entrance into the large main drain at the margin of the arable land.

(866.) Another sort of sheep-drain is formed as represented in fig. 147. A cut is made 6 inches wide at bottom, 16 inches deep, and 18 inches wide at top. The upper turf *a* is taken out whole across the cut, as deep as the spade can wield it. Two men will tak out such a turf better than one. It is laid on its grassy face upon the higher side of the drain, and the earth pared away from the other side with the spade, leaving the turf of a trapezoidal shape. While one man is doing this, the other is casting out with a narrow spade the bottom of the cut *b*. The earth and shovelling should be spread abroad over the grass; and the large turf *a* then replaced in its natural position, and tramped down, thereby leaving an open space *b* below it for the water to pass along.

Fig. 147.

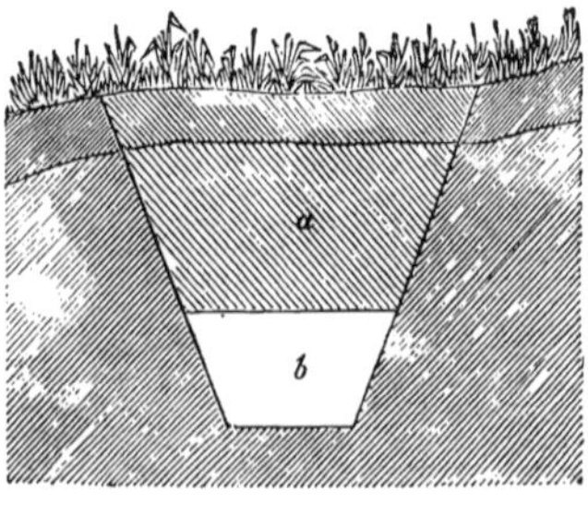

A COVERED SHEEP DRAIN IN GRASS.

This is not so permanent a form of sheep-drain as the last, nor is it at all suitable in pasture where cattle graze, as they would inevitably trample down the turf to the bottom of the drain. It is also a temptation for moles to run along; and when any obstruction is occasioned by them or any other burrowing animal, the part obstructed cannot be seen until the water overflows the lower side of the drain, when the turfs have again to be taken up, and the obstruction removed. It forms, however, a neat drain, and possesses the advantage of retaining the surface whole where sheep alone are grazed. Figs. 146 and 147 are drawn on a scale of $\frac{1}{8}$ inch to 2 inches.

(867.) Having described the various modes of pure *surface*-draining, and traced the origin of springs, immediately connected with which arises the necessity for the sheep-drains just described, I shall now proceed to describe to you the *deep*, or Elkington's, method of draining, which is peculiarly well adapted for draining *isolated hollow spots of ground.* These are usually formed by water standing in winter on an impervious clay subsoil, the water being either entirely derived from rain—in which case the pool becomes dry in summer—but most frequently partly from rain, and partly from springs in the subjacent strata fed from a higher source. Such pools are drained either by boring holes through the impervious clay into a porous stratum below,—should such a stratum exist,—or by a deep drain, having an efflux at a lower level.

(868.) I shall give you an account of the successful draining of such a pool. It was covered with water in winter to the extent of about 2 acres, in the centre of a field of 25 acres; and though no water was visible in summer, its site was always swampy. It obtained the name of the "Duck-mire," wild ducks being in the habit of frequenting it every season. On taking a level from its water, it was found that a drain of 10 feet in depth would be required to carry it away in a $2\frac{1}{2}$-feet-deep drain through the pool. The outlet was on the top of a clay-bank about 150 yards distant from the nearest margin of the pool, rising perpendicularly 40 or 50 feet above the bed of a small river, and was the nearest point for a fall from the pool. The operations were performed in summer, when the pool was comparatively dry. The deep cut of 10 feet was first executed; and to render it ever after secure, a conduit of 9 inches in width by 12 inches in height was built and covered with land stones obtained from the field by trench-ploughing, above which about 2 feet of stones were placed and covered with turf before the earth was returned into the deep cut. The continuation of the main drain was carried right through the centre of the pool, where it could only be formed 30 inches deep, in order to preserve the requisite fall. Another drain, of 3 feet in depth, encircled the area of the pool a little above the water-mark, and was let by each end into the main drain. Both these drains were made 9 inches wide at bottom, to contain a coupled duct of 4 inches in width ; and filled with small round stones, admirably adapted for the purpose, none exceeding the size of a goose's egg, gathered from the surface of the field. The stones were blinded with withered wrack, and the earth returned above them, first with the spade and then with the plough. The pool was at once determined to be drained in this manner, because the high bank of clay above the river,—and which formed the entire subsoil of the field,—forbade any attempt at boring to a porous stratum below.

(869.) But a difficulty occurred in passing the drain through the centre of the pool, which was not foreseen. A complete quicksand was met with, the bottom of which, resting on the clay, was much below that of the deep cut. To have effectually drained the quicksand, the cut should have been made at least 13 feet in depth ; so that about 2 feet deep of quicksand were obliged to be left beneath the drain ; and how to construct a lasting drain upon such a foundation, was a puzzling thing, as the wet sand thrown out by the spade was followed by larger quantities sliding down from each side of the drain, and filling up the emptied space.

(870.) It is here worthy of remark, that I committed a mistake in not ascertaining the existence of the quicksand, and of its depth, before beginning to cast the deep main drain; for I had only thought of making such an outlet as would enable me to make a drain of such a depth through the centre of the pool as would drain it; whereas I ought to have ascertained, in the first place, the nature of the strata under the pool, which would have made me acquainted with the depth of the quicksand; and the drain and outlet should then have been made of the depth to deprive the quicksand entirely of its water. However, as matters were, I was obliged to do the best to form a drain in the quicksand, and this was found to be a rather troublesome operation. Thick tough turfs were provided, to lay upon the sand in the bottom of the drain, and upon these were laid flat stones, to form a foundation on which to build a conduit of stones, having an opening of 6 inches in width and 6 or 7 inches in height. The back of the conduit, when building, was completely packed with turf, to prevent the sand finding its way into it from the sides of the drain; and the packing was continued behind the few small rubble stones that were placed over the cover of the conduit. A thick covering of turf was then laid over the stones, so that the whole stones of the drain were completely encased in turf, before the earth was returned upon them. The filling up was entirely executed with the spade, in case the trampling of the horses should have displaced any of the stones; but these extraordinary precautions were only used as far as the quicksand was found to be annoying. After all the drains were finished, a large quantity of water flowed out of the main drain during the succeeding autumn and winter; but by spring the land was quite dry, the blue unctuous clay forming the bottom of the pool became friable, and on the soil and subsoil being intermixed by deep ploughing, the new and fresh soil, with proper management, ever after bore fine luxuriant crops.

(871.) A 12-acre field of good deep land on the farm of Frenchlaw in Berwickshire was rendered swampy by springs and oozings of water from the surrounding rising ground being retained upon the clay subsoil. A 4-feet drain was formed all round the base of the rising ground immediately above the line of wet, and several drains of 3 feet in depth were run through the flat part of the field. The outlet was obliged to be cut through a part of a field on the adjoining farm to the depth of 13 feet, conduited and covered over. The swampiness of the ground was completely removed, and the crops ever after were excellent.

(872.) Another application of Elkington's system may be successfully made in draining the *springs or oozings of water around gravelly eminences standing isolated in single fields, or across more than one field, upon a bed of clay or other impervious matter.* A circumvallation of drain around the base of the eminence, begun in the porous and carried into the impervious substance, having a depth of perhaps from 5 to 7 feet, and connected with a main drain along the lowest quarter of the field, will most effectually dry all the part of it that was made wet by the springs or oozings.

(873.) *Bogs* and *marshes* have been drained with great effect by Elkington's method. These almost always rest on basin-shaped hollows in clay; and when this is of considerable depth, the only way of draining them is by bringing up a deep cut from the lowest ground and passing it through the dam-like barrier of clay. But it not unfrequently happens, that gravel or sand is found at no great depth below the clay on which bogs rest; in which case, the most ready and economical plan is to bore a hole or holes in the first instance through the clay, with an auger 5 inches in diameter; and, after the water has almost subsided, to finish the work by sinking wells through the clay, and filling them up with small stones to within 2 feet of the top.

(874.) I have never seen an instance of the draining of bog by *boring* or by *wells;* but the late Mr George Stephens, land-drainer, instances two or three cases of bogs being successfully drained in Sweden by means of boreholes and wells in connection with drains; and the late Mr Johnstone adduces many as successful instances in this country.*

(875.) I have seen extensive and successful effects of drying bogs in Ireland, by ordinary drains, especially Carrick Bog, at Castle Rattan, belonging to Mr Featherstonehaugh, in the county of Meath. The plan consists of dividing the bog into divisions of 60 yards in breadth by open ditches of 4 feet in depth and 4 feet wide at top, allowance being made for the sliding in of the sides and subsidence by drying, and which movements have the effect of considerably diminishing the size of the drains; and these ditches are connected by parallel drains at right angles 3 feet 3 inches in depth and 18 inches in width. Fig. 148 is a plan of these drains, where *a* are the large ditches and *b* the small drains.

Fig. 148.

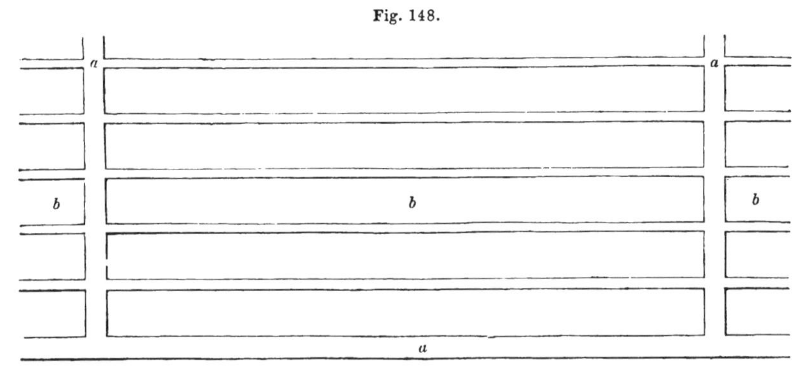

A PLAN OF DRAINS FOR BOGS AS PRACTISED IN IRELAND.

The ditch *a* at the bottom is that which takes away all the water to some large ditch, river, or lake. The fall in the ditches and drains is produced by the natural upheaving of the moss above the level of the circumjacent ground, and, of course, this peculiarity causes all the drainage of the bog to flow towards the land.

(876.) The small drains *b*, fig. 148, are made in this manner. A garden line is stretched at right angles across the division from the large

* See Stephens' Practical Irrigator and Drainer, pp. 169-184, edition of 1834; and Johnstone's Systematic Treatise on Draining, 4to edition of 1834, p. 75; both excellent works on the subject of deep draining.

open drain *a* to *a* 60 yards. The upper rough turf is rutted in a perpendicular direction along the line with a short edging-iron. The line is then shifted 18 inches, the width of the top of the drain, and another rut is made by the edging-iron. While one man is employed at this, another cuts out a thick turf across the drain with the broad-mouthed shovel, fig. 149, and if any inequalities or ruggedness is observed in the wet turf, he makes them smooth and square with a stroke or two with the back of the shovel. The drain is thus left for 2 months to allow the water to run off, the moss to subside, and the turf to dry and harden.

(877.) At the end of that time the long edging-iron, fig. 150, is employed to cut down the sides of the drain in a perpendicular direction 2 feet 3 inches (see fig. 153), and the flat shovel is also again employed to cut the moss into square turfs, which in this case are not thrown out with the shovel, as on account of their wet state they cannot remain on its clear wet face, when used so far below the hand, but are seized by another man with the small graip, fig. 151, and thrown on the surface to

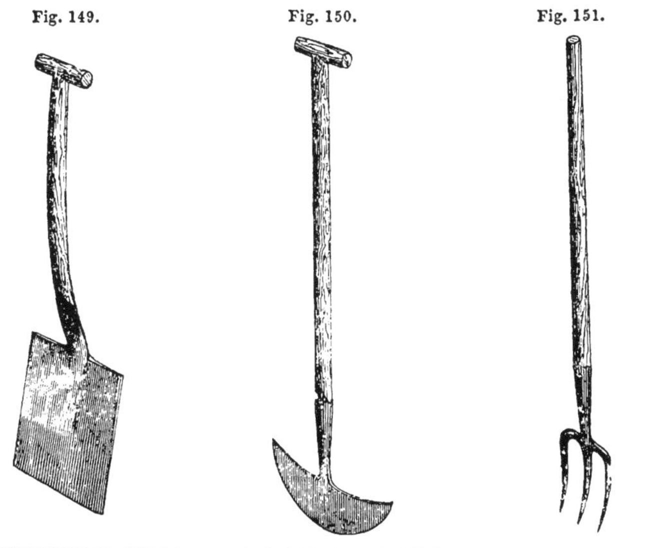

Fig. 149. THE BROAD-MOUTHED SHOVEL. Fig. 150. THE LONG EDGING-IRON. Fig. 151. THE SMALL GRAIP.

dry. The work is again left for 2 months more to allow time for the water to drain off and the turfs to dry and harden.

(878.) In these four months the moss subsides about 1 foot. After the two spits of the shovel, the longest edging-iron is again employed to cut down the last spit, which is done by leaving a shoulder *e e*, 5 inches broad, on each side of the drain, fig. 153. The scoop, fig. 152, is then employed to cut under the last narrow spit, which is removed from its position by the small graip. The scoop pares, dresses, and finishes the

Fig. 152.

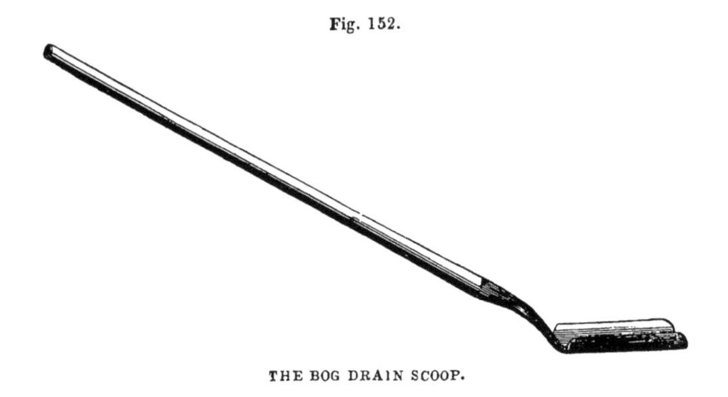

THE BOG DRAIN SCOOP.

narrow bottom of the drain, with a few strokes with its back, making the duct *d* 1 foot deep.

(879.) The filling of the drain is performed at this time, and it is done in this manner. The large turf *b*, fig. 153, which was first taken out, and is now dry, is lifted by the hand and placed, grass side undermost, upon the shoulders *e e* of the drain, and tramped firmly down with the feet. The second large turf *a*, which is not so dry or light as the first, is lifted by the graip and put into the middle of the drain, and the long narrow stripes of turf *c c* separated by the scoop from the bottom, along with other broken pieces, are also placed by the graip along both sides and top of the drain, and all the sods just fill up the subsided drain.

Fig. 153.

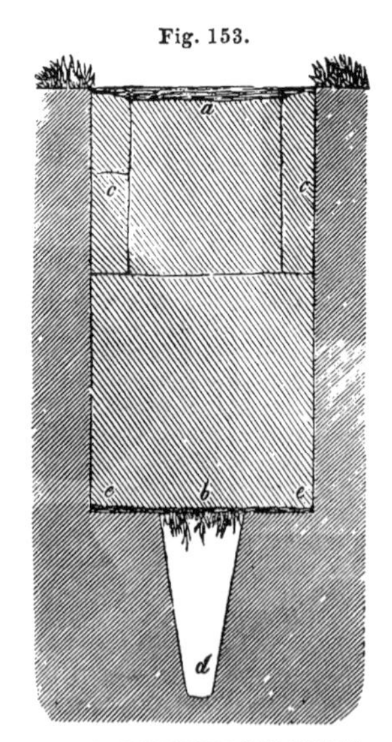

THE SHOULDERED BOG DRAIN.

(880.) Fig. 153 represents the drain thus finished, which is well suited for the drying of bog, and in its construction possesses the advantage of having all the materials for filling it upon the spot. It is a well known property of dried moss that it resists the action of water with impunity, and the mode just described of making drains affords ample time for the drying and hardening of the turfs cast out of the drains; but it is not requisite for the efficiency of the turfs that they be dried, as they answer the same purpose quite well in a wet state; but the time allowed for the subsidence of the moss itself is a great advantage to the drain, such materials being never again disturbed in a subsided bog drain. A bog drain requires no other materials, such as wood or tiles, to fill it, there being no material so appropriate or more durable than the moss itself, the slightest subsidence in the drain destroying the continuity of the soles and tiles, whether of wood or clay, while those made of the latter substance will gravitate in the moss by their own weight. To expedite the subsidence of the moss, the cutting of the drains is most successfully practised in summer, when the drought not only dries the turfs, but gets quit of a large proportion of the water by evaporation. The scale of this figure is $\frac{1}{8}$ to 2 inches, or $\frac{3}{4}$ inch to 1 foot.

(881.) These are all the cases, as I conceive, in which Elkington's method of draining can be applied, and even in them all it will not be attended with certain success, certainly not with equal success. I have frequently made lines of drains across the spouty sloping faces of fields, to the depth of even 6 feet, and never less than 4, without drying more than the breadth which they covered. In these cases I considered the cost of making them just thrown away; whilst in other cases, 4-feet drains have completely removed the spouts, though the subsoil was apparently identically the same in them all. It is possible that the small veins of sand which were intersected by the cutting might, in the unsuccessful cases, dip away from the drains, and the water in them had perhaps ceased to flow in the same direction after their bisection, and in the successful cases the sand veins may have dipped with even a more favourable inclination for discharging their contents into the drains. Whatever difference of distribution there might have been in the component parts of the strata, in these opposite cases, there is little doubt that it was not sufficiently great to be indicated on the surface of the ground; and it is questionable, that even the most minute investigation of apparently similar veins of sand, in similar strata, would acquaint us with their real positions, as it is not impossible that the most trifling difference in the relative positions of such veins may produce very different effects upon the course of the water in the subsoil.

(882.) It is now necessary to describe to you the mode to be adopted in forming drains on Elkington's method. Before determining on the direction in which the lines of drains should run in the field proposed to be drained, it has been recommended to sink pits here and there, of such dimensions as to allow a man to work in them easily, and to a depth which will secure the exposure of the subjacent strata and the greatest flow of water, the depth varying perhaps from 5 to 7 feet A previous examination of the underground is certainly requisite, and pits will certainly acquaint you with the arrangement of the substrata; and had I pitted the bottom of the pool, the drainage of which I have described above

(870), the depth of the quicksand would have been easily ascertained, and the main drain made commensurate with the circumstances of the case. But I agree with the late Mr Wilson of Cumledge, Berwickshire, that the driving of lines of drains from the bottom to the top of the field is the most satisfactory method of obtaining an enlarged view of the disposition of the subjacent strata, and of course of the depth to which the drains should be sunk.* Such lines of drains will not be useless; on the contrary they will form the outlets of the system of drains connected with each of them, and for that purpose they should be made in the lowest parts of the field.

(883.) Having thus ascertained the nature of the underground, the lines of the drains which run *across* from the mains should be marked off. This can be done by drawing a furrow-slice along each line; but a neater plan, and one which will not spend the time of horses at all, is to set them off by means of short stakes driven into the ground, or, if the field is in grass, by small holes made in the ground with three or four notches of the spade, and the turf turned over on its grassy face beside each hole.

(884.) It is very desirable that the stones for filling the drains should be laid down along the lines in the order the drains are to be opened up, not only on account of having them at hand when the filling process is to commence, and of thereby, perhaps, saving the labour of throwing out the earth that may have fallen down from the sides of the drain, when waiting for the stones, and of procuring additional stones for filling up the spaces thus enlarged, but of saving the horses much trouble in backing and forwarding the cart on the ground when it is necessarily much confined at the side of an opened drain. The stones should be laid down on the upper or higher side of the ground, if there be one, that the earth from the drain may be thrown upon the lower side.

(885.) Suppose that it has been determined to make the drains 6 feet deep. For this depth a width at top of 30 inches, and one at bottom of 18 inches, will be quite sufficient for the purpose of drainage, and for room to men to work in easily. This particular, in regard to the dimensions of the contents of a drain should always be kept in view when cutting one; as even a small unnecessary addition either to the depth or width, and especially to both, of a deep drain, makes a considerable difference in the quantity of matter to be thrown out, and of course in the quantity of stones required for again filling up the excavated space. A simple calculation will at once shew you the great difference there is in the contents

* Prize Essays of the Highland and Agricultural Society, vol. vii. p. 243.

of a drain a little wider and narrower than another; and the difference is much greater than you would imagine at first sight. A drain of the above dimensions, namely of 6 feet deep, 2½ feet wide at top, and 1½ foot at bottom, gives an area by a vertical section of 22½ square feet, and in a rood of 6 yards in length, a capacity of 405 cubic feet; whereas a drain of 6 feet deep, 3 feet wide at top, and 2 feet wide at bottom, as recommended in a particular instance by the late Mr Stephens,* would give a vertical section of 36 square feet, and a capacity of 644 cubic feet, creating more than 50 per cent. of additional work And you should bear in mind, that, provided the parts of a drain are substantially executed, its *width*, beyond that which will secure efficacy, cannot render it more efficacious. The rule for the width of a drain is very well determined by the ease with which men are able to work at the bottom; and, indeed, men working by the piece, when their work is measured longitudinally, will always prefer narrow to wide drains.

(886.) The cutting of drains should always be contracted for at so much per rood of 6 yards. The size of drain which I have just recommended (885) may be cut for from 1s. 6d. to 2s. per rood, according to the hardness or other difficulties of removing the subsoil. Where clay is very hard and dry, or very spongy, tough, and wet, or where many boulders interfere, the larger sum is not too much; but where the subsoil can be loosened with ordinary picking, and is mixed with small sand veins and stones, the smaller sum will suffice. In such a contract it should always be understood that the first portion of the earth in the refilling shall be returned into the drain by the contractor, and that he shall provide himself with all the tools necessary for the work.

(887.) The first operation in breaking ground is to stretch the garden line for setting off the width of the top of the drain, 30 inches, the drain being begun at the lowest part of the ground, and each division thus lined off consists of about 4 roods or 24 yards. Three men are the most efficient number for carrying on the most expeditious cutting of drains. Whilst the principal workman is rutting off the second side of the top of the drain with the common spade, the other two begin to dig and shovel out the mould-earth, face to face, throwing it upon the lower and opposite side from the stones. The first spit of the spade most likely removing all the mould, the first man commences the picking of the subsoil with the foot-pick, fig. 37, or if the mould is too deep to be removed by one spit, and requires no picking, the first man digs and shovels out the remainder of it by himself with the spade. The mould is thus all removed from the

* Prize Essays of the Highland and Agricultural Society, vol. vii. p. 222.

lined off break or division of the drain. When the picking commences one man uses the foot-pick, working backwards, another follows him with his back with a spade and digs out the picked earth, while the contractor comes forward with the shovel, fig. 38, with his face to the last man, and takes up all the loose earth and trims the sides of the drain. In this way the first spit of the subsoil is removed. Should the drain prove very wet, and

Fig. 154.

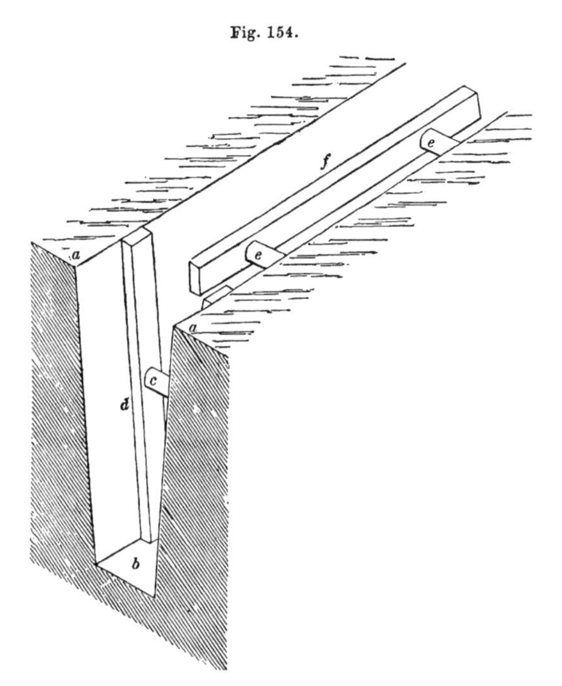

THE POSITIONS OF PLANKS AND WEDGES TO PREVENT THE SIDES OF DRAINS FALLING IN.

danger be apprehended of the sides falling in, the whole division should be taken out to the bottom without stopping, in order to have the stones laid in it as quickly as possible. Should the earth have a tendency to fall in before the bottom is reached, short thick planks should be provided, and placed against the loose parts of both sides of the drain, in a perpendicular or horizontal position, according to the form of the loose earth, and there kept firm by short stakes acting as wedges between the planks on both sides of the drain, as represented in fig. 154, where *a a* are the sides of the drain, *d* planks placed perpendicularly against them, and kept in their places by the short stake or wedge *c*; and where *f* are planks placed horizontally and kept secure by the wedges *e e*.

(888.) But if the earth in the drain be moderately dry and firm, another division of 4 roods may be lined off at top, and the subsoil removed as low as the depth of the former division. Before proceeding, however, to line off a third division, the first division should be cleared out for the builder of the conduit. The object of this plan is to give room to separate the diggers of the earth from the builders of the stones, so as there may be no interference with one another's work, and also to give advantage of the half thrown out earth of the second division as a stage upon which to receive the larger stones, such as the covers of the conduit, to their being easily handed to the builder, as he proceeds in the laying of the conduit in the first division. On throwing out the earth to the bottom of the first break, special care should be taken to clear out the bottom square to the sides, to make its surface even, and to preserve the fall previously determined on.

(889.) When a division of the drain has thus been completely cleared out, you yourself, or the farm-steward, should ascertain that the dimensions and fall have been preserved correct as contracted for, before any of the stones are placed in the bottom. I have seen it recommended that the person appointed to build the conduit should ascertain if these particulars have been attended to; but it is always an invidious task for one class of workmen to check the workmanship of another, and on this account such a duty should always be performed by the farmer himself, or by any other authorized person.

(890.) Instead of measuring the dimensions of the drain with a tape-line or foot-rule, which are both inconvenient for the purpose, a *rod* of the form of fig. 155, will be found most convenient, most certain, and most quickly applied. The rod, divided into feet and inches, is put down to ascertain the depth of the drain, and then turned partially round while resting on its end on the bottom of the drain, until the ends of its arms touch the earth on both sides. If the arms cannot come round square to the sides of the drain, the drain is narrower than intended; and if they cannot touch both sides, it is wider than necessary. When the drain is made narrower than intended, you may take it off the contractor's hands, for the men having been able to work in it with ease to themselves, shews that the width is sufficient; but if the drain is wider than necessary, you should object to it to prevent similar enlargements in other places, for although the contract may have been formed by the longitudinal measurement, and not by the cubical contents, the larger space involves you in greater expense to fill up with stones.

Fig. 155.

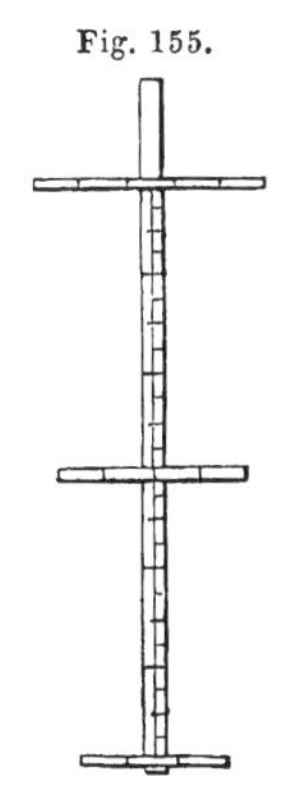

THE DRAIN-GAUGE.

(891.) All deep drains should be furnished with *built conduits*, that the water may have a free passage in all circumstances, and thereby escape being choked up, and save the consequent expense of relifting and relaying its materials. The relifting of a drain that has *blown*, that is, of one in which the water is forced to the surface of the ground, in consequence of a deposition of mud amongst the stones preventing its flow under ground, is a dirty and disagreeable business for work-people, and an expensive one for their employer, as it costs at least 9d., and the filling in again of the earth 1d. more per rood of 6 yards;* besides, additional stones are required to fill the enlarged space occasioned by the unavoidable removal of wet earth along with the stones.

(892.) The *building of the conduit should be contracted for in a separate item from the cutting of the drains.* If both are undertaken by the same party, there is risk of the two sorts of work being so carried on together, to suit the convenience of the contractor and his men, as to deceive even the inspector; whereas, if each sort is inspected and passed before another is allowed to be begun, then both may be executed in a satisfactory manner. The building of the conduit will cost from 1d. to 2d. per rood, according to the adaptation of the stones for the purpose.† Flat handy stones can be built firmly and quickly, whereas round-shaped ones will require dressing with the hammer to bring them into proper shape, and much pinning to give them stability. The stones are furnished to the builder, and a labourer is also usually provided for him, to supply the stones as he requires them. But circumstances may occur in which it will be more convenient for you to contract with the builder to quarry the stones, supply himself with a labourer and build the conduit, and you to undertake only the carriage of the stones. A dry-stone builder of dykes is a better hand at building conduits for drains than a common mason, as he does not depend upon mortar for giving steadiness to his work.

(893.) Should the ground be firm, and the drain made in summer, and the length of any particular drain not very great, the conduit is most uniformly built when begun at the top and finished at the bottom of the line of drain; but in ground liable to fall down in the sides, or in winter, when the weather cannot be depended upon for two days together, or when the drain extends to many roods in length, the safest plan is to build the conduit immediately after the earth is taken out to the bottom.

(894.) A very convenient article in the building of conduits in a deep

* Stephens' Practical Irrigator and Drainer, p. 105.

† Prize Essays of the Highland and Agricultural Society, vol. vii. p. 242.

drain is a plank of 5 inches in breadth, and of from 6 to 9 feet in length, to put down in the middle of the bottom of the drain, to afford a dry and firm footing to the builder, and to answer the purpose, at the same time, of a gauge of the breadth of the conduit, a space of ½ inch on each side of the plank giving a breadth of 6 inches to the conduit. This plank can be easily removed by two short rope-ends, one attached near each end to an iron staple.

(895.) Suppose the plank set down at the mouth of the drain in the middle of the cut, the dyker begins by leaving a conduit at the mouth of 6 inches wide, having 6 inches of breadth of building on each side of it, and 6 inches high, and using the plank as his foot-board. When the building of these dimensions is finished to the length of the plank, this is carried or pushed by the ropes another length up the drain, and so on, length after length, until the whole space of drain, when cleared out to the bottom, is built upon. The stones are handed down from the surface to the dyker by the labourer, who, in this case, may be a female field-worker, until the building is finished. The plank is then removed out of the way, the dyker clears the bottom of the conduit of all loose earth, stones, and other matter, with a hand-draw-hoe 5 inches wide in the face. Immediately after this, he lays the flat covers, which extend at least 3 inches on each side over the conduit, they being from 2 to 3 inches in thickness; and they lie ready for him on the half cast out division of the drain, from which they are handed to him as he works backwards. The open space left between the meetings of the covers, which will not probably have square ends, should be covered with flat stones, and the space from the ends of the covers and flat stones to each side of the drain should be filled up and neatly packed with small stones. In this way the dyker proceeds to finish the conduit in every division of drain. To keep the finished conduit clear of all impediments, the dyker makes a firm wisp of wheat or oat straw large enough to fill the bore of the conduit; and which, while permitting the water to pass through, deprives it of all earthy impurities.

(896.) Before the conduit is entirely finished, the drainers throw out the earth of the adjoining division of the drain to the bottom, and the conduit is then built upon it in the same manner as the one just described. Should the labourer have any spare time from supplying the builder with materials, he throws in stones promiscuously upon the covers, until they reach a height of 2 feet above the bottom of the drain, where they are levelled to a plain surface. They have been recommended to reach the height of 4 feet, and when the drain is filled with rubble stones entirely, this height is desirable, to give the water plenty of room to find its way into it; but with a conduit such as in fig. 156, more than 2 feet seems an unnecessary supply of stones, unless in places where water is more than usually abundant. It has also been recommended to break this upper covering of stones as small as road-metal;* but in deep draining, such as this, there seems no good reason for the adoption of such a practice, while it enhances the cost very considerably. Ordinary land stones or quarry rubbish are quite suitable for the purpose, and should any of the stones be unusually large, they can be broken smaller with a sledge-hammer. This the dyker might be employed in occasionally, as he will break stones much more easily than a labourer, and the work might be included in the contract with him. Should the stones be brought as they are required, the process of filling would be greatly expedited were they emptied at once out of the cart into the drain. This could be done by backing the cart to the edge of the drain, and letting the shafts or movable body of the cart rise so gently as to pour out the stones by degrees. To save the edge of the drain, and break the fall of the stones, a strong broad board should be laid along the side of the drain, with its edge projecting so far as to cause the stones to fall down into the middle of it. A short log of wood placed in front of the board will prevent the wheels of the cart coming farther back than itself. I am aware that this mode of filling drains has been objected to by a competent authority in these matters, the late Mr Stephens, as being a dangerous practice for the safety of the drain, especially as stones carry much earth along with them.† But in the case of deep and conduited drains I am sure no danger can arise from its adoption; because I have pursued the plan myself to a large extent with perfect impunity, and can vouch for its expedition and economy, and also for its safeness. To prevent the stones doing injury to thin covers, they should not be allowed to fall direct upon *them*, but *upon the end of the stones previously thrown in*, from which position numbers will roll down of themselves upon the covers without force, and the remainder can be levelled down with the hand before the next cart-load is emptied. There is a very considerable saving in the expense of filling drains in this way, provided it be done in the cautious manner just described, compared with the usual plan of laying down the stones when the drain is ready to receive them, and then throwing them singly in by the hand. Were it convenient to lay the stones down before the drain was begun to be cut, the plan would be inapplicable. As to the stones

* Prize Essays of the Highland and Agricultural Society, vol. vii. p. 223 and 230.

† Quarterly Journal of Agriculture, vol. iii. p. 286, *note*.

having earth amongst them, as much care can be taken to avoid that when they are each thrown or shovelled into the cart, as when put into the drain.

(897.) The levelled surface of the stones should be covered with some *dry material* before the earth is put over them. The best substance for the purpose is undoubtedly turf, but it is expensive to prepare and carry from a distance; but should the field be in grass when it is drained, the turf over the drain could be laid aside at hand by the drainers, and used for covering the stones. Other materials answer well enough, such as withered wrack, dried leaves, coarse grass, broken moss, tanners' refuse bark or straw; but I much dislike to see good straw wasted for such a purpose, when manure is usually too scanty upon a farm. The object of placing any thing upon the stones is to prevent the loose earth finding its way among them; and although it is not to be supposed that any of the substances recommended will continue long undecomposed, they, however, preserve their consistence until the earth above them becomes so consolidated as to retain its firmness ever afterwards. You will learn, in the course of this article, how stones themselves are prepared to answer the purpose of a covering to those below them.

(898.) After the drain has been sufficiently filled with stones, the *earth* which was taken out of it should be *returned* as quickly as possible, in case rain fall and wash the earth down its sides among the stones. The filling in of the first earth of a deep drain is usually included in the contract made with the drainer, and done with the spade, because no horse can assist in that operation until the earth has been put in to such a height as to enable him to walk upon it nearly on a level with the ground. The men may either put in all the earth with the spade, or they may put in so much as to allow the plough to do the remainder, but in both cases a little is left elevated immediately over the drain, to subside to the usual level of the ground. There will be much less earth left over the filling than you would imagine from the quantity thrown out at first, and the space occupied by the stones; and it soon consolidates in a drain, especially in rainy weather.

(899.) The section of such a drain as I have been describing, is seen in fig. 156, where *a* is the opening of the conduit 6 inches square, built with dry masonry, and covered with a flat stone at least 2 inches thick; and above it is a stratum of loose round stones *b*, 16 or 18 inches in thickness. The covering above the stones is *c*, and the earth returned into the drain is *d*, with the portion *e* raised a few inches above the ordinary level of the ground. The mouths of such conduits, when forming outlets, should be protected against the inroads of vermin by close iron gratings.

(900.) Should water be supposed or known to exist in quantity below the reach of even a 6-feet drain, means should be used to render the drain available for its abstraction, and these means are, sinking wells

Fig. 156.

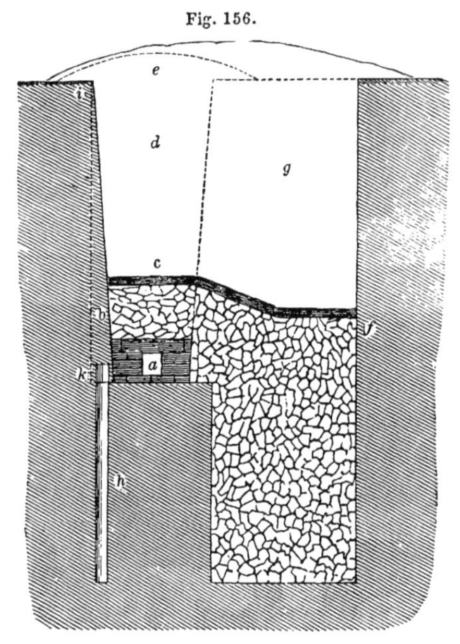

THE DEEP CONDUITED DRAIN, WITH WELL AND AUGER BORE.

and boring holes into the substrata. A *well* is made as represented by a part of fig. 156, where a pit *g* of the requisite depth is cast out on the lower side of the drain *a*, if the ground is not level A circular or square opening, of 3 feet in diameter, or 3 feet in the side, will suffice for a man to work down several feet by the side of the open drain *d*, and when the stratum which supplies the water is reached, the well should be filled with small stones to about the height of those in the drain, as at *f*, and the whole area of the drain and well should be covered with dry substances from *f* to *c*, and the earth is filled in again above all, as at *g*. In making such wells, a small scarcement of solid ground on a level with the bottom of the building of the conduit *a* should be preserved, so that the building may have a firm foundation to stand upon, and run no risk of being shaken, by the operations connected with making the well. I fear this precaution is less attended to in the making of drain wells than it deserves. Such a well should be sunk *wherever* water has been ascertained to be in *quantity* at a lower depth than the drain.

(901.) Or the *auger* may be used instead of the well for the same purpose, by boring through a retentive stratum into a porous, whereby confined water may be brought up into the bottom of the drain, by altitudinal pressure, and escape; or free water may pass down through the bore and be absorbed by the porous stratum below. In the first case, the retreat of the water has to be discovered in making the passage for it to pass away; in the second, it is got rid of by a simple bore. In boring for water at the bottom of a drain, the bore should be made at one side rather than in the middle of the bottom, because any sediment in the water might enter the bore at the latter place and choke it, when the water happened to come up with a small force. In preparation of the bore let a cut *i k*, fig. 156, be made down the side of the drain, and inserting the auger at *k*, let the bore be made down through the solid ground, in the direction of *b h*, as far as necessary, the orifice of the bore being made at a little higher level than the bottom of the drain, and an opening left in the building there, to permit the water from the bore to flow easily into and join the water of the drain.

(902.) As *boring-irons* may be as useful to you for finding water for fields, or for draining a bog, or for ascertaining the depth and contents of a moss, as for ordinary draining, it is proper to give a description of them. The *auger*, *a*, fig. 157, is from 2½ to 3½ inches in diameter, and

Fig. 157.

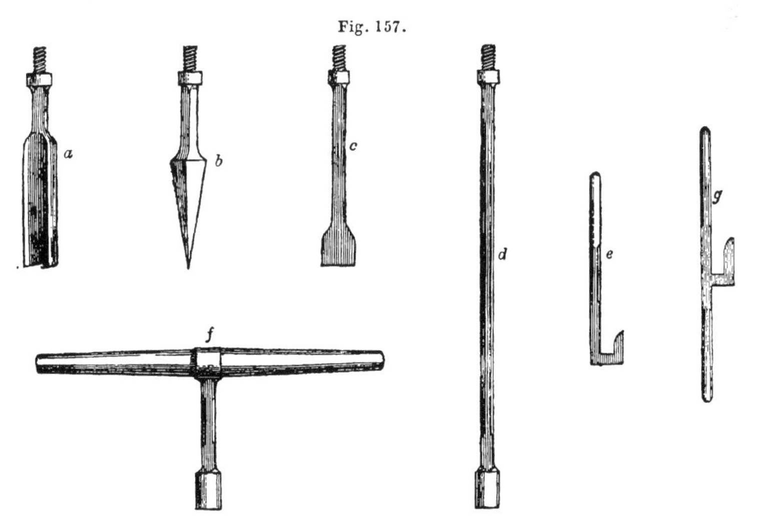

THE INSTRUMENTS FOR BORING THE SUBSTRATA OF DEEP DRAINS.

about 16 inches in length in the shell, the sides of which are brought pretty close together; and it is used for excavating the earth through which it passes, and bringing it up. When more indurated substances than earth are met with, such as hardened gravel or thin soft rock, a *punch b* is used instead, to penetrate into and make an opening for the auger. When rock intervenes, then the chisel or jumper *c* must be used to cut through it; and its face should be of greater breadth than the diameter of the auger used. There are *rods* of iron *d*, each 3 feet long, 1 inch square iron, unless at the joints, where they are 1½ inch and round, with a male screw at one end, and a female at the other, for screwing into either of the instruments, or into one another, to allow them to descend as far as requisite. The short iron *key e* is used for screwing and unscrewing the rods and instruments when required. A *cross-handle* of wood *f*, having a piece of rod attached to it, with a screw to fasten it to the top of the uppermost rod, is used for the purpose of wrenching round the rods and auger, when the latter only is used, or for lifting up and letting fall the rods and jumper or punch, when they are used. The long iron key *g* is used to support the rods and instruments as they are let down and taken up, while the rods are screwed on or off with the short key *e*. Three men are as many as can conveniently work at the operation of boring drains.

(903.) As I have never witnessed the use of the auger in draining, I will give a description of the manner of using it from a competent authority. "Two men," says Mr Johnstone, "stand above, one on each side of the drain, who turn the auger round by means of the wooden handle; and when the auger is full of earth they draw it out, and the man in the bottom of the drain clears out the earth, assists in pulling it out, and directing it into the hole. The workmen should be cautious, in boring, not to go deeper at a time, without drawing, than the exact depth that will fill the shell of the auger, otherwise the earth, through which it is boring, after the shell is full, makes it more difficult to pull out. For this purpose the exact length of the auger should be regularly marked on the rods from the bottom upward. Two flat boards, with a hole cut into the side of one of them, and laid alongside of one another over the drain, in time of boring, are very useful for directing the rods in going down perpendicularly, for keeping them steady in boring, and for the men standing on when performing the operation."*

(904.) The *principles* of Elkington's mode of draining seem to depend on these three alleged facts. 1. That water from springs is the principal cause of the wetness of land, which, if not removed, nothing effectual in draining can be accomplished. 2. That the bearings of springs to one another must be ascertained before it can be determined where the lines of drains should be opened; and by the bearings of springs is

* Johnstone on Elkington's Mode of Draining, p. 111, 8vo edition.

meant that line which would pass through the seats of *true* springs in any given locality. Springs are characterized as true which continue to flow and retain their places at all seasons; and temporary springs consist of bursts of water, occasioned either by heavy rains causing it to appear to the day sooner or at a *higher* level than permanent springs, or by true springs leaking water, and causing it to appear to day at a *lower* level than themselves, and if such springs are weak, their leakage may be mistaken for themselves. It is evident that if drains are formed through these *bursts* of water, no effectual draining takes place, and which can only be accomplished by the drain passing through the line of true springs. 3. That tapping the spring with the auger is a necessary expedient, when the drain cannot be cut deep enough to intercept it.* From these three averments it would appear that the seats of true springs are neither at the top nor in the base of a rising ground, but that temporary springs may be at both; and, of course, the more extensive the height, the more numerous will be the springs, whether true or temporary. In the case of true springs in the side of rising ground, a system of branched drains will be required to remove them; but in the case of their being situated near the base, their leakage will originate bogs or swampy grounds; and hence Elkington's mode of draining is only adapted to these peculiarities. It has been very extensively and, I must add, successfully practised in Scotland, for the removal of both these sources of annoyance to land. The system would have ample scope in Ireland, where bog land still exists to an incredible extent; and in England also, where the regularity of alluvial deposites in many of the western and southern counties, might give employment to the auger to great advantage in removing the largest proportion of the water which is doing injury; but in Scotland the system of tapping is inapplicable in irregular superficial deposites, though it might be tried in the few bogs which rest on regular strata.

(905.) In so far as the soil of Scotland is affected with water, there is no doubt that it is *not now most injured by springs* What injury it suffered in that way has long been removed, by the extensive application of Elkington's mode of draining; and as in the pursuance of that system experience soon indicated that injury was sustained by the land from other water than that issuing from springs, a modification was introduced into the system, which, not being in accordance with its principles, can excite no surprise that it failed in many instances; and the misguided failures had the effect of bringing disrepute upon otherwise an excellent and

* Johnstone on Elkington's Mode of Draining, p. 11. 8vo edition.

efficient mode of draining. The modification I allude to, which brought obloquy upon Elkington's system, was the cutting of *deep* drains in every direction, irrespective of the arrangement of the subjacent strata, and the filling them nearly full of stones of any size and in any order. Much expense was in the first instance incurred by this practice, and when its effects were not commensurate with the outlay, disappointment was the result, and blame was imputed to the system, instead of to the mode of practising it.

(906.) The chief injury now sustained by the soil of Scotland arises from the *stagnation of rain-water* upon an impervious subsoil. Most of the soil of that country consists of loam, of different consistence, resting on clayey subsoil sufficiently tenacious to retain water, the arable part of which is of unequal depth;—where it is shallowest, it is itself injured by the stagnant water immediately below it; and where it is deepest, the plants upon it are injured by chilly exhalations.

(907.) The injury done by stagnant water to arable soil may be estimated by these effects. While hidden water remains, manure, whether putrescent or caustic, imparts no fertility to the soil; the plough, the harrow, and even the roller, cannot pulverize it into fine mould; new grass from it contains little nutriment for live-stock; when old, the finer sorts disappear, and are succeeded by coarse sub-aquatic plants. The stock never receive a hearty meal of grass, hay, or straw, from land in that state; they are always hungry and dissatisfied, and of course in low condition. Trees acquire a hard bark and stiffened branches, and become a prey to parasitic plants. The roads in the neighbourhood are constantly soft, and apt to become rutted; while ditches and furrows are either plashy, or like a wet sponge ready to absorb water. The air always feels damp and chilly, and, from early autumn to late in spring, the hoar-frost meets the face like a damp cloth. In winter the slightest frost encrusts every furrow and plant with ice, not strong enough to bear one's weight, but just weak enough to give way at every step. while snow lies long lurking behind the sun in corners and crevices; and in summer musquitoes, green-flies, midges, gnats, and gadflies, torment the cattle, and the ploughman and his horses, from morning to night; whilst, in autumn, the sheep get scalded heads, and are eaten up by maggots, during the hot blinks of sunshine. These are no exaggerated statements, but such as I have witnessed in every similar situation; and they may be observed in every county in Scotland, in hill, valley, and plain.*

* See a paper by me on this subject in vol. vi. p. 325, of the Quarterly Journal of Agriculture.

(908.) The only plan of draining fitted to remove the wetness which produces this state of things, is the one which allows stagnant water to flow easily away through moderately deep and numerous drains; for deep drains cannot take away stagnant water from impervious subsoil at the distances they are usually made. This constitutes the second mode of surface-draining alluded to in a former paragraph, (853), and which has now generally obtained the appellation of *thorough-draining;* and the treatment of which must now receive your attention.

(909.) What should be the exact *size* of these shallow and numerous drains, is not easily determined. It would be one step towards the settlement of this point were the *minimum size* determined, which I shall endeavour to do. A drain is not a mere ditch for conveying away water; were it only this, its size would be easily determined by calculation, or experiment, of the quantity of water it would have to convey in a given time. But the principal function of a drain is to *draw* water towards it from every direction; and its secondary purpose is to convey it away when collected; though both properties are required to be present, to the drain performing its entire functions. These being its functions, it is obvious that the greater the area its sides can present to the matter out of which it draws water, it should prove the more efficacious, and it is also obvious, that this efficiency is not so much dependent upon the breadth as upon the depth of the drain, so that, other things being equal, the deeper a drain is, it should prove the more efficient. Now, what are the circumstances that necessarily regulate the depth of drains? In the first place, the culture of the ground affects it; for were land never ploughed, but in perpetual pasture, no more earth than would support the pasture grasses would be required over a drain, and this need not perhaps exceed 3 inches in depth. The plough, however, requires more room; for the ordinary depth of a furrow slice is seldom less than 7 inches, and, in cross-furrowing, 8 inches are reached, and 2 inches more than that, or 10 inches in all, may suffice for ordinary ploughing; but in some instances, land is ploughed with 4 horses instead of 2, in which case the furrow will reach 12 inches in depth, so that 14 inches of depth will be required to place the materials of the drain beyond the danger of an extraordinary furrow. But further still, subsoil and trench ploughing are sometimes practised, and these penetrate to 16 inches below the surface, so that 18 inches of earth at least, you thus see, will require to be left on the top of a drain, to place its materials beyond the dangers arising from ploughing. This depth having been thus determined by reference to practice, it should not be regarded as a source from which a supply of moisture is afforded to the drain by its drawing-power, the water only passing through it by absorption; for it is certain that ploughed land will absorb moisture, whether there be any drain below it or not. The *drawing* portion of the drain must, therefore, lie entirely below 18 inches from the surface. Now it will be requisite to make the drain below this as deep as will afford a sufficient area for drawing-powers of the lowest degree amongst subsoils. And what data do we possess to determine this critical point? In the first place, it is evident that a subsoil of porous materials will exhaust all its water in a shorter time than one of an opposite nature. Judging from observation, I should say, that 1 inch thick of porous materials will discharge as much water in a given time, as 6 inches of a tilly, or any number of inches of a truly tenacious subsoil. What conclusions, then, ought we to draw from these data? Certainly these, that no depth beyond the upper 18 inches, farther than what is required for the materials of the drain, will draw water from a truly tenacious subsoil, and that it is therefore unnecessary to go any deeper in such a subsoil; that it is also unnecessary to go any deeper in a subsoil of porous materials, because a small depth in it will draw freely; and that it is only requisite to go deeper in the intermediate kinds of subsoil. Still you have to inquire what should be the specific depths in each of these cases? In the case of really tenacious subsoil, the size of the duct for the water depends on the quantity to pass through it, but, giving the largest allowance of 6 inches with a sole beneath and covering above, 1 foot seems ample depth for these materials to occupy, so that a drain of 2½ feet seems sufficient for the circumstances attending such a subsoil, that is, its minimum depth, which, in such a case, may also be held to be a maximum. In the case of a porous subsoil, it is absolutely necessary for the preservation of its loose materials in their proper position, to have a lining of artificial materials as far as these extend; and as such a lining can hardly be constructed of sufficient strength of less depth than 1 foot, it follows that 2½ feet is the minimum depth also in such a subsoil; but there is this difference betwixt this subsoil and the tenacious one, that the porous may be made as deep as you please, provided you apply sufficient materials for the support of the loose materials. With regard to tilly subsoils, since 1 foot is requisite for the safety of the filling materials, it does not seem an overstretch of liberality to give 6 inches more for extension of the drawing surface, so that the minimum depth in this case seems to be 3 feet, and as much more as the peculiar state of the subsoil in regard to tenacity and porosity will warrant you to go. There is another way of arriving at the same conclusions, and it is this.

(910.) It must be admitted by all drainers, that the part of the drain which is intended to draw water under the earth should be occupied with such loose materials as will easily permit the water to pass through them. It is therefore consonant with reason to give a large area to the sides of a drain in a subsoil that draws water rather slowly, and by consequence a smaller area to one in materials that draw freely, whilst a drain in pure clay will act chiefly as a channel to convey away the water that is permitted to percolate into it through the superincumbent materials. Keeping these important distinctions in subsoils in view, you shall soon learn what use may be made of them in the construction of efficient drains. I guard myself by saying *efficient* drains; for drains can be ill made although planned on the most correct principles; and to guard myself against further misconception, you should bear in mind, that the depths which I have just specified are the *minimum* depths which are considered suitable for the respective circumstances of the drains.

(911.) Viewing drains as mere *channels for the conveyance of water*, it is obvious, that the quicker they promote its emission without injuring themselves or the land, they act the more characteristically; and it is also evident, that an open duct will give a freer passage to water than a mass of loose stones, however large or small they may be used. These obvious points being conceded, it follows as a corollary, that a drain will act the better of being provided with a duct, along with porous material. Viewing drains as a drawer or *gravitator* of water, it is also clear that the more porous the materials, and the greater the quantity used, they will allow the water an easier passage through them. So, it is also requisite on this account to have a duct for the water to pass quickly away. I wish you to pay particular attention to this mode of reasoning in support of the use of ducts, as I conceive that very erroneous opinions prevail amongst farmers regarding their utility; but I believe such opinions are prompted more on account of the cost incurred by the use of ducts, than from any valid objection that can be urged against their efficacy.

(912.) There are various substances which may be employed as ducts, 1*st*, dry stones, built as you have seen at *a*, in fig. 156; 2*d*, a coupling of flat stones set up against each other as a triangle, or in a more rude way two round stones, set one on each side of the drain, with a flat one, or a large round one, to cover them; 3*d*, tiles made for the purpose. One or all of these forms of ducts answer the purpose well, and should be selected according to the facility of obtaining the materials of which they are composed.

(913.) I must now direct your serious attention to another consideration in the construction of drains. It is a well known fact, that over whatever kind of substance water flows, it has the power of abrading it; for besides earthy matter, it will in time wear down by friction the hardest rock. This it is enabled to do, not only by its own physical properties, but by the assistance afforded it by the foreign matters which it almost always holds both in solution and suspension, so that both physically and chemically it has the power to produce destructive effects. It seems, however, to be a very prevalent opinion amongst farmers, that hard clay can for any length of time withstand the action of water in a drain. They judge of the hardness of the clay from the state it is in when laid bare to the sight on the drain being opened, imagining that it will remain in the same state, but seeming to forget that water can both soften and scrub against substances. Were clay, indeed, always to retain the hardness it at first exhibits, it would require no protection from the abrading action of water, but when it is known that it cannot possibly remain so, the safest practice is to afford it protection by a covering which may be fashioned to suit the purpose, such as a flat stone or tile, both of which obtain the name of *drain-soles*. If water can affect even the hardest clay, it will, of course, have a much greater effect upon softer earth. The effects usually produced by water on clay subsoils are, that the lower stratum of stones and the tiles become embedded in it to a considerable depth, as has been found to be the case when drains that have *blown* have been re-opened, and as in the first sets of tile-drains made in Ayrshire. In somewhat softer subsoils, the sandy particles are carried along with the water, and deposited in heaps in the curves and joinings of drains; and where the subsoil happens to be more sandy than clayey, the foundation which supports the building or tile gives way, and the matter thus displaced forms obstructions at parts which render the drain above them almost useless. Water also carries sand down the sides of the drain, and, where there is no duct, deposites it among the lowest stratum of stones. You thus see that various risks of derangement occur in a drain, where there are no soles to protect its bottom. On this account, I am a strenuous advocate for drain-soles in all cases; and even where they may really prove of little use, I would rather use too many than too few precautions in draining, because, even in the most favourable circumstances, we cannot tell what change may take place beyond our view of the interior of a drain, which we are never again permitted, and which we have no desire, to see.

(914.) Porous materials, which are the next things he requires for filling drains, are few at the command of the farmer *on his farm*, consisting only, 1*st*, Of small stones gathered from the surface of the land by the hand: 2*d* Small stones so prepared in a quarry by the use of the hammer; and, 3*d*, Gravel, obtained either from the bed of a river, the sea-beach, or a gravelly knoll.

(915.) Before beginning to break ground for thorough draining, it should be considered what quantity of water the drains will have to convey, and as the water in the soil is entirely derived from the rain that falls and is absorbed by the soil, its quantity depends upon the climate of the locality in which the drains are desired to be made. Such an investigation is unnecessary in commencing Elkington's mode, as the springs shew at once the quantity of water to be conveyed away. In pursuance of the investigation, it is well known that more rain falls on the W than the E. coast of this country in the ratio of 5 : 3; so that, under the same circumstances of soil, nearly double the number or capacity of drains will be required to keep the soil in the same state of dryness in the western as in the eastern coast. With a view to ascertain the quantity, it has been, in the first instance, "ascertained that the water which flows from a drain is considerably less at any one time than what formerly ran on the surface;" and this is an expected result, for evaporation and vegetation together must dissipate much of the water that falls on the ground before it sinks into the soil.

(916.) In order, however, to obtain accurate data on this subject, Mr James Carmichael, Raploch Farm, Stirlingshire, one of the midland counties, and therefore experiencing about the average fall of rain in Scotland, ascertained that, in a "length of 200 yards, and the distance from drain to drain 18 feet, the *square feet of surface* receiving rain-water for each drain amounts to 10,800; this, at 2 inches of rain in 24 hours, will give 1800 cubic feet of rain water, and taking the sectional area of the smallest tile of 2½ by 3 inches at 7.5 inches, and the water moving in this aperture at the rate of 1 mile per hour, the number of cubic feet discharged by the drain in 24 hours will be 6600, or nearly four times as much as is necessary to carry off so great a fall of rain as 2 inches in 24 hours;" and this besides what would be carried off by evaporation and absorbed by vegetation. Mr Stirling of Glenbervie, also in Stirlingshire, has given similar testimony of his experience in regard to the capability of drains to let off water. "I have only three sets of drains," he says, "in which I know the exact fall in the mains near the mouths and the area drained. The land is mostly stiff clay, having in some places a fall of 1 in 6, and for 50 yards from the mouths of the mains only 1 in 140; is drained at 15 feet; the main-tiles are 2¾ by 3½ inches, and the rain which falls on 5 superficial roods is discharged at each mouth. I find the tiles nearly ⅔ full after very heavy rain; therefore that size of tile would, with the same declivity, pass the rain which falls on nearly 2 acres; and if the fall in the side drains were less, the water would never stand so high in the mains."*

(917.) It should be borne in mind, that these calculations are founded on data obtained from strong clay soil, from which, it may reasonably be supposed, much of the rain that fell had run off, and, consequently, that by a porous soil much more rain will be absorbed; but although this is doubtless the case, it is obvious that a small orifice will be quite sufficient to carry off much more water than can possibly fall from the heavens in these latitudes in any given time; and that in ordinary rain the drains will be little more than wetted. Still the *drainage should be made to carry off the greatest quantity that falls, although it should occur only once in a lifetime.*

(918.) Having thus calculated the probably greatest quantity of rain that may fall in the locality of your farm, the next step is to *drain each field in succession.* It may seem too indiscriminate an instruction to recommend the draining of every field; for it is possible that some of the fields in your farm may be so dry as not to require entire drainage, but it is scarcely possible but that every field will require draining to a certain degree in some part of it. Be that as it may, in pursuing a system of drainage every field should be thoroughly examined in regard to its state of wetness throughout the year, for that land is in a bad state which is soaking in winter, though it should be burnt up in summer; but the truth is, burning land requires draining as well as soaked land, because drains will supply moisture to burning land in summer, while it will render soaked land dry in winter. Should your farm be pretty level, it matters not at what side you commence operations; but should it have a decided inclination one way, the lowest portion should first be drained, and if it inclines in more than one direction, then each plane of inclination should have a system of drains for itself. It deserves consideration, however, in choosing the fields for draining, that as drains are more conveniently made at one member of the rotation of crops than another, it may happen that the field ready in this respect for drainage is not the one situate at the lowest part of the farm, in which case care must be taken to give the water from the drained field such an outlet as will not make the ground below it wetter, and this may be effected either by clearing a ditch along the side of the lower field, or by forming a new ditch, or by leading the water to a ditch, drain, or rivulet at some distance.

(919.) The field having thus been fixed upon, the first consideration is

* Prize Essays of the Highland and Agricultural Society, vol. xii. p. 94 and 100.

the position of those drains that receive the water from the drains that are immediately supplied from the soil; and these are called *main-drains*. In every case they should be provided with a duct, and the ducts may be formed either of stone or of tile,—of stone when that material is abundant on the farm, or can be obtained at a short distance,—of tile where stone cannot be easily procured; but if tiles cannot be found at hand, they should be procured from a distance rather than not be obtained at all where stones are scarce.

(920.) *Ducts of stone* may be formed in various ways, the strongest of which are built with masonry and covered with strong flat stones, as in fig. 156.

(921.) Two flat stones placed against each other at the bottom of the drain with another covering both, as at *a*, fig. 158, form an equilateral duct of 6 inches in the side, resting on its apex. It should be held down in its position by small stones *b* gathered from the land, or broken for the purpose, to a height of 18 inches, then covered with turf or other dry substance *c*, and the earth *d* returned above them. Where stones are found in sufficient quantity for such a drain, it is highly probable that the subsoil will consist of clay, intermixed with small stones and veins of sand, which, requiring a large area of drawing surface, will fix the depth of the drain at 3 feet. In making this form of duct the drain will require to be 18 inches wide at top to allow the drainer room to work while standing on the narrow triangular space at the bottom. Placing the apex of the triangle undermost, gives the water power to sweep away any sediment along the narrow bottom; but it possesses the disadvantage of permitting the water to descend by its own gravity

Fig. 158.

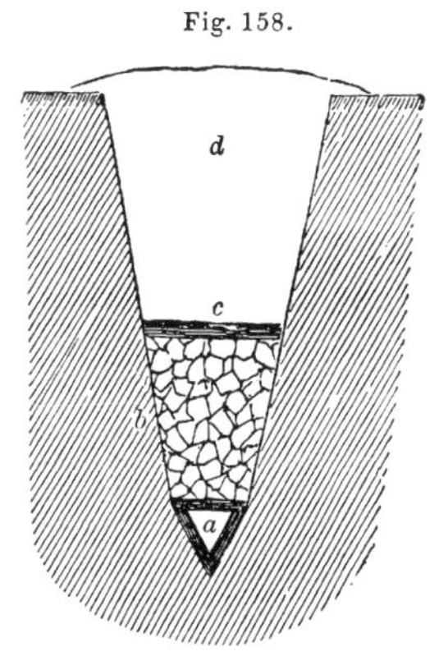

THE TRIANGULAR STONE DUCT.

Fig. 159.

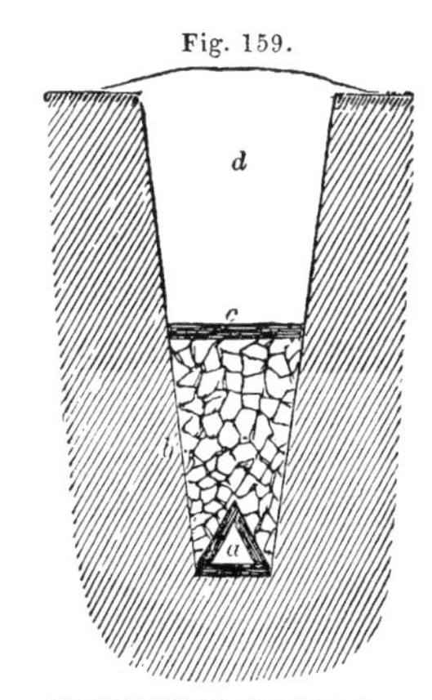

THE COUPLED STONE DUCT.

between the joining of the stones to the subsoil which runs the risk of being softened into a pulp, or of its sandy portion being carried away, and it is possible for a stone to get jammed in the narrow gutter and form a damming.

(922.) Another form of duct, which I prefer to this, and which is also constructed of stone, may be seen beside it in fig. 159, where *a* is the duct consisting of a sole lying on the ground supporting 2 stones meeting at the top, forming an equilateral triangle of 6 inches a side. This form encourages a deposition of sediment to a greater degree than the former, but it prevents, to any dangerous extent, the descent of the water under the sole. Having a flat bottom, the drain can easily be cast out with a width at top of only 15 inches to a depth of 3 feet. The slanting stones of the duct are held in their position by selected stones being placed on each side, which act as wedges between them and the earth, and the whole structure is retained in its place by 18 inches of small stones above them *b*, covered with turf *c*, and the earth *d* returned above them.

(923.) A more perfect duct than either of these is made by a tile and sole. In all main drains, formed of whatever materials, capable of conveying a considerable body of water, a sole is absolutely requisite to protect the ground from being washed away by the water, and a more effectual protection cannot be given to it than by tile and sole. A *main-tile*, which the tiles in main drains are called, of 4 inches wide and 5 inches high, will contain a large body of water, but should 1 such tile be considered insufficient for the purpose, 2 may be placed side by side, as represented by *a* and *b* in fig. 160. Should a still larger space be required, 1 or 2 soles may be placed above these tiles, and other tiles set on them,

Fig. 160.

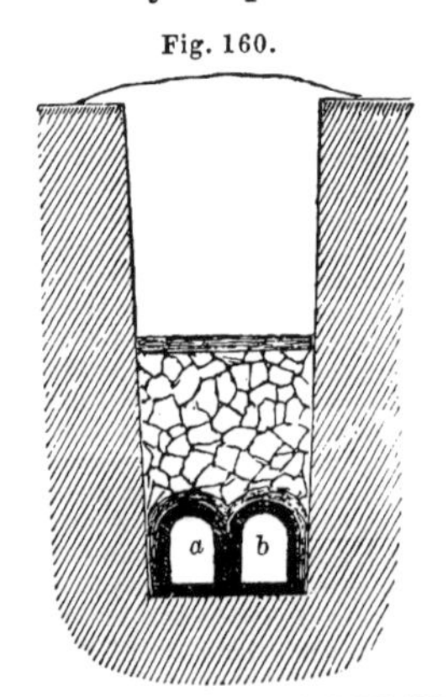

THE DOUBLE TILED MAIN DRAIN.

Fig. 161.

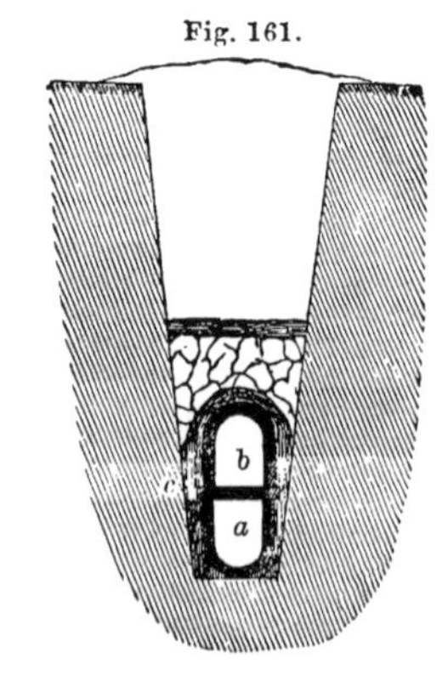

THE INVERTED DOUBLE TILED MAIN DRAIN.

as *a* and *b* are. Or should a still deeper and heavier body of water be required to pass through a main drain, 1 or 2 tiles can be inverted on the ground on their circular top, as *a*, fig. 161, bearing each a sole *c* upon its open side, and this again surmounted by another tile *b* in its proper position. In such an arrangement, there is some difficulty in making the undermost tile *a* steady on its top ; for which purpose, the earth is taken out of a rounded form, and the tile carefully laid and wedged round with stones or earth ; but there is greater difficulty in making the uppermost tile *b* stand in that position without a sole, as is recommended by some writers on draining, because the least displacement of either tile will cause the upper one to slip off the edge of the under, and fall into it. In the narrowest of these cases of main drains with tiles, the drains can be easily cut at 15 inches wide at top to the depth of 3 feet. Small stones should be put above the tiles, if at all procurable, to the height of 18 inches above the bottom ; if not procurable, gravel will answer the same purpose ; and if both are beyond reach, they should be enveloped with thin tough turf, as shewn afterwards.

(924.) Having thus determined on the construction of main drains, according to circumstances in which the water is to be conveyed away, the next thing is to *fix the place they should occupy in the field.* As they are intended to carry away accumulations of water beyond what they can themselve draw, they should *occupy the lowest parts of a field,* whether along the bottom of a declivity, the end, or the middle of a field. If the field is so flat as to have very little fall, the water may be drawn towards the main drains by making them deeper than the other drains, and as deep as the fall of the outlet will allow. If the field have a uniform declivity one way, one main drain at the bottom will answer every purpose ; but should it have an undulating surface, every hollow of any extent, and every deep hollow of however limited extent, should be furnished with a main drain. No main drain should be put nearer than 5 yards to any tree or hedge, that may possibly push its roots towards it ; but although the ditch of a hedge, whose roots lie in the opposite direction, merely receive the surface water from the field at the lowest end, it should not be converted into a main drain, that should be cut out of the solid ground, and not be nearer than 3 yards to the ditch lip ; and the old ditch should be occupied by a small drain, and filled up with earth from the head-ridge.

(925) As main-drains thus occupy the lowest parts of fields, the *fall* in them cannot be so great as in other parts of the field, though it should be kept quite sufficient for drainage. In the case of a level field the fall may entirely depend on cutting them deeper at the lowest end than at other places ; but when the fall is small, the duct should be larger than when it is considerable ; because the same body of water will require a longer time to flow away. Should the fall vary in the course of the drain, the

least rapid parts should be provided with the largest sized tiles; and in any case I would recommend an increase of fall on the last few yards towards the outlet, to expedite the egress of the water, and promote an accelerated speed along the whole length of the drain; but where the fall is rapid enough throughout, there is the less necessity for an increase of acceleration at the termination. It is surprising what a small descent is required for the flow of water in a well constructed duct. "People frequently complain," says Mr Smith, "that they cannot find a sufficient fall or *level*, as they sometimes term it, to carry off the water from their drains. There are few situations where a sufficient fall cannot be found if due pains are exercised. It has been found in practice that a water-course 30 feet wide and 6 feet deep, giving a transverse sectional area of 180 square feet, will discharge 300 cubic yards of water per minute, and will flow at the rate of 1 mile per hour with a fall of no more than 6 *inches per mile*."* On the principle of the acceleration of water from drains, main drains, where practicable, should be 6 inches deeper than those which fall into them, and the greater depth has the additional advantage of keeping the drains clear of sand, mud, or other substances which might lodge, and not only impede but dam back the water in the drains. Should it so happen, from the nature of the ground, that the fall in the main drains is too rapid for the safety of the materials which construct them, it is easy to cut such a length of the proper fall as the extent of the ground will admit, cutting length after length, and joining every two lengths by an inclined plane. The inclined planes could be furnished with ducts like the rest of the drain, or what is better, in order to break the force of the water, like steps of stairs, of brick or stone masonry, built dry. Fig. 162 will illustrate this method at once, where *a b* represents the line of the lowest fall that can be obtained for a main drain in a field, but which, you will observe, is very considerable, and much more so than a main drain should have which has to convey, at any time, a considerable quantity of water. To lessen the fall, let the drain be cut in the form represented by the devious line *c h*, which consists of, first, a level part at the highest end *c d*; then of an inclined plane, *d e*; again of a level part, *e f*; again of an inclined plane, *f g*; and lastly, of a less level part *g h*, to allow the water to flow rapidly away at the outlet, and this part may be parallel with the inclination of the ground.

(926.) The inclined parts may be filled with materials in different

* Smith's Remarks on Thorough-Draining, p. 6, *note*.

ways. One way is with tiles, as seen from *k* to *l*, where it is obvious, that, as drain-tiles are formed square at the ends, those in the inclined plane *k l* cannot conjoin with those on the level above and below; and must, therefore, be broken so as to fit the others at *k* and *l*. In constructing tiles in this way, it is absolutely necessary that the inclined plane be protected with soles, firmly secured from sliding down, at the lowest end at *l*; by having there a strong stone abutting against the

Fig. 162.

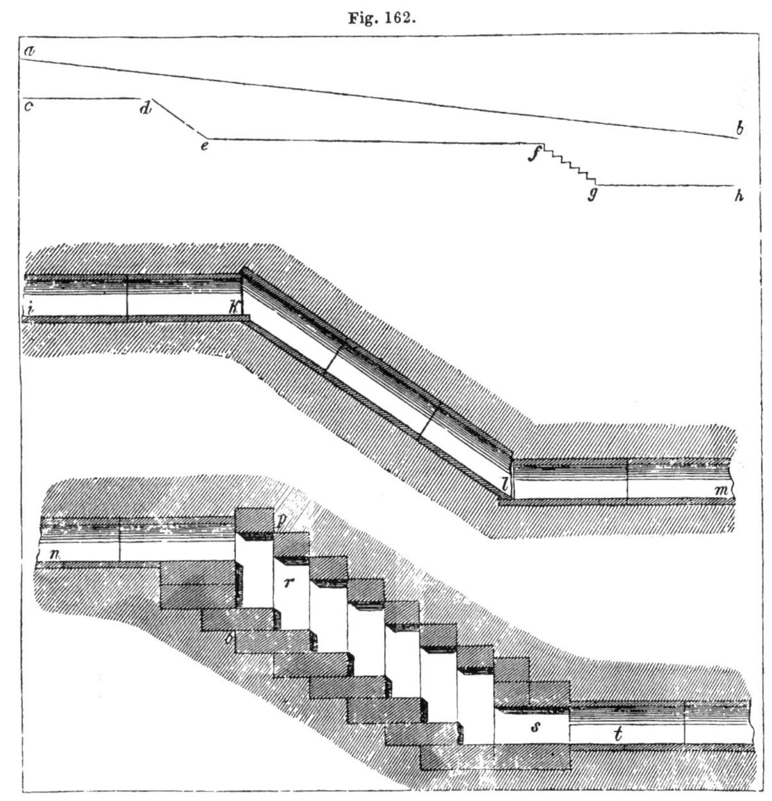

THE DIFFERENT FORMS OF CONDUITS IN THE INCLINED PLANES OF DRAINS.

lowermost sole; or a better plan would be to line the inclined plane with troughs of hewn stone, which will last for ever.

(927.) Instead of tiles, or hewn troughs, stones may form a conduit upon the inclined plane; and ducts of this material, in such a situation, and built dry with selected stones, would certainly be preferable to tiles, even although they could be obtained of the peculiar form required.

(928.) Or the inclined plane could be conduited with brick, as represented from *r* to *s*. The bricks could be built dry as well as stones.

and could form either a smooth inclined sole like tile-soles, or a series of steps, as represented in the figure, where they are set two a-side lengthways on bed to form the bottom, as at *o*; set on end upon these for the sides of the conduit, as at *r*; and set lengthways across the conduit upon the upright ones, for the cover, as at *p*. Tiles on the level above connect themselves easily with the bricks, as from *n*; as also on the level below, as at *t*. Should a considerable run of water be expected at times, the step form is preferable to the smooth, in order to break the fall and impede the velocity of the water, especially towards the lower extremity of the drain, where it may acquire too much momentum without a preventive-check of this kind. Although much water is expected to flow through the drain, it would not be prudent to build the steps with lime-mortar, as it is too easily removed, and would not prevent the water finding its way to the foundation; but, in every case, it is proper to build the duct on the inclined planes, with selected materials skilfully put together.

Fig. 163.

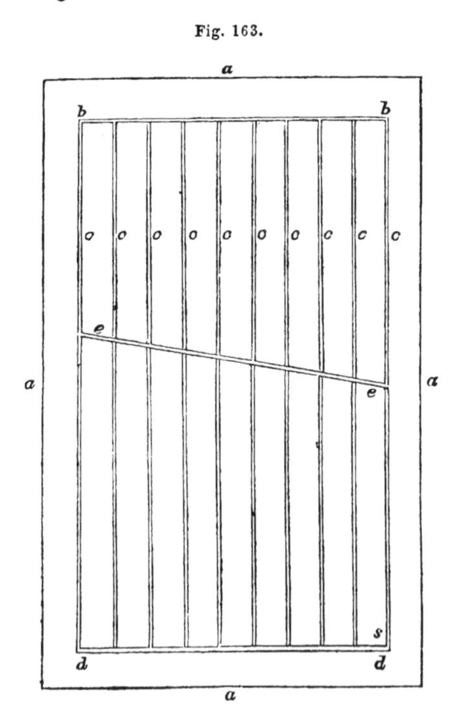

PARALLEL DRAINS IN THE SAME PLANE OF INCLINATION OF THE GROUND.

(929.) After having fixed the position of the main drains, and determined their levels and depths as here described, the next thing is the laying off of the *small drains*, which are so placed, or should be so constructed, as to have an easy descent towards the main drains into which they individually discharge their waters. They are usually cut in parallel lines down the declination of the ground ; not that all the drains of the same field should be parallel to one another, but only those in the same plane, whatever number of different planes the field may consist of. In a field of one plane, there can be no difficulty in setting off the small drains, as they should all be parallel and all terminate in the same main drain, whether the field is nearly level or has a descent. Thus, in fig. 163, *a* are the fences of the field ; *d d* is the main drain whether the field is a level or inclined towards *d* ; and *s* is its outlet. In this case, all the drains *c* run parallel to one another, from the one end *b b*, which may be the upper, to the other end *d d*, which may be the lower end ; and which convey all the water by the outlet *s*.

(930.) But when the field has an undulating surface, though the same principle of parallelism is maintained, a different arrangement is followed in regard to it. I have already intimated in a former paragraph (924), that where an undulating surface occurs in a field, a main drain is carried up the hollowest part of it, and the small drains are brought in parallels down the inclination to it. This very favourable arrangement for the speedy riddance of water after it has reached the drain, is not frequently enough attended to. Thus, the common practice is to run the small drains *b c d e b*, in fig. 164, parallel to one another, throughout the whole field, al-

Fig. 164.

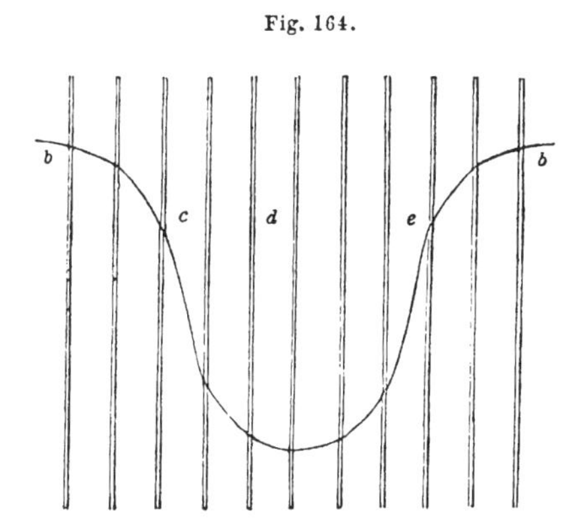

DRAINS IMPROPERLY MADE PARALLEL IRRESPECTIVE OF THE SLOPE OF THE GROUND.

though its undulating surface, as supposed to be represented by the curved line *b c e b*, would cause the so arranged parallelism of the drains at *c* and *e* to run along the sides of the rising ground, where, if any vein of sand occur, it may escape being cut by the drain running parallel along its line either above or below it, instead of being divided across its dip; and even were the sand-vein severed along its length, it would be apt to slip down from the higher side, and render the drain along it inoperative

(931.) Such drains should be cut, as in fig. 165, up and down the inclined surface *b b*, towards the main drain, which would occupy the line

Fig. 165.

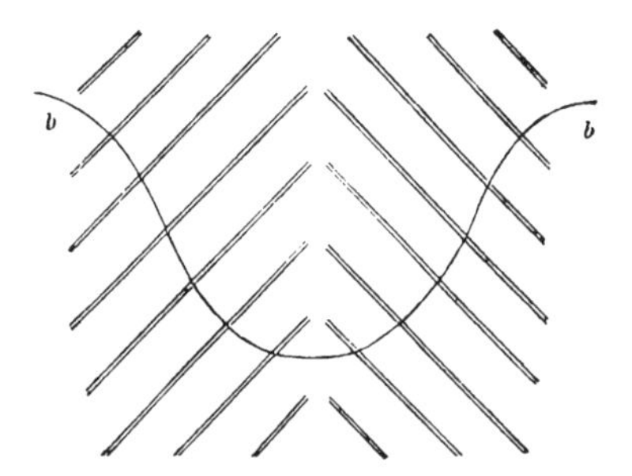

PARALLEL DRAINS IN ACCORDANCE WITH THE SLOPE OF THE GROUND.

along the points of junction of the drains *b b*. This specific plan is just as easily executed as the other more indiscriminate one of making the direction of every drain of every field alike.

(932.) The next step is to fix the *depth* of drain most suitable for draining the particular field; and this can only be done by having a thorough knowledge of the nature of its subsoil. I have already given reasons for fixing the minimum depth of drains in the different kinds of subsoil, in paragraph (909); but as the reasoning given there only establishes the principle, it is not sufficient to determine the most proper depth for every peculiarity of circumstances; for this must be determined by the nature of the subsoil which guides the whole affair. If the field present an uniform surface, but inclining, let at least 2 exploratory drains be cut from the bottom to the top of the field, if its extent does not exceed 10 acres, and as many more as it is proportionally larger; and if the subsoil of both is found at once tilly, that is, drawing a little water, let the cut be made 3 feet deep without hesitation. On proceeding up the rising ground, the depth may be increased to 4 feet, to ascertain if that depth will not draw a *great deal more water* than the other. Should the subsoil prove of porous materials, 2½ feet—the minimum—may suffice; though, on going up the rising ground, it may be increased to 3 feet, to see the effect; but should it, on the other hand, prove a pure tenacious clay, 2 feet will suffice at first, increasing the depth in the rising ground to

2½ and even 3 feet; for it may turn out that the stratum under the tenacious clay is porous. Where the surface is in small undulations, the drain should be cut right through both the flat and rising parts. In very flat ground, any considerable variation of depth is impracticable, and only allowable to preserve the fall. From such experimental drains data should be obtained to fix the proper dimensions of the other drains.

(933.) If you find the substratum pretty much alike in all the experimental drains, you may reasonably conclude that the subsoil of the whole field is nearly alike, and that all the drains should be of the same depth; but should the subsoil prove of different natures in different parts, then the drain should be made of the depth best suited to the nature of the subsoil. A correct judgment, however, of the true nature of the subsoil, cannot be formed immediately on opening a cut; time must be given to the water in the adjoining ridges to find its way to the drain, which, when it has reached, will satisfactorily shew the place which supplies the most water; and if one set of men open all the cuts, by the time the last one has been finished, the first will probably have exhibited its powers of drawing; for it is a fact, that drains do not exhibit their powers, until some hours after they have been opened. When you are satisfied that the drains have drawn in dry weather as much water as they can, you will be able to see whether or not the shallowest parts have drawn as much as the deepest; and you should then determine on cutting the remainder to the depth which has operated most effectually. If rainy weather ensue during the experiment, still you can observe the comparative effects of the drains, and abide by the results. Never mind though parts of the sides of the cuts fall down during dry or wet weather; they need not be regretted, as they afford excellent indications of the nature of the subsoil, the true structure of which being left by the fall in a much better state for examination than where cut by the spade; and you may then observe whether most water is coming out of the highest or lowest part of the subsoil. It is essential for the durability of drains to bear in mind, that they should always stand, if practicable, upon impervious matter, to prevent the escape of the water from the drain by any other channel than the duct.

(934.) You should be made aware, that this is not the usual method adopted by farmers for ascertaining the depth to which drains should be cut. The common practice is, knowing that the field stands on tilly bottom, the drains are made of a predetermined depth, and the contract with the labourers is made on that understanding, be the guess true or false, as it may happen. Now, the considerate plan which I have recommended, incurs no additional expense, as all the experimental drains will serve their purpose afterwards as well as the others; and even although they should cost more than the same extent of other drains, the satisfaction afforded to the mind of having ascertained the true state of the subsoil, more than compensates for any trifling addition of expense which may have been incurred; and be it remembered, that any extra expense consists of only scouring out the earth (if any) that may have fallen down, and of supplying more materials to fill up the chasms thereby occasioned. But the ascertainment of the most proper depths for drains in any sort of subsoil is a much more important matter than many farmers seem, to judge from their practice, to be aware of; for by neglecting to descend only ½ a foot, nay, perhaps 3 inches more, many of the benefits of draining may be unattained. I quite agree with the late Mr Stephens on this subject, when he states, that "land may be filled full of small drains, so that the surface shall appear to be dry; but the land thus attempted to be drained will never produce a crop, either in quality or quantity, equal to land that has been *perfectly* drained,"* where a different kind of draining should have been resorted to.

(935.) A very important particular in the art of thorough draining now claims your attention, which is the determining the *distance* that should be left between the drains. It is evident that this point can only be satisfactorily determined after the depths of the drains have been fixed upon, as drains in a porous substratum, which draws water from a long distance, need not, of course, be placed so close together as where the substratum yields water in small quantities; and as drains may be of different depths in the same field, according to the draining powers of the substratum, so they should be placed at different distances in the same field. It is the common practice to fix on the open furrows between the ridges, for the sites of drains; because the hollow of the open furrow saves a little cutting, though such saving is a trifling consideration compared to the advantage of executing the drains in the best manner. For my part, I can see no greater claim for a drain in the furrow than in any other part of the ridge, especially as most of the water should be received from the subsoil rather than the surface except in pure clay-soils; and it is, of course, as easy to make them in any other part of the ridge as in the open furrow. These observations of Mr Smith on this subject court remark. "When the ridges of the field," says he, "have been formerly much raised, it suits very well to run a drain up every furrow, which saves some depth of cutting. The feering being thereafter made over the drains, the hollow is filled up, and the general surface ultimately becomes level." This is all very well for the purpose of level-

* Quarterly Journal of Agriculture, vol. iii. p. 290.

ling the ground; but mark what follows? "When the field is again ridged," he continues, "the drains may be kept in the crowns or middle of the ridges; but if it be intended to work the field so as to alternate the crowns and furrows, then the ridges should be of a breadth equal to *double* the distance from drain to drain; and by setting off the furrows in the middle betwixt two drains, the crowns will be in the same position; so that when the furrows take the places of the crowns, they will still be in the middle betwixt two drains, which will prevent the risk of surface-water getting access to the drain from the water-furrows by any direct opening."* No doubt, it is easy to transpose furrows into crowns, and *vice versa;* but how would the transposition be effected in these circumstances, since the drains were made in each former furrow, and it is proposed to make the crowns of the ridges between the drains, the transposition of the crowns could only be effected by adopting the unfarmerlike plan of leaving, in a finished field, a half of the breadth of the ridge adopted at each side; and rather than practise such slovenliness, would it not be better to cut the drains in the middle of the ridges, and preserve each ridge unbroken?

(936.) With regard to distances between drains, in a partially impervious subsoil, 15 feet are as great a distance as a 3-feet drain can be expected to draw; and in some cases, I have no doubt that a 4-feet one will be required. In more porous matter, a 3-feet drain will probably draw 20 feet, with as great if not greater effect; and in the case of a mouldy, deep soil, resting on an impervious subsoil,—which is not an uncommon combination of soils in the turnip-districts of this country,—a drain passing through the mould, and resting perhaps 3 or 4 inches in the impervious clay,—which may altogether make it 4 feet deep,—will draw, I have no doubt, a distance of 30 feet. More than 30 feet distant, I would feel exceeding reluctance to recommend drains being made, unless the circumstances were remarkably singular, when, of course, a special thing must be done for a special case, such as an entirely porous subsoil containing somewhat indurated portions, when a drain through each of these, at whatever distance, will suffice to keep the whole dry.

(937.) The distance at which ordinary drains in tilly subsoils will *not* draw is not left to conjecture, but has partially been determined by experiment. Conceiving that a drain in every furrow, in a tilly subsoil, is attended with more expense than any anticipated increase of produce from the soil would warrant, a farmer in East Lothian put a drain in every *fourth* furrow; and that they might, as he conceived, have a chance of drawing at that distance, he caused them to be cut 4 feet deep. A figure will best

* Smith's Remarks on Thorough Draining, p. 7-8, 4th edition.

illustrate the results, where the black lines *a*, fig. 166, are the drains between every fourth furrow, and the dotted lines represent the intermediate undrained furrows, and where it is evident, at the first glance, that the drains *a* have to dry 2 ridges on each side *b c* and *d e*, of which we should expect that the 2 ridges *b* and *d*, being nearest to *a*, should be more dried,

Fig. 166.

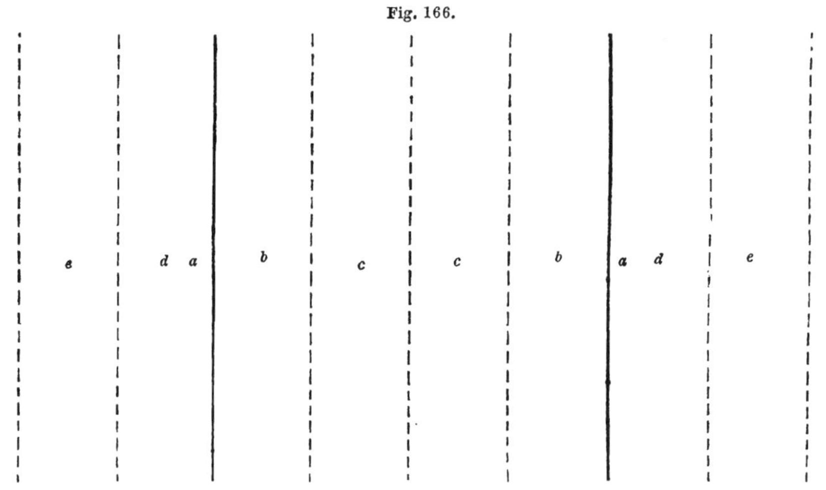

THE EFFECTS OF TOO GREAT A DISTANCE BETWIXT DRAINS.

in the same time, than the 2 furthest ridges *c* and *e*, and the result agrees with expectation; but still, had the subsoil been of an entirely porous nature, both ridges might have been sufficiently dried by *a*. Trusting to similar contingency, it is not an unusual expectation, entertained by many farmers, that a drain will sufficiently dry 2 ridges on each side, or at least 1 ridge on each side, without ascertaining the exact nature of the subsoil. But mark the results of this particular experiment, which was conducted with the usual expectations. The 2 ridges *b* and *d*, nearest to *a*, actually produced 9 bushels of corn more per acre than the 2 more distant ridges *c* and *e*. This is a great difference of produce from adjoining grounds under the same treatment, and yet it does not shew the entire advantage that may be obtained by drained over undrained land, because it is possible that the drain *a* also partially drained the distant ridges *c* and *e*; and this being possible, together with the circumstance that none of the ridges had a drain on each side, it cannot be maintained that either the absolute or the comparative drying power of these 4-feet drains was exactly ascertained by this experiment.* It may be conceived, however, that if the drains had been put into every other, instead of every fourth, furrow, that the produce of all the ridges

* Quarterly Journal of Agriculture, vol. viii. p. 539.

would have been alike; inasmuch as every ridge would then have been placed in the same relative position to a drain; and the conjecture seems so reasonable, that most farmers, from what I observe of their practice, act upon this plan as from a settled opinion. But such a conjecture, not having been founded upon experience, cannot have the force of an opinion, especially when opposed to the great probability that, *cæteris paribus*, land must be more effectually drained by a drain in every furrow than at greater distances; as it is not supposable that the open furrows of *b* and *d* can be so thoroughly drained as the furrow *a*, which contains the drain itself; because it is obvious, that the one side of a ridge should be *less* effectually drained than the other, which, if of a *retentive subsoil*, may not be affected at all. All, then, that has been *demonstrated* by this experiment is this, and the proof I consider is important, that a drain—a deep one though it be—will draw water more effectually across one than across two ridges; and it should be useful to you as a guide against imitating the practice of those who seem to believe that a drain cannot have too much to do.

(938.) Whilst taking this view of the subject, I cannot agree in the advice which Mr Smith gives when he says,—"In cases where time or capital are awanting to complete the drainage at once, each alternate drain may be executed in the first instance, and the remainder can be done in the next time the field is to be broken up."* I would much rather use the words of Mr Stirling of Glenbervie, where he says, that "I think it a *great error* to make the half the number of drains required at first, with the intention of putting one between each at a future period. Let what is drained be done as thoroughly as the farmer's exchequer will allow; the farm will be gone over in as short a time, and much more profitably." The reason which Mr Stirling gives for holding this opinion is a true and practical one; namely, because "a tid (or proper condition of the ground for harrowing) cannot be taken advantage of on the drained furrow until the other is dry, and the benefit of an extended period for performing the various operations of the farm is thus lost."† Every farmer who has studied the influence which soil possesses over crops, will be ready to allow that wet soil does much more injury to the dry soil in its neighbourhood, than dry soil does good to the wet. I would, under every circumstance of season and soil, prefer having the half of my farm thoroughly drained, than the whole of it only half drained.

(939.) At whatever distances drains are placed, they should run *nearly*

* Smith's Remarks on Thorough Draining, p. 17, 4th edition.

† Prize Essays of the Highland and Agricultural Society, vol. xii. p. 102.

at right angles to the main drains. Excepting in confined hollows, having steep ascents on both sides, the drains should run parallel with the ridges, and always parallel with themselves, in the drainage of the same plane of the field. Drains should be carried through the whole length of the field, irrespective of the wet or dry appearances of parts of it; because uniform and complete dryness is the object aimed at by draining, and portions of land that seem dry at one time, may be injuriously wet at others, and these may seem dry on the surface when the subsoil may be in a state of injurious wetness.

(940.) Regarding the *direction which the drains should run in reference to the inclination of the ground*, so as to dry the land most effectually, much diversity of opinion at one time existed; but I believe most farmers are now of the opinion that it should follow the inclination of the ground. The late Mr Stephens maintained, and as I think erroneously, that as it is evident that water within the earth, or on the surface, seeks a level where the fall through the porous subsoil is greatest; *therefore* a drain made across the slope or declivity of a field, or any piece of land, will undoubtedly intercept more water than when it is carried straight up the bank or rising ground, and this principle, he says, holds good in every case, whether "the drain be made to receive surface or subterraneous water." I confess I cannot arrive at the conclusion from the premises. He reiterates the same opinion more generally, and apparently more practically, in these words. "Drains winding across the slope or declivity of a field, whatever their number or depth may be, their effect upon tenacious or impervious substrata will be much greater than if they were made straight up and down the slope; and when the soil is mixed with thin strata of fine sand, which is the case in nine times out of ten, the effect will be increased in proportion, and accordingly, a much less number will answer the purpose, the expense will be greatly lessened, and the land and occupier much more benefited in every respect."* Mr Smith opposes this opinion, and, what is remarkable, uses the same illustration to refute it, in regard to the property of water and the structure of the substratum, as Mr Stephens did in support of his views. "Drains," says he, "drawn across a steep, cut the strata or layers of subsoil transversely, and as the stratification generally lies in sheets at an angle to the surface (see fig. 169), the water passing in or between the strata, immediately below the bottom of one drain, nearly comes to the surface before reaching the next lower drain. But as water seeks the lowest level in all directions, if the strata be cut longitudinally by a drain directed down the steeps, the bottom of which

* Stephens' Practical Irrigator and Drainer, p. 103.

cuts each stratum to the same distance from the surface, the water will flow into the drain at the intersecting point of each sheet or layer, on a level with the bottom of the drain, leaving one uniform depth of dry soil."* Without taking any other element at present into the argument than the single proposition in hydraulics, that water seeks the lowest level in all directions, adduced by Mr Stephens himself, I shall prove the accuracy of Mr Smith's conclusions, by simply referring to fig. 167, which represents a part of a field all having the same, and that a steep acclivity, and which is laid off in the ridges *a b c d e f*, up and down the slope, but the 3 ridges *a b c* have drains across them, and the other 3 ridges have drains parallel with them, the oblique drains being made at the same distance from each other as the up and down ones, whatever that distance may be. Now, when rain falls on, and is absorbed by the ridges *a b c d e f*, it will naturally make its way to the lowest level, that

Fig. 167.

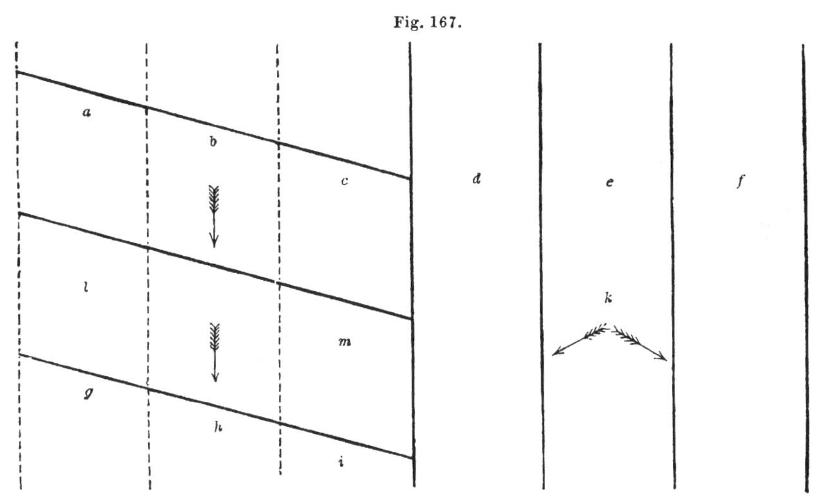

THE COMPARATIVE EFFICACY OF DRAINS ACROSS AND ALONG RIDGES ON A DECLIVITY.

is, to the bottom of the drains, and as the ground has the same declivity, the water will descend according to the circumstances which are presented to it by the positions of the respective systems of drains. On the ridges *d e f*, having the drains parallel to them, and up and down the inclination of the ground, the water will take a diagonal direction towards the bottom of the drains, as indicated by the deflected arrows at *k*; and as ground has seldom only one plane of declination, such as straight up and down, but more commonly two, another in the direction either from *a* to *f* or from *f* to *a*, it follows that the one side, that is,

* Smith's Remarks on Thorough-Draining, p. 9.

the lower side of a ridge thus situated, will be sooner drained than the other; but both sides will be soon drained, as may be seen in fig. 168, where *a b* are vertical sections of small drains, each 30 inches deep; *c* 1 foot of mould, in which the rain is absorbed as fast as it falls upon the ridge, 15 feet broad, betwixt *a* and *b*. On being absorbed, the rain,

Fig. 168.

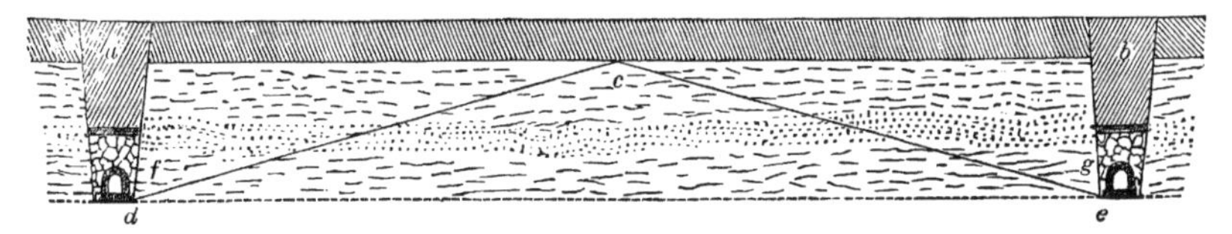

THE DESCENT OF WATER FROM A RIDGE INTO A DRAIN ON EACH SIDE.

seeking the lowest level, will be hastened towards the drains *a* and *b* in the direction of *c d* and *c e*, that is, by a fall of 30 inches in about 8 feet, which is a rapid fall of rather more than 1 in 3, and which rapid fall, as is well known, will clear water quickly, and in the clearance of which the drains have only each to draw a distance of half a ridge, or 7½ feet. Whereas on the ridges *a b c*, which have oblique drains, *a*, *l*, *g*, fig. 167, the water will have to run in the direction of the arrows *b* and *h*, in doing which it will have to traverse the entire breadth of the ground betwixt *a* and *l* or *l* and *g*, that is, 15 feet, just double the distance the other drains have. But take the superficial view of the case, and suppose that *d*, *e*, *f*, and *a*, *l*, *g*, are not drains, but open furrows, it is clear that when rain falls, the water will flow towards *d*, *e*, or *f*, as indicated by the arrows at *k*, that is, 7½ feet towards each furrow; whereas the water that falls on *a c*, *l m*, or *g i*, will have to run across the entire breadth of the ridge from *a* to *l*, or from *l* to *g*, that is, 15 feet, just double the distance of the other, before it can reach the open furrows. Or rather take the more profound case, and trace the progress of the water through the substrata. Mr Thomson, Hangingside, Linlithgowshire, drained 150 acres of land having an inclination varying from 1 in 10 to 1 in 30. Portions of 3 fields had drains put into them in 1828, 1829, and 1830, in the oblique direction, and, finding them unsuccessful, he put them in the direction of the slope, like the rest of the fields. "In order," says he, "to ascertain the cause of these failures, a cut was made in the field first referred to, entering at a given point, and carrying forward a level to a considerable depth, when it was clearly seen that the substrata, instead of taking in any degree the inclination of the surface, lay horizontally, as represented in fig. 169. It is therefore obvious," he continues, "that in making drains *across* a sloping surface, unless they are put in at the precise point where the substrata crop out (and these are exceedingly irregular in point of thickness), they may in a great measure prove nugatory; because, although one drain is near another, from the rise of

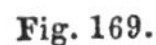

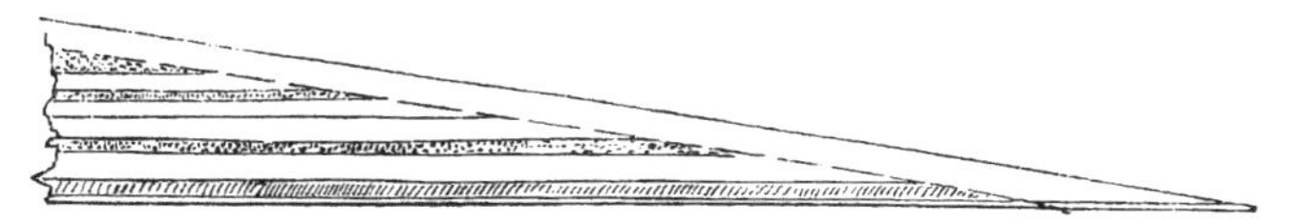

Fig. 169.

THE USUAL POSITION OF SUBSTRATA IN REFERENCE TO THE SURFACE SOIL.

the ground, none of them may reach the point sought; whereas, in carrying a drain right up the direction of a slope, it is impossible to miss the extremity of every substratum passed through."* And although a drain in the oblique direction should cut through a vein of sand as at *f*, fig. 168, and thereby carry off the water it contains, yet it cannot be denied that the drains *a* and *b* will also cut through the said vein, which, when they do, what is there to prevent the water in the vein running towards the drains *a* and *b* on each side of the ridge towards *f* and *g*? These observations of Mr Thomson corroborate Mr Smith's views, in which I entirely concur.

(941.) In all cases of thorough-draining there should a small drain connect the tops of the drains at the upper end of the field. The object of this drain is, in the first instance, to dry the upper head-ridge, and also to protect the upper ends of the ridges from any oozings of water that might come from the fence ditch, or from any rising ground beyond that end of the field. If the fence ditch conveys no current of water, and the hedge-roots lie away from the field, and there are no hedge-row trees near at hand, this drain may be made in the ditch itself, and the ends of the furrow-drains brought across the head-ridge to it; but should water or trees be connected with the ditch, the drain should be made on the head-ridge not nearer than 3 yards from the ditch lip; and it should be of the same depth, though not deeper than the other drains.

(942.) When drains have a course along very long ridges, it is recommended to run a *sub-main* drain in an oblique direction from side to side, or rather only across all the long ridges of the field, as represented by *e e* in fig. 163. The length of any drain, it is maintained, should not exceed 200 yards, without a sub-main drain to assist in carrying off the water; and the reasons assigned by Mr Carmichael for requiring the assistance of such a drain are, "because, if the fall is considerable, the bottom may be endangered by the velocity and volume of water collected during continued rain; or if the declivity be very limited, and

* Prize Essays of the Highland and Agricultural Society, vol. xiii. p. 295.

the aperture small, the drain is in danger of bursting from an impeded discharge, but a complete answer to these apprehensions is found in the very next sentence, namely, " the rule is to apportion the area of all drains to their length, declivity, and distance from each other."* It is quite true what Mr Smith says on the subject, that " some people are still prone to the practice of throwing in a cross drain, or to branches going off at right angles, which are of no farther avail in drying the land, whilst they increase the length of drain without a proportionate increase of the area drained."† Should the want, however, of proper sized tiles, in any particular part of a field, where the quantity of water is greater than over the ordinary surface of the farm, induce you to incur the expense of a sub-main drain, rather than run the risk of injuring the land by the dreaded insufficiency of the drains below, it should be directed across the field as shewn by *e* in fig. 163, where, if cut of the same depth as the other small drains, those below should be disjoined from it by a narrow stripe of ground in the line of *e* to *e*; but a much better plan is to make the sub-main 6 inches deeper than the rest of the drains, where it can be so deepened, and it will intercept the water coming from the ground above, while the drains will pass continuously over it. In such a case, when the sub-main *e* falls into the small drain *b d* at the side of the field at *e*, that part of the latter below *e* to *s* should be converted into a sub-main, which should be larger than small drains, though sub-mains need not be so capacious as main drains; but in truth, in such an arrangement as this, sub-mains become mains, inasmuch as they convey as great a quantity of water.

(943.) The *experimental cuts* having been made, you become acquainted with the nature of the subsoil, and determine upon the depth of the drains; then cutting should be proceeded with forthwith, and this part of the work is best and most satisfactorily done by contracting with an experienced spadesman, at so much per rood of 6 yards.‡ The rates of cutting are generally well understood in the country. Let me impress upon you, in the matter of making a contract, the great satisfaction you will feel in engaging stout, active, and *skilful* men; for although you may find men able to work a hard day's work, if they are nevertheless unskilful and inexperienced, you will experience many difficulties. Such men willingly take on work at low rates; but you will find it conducive to

* Prize Essays of the Highland and Agricultural Society, vol. xii. p. 94.

† Smith's Remarks on Thorough Draining, p. 9.

‡ It would be extremely convenient and highly satisfactory were the lineal measure of the *rood*, in which all country work is estimated, fixed of the same length throughout the kingdom, as the great diversities existing in this measure are truly perplexing. I cannot see the utility of a general law on weights and measures, if such anomalies as this, and many others, are alowed to exist.

your interest rather to give such rates as will enable skilful workmen to earn good wages, than save a little money by employing rough bungling hands; for there is no comparison between the advantages derivable from good and bad work.

(944.) The cutting of the drains is commenced by that of the main drain which terminates at the outlet, and the operation is commenced at the outlet, or lowest part of the field. The commencement of the operation is done in the same way as pointed out in the drains of the Elkington method; namely, by stretching the garden-line, and rutting off the breadth at top with the common spade by the principal man of the party. A second man then removes the top-mould with the spade; and if the subsoil is of strong clay, or tiles alone are to be used in filling the drains, he lays the mould on one side of the drain, and the subsoil on the other. In other kinds of soils and subsoils, and where stones are to be used in conjunction with tiles, the separation of the soils is not necessary. The reasons for this distinction in the use of the soils will be given a little farther on. The principal man, or contractor, follows, and shovels off all the mould, working with his face to the first man. A third man—for the gang or set of drainers should consist of 3, for expeditious and clean work—loosens the top of the subsoil with the tramp-pick, fig. 37, and proceeds backwards with the picking, whilst the other men are removing the mould along the break or division measured off by the line, perhaps 60 or 70 yards. The second man then removes the loosened subsoil with the spade in fig. 170, which is narrower than the common spade, being 6 inches wide at the point, digging with his back to the face of the picker, that is, working backwards; and the leading man follows with a narrow pointed shovel, fig. 38, called the ditcher's or hedger's shovel, with which he trims the sides of the drain, and shovels out the loose part of the subsoil left by the digger.

Fig. 170.

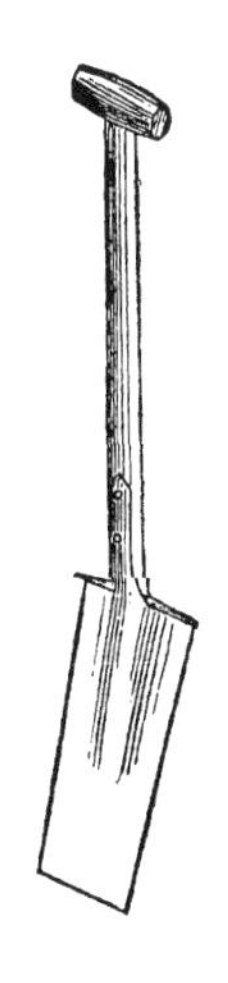

THE NARROW DRAIN SPADE.

(945.) Should the drain be very wet, owing to a great fall of rain, or the cut draw much water from the porosity of the subsoil, to secure a proper consistence to the drain, it is better to leave off the digging at this stage of the work, and proceed to set off another length of line at the top; and, indeed, in such circumstances, it would be expedient to remove the top of the whole length of the particular drain *in hand*, to allow the water time to run off, and the sides of the drain to harden, as perseverance in digging to the bottom, in the circumstances, would be attended with risk of the sides falling in to a considerable extent. This precaution in digging drains is the more necessary to be adopted in digging narrow shallow drains than deep ones, as planks cannot be used in them to support the falling sides, as in fig. 154; because the men could not find room in small drains to work *below* the wedges which keep up the planks. Should the ground be firm, or no inconvenient quantity of water be present in the drain, the digging, of course, may properly be proceeded with to the bottom at once.

(946.) To effect this, the picking is renewed at the lower part of the drain, and another spit of earth thrown out with a still narrower though of the same form of spade as in the last figure, being only 4 inches wide at the point. The leading man trims down the sides of the drain

Fig. 171.

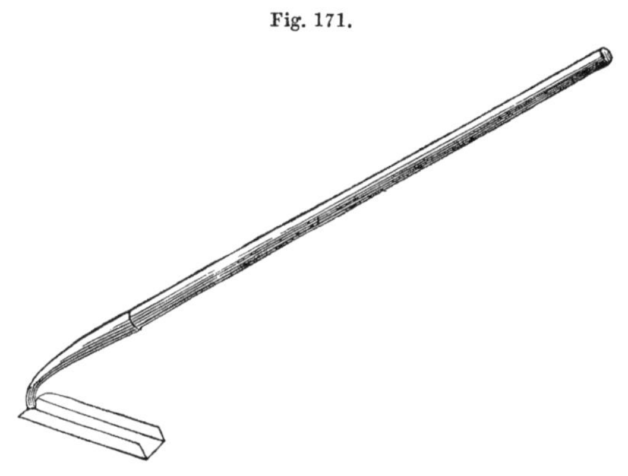

THE EARTH DRAIN SCOOP.

with this spade, and pulls out the remaining loose earth towards him with the scoop, such as in fig. 171; or throws it out with such a scoop as in fig. 152; and thus finishes the bottom and sides in a neat, even, clean, square, and workmanlike style.

(947.) What with the experimental cuts, and these first two spits of digging below the mould, you will be easily able to determine the drawing property of the subsoil, and, consequently, the depth the drain should go. If the subsoil prove tilly, but still drawing a little water below the mould downwards, the drain should certainly be 3 feet deep and 15 inches wide at top; if of intermixed and minute veins of sand, and otherwise of good drawing materials, then 30 inches of depth will suffice, and 12 inches of width at top; if of quite impervious clay, 2 feet deep, and 10 inches of width at top will be found sufficient. It is right to cut the drain a little deeper where there is any sudden rise of the surface, and a little shallower where there are any sudden hollows, than to follow the undulations of the ground where these are trifling. As to the distances betwixt the drains in the first case of a tilly but drawing bottom, 15 feet asunder is, in my opinion, quite wide enough. In the second case of a drawing subsoil, drains at 30 feet asunder will effect as much as in the former case. And as to pure clays, as 15 feet is too wide a distance, I would prefer 12 feet; but to suit the ridges, there should be a drain in every open furrow, whatever distance asunder these may be.

(948.) In *filling* drains it is a common practice with farmers to put in the materials as the drain proceeds in the digging, which, I conceive, is an objectionable proceeding. I think the whole length of the particular drain in hand should be entirely cleared out to the specified dimensions before the filling commence; because it is necessary, in the first place, that the state of the work be inspected, in accordance with the specification, before taking it off the contractor's hands, and inspection implies measurement of the contents in depth and breadth and the fall of the bottom, whether it be regular throughout, where the slope of the ground is regular, or sufficient, where the general fall of the ground is small; or whether the fall is preserved in all the places where the ground is irregular. These are not trifling considerations, but essential; so much so, indeed, that the very efficacy of a drain as a conductor of water entirely depends upon them.

(949.) The *fall of the ground* can at any time be ascertained by the workmen by a simple contrivance. As the bottom of the drain is cleared out, a damming of 4 to 6 inches high will intercept and collect the water seeking its way along the bottom, and by this it can be seen whether the level line of the water cuts the bottom of the drain as far up as it should do according to the specified fall; and a succession of such dammings will preserve the fall all the way up the drain. When the weather is very dry, and a sufficiency of water awanting in the drain to adopt this mode of testing the fall, a few buckets of water thrown in will detect it, and of course it is only on comparatively level ground that such expedients as these are at all required.

(950.) Another reason for filling drains in this shallow mode of draining, where they are necessarily numerous, is from the upper to the lower end, and not from the lower to the upper, as is too commonly the practice, that the bottom of the drain should be cleared out most effectually with the scoop before the materials are put in, and this is best and most easily done down the natural declivity of the ground; and besides, in doing this it is at once seen whether the fall has been preserved, by the following of the water down the declivity. In deep-draining the case is otherwise, because in that case the drains being few in number, and each possessing importance, the falls should be previously determined by levelling, and the amount of each levelling marked, by which means they can be preserved as the filling proceeds; and, besides, there would be risk of a deep drain, which may be of considerable length, and take a long time to throw out, falling in, to allow it to remain open for a length of time.

(951.) Of the materials for filling drains I shall first notice *stones*, not only because they have hitherto been the most common material, but have been for the longest time employed for the purpose. Drain stones are usually derived from two sources, 1. From the surface of the land, and when they are small and round, not exceeding the size of a goose's egg, no other material is equal to them in durability for the purposes of a drain; and, 2. From the quarry, where they must be broken with hammers, like road-metal, to the smallness of from 2½ to 4 inches in diameter. It is a pernicious, and, indeed, an obviously absurd practice, to mix promiscuously stones of different sizes in a drain, as such can never assort together, and nothing can be more absurd than to throw in a stone which nearly fills up the bottom of a drain, and is sure to make a dam across it to intercept water. All large land-stones should be broken into small pieces, and any large angular piece should not be put near the bottom, which should be kept as open as possible. Stones broken in the quarry are always angular, and in so far they are of an objectionable shape, because on fitting together, face to face, they can become a more compact body than round stones possibly can. No doubt, no ordinary pressure upon a body of earth 18 inches deep could squeeze small broken stones together so as entirely to compress the spaces between them; but gravity, continually acting on loose bodies, will in time consolidate small stones more and more; and heavy labour on the surface, and subsidence of water through the earth, assist by their action to produce a similar result; and we all know that macadamization makes a much more compact road than the old-fashioned large round stones.

(952.) Stones should never be broken at the side of the drain. I quite agree with Mr Stirling when he says that "I prefer breaking stones in a *bin*. It is more easy to check the size, and it is done cheaper, as otherwise each heap has to be begun on the sward, and many of the stones are forced into the ground, which adds to the difficulty of lifting them. There will be a saving in carting the stones large, but it will be fully balanced by this disadvantage. I would deprecate of all practice that of breaking the stones in the field, and filling by the chain. This may be contracted for at a low rate, but it is easy to guess how the contractor makes wages."* But although I would greatly prefer small round stones to angular ones for drains, yet as the places that afford small round stones naturally are very limited in number, and draining, if confined to such localities, would be as limited, it is far better to take any sort of quarried stones than leave land undrained, and there is no doubt that almost every sort of stones forms an efficient and durable drain if employed in a proper manner.

(953.) As I am acquainted with no drainer who has bestowed so much pains in the breaking, preparing, and putting in stones into drains as Mr Roberton, I shall describe his method of managing

Fig. 172.

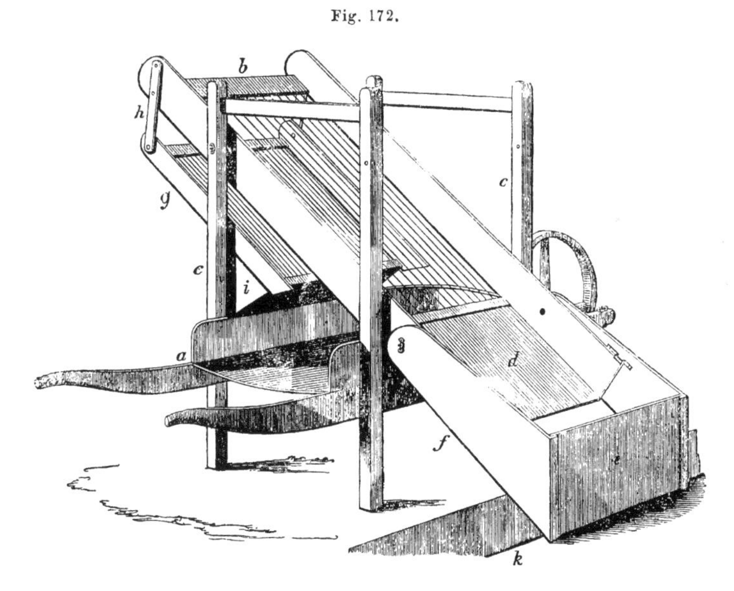

THE DRAIN STONE HARP OR SCREEN.

quarried stones; and first in regard to the implements used by him for that purpose. 1. There is a portable *screen* or *harp* for riddling and depositing the stones, as seen in fig. 172, which consists of " a wheelbarrow *a*, over and across which is suspended a screen *b*, having the bars more or less apart, according to the description of materials intended to be used. The upper end is hung upon two posts *c c* about

* Prize Essays of the Highland and Agricultural Society, vol. xii. p. 110.

3 feet above the barrow, the lower end rests upon the opposite side of the barrow. To this lower end is affixed a spout *d*, attached about 10 inches from the lower extremity of which is a board *e*, by means of two arms *f*. Another screen *g*, about one half the length, and having the bars about half an inch apart, is hung parallel, about 10 inches below the larger one. The upper end of *g* is fixed by means of two small iron bars *h* to the upper end of the larger screen; the lower end rests upon a board *i* sloping outwards upon the side of the barrow opposite to that on which the spout *d* is situate." 2. A movable trough, or as it is commonly called, a *tail-board a*, fig. 173, is attached to the hind part of

Fig. 173.

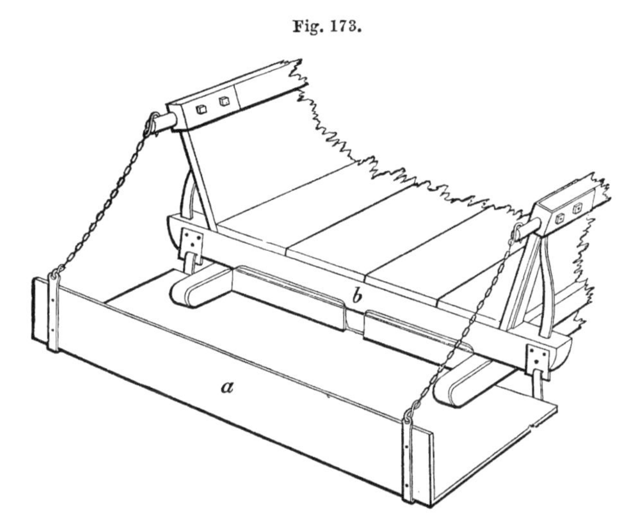

THE TAIL-BOARD TROUGH FOR RECEIVING THE DRAIN STONES IN THEIR FALL.

a cart, for the purpose of receiving any stones that may drop while the workmen are shovelling them out of the cart. A portion of the hind part of a cart *b* shews the manner in which it is affixed to it. 3. Fig. 174

Fig. 174.

THE DRAIN STONE RAKE.

is a small iron *rake* used by the workman in charge of the screen, "for the purpose of making the surface of the larger stones of a uniform height before being covered with the smaller." 4. Fig. 175 is called a "*beater*, which is a square piece of wood, the width of the drain, used for beating the smaller stones into the interstices of the larger ones, and thus levelling the surface of the drain."*

Fig. 175.

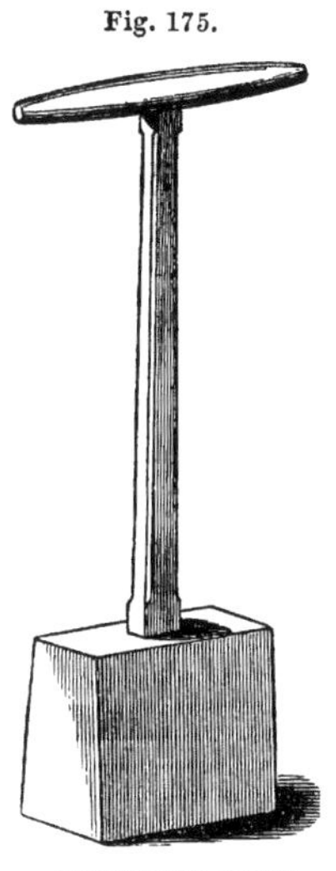

THE DRAIN STONE BEATER.

(954.) The *stones are put in* in this manner. The earth is all put on one side of the drain. The barrow-screen is placed on the other, so as the board *e*, fig. 172, attached to the lower end of the spout *d* shall reach the opposite side of the drain *k*. The cart with a load of broken stones from the bin is brought to the same side of the drain as the barrow, and a little in advance, and there the tail-board *a*, fig. 173, is attached to the hinder part of it. The carter then shovels the stones out of the cart, and empties them over the top of the screen. In doing this, some care is requisite; for if the stones are thrown over the screen with force, they will not alight sooner than half-way down the screen, and thus its screening efficacy will be impaired. The proper method is to rest the shovel on the top of the screen, which part should be shod with plate-iron, and merely turn it over, by which a separation of the stones is at once effected, the larger ones, rolling down, strike against the board *e*, fig. 172, and drop into the middle of the drain, without disturbing the earth on either side. The smaller ones, at the same time, pass through the upper screen *b*, and being separated from the rubbish by falling on the lower screen *g*, roll down into the barrow *a*, whilst the rubbish descends to the ground on the side of the barrow farthest from the drain.

(955.) The best form of shovel for putting the stones over the top

Fig. 176.

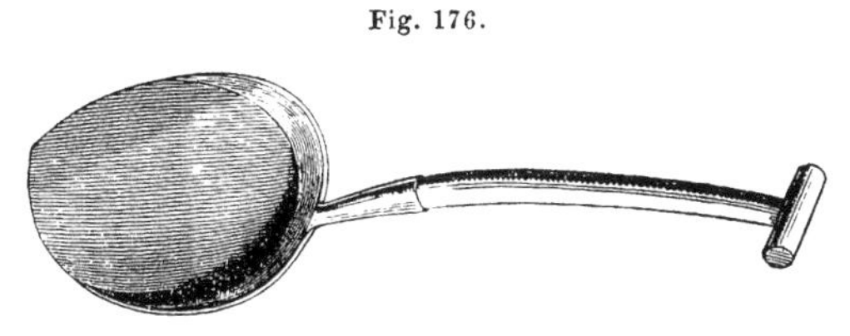

THE FRYING-PAN OR LIME SHOVEL.

of the screen is what is called a frying-pan or lime shovel, represented

* Prize Essays of the Highland and Agricultural Society, vol. xiv. p. 37.

by fig. 176, the raised back of which keeps the stones in a collected form until they are turned over the screen, and its point secures an easy access along the bottom of the cart under the stones. Such shovels are much in use for spreading lime and shovelling up the bottoms of dunghills in the border counties of Scotland, and they cost 3s. 10d. each of medium size, ready for use.

(956.) One man takes charge of the filling of the drain. His duties are to move the barrow forward along its side as the larger stones are filled to the required height; to level them with the rake, fig. 174; to shovel the smaller stones from the barrow, spread them regularly over the top of the larger, and beat them down with the beater, fig. 175, so as to form a close and level surface through which no earth may pass. When the stones are broken in the quarry so as to pass through a ring 4 inches in diameter, a quarter of them is so small, or should be made so small, as to pass through the wires of the upper screen *b*, fig. 172, which are 1¾ inch apart, and they then will be found sufficient to give the top of the drain a covering of 2 or 3 inches deep, which being beaten closely down, requires neither straw, turf, or any thing else to cover them.

(957.) With regard to *covering with vegetable substances*, Mr Roberton says with much probable truth, that "the only possible use of a covering of straw or turf is to prevent any of the earth, when thrown back into the drain, getting down among the stones; but it is evident that such a covering will soon decay, and then it becomes really injurious; because, being lighter (and finer) than the soil, it will, when decomposed, be easily carried down by any water that may fall directly upon the drain, and if the surface of the stones has been broken so small as to prevent the drain sustaining any injury in this way, then the covering itself must be altogether superfluous. But farther, it will be found that the effect of this practice, in many cases, is still more injurious. When drains are filled in the usual way, whether with land or quarried stones, a man, or sometimes a woman, is appointed to level the surface and put on the straw or turf; and the person appointed to this duty knows that his master expects him to do a certain number of roods per day, and finding the stones difficult to break, he too frequently contents himself with merely levelling the surface, and by means of the covering the fault is effectually concealed. By the method, however, of separating the small stones from the large, the whole expense of this sort of breaking is saved, and a covering is given to the drain on which time will produce no change."* I have often grudged fine straw being wasted

* Prize Essays of the Highland and Agricultural Society, vol. xiv. p. 40.

in covering drains, when less valuable materials might have been collected for the purpose, such as dry leaves, dry quickens, tanner's refuse bark when near towns, coarse bog hay, broken moss, &c. I never would suffer a particle of good straw to be wasted in covering drains.

(958.) A drain completed in this manner with stones may be seen in fig 177. The dimensions given by Mr Roberton are 33 inches deep, 7 inches wide at bottom, and 9 inches wide at the height of the stones, which is 15 inches, and within these dimensions 15 cubic feet of stones will fill a rood of 6 yards of drain. Mr Stirling has 30 inches deep in the furrows, 5 inches wide at bottom, and 8 inches wide at 15 inches from the bottom; the contents of a rood of 6 yards being rather more than 12 cubic feet. The figure here represents a drain 36 inches deep, 9 inches wide at bottom, 12 inches at the top of the stones, and the stones 18 inches deep. These dimensions give cubical contents of 23½ feet per rood of 6 yards; that is, about half as many stones more than the drains of Mr Roberton, and of course so much more expensive. I own I am partial to the breadth of the common spade as a gauge for the width of the bottom of a drain that is to be filled with *stones*, because it gives plenty of room to them to form a durable stony filter, which 7 inches can scarcely do so well, especially when they are broken to 4 inches in diameter. I am quite persuaded, nevertheless, that the permanency of a drain does not depend so much on the quantity as upon the manner in which the stones are put into it, and I am as well persuaded that it is no matter what description of materials are used, provided there is always left an open and large enough space at the bottom to contain the greatest quantity of water that the drain can possibly have to receive, and provided also that the opening shall be protected from any earth or mud getting in to intercept the flow of water. Yet I agree with Mr Stirling that our experience is not sufficient to prove what is the *smallest* size that a drain might be to be *permanent.* In which uncertainty it should be of sufficient breadth to prevent moles pushing across it; and this consideration regarding moles acquires greater importance the more the land is drained, for the deeper we confine water *under* the ground, the deeper will the worms be obliged to go in search of it, and of course the nearer the bottom of the drains will the moles be disposed

Fig. 177.

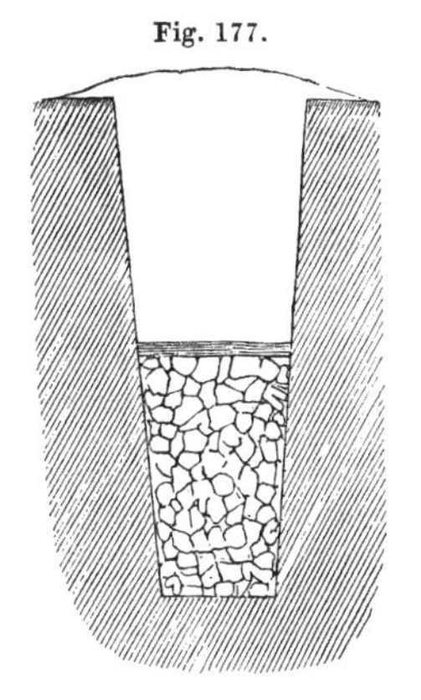

THE SMALL DRAIN FILLED WITH SMALL BROKEN STONES.

to burrow in search of their food. Mr Stirling proposes only to make the bottom of the drain 5 inches, but then he directs the stones to be broken to pass through a ring of 2½ inches diameter. Such diversity of opinion on the same subject shew you either that experience has not as yet proved what capacity of drain is the best, or that it is immaterial to the draining of land of what breadth drains are made. The principle I maintain in the making of drains is, that, being *permanent* works, they ought to be made in the most substantial manner. It has not yet been ascertained by experiment what dimension, in given circumstances, afford *sufficient* permanency, and until that point has been settled, it is wisdom rather to exceed than to curtail the dimensions; and although in the mean time the wisdom may be "dear bought," the question of cost is a secondary one to efficiency and permanency.

(959.) With regard to the *quantity of stones used in such drains, and the time required for putting them in,* Mr Roberton's experience is, in drains of the above dimensions, namely, 33 inches deep, 7 inches wide at bottom, 15 inches filled with stones, and 9 inches wide at the top of the stones—the cubical contents being 15 feet per rood of 6 yards—supposing that a set of carts, driven by boys or women, are able to keep a man employed in unloading them, and another man taking charge of the screen-barrow, 60 to 70 roods can be filled in a summer day of 10 hours; but as the lineal length depends on the dimensions of the drain, the work, reduced to cubical contents, gives 3½ cubic yards per hour. These data were derived from whole pieces of work, such as in 1840 Mr Roberton contracted for, for the execution of 4000 roods, the filling to commence on the 1st July and to be completed on the 12th August. There were 2 sets of carts and 2 screens employed, and the contractors had some stones ready, and part of the drains half executed by the 1st July. When the filling commenced 66 roods were finished every day, that is, as it happened, a stretch of drain of exactly 400 yards; but as the weather was very unfavourable for the work, only 3300 roods, instead of 4000, were executed, in which about 2000 cubic yards of stones were buried. In 1839, of drains of 28 inches deep, 10 to 12 inches of stones in depth, and about 10 cubic feet contents per rood, 2100 roods, or from 90 to 110 roods per day were filled, with 1 set of carts and 1 screen, from 1st July to 5th August.

(960.) In Mr Stirling's case of the drains mentioned above, namely, 30 inches deep in the furrow, 5 inches wide at bottom, and 8 inches at the top of the stones,—which were 15 inches deep, and their cubical contents 12.3 feet per rood of 6 yards, the stones, being supposed to be carted 1 mile,—2 men filled 60 carts of broken stones each day, allowing for loss of time in backing into the bin of stones; a man emptied a cart-load into the drain in 15 minutes, and was ready to return with the cart in 2 minutes more, the horse being supposed to walk at the rate of 3 miles per hour. In this way, a chain of 22 yards, or 3.66 roods, required 3 carts of stones.

(961.) So much for stone, and now for the cost of *tile-draining.* The *dimensions of tile-drains* depends entirely on the mode they are to be constructed. If no soles are to be employed, they may be the narrower; and if nothing else but tile and sole are to be put into them before the earth is returned, they may be the shallower. If the same rule be followed in regard to them as with stone-drains,—that is, if 18 inches of earth should be retained over the hard materials, to give liberty to deep ploughing,—then 18 inches, added to the tile and covering, is the *least depth* that a tile-drain should have; and its *least breadth* is determined by the breadth of sole that is used.

(962.) As the dimensions of these drains depend on the use of *soles,* the necessity for their adoption should be settled at once. It seems to be the uniform opinion of all writers on tile-draining, that, "in hard-bottomed land, the sole-tile is unnecessary;" but why unnecessary, as I have before observed, no one has proved to *my* satisfaction. Water being the substance to whose use drains are appropriated, I may mention in regard to the quantity that may sometimes be found in drains, that Mr Stirling has found that, after a very heavy fall of rain, tiles of $2\frac{3}{4}$ by $3\frac{1}{2}$ inches are filled with water nearly $\frac{2}{3}$ full;* and yet writers on draining wish to persuade you that such a body of water will not at all affect a clay subsoil or endanger the stability of tiles. I advise you to believe no such assertions, but take for granted that all drains, having an earthy bottom of whatever nature, intended to be occupied by tiles, should have soles, or something equivalent,—such as slates,—under the tiles, to protect the earth from the destructive effects of water. Mr George Bell, Woodhouselees, Dumfriesshire, has used Welsh slates instead of tile-soles, and found them equally efficacious and much cheaper.† Grey slate and pavement quarries, such as abound in Forfarshire, would supply an abundance of excellent materials for the soles of drains.

(963.) The *breadth of the sole, then, determines the width of the bottom of the drain;* and should the breadth vary in different parts of the

* Prize Essays of the Highland and Agricultural Society, vol. xii. p. 100.

† Ibid., vol. xiii. p. 509.

country, the width must in practice be made to suit the sole, but it is probable that soles will be made to suit the proper breadth of drains, when that has been determined by experience. But as that point has not yet been determined by experience, and soles are made of sizes most convenient for their manufacture, the drains must continue to be made of the dimensions suited to the materials by which they are to be filled, until a better order of things arrive. I perceive that the breadth of soles made in the neighbourhood of Kilmarnock, at the tile-kilns belonging to the Duke of Portland in Ayrshire, as well as those made by Mr Boyle, tile-maker in Ayr, is 7 inches; and this breadth is made to answer tiles varying from 4 to 3 inches in width, inside measure. For a 4-inch tile, a narrower width than 7 inches would not answer; as the tile is $\frac{3}{4}$ of an inch thick, only $\frac{3}{4}$ of an inch is left beyond each side of the tile when placed on the sole, which is as little space as it can stand on securely. For the smaller sized tile of 3 inches, the width is ample; but still, it is no disadvantage to a tile to have plenty of room on a sole, as its position can easily be fixed by wedging in stones on each side against the walls of the drain, when stones are used above the tiles; or it leaves sufficient room for a lapping of turf over, and wedging of earth on each side of, the top of the tile. In the case of a 5-inch-wide drain at bottom, the smallest size of tile, $2\frac{3}{4}$ inches wide inside, must be used, as only $\frac{3}{8}$ of an inch would be left on each side of that width of tile. I am aware, that to press the tile into the drain, made tight to fit it, without a tile-sole, is a very common practice amongst drainers; but the practice of pressing hard against the sides of the drain is, in my opinion, objectionable, inasmuch as it is not the hard tile, but the free side of the drain, that draws the water from the land; and to press a hard substance like a tile against the earth in a *shallow* cut, is very like an attempt to curtail the extent of drawing surface. The inducement to use such expedients would be greatly removed, were soles made to suit each description of tile; and, what would be still better, were the sizes of tiles more limited in their range, and more uniformly alike; for as at present made, a great diversity of sizes exist throughout the country, in the area of vertical section as well as in length, so that the prices quoted afford no true criterion of their intrinsic worth

(964.) Soles are usually made flat, but Mr Boyle makes them *curved;* not because theyare better suitedfor the purpose, but merely because they are more easily dried in the sheds; but a curved sole is objectionable, as it is more difficult to form a smooth bed for it to lie upon, and it is more apt to break when it happens not to be firmly laid upon its bed than a flat sole.

(965.) As to *tiles*, their perfect form is thus well described by Mr Boyle: "All tiles should be a *fourth* higher than wide; the top rather quickly turned, and the sides nearly perpendicular. Tiles which are made to spread out at the lower edge and flat on the top, are weak, and bad for conveying water. Some people prefer tiles with flanges instead of soles; but if placed, even in a drain with a considerably hard bottom, the mouldering of the subsoil by the currents of air and water causes them to sink and get deranged."* Tiles should be smooth on the surface, heavy, firm, and ring like cast-iron when struck with the knuckle. They should be so strong when set, as to allow a man not only to stand, but to leap upon them without breaking. The introduction of machinery into the manufacture of drain-tiles, by compressing the clay, and working it thoroughly in a pug-mill to prepare it for being compressed, has greatly tended to increase the strength of tiles. I have seen drain-tiles so rough, spongy, crooked, and thin, as to be shivered to pieces by a night's frost when laid down beside the drain. The use of machinery has caused a great deal more clay to be put into them, and their greater substance has been the cause of improvement in the construction of kilns, in which they are now burned to a uniform texture, as well as some avoidance of breakage in the manufacture, by all which, of course, their cost is lessened. An under-burnt as well as an over-burnt tile is bad, the former being spongy and absorbing water, and ultimately falling down; and the latter is so brittle, as to break when accidentally struck against any object.

(966.) The *length* of drain-tiles varies in different parts of the country. Mr Boyle's are 13 inches; the Duke of Portland's, in Ayrshire, and Mr Beart's, Godmanchester, Hertfordshire, 12 inches; and those from the Marquis of Tweeddale's machine, 14 inches, when burnt. If the price is the same per 1000, of course, the 14-inch tile is cheaper than the 12-inch; but otherwise, the 12-inch is the handiest article in the manufacture, as being less apt to waste in handling, and twist when in the kiln; and their number is much more easily calculated in any given length of drain. The following table shews the numbers of tiles required for an imperial acre, of the different lengths made, and placed at the stated distances.

* Prize Essays of the Highland and Agricultural Society, vol. xii. p. 20.

	12 in.	13 in.	14 in.	15 in.	
Drains at 12 feet apart require	3630	3351	3111	2904	per acre.
... 15	2904	2681	2489	2323	...
... 18	2420	2234	2074	1936	...
... 21	2074	1914	1777	1659	...
... 24	1815	1675	1556	1452	...
... 27	1613	1480	1383	1291	..
... 30	1452	1340	1245	1162	...
... 33	1320	1218	1131	1056	...
... 3	1210	1117	1037	968	...

The numbers of each length of tile required at intermediate distances can easily be calculated from these data.

(967.) I give here a representation of a well formed drain-tile, and how tiles should be set on soles, as in fig. 178, where *a* and *b* are two 12-inch

Fig. 178.

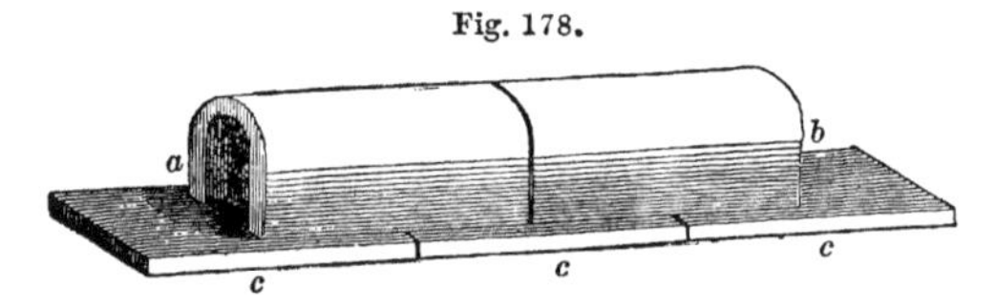

THE DRAIN-TILES PROPERLY SET UPON TILE-SOLES.

tiles, of the correct shape described in paragraph (965.), by Mr Boyle. They are represented as set upon the sole-tiles *c*; and to ensure a continuation of the same relation between tile and sole, the former should stand upon part of two of the latter, making the joinings of the tiles intermediate with those of the soles, the latter being also 12 inches in length. The drain-tiles used for draining the estate of Netherby in Cumberland, belonging to Sir James Graham, Bart., and represented in vol. vii. p. 392 of the Prize Essays of the Highland and Agricultural Society, are more pointed in the arch than these; but, on that account, are not so strong in the shoulder to bear a weight upon them. It is the practice of some tile-drainers to put a ½ sole under every joining of 2 tiles, leaving the intermediate space of the bottom without any sole, imagining that this will ensure sufficient steadiness to tiles on what they call hard clay, whilst only half the number of soles are used; but I hope I have said enough on the *hardness* of clay when in contact with water, for you to avoid so precarious a practice.

(968.) There is a mode of joining tiles in drains that meet one another, that deserves attention. The usual practice is to break a piece off the corner of 1 or 2 main-drain tiles, where the tiles of the common drains should be connected with them. In breaking off corners, there is risk of breaking the entire tile; and, no doubt, many are broken when subjected to this treatment. Another plan is to set 2 main-drain tiles so far asunder as the inside width of a common-drain tile, and the opening on the other side of the tiles, if not occupied in the same manner by the tiles of another drain, is filled up with pieces of broken tiles or stones, or any other hard substance. It is possible that the broken piece of tile, so placed, may be farther broken or dislodged by the returning of the earth and the action of moles, which may push in earth at that part, and render all above it useless. This is perhaps a better plan than running the risk of breaking a number of tiles, and, after all, failing in making the opening suitable for the reception of the adjoining drain-tiles. Both plans, however, are highly objectionable, and should never be resorted to where tiles, formed for the purpose of receiving others in their sides can be procured. Mr Boyle of Ayr makes main-drain tiles with openings on purpose to receive the shouldered end of the furrow-tiles;* and to answer a similar purpose in particular situations, where such tiles cannot be conveniently joined, he makes ½ and ¼ lengths of main and furrow tiles, which may be so arranged in regard to one another's position, as to conjoin the openings of both at the same place. Fig. 179 represents the mode of joining a common drain with a main-drain tile, having an opening in its side. The common tile *b* is not inserted entirely into the main-drain tile *a*, but only placed against it, with a small shoulder, that the openings of both tiles may be always in conjunction.

Fig. 179.

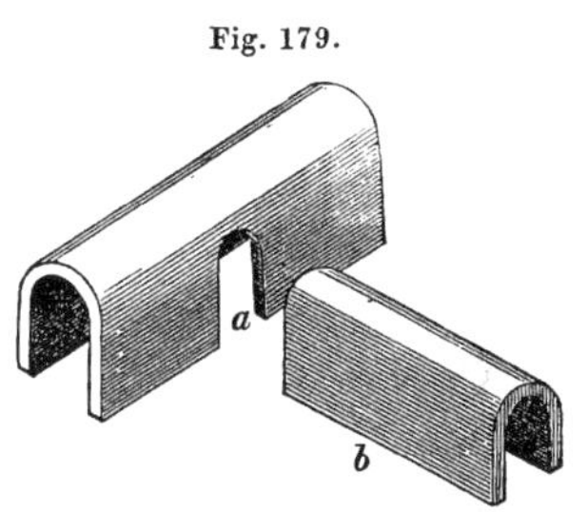

THE JUNCTION OF A COMMON TILE WITH A MAIN DRAIN ONE.

(969.) The *outlet* forms the end of the main drain, and its proper place deserves serious consideration. There should be a decided fall from the outlet, whether it is affected by natural or artificial means. If it be very small, and I have already stated (925.) that a small fall is all that is requisite, that is, 1 foot in 150 feet, or 3 feet in the mile, as indicated by the spirit level, the open ditch into which the main drain issues should be scoured deep enough for the purpose, even for a considerable distance; and when this expedient is adopted, it will be requisite to see every year that the outlet is kept open; and the ditch scoured as often as necessary for the purpose.

(970.) It is a frequent charge of neglect against farmers, that they allow open ditches almost to fill up before they are again scoured out, and a not unfrequent excuse for the neglect is, that scouring of ditches

* See Prize Essays of the Highland and Agricultural Society, vol. xii. Plate I., for figure of this tile.

to any extent incur considerable labour and expense. No doubt they do, and no wonder, since so much work has to be done, when it is done. Were the ditches scoured out when they actually required it, nay every year, if that is found necessary for the welfare of stock, fences, or drains, so little expense would be incurred at one time, as to remove every complaint against the labour as a burden; but much better, in every case where it can be done, to incur the expense at once of converting an open ditch into a covered drain, than grudge the expense of keeping it in a proper state.

(971.) Should the fall from the mouth of the main drain to a river be too small, and there be risk, at times, of the overflowings of the river sending back-water into the drain, the drain should be carried down as far by the side of the river as will secure a sufficient fall for the outlet. Rather be at the expense of carrying the drain *under* a mill-course or rivulet than permit back-water to enter it.

(972.) A *spirit level*, such as fig. 180, I have found a very convenient instrument for ascertaining such a point, and generally for taking levels in fields. It is furnished with eye-sights *a b*, and when in use is placed into a framing of brass, which operates as a spring to adjust it to the level position *d*, by the action of the large headed brass screw *c*. A stud is affixed to the framing, and pushed firmly into a gimblet hole in the top of the short rod *e*, which is pushed or driven into the ground at the spot from whence the level is desired to be ascertained. I need scarcely mention that the height of the eye-sight from the ground is deducted from the height of observation, and which quantity is easily obtained by having the rod marked off in inches and feet; but I may mention that you should use this instrument in all cases of draining on level ground, even where you are confident that you know the fall of the ground, for the eye is a very deceitful monitor for informing you of the levelness of ground. In one case of my own, I was pretty sure by the eye that the outlet to a division of drains in a field should fall, at some yards off, into an open ditch, which constantly contained spring water. The contractor of the drains was of the same opinion. On testing with the spirit level, however, we found that the bottom of the outlet would have been 8 inches below

Fig. 180.

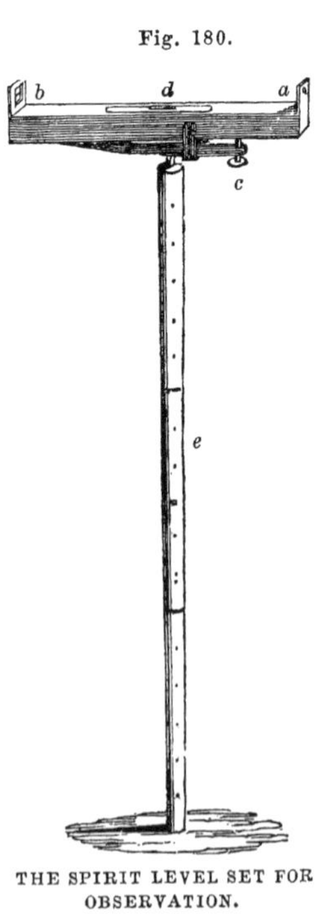

THE SPIRIT LEVEL SET FOR OBSERVATION.

the bottom of the ditch instead of above it. As, in this particular case, it would have occasioned a cutting of 200 yards to get a proper fall for the outlet in another direction, I caused a narrow well to be sunk on the spot, 8 feet deep, to the stratum of gravel below, and on being filled with stones, the gravel absorbed all the water from the drains. Such a spirit level, well finished, costs 15s. When not in use, the framing is concealed, and the spirit-tube protected by a movable cover; and the whole instrument, being only 8 inches in length, $1\frac{3}{4}$ inches deep, and 1 inch broad, and light withal, can be easily carried in the pocket, whilst its rod may be used as a staff.

(973.) It may happen that, through the undulatory nature of the ground, more than one outlet will be required to clear a field of water, that is, one division of drains may be let more easily out in one place, and another division more easily in another. In such a case, it should be well considered whether both outlets should be joined together or carried away separately, the latter being the less objectionable mode.

(974.) The *cutting* of the main drain should be *entirely finished* before the tiles are laid in it; and immediately after it is finished, it should be measured with the drain-gauge, fig. 155, to ascertain if it contains the specified dimensions and fall.

(975.) Whilst the earth is throwing out towards the narrowest side of the head-ridge, that is, next the fence, the carts should be laying down the tiles and soles along the open side next the field; or they can be laid down before the drain is begun to be opened, and after its line of direction has been fixed. To be certain that the number of tiles and soles are laid down, they should each be placed end to end respectively along the whole line, the soles nearest the drain lying against the tiles, amongst which, of course, broken ones are not counted, though a sole fractured in two will lay down well enough in a good bed between two whole ones. The tiles with the opening in the side, along with its conjunctive small tile, fig. 179, should be laid down at the distances determined on for the small drains to enter the main drain. These preliminary arrangements should be carefully attended to, or much inconvenience may be occasioned in carrying tiles and soles to and fro to the person who lays them in. It is necessary beforehand to instruct the ploughman who is to lay them down out of the cart, of the plan, as some mistake will inevitably ensue, if he is merely told to lay down the tiles and soles by the drain; for few ploughmen reflect on the consequences of what they are doing. If, by inadvertence to these minutiæ of practice, more or fewer tiles or soles are laid down than required, part of the time of the yoking of a pair of horses is lost in laying them down, and part of another is also lost in leading them away to another place, while the unused tiles are in danger of being broken by frequent lifting, and all this waste of time arising from want of forethought.

(976.) The *person* entrusted with the laying of the soles and tiles into the drains, should be one who has been long accustomed to that kind of work, and otherwise a good workman, possessing judgment and common sense. If he is not a hired servant, he should be paid by day's-wages, that he may have no temptation to execute the work ill; and to enable him to do it well let him take even more time than you imagine is necessary, especially at first, provided he executes what he does to the satisfaction of his employer. You will soon be able to ascertain how much work of this kind a man should do in a day, according to the circumstances of the case, and you can then judge whether he has been putting off his time, and admonish and encourage him accordingly.

(977.) This person should remain constantly at the bottom of the drains; and, to enable him to do so, he should have an *assistant*, to hand him the materials from the ground. The best assistant he can have, in my opinion, is a female field-worker. Such a one not only receives cheaper wages, but is dexterous in handling light materials, and quite able to lift tiles, soles, and turf easily.

(978.) Immediately before proceeding to *lay the sole-tiles*, the man should remove any wet sludgy matter from the bottom of the drain with a scoop, fig. 171, and dry earth and small stones can be removed with a narrow draw-hoe, as in fig. 181, with a 2-feet handle *b*, and

Fig. 181.

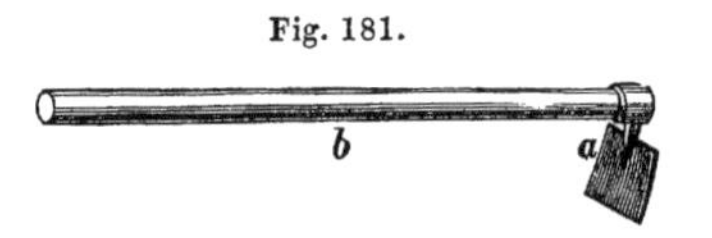

THE NARROW DRAW-HOE FOR DRAINS.

Fig. 182.

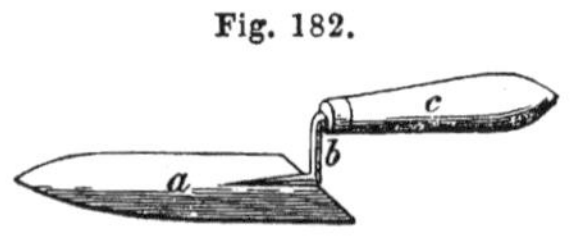

THE TROWEL FOR DRAINS.

mouth *a* 3 inches in width, cost 1s. The sole is firmly laid and imbedded a little into the earth. Should it ride upon any point, such as a small stone or hard lump of earth, that should be removed; and a very convenient instrument for the purpose, and otherwise making the bed for the soles, is a mason's narrow trowel, as in fig. 182, 7 inches long in the blade *a*, 5 inches in the handle *c*, and 1½ inch at *b*, and if of cast-steel will cost 2s., of common 1s. 3d. If a single sole has been determined to be laid on the ground, as in fig. 178, or a double one side by side, as in fig. 160, he lays them accordingly. After laying 3 soles in length, he examines to see if they are straight in the face, and neither rise nor fall more than the fall of the drain. As a safe guide to him, in cases where the fall is not decidedly cognizable by the senses, a mason's plumb-level, such as fig. 183, will be found a convenient instrument.

Fig. 183.

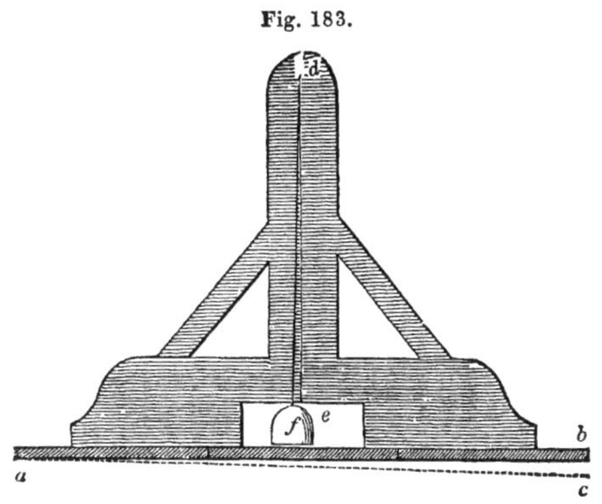

THE DRAINER'S PLUMB-LEVEL.

A mark at which the plummet-line *d f* will subtend an angle with the plumb-line *d e*, equal to the angle of the fall of the drain, should be made on the top of the opening *e*, which, in this case, may be supposed to be where the plumb *f* at present hangs; by which arrangement it is demonstrable that the angle *e d f* is always equal to the angle *b a c*, which is the angle of inclination of the fall. The breadth of the sole or soles, as the case may be, should occupy the exact width of the drain, and in the case of a main drain the soles are each 10 inches broad.

(979.) After 3 soles are thus placed, 2 tiles are set upon them, as represented in fig. 178, that is, the tiles *a* and *b* are so placed as that their joinings shall meet on the intermediate spaces *between* the joinings of the soles *c*; and this is done for the obvious reason, that, should any commotion disturb one of the soles, neither of the tiles, partially standing upon it, should be disturbed. In ordinary cases of water in a main drain, a tile of 4 inches wide and 5 inches high inside is a good size; and from this size they vary to $5\frac{3}{4}$ inches in width and $6\frac{1}{2}$ inches in height. Although the size of the tile varies, that of the main drain sole is always the same, that is, 10 inches wide and 12 inches long. Taking the useful tile of 4 inches in width and 5 inches in height, its thickness being $\frac{3}{4}$ inch, there will be a space left in each side of $2\frac{1}{4}$ inches.

(980.) The *covering*, of whatever substance, should be laid in a row or in heaps along the line of the tiles. Turf is the best covering, and it is put over the tiles saddle-wise. If the turf were cut 12 inches broad and 18 inches in length, it would just lap over the size of tile mentioned above, and rest its end upon the sole on both sides; and, if it be from 2 to 2½ inches in thickness, the small space left on each side between the turf and the walls of the drain would be filled up. It is as easy to cut the turfs of the exact sizes required as any other, by rutting off the swarded ground in regular breadths; and it would be as easy to cast the turfs in regular oblongs, as in the irregular pieces usually raised according to the whim of the spadesman. The old *flauchter-spade* of Scotland has long been used to cast turf, but it is a rude instrument at best, and not nearly so good as the common spade for a neat job. When cast, the turfs should be laid one above another in neat bundles of 3 or 4 turfs, which can be easily taken up, and placed safely into the cart, and not thrown singly in, to the risk of their being torn, broken, or put out of shape on being doubled up. They should be as carefully taken out of the cart, in the same bundles they were put in, and if not used immediately, should be put in large bundles to keep them supple and moist; but not so kept a long time, in case of their heating and fermenting. If used in summer, in very dry weather, some water should be thrown upon them to keep them moist, but water in winter might injure their texture by frost. If, on the other hand, they are used immediately, they should be laid down along the outside of the tiles, not in a single row like them, because taking them from the cart and lifting them up again is apt to tear them, but in the small bundles, which are placed as far asunder as the space the turfs would occupy were they laid singly along in line. Judging from the usual treatment which it receives, turf seems to be very little valued, being crumpled up, thrown down, and kicked about, until it becomes much broken and bruised, when it is not nearly so fit for a *covering for tile* as when raised from the ground. I need scarcely add, that smooth turf is much better than tufty or heathery clods. Good turf is an expensive article, and not to be obtained every where. A man will cast from 4 to 6 cart loads, of 1 ton each, per day, according to the smoothness and softness of the ground. Its usual thickness is about 3 inches, when 1 square yard will weigh about 54 lb., and of course 1 ton will cover about 40 square yards, or 40 roods of 6 yards with turfs of 1 foot by 1½ foot. In the country carriage is the heaviest charge against turf; in towns it is charged from 8s. to 20s. a ton, and 8s. per square yard is charged for casting, carting, and laying turf for greens and borders.

(981.) On being handed to him, the man lays the turf, grass side down, over the tiles in a firm manner, taking care to cause the joinings of the turf to meet as near the middle of the tiles as practicable, and not over the joinings. Were the turf cut of the same breadth as that of the tiles used, the covering of a drain would proceed not only rapidly, but neatly and satisfactorily. He takes care not to displace the tiles in the least when the turf is being put over; and to secure the tiles in their respective places, he puts earth firmly between the covering and the sides of the drain as high as the turf over the tile. This earth is obtained from the soil that was thrown out; and if the subsoil is a strong clay, the surface soil is the best, but a porous subsoil anwers the purpose. When all these things which I have described have been done, the drain will appear like the small drain, fig. 184, where the sole and the tile set upon it, the turf wrapped round the top of the tile, and the stuffing of earth on each side of the tile may all be easily observed.

(982.) The preparations for the junction with the small drains should be made during the completion of the main drain, for if the main tiles are taken up when the small drains are forming, in order to accommodate the small tiles, they will run the risk of being displaced, and of otherwise disturbing the current of water when it is to run in it. Whichever plan is adopted for letting in the small tiles, and be it ever remembered that the tiles with the open side are the best for the purpose, the man should never forget to make the openings at the stated distances the small drains should enter, and for this purpose he should be provided with a 6-feet rod, marked off in feet and inches, to measure the distances as near as he can, in regard to the fitting of the tiles. The covering of turf should, of course, not be put over the openings left for the small tiles, but the openings should not be left wholly unprotected after the main drain is finished, in case any thing should thrust earth or any other substance into the tile-duct, that might close up or otherwise injure the drain. A bundle of straw, or rather a turf, until the small drains are connected with them, will be sufficient to protect the openings against injury of this kind.

(983.) The *mouth of the main drain* at its outlet, whether in a ditch or river, should be protected with masonry, and dry masonry will do. The last sole, which should be of stone, should project as far beyond the mouth as to throw the water either directly upon the bottom, or upon masonry built up by the side of the ditch. The masonry should be founded below the bottom of the ditch, and built in a perpendicular recess in its side, with the outer face sloping in a line with the slope of the ditch. The sloping face can be made either straight, which will allow the water to slip down it into the ditch, or like steps of a stair, over which the water will descend with broken force. It would be proper to have an iron grating on the end of the outlet, to prevent vermin creeping up the drain; not that they can injure tiles while alive, but in creeping too far up, they may die, and cause for a time a stagnation of water above them in the drain.

(984.) If the ground fall uniformly towards the main drain over the whole field, the small drains should be proceeded with immediately after the main drain is finished ; but should any hollow ground occur in the field too deep for its waters to find their way direct to the main drain, then a *sub-main drain* should be made along the lowest part of the hollow, to receive all the drainage of the ground around it, in order to transmit it to the main drain. The size of sub-main drains is determined by the extent of drainage they have to effect, and should they have as much to do as the main, they should have the same capacity, but if not, they should have less.

(985.) Sub-main drains are made in all respects in the same manner as main drains; but there may be this peculiarity in regard to them, that they will most probably have to receive small drains on both sides, on account of the position they may occupy in the area of a field, when they will require just double the number of tiles with openings in the side than the main. In order to avoid the interference of sediment from opposite small drains, these should not enter the sub-main directly opposite to each other, nor should their ends enter at right angles, but at an acute angle.

(986.) The sub-main drain should be as far below the small drains as the main itself, when it receives the small drains directly, and for the same reasons; and the main should be as far below the sub-main as the latter is below the small drains. The simple way to effect both these purposes is, to make the main drain deeper after its junction with the sub-main.

(987.) There is nothing now to prevent you proceeding with the *small drains*. In a field having a uniform surface, there is no difficulty or irregularity of work to be encountered in bringing the drains directly down the inclined ground into the main drain. Where sub-mains are employed in particular hollows, the ground comprehending the drainage belonging to each hollow should be distinctly marked off from the rest, that no confusion in the direction of the other small drains may ensue in the execution of the work. These markings should be made in the *water-shed of the ground*, from which the fall tends towards each sub-main, if more than one is required, and it may also tend towards the main drain. The markings can be made with pins driven in the lines determined by the water-shed.

(988.) In commencing the small drains from a fence on one side of the field, supposing that the ridges are 15 feet wide, and keeping in mind that, if the soil of the field is not strong clay, the drains need not be formed in the open furrows, it is requisite to measure the distance of the first drain from the fence, whatever that fence may be, at 16 feet. This space of 16 feet gives 2 feet for the fence-side, 14 feet from the fence-side to the drain, and one foot beyond the drain for the open furrow of the 15-feet ridge. Keeping the distance of every other drain from each other at the breadth of one ridge of 15 feet, or at any other multiple of that breadth, it is clear that every drain will fall within one foot of an open furrow. If the subsoil draws slowly, the drains should *not exceed* 15 *feet asunder*, and the *depth*, I should say, *not less than* 3 *feet.*

(989.) I know it is a common impression among farmers, that if a subsoil cannot draw water, there is no use of making drains *in* it, and this opinion I conceive to be quite correct in regard to pure clay subsoils, which cannot draw water at all. But the view I take of the matter is this, that pure clay subsoils are very limited in extent, and that many clays which *seem* quite impervious may draw water notwithstanding. Admitting that the subsoil draws water at all, which is the supposition in the present case, it is clear, that the larger the area is extended for drawing it, the more water will be drawn into the drain. Now, a large area can only be secured by making drains deep and close together; and in the case supposed above, it appears to me that 3 feet in depth, with 15 feet asunder, will not give a greater area than is requisite for drawing water out of such ground. When, on the other hand, the subsoil is free, and discharges water as freely, so large an area is not required to dry the subsoil, and drains of less depth and at greater distance will answer the same purpose as in the other case, such as 30 inches in depth and 30 feet asunder. You must endeavour to make the depths and distances of the small drains suit the nature of the subsoil, for it is impossible for me to lay down here any absolute rule in a matter which admits of such diversity of character.

(990.) Small drains, as well as mains and sub-mains, should be completely cast out, gauged, and examined for the fall, before being attempted to be filled up; and the materials for doing so should be laid down beside them, as well as in the case of mains. The tiles for small drains are smaller than for mains and sub-mains, being 3 inches wide and 4 inches high, inside measurement, which may be considered a large tile in places where those of $2\frac{3}{4}$ inches wide by $3\frac{1}{2}$ inches high are used; but so small ones are not made everywhere. There is this consideration in regard to the size of tiles which should be kept in view, that a substantial tile will have the chance of lasting much longer than a slight one, and the probability is, that the larger ones are the more substantial, which, however, may not actually be the case, but it is proper to examine whether they are heavy and firm, before you purchase your tiles. Be guided in your choice of them more on account of substantiality than cheapness, which, as I have said before, is quite of secondary consideration when brought into comparison with durability. Soles will also be required for small drains, for don't give credence to the absurd assumption, that clay will retain its hardness at the bottom of a drain, because it happened to be hard when first laid open to the day. Soles for small drains are of different breadths, being 5 inches at one place, and 7 inches at another: the former, 5 inches, I should conceive *too narrow* for most purposes; for take even the narrowest tiles that are made, $2\frac{3}{4}$ inches inside—these are moulded at 6-8ths inch thick, and allowing them to shrink 1-8th in the kiln, their thickness will be $1\frac{1}{4}$ inch; the outside breadth of the tile being thus 4 inches, leaves only $1\frac{1}{4}$ inch to divide between the two sides of the tile on a 5 inch sole, or just $\frac{1}{2}$ an inch on each side, a small enough space certainly. But as most soles for small drains are made of the same breadth, take a 3-inch tile, and it will be found by the same mode of calculation that only $\frac{1}{4}$ inch on each side of a 5-inch sole will be left, which is a much too narrow space to afford perfect steadiness to the tile. I would prefer the 7-inch soles as made in Ayrshire, and, of course, the breadth of the bottom of the drain should also be 7 inches. In other respects, the filling of the small drains is conducted in the same manner as the mains and sub-mains, and they are finished as represented by fig. 184.

Fig. 184.

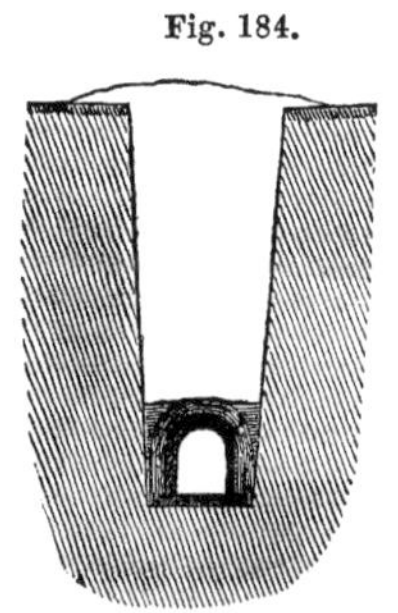

THE SMALL TILE-DRAIN.

(991.) While casting out the bottom of the end of each small drain, care should be taken in communicating it with the main or sub-main with which it is to be connected, that no displacement of tiles takes place in either; and when the bottom is cleared out, the turf or small bundle of straw left in the openings of the sides of the tiles is removed, and the opening examined, and any extraneous matter that may have got into the tiles removed. The places for the entrance of the small drain tiles having been prepared while constructing the main and sub-mains, there will be no difficulty of effecting the junction between the respective sorts of drains. Thus one small drain after another is finished, until the field, having been begun at one side, is furnished with drains by the time the other is reached. The small drain connecting the tops of all the small drains along the upper end of the field, should not be neglected. (941.)

(992.) The next procedure is the *filling up of the drains with the earth that was thrown out of them*, which is returned either with the spade or the plough, or both. When drains are furnished with stones, the plough may be used from the first, giving it as much *land* for the first bout or two as it can work with. If the earth has been thrown out on both sides, a strong furrow on each side of the top of the drain will fill in a considerable quantity of the earth; but, as the earth is generally thrown out on one side of the drain, and the plough can only advance the earth towards the drain while going in one direction, that is, going every other landing *empty*, or without a furrow, a more expeditious mode of levelling the ground, which, in the considerable labour of returning the earth into all the small drains of a field, is a matter of some importance, is to cleave down the mound of earth thrown out, and then take in a breadth of land on both sides of the drain, and gather it up twice or thrice towards the middle of the drain, which will constitute a prepared feering, after which the harrows will make the ground sufficiently level. This species of work, however, is only required when much earth has been thrown out, and thrown a distance from the drain, in deep draining; but in thorough-draining, what is accomplished by the plough is done with much less trouble. When the plough alone is used for this purpose, the first two furrows are taken round the mouth of the drain, and fall into it with considerable force; and, where tiles alone are used, such a fall of earth may be apt to break or displace them; and even the steadiest horses, which should only be employed at this work, run the risk of slipping in a hind foot into the drain, which, in attempting to recover, may be overstrained; and such an accident, trifling as it may seem, may be attended with serious injury to the animal. The safest mode, therefore, both for horses and tiles, is, in all cases, to put the first portion of earth into the drain with the spade, and this provision can be made in the agreement with the contractor; and there is this advantage attending the use of the spade that a better choice can be made, if desired, of the earth to be returned, the surface earth may first be put in before the poorer subsoil. (944.)

(993.) In regard to the quality of the earth which is employed to fill up the drains, some considerations are requisite. All *deep* drains, whether furnished with stones or tiles, should receive their supply of water from *below*, and not immediately from above through the soil; and all drains that receive their supply of water in this manner should be denominated deep drains, in reference to the nature of their functions, whatever may be their respective depths.

(994.) Were drains *entirely* filled with loose mould, or other loose materials, it is evident that the rain, percolating directly through them, will arrive in the drain loaded with as many of the impurities that the soil may contain as it could carry along with it in its downward course; but a primary object with drainers is to prevent impurities getting into the ducts of drains, because in time they might either collect in quantities in the ducts, or fill up the interstices between the stones; and the smaller the stones were broken, their upper stratum at least would the more easily be rendered inoperative as a drain. To prevent one and all of these mischances, the practicable way is to return the clayey subsoil into the drain, where it will again soon consolidate, and resist the direct gravity of rain.

(995.) Keeping these distinctions in view, and applying them first to the case of strong clay soil, such as in the Carse of Gowrie, which does not draw water at all, were they filled up above the tiles with pure clay, the ultimate effect would be, that the duct would remain open, but no water would ever enter it. To make them draw at all, there must loose materials be put above the tiles, within 2 or 3 inches of the plane upon which the sole of the plough moves; and to obtain the greatest depth of loose materials for such drains, they should be made in the open furrows. As they cannot draw but through the loose materials, and are, in fact, covered ditches, they must receive their supply of water like any other ditch from above; but here the analogy ceases, for instead of receiving their water direct from the top like a ditch, they should receive it by percolation through the ploughed soil, and when the water has descended through the soil, deprived of most of its impurities, it meets the retentive subsoil across the whole area of the ridge, upon which it moves under the arable soil until it meets with the loose materials in the drains, by which it is taken down into the ducts to be conveyed away. The loose materials may be gravel, sand, peaty earth, scoriæ from furnaces, refuse tanners' bark, and such like.

(996.) In a subsoil that draws only a little water, were the clayey subsoil returned immediately above the *tiles*, it would have the effect of counteracting the purpose for which the drains were made, because it would curtail the drawing surface to only the height of the tiles themselves. The method, therefore, to fill such drains is to put loose materials immediately above the tiles, to a height not so far as in the case of pure clay drains, but to within ½ a foot of the plane of the plough's sole-shoe. Were the drains in such a subsoil, however, filled with *stones*, the case would be different, for these would secure a sufficient drawing surface, and the clayey subsoil may be returned immediately on their top with perfect propriety.

(997.) In the case of a free drawing subsoil to the bottom of the drain, the most retentive portion of the earth may be returned immediately above even *tiles*, for such a subsoil would still draw the moisture towards them; and were *stones* used, there would be left ample room for drawing with the most retentive part of the earth returned above them. But should the part of the drain occupied by the tiles or stones be of strong impervious clay, although the soil above it be of the best drawing materials, as much of the loose subsoil should be placed above the tiles or stones as would give an easy access to the water, and all the space above that may consist of the strongest part of the clay.

(998). The general rule, then, for filling the drains with the earth that has been thrown out of them is, that, with the exception of strong clay soils,—the drains in which should be filled with porous materials, that the water on the surface may descend through them into the duct below, and be thence carried away,—that, with this exception, every kind of drain should be filled near its top with the strongest soil afforded by the drain, in order to *prevent the descent of the water into the drain by the top*, but rather that the water shall seek its way through the ploughed ground, and thence by the porous materials above the duct, and under the clay put in above them into the duct at the bottom. Through such a channel of filtration the water will have every chance of entering the duct in a comparatively pure state.

(999.) But the best mode, in my opinion, of draining land of any that has yet been described, has to be brought before your notice, and that is by the *union of stones and tiles* in the same drain. This method is represented in fig. 185, where a tile *a* rests on a sole; small stones are packed around the tile by the hand until they cover it as at *b*; the remaining small stones *c* are put in by any of the methods described above, but especially by the drain-screen; a covering is either put above them or small stones beaten down, as in the case of the stone drain, with the beater, and the earth returned upon them in either of the modes just described. The width of the bottom is 7 inches the width of a good sole, width of the top 12 inches, depth 2½ feet, composed of 18 inches of earth, and 12 inches to the top of the covering of the stones. This drain is con-

Fig. 185.

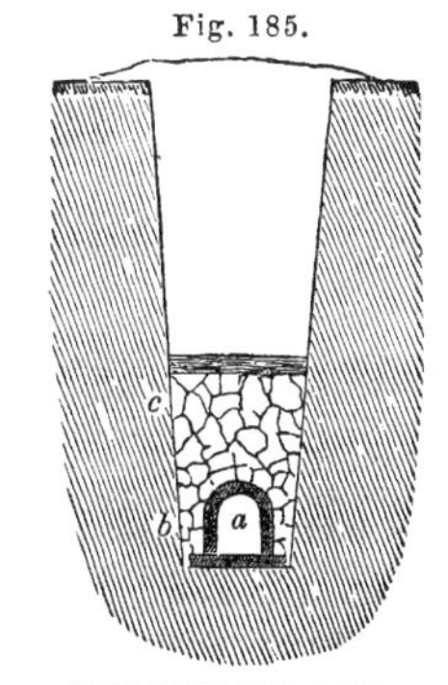

THE TILE AND STONE DRAIN.

structed very similarly to the tile drains that have been described, by first laying the sole at the bottom and the tile upon it; but instead of covering the tile immediately with turf, small stones are packed by the hand on both sides until they cover its top. As these stones should be packed in as the laying of the tiles proceeds, they should be laid down in heaps, immediately after the tiles have been laid down, as near the drain as possible, so as they may be filled in baskets by the assistant, and handed down in them to the man in the drain. Two baskets are required for this purpose, one to be filled by the assistant when the other is emptying by the drainer. In filling up with stones afterwards to their proper height as to *c*, I would be afraid of using the drain-screen at first, in case the fall of the first stones upon those which were laid in by the hand, as at *b*, should by any chance fracture the *tiles* below them. I would rather fill up a few yards of the drain as high as required by the hand, and then use the drain-screen to let fall the stones upon the end of those previously filled in, from which they could be shovelled (fig. 38.) or raked (fig. 174.) down gently upon the stones over the tiles; or the stones could be filled in by the hand at first so high, while laying those at *b*, as to remove all danger from those falling in small quantities from the screen. The filling in from the drain-screen and carts should not be proceeded with until as much of the drain has been laid with tiles and packed in with stones by the hand, as to employ *at least* 2 single horse carts for one yoking, and should the weather seem favourable, not until that number of horses can be employed a whole day, because otherwise the time of the horses would be wasted. If the draining is of such an extent as to keep a pair of horses thus constantly employed, so much the better. In such a case, other hands than those employed in cutting the drain and laying the tiles should be employed in filling in the upper layer of stones with the screen, and beating down the small riddlings as a covering upon them. On the earth being returned into the drain the operation is completed.

(1000.) This construction of drain is declared by every writer on and practitioner of draining, to be the *ne plus ultra* of the art, though I believe very few farmers have adopted it, not because there can the slightest objection be urged against it, but because, in cases where stones have to be quarried and broken, it is an expensive mode, and in other cases stones cannot be obtained at all. This last reason is a very good one, but that of the expense must fall to the ground where there is abundance of stones, as the advantage derived from their use along with the tile will be more than counterbalanced by the additional cost. The durability and efficiency of such a drain is undoubted. It is a perfect piece of work, inasmuch as the duct formed of the tile and sole presents the smoothest passage imaginable for carrying off water, and it is proof against the efforts of vermin; whilst the stones not only secure the duct in its place, but impart durability to the whole structure, which at the same time presents an extensive area to the subsoil. What other property that a good drain should have does this one not possess?

(1001.) It may be satisfactory to you to have a general idea of thorough draining a field by a sketch of a ground plan, which is represented in fig. 186, where *a b* is the main drain formed in the lowest head-ridge; and if the field were of a uniform surface, the drains would run parallel to one another from the top to the bottom into the main drain, as those do from *a* to *c*, connected as they should be at the top with the drain *d e* running along the upper head-ridge. But as there may be inequalities in the ground, a very irregular surface cannot be drained in this manner, and must therefore be provided with sub-main drains, as *f g*

Fig. 186.

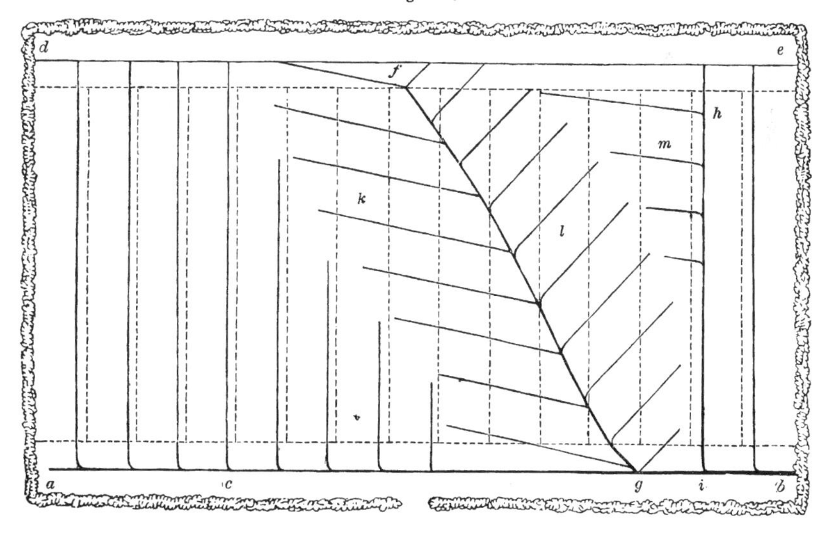

A PLAN OF A THOROUGH-DRAINED FIELD.

and *h i*, which are each connected with a system of drains belonging to itself, and which may differ in character from each other, as *f g* with a large double set *k l* in connection with it, and *h i* with only a small single set *m*; the sub-main *f g* is supposed to run up the lowest part of a pretty deep hollow in the ground, and the drains *k* and *l* on either side of it are made to run down the faces of the acclivities as nearly at right angles to the sub-main as the nature of the inclination of the ground will allow, so as always to preserve the natural tendency of water to find its way down the hollow. There is also a supposed fall of the ground from the height above *l* towards *h*, which causes the drain at *m* to run down and fall into what would be a common drain *h i*, were it not, from this circumstance, obliged to be converted into a sub main. The sub-main *f g* may be made as large as the main drain *a b*, as both have much to do; but the sub-main *h i* may be made comparatively smaller, and not larger, from the top of the field, than a common drain, until it reaches the point *h*, where the collateral drains begin to join it. The main drain should be made larger below *g* to *i* than above it, and still larger from *i* to *b*, which is its outlet. It will be observed, that all the common drains along *a* and *c*, and at *l* and *m*, have their ends curved, those at *k* not requiring that assistance, as they enter more obliquely into the main, from the position of the slope of the ground. The dotted lines represent the upper and lower head-ridges, and the open furrows of the ridges of the field; and it will be observed that the drains are not made to run in the open furrows—that is, the black lines in conjunction with the dotted, but along the furrow brows of the ridges. This is done with the view of not confounding the open furrows and drains in the figure; but it is a plan which may be followed with propriety in subsoils otherwise than of strong clay; that is, of a light loam resting on a rather retentive subsoil; the water falling upon which should not be drained away by the small drains receiving it through their tops, but rather by the absorption of the water towards them from below the ploughed soil, as far as the subsoil is porous. A hollow, such as that occupied by the sub-main drain *f g*, also indicates that the soil is a loam, and not strong clay. Although the ridges are supposed to be 15 feet wide, and they have been set off here at quarters of an inch, they bear no true relation to the size of the field; so that this diagram should not be considered as shewing the relative proportions of the distances betwixt the drains and the size of the field.

(1002.) The period of the rotation of cropping at which draining should be executed, requires consideration; but I believe it is now generally allowed to be best performed when the ground is in grass, and before the grass is ploughed up. There are several advantages attending this period of cropping over every other. 1. Turf can be obtained at hand for covering the tiles; and although one year's grass may not afford very good turf for the purpose, yet, if the turfs are carefully raised by the spade, and as carefully laid aside until used—not heaped upon one another to run the risk of rotting, but set down in a row with the grass-side up—and as carefully handled when about to be used, it will answer very well. In 2 or 3 years' old grass, the turf is better; and in old pasture or meadow ground, it is as good as can be procured elsewhere. At whatever age the turf is used, it should not be too rough or too thick, as it will not clap so closely over the tile in either state as it should. Sheep are the best stock for eating down the forage, and preparing the turf for this purpose. 2. Another advantage which grass-land possesses is the firm surface which it presents to cartage of materials, whether stones or tiles. If the stones are put in with the screen, the cart and barrow will pass lightly along the side of the drain; and if tiles are used, the grass forms clean ground for them to be laid down upon. 3. In grass, the filling in of the earth with the spade makes very neat work.

(1003.) When it is determined to drain the land while in grass, the *season* of the year in which the drains should be opened is thereby in a great degree determined. It would scarcely be prudent to sacrifice the pasturage in summer, and no stock should be allowed to roam about a field that is in the act of being drained, not only on account of the possibility of their injuring themselves by slipping into the drains, but of injuring the drains by breaking down their edges, fracturing the tiles, or displacing the stones. It is therefore expedient to take the use of the summer's grass; but that the operation may commence soon in autumn, the grass should be by that time eaten down bare by an extra quantity of stock. These preliminary arrangements, then, being made, and the materials laid down as long as the weather is dry and the ground hard, the draining operations may be carried on through the winter, and as far into spring as to give time for the land to be ploughed for the reception of the seed. Whether there are one or more sets of men engaged in cutting the drains, they should all work in the same field at the same time, as it invariably entails loss of time to drive materials with horses over different fields. With concentrated work, one field is drained after another, and this regularity of the order permits the eating down of the grass in succession, as regularly as the draining proceeds, so that none of the aftermath is sacrificed.

(1004.) It should be endeavoured to drain the entire division occupied by oats after lea every year, until the whole farm is gone over, which, in this way, it will be in as many years as there are years in the rotation followed. But even more land than this may be drained in any one year, if desired; for a portion of the fallow-break may be set apart for that purpose, as well as the lea, and bare-fallowed for wheat. Indeed, some farmers prefer draining in summer to any other season, because the land can then be easily carted on, every thing is done more cleanly, and the days being long, a good day's work can be done. These reasons are no doubt all correct; but unless the whole fallow-break is bare-fallowed, there cannot be drained, in this way, a large extent of ground every year; and if there be not, a long time will elapse ere the whole farm can be drained. There would be no time to drain the portions of the fallow-break occupied by potatoes and turnips, by the time these crops should be put into the ground; and it is equally inexpedient to carry on a large extent of drainage after they have been removed from the ground. At both these times, too, no advantages are derived as from summer-work; besides of its being very slovenly practice to poach ground, which draining cannot fail to occasion, after it has been dunged in the fallow-break, and prepared to undergo a whole rotation. A few drains at a particular spot may be executed after potatoes in autumn, or turnips in spring, but to no farther extent. The lea ground, therefore, presents the largest extent of surface for drainage, with the least interference with growing crops and prepared ground.

(1005.) I come now to a most important particular regarding draining, and that is its *cost*. 1. With regard to Elkington's mode, as it covers more or less of the surface of the field, its cost is usually not estimated by the *acre*, but only by the *rood* of the respective depths of drain employed; and as those depths vary from 4 to 7 feet, the cost will vary from 1s. to 2s. per rood of 6 yards, according as the subsoil is more or less difficult to labour.* 2. On the other hand, as thorough draining occupies so large a space of the surface of a field, its cost *per acre* may be ascertained; and fortunately there are sufficient data extant to satisfy the inquiries of drainers on this point.

(1006.) The great expense of executing very deep drains has been urged as an objection to the adoption of Elkington's method. "A general answer to this," however, as Mr Black truly says, in his account of the draining of the estate of Spottiswoode in Berwickshire some years ago, "might be, that the practice which is ineffectual can never be a cheap one. But even in the mere matter of cost, the balance will probably as often be found to turn in favour of the larger as of the smaller drains. If the first be larger in size, the latter must be more numerous; and a single good drain, well laid out, will be often seen to do that which a hundred minor ones would fail to effect. The chief difference of expense is in digging the drains; for, in regard to the materials of filling, it is to be observed that the larger drains are not at all filled in the same proportion to their size as the lesser; which circumstance, combined with the com-

* Stephens' Practical Drainer, p. 105; and Prize Essays of the Highland and Agricultural Society, vol. vii., p. 242.

parative smallness of their number, will, in this particular, generally shew the balance of saving in expense to be on their side. The quantity of materials indeed," and this remark is worth your serious attention, "which has been consumed in these smaller drains, in a few of the earliest improved tillage counties of Scotland, is surprising. Instances are constantly occurring, where new drains are in the course of construction, of their lines intersecting innumerable smaller drains, long since forgotten and choked up, and serving no useful purpose as conductors of water."* The smaller drains alluded to had been imperfectly formed, and this will ultimately be the fate of *all* drains that are so constructed.

(1007.) With regard to the cost of thorough draining, the account of expenses incurred by Mr Roberton I will here give in detail. The drains were placed from 30 to 36 feet apart, as the nature of the subsoil was favourable to drainage, which is equal to 70 roods of drains of 6 yards in the imperial *acre*.

Item	L.	s.	d.
Opening drains 33 inches deep and 7 inches wide at bottom, at 5½d. per rood of 6 yards,	L.1	12	1
Preparing stones, 4 inches diameter, at 4d. per ditto,	1	3	4
Carriage of stones, at 4½d. per ditto,	1	6	3½
Unloading carts and moving screen-barrow, ¾d. per ditto,	0	4	4½
Filling in earth, ¼d. per ditto,	0	1	5½
Extra expense in the main drains,	0	10	0
Per acre of 70 roods,	L.4	17	6½

Item	L.	s.	d.
Opening drains 28 inches deep and 7 inches wide at bottom, at 4d. per rood of 6 yards,	L.1	3	4
Preparing stones, at 2½d. per ditto,	0	14	7
Carriage of stones, at 2¾d. per ditto,	0	16	0½
Unloading carts and moving screen-barrow, at ½d. per ditto,	0	2	11
Filling in earth, at ¼d. per ditto,	0	1	5½
Extra expense in the main drains,	0	10	0
Per acre of 70 roods,	L.3	8	4†

(1008.) Mr Stirling of Glenbervie's expenses of draining with stones, per rood of 6 yards, are the following; the stones being supposed to be carted ½ a mile, the hire of the horse being 3s. 4d., the man's wages 1s. 8d., and that of the driver 10d., per day.

* Prize Essays of the Highland and Agricultural Society, vol. vii., p. 239.

† Ibid. vol. xiv. p. 43.

Cutting drain 30 inches deep in the furrow, 5 inches wide at bottom, and 8 inches wide at 15 inches from the surface, at (according to the soil) from $2\frac{1}{2}\frac{6}{22}$d. to $5\frac{1}{4}\frac{18}{22}$d. average $3\frac{3}{4}\frac{6}{22}$d. per *rood* of 6 yards, ...	L.0	0	$3\frac{3}{4}\frac{6}{22}$
Preparing $12\frac{9}{11}$ cubic feet of stones, screened, per rood, at 9d. per cubic yard, ...	0	0	$4\frac{1}{4}$
2 carts filling, carting, and emptying, ...	0	0	$1\frac{3}{4}\frac{12}{22}$
2 carts filling into drain with screen, ...	0	0	$0\frac{3}{4}\frac{6}{22}$
Returning earth with the plough, ...	0	0	$0\ \frac{5}{22}$
Per rood of 6 yards,	L.0	0	$10\frac{3}{4}\frac{7}{22}$

Cutting the same size of drain, and at the same cost per rood,	L.0	0	$3\frac{3}{4}\frac{6}{22}$
Preparing $12\frac{9}{11}$ cubic feet of stones, riddled at the bin, at 9d. per cubic yard, ...	0	0	$4\frac{1}{4}$
2 carts, riddling, filling, carting, and putting stones into drain, .	0	0	$2\frac{3}{4}$
Putting on flauchter-turf, and returning the earth, . . .	0	0	$0\ \frac{5}{22}$
Per rood of 6 yards,	L.0	0	$10\frac{3}{4}\frac{11}{22}$

The expense of these two sorts of drains will thus stand, per imperial acre.

Distance between the Drains, in feet.	Number of roods, per acre.	Expense per imperial acre.					
		At $10\frac{3}{4}\frac{7}{22}$d. per rood.			At $10\frac{3}{4}\frac{11}{22}$d. per rood.		
		L.	S.	D.	L.	S.	D.
14	$172.84\frac{4}{6}$	7	18	4	8	2	$5\frac{1}{2}$
16	151.25	6	18	$6\frac{1}{2}$	7	2	$1\frac{3}{4}$
18	134.42	6	3	1	6	6	3
20	121.00	5	10	10	5	13	$8\frac{1}{2}$*

(1009.) Mr Smith of Deanston's principal experience has been in stone-draining. The dimensions of his drains are 13 or 14 inches wide at top, 3 or 4 inches wide at bottom, and from 2 to $2\frac{1}{2}$ feet deep, the latter being always preferred. The cutting costs from 3d. to 5d. per rood of 6 yards, according to the hardness of the subsoil. As much sandstone as will fill a rood with broken stones can, in most circumstances, be quarried, carted a mile, and broke to pieces through a $2\frac{1}{2}$-inch ring, for 7d ; if the stones have been collected in the adjoining field, they will cost from 2d. to 3d. per rood. It is estimated, that about $1\frac{1}{2}$ cubic yard of broken stones will fill 6 roods, of 6 yards each, of a narrow and well cut drain. The putting in of the stones may be calculated to cost $\frac{1}{2}$d. per rood, and the turfing $\frac{2}{3}$ of a penny, and the filling in of the earth over the stones with the plough about as much. The whole cost of

* Prize Essays of the Highland and Agricultural Society, vol. xii. p. 111-2.

common drains may be taken at 9⅓d, or, including a charge to cover the proportion of main drains, 10d. per rood. Upon these data the following table has been constructed, the rood being 6 yards.*

Subsoils to which the distances are applicable.	Distances between the drains, in feet.	Roods per acre.	Cost per rood, in pence.	Cost per acre. L.	S.	D.
For hard till subsoil, ...	10	228	10	9	10	0
	11	207	...	8	12	6
	12	190⅓	...	7	18	9
Stiff clay, ...	13	175⅓	...	7	6	3
	14	163⅓	...	6	16	3
Sandy clay, ...	15	152	...	6	6	7
	16	144	...	6	0	0
	17	135	...	5	12	6
	18	127⅓	...	5	6	3
	19	120	...	5	0	0
	20	114	...	4	15	0
Free stony bottom, ...	21	108	...	4	10	0
	22	103⅓	...	4	6	3
	23	99	...	4	2	6
	24	96	...	4	0	0
	25	91⅓	...	3	16	3
	26	87	...	3	12	2
	27	84	...	3	10	0
	28	81	...	3	7	6
	29	78	...	3	4	0
More open bottom, ...	30	75	...	3	2	6
	31	73⅓	...	3	1	3
	32	72	...	3	0	0
	33	69	...	2	17	6
	34	67⅓	...	2	16	3
	35	66	...	2	15	0
	36	64⅓	...	2	13	9
	37	61⅓	...	2	11	3
Irregular beds of gravel or sand, and irregular open rocky stratifications, ...	38	60	...	2	10	0
	39	58	...	2	8	9
	40	57	...	2	7	6†

(1010.) Mr James Carmichael, Raploch Farm, Stirlingshire, gives this tabular view of the expense of stone draining. He also calculates

* Mr Smith calculates by the Stirlingshire rood of 36 yards.

† Smith's Remarks on Thorough-draining, p. 12–16.

by the Stirlingshire rood of 36 yards, but I have reduced them in this, as in the case above, to the ordinary rood of 6 yards. The expense of carriage is taken at 5s. per day for man and horse, and the stones are supposed to be so far distant as only 5 loads can be fetched in a day:—

	Distance of drains apart, in feet.	Depth of drain, in inches.	Width of bottom, in inches.	Roods of 6 yards, per acre.	Cost of carting and filling, per acre.	Cart-loads of stones, per acre.	Cost of carriage, per acre.	Total cost per acre.
					L. S. D.		L. S. D.	L. S. D.
Aluminous clay.	18	20	5	134⅓	3 7 2	44⅘	2 4 9	5 11 11¼
	18	24	5	134⅓	3 12 10	44⅘	2 4 9	5 17 7½
	18	27	5	134⅓	3 18 4	44⅘	2 4 9	6 3 1½*

(1011.) As tiles themselves form an important item in the expense of *tile-draining*, it is necessary to state the cost of that indispensable article before detailing the expense of draining with them. Tiles may either be made by the drainer himself or purchased for the purpose from tile-makers who undertake to supply the market.

(1012.) Of those who have supplied themselves with tiles for draining, Sir James Graham of Netherby is a successful example. Before 1829 he erected a complete establishment for their manufacture, and also of bricks, and made an agreement with a tile-burner to supply him with the requisite number. He gave the contractor a cottage and garden, the use of tools, moulds, &c., belonging to the kiln, rent-free, all which he was bound to keep and leave in good order, and prepare the clay, provide coal and every thing necessary at his own expense, and furnish Sir James with the best made draining tiles at the following prices:—

3-inch tiles per 1000,	. . . . .	L.1 4 0
4	. . . . . .	1 8 0
6	. . . . . .	1 17 0
8	. . . . . .	3 0 0

As a means of comparison with prices paid for tiles at the time at the sale-kilns of Carlisle and Wigton, from whence a very considerable quantity were used by farmers, the following statement may prove interesting:—

3-inch tiles per 1000,	. . . . .	L.2 2 0
4	. . . . . .	2 12 0
6	. . . . . .	4 4 0
8	. . . . . .	8 8 0†

These tiles, however, were of the extraordinary length of 18 inches each.

* Prize Essays of the Highland and Agricultural Society, vol. xii. p. 98.

† Ibid , vol. xii., p. 394

(1013.) The Duke of Buccleuch has erected tile-works on most of his extensive estates, from which his tenants are supplied at prime cost, namely, 3 inch tiles at 25s., and 4 inch at 32s. per 1000.*

(1014.) So long ago as 1823, the Duke of Portland introduced the manufacture of drain-tiles in Ayrshire. At that time they were sold for L.3 per 1000; in 1835 their price was reduced to 26s. 6d., and since then, by several important improvements which have been introduced into the manufacture, a still farther reduction has taken place. "It is not easy to establish a general rule for the selling price," says Mr James Taylor, factor to the Duke of Portland at Kilmarnock, "so as to meet every expense, as that must depend on the value of the land occupied by the work, the extent of ground taken up by roads, and many other incidents, such as the surface where the clay is taken from being rendered useless for cropping ever after, but which might have let for 30s. a year per acre. Taking the land at this value, estimating a road to be made of ¼ of a mile, and supposing the clay to last 10 years, I consider that tiles may be sold at the following rates, after making allowance for every possible expense :—

No. 1 tiles, 12 inches long, 5¾ inches wide, and 6½ inches high, inside measure, per 1000,	L.3	5	0
No. 2 tiles, 12 inches long, 5 inside, and 6 high,	3	0	0
No. 3 ... 12 ... ... 4 ... 5	2	10	0
No. 4 ... 12 ... ... 3 ... 4	1	5	0
No. 5 ... 12 ... ... 3 ... 3½	1	2	6
Large soles for Nos. 1 and 2 tiles, 12 inches long and 10 inches broad, per 1000,	1	5	0
Small soles for Nos. 3, 4 and 5 tiles, 12 inches long and 7 inches broad,	1	2	6

Nos. 1, 2, and 3 are tiles for main and sub-main drains, and Nos. 4 and 5 are those for common drains."†

(1015.) The prices of drain-tiles may be learned from what the manufacturers themselves state. Those demanded by Mr Robert Boyle, Ayr, were, in

	1836				1837		
For large sewer tiles,	L.4	0	0	and	L.4	4	0
... main drain do.	2	13	0	...	3	0	0
... furrow-drain do.	1	6	0	...	1	7	6
... main drain soles,	1	10	0	...	1	12	6
... furrow-drain do.	1	0	0	...	1	2	6

The rise of price in 1837 was owing to a rise of price in coal. Mr Boyle makes these sensible remarks in regard to the market price of tiles. "The price of tiles," he says, "is of less importance than their durability, as *on this alone* their preference ought to depend. The best method, therefore, of making and burning them is of greater importance than their price, and a remunerating price must always be received,

* Prize Essays of the Highland and Agricultural Society, vol. xiii., p. 509.

† Ibid., vol. xii., p. 36.

else the manufacturer will soon desist from working, or he will furnish an inferior article."* The tiles made by Mr Boyle are 13 inches long.

(1016.) Mr Beart, Godmanchester, near Huntingdon, enters minutely into the particulars of manufacture, in order to arrive at a fair estimate of the selling price of tiles. He says, "The price at which tiles can be produced and sold by the manufacturer depends upon the system pursued, and the convenience for making a large quantity during the season. Where the system detailed in this essay is practised, and there is a sufficient extent of drying-shelves to keep a machine (one invented by Mr Beart himself) at work, the following is a statement of the average cost per 1000:—The expense of raising and preparing the clay and cost of fuel will vary; but the average expense of producing tiles per 1000, under ordinary cases, each tile to contain 100 cubic inches of clay, making a proportionate allowance for tiles containing less, and the price of coals being calculated at 17s. 6d. per ton, is as follows:—

Raising the clay, per 1000,	L.0 2 0	
Turning the same once over with water,	0 0 6	
Straw or sand for covering over the clay,	0 0 6	
		L.0 3 0
Grinding, and barrowing to the machine,	L.0 1 0	
Moulding by the machine, per 1000,	0 2 0	
		0 3 0
Setting and unloading the kiln, per 1000,	L.0 1 6	
Burning,	0 1 0	
Waste,	0 1 0	
		0 3 6
Cost of fuel per 1000, 1 ton of coal at 17s. 6d. per ton calculated to burn 3500 tiles,		0 5 0
Expense in the yard per 1000,		L.0 14 6

To which must be added rent, interest of money, and incidental expenses, say 2s. 6d. per 1000, making the price 17s. per 1000, to which should be added 25 per cent. for manufacturer's profit, if the tiles are intended for sale, or 21s. 3d. per 1000. Where clay is of so mild a nature that it can be ground as it is raised, and in the neighbourhood of coal-works, the following deductions from the above estimate should be made:—

In raising and grinding, per 1000,	L.0 1 0
... straw,	0 0 6
... cost of fuel, from 1s. to 3s.	0 3 0
	0 4 6
Making the expense in the yard per 1000,	0 10 0
	L.0 14 6"†

* Prize Essays of the Highland and Agricultural Society, vol. xii., p. 26.

† Prize Essays of the Highland and Agricultural Society, vol. xii., p. 44-5; and for a figure and description of Mr Beart's tile-machine, see p. 138 of the same volume.

While giving Mr Beart's own statement, I should mention that his tiles are only 12 inches long, and that those made with his machines in Fife and Mid Lothian are 15 inches, which would raise his price to 26s. 7d. per 1000. I should also mention, that doubts have been entertained of his estimates, from the circumstance that, though he has sent men to Scotland, who have built kilns on the plan which he recommends as a means of saving to the extent of 4s. or 5s. per 1000, yet in all cases they have failed of doing so.

(1017.) The important tile machine invented by the Marquis of Tweeddale makes tiles at the rate of 10,000 tiles a-day.† It has been assigned to a company, under the title of the Yester Patent Drain-Tile Company, who have erected several works throughout the kingdom: the one erected by them at Swinton, in Berwickshire, is on an extensive scale, and situate on a bed of clay of excellent quality for tile-making. A modification of the Yester machine has been, I believe, in use near Morpeth for some time past.

(1018.) Amongst the machines recently introduced for the manufacture of drain-tiles, that under the patent of Mr Ainslie, Redheugh, Mid-Lothian, stands pre-eminent, whether as regards the amount of its production, or for the quality of the article which it produces. There is a directness in the principle on which tiles are formed by this machine, that gives them at once greater solidity and soundness of texture than any process hitherto adopted. The principle of its action is this: The clay, prepared in the usual way by lifting and turning, is thrown into the hopper of the machine, and passing between a pair of smooth metal rollers, which mix and amalgamate the mass, besides crushing any stones that may be in the clay, it passes thence into a cylinder, where it is received into the coils of an endless screw, and by it is strongly pressed into a small chamber. The front of this chamber is changeable, and in it are formed the matrices, or rather *draw-plate* orifices, through which the continuous lines of tiles are expressed. This draw-plate may contain from 2 to 5 orifices, according to the size of tile, each orifice presenting an exact transverse section of the tile which it forms. The clay, then, on being pressed into the chamber at one side, is expressed through the orifice at the other side under great pressure; and as the tile receives at once the intended shape, there is no bending or fracture by any ulterior operation. The process, as here described, would produce a tile of indefinite length, but the machine is provided with an apparatus, driven by the tiles themselves that are being thus expressed,

* For a figure and description of which, see p. 50, vol. xii. of the Prize Essays of the Highland and Agricultural Society.

which, by the passage of a wire across the lines of tile, cuts them off at a uniform length; they are then removed to the drying sheds, which are, for the purposes of this machine, made movable on railways, each shed containing a thousand tiles. Tiles of any size, from a 9-inch main-drain down to the smallest conduit, can be made by this machine, at rates varying from 14 large mains to 36 small conduit-tiles per minute, or from 8000 to 20,000 per day.

(1019.) A sort of drain-tile has lately been introduced by Lord James Hay of Seaton, Aberdeenshire. The composition of which it is formed is a *concrete*, consisting of *good* lime, *sharp* sand and gravel, which are mixed in the proportion of 1 bushel of lime shells to 2½ bushels of sand and 4 bushels of gravel, which in swelling give 8 bushels of composition that will make 120 tiles. The composition is run into moulds, in which it soon sets firm enough to be placed on boards, and the tiles become in a short time, according to the state of the air, in a sufficiently indurated state to be used. One man, aided with perhaps 4 others to supply the materials, will make 5000 tiles a day; but when the quantity of boarding is taken into consideration, I have great doubts of this process affording so cheap a tile as is represented of it: at all events it can only be practised in those localities which afford *sharp* sand and gravel in abundance,—substances which cannot be carried to a distance but at great expense; and experience has not yet sufficiently tested their durability even in the most favourable circumstances.

(1020.) With all these facilities for obtaining tiles, and the experience already acquired of making them suitable to particular purposes, the expense of tile-draining will be rendered considerably less than formerly. The current cost of using them, as well as stones, will, however, be best ascertained from the experience of drainers in the locality in which you may select your farm.

(1021.) In respect to the expense of draining by the Elkington method, no definite sum can be named which will apply to a definite extent of ground, such as an acre, as the extent of drainage in that system entirely depends on the quantity and direction in which water is met with under the surface of the ground. The cost, therefore, must be entirely estimated by the lineal rood, and the dimensions of the drains actually cut, and the difficulty or facility experienced in obtaining materials to fill them. These particulars, it is obvious, must vary according to circumstances, particularly in regard to the supply of tiles and stones, as the labour of cutting the ground does not much differ throughout the country.

(1022.) According to Mr Wilson's experience, the expense of the Elkington method of draining a retentive clay loam upon a retentive substratum of clay, with drains from 5 to 8 feet in depth, is on the average as follows:—

Expense of cutting 6 feet deep drains, 2½ feet wide at top, and 16 inches wide at bottom, the rood of 6 yards,	.	L.0 2 0
... of making the conduit, per rood,	.	0 0 2
... of quarrying, gathering, and carting 5 loads of stones, which cost (according to distance of carriage) from 8d. to 1s. 4d., average 1s. the load per rood,	.	0 5 0
... of filling in small stones, and the earth,	.	0 0 6
Average cost of rood,	.	L.0 7 8*

This sum may be considered as a fair charge for the Elkington method of draining by the rood of 6 yards.

(1023.) The expense of draining with tiles depending so much on the number and size of the drains, and the means of obtaining the materials for filling them, the subject will require to be considered somewhat in detail.

(1024.) The first instance I shall adduce of the cost of draining with *tiles* is derived from the experience of Sir James Graham of Netherby, Cumberland, who had drained with them to great extent prior to March 1829, when the following statement was published. I have reduced the expense into the *rood of* 6 *yards*.

With 3-inch tiles. Expense of cutting the drain on an average of 2 feet 9 inches deep, laying the tiles on slate or refuse tile, cutting and laying a turf over the tile, reversing and returning the surface soil, per rood of 6 yards,	L.0 0 3½
Expense of 18 tiles to the rood at the price paid at Netherby for 3-inch tiles, viz. 24s. per 1000,	0 0 5¼
Cost of carriage of tiles at an average distance of 3 miles, 3 rakes of a horse and cart and man a day, at 5s. a-day, the cart carrying 250 tiles each time,	0 0 1½
Cost of refuse slate or broken tile, and carriage,	0 0 0½
	L.0 0 10¾

With 4-inch tiles. Expense of cutting from 4½ to 5 feet deep drains, and in other respects the same as above,	L.0 0 5½
Expense of tiles, 18 to the rood, at 28s. per 1000,	0 0 6¼
Cost of carriage same as above,	0 0 1½
Cost of refuse slate or broken tile, and carriage,	0 0 0½
	L.0 1 1¾

* Prize Essays of the Highland and Agricultural Society, vol. vii. p. 242.

With 6-inch tiles. Expense of cutting the same depth of drain as in the last case,	L.0	0	5½
Cost of tiles, 37s. per 1000,	0	0	8
Cost of carriage,	0	0	1¾
Cost of refuse slate or broken tile, and carriage,	0	0	0½
	L.0	1	3¾

Had the tiles been bought at that time at the public tile-works, the draining with the 3-inch tiles would have cost 1s. 2¼d., with the 4-inch tiles 1s. 6½d., and with the 6-inch tiles 2s. 1¾d., the rood of 6 yards.*

(1025) The next instance I shall adduce of the cost of draining with tiles, is from the observations of Mr James Carmichael, Raploch Farm, Stirlingshire. The results are thrown into the tabular form, for the sake of easy reference, the rood being reduced to that of 6 yards, and the expense of carriage taken at 5s. a-day for man and horse and cart.

Soil.	Space between the drains, in feet.	Depth of drain, in inches.	Breadth of drain at the bottom, in inches.	Yards in the acre.	Cost of cutting and laying per rood of 6 yds., in pence.	Number of tiles per acre, at 3s. the 100.	Number of soles per acre, at 1s. 6d. per 100.	Cost of carriage per acre, in shillings.	Total cost. L.	S.	D.
Aluminous clay.	15	20	5	968	$1\frac{1}{2}\ \frac{8}{12}$	2500	1250	11	6	7	1¾
	15	22	5	968	$1\frac{3}{4}\ \frac{4}{12}$	2500	1250	11	6	9	4½
	15	24	5	968	$2\ \frac{8}{12}$	2500	2500	12	7	13	7½
	18	20	5	806	$1\frac{1}{2}\ \frac{8}{12}$	2080	1040	8	5	4	8
	18	22	5	806	$1\frac{3}{4}\ \frac{4}{12}$	2080	1040	8	5	6	6¼
	18	24	5	806	$2\ \frac{8}{12}$	2080	2080	10	6	7	10
	21	20	5	691	$1\frac{1}{2}\ \frac{8}{12}$	1780	890	7	4	9	8½
	21	22	5	691	$1\frac{3}{4}\ \frac{4}{12}$	1780	890	7	4	11	3¾
	21	24	5	691	$2\ \frac{8}{12}$	1780	1780	8	5	8	11¾
Mixed clay.	15	18	5	968	$2\frac{1}{4}\ \frac{4}{12}$	2500	...	8	5	14	4
	15	20	5	968	$2\frac{1}{2}\ \frac{8}{12}$	2500	...	8	5	18	10
	15	22	5	968	$2\frac{3}{4}\ \frac{6}{12}$	2500	...	8	6	1	8
	15	24	5	968	$3\frac{1}{4}$	2500	1250	10	7	6	10
	18	18	5	806	$2\frac{1}{4}\ \frac{4}{12}$	2080	...	7	4	15	6
	18	20	5	806	$2\frac{1}{2}\ \frac{8}{12}$	2080	...	7	4	19	1
	18	22	5	806	$2\frac{3}{4}\ \frac{6}{12}$	2080	...	7	5	1	6
	18	24	5	806	$3\frac{1}{4}$	2080	1040	8	6	4	2†

It will be observed, in the above statement, that where soles are men-

* Prize Essays of the Higland and Agricultural Society, vol. vii. p. 397. † Ibid. vol. xii. p. 98.

tioned, their number is set down at only half of that of the tiles; and, in some instances, the soles are omitted altogether, thereby implying that they are not necessarily required in mixed clay. I trust I have said enough to dissuade you from adopting the opinion that soles can be dispensed with in any instance of tile-draining. (913.)

(1026.) The experience of Mr Stirling of Glenbervie, Stirlingshire, in draining with tiles, gives the following results. I have retained the calculations by the *chain*, in order to shew you that there are various ways practised in this country of measuring drain-work. The drains are 30 inches deep in the furrow, 5 inches broad at the bottom, and 8 inches wide at 15 inches from the surface. The cost of cutting such a drain will vary from 8d. to 1s. 8d. the imperial chain of 66 feet, or $3\frac{2}{3}$ roods of 6 yards. The reason assigned by Mr Stirling for recommending this size of drain instead of a narrower is, that experience has not yet sufficiently proved what is the *smallest size that will be permanent.* The cost is estimated by Mr Stirling on the fact that 1 man and 2 horses will bring and string along the drains 960 tiles and soles a-day, from a distance varying from 4 to 5 miles. The prices of tiles and soles are taken at 40s. the 1000, of which 57 will lay a chain of 66 feet. The whole cost stands thus:—

Cost of cutting drain, per chain, . . .	L.0	1	2
... of 57 tiles and soles and carriage, . .	0	2	$9\frac{1}{2}$
... of returning earth, ...	0	0	$1\frac{5}{20}$
... of throwing on furrow-slice from between drains,	0	0	$0\frac{1}{2}$
	L.0	4	$1\frac{5}{20}$

In a tabular form the cost will stand thus by the imperial acre:—

Distance between the drains, in feet.	Number of chains, per acre.	Expense, per imperial acre.		
		L.	S.	D.
14	47.14	9	13	$5\frac{3}{4}$
16	41.25	8	9	$3\frac{1}{2}$
18	36.66	7	10	6
20	33.00	6	15	$5\frac{1}{4}$*

(1027.) A more recent authority on the expense of draining with tiles, as recent as October 1839, is the Marquis of Tweeddale, who has not only tile-drained extensively, but paid very great attention to every particular connected with it. His lordship's experience is embodied in the following table.†

* Prize Essays of the Highland and Agricultural Society, vol. xii. p. 111-12.

† Quarterly Journal of Agriculture, vol. x. p. 439.

Depth of drains in feet.	Cost of cutting the rood of 6 yards lineal, in pence.	Distance between the drains in feet.	Roods of 6 yards in the acre.	Cost of cutting drains per acre.	Cost of filling in earth per rood of 6 yards, in pence.	Cost of filling in earth per acre.	Cost of laying tiles per rood of 6 yards.	Cubic yards in the drains per rood of 6 yards.	Cubic yards in the drain per acre.	Number of tiles per acre, of 14 inches in length.	Cost of tiles per acre, at 30s. the 1000.	Number of half-soles per acre.	Cost of soles per acre, at 15s. the 1000.	Total expense.
				£ s. d.		s. d.	s. d.				£ s. d.		s. d.	£ s. d.
2	3	15	161⅓	2 0 4	¾	10 1	4 0	1	161½	2489	3 14 8	1245	18 8	7 7 9
2	3	18	134⅔	1 13 7	¾	8 4¾	3 6	1	134¾	2072	3 2 1¾	1036	15 6¼	6 3 1¾
2	3	24	100⅚	1 5 2½	¾	6 3½	2 6	1	100⅝	1556	2 6 8	778	11 8	4 12 4
2	3	30	80⅔	1 0 2	¾	5 0	2 0	1	80¾	1244	1 17 3¾	622	9 3¾	3 13 10
2½	4½	15	161⅓	3 0 6	1	13 5½	4 0	1 10/27	221	2489	3 14 8	1245	18 8	8 11 3½
2½	4½	18	134⅔	2 10 4½	1	11 2½	3 6	1 10/27	184	2072	3 2 1¾	1036	15 6¼	7 2 9
2½	4½	24	100⅚	1 17 9¾	1	8 4¾	2 6	1 10/27	138	1556	2 6 8	778	11 8	5 7 0½
2½	4½	30	80⅔	1 10 3	1	6 8¾	2 0	1 10/27	112	1244	1 17 3¾	622	9 3¾	4 5 7¼
3	5½	15	161⅓	3 13 11	1¼	16 9½	4 0	1 20/27	282	2489	3 14 8	1245	18 8	9 8 0½
3	5½	18	134⅔	3 1 6½	1¼	13 11½	3 6	1 20/27	235	2072	3 2 1¾	1036	15 6¼	7 16 8
3	5½	24	100⅚	2 6 2½	1¼	10 5½	2 6	1 20/27	176	1556	2 6 8	778	11 8	5 17 6
3	5½	30	80⅔	1 6 11½	1¼	8 4½	2 0	1 20/27	141	1244	1 17 3¾	622	9 3¾	4 13 11 8/4
3½	7	15	161⅓	4 14 1	1½	20 2	4 0	2⅑	345	2489	3 14 8	1245	18 8	10 11 7
3½	7	18	134⅔	3 18 4	1½	16 9½	3 6	2⅑	287	2072	3 2 1¾	1036	15 6¼	8 16 3½
3½	7	24	100⅚	2 18 10	1½	12 7	2 6	2⅑	215	1556	2 6 8	778	11 8	6 12 2
3½	7	30	80⅔	2 7 0½	1½	10 1	2 0	2⅑	172	1244	1 17 3¾	622	9 3¾	5 5 9

(1028.) The only other instance I shall adduce of the expense of draining with tiles is derived from the experience of Mr George Bell, Woodhouselees, Dumfriesshire, one of the Duke of Buccleuch's tenants on the Langholm estate. The soil drained is that which is provincially termed "black-top," that is, a black mossy earth resting on a retentive clay subsoil, the upper soil being 10 or 18 inches in thickness. The drains are 30 inches deep in the furrows, and 15 feet apart, and were executed in November 1837 and 1838. One instance of draining only, out of several, shall be adduced, and I shall select the most costly, namely that executed over 13 acres in 1837. It is proper to premise, that the retentive clay subsoil, when dry, was thrown over the surface to mix with the mossy soil, and not returned into the drain. The cutting of the drains was contracted for, but the laying of tiles and the filling in of earth were done by the grieve on the farm, when the *soil was in a dry state;* this done, a furrow of the top soil, on each side of the drain, was ploughed in, as being an economical mode of filling in the earth. The soles consisted of Welsh slates, which were obtained in quantity at 16s. per 1000. The statement stands thus :—

	L.	s.	d.
Cost of 38,000 of 3-inch tiles, at 25s. the 1000, ...	L.47	10	0
... 1,557 of 4-inch tiles, at 32s.	2	10	5
... Cutting 2003 roods of drains of 6 yards each, at 3d. the rood,	26	0	9
... Slates for soles, ...	1	5	0
	L.77	6	2
... Carriage of 38,000 tiles, at 3s. 4d. the 1000, ...	6	6	8
... ... 1,557 ... 5s.	0	7	10
... 31 days' work of man and horse laying down tiles, straw and for covering them, at 5s. 6d. per day, ...	8	10	6
... Women loading and unloading the carts, ...	2	3	0
... 30 days' work of a man laying tiles and soles, ...	2	5	0
... 30 days' work of a woman, at 8d. per day, ...	1	0	0
... 3 days of plough-work, at 10s. per day, ...	1	10	0
Cost of draining 13 acres, ...	L.99	9	2
... ... 1 acre, ...	L.7	13	0

(1029.) If you carefully compare these statements of draining land with stones and with tile, you will find data most probably applicable to every circumstance which you may meet with in draining your own land. Should you not be able to find the individual fact you are in quest of, you will be able to arrive at it by calculation or inference from those given, and this is as near an approach as any general statement can make towards particular cases.

(1030.) In regard to the *comparative advantages of stone and tile drains*, it is impossible, in the present state of experience, to decide upon the superiority (if any) of either. I believe it to be quite possible to make a drain of either material to be permanent, and this being the case, the only question betwixt them is one of expense, which is partly dependent upon contingent circumstances, connected with locality. In one place stones are so plentiful, and tiles so distant, that it would be inconsistent to reject the former and procure the latter material; and, on the other hand, there are localities where tiles can be made on the spot, and stones cannot be obtained within many miles. But although the case of distance may be the same with the two sorts of materials, they are nevertheless not placed exactly in the same predicament, for tiles may be brought from a considerable distance to the locality in want of them at much less cost than stones. In the difference of the cost of carriage between the two sorts of materials, Mr Carmichael has shewn, by adducing the case of a man with a horse and cart being employed to draw the same quantity, say 5 loads a day, of both kinds of materials, that 1 cart-load of tiles and soles, each 14 inches in length, will lay upwards of 100 yards of a drain, 6 inches wide and of any depth; whereas, 1 cart-load, or cubic yard, of stones will only fill 18 yards of a drain 6 inches wide, to a depth of 12 inches, being an amount of carriage nearly 6 to 1 in favour of the tiles; and as carriage is the most laborious item in the cost of draining, it constitutes an important point for consideration, when you are about to undertake the drainage of your farm.

(1031.) The *next* important point for consideration is, whether the great outlay upon land occasioned by draining can be compensated for by increase of produce? for if no increase of produce, adequate to repay the large outlay, can be guaranteed, draining will not be persevered in. No one, beforehand, can give such a guarantee; but the experience of enterprising drainers, who have vested their capital in the experiment, has proved that draining—that is, effectual or thorough-draining, by whatever means that object is attained—not only compensates for the outlay incurred, but also improves the quality of the land and every thing that grows upon it. Examples of amelioration, as well as of profit, effected by draining, inspiring confidence and stimulating imitation, I shall adduce.

(1032.) The existence of moisture in the soil being most easily detected by its injurious effects on the crops usually grown upon it, the benefits of draining are also first indicated by the crops. On drained land, the straw of white crops shoots up steadily from a vigorous braird, strong, long, and at the same time so stiff as not to be easily lodged with wind or rain. The grain is plump, large, bright coloured, and thin skinned. The crop ripens uniformly, is bulky and prolific, more quickly won for stacking in harvest, more easily thrashed, winnowed, and cleaned, and produces fewer small and light grains. The straw also makes better fodder for live stock. Clover, in such land, becomes rank, long, and juicy, and the flowers are large and of bright colour. The hay from it wons easily, and weighs heavy to its bulk. Pasture-grass shoots out in every direction, covering the ground with a thick sward, and produces fat and milk of the finest quality. Turnips become large, plump, as if fully grown, juicy, and with a smooth and oily skin. Potatoes push out long and strong stems, with enlarged tubers, having skins easily peeled off, and a meally substance when boiled. Live stock of every kind thrive, become good tempered, are easily fattened, and of fine quality. Land is less occupied with weeds, the increased luxuriance of all the crops checking their growth. Summer fallow is more easily cleaned, and much less work is required to put the land in proper trim for the manure and seed; and all sorts of manures incorporate more quickly and thoroughly with the soil.

(1033.) Thorough-drained land is easily worked with all the common implements. Being all alike dry, its texture becomes uniform, and, in consequence, the plough passes through it with uniform freedom; and even where pretty large sized stones are found, the plough can easily dislodge them; and moving in freer soil, it is able to raise a deeper furrow-slice; and the furrow-slice, on its part, though heavy, crumbles down and yields to the pressure and friction of the plough, forming a friable, mellow, rich-looking mould. The harrows, instead of being held back at times, and starting forward, and oscillating sideways, swim smoothly along, raking the soil into an uniform surface and entirely obliterating foot-marks. The roller compresses and renders the surface of the soil smooth, but leaves what is below in a mellow state for the roots of plants to expand in. All the implements are much easier drawn and held; and hence, all the operations can be executed with less labour, and of course more economically and satisfactorily on drained than undrained land.* All these effects of draining I have observed from my own experience.

(1034.) "It is gratifying," says Mr James Black, in reference to the effects of the Elkington mode of draining on the estate of Spottiswoode in Berwickshire, "to be enabled to state, that the general result of the operations has been such as to bear out the calculations of the engineer,

* See papers by me on this subject in the Quarterly Journal of Agriculture, vol. vi. p. 526, and vol. viii. p. 171-2.

and to justify the most sanguine hopes that could have been formed of a valuable improvement. Bursts and springs, which formerly disfigured entire fields, and which rendered tillage precarious and unprofitable, are now not to be seen; and swamps, which were not only useless in themselves, but which injured all the land around them, have been totally removed. The consequence is, that tillage can now in those parts be carried on without interruption, and with nothing beyond the ordinary expenditure of labour and manure; and a sward of the best grasses, raised and continued on spots which formerly only produced the coarsest and least valued herbage."

(1035.) "Besides those effects," he continues, "which were, in a certain degree, to be expected as a consequence of laying land dry, others have resulted, which, it must be confessed, were not at first so clearly contemplated. The hurtful effect of rime or hoar-frost on vegetation is a circumstance familiar to all who have had experience of cold and elevated districts, or of low lands subject to exhalations, or excluded from the influence of the sun and currents of air. The rime, in these swampy hollows of which mention has been made, was found, even in the warmest seasons, to be productive of serious inconvenience and injury to the growing crops; and that chiefly at the period when the grain was approaching to its mature state. This evil, it may be said, has been removed, or at least is now so little felt, that the grain produced in these very hollows has, for many years, escaped the smallest perceptible injury from this cause."

(1036.) "Another effect," he adds, "which was still less contemplated, and has not less agreeably resulted from the drainage undertaken, has been the improvement of the trees and woodlands in the property. Considerable difficulty was experienced in nursing up the trees in the first stages of their growth; and often individual trees grew up with stunted stems, and covered with parasitical plants, which always indicate unhealthy growth. Latterly this evil has been infinitely less felt, owing, in a material degree certainly, to the superior management of the woods themselves, but obviously also, in a certain degree, to the greater dryness of the ground. Since several of the woods have been laid dry by under-drainage, the ground, in many of the hollows, has sunk so much, that the roots of the trees have been left standing up bare above the surface, with the appearance of crows' feet; and parts which were boggy and marshy, and in which sportsmen used to stick fast in hunting, are now perfectly solid, with a good sward of grass, over which they may now gallop with freedom."*

* Prize Essays of the Highland and Agricultural Society, vol. vii. p. 234-6.

(1037.) All these characteristics of draining are nothing more nor less than the properties of *good* land, which are here observed on the same soil that formerly exhibited the properties of *bad;* thus proving that draining places bad land—that is, natural land that rests on so retentive a subsoil as to detain surface-water until it stagnates—in the same state as naturally good land,—that is, natural land that rests on a subsoil naturally pervious to surface-water. Draining, in thus curtailing the limits of bad, produces the immediate effect of extending the limits of good soil.

(1038.) But draining has been found beneficial not only to the soil itself, to the processes of labouring it, to the climate in reference to crops, and to the growth of trees, but also to the health of the labouring population. Dr Charles Wilson, Kelso, when comparing the health of the labouring population of the district of Kelso in two decennial periods, from 1777 to 1787 and from 1829 to 1839, came to this conclusion in regard to the effect of draining, that "our attention is here justly attracted by the extraordinary preponderance of cases of ague in the first decennium, where they present an average of $\frac{1}{7}$ of all cases of disease coming under treatment; and a closer examination of the separate years shews this proportion rising more than once to even as high as $\frac{1}{5}$; while, in the second decennium, the average proportion is only $\frac{6}{100}$ of the general mass of disease. Ague, then, as is well known to the older inhabitants of the district, was *at one time regularly endemic amongst us;* affecting every year a varying, but always a considerable portion of population, and occasionally, in seasons of unusual coldness and moisture, spreading itself extensively as an endemic, and shewing its ordinary tendency, under such circumstances, of passing into a continued and more dangerous type. Ague was not usually in itself a disease of great fatality, the deaths recorded at the Dispensary having been only 1.81 per cent. of the cases treated,—a sum which denotes its absolute mortality, whilst its relative mortality was 0.26, when viewed in connection with that from all other diseases. Still, if we keep in view how frequently it was known to degenerate into fevers of a worse form, and how often it terminated in jaundice, "obstruction of the viscera of the abdomen," and consequent dropsies; or even if we take into consideration the frequency of its recurrence, and the lengthened periods during which it racked its victims, we shall see much reason to be thankful that a plague so universal and so pernicious has been almost wholly rooted out from amongst us. Those who recollect what has been stated of the former swampy nature of the soil in our vicinity, and of the *extensive means which have been adopted for its drainage*, will, of course, have no difficulty in understanding why ague was once so prevalent, and under what agency it should now have disappeared; and will gratefully acknowledge the *twofold value of those improvements, which have at once rendered our homes more salubrious, and our fields more fruitful.*"*

(1039.) But the most palpable advantage of draining land is the *profit* which it returns to the farmer. A few authenticated instances of the profits actually derived from draining will suffice to convince any occupier of land of the benefits to be derived from it. "I am clearly of opinion," says Mr North Dalrymple of Cleland, Lanarkshire, "that well-authenticated facts on economical draining, accompanied with details of the expenses, value of succeeding crops, and of the land before and after draining, will be the means of stimulating both landlords and tenants to pursue the most important, judicious, and *remunerating* of all land improvements. The statements below will prove the advantages of furrow-draining; and as to the *profits* to be derived from it, they are *great*, and a farmer has only to drain a 5-acre field to have ocular proof upon the point."†

(1040.) Without entering into all the minutiæ of the statements given by Mr Dalrymple, it will suffice here to exhibit the general results. 1. One field containing 54 Scots acres cost L.303, 7s. to drain, or L.5, 12s. per acre. The wheat off a part of it was sold for L.11, and the turnips off the remainder for L.25 : 13 : 4 per acre. The soil was a stiff chattery clay, and let in grass for 20s. an acre; but in 1836, after having been drained, it kept 5 cheviot ewes, with their lambs, upon the acre. 2. Another field of 18 acres cost L.5, 9s. the acre to drain. The wheat off a part of it fetched L.13, the potatoes off another part L.15, 15s., and the turnips off the remainder L.21 per acre. The land was formerly occupied with whins and rushes, and let for 12s. the acre; but when let for pasture after being drained, Mr Dalrymple expected to get 50s. an acre for it. It may be mentioned, that the drains made by Mr Dalrymple were narrow ones, 30 inches in depth, filled 18 inches high with stones or scoriæ from a furnace, and connected with main drains, 36 inches deep, furnished with tiles and soles.‡

(1041.) Mr James Howden, Wintonhill, near Tranent, in East Lothian, asserts from his experience, that although drains should cost as much as

* Quarterly Journal of Agriculture, vol. xii., p. 328.

† Ibid., vol. viii., p. 319.

‡ Ibid., vol. viii. p. 320.

L.7 the acre, yet on damp heavy land thorough draining will repay from 15 to 20 per cent. on the outlay.*

(1042.) A farmer in Lanarkshire, who thorough-drained one-half of a 4-acre field, and left the other half undrained in 1838, planted the whole field with potatoes, and from the drained portion realized L.45, whilst the undrained only realized L.13, the Scotch acre.†

(1043.) A very successful instance of drainage is related to have taken place on the estate of Teddesley Hay, near the river Penk, in Staffordshire, belonging to Lord Hatherton, under the direction of his agent Mr Bright. The soil is represented of a light nature, resting on a subsoil of stiff clay. The results are these :

Quantity of land drained.	Value of the land in its original state.		Cost of draining.	Value of the land in its present state.	
	Per acre.	Annual value.		Per acre.	Annual value.
A. R. P.	S.	L. S. D.	L. S. D.	S.	L. S. D.
78 1 36	10	39 4 3	262 15 0	27	105 18 9
19 1 32	10	9 14 6	74 9 8	35	34 0 9
38 0 3	16	30 8 3	52 14 2	40	76 0 9
82 2 2	15	61 17 8	346 16 4	30	123 15 4
30 3 24	10	15 9 0	121 5 8	35	54 1 6
81 1 34	8	32 11 8	153 16 4	22	89 12 2
36 3 16	10	18 8 6	142 8 0	30	55 5 6
33 0 0	8	13 4 0	80 5 2	26	42 18 0
10 2 33			90 8 0	50	26 15 3
10 0 8				21	10 11 0
9 0 0	12	5 8 0	76 9 8	30	13 10 0
15 0 11	16	12 1 0	41 9 4	33	24 17 3
21 2 10	15	16 3 5	66 0 0	30	32 6 10
467 0 9		254 10 9	1508 17 4		689 13 1

Here is an increase of L.435 : 2 : 4 a-year by draining, with an expenditure of only L.1508 : 17 : 4, or 29 per cent. on the capital expended.‡

(1044.) Mr George Bell's experience of the good effects of thorough draining on turnips gave, in the instance of Aberdeenshire yellow bullock turnips, which were raised from bone-dust in 1838, a crop of 16 tons 16 cwt, on 2 acres; whereas the same extent of undrained land

* Quarterly Journal of Agriculture, vol. viii., p. 321.

† Ibid., vol. x., p. 271.

‡ On Land-Drainage, &c., p. 12.

only produced 6 tons 4 cwt. the acre. In 1839, the produce of potatoes on drained land was 175 cwt. the acre, whereas that on undrained land was only 70 cwt.

(1045.) I should here remark that, when drains are executed on stubble or lea ground, the first corn crop after draining is not sensibly increased in produce; but after the ground has been fallowed, that is, ploughed, properly wrought, and manured, a very sensible increase of crop takes place. Thus, in the instance of Mr Bell's experience, in 1838, the increase on the oat crop was only 5 bushels, on 2 acres, more on the drained than the undrained land; and in 1839, 9 acres drained produced 258 bolls, and 6¾ acres undrained produced 192 bolls. These results are very much less than those obtained from green crops when the land had been effectually laboured after the operation of draining.

(1046.) Other instances of successful draining could be adduced, such as the improvements of Mr Denison on his property of Kilnwick Percy, and on Hutten Bushel by the Rev. Mr Croft,* and last, though not least, by Sir James Graham of Netherby,† and the Marquis of Tweeddale at Yester; and I might adduce my own humble doings in that way, but enough, I presume, has been already stated to shew you the value of draining.

(1047.) But although remarkable instances of increase and of profit are immediately derived from draining land, it must not be received as an undoubtedly established fact, that the great increase will continue ever afterwards without diminution. Effectual draining makes the greatest impression at first on soils much under the influence of water, whether they be naturally good or bad; but from the nature of things, naturally good land should possess more stamina than bad, and accordingly, experience has long since proved, that good land effectually drained maintains its superiority over bad for a period of years, even although the inferior should exert itself more for a few years after being drained. Although I express myself in these terms, I by no means acquiesce in the opinion expressed on a similar view of the subject by Mr Peter Thomson, Hangingside, Linlithgowshire; yet there is doubtless much truth in what he states, and such sentiments you should keep in mind, in order to check over sanguine expectations excited by recent improvements. "Thorough-draining, like every other improvement," says Mr Thomson, "has the best return from good soil. When executed on bad

* Journal of the Royal Agricultural Society of England, vol. ii., p. 35.

† Ibid., vol. i., p. 32; and Prize Essays of the Highland and Agricultural Society, vol. vii., p. 388.

land, the outlay will not be repaid, and no little disappointment will be the certain consequence of much that has been already done upon weak soils. Weak land, upon being relieved from an excess of moisture, makes an extraordinary exertion, and in the course of the first rotation of crops yields considerably beyond what it formerly did; but in the course of the second rotation, the produce becomes considerably diminished, and when laid down to pasture, the finer description of grasses give way to those indigenous to the soil." These remarks I conceive to be more applicable to the abuse than to the proper use of draining, for I cannot coincide with the opinion that any bad land will not repay the expense of *thorough*-draining, because experience hitherto leads our convictions the other way; and although the coarser grasses may predominate on bad land after drainage, they will only do so in permanent and not in arable pasture, and even there they will be finer than they were; and it is any thing but good farming to allow land that is naturally weak to remain long in grass, immediately after being first drained. Here is an instructive table, constructed by Mr Thomson, to shew the produce of an imperial acre of both inferior and good land, beyond the first rotation of cropping, before and after thorough-draining; and the results are, that the produce fell off in both conditions of soil in the second rotation, though the falling off was less on the good than the inferior soil; but even on the inferior soil the return, on the average, from all the species of crops, is equivalent to at least 10 per cent. on the largest sum that is incurred in thorough-draining.

Kinds of Crops.	On inferior land.			On good land.		
	Before being drained.	After being drained.		Before being drained.	After being drained.	
		In the 1st rotation.	In the 2d rotation.		In the 1st rotation.	In the 2d rotation.
	Bush. Pks.	Bush. Pks.	Bush. Pks.	Bush. Pks.	Bush. Pks.	Bush. Pks.
Barley, .	23 3	33 1	29 1¼	27 3	38 0	36 2
Oats, . .	35 2¾	47 2¼	44 1½	38 0	52 1¼	50 0
	L. S. D.	L. S. D.	L. S. D.	L. S. D.	L. S. D.	L. S. D.
Grass by the acre.	1 3 9	2 11 6	1 19 8	1 11 8½	3 19 3	3 11 4*

It would be of essential service to future drainers were those of the present day to ascertain the comparative produce derived from drained

* Prize Essays of the Highland and Agricultural Society, vol. xiii. p. 297-8.

good and bad land, for a series of rotation of crops, so as the smallest amount of expenditure which bad land would require to be laid out in draining it, to render it profitable to the drainer, may be clearly ascertained.

(1048.) An important precaution in regard to draining must be given you in regard to the *mode of conducting* draining operations. I have frequently observed in bad weather in winter a great extent of drains cut and left open for an indefinite length of time, in the intervals of which rain and snow have fallen and brought down parts of the sides into the bottom. The spade-work, too, is frequently roughly and slovenly executed, whereas it should be done neatly and correctly in every size of drain. I have also observed drains circumscribe comparatively small boulder stones, instead of the stones being removed, and the drain carried forward in a straight line. The most retentive part of the earth from the bottom of the drain is often thrown upon the edge of the drain, whereas being put into the drain after some of the more open portions, it, of course, should be thrown at first farthest from the edge. The tiles are frequently laid down in a very careless manner, instead of being placed as near the hand of the person who lays them as possible, on the opposite side of the drain on which the earth is thrown out. Soles of any kind are too frequently neglected to be used. And to reach the climax of negligence in the whole process, a long time is frequently allowed to elapse before the earth is returned again into the drain. Every one of these negligent practices you should scrupulously avoid; and as they entirely originate in neglecting to exercise a strict superintendence over the labourers who have undertaken to perform the work, either by day's wages or by the piece, the farmer himself is to blame in allowing them to exist; and constant superintendence is required to avoid them. For example. If the same set of men undertake to cut the drains and lay the tiles, which is by far too common a practice, a wet state of weather is pleasanter for them to cut the solid ground than to lay the tiles, and so they continue, day after day, as if they had nothing else to do but to cut the drains. The consequence is, that a large extent of drain is left exposed to the weather, which being supposed to be wet, the chances are that much of the sides fall in. If the rain continue, the workmen can neither bottom out the drain nor lay the tiles, and the matter becomes worse daily. Then a sudden frost comes, and moulders down still more of the earth from both sides, which, absorbing the rain that falls, is converted into sludge that cannot be taken out until it becomes firm. A fine day or two succeed, which induce the men to lay the soles and tiles, and they continue laying them, as if they were certain that the dry weather will continue, until they are ready to return the earth into the drain. This earth they find too wet one day to put into the drain, and too hard with frost in another, and so the laid tiles get leave to lie exposed to whatever change of weather may happen to come next, with a slight sprinkling of straw or other substance above them. In all these various states I have seen drains exposed for weeks together.

(1049.) Now, it is certain that the occurrence of all this negligence would be prevented were a strict superintendence exercised over the workmen. When left to the dictates of their own will, they will naturally execute that part of the work which, in reference to the state of the weather, is most conducive to their own interest, if they are working by the piece, or which is pleasantest to their own feelings, if working on day's wages, irrespective of the ultimate consequences in which their choice may involve the drain. They would not willingly see their work injured; but as they are unable to predict the state of the weather beyond the day before them, it is surely worse than folly, on the part of the farmer, to grudge the cost of constant superintendence over one of the most permanent operations that can be performed on a farm. The time of a grieve or steward is considered thrown away when superintending drainers. No doubt the grieve's time can be fully occupied elsewhere, and there is little fear of men on piece-work doing less work each day than will secure them good wages, but it is not the quantity of work done in draining which constitutes the most material consideration for the farmer; it is its *quality* and *efficiency;* and to obtain these, proper superintendence over workmen is requisite. If the grieve have not sufficient leisure, let another and competent person be appointed to superintend, and if he also undertake to lay the tiles, in so far a saving will be effected in that part of the operations, whilst his superintendence will oblige the workmen to cut the drains and return the earth whenever the state of the drains is best adapted for each operation; but if they are not bound to return the earth, he should have the power to direct the steward of the farm to send ploughs for the purpose when required. When such a system of superintendence is begun and persevered in, it is much easier to conduct the whole work by it than when work is done in an irregular manner, and it possesses the great advantage of securing every part of the work, in the most proper time against the effects of weather, and also in the most satisfactory condition.

(1050.) Besides the methods of draining land with stones and tiles as have just been described to you at much length, there are other methods which deserve your attention, because they may be practised in particular situations in an economical manner. I do not believe that the methods I am about to mention are so effectual as those I have described, still I have no doubt any one of them may be made effectual in situations where the materials recommended are abundant. Besides, it is well to have a choice of methods of performing the same operation, that your judgment may be exercised in adopting the one most advisable in the circumstances in which you are placed; whilst, at the same time, you should never lose sight of this maxim in agriculture, that that operation is most economically executed, or, at all events, affords most satisfaction in the end, which is executed in the most efficient manner, both as regards materials and workmanship, and the maxim applies to no operation so strongly as to draining, because of its permanent nature. The methods of draining which I am about to mention apply to every species of soil, from light loam, the heaviest clay, to bog.

(1051.) The first method which I shall notice is applicable to a *tilly subsoil which draws water* a little, situate in a locality in which *flat stones are plentiful and sufficiently cheap.* Suppose a piece of land, containing 2 ridges of 15 feet in width, which had been gathered up from the flat, and in this form of ploughing, as you have already learned, there is an open furrow on each side of a ridge (824.). The drains are made in this manner: Gather up the land twice, by splitting out a feering in the crown of each ridge, and do it with a strong furrow. Should the 4-horse plough have been used for the purpose, the open furrow will be left 16 inches wide at bottom, and if the furrow have been turned over 12 inches in depth, and the furrow-slice laid over at the usual angle of 45°, the tops of the furrow-slices on the furrow-brow will be 32 inches apart, as from *a* to *a*, fig. 187. After this ploughing the spade takes out a trench from the bottom of the open-furrow 8 inches wide at top *e*, 16 inches deep by *f*, and 3 inches wide at bottom at *g*. The depth of the drain will thus be 32 inches in all below the crowns of the gathered up ridges. The drain is filled by two flags *h h* being set up against its sides and meeting in the bottom at *g*; and they are kept asunder by a large stone of any shape, as a wedge, but large enough to be prevented by *h h* descending farther than to leave a conduit *g* for the water. The remainder of the drain is filled to *e* with small riddled stones with Mr Roberton's drain-screen or with clean gravel. The stones are covered over with turf and earth like any other drain, or with small stones beaten down firmly. The expense of this method of draining is small: the spade work may be executed at 1d. the rood of 6 yards, and of an imperial acre, containing 161⅓ of such roods, the cutting will cost 13s. 5 4/12d. The flags, at 1 inch thick and 6 inches broad, will make 15 tons per acre, at 4d. the ton, will cost 5s. more. The broken stones, to fill 9 cubic feet in the rood of 6 yards, at 2¼d. per rood, will cost L.1 : 10 : 3½ more; making in all about L.2 : 8 : 8 the acre, exclusive of carriage and ploughing, which, though estimated, will yet make this a cheap mode of draining land so closely as 15 feet apart.*

Fig. 187.

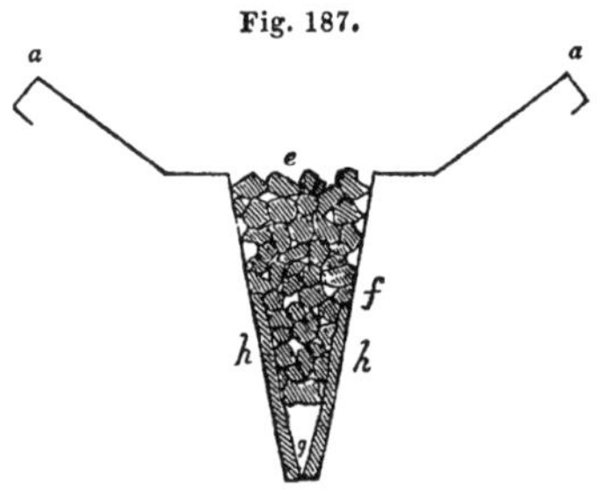

THE FLAT STONE DRAIN.

(1052.) The draining of *mossy light soils* where *peat is plentiful* may be

* Quarterly Journal of Agriculture, vol. vii. p. 245.

effected in this way. The peats are made somewhat of the shape of drain-tiles but more massive, as may be seen in fig. 188. They are laid in the drain one *a* like a tile-sole, and another inverted upon it, as *b*, like a drain-tile, leaving a round opening between them for the passage of the water. These peats are cut out with a spade-tool, contrived some years ago by Mr Hugh Calderwood, Blacklyres, Ayrshire. The spade is easily worked, and forms a peat with one cut, without any waste of materials; that is, the exterior semi-circle *b* is is cut out of the interior semi-circle of *a*. A man can cut out from 2000 to 3000 peats a-day with such a spade. The peats are dried in the sun in summer, with their hollow part upon the ground, and are stacked until used; and those used in drains have been found to remain quite hard. The invention of this spade, of which a figurè, 189, is here given, tends to make the draining of moorish soils more practicable than heretofore, and it may be done at $\frac{1}{3}$ or $\frac{1}{4}$ of the expense of ordinary drain tiles. The frequent want of clay in upland moory districts renders the manufacture of drain-tiles on the spot impracticable, and their carriage from a distance a serious expense.*

Fig. 188.

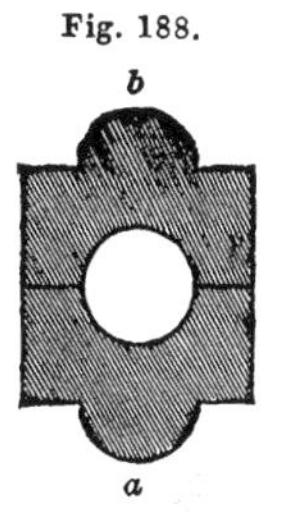

THE PEAT-TILE FOR DRAINS.

(1053.) Sir Joseph Banks alludes to the filling up of drains in bogs, which had been executed at great expense at Woburn, by the growth of the marestail (*Equisetum palustre*). On examining the plant, Sir Joseph found "its stem under ground a yard or more in length, and in size like a packthread; from this a root of twice the size of the stem runs horizontally in the ground, taking its origin from a lower root, which strikes down perpendicularly to a depth I have not hitherto been able to trace, as thick as a small finger."† I have frequently met with the roots or stems of the marestail under ground, which, on being bisected by the drains, poured out a constant run of water for some time, but, when fairly emptied of it, and no longer receiving support by a due supply of moisture from above, they withered away. Although there is no doubt that in the case mentioned by Sir Joseph Banks, that the roots of the marestail penetrated deeper than the drains, yet the circumstance of their sending upwards shoots which grew "along the openings left for the passage of water," proves that sufficient moisture had been left near the surface of the bog, notwithstanding the draining, to support the plant in life; in short, that the bog had been insufficiently drained, otherwise the rivation of support by moisture to the stems at the surface would inevitably have destroyed the vitality of the roots below.

Fig. 189.

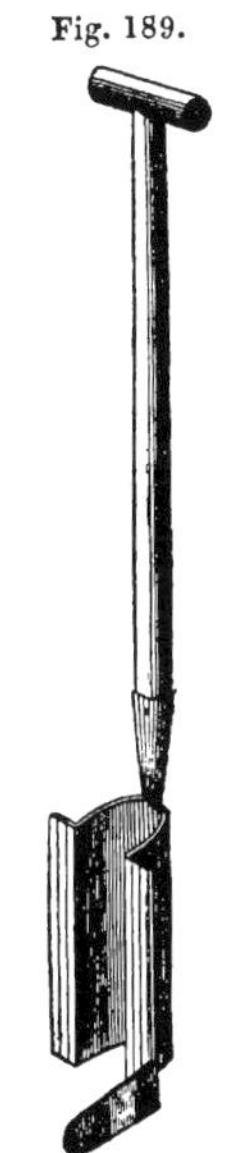

THE CALDERWOOD PEAT-TILE SPADE.

(1054.) A plan similar to that described in (1051) may be practised on *strong clay land*. The open-furrow is formed in the same manner with the plough, and being left 16 inches in width, the spade work is conducted in this manner. Leave a scarcement of 1 inch on each side of the open-furrow left by the plough, as seen below *a a*, fig. 190, and cut out the earth, 14 inches wide, perpendicularly, and 10 inches deep, as at *b b*. Then cast out from the bottom of this cut

* Quarterly Journal of Agriculture, vol. vii. p. 247.

† Communications to the Board of Agriculture, vol. ii. p. 349.

with a spade 3 or 4 inches wide, a cut 5 inches or more in depth *c*, leaving a scarcement of 5 inches on each side of the bottom of the former cut *b b*. The bottom of the small cut will be found to be 32 inches below the crowns of the ridges, when twice gathered up with a strong furrow. The drain is filled up in this way: Take flag-stones of 2 or 3 inches in thickness, as *d*, and place them across the opening of *c* upon the 5-inch scarcements, left by the narrow spade; they need not be dressed at the joints, as one stone can overlap the edges of the two adjoining, and they thus form the top of a conduit of pure clay in which the water may flow. As the water is made to flow immediately upon the clay, it is clear that this form of drain can not be regarded as a permanent one; though a flag or tile sole laid on the bottom of the cut *c* would render it much more durable. The cutting of this form of drain, the workmen having to shift from one tool to another, will cost 1½d. the rood of 6 yards, which at 15 feet apart make 20s. 2d. the acre. The flags for covers will be 12 tons at 4d. per ton, 4s. more, in all 24s. 2d., but with 10 tons of soles the cost will be 3s. 4d. more, or 27s. 6d. the acre, exclusive of the carriage of stones and the labour of the plough. After the *joinings* of the flags are covered over with turf, the earth may be returned into the drain with the plough, but with precaution, and probably with the previous assistance of the spade; but, after all, the probability is, that *flat* stones cannot be easily obtained in the neighbourhood of strong clay, though this *form* of drain may be adopted in any subsoil where flat stones are abundant.*

Fig. 190.

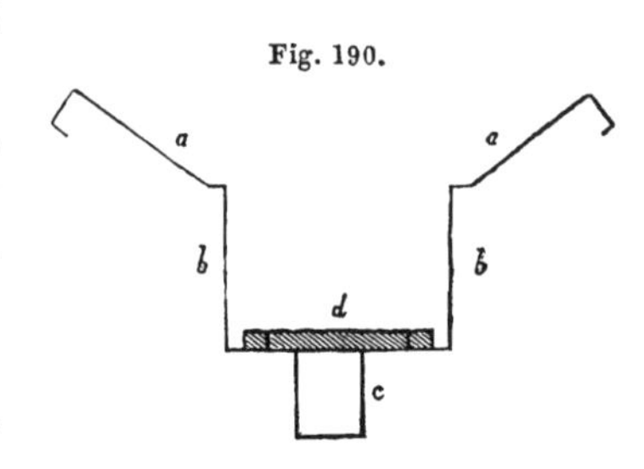

THE CLAY-LAND SHOULDER DRAIN.

(1055.) A somewhat analogous mode to this last of draining heavy clay land is with the *wedge* or *plug*. As this mode of draining requires a very peculiar form of tools, they will be described as required for use.

(1056.) The first remarkable implement used in this operation is the *bitting-iron*, represented by fig. 191, where *a* is the mouth, 1¾ inch wide; *b* the bit 6 inches in length; *c* the width of the bit 4½ inches. The bit is worked out of the body of the instrument, and laid with the best tempered steel; *e* is the tramp of the implement, placed 18 inches *d* from the mouth *a*; it would perhaps strengthen the power of the implement to have the tramp on the same side as the bit *c*; and *f* is the helve, which is of the length of that of a common spade.

Fig. 191.

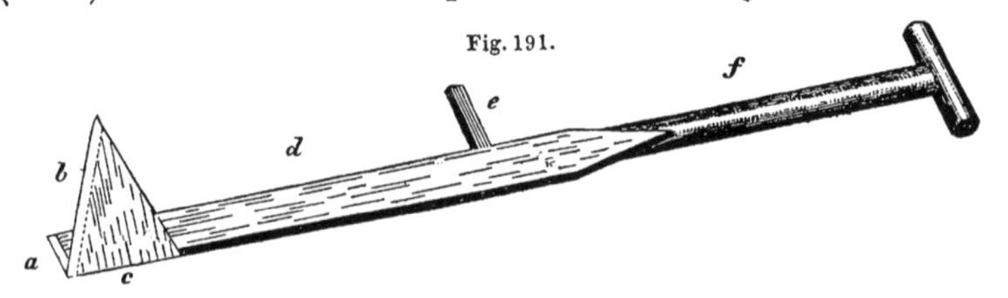

THE BITTING-IRON IN PLUG-DRAINING.

(1057.) This species of draining is represented by those who have practised

* Quarterly Journal of Agriculture, vol. vii., p. 246.

it to be applicable to all soils that have a various and uncertain depth of vegetable mould, incumbent on a subsoil of tenacious clay, exceedingly impervious to water, and never dry but by evaporation. It is, however, more suitable to pasture than to arable land, although it will suit all heavy soils that are far removed from stones, or where tiles cannot be conveniently made; but I would remark on this last observation, that I would advise you to prefer *tile* draining to this mode, even although the tiles be very dear, either from distance of carriage or difficulty of manufacture on the spot.

(1058.) The first process is to remove the surface turf, 12 inches in width, and 6½ inches in depth, with the common spade, and to place it on the right hand side of the workman, with the grass side uppermost. A cut is then made in the clay, on each side of the drain, with an edging iron, the circular-mouthed spade, as fig. 150, but a common spade will answer the purpose well enough, and it requires some skill and dexterity to remove this second cut properly. The first cut having been made with the spade 12 inches wide, the second should be made at such an angle down both sides of the drain, 9 inches deep, as that the breadth at the bottom shall be the exact width of the top of the plug *h*, fig. 192, that is, 4 inches wide. Carelessness in expert, or blundering in inexperienced workmen, in this part of the operation, has caused this kind of drain to fail. The bitting-iron then completes the cuttings, by taking out the last cut 9 inches deep, and 1¾ inch wide at the bottom. This instrument is used in this manner: The workman gives its shaft such an angle with the ground line that when pushed down to the requisite depth it continues the cut made by the spade or edging-iron used previously, on the right hand side of the drain; and he does exactly the same on the opposite side of the drain, using his foot in both cases on the tramp *e*, fig. 191. On being forced down on the second side of the drain, the clay that is now separated all round by the bit *b*, leans against the stem of the iron, and is easily lifted out, so that each bitful of the clay taken out by this instrument will have the form of an oblique parallelopepidon. If this part of the operation is performed inaccurately the drain cannot succeed; because the angle and depth made by this instrument are of the utmost consequence in forming the bed which is to be occupied by the plug. Considerable accuracy of hand and eye are requisite, which indeed cannot well be acquired by workmen without much experience, but both may be soon acquired. The clay from the two last cuttings should be placed on the left hand side of the workmen, or the opposite side to that on which the upper turf was laid; and from the last cutting being uppermost, it will come readily to hand when first returned into the drain. Any loose soil that may happen to remain at the bottom should be carefully taken out by a scoop spade, such as fig. 152, so as to leave the drain perfectly clean before the farther operations are effected.

(1059.) The next implement used is the *suter* or *plug*, fig. 192, which consists of three or more pieces of wood *i*, 8½ inches in height, 6 inches in length, 4 inches wide at the top *h*, and 1¾ inch wide at the bottom *g*, joined together by means of iron links *l* sunk into the sides which allow them to pass in a cut with a slight curve. A single suter of 18 or 24 inches long would answer the same or perhaps better purpose. These dimensions are the guage of the opening of the drain described above.

(1060.) The next step in the process is the placing of the plugs on their narrow edges in the bottom of the drain, which they will exactly fit, if the drains have been properly cut out. The most important part of the process is now to be done. The clay that was last taken out with the bitting-iron is well

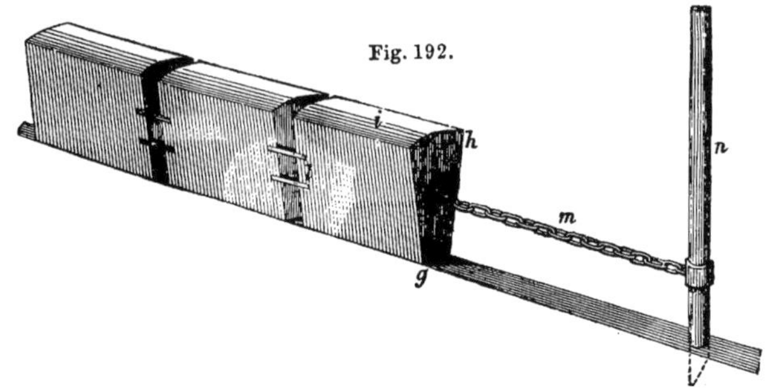

THE SUTERS OR PLUGS IN PLUG-DRAINING.

rammed down upon the plugs, the pieces of the clay being perfectly incorporated into one mass; then the next portion that was cut is returned, and equally well rammed down; and lastly, the turf is placed in the order it was taken out, and fixed in its original position. The whole earth and the turf are rammed down to the full length of the plug, with a rammer made for the purpose, or with such a one as is represented by fig. 175. The operation of ramming being finished, the lever *n*, fig. 192, is then struck into the bottom of the drain, and the plugs drawn forward to within 8 inches of their entire length by the power of the lever on the chain *m*, which is hooked to a staple in the end of the nearest plug. The work of ramming proceeds thus step by step until the whole drain is completed.

(1061.) The finished drain is represented in section in fig. 193, where *o* is the duct left in the clay by the plugs, 8½ inches high; *p* is the clay that was rammed down above the plugs, 9 inches deep; and *r* is the returned turf, with the grassy side uppermost, 6½ inches, which again makes the surface smooth, making a drain of 2 feet in depth. These two figures are drawn to the scale of ⅛ of an inch to 2 inches.

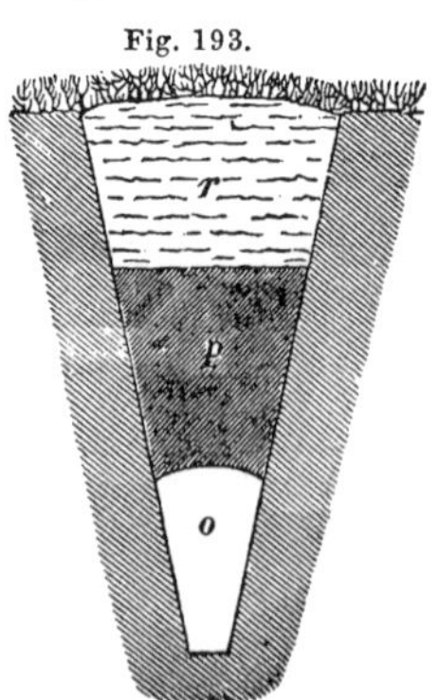

THE SECTION OF A PL UG DRAIN.

(1062.) Some particulars in the conducting of the work should be attended to. 1. Care should be taken to return *all* the earth that was cast out of the drain. This is a criterion of good work; and for this purpose, the ramming being the most laborious part of the operation, the workmen are apt to execute it in an inefficient manner, and should therefore be strictly superintended in its execution. Four men and a boy are the best number of people for carrying on the work expeditiously; and only stout people should be employed, as the ramming is really a laborious process. 2. As few main drains should be made as possible, and the open ends of all should be protected against the inroads of vermin; or what is a better finish, the lowest end of a plug drain should be furnished with tile and sole or stone. The main drains, of course, should be made larger than the ordinary drains, and they will have to be provided with proportionally larger plugs. The drains should be at a distance from each other, in proportion to the drawing nature of the subsoil. 3. No stock whatever should be allowed to enter the field while under this treatment, and even not until the earth over the drains has again become somewhat firm. After the drains of a field are all finished, the ground should be rolled with a heavy roller. 4. This sort of drain should not be made in frosty, snowy, or very rainy weather, as the earth to be rammed in will then be either too hard, crumbly, or too soft. A strict superintendence of the work when it is going on is the only guarantee for efficiency of work; for as to the expedient of imposing fines upon poor workmen, they cannot be exacted without hardship, and perhaps injustice.

(1063.) Mr W. S. Evans, of Selkirk House, near Cheltenham, Gloucestershire, executed 300 miles of this kind of drain in 4 years, and is well pleased with its effects upon the land that has been subjected to it.

(1064.) It is not so inexpensive a mode of draining as it at first sight appears, costing 1¼d. the lineal yard, or L.5 : 0 : 10 the acre, according to Mr Evans' experience; but according to another account, the expense is 4d. the rood of 6 yards, or L.2 : 13: 9¾ the acre.

(1065.) The principle of this mode of draining is said to have succeeded well on the tops of the Gloucestershire hills, where the bottoms of the drains descend to and are cut through rock, and where the bitting-iron and plug have been laid aside for the pick-axe, the channel formed by which is covered with flat stones; and the whole covered with clay rammed down as before described. *This* may be a permanent mode of draining; but in plug-draining in clay, I have no doubt that water will have the effect of softening the sides of the duct, and causing the rammed wedge of clay above to slip downwards; and should the water ever reach to the wedge, the latter will inevitably crumble down, and either entirely fill up, or form a dam across the duct.*

(1066.) An imperfect form of wedge-draining is practised in some parts of England on strong clay soils, under the name of *sod*-draining. It is executed by removing the upper turf with the common spade, and laying it aside, for the purpose of making it the wedge at a subsequent part of the operation; and if the turf is tough, so much the better for the durability of the sod-drain. Another spit is made with the narrow spade, fig. 170, and the last or undermost one is taken out with the narrowest spade represented in fig. 194, which is only 2½ inches wide at the mouth, and as its entire narrowness cannot allow a man's foot being used upon it in the usual manner, a stud or spur is placed in front at the bottom of the helve, upon which the workman's heel is pressed, and pushes down the spade and cuts out the spit. The depth may be to any desired extent. The upper turf is then put in and trampled or beaten down into the narrow drain, in which it becomes wedged against the small shoulder left on each side of the drain, before it can reach the narrow channel formed by the last-mentioned spade, fig. 194, and the channel below the turf being left open, constitutes the duct for the water. It will readily be perceived, that this is a temporary form of drain under any circumstances, though it may last some time in grass land, but it seems quite unsuited for arable ground, which is more liable to be affected by dashes of rain than grass land,

Fig. 194.

THE NARROWEST SPADE FOR SOD-DRAINS.

* Quarterly Journal of Agriculture, vol. iv. p. 501, and vol. xi. p. 68.

and in any situation the clay in contact with water will run the risk of being so much softened as to endanger the existence of the dust.

(1067.) Another method of draining is performed on strong clay land by the *mole plough*. This implement is almost unknown in Scotland, its use being confined to some parts of England, particularly in those parts where grass land on a clay subsoil abounds. It was, I believe, first introduced to the notice of Scottish agriculturists by the Duke of Hamilton, who caused it to be exhibited publicly on the occasion of the Highland and Agricultural Show at Glasgow in 1838. The day after the Show, I saw it exhibited in operation on a farm in the neighbourhood of Glasgow, of strong clay land, for it seems to be best suited to operate in that kind of soil. Its object is to make a small opening in the soil at a given distance from the surface, in the form of a mole-run, to act as a duct for the water that may find its way into it; hence its name of *mole* plough. It makes the pipe or opening in the soil by means of an iron-pointed cone, drawn through the soil by the application of a force, considerably greater than that applied to a common plough.

(1068.) The mole-plough as a draining machine can never be of much utility in a country like Scotland, whose alluvial formations, though not deficient in extent, are characterized more by the abundance of their stony matters than by their clays as occupying the place of subsoils; and it is only in the few patches

Fig. 195.

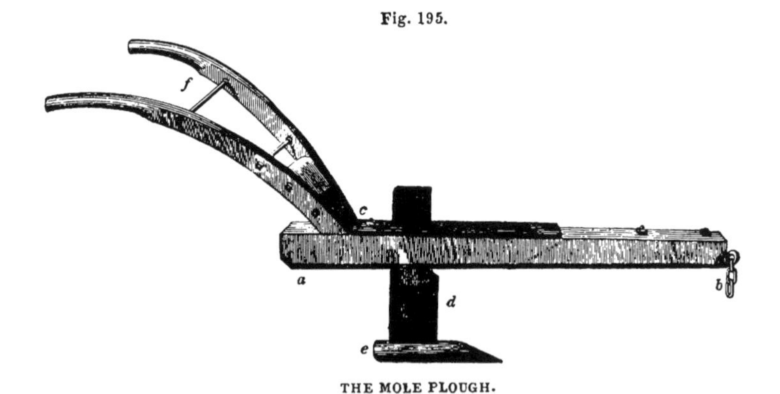

THE MOLE PLOUGH.

of *carse-land* that such clays occur as can be brought under the action of the mole-plough. In all those subsoils where boulders occur, whether large or small, the mole-plough is so inapplicable, its usefulness is limited to such subsoils as consist of pure alluvial clays. In England, and where extensive flat districts of country occur, there the alluvium may be found which are the proper sphere of action for the mole-plough.

(1069.) This plough is of extremely simple construction, as will appear from fig. 195, which is a view of it in perspective. It consists of a beam of oak or ash wood 6½ feet in length, and measuring 6 by 5 inches from the butt-end forward to 4 inches square at the bridle *b*. As the beam when in operation lies close upon the ground, and is indeed the only means of regulating the depth at which the conduit is to be formed, the lower side is sheathed all over with a plate of iron about ½ inch thick. This plate at the proper place (4 feet 4 inches, or thereby, from the point of the beam) is perforated for the coulter-box; its fore-end is worked into an eye, which serves as a bridle, and is altogether strongly bolted to the beam. At the distance of a foot behind the coulter-box a strong stub of wood is mortised into the beam at *c*, standing at the rake and spread which is to be given to the handles. Another plate of iron, of about 3 feet in length and ½ inch thick, is applied on the upper side of the beam; the coulter-box is also formed through this plate, and the hind-part is kneed at *c*, to fit upon and support the stub, to which, as well as to the beam, the plate is firmly bolted. The two stilts or handles *c f* are simply bolted to the stub, which last is of such breadth as to admit of several bolt-holes, by which the *height* of the handles can be adjusted. That which may be termed the head of the plough is a malleable iron plate of about 2 feet in length; that part of it which passes through the beam, and is there fastened by means of wedges like the common coulter, is 7 inches broad and ¾ inch thick. The part *d* below the beam that performs the operation of a coulter, is 9 inches broad, ¾ inch thick in the back edge, and thinned off to a knife-edge in the front. The share or *mole*, is a solid of malleable iron, welded or riveted to the head; its length in the sole is about 15 inches, and in its cross section (which is a triangle with curved sides and considerably blunted on the angles) it measures about 3 inches broad at the sole, and 3½ inches in height. A cylinder is, however, a better form than a triangle; but in either case, the fore-part of the share is worked into a conical form, the apex being in the line of the sole, or nearly so. This, while it enables the share to penetrate the earth more freely, prevents a tendency to rising out of the ground. The tendency to rise is, however, not so great as may be supposed, for the centre of motion in this implement being very low, not less than 12 inches under the surface of the ground, and the draft being applied horizontally, there is a strong tendency in the point of the beam and of the share, as in all similar cases of oblique draft, to sink into the ground, (804.)–(808.); the effect of which, if not properly balanced by the effects of *form* in the parts, will give the mole-plough much unnecessary resistance.

(1070.) In working this plough, the draft-chain is attached to the bridle-eye at *b*, and it is usually drawn by two horses walking in a circular course, giving motion to a portable horse capstan, that is constructed on a small platform movable on low carriage-wheels, and which is moored by anchors at convenient reaches of 50 to 60 yards. The mechanical advantage yielded by the horse capstan gives out a power of about 10 to 1, or, deducting friction, equal to a force of about 14 horses.

(1071.) When the plough is entered into the soil and moved forward, the broad coulter cuts the soil with its sharp edge, and the sock makes its way through the clay subsoil by compressing it on all sides, and the tenacity of the clay keeps not only the pipe thus formed open, but the slit which is made by the broad coulter permits the water that is in the soil to find its way directly into the pipe. The plough is found to work with the greatest steadiness at 15 inches below the surface. The upper turf is sometimes laid over beforehand by the common plough, when the mole plough is made to pass along the bottom of its furrow, and the furrow-slice or turf is again carefully replaced. This is the preferable mode of working this plough, as it serves to preserve the slit made by the coulter longer open than when it terminates at the surface of the turf, where, of course, it is liable to be soon closed up; but the least trouble is incurred when the plough is made to pass through the turf unploughed.

(1072.) To work the whole apparatus efficiently 2 horses and 3 men are required; and if the common estimate of 10s. a-day for 2 horses and 1 man is taken, but which is too high, as you shall have occasion afterwards to learn, and 3s. 6d. for the other 2 men, an acre of ground can be mole-drained for 13s. 6d. exclusive of the first cost and tear and wear of this apparatus, the cost of which cannot be less than L.50. At this rate, this is the cheapest of all the modes of draining that you have yet heard of.

(1073.) If the mole plough is put in motion in soft clay, the slit made by the broad coulter will not remain open even for a single day; and though it may again open in severe drought, it will close again whenever the clay becomes moist. This plough seems fitted for action only in pure clay subsoils, and when such are found under old grass, it may partially drain the ground with comparative economy; and the process being really economical, it may be repeated in the course of years in the same ground. In my estimation, this mode of draining cannot bear a comparison for efficacy to tile-draining, although it is employed in some parts of England, where its effects are highly spoken of.*

(1074.) It has lately been proposed by Mr Scot of Craigmoy, Stewartry of Kirkcudbright, to substitute tubes of larch wood for drain-tiles, in situations where larch is plentiful, and consequently cheap, and drain-tiles dear, and he considers that they would be equally efficient with tiles in many situations, and especially in mossy soils. Were larch tubes confined to draining mossy soils, I conceive they would answer the purpose well, not only on account of their length maintaining their original position in the drain; but on account of the durable nature of larch where water is constantly present, as is instanced in cases of great antiquity, such as the piles of larch upon which the city of Venice is founded. The larch tree that is felled in winter, and allowed to dry with the bark on, is much more durable and useful for every purpose, and infinitely more free of splits and cracks than that which is cut down in sap, and immediately deprived of its bark for tan.

(1075.) The tube finished, fig. 196, presents a square of 4 inches outside, with a clear water-way of 2 inches. To those who wish to know how they are made I refer to Mr Scot's published statement;† but in doing this I must remark that the cost of these tubes will exceed that of clay tiles. For, take the cost of drain tiles at 30s. per 1000 including carriage, that will be 1½ farthing the lineal foot. Now, a lineal foot of larch tube contains say 1 superficial foot of timber at 1 inch thick, which will cost for carriage and sawing the timber 1 farthing; the fitting, boring, and pins will cost other 2 farthings; and the timber, at 6d. the cubic foot, will increase the cost 2 farthings more, which altogether make the tube more than 3 times dearer than tiles; and if the cost of the timber is thrown into the bargain, still they will be double the price of tiles.

Fig. 196.

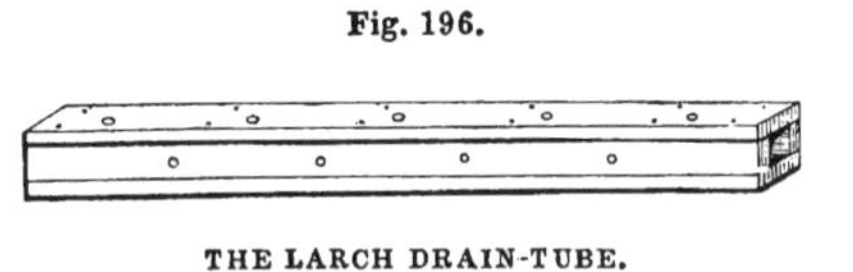

THE LARCH DRAIN-TUBE.

(1076.) The recommendation of wooden tubes for the purpose of draining land, reminds me of many expedients which are practised to fill drains, among which are brushwood, thorns, trees, and even straw-ropes. With the exception

* See the Agricultural Surveys of Middlesex and Essex.

† Prize Essays of the Highland and Agricultural Society, vol. xiv. p. 99-109, where the machinery for making these tubes is figured and minutely described.

of the trunks of small trees, which, when judiciously laid down in drains, may last a considerable time, it is not to be imagined that brushwood of any kind can be durable. Hence drains filled with them soon fall in. It could only be dire necessity that would induce any man to fill drains with straw twisted into ropes; and it could only have been the same cause, in situations where stones were scarce, and at a time when drain-tiles were little known in Scotland, such as was the case during the late war, that could have tempted farmers to fill drains with thorns. No doubt, the astringent nature of thorn wood and bark may preserve their substance from decay under ground for a considerable time, but the sinking of holes in such drains, as I have seen, were infallible symptoms of decay. Only conceive what a mess such a drain must be that is " filled up to the height of 8 or 10 inches either with brushwood, stripped of the leaves—oak, ash, or willow twigs being the best—and covered with long wheat straw, twisted into bands, which are put in with the hand, and afterwards forced down with the spade, care being taken," the only case of it evinced in the whole operation, " that none of the loose mould is allowed to go along with them. The trench is then entirely filled up with earth, the first layer of which is closely trampled down, and the remainder thrown in loosely."* And yet such is the practice in several of the south-eastern and midland counties of England.

(1077.) Of the *durability of common brick* when used in drains, there is a remarkable instance mentioned by Mr George Guthrie, factor to the Earl of Stair, on Culhorn, Wigtonshire. In the execution of modern draining on that estate, some brick-drains, on being intersected, emitted water very freely. According to documents which refer to these drains, it appears that they had been formed by the celebrated Marshal, Earl Stair, *upwards of a hundred years ago*. They were found between the vegetable mould and the clay upon which it rested, between the "wet and the dry," as the country phrase has it, and about 31 inches below the surface. They presented two forms; one consisting of 2 bricks set asunder on edge, and the other 2 laid lengthways across them, leaving between them an opening of 4 inches square for water, but having no soles. The bricks had not sunk in the least through the sandy clay bottom upon which they rested, as they were 3 inches broad. The other form was of 2 bricks laid side by side, as a sole, with 2 others built on bed on each other at both sides, upon the solid ground, and covered with flat stones, the building being packed on each side of the drain with broken bricks.†

(1078.) Various attempts have been made to *lessen the cost of cutting drains*. One of these is to cut the drains narrower than they used to be, for the obvious reason, that the drawing power of drains lies more in their depth than breadth; and the cubical contents of drains, of any given length, have in consequence been much decreased, and the cost of digging them of course much lessened.

(1079.) An attempt has been made with this view by Mr Peter M'Ewan, Blackdub, Stirlingshire. His invention consists of the application of the plough in casting out the contents of drains, and it certainly displays much mechanical ingenuity, and really performs the work with a considerable degree of perfection. This application of the plough, however, is by no means adapted to every species of subsoil, the most common one, of a tilly clay, containing small stones and occasional boulders, presenting insuperable difficulties to its progress, whilst in pure unctuous clay it cuts its way with ease, and lays aside the tenacious furrow-slice

* British Husbandry, vol. i. p. 457.

† Prize Essays of the Highland and Agricultural Society, vol. xiv. p. 45.

with a considerable degree of regularity. The instrument has thus a limited application, but a greater objection exists against it, inasmuch as it requires an inordinate amount of power to set it in motion, consisting of that of 12 horses. This circumstance alone still more limits its application, for there are comparatively few farms which employ 6 pairs of horses at work; and besides, it is almost impossible to yoke 12 horses together, so as to derive the amount of labour from them, as when yoked in pairs. It is truly distressing to see the horses working with this plough, as I once had the opportunity of witnessing in a field, of favourable subsoil too, in the neighbourhood of Glasgow in 1838, on the occasion of the Highland and Agricultural Society's Show.

(1080.) Mr Smith, Deanston, has given a description of Mr M'Ewan's draining plough, which it is not necessary to particularise farther than that the horses go in two divisions, one on each side of the line of draught, yoked to a strong master-tree 10 feet long, arranged so as to have 4 abreast, when 8 horses are used, and 6 abreast when 12 horses are yoked.

(1081.) With regard to the state of the work left by this plough, men follow with spades, and take out a bed for tiles or broken stones, and correct any deviation from a uniform fall in the bottom, occasioned by unevenness of ground. The tiles or stones are then put in in the usual manner, and the earth is returned into the drain by the plough.

(1082.) This drain-plough is made of two sizes, one weighing 5 cwt., costing L.11, the other weighing 4 cwt., and costing L.8, 8s., and the bars or swingle-trees, necessary to accompany each plough, are 2 six-horse, 4 three-horse, and a strong chain, the whole costing L.4, 4s.

(1083.) With regard to the length of drain cut by this plough, Mr Smith estimates the time spent at 2 miles per hour for 8 hours; and allowing $\frac{1}{3}$ of it to be lost in turnings, the actual quantity of work done in 8 hours he takes at 3126 roods of 6 yards, or about 19½ acres, at 15 feet asunder, the drains being cut from 18 to 22 inches in depth. This quantity of work is corroborated by Mr John Glen, Hilton, Clackmannanshire, who states that "we drain 400 Scotch chains in 9 hours," going down hill with the furrow, and up empty.

(1084.) The rate of walking taken by Mr Smith, at 2 miles the hour, is too great, as the distance travelled in ploughing 1 imperial acre of ground, in the usual way, in a day of 10 hours, which constitutes a good rate of work, is 9⅞ miles, or only 1742 yards per hour, including of course turnings. There is also a discrepancy in Mr Glen's statement of draining nearly half the extent of his land in 9 hours, going half the time empty, with another statement where he says, "we have used Mr M'Ewan's drain-plough for the last 4 months, and have drained 837 chains, Scotch measure, with it;" that is, only 2 days' work in 4 months, with 6 horses, the drain being 18½ inches wide at top and 8 inches wide at bottom, and from 15 to 17 inches in depth.

(1085.) The cost of employing this drain-plough is thus given by Mr Smith:

12 horses at 4s. a-day each, ...	L.2	8	0
8 men at 2s. a-day each, ...	0	16	0
To cover interest of cost, and tear and wear of plough, say 1s. the hour, ...	0	8	0
	L.3	12	0

which is only $1\frac{1}{3}$ farthing per rood of 6 yards.*

* Smith's Remarks on Thorough-Draining, pp. 26–31.

(1086.) Other ploughs have been invented for making drains, which have attracted attention, and engaged the advocacy of friends in the immediate locality in which they originated, but seem never to have extended farther.

(1087.) In 1832, Mr Robert Green, a farmer in Cambridgeshire, published an account of a drain-plough of his invention. It cuts the ground 23 inches deep and 8 inches wide at top, and 2 inches at bottom, at three cuts; the first being 9 inches, the second 8 inches, and the third 6 inches deep. It is said to take the earth out clean, leaving none to shovel out. It cuts about 500 or 600 poles or rods of the above dimensions, at three times. It requires 4 horses the first time, and 6 horses the other two, and 2 men and a boy to work them, at L.1, 10s. a-day. The price of this plough is quoted at L.15.*

(1088). In 1833, Mr Thomas Law Hodges published an account of a drain-plough invented by Mr John Pearson, Frotterden, near Cranbrook in Kent. The drain is taken out by it at three turns. Men follow with narrow scoops, and throw out all the loose earth clean, which finishes the drain at 26 inches deep, at an expense of 1d. the rod.

(1089.) Both these implements are best adapted to strong clay subsoils, and best for plug-draining, especially Pearson's, when, after its operation, a long narrow plug or slide of wood is used, the clay being rammed down upon which, it is then drawn forward by means of a windlass and rope. This plough is estimated to cost L.9, 5s., but with spades, scoops, and rammers, it costs L.18.†

(1090.) I am now arrived at a very important question connected with the draining of land, namely, Whether *landlords should undertake part of the expense?* This question cannot be satisfactorily answered without taking into consideration the object and effect of draining land, and the cost attending it. The object of draining land is simply to make it dry, but in doing that, the fertility of the soil is found to be increased, not merely for a year or two, or even for a rotation of crops, which manure only affects to embrace, but *at least* for the duration of a 19 years' lease, and probably for a much longer period, and possibly for an indefinite length of time. Here, then, is an operation which is capable of making land better, not merely in a temporary, but in a permanent manner, and hence its intrinsic worth is to increase the permanent value of land. This being the case, the question simply resolves itself into this: Ought landlords to allow other parties to enhance the permanent value of their land, or, permitting it, ought they to accept a permanent increase of rent for land whose permanent value they have in no way contributed to enhance? Can they in honour refuse to assist in the permanent improvement of their land, and yet exact the highest rent the land is worth, in consequence of those improvements? I think, in honour, they cannot act thus; it would be unfair to do so. Improvement effected by judicious draining is acknowledged to be permanent, that effected by good husbandry is acknowledged to be temporary. In the latter case, the landlord is quite entitled to derive every additional advantage arising from good management, because it is in the power of the tenant, if he chooses, to avail himself of all its good effects during his lease, and if he leave any remarkable advantage to his landlord, it is the act of his own free will; but in the permanent improvement of draining, he cannot avail himself of its entire advantages. Some of these, and indeed the whole value of these advantages may be given over to the landlord at the end of the lease; and this being practically the case, the landlord in fairness should not accept of an improvement

* Green on Underdraining Wet and Cold Land.

† Hodges on the Use and Advantages of Pearson's Draining Plough.

in his condition effected by a process to which he has in no degree contributed. To enable him to accept such an effect with honour, he should insist on becoming a party in the process of acquiring it along with his tenant. This is the question regarding draining in reference to the landlord, but there is one also in connection with the tenant, namely, ought he to spend his money in draining his landlords' land without assistance? In fairness to himself, he ought not to do so; and, at any rate, it is improper in him to do it without, in the first instance, obtaining his landlord's consent. Nevertheless, in regard to both questions, there are landlords who refuse to drain, and there are tenants who do drain, farms, at their own risk, the tenants thereby gratuitously, as it were, creating an increase of income to their landlords, without receiving an equivalent in return. When the subject of draining is placed only in this light before the tenant, the chief and indeed only consideration with him is, whether the outlay he will incur by it will be returned to him during the currency of his lease? and if the trouble and cost he will be at will no more than accomplish this, his condition will remain unimproved; for, to improve his condition, he would require to receive a larger return than the mere amount of the money he expends. I believe most of the draining executed in this country of late years has been conducted by the tenant in the hope that he will have his outlay returned to him before the expiry of his lease. But this is an unsatisfactory state for a tenant to be placed in, because it secures neither the permanent improvement of the soil, nor insures the co-operation of its owner, whilst it diverts a large proportion of the capital of the tenant into a channel from which there may possibly flow no advantage to him; because, though there is, in every case, little doubt of the land deriving benefit from draining, there is a well-grounded apprehension whether the tenant will have time to receive back all the money he expends, and whether at the same time he will be remunerated for the trouble of conducting the operation, for which he is entitled to be so as much as any other man who is engaged in business. This apprehension is strengthened from the circumstance that a large sum is required to drain land in an efficient manner; that from L.3 to L.10 an acre are required to do it; can the tenant therefore with prudence solely undertake so expensive a system of improvement, since it is clear that the landlord will derive advantage from it, whether he participate in the outlay or not. This being the state of things, the landlord has no direct motive in offering to participate in the expense; but the tenant has a direct one for requesting him to do it. It is, therefore, not improbable, that where the landlord does not assist his tenant in draining, the fault rests with the tenant in neglecting to request his co-operation; for in the circumstances, it would require a landlord to be actuated by a very high sense of honour and justice, before he would voluntarily offer to participate in an expense, the benefits accruing from which he will enjoy as much without the outlay. It is feared that in such circumstances the inevitable consequence should be, that the assistance of the landlord must be requested, or the tenant undertake the whole outlay himself.

(1091.) I have hitherto conducted this argument on the supposition of landlords refusing to incur any part of the expense of draining land; but were they to undertake, as a matter of course, the proportion which really belongs to them in the relation in which they stand with their tenants, the inconvenience to the tenants of having to disburse a large sum of money would be avoided, and they would then require to possess no larger capitals than what would fully stock their farms, and all the operations connected with draining would be executed in the most substantial manner. Landlords would then be fairly entitled to receive the full increase of value which would be derived from draining. As the true relation of the landlord and tenant in regard to draining has hitherto not been so clearly illustrated as it deserves, I shall endeavour to show the proper positions of both parties, by proving that it is more a landlord's than a tenant's question, even in the low view of pecuniary remuneration, which is probably the most practical way of viewing the subject; and in doing this I shall first consider the opinions of some practical men who have expressed their sentiments on this interesting inquiry.

(1092.) Mr Roberton, Ladyrig, who has drained much, and considered the relation of landlord and tenant in regard to the prosecution of that operation, expresses himself on the subject in judicious terms. While commenting on the different style of draining which is executed by the tenant himself, from that which is undertaken conjointly with the landlord, he says, " that the immediate effect in both cases is much the same; and to serve merely the temporary purpose of the tenant, I have no doubt that the one will prove as beneficial as the other. To the proprietor, however, the case is very different; because, by the latter method, an improvement is effected which may be guaranteed to endure for several leases. It is very doubtful whether, by the former mode, it can be ensured much beyond the existing lease. That the proprietor should at all times become a party, and thereby secure the permanent improvement of his estate, is now very generally admitted; and yet the plan is not always acted upon. It may, however, be asserted, without much fear of contradiction, that improvements by thorough-draining will never become general, or be made permanent, unless the assistance of the landlord be obtained. When left altogether to the tenant, want of capital and the shortness of the lease will tend at all times to limit the extent of improvements, and will seldom be made permanent; because the true interest of the tenant is to execute the work only in such a manner as will secure his own temporary purpose. To the proprietor, among the many inducements to improve his estate by draining, the greatest, at least the most satisfactory, is, that it yields an immediate and large return. If he has no spare money, he has only to borrow it at 4 per cent. and lend it out at 6 per cent.; a per centage which no tenant will refuse to pay, and upon a security, too, undoubted—that of his own property. No one will deny that a proprietor is as justly entitled to receive a fair return for money laid out in the improvement of his estate, as he is for that laid out on the original purchase of it. Hence, I would assume, as a general principle, that for every penny laid out by a proprietor upon ameliorations of any kind, he shall have an assurance of a return, either immediate or prospective—immediate, in the form of interest or of additional rent; prospective, in the increased value of his property, by which, in after leases, it will yield such an increase of rent as will repay the present outlay. Again, as regards a tenant, I will assume that he will make every improvement the subject of a calculation of profit or loss for *one lease only*, and that he will not lay out any money *merely for the purpose* of making improvements to extend beyond that period. Let him even have an assurance of a renewal of his lease, still, before that takes place, a valuation will be made of his farm, and in that valuation will be included his improvements; so that, while he originally disbursed the whole expense of them, he will in reality have to pay for them again in the shape of additional rent."

(1093.) In the instances of the cost of draining given a few pages back, that incurred by Mr Roberton varied from L.4 : 17 : 6 to L.3 : 8 : 4 the acre. In the first example, Mr Roberton informs us that the proprietors of his farm, the Governors of the Merchant Maiden Hospital in Edinburgh, bore the expense of opening the drain, and the work was executed in a manner that, case, they were wholly executed at his own expense, upon a lease of only 12 years' duration, and were therefore more superficially executed. "In the preceding examples," he proceeds to say, "both methods have been tried, and both have succeeded. And I think they tend to prove, in the first place, that the difference in the expense of the two methods is very nearly equal to what may be deemed a fair allowance for the landlord; and when it is taken into consideration that, by the cheaper mode, the improvement of a greater extent of land is completed in a given time without materially increasing the number of horses upon the farm, it is doubtful whether, in the end, it may not prove the more profitable one for the tenant; and, in the second place, it proves that, to a tenant of capital, the assistance of the landlord is by no means so essential a matter as to deter him from engaging in an improvement of the kind. For, as a mere speculation, he may embark in it with confidence; and let the prices of produce vary as they may, the money expended in this way will always yield him a fair return."*

(1094.) In a table of the relative proportion which landlords and tenants should bear in the making of drains, Mr Smith, Deanston, has taken that of $\frac{2}{3}$ for the landlord and $\frac{1}{3}$ for the tenant,—being the reverse of what Mr Roberton's remarks seem to indicate.

Cost of draining the acre,			Landlord's share.			Tenant's share.		
L.	S.	D.	L.	S.	D.	L.	S.	D.
9	10	0	6	6	8	3	3	4
8	12	7	5	15	0	2	17	6
7	18	9	5	5	10	2	12	11
7	6	3	4	17	6	2	8	9
6	16	3	4	10	10	2	5	5
6	6	7	4	4	5	2	2	2
6	0	0	4	0	0	2	0	0
5	12	6	3	15	0	1	17	6
5	6	3	3	10	10	1	15	5
5	0	0	3	6	8	1	13	4
4	15	0	3	3	4	1	11	8
4	10	0	3	0	0	1	10	0
4	6	3	2	17	6	1	8	9
4	2	6	2	15	0	1	7	6
4	0	0	2	13	4	1	6	8
3	16	3	2	10	10	1	5	5
3	12	2	2	8	4	1	4	6
3	10	0	2	6	8	1	3	4
3	7	6	2	5	0	1	2	6
3	4	0	2	3	4	1	1	5
3	2	6	2	1	8	1	0	10
3	1	3	2	0	10	1	0	5
3	0	0	2	0	0	1	0	0
2	17	6	1	18	4	0	19	2
2	16	3	1	17	6	0	18	9
2	15	0	1	16	8	0	18	4
2	13	9	1	15	10	0	17	11
2	11	3	1	14	2	0	17	1
2	10	0	1	13	4	0	16	8
2	8	6	1	12	6	0	16	3
2	7	9	1	11	8	0	15	10†

* Prize Essays of the Highland and Agricultural Society, vol. xiv. p. 43–5.
† Smith's Remarks on Thorough-Draining, p. 16.

(1095.) The statement of Mr George Bell, Woodhouselees, of the cost of tile-draining (1028.), shews the actual proportions borne by his landlord the Duke of Buccleuch and by himself, in the draining of his farm. The proportions are relatively these:—

By the landlord—			
38,000 3-inch tile, at 25s.		L.47 10 0	
1,577 4-inch ... 32s.		2 10 5	
Cutting 2003 roods of 6 yards, at 3d. the rood, ...		26 0 9	
Slates for soles, ...		1 5 0	
Total cost by the landlord,		L.77 6 2	or, per acre, L.5 18 11
By the tenant—			
Leading 38,000 3-inch tiles, at 3s. 4d. per 1000, ...	L.6 6 8		
Leading 1577 4-inch tiles, at 5s. the 1000, ...	0 7 10		
31 days' work of man and horse laying down tiles, straw for covering them, &c. at 5s. 6d. per day, ...	8 10 6		
Women loading and unloading carts, ...	2 3 0		
31 days of a man setting tiles,	2 5 0		
31 days of a woman assisting him, ...	1 0 0		
3 days of a plough, and horses and man, ...	1 10 0		
		L.22 3 0	or, per acre, L.1 14 1
Total cost by landlord and tenant,		L.99 9 2	
Total cost per acre, ...			L.7 13 0

Taking Mr Smith's proportion of $\frac{2}{3}$ for the landlord, the ratio which the Duke of Buccleuch should pay of the total cost of L.99 : 9 : 2 should be L.66 : 6 : 1$\frac{1}{4}$; but he actually paid L.77 : 6 : 2, being more than $\frac{3}{4}$, that being L.74 : 11 : 0$\frac{1}{2}$, and nearly $\frac{4}{5}$, which is L.79 : 11 : 4.

(1096.) In every case, the landlord should, as I think, follow the above example, and disburse the expense of cutting the drains and the cost of the materials for filling them, though these should be brought from a distance, or inaccessible without much labour. The tenant should afford carriage of all sorts, and pay, besides, the legal rate of interest, on the landlord's entire outlay. On these conditions, with the expense, mutually borne, of an experienced man to superintend the execution of the drains, according to specifications previously agreed on betwixt landlord and tenant, the drains will be executed in so efficient a manner as to last for an indefinite period of years. It may be seen, from this statement of Mr Bell, that, in fulfilment of these conditions, the landlord should incur $\frac{4}{5}$ and the tenant only $\frac{1}{5}$ of the expenses, proportions which differ very materially in favour of the tenant from those laid down by Mr Smith, and still more so than those experienced by Mr Roberton. It appears, therefore, that on fixed rule has yet been established on this subject; though it is desirable that there should be, and let us endeavour to discover a rule that shall deserve to be established.

(1097.) Suppose, then, that a landlord determines on thorough-draining a farm, and that for the purpose he takes the farm into his own hands, and disburses every cost, including carriages, attending the operation. When his purpose has been attained, and he wishes to let it in a drained state, it is no more than reasonable of him to desire to receive back his disbursements, principal and interest, during the currency of the 19 years' lease which he is about to enter into with a tenant; because, on the one hand, if the land will not repay the expense of its improvement in a reasonable time, and surely 19 years is a long enough time in which it should be repaid, there will be no advantage to either party in the improving of it, and, on the other hand, if a tenant receive an improved farm, he cannot expect to hire it on the same terms as when it was unimproved. Now, that a landlord may receive back all his disbursements, principal and interest, during a 19 years' lease, he would require to receive from the tenant 8 per cent. on them.

(1098.) Suppose, on the other hand, that the tenant disbursed every expense of draining, then, of course, it is equally reasonable that he should receive 8 per cent. on his outlay during the lease, in order to receive the entire sum back.

(1099.) But the positions of the two parties, landlord and tenant, in regard to expending the same amount in draining a farm, are widely different. The tenant is entitled to receive back not only all the money he has laid out, that is, to receive 8 per cent., but he is also entitled to receive at least 10 if not 15 per cent. more for his personal trouble in undertaking the task of draining another man's land, and for the risk incurred in laying out money on an undertaking attended with contingencies; because, in similar circumstances, commercial people expect 15 per cent. Thus the tenant, being a temporary lessee, should receive *at least* 18 per cent. for his disbursements, whereas the landlord, being a permanent owner, should be satisfied with *at most* 8 per cent. for the same amount of outlay. For in regard to the tenant, the period of his agreement, namely, 19 or any other number of years, is the longest period that he can calculate upon to receive back the money, and it is no matter though the lease should then be renewed, because the new conditions will be made as if the sitting tenant were a stranger; and on this account matters should be finally settled between him and his landlord at the end of the lease, which can only be accomplished by the tenant receiving from the farm 18 per cent. on his outlay; but in the relation of the landowner to his land, whatever improvement he effects upon it produces results to him to an indefinite period of time, and this being the case, all that he can expect in return for his outlay is the common rate of interest which he would receive were he to invest his money in any other ordinary security, and which, in such a case, never exceeds 5 per cent.

(1100.) Thus then when a tenant drains his farm thoroughly, he should receive at least 18 per cent. for his outlay, and when a landlord does it he should only receive 5 per cent. Now, what conclusion should be drawn from these premises? Clearly that the landlord should undertake the entire expense of draining his land; because his interest in the improvement is permanent, he has the strongest motives for improving it—his demands upon the land are moderate, amounting only to the usual rate of interest—and in his disbursing a portion of his capital a smaller portion of the capital of the country is placed in less jeopardy than when the tenant undertakes to fulfil the landlords' obligations.

(1101.) In both these suppositions the landlord and tenant are each supposed to have effected the entire drainage, but when a mutual understanding exists betwixt them on the subject, its condition would justly be based on the principles advocated in (1096.), and as the understanding betwixt the parties is only for a definite period, both parties expect and should receive, during that period, their respective amounts of interest or return on the outlay which each has incurred, namely, the landlord 8 per cent. and the tenant 18 per cent; and to attain this desirable end the tenant should not grudge his landlord his interest of 8 per cent., nor should the landlord exact a greater rent than what will enable the farm to pay the tenant 18 per cent. on his portion of the outlay, and either will not amount to a large annual sum. For example, suppose that $\frac{4}{5}$ or L.80 out of every L.100 are expended by the landlord, he should receive L.6, 8s. a-year to get his 8 per cent., and to give the tenant 18 per cent. on his $\frac{1}{5}$ or L.20 he would require to receive L.3 : 11 : 8 a-year, both sums making together 10 per cent. on the whole outlay, which, if exacted in the shape of an annual tribute from the land, would amount only to 4s. per acre on land worth 40s.,—a sum which thorough-draining would easily repay.

(1102.) [The mechanical principles of draining have been already so fully discussed that I need not detain you a moment with their examination : but this will be the best place for considering a most interesting subject connected with soil, upon which the whole *necessity* of draining depends, I refer to the manner in which an excess of water proves injurious to the fertility of the soil.

(1103.) In considering this subject it will be advisable to examine into the effects of water, 1*st* upon the mechanical condition of the soil, and 2*d*, upon its chemical constituents, reserving the influence which it exerts directly upon vegetation to be discussed on some future occasion.

(1104.) If you call to mind what I have said regarding the mechanical constitution of soil (516.), you will at once perceive that a soil *in situ* might not inaptly be compared to a porous solid permeated by innumerable tortuous channels, these channels being formed by the interstitial spaces occurring between the various particles composing the soil.

(1105.) If water is added gradually to soil, the first effect will be doubtless to fill these channels, but from the attraction which the various components of soil have for water, they speedily draw it into their pores, and thus empty the channels so that even after a considerable addition, the soil, *taken as a whole*, does not lose its porosity although each particle *has its individual pores* filled with water. This is the healthy condition of soil, it is what I shall call *moist*, in contradistinction to *wet*. Soil in this state can be crumbled down in the hands without making them muddy, although it feels distinctly *damp*, and will lose, when heated to 212° F., from 20 to 50 per cent. of water.

(1106.) If now more water should be added, the channels will be again filled, and as the pores of each particle are already saturated with moisture, they can again be emptied only by one of the two following methods : 1*st*, either very gradually by evaporation from the surface, as in *undrained soil*, or 2*d*, much more rapidly and effectually by the channels having communication with some larger channel in a relatively lower level, as is the case in *drained soil*. Soil in which all the interstices between its particles are more or less filled with water may be called *wet* soil, and all such land must be drained before it can be properly and advantageously cultivated.

(1107.) You will thus perceive that water does no harm, in fact it is absolutely necessary in soil so long as it does not alter its mechanical condition ; but whenever it fills up the interstitial channels it becomes injurious for the following reasons:—1*st*, it prevents the circulation of air through the soil, as this takes place entirely through the medium of these channels,—2*d*, it impoverishes the soil by permitting soluble matter to soak through; because until these channels are filled there is no flow of liquid in the soil, except a very gentle current from below upwards, produced by capillary attraction towards the drier particles near the surface.*

(1108.) Again, an excess of water acts most injuriously in soil by reducing its temperature. This is owing to the extremely slight conducting power of water for heat; as compared to earthy matter, assisted also by the cold produced by continued evaporation. According to some experiments which I performed,—the diminution of heat produced in this way amounts, in summer, on an average to 6½ degrees of Fahrenheit, which, according to Sir John Leslie's mode of calculating elevation by the mean temperature, is equivalent to a difference of 1950 feet. When we consider the effects of elevation upon the nature and amount of produce, we shall have good reason to see the baneful effects of such a change as this represents.

(1109.) Besides the above injuries inflicted by an excess of water, there are numerous effects upon the chemical changes in the soil, and also upon the plants themselves, all of which must be considered in their proper place. I trust, however, that what I have advanced will serve to impress sufficiently on your minds the evident necessity of thorough-draining in all situations where the soil is *wet*.—H. R. M.]

(1110.) After pointing out the effects of draining in ameliorating the soil and promoting a healthy condition of vegetation, Professor Johnston proceeds to shew the effects of water upon clay soil. "I shall add one important remark," he says, "which will readily suggest itself to the geologist who has studied the action of air and water on the various clay beds that occur here and there as members of the series of stratified rocks. There are *no clays* which do *not* gradually *soften* under the united influence of air and of running water. *It is false economy, therefore, to lay down tiles without soles, however hard and stiff the clay subsoil may appear to be.* In the course of 10 or 15 years, the stiffest clays will soften, so as to allow the tile to sink, and many very much sooner. The passage for the water is thus gradually removed; and when the tile has sunk a couple of inches, the whole must be taken up. Thousands of miles of drains have been thus laid down, both in the low country of Scotland and in the southern counties of England, which have now become nearly useless; and yet the system still goes on. It would appear even as if the farmers and proprietors of each district, unwilling to believe in or to be benefited by the experience of others, were determined to prove the matter in their own case also, before they will consent to adopt that surer system which, though demanding a slightly greater outlay at first, will return upon the drainer with no after-calls for either time or capital. If my reader," continues the Professor, "lives in a district where this practice is now exploded, and if he be inclined to doubt if other counties be farther behind the advance of knowledge than his own, I would invite him to spend a week in crossing the county of Durham, where he may find op-

* See Prize Essay on this subject by me in the Prize Essays of the Highland and Agricultural Society, vol. xiii. p. 141.

† Ibid., vol. xiv. p. 227.

portunities not only of satisfying his own doubts, but of scattering here and there a few words of useful advice among the more intelligent of our practical farmers."*

(1111.) As the preservation of the fall in a drain on nearly level ground is of great importance in drying it, it may be satisfactory to have a demonstration of the fact that the angle subtended by the plumb-line *d f*, in fig. 183, is equal to the angle of inclination of the drain *b a c*. The rule is, as radius : *a b* :: sine of the angle, *b a c* : *b c*, the height of the fall : Or, multiply the natural sine of the angle *b a c* by the length of the fall *a b*, and the same result will be obtained.†

(1112.) The Romans practised draining both with open and covered drains, the former in clay and the latter in porous soils. The instructions given by Palladius for the formation of drains may be received with surprise by modern practisers of the art on account of their correctness, and when their great antiquity is held in remembrance. "If the land is wet," he says, "it may be dried by drains drawn from every part. Open drains are well known; covered drains are made in this manner: Ditches are made across the field 3 feet deep; afterwards they are filled half-way up with small stones or gravel, and then filled to the surface with the earth that was thrown out. These covered drains are let to an open one to which they descend, so that the water is carried off, and destroys no part of the field. If stones cannot be got, branches, or straw, or any kind of twigs, may be used in their place."‡

---

28. OF YOKING AND HARNESSING THE PLOUGH, AND OF SWING-TREES.

"No wheels support the diving pointed share;
No groaning ox is doomed to labour there;
No helpmates teach the docile steed his road;
Alike unknown the plough-boy and the goad;
But, unassisted through each toilsome day,
With smiling brow, the ploughman cleaves his way."

BLOOMFIELD.

(1113.) Having inspected the varieties of soil within the sphere of your observation, and been told of the various modes in which the land may be stirred by the plough in winter, it will be proper for you to know the simple and efficient method by which horses are attached to and driven in the plough in Scotland, before the winter-ploughing of the soil is begun, and to enable you to conceive the process more vividly,

* Johnston's Elements of Agricultural Chemistry, p. 125–6.

† See the practical application of this rule on a large scale illustrated in Denton on Model-Mapping, p. 35.

‡ Dickson's Husbandry of the Ancients, vol. i. p. 370.

you will find a pretty accurate representation of a plough at work in Plate XIII.

(1114.) The first thing that will strike you is the extreme simplicity of the whole arrangement of the horses, harness, plough, and man, impressing you with the satisfactory feeling that no part of it can go wrong, and affording you a happy illustration of a complicated arrangement performing complicated work by a simple action. On examining particulars, you will find the *collar*, better seen in fig. 197, around the horse's neck, serving as a padding to preserve his shoulders from injury while pressing forward to the draught. Embracing a groove in the anterior part of the collar, are the *haims*, composed of two pieces of wood, curved towards their lower extremities, which are hooked and attached together by means of a small chain, and their upper extremities held tight by means of a leather strap and buckle; and they are moreover provided on each side with an iron hook, to which the object of draught is attached. The horse is yoked to the swing-trees by light chains, called *trace-chains*, which are linked on one end to the hooks of the haims, and hooked at the other into the eyes of the swing-trees. A *back-band* of leather put across the back, near the groins of the horse, supports the trace-chains by means of simple hooks. The *bridle* has blinders, and while the horse is in draught, it is customary to hang the *bearing-reins* over the tops of the haims. In some parts of the country, there are no *blinders;* and there is no doubt that many horses so brought up will work very well without them. But in cases of horses of so timid a nature as to be easily frightened at distant objects, and those of so careless a disposition as to look much about them, they are useful in keeping the attention of the horse to his work. You observe there are two horses, the draught of the common plough requiring that number, which are yoked by the trace-chains to the *swing-trees*, which, on being hooked to the draught-swivel of the bridle of the plough, enable the horses to exercise their united strength on that single point; and being yoked a-breast, they are enabled to exert their united strength much more effectually than if yoked a-trip—that is, one before the other. The two horses are kept together either by a *leather-strap*, buckled at each end to the bridle-ring, or by a *short rein* of rope passed from the bridle-ring to the shoulder of each horse, where it is fastened to the end of the trace-chain with a knot. The strap prevents the horses separating beyond its length, but allows their heads to move about loosely; the short reins prevent them not only separating, but keep their heads steady; and on this account, horses fastened with reins can be turned round more quickly and simultaneously than with the strap. The ploughman guides the horses with *plough-reins*, made of rein-rope, which pass from both stilts to the bridle-ring of each horse, along the outermost side of the horse, threading in their way a ring on the back-band and sometimes another on the haims. The reins are looped at the end next the ploughman, and conveniently placed for him under the ends of pieces of hard leather screwed to the foremost end of the helves; or small rings are sometimes put there to fasten the reins to. In many places, only one rein is attached to the near-side horse, and in others the horses are guided solely by the voice. It is perfectly obvious that the ploughman must have a better and quicker command over his horses with a double than a single rein, and very much more so than by the voice alone.

(1115.) Thus harnessed, each horse has not much weight to bear, nor is its harness costly, though made of the strongest harness leather, as this statement will shew :—

	Weight.		Value.		
Collar, ...	15 lb.		L.1	0	0
Haims, when covered with plate-iron, and with a strap, .	7		0	5	6
Bridle, ...	4½		0	10	0
Back-band, ...	3½		0	8	0
Chains, ...	8	at 7d. per lb.,	0	4	8
Total, . .	38 lb	, and for each horse,	L.2	8	2

When compared with the weight of English harness, these are little more than feather-weight.

(1116.) The *collars* are differently mounted in the *cape* in different parts of the country. The use of the cape is to prevent rain falling upon the top of the shoulder, and getting between the collar and shoulder, where, in draught, it would heat and blister the skin. In the Lothians, the cape of the form of fig. 197 is both neat and convenient. In Forfarshire, and somewhat more northerly, it is of the form of fig. 198, which lies flatter and comes farther back than the former; and it is certainly a complete protection from rain; but it makes the collar rather heavy, and its own weight is apt to loosen the sewing of white sheep-skin with which it is attached to the body of the collar. Fig. 199 is a form of cape common in England, which answers no purpose of protection from rain, but rather to catch the wind, and thereby obstruct the progress of the horse. Such a cape is frequently ornamented with flaring-coloured red worsted fringes round the edge, or with large tassels from the corner and middle, or even with bells.

(1117.) With regard to ornamenting farm harness, it never appears, in my estimation, to greater advantage than when quite plain, and of

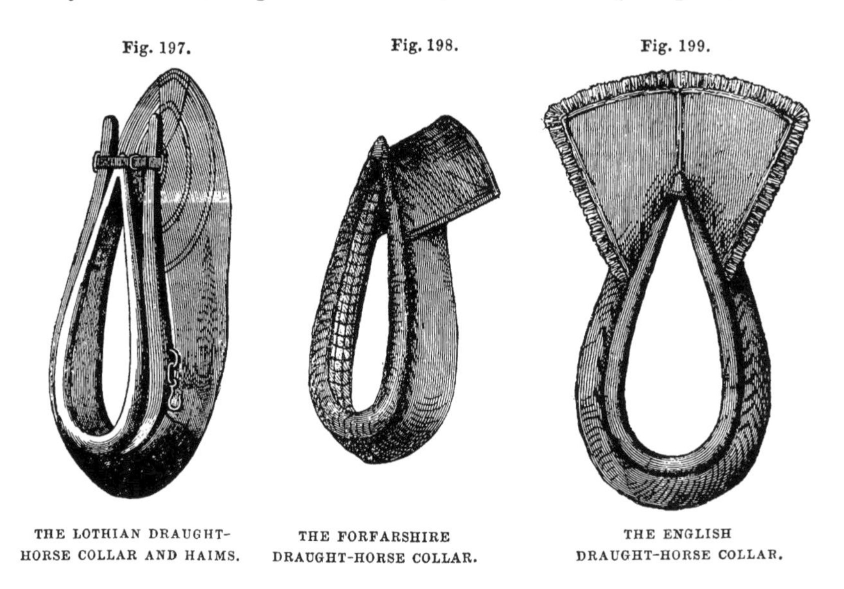

Fig. 197. THE LOTHIAN DRAUGHT-HORSE COLLAR AND HAIMS.

Fig. 198. THE FORFARSHIRE DRAUGHT-HORSE COLLAR.

Fig. 199. THE ENGLISH DRAUGHT-HORSE COLLAR.

good materials and excellent workmanship. Brass or plated buckles and brow-bands, worsted rosettes, and broad bands of leather tattooed with filligree sewing, serve only to load and cover the horses when at work, and display a wasteful and vulgar taste in the owner. Whatever temptation there may be in towns to shew off the grandeur of teams, you should shun such display of weakness in the country.

(1118.) The English farmer is not unfrequently recommended by writers on agriculture to adopt the 2-horse plan of working the plough; but the recommendation is never accompanied with such a description of the plough as any farmer could understand it, who had never seen a plough with 2 horses at work; and it is not enough to tell people to adopt this or that plan, without putting it in their power to understand what is recommended. To enable the English farmer, who may never have chanced to see a two-horse plough at work, and to facilitate the understanding of its arrangements by those who may have seen, but not have paid sufficient attention to it, the figure on Plate XIII. has been executed with a regard to shew the just proportions of the various parts of the plough and the harness. The plough has been sufficiently well explained already; and keeping in mind the relative proportions of its parts, those of the horse and harness may be ascertained from this plate; for so practically correct are those proportions, that any one desirous of mounting a plough in a similar manner may easily do so from this figure before them.

(1119.) Although the reins alone are sufficient to guide the horses in the direction they should go, and I have seen a ploughman both deaf and dumb manage a pair of horses with uncommon dexterity, yet the voice is a ready assistance to the hands, the intonations of which horses obey with celerity, and the modulations of which they understand, whether expressive of displeasure or otherwise. Indeed, in some of the midland counties of Scotland it is no uncommon occurrence to observe the ploughmen guiding their horses, both in the field and on the road, with nothing but the voice ; but the practice is not commendable, inasmuch as those accustomed to it fall into the practice of constantly roaring to their horses, which at length become regardless of the noise, especially at the plough ; and on the road, the driver has no command over them, in any case even of the slightest emergency, when he is obliged to hurry and seize the bridle of the horse nearest to him at the time; and should one or both horses evince restiveness, when he can only have the command of one by the bridle, he runs the risk of being overcome by the other or by the cart.

(1120.) The language addressed to horses varies as much as even the dialects are observed to do in different parts of the country. One word, *Wo*, to stop, seems, however, to be in general use. The motions required to be performed by the horse at work, are, to go forward, to go backward, to go from you, and to come towards you, and the cessation of all these, namely, to stop or stand still.

To lessen or cease motion.—The word *Wo*, is the common one for a cessation of motion ; and it is also used to the making any sort of motion slower ; and it also means to be careful, or cautious, or not be afraid, when it is pronounced with some duration, such as *Wo-o-o*. In some parts, as in Forfarshire, *Stand* has a similar signification ; but to stand without any movement at all, the word *Still* is there employed. In England, *Wo* is to stop.

To go forward.—The name of the leader is usually pronounced, as also the well-known *Chuck, Chuck,* made with the tongue at the side of the mouth, while impelling the breath.

To step backward.—*Back* is the only word I can remember to have heard for this motion.

To come towards you.—*Hie* is used in all the border counties of England and Scotland ; *Hie here*, *Come ather*, are common in the midland counties of Scotland. In towns one hears frequently *Wynd* and *Vane*. In the west of England *Wo-e* is used.

To go from you.—*Hup* is the counterpart to hie in the southern counties, whilst *haud aff* is the language of the midland counties; and in towns, *Haap* is used where wynd is heard, and *Hip* bears a similar relation to vane. In the west of England *Gee agen* is used.

In all these cases, the speaker is supposed to be on what is called the *near-side* of the horse, that is, on the horse's left side. As a single word is more convenient to use than a sentence, I shall employ the simple and easily pronounced words *hup* and *hie* when having occasion to describe any piece of work, in which horses are employed.

(1121.) [The *swingle* or *swing-trees*, *whipple-trees*, *draught-bars*, or simply *bars*, for by all these names are they known, are those bars by which horses are yoked to the plough, harrows, and other implements. In the plough yoke a set of swing-trees consist of 3, as represented in fig. 200, where *a* points out the bridle of the plough, *b b* the main swing-tree attached immediately to

Fig. 200.

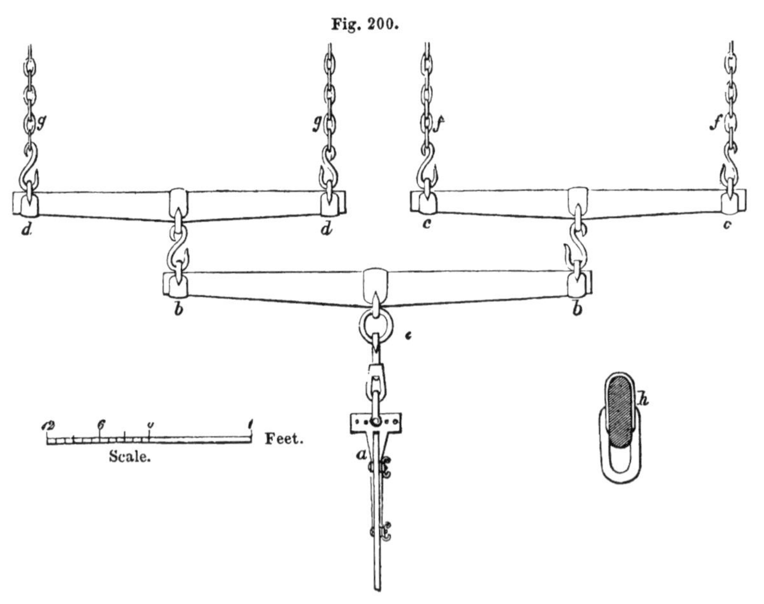

THE SWING-TREES FOR TWO HORSES.

the bridle, *c c* the furrow or off-side little swing-tree, and *d d* the land or nigh-side little tree, arranged in the position in which they are employed in working. The length of the main-tree, between the points of attachment for the small trees, is generally 3½ feet, but this may be varied more or less, the length of the little trees is usually 3 feet between the points of attachment of the trace chain, but this also is subject to variation.

(1122.) Swing-trees are for the most part made of wood, oak or ash being most generally used; but the former, if sound English oak, is by much the most durable, though good Scotch ash is the strongest, so long as it remains sound, but it is liable, by long exposure, to a species of decay resembling dry-rot. As it is always of importance to know the why and wherefore of every thing, I shall here point out how it may be known when a swing-tree is of a proper degree of strength. A swing-tree, when in the yoke, undergoes a strain similar in practice to that of a beam supported at both ends and loaded at the middle, and the strength of beams or of swing-trees in this state are proportional to their breadths multiplied into the square of their depths and divided by their lengths. It is to be understood that the *depth* here expressed is that dimension of the swing-tree that lies in the direction of the strain, or what in the language of agricultural mechanics is called the *breadth* of the swing-tree. To apply the above expression to practice, suppose a swing-tree of 3 feet in length between the points of attachment for the draught, that its breadth is $1\frac{1}{2}$ inches and depth 3 inches, and another of the same breadth and depth but whose length is 6 feet, then in the case of the first we have $\frac{1.5 \times 3 \times 3}{3 \text{ feet}} = 4.5$; and in the second we have $\frac{1.5 \times 3 \times 3}{6} =$ 2.25, the strength of these two being as 2 to 1; and to make the 6 feet swing-tree of equal strength with the other the *breadth* must be increased directly as the length, that is to say, doubled, or the depth increased, so that its *square* shall be double that of the former. Hence a swing-tree of 6 feet long, and having a breadth of $1\frac{1}{2}$ inch and depth $4\frac{1}{2}$ inches, will be equal in strength to the 3 feet swing-tree with a breadth of $1\frac{1}{2}$ and depth of 3 inches; but the depth remaining equal, the breadth is required to be *doubled* or made 3 inches for the 6-feet swing-tree.

(1123.) To find the absolute strength of a bar or beam, situate as above described, we have this rule. Multiply the breadth in inches by the square of the depth in inches, divide the product by the length in feet, and multiply the quotient by the constant 660 if for oak, or by 740 if for ash, the product will be the force in pounds that would break the swing-tree or the beam.* Here, then, taking the former dimensions as of a small swing-tree, $\frac{1.5 \times 3^2 \times 740}{3} = 3333$ lb. the absolute force that would break the tree, but taking into account the defect that all woods are liable to break from crossing the fibres and other contingent defects, we may allow $\frac{1}{2}$ to go for security against such contingencies, leaving a disposable strength equal to 1666 lb. It has been shewn (808.) that the usual force exerted by a horse in the plough does not exceed 168 lb , but it occasionally rises to 300 lb., and on accidental occasions even to 600 lb.; but this is not much beyond $\frac{1}{3}$ of the disposable strength of the 3 feet swing-tree when its breadth and depth are $1\frac{1}{2}$ and 3 inches. The depth of such trees may therefore be safely reduced to $2\frac{1}{2}$ inches, and still retain a sufficient degree of strength to resist any possible force that can come upon it. In the large swing-tree the same rule applies; suppose its length between the points of attachment to be 3 feet 9 inches, its breadth $1\frac{3}{4}$ inch, and depth $3\frac{1}{2}$ inches, the material being ash as before; then $\frac{1.75 \times 3.5^2 \times 740}{3.75} = 4230$ lb.; reducing this $\frac{1}{2}$ for security, there remain 2115 lb., but the greatest force that may be calculated upon from 2 horses is 1200 lb.; we have, therefore, nearly double security in this size of large swing-tree.

(1124.) In proportioning the strength of swing-trees to any particular draught,

* Tredgold's Carpentery, art. 110.

let the greatest possible amount of force be calculated that can be applied to each end of the tree, the sum of these will be the opposing force as applied at the middle, and this may be taken as above (1123.) at 600 lb. for each horse, but for security let it be 3 times or 1800 lb. each horse H, any number of horses being m H, and having fixed upon a breadth B for the tree, and L the length, C being the constant as before, then the depth D will be found thus, $\frac{L \times m H}{B \times C} = D^2$, or, in words, multiply the length into as many times 1800 lb. as there are to be horses applied to the tree, divide the product by the *constant* (740 for ash, or 660 for oak) multiplied into the breadth, the quotient will be the square of the depth, and the square-root of this will be the depth of the swing-tree with ample allowance for assurance strength. In all cases the depth at the ends may be reduced to $\frac{3}{4}$ of that of the middle.

(1125.) Wooden swingtrees ought always to be fitted up with clasp and eye mounting of the best wrought iron, from 2 to $2\frac{1}{2}$ inches broad, about $\frac{5}{16}$ inch thick in the middle parts, and worked off to a thin edge at the sides; the part forming the eye may range from $\frac{1}{2}$ inch diameter in the centre eye of the large tree to $\frac{3}{8}$ inch in the end clasps of the small trees; and they are applied to the wood in a hot state, which, by cooling, makes them take a firm seat. In the main tree, the middle clasp has usually a ring or a link *e* welded into it, by which the set is attached to the hook of the plough's bridle; the two end clasps have their eyes on the opposite edge of the swing-trees, with sufficient opening in the eyes to receive the S hooks of the small tree. The small are trees furnished with the S hooks, by which they are appended to the ends of the main trees; and end clasps are adapted to receive the hooks of the trace-chains *ff*, *g g*, a small part only of which are shewn in the figure. The detached figure *h* is a transverse section of a tree shewing the form of the clasps; the scale of which is double the size of the principal figure in the cut.

(1126.) Though wood has hitherto been the material chiefly used for swing-trees, there have been some successful trials of malleable iron for the purpose. These have been variously constructed, in some cases entirely of sheet iron turned round into a form somewhat resembling the wooden trees; but in this form, either the iron must be thin, or the bar must be inconveniently heavy; if the former, durability becomes limited, by reason of the oxidation of the iron acting over a large surface, and soon destroying the fabric. Another method has been to form a diamond-shaped truss of solid iron rods, the diamond being very much elongated, its length being 3 feet, and its breadth about 4 inches, with a stretcher between the obtuse angles. A third has been tried, consisting of a straight welded tube of malleable iron, about 3 feet long and $\frac{3}{4}$ inch diameter. In this tube, acting as a strut, a tension rod, also of malleable iron, is applied with a deflection of 4 inches, the extremities of the tension-rod being brought into contact by welding or rivetting with the ends of the tubular strut, and eyes formed at the ends and middle, for the attachment of the hooks and chains. A tree thus formed is sufficiently strong for every purpose to which it is applied, while its weight does not exceed 7 lb, and the weight of a wooden tree, with its mounting, frequently weighs 8 lb. The price of a set of common wooden trees, with the iron mounting, is 12s., and of the iron trees 18s.

(1127.) The foregoing remarks apply, so far as arrangement goes, to the common 2-horse swing-trees; but the various modes of applying horse-power, both as regards number and position of the horses. require further illustration.

The next I shall notice, therefore, is the 3-*horse yoke*, of which there are various modes, the simplest of which is, first, a pair, working in the common trees, fig. 200; and for the third horse, a light chain is attached by a shackle to the middle of the main bar *b b*. To this chain the third horse is yoked, taking his place in front of the other two, in unicorn fashion. This yoke is defective, inasmuch as there are no means of equalizing the draught of the third horse.

(1128.) Perhaps the most perfect method of yoking a 3-horse team, whether abreast or unicorn-fashion, is that by the compensation levers, fig. 201—a

Fig. 201.

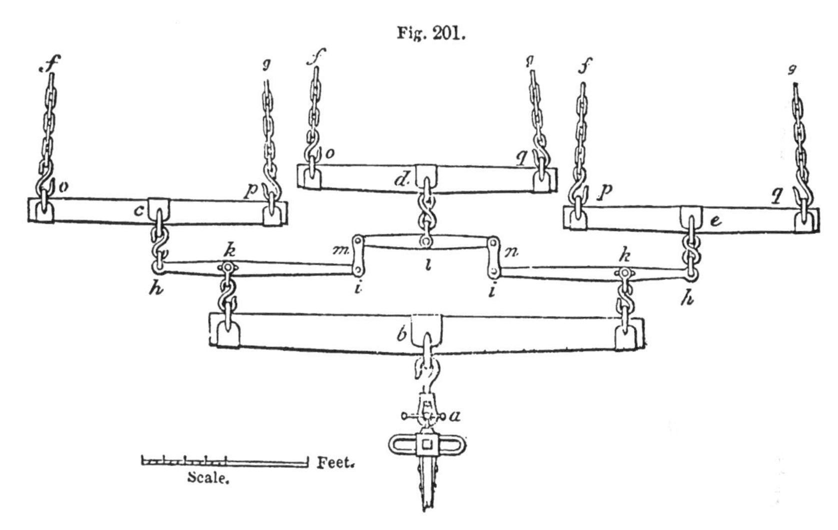

THE SWING-TREES FOR THREE HORSES.

statical combination, which is at once correct in its equalisation, scientific in its principles, and elegant in its arrangement; and I have to regret my inability to single out the person who first applied it. The apparatus in the figure is represented as applied to the subsoil plough; *a* being the bridle of that plough; *b* is a main swing-tree, 5 feet in length, and of strength proportioned to the draught of 3 horses; and *c d e* are three small common trees, one for each horse. The trace-chains are here broken off at *f*, *g*, respectively, but are to be conceived as extending forward to the shoulders of the horses. Between the main swing-tree and the three small ones the compensating apparatus is placed, as in the figure, consisting of three levers, usually constructed of iron. Two of these, *h i* and *h i*, are levers of the first order, but with unequal arms, the fulcrum *k* being fixed at $\frac{1}{3}$ of the entire length from the outward end of each; the arms of these levers are therefore in the proportion of 2 to 1, and the entire length of each between the points of attachment is 27 inches. A connecting lever *l*, of equal arms, and 20 inches in length, is jointed to the longer arms *i i* of the former, by means of the double short links *m*, *n*. The two levers *h i*, *h i*, are hooked by means of their shackles at *k* to the main swing-tree *b*; and the three small swing-trees *c*, *d*, *e*, are hooked to the compensation lever at *h*, *h* and *l*. From the mechanical arrangement of these levers, if the whole resistance at *a* be taken at 600 lb., *k* and *k* will each require an exertion of 300 lb. to overcome the resistance. But these two forces fall to be subdivided in the proportion of the arms of the levers *h i*,

$\frac{2}{3}$ of each, or 200 lb., being allotted to the arms *h*, and the remaining $\frac{1}{3}$, 100 lb. to the arms *i*, which brings the system to an equilibrium. The two forces *i*, *i*, being conjoined by means of the connecting levers *m*, *n*, their union produces a force of 200 lb., thus equalizing the three ultimate forces *h l h* to 200 lb. each, and these three combined are equal to the whole resistance *a*; and the 3 horses that are yoked to the swing-tree *c*, *d*, *e*, are subjected to equal exertion, whatever may be the amount of resistance at *a* which has to be overcome.

(1129.) The judicious farmer will frequently see the propriety of lightening the labour of some individual horse; and this is easily accomplished by the compensation apparatus. For this purpose, one or more holes are perforated in the levers *h i*, on each side of the true fulcrum *k*, to receive the bolt of the small shackles *k*. By shifting the shackle and bolt, the relation of the forces *h* and *i* are changed, and that in any proportion that may be desired; but it is necessary to observe that the *distance* of the additional holes, on either side of the central hole or fulcrum of equilibrium in the system, should be in the same proportion as the length of the arms in which the holes are perforated. Thus, if the distance between those in the short arm is half an inch, those in the longer arm should be an inch. By such arrangement, every increase to the exertion of the power, whether on the long or the short arm, would be equal.

(1130.) The same principle of compensation has been applied to various ways of yoking, one of which is a complicated form of that just described. The main swing-tree and the compensation levers are the same, except that they may be a few inches shorter in all the arms, and the middle one of the three small swing-trees also shorter. The yoking is performed in this manner. The nigh trace-chain of the nigh horse is hooked to the end *o* of the swing-tree *c*, and his off-side trace-chain to the end *o* of the swing-tree *d*. The middle horse has his nigh-side chain hooked to the end *p* of the swing-tree *c*; while his off-side chain goes to the end *p* of the swing-tree *e*, and the off-side horse has his nigh-side chain attached to the end *q* of the middle swing-tree *d*, and his off-side to *q* of the swing tree *e*. This system of yoking is complicated, and though in principle it equalizes the forces so long as all the horses keep equally a-head, yet it is in some degree faulty. Whenever the middle horse gets either behind or before his proper station,—or out of that position which keeps all the swing-trees parallel to each other,—the outside horses have a larger share of the draught upon one shoulder than upon the other, and as this produces an unnecessary fatigue to the animal, it should be avoided. Such irregularity cannot occur with the simple mode of giving each horse his own swing-tree.

(1131.) A modification of this compensation yoke has been contrived, as I am informed, by Mr Bauchop, Bogend, Stirlingshire. The compensation levers are formed of wood, and in place of the connecting levers *l*, fig. 201, a chain, 2 feet in length, connects the ends *i i* of the levers *h i*; and in the bight of the chain, as at *k*, a pulley and strap are placed, to which a *soam* chain is hooked; the pulley from it oscillating in the bight of the chain serves the same purpose as the connecting lever *l*. In this mode of yoking, the horses work in unicorn-team, the middle horse pulling by the soam-chain.

(1132.) *In the yoking of* 4 *horses*, various modes are also adopted. The old and simple method is for the plough horses to draw by a set of common swing-trees, fig. 200; and to the centre of the main swing-tree at *e* a soam-chain is hooked by means of a shackle or otherwise. The leading horses are thus yoked by a second set of common swing-trees to the end of the soam. This is now seldom employed, but an improved method of applying the soam has been adopted in its place, which is represented by fig. 202, where *a* is the bridle of the plough, with its swivel hook. A pulley *b* of cast iron, 6 inches diameter

Fig. 202.

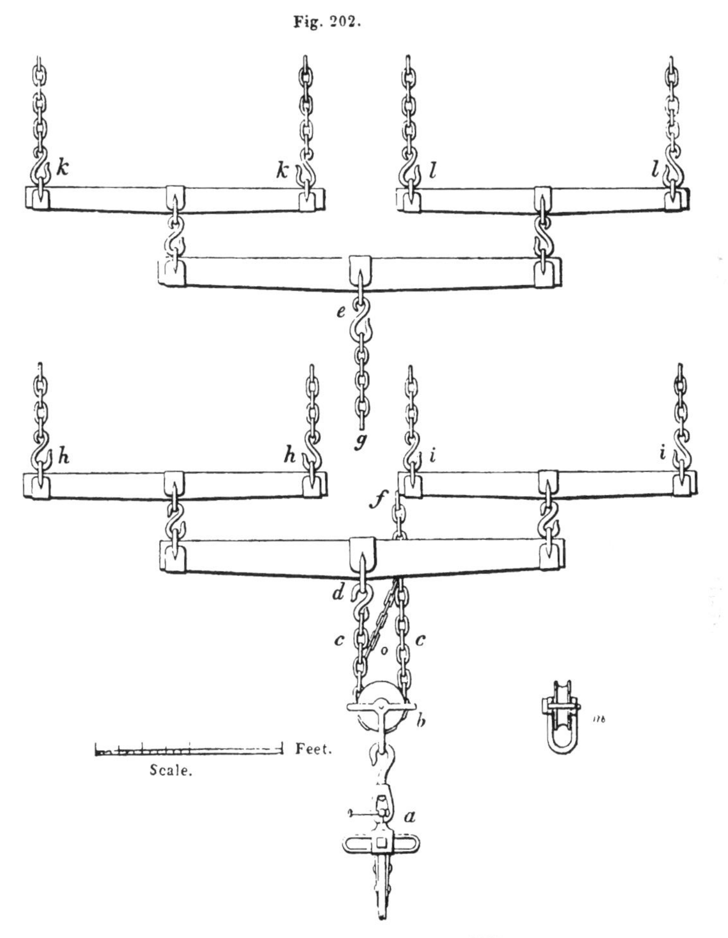

THE SWING-TREES FOR FOUR HORSES.

mounted in an iron frame, of which an edge-view is given at *m*, is attached to the hook of the bridle. A link chain *c* is rove through the frame of the pulley; and to one end of it, the short end, is hooked the main swing-tree *d* of a set of common trees for the plough horses. The other end of the chain passes forward to a sufficient distance to allow the leading horses room to work; and to it is hooked the second set of common swing-trees at *e* for the leaders. In the figure, a part of the chain, from *f* to *g*, is broken off; but the full length is about 11 feet. In this yoke, the trace-chains of the nigh-side hind horse are hooked to the swing-trees at *h h*, and those of the off-side horse at *i i*, the leaders being yoked at *k k* and *l l* respectively. In this arrangement, the balance of forces is perfectly preserved; for the hind horses and the leaders, as they pull at opposing ends of the chain passing round a pulley, which must inevitably be always in equilibrium, each pair of horses has an equal share of the draught ; and from the principles of the common swing trees through which each pair acts, the individual horses must have an equally perfect division of the labour, unless this equilibrium has been removed for the purpose of easing a weaker horse. In order to prevent either the hind horses or the leaders from slipping too much a-head, it is common to apply a light check-chain *o*, of about 15 inches long, connecting the two parts of the main-chain, so as to allow only a short oscillation round the pulley, which is limited by the check-chain. When this is adopted, care should be taken never to allow the check-chain to remain upon the stretch ; for if it do so, the advantage of equalization in the yoke is lost, and it becomes no better than the simple soam. In all cases of using a chain, that part of it which passes forward between the hind horses must be borne up by means of attachment to their back bands, or suspended from their collars.

(1133.) Mr Stirling of Glenbervie, Stirlingshire, recommends a method of yoking a team of four horses in pairs, the arrangements of which are represented in fig. 203 ; *a* is part of a main swing-tree of the common length, *b* a small swing-tree about 4 inches longer than the usual length, but both mounted

Fig. 203.

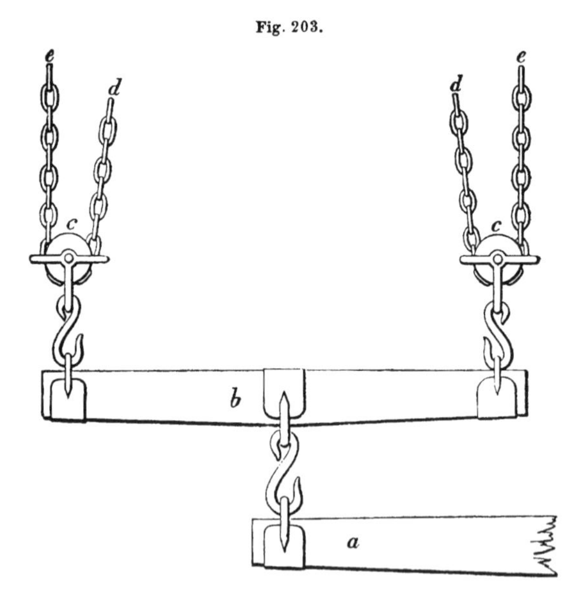

THE SWING-TREES ALSO FOR FOUR HORSES.

in the usual form, except that, at each end of the small swing-trees, cast-iron pulleys *c c*, of 3 or 4 inches diameter, and set in an iron frame, are hooked on to the eyes of the swing tree. The common trace-chains are rove through the frames of these pulleys, as in the figure, the ends *d d* of the chains are prolonged forward to the proper length for the nigh hind horse, and the ends *e e* are extended to the nigh leader. At the opposite end of the main swing-tree, which, in this figure, is cut off, the same arrangement is repeated for the off-side horses. The principle of action in this yoke is simple and effective, though different in effect from the former. There the two hind horses are equalized through the medium of their set of common swing-trees. The leading horses are alike equalized by their set, and thus the two pairs balance each other through the medium of the soam. Here, on the other hand, the two nigh side horses have their forces equalized through the trace-chains which are common to both by passing over the pulleys *c c*, and the same holds in respect to the two off-sides. The couple of nigh-side and of off-side horses, again, are equalized through the medium of the one set of swing-trees. In both, therefore, the principle of equalization is complete, but there is a trifling difference in their economy. In the yoke, fig. 202, which I call the *cross balance yoke*, the soam-chain and pulley are the only articles required in addition to the every-day geer. In that of fig. 203, which I call the *running balance yoke*, there is first the set of swing-trees, which, as they have to resist the force of 4 horses, must in all their parts be made stronger than the common set, agreeably to the rules before laid down; and to which is added the 4 pulleys, all of which are applicable only to this yoke. The trace-chain, though not necessarily stronger than those for common use, is required about three times longer than single horse-chains, that is to say, four horses will require the chains of six; but the chains of the leaders are more conveniently supported when they pass along the sides of the hind horses, and it is free of the set of swing-trees which dangle behind the leaders, of the method fig. 202.

(1134.) In cases where 6, 8, and even 12 horses are required, such as for trenching, subsoil-ploughing, and especially draining with the plough, the yoking is accomplished by modifications and extension of the principles here laid down; for example, a team of 6 can be very conveniently applied with equalized effect by employing the compensation levers of fig. 202, along with 3 single swing-trees with pulleys at each end and running trace-chains, as in fig. 203.—J. S.]

---

29. OF PLOUGHING STUBBLE AND LEA GROUND.

"'Tis time to clear your ploughshare in the glebe."

GRAHAM.

(1135.) When you take an extensive glance over the fields immediately after harvest, when the crop has been gathered into the stackyard, you perceive that a large proportion of them are in stubble, whilst others are occupied by grass, turnips, and young wheat. On examining the stubbled fields particularly, you will observe young grass amongst the stubble in some fields, and nothing but stubble in others. You could not, of yourself, discover at once, that these various states of the fields bear a certain proportion to one another, though they really do; and the cause of their being in those proportions, is, that they are cultivated under what is termed a "regular rotation of crops," which, when followed out, necessarily causes every field, in its turn, to carry the same series of crops. The numbers composing the series depend on the nature of the soil, and it shall be my duty to make you acquainted with them in due time. Meantime, suffice it to intimate, that when the stubble is in that state, the beginning of the agricultural year is arrived, when certain parts of it must undergo a change, and be transformed into those which follow the ones you find them in. Now, that part of the stubble-land which is devoid of any crop is the first to undergo a change, and it is effected by the plough, not at random, but by the application of those principles which have already been explained to you when we considered the "various modes of ploughing land into ridges," from pages 464 to 481, where, as you may remember, the mode of ploughing was said to be determined by the nature of the soil and subsoil. The stubble-land is generally all ploughed before the lea is commenced with, and that part which is to bear the potato-crop next spring is first ploughed, then that for the turnip-crop, and last of all for the bare fallow, when there is any.

(1136.) On *clay soil* you will find the stubbled ridges of a rounded form, having been at least twice gathered up, fig. 139; and the way to keep them in a dry state during winter, on a considerable declivity, is to cleave them down without a gore-furrow, fig. 140, and without a mould-furrow, fig. 134, or to cleave them down with gore-furrows, fig. 141, and mould-furrows, when clay-land is flat. On *less strong soil*, casting with a gore-furrow (831.) will preserve land dry whether it be flat or on a declivity. On *light loams*, casting without gore-furrows, fig. 135, will serve the purpose. And on *sandy* and *gravelly soils*, crown and furrow (827) is the most appropriate mode of ploughing stubble. It is rare that stubble-land is subjected to any other mode of ploughing in winter. Snow should never be ploughed in, nor the ground turned over when affected by frost, nor should strong clay soil be stirred when very wet, as it is apt to become very hard in spring, and of course more difficult to work.

(1137.) In every variety of soil, ploughed in the forms just described for winter care should be taken to have plenty of channels, or *gaws* or *grips*, as they are usually termed in Scotland, cut in the hollowest places, so as surface-water may have them at every point by which to escape into the nearest open ditch. The gaws are first drawn by the plough laying them open like a feering, taking, in all cases, the hollowest parts of the ground, whether these may happen to cross the ridges or go along the open furrows ; and they are immediately afterwards cleared out with the spade of the *loose earth* left by the plough, and cast abroad over the surface. The fall in the gaws is made to tend towards a point or points best adapted to carry off surface-water by the shortest route, and do the least injury to the soil. The ends of the open furrows which terminate at the furrow along the side of the lowest head-ridge, as well as this furrow itself, should be cleared out with the spade, and cuts made at the hollowest places across the head-ridge into the ditch. This precaution of gaw-cutting should never be neglected in winter in any kind of soil, the stronger soils requiring more gaws than the lighter; for as there is no foreseeing the injuries which a single deluge of rain may commit, it is never neglected by the provident farmer, though many small farmers, to their own loss, pay little heed to the necessity of its observance.

(1138.) With regard to the ploughing of *lea ground*, the most usual form in *strong soil* is to cast with a gore-furrow, fig. 136, and on *less strong soil* the same form of ploughing without a gore-furrow, whilst on the lightest soils of all, the crown and furrow is in most common use (827.). Gathering up is a rare form of furrow for lea, though it is occasionally practised on strong soil after gathered up or cast ridges, when it is a rather difficult operation to plough the furrow-brows and open furrows as they should be. The oldest lea is first ploughed, that the slices may have time to mellow by exposure to the winter air, and that which is on the strongest land is for the same reason ploughed before that on light. Lea should never be ploughed in frosty weather, that is, as long as the ground is at all affected by frost, nor when there is rime on the grass, nor when the ground is very soft with rain; because when ice or rime is ploughed down, the non-conducting property of grass and earth, in regard to heat and cold, preserves the ice in an unaltered state so long as to chill the ground to a late period of the season, and when the ground is too soft, the horses not only cut it into pieces with their feet, but the furrow-slice is apt to be squeezed out of its proper shape by the mould-board. Nor should lea be ploughed when hard with drought, as the plough in that case will take too shallow a furrow-slice, and raise the ground in broad thin slabs instead of proper furrow-slices. A semi-moist state of the ground in fresh weather is that which should be chosen for ploughing lea. Gaws should not be neglected to be cut after lea-ploughing, especially in the fields first ploughed, and in strong land, always whether early or late ploughed.

(1139.) It is a slovenly though too common a practice to allow the headridges to remain unploughed for a considerable time after the rest of the field has been finished ploughing, and the neglect is most frequently observed on stubble ground. The reasoning on the matter is, that as all the draughts cannot be employed on the headridges, it is a pity to break their number in beginning another entire field, and this reason would be a good one in summer when there is little chance of bad weather occurring; but in winter it has no force at all, for the gaw cuts cannot be properly executed until the field is entirely ploughed, and to leave a ploughed field to the risk of injury from wet weather, even for a day longer than you can help, shews little regard to future consequences, which may turn out far more serious than the beginning to plough a new field without all the draughts. No doubt, when land has been thorough-drained, there is less dread of ill consequences from the neglect of gaw-cutting; but even in the most favoured circumstances of drained land, I think it imprudent to leave isolated hollows in fields, and such are to be found in numbers on every farm, without the means of getting rid of any torrent of water that may fall at an unexpected time. Let, therefore, as many draughts remain in the field as will plough both headridges during the next day at longest, and if they can be finished in one yoking so much the better.

(1140.) With regard to the mode of ploughing headridges for a winter furrow some consideration is requisite. In stubble, should the former furrow have been cast with or without a gore-furrow, then on reversing the casting, a ridge will be left on each side of the field, which will be most conveniently ploughed along with the headridges by the plough going round parallel to all the fences of the field, and laying the furrow-slices towards them. The same plan could be adopted in ploughing lea in the same circumstances. Should the furrow given to the stubble have been a cleaving down with or without gore-furrows, then the headridges should be cloven down with a gore-furrow along the ends of the ridges, and mould furrows along their own crowns. On the ridges having been crown and furrowed, the headridges may be gathered up in early and late lea ploughing and in stubble, they may be cloven down without a gore-furrow along the ends of the ridges, especially in the upper headridge, and the half-ridge left on each side of the field may be ploughed by going the half of every bout empty; but a better plan would be, *only if the ridges of the field are short*, to plough half of each headridge towards the ends of the ridges, going the round of the field, and passing up and down upon the half-ridge on each side empty, and then to plough those half-ridges with the other half of the headridges in a circuit, laying the furrow-slice still towards the ridges, all which will have the effect of casting the headridges, towards the ends of the ridges. When the ridges have been ploughed in a completed form, a convenient mode of ploughing the headridges on strong land is to gather them up, first making an open feering along the crowns.

(1141.) Whatever mode of ploughing the land is subjected to, you should take special care that it be ploughed for a winter furrow in the best manner. The furrow-slice should be of the requisite depth, whether of 5 inches on the oldest lea, or 7 inches on the most friable ground; and it should also be of the requisite breadth of 9 inches in the former case, and of 10 in the latter; but as ploughmen incline to hold a shallower furrow than it should be, to make the labour easier to themselves, there is less likelihood of their making a narrower furrow than it should be, a shallow and broad furrow conferring both ease on themselves, and getting over the ground quickly. A proper furrow-slice in land not in grass, or, as it is termed, in *red* land, should never be less than 9 inches in breadth and 6 inches in depth on the strongest soil, and 10 inches in breadth and 7 inches in depth on lighter soils. On grass-land of strong soil, or on land of any texture that has lain long in grass, 9 inches of breadth and 5 inches of depth is as large a furrow-slice as may possibly be obtained, but on lighter soil, with comparatively young grass, a furrow-slice of 10 inches by 6 and even 7 is easily turned over. At all seasons, but especially for a winter furrow, you should endeavour to establish for yourself a character for deep and correct ploughing.

(1142.) *Correct ploughing* possesses these characteristics:—The furrow-slices should be quite straight; for a ploughman that cannot hold a straight furrow is unworthy of his charge. The furrow-slices should be quite parallel in length, and this property shews that they have been turned over of an uniform thickness, for thick and thin slices lying together present irregularly horizontal lines. The furrow-slices should be of the same height, which shews that they have been cut of the same breadth, for slices of different breadths, laid together at whatever angle, present unequal vertical lines. The furrow-slices should present to the eye a similar form of crest and equal surface; because where one furrow-slice exhibits a narrower surface than it should have, it has been covered with a broader slice than it should be; and where it displays a broader surface than it should, it is so exposed by a narrower slice than it should be lying upon it. The furrow-slices should have their back and face parallel, and to discover this property requires rather minute examination after the land has been ploughed; but it is easily ascertained at the time of ploughing. The ground, on being ploughed, should feel equally firm under the foot at all places, for slices in a more upright position than they should be, not only feel hard and unsteady, but will allow the seed-corn to fall down between them and become buried. Furrow-slices in too flat a state always yield considerably to the pressure of the foot; and they are then too much drawn, and afford insufficient mould for the seed. Furrow-slices should lie over at the same angle, and it is demonstrable that the largest extent of surface exposed to the action of the air is when they are laid over at an angle of 45°, thus presenting crests in the best possible position for the action of the harrows. Crowns of ridges formed by the meeting of opposite furrow slices, should neither be elevated nor depressed in regard to the rest of the ridge, although ploughmen often commit the error of raising the crowns too high into a crest, the fault being easily committed by not giving the feered furrow-slices sufficient room to meet, and thereby pressing them upon one another. The furrow brows should have slices uniform with the rest of the ridge, but ploughmen are very apt to miscalculate the width of the slices near the sides of the ridges, for if the specific number of furrow-slices into which the whole ridge should be ploughed are too narrow, the last slice of the furrow-brow will be too broad, and will therefore lie over too flat; and should this too broad space be divided into two furrows, each slice will be too narrow and stand too upright. When the furrow-brows are ill made, the mould furrows cannot be proportionately ploughed out; because, if the space between the furrow-brows is too wide, the mould-furrows must be made too deep to fill up all the space, and *vice versa*. If the furrow-brow slices are laid too flat, the mould-furrows will be apt to throw too much earth upon their edges next the open furrow, and there make them too high. When the furrow-brows of adjoining ridges are not ploughed alike, one side of the open-furrow will require a deeper mould-furrow than the other.

(1143.) You thus see that many particulars have to be attended to in ploughing land into a ridge of the most perfect form. Ploughmen differ much in bestowing attention on these particulars; some can never make a good crown, others a good furrow-brow and open furrow, whilst others will make them all in a passable, but still objectionable manner. This last class of ploughmen, however, is preferable to the other, because the injurious effects of the bad ploughing of the former are obvious; whereas the effects of mediocre compared with first-rate ploughing are not easy to ascertain, though no doubt the difference of their effects must be considerable in many respects. "It is well known," observes Sir John Sinclair, "that the horses of a good ploughman suffer less from the work than those intrusted to an awkward and unskilful hand, and that a material difference will be found in the crops of those ridges tilled by a bad ploughman, when compared to any part of the field where the operation has been judiciously performed."* Marshall contends that want of good tillage incurs a loss of as much as $\frac{1}{4}$ of the crops throughout the kingdom,† which may be an approximation to the truth in his day; but ploughing is certainly now better performed in Scotland than it was, though it must be owned that by far the greatest part of the process is yet of a mediocre description, and the reasons for the mediocrity of the work are not difficult to find.

(1144.) *Ploughmen* cannot learn their profession at a very early age, when every profession ought to be acquired to attain a high degree of perfection in it, because ploughing requires a considerable amount of physical power, even from the most expert ploughmen, and it exacts the greatest exertion of strength by comparison from the youngest in years, and the least initiated in the art; and after young men possess sufficient strength to hold the plough, they are left to acquire a knowledge of ploughing more through sheer experience than by any tuition given them by those who are better acquainted with the art; and as excellence acquired in it cannot be bequeathed to the rising generation, its knowledge must be acquired *ab initio* by every generation. For example, to teach *boys* to plough it has been recommended "to put a cross-bar between the cheeks of the bridle, so as to keep them precisely at the same distance from each other, and then setting up a pole at the end of a furrow, exactly measured to the same line as that from which he starts, fixes his eye steadily upon it, and carries the plough in a direction precisely to that point."‡ To do all this implies that the *boy* has sufficient strength to hold a plough, which if he have, he will have come the length of a stout lad; and to "fix the eye steadily" upon a pole at a distance, while holding the plough with a staggering gait, and unable for want of breath to speak even a word to the horses, far less to guide them with the reins, is much beyond the power of any *lad*, instead of a *boy:* for it would require a very expert ploughman to do that, for all that is nothing short of feering, and none but the expertest of the ploughmen on a farm is intrusted to feer land; and, besides, no single pole always before the spectator can possibly guide any one in a straight line, for he may imagine he is moving by it in a straight line, while all the while he may be deviating very widely from it. The truth is, the young man who is desirous of becoming a ploughman in a short time should be taught day by day by an experienced ploughman to temper the irons, and guide his plough according to his strength

* Sinclair's Code of Agriculture, p. 298.

† Marshall's Gloucestershire, vol. i. p. 72.

‡ British Husbandry. vol. ii. p. 39.

and talents. Very few young men have, or are permitted to have such opportunities of learning, and the consequence is, that, as my observation confirms, the best ploughmen are generally those who have been taught directly by their fathers, and work constantly upon their fathers' farms.

(1145.) Were all the particulars of good ploughing mentioned above (1142.) constantly attended to, there would be no *high crowned* ridges as at *a*, fig. 204, by bringing the two feering, or the two open furrows,

Fig. 204.

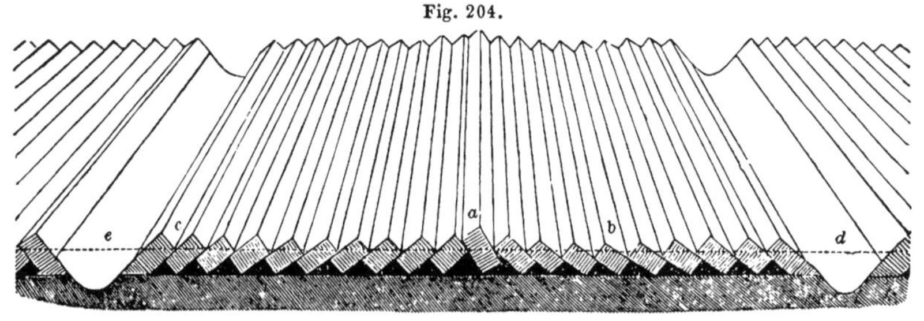

AN EXAMPLE OF BAD PLOUGHING.

too close together, thereby causing the corn sown upon it to slip down both sides, and leave a space bare of seed on the best land of the ridge. There would be no *lean* flanks as at *b*, by making the furrow-slices there broader than they should be, with a view to ploughing the ridge as fast as possible, and thereby constituting a hollow which becomes a receptacle for surface-water that sours the land ; or when the soil is strong, it becomes so consolidated, that it is almost sure to resist the action of the harrows, especially when passed across the ridge ; or in light soil it is filled up with the loose soil drawn by the harrows from the surrounding heights. There would be no *proud furrow-brows* as at *c*, by setting up the furrow slices there more upright than they should be, to the risk of being drawn wholly into the open furrows when the harrows catch them too forcibly on leaving the ridge when cross-harrowed. And there would be no *unequal* open furrows, as at *d*, by turning over a flatter mould-furrow on the one side than the other, which cannot fail to retain the greater quantity of seed. To extend this lengthened catalogue of ills accompanying bad ploughing, I may mention that every sort of crop grows unequally on an ill-ploughed ridge, because the soil is more kindly on the better ploughed parts ; but the evils of bad ploughing are not confined to the season in which it is performed, as it renders land unequal when broken up again, and the thinner and harder portions cannot yield so abundantly as the deeper and more kindly. The line *d e*, fig. 204, shews the position of the surface before the land was ploughed, and the furrow-slices, in relation to that line, shew the unequal manner in which the ridge had been ploughed.

(1146.) It seems to be a prevalent opinion among agricultural writers,* that land when ploughed receives a curvature of surface; whereas, correct ploughing, that is, making the furrow-slices on the same ridge all alike, cannot possibly give the surface any other *form* than it had before it was ploughed. If the former surface were curved, then the newly ploughed surface would also be curved; but if it were flat, the new surface will be flat also. No doubt, in gathering up a ridge, the earth displaced by the plough occupies a smaller area than it did before, but as the displacement only elevates it above its former level, the act of elevating it does not necessarily impart any curvature to it. It is quite true, however, that a ridge on being cross-harrowed, becomes curved, inasmuch as it becomes highest at the crown, because the harrows, in crossing, have a tendency to draw the soil towards the open sides of the ridge, that is, into the open furrows, where the least resistance is presented, and which will alter the uniformity of surface left by the plough; but this effect has no connection with the ploughing. Seeing this external effect produced without knowing its cause, it is equally true that most ploughmen endeavour to give the ridge a curvature, and this they accomplish by what I would designate bad ploughing; that is, they give a slight cresting to the crown, which they support with a bout or two of well-proportioned furrow-slices: they then plough the flanks with narrow and rather deep slices set up a little high, to maintain the curvature, for about four bouts more, giving the last of these bouts rather less depth and height than the rest, and the remaining three bouts next the furrow are gradually flattened towards the open furrows, which are endeavoured to be finished off to the desired curved form by the mould-furrows. This artfulness produces a ridge of pleasing enough curvature, though it is exercised by the ploughman with no intention to deceive; he, on the contrary, conceives all the while that he is displaying great skill in his art by so doing, and if he is not instructed better he will continue to practise it as an accomplishment. Such a device, however, sacrifices correct ploughing to a fancied superiority of external appearance, as much as the crested furrow formerly spoken of (764.), fig. 109. A thoroughly good ploughman, and I have known a few, but only a few, of such valuable men, avoids so objectionable a practice, and ploughs always a true sound furrow, making it larger or smaller as the particular state of the work may require.

(1147.) Without putting much value on the information, it may serve as a fact to refer to, in case it should be wanted, to state the weight of earth turned over in ploughing. If 10 inches are taken as a fair breadth for a furrow-

* Low's Elements of Practical Agriculture, p. 152, and British Husbandry, vol. ii. p. 45.

slice, there will be 18 such slices across a ridge of 15 feet in breadth; and taking 7 inches as a proper depth for such a furrow-slice, a cross section of the slice will have 70 square inches. A cubic foot of earth is thus turned over in every 24½ inches and a little more of length of such a slice; and taking 2.7 as the specific gravity of ordinary soil, every 24½ inches and a fraction more of such a slice will weigh 12 stones 1 lb. imperial.

(1148.) The usual *speed* of horses at the plough may be ascertained in this way. A ridge of 5 yards in breadth will require a length of 968 yards to contain an imperial acre; and to plough which at 9 bouts, of 10-inch breadth of furrow-slice, counting no stoppages, will make the horses walk 9⅞ miles, which in 10 hours gives a speed of 1742½ yards per hour. But as ridges are not made of 968 yards in length, and as horses cannot draw a plough that distance without being affected in their wind, and as allowance must be made for time lost in turning at the ends of the ridges, as well as for affording rest to the horses, that speed will have to be considerably increased to do that quantity of work in the time. By experiment it has been found, that 1 hour 19 minutes, out of 8 hours, are lost by turnings while ploughing an acre on ridges of 274 yards in length, with an 8-inch furrow-slice.* Hence, in ploughing an acre on ridges of 250 yards in length, which is the length of ridge I recommended as the best for horses in draught, when speaking of enclosures (585.), in 10 hours, with a 10-inch furrow-slice, the time lost by turnings is 1 hour 22 minutes. I presume that the experiment alluded to does not include the necessary stoppages for rest to the horses, but which should be included; for however easy the length of ridge may be made for draught, horses cannot go on walking in the plough for 5 hours together (one yoking) without taking occasional rests. Now 250 yards of length of ridge give nearly 4 ridges to the acre, or 36 bouts; and allowing a rest of one minute in every other bout, 18 minutes will have to be added to the 1 hour 22 minutes lost, or very nearly 1¾ hour of loss of time, out of the 10 hours, for turnings and rest. Thus 18,000 yards will be ploughed in 8¼ hours, or at the rate of 1 mile 422 yards per hour. I think this result is near the truth in regard to the ploughing of lea in spring; it is too little in ploughing red land in summer, and perhaps too much in ploughing stubble land in winter; but, as lea-ploughing is the criterion by which all others are estimated, this result may be taken as a near approximation to the truth.

(1149.) The comparative time lost in turning at the ends of long and short ridges may be seen from the following table, constructed from data furnished by the experiment above alluded to:—

Length of ridge.	Breadth of furrow-slice.	Time lost in turning.	Time devoted to ploughing.	Hours of work.
Yards.	Inches.	H. M.	H. M.	H.
78	10	5 11	4 4	10
149	...	2 44	7 16	...
200	...	2 1	7 59	...
212	...	1 56½	8 3½	...
274	...	1 28	8 32	...

* Sinclair's Code of Agriculture, p. 306.

Thus it appears that a ridge of no more than 78 yards in length requires 5 hours 11 minutes of time to turn at the landings, to plough an acre in 10 hours, with a 10-inch furrow-slice; whereas a ridge of 274 yards in length only requires 1 hour 28 minutes for the same purpose, making a difference of 3 hours 43 minutes in favour of the long ridge in regard to saving of time. Consequently, in the case of the shortest ridge, only 4 hours 49 minutes out of the 10 can be appropriated to ploughing, whereas in that of the long ridge, 8 hours 32 minutes may be devoted to the purpose. Hence so very short ridges require double the time of long ones to plough, and are thus a decided loss to the farmer. This is a subject well worth your experimenting on, by ascertaining the time usually taken in ploughing and turning and resting on ridges of different lengths, in the different seasons, and in different soils. A watch with a good seconds-hand to mark the time will be required, and the observations should be made unknown to the ploughmen at their usual rate of work; for if you be constantly in the presence of the men, more than the usual work will be done, and less than the usual rests taken.

(1150.) There is another circumstance on some farms which also greatly affect the speed of horses at work, I mean the *great steepness of the ground;* and it is not unusual to see the ridges traversing such steeps straight up and down. Ridges in such a position are laborious to plough, to cart upon, to manure, and for every operation connected with farming. The water runs down the furrows when the land is under the plough, and carries to the bottom of the declivity the finest portion of the soil. In such a position a ridge of 250 yards is much too long to plough without breathing the horses. But although the general rule of making the ridges run N. and S. is the correct one, yet in such a situation as a steep acclivity, they should be made to slope along the face of the hill instead of running right up and down the acclivity, and the slope will not only be easier to labour in every respect, but the soil will be saved being washed so much away in the furrows; but the direction of the slope should not be made at random: it should go away to the right hand in looking up the acclivity, because the plough will then lay the furrow-slice down the hill when it is in the act of climbing the steep, and on coming down the hill the horses will be the better able to lay the slice even against the inclination of the ground. What the exact length of the ridges on such an acclivity should be, even with the assistance of the slope, I cannot positively say, but should imagine that 100 or 150 yards would be sufficient for the horses; but, at all events, there can be no doubt that it would be much better for the labour of the farm, as well as for the soil, that there should be 2 fields 100 yards broad each, one higher up than the other, than that the whole ground should be in one field 200 yards in breadth. I have all along been referring to very steep ascents.

(1151.) There is still another arrangement of ridges which may materially affect the time required to labour them; I mean that where, by reason of irregularities in the fences or surface of the ground, ridges from opposite directions meet in a common line in the same field; and the question is, Whether the ridges should meet in an imaginary line or at a common headridge? Professor Low, when alluding to such an arrangement of ridges, says, that "the part where the opposite sets of furrows meet, may be made an open furrow, *or* a raised up ridge or headland, as circumstances may require." * When

* Low's Elements of Practical Agriculture, p. 156.

ridges meet from opposite directions, it is clear that they cannot be ploughed at the same time without the risk of the horses encountering one another even upon a headridge; and where there is no headridge, should one set of ridges be ploughed before the other, in the ploughing of the second set, the end of the ploughed land of the first will be completely trampled down. At the least, therefore, there should be one headridge betwixt two sets of ridges, that one set may be ploughed before the other. But the most independent way in all respects with such a form of surface, is to treat it as if each set of ridges belonged to separate fields, and let each have a headridge of its own.

(1152.) When *horses are driven in the plough beyond their step*, they draw very unequally together, and, of course, the plough is then held unsteadily. In that case, the plough has a tendency to take too much land; to obviate which the ploughman leans the plough over to the left, in which position it raises a thin broad furrow-slice, and lays it over at too low an angle. On the other hand, when the ploughman allows the horses to move at too slow a pace, he is apt to forget what he is about, and the furrow-slices most probably will then be made both too narrow and too shallow, and though they may be laid over at the proper angle, and the work appear externally well enough executed, yet there will be a want of mould in the ploughed soil.

(1153.) [The whole value of ploughing, scientifically speaking, depends upon its having the effect of loosening the texture of the soil, and thus permitting a free circulation of air and moisture through its interstices, for the double purpose of increasing the rapidity of the disintegration of its stony portions, and of re-reducing to powder what had formerly been pulverised, but which, from the joint action of pressure, and the binding effect of root-fibres, had become agglutinated together.

(1154.) Sufficient has already been said to draw your attention to the point of pulverising the soil; in it lies one of the most important secrets of good farming. However well you may manure your land, however thoroughly you may drain it, you will never obtain the crops it is capable of yielding, unless you pulverise it; nay, so important did Jethro Tull think this, that he felt firmly persuaded that if you pulverised your soil well, you need not manure at all. I need hardly tell you, that we shall prove hereafter Jethro Tull to have carried his conclusions too far; but still so direct and unqualified a statement, from such a writer, should have its full influence upon all who wish to learn thoroughly the art of agriculture. Always bear in mind that the *impalpable powder* is the active part of soil, and that no other portion has any *direct* influence upon vegetation, and you will then, at all times, be sufficiently impressed with the necessity of thorough ploughing, harrowing, &c.; indeed, you may rest assured that, except upon some few very light sands, you cannot pulverise the soil too much—economy alone must fix the limit of this useful operation.

(1155.) But were I to stop here, you might naturally suppose that any season of the year would do equally well for ploughing, provided it was before seedtime, and that the fixing of the time was regulated entirely with a view to economise labour. It is certainly true, that, to a considerable extent, the time of ploughing may be varied; but you may rest assured, that, as a general rule, the sooner you plough after the removal of the crop, the better condition will your soil be in at the commencement of spring.

(1156.) Several chemical processes of considerable consequence as respects the fertility of soil, occur after it has been ploughed, which either take place very slowly, or not at all, while it lies unstirred; and, moreover, some of these take place to the greatest advantage during winter.

(1157.) This is especially the case with the disintegration of mineral masses, nothing tending so powerfully to reduce even the hardest stones to powder as sudden changes of temperature, combined with the presence of much moisture. During rain or thaw after snow all the clods of earth and the pores of the more loosely aggregated stones become filled with water, which, of course, freezes, if the temperature is sufficiently reduced; and from its expansion during solidification (353.) (354.) a peculiar property possessed in a marked degree by water, the particles of earth or stone, as the case may be, are pushed so far asunder, that when the thaw returns, it crumbles into fragments, which are again and again acted on until reduced to the state of soil.

(1158.) This crumbling by frost is of the greatest importance in the case of stiff clays, for two reasons, 1*st*, because they are thus reduced much more easy to work, and, 2*d*, which is of far greater consequence, they are enabled to give up their alkalies more readily to water; and clayey minerals are fortunately the quickest to disintegrate, or rather to *decompose* by the action of the weather; and hence every means that facilitates that process is valuable, because, as we have already seen, that those most valuable ingredients of soil, potass and soda, are of no use to plants, unless they are soluble in water, and that they do not obtain this property until the mineral with which they have been associated becomes completely decomposed.—H. R. M.]

(1159.) [In the previous remarks on the plough were embraced its construction, its principles of action, the principles on which its draught is exerted, and the resistance which it presents to the draught, as also some remarks on the system of ploughing that each of the three leading varieties of ploughs have given rise to; and on this last branch of the subject I feel constrained to offer some further remarks.

(1160.) In treating of the form of the furrow-slice I have sufficiently evinced the preference that I give to the rectangular slice; and this I do on the broad principle that *deep ploughing* ought to be the *rule*, and any other practice the *exception*. The exception may apply in a variety of cases, so well known to practical farmers that it would be presumptuous in me to point them out; but our " Book of the Farm" being peculiarly addressed to young farmers, the pointing out of a few of these cases of exception becomes more in place.

(1161.) Shallow ploughing, then, may be admissible in the case of a field that has been depastured with sheep, and to be simply turned up for a seed-furrow. The reason usually assigned for this is, that the droppings of the sheep forming only a top-dressing, has given rise to the notion that a deep furrow would bury the manure to a depth at which its beneficial effects could not be reached by the plants of the crop that may be sown upon this field. While I allow that this is an admissible case. the *rationale* of the reasons assigned for it, by practical men, may, on very fair grounds, be called in question. Thus, it is well known that the roots of vegetables in general push themselves out in pursuit of their nutriment, and with an instinctive perseverance they will pass over or through media which afford little or no nutriment, in order to reach a medium in which they can luxuriate at will. With the larger vegetable productions this is remarkably the case; and though, amongst those plants which the farmer cultivates, the necessity of hunting, as it were, for food cannot occur to a great extent, yet we are well aware that the roots of the cereal grasses may extend from 6 to 12 or more inches; and there is good reason to believe that their length depends upon the depth of the penetrable soil, and that the luxuriance of growth in the plant will in general be proportioned to that depth, soil and climate being the same.

(1162.) Another case of exception to deep ploughing, is in some of the courses of fallow ploughing, where a deep furrow might be injurious; these occurring in the later courses. And a third is that of a seed-furrow, though in many cases this last is of doubtful recommendation.

(1163.) In some of the clay districts, a system of shallow and narrow ploughing is practised, under the impression that the exposure of the soil, thus cut up in thin slices, tends more to its amelioration than a system of deep and broad ploughing could effect. This supposition may, to a certain extent, be true, as a certain portion of the soil thus treated will undergo a stage of improvement; but allowing that it does so, the improvement is but a half measure. Soils of this kind are frequently deep, and, though apparently poor, they afford the stamina out of which may be formed the best artificial soils—the clay loam—which may be brought about by the due application of manure, and a proper, well-directed, and continued system of ploughing. On lands of this kind, the system of deep ploughing will be always attended with beneficial effects; and instead of the apparently thin and hungry soil which the shallow system is more likely to perpetuate, the result might be a deep and strong clay loam. To effect this, however, there must be no sparing of expense or of labour, the draining must be efficient, and the manuring, especially with those substances that will tend to sharpen and yield porosity to the clay, must be abundantly supplied.

(1164.) The most extensive suite of cases where a departure from the rule is admissible are those lands where a naturally thin soil rests on a subsoil of sand or gravel variously impregnated with oxides of iron. To plough deep at once in such situations would run the risk of serious injury to the sparing quantity of soil naturally existing. But it is to be observed of soils of this kind, that the subsoil has always a tendency to *pan*, and if such do exist, the deep system should again come into requisition in the form of subsoil ploughing, which, by destroying the pan—that frequent cause of sterility in soils of this kind—opens a way to the amelioration of both soil and subsoil.

(1165.) There appears, in short, every reason for inculcating the system of deep ploughing, not only where existing circumstances admit of its adoption, but where its ultimate effects are likely to induce a gradual improvement on the soil and all its products, admitting always that a variation in depth is proper and necessary under the varying circumstances of crops and seasons.

(1166.) Though the Scotch swing plough has afforded the principal subject of what has been here given on this implement, it must not be lost sight of that numerous varieties of this important implement are to be found in other parts of the kingdom, many of which possess a high degree of excellence; and England is especially remarkable for these varieties. It has been already noticed (661.) that the germ of improvement in the Scotch implements appear to have been obtained through England; but, like many other importations from that quarter, the necessities arising from circumstances of climate, of soil, and, perhaps not the least important, the paucity of pecuniary means, obliged the Scottish agriculturist to husband all his resources, and to call forth all his energies, in making the best and most economical use of his new acquisitions, so as in the end to outstrip his more favoured brethren of the south. This will be found to have occurred, not only in the plough, but in the introduction of the turnip, of bone manure, and many other similar acquisitions.

(1167.) It is remarkable, too, that the decided step taken in Scotland in regard to the rapid extension of the use of the improved plough, was long in retracing its steps back to England, and that the retrograde movement was gradual from the northern counties southward. In nearly half a century, this retrogression appears to have made very slow progress; and, like many other improvements which linger until some master-mind takes them in hand, the extension of the use of an improved plough met with little encouragement. In due time, this subject was taken up by the Messrs Ransome of Ipswich, and through their exertions, such changes have been produced in the plough as place the English agriculturist in possession of a command of these implements in such a variety of forms that no other country can boast of from the hands of one maker.

(1168.) The numerous varieties (amounting to at least 100) of the ploughs constructed by the Messrs Ransome, seem to be chiefly adapted to the soils of England, and to the practice of her agriculturists; for we do not find that, when brought into Scotland, and placed in direct competition with the Scotch plough, that they ever gain a preference. There can be no question, however, that some of the varieties of these ploughs perform well, exhibiting work, when conducted by a skilful hand, that for its usefulness may compare with that of any implement now employed. The system of ploughing in England being generally of the shallow character, and the modern plough for the most part of a light construction, adapted to the practice, it has been found that these ploughs were unable to resist the force required where the deep-ploughing system is followed, as in many parts of Scotland. But a more serious objection to the introduction of these ploughs into Scotland lies in the frequent application to them of wheels. No ploughman who has been able to wield the swing plough, will ever suffer himself to be incommoded with the addition of wheels to his plough (for he will always consider wheels an inconvenience) and this he does not from a conviction that wheels increase the labour of his horses, but because to himself they appear a source of annoyance; and here it may be further remarked, as regards wheel-ploughs, that, since the wheels must always have a tendency to increase the draught (810.), and on that account are objectionable, so also, if a plough can be wielded with equal and perhaps better effect without wheels than with them, the excuse that a wheel-plough may be wielded by a man of inferior qualifications is of small value. Any man may be trained to handle a plough, though every man will not be equally successful; and since in the whole of Scotland not a wheel-plough is to be found, except as a curiosity, while her ploughing is at least not inferior to that of any part of the kingdom, and as the chances are surely equal that the ploughmen are not all equally good, it is evident that ploughing can be satisfactorily performed without wheels. If ploughing can thus be performed over one part of the kingdom with an implement of the simplest form, and in a satisfactory and economical manner, there can be no necessity for using a more complicated and more expensive machine to perform the same work in another part of the kingdom, where it is at least not *better* done or done at less expense.

(1169.) Having adverted to the ploughs of England, and particularly to those of the Messrs Ransome, and though still impressed with the opinion that the simple Scotch swing plough is preferable as an implement to the wheel-ploughs in their most improved form, and perhaps even to the *swing* ploughs of England, it is proper to describe generally at least one example out of the many.

Fig. 205.

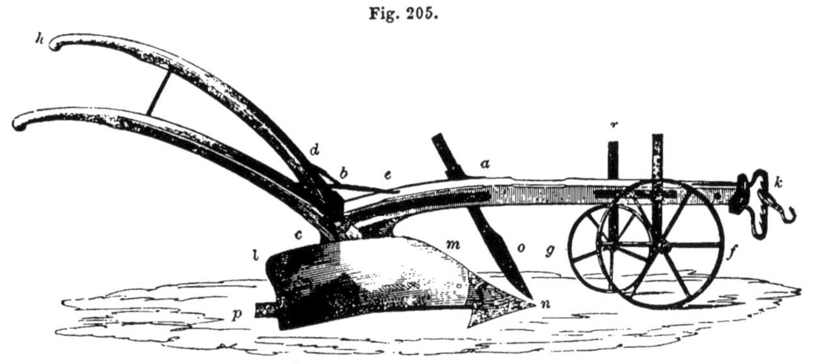

RANSOME'S F F, OR BEDFORDSHIRE PLOUGH.

(1170.) The example chosen for the purpose of illustration is Ransome's F F or Bedfordshire plough, represented in fig. 205. This plough has attained a high character for its general usefulness, and may be considered as the most perfect of modern English ploughs.

(1171.) Without going into such a minute detail of its parts as has been done in the case of the three leading Scotch ploughs, I cannot avoid giving a short description of it. Like the greater part of modern English ploughs, it is constructed partly of wood and partly of iron. The body is of cast iron, and is ingeniously formed for the attachment of the beam and handles. These are simply bolted to the body, a practice which leaves the parts in possession of their full strength, instead of being weakened by the morticing, as is the case in the joining of the beam and left handle of the Scotch wooden plough. The body-frame rises from the middle of the sole bar to the full height of the upper edge of the beam, and the two are bolted together, the body being applied to the landside of the beam, where its upper edge is seen at *a b*. The landsides of the beam and of the body lie, therefore, in one plane behind; but the beam, at the point, lies 1½ inch to the right of the body-plane. The handles are bolted to a vertical flange that projects from the hind part of the body; and as an additional security to the right handle, a bar of cast iron, extending from *a* to *c*, is laid upon the right hand side of the beam, as seen in the figure, and fixed by the same bolts that connect the beam and the body. The hind part of this bar is also formed to embrace the root of the right handle, and is also secured by bolts A further security is effected by the application of the iron stay-bar *d e*, tying the beam and handles together. When the landside of the plough is vertical, the left handle *h* stands 10 inches to the left of the line of the land-side, and the width between the handles *h i* is 26 inches. Following the same rule as has been adopted in giving the details of the Scotch ploughs, we have the zero of the FF, figs. 121 and 122, Plate XII., at 27 inches behind the point of the share *n*, and the heel *p*, 11 inches behind the zero. The extremity of the handles is 4 feet 3 inches behind, and the point of the beam 4 feet 5 inches before the zero. making the horizontal length of the plough only

8 feet 8 inches. The height of the handles above the base line is 2 feet 10 inches; the height of the body, at the junction *b* of the beam and handles, is 14 inches; the height of the beam, at the coulter-box, is 17 inches, and at the point 16 inches; these heights being all as measured to the upper edge of the beam. The bridle *k* of this plough is similar to many others of this much-varied member, but differs in the material of which it is composed, being formed of cast-iron. In fig. 148 the plough is represented with two wheels *f* and *g*, which are mounted on stems *r s*; these move vertically in separate boxes, one on each side of the beam, and are held in position by clamp screws. The larger wheel *f* runs in the furrow, and bears against the *land*, thus regulating the landing of the plough, while the wheel *g* runs *upon the land*, and regulates the earthing of the plough.

(1172.) The active parts of the plough are also peculiar. The mould-board *l m* has been already given in detail in Plate XII., figs. 121 and 122; it is only necessary to add, that its form indicates a medium of the convex and concave surfaces, and that its height points out its inapplicability to deep ploughing. The share *n*, as in a large proportion of all ploughs made by the Messrs Ransome, is of cast-iron, but is very judiciously hardened at the point and along the edge of the feather on the lower surface only, which has the effect of throwing all the wear of the metal on the upper surface, thereby keeping the edge sharp below so long as the share lasts. This share has great breadth, being seldom under 7 inches at the broadest part. In the clays and chalky soils of England, the cast-iron share is both convenient and economical, though it is doubtful how they might answer in gravelly and stony soils, especially in the latter. The price of a cast-iron share is about 1s. 2d., and an allowance is made for them when worn out and returned, of about 6d.; their duration may be taken at from 4 to 14 days, depending much on the texture of the soil. The coulter *o* in this plough, as in most others of the class, is fixed in a metal box bolted in the land-side of the beam. The land-side plane of the coulter, therefore, instead of crossing that of the plough's body, as in the Lanarkshire and other Scotch ploughs, is parallel to it, and stands altogether to landward of the land-side plane of the plough from top to bottom, and in some cases forms a small angle from the point landward. The body is frequently left entirely open on the land-side, except in so far as it is covered by the land-side flange of the sole-shoe, which is not more than 2 inches high, and it stands 1½ inch to landward of the body frame, which last arrangement virtually brings the land-side plane of the body and of the fore part of the beam to coincide.

(1173.) Having in a general way described the construction of the framework and the acting parts of this plough, there remains for me to say a few words on the wheels with which it is furnished. I have already (810–812.) adverted to wheels, as they appear to me to affect the draught of ploughs, and have expressed myself in sufficiently distinct language to shew that, in my opinion, they must in all cases be injurious, and tend to increase the resistance of the plough to which they are appended, whether they be applied within the body, or under the front, or any other part of the beam. That wheels may be of advantage for the working of a plough in the hands of an unskilful ploughman may be true; but if this advantage is acquired by a certain additional expenditure of horse power, which, however much the proprietor of the team may blind himself to, will ultimately, though probably unheeded, tell on his profit and loss account, there will be no gain, but an ultimate loss. It must be admitted, even by the advocates of the wheel-plough, that though they may be handled with perfect regularity in ploughing *along* ridges, whether the holder be an experienced ploughman or not, yet in *cross* ploughing they cannot by any means be brought so handily to follow the undulations of the surface. In leaving one ridge, the share will pass too shallow, and in entering on the brow of the next, it will go too deep, or at least deeper than the average of the ploughing. There is also the element of time, which in all farming operations is an important one; and here wheel-ploughs are found to come short by about 25 per cent. as compared with swing-ploughs. Mr Pusey, in his paper on the draught of ploughs, incidentally observes: "While the work of our ploughing teams is at best but $\frac{3}{4}$ of an acre upon strong ground (and sometimes as much as 1 acre upon the lightest), the daily task performed by two Scotch horses upon strong land is $1\frac{1}{4}$ acre."* This deficiency of effect cannot be attributed to want of power in the horses, for English horses are at least not inferior to those employed in Scotland for agricultural purposes, neither can it be from unskilfulness in the ploughmen, for even the most skilful seem to come short in this respect, by not being able to plough more than $\frac{3}{4}$ of an acre in a day, while with the swing-plough almost any ploughman will turn over his acre a-day. From the remarks of the same writer,† it is to be inferred that a Scotch swing-plough was incapable of being drawn through a certain clay soil by two horses, while the wheel-ploughs were found to perform the work with tolerable ease, though still a heavy draught. There may be such cases; but from the conditions of this particular case, where the draught that baffled the horses in the swing-plough seems not to have exceeded 52 stones, there is an ambiguity in the matter that leads to doubts of the accuracy on the part of the observers of the experiment. We know well that in working the Scotch swing-plough in an 8 or 9 inch furrow on stiff land, the draught is not unfrequently as high as 7 cwt. or 56 stones; but two good horses never shrink from the task; and how a less draught, whatever be the soil, should have baffled the exertions of two good horses in a swing-plough, even in the Oxford clay, requires some further investigation to be satisfactory.

(1174.) Under all the circumstances, then, whether we take expenditure of horse power compared with the small saving in the pay of an inferior workman, the disadvantages attending the more complicated operation of ploughing, compared with the celerity with which the swing plough can be made to accommodate itself to all irregularities of ground; the loss of time, which is equivalent with capital, in ploughing a given surface, when compared with the extent turned over by the swing-plough, and the probability that even the solitary instance of an apparent superiority in a wheel-plough, may rest upon some oversight in observation, all seem to conspire to produce a conviction that a superiority exists in the swing-plough which is in some measure due to its deserving that appellation from an absence of wheels. And certainly, whatever be the merits of the modern improvements on English ploughs, they may be ascribed to any other cause than their possessing wheels, in whatever position they may be placed in the plough.

* Journal of the Royal Agricultural Society of England, vol. i., p. 239.

† Ibid., vol. i., p. 225.

(1175.) The plough under consideration is furnished with two wheels, see again fig. 205. The land-side wheel is 12 inches diameter, with a rim not exceeding 1 inch in breadth. The only purpose to which this wheel is applied is to regulate the depth of the furrow, for which purpose it runs upon the solid land. The furrow-wheel is 18 inches in diameter, with a breadth of rim equal to the former; its object is twofold, serving in some measure to regulate the depth, by running on the bottom of the previously formed furrow, but its chief duty is, by bearing against the edge of the furrow-slice that is about to be raised, to regulate the *breadth* of the slice, at the desired height, by means of pinching-screws.

(1176.) It is evident that both wheels perform a duty that either of them alone could do with perhaps equal effect, namely, the regulation of the depth; but the furrow-wheel performs a second office, regulating the breadth, which it can also do without interfering with its other duty. It would appear, therefore, that the land-side wheel may be set aside without impairing the efficiency of the plough; and we find, accordingly, that these ploughs are frequently used with only one wheel, which in itself performs both duties.

(1177.) The consideration of these wheels, and their effects on the plough, suggests a further objection to their utility in respect of the increased resistance they produce to the draught. If these wheels are to produce any effect at all, the plough irons and yoke must be set so as to give the plough a bias both to *earth* and *land*. If the plough has not this, then whether it swim evenly, or have a bias, *from* both earth and land, in either case the wheels are ineffective, as they will neither bear upon the sole nor the edge of the furrow, but let the plough have the bias as proposed to both *earth* and *land*, the wheels will then both bear, and exert their efforts by reaction to counteract the tendency of the plough; on the one hand to sink deeper in the furrow, and on the other to cut a broader slice; and since " action and reaction are alike and in opposite directions," these antagonist forces will be in constant operation to a greater or less amount. Such effects will thereby increase the friction and consequent resistance in proportion to the amount of bias which has been given to the plough; and hence the conclusion is strengthened, that in all cases wheels are an incumbrance and a source of increased resistance to the plough.

(1178.) Amongst the numerous makers of ploughs in England whose works have come under our observation, besides those of Messrs Ransome, I cannot omit to notice the names of Hart, of King, of Parker, and of Crosskill, all of whom take a high standing as plough-makers after the English fashions, and many of their productions are mounted with wheels. It is unnecessary to repeat any of the observations on that head, but should the preceding remarks come under the observation of any of the makers referred to, or of any other person who may take an interest in the subject, it will be gratifying to find that they endeavour to shew how wheel-ploughs can be rendered more advantageous than swing-ploughs, and in doing so, either practically or demonstratively, in a satisfactory manner, I shall be open to conviction, and ready to yield up that system which appears to me at present as the only tenable one; but it would, of course, be still more satisfactory to learn that these very humble efforts shall be of any use in satisfying those who take the trouble to inquire, that an extended application of the swing-plough practice might either be of individual or general importance.

(1179.) Amongst the other numerous varieties, I cannot pass over the *two-furrow plough*, which, though seldom, if ever, seen in the hands of a Scotch farmer, is now rather extensively employed in some of the eastern counties of England, but more especially in Lincolnshire. These ploughs are constructed of a very effective and convenient form by Ransome and others, and are held to be very economical in point of draught, a pair of good horses being capable of working a two-furrow plough, or in cases of heavier soil three horses; the saving of labour in the one case being one-half, in the other one-fourth. They are also mounted with wheels, and in the districts where they are employed, and the ploughman accustomed to the implement, they make very fair work, the two furrows being in general laid very nearly alike. It must be conceded, however, that in the districts where these ploughs are used the work is done with a very shallow furrow, seldom exceeding 3 or 4 inches, which may allow of 2 horses taking the draught. Where the deep-ploughing system is followed, a two-furrow-plough could not be drawn by fewer than 4 horses, which, as it would afford no saving, but rather the contrary, can never be expedient, or in any way advantageous; for though it may be urged, that when a light furrow only was required the two-furrow plough might offer some advantage, yet if it could not be applicable in every case, the inference is, that two sets of ploughs, double and single furrow, must be retained—a practice which cannot, under any circumstances, be recommended. The conclusion to be drawn from these remarks is, that though expedients, such as the two-furrow plough, may be very advantageously employed under a particular climate and soil, the practice cannot be held up as one of general application, or that could be rendered economical and advantageous under all circumstances.—J. S.]

(1180.) This seems to me a befitting place to say a few words on *ploughing matches*. I believe it admits of no doubt that, since the institution of ploughing matches throughout the country, the character of our farm-servants as ploughmen has risen to considerable celebrity, not but that individual ploughmen could have been found before the practise of matches existed as dexterous as any of the present day, but the general diffusion of good ploughing must be obvious to every one who has been in the habit of observing the ploughed surface of the country. This improvement is not to be ascribed to the institution of ploughing matches alone, because superior construction of implements, better kept, better matched, and superior race of horses; and superior judgment and taste in field labour in the farmer himself are too important elements in influencing the conduct of ploughmen, to be overlooked in a consideration of this question.

(1181.) But be the primary motive for improvement in the most important branch of field labour as it may, there cannot be a doubt that a properly regulated emulation amongst workmen of any class, proves a strong incentive to the production of superior workmanship, and the more generally the inducement is extended, the improvement arising from it may be expected to be the more generally diffused; and on this account the *plough medals* of the Highland and Agricultural Society of Scotland being open for competition to all parts of Scotland every year, have perhaps excited a spirit of emulation among ploughmen, by rewarding those who excel, beyond any thing to be seen in any other country Wherever 15 ploughs can be gathered together for competition at any time and place, there the ploughman who obtains the first premium offered by those interested in the exhibition, is entitled to receive, over and above, the Society's plough medal of silver, bearing a suitable inscription, with the gainer's name.

About 40 applications are made for the medals every year, so that at least 600 ploughmen annually compete for them; but the actual number far exceeds that number; as, in many instances, matches comprehend from 40 to 70 ploughs, instead of the minimum number of 15. The matches are usually occasioned by the welcome which his neighbours are desirous of giving an incoming tenant to his farm, and its heartiness is shewn in the extent of the assistance which they give him in ploughing a field or fields at a time when he has not yet collected a working stock sufficient for the purpose.

(1182.) Ploughing matches are generally very fairly conducted in Scotland. They usually take place on lea ground, the ploughing of which is considered the best test of a ploughman's skill, though I hold that drilling is much more difficult to execute correctly. The best part of the field is usually selected for the purpose, if there be such, and the same extent of ground, usually from 2 to 4 ridges, according to the length, is allotted to each portion of ground to be ploughed. A pin, bearing a number, is pushed into the ground at the end of each lot, of which there are as many marked off as there are ploughs entered in competition. Numbers corresponding to those on the pins are drawn by the competing ploughmen, who take possession of the lots as they are drawn. Ample time is allowed to finish the lot, and in this part of the arrangements, I am of opinion that too much time is usually allowed, to the annoyance of the spectators. Although shortness of time in executing the same extent of work is not to be compared to excellency of execution, yet it should enter as an important element into the decision of the question of excellence. Every competitor is obliged to feer his own lot, guide his own horses, and do every other thing connected with the work, such as assorting his horses, and trimming his plough-irons, without the least assistance.

(1183.) The judges, who have been brought from a distance, and have no personal interest in the exhibition, are requested to inspect the ground after all the ploughs have been removed, having been kept away from the scene during the time the ploughs were engaged. Now, this appears to me a very objectionable part of the arrangements, and it is made on the plea, that were the judges to see the ploughs at work, some particular ones might be recognised by them as belonging to friends, and their minds might thereby be biased by the circumstance. Such a plea pays but a poor compliment to the integrity of the judge; and any farmer who accepts of the responsible and honoured office of judge, who would allow himself to be influenced by so pitiful a consideration, would deserve not only not to be employed in a similar arbitration again, but to be scouted out of society. One consequence of the exaction of this rule is, that the spectators evince impatience—the spectators, not the ploughmen who have been competitors, for they are busily and happily occupied at the time in replenishing the inner man with rations of cheese and bread and ale provided to them by the possessor of the field who is to enjoy the profits of their labour—while the judges are taking no more than the proper time for deciding the ploughing of, it may be, a large extent of ground. The judges ought, therefore, to be present during the whole time devoted to the competition, when they could calmly and certainly ascertain the nature and depth of the furrow-slices, and have leisure to mature their thoughts on points which may turn the scale against first impressions. That the bare inspection of the finished surface cannot inform them, in a satisfactory manner, whether the land has been correctly ploughed or not, which can only be done by comparison of the soles of the furrows while the land is ploughing, I shall endeavour to make clear to you by figures in a supposed case.

(1184.) You have seen the action of different ploughs, which may be all employed in the same match; and you have seen that the East Lothian form of plough lays over a slice of one form, as in fig. 108, and that the Lanarkshire plough lays over a slice of another form, as in fig. 109, and paragraph (765.) acquaints you, that the latter form of slice, namely, that with the high crest and serrated furrow sole, contains $\frac{1}{7}$ less earth than the other. Now, were the surface work only to be judged of, which must be the case when judges are prohibited seeing the work done in the course of execution, the serrated extent of the furrow-sole cannot be ascertained by removing portions of the ploughed ground here and there, so well as by constant inspection. As equal ploughing consists in turning over equal portions of soil in the same extent of ground, other things being equal, a comparison of the quantity of earth turned over by these two ploughs may be made in this way. Suppose a space of 1 square yard, turned over by each of the two kinds of ploughs specified, taking a furrow-slice in both cases of 10 inches in breadth and 7 inches in depth, and taking the specific gravity of soil at 2.7, the weight of earth turned over by the East Lothian plough would be 63 stones, while the Lanarkshire plough would only turn over 54 stones, making a difference of 9 stones of 14 lb. in the small area of one square yard. In these circumstances, is it fair to say, that the horses yoked to the East Lothian plough have done no more work than those yoked to the Lanarkshire, or that the crop for which the land has been ploughed will receive the same quantity of loosened mould to grow in in both these cases? The prohibitory rule against the judges making their inspection during the ploughing has been relaxed in several instances; but I fear more from the circumstance of the spectators losing their patience, while waiting for the decision after the excitement of the competition is over, than from regard to the justness of the principle. Thus far is the obvious view of the question regarding the mode in which ploughing-matches is usually conducted; but in what follows will be found a more important view as affecting the integrity of good ploughing.

(1185.) [The primary objects of the institution of ploughing matches must have been to produce the best examples of ploughmanship—and by the best, must be understood that kind of ploughing which shall not only *appear* to be well done, but must be thoroughly and essentially well done. In other words, the award should be given to the plough that produces not only work of a proper surface finish, but which will exhibit, along with the first, the property of having turned up the greatest quantity of soil and in the best manner. That this combination of qualities has ceased to be the object of reward, is now sufficiently apparent to any one that will examine for himself the productions and rewards of recent ploughing matches, and the causes of such dereliction is this:—

(1186.) The introduction by Wilkie of the Lanarkshire plough, gave rise, as is supposed, to the high-crested furrow-slice. It cannot be denied that the ploughs made on that principle produce work on lea land that is highly satisfactory to the eye of a ploughman, or to any person, indeed, whose eye can appreciate regularity of form; and, as there are many minds who can dwell with pleasure on the beauty of form, but who do not combine with that idea its adaptation to usefulness, it is no wonder that ploughs which could thus affect the mind through the sense of sight, should become favourites. While the crested system of ploughing kept within bounds, it was all very good, but in course of time, the taste for this practice became excessive; and losing sight of the useful, a depraved taste, of its kind, sacrificed utility to the beautiful, in so far as ploughing can be said to produce that impression. This taste came gradually to spread itself over certain districts, and plough-makers came to vie with each other in producing machines that should excel in that particular point of cresting. A keen spirit of emulation amongst ploughmen kept up the taste amongst their own class, and very frequently the sons of farmers became successful competitors in the matches, which circumstance gave the taste a higher step in the social scale. Thus, by degrees, the taste for this mode of ploughing spread wider and wider, until, in certain districts, it came to pervade all classes of agriculturists. At ploughing matches in those districts, the criterion of good ploughing became generally to be taken entirely from the appearance of the surface; furrow-slices, possessing the highest degree of parallelism, *exposing* faces of equal breadth, and, above all, a high crest, carried off the palm of victory. I have seen a quorum of plough judges "plodding their weary way" for two hours together over a field, measuring the breadth of faces, and scanning the parallelism of slices, but who never seemed to consider the underground work of any importance, in enabling them to come to a decision. Under such a system, it is not surprising that ploughmen devote their energies to produce work that might satisfy this depraved taste, and that plough-makers find it their interest to minister to those desires, by going more and more into that construction of parts of the plough that would yield the so much desired results. Thus have those valuable institutions of ploughing-matches, in the districts alluded to, been unwittingly brought to engender a practice which, though beautiful as an object of sight, and when within due bounds, also of utility, has induced a deterioration in the really useful effects of the plough.

(1187.) But it is not yet too late to retrieve what has been lost. Let the Highland and Agricultural Society of Scotland, and all local agricultural associations, take up the subject, and institute a code of rules by which the judges of ploughing matches shall be guided in delivering their awards. Let these rules direct attention to what is truly beneficial to the land, as well as what may be satisfactory to sight in ploughing. When such rules shall have been promulgated from competent authority, we may hope to see ploughing-matches restored to their pristine integrity—doing good to all who are concerned in them, and resting that confidence in their usefulness which is at present on the wane, but distrust in which has only arisen from an accidental misdirection of their main objects.

(1188.) In connection with that part of the subject which has given rise to the foregoing remarks on ploughing matches, it is not a little curious to find, that instead of the high-crested furrow being a modern innovation, it is as old as the days of Blith in 1652; and he, like the moderns, had entertained the same false notions of its advantages. In his curious work under the section, "How to plough as it may yeeld most mould," he, in his quaint style says— "As for your ordinary seasons of ploughing, your land being in good tillage, any well ordered and truly compassed plough will do, you may help yourself sufficiently in the making of your irons, if you would have the edge of your lying furrow lye up higher, which will yeeld most mould, then set your sharephin the shallower, and set your plough the broader, and hold it the more ashore, the plough-man going upon the land, and it will lay it with a sharp edge, which is a gallant posture for almost any land, especially for the lay turf beyond compare."*

(1189.) The setting of the share-phin (feather) as here described, is precisely what is done in the modern ploughs to make them produce the high-crested furrow (764.) Blith seems to consider that holding the plough "ashore" (to landward), aids the effect; it will make a slice thinner at one edge, but not more acute in the crest.—J. S.]

---

30. OF TRENCH AND SUBSOIL-PLOUGHING, AND OF MOOR-BAND PAN.

"If deep you wish to go, or if the soil
Be stiff and hard, or not yet cleared of stones,
The Scottish plough, drawn by a team four strong,
Your purpose best will suit;———"

GRAHAM.

(1190.) Trenching of land with the spade has been a favourite operation in gardening for many ages; and since the plough became the substitute for the spade in field culture, it has been employed for the same purpose, of deepening the friable portion of the soil, and affording to the roots of plants a wider range in which to search for food. It is highly probable, however, that the plough could not have closely imitated the trenching of ground with the spade until after the introduction of the mould-board, which, comparatively speaking, is of very recent date, the ancient plough retaining its primitive simplicity of form until within a few centuries. Indeed, until the mould-board was added, it was scarcely in the power of the plough to trench the soil, that is, to reverse the position of the furrow-slice and mix the upper and lower soils together. When it was added, may now be difficult to ascertain; but fully two centuries ago, Hartlib, in his Legacie, intimates the practice of very deep ploughing, with the mould-board in use, when he says, "There is an ingenious yeoman in Kent who hath two ploughs fastened together very finely, by the which he plougheth two furrows at once, *one under the other*, and so stirreth up the land 12 or 14 inches deep, which in deep land is good." This is essentially trench ploughing.

(1191.) Within a very recent date, it has been recommended to plough land as deep as trenching, but so as to retain the stirred soil below the surface. Mr Smith, Deanston, by the invention of his subsoil plough, has been the means of directing the attention of agriculturists to this

* Blith's Improver Improved, p. 216, edition 1652.

peculiar and apparently new process, which has obtained the appellation of *sub*soil ploughing. A figure and description of his *subsoil plough* is given below. After the introduction of the mould-board subsoil ploughing could not have been practised; but prior to that improvement it is not improbable that the process was known and practised, and so long ago even as by the Romans. It is uncertain what was the depth of the furrow usually made by the Roman plough, some commentators supposing, from a particular phrase used by Pliny, that it was as much as 9 inches, but at all events he designates a depth of furrow of 3 inches as a mere scarification of the soil. There is no doubt, however, from a passage of Columella, that the Roman farmers occasionally gave a deep furrow to good deep land, when he says, " Nor ought we to content ourselves with viewing the surface, but the *quality of the matter below* should be diligently inquired into, whether or no it is of earth. It is sufficient for corn if the land is equally good 2 feet deep." If they imagined that corn received benefit from the soil at the distance of 2 feet below the surface, they would consider it as an advantage to plough as deep as their cattle were capable of, and their plough could go.* As the Roman plough had no mould-board, any *deep* ploughing effected by it would partake much more of the character of a subsoil than of a trench ploughing.

(1192.) The effect of subsoil ploughing being merely to stir the subsoil without affecting its relative position, the best way of performing the operation is, as I conceive, in the following manner; and it may be executed either in winter or in summer according as it is made to form a part of the spring or summer's operations. It is best executed *across the ridges*; let, therefore, a feering of 30 yards in width be taken across them with the common plough from the upper fence of the field; and this is most easily effected by opening out feering furrow-slices parallel with and close to the fence, if it be straight, and another at 30 paces distant, and let the subsoil-plough follow in both the open feerings. The plough then closes the feerings, and so ploughs from one feering to another until the open furrow is formed in the middle of the feered space between them, followed implicitly all the time by the subsoil plough, which is held by one man, and the horses are driven by another. Feering after feering is thus made and ploughed with the common plough, and followed by the subsoil until the whole field is gone over, with the exception of about the breadth of a ridge at each side of the field, upon which the horses had turned, and the neglect of which is probably of no great importance. Fig. 206 is given as a representation of the operation, where the ploughs and horses appear in black, and where the common plough

* Dickson's Husbandry of the Ancients, vol. i. p. 442.

with 2 horses precedes the subsoil one with 4. The depth taken by the plough is the usual one of 7 inches in stubble, which is seen as the upper furrow, succeeded by the subsoil-plough, which takes usually 9 inches

Fig. 206.

THE TRENCH OR SUBSOIL PLOUGHING.

in such a position, and whose furrow is seen in section below that of the other plough, making both furrows 16 inches deep. Care should be specially taken not to allow the subsoil plough to approach within 2 inches of the covering of any drain, otherwise the drain will be torn up and materially injured. The drains in the figure are supposed to be 36 inches deep, filled 12 inches with tile and sole and small stones, and placed in every open furrow at 15 feet as under, the curved form of the ground between them representing the ridges. This figure is not meant to give the exactly relative proportions of the different objects composing it.

(1193.) The immediate effect of subsoil ploughing being to deepen the friable portion of the soil, it is evident that where the subsoil ploughed soil rests upon impervious or even retentive matter, that the operation will increase the depth, and, of course, the capacity of the soil for holding water, and on this account, in so far as respects itself, the operation after wet weather, would do more injury than good to the crops growing upon it. This is a very important fact in regard to the effects of subsoil ploughing, considered in itself, and demands your serious consideration, because a misconception and disbelief of it continues to exist in some parts of the country, especially in England, and injury may thereby be inflicted on land which will require a considerable time to recover. But if injurious effects accompany subsoil ploughing, when it occasions excess of water, it is evident that were drains formed to give the water an opportunity to escape, it would do no injury to plough land to any depth. The misconception which I have alluded to as existing may not be easily dispelled, as the unusual depth to which subsoil ploughing is executed operates in the first instance as a drier of the *surface* of the ground, even when there has been no previous draining, and it also renders drained ground drier; and these immediate effects are regarded by improvers of land as all that are required to be effected by the operation, and, consequently, when it is easily ascertained that subsoil ploughing is a much cheaper operation than draining, and seems to be equally efficacious, they are content to abide by it alone. I have no doubt that much of the land that has been subsoil ploughed in England has been so in consequence of the adoption of this opinion by farmers, upon whose attention the great comparative economy attending the process was so earnestly pressed some years ago by people of influence. They, however, who understood the nature and capability of subsoil ploughing, and Mr Smith himself at their head, both published and publicly stated, that to employ the subsoil plough upon land having a retentive subsoil, without draining it in the first instance, would only aggravate the evil they wished to avoid. It is true that the subsoil plough might penetrate through the retentive matter to an open substratum through which the water would escape; but the chance of meeting with such a rare arrangement of strata, forming the exception to the general structure of clayey subsoil, cannot afford a sufficient excuse for an indiscriminate use of the subsoil plough.

(1194.) It should therefore be laid down as a general rule, that no land ought to be subsoil-ploughed unless it has been previously drained, for where the subsoil is so porous naturally as not to require draining, neither will it require subsoil ploughing. After being thoroughly drained, any sort of land may be subsoil-ploughed with safety, that is, no harm will accrue from it, but all sorts of land will not derive equal advantage from the operation. Taking it, therefore, for granted, that draining should precede the subsoil plough, the interesting inquiry arises, in what quality of subsoil does subsoil ploughing confer the greatest (if any) benefit to land? the correct answer to which can alone determine the extent to which this operation should be carried. In the first place, in pure plastic clay, any opening made by the subsoil plough passing through it would probably soon collapse together behind the implement. Through such a clay, in a dry state, the operation would be performed with great difficulty, if not prove impracticable. In what is usually called *till*, that is, clay containing sand veins, small stones, or small boulders, the subsoil plough will pass sufficiently well, though slowly, and it will displace even pretty large stones, and the clay be afterwards kept open for a time. Hardened masses of gravelly clay may be entirely broken up by this operation. I believe experience has established the effect of the subsoil plough in these respects. It thus appears that the sphere of the subsoil plough, as an operation of permanent utility, is limited to the breaking up of hard gravelly subsoils; because it is scarcely supposable that it can keep pure clay always open, and it certainly admits of doubt that it will keep a tilly bottom constantly open, as experience has proved, that percolation of water through a somewhat porous clay, renders it more firm, by the well-known fact that such a soil, returned above a drain, soon becomes as firm as any other part of the field. Hard, chalky, gravelly matter, and moorband-pan are the only subsoils on which one would feel confident that subsoil ploughing would confer permanent benefit. I say *permanent* benefit; for I believe it is acknowledged that the process confers an immediate benefit in almost every case in which it has been tried; and on this account, its keener advocates have claimed for it much, if not the entire, advantages derived from its precursor—thorough-draining; and there seems some ground for the claim, inasmuch as subsoil ploughing is executed so soon after thorough-draining that it would be impossible to assert the superior claims of draining, were it not for its occurrence being more common without than with subsoil ploughing; whereas, when the latter is taken by itself, it cuts but a sorry figure. In vindication of his own invention, Mr Smith endeavours to explain in general terms *why* indurated subsoil, when drained, should preserve the friability imparted to it by subsoil ploughing. "When drains have been some time executed," he says, "innumerable small fissures will be found in the subsoil, extending from drain to drain; these are caused by the contraction of the substance of the soil arising from its drier state. The contraction being greatest in the stiffest clays, the operation of the subsoil plough admitting the air to a greater depth, the fissures take place under its operations, and generally reach to the level of the bottom of the drains." This is a natural enough explanation of the almost immediate effect of draining wet subsoils. and also of the almost immediate extension of its effects by a subsequent subsoil ploughing. "These fissures," he continues, "will get more or less silted or glutted up, from time to time, by the minute alluvial particles carried down and left in filtration by the rain-water," which is also a natural effect; but he adds, "the constant expansion and contraction of the unremoved subsoil, by the alternations of wet and dry, has a perpetual tendency to renew them;" and it is this effect which I question, because, before such expansion and contraction can be kept up, it must be assumed that the subsoil, after being subsoil ploughed, has no tendency to consolidate into its original state, whether of strong clay or any other substance; and yet the conviction, as I conceive, of all drainers must be, that every sort of subsoil, except hard rock, consolidates, however well it may have been stirred, though perhaps not to the degree of impermeability it may have possessed before; but, at all events, the more friable it becomes in its condition, it will be the less affected by the "alternations of wet and dry." *

* Smith's Remarks on Thorough-Draining. p. 25.

(1195.) It is allowed by all who have used the subsoil plough, that it requires much greater exertion from the horses to work it than the common plough; and that horses do not work well together in it for some time. With regard to the quantity of ground which a plough will subsoil in a day, in a long day in summer, 1 imperial acre may be calculated on being accomplished in favourable circumstances; but should obstructions occur, such as large boulder stones, ¾ of an acre is a very good day's work; and in winter ¾ is a good day's work without obstructions.

(1196.) The great force required to work even the lightest of the Deanston subsoil ploughs, which weighs 18½ stones, the heaviest weighing 28½ stones of 14 lb., and the insuperable bar which this circumstance places against its employment on farms working less than 3 pairs of horses, have induced people to contrive what they designate subsoil ploughs to be used as a substitute for the Deanston one; but in every modification which I have seen proposed, their effect is quite different from what Mr Smith proposes that his should produce. The Deanston subsoil plough not only penetrates the subsoil to a determinate depth, but by the simple contrivance of the feather, the subsoil is not only stirred, but pushed a little aside, and thereby partially mixed with the portion adjoining it. In doing this there is little doubt that it is the action of the feather which causes the principal weight of the draught complained of in this plough. To avoid this redundancy of draught, as it is supposed to be, a feather is discarded. and simply a large tine bent forward at the point, as in the case of Gabell's subsoil plough,* or a small scarifier, as in the case of the Charlbury one,† is substituted as its principal feature, a furrow being opened by the common plough preceding, as in the case of the subsoil one. But as the subsoil plough makes a demand on the horses of the farm for a common plough as well as itself, it is proposed in the Charlbury one, to have a small plough attached to the beam to lay over the furrow slice, in order to prepare it for the tine or scarifier to pass along. But although a lightness of draught has been attained in both these instances, and a pair of horses have been said to be able to work Gabell's to the depth of 18 inches, it requires 4 horses to work the Charlbury to 12 inches, which as a saving of labour is of no great importance, except as regards the employment of the common plough in preparing the way; for the difference in the nature of the work performed by them differs so widely from that of the Deanston

* Journal of the Royal Agricultural Society of England, vol. ii. p. 421.

† Ibid. vol. i. p. 434.

plough, that they cannot be said to be its substitutes, inasmuch as they only make ruts in the subsoil at the distance of the breadth of a furrow-slice from one another, namely, 8 inches at the least, most probably 9 inches, and not improbably 10 inches, and which of course leave ribs of hard land standing untouched in the subsoil. It is acknowledged by the proposers of these substitutes, that the Deanston is more efficient than either; and as Mr Smith's opinion is that the heaviest of his ploughs does the most satisfactory work, it is clear that they can never be a substitute for his, provided he is correct in his views regarding the utility of *thorough* subsoil ploughing, which these substitutes certainly do not even profess to perform. The conclusion I would draw from the inefficiency of these modifications and substitutes for the Deanston subsoil plough is, that none of them are likely to be used on farms employing less than 3 pairs of horses, such employment being the only object their contrivers had in offering them to public notice.

(1197). A modification has been proposed and practised in the use of Mr Smith's own subsoil plough, which is, that instead of passing it in every furrow of the preceding small plough, it should pass in every other furrow. The advantages said to be derived from this plan are, that it is cheaper, speedier, and the subsoil is not so much broken, though broken enough to allow the water to escape to the drains; but it is obvious that it is this very defective mode of operation which constitute the great objection to the English substitution of the Deanston plough.

(1198.) Instances are not awanting to prove that benefits have been derived from the conjoint operations of thorough-draining and subsoil-ploughing,* but as in almost every recorded case, the combined effects of both operations are reported, it is impossible to ascertain the advantages derived from each. In a memorandum which I made some time ago, but now forget where the circumstance happened, I find it stated, that a field of lea was drained in 1838, and the crop of oats from it in 1839 did not exceed 13 bushels per acre imperial; whereas, after it was subsoil-ploughed, another crop of oats in 1840 gave 32 bushels per acre. It is well understood that the first crop of oats from lea newly thorough-drained never yields an increase; but in this instance, I have no doubt that the second crop of oats would have been better than the first, without the use of the subsoil-plough, especially if the lea were old. In Mr Laing's experience on Campend, Mid-Lothian, he has "found land to be more thoroughly dried after subsoil-ploughing (especially when there was any approach to clay in the subsoil), with a drain in every alternate furrow, than with a drain in every furrow

* Journal of the Royal Agricultural Society of England, vol. i. p. 29, 33, 38: vol. ii. p. 346; vol. iii. p. 18.

without it; in fact, on a stiff clay subsoil I have seen drains of little service, the water for some time standing on the top of them till evaporated, while in the very next field which had been subsoil-ploughed, there was an immense flow of water in every drain, and not a drop to be seen on the surface." Such an effect is not at all surprising, as it is well understood that subsoil-ploughing greatly assists thorough-draining at first in drying land, and that effect appears the more striking, when the land has not been so well drained as it should have been, which it certainly would not be, with a drain in every alternate furrow, when it is so strong as that mentioned by Mr Laing; where he says of a field of 10 acres that was subsoil-ploughed in November 1836, a wet season certainly, that it "was at the time, and during the whole operation, so saturated with rain, that the horses' feet sunk in the unploughed ground from 4 to 6 inches, which shewed, though there was a drain in every alternate furrow, they had not drawn the water from the stiff retentive subsoil. This circumstance," continues Mr Laing, "convinced me the more of the necessity of persevering in subsoil-ploughing, which *alone* enabled me to accomplish my object of thoroughly drying the soil."* The conclusion come to is scarcely a fair inference from the premises, which should rather, in the first instance, have brought conviction, from the nature and wet state of the soil, of the necessity of persevering in thorough-draining, by making a drain in every, instead of every alternate, furrow; and it was after *thorough*-draining had failed, that the drainer would be entitled to say, "that subsoil-ploughing *is an indispensable* accompaniment to furrow-draining," "or that *it alone* enabled him to accomplish his object of thoroughly drying the soil." I cannot refrain from making a passing remark here, that there is a strong propensity in farmers generally to laud the good properties of its auxiliaries at the expense of thorough-draining, and I can only account for the prevalence of the feeling, from the *fact* being well known to them, that it is *cheaper* to subsoil-plough land than to thorough-drain it, the amount of labour to put it in the condition of being thoroughly dry, depending upon its nature.

(1199.) Mr Melvin, Ratho Mains, Mid-Lothian, says what will readily be believed in Scotland, that "I have never seen *any* benefit from the use of the subsoil plough upon damp-bottomed land that had not been drained;" and after a fair trial in a particular field of deep, soft, damp soil, of both operations conjointly, he expresses himself in terms which places the art of subsoil ploughing in nearly its proper position. "Much, no doubt, of the improvement in the condition of this field, is to be at-

* Prize Essays of the Highland and Agricultural Society vol. xii. p. 514.

tributed to draining, still, the quick absorption of the water in the furrows between the drains (the land being cast), the decided improvement of the drier part, and the uniformly equal crop, sufficiently attest the merits of subsoil ploughing." I have said that, in these remarks, Mr Melvin has placed subsoil ploughing in *nearly*, but as I conceive, not altogether its proper position; because the field was drained in the alternate furrows, and the drier part of it was not drained at all. Now, had every furrow been drained, would not the water have been quickly absorbed; and had the drier part been drained, would it have required subsoil ploughing at all?

(1200.) With regard to the expense of subsoil ploughing, it may be fairly taken at the cost of 3 pairs of horses and 3 men, and wear and tear of implements per day for every ¾ of an acre imperial ploughed; and Mr Pusey instances a case of a farm of not 600 acres of cold clay, the subsoil ploughing of which was estimated to cost L.1300, but how this sum was made out does not appear.* The returns of grain crops seem to imply an increase of 25 per cent. at most, and in regard to green crops, an instance is given of a yield of turnips off peaty soil, resting on stiff clay and hard sand and gravel at Drayton in Staffordshire, belonging to Sir Robert Peel, of "four times the quantity in weight ever produced in the same field at any previous time," the large crop alluded to being 27 tons per acre including tops.†

(1201.) With regard to *trenching* the ground, it has long been practised by gardeners with the spade, and its object is to bury the exhausted soil on the surface with all its seeds of weeds and eggs of insects, and bring up to the surface a comparatively fresh and unexhausted soil, not so rich with manure as the one buried down, but more capable, by its fresh properties, to make a better use of the manure put into it. Trenching with the spade is also practised on farms on a large scale. From experience in both ways, I can maintain that it is cheaper to trench rough stony ground with the spade than with the plough, giving consideration to the state of the soil when left by the two implements. The plough with 4 horses will turn over and rip up a strong furrow, and where there are no stones and roots, it will answer the purpose well enough; but where stones, though small but numerous, and if large, are encountered, the furrow becomes very uneven and unequal, the horses jaded, the men fatigued, the implement broken, and the work very imperfectly done. It is the same case with the roots of trees, and even of bushes, against which, when the plough comes, horses pull with vehemence, so as either to injure themselves, or break their tackling. At

* Journal of the Royal Agricultural Society of England, vol. i. p. 433.

† Ibid. vol. iii. p. 21.

such work, I had two valuable horses so much injured in their wind, as to become unfit for ordinary farm work ; and finding so I abandoned the plough for this purpose altogether. The same work, on the other hand, can be much better done with the spade, and when it is undertaken by a contractor who remains constantly with the spadesmen, it will be your own fault in superintendence, if the work be ill executed.

(1202.) I have found this plan succeed in making good trenching. Let the ground to be trenched be laid off in lots with pins ; and let the lots contain equal areas of five yards in breadth. The trench to be 14 inches in perpendicular depth in the solid ground on the average over the lot, the surface being left even with the general inclination of the field that is to be. The 14 inches out of the solid will give a depth of 16 inches in the trenched part of the ground. The contractors should be obliged to remove all stones, large and small, all roots, large and small, and every other thing that is likely to obstruct the future course of the plough, and lay them upon the surface of the trenched ground ; and should large boulders be found a little below the surface, these must either be blown to pieces by gunpowder, and the fragments left on the surface, or further sunk in the earth so as to be out of the reach of the plough in future, according as you find that you may have use for the stones for drains or foundations of fence dykes. The trenching is begun at the utmost limit of the rough ground, by each man rutting some breadths of 12 or 15 inches wide across his lot, and making a trench of the required depth of 14 inches, gauged by a stick kept constantly in his possession to guide him in the depth, that he may not have the plea of ignorance to urge in extenuation of his cupidity. The upper turf or spading is put on its back in the bottom of the trench ; the soil is then dug and thrown upon it, care being taken to make the new ground level and even ; and, lastly, shovelling the loose earth over the surface, and leaving no inequalities in the bottom of the new trench. After one set of allotted spaces have been trenched in this way, another is ready marked off by the contractor for the men to enter upon as they finish their lots, and the second set should be marked off either along one end or one side of the field, whichever is found most convenient for the future operations of removing the trenched-up materials to their destination, that a whole piece of ground may be cleared for future operations without interfering with the progress of the trenching, the workmen employed in which should be called upon to do nothing else than their appointed tasks.

(1203.) Ground that has lain in this rough state for years will no doubt require draining, and should be drained before or after being trenched, according to circumstances. It should be examined beforehand, by pits sunk here and there, whether the subsoil will afford a sufficient quantity of stones to thorough-drain the ground. If it is supposed or certain that it will, the ground should first be trenched to obtain the stones, and they being on the spot, the drains will be easily filled with them. If the stones be only to that amount as to form an ordinary covering to tiles, then tiles and soles should be used as the principal materials, and, in this case as well as the other, the ground should first be trenched. But if stones are plentiful near at hand, though not in the particular field under improvement, from a quarry hard by for instance, then the drains should be opened and filled to the requisite depth before the surface of the old ground is broken up, that the cartage of the stones may first be borne by it; and the trenchers in that case should be obliged to cover the stones of the drains with turf, and level the ground over them as they proceed with the trenching.

(1204.) The expense of trenching rough ground at 14 inches deep—and it should never be shallower, in order to insure a good plough-furrow ever after—is from 10d. to 1s. per pole, according to the roughness of the ground. I have had very rough ground, consisting of large roots of trees in a scattered wood, with brushwood of birch, alder, whin, and broom, and containing as many stones as would have half-drained the ground, trenched 14 inches deep for 1s. per fall, Scotch measure, which is equal to L.6 : 13 : 3 the imperial acre, or rather more than 9½d. per pole, a large sum undoubtedly, independent of draining, clearing away rubbish, and other horse and manual labour; but then the ground was rendered at once from a state of wilderness to one in which manure could be applied and covered in with an ordinary furrow-slice of mould. If this is not the *cheapest* mode, in a pecuniary point of view, of rendering ground available to cultivation, it is at all events the most pleasant to the feelings in the doing, and the most satisfactory when done.

(1205.) But there is a mode of trenching ground which is best done with the plough, its object being to imitate the work of the spade by descending deeper than the ordinary depth of furrow, and of commixing part of the subsoil with the surface soil, which has been probably rendered effete by overcropping. Ground can be trenched with the plough in two ways, either with a large sized common plough drawn by 4 horses in one of the ways pointed out before, fig. 202, or with one plough going before and turning over an ordinary furrow-slice, and another following in the same furrow drawn by 2 or more, usually with 3 horses, or both ploughs drawn by 3 horses each. It is best performed across the ridges. In either of the above ways the same effect is produced in similar soil, breaking up indurated gravel, deepening thin clays, ameliorating stiff days by exposure to the air, and mixing old and new soils together, the ultimate effect on all being to *deepen* that portion of the soil which is used by the cultivated crops.

(1206.) In one respect trenching has the same effect as subsoil ploughing, namely, the stirring of the ground to the same depth, the first plough turning over a furrow of 7 inches in depth, and the second going 8 or 9 inches deeper, making in all a furrow of 15 or 16 inches in depth; but in another respect the two operations leave the soil in very different states—the subsoil plough stirs the soil to the depth named, but brings none of it to the surface, whilst the trench plough does not altogether bring that which was undermost to the surface, but commixes the under and upper soils together. This latter practice has long been known in the midland counties of England, but the former has only been presented to the notice of the Scottish agriculturist since 1829.

(1207.) It has been made a question, which is the better mode, if both are not alike, of making the soil fertile?—the advocates of subsoil ploughing alleging that it is better to ameliorate the subsoil while under the soil by the admission to it of air and moisture; while those of the trench plough answer, that if the object of both operations is to ameliorate the subsoil, it will become sooner so by being brought to the surface, in contact with atmospheric air and moisture. But, say the promoters of subsoil ploughing, there are subsoils of so pernicious a nature, having the salts of iron and of magnesia in them, that the upper soil would be much injured by its admixture with such substances. No doubt, answer the trench ploughers, if the subsoil that contained these noxious ingredients in a large proportion were brought up in quantity, when compared with the bulk of the upper soil, injury would be done to it for a time, but they say it is not the abuse but the proper use of trench ploughing which they advocate; and of *such a subsoil*, they would use the discretion to bring up only a little at a time, which they have it in their power to do, until they accomplish their end, namely, that of ameliorating the whole depth of subsoil. But they maintain, that by far the greatest proportion of subsoils do not contain those noxious ingredients; and, besides, the very best and quickest way of getting rid of even these is to bring them at once to the surface, for any of the acids, or the salts of iron, are easily neutralized by the action of lime, which is always applied to the surface; and those of magnesia are most easily reduced on free exposure to the air. And, moreover, they ask, If subsoils shall be ameliorated by air and moisture when stirred by a subsoil, why should they not also be ameliorated when stirred by a trench plough? And they urge further, that trenching may be practised more safely without previous thorough-draining, than subsoil ploughing.

(1208.) I have no hesitation in expressing my preference of trench to subsoil ploughing; and I cannot see a single instance, with the sole exception of turning up a very bad subsoil in large quantity, there is any advantage attending subsoil, that cannot be enjoyed by trench ploughing; and for this single drawback of a very bad subsoil, trenching has the advantage of being performed in perfect safety, where subsoil ploughing could not be, without previous draining. Mr Melvin, Ratho Mains, mentions an instance of a field containing both damp and dry ground, the dry was trench-ploughed in the autumn of 1836, an inch or two of the sandy gravel being brought up, and "was decidedly increased in fertility," both in the turnip and barley crops which followed.* I trench-ploughed a field of 25 acres of deep black mould which had been worn out, with a 4-horse plough, taking and clearing a furrow from 14 to 16 inches deep in the solid land, and bringing up almost in every part a portion of the tilly subsoil, which was only drained to the extent of a few roods put in the face of a slope exhibiting spouts of water. The turnips that followed were excellent; the barley yielded upwards of 50 bushels per acre imperial, and the year after a part was measured off and fenced, containing 6 acres, to stand for hay, which yielded of good hay 1999 stones of 22 lb. Another field, the year after, that was not drained, suffered injury after trench ploughing; but that was in consequence of having been caught with a premature fall of rain in the autumn before the trenched land could be ridged up, and it lay in the trenched furrow al winter. It is stated that Mr Scott, Craiglockart, Mid-Lothian, "trench-ploughed, in the winter of 1833-4, with one common plough following another, a field of 20 acres, every two alternate ridges, and he has never observed on any of the crops the slightest difference."† This is, as I conceive, an unsatisfactory mode of testing the value of any sort of ploughing land, as it is possible that the untrenched ridges derived a certain, and it might be a sufficient, advantage, in regard to drying, from the adjoining trenched ridges.

(1209.) But whilst giving a preference to trench-ploughing over subsoil, I am of opinion that it should not be generally attempted under any circumstances, however favourable, without previous thorough-draining, any more than subsoil-ploughing, but when so drained there is no mode of management, in my opinion, that will render land so soon amenable to the means of putting it in a high degree of fertility as trench-ploughing. Mr Smith himself acknowledges the necessity of trench-ploughing land in a rotation or so after the subsoil has been subsoil-ploughed, in order to insure to it the greatest degree of fertility.‡ The experi-

* Prize Essays of the Highland and Agricultural Society, vol. xii. p. 522.

† Ibid., vol. xii. p. 526.

‡ Smith's Remarks on Thorough Draining. p. 25.

ence in trench-ploughing after thorough-draining of the Marquis of Tweeddale at Yester, East Lothian, may with great confidence be adduced in favour of the system. I have seen a field on Yester farm under the operation of draining which did not carry a single useful pasture plant, but which afterwards admitted of the turnips being drilled across the face of inclining ground, and of presenting to sheep in winter as dry a bed as they could desire; and no farther gone than the spring of 1841, after the Swedish turnip seed had been sown, a field was trench-ploughed with 3 powerful horses in each plough, bringing up white and yellow tilly subsoil, as unpromising in appearance as possible. The weather being very dry, this till became so hard, that part of the field had to be rolled four times, before they were reduced to powder, and after all the operations, there was apparently no sap left in the ground. White turnips were sown, came away, one half being eaten off by sheep; and when the land was ploughed up in spring 1842, it turned up to appearance a fine rich dark mould, rising in friable clods, and not a particle of till to be seen. No one need be afraid to bring up subsoil of any kind on thorough-drained land after the experience at Yester.

(1210.) The advocates of subsoil ploughing seem to lay great stress on the laying of ground quite flat after that operation has followed throrough-draining, and of showing no open furrows in the field; because an uniform surface is the best for absorbing the rain, and transmitting it in the purest state to the drains. All this, however, is not peculiar to subsoil ploughing, for trenched land can be so treated, if desired. But as to dispensing with open furrows, the plan savours more of conceit than of possessing real utility. There is no way that has been contrived of ploughing land so conveniently as in ridges, a portion of ground being allotted to each ploughman, who is responsible for his own work; and the operations of sowing and reaping are easily marked off in equal distances to the work-people; and if in conducting all these operations few open furrows seem desirable, there is the mode of ploughing by two-out-and-two-in, fig. 138, which only leaves one open furrow in every four ridges, and the ground as flat as you please. But the truth is, that a field cannot be ploughed without making an open furrow, but with either one plough making a feering in the middle and turning over the whole ground, or, if more than one plough is employed, they must follow one another in adjoining furrows,—a plan inimical to good ploughing, inasmuch as no ploughman can hold so steady a furrow as when following up his own method of ploughing, and few ploughs are exactly of the same gauge on the furrow-sole; or the land must be ploughed with a turn-wrest plough, beginning at one end and finishing at the other of the field, ploughing the whole of it itself, or followed by others of the same sort; but where such ploughs are used for such a purpose, other common ploughs must be provided on the same farm, as land for turnips or potatoes cannot be drilled up with the turn-wrest plough, as you will learn by and by.

(1211.) The nature of *moor-band pan* is given below, and as to its destruction, although I have not had much experience of its obduracy, any case within my experience not exceeding 2 or 3 inches in thickness, which were easily ripped up with the 4-horse plough, and as easily mouldered down to dust on exposure to the winter's frost, yet there are places, such as in Aberdeenshire and Morayshire, where it is so deep and hard that extraordinary means are required to break it up. A remarkable and extensive band of this substance was encountered by Mr Roderick Gray, Peterhead, when improving a part of the property of the Governors of the Merchants' Maiden Hospital of Edinburgh in that neighbourhood. The moory surface was ploughed with 4 horses. "At first the plough ran upon the pan, which it seemed impossible to penetrate; various trials were made, and the plan which ultimately succeeded was to have 4 men employed at the plough, and these were engaged as follows:—One with a pick and spade made a hole where necessary, until it reached below the pan, and entered the plough at this hole; another held the plough; the third held down the beam, and kept the plough below the pan; and the fourth took care of the horses. In this way the upper stratum and pan were broken, and afterwards they were brought into a sort of mould by the grubber and harrows."* However obdurate this substance may be to break up, it will yield to the air, and moulder down into an innocuous powder of sand and gravel; but I should suppose that, after the plough was fairly entered below the crust, it would not require to be held down.

(1212.) [In describing the simple construction of the subsoil plough, I shall not go to any length into its history. The implement, as now used, is generally known as Smith's subsoil plough, having been brought into the present form by Mr Smith, Deanston Works, who, in the year 1829, exhibited this plough at the Highland and Agricultural Society's Show at Dumfries, and obtained a premium from the Society for his invention and application of this useful implement.†

(1213.) There is no doubt that ploughs, acting on the principle of Mr Smith's, penetrating into, breaking, and stirring up the subsoil, without bringing it to the surface, or mixing it in the first instance with the incumbent soil, have been long known. Mr Holt, in his View of the Agriculture of the County of Lancaster, rendered in 1794 to the Board of Agriculture, when treating of the ploughs of that county, says, "Another instrument has been lately introduced,

* Prize Essays of the Highland and Agricultural Society, vol. viii. p. 169.

† Ibid., vol. viii. p. 206.

which Mr Eccleston with propriety calls the *Miner*, which is a ploughshare fixed in a strong beam, without mould boards, and drawn by four or more horses, and follows in the furrow the plough [the common plough] has just made; and, without turning up the substratum, penetrates into and loosens from 8 to 12 inches deeper than the plough has before gone; which operation, besides draining the land, causes the water to carry along with it any vitriolic or other noxious matter by the substratum thus loosened. The roots of plants may penetrate deeper; and, in course of time, that which is but a barren substance, may become fertile soil." This is truly the subsoil plough of Mr Smith, invented, laid aside, and forgotten for a period of 35 years.

(1214.) Recent experience points out the reason why the earlier introduction of the subsoil plough did not meet with the success which has attended Mr Smith's, which, from the above description, appears to be the same implement, for they appear in the essential parts to be almost exactly alike; yet the one has been lost sight of, while the other has come into all that notice which it deserves. The reason is now obvious: Without the necessary improvement of thorough-draining, subsoil ploughing is thrown away; and though thorough, or at least furrow, draining, has been practised in England for a long period,* the idea of combining the two seems not to have occurred to the agriculturists of that day. To Mr Smith, therefore, is still due the merit of having brought these two powerful auxiliaries of agriculture into effective co-operation.

(1215.) Since its first appearance in 1829, Mr Smith's plough has undergone various slight alterations, not affecting, however, its essential character, but chiefly in lightening its construction. The implement at first was made of enormous weight, sometimes so much as 5 cwt., but a few years' experience served to show that all its objects could be achieved with a plough of little more than half that weight; they are accordingly now generally made from 2 to 3 cwt. Fig. 207 represents one of the modifications of the subsoil plough as now manufactured by James Slight & Co., Edinburgh. It retains all the acting parts of Mr

Fig. 207.

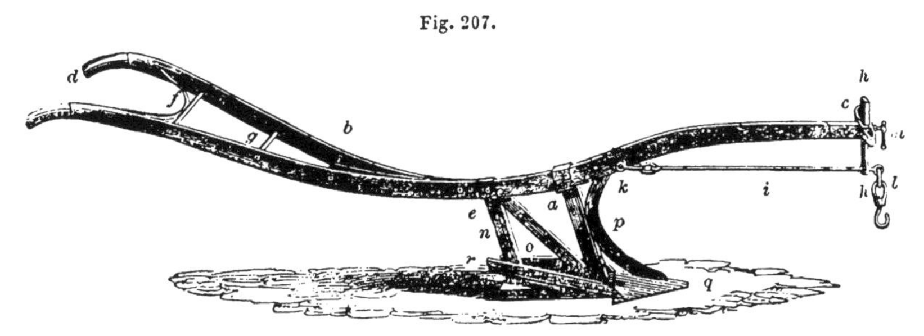

THE DEANSTON SUBSOIL PLOUGH.

Smith's without material change, except in weight, though in other respects it deviates slightly from the original. The beam, which is from 3 to 3½ inches deep at the fore sheath or slot, *a*, and 1 to 1¼ inches thick, extends from *b* to *c*, a length of 7 feet 4 inches; at *c*, the point, it is diminished to 2¼ by ¾ inches, and at *b* to about the same dimensions. The two handles, extending from *d* to

* See Sir James Graham's observations on the subject in vol. i. p. 30 of the Journal of the Royal Agricultural Society of England.

e, are 6 feet 9 inches in length. They are thinned off at *e*, and bolted, one on each side, to the beam; the depth of the handles is 2 to 2¼ inches, and are ⅝ to ½ inch thick, worked into sockets at *d* in the usual manner for the reception of a wooden helve. The beam and handles are further connected by stretcher-tubes and bolts, the latter passing through all three at *b*, and binding them firmly together; the handles are also further supported by the stretcher-bolts and bow, *f* and *g*. The beam is mounted at *c* with the bridle, which is at least 2 inches by ½ inch, bolted on the point of the beam, being first formed into an oblong loop of 8 inches in length, standing at right angles to the beam, and having the opening vertical. To the front part of the loop is fitted a stout clasp, the two arms of which embrace the loop above and below, and admit of the slot *h h* to pass at once through them and the loop. The clasp and slot together have a motion along the loop right and left, and the slot itself has a motion vertically. The chain-bar, *i*, is attached to the beam at *k*, and passes through an eye in the lower end of the slot *h*; to the chain-bar is then attached the draught hook *l*, to which the yoke is applied. The motion above described of the slot *h*, and consequently of the chain-bar and draught hook, afford ready means of adjusting the earthing and landing of the plough, and the position is retained by means of the pinching screw *m*, which, by being screwed into the clasp, acts against the outside of the loop, drawing the slot and the loop into firm contact. The body consists of the two slots *a* and *n*, the first about 3 inches broad, the last about 2½ inches, and each ¾ inch thick; they are welded to a sole bar 2 inches square, and 30 inches long, flush on the land side. The head of the slots is worked into a kneed palm, which is strongly bolted to the beam, and the diagonal brace *o*, is fitted in to resist the strain that tends to derange the form of the body. The coulter-bar *p* is 3 inches broad, ¾ inch thick at the back in the upper parts, becoming thinner downwards, and is finished with a blunt edge and point; it is simply held in its place by being tongued into the beam, the fore slot, and the share. The share *q* is made after the same form as that of the common plough, having a feather to the furrow side, and is spear pointed. The length of the share is from 14 to 16 inches, and the breadth over the feather about 6 inches. It is fitted upon the prolongation of the sole bar, and its socket is usually furnished with a short ear, by which it is fixed to the sole bar to prevent its falling off, as the fixture of the coulter depends upon the share keeping its place. The feather *r* is a thin edged bar, 3 inches deep and about ½ inch thick, thinned off on the upper edge; it is tapered off at the fore end where it joins the share, and is held in contact by being notched into it; but its chief supports are two palms, by which it is bolted to the sole bar; and a sole shoe of cast iron, having a flange rising 6 inches on the land side, completes the subsoil plough, which, with the exception of the sole shoe, is constructed entirely of malleable iron. The length of the plough over all is about 13 feet; the length of the sole 3 feet 3 inches; the height of the handles 3 feet 6 inches; and at the point of the beam 2 feet 4 inches.—J. S.]

(1216.) [Not much need be said regarding the efficacy of subsoil-ploughing. After what I have stated of the immense value of a mixture of impalpable matter, and larger particles, in the form of a porous mass, I need scarcely say, that anything capable of increasing the depth to which this porosity extends, must of necessity be advantageous. This, however, does not shew any difference betwen sub-soil and trench-ploughing—in my opinion, the latter is the best in most instances, and this for the following reasons. All subsoils require ameliorating by exposure to air, before they are capable of acting beneficially to plants—this is owing to certain chemical changes which are produced by the joint action of air and water, and it is very evident that all these must take place much more rapidly, when the subsoil, as in trench-ploughing, is laid *upon the surface* of the field, and freely exposed throughout the winter, than when the air is merely admitted more freely by the subsoil being *broken up* while it still remains *under the surface*. It may be averred that the trench-plough does not go so deep into the soil as the subsoil-plough, but still I cannot help thinking that notwithstanding this disadvantage (if any such exists), it is in most cases the most advisable of the two methods, if employed for *deepening* the soil. Not so, however, if used to assist in *draining the subsoil*. To prove its value for this purpose, I would earnestly direct your attention to the following valuable remarks of Professor Johnston:—" The subsoil plough is an *auxiliary* to the drain—in very stiff clay subsoils it is most advantageous in loosening the under layers of clay, and allowing the water to find a ready escape downwards, and to either side until it reach the drains. It is well known that if a piece of stiff clay be cut into the shape of a brick, and then allowed to dry, it will contract and harden—cut up *while wet*, it will only be divided into so many pieces, each of which will harden when dry, or the whole of which will again attach themselves, and stick together if exposed to pressure. But tear it asunder *when dry*, and it will fall into many pieces, will more or less crumble, and will readily admit the air into its inner parts. So it is with a clay subsoil. After the land is provided with drains, the subsoil being very retentive, the subsoil-plough is used to open it up—to *let out the water*, and to let in the air. If this is not done, the stiff under-clay will contract and *bake as it dries*, but it will neither sufficiently admit the air"—nor let out the water—" nor open a free passage for the roots. But let this operation be performed when the clay is still too wet, a good effect will follow in the first instance; but after a while the cut clay will again *cohere*, and the farmer will pronounce subsoiling to be a useless expense *upon his land*. Defer the use of the subsoil-plough till the clay is dry—it will then *tear* and *break* instead of *cutting*, and the openness will remain. Once give the air free access, and it, after a time, so modifies the drained clay, that it has no longer an equal tendency to cohere. Mr Smith of Deanston very judicially recommends that the subsoil-plough should *never* be used till at least *a year* after the land has been thoroughly drained. To attain those benefits which attend the adoption of improved methods of culture, . . . let the practical man make his trial *in the ways and with the precautions recommended by the author of the method*, before he pronounce its condemnation."* Thus you perceive that subsoil-ploughing *when properly performed*, will always be found useful in assisting the action of *drains*, but cannot be considered equal to deep or trench-ploughing, if an alteration is desired in the *depth of the soil*.

(1217.) Another alleged advantage of subsoiling is the breaking in pieces the *moor-band pan*. I will therefore now say a few words respecting this enemy to good farmers. This ferruginous deposite which so frequently occurs in particular localities between the soil and subsoil is extremely hard and compact, and almost completely impermeable to water. Very much has been written concerning this substance, by persons who have but little knowledge of chemistry,

* Johnston's Elements of Agricultural Chemistry, p. 126.

and in their endeavours to prove the manner in which the deposite had been produced, and likewise the cause of its injurious action upon vegetation when newly brought to the surface, have made so many chemical errors, that the whole subject appears at first sight wrapped in doubt, whereas, we believe, that for all practical purposes its nature is already sufficiently well known.

(1218.) Moor-band pan belongs to a class of bodies known to chemists under the name of *ochrey deposites.* These deposites, which so frequently occur in the beds of chalybeate springs, were carefully examined by Berzelius in 1832 ; and were found to consist of the two oxides of iron in chemical combination with two new organic acids, which he denominated the *crenic* and *apocrenic acids.* Feeling certain from various circumstances, that moor-band pan belonged to this class, I undertook an analysis to ascertain whether it contained these acids, and find that in each of two specimens of pan, sent to me for the purpose, there exists a large proportion of *crenic acid*, in one *apocrenic* also, and in the other *humic acid ;* there can therefore be no longer any doubt about the composition of this substance : and, instead of attempting to prove its injurious effects by relating the difference between the protoxide and peroxide of iron, and the fact of the peroxide being generally combined with water forming *hydrate*, none of which facts throw the least light upon the subject; we can readily explain ah by reference to the chemical properties of the compounds of these two acids with iron. It is well known that iron *in solution* acts injuriously upon vegetation ; and Berzelius has shewn, that the *crenate* and *apocrenate* of the protoxide of iron are both *soluble in water ;* and that the same salts of the peroxide, although of themselves insoluble, are easily rendered so by ammonia, which substance is always produced in fertile soil ; it follows, therefore, that moor-band pan must continue injurious to vegetation so long as the *crenates* and *apocrenates* of iron remain undecomposed. In the course of time, various chemical changes are effected by the joint action of air and moisture which decompose these compounds, and give rise to new ones having no injurious effect upon vegetation.—H. R. M.]

END OF VOLUME I.

PRINTED BY NEILL AND CO., OLD FISHMARKET, EDINBURGH.

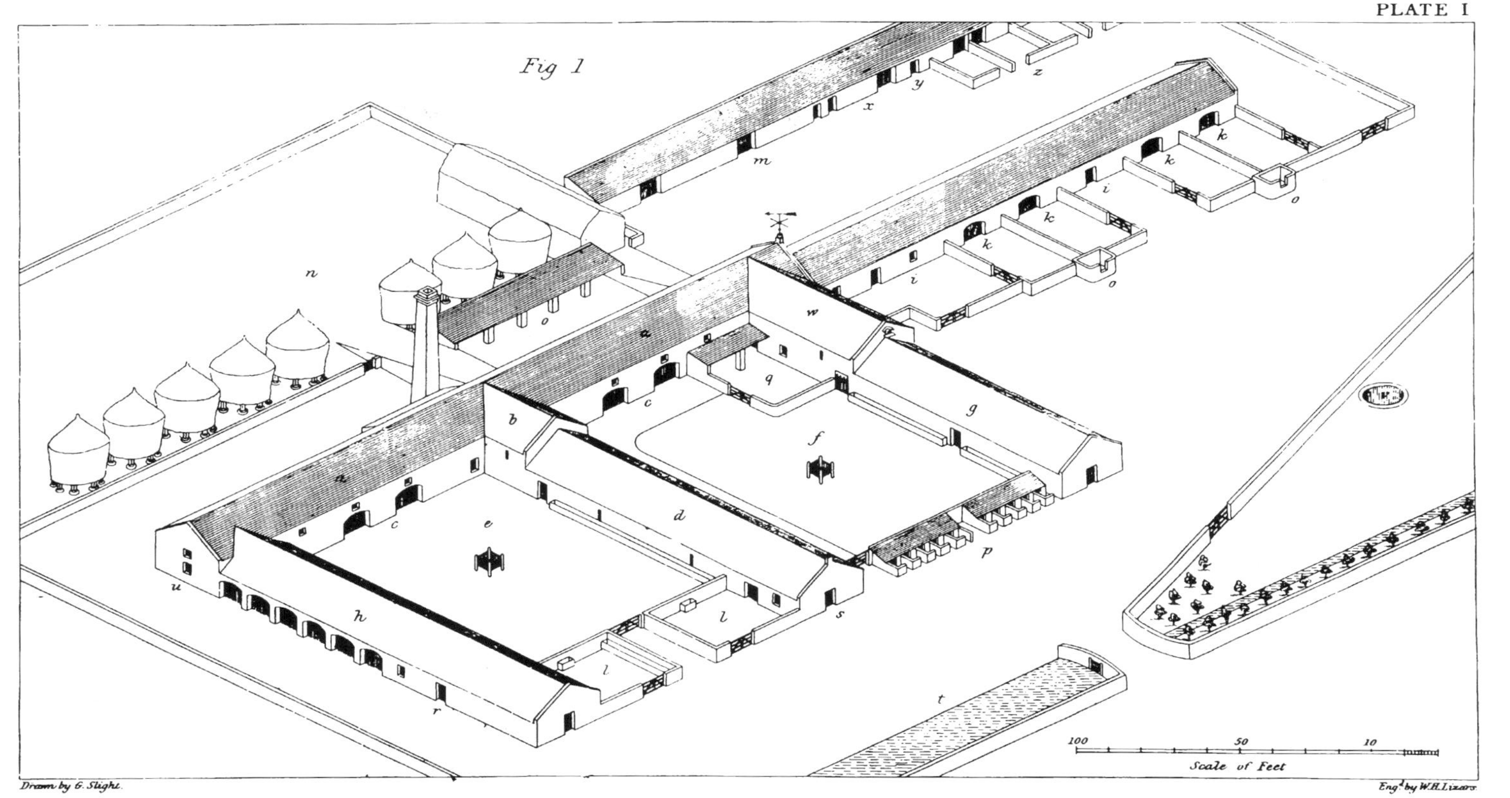

ISOMETRICAL VIEW OF AN EXISTING STEADING

PLATE II

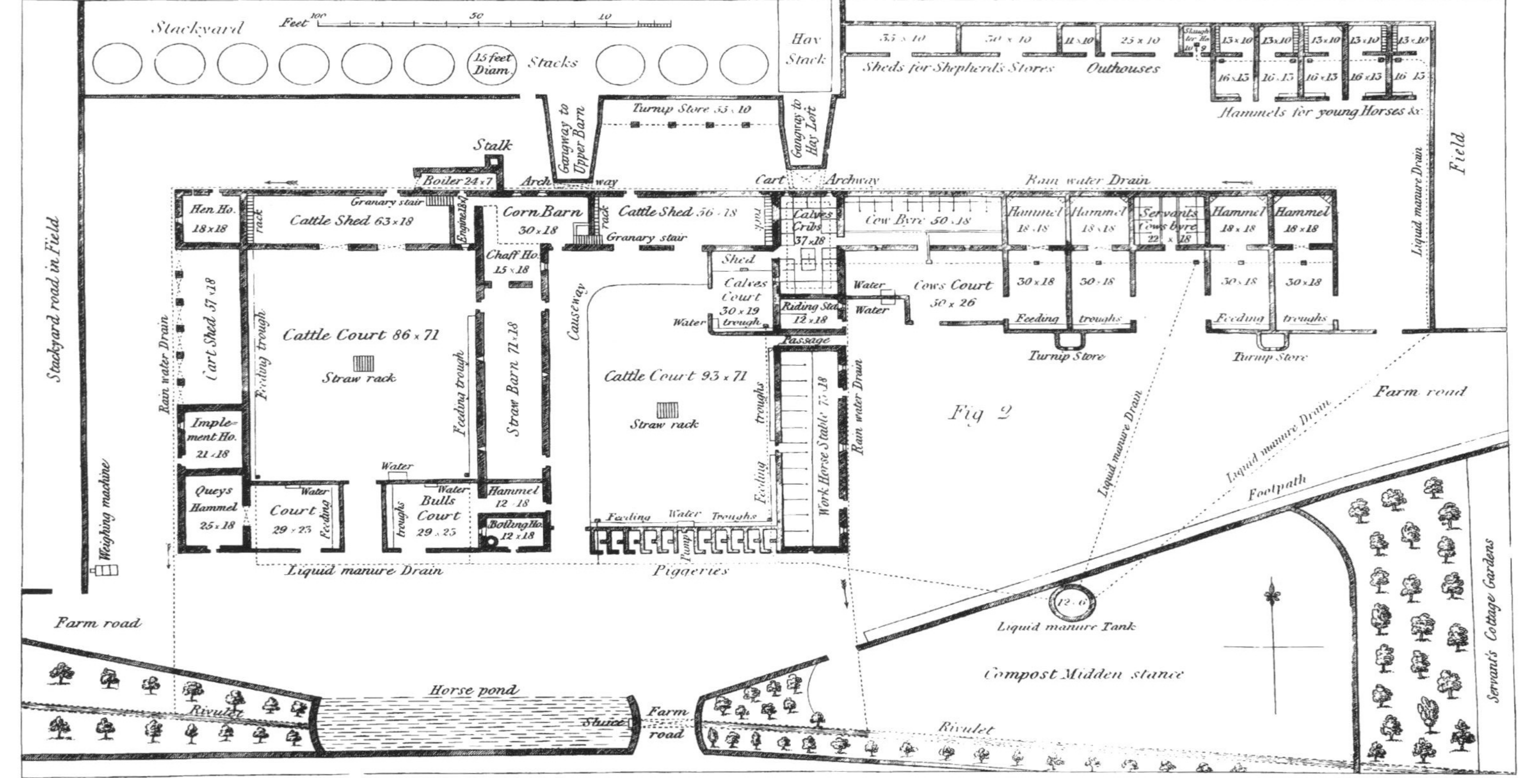

GROUND PLAN OF AN EXISTING STEADING.

PLATE III.

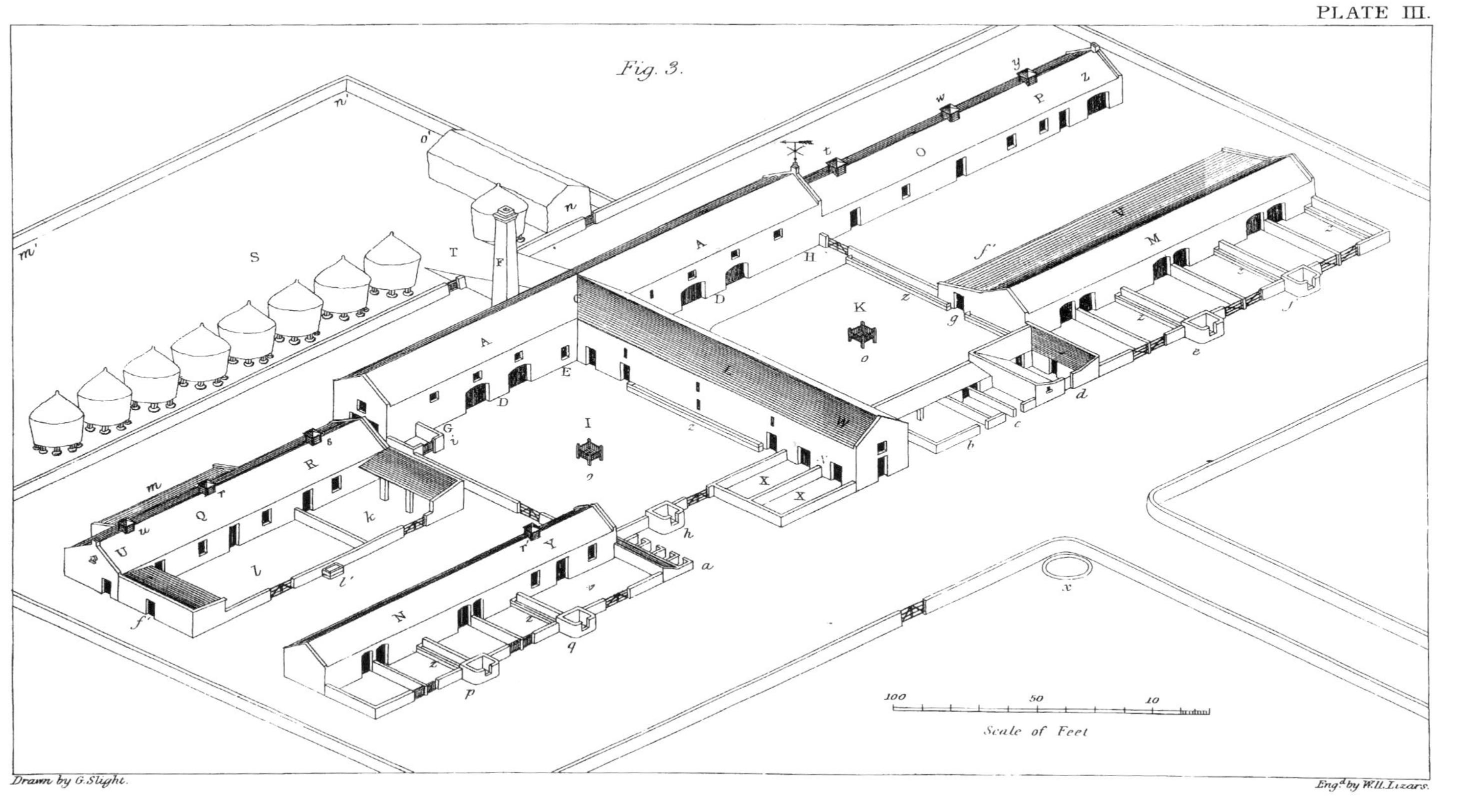

Drawn by G. Slight.

Engd. by W.H. Lizars.

ISOMETRICAL VIEW OF A PROPOSED STEADING.

PLATE IV.

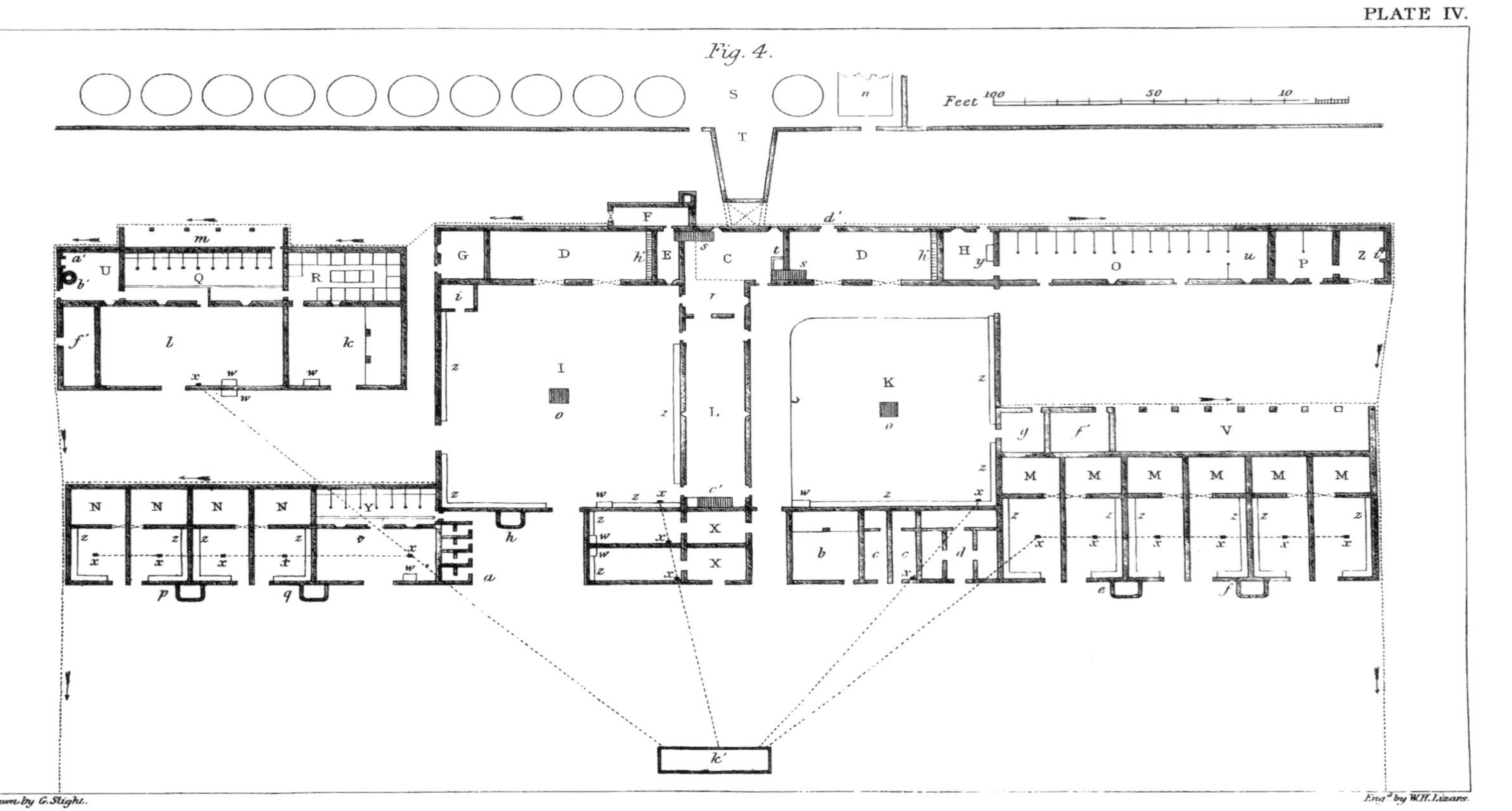

GROUND PLAN OF A PROPOSED STEADING.

EAST LOTHIAN OR SMALL'S PLOUGH.

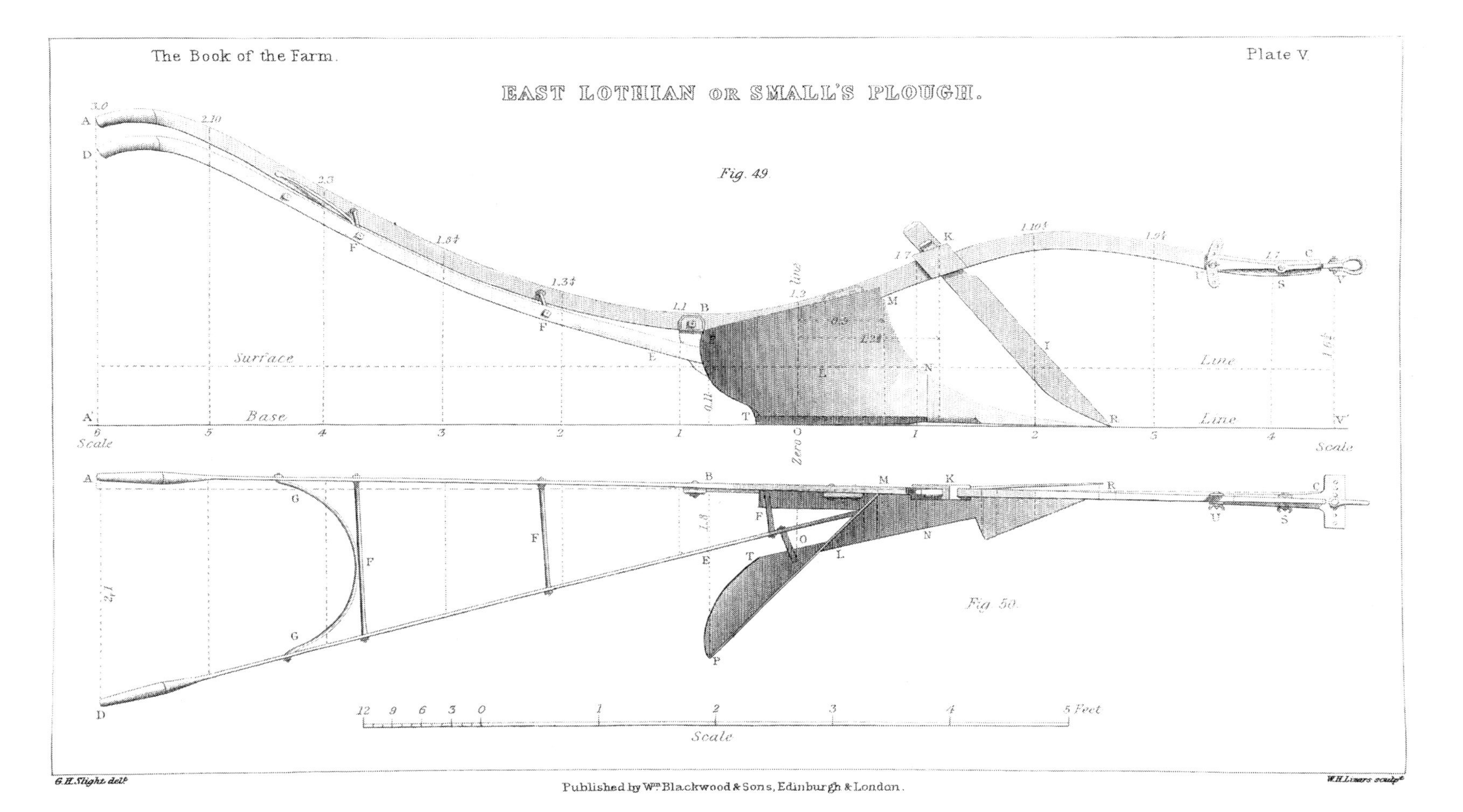

G. H. Slight delt.

W. H. Lizars sculpt.

Published by Wm. Blackwood & Sons, Edinburgh & London.

SHORT-HORN OX.

THE PROPERTY OF JOHN WILSON, ESQ. OF CUMLEDGE BERWICKSHIRE.

Published by Wm Blackwood & Sons Edinburgh & London.

DRAUGHT HORSE,

THE PROPERTY OF MESSRS HOWEY & Co EDINBURGH.

Published by Wm Blackwood & Sons Edinburgh & London.

BROOD SOW.

THE PROPERTY OF HIS GRACE THE DUKE OF BUCCLEUCH.

LANARKSHIRE OR WILKIE'S PLOUGH.

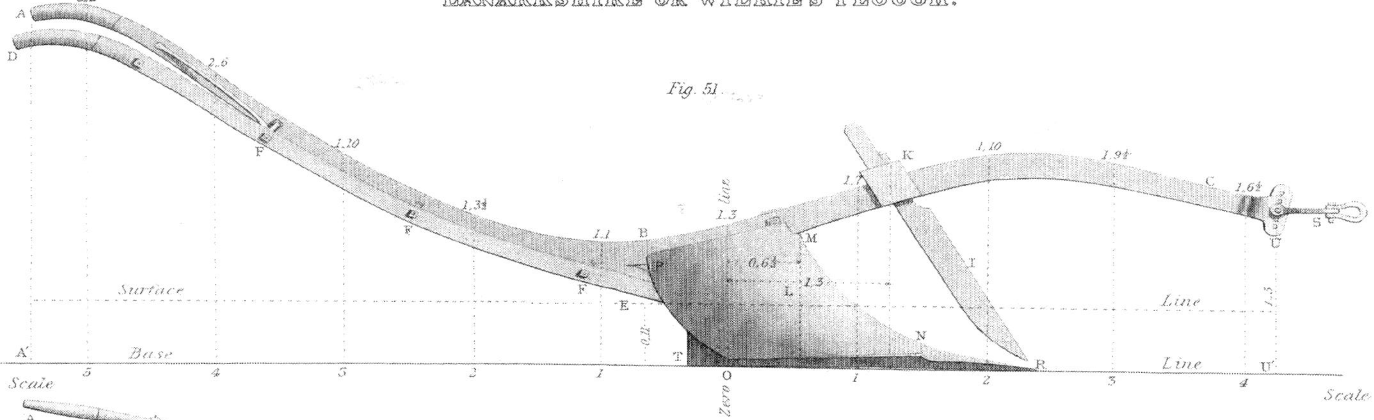

Fig. 51.

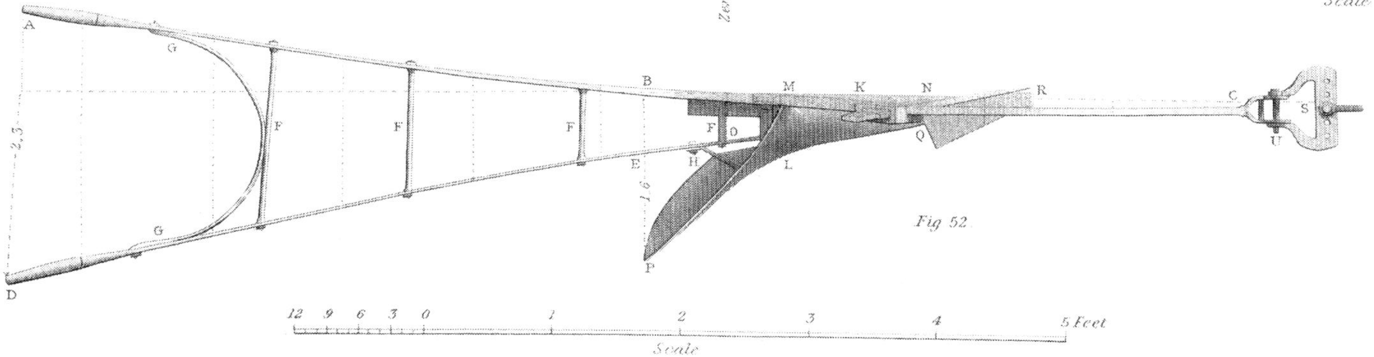

Fig 52.

G. H. Slight del.
W. H. Lizars sculp.
Published by Wm Blackwood & Sons, Edinburgh & London.

MID LOTHIAN OR CURRIE PLOUGH.

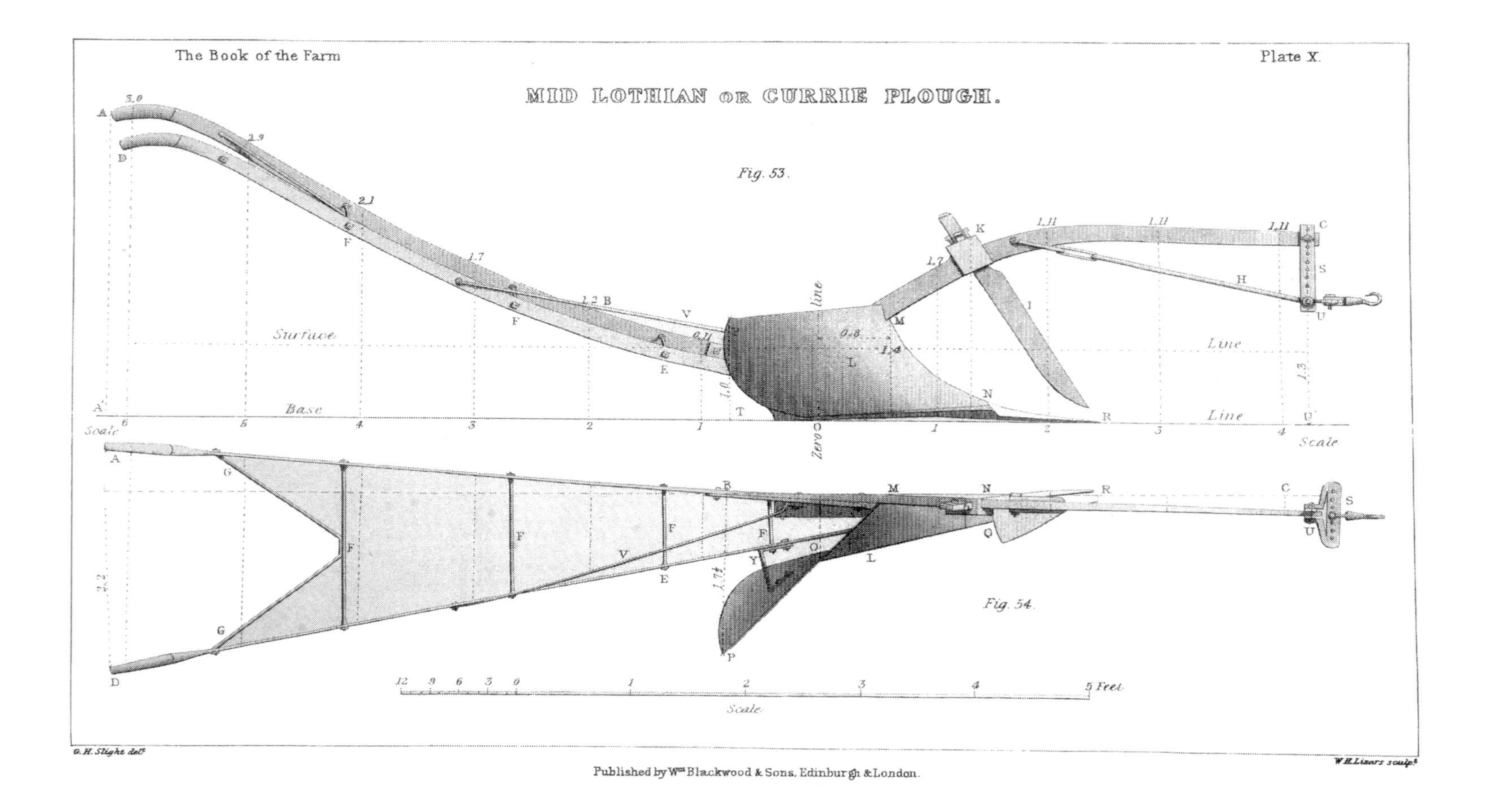

G. H. Slight delt
W. H. Lizars sculpt
Published by Wm Blackwood & Sons, Edinburgh & London.

ANALYTICAL SECTIONS,

OF MOULD BOARDS.

The East Lothian.

Fig. 111.

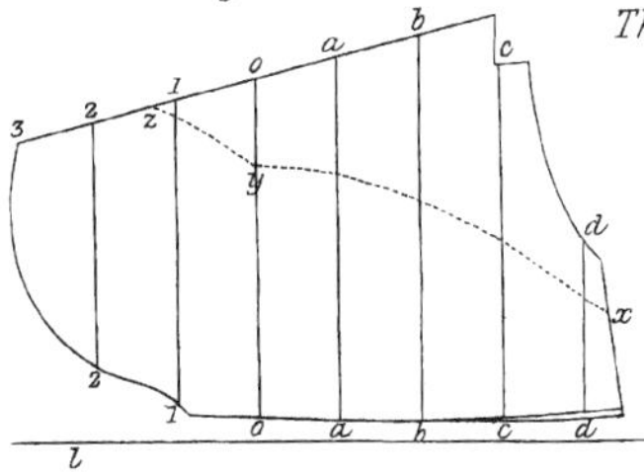

Fig. 112

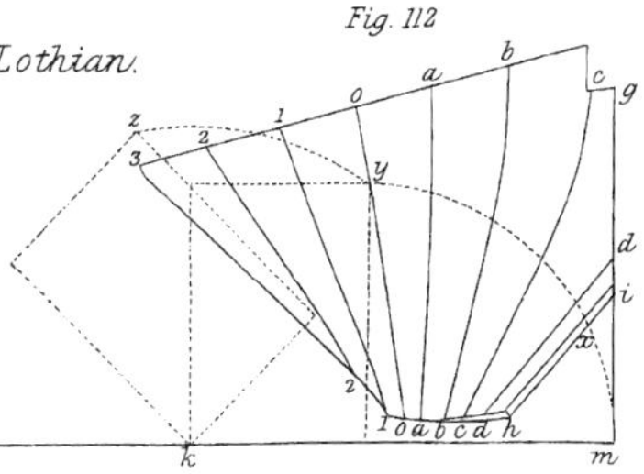

The Mid Lothian.

Fig. 113.

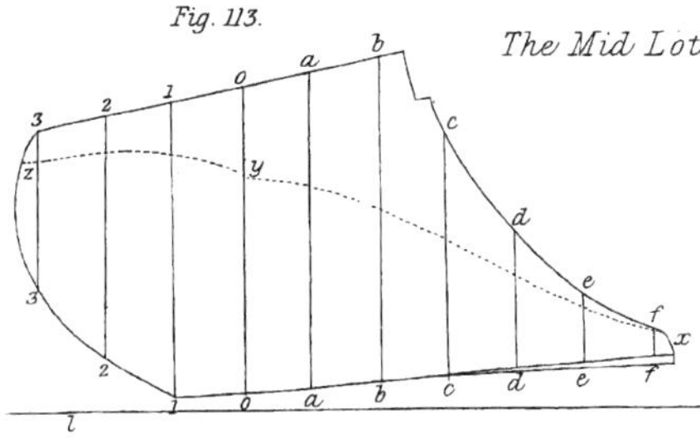

Fig. 114

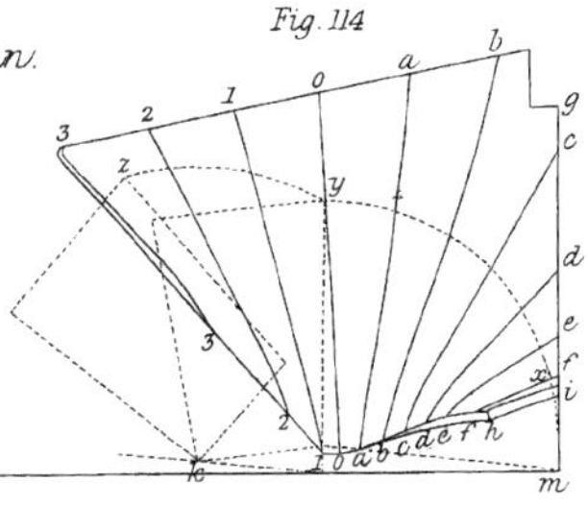

The Berwickshire.

Fig. 115

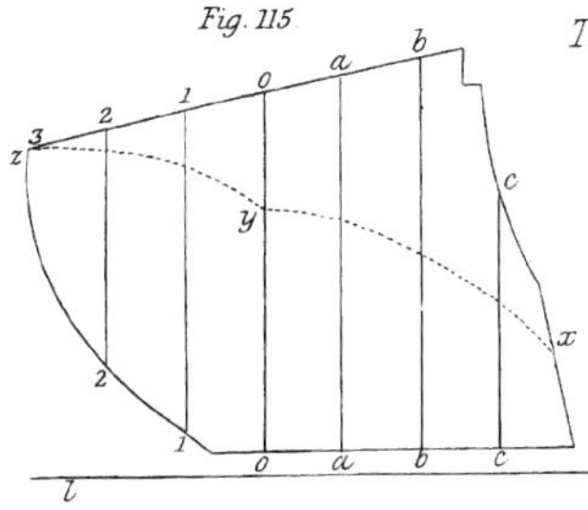

Fig. 116.

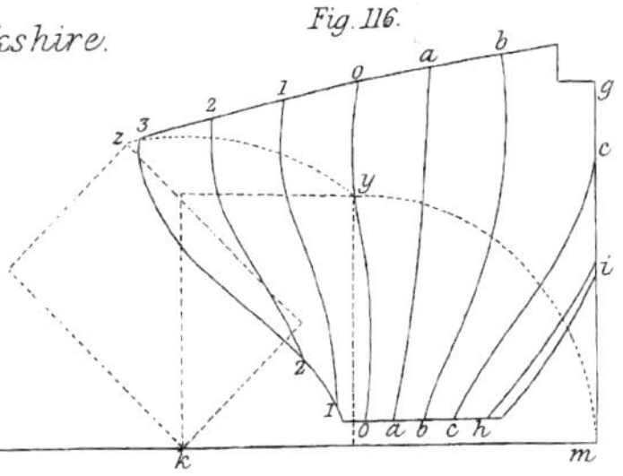

The Lanarkshire.

Fig. 117.

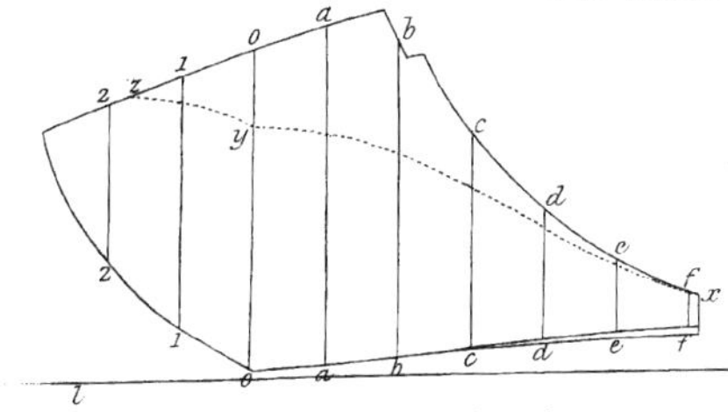

Fig. 118

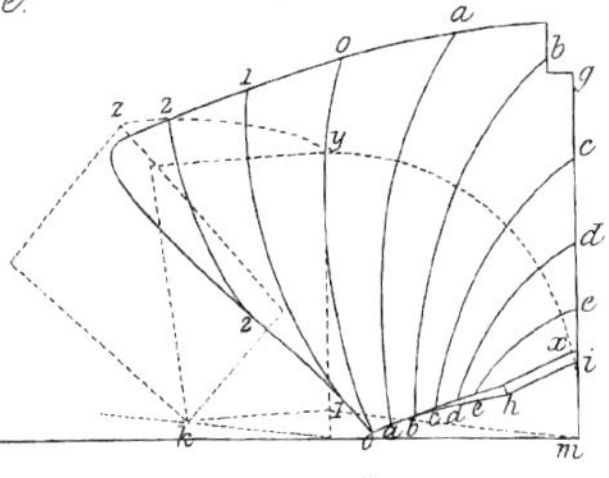

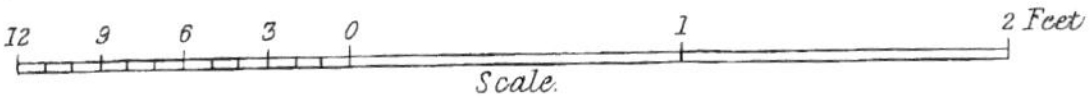

12 9 6 3 0 1 2 Feet

Scale.

G.H. Slight delt. W.H. Lizars sculpt.

Published by Wm. Blackwood & Sons, Edinburgh & London.

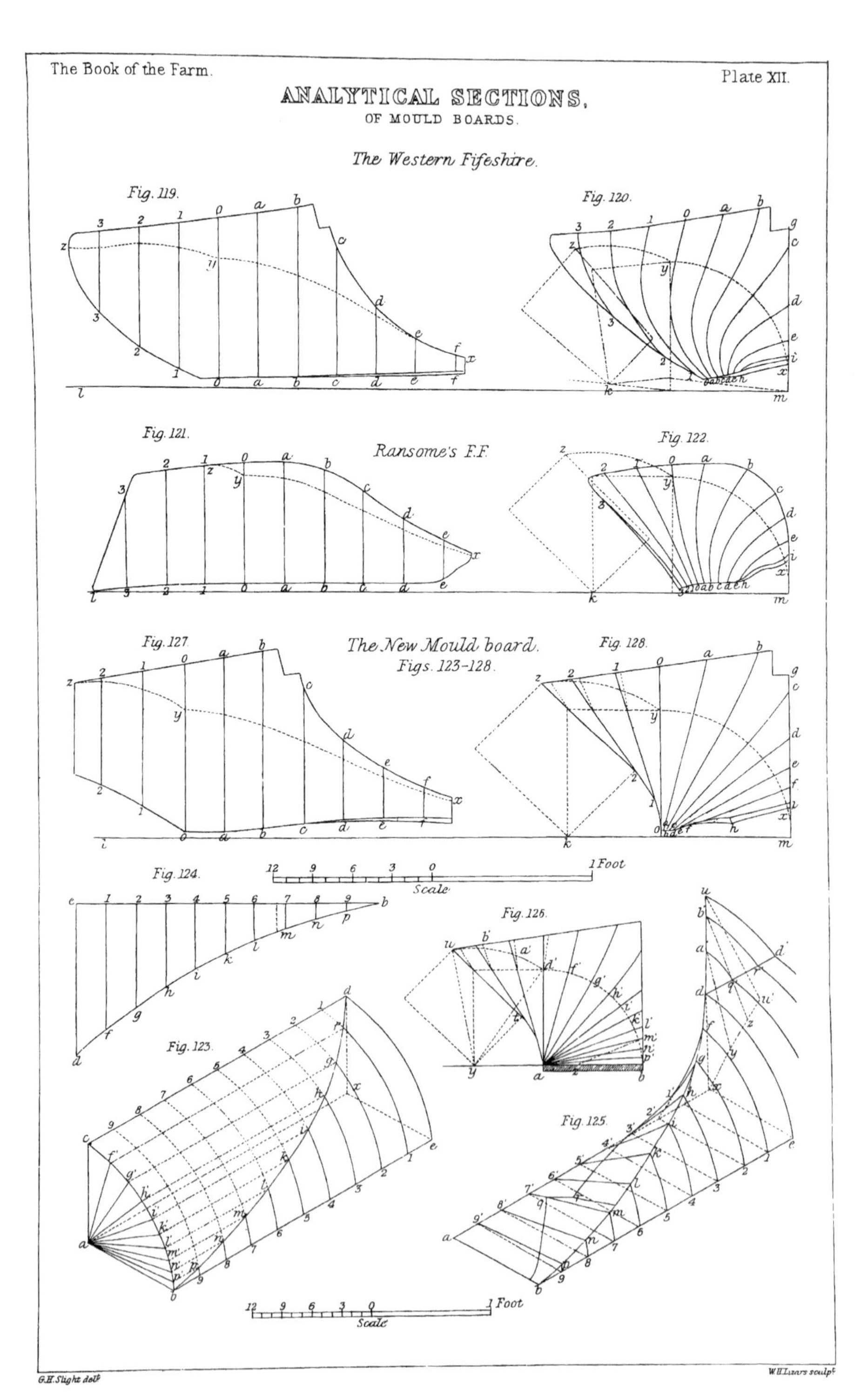

Published by Wm Blackwood & Sons Edinburgh & London.

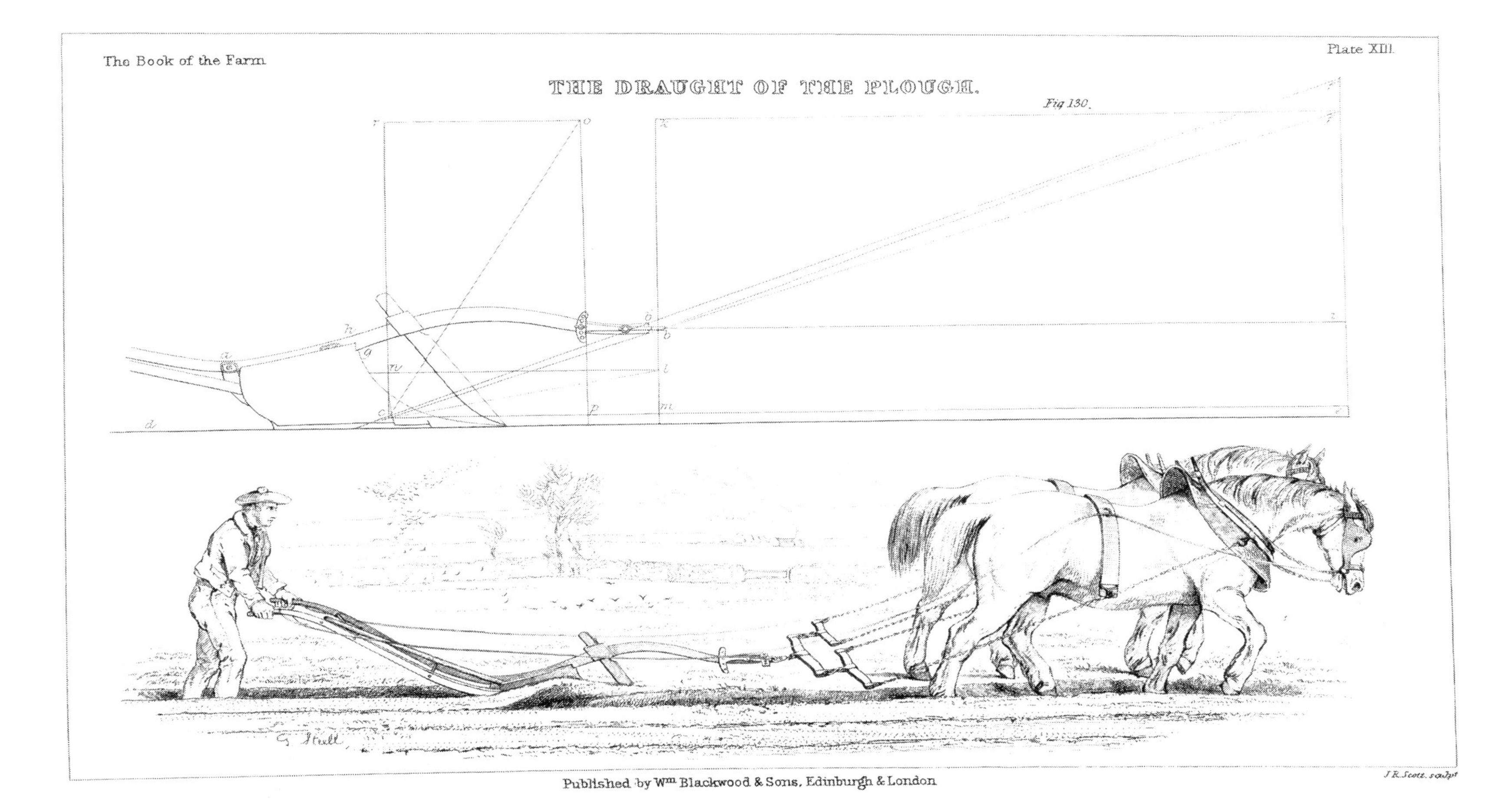

THE DRAUGHT OF THE PLOUGH.

Fig 130.

G. Hull

J. R. Scott, sculpt

Published by Wm Blackwood & Sons, Edinburgh & London

John Sheriff A.R.S.A. Thos. Landseer

LEICESTER EWE AND LAMBS,

THE PROPERTY OF MR. JOHN BRODIE, EAST LOTHIAN.

Published by Wm. Blackwood & Sons, Edinburgh & London.

John Sheriff A.R.S.A.   Thos Landseer.

SHORT-HORN COWS.

THE PROPERTY OF HIS GRACE THE DUKE OF BUCCLEUCH.

Published by Wm. Blackwood & Sons, Edinburgh & London.

DRAUGHT-HORSE,

THE PROPERTY OF MR JAMES STEEDMAN, BOGHALL.

Published by Wm Blackwood & Sons, Edinburgh & London

DRAUGHT-MARE.

THE PROPERTY OF MR BAGRIE, MONKTON, MIDLOTHIAN.

Published by Wm Blackwood & Sons, Edinburgh & London.

Printed in Great Britain
by Amazon